THE
OXFORD ANTHOLOGY
OF
AMERICAN LITERATURE

CHOSEN AND EDITED BY

WILLIAM ROSE BENÉT

AND

NORMAN HOLMES PEARSON

IN TWO VOLUMES
Volume II

OXFORD UNIVERSITY PRESS

New York

PREFACE

THE OXFORD ANTHOLOGY OF AMERICAN LITERATURE *is an historical selection from the literary expression of the American people.*

A man may look at writing as he chooses. We have regarded it as literature. Undoubtedly by the introduction of a social approach, an interest in the history of American letters has been enormously stimulated. This has been occasioned partly by a general concern with social matters and social history; but it has been mostly seized on with a defensive enthusiasm for one quality when the presence of another, the purely literary, was not certain. While the endowment of a novel with proletarian significance, or the identification of an essay with the deistic movement, or the recognition of the spirit of democracy in a poem may form the basis of useful estimates, they leave unanswered the stubborn question of literary values.

The writing of prose and poetry is primarily a conscious art, and for this reason an attempt has been made to express the literary life of this country. The seventeenth century has been comprehensively represented in the variety of its creative efforts; what has been generally regarded as odd will now assume validity as an American adaptation of suitable literary forms. In the nineteenth century, when America's first purely literary figures began to appear, no significant development has been ignored, and an effort has been made to represent its chief writers generously enough to permit their study as stylists and experimenters. There has been no effort to be all-inclusive, and no timidity in adjusting selections to valuations now generally accepted. Nor has there been hesitation to place on literature of the present that emphasis which its excellence demands. We have tried not to be satisfied with a puzzled gesture in this direction. These are the works which have interested literary figures of our own time, and through them the reader may understand that literature is a versatile and ever-changing art. The intent of the annotation and the somewhat informal commentary has been to show the directions of this change, and, when possible, to let men speak for themselves.

In all cases we have attempted to make use of the most satisfactory texts. Most of the colonial selections have been modernized, lest literary merit be veiled in quaintness. In such cases the change has been indicated. References have been made to the most accessible editions, though the texts do not always come from them. At the conclusion of each selection the dates of composition and of first appearance in book-form have, when known, been added.

WILLIAM ROSE BENÉT

NORMAN HOLMES PEARSON

New Haven,

August, 1938

ACKNOWLEDGMENTS

The editors and publisher wish to offer thanks to those who have given permission to include copyright material:

To The Alcestis Press for 'The Yachts' and 'Fine Work with Pitch and Copper,' and to the author, William Carlos Williams, for nine other poems.

To Albert and Charles Boni, Inc., Publishers, for a selection from *The Woman of Andros* by Thornton Wilder, and for the selections by Ambrose Bierce.

To The John Day Company for 'Country Summer,' 'The River in the Meadows,' 'Word for Harvest,' and 'The Mount,' from *High Falcon* by Léonie Adams.

To Dodd, Mead and Company for the poems of Richard Hovey.

To Doubleday, Doran and Company for selections from *Leaves of Grass* by Walt Whitman, copyright 1924 by the publishers; for a selection from *Strictly Business* by O.Henry, copyright 1931 by the publishers; and for a selection from *The Octopus* and *The Pit* by Frank Norris, used by permission of Charles Norris and the publishers.

To Farrar and Rinehart for two poems from *A Draft of XXX Cantos* by Ezra Pound, reprinted by permission of the publishers; for 'Pole Star for This Year,' and 'Speech to Those Who Say Comrade' from *Public Speech* by Archibald MacLeish, copyright 1936 and reprinted by permission of the publishers; for three poems from *The Selected Poems of Lizette Woodworth Reese*, copyright 1926 and reprinted by permission of the publishers; and for 'A Puritan Lady,' reprinted by permission of Norman Remington and Company of Baltimore, Remington-Putnam Book Company, Successors, and Farrar and Rinehart.

To Harcourt, Brace and Company for the poetry and prose of T.S.Eliot; for poems by Carl Sandburg from *The People, Yes*; *Smoke and Steel*, and *Slabs of the Sunburnt West*; and for a selection from *Main Street* by Sinclair Lewis.

To Harper and Brothers for a selection from *The American Scene* by Henry James; for a selection from *Chita* by Lafcadio Hearn; for

a selection from *Giants in the Earth* by Ole Rölvaag; for a selection from *Life on the Mississippi* and for *The Man That Corrupted Hadleyburg* by Mark Twain, and for 'Little Bessie Would Assist Providence' from Paine's *Mark Twain: A Biography*.

To Harvard University Press for a selection from Thomas Hutchinson's *History of Massachusetts Bay*.

To Henry Holt for the poems of Robert Frost from *Collected Poems* and *A Further Range*; and for the poems of Carl Sandburg from *Chicago Poems* and *Cornhuskers*.

To the Houghton Mifflin Company for a selection from *A Modern Instance* by William Dean Howells; for a selection from *The Country of the Pointed Firs* by Sarah Orne Jewett; for two selections from *The Education of Henry Adams* by Henry Adams; for 'Criticism' from *Shelburne Essays* by Paul Elmer More; for two poems, 'Memory' and 'Heredity,' by Thomas Bailey Aldrich; for 'A Friend's Song for Simoisius' from *Happy Ending* and 'The Wild Ride' by Louise Imogen Guiney; for 'Menagerie' and 'Gloucester Moors' by William Vaughn Moody; for nine poems of Amy Lowell; for twelve poems of Archibald MacLeish; for a poem from *Hippolytus Temporizes* by Hilda Doolittle.

To the Huntington Library for permission to reprint a part of the text of Benjamin Franklin's *Autobiography* as it was printed in *Major American Writers* by Jones and Leisy, and to the publishers, Harcourt, Brace and Company.

To the International Publishers Company for a selection from *Ten Days That Shook the World* by John Reed.

To Little, Brown and Company for 32 poems from *The Poems of Emily Dickinson*, Centenary Edition, edited by Martha Dickinson Bianchi and Alfred Leete Hampson.

To Liveright Publishing Corporation for thirteen poems from *Personae, The Collected*

viii ACKNOWLEDGMENTS

Poems of Ezra Pound; for thirteen poems by Hilda Doolittle from *Collected Poems of H.D.*; for the poems of Hart Crane.

To The Macmillan Company for ten poems from *Collected Poems* by Edwin Arlington Robinson; for the poems of Vachel Lindsay from *Collected Poems*; for six poems by Sara Teasdale from *Flame and Shadow, Rivers to the Sea*, and *Love Songs*; for eleven poems by Marianne Moore from *Selected Poems*; for 'The Art of Fiction' from *Partial Portraits* by Henry James.

To Robert M.McBride and Company for 'An Old Spell' and 'Said of the Earth and the Moon' from *These Not Elect* by Léonie Adams; for 'The Demiurge' from *The Silver Stallion* by James Branch Cabell.

To W.W.Norton and Company, the publishers, and to Mrs.Grace Hart Crane for permission to reprint 'General Aims and Theories' from Philip Horton's *Hart Crane, A Biography*.

To Random House, Inc. for permission to reprint *Lazarus Laughed* by Eugene O'Neill; 'Dry September' from *These Thirteen* by William Faulkner; 'The Life of Juan Gris' by Gertrude Stein; *The Tower Beyond Tragedy* and other poems from *Cawdor, Roan Stallion, Solstice, Such Counsels*, and *Tamar* by Robinson Jeffers; six selections from 'Via Ignis' by Lola Ridge.

To Charles Scribner's Sons for five poems from *Poems* by George Santayana and for prose selections from Santayana's *Little Essays on Art and Poetry* and *Soliloquies in England*; for the poems by Conrad Aiken; for 'Belles Desmoiselles Plantation' from *Creole Days* by George Washington Cable; for 'Crapy Cornelia' from *The Finer Grain* and selections from *The Wings of the Dove* and *The Golden Bowl* by Henry James; for 'The Other Two' from *The Descent of Man* by Edith Wharton; for 'Golden Honeymoon' from *How to Write Short Stories* by Ring Lardner; for 'The Undefeated' from *Men Without Women* by Ernest Hemingway; for 'The Death of Stoneman Gant' from *Of Time and the River* by Thomas Wolfe; for ten poems by Sidney Lanier; for six poems from *Town down the River* and *Children of the Night* by Edwin Arlington

Robinson; for four poems from *Selected Poems* by Allen Tate.

To The Viking Press, Inc. for 'Sonnets' and 'Indian Summer' from *Two Lives* by William Ellery Leonard, copyright 1922 and 1925, and for 'Tom Mooney' from *A Son of Earth* by William Ellery Leonard, copyright 1928; for 'Faces' from *The Ghetto* by Lola Ridge, copyright 1918, and for 'Sons of Belial' and 'Reveille' from *Sun-Up* by Lola Ridge, copyright 1920.

To Yale University Press for 'A Snow Storm' by Hector St. Jean de Crèvecœur from *Sketches of Eighteenth Century America*.

To *The New England Quarterly* and to Thomas H.Johnson for 'Huswifery' and excerpts from 'God's Determination' and 'Meditations' by Edward Taylor.

To *The Choate Literary Magazine* for 'How Writing Is Written' by Gertrude Stein.

The following selections are used by permission of, and by special arrangement with, Alfred A.Knopf, Inc., the authorized publishers: six poems from *The Sonnets* by Frederick Goddard Tuckerman; poems from *The Collected Poems* by Stephen Crane; 'The Worms at Heaven's Gate,' 'Emperor of Ice-Cream,' 'Sunday Morning,' 'The Bird with the Coppery, Keen Claws,' 'To the One of Fictive Music,' 'Peter Quince at the Clavier,' 'Sea Surface Full of Clouds,' 'The Idea of Order at Key West,' 'A Postcard from a Volcano,' and selections from 'Owl's Clover' and 'A Thought Revolved' by Wallace Stevens; 'Spectral Lovers,' 'Old Man Playing with Children,' and 'Philomela' by John Crowe Ransom; thirty-four poems by Elinor Wylie from *Collected Poems* and a selection from *Mr. Hodge and Mr. Hazard, Collected Prose of Elinor Wylie*; 'Grenstone River,' 'Grieve Not for Beauty,' 'A Tent Song,' 'Passing Near,' 'Tiles,' 'The Old Men and the Young Men,' and 'A Dance for Rain' by Witter Bynner; 'Bryan' from *Selected Prejudices* by Henry L. Mencken; and a selection from *Death Comes for the Archbishop* by Willa Cather, also used by permission of Houghton Mifflin Company.

Thanks are also due:

To Sherwood Anderson for 'Death in the Woods'; to Stephen Vincent Benét and to the publishers, Farrar and Rinehart, Inc., for 'King David' and 'The Mountain Whippoorwill' from *Ballads and Poems*, copyright 1931 by the author, for poems from *John Brown's Body*, copyright 1928 by the author, and for 'Litany for Dictatorships' from *Burning City*, copyright 1936 by the author; to E.E.Cummings for 'All in green went my love riding,' 'of evident invisibles,' 'it is at moments after i have dreamed,' and 'Buffalo Bill's defunct' from *Tulips and Chimneys*, copyright 1923 by the author, for 'this is the garden: colours come and go,' 'Picasso,' 'O Thou to whom the musical white spring,' and From 'La Guerre'— 'II Humanity i love you' from *XLI Poems*, copyright 1925 by the author, for 'somewhere i have never travelled, gladly beyond' from *Viva*, copyright 1931 by the author, for 'gee i like to think of dead' from *&* (*Ampersand*), copyright 1925 by the author, for 'since feeling is first,' 'it really must,' 'here's a little mouse) and,' and 'along the brittle treacherous bright streets' from *Is 5*, published by Boni and Liveright, copyright 1926 by the publishers; to John Dos Passos for 'Tin Lizzie' from *The Big Money*, published by Harcourt, Brace & Company, Inc., copyright 1936 by the author; to Theodore Dreiser for a selection from *An American Tragedy*; to John Gould Fletcher and to Horace Gregory for their poems; to Lucien Harris for the selections from *Uncle Remus* by Joel Chandler Harris and to D.Appleton-Century Company, the publishers; to Mildred Howells for a selection from *Criticism and Fiction* by William Dean Howells, copyright 1891 by Harper and Brothers and 1918 by Mildred Howells and John Mead Howells; to Virgil Markham for 'The Man with the Hoe' by Edwin Markham; to Edgar Lee Masters for his poems and also to the publishers, The Macmillan Company; to Edna St. Vincent Millay and to the publishers, Harper and Brothers, for 'I shall forget you presently, my dear' from *A Few Figs from Thistles*, copyright 1922 by the author, for 'When the Year Grows Old' from *Renascence*, copyright 1917 by the author, for 'The Poet and His Book,' 'And you as well must die, beloved dust,' 'Lament,' 'Elegy' (From 'Memorial to D. C.'), from *Second April*, copyright 1921 by the author, for 'Pity me not because the light of day,' and 'Euclid alone has looked on Beauty bare' from *The Harp Weaver and Other Poems*, copyright 1923 by the author, for 'Dirge Without Music,' 'The Cameo,' and 'On Hearing a Symphony of Beethoven' from *The Buck in the Snow*, copyright 1928 by the author, for 'The Return,' 'Where Can the Heart Be Hidden in the Ground?', 'How Naked, How Without a Wall,' 'Only the Diamond and the Diamond's Dust,' and 'Here lies, and none to mourn him but the sea' from *Wine from These Grapes*, copyright 1934 by the author, for 'I dreamed I moved among the Elysian fields' and 'Oh, sleep forever in the Latmian cave' from *Fatal Interview*, copyright 1931 by the author; to Abbie and Juanita Miller and also to Putnam's Sons, the publishers, for permission to use the poems of Joaquin Miller; to Ezra Pound for 'A Retrospect' from *Pavannes, and Divisions*; to Gertrude Stein for 'When They Are a Little Older' from *A Long Gay Book*; to Harry Robertson for three poems by George Sterling; to Henry A.Stickney and William W. Mathewson for the poems of Trumbull Stickney; to Francis Litz for the poems of John Banister Tabb from *The Poetry of Father Tabb*, published by Dodd, Mead and Company; to William Carlos Williams for permission to use his poems; to Colonel Charles Erskine Scott Wood for permission to use 'First Snow' and poems from *The Poet in the Desert*.

They also wish to thank the many publishers by whom permission was given to include material in the annotation and Commentaries. Short excerpts were used from the following books:

The Locomotive God by William Ellery Leonard, published by the D.Appleton-Century Company; *The Orient in American Transcendentalism* by Arthur Christy, published by Columbia University Press; *Fifty Poets* by William Rose Benét, published by Dodd, Mead and Company; *Diedrich Knickerbocker's History of New York*, edited by Stanley Williams and Tremaine McDowell, and *Selections from Cotton Mather* by Kenneth B. Murdock, published by Harcourt, Brace and Company; *Mark Twain* by Albert Bigelow Paine, published by Harper and Broth-

CONTENTS

Robert Frost (1875——)

Vachel Lindsay (1879–1931)

Edgar Lee Masters (1869——)

Carl Sandburg (1878——)

CONTENTS

ALPHABETICAL LIST OF AUTHORS

The figures in brackets indicate the page number of the commentary and bibliography.

THE OXFORD ANTHOLOGY OF
AMERICAN LITERATURE
VOLUME II

THE
OXFORD ANTHOLOGY
OF
AMERICAN LITERATURE

THE Civil War marked the conclusion to a period of American literature. The New England Renaissance of such writers as Hawthorne, Emerson, Longfellow, and Holmes was over; although it still lingered in the odd freshness of Emily Dickinson and the uncreative power of writers and editors whose standards were set by a departed age. When a friend wrote to Walt Whitman in 1884, 'I find a solid line of enemies to you everywhere,' he expressed the obvious fact that it takes both public and publisher a long time to recognize the signs of death.

The new and somewhat motley group which took over the leadership from the New Englanders possessed their own individual powers. But these figures are equally interesting and significant because of the indications of present-day technique to be found in their writing; and their examination becomes particularly important in view of the fact that we are now in the midst of America's second great period of literary creation.

WALT WHITMAN
1819–1892

A BACKWARD GLANCE O'ER TRAVEL'D ROADS [1]

PERHAPS the best of songs heard, or of any and all true love, or life's fairest episodes, or sailors', soldiers' trying scenes on land or sea, is the *résumé* of them, or any of them, long afterwards, looking at the actualities away back past, with all their practical excitations gone. How the soul loves to float amid such reminiscences!

So here I sit gossiping in the early candle-light of old age—I and my book—casting backward glances over our travel'd road. After completing, as it were, the journey—(a varied jaunt of years, with

[1] The essay served as preface to *November Boughs* (Philadelphia, 1888).

many halts and gaps of intervals—or some lengthen'd ship-voyage, wherein more than once the last hour had apparently arrived, and we seem'd certainly going down—yet reaching port in a sufficient way through all discomfitures at last)—After completing my poems, I am curious to review them in the light of their own (at the time unconscious, or mostly unconscious) intentions, with certain unfoldings of the thirty years they seek to embody. These lines, therefore, will probably blend the weft of first purposes and speculations, with the warp of that experience afterwards, always bringing strange developments.

Result of seven or eight stages and struggles extending through nearly thirty years, (as I nigh my three-score-and-ten I live largely on memory,) I look upon *Leaves of Grass*, now finish'd to the end of its opportunities and powers, as my definitive *carte visite* to the coming generations of the New World,[1] if I may assume to say so. That I have not gain'd the acceptance of my own time, but have fallen back on fond dreams of the future—anticipations—('still lives the song, though Regnar dies')—That from a worldly and business point of view *Leaves of Grass* has been worse than a failure—that public criticism on the book and myself as author of it yet shows mark'd anger and contempt more than anything else—('I find a solid line of enemies to you everywhere,'—letter from W.S.K., Boston, May 28, 1884)—And that solely for publishing it I have been the object of two or three pretty serious special official buffetings—is all probably no more than I ought to have expected. I had my choice when I commenc'd. I bid neither for soft eulogies, big money returns, nor the approbation of existing schools and conventions. As fulfill'd, or partially fulfill'd, the best comfort of the whole business (after a small band of the dearest friends and upholders ever vouchsafed to man or cause—doubtless all the more faithful and uncompromising—this little phalanx!—for being so few) is that, unstopp'd and unwarp'd by any influence outside the soul within me, I have had my say entirely my own way, and

put it unerringly on record—the value thereof to be decided by time.

In calculating that decision, William O'Connor and Dr. Bucke are far more peremptory than I am. Behind all else that can be said, I consider *Leaves of Grass* and its theory experimental—as, in the deepest sense, I consider our American republic itself to be, with its theory. (I think I have at least enough philosophy not to be too absolutely certain of anything, or any results.) In the second place, the volume is a *sortie*—whether to prove triumphant, and conquer its field of aim and escape and construction, nothing less than a hundred years from now can fully answer. I consider the point that I have positively gain'd a hearing, to far more than make up for any and all other lacks and withholdings. Essentially, *that* was from the first, and has remain'd throughout, the main object. Now it seems to be achiev'd, I am certainly contented to waive any otherwise momentous drawbacks, as of little account. Candidly and dispassionately reviewing all my intentions, I feel that they were creditable—and I accept the result, whatever it may be.

After continued personal ambition and effort, as a young fellow, to enter with the rest into competition for the usual rewards, business, political, literary, &c.—to take part in the great *mêlée*, both for victory's prize itself and to do some good—After years of those aims and pursuits, I found myself remaining possess'd, at the age of thirty-one to thirty-three, with a special desire and conviction. Or rather, to be quite exact, a desire that had been flitting through my previous life, or hovering on the flanks, mostly indefinite hitherto, had steadily advanced to the front, defined itself, and finally dominated everything else. This was a feeling or ambition to articulate and faithfully express in literary or poetic form, and uncompromisingly, my own physical, emotional, moral, intellectual, and æsthetic Personality, in the midst of, and tallying, the momentous spirit and facts of its immediate days, and of current America—and to exploit that Personality, identified with place and date, in a far more candid and comprehensive sense than any hitherto poem or book.

Perhaps this is in brief, or suggests, all I

---

[1] 'When Champollion, on his death-bed, handed to the printer the revised proof of his *Egyptian Grammar*, he said gayly, "Be careful of this—it is my *carte de visite* to posterity." ' Author's note, ibid.,5.

have sought to do. Given the Nineteenth Century, with the United States, and what they furnish as area and points of view, *Leaves of Grass* is, or seeks to be, simply a faithful and doubtless self-will'd record. In the midst of all, it gives one man's—the author's—identity, ardors, observations, faiths, and thoughts, color'd hardly at all with any decided coloring from other faiths or other identities. Plenty of songs had been sung—beautiful, matchless songs —adjusted to other lands than these— another spirit and stage of evolution; but I would sing, and leave out or put in, quite solely with reference to America and to-day. Modern science and democracy seem'd to be throwing out their challenge to poetry to put them in its statements in contradistinction to the songs and myths of the past. As I see it now (perhaps too late,) I have unwittingly taken up that challenge and made an attempt at such statements— which I certainly would not assume to do now, knowing more clearly what it means.

For grounds for *Leaves of Grass*, as a poem, I abandon'd the conventional themes, which do not appear in it: none of the stock ornamentation, or choice plots of love or war, or high, exceptional personages of Old-World song; nothing, as I may say, for beauty's sake—no legend, or myth, or romance, nor euphemism, nor rhyme. But the broadest average of humanity and its identities in the now ripening Nineteenth Century, and especially in each of their countless examples and practical occupations in the United States to-day.

One main contrast of the ideas behind every page of my verses, compared with establish'd poems, is their different relative attitude towards God, towards the objective universe, and still more (by reflection, confession, assumption, &c.) the quite changed attitude of the ego, the one chanting or talking, towards himself and towards his fellow-humanity. It is certainly time for America, above all, to begin this readjustment in the scope and basic point of view of verse; for everything else has changed. As I write, I see in an article on Wordsworth, in one of the current English magazines, the lines, 'A few weeks ago an eminent French critic said that, owing to the special tendency to science and to its all-devouring force, poetry would cease to be read in fifty years.' But I anticipate the very contrary. Only a firmer, vastly broader, new area begins to exist—nay, is already form'd—to which the poetic genius must emigrate. Whatever may have been the case in years gone by, the true use for the imaginative faculty of modern times is to give ultimate vivification to facts, to science, and to common lives, endowing them with the glows and glories and final illustriousness which belong to every real thing, and to real things only. Without that ultimate vivification—which the poet or other artist alone can give—reality would seem incomplete, and science, democracy, and life itself, finally in vain.

Few appreciate the moral revolutions of our age, which have been profounder far than the material or inventive or war-produced ones. The Nineteenth Century, now well towards its close (and ripening into fruit the seeds of the two preceding centuries[1])—the uprisings of national masses and shiftings of boundary-lines— the historical and other prominent facts of the United States—the war of attempted Secession—the stormy rush and haste of nebulous forces—never can future years witness more excitement and din of action —never completer change of army front along the whole line, the whole civilized world. For all these new and evolutionary facts, meanings, purposes, new poetic messages, new forms and expressions, are inevitable.

My Book and I—what a period we have presumed to span! those thirty years from 1850 to '80—and America in them! Proud, proud indeed may we be, if we have cull'd enough of that period in its own spirit to worthily waft a few live breaths of it to the future!

Let me not dare, here or anywhere, for my own purposes, or any purposes, to attempt the definition of Poetry, nor answer the question what it is. Like Religion, Love, Nature, while those terms are indis-

1 'The ferment and germination even of the United States to-day, dating back to, and in my opinion mainly founded on, the Elizabethan age in English history, the age of Francis Bacon and Shakspere. Indeed, when we pursue it, what growth or advent is there that does not date back, back, until lost—perhaps its most tantalizing clues lost—in the receded horizons of the past?' Author's note, ibid.,8.

pensable, and we all give a sufficiently accurate meaning to them, in my opinion no definition that has ever been made sufficiently encloses the name Poetry; nor can any rule or convention ever so absolutely obtain but some great exception may arise and disregard and overturn it.

Also it must be carefully remember'd that first-class literature does not shine by any luminosity of its own; nor do its poems. They grow of circumstances, and are evolutionary. The actual living light is always curiously from elsewhere—follows unaccountable sources, and is lunar and relative at the best. There are, I know, certain controling themes that seem endlessly appropriated to the poets—as war, in the past—in the Bible, religious rapture and adoration—always love, beauty, some fine plot, or pensive or other emotion. But, strange as it may sound at first, I will say there is something striking far deeper and towering far higher than those themes for the best elements of modern song.

Just as all the old imaginative works rest, after their kind, on long trains of presuppositions, often entirely unmention'd by themselves, yet supplying the most important bases of them, and without which they could have had no reason for being, so *Leaves of Grass*, before a line was written, presupposed something different from any other, and, as it stands, is the result of such presupposition. I should say, indeed, it were useless to attempt reading the book without first carefully tallying that preparatory background and quality in the mind. Think of the United States to-day—the facts of these thirty-eight or forty empires solder'd in one—sixty or seventy millions of equals, with their lives, their passions, their future —these incalculable, modern, American, seething multitudes around us, of which we are inseparable parts! Think, in comparison, of the petty environage and limited area of the poets of past or present Europe, no matter how great their genius. Think of the absence and ignorance, in all cases hitherto, of the multitudinousness, vitality, and the unprecedented stimulants of to-day and here. It almost seems as if a poetry with cosmic and dynamic features of magnitude and limitlessness suitable to the human soul, were never possible before. It is certain that a poetry of absolute faith and equality for the use of the democratic masses never was.

In estimating first-class song, a sufficient Nationality, or, on the other hand, what may be call'd the negative and lack of it, (as in Goethe's case, it sometimes seems to me,) is often, if not always, the first element. One needs only a little penetration to see, at more or less removes, the material facts of their country and radius, with the coloring of the moods of humanity at the time, and its gloomy or hopeful prospects, behind all poets and each poet, and forming their birth-marks. I know very well that my *Leaves* could not possibly have emerged or been fashion'd or completed, from any other era than the latter half of the Nineteenth Century, nor any other land than democratic America, and from the absolute triumph of the National Union arms.

And whether my friends claim it for me or not, I know well enough, too, that in respect to pictorial talent, dramatic situations, and especially in verbal melody and all the conventional technique of poetry, not only the divine works that to-day stand ahead in the world's reading, but dozens more, transcend (some of them immeasurably transcend) all I have done, or could do. But it seem'd to me, as the objects in Nature, the themes of æstheticism, and all special exploitations of the mind and soul, involve not only their own inherent quality, but the quality, just as inherent and important, of *their point of view*,[1] the time had come to reflect all themes and things, old and new, in the lights thrown on them by the advent of America and democracy— to chant those themes through the utterance of one, not only the grateful and reverent legatee of the past, but the born child of the New World—to illustrate all through the genesis and ensemble of to-day; and that such illustration and ensemble are the chief demands of America's prospective imaginative literature. Not to carry out, in the approved style, some choice plot of fortune or misfortune, or fancy, or fine thoughts, or incidents, or courtesies—all of which has been done overwhelmingly and well, probably never to be excell'd— but that while in such æsthetic presenta-

1 'According to Immanuel Kant, the last essential reality, giving shape and significance to all the rest.' Author's note, ibid.,10.

tion of objects, passions, plots, thoughts, &c., our lands and days do not want, and probably will never have, anything better than they already possess from the bequests of the past, it still remains to be said that there is even towards all those a subjective and contemporary point of view appropriate to ourselves alone, and to our new genius and environments, different from anything hitherto; and that such conception of current or gone-by life and art is for us the only means of their assimilation consistent with the Western world.

Indeed, and anyhow, to put it specifically, has not the time arrived when, (if it must be plainly said, for democratic America's sake, if for no other) there must imperatively come a readjustment of the whole theory and nature of Poetry? The question is important, and I may turn the argument over and repeat it: Does not the best thought of our day and Republic conceive of a birth and spirit of song superior to anything past or present? To the effectual and moral consolidation of our lands (already, as materially establish'd, the greatest factors in known history, and far, far greater through what they prelude and necessitate, and are to be in future)—to conform with and build on the concrete realities and theories of the universe furnish'd by science, and henceforth the only irrefragable basis for anything, verse included—to root both influences in the emotional and imaginative action of the modern time, and dominate all that precedes or opposes them—is not either a radical advance and step forward, or a new verteber of the best song indispensable?

The New World receives with joy the poems of the antique, with European feudalism's rich fund of epics, plays, ballads—seeks not in the least to deaden or displace those voices from our ear and area—holds them indeed as indispensable studies, influences, records, comparisons. But though the dawn-dazzle of the sun of literature is in those poems for us of to-day—though perhaps the best parts of current character in nations, social groups, or any man's or woman's individuality, Old World or New, are from them—and though if I were ask'd to name the most precious bequest to current American civilization from all the hitherto ages, I am not sure but I would

name those old and less old songs ferried hither from east and west—some serious words and debits remain; some acrid considerations demand a hearing. Of the great poems receiv'd from abroad and from the ages, and to-day enveloping and penetrating America, is there one that is consistent with these United States, or essentially applicable to them as they are and are to be? Is there one whose underlying basis is not a denial and insult to democracy? What a comment it forms, anyhow, on this era of literary fulfilment, with the splendid dayrise of science and resuscitation of history, that our chief religious and poetical works are not our own, nor adapted to our light, but have been furnish'd by far-back ages out of their arriere and darkness, or, at most, twilight dimness! What is there in those works that so imperiously and scornfully dominates all our advanced civilization, and culture?

Even Shakspere, who so suffuses current letters and art (which indeed have in most degrees grown out of him,) belongs essentially to the buried past. Only he holds the proud distinction for certain important phases of that past, of being the loftiest of the singers life has yet given voice to. All, however, relate to and rest upon conditions, standards, politics, sociologies, ranges of belief, that have been quite eliminated from the Eastern hemisphere, and never existed at all in the Western. As authoritative types of song they belong in America just about as much as the persons and institutes they depict. True, it may be said, the emotional, moral, and æsthetic natures of humanity have not radically changed—that in these the old poems apply to our times and all times, irrespective of date; and that they are of incalculable value as pictures of the past. I willingly make those admissions, and to their fullest extent; then advance the points herewith as of serious, even paramount importance.

I have indeed put on record elsewhere my reverence and eulogy for those never-to-be-excell'd poetic bequests, and their indescribable preciousness as heirlooms for America. Another and separate point must now be candidly sta_ed. If I had not stood before those poems with uncover'd head, fully aware of their colossal grandeur and beauty of form and spirit, I could not have written *Leaves of Grass*. My verdict and conclusions as illustrated in its pages are arrived at through the temper and inculcation of the old works as much as through anything else—perhaps more than through anything else. As America fully and fairly construed is the legitimate result and evolutionary outcome of the past, so I would dare to claim for my verse. Without stopping to qualify the averment, the Old World has had the poems of myths, fictions, feudalism, conquest, caste, dynastic wars, and splendid exceptional characters and affairs, which have been great; but the New World needs the poems of realities and science and of the democratic average and basic equality, which shall be greater. In the centre of all, and object of all, stands the Human Being, towards whose heroic and spiritual evolution poems and everything directly or indirectly tend, Old World or New.

Continuing the subject, my friends have more than once suggested—or may be the garrulity of advancing age is possessing me—some further embryonic facts of *Leaves of Grass*, and especially how I enter'd upon them. Dr. Bucke has, in his volume, already fully and fairly described the preparation of my poetic field, with the particular and general plowing, planting, seeding, and occupation of the ground, till everything was fertilized, rooted, and ready to start its own way for good or bad. Not till after all this, did I attempt any serious acquaintance with poetic literature. Along in my sixteenth year I had become possessor of a stout, well-cramm'd one thousand page octavo volume (I have it yet,) containing Walter Scott's poetry entire—an inexhaustible mine and treasury of poetic forage (especially the endless forests and jungles of notes)—has been so to me for fifty years, and remains so to this day.[1]

Later, at intervals, summers and falls, I used to go off, sometimes for a week at a stretch, down in the country, or to Long Island's seashores—there, in the presence of outdoor influences, I went over thoroughly the Old and New Testaments, and absorb'd (probably to better advantage for me than in any library or indoor room—it makes such difference *where* you read,) Shakspere, Ossian, the best translated versions I could get of Homer, Eschylus, Sophocles, the old German *Nibelungen*, the ancient Hindoo poems, and one or two other masterpieces, Dante's among them. As it happen'd, I read the latter mostly in an old wood. The *Iliad* (Buckley's prose version) I read first thoroughly on the peninsula of Orient, northeast end of Long Island, in a shelter'd hollow of rocks and sand, with the sea on each side. (I have wonder'd since why I was not overwhelm'd by those mighty masters. Likely because I read them, as described, in the full presence of Nature, under the sun, with the far-spreading landscape and vistas, or the sea rolling in.)

Toward the last I had among much else look'd over Edgar Poe's poems—of which I was not an admirer, tho' I always saw that beyond their limited range of melody (like perpetual chimes of music bells, ringing from lower *b* flat up to *g*) they were melodious expressions, and perhaps never excell'd ones, of certain pronounc'd phases of human morbidity. (The Poetic area is very spacious—has room for all—has so many mansions!) But I was repaid in Poe's prose by the idea that (at any rate for our occasions, our day) there can be no such thing as a long poem. The same thought had been haunting my mind before, but Poe's argument, though short, work'd the sum out and proved it to me.

Another point had an early settlement, clearing the ground greatly. I saw, from the time my enterprise and questionings positively shaped themselves (how best can I express my own distinctive era and surroundings, America, Democracy?) that the trunk and centre whence the answer was to radiate, and to which all should

1 'Sir Walter Scott's *Complete Poems*; especially including "Border Minstrelsy"; then "Sir Tristrem"; "Lay of the Last Minstrel"; "Ballads from the German"; "Marmion"; "Lady of the Lake"; "Vision of Don Roderick"; "Lord of the Isles"; "Rokeby"; "Bridal of Triermain"; "Field of Waterloo"; "Harold the Dauntless"; all the Dramas; various Introductions, endless interesting Notes, and Essays on Poetry, Romance, &c.

'Lockhart's 1833 (or '34) edition with Scott's latest and copious revisions and annotations. (All the poems were thoroughly read by me, but the ballads of the "Border Minstrelsy" over and over again.)' Author's note, ibid.,12.

return from straying however far a distance, must be an identical body and soul, a personality—which personality, after many considerations and ponderings I deliberately settled should be myself—indeed could not be any other. I also felt strongly (whether I have shown it or not) that to the true and full estimate of the Present both the Past and the Future are main considerations.

These, however, and much more might have gone on and come to naught (almost positively would have come to naught,) if a sudden, vast, terrible, direct and indirect stimulus for new and national declamatory expression had not been given to me. It is certain, I say, that, although I had made a start before, only from the occurrence of the Secession War, and what it show'd me as by flashes of lightning, with the emotional depths it sounded and arous'd (of course, I don't mean in my own heart only, I saw it just as plainly in others, in millions) —that only from the strong flare and provocation of that war's sights and scenes the final reasons-for-being of an autochthonic and passionate song definitely came forth.

I went down to the war fields in Virginia (end of 1862), lived thenceforward in camp —saw great battles and the days and nights afterward—partook of all the fluctuations, gloom, despair, hopes again arous'd, courage evoked—death readily risk'd—*the cause*, too—along and filling those agonistic and lurid following years, 1863–'64–'65— the real parturition years (more than 1776– '83) of this henceforth homogeneous Union. Without those three or four years and the experiences they gave, *Leaves of Grass* would not now be existing.

But I set out with the intention also of indicating or hinting some point-characteristics which I since see (though I did not then, at least not definitely) were bases and object-urgings toward those *Leaves* from the first. The word I myself put primarily for the description of them as they stand at last, is the word Suggestiveness. I round and finish little, if anything; and could not, consistently with my scheme. The reader will always have his or her part to do, just as much as I have had mine. I seek less to state or display any theme or thought, and more to bring you, reader, into the atmosphere of the theme or thought—there to pursue your own flight. Another impetus-word is Comradeship as for all lands, and in a more commanding and acknowledg'd sense than hitherto. Other word signs would be Good Cheer, Content, and Hope.

The chief trait of any given poet is always the spirit he brings to the observation of Humanity and Nature—the mood out of which he contemplates his subjects. What kind of temper and what amount of faith report these things? Up to how recent a date is the song carried? What the equipment, and special raciness of the singer— what his tinge of coloring? The last value of artistic expressers, past and present— Greek æsthetes, Shakspere—or in our own day Tennyson, Victor Hugo, Carlyle, Emerson—is certainly involv'd in such questions. I say the profoundest service that poems or any other writings can do for their reader is not merely to satisfy the intellect, or supply something polish'd and interesting, nor even to depict great passions, or persons or events, but to fill him with vigorous and clean manliness, religiousness, and give him *good heart* as a radical possession and habit. The educated world seems to have been growing more and more ennuyed for ages, leaving to our time the inheritance of it all. Fortunately there is the original inexhaustible fund of buoyancy, normally resident in the race, forever eligible to be appeal'd to and relied on.

As for native American individuality, though certain to come, and on a large scale, the distinctive and ideal type of Western character (as consistent with the operative political and even money-making features of United States' humanity in the Nineteenth Century as chosen knights, gentlemen and warriors were the ideals of the centuries of European feudalism) it has not yet appear'd. I have allow'd the stress of my poems from beginning to end to bear upon American individuality and assist it— not only because that is a great lesson in Nature, amid all her generalizing laws, but as counterpoise to the leveling tendencies of Democracy—and for other reasons. Defiant of ostensible literary and other conventions, I avowedly chant 'the great pride of man in himself,' and permit it to be more or less a *motif* of nearly all my verse. I think this pride indispensable to an American. I think it not inconsistent with obedience, humility, deference, and self-questioning.

Democracy has been so retarded and jeopardized by powerful personalities, that its first instincts are fain to clip, conform, bring in stragglers, and reduce everything to a dead level. While the ambitious thought of my song is to help the forming of a great aggregate Nation, it is, perhaps, altogether through the forming of myriads of fully develop'd and enclosing individuals. Welcome as are equality's and fraternity's doctrines and popular education, a certain liability accompanies them all, as we see. That primal and interior something in man, in his soul's abysms, coloring all, and, by exceptional fruitions, giving the last majesty to him—something continually touch'd upon and attain'd by the old poems and ballads of feudalism, and often the principal foundation of them—modern science and democracy appear to be endangering, perhaps eliminating. But that forms an appearance only; the reality is quite different. The new influences, upon the whole, are surely preparing the way for grander individualities than ever. To-day and here personal force is behind everything, just the same. The times and depictions from the *Iliad* to Shakspere inclusive can happily never again be realized—but the elements of courageous and lofty manhood are unchanged.

Without yielding an inch the working-man and working-woman were to be in my pages from first to last. The ranges of heroism and loftiness with which Greek and feudal poets endow'd their god-like or lordly born characters—indeed prouder and better based and with fuller ranges than those—I was to endow the democratic averages of America. I was to show that we, here and to-day, are eligible to the grandest and the best—more eligible now than any times of old were. I will also want my utterances (I said to myself before beginning) to be in spirit the poems of the morning. (They have been founded and mainly written in the sunny forenoon and early midday of my life.) I will want them to be the poems of women entirely as much as men. I have wish'd to put the complete

Union of the States in my songs without any preference or partiality whatever. Henceforth, if they live and are read, it must be just as much South as North—just as much along the Pacific as Atlantic—in the valley of the Mississippi, in Canada, up in Maine, down in Texas, and on the shores of Puget Sound.

From another point of view *Leaves of Grass* is avowedly the song of Sex and Amativeness, and even Animality—though meanings that do not usually go along with those words are behind all, and will duly emerge; and all are sought to be lifted into a different light and atmosphere. Of this feature, intentionally palpable in a few lines, I shall only say the espousing principle of those lines so gives breath of life to my whole scheme that the bulk of the pieces might as well have been left unwritten were those lines omitted. Difficult as it will be, it has become, in my opinion, imperative to achieve a shifted attitude from superior men and women towards the thought and fact of sexuality, as an element in character, personality, the emotions, and a theme in literature. I am not going to argue the question by itself; it does not stand by itself. The vitality of it is altogether in its relations, bearings, significance—like the clef of a symphony. At last analogy the lines I allude to, and the spirit in which they are spoken, permeate all *Leaves of Grass*, and the work must stand or fall with them, as the human body and soul must remain as an entirety.

Universal as are certain facts and symptoms of communities or individuals all times, there is nothing so rare in modern conventions and poetry as their normal recognizance. Literature is always calling in the doctor for consultation and confession, and always giving evasions and swathing suppressions in place of that 'heroic nudity' [1] on which only a genuine diagnosis of serious cases can be built. And in respect to editions of *Leaves of Grass* in time to come (if there should be such) I take occasion now to confirm those lines with the settled convictions and deliberate renewals

---

1 'Nineteenth Century, July, 1883.' Author's note, ibid., 16. Whitman evidently refers to an article by W.C. Perry, 'The Sirens in Ancient Literature and Art,' in which various representations of the mythological Sirens are discussed.

of thirty years, and to hereby prohibit, as far as word of mine can do so, any elision of them.

Then still a purpose enclosing all, and over and beneath all. Ever since what might be call'd thought, or the budding of thought, fairly began in my youthful mind, I had had a desire to attempt some worthy record of that entire faith and acceptance ('to justify the ways of God to man' is Milton's well-known and ambitious phrase) which is the foundation of moral America. I felt it all as positively then in my young days as I do now in my old ones; to formulate a poem whose every thought or fact should directly or indirectly be or connive at an implicit belief in the wisdom, health, mystery, beauty of every process, every concrete object, every human or other existence, not only consider'd from the point of view of all, but of each.

While I cannot understand it or argue it out, I fully believe in a clue and purpose in Nature, entire and several; and that invisible spiritual results, just as real and definite as the visible, eventuate all concrete life and all materialism, through Time. My book ought to emanate buoyancy and gladness legitimately enough, for it was grown out of those elements, and has been the comfort of my life since it was originally commenced.

One main genesis-motive of the *Leaves* was my conviction (just as strong to-day as ever) that the crowning growth of the United States is to be spiritual and heroic. To help start and favor that growth—or even to call attention to it, or the need of it—is the beginning, middle and final purpose of the poems. (In fact, when really cipher'd out and summ'd to the last, plowing up in earnest the interminable average fallows of humanity—not 'good government' merely, in the common sense—is the justification and main purpose of these United States.)

Isolated advantages in any rank or grace or fortune—the direct or indirect threads of all the poetry of the past—are in my opinion distasteful to the republican genius, and offer no foundation for its fitting verse. Establish'd poems, I know, have the very great advantage of chanting the already perform'd, so full of glories, reminiscences dear to the minds of men. But my volume is a candidate for the future. 'All original art,' says Taine, anyhow, 'is self-regulated, and no original art can be regulated from without; it carries its own counterpoise, and does not receive it from elsewhere—lives on its own blood'—a solace to my frequent bruises and sulky vanity.

As the present is perhaps mainly an attempt at personal statement or illustration, I will allow myself as further help to extract the following anecdote from a book, *Annals of Old Painters*, conn'd by me in youth. Rubens, the Flemish painter, in one of his wanderings through the galleries of old convents, came across a singular work. After looking at it thoughtfully for a good while, and listening to the criticisms of his suite of students, he said to the latter, in answer to their questions (as to what school the work implied or belong'd,) 'I do not believe the artist, unknown and perhaps no longer living, who has given the world this legacy, ever belong'd to any school, or ever painted anything but this one picture, which is a personal affair—a piece out of a man's life.'

Leaves of Grass indeed (I cannot too often reiterate) has mainly been the outcropping of my own emotional and other personal nature—an attempt, from first to last, to put *a Person*, a human being (myself, in the latter half of the Nineteenth Century, in America,) freely, fully and truly on record. I could not find any similar personal record in current literature that satisfied me. But it is not on *Leaves of Grass* distinctively as *literature*, or a specimen thereof, that I feel to dwell, or advance claims. No one will get at my verses who insists upon viewing them as a literary performance, or attempt at such performance, or as aiming mainly toward art or æstheticism.

I say no land or people or circumstances ever existed so needing a race of singers and poems differing from all others, and rigidly their own, as the land and people and circumstances of our United States need such singers and poems to-day, and for the future. Still further, as long as the States continue to absorb and be dominated by the poetry of the Old World, and remain unsupplied with autochthonous song, to express, vitalize and give color to and define their material and political success, and minister to them distinctively, so long will they stop short of first-class Nationality and remain defective.

In the free evening of my day I give to you, reader, the foregoing garrulous talk, thoughts, reminiscences,

As idly drifting down the ebb,
Such ripples, half-caught voices, echo from
     the shore.

Concluding with two items for the imaginative genius of the West, when it worthily rises—First, what Herder taught to the young Goethe, that really great poetry is always (like the Homeric or Biblical canticles) the result of a national spirit, and not the privilege of a polish'd and select few; Second, that the strongest and sweetest songs yet remain to be sung.

                                        1888

FROM SPECIMEN DAYS
DIARY-JOTTINGS [1]

A Happy Hour's Command.
    Down in the Woods, July 2d, 1882.—If I do it at all I must delay no longer. Incongruous and full of skips and jumps as is that huddle of diary-jottings, war-memoranda of 1862-'65, Nature-notes of 1877-'81, with Western and Canadian observations afterwards, all bundled up and tied by a big string, the resolution and indeed mandate comes to me this day, this hour,—(and what a day! what an hour just passing! the luxury of riant grass and blowing breeze, with all the shows of sun and sky and perfect temperature, never before so filling me, body and soul),—to go home, untie the bundle, reel out diary-scraps and memoranda, just as they are, large or small, one after another, into print-pages,[2] and

let the melange's lackings and wants of connection take care of themselves. It will illustrate one phase of humanity anyhow; how few of life's days and hours (and they not by relative value or proportion, but by chance) are ever noted. Probably another point, too, how we give long preparations for some object, planning and delving and fashioning, and then, when the actual hour for doing arrives, find ourselves still quite unprepared, and tumble the thing together, letting hurry and crudeness tell the story better than fine work. At any rate I obey my happy hour's command, which seems curiously imperative. May-be, if I don't do anything else, I shall send out the most wayward, spontaneous, fragmentary book ever printed.

A Night Battle, Over a Week Since.
    May 12.—There was part of the late battle at Chancellorsville, (second Fredericksburgh,) a little over a week ago, Saturday, Saturday night and Sunday, under Gen. Joe Hooker, I would like to give just a glimpse of—(a moment's look in a terrible storm at sea—of which a few suggestions are enough, and full details impossible.) The fighting had been very hot during the day, and after an intermission the latter part, was resumed at night, and kept up with furious energy till 3 o'clock in the morning. That afternoon (Saturday) an attack sudden and strong by Stonewall Jackson had gain'd a great advantage to the southern army, and broken our lines, enter-

---

1 These impressionistic jottings are selections from the first section of Whitman's *Specimen Days and Collect* (Philadelphia, 1882–83). The title has been given by the editors.

2 '. . . Following, I give some gloomy experiences. The war of attempted secession has, of course, been the distinguishing event of my time. I commenced at the close of 1862, and continued steadily through '63, '64 and '65, to visit the sick and wounded of the army, both on the field and in the hospitals in and around Washington city. From the first I kept little note-books for impromptu jottings in pencil to refresh my memory of names and circumstances, and what was especially wanted, &c. In these, I brief'd cases, persons, sights,

occurrences in camp, by the bed-side, and not seldom by the corpses of the dead. Some were scratch'd down from narratives I heard and itemized while watching, or waiting, or tending somebody amid those scenes. . . . I leave them just as I threw them by after the war, blotch'd here and there with more than one bloodstain, hurriedly written, sometimes at the clinique, not seldom amid the excitement of uncertainty, or defeat, or of action, or getting ready for it, or a march. . . . Very different are most of the memoranda that follow. Some time after the war ended I had a paralytic stroke, which prostrated me for several years. In 1876 I began to get over the worst of it. From this date, portions of several seasons, especially summers, I spent at a secluded haunt down in Camden county, New Jersey— Timber creek, quite a little river (it enters from the great Delaware, twelve miles away)—with primitive solitudes, winding stream, recluse and woody banks, sweet-feeding springs, and all the charms that birds, grass, wild-flowers, rabbits and squirrels, old oaks, walnut trees, &c., can bring.' Author's note, *Specimen Days and Collect, Complete Prose Works*(Boston, 1898),1–2.

ing us like a wedge, and leaving things in that position at dark. But Hooker at 11 at night made a desperate push, drove the secesh forces back, restored his original lines, and resumed his plans. This night scrimmage was very exciting, and afforded countless strange and fearful pictures. The fighting had been general both at Chancellorsville and northeast at Fredericksburgh. (We hear of some poor fighting, episodes, skedaddling on our part. I think not of it. I think of the fierce bravery, the general rule.) One corps, the 6th, Sedgewick's, fights four dashing and bloody battles in thirty-six hours, retreating in great jeopardy, losing largely but maintaining itself, fighting with the sternest desperation under all circumstances, getting over the Rappahannock only by the skin of its teeth, yet getting over. It lost many, many brave men, yet it took vengeance, ample vengeance.

But it was the tug of Saturday evening, and through the night and Sunday morning, I wanted to make a special note of. It was largely in the woods, and quite a general engagement. The night was very pleasant, at times the moon shining out full and clear, all Nature so calm in itself, the early summer grass so rich, and foliage of the trees—yet there the battle raging, and many good fellows lying helpless, with new accessions to them, and every minute amid the rattle of muskets and crash of cannon, (for there was an artillery contest too,) the red life-blood oozing out from heads or trunks or limbs upon that green and dew-cool grass. Patches of the woods take fire, and several of the wounded, unable to move, are consumed—quite large spaces are swept over, burning the dead also—some of the men have their hair and beards singed—some, burns on their faces and hands—others holes burnt in their clothing. The flashes of fire from the cannon, the quick flaring flames and smoke, and the immense roar—the musketry so general, the light nearly bright enough for each side to see the other—the crashing, tramping of men—the yelling—close quarters—we hear the secesh yells—our men cheer loudly back, especially if Hooker is in sight—hand to hand conflicts, each side stands up to it, brave, determin'd as demons, they often charge upon us—a thousand deeds are done

worth to write newer greater poems on—and still the woods on fire—still many are not only scorch'd—too many, unable to move, are burn'd to death.

Then the camps of the wounded—O heavens, what scene is this?—is this indeed *humanity*—these butchers' shambles? There are several of them. There they lie, in the largest, in an open space in the woods, from 200 to 300 poor fellows—the groans and screams—the odor of blood, mixed with the fresh scent of the night, the grass, the trees—that slaughter-house! O well is it their mothers, their sisters cannot see them—cannot conceive, and never conceiv'd, these things. One man is shot by a shell, both in the arm and leg—both are amputated—there lie the rejected members. Some have their legs blown off—some bullets through the breast—some indescribably horrid wounds in the face or head, all mutilated, sickening, torn, gouged out—some in the abdomen—some mere boys—many rebels, badly hurt—they take their regular turns with the rest, just the same as any—the surgeons use them just the same. Such is the camp of the wounded —such a fragment, a reflection afar off of the bloody scene—while all over the clear, large moon comes out at times softly, quietly shining. Amid the woods, that scene of flitting souls—amid the crack and crash and yelling sounds—the impalpable perfume of the woods—and yet the pungent, stifling smoke—the radiance of the moon, looking from heaven at intervals so placid—the sky so heavenly—the clear-obscure up there, those buoyant upper oceans—a few large placid stars beyond, coming silently and languidly out, and then disappearing—the melancholy, draperied night above, around. And there, upon the roads, the fields, and in those woods, that contest, never one more desperate in any age or land—both parties now in force—masses—no fancy battle, no semi-play, but fierce and savage demons fighting there—courage and scorn of death the rule, exceptions almost none.

What history, I say, can ever give—for who can know—the mad, determin'd tussle of the armies, in all their separate large and little squads—as this—each steep'd from crown to toe in desperate, mortal purports? Who know the conflict, hand-to-hand—the many conflicts in the dark, those shadowy-tangled, flashing moonbeam'd woods—the writhing groups and squads—the cries, the din, the cracking guns and pistols—the distant cannon—the cheers and calls and threats and awful music of the oaths—the indescribable mix—the officers' orders, persuasions, encouragements—the devils fully rous'd in human hearts—the strong shout, *Charge, men, charge*—the flash of the naked sword, and rolling flame and smoke? And still the broken, clear and clouded heaven—and still again the moonlight pouring silvery soft its radiant patches over all. Who paint the scene, the sudden partial panic of the afternoon, at dusk? Who paint the irrepressible advance of the second division of the Third corps, under Hooker himself, suddenly order'd up—those rapid-filing phantoms through the woods? Who show what moves there in the shadows, fluid and firm—to save, (and it did save,) the army's name, perhaps the nation? as there the veterans hold the field. (Brave Berry falls not yet—but death has mark'd him—soon he falls.)

Unnamed Remains the Bravest Soldier.

Of scenes like these, I say, who writes—whoe'er can write the story? Of many a score—aye, thousands, north and south, of unwrit heroes, unknown heroisms, incredible, impromptu, first-class desperations—who tells? No history ever—no poem sings, no music sounds, those bravest men of all —those deeds. No formal general's report, nor book in the library, nor column in the paper, embalms the bravest, north or south, east or west. Unnamed, unknown, remain, and still remain, the bravest soldiers. Our manliest—our boys—our hardy darlings; no picture gives them. Likely, the typic one of them (standing, no doubt, for hundreds, thousands,) crawls aside to some bush-clump, or ferny tuft, on receiving his death-shot—there sheltering a little while, soaking roots, grass and soil, with red blood—the battle advances, retreats, flits from the scene, sweeps by—and there, haply with pain and suffering (yet less, far less, than is supposed,) the last lethargy winds like a serpent round him—the eyes glaze in death —none recks—perhaps the burial-squads, in truce, a week afterwards, search not the secluded spot—and there, at last, the Bravest Soldier crumbles in mother earth, unburied and unknown.

Some Specimen Cases.

June 18th.—In one of the hospitals I find Thomas Haley, company M, 4th New York cavalry—a regular Irish boy, a fine specimen of youthful physical manliness—shot through the lungs—inevitably dying—came over to this country from Ireland to enlist—has not a single friend or acquaintance here—is sleeping soundly at this moment, (but it is the sleep of death)—has a bullet-hole straight through the lung. I saw Tom when first brought here, three days since, and didn't suppose he could live twelve hours—(yet he looks well enough in the face to a casual observer). He lies there with his frame exposed above the waist, all naked, for coolness, a fine built man, the tan not yet bleach'd from his cheeks and neck. It is useless to talk to him, as with his sad hurt, and the stimulants they give him, and the utter strangeness of every object, face, furniture, &c., the poor fellow, even when awake, is like some frighten'd, shy animal. Much of the time he sleeps, or half sleeps. (Sometimes I thought he knew more than he show'd.) I often come and sit by him in perfect silence; he will breathe for ten minutes as softly and evenly as a young babe asleep. Poor youth, so handsome, athletic, with profuse beautiful shining hair. One time as I sat looking at him while he lay asleep, he suddenly, without the least start, awaken'd, open'd his eyes, gave me a long steady look, turning his face very slightly to gaze easier —one long, clear, silent look—a slight sigh—then turn'd back and went into his doze again. Little he knew, poor death-stricken boy, the heart of the stranger that hover'd near.

W.H.E., Co. F., 2nd N.J.—His disease is pneumonia. He lay sick at the wretched hospital below Aquia creek, for seven or eight days before brought here. He was detail'd from his regiment to go there and help as nurse, but was soon taken down himself. Is an elderly, sallow-faced, rather gaunt, gray-hair'd man, a widower, with children. He express'd a great desire for good, strong green tea. An excellent lady, Mrs. W., of Washington, soon sent him a package; also a small sum of money. The doctor said give him the tea at pleasure; it lay on the table by his side, and he used it every day. He slept a great deal; could not talk much, as he grew deaf. Occupied bed 15, ward I, Armory. (The same lady above, Mrs.W., sent the men a large package of tobacco.)

J.G. lies in bed 52, ward I; is of company B, 7th Pennsylvania. I gave him a small sum of money, some tobacco, and envelopes. To a man adjoining also gave twenty-five cents; he flush'd in the face when I offer'd it—refused at first, but as I found he had not a cent, and was very fond of having the daily papers to read, I prest it on him. He was evidently very grateful, but said little.

J.T.L., of company F., 9th New Hampshire, lies in bed 37, ward I. Is very fond of tobacco. I furnish him some; also with a little money. Has gangrene of the feet; a pretty bad case; will surely have to lose three toes. Is a regular specimen of an old-fashion'd, rude, hearty, New England countryman, impressing me with his likeness to that celebrated singed cat, who was better than she look'd.

Bed 3, ward E, Armory, has a great hankering for pickles, something pungent. After consulting the doctor, I gave him a small bottle of horse-radish; also some apples; also a book. Some of the nurses are excellent. The woman-nurse in this ward I like very much. (Mrs. Wright—a year afterwards I found her in Mansion house hospital, Alexandria—she is a perfect nurse.)

In one bed a young man, Marcus Small, company K, 7th Maine—sick with dysentery and typhoid fever—pretty critical case—I talk with him often—he thinks he will die—looks like it indeed. I write a letter for him home to East Livermore, Maine—I let him talk to me a little, but not much, advise him to keep very quiet—do most of the talking myself—stay quite a while with him, as he holds on to my hand —talk to him in a cheering, but slow, low and measured manner—talk about his furlough, and going home as soon as he is able to travel.

Thomas Lindly, 1st Pennsylvania cavalry, shot very badly through the foot— poor young man, he suffers horribly, has to be constantly dosed with morphine, his face ashy and glazed, bright young eyes—I give him a large handsome apple, lay it in sight, tell him to have it roasted in the morning, as he generally feels easier then, and can eat a little breakfast. I write two letters for him.

Opposite, an old Quaker lady sits by the side of her son, Amer Moore, 2d U.S. artillery—shot in the head two weeks since, very low, quite rational—from hips down paralyzed—he will surely die. I speak a very few words to him every day and evening—he answers pleasantly—wants nothing—(he told me soon after he came about his home affairs, his mother had been an invalid, and he fear'd to let her know his condition.) He died soon after she came.

Death of President Lincoln.

April 16, '65.—I find in my notes of the time, this passage on the death of Abraham Lincoln: He leaves for America's history and biography, so far, not only its most dramatic reminiscence—he leaves, in my opinion, the greatest, best, most characteristic, artistic, moral personality. Not but that he had faults, and show'd them in the Presidency; but honesty, goodness, shrewdness, conscience, and (a new virtue, unknown to other lands, and hardly yet really known here, but the foundation and tie of all, as the future will grandly develop,) UNIONISM, in its truest and amplest sense, form'd the hard-pan of his character. These he seal'd with his life. The tragic splendor of his death, purging, illuminating all, throws round his form, his head, an aureole that will remain and will grow brighter through time, while history lives, and love of country lasts. By many has this Union been help'd; but if one name, one man, must be pick'd out, he, most of all, is the conservator of it, to the future. He was assassinated—but the Union is not assassinated—*ça ira!* One falls and another falls. The soldier drops, sinks like a wave—but the ranks of the ocean eternally press on. Death does its work, obliterates a hundred, a thousand— President, general, captain, private,—but the Nation is immortal.

Three Years Summ'd Up.

During those three years in hospital, camp or field, I made over six hundred visits or tours, and went, as I estimate, counting all, among from eighty thousand to a hundred thousand of the wounded and sick, as sustainer of spirit and body in some degree, in time of need. These visits varied from an hour or two, to all day or night; for with dear or critical cases I generally watch'd all night. Sometimes I took up my quarters in the hospital, and slept or watch'd there several nights in succession. Those three years I consider the greatest privilege and satisfaction, (with all their feverish excitements and physical deprivations and lamentable sights), and, of course, the most profound lesson of my life. I can say that in my ministerings I comprehended all, whoever came in my way, northern or southern, and slighted none. It arous'd and brought out and decided undream'd-of depths of emotion. It has given me my most fervent views of the true ensemble and extent of the States. While I was with wounded and sick in thousands of cases from the New England States, and from New York, New Jersey, and Pennsylvania, and from Michigan, Wisconsin, Ohio, Indiana, Illinois, and all the Western States, I was with more or less from all the States, North and South, without exception. I was with many from the border States, especially from Maryland and Virginia, and found, during those lurid years 1862-63, far more Union southerners, especially Tennesseans, than is supposed. I was with many rebel officers and men among our wounded and gave them always what I had, and tried to cheer them the same as any. I was among the army teamsters considerably, and, indeed, always found myself drawn to them. Among the black soldiers, wounded or sick, and in the contraband camps, I also took my way whenever in their neighborhood, and did what I could for them.

The Million Dead, Too, Summ'd Up.

The dead in this war—there they lie, strewing the fields and woods and valleys and battlefields of the south—Virginia, the Peninsula—Malvern hill and Fair Oaks—the banks of the Chickahominy—the terraces of Fredericksburgh—Antietam bridge—the grisly ravines of Manassas—the bloody promenade of the Wilderness—the varieties of the *strayed*

dead, (the estimate of the War department is 25,000 national soldiers kill'd in battle and never buried at all, 5,000 drown'd—15,000 inhumed by strangers, or on the march in haste, in hitherto unfound localities—2,000 graves cover'd by sand and mud by Mississippi freshets, 3,000 carried away by caving-in of banks, &c.,)—Gettysburgh, the West, Southwest—Vicksburgh—Chattanooga—the trenches of Petersburgh—the numberless battles, camps, hospitals everywhere—the crop reap'd by the mighty reapers, typhoid, dysentery, inflammations—and blackest and loathesomest of all, the dead and living burial-pits, the prison-pens of Andersonville, Salisbury, Belle-Isle, &c., (not Dante's pictured hell and all its woes, its degradations, filthy torments, excell'd those prisons)—the dead, the dead, the dead—*our* dead—or South or North, ours all, (all, all, all, finally dear to me)—or East or West—Atlantic coast or Mississippi valley—somewhere they crawl'd to die, alone, in bushes, low gullies, or on the sides of hills—(there, in secluded spots, their skeletons, bleach'd bones, tufts of hair, buttons, fragments of clothing, are occasionally found yet)—our young men once so handsome and so joyous, taken from us—the son from the mother, the husband from the wife, the dear friend from the dear friend—the clusters of camp graves, in Georgia, the Carolinas, and in Tennessee—the single graves left in the woods or by the roadside, (hundreds, thousands, obliterated)—the corpses floated down the rivers, and caught and lodged, (dozens, scores, floated down the upper Potomac, after the cavalry engagements, the pursuit of Lee, following Gettysburgh)—some lie at the bottom of the sea—the general million, and the special cemeteries in almost all the States—the infinite dead—(the land entire saturated, perfumed with their impalpable ashes' exhalation in Nature's chemistry distill'd, and shall be so forever, in every future grain of wheat and ear of corn, and every flower that grows, and every breath we draw)—not only Northern dead leavening Southern soil—thousands, aye tens of thousands, of Southerners, crumble to-day in Northern earth.

And everywhere among these countless graves—everywhere in the many soldier

Cemeteries of the Nation, (there are now, I believe, over seventy of them)—as at the time in the vast trenches, the depositories of slain, Northern and Southern, after the great battles—not only where the scathing trail passed those years, but radiating since in all the peaceful quarters of the land—we see, and ages yet may see, on monuments and gravestones, singly or in masses, to thousands or tens of thousands, the signifi-cant word UNKNOWN.

(In some of the cemeteries nearly *all* the dead are unknown. At Salisbury, N.C., for instance, the known are only 85, while the unknown are 12,027, and 11,700 of these are buried in trenches. A national monu-ment has been put up here, by order of Congress, to mark the spot—but what vis-ible, material monument can ever fittingly commemorate that spot?)

The Real War Will Never Get in the Books.

And so good-bye to the war. I know not how it may have been, or may be, to others —to me the main interest I found, (and still, on recollection, find,) in the rank and file of the armies, both sides, and in those specimens amid the hospitals, and even the dead on the field. To me the points illus-trating the latent personal character and eligibilities of these States, in the two or three millions of American young and middle-aged men, North and South, em-bodied in those armies—and especially the one-third or one-fourth of their number, stricken by wounds or disease at some time in the course of the contest—were of more significance even than the political interests involved. (As so much of a race depends on how it faces death, and how it stands per-sonal anguish and sickness. As, in the glints of emotions under emergencies, and the indirect traits and asides in Plutarch, we get far profounder clues to the antique world than all its more formal history.) Future years will never know the seeth-ing hell and the black infernal background of countless minor scenes and interiors, (not the official surface-courteousness of the Generals, not the few great battles) of the Secession war; and it is best they should not—the real war will never get in the books. In the mushy influences of current times, too, the fervid atmosphere and typical events of those years are in danger of being totally forgotten. I have at night watch'd by the side of a sick man in the hos-pital, one who could not live many hours. I have seen his eyes flash and burn as he raised himself and recurr'd to the cruelties on his surrender'd brother, and mutilations of the corpse afterward. (See in the preced-ing pages, the incident at Upperville—the seventeen kill'd as in the description, were left there on the ground. After they dropt dead, no one touch'd them—all were made sure of, however. The carcasses were left for the citizens to bury or not, as they chose.)

Such was the war. It was not a quadrille in a ball-room. Its interior history will not only never be written—its practicality, minutiæ of deeds and passions, will never be even suggested. The actual soldier of 1862-'65, North and South, with all his ways, his incredible dauntlessness, habits, practices, tastes, language, his fierce friend-ship, his appetite, rankness, his superb strength and animality, lawless gait, and a hundred unnamed lights and shades of camp, I say, will never be written—perhaps must not and should not be.

The preceding notes may furnish a few stray glimpses into that life, and into those lurid interiors, never to be fully convey'd to the future. The hospital part of the drama from '61 to '65, deserves indeed to be recorded. Of that many-threaded drama, with its sudden and strange surprises, its confounding of prophecies, its moments of despair, the dread of foreign interference, the interminable campaigns, the bloody battles, the mighty and cumbrous and green armies, the drafts and bounties—the immense money expenditure, like a heavy-pouring constant rain—with, over the whole land, the last three years of the strug-gle, an unending, universal mourning-wail of women, parents, orphans—the marrow of the tragedy concentrated in those Army Hospitals—(it seem'd sometimes as if the whole interest of the land, North and South, was one vast central hospital, and all the rest of the affair but flanges)—those forming the untold and unwritten history of the war—infinitely greater (like life's) than the few scraps and distortions that are ever told or written. Think how much, and of importance, will be—how much, civic and military, has already been—buried in the grave, in eternal darkness.

An Interregnum Paragraph.

Several years now elapse before I resume my diary. I continued at Washington working in the Attorney-General's department through '66 and '67, and some time afterward. In February '73 I was stricken down by paralysis, gave up my desk, and migrated to Camden, New Jersey, where I lived during '74 and '75, quite unwell—but after that began to grow better; commenc'd going for weeks at a time, even for months, down in the country, to a charmingly recluse and rural spot along Timber creek, twelve or thirteen miles from where it enters the Delaware river. Domicil'd at the farm-house of my friends, the Staffords, near by, I lived half the time along this creek and its adjacent fields and lanes. And it is to my life here that I, perhaps, owe partial recovery (a sort of second wind, or semi-renewal of the lease of life) from the prostration of 1874–'75. If the notes of that outdoor life could only prove as glowing to you, reader dear, as the experience itself was to me. Doubtless in the course of the following, the fact of invalidism will crop out, (I call myself *a half-Paralytic* these days, and reverently bless the Lord it is no worse,) between some of the lines—but I get my share of fun and healthy hours, and shall try to indicate them. (The trick is, I find, to tone your wants and tastes low down enough, and make much of negatives, and of mere daylight and the skies.)

New Themes Entered Upon.

1876, '77.—I find the woods in mid-May and early June my best places for composition.[1] Seated on logs or stumps there, or resting on rails, nearly all the following memoranda have been jotted down. Wherever I go, indeed, winter or summer,

---

[1] 'Without apology for the abrupt change of field and atmosphere, . . . —temporary episodes, thank heaven! —I restore my book to the bracing and buoyant equilibrium of concrete outdoor Nature, the only permanent reliance for sanity of book or human life.

'Who knows, (I have it in my fancy, my ambition,) but the pages now ensuing may carry ray of sun, or smell of grass or corn, or call of bird, or gleam of stars by night, or snow-flakes falling fresh and mystic, to denizen of heated city house, or tired workman or workwoman?—or may-be in sick-room or prison—to serve as cooling breeze, or Nature's aroma, to some fever'd mouth or latent pulse.' Author's note, ibid., 75–76.

city or country, alone at home or traveling, I must take notes—(the ruling passion strong in age and disablement, and even the approach of—but I must not say it yet.) Then underneath the following excerpta—crossing the *t*'s and dotting the *i*'s of certain moderate movements of late years—I am fain to fancy the foundations of quite a lesson learn'd. After you have exhausted what there is in business, politics, conviviality, love, and so on—have found that none of these finally satisfy, or permanently wear—what remains? Nature remains; to bring out from their torpid recesses, the affinities of a man or woman with the open air, the trees, fields, the changes of seasons—the sun by day and the stars of heaven by night. We will begin from these convictions. Literature flies so high and is so hotly spiced, that our notes may seem hardly more than breaths of common air, or draughts of water to drink. But that is part of our lesson.

Dear, soothing, healthy, restoration-hours—after three confining years of paralysis—after the long strain of the war, and its wounds and death.

Summer Sights and Indolences.

June 10th.—As I write, 5½ P.M., here by the creek, nothing can exceed the quiet splendor and freshness around me. We had a heavy shower, with brief thunder and lightning, in the middle of the day; and since, overhead, one of those not uncommon yet indescribable skies (in quality, not details or forms) of limpid blue, with rolling silver-fringed clouds, and a pure-dazzling sun. For underlay, trees in fulness of tender foliage—liquid, reedy, long-drawn notes of birds—based by the fretful mewing of a querulous cat-bird, and the pleasant chippering-shriek of two kingfishers. I have been watching the latter the last half hour, on their regular evening frolic over and in the stream; evidently a spree of the liveliest kind. They pursue each other, whirling and wheeling around, with many a jocund downward dip, splashing the spray in jets of diamonds—and then off they swoop, with slanting wings and graceful flight, sometimes so near me I can plainly see their dark-gray feather-bodies and milk-white necks.

A July Afternoon by the Pond.

The fervent heat, but so much more endurable in this pure air—the white and pink pond-blossoms, with great heart-shaped leaves; the glassy waters of the creek, the banks, with dense bushery, and the picturesque beeches and shade and turf; the tremulous, reedy call of some bird from recesses, breaking the warm, indolent, half-voluptuous silence; an occasional wasp, hornet, honey-bee or bumble (they hover near my hands or face, yet annoy me not, nor I them, as they appear to examine, find nothing, and away they go)—the vast space of the sky overhead so clear, and the buzzard up there sailing his slow whirl in majestic spirals and discs; just over the surface of the pond, two large slate-color'd dragon-flies, with wings of lace, circling and darting and occasionally balancing themselves quite still, their wings quivering all the time, (are they not showing off for my amusement?)—the pond itself, with the sword-shaped calamus; the water snakes—occasionally a flitting blackbird, with red dabs on his shoulders, as he darts slantingly by—the sounds that bring out the solitude, warmth, light and shade—the quawk of some pond duck—(the crickets and grasshoppers are mute in the noon heat, but I hear the song of the first cicadas;)—then at some distance the rattle and whirr of a reaping machine as the horses draw it on a rapid walk through a rye field on the opposite side of the creek—(what was the yellow or light-brown bird, large as a young hen, with short neck and long-stretch'd legs I just saw, in flapping and awkward flight over there through the trees?)—the prevailing delicate, yet palpable, spicy, grassy, clovery perfume to my nostrils; and over all, encircling all, to my sight and soul, the free space of the sky, transparent and blue—and hovering there in the west, a mass of white-gray fleecy clouds the sailors call 'shoals of mackerel'—the sky, with silver swirls like locks of toss'd hair, spreading, expanding—a vast voiceless, formless simulacrum—yet maybe the most real reality and formulator of everything—who knows?

Autumn Side-Bits.

Sept. 20.—Under an old black oak, glossy and green, exhaling aroma—amid a grove the Albic druids might have chosen—envelop'd in the warmth and light of the noonday sun, and swarms of flitting insects—with the harsh cawing of many crows a hundred rods away—here I sit in solitude, absorbing, enjoying all. The corn, stack'd in its cone-shaped stacks, russet-color'd and sere—a large field spotted thick with scarlet-gold pumpkins—an adjoining one of cabbages, showing well in their green and pearl, mottled by much light and shade—melon patches, with their bulging ovals, and great silver-streak'd, ruffled, broad-edged leaves—and many an autumn sight and sound beside—the distant scream of a flock of guinea-hens—and pour'd over all the September breeze, with pensive cadence through the tree tops.

Another Day.—The ground in all directions strew'd with *débris* from a storm. Timber creek, as I slowly pace its banks, has ebb'd low, and shows reaction from the turbulent swell of the late equinoctial. As I look around, I take account of stock—weeds and shrubs, knolls, paths, occasional stumps, some with smooth'd tops, (several I use as seats of rest, from place to place, and from one I am now jotting these lines,)—frequent wild-flowers, little white, star-shaped things, or the cardinal red of the lobelia, or the cherry-ball seeds of the perennial rose, or the many-threaded vines winding up and around trunks of trees.

Oct. 1, 2 *and* 3.—Down every day in the solitude of the creek. A serene autumn sun and westerly breeze to-day (3d) as I sit here, the water surface prettily moving in wind-ripples before me. On a stout old beech at the edge, decayed and slanting, almost fallen to the stream, yet with life and leaves in its mossy limbs, a gray squirrel, exploring, runs up and down, flirts his tail, leaps to the ground, sits on his haunches upright as he sees me, (a Darwinian hint?) and then races up the tree again.

Oct. 4.—Cloudy and coolish; signs of incipient winter. Yet pleasant here, the leaves thick-falling, the ground brown with them already; rich coloring, yellows of all hues, pale and dark-green, shades from lightest to richest red—all set in and toned down by the prevailing brown of the earth and gray of the sky. So, winter is coming; and I yet in my sickness. I sit here amid all these fair sights and vital influences, and abandon myself to that thought, with its wandering trains of speculation.

The Sky—Days and Nights—Happiness.

Oct. 20.—A clear, crispy day—dry and breezy air, full of oxygen. Out of the sane, silent, beauteous miracles that envelope and fuse me—trees, water, grass, sunlight, and early frost—the one I am looking at most to-day is the sky. It has that delicate, trans-parent blue, peculiar to autumn, and the only clouds are little or larger white ones, giving their still and spiritual motion to the great concave. All through the earlier day (say from 7 to 11) it keeps a pure, yet vivid blue. But as noon approaches the color gets lighter, quite gray for two or three hours—then still paler for a spell, till sun-down—which last I watch dazzling through the interstices of a knoll of big trees—darts of fire and a gorgeous show of light-yellow, liver-color and red, with a vast silver glaze askant on the water—the transparent shadows, shafts, sparkle, and vivid colors beyond all the paintings ever made.

I don't know what or how, but it seems to me mostly owing to these skies, (every now and then I think, while I have of course seen them every day of my life, I never really saw the skies before,) I have had this autumn some wondrously con-tented hours—may I not say perfectly happy ones? As I've read, Byron just before his death told a friend that he had known but three happy hours during his whole existence. Then there is the old German legend of the king's bell, to the same point. While I was out there by the wood, that beautiful sunset through the trees, I thought of Byron's and the bell story, and the notion started in me that I was having a happy hour. (Though perhaps my best moments I never jot down; when they come I cannot afford to break the charm by inditing memoranda. I just abandon my-self to the mood, and let it float on, carrying me in its placid extasy.)

What is happiness, anyhow? Is this one of its hours, or the like of it?—so impal-pable—a mere breath, an evanescent tinge? I am not sure—so let me give myself the benefit of the doubt. Hast Thou, pellu-cid, in Thy azure depths, medicine for case like mine? (Ah, the physical shatter and troubled spirit of me the last three years.) And dost Thou subtly mystically now drip it through the air invisibly upon me?

Night of Oct. 28.—The heavens unusually transparent—the stars out by myriads—the great path of the Milky Way, with its branch, only seen of very clear nights—Jupiter, setting in the west, looks like a huge hap-hazard splash, and has a little star for companion.

Clothed in his white garments,
Into the round and clear arena slowly
    entered the brahmin,
Holding a little child by the hand,
Like the moon with the planet Jupiter in a
    cloudless night-sky.
                    Old Hindu Poem.

Early in November.—At its farther end the lane already described opens into a broad grassy upland field of over twenty acres, slightly sloping to the south. Here I am accustom'd to walk for sky views and effects, either morning or sundown. To-day from this field my soul is calm'd and ex-panded beyond description, the whole fore-noon by the clear blue arching over all, cloudless, nothing particular, only sky and daylight. Their soothing accompaniments, autumn leaves, the cool dry air, the faint aroma—crows cawing in the distance—two great buzzards wheeling gracefully and slowly far up there—the occasional mur-mur of the wind, sometimes quite gently, then threatening through the trees—a gang of farm-laborers loading corn-stalks in a field in sight, and the patient horses wait-ing.

Colors—A Contrast.

Such a play of colors and lights, different seasons, different hours of the day—the lines of the far horizon where the faint-tinged edge of the landscape loses itself in the sky. As I slowly hobble up the lane toward day-close, an incomparable sunset shooting in molten sapphire and gold, shaft after shaft, through the ranks of the long-leaved corn, between me and the west.

Another day.—The rich dark green of the tulip-trees and the oaks, the gray of the swamp-willows, the dull hues of the syca-mores and black-walnuts, the emerald of the cedars (after rain,) and the light yellow of the beeches.

Sea-Shore Fancies.

Even as a boy, I had the fancy, the wish, to write a piece, perhaps a poem, about the sea-shore—that suggesting, dividing line, contact, junction, the solid marrying the liquid—that curious, lurking something, (as doubtless every objective form finally becomes to the subjective spirit,) which means far more than its mere first sight, grand as that is—blending the real and ideal, and each made portion of the other. Hours, days, in my Long Island youth and early manhood, I haunted the shores of Rockaway or Coney island, or away east to the Hamptons or Montauk. Once, at the latter place, (by the old lighthouse, nothing but sea-tossings in sight in every direction as far as the eye could reach,) I remember well, I felt that I must one day write a book expressing this liquid, mystic theme. Afterward, I recollect, how it came to me that instead of any special lyrical or epical or literary attempt, the sea-shore should be an invisible *influence*, a pervading gauge and tally for me, in my composition. (Let me give a hint here to young writers. I am not sure but I have unwittingly follow'd out the same rule with other powers besides sea and shores—avoiding them, in the way of any dead set at poetizing them, as too big for formal handling—quite satisfied if I could indirectly show that we have met and fused, even if only once, but enough—that we have really absorb'd each other and understand each other.)

There is a dream, a picture, that for years at intervals, (sometimes quite long ones, but surely again, in time,) has come noiselessly up before me, and I really believe, fiction as it is, has enter'd largely into my practical life—certainly into my writings, and shaped and color'd them. It is nothing more or less than a stretch of interminable white-brown sand, hard and smooth and broad, with the ocean perpetually, grandly, rolling in upon it, with slow-measured sweep, with rustle and hiss and foam, and many a thump as of low bass drums. This scene, this picture, I say, has risen before me at times for years. Sometimes I wake at night and can hear and see it plainly.

An Hour on Kenosha Summit.

Jottings from the Rocky Mountains, mostly pencill'd during a day's trip over the South Park R.R., returning from Leadville, and especially the hour we were detain'd, (much to my satisfaction,) at Kenosha summit. As afternoon advances, novelties, far-reaching splendors, accumulate under the bright sun in this pure air. But I had better commence with the day.

The confronting of Platte cañon just at dawn, after a ten miles' ride in early darkness on the rail from Denver—the seasonable stoppage at the entrance of the cañon, and good breakfast of eggs, trout, and nice griddle-cakes—then as we travel on, and get well in the gorge, all the wonders, beauty, savage power of the scene—the wild stream of water, from sources of snows, brawling continually in sight one side—the dazzling sun, and the morning lights on the rocks—such turns and grades in the track, squirming around corners, or up and down hills—far glimpses of a hundred peaks, titanic necklaces, stretching north and south—the huge rightly-named Dome-rock—and as we dash along, others similar, simple, monolithic, elephantine.

An Egotistical 'Find.'

'I have found the law of my own poems,' was the unspoken but more-and-more decided feeling that came to me as I pass'd, hour after hour, amid all this grim yet joyous elemental abandon—this plenitude of material, entire absence of art, untrammel'd play of primitive Nature—the chasm, the gorge, the crystal mountain stream, repeated scores, hundreds of miles—the broad handling and absolute uncrampedness—the fantastic forms, bathed in transparent browns, faint reds and grays, towering sometimes a thousand, sometimes two or three thousand feet high—at their tops now and then huge masses pois'd, and mixing with the clouds, with only their outlines, hazed in misty lilac, visible. ('In Nature's grandest shows,' says an old Dutch writer, an ecclesiastic, 'amid the ocean's depth, if so might be, or countless worlds rolling above at night, a man thinks of them, weighs all, not for themselves or the abstract, but with reference to his own personality, and how they may affect him or color his destinies.')

New Senses: New Joys.

We follow the stream of amber and bronze brawling along its bed, with its frequent cascades and snow-white foam. Through the cañon we fly—mountains not only each side, but seemingly, till we get near, right in front of us—every rood a new view flashing, and each flash defying description—on the almost perpendicular sides, clinging pines, cedars, spruces, crimson sumach bushes, spots of wild grass—but dominating all, those towering rocks, rocks, rocks, bathed in delicate vari-colors, with the clear sky of autumn overhead. New senses, new joys, seem develop'd. Talk as you like, a typical Rocky Mountain cañon, or a limitless sea-like stretch of the great Kansas or Colorado plains, under favoring circumstances, tallies, perhaps expresses, certainly awakes, those grandest and subtlest element-emotions in the human soul, that all the marble temples and sculptures from Phidias to Thorwaldsen—all paintings, poems, reminiscences, or even music, probably never can.

After Trying a Certain Book.

I tried to read a beautifully printed and scholarly volume on 'the Theory of Poetry,' received by mail this morning from England—but gave it up at last for a bad job. Here are some capricious pencillings that follow'd, as I find them in my notes:

In youth and maturity Poems are charged with sunshine and varied pomp of day; but as the soul more and more takes precedence, (the sensuous still included,) the Dusk becomes the poet's atmosphere. I too have sought, and ever seek, the brilliant sun, and make my songs according. But as I grow old, the half-lights of evening are far more to me.

The play of Imagination, with the sensuous objects of Nature for symbols and Faith—with Love and Pride as the unseen impetus and moving-power of all, make up the curious chess-game of a poem.

Common teachers or critics are always asking 'What does it mean?' Symphony of fine musician, or sunset, or sea-waves rolling up the beach—what do they mean? Undoubtedly in the most subtle-elusive sense they mean something—as love does, and religion does, and the best poem;—but who shall fathom and define those meanings? (I do not intend this as a warrant for wildness and frantic escapades—but to justify the soul's frequent joy in what cannot be defined to the intellectual part, or to calculation.)

At its best, poetic lore is like what may be heard of conversation in the dusk, from speakers far or hid, of which we get only a few broken murmurs. What is not gather'd is far more—perhaps the main thing.

Grandest poetic passages are only to be taken at free removes, as we sometimes look for stars at night, not by gazing directly toward them, but off one side.

(*To a poetic student and friend.*)—I only seek to put you in rapport. Your own brain, heart, evolution, must not only understand the matter, but largely supply it.

Final Confessions—Literary Tests.

So draw near their end these garrulous notes. There have doubtless occurr'd some repetitions, technical errors in the consecutiveness of dates, in the minutiæ of botanical, astronomical, &c., exactness, and perhaps elsewhere;—for in gathering up, writing, peremptorily dispatching copy, this hot weather, (last of July and through August, '82,) and delaying not the printers, I have had to hurry along, no time to spare. But in the deepest veracity of all—in reflections of objects, scenes, Nature's outpourings, to my senses and receptivity, as they seem'd to me—in the work of giving those who care for it, some authentic glints, specimen-days of my life—and in the *bona fide* spirit and relations, from author to reader, on all the subjects design'd, and as far as they go, I feel to make unmitigated claims.

The synopsis of my early life, Long Island, New York city, and so forth, and the diary-jottings in the Secession war, tell their own story. My plan in starting what constitutes most of the middle of the book, was originally for hints and data of a Nature-poem that should carry one's experiences a few hours, commencing at noon-flush, and so through the after-part of the day—I suppose led to such idea by my own life-afternoon now arrived. But I soon found I could move at more ease, by giving the narrative at first hand. (Then there is a humiliating lesson one learns, in serene hours, of a fine day or night. Nature seems to look on all fixed-up poetry and art as something almost impertinent.)

Thus I went on, years following, various seasons and areas, spinning forth my thought beneath the night and stars, (or as I was confined to my room by half-sickness,) or at midday looking out upon the sea, or far north steaming over the Saguenay's black breast, jotting all down in the loosest sort of chronological order, and here printing from my impromptu notes, hardly even the seasons group'd together, or anything corrected—so afraid of dropping what smack of outdoors or sun or starlight might cling to the lines, I dared not try to meddle with or smooth them. Every now and then, (not often, but for a foil,) I carried a book in my pocket—or perhaps tore out from some broken or cheap edition a bunch of loose leaves; most always had something of the sort ready, but only took it out when the mood demanded. In that way, utterly out of reach of literary conventions, I re-read many authors.

I cannot divest my appetite of literature, yet I find myself eventually trying it all by Nature—*first premises* many call it, but really the crowning results of all, laws, tallies and proofs. (Has it never occur'd to any one how the last deciding tests applicable to a book are entirely outside of technical and grammatical ones, and that any truly first-class production has little or nothing to do with the rules and calibres of ordinary critics? or the bloodless chalk of Allibone's Dictionary? I have fancied the ocean and the daylight, the mountain and the forest, putting their spirit in a judgment on our books. I have fancied some disembodied human soul giving its verdict.)

Nature and Democracy—Morality.

Democracy most of all affiliates with the open air, is sunny and hardy and sane only with Nature—just as much as Art is. Something is required to temper both—to check them, restrain them from excess, morbidity. I have wanted, before departure, to bear special testimony to a very old lesson and requisite. American Democracy, in its myriad personalities, in factories, workshops, stores, offices—through the dense streets and houses of cities, and all their manifold sophisticated life—must either be fibred, vitalized, by regular contact with out-door light and air and growths, farm-scenes, animals, fields, trees, birds, sun-warmth and free skies, or it will certainly dwindle and pale. We cannot have grand races of mechanics, work people, and commonalty, (the only specific purpose of America,) on any less terms. I conceive of no flourishing and heroic elements of Democracy in the United States, or of Democracy maintaining itself at all, without the Nature-element forming a main part—to be its health-element and beauty-element—to really underlie the whole politics, sanity, religion and art of the New World.

Finally, the morality: 'Virtue,' said Marcus Aurelius, 'what is it, only a living and enthusiastic sympathy with Nature?' Perhaps indeed the efforts of the true poets, founders, religions, literatures, all ages, have been, and ever will be, our time and times to come, essentially the same—to bring people back from their persistent strayings and sickly abstractions, to the costless average, divine, original concrete.

1882–1883

ONE'S–SELF I SING

ONE'S-SELF I sing, a simple separate person,
Yet utter the word Democratic, the word En-Masse.

Of physiology from top to toe I sing,
Not physiognomy alone nor brain alone is worthy for the Muse, I say the Form complete is
    worthier far,
The Female equally with the Male I sing.

Of Life immense in passion, pulse, and power,
Cheerful, for freest action form'd under the laws divine,
The Modern Man I sing.

1867

I HEAR AMERICA SINGING

I HEAR America singing, the varied carols I hear,
Those of mechanics, each one singing his as it should be blithe and strong,
The carpenter singing his as he measures his plank or beam,
The mason singing his as he makes ready for work, or leaves off work,
The boatman singing what belongs to him in his boat, the deck-hand singing on the
        steamboat deck,
The shoemaker singing as he sits on his bench, the hatter singing as he stands,
The wood-cutter's song, the ploughboy's on his way in the morning, or at noon intermission
        or at sundown,
The delicious singing of the mother, or of the young wife at work, or of the girl sewing or
        washing,
Each singing what belongs to him or her and to none else,
The day what belongs to the day—at night the party of young fellows, robust, friendly,   10
Singing with open mouths their strong melodious songs.

1860

SONG OF MYSELF

1

I CELEBRATE myself, and sing myself,
And what I assume you shall assume,
For every atom belonging to me as good belongs to you.

I loafe and invite my soul,
I lean and loafe at my ease observing a spear of summer grass.

My tongue, every atom of my blood, form'd from this soil, this air,
Born here of parents born here from parents the same, and their parents the same,
I, now thirty-seven years old in perfect health begin,
Hoping to cease not till death.

Creeds and schools in abeyance,   10
Retiring back a while sufficed at what they are, but never forgotten,
I harbor for good or bad, I permit to speak at every hazard,
Nature without check with original energy.

2

Houses and rooms are full of perfumes, the shelves are crowded with perfumes,
I breathe the fragrance myself and know it and like it,
The distillation would intoxicate me also, but I shall not let it.

The atmosphere is not a perfume, it has no taste of the distillation, it is odorless,
It is for my mouth forever, I am in love with it,
I will go to the bank by the wood and become undisguised and naked,
I am mad for it to be in contact with me.   20

The smoke of my own breath,
Echoes, ripples, buzz'd whispers, love-root, silk-thread, crotch and vine,
My respiration and inspiration, the beating of my heart, the passing of blood and air through
        my lungs,
The sniff of green leaves and dry leaves, and of the shore and dark-color'd sea-rocks, and of
        hay in the barn,
The sound of the belch'd words of my voice loos'd to the eddies of the wind,

A few light kisses, a few embraces, a reaching around of arms,
The play of shine and shade on the trees as the supple boughs wag,
The delight alone or in the rush of the streets, or along the fields and hill-sides,
The feeling of health, the full-noon trill, the song of me rising from bed and meeting the
    sun.

Have you reckon'd a thousand acres much? have you reckon'd the earth much?   30
Have you practis'd so long to learn to read?
Have you felt so proud to get at the meaning of poems?

Stop this day and night with me and you shall possess the origin of all poems,
You shall possess the good of the earth and sun, (there are millions of suns left,)
You shall no longer take things at second or third hand, nor look through the eyes of the dead,
    nor feed on the spectres in books,
You shall not look through my eyes either, nor take things from me,
You shall listen to all sides and filter them from your self.

3

I have heard what the talkers were talking, the talk of the beginning and the end,
But I do not talk of the beginning or the end.

There was never any more inception than there is now,   40
Nor any more youth or age than there is now,
And will never be any more perfection than there is now,
Nor any more heaven or hell than there is now.

Urge and urge and urge,
Always the procreant urge of the world.
Out of the dimness opposite equals advance, always substance and increase, always sex,
Always a knit of identity, always distinction, always a breed of life.

To elaborate is no avail, learn'd and unlearn'd feel that it is so.

Sure as the most certain sure, plumb in the uprights, well entretied, braced in the beams,
Stout as a horse, affectionate, haughty, electrical,   50
I and this mystery here we stand.

Clear and sweet is my soul, and clear and sweet is all that is not my soul.

Lack one lacks both, and the unseen is proved by the seen,
Till that becomes unseen and receives proof in its turn.

Showing the best and dividing it from the worst age vexes age,
Knowing the perfect fitness and equanimity of things, while they discuss I am silent, and go
    bathe and admire myself.

Welcome is every organ and attribute of me, and of any man hearty and clean,
Not an inch nor a particle of an inch is vile, and none shall be less familiar than the rest.

I am satisfied—I see, dance, laugh, sing;
As the hugging and loving bed-fellow sleeps at my side through the night, and withdraws at
    the peep of the day with stealthy tread,   60
Leaving me baskets cover'd with white towels swelling the house with their plenty,
Shall I postpone my acceptation and realization and scream at my eyes,
That they turn from gazing after and down the road,

And forthwith cipher and show me to a cent,
Exactly the value of one and exactly the value of two, and which is ahead?

4

Trippers and askers surround me,
People I meet, the effect upon me of my early life or the ward and city I live in, or the nation,
The latest dates, discoveries, inventions, societies, authors old and new,
My dinner, dress, associates, looks, compliments, dues,
The real or fancied indifference of some man or woman I love,
The sickness of one of my folks or of myself, or ill-doing or loss or lack of money, or
        depressions or exaltations,
Battles, the horrors of fratricidal war, the fever of doubtful news, the fitful events;
These come to me days and nights and go from me again,
But they are not the Me myself.

Apart from the pulling and hauling stands what I am,
Stands amused, complacent, compassionating, idle, unitary,
Looks down, is erect, or bends an arm on an impalpable certain rest,
Looking with side-curved head curious what will come next,
Both in and out of the game and watching and wondering at it.

Backward I see in my own days where I sweated through fog with linguists and contenders, 80
I have no mockings or arguments, I witness and wait.

5

I believe in you my soul, the other I am must not abase itself to you,
And you must not be abased to the other.

Loafe with me on the grass, loose the stop from your throat,
Not words, not music or rhyme I want, not custom or lecture, not even the best,
Only the lull I like, the hum of your valvèd voice.

I mind how once we lay such a transparent summer morning,
How you settled your head athwart my hips and gently turn'd over upon me,
And parted the shirt from my bosom-bone, and plunged your tongue to my bare-stript heart,
And reach'd till you felt my beard, and reach'd till you held my feet. 90

Swiftly arose and spread around me the peace and knowledge that pass all the argument of the
        earth,
And I know that the hand of God is the promise of my own,
And I know that the spirit of God is the brother of my own,
And that all the men ever born are also my brothers, and the women my sisters and lovers,
And that a kelson of the creation is love,
And limitless are leaves stiff or drooping in the fields,
And brown ants in the little wells beneath them,
And mossy scabs of the worm fence, heap'd stones, elder, mullein and poke-weed.

6

A child said *What is the grass?* fetching it to me with full hands,
How could I answer the child? I do not know what it is any more than he. 100

I guess it must be the flag of my disposition, out of hopeful green stuff woven.

Or I guess it is the handkerchief of the Lord,
A scented gift and remembrancer designedly dropt,

Bearing the owner's name someway in the corners, that we may see and remark, and say
    Whose?

Or I guess the grass is itself a child, the produced babe of the vegetation.

Or I guess it is a uniform hieroglyphic,
And it means, Sprouting alike in broad zones and narrow zones,
Growing among black folks as among white,
Kanuck, Tuckahoe, Congressman, Cuff, I give them the same, I receive them the same.

And now it seems to me the beautiful uncut hair of graves.   110

Tenderly will I use you curling grass,
It may be you transpire from the breasts of young men,
It may be if I had known them I would have loved them,
It may be you are from old people, or from offspring taken soon out of their mothers' laps,
And here you are the mothers' laps.

This grass is very dark to be from the white heads of old mothers,
Darker than the colorless beards of old men,
Dark to come from under the faint red roofs of mouths.
O I perceive after all so many uttering tongues,
And I perceive they do not come from the roofs of mouths for nothing.   120

I wish I could translate the hints about the dead young men and women,
And the hints about old men and mothers, and the offspring taken soon out of their laps.

What do you think has become of the young and old men?
And what do you think has become of the women and children?

They are alive and well somewhere,
The smallest sprout shows there is really no death,
And if ever there was it led forward life, and does not wait at the end to arrest it,
And ceas'd the moment life appear'd.

All goes onward and outward, nothing collapses,
And to die is different from what any one supposed, and luckier.   130

7

Has any one supposed it lucky to be born?
I hasten to inform him or her it is just as lucky to die, and I know it.

I pass death with the dying and birth with the new-wash'd babe, and am not contain'd between
    my hat and boots,
And peruse manifold objects, no two alike and every one good,
The earth good and the stars good, and their adjuncts all good.

I am not an earth nor an adjunct of an earth,
I am the mate and companion of people, all just as immortal and fathomless as myself,
(They do not know how immortal, but I know.)

Every kind for itself and its own, for me mine male and female,
For me those that have been boys and that love women,
For me the man that is proud and feels how it stings to be slighted,
For me the sweet-heart and the old maid, for me mothers and the mothers of mothers,   140

For me lips that have smiled, eyes that have shed tears,
For me children and the begetters of children.

Undrape! you are not guilty to me, nor stale nor discarded,
I see through the broadcloth and gingham whether or no,
And am around, tenacious, acquisitive, tireless, and cannot be shaken away.

8

The little one sleeps in its cradle,
I lift the gauze and look a long time, and silently brush away flies with my hand.

The youngster and the red-faced girl turn aside up the bushy hill,   150
I peeringly view them from the top.

The suicide sprawls on the bloody floor of the bedroom,
I witness the corpse with its dabbled hair, I note where the pistol has fallen.

The blab of the pave, tires of carts, sluff of boot-soles, talk of the promenaders,
The heavy omnibus, the driver with his interrogating thumb, the clank of the shod horses on
      the granite floor,
The snow-sleighs, clinking, shouted jokes, pelts of snow-balls,
The hurrahs for popular favorites, the fury of rous'd mobs,
The flap of the curtain'd litter, a sick man inside borne to the hospital,
The meeting of enemies, the sudden oath, the blows and fall,
The excited crowd, the policeman with his star quickly working his passage to the centre
      of the crowd,   160
The impassive stones that receive and return so many echoes,
What groans of over-fed or half-starv'd who fall sunstruck or in fits,
What exclamations of women taken suddenly who hurry home and give birth to babes,
What living and buried speech is always vibrating here, what howls restrain'd by decorum,
Arrests of criminals, slights, adulterous offers made, acceptances, rejections with convex lips,
I mind them or the show or resonance of them—I come and I depart.

9

The big doors of the country barn stand open and ready,
The dried grass of the harvest-time loads the slow-drawn wagon,
The clear light plays on the brown gray and green intertinged,
The armfuls are pack'd to the sagging mow.   170

I am there, I help, I came stretch'd atop of the load,
I felt its soft jolts, one leg reclined on the other,
I jump from the cross-beams and seize the clover and timothy,
And roll head over heels and tangle my hair full of wisps.

10

Alone far in the wilds and mountains I hunt,
Wandering amazed at my own lightness and glee,
In the late afternoon choosing a safe spot to pass the night,
Kindling a fire and broiling the fresh-kill'd game,
Falling asleep on the gather'd leaves with my dog and gun by my side.

The Yankee clipper is under her sky-sails, she cuts the sparkle and scud,   180
My eyes settle the land, I bend at her prow or shout joyously from the deck.

The boatmen and clam-diggers arose early and stopt for me,
I tuck'd my trowser-ends in my boots and went and had a good time;
You should have been with us that day round the chowder-kettle.

I saw the marriage of the trapper in the open air in the far west, the bride was a red girl,
Her father and his friends sat near cross-legged and dumbly smoking, they had moccasins to
    their feet and large thick blankets hanging from their shoulders,
On a bank lounged the trapper, he was drest mostly in skins, his luxuriant beard and curls
    protected his neck, he held his bride by the hand,
She had long eyelashes, her head was bare, her coarse straight locks descended upon her
    voluptuous limbs and reach'd to her feet.

The runaway slave came to my house and stopt outside,
I heard his motions crackling the twigs of the woodpile,   190
Through the swung half-door of the kitchen I saw him limpsy and weak,
And went where he sat on a log and led him in and assured him,
And brought water and fill'd a tub for his sweated body and bruis'd feet,
And gave him a room that enter'd from my own, and gave him some coarse clean clothes,
And remember perfectly well his revolving eyes and his awkwardness,
And remember putting plasters on the galls of his neck and ankles;
He staid with me a week before he was recuperated and pass'd north,
I had him sit next me at table, my fire-lock lean'd in the corner.

11

Twenty-eight young men bathe by the shore,
Twenty-eight young men and all so friendly;   2co
Twenty-eight years of womanly life and all so lonesome.

She owns the fine house by the rise of the bank,
She hides handsome and richly drest aft the blinds of the window.

Which of the young men does she like the best?
Ah the homeliest of them is beautiful to her.

Where are you off to, lady? for I see you,
You splash in the water there, yet stay stock still in your room.

Dancing and laughing along the beach came the twenty-ninth bather,
The rest did not see her, but she saw them and loved them.

The beards of the young men glisten'd with wet, it ran from their long hair,   210
Little streams pass'd all over their bodies.

An unseen hand also pass'd over their bodies,
It descended tremblingly from their temples and ribs.

The young men float on their backs, their white bellies bulge to the sun, they do not ask who
    seizes fast to them,
They do not know who puffs and declines with pendant and bending arch,
They do not think whom they souse with spray.

12

The butcher-boy puts off his killing-clothes, or sharpens his knife at the stall in the
    market,
I loiter enjoying his repartee and his shuffle and break-down.

Blacksmiths with grimed and hairy chests environ the anvil,
Each has his main-sledge, they are all out, there is a great heat in the fire.   220

From the cinder-strew'd threshold I follow their movements,
The lithe sheer of their waists plays even with their massive arms,
Overhand the hammers swing, overhand so slow, overhand so sure,
They do not hasten, each man hits in his place.

13

The negro holds firmly the reins of his four horses, the block swags underneath on its tied-over chain,
The negro that drives the long dray of the stone-yard, steady and tall he stands pois'd on one leg on the string-piece,
His blue shirt exposes his ample neck and breast and loosens over his hip-band,
His glance is calm and commanding, he tosses the slouch of his hat away from his forehead,
The sun falls on his crispy hair and mustache, falls on the black of his polish'd and perfect limbs.

I behold the picturesque giant and love him, and I do not stop there,   230
I go with the team also.

In me the caresser of life wherever moving, backward as well as forward sluing,
To niches aside and junior bending, not a person or object missing,
Absorbing all to myself and for this song.

Oxen that rattle the yoke and chain or halt in the leafy shade, what is that you express in your eyes?
It seems to me more than all the print I have read in my life.

My tread scares the wood-drake and wood-duck on my distant and day-long ramble,
They rise together, they slowly circle around.

I believe in those wing'd purposes,
And acknowledge red, yellow, white, playing within me,   240
And consider green and violet and the tufted crown intentional,
And do not call the tortoise unworthy because she is not something else,
And the jay in the woods never studied the gamut, yet trills pretty well to me,
And the look of the bay mare shames silliness out of me.

14

The wild gander leads his flock through the cool night,
Ya-honk he says, and sounds it down to me like an invitation,
The pert may suppose it meaningless, but I listening close,
Find its purpose and place up there toward the wintry sky.

The sharp-hoof'd moose of the north, the cat on the house-sill, the chickadee, the prairie-dog,
The litter of the grunting sow as they tug at her teats,
The brood of the turkey-hen and she with her half-spread wings,
I see in them and myself the same old law.

The press of my foot to the earth springs a hundred affections,
They scorn the best I can do to relate them.

I am enamour'd of growing out-doors,
Of men that live among cattle or taste of the ocean or woods,

Of the builders and steerers of ships and the wielders of axes and mauls, and the drivers of
      horses,
I can eat and sleep with them week in and week out.

What is commonest, cheapest, nearest, easiest, is Me,
Me going in for my chances, spending for vast returns, 260
Adorning myself to bestow myself on the first that will take me,
Not asking the sky to come down to my good will,
Scattering it freely forever.

15

The pure contralto sings in the organ loft,
The carpenter dresses his plank, the tongue of his foreplane whistles its wild ascending lisp,
The married and unmarried children ride home to their Thanksgiving dinner,
The pilot seizes the king-pin, he heaves down with a strong arm,
The mate stands braced in the whale-boat, lance and harpoon are ready,
The duck-shooter walks by silent and cautious stretches,
The deacons are ordain'd with cross'd hands at the altar, 270
The spinning-girl retreats and advances to the hum of the big wheel,
The farmer stops by the bars as he walks on a First-day loafe and looks at the oats and rye,
The lunatic is carried at last to the asylum a confirm'd case,
(He will never sleep any more as he did in the cot in his mother's bed-room;)
The jour printer with gray head and gaunt jaws works at his case,
He turns his quid of tobacco while his eyes blurr with the manuscript;
The malform'd limbs are tied to the surgeon's table,
What is removed drops horribly in a pail;
The quadroon girl is sold at the auction-stand, the drunkard nods by the bar-room stove,
The machinist rolls up his sleeves, the policeman travels his beat, the gate-keeper marks who
      pass, 280
The young fellow drives the express-wagon, (I love him, though I do not know him;)
The half-breed straps on his light boots to compete in the race,
The western turkey-shooting draws old and young, some lean on their rifles, some sit on logs,
Out from the crowd steps the marksman, takes his position, levels his piece;
The groups of newly-come immigrants cover the wharf or levee,
As the woolly-pates hoe in the sugar-field, the overseer views them from his saddle,
The bugle calls in the ball-room, the gentlemen run for their partners, the dancers bow to each
      other,
The youth lies awake in the cedar-roof'd garret and harks to the musical rain,
The Wolverine sets traps on the creek that helps fill the Huron,
The squaw wrapt in her yellow-hemm'd cloth is offering moccasins and bead-bags for sale,
The connoisseur peers along the exhibition-gallery with half-shut eyes bent sideways, 291
As the deck-hands make fast the steamboat the plank is thrown for the shore-going
      passengers,
The young sister holds out the skein while the elder sister winds it off in a ball, and stops now
      and then for the knots,
The one-year wife is recovering and happy having a week ago borne her first child,
The clean-hair'd Yankee girl works with her sewing-machine or in the factory or mill,
The paving-man leans on his two-handed rammer, the reporter's lead flies swiftly over the
      note-book, the sign-painter is lettering with blue and gold,
The canal boy trots on the tow-path, the book-keeper counts at his desk, the shoemaker waxes
      his thread,
The conductor beats time for the band and all the performers follow him,
The child is baptized, the convert is making his first professions,
The regatta is spread on the bay, the race is begun, (how the white sails sparkle!) 300
The drover watching his drove sings out to them that would stray,

The pedler sweats with his pack on his back, (the purchaser higgling about the odd cent;)
The bride unrumples her white dress, the minute-hand of the clock moves slowly,
The opium-eater reclines with rigid head and just-open'd lips,
The prostitute draggles her shawl, her bonnet bobs on her tipsy and pimpled neck,
The crowd laugh at her blackguard oaths, the men jeer and wink to each other,
(Miserable! I do not laugh at your oaths nor jeer you;)
The President holding a cabinet council is surrounded by the great Secretaries,
On the piazza walk three matrons stately and friendly with twined arms,
The crew of the fish-smack pack repeated layers of halibut in the hold,   310
The Missourian crosses the plains toting his wares and his cattle,
As the fare-collector goes through the train he gives notice by the jingling of loose change,
The floor-men are laying the floor, the tinners are tinning the roof, the masons are calling for mortar,
In single file each shouldering his hod pass onward the laborers;
Seasons pursuing each other the indescribable crowd is gather'd, it is the fourth of Seventh-month, (what salutes of cannon and small arms!)
Seasons pursuing each other the plougher ploughs, the mower mows, and the winter-grain falls in the ground;
Off on the lakes the pike-fisher watches and waits by the hole in the frozen surface,
The stumps stand thick round the clearing, the squatter strikes deep with his axe,
Flatboatmen make fast towards dusk near the cotton-wood or pecan-trees,
Coon-seekers go through the regions of the Red river or through those drain'd by the Tennessee, or through those of the Arkansas,   320
Torches shine in the dark that hangs on the Chattahooche or Altamahaw,
Patriarchs sit at supper with sons and grandsons and great grandsons around them,
In walls of adobie, in canvas tents, rest hunters and trappers after their day's sport,
The city sleeps and the country sleeps,
The living sleep for their time, the dead sleep for their time,
The old husband sleeps by his wife and the young husband sleeps by his wife;
And these tend inward to me, and I tend outward to them,
And such as it is to be of these more or less I am,
And of these one and all I weave the song of myself.

16

I am of old and young, of the foolish as much as the wise,   330
Regardless of others, ever regardful of others,
Maternal as well as paternal, a child as well as a man,
Stuff'd with the stuff that is coarse and stuff'd with the stuff that is fine,
One of the Nation of many nations, the smallest the same and the largest the same,
A Southerner soon as a Northerner, a planter nonchalant and hospitable down by the Oconee I live,
A Yankee bound my own way ready for trade, my joints the limberest joints on earth and the sternest joints on earth,
A Kentuckian walking the vale of the Elkhorn in my deer-skin leggings, a Louisianian or Georgian,
A boatman over lakes or bays or along coasts, a Hoosier, Badger, Buckeye;
At home on Kanadian snow-shoes or up in the bush, or with fishermen off Newfoundland,
At home in the fleet of ice-boats, sailing with the rest and tacking,   340
At home on the hills of Vermont or in the woods of Maine, or the Texan ranch,
Comrade of Californians, comrade of free North-Westerners, (loving their big proportions,)
Comrade of raftsmen and coalmen, comrade of all who shake hands and welcome to drink and meat,
A learner with the simplest, a teacher of the thoughtfullest,
A novice beginning yet experient of myriads of seasons,
Of every hue and caste am I, of every rank and religion,

A farmer, mechanic, artist, gentleman, sailor, quaker,
Prisoner, fancy-man, rowdy, lawyer, physician, priest.

I resist any thing better than my own diversity,
Breathe the air but leave plenty after me, 350
And am not stuck up, and am in my place.

(The moth and the fish-eggs are in their place,
The bright suns I see and the dark suns I cannot see are in their place,
The palpable is in its place and the impalpable is in its place.)

17

These are really the thoughts of all men in all ages and lands, they are not original with me,
If they are not yours as much as mine they are nothing, or next to nothing,
If they are not the riddle and the untying of the riddle they are nothing,
If they are not just as close as they are distant they are nothing.

This is the grass that grows wherever the land is and the water is,
This the common air that bathes the globe. 360

18

With music strong I come, with my cornets and my drums,
I play not marches for accepted victors only, I play marches for conquer'd and slain persons.

Have you heard that it was good to gain the day?
I also say it is good to fall, battles are lost in the same spirit in which they are won.

I beat and pound for the dead,
I blow through my embouchures my loudest and gayest for them.

Vivas to those who have fail'd!
And to those whose war-vessels sank in the sea!
And to those themselves who sank in the sea!
And to all generals that lost engagements, and all overcome heroes! 370
And the numberless unknown heroes equal to the greatest heroes known!

19

This is the meal equally set, this the meat for natural hunger,
It is for the wicked just the same as the righteous, I make appointments with all,
I will not have a single person slighted or left away,
The kept-woman, sponger, thief, are hereby invited,
The heavy-lipp'd slave is invited, the venerealee is invited;
There shall be no difference between them and the rest.

This is the press of a bashful hand, this the float and odor of hair,
This the touch of my lips to yours, this the murmur of yearning,
This the far-off depth and height reflecting my own face, 380
This the thoughtful merge of myself, and the outlet again.

Do you guess I have some intricate purpose?
Well I have, for the Fourth-month showers have, and the mica on the side of a rock has.

Do you take it I would astonish?
Does the daylight astonish? does the early redstart twittering through the woods?
Do I astonish more than they?

This hour I tell things in confidence,
I might not tell everybody, but I will tell you.

20

Who goes there? hankering, gross, mystical, nude;
How is it I extract strength from the beef I eat?   390

What is a man anyhow? what am I? what are you?

All I mark as my own you shall offset it with your own,
Else it were time lost listening to me.

I do not snivel that snivel the world over,
That months are vacuums and the ground but wallow and filth.

Whimpering and truckling fold with powders for invalids, conformity goes to the fourth-
      remov'd,
I wear my hat as I please indoors or out.

Why should I pray? why should I venerate and be ceremonious?

Having pried through the strata, analyzed to a hair, counsel'd with doctors and calculated close,
I find no sweeter fat than sticks to my own bones.   400

In all people I see myself, none more and not one a barley-corn less,
And the good or bad I say of myself I say of them.

I know I am solid and sound,
To me the converging objects of the universe perpetually flow,
All are written to me, and I must get what the writing means.

I know I am deathless,
I know this orbit of mine cannot be swept by a carpenter's compass,
I know I shall not pass like a child's carlacue cut with a burnt stick at night.

I know I am august,
I do not trouble my spirit to vindicate itself or be understood,   410
I see that the elementary laws never apologize,
(I reckon I behave no prouder than the level I plant my house by, after all.)

I exist as I am, that is enough,
If no other in the world be aware I sit content,
And if each and all be aware I sit content.

One world is aware and by far the largest to me, and that is myself,
And whether I come to my own to-day or in ten thousand or ten million years,
I can cheerfully take it now, or with equal cheerfulness I can wait.

My foothold is tenon'd and mortis'd in granite,
I laugh at what you call dissolution,   420
And I know the amplitude of time.

21

I am the poet of the Body and I am the poet of the Soul,
The pleasures of heaven are with me and the pains of hell are with me,

The first I graft and increase upon myself, the latter I translate into a new tongue.

I am the poet of the woman the same as the man,
And I say it is as great to be a woman as to be a man,
And I say there is nothing greater than the mother of men.

I chant the chant of dilation or pride,
We have had ducking and deprecating about enough,
I show that size is only development.   430

Have you outstript the rest? are you the President?
It is a trifle, they will more than arrive there every one, and still pass on.

I am he that walks with the tender and growing night,
I call to the earth and sea half-held by the night.

Press close bare-bosom'd night—press close magnetic nourishing night!
Night of south winds—night of the large few stars!
Still nodding night—mad naked summer night.

Smile O voluptuous cool-breath'd earth!
Earth of the slumbering and liquid trees!
Earth of departed sunset—earth of the mountains misty-topt!
Earth of the vitreous pour of the full moon just tinged with blue!   440
Earth of shine and dark mottling the tide of the river!
Earth of the limpid gray of clouds brighter and clearer for my sake!
Far-swooping elbow'd earth—rich apple-blossom'd earth!
Smile, for your lover comes.

Prodigal, you have given me love—therefore I to you give love!
O unspeakable passionate love.

                                   22

You sea! I resign myself to you also—I guess what you mean,
I behold from the beach your crooked inviting fingers,
I believe you refuse to go back without feeling of me,
We must have a turn together, I undress, hurry me out of sight of the land,
Cushion me soft, rock me in billowy drowse,
Dash me with amorous wet, I can repay you.

Sea of stretch'd ground-swells,
Sea breathing broad and convulsive breaths,
Sea of the brine of life and of unshovell'd yet always-ready graves,
Howler and scooper of storms, capricious and dainty sea,
I am integral with you, I too am of one phase and of all phases.

Partaker of influx and efflux I, extoller of hate and conciliation,
Extoller of amies and those that sleep in each others' arms.

I am he attesting sympathy,
(Shall I make my list of things in the house and skip the house that supports them?)

I am not the poet of goodness only, I do not decline to be the poet of wickedness also.

What blurt is this about virtue and about vice?

Evil propels me and reform of evil propels me, I stand indifferent,
My gait is no fault-finder's or rejecter's gait,
I moisten the roots of all that has grown.

Did you fear some scrofula out of the unflagging pregnancy?
Did you guess the celestial laws are yet to be work'd over and rectified?

I find one side a balance and the antipodal side a balance,
Soft doctrine as steady help as stable doctrine,
Thoughts and deeds of the present our rouse and early start.

This minute that comes to me over the past decillions,
There is no better than it and now.

What behaved well in the past or behaves well to-day is not such a wonder,
The wonder is always and always how there can be a mean man or an infidel.

23

Endless unfolding of words of ages!
And mine a word of the modern, the word En-Masse.

A word of the faith that never balks,
Here or henceforward it is all the same to me, I accept Time absolutely.   48c

It alone is without flaw, it alone rounds and completes all,
That mystic baffling wonder alone completes all.

I accept Reality and dare not question it,
Materialism first and last imbuing.

Hurrah for positive science! long live exact demonstration!
Fetch stonecrop mixt with cedar and branches of lilac,
This is the lexicographer, this the chemist, this made a grammar of the old cartouches,
These mariners put the ship through dangerous unknown seas,
This is the geologist, this works with the scalpel, and this is a mathematician.

Gentlemen, to you the first honors always!   490
Your facts are useful, and yet they are not my dwelling,
I but enter by them to an area of my dwelling.

Less the reminders of properties told my words,
And more the reminders they of life untold, and of freedom and extrication,
And make short account of neuters and geldings, and favor men and women fully equipt.
And beat the gong of revolt, and stop with fugitives and them that plot and conspire.

24

Walt Whitman, a kosmos, of Manhattan the son,
Turbulent, fleshy, sensual, eating, drinking and breeding,
No sentimentalist, no stander above men and women or apart from them,
No more modest than immodest.   500

Unscrew the locks from the doors!
Unscrew the doors themselves from their jambs!

Whoever degrades another degrades me,
And whatever is done or said returns at last to me.

Through me the afflatus surging and surging, through me the current and index.

I speak the pass-word primeval, I give the sign of democracy,
By God! I will accept nothing which all cannot have their counterpart of on the same terms.

Through me many long dumb voices,
Voices of the interminable generations of prisoners and slaves,
Voices of the diseas'd and despairing and of thieves and dwarfs,   510
Voices of cycles of preparation and accretion,
And of the threads that connect the stars, and of wombs and of the father-stuff,
And of the rights of them the others are down upon,
Of the deform'd, trivial, flat, foolish, despised,
Fog in the air, beetles rolling balls of dung.

Through me forbidden voices,
Voices of sexes and lusts, voices veil'd and I remove the veil,
Voices indecent by me clarified and transfigur'd.

I do not press my fingers across my mouth,
I keep as delicate around the bowels as around the head and heart,   520
Copulation is no more rank to me than death is.

I believe in the flesh and the appetites,
Seeing, hearing, feeling, are miracles, and each part and tag of me is a miracle.

Divine am I inside and out, and I make holy whatever I touch or am touch'd from,
The scent of these arm-pits aroma finer than prayer,
This head more than churches, bibles, and all the creeds.

If I worship one thing more than another it shall be the spread of my own body, or any part of it,
Translucent mould of me it shall be you!
Shaded ledges and rests it shall be you!
Firm masculine colter it shall be you!   530
Whatever goes to the tilth of me it shall be you!
You my rich blood! your milky stream pale strippings of my life!
Breast that presses against other breasts it shall be you!
My brain it shall be your occult convolutions!
Root of wash'd sweet-flag! timorous pond-snipe! nest of guarded duplicate eggs! it shall be
      you!
Mix'd tussled hay of head, beard, brawn, it shall be you!
Trickling sap of maple, fibre of manly wheat, it shall be you!
Sun so generous it shall be you!
Vapors lighting and shading my face it shall be you!
You sweaty brooks and dews it shall be you!   540
Winds whose soft-tickling genitals rub against me it shall be you!
Broad muscular fields, branches of live oak, loving lounger in my winding paths, it shall be you!
Hands I have taken, face I have kiss'd, mortal I have ever touch'd, it shall be you.

I dote on myself, there is that lot of me and all so luscious,
Each moment and whatever happens thrills me with joy,
I cannot tell how my ankles bend, nor whence the cause of my faintest wish,
Nor the cause of the friendship I emit, nor the cause of the friendship I take again.

That I walk up my stoop, I pause to consider if it really be,
A morning-glory at my window satisfies me more than the metaphysics of books.

To behold the day-break!   55c
The little light fades the immense and diaphanous shadows,
The air tastes good to my palate.

Hefts of the moving world at innocent gambols silently rising, freshly exuding,
Scooting obliquely high and low.

Something I cannot see puts upward libidinous prongs,
Seas of bright juice suffuse heaven.

The earth by the sky staid with, the daily close of their junction,
The heav'd challenge from the east that moment over my head,
The mocking taunt, See then whether you shall be master!

25

Dazzling and tremendous how quick the sun-rise would kill me,   56c
If I could not now and always send sun-rise out of me.

We also ascend dazzling and tremendous as the sun,
We found our own O my soul in the calm and cool of the daybreak.

My voice goes after what my eyes cannot reach,
With the twirl of my tongue I encompass worlds and volumes of worlds.

Speech is the twin of my vision, it is unequal to measure itself,
It provokes me forever, it says sarcastically,
Walt you contain enough, why don't you let it out then?

Come now I will not be tantalized, you conceive too much of articulation,
Do you not know O speech how the buds beneath you are folded?   57c
Waiting in gloom, protected by frost,
The dirt receding before my prophetical screams,
I underlying causes to balance them at last,
My knowledge my live parts, it keeping tally with the meaning of all things,
Happiness, (which whoever hears me let him or her set out in search of this day.)

My final merit I refuse you, I refuse putting from me what I really am,
Encompass worlds, but never try to encompass me,
I crowd your sleekest and best by simply looking toward you.

Writing and talk do not prove me,
I carry the plenum of proof and every thing else in my face,   58c
With the hush of my lips I wholly confound the skeptic.

26

Now I will do nothing but listen,
To accrue what I hear into this song, to let sounds contribute toward it.

I hear bravuras of birds, bustle of growing wheat, gossip of flames, clack of sticks cooking my
      meals.
I hear the sound I love, the sound of the human voice,
I hear all sounds running together, combined, fused or following,

Sounds of the city and sounds out of the city, sounds of the day and night,
Talkative young ones to those that like them, the loud laugh of work-people at their meals,
The angry base of disjointed friendship, the faint tones of the sick,
The judge with hands tight to the desk, his pallid lips pronouncing a death-sentence,   590
The heave'e'yo of stevedores unlading ships by the wharves, the refrain of the anchor-lifters,
The ring of alarm-bells, the cry of fire, the whirr of swift-streaking engines and hose-carts with
    premonitory tinkles and color'd lights,
The steam-whistle, the solid roll of the train of approaching cars,
The slow march play'd at the head of the association marching two and two,
(They go to guard some corpse, the flag-tops are draped with black muslin.)

I hear the violoncello, ('tis the young man's heart's complaint,)
I hear the key'd cornet, it glides quickly in through my ears,
It shakes mad-sweet pangs through my belly and breast.

I hear the chorus, it is a grand opera,
Ah this indeed is music—this suits me.   600

A tenor large and fresh as the creation fills me,
The orbic flex of his mouth is pouring and filling me full.

I hear the train'd soprano (what work with hers is this?)
The orchestra whirls me wider than Uranus flies,
It wrenches such ardors from me I did not know I possess'd them,
It sails me, I dab with bare feet, they are lick'd by the indolent waves,
I am cut by bitter and angry hail, I lose my breath,
Steep'd amid honey'd morphine, my windpipe throttled in fakes of death,
At length let up again to feel the puzzle of puzzles,
And that we call Being.   610

27

To be in any form, what is that?
(Round and round we go, all of us, and ever come back thither,)
If nothing lay more develop'd the quahaug in its callous shell were enough.

Mine is no callous shell,
I have instant conductors all over me whether I pass or stop,
They seize every object and lead it harmlessly through me.

I merely stir, press, feel with my fingers, and am happy,
To touch my person to some one else's is about as much as I can stand.

28

Is this then a touch? quivering me to a new identity,
Flames and ether making a rush for my veins,   620
Treacherous tip of me reaching and crowding to help them,
My flesh and blood playing out lightning to strike what is hardly different from myself,
On all sides prurient provokers stiffening my limbs,
Straining the udder of my heart for its withheld drip,
Behaving licentious toward me, taking no denial,
Depriving me of my best as for a purpose,
Unbuttoning my clothes, holding me by the bare waist,
Deluding my confusion with the calm of the sunlight and pasture-fields,
Immodestly sliding the fellow-senses away,
They bribed to swap off with touch and go and graze at the edges of me,   630
No consideration, no regard for my draining strength or my anger.

Fetching the rest of the herd around to enjoy them a while,
Then all uniting to stand on a headland and worry me.

The sentries desert every other part of me,
They have left me helpless to a red marauder,
They all come to the headland to witness and assist against me.

I am given up by traitors,
I talk wildly, I have lost my wits, I and nobody else am the greatest traitor,
I went myself first to the headland, my own hands carried me there.

You villain touch! what are you doing? my breath is tight in its throat,   640
Unclench your floodgates, you are too much for me.

29

Blind loving wrestling touch, sheath'd hooded sharp-tooth'd touch!
Did it make you ache so, leaving me?

Parting track'd by arriving, perpetual payment of perpetual loan,
Rich showering rain, and recompense richer afterward.

Sprouts take and accumulate, stand by the curb prolific and vital,
Landscapes projected masculine, full-sized and golden.

30

All truths wait in all things,
They neither hasten their own delivery nor resist it,
They do not need the obstetric forceps of the surgeon,   650
The insignificant is as big to me as any,
(What is less or more than a touch?)

Logic and sermons never convince,
The damp of the night drives deeper into my soul.

(Only what proves itself to every man and woman is so,
Only what nobody denies is so.)

A minute and a drop of me settle my brain,
I believe the soggy clods shall become lovers and lamps,
And a compend of compends is the meat of a man or woman,
And a summit and flower there is the feeling they have for each other,   660
And they are to branch boundlessly out of that lesson until it becomes omnific,
And until one and all shall delight us, and we them.

31

I believe a leaf of grass is no less than the journey-work of the stars,
And the pismire is equally perfect, and a grain of sand, and the egg of the wren,
And the tree-toad is a chef-d'œuvre for the highest,
And the running blackberry would adorn the parlors of heaven,
And the narrowest hinge in my hand puts to scorn all machinery,
And the cow crunching with depress'd head surpasses any statue,
And a mouse is miracle enough to stagger sextillions of infidels.

I find I incorporate gneiss, coal, long-threaded moss, fruits, grains, esculent roots,   670
And am stucco'd with quadrupeds and birds all over,

And have distanced what is behind me for good reasons,
But call any thing back again when I desire it.

In vain the speeding or shyness,
In vain the plutonic rocks send their old heat against my approach,
In vain the mastodon retreats beneath its own powder'd bones,
In vain objects stand leagues off and assume manifold shapes,
In vain the ocean settling in hollows and the great monsters lying low,
In vain the buzzard houses herself with the sky,
In vain the snake slides through the creepers and logs,   580
In vain the elk takes to the inner passes of the woods,
In vain the razor-bill'd auk sails far north to Labrador,
I follow quickly, I ascend to the nest in the fissure of the cliff.

32

I think I could turn and live with animals, they're so placid and self-contain'd,
I stand and look at them long and long.

They do not sweat and whine about their condition,
They do not lie awake in the dark and weep for their sins,
They do not make me sick discussing their duty to God,
Not one is dissatisfied, not one is demented with the mania of owning things,
Not one kneels to another, nor to his kind that lived thousands of years ago,   590
Not one is respectable or unhappy over the whole earth.

So they show their relations to me and I accept them,
They bring me tokens of myself, they evince them plainly in their possession.

I wonder where they get those tokens,
Did I pass that way huge times ago and negligently drop them?

Myself moving forward then and now and forever,
Gathering and showing more always and with velocity,
Infinite and omnigenous, and the like of these among them,
Not too exclusive toward the reachers of my remembrancers,
Picking out here one that I love, and now go with him on brotherly terms.   700

A gigantic beauty of a stallion, fresh and responsive to my caresses,
Head high in the forehead, wide between the ears,
Limbs glossy and supple, tail dusting the ground,
Eyes full of sparkling wickedness, ears finely cut, flexibly moving.

His nostrils dilate as my heels embrace him,
His well-built limbs tremble with pleasure as we race around and return.

I but use you a minute, then I resign you, stallion,
Why do I need your paces when I myself out-gallop them?
Even as I stand or sit passing faster than you.

33

Space and Time! now I see it is true, what I guess'd at,
What I guess'd when I loaf'd on the grass,
What I guess'd while I lay alone in my bed,
And again as I walk'd the beach under the paling stars of the morning.

My ties and ballasts leave me, my elbows rest in sea-gaps,
I skirt sierras, my palms cover continents,
I am afoot with my vision.

By the city's quadrangular houses—in log huts, camping with lumbermen,
Along the ruts of the turnpike, along the dry gulch and rivulet bed,
Weeding my onion-patch or hoeing rows of carrots and parsnips, crossing savannas, trailing
    in forests,
Prospecting, gold-digging, girdling the trees of a new purchase,   720
Scorch'd ankle-deep by the hot sand, hauling my boat down the shallow river,
Where the panther walks to and fro on a limb overhead, where the buck turns furiously at the
    hunter,
Where the rattlesnake suns his flabby length on a rock, where the otter is feeding on fish,
Where the alligator in his tough pimples sleeps by the bayou,
Where the black bear is searching for roots or honey, where the beaver pats the mud with his
    paddle-shaped tail;
Over the growing sugar, over the yellow-flower'd cotton plant, over the rice in its low moist
    field,
Over the sharp-peak'd farm house, with its scallop'd scum and slender shoots from the
    gutters,
Over the western persimmon, over the long-leav'd corn, over the delicate blue-flower flax,
Over the white and brown buckwheat, a hummer and buzzer there with the rest,
Over the dusky green of the rye as it ripples and shades in the breeze;   730
Scaling mountains, pulling myself cautiously up, holding on by low scragged limbs,
Walking the path worn in the grass and beat through the leaves of the brush,
Where the quail is whistling betwixt the woods and the wheat-lot,
Where the bat flies in the Seventh-month eve, where the great gold-bug drops through the
    dark,
Where the brook puts out of the roots of the old tree and flows to the meadow,
Where cattle stand and shake away flies with the tremulous shuddering of their hides,
Where the cheese-cloth hangs in the kitchen, where andirons straddle the hearth-slab, where
    cobwebs fall in festoons from the rafters;
Where trip-hammers crash, where the press is whirling its cylinders,
Where the human heart beats with terrible throes under its ribs,
Where the pear-shaped balloon is floating aloft, (floating in it myself and looking composedly
    down,)   740
Where the life-car is drawn on the slip-noose, where the heat hatches pale-green eggs in the
    dented sand,
Where the she-whale swims with her calf and never forsakes it,
Where the steam-ship trails hind-ways its long pennant of smoke,
Where the fin of the shark cuts like a black chip out of the water,
Where the half-burn'd brig is riding on unknown currents,
Where shells grow to her slimy deck, where the dead are corrupting below;
Where the dense-starr'd flag is borne at the head of the regiments,
Approaching Manhattan up by the long-stretching island,
Under Niagara, the cataract falling like a veil over my countenance,
Upon a door-step, upon the horse-block of hard wood outside,   750
Upon the race-course, or enjoying picnics or jigs or a good game of base-ball,
At he-festivals, with blackguard gibes, ironical license, bull-dances, drinking, laughter,
At the cider-mill tasting the sweets of the brown mash, sucking the juice through a straw,
At apple-peelings wanting kisses for all the red fruit I find,
At musters, beach-parties, friendly bees, huskings, house-raisings;
Where the mocking-bird sounds his delicious gurgles, cackles, screams, weeps,
Where the hay-rick stands in the barn-yard, where the dry-stalks are scatter'd, where the
    brood-cow waits in the hovel,

Where the bull advances to do his masculine work, where the stud to the mare, where the cock
    is treading the hen,
Where the heifers browse, where geese nip their food with short jerks,
Where sun-down shadows lengthen over the limitless and lonesome prairie,   760
Where herds of buffalo make a crawling spread of the square miles far and near,
Where the humming-bird shimmers, where the neck of the long-lived swan is curving and
    winding,
Where the laughing-gull scoots by the shore, where she laughs her near-human laugh,
Where bee-hives range on a gray bench in the garden half hid by the high weeds,
Where band-neck'd partridges roost in a ring on the ground with their heads out,
Where burial coaches enter the arch'd gates of a cemetery,
Where winter wolves bark amid wastes of snow and icicled trees,
Where the yellow-crown'd heron comes to the edge of the marsh at night and feeds upon
    small crabs,
Where the splash of swimmers and divers cools the warm noon,
Where the katy-did works her chromatic reed on the walnut-tree over the well,   770
Through patches of citrons and cucumbers with silver-wired leaves,
Through the salt-lick or orange glade, or under conical firs,
Through the gymnasium, through the curtain'd saloon, through the office or public
    hall;
Pleas'd with the native and pleas'd with the foreign, pleas'd with the new and old,
Pleas'd with the homely woman as well as the handsome,
Pleas'd with the quakeress as she puts off her bonnet and talks melodiously,
Pleas'd with the tune of the choir of the whitewash'd church,
Pleas'd with the earnest words of the sweating Methodist preacher, impress'd seriously at the
    camp-meeting;
Looking in at the shop-windows of Broadway the whole forenoon, flatting the flesh of my
    nose on the thick plate glass,
Wandering the same afternoon with my face turn'd up to the clouds, or down a lane or along
    the beach,   780
My right and left arms round the sides of two friends, and I in the middle;
Coming home with the silent and dark-cheek'd bush-boy, (behind me he rides at the drape of
    the day,)
Far from the settlements studying the print of animals' feet, or the moccasin print,
By the cot in the hospital reaching lemonade to a feverish patient,
Nigh the coffin'd corpse when all is still, examining with a candle;
Voyaging to every port to dicker and adventure,
Hurrying with the modern crowd as eager and fickle as any,
Hot toward one I hate, ready in my madness to knife him,
Solitary at midnight in my back yard, my thoughts gone from me a long while,
Walking the old hills of Judæa with the beautiful gentle God by my side,   790
Speeding through space, speeding through heaven and the stars,
Speeding amid the seven satellites and the broad ring, and the diameter of eighty thousand
    miles,
Speeding with tail'd meteors, throwing fire-balls like the rest,
Carrying the crescent child that carries its own full mother in its belly,
Storming, enjoying, planning, loving, cautioning,
Backing and filling, appearing and disappearing,
I tread day and night such roads.

I visit the orchards of spheres and look at the product,
And look at quintillions ripen'd and look at quintillions green.

I fly those flights of a fluid and swallowing soul,   800
My course runs below the soundings of plummets.

I help myself to material and immaterial,
No guard can shut me off, no law prevent me.

I anchor my ship for a little while only,
My messengers continually cruise away or bring their returns to me.

I go hunting polar furs and the seal, leaping chasms with a pike-pointed staff, clinging to
    topples of brittle and blue.

I ascend to the foretruck,
I take my place late at night in the crow's-nest,
We sail the arctic sea, it is plenty light enough,
Through the clear atmosphere I stretch around on the wonderful beauty,   810
The enormous masses of ice pass me and I pass them, the scenery is plain in all directions,
The white-topt mountains show in the distance, I fling out my fancies toward them,
We are approaching some great battle-field in which we are soon to be engaged,
We pass the colossal outposts of the encampment, we pass with still feet and caution,
Or we are entering by the suburbs some vast and ruin'd city,
The blocks and fallen architecture more than all the living cities of the globe.

I am a free companion, I bivouac by invading watchfires,
I turn the bridegroom out of bed and stay with the bride myself,
I tighten her all night to my thighs and lips.

My voice is the wife's voice, the screech by the rail of the stairs,   820
They fetch my man's body up dripping and drown'd.

I understand the large hearts of heroes,
The courage of present times and all times,
How the skipper saw the crowded and rudderless wreck of the steamship, and Death chasing
    it up and down the storm,
How he knuckled tight and gave not back an inch, and was faithful of days and faithful of
    nights,
And chalk'd in large letters on a board, *Be of good cheer, we will not desert you*;
How he follow'd with them and tack'd with them three days and would not give it up,
How he saved the drifting company at last,
How the lank loose-gown'd women look'd when boated from the side of their prepared
    graves,
How the silent old-faced infants and the lifted sick, and the sharp-lipp'd unshaved men;   830
All this I swallow, it tastes good, I like it well, it becomes mine,
I am the man, I suffer'd, I was there.

The disdain and calmness of martyrs,
The mother of old, condemn'd for a witch, burnt with dry wood, her children gazing on,
The hounded slave that flags in the race, leans by the fence, blowing, cover'd with sweat,
The twinges that sting like needles his legs and neck, the murderous buckshot and the
    bullets,
All these I feel or am.

I am the hounded slave, I wince at the bite of the dogs,
Hell and despair are upon me, crack and again crack the marksmen,
I clutch the rails of the fence, my gore dribs, thinn'd with the ooze of my skin,   840
I fall on the weeds and stones,
The riders spur their unwilling horses, haul close,
Taunt my dizzy ears and beat me violently over the head with whip-stocks.

Agonies are one of my changes of garments.
I do not ask the wounded person how he feels, I myself become the wounded
    person,
My hurts turn livid upon me as I lean on a cane and observe.

I am the mash'd fireman with breast-bone broken,
Tumbling walls buried me in their debris,
Heat and smoke I inspired, I heard the yelling shouts of my comrades,
I heard the distant click of their picks and shovels,   850
They have clear'd the beams away, they tenderly lift me forth.
I lie in the night air in my red shirt, the pervading hush is for my sake,
Painless after all I lie exhausted but not so unhappy,
White and beautiful are the faces around me, the heads are bared of their fire-caps,
The kneeling crowd fades with the light of the torches.

Distant and dead resuscitate,
They show as the dial or move as the hands of me, I am the clock myself.

I am an old artillerist, I tell of my fort's bombardment,
I am there again.

Again the long roll of the drummers,   860
Again the attacking cannon, mortars,
Again to my listening ears the cannon responsive.

I take part, I see and hear the whole,
The cries, curses, roar, the plaudits for well-aim'd shots,
The ambulanza slowly passing trailing its red drip,
Workmen searching after damages, making indispensable repairs,
The fall of grenades through the rent roof, the fan-shaped explosion,
The whizz of limbs, heads, stone, wood, iron, high in the air.

Again gurgles the mouth of my dying general, he furiously waves with his hand,
He gasps through the clot *Mind not me—mind—the entrenchments.*   870

34

Now I tell what I knew in Texas in my early youth,
(I tell not the fall of Alamo,
Not one escaped to tell the fall of Alamo,
The hundred and fifty are dumb yet at Alamo,)
'Tis the tale of the murder in cold blood of four hundred and twelve young men.

Retreating they had form'd in a hollow square with their baggage for breastworks,
Nine hundred lives out of the surrounding enemy's, nine times their number, was the price
    they took in advance,
Their colonel was wounded and their ammunition gone,
They treated for an honorable capitulation, receiv'd writing and seal, gave up their arms and
    march'd back prisoners of war.

They were the glory of the race of rangers,   880
Matchless with horse, rifle, song, supper, courtship,
Large, turbulent, generous, handsome, proud, and affectionate,
Bearded, sunburnt, drest in the free costume of hunters,
Not a single one over thirty years of age.

The second First-day morning they were brought out in squads and massacred, it was
     beautiful early summer,
The work commenced about five o'clock and was over by eight.

None obey'd the command to kneel,
Some made a mad and helpless rush, some stood stark and straight,
A few fell at once, shot in the temple or heart, the living and dead lay together,
The maim'd and mangled dug in the dirt, the new-comers saw them there,   890
Some half-kill'd attempted to crawl away,
These were despatch'd with bayonets or batter'd with the blunts of muskets.
A youth not seventeen years old seiz'd his assassin till two more came to release him,
The three were all torn and cover'd with the boy's blood.

At eleven o'clock began the burning of the bodies;
That is the tale of the murder of the four hundred and twelve young men.

35

Would you hear of an old-time sea-fight?
Would you learn who won by the light of the moon and stars?
List to the yarn, as my grandmother's father the sailor told it to me.

Our foe was no skulk in his ship I tell you, (said he,)   900
His was the surly English pluck, and there is no tougher or truer, and never was, and never
     will be;
Along the lower'd eve he came horribly raking us.

We closed with him, the yards entangled, the cannon touch'd,
My captain lash'd fast with his own hands.

We had receiv'd some eighteen pound shots under the water,
On our lower-gun-deck two large pieces had burst at the first fire, killing all around and blow-
     ing up overhead.

Fighting at sun-down, fighting at dark,
Ten o'clock at night, the full moon well up, our leaks on the gain, and five feet of water
     reported,
The master-at-arms loosing the prisoners confined in the after-hold to give them a chance for
     themselves.

The transit to and from the magazine is now stopt by the sentinels,   910
They see so many strange faces they do not know whom to trust.

Our frigate takes fire,
The other asks if we demand quarter?
If our colors are struck and the fighting done?

Now I laugh content, for I hear the voice of my little captain,
We have not struck, he composedly cries, *we have just begun our part of the fighting.*

Only three guns are in use,
One is directed by the captain himself against the enemy's main-mast,
Two well serv'd with grape and canister silence his musketry and clear his decks.

The tops alone second the fire of this little battery, especially the main-top,   920
They hold out bravely during the whole of the action.

Not a moment's cease,
The leaks gain fast on the pumps, the fire eats toward the powder-magazine.

One of the pumps has been shot away, it is generally thought we are sinking.

Serene stands the little captain,
He is not hurried, his voice is neither high nor low,
His eyes give more light to us than our battle-lanterns.

Toward twelve there in the beams of the moon they surrender to us.

36

Stretch'd and still lies the midnight,
Two great hulls motionless on the breast of the darkness,   930
Our vessel riddled and slowly sinking, preparations to pass to the one we have conquer'd,
The captain on the quarter-deck coldly giving his orders through a countenance white as a
          sheet,
Near by the corpse of the child that serv'd in the cabin,
The dead face of an old salt with long white hair and carefully curl'd whiskers,
The flames spite of all that can be done flickering aloft and below,
The husky voices of the two or three officers yet fit for duty,
Formless stacks of bodies and bodies by themselves, dabs of flesh upon the masts and spars,
Cut of cordage, dangle of rigging, slight shock of the soothe of waves,
Black and impassive guns, litter of powder-parcels, strong scent,
A few large stars overhead, silent and mournful shining,   940
Delicate sniffs of sea-breeze, smells of sedgy grass and fields by the shore, death-messages
          given in charge to survivors,
The hiss of the surgeon's knife, the gnawing teeth of his saw,
Wheeze, cluck, swash of falling blood, short wild scream, and long, dull, tapering groan,
These so, these irretrievable.

37

You laggards there on guard! look to your arms!
In at the conquer'd doors they crowd! I am possess'd!
Embody all presences outlaw'd or suffering,
See myself in prison shaped like another man,
And feel the dull unintermitted pain,

For me the keepers of convicts shoulder their carbines and keep watch,   950
It is I let out in the morning and barr'd at night.

Not a mutineer walks handcuff'd to jail but I am handcuff'd to him and walk by his side,
(I am less the jolly one there, and more the silent one with sweat on my twitching lips.)

Not a youngster is taken for larceny but I go up too, and am tried and sentenced.

Not a cholera patient lies at the last gasp but I also lie at the last gasp,
My face is ash-color'd, my sinews gnarl, away from me people retreat.

Askers embody themselves in me and I am embodied in them,
I project my hat, sit shame-faced, and beg.

38

Enough! enough! enough!
Somehow I have been stunn'd. Stand back!   960

Give me a little time beyond my cuff'd head, slumbers, dreams, gaping,
I discover myself on the verge of a usual mistake.

That I could forget the mockers and insults!
That I could forget the trickling tears and the blows of the bludgeons and hammers!
That I could look with a separate look on my own crucifixion and bloody crowning!

I remember now,
I resume the overstaid fraction,
The grave of rock multiplies what has been confided to it, or to any graves,
Corpses rise, gashes heal, fastenings roll from me.

I troop forth replenish'd with supreme power, one of an average unending procession,   970
Inland and sea-coast we go, and pass all boundary lines,
Our swift ordinances on their way over the whole earth,
The blossoms we wear in our hats the growth of thousands of years.

Eleves, I salute you! come forward!
Continue your annotations, continue your questionings.

39

The friendly and flowing savage, who is he?
Is he waiting for civilization, or past it and mastering it?

Is he some Southwesterner rais'd out-doors? is he Kanadian?
Is he from the Mississippi country? Iowa, Oregon, California?
The mountains? prairie-life, bush-life? or sailor from the sea?   980

Wherever he goes men and women accept and desire him,
They desire he should like them, touch them, speak to them, stay with them.

Behavior lawless as snow-flakes, words simple as grass, uncomb'd head, laughter, and naivetè,
Slow-stepping feet, common features, common modes and emanations,
They descend in new forms from the tips of his fingers,
They are wafted with the odor of his body or breath, they fly out of the glance of his eyes.

40

Flaunt of the sunshine I need not your bask—lie over!
You light surfaces only, I force surfaces and depths also.

Earth! you seem to look for something at my hands,
Say, old top-knot, what do you want?   990

Man or woman, I might tell how I like you, but cannot,
And might tell what it is in me and what it is in you, but cannot,
And might tell that pining I have, that pulse of my nights and days.

Behold, I do not give lectures or a little charity,
When I give I give myself.

You there, impotent, loose in the knees,
Open your scarf'd chops till I blow grit within you,
Spread your palms and lift the flaps of your pockets,
I am not to be denied, I compel, I have stores plenty and to spare,
And any thing I have I bestow.   1000

I do not ask who you are, that is not important to me,
You can do nothing and be nothing but what I will infold you.

To cotton-field drudge or cleaner of privies I lean,
On his right cheek I put the family kiss,
And in my soul I swear I never will deny him.

On women fit for conception I start bigger and nimbler babes,
(This day I am jetting the stuff of far more arrogant republics.)

To any one dying, thither I speed and twist the knob of the door,
Turn the bed-clothes toward the foot of the bed,
Let the physician and the priest go home.   1010

I seize the descending man and raise him with resistless will,
O despairer, here is my neck,
By God, you shall not go down! hang your whole weight upon me.

I dilate you with tremendous breath, I buoy you up,
Every room of the house do I fill with an arm'd force,
Lovers of me, bafflers of graves.

Sleep—I and they keep guard all night,
Not doubt, not disease shall dare to lay finger upon you,
I have embraced you, and henceforth possess you to myself,
And when you rise in the morning you will find what I tell you is so.   1020

                              41

I am he bringing help for the sick as they pant on their backs,
And for strong upright men I bring yet more needed help.

I heard what was said of the universe,
Heard it and heard it of several thousand years;
It is middling well as far as it goes—but is that all?

Magnifying and applying come I,
Outbidding at the start the old cautious hucksters,
Taking myself the exact dimensions of Jehovah,
Lithographing Kronos, Zeus his son, and Hercules his grandson,
Buying drafts of Osiris, Isis, Belus, Brahma, Buddha,   1030
In my portfolio placing Manito loose, Allah on a leaf, the crucifix engraved,
With Odin and the hideous-faced Mexitli and every idol and image,
Taking them all for what they are worth and not a cent more,
Admitting they were alive and did the work of their days,
(They bore mites as for unfledg'd birds who have now to rise and fly and sing for themselves,)
Accepting the rough deific sketches to fill out better in myself, bestowing them freely on each
          man and woman I see,
Discovering as much or more in a framer framing a house,
Putting higher claims for him there with his roll'd-up sleeves driving the mallet and chisel,
Not objecting to special revelations, considering a curl of smoke or a hair on the back of my
          hand just as curious as any revelation,
Lads ahold of fire-engines and hook-and-ladder ropes no less to me than the gods of the
          antique wars,   1040
Minding their voices peal through the crash of destruction,

Their brawny limbs passing safe over charr'd laths, their white foreheads whole and unhurt
    out of the flames;
By the mechanic's wife with her babe at her nipple interceding for every person born,
Three scythes at harvest whizzing in a row from three lusty angels with shirts bagg'd out at
    their waists,
The snag-tooth'd hostler with red hair redeeming sins past and to come,
Selling all he possesses, traveling on foot to fee lawyers for his brother and sit by him while he
    is tried for forgery;
What was strewn in the amplest strewing the square rod about me, and not filling the square
    rod then,
The bull and the bug never worshipp'd half enough,
Dung and dirt more admirable than was dream'd,
The supernatural of no account, myself waiting my time to be one of the supremes,   1050
The day getting ready for me when I shall do as much good as the best, and be as prodigious;
By my life-lumps! becoming already a creator,
Putting myself here and now to the ambush'd womb of the shadows.

42

A call in the midst of the crowd,
My own voice, orotund sweeping and final.

Come my children,
Come my boys and girls, my women, household and intimates,
Now the performer launches his nerve, he has pass'd his prelude on the reeds within.

Easily written loose-finger'd chords—I feel the thrum of your climax and close.

My head slues round on my neck,   1060
Music rolls, but not from the organ,
Folks are around me, but they are no household of mine.

Ever the hard unsunk ground,
Ever the eaters and drinkers, ever the upward and downward sun, ever the air and the
    ceaseless tides,
Ever myself and my neighbors, refreshing, wicked, real,
Ever the old inexplicable query, ever that thorn'd thumb, that breath of itches and thirsts,
Ever the vexer's *hoot! hoot!* till we find where the sly one hides and bring him forth,
Ever love, ever the sobbing liquid of life,
Ever the bandage under the chin, ever the trestles of death.

Here and there with dimes on the eyes walking,   1070
To feed the greed of the belly the brains liberally spooning,
Tickets buying, taking, selling, but in to the feast never once going,
Many sweating, ploughing, thrashing, and then the chaff for payment receiving,
A few idly owning, and they the wheat continually claiming.

This is the city and I am one of the citizens,
Whatever interests the rest interests me, politics, wars, markets, newspapers, schools,
The mayor and councils, banks, tariffs, steamships, factories, stocks, stores, real estate and
    personal estate.

The little plentiful manikins skipping around in collars and tail'd coats,
I am aware who they are, (they are positively not worms or fleas,)
I acknowledge the duplicates of myself, the weakest and shallowest is deathless with me,   1080

What I do and say the same waits for them,
Every thought that flounders in me the same flounders in them.

I know perfectly well my own egotism,
Know my omnivorous lines and must not write any less,
And would fetch you whoever you are flush with myself.

Not words of routine this song of mine,
But abruptly to question, to leap beyond yet nearer bring;
This printed and bound book—but the printer and the printing-office boy?
The well-taken photographs—but your wife or friend close and solid in your arms?
The black ship mail'd with iron, her mighty guns in her turrets—but the pluck of the captain
    and engineers?   1090
In the houses the dishes and fare and furniture—but the host and hostess, and the look out of
    their eyes?
The sky up there—yet here or next door, or across the way?
The saints and sages in history—but you yourself?
Sermons, creeds, theology—but the fathomless human brain,
And what is reason? and what is love? and what is life?

43

I do not despise you priests, all time, the world over,
My faith is the greatest of faiths and the least of faiths,
Enclosing worship ancient and modern and all between ancient and modern,
Believing I shall come again upon the earth after five thousand years,
Waiting responses from oracles, honoring the gods, saluting the sun,   1100
Making a fetich of the first rock or stump, powowing with sticks in the circle of obis,
Helping the llama or brahmin as he trims the lamps of the idols,
Dancing yet through the streets in a phallic procession, rapt and austere in the woods a
    gymnosophist,
Drinking mead from the skull-cup, to Shastas and Vedas admirant, minding the Koran,
Walking the teokallis, spotted with gore from the stone and knife, beating the serpent-skin drum,
Accepting the Gospels, accepting him that was crucified, knowing assuredly that he is divine,
To the mass kneeling or the puritan's prayer rising, or sitting patiently in a pew,
Ranting and frothing in my insane crisis, or waiting dead-like till my spirit arouses me,
Looking forth on pavement and land, or outside of pavement and land,
Belonging to the winders of the circuit of circuits.   1110

One of that centripetal and centrifugal gang I turn and talk like a man leaving charges before
    a journey.

Down-hearted doubters dull and excluded,
Frivolous, sullen, moping, angry, affected, dishearten'd, atheistical,
I know every one of you, I know the sea of torment, doubt, despair and unbelief.

How the flukes splash!
How they contort rapid as lightning, with spasms and spouts of blood!

Be at peace bloody flukes of doubters and sullen mopers,
I take my place among you as much as among any,
The past is the push of you, me, all, precisely the same,
And what is yet untried and afterward is for you, me, all precisely the same.   1120

I do not know what is untried and afterward,
But I know it will in its turn prove sufficient, and cannot fail.

Each who passes is consider'd, each who stops is consider'd, not a single one can it fail.

It cannot fail the young man who died and was buried,
Nor the young woman who died and was put by his side,
Nor the little child that peep'd in at the door, and then drew back and was never seen again,
Nor the old man who has lived without purpose, and feels it with bitterness worse than gall,
Nor him in the poor house tubercled by rum and the bad disorder,
Nor the numberless slaughter'd and wreck'd, nor the brutish koboo call'd the ordure of
          humanity,
Nor the sacs merely floating with open mouths for food to slip in,   1130
Nor any thing in the earth, or down in the oldest graves of the earth,
Nor any thing in the myriads of spheres, nor the myriads of myriads that inhabit them,
Nor the present, nor the least wisp that is known.

44

It is time to explain myself—let us stand up.

What is known I strip away,
I launch all men and women forward with me into the Unknown.

The clock indicates the moment—but what does eternity indicate?

We have thus far exhausted trillions of winters and summers,
There are trillions ahead, and trillions ahead of them.

Births have brought us richness and variety,   1140
And other births will bring us richness and variety.

I do not call one greater and one smaller,
That which fills its period and place is equal to any.

Were mankind murderous or jealous upon you, my brother, my sister?
I am sorry for you, they are not murderous or jealous upon me,
All has been gentle with me, I keep no account with lamentation,
(What have I to do with lamentation?)

I am an acme of things accomplish'd, and I an encloser of things to be.

My feet strike an apex of the apices of the stairs,
On every step bunches of ages, and larger bunches between the steps,   1150
All below duly travel'd, and still I mount and mount.

Rise after rise bow the phantoms behind me,
Afar down I see the huge first Nothing, I know I was even there,
I waited unseen and always, and slept through the lethargic mist,
And took my time, and took no hurt from the fetid carbon.

Long I was hugg'd close—long and long.

Immense have been the preparations for me,
Faithful and friendly the arms that have help'd me.

Cycles ferried my cradle, rowing and rowing like cheerful boatmen,
For room to me stars kept aside in their own rings,   1160
They sent influences to look after what was to hold me.

Before I was born out of my mother generations guided me,
My embryo has never been torpid, nothing could overlay it.

For it the nebula cohered to an orb,
The long slow strata piled to rest it on,
Vast vegetables gave it sustenance,
Monstrous sauroids transported it in their mouths and deposited it with care.

All forces have been steadily employ'd to complete and delight me,
Now on this spot I stand with my robust soul.

45

O span of youth! ever-push'd elasticity.   1170
O manhood, balanced, florid and full.

My lovers suffocate me,
Crowding my lips, thick in the pores of my skin,
Jostling me through streets and public halls, coming naked to me at night,
Crying by day *Ahoy!* from the rocks of the river, swinging and chirping over my head,
Calling my name from flower-beds, vines, tangled underbrush,
Lighting on every moment of my life,
Bussing my body with soft balsamic busses,
Noiselessly passing handfuls out of their hearts and giving them to be mine.

Old age superbly rising! O welcome, ineffable grace of dying days!   1180

Every condition promulges not only itself, it promulges what grows after and out of itself,
And the dark hush promulges as much as any.

I open my scuttle at night and see the far-sprinkled systems,
And all I see multiplied as high as I can cipher edge but the rim of the farther systems.

Wider and wider they spread, expanding, always expanding,
Outward and outward and forever outward.

My sun has his sun and round him obediently wheels,
He joins with his partners a group of superior circuit,
And greater sets follow, making specks of the greatest inside them.

There is no stoppage and never can be stoppage,   1190
If I, you, and the worlds, and all beneath or upon their surfaces, were this moment reduced
        back to a pallid float, it would not avail in the long run,
We should surely bring up again where we now stand,
And surely go as much farther, and then farther and farther.

A few quadrillions of eras, a few octillions of cubic leagues, do not hazard the span or make
        it impatient,
They are but parts, any thing is but a part.

See ever so far, there is limitless space outside of that,
Count ever so much, there is limitless time around that.

My rendezvous is appointed, it is certain,
The Lord will be there and wait till I come on perfect terms,
The great Camerado, the lover true for whom I pine will be there.   1200

46

I know I have the best of time and space, and was never measured and never will be measured.

I tramp a perpetual journey, (come listen all!)
My signs are a rain-proof coat, good shoes, and a staff cut from the woods,
No friend of mine takes his ease in my chair,
I have no chair, no church, no philosophy,
I lead no man to a dinner-table, library, exchange,
But each man and each woman of you I lead upon a knoll,
My left hand hooking you round the waist,
My right hand pointing to landscapes of continents and the public road.

Not I, not any one else can travel that road for you,   1210
You must travel it for yourself.

It is not far, it is within reach,
Perhaps you have been on it since you were born and did not know,
Perhaps it is everywhere on water and on land.

Shoulder your duds dear son, and I will mine, and let us hasten forth,
Wonderful cities and free nations we shall fetch as we go.

If you tire, give me both burdens, and rest the chuff of your hand on my hip,
And in due time you shall repay the same service to me,
For after we start we never lie by again.

This day before dawn I ascended a hill and look'd at the crowded heaven,   1220
And I said to my spirit *When we become the enfolders of those orbs, and the pleasure and*
   knowledge of every thing in them, shall we be fill'd and satisfied then?
And my spirit said *No, we but level that lift to pass and continue beyond.*

You are also asking me questions and I hear you,
I answer that I cannot answer, you must find out for yourself.

Sit a while dear son,
Here are biscuits to eat and here is milk to drink,
But as soon as you sleep and renew yourself in sweet clothes, I kiss you with a good-by kiss
   and open the gate for your egress hence.

Long enough have you dream'd contemptible dreams,
Now I wash the gum from your eyes,
You must habit yourself to the dazzle of the light and of every moment of your life.   1230

Long have you timidly waded holding a plank by the shore,
Now I will you to be a bold swimmer,
To jump off in the midst of the sea, rise again, nod to me, shout, and laughingly dash with
   your hair.

47

I am the teacher of athletes,
He that by me spreads a wider breast than my own proves the width of my own,
He most honors my style who learns under it to destroy the teacher.

The boy I love, the same becomes a man not through derived power, but in his own right,
Wicked rather than virtuous out of conformity or fear,

Fond of his sweetheart, relishing well his steak,
Unrequited love or a slight cutting him worse than sharp steel cuts,   1240
First-rate to ride, to fight, to hit the bull's eye, to sail a skiff, to sing a song or play on the banjo,
Preferring scars and the beard and faces pitted with small-pox over all latherers,
And those well-tann'd to those that keep out of the sun.

I teach straying from me, yet who can stray from me?
I follow you whoever you are from the present hour,
My words itch at your ears till you understand them.

I do not say these things for a dollar or to fill up the time while I wait for a boat,
(It is you talking just as much as myself, I act as the tongue of you,
Tied in your mouth, in mine it begins to be loosen'd.)

I swear I will never again mention love or death inside a house,   1250
And I swear I will never translate myself at all, only to him or her who privately stays with me
          in the open air.

If you would understand me go to the heights or water-shore,
The nearest gnat is an explanation, and a drop or motion of waves a key,
The maul, the oar, the hand-saw, second my words.

No shutter'd room or school can commune with me,
But roughs and little children better than they.

The young mechanic is closest to me, he knows me well,
The woodman that takes his axe and jug with him shall take me with him all day,
The farm-boy ploughing in the field feels good at the sound of my voice,
In vessels that sail my words sail, I go with fishermen and seamen and love them.   1260

The soldier camp'd or upon the march is mine,
On the night ere the pending battle many seek me, and I do not fail them,
On that solemn night (it may be their last) those that know me seek me.

My face rubs to the hunter's face when he lies down alone in his blanket,
The driver thinking of me does not mind the jolt of his wagon,
The young mother and old mother comprehend me,
The girl and the wife rest the needle a moment and forget where they are,
They and all would resume what I have told them.

48

I have said that the soul is not more than the body,
And I have said that the body is not more than the soul,   1270
And nothing, not God, is greater to one than one's self is,
And whoever walks a furlong without sympathy walks to his own funeral drest in his shroud,
And I or you pocketless of a dime may purchase the pick of the earth,
And to glance with an eye or show a bean in its pod confounds the learning of all times,
And there is no trade or employment but the young man following it may become a hero,
And there is no object so soft but it makes a hub for the wheel'd universe,
And I say to any man or woman, Let your soul stand cool and composed before a million
          universes.

And I say to mankind, Be not curious about God,
For I who am curious about each am not curious about God,
(No array of terms can say how much I am at peace about God and about death.)   1280

I hear and behold God in every object, yet understand God not in the least,
Nor do I understand who there can be more wonderful than myself.

Why should I wish to see God better than this day?
I see something of God each hour of the twenty-four, and each moment then,
In the faces of men and women I see God, and in my own face in the glass,
I find letters from God dropt in the street, and every one is sign'd by God's name,
And I leave them where they are, for I know that wheresoe'er I go,
Others will punctually come for ever and ever.

49

And as to you Death, and you bitter hug of mortality, it is idle to try to alarm me.

To his work without flinching the accoucheur comes,   1290
I see the elder-hand pressing receiving supporting,
I recline by the sills of the exquisite flexible doors,
And mark the outlet, and mark the relief and escape.

And as to you Corpse I think you are good manure, but that does not offend me,
I smell the white roses sweet-scented and growing,
I reach to the leafy lips, I reach to the polish'd breasts of melons.

And as to you Life I reckon you are the leavings of many deaths,
(No doubt I have died myself ten thousand times before.)

I hear you whispering there O stars of heaven,
O suns—O grass of graves—O perpetual transfers and promotions,   1300
If you do not say any thing how can I say any thing?

Of the turbid pool that lies in the autumn forest,
Of the moon that descends the steeps of the soughing twilight,
Toss, sparkles of day and dusk—toss on the black stems that decay in the muck,
Toss to the moaning gibberish of the dry limbs.

I ascend from the moon, I ascend from the night,
I perceive that the ghastly glimmer is noonday sunbeams reflected,
And debouch to the steady and central from the offspring great or small.

50

There is that in me—I do not know what it is—but I know it is in me.

Wrench'd and sweaty—calm and cool then my body becomes,   1310
I sleep—I sleep long.

I do not know it—it is without name—it is a word unsaid,
It is not in any dictionary, utterance, symbol.

Something it swings on more than the earth I swing on,
To it the creation is the friend whose embracing awakes me.

Perhaps I might tell more. Outlines! I plead for my brothers and sisters.

Do you see O my brothers and sisters?
It is not chaos or death—it is form, union, plan—it is eternal life—it is Happiness.

51

The past and present wilt—I have fill'd them, emptied them,
And proceed to fill my next fold of the future. 1320

Listener up there! what have you to confide to me?
Look in my face while I snuff the sidle of evening,
(Talk honestly, no one else hears you, and I stay only a minute longer.)

Do I contradict myself?
Very well then I contradict myself,
(I am large, I contain multitudes.)

I concentrate toward them that are nigh, I wait on the door-slab.

Who has done his day's work? who will soonest be through with his supper?
Who wishes to walk with me?

Will you speak before I am gone? will you prove already too late? 1330

52

The spotted hawk swoops by and accuses me, he complains of my gab and my loitering.

I too am not a bit tamed, I too am untranslatable,
I sound my barbaric yawp over the roofs of the world.

The last scud of day holds back for me,
It flings my likeness after the rest and true as any on the shadow'd wilds,
It coaxes me to the vapor and the dusk.

I depart as air, I shake my white locks at the runaway sun,
I effuse my flesh in eddies, and drift it in lacy jags.

I bequeath myself to the dirt to grow from the grass I love,
If you want me again look for me under your boot-soles. 1340

You will hardly know who I am or what I mean,
But I shall be good health to you nevertheless,
And filter and fibre your blood.

Failing to fetch me at first keep encouraged,
Missing me one place search another,
I stop somewhere waiting for you.

1855

ONE HOUR TO MADNESS AND JOY

ONE hour to madness and joy! O furious! O confine me not!
(What is this that frees me so in storms?
What do my shouts amid lightnings and raging winds mean?)

O to drink the mystic deliria deeper than any other man!
O savage and tender achings! (I bequeath them to you, my children,
I tell them to you, for reasons, O bridegroom and bride.)

O to be yielded to you whoever you are, and you to be yielded to me in defiance of the
world!
O to return to Paradise! O bashful and feminine!
O to draw you to me, to plant on you for the first time the lips of a determin'd man.

O the puzzle, the thrice-tied knot, the deep and dark pool, all untied and illumin'd!   10
O to speed where there is space enough and air enough at last!
To be absolv'd from previous ties and conventions, I from mine and you from yours!
To find a new unthought-of nonchalance with the best of Nature!
To have the gag remov'd from one's mouth!
To have the feeling to-day or any day I am sufficient as I am.

O something unprov'd! something in a trance!
To escape utterly from others' anchors and holds!
To drive free! to love free! to dash reckless and dangerous!
To court destruction with taunts, with invitations!
To ascend, to leap to the heavens of the love indicated to me!   20
To rise thither with my inebriate soul!
To be lost if it must be so!
To feed the remainder of life with one hour of fulness and freedom!
With one brief hour of madness and joy.

1860

I SAW IN LOUISIANA A LIVE–OAK GROWING

I SAW in Louisiana a live-oak growing,
All alone stood it and the moss hung down from the branches,
Without any companion it grew there uttering joyous leaves of dark green,
And its look, rude, unbending, lusty, made me think of myself,
But I wonder'd how it could utter joyous leaves standing alone there without its friend near,
for I knew I could not,
And I broke off a twig with a certain number of leaves upon it, and twined around it a little
moss,
And brought it away, and I have placed it in sight in my room,
It is not needed to remind me as of my own dear friends,
(For I believe lately I think of little else than of them,)
Yet it remains to me a curious token, it makes me think of manly love;   10
For all that, and though the live-oak glistens there in Louisiana solitary in a wide flat
space,
Uttering joyous leaves all its life without a friend a lover near,
I know very well I could not.

1860

I HEAR IT WAS CHARGED AGAINST ME

I HEAR it was charged against me that I sought to destroy institutions,
But really I am neither for nor against institutions,
(What indeed have I in common with them? or what with the destruction of them?)
Only I will establish in the Mannahatta and in every city of these States inland and seaboard,
And in the fields and woods, and above every keel little or large that dents the water,
Without edifices or rules or trustees or any argument,
The institution of the dear love of comrades.

1860

CROSSING BROOKLYN FERRY

1

FLOOD-TIDE below me! I see you face to face!
Clouds of the west—sun there half an hour high—I see you also face to face.

Crowds of men and women attired in the usual costumes, how curious you are to me!
On the ferry-boats the hundreds and hundreds that cross, returning home, are more curious
     to me than you suppose,
And you that shall cross from shore to shore years hence are more to me, and more in my
     meditations, than you might suppose.

2

The impalpable sustenance of me from all things at all hours of the day,
The simple, compact, well-join'd scheme, myself disintegrated, every one disintegrated yet
     part of the scheme,
The similitudes of the past and those of the future,
The glories strung like beads on my smallest sights and hearings, on the walk in the street and
     the passage over the river,
The current rushing so swiftly and swimming with me far away,   10
The others that are to follow me, the ties between me and them,
The certainty of others, the life, love, sight, hearing of others.

Others will enter the gates of the ferry and cross from shore to shore,
Others will watch the run of the flood-tide,
Others will see the shipping of Manhattan north and west, and the heights of Brooklyn to the
     south and east,
Others will see the islands large and small;
Fifty years hence, others will see them as they cross, the sun half an hour high,
A hundred years hence, or ever so many hundred years hence, others will see them,
Will enjoy the sunset, the pouring-in of the flood-tide, the falling-back to the sea of the
     ebb-tide.

3

It avails not, time nor place—distance avails not,   20
I am with you, you men and women of a generation, or ever so many generations hence,
Just as you feel when you look on the river and sky, so I felt,
Just as any of you is one of a living crowd, I was one of a crowd,
Just as you are refresh'd by the gladness of the river and the bright flow, I was refresh'd,
Just as you stand and lean on the rail, yet hurry with the swift current, I stood yet was
     hurried,
Just as you look on the numberless masts of ships and the thick-stemm'd pipes of steamboats,
     I look'd.

I too many and many a time cross'd the river of old,
Watched the Twelfth-month sea-gulls, saw them high in the air floating with motionless
     wings, oscillating their bodies,
Saw how the glistening yellow lit up parts of their bodies and left the rest in strong shadow,
Saw the slow-wheeling circles and the gradual edging toward the south,   30
Saw the reflection of the summer sky in the water,
Had my eyes dazzled by the shimmering track of beams,
Look'd at the fine centrifugal spokes of light round the shape of my head in the sunlit water,
Look'd on the haze on the hills southward and south-westward,
Look'd on the vapor as it flew in fleeces tinged with violet,

Look'd toward the lower bay to notice the vessels arriving,
Saw their approach, saw aboard those that were near me,
Saw the white sails of schooners and sloops, saw the ships at anchor,
The sailors at work in the rigging or out astride the spars,
The round masts, the swinging motion of the hulls, the slender serpentine pennants,   40
The large and small steamers in motion, the pilots in their pilot-houses,
The white wake left by the passage, the quick tremulous whirl of the wheels,
The flags of all nations, the falling of them at sunset,
The scallop-edged waves in the twilight, the ladled cups, the frolicsome crests and glistening,
The stretch afar growing dimmer and dimmer, the gray walls of the granite storehouses by the
    docks,
On the river the shadowy group, the big steam-tug closely flank'd on each side by the barges,
    the hay-boat, the belated lighter,
On the neighboring shore the fires from the foundry chimneys burning high and glaringly into
    the night,
Casting their flicker of black contrasted with wild red and yellow light over the tops of houses,
    and down into the clefts of streets.

4

These and all else were to me the same as they are to you,
I loved well those cities, loved well the stately and rapid river,   50
The men and women I saw were all near to me,
Others the same—others who look back on me because I look'd forward to them,
(The time will come, though I stop here to-day and to-night.)

5

What is it then between us?
What is the count of the scores or hundreds of years between us?

Whatever it is, it avails not—distance avails not, and place avails not,
I too lived, Brooklyn of ample hills was mine,
I too walk'd the streets of Manhattan island, and bathed in the waters around it,
I too felt the curious abrupt questionings stir within me.
In the day among crowds of people sometimes they came upon me,   60
In my walks home late at night or as I lay in my bed they came upon me,
I too had been struck from the float forever held in solution,
I too had receiv'd identity by my body,
That I was I knew was of my body, and what I should be I knew I should be of my
    body.

6

It is not upon you alone the dark patches fall,
The dark threw its patches down upon me also,
The best I had done seem'd to me blank and suspicious,
My great thoughts as I supposed them, were they not in reality meagre?
Nor is it you alone who know what it is to be evil,
I am he who knew what it was to be evil,   70
I too knitted the old knot of contrariety,
Blabb'd, blush'd, resented, lied, stole, grudg'd,
Had guile, anger, lust, hot wishes I dared not speak,
Was wayward, vain, greedy, shallow, sly, cowardly, malignant,
The wolf, the snake, the hog, not wanting in me,
The cheating look, the frivolous word, the adulterous wish, not wanting,
Refusals, hates, postponements, meanness, laziness, none of these wanting,
Was one with the rest, the days and haps of the rest,

Was call'd by my nighest name by clear loud voices of young men as they saw me approaching
    or passing,   79
Felt their arms on my neck as I stood, or the negligent leaning of their flesh against me as I sat,
Saw many I loved in the street or ferry-boat or public assembly, yet never told them a word,
Lived the same life with the rest, the same old laughing, gnawing, sleeping,
Play'd the part that still looks back on the actor or actress,
The same old role, the role that is what we make it, as great as we like,
Or as small as we like, or both great and small.

7

Closer yet I approach you,
What thought you have of me now, I had as much of you—I laid in my stores in advance,
I consider'd long and seriously of you before you were born.

Who was to know what should come home to me?
Who knows but I am enjoying this?   90
Who knows, for all the distance, but I am as good as looking at you now, for all you cannot
    see me?

8

Ah, what can ever be more stately and admirable to me than mast-hemm'd Manhattan?
River and sunset and scallop-edg'd waves of flood-tide?
The sea-gulls oscillating their bodies, the hay-boat in the twilight, and the belated lighter?
What gods can exceed these that clasp me by the hand, and with voices I love call me
    promptly and loudly by my nighest name as I approach?

What is more subtle than this which ties me to the woman or man that looks in my face?
Which fuses me into you now, and pours my meaning into you?

We understand then do we not?
What I promis'd without mentioning it, have you not accepted?
What the study could not teach—what the preaching could not accomplish is accomplish'd, is
    it not?   100

9

Flow on, river! flow with the flood-tide, and ebb with the ebb-tide!
Frolic on, crested and scallop-edg'd waves!
Gorgeous clouds of the sunset! drench with your splendor me, or the men and women genera-
    tions after me!
Cross from shore to shore, countless crowds of passengers!
Stand up, tall masts of Mannahatta! stand up, beautiful hills of Brooklyn!
Throb, baffled and curious brain! throw out questions and answers!
Suspend here and everywhere, eternal float of solution!
Gaze, loving and thirsting eyes, in the house or street or public assembly!
Sound out, voices of young men! loudly and musically call me by my nighest name!
Live, old life! play the part that looks back on the actor or actress!   110
Play the old role, the role that is great or small according as one makes it!
Consider, you who peruse me, whether I may not in unknown ways be looking upon you;
Be firm, rail over the river, to support those who lean idly, yet haste with the hasting current;
Fly on, sea-birds! fly sideways, or wheel in large circles high in the air;
Receive the summer sky, you water, and faithfully hold it till all downcast eyes have time to
    take it from you!
Diverge, fine spokes of light, from the shape of my head, or any one's head, in the sunlit
    water!
Come on, ships from the lower bay! pass up or down, white-sail'd schooners, sloops, lighters!

Flaunt away, flags of all nations! be duly lower'd at sunset!
Burn high your fires, foundry chimneys! cast black shadows at nightfall! cast red and yellow
      light over the tops of the houses!
Appearances, now or henceforth, indicate what you are,   120
You necessary film, continue to envelop the soul,
About my body for me, and your body for you, be hung our divinest aromas,
Thrive, cities—bring your freight, bring your shows, ample and sufficient rivers,
Expand, being than which none else is perhaps more spiritual,
Keep your places, objects than which none else is more lasting.

You have waited, you always wait, you dumb, beautiful ministers,
We receive you with free sense at last, and are insatiate henceforward,
Not you any more shall be able to foil us, or withhold yourselves from us,
We use you, and do not cast you aside—we plant you permanently within us,
We fathom you not—we love you—there is perfection in you also,   130
You furnish your parts toward eternity,
Great or small, you furnish your parts toward the soul.

                                         1856

FROM SONG OF THE BROAD-AXE

I

WEAPON shapely, naked, wan,
Head from the mother's bowels drawn,
Wooded flesh and metal bone, limb only one and lip only one,
Gray-blue leaf by red-heat grown, helve produced from a little seed sown,
Resting the grass amid and upon,
To be lean'd and to lean on.

. . . .   1856

PIONEERS! O PIONEERS!

    COME my tan-faced children,
Follow well in order, get your weapons ready,
Have you your pistols? have you your sharp-edged axes?
    Pioneers! O pioneers!

    For we cannot tarry here,
We must march my darlings, we must bear the brunt of danger,
We the youthful sinewy races, all the rest on us depend,
    Pioneers! O pioneers!

    O you youths, Western youths,
So impatient, full of action, full of manly pride and friendship,   10
Plain I see you Western youths, see you tramping with the foremost,
    Pioneers! O pioneers!

    Have the elder races halted?
Do they droop and end their lesson, wearied over there beyond the seas?
We take up the task eternal, and the burden and the lesson,
    Pioneers! O pioneers!

    All the past we leave behind,
We debouch upon a newer mightier world, varied world,
Fresh and strong the world we seize, world of labor and the march,
    Pioneers! O pioneers!   20

We detachments steady throwing,
Down the edges, through the passes, up the mountains steep,
Conquering, holding, daring, venturing as we go the unknown ways,
        Pioneers! O pioneers!

We primeval forests felling,
We the rivers stemming, vexing we and piercing deep the mines within,
We the surface broad surveying, we the virgin soil upheaving,
        Pioneers! O pioneers!

Colorado men are we,
From the peaks gigantic, from the great sierras and the high plateaus,   30
From the mine and from the gully, from the hunting trail we come,
        Pioneers! O pioneers!

From Nebraska, from Arkansas,
Central inland race are we, from Missouri, with the continental blood intervein'd,
All the hands of comrades clasping, all the Southern, all the Northern,
        Pioneers! O pioneers!

O resistless restless race!
O beloved race in all! O my breast aches with tender love for all!
O I mourn and yet exult, I am rapt with love for all,
        Pioneers! O pioneers!   40

Raise the mighty mother mistress,
Waving high the delicate mistress, over all the starry mistress, (bend your heads all,)
Raise the fang'd and warlike mistress, stern, impassive, weapon'd mistress,
        Pioneers! O pioneers!

See my children, resolute children,
By those swarms upon our rear we must never yield or falter,
Ages back in ghostly millions frowning there behind us urging,
        Pioneers! O pioneers!

On and on the compact ranks,
With accessions ever waiting, with the places of the dead quickly fill'd,   50
Through the battle, through defeat, moving yet and never stopping,
        Pioneers! O pioneers!

O to die advancing on!
Are there some of us to droop and die? has the hour come?
Then upon the march we fittest die, soon and sure the gap is fill'd,
        Pioneers! O pioneers!

All the pulses of the world,
Falling in they beat for us, with the Western movement beat,
Holding single or together, steady moving to the front, all for us,
        Pioneers! O pioneers!   60

Life's involv'd and varied pageants,
All the forms and shows, all the workmen at their work,
All the seamen and the landsmen, all the masters with their slaves,
        Pioneers! O pioneers!

All the hapless silent lovers,
All the prisoners in the prisons, all the righteous and the wicked,
All the joyous, all the sorrowing, all the living, all the dying,
    Pioneers! O pioneers!

I too with my soul and body,
We, a curious trio, picking, wandering on our way,   70
Through these shores amid the shadows, with the apparitions pressing,
    Pioneers! O pioneers!

Lo, the darting bowling orb!
Lo, the brother orbs around, all the clustering suns and planets,
All the dazzling days, all the mystic nights with dreams,
    Pioneers! O pioneers!

These are of us, they are with us,
All for primal needed work, while the followers there in embryo wait behind,
We to-day's procession heading, we the route for travel clearing,   80
    Pioneers! O pioneers!

O you daughters of the West!
O you young and elder daughters! O you mothers and you wives!
Never must you be divided, in our ranks you move united,
    Pioneers! O pioneers!

Minstrels latent on the prairies!
(Shrouded bards of other lands, you may rest, you have done your work,)
Soon I hear you coming warbling, soon you rise and tramp amid us,
    Pioneers! O pioneers!

Not for delectations sweet,
Not the cushion and the slipper, not the peaceful and the studious,   90
Not the riches safe and palling, not for us the tame enjoyment,
    Pioneers! O pioneers!

Do the feasters gluttonous feast?
Do the corpulent sleepers sleep? have they lock'd and bolted doors?
Still be ours the diet hard, and the blanket on the ground,
    Pioneers! O pioneers!

Has the night descended?
Was the road of late so toilsome? did we stop discouraged nodding on our way?
Yet a passing hour I yield you in your tracks to pause oblivious,
    Pioneers! O pioneers!   100

Till with sound of trumpet,
Far, far off the daybreak call—hark! how loud and clear I hear it wind,
Swift! to the head of the army!—swift! spring to your places,
    Pioneers! O pioneers!

          1865

FRANCE

THE 18TH YEAR OF THESE STATES

A GREAT year and place,
A harsh discordant natal scream out-sounding, to touch the mother's heart closer than any yet

I walk'd the shores of my Eastern sea,
Heard over the waves the little voice,
Saw the divine infant where she woke mournfully wailing, amid the roar of cannon, curses,
     shouts, crash of falling buildings,
Was not so sick from the blood in the gutters running, nor from the single corpses, nor those
     in heaps, nor those borne away in the tumbrils,
Was not so desperate at the battues of death—was not so shock'd at the repeated fusillades of
     the guns.

Pale, silent, stern, what could I say to that long-accrued retribution?
Could I wish humanity different?
'Could I wish the people made of wood and stone?   10
Or that there be no justice in destiny or time?

O Liberty! O mate for me!
Here too the blaze, the grape-shot and the axe, in reserve, to fetch them out in case of need,
Here too, though long represt, can never be destroy'd,
Here too could rise at last murdering and ecstatic,
Here too demanding full arrears of vengeance.

Hence I sign this salute over the sea,
And I do not deny that terrible red birth and baptism,
But remember the little voice that I heard wailing, and wait with perfect trust, no matter how
     long,
And from to-day sad and cogent I maintain the bequeath'd cause, as for all lands,   20
And I send these words to Paris with my love,
And I guess some chansonniers there will understand them,
For I guess there is latent music yet in France, floods of it,
O I hear already the bustle of instruments, they will soon be drowning all that would interrupt
     them,
O I think the east wind brings a triumphal and free march,
It reaches hither, it swells me to joyful madness,
I will run transpose it in words, to justify it,
I will yet sing a song for you ma femme.

                               1860

OUT OF THE CRADLE ENDLESSLY ROCKING

OUT of the cradle endlessly rocking,
Out of the mocking-bird's throat, the musical shuttle,
Out of the Ninth-month midnight,
Over the sterile sands and the fields beyond, where the child leaving his bed wander'd alone,
     bareheaded, barefoot,
Down from the shower'd halo,
Up from the mystic play of shadows twining and twisting as if they were alive,
Out from the patches of briers and blackberries,
From the memories of the bird that chanted to me,
From your memories sad brother, from the fitful risings and fallings I heard,
From under that yellow half-moon late-risen and swollen as if with tears,   10
From those beginning notes of yearning and love there in the mist,
From the thousand responses of my heart never to cease,
From the myriad thence-arous'd words,
From the word stronger and more delicious than any,
From such as now they start the scene revisiting,
As a flock, twittering, rising, or overhead passing,
Borne hither, ere all eludes me, hurriedly,

A man, yet by these tears a little boy again,
Throwing myself on the sand, confronting the waves,
I, chanter of pains and joys, uniter of here and hereafter, 20
Taking all hints to use them, but swiftly leaping beyond them,
A reminiscence sing.

Once Paumanok,
When the lilac-scent was in the air and Fifth-month grass was growing,
Up this seashore in some briers,
Two feather'd guests from Alabama, two together,
And their nest, and four light-green eggs spotted with brown,
And every day the he-bird to and fro near at hand,
And every day the she-bird crouch'd on her nest, silent, with bright eyes,
And every day I, a curious boy, never too close, never disturbing them, 30
Cautiously peering, absorbing, translating.

Shine! shine! shine!
Pour down your warmth, great sun!
While we bask, we two together.

Two together!
Winds blow south, or winds blow north,
Day come white, or night come black,
Home, or rivers and mountains from home,
Singing all time, minding no time,
While we two keep together. 40

Till of a sudden,
May-be kill'd, unknown to her mate,
One forenoon the she-bird crouch'd not on the nest,
Nor return'd that afternoon, nor the next,
Nor ever appear'd again.

And thenceforward all summer in the sound of the sea,
And at night under the full of the moon in calmer weather,
Over the hoarse surging of the sea,
Or flitting from brier to brier by day,
I saw, I heard at intervals the remaining one, the he-bird, 50
The solitary guest from Alabama.

Blow! blow! blow!
Blow up sea-winds along Paumanok's shore;
I wait and I wait till you blow my mate to me.

Yes, when the stars glisten'd,
All night long on the prong of a moss-scallop'd stake,
Down almost amid the slapping waves,
Sat the lone singer wonderful causing tears.

He call'd on his mate,
He pour'd forth the meanings which I of all men know. 60

Yes my brother I know,
The rest might not, but I have treasur'd every note,
For more than once dimly down to the beach gliding,

Silent, avoiding the moonbeams, blending myself with the shadows,
Recalling now the obscure shapes, the echoes, the sounds and sights after their sorts,
The white arms out in the breakers tirelessly tossing,
I, with bare feet, a child, the wind wafting my hair,
Listen'd long and long.

Listen'd to keep, to sing, now translating the notes,
Following you my brother.

Soothe! soothe! soothe!
Close on its wave soothes the wave behind,
And again another behind embracing and lapping, every one close,
But my love soothes not me, not me.

Low hangs the moon, it rose late,
It is lagging—O I think it is heavy with love, with love.

O madly the sea pushes upon the land,
With love, with love.

O night! do I not see my love fluttering out among the breakers?
What is that little black thing I see there in the white?

Loud! loud! loud!
Loud I call to you, my love!
High and clear I shoot my voice over the waves,
Surely you must know who is here, is here,
You must know who I am, my love.

Low-hanging moon!
What is that dusky spot in your brown yellow?
O it is the shape, the shape of my mate!
O moon do not keep her from me any longer.

Land! land! O land!
Whichever way I turn, O I think you could give me my mate back again if you only would,
For I am almost sure I see her dimly whichever way I look.

O rising stars!
Perhaps the one I want so much will rise, will rise with some of you.

O throat! O trembling throat!
Sound clearer through the atmosphere!
Pierce the woods, the earth,
Somewhere listening to catch you must be the one I want.

Shake out carols!
Solitary here, the night's carols!
Carols of lonesome love! death's carols!
Carols under that lagging, yellow, waning moon!
O under that moon where she droops almost down into the sea!
O reckless despairing carols.

But soft! sink low!
Soft! let me just murmur,

And do you wait a moment you husky-nois'd sea,
For somewhere I believe I heard my mate responding to me,
So faint, I must be still, be still to listen,
But not altogether still, for then she might not come immediately to me.

Hither my love!
Here I am! here!
With this just-sustain'd note I announce myself to you,
This gentle call is for you my love, for you.

Do not be decoy'd elsewhere,
That is the whistle of the wind, it is not my voice,
That is the fluttering, the fluttering of the spray,
Those are the shadows of leaves.

O darkness! O in vain!
O I am very sick and sorrowful.

120

O brown halo in the sky near the moon, drooping upon the sea!
O troubled reflection in the sea!
O throat! O throbbing heart!
And I singing uselessly, uselessly all the night.

O past! O happy life! O songs of joy!
In the air, in the woods, over fields,
Loved! loved! loved! loved! loved!
But my mate no more, no more with me!
We two together no more.

130

The aria sinking,
All else continuing, the stars shining,
The winds blowing, the notes of the bird continuous echoing,
With angry moans the fierce old mother incessantly moaning,
On the sands of Paumanok's shore gray and rustling,
The yellow half-moon enlarged, sagging down, drooping, the face of the sea almost touching,
The boy ecstatic, with his bare feet the waves, with his hair the atmosphere dallying,
The love in the heart long pent, now loose, now at last tumultuously bursting,
The aria's meaning, the ears, the soul, swiftly depositing,
The strange tears down the cheeks coursing,
The colloquy there, the trio, each uttering,
140
The undertone, the savage old mother incessantly crying,
To the boy's soul's questions sullenly timing, some drown'd secret hissing,
To the outsetting bard.

Demon or bird! (said the boy's soul,)
Is it indeed toward your mate you sing? or is it really to me?
For I, that was a child, my tongue's use sleeping, now I have heard you,
Now in a moment I know what I am for, I awake,
And already a thousand singers, a thousand songs, clearer, louder and more sorrowful than
     yours,
A thousand warbling echoes have started to life within me, never to die.

150

O you singer solitary, singing by yourself, projecting me,
O solitary me listening, never more shall I cease perpetuating you,
Never more shall I escape, never more the reverberations,

Never more the cries of unsatisfied love be absent from me,
Never again leave me to be the peaceful child I was before what there in the night,
By the sea under the yellow and sagging moon,
The messenger there arous'd, the fire, the sweet hell within,
The unknown want, the destiny of me.

O give me the clew! (it lurks in the night here somewhere,)
O if I am to have so much, let me have more!

A word then, (for I will conquer it,)   160
The word final, superior to all,
Subtle, sent up—what is it?—I listen;
Are you whispering it, and have been all the time, you sea waves?
Is that it from your liquid rims and wet sands?

Whereto answering, the sea,
Delaying not, hurrying not,
Whisper'd me through the night, and very plainly before daybreak,
Lisp'd to me the low and delicious word death,
And again death, death, death, death,
Hissing melodious, neither like the bird nor like my arous'd child's heart,   170
But edging near as privately for me rustling at my feet,
Creeping thence steadily up to my ears and laving me softly all over,
Death, death, death, death, death.

Which I do not forget,
But fuse the song of my dusky demon and brother,
That he sang to me in the moonlight on Paumanok's gray beach,
With the thousand responsive songs at random,
My own songs awaked from that hour,
And with them the key, the word up from the waves,
The word of the sweetest song and all songs,   180
That strong and delicious word which, creeping to my feet,
(Or like some old crone rocking the cradle, swathed in sweet garments, bending aside,)
The sea whisper'd me.

              1860

TO THE MAN-OF-WAR-BIRD

Thou who hast slept all night upon the storm,
Waking renew'd on thy prodigious pinions,
(Burst the wild storm? above it thou ascended'st,
And rested on the sky, thy slave that cradled thee,)
Now a blue point, far, far in heaven floating,
As to the light emerging here on deck I watch thee,
(Myself a speck, a point on the world's floating vast.)
Far, far at sea,
After the night's fierce drifts have strewn the shore with wrecks,
With re-appearing day as now so happy and serene,   10
The rosy and elastic dawn, the flashing sun,
The limpid spread of air cerulean,
Thou also re-appearest.

Thou born to match the gale, (thou art all wings,)
To cope with heaven and earth and sea and hurricane,

Thou ship of air that never furl'st thy sails,
Days, even weeks untired and onward, through spaces, realms gyrating,
At dusk that look'st on Senegal, at morn America,
That sport'st amid the lightning-flash and thunder-cloud,
In them, in thy experiences, had'st thou my soul,   20
What joys! what joys were thine!

1881

ON THE BEACH AT NIGHT

ON the beach at night,
Stands a child with her father,
Watching the east, the autumn sky.

Up through the darkness,
While ravening clouds, the burial clouds, in black masses spreading,
Lower sullen and fast athwart and down the sky,
Amid a transparent clear belt of ether yet left in the east,
Ascends large and calm the lord-star Jupiter,
And nigh at hand, only a very little above,
Swim the delicate sisters the Pleiades.   10

From the beach the child holding the hand of her father,
Those burial clouds that lower victorious soon to devour all,
Watching, silently weeps.

Weep not, child,
Weep not, my darling,
With these kisses let me remove your tears,
The ravening clouds shall not long be victorious,
They shall not long possess the sky, they devour the stars only in apparition,
Jupiter shall emerge, be patient, watch again another night, the Pleiades shall emerge,
They are immortal, all those stars both silvery and golden shall shine out again,   20
The great stars and the little ones shall shine out again, they endure,
The vast immortal suns and the long-enduring pensive moons shall again shine.

Then dearest child mournest thou only for Jupiter?
Considerest thou alone the burial of the stars?

Something there is,
(With my lips soothing thee, adding I whisper,
I give thee the first suggestion, the problem and indirection,)
Something there is more immortal even than the stars,
(Many the burials, many the days and nights, passing away,)
Something that shall endure longer even than lustrous Jupiter,   30
Longer than sun or any revolving satellite,
Or the radiant sisters the Pleiades.

1856

EUROPE

THE 72D AND 73D YEARS OF THESE STATES

SUDDENLY out of its stale and drowsy lair, the lair of slaves,
Like lightning it le'pt forth half startled at itself,
Its feet upon the ashes and the rags, its hand tight to the throats of kings.

O hope and faith!
O aching close of exiled patriots' lives!
O many a sicken'd heart!
Turn back unto this day and make yourselves afresh.

And you, paid to defile the People—you liars, mark!
Not for numberless agonies, murders, lusts,
For court thieving in its manifold mean forms, worming from his simplicity the poor man's
          wages,   10
For many a promise sworn by royal lips and broken and laugh'd at in the breaking,
Then in their power not for all these did the blows strike revenge, or the heads of the nobles
          fall;
The People scorn'd the ferocity of kings.

But the sweetness of mercy brew'd bitter destruction, and the frighten'd monarchs come
          back,
Each comes in state with his train, hangman, priest, tax-gatherer,
Soldier, lawyer, lord, jailer, and sycophant.

Yet behind all lowering stealing, lo, a shape,
Vague as the night, draped interminably, head, front and form, in scarlet folds,
Whose face and eyes none may see,
Out of its robes only this, the red robes lifted by the arm,   20
One finger crook'd pointed high over the top, like the head of a snake appears.

Meanwhile corpses lie in new-made graves, bloody corpses of young men,
The rope of the gibbet hangs heavily, the bullets of princes are flying, the creatures of power
          laugh aloud,
And all these things bear fruits, and they are good.

Those corpses of young men,
Those martyrs that hang from the gibbets, those hearts pierc'd by the gray lead,
Cold and motionless as they seem live elsewhere with unslaughter'd vitality.

They live in other young men O kings!
They live in brothers again ready to defy you,
They were purified by death, they were taught and exalted.   30

Not a grave of the murder'd for freedom but grows seed for freedom, in its turn to bear seed,
Which the winds carry afar and re-sow, and the rains and the snows nourish.

Not a disembodied spirit can the weapons of tyrants let loose,
But it stalks invisibly over the earth, whispering, counseling, cautioning.

Liberty, let others despair of you—I never despair of you.

Is the house shut? is the master away?
Nevertheless, be ready, be not weary of watching,
He will soon return, his messengers come anon.

                                                                                       1855

WHEN I HEARD THE LEARN'D ASTRONOMER

WHEN I heard the learn'd astronomer,
When the proofs, the figures, were ranged in columns before me,

When I was shown the charts and diagrams, to add, divide, and measure them,
When I sitting heard the astrónomer where he lectured with much applause in the lecture-
    room,
How soon unaccountable I became tired and sick,
Till rising and gliding out I wander'd off by myself,
In the mystical moist night-air, and from time to time,
Look'd up in perfect silence at the stars.

                                                                            1865

CAVALRY CROSSING A FORD

A LINE in long array where they wind betwixt green islands,
They take a serpentine course, their arms flash in the sun—hark to the musical clank,
Behold the silvery river, in it the splashing horses loitering stop to drink,
Behold the brown-faced men, each group, each person a picture, the negligent rest on the
    saddles,
Some emerge on the opposite bank, others are just entering the ford—while,
Scarlet and blue and snowy white,
The guidon flags flutter gayly in the wind.

                                                                            1865

COME UP FROM THE FIELDS FATHER

COME up from the fields father, here's a letter from our Pete,
And come to the front door mother, here's a letter from thy dear son.

Lo, 'tis autumn, ●
Lo, where the trees, deeper green, yellower and redder,
Cool and sweeten Ohio's villages with leaves fluttering in the moderate wind,
Where apples ripe in the orchards hang and grapes on the trellis'd vines,
(Smell you the smell of the grapes on the vines?
Smell you the buckwheat where the bees were lately buzzing?)

Above all, lo, the sky so calm, so transparent after the rain, and with wondrous clouds,
Below too, all calm, all vital and beautiful, and the farm prospers well.   10

Down in the fields all prospers well,
But now from the fields come father, come at the daughter's call,
And come to the entry mother, to the front door come right away.

Fast as she can she hurries, something ominous, her steps trembling,
She does not tarry to smooth her hair nor adjust her cap.

Open the envelope quickly,
O this is not our son's writing, yet his name is sign'd,
O a strange hand writes for our dear son, O stricken mother's soul!
All swims before her eyes, flashes with black, she catches the main words only,
Sentences broken, *gunshot wound in the breast, cavalry skirmish, taken to hospital,*   20
At present low, but will soon be better.

Ah now the single figure to me,
Amid all teeming and wealthy Ohio with all its cities and farms,
Sickly white in the face and dull in the head, very faint,
By the jamb of a door leans.

Grieve not so, dear mother, (the just-grown daughter speaks through her sobs,
The little sisters huddle around speechless and dismay'd,)
See, dearest mother, the letter says Pete will soon be better.

Alas poor boy, he will never be better, (nor may-be needs to be better, that brave and simple
       soul,)
While they stand at home at the door he is dead already,   30
The only son is dead.

But the mother needs to be better,
She with thin form presently drest in black,
By day her meals untouch'd, then at night fitfully sleeping, often waking,
In the midnight waking, weeping, longing with one deep longing,
O that she might withdraw unnoticed, silent from life escape and withdraw,
To follow, to seek, to be with her dear dead son.

                                        1865

A MARCH IN THE RANKS HARD–PREST, AND THE ROAD UNKNOWN

A MARCH in the ranks hard-prest, and the road unknown,
A route through a heavy wood with muffled steps in the darkness,
Our army foil'd with loss severe, and the sullen remnant retreating,
Till after midnight glimmer upon us the lights of a dim-lighted building,
We come to an open space in the woods, and halt by the dim-lighted building,
'Tis a large old church at the crossing roads, now an impromptu hospital,
Entering but for a minute I see a sight beyond all the pictures and poems ever made,
Shadows of deepest, deepest black, just lit by moving candles and lamps,
And by one great pitchy torch stationary with wild red flame and clouds of smoke,
By these, crowds, groups of forms vaguely I see on the floor, some in the pews laid down,   10
At my feet more distinctly a soldier, a mere lad, in danger of bleeding to death, (he is shot in
       the abdomen,)
I stanch the blood temporarily, (the youngster's face is white as a lily,)
Then before I depart I sweep my eyes o'er the scene fain to absorb it all,
Faces, varieties, postures beyond description, most in obscurity, some of them dead,
Surgeons operating, attendants holding lights, the smell of ether, the odor of blood,
The crowd, O the crowd of the bloody forms, the yard outside also fill'd,
Some on the bare ground, some on planks or stretchers, some in the death-spasm sweating,
An occasional scream or cry, the doctor's shouted orders or calls,
The glisten of the little steel instruments catching the glint of the torches,
These I resume as I chant, I see again the forms, I smell the odor,   20
Then hear outside the orders given, *Fall in, my men, fall in;*
But first I bend to the dying lad, his eyes open, a half-smile gives he me,
Then the eyes close, calmly close, and I speed forth to the darkness,
Resuming, marching, ever in darkness marching, on in the ranks,
The unknown road still marching.

                                        1865

A SIGHT IN CAMP IN THE DAYBREAK GRAY AND DIM

A SIGHT in camp in the daybreak gray and dim,
As from my tent I emerge so early sleepless,
As slow I walk in the cool fresh air the path near by the hospital tent,
Three forms I see on stretchers lying, brought out there untended lying,
Over each the blanket spread, ample brownish woolen blanket,
Gray and heavy blanket, folding, covering all.

Curious I halt and silent stand,
Then with light fingers I from the face of the nearest the first just lift the blanket;
Who are you elderly man so gaunt and grim, with well-gray'd hair, and flesh all sunken about
    the eyes?
Who are you my dear comrade?   10

Then to the second I step—and who are you my child and darling?
Who are you sweet boy with cheeks yet blooming?

Then to the third—a face nor child nor old, very calm, as of beautiful yellow-white ivory;
Young man I think I know you—I think this face is the face of the Christ himself,
Dead and divine and brother of all, and here again he lies.

1865

THE WOUND-DRESSER

1

An old man bending I come among new faces,
Years looking backward resuming in answer to children,
Come tell us old man, as from young men and maidens that love me,
(Arous'd and angry, I'd thought to beat the alarum, and urge relentless war,
But soon my fingers fail'd me, my face droop'd and I resign'd myself,
To sit by the wounded and soothe them, or silently watch the dead;)
Years hence of these scenes, of these furious passions, these chances,
Of unsurpass'd heroes, (was one side so brave? the other was equally brave;)
Now be witness again, paint the mightiest armies of earth,
Of those armies so rapid so wondrous what saw you to tell us?   10
What stays with you latest and deepest? of curious panics,
Of hard-fought engagements or sieges tremendous what deepest remains?

2

O maidens and young men I love and that love me,
What you ask of my days those the strangest and sudden your talking recalls,
Soldier alert I arrive after a long march cover'd with sweat and dust,
In the nick of time I come, plunge in the fight, loudly shout in the rush of successful charge,
Enter the captur'd works—yet lo, like a swift-running river they fade,
Pass and are gone they fade—I dwell not on soldiers' perils or soldiers' joys,
(Both I remember well—many of the hardships, few the joys, yet I was content.)

But in silence, in dreams' projections,   20
While the world of gain and appearance and mirth goes on,
So soon what is over forgotten, and waves wash the imprints off the sand,
With hinged knees returning I enter the doors, (while for you up there,
Whoever you are, follow without noise and be of strong heart.)

Bearing the bandages, water and sponge,
Straight and swift to my wounded I go,
Where they lie on the ground after the battle brought in,
Where their priceless blood reddens the grass the ground,
Or to the rows of the hospital tent, or under the roof'd hospital,
To the long rows of cots up and down each side I return,   30
To each and all one after another I draw near, not one do I miss,
An attendant follows holding a tray, he carries a refuse pail,
Soon to be fill'd with clotted rags and blood, emptied, and fill'd again.

I onward go, I stop,
With hinged knees and steady hand to dress wounds,
I am firm with each, the pangs are sharp yet unavoidable,
One turns to me his appealing eyes—poor boy! I never knew you,
Yet I think I could not refuse this moment to die for you, if that would save you.

3

On, on I go, (open doors of time! open hospital doors!)
The crush'd head I dress, (poor crazed hand tear not the bandage away,)   40
The neck of the cavalry-man with the bullet through and through I examine,
Hard the breathing rattles, quite glazed already the eye, yet life struggles hard,
(Come sweet death! be persuaded O beautiful death!
In mercy come quickly.)

From the stump of the arm, the amputated hand,
I undo the clotted lint, remove the slough, wash off the matter and blood,
Back on his pillow the soldier bends with curv'd neck and side falling head,
His eyes are closed, his face is pale, he dares not look on the bloody stump,
And has not yet look'd on it.

I dress a wound in the side, deep, deep,   50
But a day or two more, for see the frame all wasted and sinking,
And the yellow-blue countenance see.

I dress the perforated shoulder, the foot with the bullet-wound,
Cleanse the one with a gnawing and putrid gangrene, so sickening, so offensive,
While the attendant stands behind aside me holding the tray and pail.

I am faithful, I do not give out,
The fractur'd thigh, the knee, the wound in the abdomen,
These and more I dress with impassive hand, (yet deep in my breast a fire, a burning flame.)

4

Thus in silence in dreams' projections,
Returning, resuming, I thread my way through the hospitals,   60
The hurt and wounded I pacify with soothing hand,
I sit by the restless all the dark night, some are so young,
Some suffer so much, I recall the experience sweet and sad,
(Many a soldier's loving arms about this neck have cross'd and rested,
Many a soldier's kiss dwells on these bearded lips.)

                                                                                    1865

GIVE ME THE SPLENDID SILENT SUN

1

GIVE me the splendid silent sun with all his beams full-dazzling,
Give me juicy autumnal fruit ripe and red from the orchard,
Give me a field where the unmow'd grass grows,
Give me an arbor, give me the trellis'd grape,
Give me fresh corn and wheat, give me serene-moving animals teaching content,
Give me nights perfectly quiet as on high plateaus west of the Mississippi, and I looking up at
     the stars,
Give me odorous at sunrise a garden of beautiful flowers where I can walk undisturb'd,
Give me for marriage a sweet-breath'd woman of whom I should never tire,
Give me a perfect child, give me away aside from the noise of the world a rural domestic life,

Give me to warble spontaneous songs recluse by myself, for my own ears only,   10
Give me solitude, give me Nature, give me again O Nature your primal sanities!

These demanding to have them, (tired with ceaseless excitement, and rack'd by the war-
    strife,)
These to procure incessantly asking, rising in cries from my heart,
While yet incessantly asking still I adhere to my city,
Day upon day and year upon year O city, walking your streets,
Where you hold me enchain'd a certain time refusing to give me up,
Yet giving to make me glutted, enrich'd of soul, you give me forever faces;
(O I see what I sought to escape, confronting, reversing my cries,
I see my own soul trampling down what it ask'd for.)

2

Keep your splendid silent sun,   20
Keep your woods O Nature, and the quiet places by the woods,
Keep your fields of clover and timothy, and your corn-fields and orchards,
Keep the blossoming buckwheat fields where the Ninth-month bees hum;
Give me faces and streets—give me these phantoms incessant and endless along the trottoirs!
Give me interminable eyes—give me women—give me comrades and lovers by the thousand!
Let me see new ones every day—let me hold new ones by the hand every day!
Give me such shows—give me the streets of Manhattan!
Give me Broadway, with the soldiers marching—give me the sound of the trumpets and
    drums!
(The soldiers in companies or regiments—some starting away, flush'd and reckless,
Some, their time up, returning with thinn'd ranks, young, yet very old, worn, marching,
    noticing nothing;)   30
Give me the shores and wharves heavy-fringed with black ships!
O such for me! O an intense life, full to repletion and varied!
The life of the theatre, bar-room, huge hotel, for me!
The saloon of the steamer! the crowded excursion for me! the torchlight procession!
The dense brigade bound for the war, with high piled military wagons following;
People, endless, streaming, with strong voices, passions, pageants,
Manhattan streets with their powerful throbs, with beating drums as now,
The endless and noisy chorus, the rustle and clank of muskets, (even the sight of the
    wounded,)
Manhattan crowds, with their turbulent musical chorus!
Manhattan faces and eyes forever for me.   40

1865

ETHIOPIA SALUTING THE COLORS

WHO are you dusky woman, so ancient hardly human,
With your woolly-white and turban'd head, and bare bony feet?
Why rising by the roadside here, do you the colors greet?

('Tis while our army lines Carolina's sands and pines,
Forth from thy hovel door thou Ethiopia com'st to me,
As under doughty Sherman I march toward the sea.)

Me master years a hundred since from my parents sunder'd,
A little child, they caught me as the savage beast is caught,
Then hither me across the sea the cruel slaver brought.

No further does she say, but lingering all the day,   10
Her high-borne turban'd head she wags, and rolls her darkling eye,
And courtesies to the regiments, the guidons moving by.

What is it fateful woman, so blear, hardly human?
Why wag your head with turban bound, yellow, red and green?
Are the things so strange and marvelous you see or have seen?

                                                                                    1871

RECONCILIATION

WORD over all, beautiful as the sky,
Beautiful that war and all its deeds of carnage must in time be utterly lost,
That the hands of the sisters Death and Night incessantly softly wash again, and ever again,
          this soil'd world;
For my enemy is dead, a man divine as myself is dead,
I look where he lies white-faced and still in the coffin—I draw near,
Bend down and touch lightly with my lips the white face in the coffin.

                                                                                    1866

WHEN LILACS LAST IN THE DOORYARD BLOOM'D [1]

I

WHEN lilacs last in the dooryard bloom'd,
And the great star early droop'd in the western sky in the night,
I mourn'd, and yet shall mourn with ever-returning spring.

Ever-returning spring, trinity sure to me you bring,
Lilac blooming perennial and drooping star in the west,
And thought of him I love.

2

O powerful western fallen star!
O shades of night—O moody, tearful night!
O great star disappear'd—O the black murk that hides the star!
O cruel hands that hold me powerless—O helpless soul of me!   10
O harsh surrounding cloud that will not free my soul.

3

In the dooryard fronting an old farm-house near the white-wash'd palings,
Stands the lilac-bush tall-growing with heart-shaped leaves of rich green,
With many a pointed blossom rising delicate, with the perfume strong I love,
With every leaf a miracle—and from this bush in the dooryard,

[1] 'In the future of these States must arise poets immenser far, and make great poems of death. The poems of life are great, but there must be poems of the purports of life, not only in itself, but beyond itself. . . . America needs, and the world needs, a class of bards who will, now and ever, so link and tally the rational physical being of man, with the ensembles of time and space, and with this vast and multiform show, Nature, surrounding him, ever tantalizing him, equally a part, and yet not a part of him, as to essentially harmonize, satisfy, and put at rest. Faith, very old, now scared away by science, must be restored, brought back by the same power that caused her departure—restored with new sway, deeper, wider, higher than ever. Surely, this universal ennui, this coward fear, this shuddering at death, these low degrading views, are not always to rule the spirit pervading future society, as it has the past, and does the present. What the Roman Lucretius sought most nobly, yet all too blindly, negatively to do for his age and its successors, must be done positively by some great coming literatus, especially poet, who, while remaining fully poet, will absorb whatever science indicates, with spiritualism, and out of them, and out of his genius, will compose the great poem of death. Then will man indeed confront Nature, and confront time and space, both with science and *con amore*, and take his right place, prepared for life, master of fortune and misfortune.' Whitman, 'Democratic Vistas' (1871), *Complete Prose Works*(Boston, 1898), 245–46.

With delicate-color'd blossoms and heart-shaped leaves of rich green,
A sprig with its flower I break.

4

In the swamp in secluded recesses,
A shy and hidden bird is warbling a song.
Solitary the thrush,   20
The hermit withdrawn to himself, avoiding the settlements,
Sings by himself a song.

Song of the bleeding throat,
Death's outlet song of life, (for well dear brother I know,
If thou wast not granted to sing thou would'st surely die.)

5

Over the breast of the spring, the land, amid cities,
Amid lanes and through old woods, where lately the violets peep'd from the ground, spotting
    the gray debris,
Amid the grass in the fields each side of the lanes, passing the endless grass,
Passing the yellow-spear'd wheat, every grain from its shroud in the dark-brown fields
    uprisen,
Passing the apple-tree blows of white and pink in the orchards,   30
Carrying a corpse to where it shall rest in the grave,
Night and day journeys a coffin.

6

Coffin that passes through lanes and streets,
Through day and night with the great cloud darkening the land,
With the pomp of the inloop'd flags with the cities draped in black,
With the show of the States themselves as of crape-veil'd women standing,
With processions long and winding and the flambeaus of the night,
With the countless torches lit, with the silent sea of faces and the unbared heads,
With the waiting depot, the arriving coffin, and the sombre faces,
With dirges through the night, with the thousand voices rising strong and solemn,   40
With all the mournful voices of the dirges pour'd around the coffin,
The dim-lit churches and the shuddering organs—where amid these you journey,
With the tolling tolling bells' perpetual clang,
Here, coffin that slowly passes,
I give you my sprig of lilac.

7

(Nor for you, for one alone,
Blossoms and branches green to coffins all I bring,
For fresh as the morning, thus would I chant a song for you O sane and sacred death.

All over bouquets of roses,
O death, I cover you over with roses and early lilies,   50
But mostly and now the lilac that blooms the first,
Copious I break, I break the sprigs from the bushes,
With loaded arms I come, pouring for you,
For you and the coffins all of you O death.)

8

O western orb sailing the heaven,
Now I know what you must have meant as a month since I walk'd,

As I walk'd in silence the transparent shadowy night,
As I saw you had something to tell as you bent to me night after night,
As you droop'd from the sky low down as if to my side, (while the other stars all look'd on,)
As we wander'd together the solemn night, (for something I know not what kept me from
     sleep,)   60
As the night advanced, and I saw on the rim of the west how full you were of woe,
As I stood on the rising ground in the breeze in the cool transparent night,
As I watch'd where you pass'd and was lost in the netherward black of the night,
As my soul in its trouble dissatisfied sank, as where you sad orb,
Concluded, dropt in the night, and was gone.

9

Sing on there in the swamp,
O singer bashful and tender, I hear your notes, I hear your call,
I hear, I come presently, I understand you,
But a moment I linger, for the lustrous star has detain'd me,
The star my departing comrade holds and detains me.   70

10

O how shall I warble myself for the dead one there I loved?
And how shall I deck my song for the large sweet soul that has gone?
And what shall my perfume be for the grave of him I love?

Sea-winds blown from east and west,
Blown from the Eastern sea and blown from the Western sea, till there on the prairies
     meeting,
These and with these and the breath of my chant,
I'll perfume the grave of him I love.

11

O what shall I hang on the chamber walls?
And what shall the pictures be that I hang on the walls,
To adorn the burial-house of him I love?   80

Pictures of growing spring and farms and homes,
With the Fourth-month eve at sundown, and the gray smoke lucid and bright,
With floods of the yellow gold of the gorgeous, indolent, sinking sun, burning, expanding the
     air,
With the fresh sweet herbage under foot, and the pale green leaves of the trees prolific,
In the distance the flowing glaze, the breast of the river, with a wind-dapple here and there,
With ranging hills on the banks, with many a line against the sky, and shadows,
And the city at hand with dwellings so dense, and stacks of chimneys,
And all the scenes of life and the workshops, and the workmen homeward returning.

12

Lo, body and soul—this land,
My own Manhattan with spires, and the sparkling and hurrying tides, and the ships,   90
The varied and ample land, the South and the North in the light, Ohio's shores and flashing
     Missouri,
And ever the far-spreading prairies cover'd with grass and corn.

Lo, the most excellent sun so calm and haughty,
The violet and purple morn with just-felt breezes,
The gentle soft-born measureless light,
The miracle spreading bathing all, the fulfill'd noon,

The coming eve delicious, the welcome night and the stars,
Over my cities shining all, enveloping man and land.

13

Sing on, sing on you gray-brown bird,
Sing from the swamps, the recesses, pour your chant from the bushes,   100
Limitless out of the dusk, out of the cedars and pines.

Sing on dearest brother, warble your reedy song,
Loud human song, with voice of uttermost woe.

O liquid and free and tender!
O wild and loose to my soul—O wondrous singer!
You only I hear—yet the star holds me, (but will soon depart,)
Yet the lilac with mastering odor holds me.

14

Now while I sat in the day and look'd forth,
In the close of the day with its light and the fields of spring, and the farmers preparing their crops,
In the large unconscious scenery of my land with its lakes and forests,   110
In the heavenly aerial beauty, (after the perturb'd winds and the storms,)
Under the arching heavens of the afternoon swift passing, and the voices of children and
       women,
The many-moving sea-tides, and I saw the ships how they sail'd,
And the summer approaching with richness, and the fields all busy with labor,
And the infinite separate houses, how they all went on, each with its meals and minutia of
       daily usages,
And the streets how their throbbings throbb'd, and the cities pent—lo, then and there,
Falling upon them all and among them all, enveloping me with the rest,
Appear'd the cloud, appear'd the long black trail,
And I knew death, its thought, and the sacred knowledge of death.

Then with the knowledge of death as walking one side of me,   120
And the thought of death close-walking the other side of me,
And I in the middle as with companions, and as holding the hands of companions,
I fled forth to the hiding receiving night that talks not,
Down to the shores of the water, the path by the swamp in the dimness,
To the solemn shadowy cedars and ghostly pines so still.

And the singer so shy to the rest receiv'd me,
The gray-brown bird I know receiv'd us comrades three,
And he sang the carol of death, and a verse for him I love.

From deep secluded recesses,
From the fragrant cedars and the ghostly pines so still,   130
Came the carol of the bird.

And the charm of the carol rapt me,
As I held as if by their hands my comrades in the night,
And the voice of my spirit tallied the song of the bird.

Come lovely and soothing death,
Undulate round the world, serenely arriving, arriving,
In the day, in the night, to all, to each,
Sooner or later delicate death.

Prais'd be the fathomless universe,
For life and joy, and for objects and knowledge curious,   140
And for love, sweet love—but praise! praise! praise!
For the sure-enwinding arms of cool-enfolding death.

Dark mother always gliding near with soft feet,
Have none chanted for thee a chant of fullest welcome?
Then I chant it for thee, I glorify thee above all,
I bring thee a song that when thou must indeed come, come unfalteringly.

Approach strong deliveress,
When it is so, when thou hast taken them I joyously sing the dead,
Lost in the loving floating ocean of thee,
Laved in the flood of thy bliss O death.   150

From me to thee glad serenades,
Dances for thee I propose saluting thee, adornments and feastings for thee,
And the sights of the open landscape and the high-spread sky are fitting,
And life and the fields, and the huge and thoughtful night.

The night in silence under many a star,
The ocean shore and the husky whispering wave whose voice I know,
And the soul turning to thee O vast and well-veil'd death,
And the body gratefully nestling close to thee.

Over the tree-tops I float thee a song,
Over the rising and sinking waves, over the myriad fields and the prairies wide,   160
Over the dense-pack'd cities all and the teeming wharves and ways,
I float this carol with joy, with joy to thee O death.

15

To the tally of my soul,
Loud and strong kept up the gray-brown bird,
With pure deliberate notes spreading filling the night.

Loud in the pines and cedars dim,
Clear in the freshness moist and the swamp-perfume,
And I with my comrades there in the night.

While my sight that was bound in my eyes unclosed,
As to long panoramas of visions.   170

And I saw askant the armies,
I saw as in noiseless dreams hundreds of battle-flags,
Borne through the smoke of the battles and pierc'd with missiles I saw them,
And carried hither and yon through the smoke, and torn and bloody,
And at last but a few shreds left on the staffs, (and all in silence,)
And the staffs all splinter'd and broken.

I saw battle-corpses, myriads of them,
And the white skeletons of young men, I saw them,
I saw the debris and debris of all the slain soldiers of the war,
But I saw they were not as was thought,   180
They themselves were fully at rest, they suffer'd not,
The living remain'd and suffer'd, the mother suffer'd,

And the wife and the child and the musing comrade suffer'd,
And the armies that remain'd suffer'd.

16

Passing the visions, passing the night,
Passing, unloosing the hold of my comrades' hands,
Passing the song of the hermit bird and the tallying song of my soul,
Victorious song, death's outlet song, yet varying ever-altering song,
As low and wailing, yet clear the notes, rising and falling, flooding the night,
Sadly sinking and fainting, as warning and warning, and yet again bursting with joy,   190
Covering the earth and filling the spread of the heaven,
As that powerful psalm in the night I heard from recesses,
Passing, I leave thee lilac with heart-shaped leaves,
I leave thee there in the door-yard, blooming, returning with spring.

I cease from my song for thee,
From my gaze on thee in the west, fronting the west, communing with thee,
O comrade lustrous with silver face in the night.

Yet each to keep and all, retrievements out of the night,
The song, the wondrous chant of the gray-brown bird,
And the tallying chant, the echo arous'd in my soul,   200
With the lustrous and drooping star with the countenance full of woe,
With the holders holding my hand nearing the call of the bird,
Comrades mine and I in the midst, and their memory ever to keep, for the dead I loved so
        well,
For the sweetest, wisest soul of all my days and lands—and this for his dear sake,
Lilac and star and bird twined with the chant of my soul,
There in the fragrant pines and the cedars dusk and dim.

1866

O CAPTAIN! MY CAPTAIN!

O CAPTAIN! my Captain! our fearful trip is done,
The ship has weather'd every rack, the prize we sought is won,
The port is near, the bells I hear, the people all exulting,
While follow eyes the steady keel, the vessel grim and daring;
        But O heart! heart! heart!
        O the bleeding drops of red,
            Where on the deck my Captain lies,
            Fallen cold and dead.

O Captain! my Captain! rise up and hear the bells;
Rise up—for you the flag is flung—for you the bugle trills,   10
For you bouquets and ribbon'd wreaths—for you the shores a-crowding,
For you they call, the swaying mass, their eager faces turning;
        Here Captain! dear father!
        The arm beneath your head!
            It is some dream that on the deck,
            You've fallen cold and dead.

My Captain does not answer, his lips are pale and still,
My father does not feel my arm, he has no pulse nor will,
The ship is anchor'd safe and sound, its voyage closed and done,
From fearful trip the victor ship comes in with object won;   20

Exult O shores, and ring O bells!
But I with mournful tread,
    Walk the deck my Captain lies,
    Fallen cold and dead.

1866

THERE WAS A CHILD WENT FORTH [1]

THERE was a child went forth every day,
And the first object he look'd upon, that object he became,
And that object became part of him for the day or a certain part of the day,
Or for many years or stretching cycles of years.

The early lilacs became part of this child,
And grass and white and red morning-glories, and white and red clover, and the song of the
    phœbe-bird,
And the Third-month lambs and the sow's pink-faint litter, and the mare's foal and the cow's
    calf,
And the noisy brood of the barnyard or by the mire of the pond-side,
And the fish suspending themselves so curiously below there, and the beautiful curious
    liquid,
And the water-plants with their graceful flat heads, all became part of him.   10

The field-sprouts of Fourth-month and Fifth-month became part of him,
Winter-grain sprouts and those of the light-yellow corn, and the esculent roots of the garden,
And the apple-trees cover'd with blossoms and the fruit afterward, and wood-berries, and the
    commonest weeds by the road,
And the old drunkard staggering home from the outhouse of the tavern whence he had lately
    risen,
And the schoolmistress that pass'd on her way to the school,
And the friendly boys that pass'd, and the quarrelsome boys,
And the tidy and fresh-cheek'd girls, and the barefoot negro boy and girl,
And all the changes of city and country wherever he went.

His own parents, he that had father'd him and she that had conceiv'd him in her womb and
    birth'd him,
They gave this child more of themselves than that,   20
They gave him afterward every day, they became part of him.

The mother at home quietly placing the dishes on the supper-table,
The mother with mild words, clean her cap and gown, a wholesome odor falling off her person
    and clothes as she walks by,
The father, strong, self-sufficient, manly, mean, anger'd, unjust,
The blow, the quick loud word, the tight bargain, the crafty lure,
The family usages, the language, the company, the furniture, the yearning and swelling heart,
Affection that will not be gainsay'd, the sense of what is real, the thought if after all it should
    prove unreal,
The doubts of day-time and the doubts of night-time, the curious whether and how,
Whether that which appears so is so, or is it all flashes and specks?
Men and women crowding fast in the streets, if they are not flashes and specks what are they?
The streets themselves and the façades of houses, and goods in the windows,   31
Vehicles, teams, the heavy-plank'd wharves, the huge crossing at the ferries,

1 'People have often asked him the meaning of the poem "There Was a Child Went Forth," and he has always made the
same answer: "What is the meaning? I wonder what? I wonder what?" Once he said to Bronsall: "Harry, maybe it has
no meaning." ' Traubel, *With Walt Whitman in Camden*(N.Y., 1915),II,228.

The village on the highland seen from afar at sunset, the river between,
Shadows, aureola and mist, the light falling on roofs and gables of white or brown two miles off,
The schooner near by sleepily dropping down the tide, the little boat slack-tow'd astern,
The hurrying tumbling waves, quick-broken crests, slapping,
The strata of color'd clouds, the long bar of maroon-tint away solitary by itself, the spread of purity it lies motionless in,
The horizon's edge, the flying sea-crow, the fragrance of salt marsh and shore mud,
These became part of that child who went forth every day, and who now goes, and will always go forth every day.

1855

THE CITY DEAD-HOUSE

By the city dead-house by the gate,
As idly sauntering wending my way from the clangor,
I curious pause, for lo, an outcast form, a poor dead prostitute brought,
Her corpse they deposit unclaim'd, it lies on the damp brick pavement,
The divine woman, her body, I see the body, I look on it alone,
That house once full of passion and beauty, all else I notice not,
Nor stillness so cold, nor running water from faucet, nor odors morbific impress me,
But the house alone—that wondrous house—that delicate fair house—that ruin!
That immortal house more than all the rows of dwellings ever built!
Or white-domed capitol with majestic figure surmounted, or all the old high-spired cathedrals,
That little house alone more than them all—poor, desperate house!
Fair, fearful wreck—tenement of a soul—itself a soul,
Unclaim'd, avoided house—take one breath from my tremulous lips,
Take one tear dropt aside as I go for thought of you,
Dead house of love—house of madness and sin, crumbled, crush'd.
House of life, erewhile talking and laughing—but ah, poor house, dead even then,
Months, years, an echoing, garnish'd house—but dead, dead, dead.

1867

TO A COMMON PROSTITUTE

Be composed—be at ease with me—I am Walt Whitman, liberal and lusty as Nature,
Not till the sun excludes you do I exclude you,
Not till the waters refuse to glisten for you and the leaves to rustle for you, do my words refuse to glisten and rustle for you.

My girl I appoint with you an appointment, and I charge you that you make preparation to be worthy to meet me,
And I charge you that you be patient and perfect till I come.

Till then I salute you with a significant look that you do not forget me.

1860

WHO LEARNS MY LESSON COMPLETE?

Who learns my lesson complete?
Boss, journeyman, apprentice, churchman and atheist,
The stupid and the wise thinker, parents and offspring, merchant, clerk, porter and customer,
Editor, author, artist, and schoolboy—draw nigh and commence;
It is no lesson—it lets down the bars to a good lesson,
And that to another, and every one to another still.
The great laws take and effuse without argument,
I am of the same style, for I am their friend,
I love them quits and quits, I do not halt and make salaams.

I lie abstracted and hear beautiful tales of things and the reasons of things,   10
They are so beautiful I nudge myself to listen.

I cannot say to any person what I hear—I cannot say it to myself—it is very wonderful.

It is no small matter, this round and delicious globe moving so exactly in its orbit for ever and
    ever, without one jolt or the untruth of a single second,
I do not think it was made in six days, nor in ten thousand years, nor ten billions of years,
Nor plann'd and built one thing after another as an architect plans and builds a house.

I do not think seventy years is the time of a man or woman,
Nor that seventy millions of years is the time of a man or woman,
Nor that years will ever stop the existence of me, or any one else.

Is it wonderful that I should be immortal? as every one is immortal;
I know it is wonderful, but my eyesight is equally wonderful, and how I was conceived in my
    mother's womb is equally wonderful,   20
And pass'd from a babe in the creeping trance of a couple of summers and winters to articu-
    late and walk—all this is equally wonderful.

And that my soul embraces you this hour, and we affect each other without ever seeing each
    other, and never perhaps to see each other, is every bit as wonderful.

And that I can think such thoughts as these is just as wonderful,
And that I can remind you, and you think them and know them to be true, is just as
    wonderful.

And that the moon spins round the earth and on with the earth, is equally wonderful,
And that they balance themselves with the sun and stars is equally wonderful.

                                         1855

ITALIAN MUSIC IN DAKOTA

('The Seventeenth—the finest Regimental Band I ever heard.')

Through the soft evening air enwinding all,
Rocks, woods, fort, cannon, pacing sentries, endless wilds,
In dulcet streams, in flutes' and cornets' notes,
Electric, pensive, turbulent, artificial,
(Yet strangely fitting even here, meanings unknown before,
Subtler than ever, more harmony, as if born here, related here,
Not to the city's fresco'd rooms, not to the audience of the opera house,
Sounds, echoes, wandering strains, as really here at home,
Sonnambula's innocent love, trios with *Norma's* anguish,
And thy ecstatic chorus *Poliuto*;)   10
Ray'd in the limpid yellow slanting sundown,
Music, Italian music in Dakota.

While Nature, sovereign of this gnarl'd realm,
Lurking in hidden barbaric grim recesses,
Acknowledging rapport however far remov'd,
(As some old root or soil of earth its last-born flower or fruit,)
Listens well pleas'd.

                                         1881

PASSAGE TO INDIA [1]

1

SINGING my days,
Singing the great achievements of the present,
Singing the strong light works of engineers,
Our modern wonders, (the antique ponderous Seven outvied,)
In the Old World the east the Suez canal,
The New by its mighty railroad spann'd,
The seas inlaid with eloquent gentle wires;
Yet first to sound, and ever sound, the cry with thee O soul,
The Past! the Past! the Past!

The Past—the dark unfathom'd retrospect!   10
The teeming gulf—the sleepers and the shadows!
The past—the infinite greatness of the past!
For what is the present after all but a growth out of the past?
(As a projectile form'd, impell'd, passing a certain line, still keeps on,
So the present, utterly form'd, impell'd by the past.)

2

Passage O soul to India!
Eclaircise the myths Asiatic, the primitive fables.

Not you alone proud truths of the world,
Nor you alone ye facts of modern science,
But myths and fables of eld, Asia's, Africa's fables,   20
The far-darting beams of the spirit, the unloos'd dreams,
The deep diving bibles and legends,
The daring plots of the poets, the elder religions;
O you temples fairer than lilies pour'd over by the rising sun!
O you fables spurning the known, eluding the hold of the known, mounting to heaven!
You lofty and dazzling towers, pinnacled, red as roses, burnish'd with gold!
Towers of fables immortal fashion'd from mortal dreams!
You too I welcome and fully the same as the rest!
You too with joy I sing.

Passage to India!   30
Lo, soul, seest thou not God's purpose from the first?
The earth to be spann'd, connected by network,
The races, neighbors, to marry and be given in marriage,
The oceans to be cross'd, the distant brought near,
The lands to be welded together.

A worship new I sing,
You captains, voyagers, explorers, yours,

---

1 In reference to this poem, Whitman said: 'There's more of me, the essential me, in that than in any of the poems. There is no philosophy, consistent or inconsistent, in that poem—there Brinton would be right—but the burden of it is evolution—the one thing escaping the other—the unfolding of cosmic purposes.' Ibid., I,156-57.

You engineers, you architects, machinists, yours,
You, not for trade or transportation only,
But in God's name, and for thy sake O soul.   40

3

Passage to India!
Lo soul for thee of tableaus twain.
I see in one the Suez canal initiated, open'd,
I see the procession of steamships, the Empress Eugenie's leading the van,
I mark from on deck the strange landscape, the pure sky, the level sand in the distance,
I pass swiftly the picturesque groups, the workmen gather'd,
The gigantic dredging machines.

In one again, different, (yet thine, all thine, O soul, the same,)
I see over my own continent the Pacific raiiroad surmounting every barrier,
I see continual trains of cars winding along the Platte carrying freight and passengers,   50
I hear the locomotives rushing and roaring, and the shrill steam-whistle,
I hear the echoes reverberate through the grandest scenery in the world,
I cross the Laramie plains, I note the rocks in grotesque shapes, the buttes,
I see the plentiful larkspur and wild onions, the barren, colorless, sage-deserts,
I see in glimpses afar or towering immediately above me the great mountains, I see the Wind
        river and the Wahsatch mountains,
I see the Monument mountain and the Eagle's Nest, I pass the Promontory, I ascend the
        Nevadas,
I scan the noble Elk mountain and wind around its base,
I see the Humboldt range, I thread the valley and cross the river,
I see the clear waters of lake Tahoe, I see forests of majestic pines,
Or crossing the great desert, the alkaline plains, I behold enchanting mirages of waters and
        meadows,   60
Marking through these and after all, in duplicate slender lines,
Bridging the three or four thousand miles of land travel,
Tying the Eastern to the Western sea,
The road between Europe and Asia.

(Ah Genoese thy dream! thy dream!
Centuries after thou art laid in thy grave,
The shore thou foundest verifies thy dream.)

4

Passage to India!
Struggles of many a captain, tales of many a sailor dead,
Over my mood stealing and spreading they come,   70
Like clouds and cloudlets in the unreach'd sky.

Along all history, down the slopes,
As a rivulet running, sinking now, and now again to the surface rising,
A ceaseless thought, a varied train—lo, soul, to thee, thy sight, they rise,
The plans, the voyages again, the expeditions;
Again Vasco de Gama sails forth,
Again the knowledge gain'd, the mariner's compass,
Lands found and nations born, thou born America,
For purpose vast, man's long probation fill'd,
Thou rondure of the world at last accomplish'd.   80

5

O vast Rondure, swimming in space,
Cover'd all over with visible power and beauty,
Alternate light and day and the teeming spiritual darkness,
Unspeakable high processions of sun and moon and countless stars above,
Below, the manifold grass and waters, animals, mountains, trees,
With inscrutable purpose, some hidden prophetic intention,
Now first it seems my thought begins to span thee.

Down from the gardens of Asia descending radiating,
Adam and Eve appear, then their myriad progeny after them,
Wandering, yearning, curious, with restless explorations,   98
With questionings, baffled, formless, feverish, with never-happy hearts,
With that sad incessant refrain, *Wherefore unsatisfied soul?* and *Whither O mocking life?*

Ah who shall soothe these feverish children?
Who justify these restless explorations?
Who speak the secret of impassive earth?
Who bind it to us? what is this separate Nature so unnatural?
What is this earth to our affections? (unloving earth, without a throb to answer ours,
Cold earth, the place of graves.)

Yet soul be sure the first intent remains, and shall be carried out,
Perhaps even now the time has arrived.   100

After the seas are all cross'd, (as they seem already cross'd,)
After the great captains and engineers have accomplish'd their work,
After the noble inventors, after the scientists, the chemist, the geologist, ethnologist,
Finally shall come the poet worthy that name,
The true son of God shall come singing his songs.

Then not your deeds only O voyagers, O scientists and inventors, shall be justified,
All these hearts as of fretted children shall be sooth'd,
All affection shall be fully responded to, the secret shall be told,
All these separations and gaps shall be taken up and hook'd and link'd together,
The whole earth, this cold, impassive, voiceless earth, shall be completely justified,   110
Trinitas divine shall be gloriously accomplish'd and compacted by the true son of God, the poet,
(He shall indeed pass the straits and conquer the mountains,
He shall double the cape of Good Hope to some purpose,)
Nature and Man shall be disjoin'd and diffused no more,
The true son of God shall absolutely fuse them.

6

Year at whose wide-flung door I sing!
Year of the purpose accomplish'd!
Year of the marriage of continents, climates and oceans!
(No mere doge of Venice now wedding the Adriatic,)
I see O year in you the vast terraqueous globe given and giving all,   120
Europe to Asia, Africa join'd, and they to the New World,
The lands, geographies, dancing before you, holding a festival garland,
As brides and bridegrooms hand in hand.

Passage to India!
Cooling airs from Caucasus, far, soothing cradle of man,
The river Euphrates flowing, the past lit up again.

Lo soul, the retrospect brought forward,
The old, most populous, wealthiest of earth's lands,
The streams of the Indus and the Ganges and their many affluents,
(I my shores of America walking to-day behold, resuming all,)   130
The tale of Alexander on his warlike marches suddenly dying,
On one side China and on the other side Persia and Arabia,
To the south the great seas and the bay of Bengal,
The flowing literatures, tremendous epics, religions, castes,
Old occult Brahma interminably far back, the tender and junior Buddha,
Central and southern empires and all their belongings, possessors,
The wars of Tamerlane, the reign of Aurungzebe,
The traders, rulers, explorers, Moslems, Venetians, Byzantium, the Arabs, Portuguese,
The first travelers famous yet, Marco Polo, Batouta the Moor,
Doubts to be solv'd, the map incognita, blanks to be fill'd,   140
The foot of man unstay'd, the hands never at rest,
Thyself O soul that will not brook a challenge.

The mediæval navigators rise before me,
The world of 1492, with its awaken'd enterprise,
Something swelling in humanity now like the sap of the earth in spring,
The sunset splendor of chivalry declining.

And who art thou sad shade?
Gigantic, visionary, thyself a visionary,
With majestic limbs and pious beaming eyes,
Spreading around with every look of thine a golden world,   150
Enhuing it with gorgeous hues.

As the chief histrion,
Down to the footlights walks in some great scena,
Dominating the rest I see the Admiral himself,
(History's type of courage, action, faith,)
Behold him sail from Palos leading his little fleet,
His voyage behold, his return, his great fame,
His misfortunes, calumniators, behold him a prisoner, chain'd,
Behold his dejection, poverty, death.

(Curious in time I stand, noting the efforts of heroes,   160
Is the deferment long? bitter the slander, poverty, death?
Lies the seed unreck'd for centuries in the ground? lo, to God's due occasion,
Uprising in the night, it sprouts, blooms,
And fills the earth with use and beauty.)

7

Passage indeed O soul to primal thought,
Not lands and seas alone, thy own clear freshness,
The young maturity of brood and bloom,
To realms of budding bibles.

O soul, repressless, I with thee and thou with me,
Thy circumnavigation of the world begin,   170
Of man, the voyage of his mind's return,
To reason's early paradise,
Back, back to wisdom's birth, to innocent intuitions,
Again with fair creation.

8

O we can wait no longer,
We too take ship O soul,
Joyous we too launch out on trackless seas,
Fearless for unknown shores on waves of ecstasy to sail,
Amid the wafting winds, (thou pressing me to thee, I thee to me, O soul,)
Caroling free, singing our song of God,   180
Chanting our chant of pleasant exploration.

With laugh and many a kiss,
(Let others deprecate, let others weep for sin, remorse, humiliation,)
O soul thou pleasest me, I thee.

Ah more than any priest O soul we too believe in God,
But with the mystery of God we dare not dally.

O soul thou pleasest me, I thee,
Sailing these seas or on the hills, or waking in the night,
Thoughts, silent thoughts, of Time and Space and Death, like waters flowing,
Bear me indeed as through the regions infinite,   190
Whose air I breathe, whose ripples hear, lave me all over,
Bathe me O God in thee, mounting to thee,
I and my soul to range in range of thee.

O Thou transcendent,
Nameless, the fibre and the breath,
Light of the light, shedding forth universes, thou centre of them,
Thou mightier centre of the true, the good, the loving,
Thou moral, spiritual fountain—affection's source—thou reservoir,
(O pensive soul of me—O thirst unsatisfied—waitest not there?
Waitest not haply for us somewhere there the Comrade perfect?)   200
Thou pulse—thou motive of the stars, suns, systems,
That, circling, move in order, safe, harmonious,
Athwart the shapeless vastnesses of space,
How should I think, how breathe a single breath, how speak, if, out of myself,
I could not launch, to those, superior universes?

Swiftly I shrivel at the thought of God,
At Nature and its wonders, Time and Space and Death,
But that I, turning, call to thee O soul, thou actual Me,
And lo, thou gently masterest the orbs,
Thou matest Time, smilest content at Death,   210
And fillest, swellest full the vastnesses of Space.

Greater than stars or suns,
Bounding O soul thou journeyest forth;
What love than thine and ours could wider amplify?
What aspirations, wishes, outvie thine and ours O soul?
What dreams of the ideal? what plans of purity, perfection, strength,
What cheerful willingness for others' sake to give up all?
For others' sake to suffer all?

Reckoning ahead O soul, when thou, the time achiev'd,
The seas all cross'd, weather'd the capes, the voyage done,   220
Surrounded, copest, frontest God, yieldest, the aim attain'd,

As fill'd with friendship, love complete, the Elder Brother found,
The Younger melts in fondness in his arms.

9

Passage to more than India!
Are thy wings plumed indeed for such far flights?
O soul, voyagest thou indeed on voyages like those?
Disportest thou on waters such as those?
Soundest below the Sanscrit and the Vedas?
Then have thy bent unleash'd.

Passage to you, your shores, ye aged fierce enigmas!   230
Passage to you, to mastership of you, ye strangling problems!
You, strew'd with the wrecks of skeletons, that, living, never reach'd you.

Passage to more than India!
O secret of the earth and sky!
Of you O waters of the sea! O winding creeks and rivers!
Of you O woods and fields! of you strong mountains of my land!
Of you O prairies! of you gray rocks!
O morning red! O clouds! O rain and snows!
O day and night, passage to you!

O sun and moon and all you stars! Sirius and Jupiter!   240
Passage to you!

Passage, immediate passage! the blood burns in my veins!
Away O soul! hoist instantly the anchor!
Cut the hawsers—haul out—shake out every sail!
Have we not stood here like trees in the ground long enough?
Have we not grovel'd here long enough, eating and drinking like mere brutes?
Have we not darken'd and dazed ourselves with books long enough?

Sail forth—steer for the deep waters only,
Reckless O soul, exploring, I with thee, and thou with me,
For we are bound where mariner has not yet dared to go,   250
And we will risk the ship, ourselves and all.

O my brave soul!
O farther farther sail!
O daring joy, but safe! are they not all the seas of God?
O farther, farther, farther sail!

                                                                       1871

CHANTING THE SQUARE DEIFIC [1]

I

CHANTING the square deific, out of the One advancing, out of the sides,
Out of the old and new, out of the square entirely divine,
Solid, four-sided, (all the sides needed,) from this side Jehovah am I,
Old Brahm I, and I Saturnius am;
Not Time affects me—I am Time, old, modern as any,

---

[1] 'Brinton said: " 'Chanting the Square Deific' is an immortal poem: I sometimes think it is the most subtle and profound thing you have written." W. said as to that: "Many of my friends have agreed with you, Doctor, about that. It would be hard to give the idea mathematical expression: the idea of spiritual equity—of spiritual substance: the four-square

Unpersuadable, relentless, executing righteous judgments,
As the Earth, the Father, the brown old Kronos, with laws,
Aged beyond computation, yet ever new, ever with those mighty laws rolling,
Relentless I forgive no man—whoever sins dies—I will have that man's life;
Therefore let none expect mercy—have the seasons, gravitation, the appointed days, mercy?
      no more have I,   10
But as the seasons and gravitation, and as all the appointed days that forgive not,
I dispense from this side judgments inexorable without the least remorse.

2

Consolator most mild, the promis'd one advancing,
With gentle hand extended, the mightier God am I,
Foretold by prophets and poets in their most rapt prophecies and poems,
From this side, lo! the Lord Christ gazes—lo! Hermes I—lo! mine is Hercules' face,
All sorrow, labor, suffering, I, tallying it, absorb in myself,
Many times have I been rejected, taunted, put in prison, and crucified, and many times shall
      be again,
All the world have I given up for my dear brothers' and sisters' sake, for the soul's sake,
Wending my way through the homes of men, rich or poor, with the kiss of affection,   20
For I am affection, I am the cheer-bringing God, with hope and all-enclosing charity,
With indulgent words as to children, with fresh and sane words, mine only,
Young and strong I pass knowing well I am destin'd myself to an early death;
But my charity has no death—my wisdom dies not, neither early nor late,
And my sweet love bequeath'd here and elsewhere never dies.

3

Aloof, dissatisfied, plotting revolt,
Comrade of criminals, brother of slaves,
Crafty, despised, a drudge, ignorant,
With sudra face and worn brow, black, but in the depths of my heart, proud as any,
Lifted now and always against whoever scorning assumes to rule me,
Morose, full of guile, full of reminiscences, brooding, with many wiles,   30
(Though it was thought I was baffled and dispel'd, and my wiles done, but that will never be,)
Defiant, I, Satan, still live, still utter words, in new lands duly appearing, (and old ones also,)
Permanent here from my side, warlike, equal with any, real as any,
Nor time nor change shall ever change me or my words.

4

Santa Spirita, breather, life,
Beyond the light, lighter than light,
Beyond the flames of hell, joyous, leaping easily above hell,
Beyond Paradise, perfumed solely with mine own perfume,
Including all life on earth, touching, including God, including Saviour and Satan,   40
Ethereal, pervading all, (for without me what were all? what were God?)
Essence of forms, life of the real identities, permanent, positive, (namely the unseen,)
Life of the great round world, the sun and stars, and of man, I, the general soul,
Here the square finishing, the solid, I the most solid,
Breathe my breath also through these songs.

1866

entity—the north, south, east, west of the constituted universe (even the soul universe)—the four sides as sustaining the universe (the supernatural something): this is not the poem but the idea back of the poem or below the poem. I am lame enough trying to explain it in other words—the idea seems to fit its own words better than mine. You see, at the time the poem wrote itself: now I am trying to write it." ' Ibid.,I,156.

A NOISELESS PATIENT SPIDER

A NOISELESS patient spider,
I mark'd where on a little promontory it stood isolated,
Mark'd how to explore the vacant vast surrounding,
It launch'd forth filament, filament, filament, out of itself,
Ever unreeling them, ever tirelessly speeding them.

And you O my soul where you stand,
Surrounded, detached, in measureless oceans of space,
Ceaselessly musing, venturing, throwing, seeking the spheres to connect them,
Till the bridge you will need be form'd, till the ductile anchor hold,
Till the gossamer thread you fling catch somewhere, O my soul.   10

1871

THE LAST INVOCATION

AT the last, tenderly,
From the walls of the powerful fortress'd house,
From the clasp of the knitted locks, from the keep of the well-closed doors,
Let me be wafted.

Let me glide noiselessly forth;
With the key of softness unlock the locks—with a whisper,
Set ope the doors O soul.

Tenderly—be not impatient,
(Strong is your hold O mortal flesh,
Strong is your hold O love.)   10

1871

TO A LOCOMOTIVE IN WINTER

THEE for my recitative,
Thee in the driving storm even as now, the snow, the winter-day declining,
Thee in thy panoply, thy measur'd dual throbbing and thy beat convulsive,
Thy black cylindric body, golden brass and silvery steel,
Thy ponderous side-bars, parallel and connecting rods, gyrating, shuttling at thy sides,
Thy metrical, now swelling pant and roar, now tapering in the distance,
Thy great protruding head-light fix'd in front,
Thy long, pale, floating vapor-pennants, tinged with delicate purple,
The dense and murky clouds out-belching from thy smoke-stack,
Thy knitted frame, thy springs and valves, the tremulous twinkle of thy wheels,   10
Thy train of cars behind, obedient, merrily following,
Through gale or calm, now swift, now slack, yet steadily careering;
Type of the modern—emblem of motion and power—pulse of the continent,
For once come serve the Muse and merge in verse, even as here I see thee,
With storm and buffeting gusts of wind and falling snow,
By day thy warning ringing bell to sound its notes,
By night thy silent signal lamps to swing.

Fierce-throated beauty!
Roll through my chant with all thy lawless music, thy swinging lamps at night,
Thy madly-whistled laughter, echoing, rumbling like an earthquake, rousing all,   20
Law of thyself complete, thine own track firmly holding,

(No sweetness debonair of tearful harp or glib piano thine,)
Thy trills of shrieks by rocks and hills return'd,
Launch'd o'er the prairies wide, across the lakes,
To the free skies unpent and glad and strong.

1876

YEARS OF THE MODERN

YEARS of the modern! years of the unperform'd!
Your horizon rises, I see it parting away for more august dramas,
I see not America only, not only Liberty's nation but other nations preparing,
I see tremendous entrances and exits, new combinations, the solidarity of races,
I see that force advancing with irresistible power on the world's stage,
(Have the old forces, the old wars, played their parts? are the acts suitable to them closed?)
I see Freedom, completely arm'd and victorious and very haughty, with Law on one side and
    Peace on the other,
A stupendous trio all issuing forth against the idea of caste;
What historic denouements are these we so rapidly approach?
I see men marching and countermarching by swift millions,   10
I see the frontiers and boundaries of the old aristocracies broken,
I see the landmarks of European kings removed,
I see this day the People beginning their landmarks, (all others give way;)
Never were such sharp questions ask'd as this day,
Never was average man, his soul, more energetic, more like a God,
Lo, how he urges and urges, leaving the masses no rest!
His daring foot is on land and sea everywhere, he colonizes the Pacific, the archipelagoes,
With the steamship, the electric telegraph, the newspaper, the wholesale engines of war,
With these and the world-spreading factories he interlinks all geography, all lands;
What whispers are these O lands, running ahead of you, passing under the seas?   20
Are all nations communing? is there going to be but one heart to the globe?
Is humanity forming en-masse? for lo, tyrants tremble, crowns grow dim,
The earth, restive, confronts a new era, perhaps a general divine war,
No one knows what will happen next, such portents fill the days and nights;
Years prophetical! the space ahead as I walk, as I vainly try to pierce it, is full of phantoms,
Unborn deeds, things soon to be, project their shapes around me,
This incredible rush and heat, this strange ecstatic fever of dreams O years!
Your dreams O years, how they penetrate through me! (I know not whether I sleep or wake;)
The perform'd America and Europe grow dim, retiring in shadow behind me,
The unperform'd, more gigantic than ever, advance, advance upon me.   30

1865

MANNAHATTA

I WAS asking for something specific and perfect for my city,
Whereupon lo! upsprang the aboriginal name.

Now I see what there is in a name, a word, liquid, sane, unruly, musical, self-sufficient,
I see that the word of my city is that word from of old,
Because I see that word nested in nests of water-bays, superb,
Rich, hemm'd thick all around with sailships and steamships, an island sixteen miles long,
    solid-founded,
Numberless crowded streets, high growths of iron, slender, strong, light, splendidly uprising
    toward clear skies,
Tides swift and ample, well-loved by me, toward sundown,
The flowing sea-currents, the little islands, larger adjoining islands, the heights, the villas,

The countless masts, the white shore-steamers, the lighters, the ferry-boats, the black sea-
    steamers well-model'd,   10
The down-town streets, the jobbers' houses of business, the houses of business of the ship-
    merchants and money-brokers, the river-streets,
Immigrants arriving, fifteen or twenty thousand in a week,
The carts hauling goods, the manly race of drivers of horses, the brown-faced sailors,
The summer air, the bright sun shining, and the sailing clouds aloft,
The winter snows, the sleigh-bells, the broken ice in the river, passing along up or down with
    the flood-tide or ebb-tide,
The mechanics of the city, the masters, well-form'd, beautiful-faced, looking you straight in
    the eyes,
Trottoirs throng'd, vehicles, Broadway, the women, the shops and shows,
A million people—manners free and superb—open voices—hospitality—the most courageous
    and friendly young men,
City of hurried and sparkling waters! city of spires and masts!
City nested in bays! my city!   20

                  1860

WITH HUSKY–HAUGHTY LIPS, O SEA!

WITH husky-haughty lips, O sea!
Where day and night I wend thy surf-beat shore,
Imaging to my sense thy varied strange suggestions,
(I see and plainly list thy talk and conference here,)
Thy troops of white-maned racers racing to the goal,
Thy ample, smiling face, dash'd with the sparkling dimples of the sun,
Thy brooding scowl and murk—thy unloos'd hurricanes,
Thy unsubduedness, caprices, wilfulness;
Great as thou art above the rest, thy many tears—a lack from all eternity in thy content,
(Naught but the greatest struggles, wrongs, defeats, could make thee greatest—no less could
    make thee,)   10
Thy lonely state—something thou ever seek'st and seek'st, yet never gain'st,
Surely some right withheld—some voice, in huge monotonous rage, of freedom-lover pent,
Some vast heart, like a planet's, chain'd and chafing in those breakers,
By lengthen'd swell, and spasm, and panting breath,
And rhythmic rasping of thy sands and waves,
And serpent hiss, and savage peals of laughter,
And undertones of distant lion roar,
(Sounding, appealing to the sky's deaf ear—but now, rapport for once,
A phantom in the night thy confidant for once,)
The first and last confession of the globe,   20
Outsurging, muttering from thy soul's abysms,
The tale of cosmic elemental passion,
Thou tellest to a kindred soul.

                  1889

AFTER THE SUPPER AND TALK

AFTER the supper and talk—after the day is done,
As a friend from friends his final withdrawal prolonging,
Good-bye and Good-bye with emotional lips repeating,
(So hard for his hand to release those hands—no more will they meet,
No more for communion of sorrow and joy, of old and young,
A far-stretching journey awaits him, to return no more,)
Shunning, postponing severance—seeking to ward off the last word ever so little,

E'en at the exit-door turning—charges superfluous calling back—e'en as he descends the
    steps,
Something to eke out a minute additional—shadows of nightfall deepening,
Farewells, messages lessening—dimmer the forthgoer's visage and form,   10
Soon to be lost for aye in the darkness—loth, O so loth to depart!
Garrulous to the very last.

                                            1889

SO LONG!

To conclude, I announce what comes after me.

I remember I said before my leaves sprang at all,
I would raise my voice jocund and strong with reference to consummations.

When America does what was promis'd,
When through these States walk a hundred millions of superb persons,
When the rest part away for superb persons and contribute to them,
When breeds of the most perfect mothers denote America,
Then to me and mine our due fruition.

I have press'd through in my own right,
I have sung the body and the soul, war and peace have I sung, and the songs of life and death,
And the songs of birth, and shown that there are many births.   11

I have offer'd my style to every one, I have journey'd with confident step;
While my pleasure is yet at the full I whisper *So long!*
And take the young woman's hand and the young man's hand for the last time.

I announce natural persons to arise,
I announce justice triumphant,
I announce uncompromising liberty and equality,
I announce the justification of candor and the justification of pride.

I announce that the identity of these States is a single identity only,
I announce the Union more and more compact, indissoluble,   20
I announce splendors and majesties to make all the previous politics of the earth insignificant.

I announce adhesiveness, I say it shall be limitless, unloosen'd,
I say you shall yet find the friend you were looking for.

I announce a man or woman coming, perhaps you are the one, (*So long!*)
I announce the great individual, fluid as Nature, chaste, affectionate, compassionate, fully
    arm'd.

I announce a life that shall be copious, vehement, spiritual, bold,
I announce an end that shall lightly and joyfully meet its translation.

I announce myriads of youths, beautiful, gigantic, sweet-blooded,
I announce a race of splendid and savage old men.

O thicker and faster—(*So long!*)   30
O crowding too close upon me,
I foresee too much, it means more than I thought,
It appears to me I am dying.

Hasten throat and sound your last,
Salute me—salute the days once more. Peal the old cry once more.

Screaming electric, the atmosphere using,
At random glancing, each as I notice absorbing,
Swiftly on, but a little while alighting,
Curious envelop'd messages delivering,
Sparkles hot, seed ethereal down in the dirt dropping,   40
Myself unknowing, my commission obeying, to question it never daring,
To ages and ages yet the growth of the seed leaving,
To troops out of the war arising, they the task I have set promulging,
To women certain whispers of myself bequeathing, their affection me more clearly explaining,
To young men my problems offering—no dallier I—I the muscle of their brains trying,
So I pass, a little time vocal, visible, contrary,
Afterward a melodious echo, passionately bent for, (death making me really undying,)
The best of me then when no longer visible, for toward that I have been incessantly preparing.

What is there more, that I lag and pause and crouch extended with unshut mouth?
Is there a single final farewell?   50

My songs cease, I abandon them,
From behind the screen where I hid I advance personally solely to you.

Camerado, this is no book,
Who touches this touches a man,
(Is it night? are we here together alone?)
It is I you hold and who holds you,
I spring from the pages into your arms—decease calls me forth.

O how your fingers drowse me,
Your breath falls around me like dew, your pulse lulls the tympans of my ears,
I feel immerged from head to foot,   60
Delicious, enough.

Enough O deed impromptu and secret,
Enough O gliding present—enough O summ'd-up past.

Dear friend whoever you are take this kiss,
I give it especially to you, do not forget me,
I feel like one who has done work for the day to retire awhile,
I receive now again of my many translations, from my avataras ascending, while others
        doubtless await me,
An unknown sphere more real than I dream'd, more direct, darts awakening rays about me,
    So long!
Remember my words, I may again return,
I love you, I depart from materials,   70
I am as one disembodied, triumphant, dead.

                                                                  1860

AS AT THY PORTALS ALSO DEATH

        As at thy portals also death,
        Entering thy sovereign, dim, illimitable grounds,
        To memories of my mother, to the divine blending, maternity,
        To her, buried and gone, yet buried not, gone not from me,

(I see again the calm benignant face fresh and beautiful still,
I sit by the form in the coffin,
I kiss and kiss convulsively again the sweet old lips, the cheeks, the closed eyes in the
        coffin;)
To her, the ideal woman, practical, spiritual, of all of earth, life, love, to me the best,
I grave a monumental line, before I go, amid these songs,
And set a tombstone here.   10

                                                                        1881

GOOD-BYE MY FANCY!

GOOD-BYE my Fancy!
Farewell dear mate, dear love!
I'm going away, I know not where,
Or to what fortune, or whether I may ever see you again,
So Good-bye my Fancy.

Now for my last—let me look back a moment;
The slower fainter ticking of the clock is in me,
Exit, nightfall, and soon the heart-thud stopping.

Long have we lived, joy'd, caress'd together;
Delightful!—now separation—Good-bye my Fancy.   10

Yet let me not be too hasty,
Long indeed have we lived, slept, filter'd, become really blended into one;
Then if we die we die together, (yes, we'll remain one,)
If we go anywhere we'll go together to meet what happens,
May-be we'll be better off and blither, and learn something,
May-be it is yourself now really ushering me to the true songs, (who knows?)
May-be it is you the mortal knob really undoing, turning—so now finally,
Good-bye—and hail! my Fancy.

                                                                        1891

EMILY DICKINSON
1830–1886

THIRTY-TWO POEMS

1

THE soul selects her own society,
Then shuts the door;
On her divine majority
Obtrude no more.

Unmoved, she notes the chariot's pausing
At her low gate;
Unmoved, an emperor is kneeling
Upon her mat.

I've known her from an ample nation
Choose one;   10
Then close the valves of her attention
Like stone.

                                                                        1890

2

MY life closed twice before its close;
    It yet remains to see
If Immortality unveil
    A third event to me,

So huge, so hopeless to conceive,
    As these that twice befell.
Parting is all we know of heaven,
    And all we need of hell.

                                                                        1896

3

THEY say that ' time assuages,'—
    Time never did assuage;
An actual suffering strengthens,
    As sinews do, with age.

Time is a test of trouble,
    But not a remedy.
If such it prove, it prove too
    There was no malady.

                                    1896

4

JUST lost when I was saved!
Just felt the world go by!
Just girt me for the onset with eternity,
When breath blew back,
And on the other side
I heard recede the disappointed tide!

Therefore, as one returned, I feel,
Odd secrets of the line to tell!
Some sailor, skirting foreign shores,
Some pale reporter from the awful doors
Before the seal!   11

Next time, to stay!
Next time, the things to see
By ear unheard,
Unscrutinized by eye.

Next time, to tarry,
While the ages steal,—
Slow tramp the centuries,
And the cycles wheel.

                                    1891

5

I TASTE a liquor never brewed,
From tankards scooped in pearl;
Not all the vats upon the Rhine
Yield such an alcohol!

Inebriate of air am I,
And debauchee of dew,
Reeling, through endless summer
        days,
From inns of molten blue.

When landlords turn the drunken bee
Out of the foxglove's door,   10
When butterflies renounce their drams,
I shall but drink the more!

Till seraphs swing their snowy hats,
And saints to windows run,
To see the little tippler
Leaning against the sun!

                                    1890

6

I STARTED early, took my dog,
And visited the sea;
The mermaids in the basement
Came out to look at me,

And frigates in the upper floor
Extended hempen hands,
Presuming me to be a mouse
Aground, upon the sands.

But no man moved me till the tide
Went past my simple shoe,   10
And past my apron and my belt,
And past my bodice too,

And made as he would eat me up
As wholly as a dew
Upon a dandelion's sleeve—
And then I started too.

And he—he followed close behind;
I felt his silver heel
Upon my ankle,—then my shoes
Would overflow with pearl.   20

Until we met the solid town,
No man he seemed to know;
And bowing with a mighty look
At me, the sea withdrew.

                                    1891

7

IF you were coming in the fall,
I'd brush the summer by
With half a smile and half a spurn,
As housewives do a fly.

If I could see you in a year,
I'd wind the months in balls,
And put them each in separate drawers,
Until their time befalls.

If only centuries delayed,
I'd count them on my hand,   10
Subtracting till my fingers dropped
Into Van Diemen's land.

If certain, when this life was out,
That yours and mine should be,
I'd toss it yonder like a rind,
And taste eternity.

But now, all ignorant of the length
Of time's uncertain wing,
It goads me, like the goblin bee,
That will not state its sting.   20
                                                1890

8

BECAUSE I could not stop for Death,
He kindly stopped for me;
The carriage held but just ourselves
And Immortality.

We slowly drove, he knew no haste,
And I had put away
My labor, and my leisure too,
For his civility.

We passed the school where children
        played
At wrestling in a ring;   10
We passed the fields of gazing grain,
We passed the setting sun.

We paused before a house that
        seemed
A swelling of the ground;
The roof was scarcely visible,
The cornice but a mound.

Since then 'tis centuries; but each
Feels shorter than the day
I first surmised the horses' heads
Were toward eternity.   20
                                                1890

9

OUR share of night to bear,
Our share of morning,
Our blank in bliss to fill,
Our blank in scorning.

Here a star, and there a star,
Some lose their way.
Here a mist, and there a mist,
Afterwards—day!
                                                1890

10

ALTER? When the hills do.
Falter? When the sun
Question if his glory
Be the perfect one.

Surfeit? When the daffodil
Doth of the dew;

Even as herself, O friend!
I will of you!
                                                1890

11

I CANNOT live with you,
It would be life,
And life is over there
Behind the shelf

The sexton keeps the key to,
Putting up
Our life, his porcelain,
Like a cup

Discarded of the housewife,
Quaint or broken;   10
A newer Sèvres pleases,
Old ones crack.

I could not die with you,
For one must wait
To shut the other's gaze down,—
You could not.

And I, could I stand by
And see you freeze,
Without my right of frost,
Death's privilege?   20

Nor could I rise with you,
Because your face
Would put out Jesus',
That new grace

Glow plain and foreign
On my homesick eye,
Except that you, than he
Shone closer by.

They'd judge us—how?
For you served Heaven, you know,   30
Or sought to;
I could not,

Because you saturated sight,
And I had no more eyes
For sordid excellence
As Paradise.

And were you lost, I would be,
Though my name
Rang loudest
On the heavenly fame.   40

And were you saved,
And I condemned to be
Where you were not,
That self were hell to me.

So we must keep apart,
You there, I here,
With just the door ajar
That oceans are,
And prayer,
And that pale sustenance,   50
Despair!

                              1890

12

I'LL tell you how the sun rose,—
A ribbon at a time.
The steeples swam in amethyst,
The news like squirrels ran.

The hills untied their bonnets,
The bobolinks begun.
Then I said softly to myself,
'That must have been the sun!'

    . . .   .

But how he set, I know not.
There seemed a purple stile   10
Which little yellow boys and girls
Were climbing all the while

Till when they reached the other side,
A dominie in gray
Put gently up the evening bars,
And led the flock away.

                              1890

13

I NEVER saw a moor,
I never saw the sea;
Yet know I how the heather looks,
And what a wave must be.

I never spoke with God,
Nor visited in heaven;
Yet certain am I of the spot
As if the chart were given.

                              1890

14

I'M nobody! Who are you?
Are you nobody, too?
Then there's a pair of us—don't tell!
They'd banish us, you know.

How dreary to be somebody!
How public, like a frog
To tell your name the livelong day
To an admiring bog!

                              1891

15

SURGEONS must be very careful
When they take the knife!
Underneath their fine incisions
Stirs the culprit,—Life!

                              1891

16

I FOUND the phrase to every thought
I ever had, but one;
And that defies me,—as a hand
Did try to chalk the sun

To races nurtured in the dark;—
How would your own begin?
Can blaze be done in cochineal,
Or noon in mazarin?

                              1891

17

THE last night that she lived,
It was a common night,
Except the dying; this to us
Made nature different.

We noticed smallest things,—
Things overlooked before,
By this great light upon our minds
Italicized, as 'twere.

That others could exist
While she must finish quite,   10
A jealousy for her arose
So nearly infinite.

We waited while she passed:
It was a narrow time,
Too jostled were our souls to speak,
At length the notice came.

She mentioned, and forgot;
Then lightly as a reed
Bent to the water, shivered scarce,
Consented, and was dead.   20

And we, we placed the hair,
And drew the head erect;
And then an awful leisure was,
Our faith to regulate.   1890

18

I FELT a funeral in my brain,
  And mourners, to and fro,
Kept treading, treading, till it seemed
  That sense was breaking through.

And when they all were seated,
  A service like a drum
Kept beating, beating, till I thought
  My mind was going numb.

And then I heard them lift a box,
  And creak across my soul   10
With those same boots of lead, again.
  Then space began to toll

As all the heavens were a bell,
  And Being but an ear,
And I and silence some strange race,
  Wrecked, solitary, here.
                                    1896

19

I LIKE to see it lap the miles,
And lick the valleys up,
And stop to feed itself at tanks;
And then, prodigious, step

Around a pile of mountains,
And, supercilious, peer
In shanties by the sides of roads;
And then a quarry pare

To fit its sides, and crawl between,
Complaining all the while   10
In horrid, hooting stanza;
Then chase itself down hill

And neigh like Boanerges;
Then, punctual as a star,
Stop—docile and omnipotent—
At its own stable door.
                                    1891

20

HE ate and drank the precious words,
His spirit grew robust;
He knew no more that he was poor,
Nor that his frame was dust.
He danced along the dingy days,
And this bequest of wings
Was but a book. What liberty
A loosened spirit brings!
                                    1890

21

To fight aloud is very brave,
  But gallanter, I know,
Who charge within the bosom,
  The cavalry of woe.

Who win, and nations do not see,
Who fall, and none observe,
Whose dying eyes no country
Regards with patriot love.

We trust, in plumed procession,
For such the angels go,   10
Rank after rank, with even feet
And uniforms of snow.
                                    1890

22

MUCH madness is divinest sense
To a discerning eye;
Much sense the starkest madness.
'Tis the majority
In this, as all, prevails.
Assent, and you are sane;
Demur,—you're straightway dangerous,
And handled with a chain.
                                    1890

23

A DEATH-BLOW is a life-blow to some
Who, till they died, did not alive become;
Who, had they lived, had died, but when
They died, vitality begun.
                                    1891

24

IT dropped so low in my regard
  I heard it hit the ground,
And go to pieces on the stones
  At bottom of my mind;

Yet blamed the fate that fractured, less
  Than I reviled myself
For entertaining plated wares
  Upon my silver shelf.
                                    1896

25

HE preached upon 'breadth' till it argued
    him narrow,—
The broad are too broad to define;
And of 'truth' until it proclaimed him a
    liar,—
The truth never flaunted a sign.

Simplicity fled from his counterfeit
    presence
As gold the pyrites would shun.
What confusion would cover the innocent
    Jesus
To meet so enabled a man!

                1891

26

THAT such have died enables us
  The tranquiller to die;
That such have lived, certificate
  For immortality.

                1896

27

To hear an oriole sing
May be a common thing,
Or only a divine.

It is not of the bird
Who sings the same, unheard,
As unto crowd.

The fashion of the ear
Attireth that it hear
In dun or fair.

So whether it be rune,   10
Or whether it be none,
Is of within;

The 'tune is in the tree,'
The sceptic showeth me;
'No, sir! In thee!'

                1891

28

THE sky is low, the clouds are mean,
A travelling flake of snow
Across a barn or through a rut
Debates if it will go.

A narrow wind complains all day
How some one treated him;
Nature, like us, is sometimes caught
Without her diadem.

                1890

29

A ROUTE of evanescence
With a revolving wheel;
A resonance of emerald,
A rush of cochineal;
And every blossom on the bush
Adjusts its tumbled head,—
The mail from Tunis, probably,
An easy morning's ride.

                1891

30

THE thought beneath so slight a film
Is more distinctly seen,—
As laces just reveal the surge,
Or mists the Apennine.

                1891

31

NOT with a club the heart is broken,
    Nor with a stone;
A whip, so small you could not see it,
    I've known

To lash the magic creature
    Till it fell,
Yet that whip's name too noble
    Then to tell.

Magnanimous of bird
    By boy descried,   10
To sing unto the stone
    Of which it died.

                1896

32

PAIN has an element of blank;
It cannot recollect
When it began, or if there were
A day when it was not.

It has no future but itself,
Its infinite realms contain
Its past, enlightened to perceive
New periods of pain.

                1890

THOMAS BAILEY ALDRICH
1836–1907

FREDERICKSBURG

THE increasing moonlight drifts across my
    bed,
And on the churchyard by the road, I know
It falls as white and noiselessly as
    snow. . . .
'Twas such a night two weary summers
    fled;
The stars, as now, were waning overhead.
Listen! Again the shrill-lipped bugles blow
Where the swift currents of the river flow
Past Fredericksburg;—far off the heavens
    are red
With sudden conflagration; on yon height,
Linstock in hand, the gunners hold their
    breath;   10
A signal-rocket pierces the dense night,
Flings its spent stars upon the town
    beneath;
Hark!—the artillery massing on the right,
Hark!—the black squadrons wheeling
    down to Death!

                  1865

IDENTITY

SOMEWHERE—in desolate wind-swept
    space—
  In Twilight-land—in No-man's-land—
Two hurrying Shapes met face to face,
  And bade each other stand.

'And who are you?' cried one a-gape,
  Shuddering in the gloaming light.
'I know not,' said the second Shape,
  'I only died last night!'

                  1877

HEREDITY

A SOLDIER of the Cromwell stamp,
With sword and psalm-book by his side,
At home alike in church and camp:
Austere he lived, and smileless died.

But she, a creature soft and fine—
From Spain, some say, some say from
    France;
Within her veins leapt blood like wine—
She led her Roundhead lord a dance!

In Grantham church they lie asleep;
Just where, the verger may not know.   10
Strange that two hundred years should keep
The old ancestral fires aglow!

In me these two have met again;
To each my nature owes a part:
To one, the cool and reasoning brain,
To one, the quick, unreasoning heart.

                  1885

MEMORY

MY mind lets go a thousand things,
Like dates of wars and deaths of kings,
And yet recalls the very hour—
'Twas noon by yonder village tower,
And on the last blue noon in May—
The wind came briskly up this way,
Crisping the brook beside the road;
Then, pausing here, set down its load
Of pine-scents, and shook listlessly
Two petals from that wild-rose tree.   10

                  1891

BAYARD TAYLOR
1825–1878

ARIEL IN THE CLOVEN PINE

Now the frosty stars are gone:
I have watched them, one by one,
Fading on the shores of Dawn.
Round and full the glorious sun
Walks with level step the spray,

Through his vestibule of Day,
While the wolves that late did
    howl
Slink to dens and coverts foul,
Guarded by the demon owl,
Who, last night, with mocking croon,   10
Wheeled athwart the chilly moon,

And with eyes that blankly glared
On my direful torment stared.

The lark is flickering in the light;
Still the nightingale doth sing;—
All the isle, alive with Spring,
Lies, a jewel of delight.
On the blue sea's heaving breast:
Not a breath from out the West,
But some balmy smell doth bring   20
From the sprouting myrtle buds,
Or from meadowy vales that lie
Like a green inverted sky,
Which the yellow cowslip stars,
And the bloomy almond woods,
Cloud-like, cross with roseate bars.
All is life that I can spy,
To the farthest sea and sky,
And my own the only pain
Within this ring of Tyrrhene main.   30

In the gnarled and cloven Pine
Where that hell-born hag did chain me,
All this orb of cloudless shine,
All this youth in Nature's veins
Tingling with the season's wine,
With a sharper torment pain me.
Pansies in soft April rains
Fill their stalks with honeyed sap
Drawn from Earth's prolific lap;
But the sluggish blood she brings   40
To the tough Pine's hundred rings,
Closer locks their cruel hold,
Closer draws the scaly bark
Round the crevice, damp and cold,
Where my useless wings I fold,—
Sealing me in iron dark.
By this coarse and alien state
Is my dainty essence wronged;
Finer senses that belonged
To my freedom, chafe at Fate,   50
Till the happier elves I hate,
Who in moonlight dances turn
Underneath the palmy fern,
Or in light and twinkling bands
Follow on with linkèd hands
To the Ocean's yellow sands.

Primrose-eyes each morning ope
In their cool, deep beds of grass;
Violets make the airs that pass
Telltales of their fragrant slope.   60
I can see them where they spring
Never brushed by fairy wing.

All those corners I can spy
In the island's solitude,
Where the dew is never dry,
Nor the miser bees intrude.
Cups of rarest hue are there,
Full of perfumed wine undrained,—
Mushroom banquets, ne'er profaned,
Canopied by maiden-hair.   70
Pearls I see upon the sands,
Never touched by other hands,
And the rainbow bubbles shine
On the ridged and frothy brine,
Tenantless of voyager
Till they burst in vacant air.
O, the songs that sung might be,
And the mazy dances woven,
Had that witch ne'er crossed the sea
And the Pine been never cloven!   80

Many years my direst pain
Has made the wave-rocked isle complain.
Winds, that from the Cyclades
Came, to blow in wanton riot
Round its shore's enchanted quiet,
Bore my wailings on the seas;
Sorrowing birds in Autumn went
Through the world with my lament.
Still the bitter fate is mine,
All delight unshared to see,   90
Smarting in the cloven Pine,
While I wait the tardy axe
Which, perchance, shall set me free
From the damned Witch Sycorax.

1848

BEDOUIN SONG

FROM the Desert I come to thee
   On a stallion shod with fire;
And the winds are left behind
   In the speed of my desire.
Under thy window I stand,
   And the midnight hears my cry:
I love thee, I love but thee,
   With a love that shall not die
     Till the sun grows cold,
     And the stars are old,   10
     And the leaves of the Judgment
     Book unfold!

Look from thy window and see
   My passion and my pain;
I lie on the sands below,
   And I faint in thy disdain.

Let the night-winds touch thy brow
  With the heat of my burning sigh,
And melt thee to hear the vow
  Of a love that shall not die   20
    Till the sun grows cold,
    And the stars are old,
    And the leaves of the Judgment
      Book unfold!

My steps are nightly driven,
  By the fever in my breast,   1853

To hear from thy lattice breathed
  The word that shall give me rest.
Open the door of thy heart,
  And open thy chamber door,   30
And my kisses shall teach thy lips
  The love that shall fade no more.
    Till the sun grows cold,
    And the stars are old,
    And the leaves of the Judgment
      Book unfold!
                  1854

EDMUND CLARENCE STEDMAN
1833–1908

HOW OLD BROWN TOOK
HARPER'S FERRY

JOHN BROWN in Kansas settled, like a
  steadfast Yankee farmer,
Brave and godly, with four sons, all
  stalwart men of might.
There he spoke aloud for freedom, and the
  Border-strife grew warmer,
Till the Rangers fired his dwelling, in his
  absence, in the night;
    And Old Brown,
    Osawatomie Brown,
Came homeward in the morning—to find
  his house burned down.

Then he grasped his trusty rifle and boldly
  fought for freedom;
Smote from border unto border the
  fierce, invading band;   9
And he and his brave boys vowed—so
  might Heaven help and speed 'em!—
They would save those grand old prairies
  from the curse that blights the land;
    And Old Brown,
    Osawatomie Brown,
Said, 'Boys, the Lord will aid us!' and he
  shoved his ramrod down.

And the Lord *did* aid these men, and they
  labored day and even,
Saving Kansas from its peril; and their
  very lives seemed charmed,
'Till the ruffians killed one son, in the
  blessed light of Heaven,—
In cold blood the fellows slew him, as he
  journeyed all unarmed;

    Then Old Brown,
    Osawatomie Brown,   20
Shed not a tear, but shut his teeth, and
  frowned a terrible frown!

Then they seized another brave boy,—not
  amid the heat of battle,
  But in peace, behind his ploughshare,—
    and they loaded him with chains,
And with pikes, before their horses, even as
  they goad their cattle,
Drove him cruelly, for their sport, and at
  last blew out his brains;
    Then Old Brown,
    Osawatomie Brown,
Raised his right hand up to Heaven, calling
  Heaven's vengeance down.

And he swore a fearful oath, by the name of
  the Almighty,
He would hunt this ravening evil that
  had scathed and torn him so;   30
He would seize it by the vitals; he would
  crush it day and night; he
Would so pursue its footsteps, so return it
  blow for blow,
    That Old Brown,
    Osawatomie Brown,
Should be a name to swear by, in backwoods
  or in town!

Then his beard became more grizzled, and
  his wild blue eye grew wilder,
And more sharply curved his hawk's-nose,
  snuffing battle from afar;
And he and the two boys left, though the
  Kansas strife waxed milder,

Grew more sullen, till was over the
    bloody Border War,
      And Old Brown,   40
      Osawatomie Brown,
Had gone crazy, as they reckoned by his
    fearful glare and frown.

So he left the plains of Kansas and their
    bitter woes behind him,
    Slipt off into Virginia, where the states-
    men all are born,
Hired a farm by Harper's Ferry, and no one
    knew where to find him,
    Or whether he'd turned parson, or was
    jacketed and shorn;
      For Old Brown,
      Osawatomie Brown,
Mad as he was, knew texts enough to wear a
    parson's gown.

He bought no ploughs and harrows, spades
    and shovels, and such trifles;   50
    But quietly to his rancho there came, by
    every train,
Boxes full of pikes and pistols, and his well-
    beloved Sharp's rifles;
    And eighteen other madmen joined their
    leader there again.
      Says Old Brown,
      Osawatomie Brown,
'Boys, we've got an army large enough to
    march and take the town!

'Take the town, and seize the muskets, free
    the negroes, and then arm them;
    Carry the County and the State, ay, and
    all the potent South.
On their own heads be the slaughter, if
    their victims rise to harm them—
    These Virginians! who believed not, nor
    would heed the warning mouth.' 60
      Says Old Brown,
      Osawatomie Brown,
'The world shall see a Republic, or my
    name is not John Brown.'

'Twas the sixteenth of October, on the
    evening of a Sunday:
    'This good work,' declared the captain,
    'shall be on a holy night!'
It was on a Sunday evening, and before the
    noon of Monday,
    With two sons, and Captain Stephens,
    fifteen privates—black and white,
      Captain Brown,

      Osawatomie Brown,
Marched across the bridged Potomac, and
    knocked the sentry down;   70

Took the guarded armory-building, and the
    muskets and the cannon;
    Captured all the county majors and the
    colonels, one by one;
Scared to death each gallant scion of
    Virginia they ran on,
    And before the noon of Monday, I say,
    the deed was done.
      Mad Old Brown,
      Osawatomie Brown,
With his eighteen other crazy men, went in
    and took the town.

Very little noise and bluster, little smell of
    powder made he;
    It was all done in the midnight, like the
    Emperor's *coup d'état.*
'Cut the wires! Stop the rail-cars! Hold the
    streets and bridges!' said he,   80
    Then declared the new Republic, with
    himself for guiding star,—
      This Old Brown,
      Osawatomie Brown;
And the bold two thousand citizens ran off
    and left the town.

Then was riding and railroading and
    expressing here and thither;
    And the Martinsburg Sharpshooters and
    the Charlestown Volunteers,
And the Shepherdstown and Winchester
    Militia hastened whither
    Old Brown was said to muster his ten
    thousand grenadiers.
      General Brown!
      Osawatomie Brown! !   90
Behind whose rampant banner all the
    North was pouring down.

But at last, 'tis said, some prisoners escaped
    from Old Brown's durance,
    And the effervescent valor of the Chivalry
    broke out,
When they learned that nineteen madmen
    had the marvellous assurance—
    Only nineteen—thus to seize the place
    and drive them straight about;
      And Old Brown,
      Osawatomie Brown,
Found an army come to take him,
    encamped around the town.

But to storm with all the forces I have
    mentioned, was too risky;
  So they hurried off to Richmond for the
    Government Marines,   100
Tore them from their weeping matrons,
    fired their souls with Bourbon
    whiskey,
Till they battered down Brown's castle
    with their ladders and machines;
        And Old Brown,
        Osawatomie Brown,
Received three bayonet stabs, and a cut on
    his brave old crown.

Tallyho! the old Virginia gentry gather to
    the baying!
  In they rushed and killed the game,
    shooting lustily away;
And whene'er they slew a rebel, those who
    came too late for slaying,
  Not to lose a share of glory, fired their
    bullets in his clay;
        And Old Brown,   110
        Osawatomie Brown,
Saw his sons fall dead beside him, and
    between them laid him down.

How the conquerors wore their laurels;
    how they hastened on the trial;
  How Old Brown was placed, half-dying,
    on the Charlestown court-house
    floor;
How he spoke his grand oration, in the
    scorn of all denial;
  What the brave old madman told them,—
    these are known the country o'er.
        'Hang Old Brown,
        Oswatomie Brown,'
Said the judge, 'and all such rebels!' with
    his most judicial frown.

But, Virginians, don't do it! for I tell you
    that the flagon,   120
  Filled with blood of Old Brown's
    offspring, was first poured by
    Southern hands;
And each drop from Old Brown's life-
    veins, like the red gore of the dragon,
  May spring up a vengeful Fury, hissing
    through your slave-worn lands!
        And Old Brown,
        Osawatomie Brown,
May trouble you more than ever, when
    you've nailed his coffin down!

1859

KEARNY AT SEVEN PINES

So that soldierly legend is still on its
    journey,—
  That story of Kearny who knew not to
    yield!
'Twas the day when with Jameson, fierce
    Berry, and Birney,
  Against twenty thousand he rallied the
    field.
Where the red volleys poured, where the
    clamor rose highest,
  Where the dead lay in clumps through
    the dwarf oak and pine,
Where the aim from the thicket was surest
    and nighest,—
  No charge like Phil Kearny's along the
    whole line.

When the battle went ill, and the bravest
    were solemn,
  Near the dark Seven Pines, where we
    still held our ground,   10
He rode down the length of the withering
    column,
  And his heart at our war-cry leapt up
    with a bound;
He snuffed, like his charger, the wind of
    the powder,—
  His sword waved us on and we answered
    the sign:
Loud our cheer as we rushed, but his laugh
    rang the louder,
  'There's the devil's own fun, boys, along
    the whole line!'

How he strode his brown steed! How we
    saw his blade brighten
  In the one hand still left,—and the reins
    in his teeth!
He laughed like a boy when the holidays
    heighten,
  But a soldier's glance shot from his visor
    beneath.   20
Up came the reserves to the mellay
    infernal,
  Asking where to go in,—through the
    clearing or pine?
'O, anywhere! Forward! 'Tis all the same,
    Colonel:
  You'll find lovely fighting along the
    whole line!'

O, evil the black shroud of night at
    Chantilly,

1860

That hid him from sight of his brave
    men and tried!
Foul, foul sped the bullet that clipped the
    white lily,
    The flower of our knighthood, the whole
      army's pride!
Yet we dream that he still,—in that
    shadowy region

Where the dead form their ranks at the
    wan drummer's sign,—   30
Rides on, as of old, down the length of his
    legion,
And the word still is Forward! along the
    whole line.

1877

BRET HARTE

1836–1902

THE OUTCASTS OF POKER FLAT [1]

As Mr. John Oakhurst, gambler, stepped into the main street of Poker Flat on the morning of the 23d of November, 1850, he was conscious of a change in its moral atmosphere since the preceding night. Two or three men, conversing earnestly together, ceased as he approached, and exchanged significant glances. There was a Sabbath lull in the air, which, in a settlement unused to Sabbath influences, looked ominous.

Mr. Oakhurst's calm, handsome face betrayed small concern in these indications. Whether he was conscious of any predisposing cause was another question. 'I reckon they're after somebody,' he reflected; 'likely it's me.' He returned to his pocket the handkerchief with which he had been whipping away the red dust of Poker Flat from his neat boots, and quietly discharged his mind of any further conjecture.

In point of fact, Poker Flat was 'after somebody.' It had lately suffered the loss of several thousand dollars, two valuable horses, and a prominent citizen. It was experiencing a spasm of virtuous reaction, quite as lawless and ungovernable as any of the acts that had provoked it. A secret committee had determined to rid the town of all improper persons. This was done permanently in regard of two men who were then hanging from the boughs of a sycamore in the gulch, and temporarily in the banishment of certain other objectionable characters. I regret to say that some of these were ladies. It is but due to the sex, however, to state that their impropriety was professional, and it was only in such easily established standards of evil that Poker Flat ventured to sit in judgment.

Mr. Oakhurst was right in supposing that he was included in this category. A few of the committee had urged hanging him as a possible example and a sure method of reimbursing themselves from his pockets of the sums he had won from them. 'It's agin justice,' said Jim Wheeler, 'to let this yer young man from Roaring Camp—an entire stranger—carry away our money.' But a crude sentiment of equity residing in the breasts of those who had been fortunate

[1] Of himself, Harte wrote: 'But he deems it worthy of consideration that during this period, i.e., from 1862 to 1866, he produced . . . his first efforts toward indicating a peculiarly characteristic Western American literature. He would like to offer these facts as evidence of his very early, half-boyish, but very enthusiastic, belief in such a possibility—a belief which never deserted him, and which, a few years later, from the better-known pages of the *Overland Monthly*, he was able to demonstrate to a larger and more cosmopolitan audience in the story of "The Luck of Roaring Camp" and the poem of the "Heathen Chinee." But it was one of the anomalies of the very condition of life that he worked amidst, and endeavoured to portray, that these first efforts were rewarded by very little success; and . . . even "The Luck of Roaring Camp" depended for its recognition in California upon its success elsewhere. Hence the critical reader will observe that the bulk of these earlier efforts . . . were marked by very little flavour of the soil, but were addressed to an audience half foreign in their sympathies, and still imbued with Eastern or New England habits and literary traditions. "Home" was still potent with these voluntary exiles in their moments of relaxation. Eastern magazines and current Eastern literature formed their literary recreation, and the sale of the better class of periodicals was singularly great. Nor was the taste confined to American literature. The illustrated and satirical English journals were as frequently seen in California as in Massachusetts; and the author records that he has experienced more difficulty in procuring a copy of *Punch* in an English provincial town than was his fortune at "Red Dog" or "One-Horse Gulch."' Harte, Introduction, *Works* (Boston, 1882), I, 2–3.

enough to win from Mr. Oakhurst over-ruled this narrower local prejudice.

Mr. Oakhurst received his sentence with philosophic calmness, none the less coolly that he was aware of the hesitation of his judges. He was too much of a gambler not to accept fate. With him life was at best an uncertain game, and he recognized the usual percentage in favor of the dealer.

A body of armed men accompanied the deported wickedness of Poker Flat to the outskirts of the settlement. Besides Mr. Oakhurst, who was known to be a coolly desperate man, and for whose intimidation the armed escort was intended, the expatri-ated party consisted of a young woman fa-miliarly known as 'The Duchess;' another who had won the title of 'Mother Shipton;' and 'Uncle Billy,' a suspected sluice-robber and confirmed drunkard. The cavalcade provoked no comments from the spectators, nor was any word uttered by the escort. Only when the gulch which marked the ut-termost limit of Poker Flat was reached, the leader spoke briefly and to the point. The exiles were forbidden to return at the peril of their lives.

As the escort disappeared, their pent-up feelings found vent in a few hysterical tears from the Duchess, some bad language from Mother Shipton, and a Parthian volley of expletives from Uncle Billy. The philo-sophic Oakhurst alone remained silent. He listened calmly to Mother Shipton's desire to cut somebody's heart out, to the repeated statements of the Duchess that she would die in the road, and to the alarming oaths that seemed to be bumped out of Uncle Billy as he rode forward. With the easy good humor characteristic of his class, he insisted upon exchanging his own riding-horse, 'Five-Spot,' for the sorry mule which the Duchess rode. But even this act did not draw the party into any closer sympathy. The young woman readjusted her some-what draggled plumes with a feeble, faded coquetry; Mother Shipton eyed the pos-sessor of 'Five-Spot' with malevolence, and Uncle Billy included the whole party in one sweeping anathema.

The road to Sandy Bar—a camp that, not having as yet experienced the regenerating influences of Poker Flat, consequently seemed to offer some invitation to the emi-grants—lay over a steep mountain range. It was distant a day's severe travel. In that ad-vanced season the party soon passed out of the moist, temperate regions of the foothills into the dry, cold, bracing air of the Sierras. The trail was narrow and difficult. At noon the Duchess, rolling out of her saddle upon the ground, declared her intention of going no farther, and the party halted.

The spot was singularly wild and impres-sive. A wooded amphitheatre, surrounded on three sides by precipitous cliffs of naked granite, sloped gently toward the crest of another precipice that overlooked the valley. It was, undoubtedly, the most suitable spot for a camp, had camping been advisable. But Mr. Oakhurst knew that scarcely half the journey to Sandy Bar was accom-plished, and the party were not equipped or provisioned for delay. This fact he pointed out to his companions curtly, with a philosophic commentary on the folly of 'throwing up their hand before the game was played out.' But they were furnished with liquor, which in this emergency stood them in place of food, fuel, rest, and pre-science. In spite of his remonstrances, it was not long before they were more or less un-der its influence. Uncle Billy passed rapidly from a bellicose state into one of stupor, the Duchess became maudlin, and Mother Shipton snored. Mr. Oakhurst alone re-mained erect, leaning against a rock, calmly surveying them.

Mr. Oakhurst did not drink. It interfered with a profession which required coolness, impassiveness, and presence of mind, and, in his own language, he 'couldn't afford it.' As he gazed at his recumbent fellow exiles, the loneliness begotten of his pariah trade, his habits of life, his very vices, for the first time seriously oppressed him. He bestirred himself in dusting his black clothes, wash-ing his hands and face, and other acts char-acteristic of his studiously neat habits, and for a moment forgot his annoyance. The thought of deserting his weaker and more pitiable companions never perhaps occurred to him. Yet he could not help feeling the want of that excitement which, singularly enough, was most conducive to that calm equanimity for which he was notorious. He looked at the gloomy walls that rose a thou-sand feet sheer above the circling pines around him, at the sky ominously clouded, at the valley below, already deepening into shadow; and, doing so, suddenly he heard his own name called.

A horseman slowly ascended the trail. In the fresh, open face of the newcomer Mr. Oakhurst recognized Tom Simson, otherwise known as 'The Innocent,' of Sandy Bar. He had met him some months before over a 'little game,' and had, with perfect equanimity, won the entire fortune—amounting to some forty dollars—of that guileless youth. After the game was finished, Mr. Oakhurst drew the youthful speculator behind the door and thus addressed him: 'Tommy, you're a good little man, but you can't gamble worth a cent. Don't try it over again.' He then handed him his money back, pushed him gently from the room, and so made a devoted slave of Tom Simson.

There was a remembrance of this in his boyish and enthusiastic greeting of Mr. Oakhurst. He had started, he said, to go to Poker Flat to seek his fortune. 'Alone?' No, not exactly alone; in fact (a giggle), he had run away with Piney Woods. Didn't Mr. Oakhurst remember Piney? She that used to wait on the table at the Temperance House? They had been engaged a long time, but old Jake Woods had objected, and so they had run away, and were going to Poker Flat to be married, and here they were. And they were tired out, and how lucky it was they had found a place to camp, and company. All this the Innocent delivered rapidly, while Piney, a stout, comely damsel of fifteen, emerged from behind the pine-tree, where she had been blushing unseen, and rode to the side of her lover.

Mr. Oakhurst seldom troubled himself with sentiment, still less with propriety; but he had a vague idea that the situation was not fortunate. He retained, however, his presence of mind sufficiently to kick Uncle Billy, who was about to say something, and Uncle Billy was sober enough to recognize in Mr. Oakhurst's kick a superior power that would not bear trifling. He then endeavored to dissuade Tom Simson from delaying further, but in vain. He even pointed out the fact that there was no provision, nor means of making a camp. But, unluckily, the Innocent met this objection by assuring the party that he was provided with an extra mule loaded with provisions, and by the discovery of a rude attempt at a log house near the trail. 'Piney can stay with Mrs. Oakhurst,' said the Innocent, pointing to the Duchess, 'and I can shift for myself.'

Nothing but Mr. Oakhurst's admonishing foot saved Uncle Billy from bursting into a roar of laughter. As it was, he felt compelled to retire up the cañon until he could recover his gravity. There he confided the joke to the tall pine-trees, with many slaps of his leg, contortions of his face, and the usual profanity. But when he returned to the party, he found them seated by a fire —for the air had grown strangely chill and the sky overcast—in apparently amicable conversation. Piney was actually talking in an impulsive girlish fashion to the Duchess, who was listening with an interest and animation she had not shown for many days. The Innocent was holding forth, apparently with equal effect, to Mr. Oakhurst and Mother Shipton, who was actually relaxing into amiability. 'Is this yer a d—d picnic?' said Uncle Billy, with inward scorn, as he surveyed the sylvan group, the glancing firelight, and the tethered animals in the foreground. Suddenly an idea mingled with the alcoholic fumes that disturbed his brain. It was apparently of a jocular nature, for he felt impelled to slap his leg again and cram his fist into his mouth.

As the shadows crept slowly up the mountain, a slight breeze rocked the tops of the pine-trees and moaned through their long and gloomy aisles. The ruined cabin, patched and covered with pine boughs, was set apart for the ladies. As the lovers parted, they unaffectedly exchanged a kiss, so honest and sincere that it might have been heard above the swaying pines. The frail Duchess and the malevolent Mother Shipton were probably too stunned to remark upon this last evidence of simplicity, and so turned without a word to the hut. The fire was replenished, the men lay down before the door, and in a few minutes were asleep.

Mr. Oakhurst was a light sleeper. Toward morning he awoke benumbed and cold. As he stirred the dying fire, the wind, which was now blowing strongly, brought to his cheek that which caused the blood to leave it,—snow!

He started to his feet with the intention of awakening the sleepers, for there was no time to lose. But turning to where Uncle Billy had been lying, he found him gone. A suspicion leaped to his brain, and a curse to his lips. He ran to the spot where the mules had been tethered—they were no longer there. The tracks were already rapidly disappearing in the snow.

The momentary excitement brought Mr. Oakhurst back to the fire with his usual calm. He did not waken the sleepers. The Innocent slumbered peacefully, with a smile on his good-humored, freckled face; the virgin Piney slept beside her frailer sisters as sweetly as though attended by celestial guardians; and Mr. Oakhurst, drawing his blanket over his shoulders, stroked his mustaches and waited for the dawn. It came slowly in a whirling mist of snowflakes that dazzled and confused the eye. What could be seen of the landscape appeared magically changed. He looked over the valley, and summed up the present and future in two words, 'Snowed in!'

A careful inventory of the provisions, which, fortunately for the party, had been stored within the hut, and so escaped the felonious fingers of Uncle Billy, disclosed the fact that with care and prudence they might last ten days longer. 'That is,' said Mr. Oakhurst *sotto voce* to the Innocent, 'if you're willing to board us. If you ain't—and perhaps you'd better not—you can wait till Uncle Billy gets back with provisions.' For some occult reason, Mr. Oakhurst could not bring himself to disclose Uncle Billy's rascality, and so offered the hypothesis that he had wandered from the camp and had accidentally stampeded the animals. He dropped a warning to the Duchess and Mother Shipton, who of course knew the facts of their associate's defection. 'They'll find out the truth about us *all* when they find out anything,' he added significantly, 'and there's no good frightening them now.'

Tom Simson not only put all his worldly store at the disposal of Mr. Oakhurst, but seemed to enjoy the prospect of their enforced seclusion. 'We'll have a good camp for a week, and then the snow'll melt, and we'll all go back together.' The cheerful gayety of the young man and Mr. Oakhurst's calm infected the others. The Innocent, with the aid of pine boughs, extemporized a thatch for the roofless cabin, and the Duchess directed Piney in the rear-

rangement of the interior with a taste and tact that opened the blue eyes of that provincial maiden to their fullest extent. 'I reckon now you're used to fine things at Poker Flat,' said Piney. The Duchess turned away sharply to conceal something that reddened her cheeks through their professional tint, and Mother Shipton requested Piney not to 'chatter.' But when Mr. Oakhurst returned from a weary search for the trail, he heard the sound of happy laughter echoed from the rocks. He stopped in some alarm, and his thoughts first naturally reverted to the whiskey, which he had prudently cachéd. 'And yet it don't somehow sound like whiskey,' said the gambler. It was not until he caught sight of the blazing fire through the still blinding storm, and the group around it, that he settled to the conviction that it was 'square fun.'

Whether Mr. Oakhurst had cachéd his cards with the whiskey as something debarred the free access of the community, I cannot say. It was certain that, in Mother Shipton's words, he 'didn't say "cards" once' during that evening. Haply the time was beguiled by an accordion, produced somewhat ostentatiously by Tom Simson from his pack. Notwithstanding some difficulties attending the manipulation of this instrument, Piney Woods managed to pluck several reluctant melodies from its keys, to an accompaniment by the Innocent on a pair of bone castanets. But the crowning festivity of the evening was reached in a rude camp-meeting hymn, which the lovers, joining hands, sang with great earnestness and vociferation. I fear that a certain defiant tone and Covenanter's swing to its chorus, rather than any devotional quality, caused it speedily to infect the others, who at last joined in the refrain:

'I'm proud to live in the service of the Lord,
And I'm bound to die in His army.'

The pines rocked, the storm eddied and whirled above the miserable group, and the flames of their altar leaped heavenward, as if in token of the vow.

At midnight the storm abated, the rolling clouds parted, and the stars glittered keenly above the sleeping camp. Mr. Oakhurst, whose professional habits had enabled him to live on the smallest possible amount of sleep, in dividing the watch with Tom Simson somehow managed to take upon himself the greater part of that duty. He excused himself to the Innocent by saying that he had 'often been a week without sleep.' 'Doing what?' asked Tom. 'Poker!' replied Oakhurst sententiously. 'When a man gets a streak of luck,—nigger-luck,— he don't get tired. The luck gives in first. Luck,' continued the gambler reflectively, 'is a mighty queer thing. All you know about it for certain is that it's bound to change. And it's finding out when it's going to change that makes you. We've had a streak of bad luck since we left Poker Flat,— you come along, and slap you get into it, too. If you can hold your cards right along you're all right. For,' added the gambler, with cheerful irrelevance—

' "I'm proud to live in the service of the
    Lord,
And I'm bound to die in His army." '

The third day came, and the sun, looking through the white-curtained valley, saw the outcasts divide their slowly decreasing store of provisions for the morning meal. It was one of the peculiarities of that mountain climate that its rays diffused a kindly warmth over the wintry landscape, as if in regretful commiseration of the past. But it revealed drift on drift of snow piled high around the hut,—a hopeless, uncharted, trackless sea of white lying below the rocky shores to which the castaways still clung. Through the marvelously clear air the smoke of the pastoral village of Poker Flat rose miles away. Mother Shipton saw it, and from a remote pinnacle of her rocky fastness hurled in that direction a final malediction. It was her last vituperative attempt, and perhaps for that reason was invested with a certain degree of sublimity. It did her good, she privately informed the Duchess. 'Just you go out there and cuss, and see.' She then set herself to the task of amusing 'the child,' as she and the Duchess were pleased to call Piney. Piney was no chicken, but it was a soothing and original theory of the pair thus to account for the fact that she didn't swear and wasn't improper.

When night crept up again through the gorges, the reedy notes of the accordion rose and fell in fitful spasms and long-drawn gasps by the flickering campfire. But music failed to fill entirely the aching void left by insufficient food, and a new diversion was proposed by Piney,—story-telling. Neither Mr. Oakhurst nor his female companions caring to relate their personal experiences, this plan would have failed too, but for the Innocent. Some months before he had chanced upon a stray copy of Mr. Pope's ingenious translation of the Iliad. He now proposed to narrate the principal incidents of that poem—having thoroughly mastered the argument and fairly forgotten the words —in the current vernacular of Sandy Bar. And so for the rest of that night the Homeric demigods again walked the earth. Trojan bully and wily Greek wrestled in the winds, and the great pines in the cañon seemed to bow to the wrath of the son of Peleus. Mr. Oakhurst listened with quiet satisfaction. Most especially was he interested in the fate of 'Ash-heels,' as the Innocent persisted in denominating the 'swift-footed Achilles.'

So, with small food and much of Homer and the accordion, a week passed over the heads of the outcasts. The sun again forsook them, and again from leaden skies the snowflakes were sifted over the land. Day by day closer around them drew the snowy circle, until at last they looked from their prison over drifted walls of dazzling white, that towered twenty feet above their heads. It became more and more difficult to replenish their fires, even from the fallen trees beside them, now half hidden in the drifts. And yet no one complained. The lovers turned from the dreary prospect and looked into each other's eyes, and were happy. Mr. Oakhurst settled himself coolly to the losing game before him. The Duchess, more cheerful than she had been, assumed the care of Piney. Only Mother Shipton—once the strongest of the party— seemed to sicken and fade. At midnight on the tenth day she called Oakhurst to her side. 'I'm going,' she said, in a voice of querulous weakness, 'but don't say anything about it. Don't waken the kids. Take the bundle from under my head, and open it.' Mr. Oakhurst did so. It contained Mother Shipton's rations for the last week, untouched. 'Give 'em to the child,' she said, pointing to the sleeping Piney. 'You've starved yourself,' said the gambler. 'That's what they call it,' said the woman querulously, as she lay down again, and, turning her face to the wall, passed quietly away.

The accordion and the bones were put aside that day, and Homer was forgotten. When the body of Mother Shipton had been committed to the snow, Mr. Oakhurst took the Innocent aside, and showed him a pair of snowshoes, which he had fashioned from the old pack-saddle. 'There's one chance in a hundred to save her yet,' he said, pointing to Piney; 'but it's there,' he added, pointing toward Poker Flat. 'If you can reach there in two days she's safe.' 'And you?' asked Tom Simson. 'I'll stay here,' was the curt reply.

The lovers parted with a long embrace. 'You are not going, too?' said the Duchess, as she saw Mr. Oakhurst apparently waiting to accompany him. 'As far as the cañon,' he replied. He turned suddenly and kissed the Duchess, leaving her pallid face aflame, and her trembling limbs rigid with amazement.

Night came, but not Mr. Oakhurst. It brought the storm again and the whirling snow. Then the Duchess, feeding the fire, found that some one had quietly piled beside the hut enough fuel to last a few days longer. The tears rose to her eyes, but she hid them from Piney.

The women slept but little. In the morning, looking into each other's faces, they read their fate. Neither spoke, but Piney, accepting the position of the stronger, drew near and placed her arm around the Duchess's waist. They kept this attitude for the rest of the day. That night the storm reached its greatest fury, and, rending asunder the protecting vines, invaded the very hut.

Toward morning they found themselves unable to feed the fire, which gradually died away. As the embers slowly blackened, the Duchess crept closer to Piney, and broke the silence of many hours: 'Piney, can you pray?' 'No, dear,' said Piney simply. The Duchess, without knowing exactly why, felt relieved, and, putting her head upon Piney's shoulder, spoke no more. And so reclining, the younger and purer pillowing the head of her soiled sister upon her virgin breast, they fell asleep.

The wind lulled as if it feared to waken them. Feathery drifts of snow, shaken from the long pine boughs, flew like white-winged birds, and settled about them as they slept. The moon through the rifted clouds looked down upon what had been the camp. But all human stain, all trace of earthly travail, was hidden beneath the spotless mantle mercifully flung from above.

They slept all that day and the next, nor did they waken when voices and footsteps broke the silence of the camp. And when pitying fingers brushed the snow from their wan faces, you could scarcely have told from the equal peace that dwelt upon them which was she that had sinned. Even the law of Poker Flat recognized this, and turned away, leaving them still locked in each other's arms.

But at the head of the gulch, on one of the largest pine-trees, they found the deuce of clubs pinned to the bark with a bowie-knife. It bore the following, written in pencil in a firm hand:

✝

BENEATH THIS TREE
LIES THE BODY
OF
JOHN OAKHURST,
WHO STRUCK A STREAK OF BAD LUCK
ON THE 23D OF NOVEMBER, 1850,
AND
HANDED IN HIS CHECKS
ON THE 7TH DECEMBER, 1850.

↓

And pulseless and cold, with a Derringer by his side and a bullet in his heart, though still calm as in life, beneath the snow lay he who was at once the strongest and yet the weakest of the outcasts of Poker Flat.

1868   1870

PLAIN LANGUAGE FROM TRUTHFUL JAMES

(TABLE MOUNTAIN, 1870)

WHICH I wish to remark,
    And my language is plain,
That for ways that are dark
    And for tricks that are vain,
The heathen Chinee is peculiar,
    Which the same I would rise to explain.

Ah Sin was his name;
  And I shall not deny,
In regard to the same,
  What that name might imply;   10
But his smile it was pensive and childlike,
  As I frequent remarked to Bill Nye.

It was August the third,
  And quite soft was the skies;
Which it might be inferred
  That Ah Sin was likewise;
Yet he played it that day upon William
  And me in a way I despise.

Which we had a small game,
  And Ah Sin took a hand: 20
It was Euchre. The same
  He did not understand;
But he smiled as he sat by the table,
  With the smile that was childlike and
    bland.

Yet the cards they were stocked
  In a way that I grieve,
And my feelings were shocked
  At the state of Nye's sleeve,
Which was stuffed full of aces and bowers,
  And the same with intent to deceive.   30

But the hands that were played
  By that heathen Chinee,
And the points that he made,
  Were quite frightful to see,—
Till at last he put down a right bower,
  Which the same Nye had dealt unto
    me.

Then I looked up at Nye,
  And he gazed upon me;
And he rose with a sigh,
  And said, 'Can this be?   40
We are ruined by Chinese cheap labor,'—
  And he went for that heathen Chinee.

In the scene that ensued
  I did not take a hand,
But the floor it was strewed
  Like the leaves on the strand
With the cards that Ah Sin had been hiding,
  In the game 'he did not understand.'

In his sleeves, which were long,
  He had twenty-four packs,—   50
Which was coming it strong,
  Yet I state but the facts;

And we found on his nails, which were taper,
  What is frequent in tapers,—that's wax.

Which is why I remark,
  And my language is plain,
That for ways that are dark
  And for tricks that are vain,
The heathen Chinee is peculiar,—
  Which the same I am free to maintain.   60
1870   1871

DICKENS IN CAMP [1]

(1812–1870)

ABOVE the pines the moon was slowly
    drifting,
  The river sang below;
The dim Sierras, far beyond, uplifting
  Their minarets of snow.

The roaring camp-fire, with rude humor,
    painted
  The ruddy tints of health
On haggard face and form that drooped and
    fainted
  In the fierce race for wealth;

Till one arose, and from his pack's scant
    treasure
  A hoarded volume drew,   10
And cards were dropped from hands of list-
    less leisure
  To hear the tale anew.

And then, while round them shadows gath-
    ered faster,
  And as the firelight fell,
He read aloud the book wherein the Master
  Had writ of 'Little Nell.'

Perhaps 'twas boyish fancy,—for the reader
  Was youngest of them all,—
But, as he read, from clustering pine and
    cedar
  A silence seemed to fall;   20

The fir-trees, gathering closer in the
    shadows,
  Listened in every spray,

1 'When news of the death of Dickens reached Bret
Harte he was camping in the Foot-Hills, far from
San Francisco, but he sent a telegram to hold back for
a day the printing of the *Overland*, then ready for the
press, and his poem was written that night and for-
warded the next morning.' Merwin, *The Life of Bret
Harte* (Boston, 1911), 312n.

While the whole camp with 'Nell' on
    English meadows
Wandered and lost their way.

And so in mountain solitudes—o'ertaken
    As by some spell divine—
Their cares dropped from them like the
    needles shaken
    From out the gusty pine.

Lost is that camp and wasted all its
    fire;
    And he who wrought that spell?   30
Ah! towering pine and stately Kentish
    spire,
    Ye have one tale to tell!

Lost is that camp, but let its fragrant
    story
    Blend with the breath that thrills
With hop-vine's incense all the pensive
    glory
    That fills the Kentish hills.

And on that grave where English oak and
    holly
    And laurel wreaths entwine,
Deem it not all a too presumptuous folly,
    This spray of Western pine!   40
1870   1871

'JIM'

SAY there! P'r'aps
Some on you chaps
    Might know Jim Wild?
Well,—no offense:
Thar ain't no sense
    In gittin' riled!

Jim was my chum
    Up on the Bar:
That's why I come
    Down from up yar,   10
Lookin' for Jim.
Thank ye, sir! *You*
Ain't of that crew,—
    Blest if you are!

Money? Not much:
    That ain't my kind;
I ain't no such.
    Rum? I don't mind,
Seein' it's you.

Well, this yer Jim,—   20
Did you know him?
Jes' 'bout your size;
Same kind of eyes;—
Well, that is strange:
    Why, it's two year
    Since he came here,
Sick, for a change.

Well, here's to us:
    Eh?
The h— you say: 30
    Dead?
That little cuss?

What makes you star',
You over thar?
Can't a man drop
's glass in yer shop
But you must r'ar?
    It wouldn't take
    D—d much to break
You and your bar.   40

    Dead!
Poor—little—Jim!
Why, thar was me,
Jones, and Bob Lee,
Harry and Ben,—
No-account men:
Then to take *him*!

Well, thar—Good-by—
No more, sir—I—
    Eh?   50
What's that you say?
Why, dern it!—sho!—
No? Yes! By Joe!
    Sold!
Sold! Why, you limb,
You ornery,
    Derned old
Long-legged Jim.

                  1871

WHAT THE BULLET SANG

O JOY of creation
    To be!
O rapture to fly
    And be free!
Be the battle lost or won,
Though its smoke shall hide the sun,
I shall find my love,—the one
    Born for me!

I shall know him where he stands,
    All alone,   10
With the power in his hands
    Not o'erthrown;
I shall know him by his face,
By his godlike front and grace;
I shall hold him for a space,
    All my own!

It is he—O my love!
    So bold!
It is I—all thy love
    Foretold!   20
It is I. O love! what bliss!
Dost thou answer to my kiss?
O sweetheart! what is this
    Lieth there so cold?

              1882

JOHN HAY

1838–1905

JIM BLUDSO,
OF THE PRAIRIE BELLE

WALL, no! I can't tell whar he lives,
    Becase he don't live, you see;
Leastways, he's got out of the habit
    Of livin' like you and me.
Whar have you been for the last three year
    That you haven't heard folks tell
How Jimmy Bludso passed in his checks
    The night of the Prairie Belle?

He weren't no saint,—them engineers
    Is all pretty much alike,—   10
One wife in Natchez-under-the-Hill
    And another one here, in Pike;
A keerless man in his talk was Jim,
    And an awkward hand in a row,
But he never flunked, and he never lied,—
    I reckon he never knowed how.

And this was all the religion he had,—
    To treat his engine well;
Never be passed on the river;
    To mind the pilot's bell;   20
And if ever the Prairie Belle took fire,—
    A thousand times he swore,
He'd hold her nozzle agin the bank
    Till the last soul got ashore.

All boats has their day on the Mississip,
    And her day come at last,—
The Movastar was a better boat,
    But the Belle she *wouldn't* be passed.

And so she come tearin' along that night—
    The oldest craft on the line—   30
With a nigger squat on her safety-valve,
    And her furnace crammed, rosin and
        pine.

The fire bust out as she clared the bar,
    And burnt a hole in the night,
And quick as a flash she turned, and made
    For that willer-bank on the right.
There was runnin' and cursin', but Jim
    yelled out,
    Over all the infernal roar,
'I'll hold her nozzle agin the bank
    Till the last galoot's ashore.'   40

Through the hot, black breath of the
    burnin' boat
Jim Bludso's voice was heard,
And they all had trust in his cussedness,
    And knowed he would keep his word.
And, sure's you're born, they all got off
    Afore the smokestacks fell,—
And Bludso's ghost went up alone
    In the smoke of the Prairie Belle.

He weren't no saint,—but at jedgment
    I'd run my chance with Jim,   50
'Longside of some pious gentlemen
    That wouldn't shook hands with him.
He seen his duty, a dead-sure thing,—
    And went for it thar and then;
And Christ ain't a going to be too hard
    On a man that died for men.

              1871

JOAQUIN MILLER

1839–1913

KIT CARSON'S RIDE[1]

ROOM! *room to turn round in, to breathe and*
  be free,
To grow to be giant, to sail as at sea
With the speed of the wind on a steed with his
  mane
To the wind, without pathway or route or a
  rein.
Room! room to be free where the white bor-
  der'd sea
Blows a kiss to a brother as boundless as he;
Where the buffalo come like a cloud on the
  plain,
Pouring on like the tide of a storm-driven
  main,
And the lodge of the hunter to friend or to foe
Offers rest; and unquestion'd you come or you
  go.   10
My plains of America! Seas of wild lands!
From a land in the seas in a raiment of foam,
That has reached to a stranger the welcome of
  home,
I turn to you, lean to you, lift you my hands.

Run? Run? See this flank, sir, and I do
  love him so!
But he's blind, badger blind. Whoa, Pache
  boy, whoa,
No, you wouldn't believe it to look at his
  eyes,
But he's blind, badger blind, and it happen'd this wise:

'We lay in the grass and the sunburnt
  clover
That spread on the ground like a great
  brown cover   20
Northward and southward, and west and
  away
To the Brazos, where our lodges lay,
One broad and unbroken level of brown.

We were waiting the curtains of night to
  come down
To cover us trio and conceal our flight
With my brown bride, won from an Indian
  town
That lay in the rear the full ride of a night.

'We lounged in the grass—her eyes were
  in mine,
And her hands on my knee, and her hair was
  as wine
In its wealth and its flood, pouring on and
  all over   30
Her bosom wine red, and press'd never by
  one.
Her touch was as warm as the tinge of the
  clover
Burnt brown as it reach'd to the kiss of the
  sun.
Her words they were low as the lute-
  throated dove,
And as laden with love as the heart when it
  beats
In its hot, eager answer to earliest love,
Or the bee hurried home by its burthen of
  sweets.

'We lay low in the grass on the broad
  plain levels,
Old Revels and I, and my stolen brown
  bride;
"Forty full miles if a foot to ride!   40
Forty full miles if a foot, and the devils
Of red Comanches are hot on the track
When once they strike it. Let the sun go
  down
Soon, very soon," muttered bearded old
  Revels
As he peer'd at the sun, lying low on his back,
Holding fast to his lasso. Then he jerk'd at
  his steed
And he sprang to his feet, and glanced
  swiftly around,
And then dropp'd, as if shot, with an ear to
  the ground;
Then again to his feet, and to me, to my
  bride,
While his eyes were like flame, his face like
  a shroud,   50
His form like a king, and his beard like a
  cloud,

---

[1] 'The bugle-call to battle, the shouts of men and the
neighing of horses, the roar of cannon, the waving
banners—here is something sinfully poetic. The
spotted cattle on the hills, the winding rivers through
the valleys, the surging white seas against the granite
shores—all life, all action that is beautiful and grand
is poetry, waiting for expression. The world is one
great poem, because it is very grand, very good, and
very beautiful.' Miller, 'What Is Poetry,' *Memorie and
Rime* (N.Y., 1884),39.

And his voice loud and shrill, as both trum-
    pet and reed,—
"Pull, pull in your lassoes, and bridle to
    steed,
And speed you if ever for life you would
    speed.
Aye, ride for your lives, for your lives you
    must ride!
For the plain is aflame, the prairie on fire,
And the feet of wild horses hard flying
    before
I heard like a sea breaking high on the
    shore,
While the buffalo come like a surge of the
    sea,
Driven far by the flame, driving fast on us
    three   60
As a hurricane comes, crushing palms in his
    ire."

'We drew in the lassoes, seized saddle and
    rein,
Threw them on, cinched them on, cinched
    them over again,
And again drew the girth; and spring we to
    horse,
With head to the Brazos, with a sound in
    the air
Like the surge of a sea, with a flash in the
    eye,
From that red wall of flame reaching up to
    the sky;
A red wall of flame and a black rolling sea
Rushing fast upon us, as the wind sweeping
    free
And afar from the desert blown hollow and
    hoarse.   70

'Not a word, not a wail from a lip was let
    fall,
We broke not a whisper, we breathed not a
    prayer,
There was work to be done, there was death
    in the air,
And the chance was as one to a thousand
    for all.

'Twenty miles! . . . thirty miles! . . . a
    dim distant speck . . .
Then a long reaching line, and the Brazos in
    sight!
And I rose in my seat with a shout of
    delight.
I stood in my stirrup, and look'd to my
    right—

But Revels was gone; I glanced by my
    shoulder
And saw his horse stagger; I saw his head
    drooping   80
Hard down on his breast, and his naked
    breast stooping
Low down to the mane, as so swifter and
    bolder
Ran reaching out for us the red-footed fire
He rode neck to neck with a buffalo bull,
That made the earth shake where he came
    in his course,
The monarch of millions, with shaggy mane
    full
Of smoke and of dust, and it shook with
    desire
Of battle, with rage and with bellowings
    hoarse.
His keen, crooked horns, through the storm
    of his mane,
Like black lances lifted and lifted again;   90
And I looked but this once, for the fire
    licked through,
And Revels was gone, as we rode two and
    two.

'I look'd to my left then—and nose, neck,
    and shoulder
Sank slowly, sank surely, till back to my
    thighs,
And up through the black blowing veil of
    her hair
Did beam full in mine her two marvelous
    eyes,
With a longing and love yet a look of
    despair
And of pity for me, as she felt the smoke
    fold her,
And flames leaping far for her glorious hair.
Her sinking horse falter'd, plunged, fell and
    was gone   100
As I reach'd through the flame and I bore
    her still on.
On! into the Brazos, she, Pache and I—
Poor, burnt, blinded Pache. I love
    him. . .
        That's why.'
1871   1871

CROSSING THE PLAINS

WHAT great yoked brutes with briskets low,
With wrinkled necks like buffalo,
With round, brown, liquid, pleading eyes,
That turn'd so slow and sad to you,

That shone like love's eyes soft with tears,
That seem'd to plead, and make replies,
The while they bow'd their necks and drew
The creaking load; and look'd at you.
Their sable briskets swept the ground,
Their cloven feet kept solemn sound.   10

Two sullen bullocks led the line,
Their great eyes shining bright like wine;
Two sullen captive kings were they,
That had in time held herds at bay,
And even now they crushed the sod
With stolid sense of majesty,
And stately stepp'd and stately trod,
As if 'twere something still to be
Kings even in captivity.

                                    1878

COLUMBUS [1]

(AUGUST 3—OCTOBER 12, 1492)

BEHIND him lay the gray Azores,
    Behind the Gates of Hercules;
Before him not the ghost of shores,
    Before him only shoreless seas.
The good mate said: 'Now must we pray,
For lo! the very stars are gone,
Brave Adm'r'l, speak; what shall I say?'
    'Why, say: "Sail on! sail on! and on!" '

'My men grow mutinous day by day;
    My men grow ghastly, wan and weak.'   10
The stout mate thought of home; a spray
    Of salt wave washed his swarthy cheek.
'What shall I say, brave Adm'r'l, say,
    If we sight naught but seas at dawn?'
'Why, you shall say at break of day:
    "Sail on! sail on! sail on! and on!" '

They sailed and sailed, as winds might
        blow,
    Until at last the blanched mate said:
'Why, now not even God would know
    Should I and all my men fall dead.   20
These very winds forget their way,
    For God from these dread seas is gone.

1 ' "Columbus" was written at "The Hights" in Oakland the first week in October, 1892. He had suffered
loss through, and disillusionment in one he had trusted
that year. Reading a translated copy of the logbook
left by Columbus, he marked—"the men mutinied,
but I sailed on." Another annotation: "Storm and
darkness; stars changed, but we sailed on." ' Daughter's note.

Now speak, brave Adm'r'l, speak and say—'
    He said: 'Sail on! sail on! and on!'

They sailed. They sailed. Then spake the
        mate:
    'This mad sea shows his teeth tonight.
He curls his lip, he lies in wait,
    With lifted teeth, as if to bite!
Brave Admiral, say but one good word:
    What shall we do when hope is gone?'   30
The words leapt like a leaping sword:
    'Sail on! sail on! sail on! and on!'

Then, pale and worn, he paced his deck,
    And peered through darkness. Ah, that
        night
Of all dark nights! And then a speck—
    A light! A light! At last a light!
It grew, a starlit flag unfurled!
    It grew to be Time's burst of dawn.
He gained a world; he gave that world
    Its grandest lesson: 'On! sail on!'   40
1892   1896

FROM A SONG OF CREATION

CANTO I

1

HIS triple star led on and on,
Led up blue, bastioned Chilkoot Pass
To clouds, through clouds, above white
        clouds
That droop with snows like beaded
        strouds—
Above a world of gleaming glass,
Where loomed such cities of the skies
As only prophets look upon,
As only loving poets see,
With prophet ken of mystery.

2

What lone, white silence, left or right,   10
What whiteness, something more than
        white!
Such steel blue whiteness, van or rear—
Such silence as you could but hear
Above the sparkled, frosted rime,
As if the steely stars kept time
And sang their mystic, mighty rune—
. . . And oh, the icy, eerie moon!

3

What temples, towers, tombs of white,
White tombs, white tombstones, left and
        right,

That pushed the passing night aside   20
To ward where fallen stars had died—
To ward white tombs where dead stars
    lay—
White tombs more white, more bright than
    they;
White tombs high heaped white tombs
    upon—
White Ossa piled on Pelion!

4

Pale, steel stars flashed, rose, fell again,
Then paused, leaned low, as pitying,
And leaning so they ceased to sing,
The while the moon, with mother care,
Slow rocked her silver rocking-chair.   30

5

Night here, mid-year, is as a span;
Thor comes, a gold-clad king of war,
Comes only as the great Thor can.
Thor storms the battlements and Thor,
Far leaping, clinging crowned upon,
Throws battle hammer forth and back
Until the walls blaze in his track
With sparks and it is sudden dawn—
Dawn, sudden, sparkling, as a gem—
A jeweled, frost-set diadem   40
Of diamond, ruby, radium.

6

Two tallest, ice-tipt peaks take flame,
Take yellow flame, take crimson, pink,
Then, ere you yet have time to think,
Take hues that never yet had name.
Then turret, minaret, and tower,
As if to mark some mystic hour,
Or ancient, lost Masonic sign,
Take on a darkness like to night,
Deep night below the yellow light   50
That erstwhile seemed some snow-white
    tomb.
Then all is set in ghostly gloom,
As some dim-lighted, storied shrine—
As if the stars forget to stay
At court when comes the kingly day.

7

And now the high-built shafts of brass,
Gate posts that guard the tomb-set pass,
Put off their crowns, rich robes, and all
Their sudden, splendid light let fall;
And tomb and minaret and tower   60
Again gleam as that midnight hour.
While day, as scorning still to wait,

Drives fiercely through the ice-built gate
That guards the Arctic's outer hem
Of white, high-built Jerusalem.

8

To see, to guess the great white throne,
Behold Alaska's ice-built steeps
Where everlasting silence keeps
And white death lives and lords alone:
Go see God's river born full grown—   70
The gold of this stream it is good:
Here grows the Ark's white gopher
    wood—
A wide, white land, unnamed, unknown,
A land of mystery and moan.

9

Tall, trim, slim gopher trees incline,
A leaning, laden, helpless copse,
And moan and creak and intertwine
Their laden, twisted, tossing tops,
And moan all night and moan all day
With winds that walk these steeps alway.   80

10

The melancholy moose looks down,
A tattered Capuchin in brown,
A gaunt, ungainly, mateless monk,
An elephant without his trunk,
While far, against the gleaming blue,
High up a rock-topt ridge of snow,
Where scarce a dream would care to go,
Climb countless blue-clad caribou,
In endless line till lost to view.

11

The rent ice surges, grinds, and groans,   90
Then gorges, backs, and climbs the shore,
Then breaks with sudden rage and roar
And plunging, leaping, foams and moans
Swift down the surging, seething stream—
Mad hurdles of some monstrous dream.

12

To see God's river born full grown,
To see him burst the womb of earth
And leap, a giant at his birth,
Through shoreless whiteness, with wild
    shout—
A shout so sharp, so cold, so dread   100
You see, feel, hear, his sheeted dead—
'Tis as to know, no longer doubt,
'Tis as to know the eld Unknown,
Aye, bow before the great white throne.

                        1903

SAMUEL CLEMENS
(Mark Twain)
1835–1910

THE CELEBRATED JUMPING FROG OF CALAVERAS COUNTY[1]

IN compliance with the request of a friend of mine, who wrote me from the East, I called on good-natured, garrulous old Simon Wheeler, and inquired after my friend's friend, *Leonidas W.* Smiley, as requested to do, and I hereunto append the result. I have a lurking suspicion that Leonidas W. Smiley is a myth; that my friend never knew such a personage; that he only conjectured that, if I asked old Wheeler about him, it would remind him of his infamous *Jim* Smiley, and he would go to work and bore me nearly to death with some infernal reminiscence of him as long and tedious as it should be useless to me. If that was the design, it certainly succeeded.

I found Simon Wheeler dozing comfortably by the bar-room stove of the old, dilapidated tavern in the ancient mining camp of Angel's, and I noticed that he was fat and bald-headed, and had an expression of winning gentleness and simplicity upon his tranquil countenance. He roused up and gave me good-day. I told him a friend of mine had commissioned me to make some inquiries about a cherished companion of his boyhood named *Leonidas W.* Smiley— Rev. *Leonidas W.* Smiley—a young minister of the Gospel, who he had heard was at one time a resident of Angel's Camp. I added that, if Mr. Wheeler could tell me anything about this Rev. Leonidas W. Smiley, I would feel under many obligations to him.

Simon Wheeler backed me into a corner and blockaded me there with his chair, and then sat me down and reeled off the monotonous narrative which follows this paragraph. He never smiled, he never frowned, he never changed his voice from the gentle-flowing key to which he tuned the initial sentence, he never betrayed the slightest suspicion of enthusiasm; but all through the interminable narrative there ran a vein of impressive earnestness and sincerity, which showed me plainly that, so far from his imagining that there was anything ridiculous or funny about his story, he regarded it as a really important matter, and admired its two heroes as men of transcendent genius in *finesse*. To me, the spectacle of a man drifting serenely along through such a queer yarn without ever smiling, was exquisitely absurd. As I said before, I asked him to tell me what he knew of Rev. Leonidas W. Smiley, and he replied as follows. I let him go on in his own way, and never interrupted him once:

There was a feller here once by the name of *Jim* Smiley, in the winter of '49—or may be it was the spring of '50—I don't recollect exactly, somehow, though what makes me think it was one or the other is because I remember the big flume wasn't finished when he first came to the camp; but any way, he was the curiosest man about always betting on any thing that turned up you ever see, if he could get any body to bet on the other side; and if he couldn't, he'd change sides. Any way that suited the other man would suit him—any way just so's he got a bet, *he* was satisfied. But still he was lucky, uncommon lucky; he most always come out winner. He was always ready and laying for a chance; there couldn't be no solitary thing mentioned but that feller'd offer to bet on it, and take any side you please, as I was just telling you. If there was a horse-race, you'd find him flush, or you'd find him busted at the end of it; if there was a dog-fight, he'd bet on it; if there was a cat-fight he'd bet on it; if there was a chicken-fight he'd bet on it; why, if there was two birds setting on a fence, he would bet you which one would fly first; or if there was a camp meeting, he would be there reg'lar, to bet on Parson Walker, which he judged to be

1 In a notebook kept at Angel's Camp, California, Clemens jotted down the following incident: 'Coleman with his jumping frog—bet a stranger $50.—Stranger had no frog and C. got him one:—In the meantime stranger filled C.'s frog full of shot and he couldn't jump. The stranger's frog won.' Across this note he wrote: 'Wrote this story for Artemus [Ward]—his idiot publisher, Carleton, gave it to Clapp's *Saturday Press*.' Paine, ed., *Mark Twain's Notebook*(N.Y., 1935),7.

the best exhorter about there, and so he was, too, and a good man. If he even seen a straddle-bug start to go anywheres, he would bet you how long it would take him to get wherever he was going to, and if you took him up, he would follow that straddle-bug to Mexico but what he would find out where he was bound for and how long he was on the road. Lots of the boys here has seen that Smiley, and can tell you about him. Why, it never made no difference to *him*—he would bet on *any* thing—the dangdest feller. Parson Walker's wife laid very sick once, for a good while, and it seemed as if they warn't going to save her; but one morning he come in, and Smiley asked how she was, and he said she was considerable better—thank the Lord for his inf'nit mercy—and coming on so smart that, with the blessing of Prov'dence, she'd get well yet; and Smiley, before he thought, says, 'Well, I'll risk two-and-a-half that she won't, any way.'

Thish-yer Smiley had a mare—the boys called her the fifteen-minute nag, but that was only in fun, you know, because, of course, she was faster than that—and he used to win money on that horse, for all she was so slow and always had the asthma, or the distemper, or the consumption, or something of that kind. They used to give her two or three hundred yards start, and then pass her under way; but always at the fag-end of the race she'd get excited and desperate-like, and come cavorting and straddling up, and scattering her legs around limber, sometimes in the air, and sometimes out to one side amongst the fences, and kicking up m-o-r-e dust, and raising m-o-r-e racket with her coughing and sneezing and blowing her nose—and always fetch up at the stand just about a neck ahead, as near as you could cypher it down.

And he had a little small bull pup, that to look at him you'd think he wa'n't worth a cent, but to set around and look ornery, and lay for a chance to steal something. But as soon as money was up on him, he was a different dog; his underjaw'd begin to stick out like the fo'castle of a steamboat, and his teeth would uncover, and shine savage like the furnaces. And a dog might tackle him, and bullyrag him, and bite him, and throw him over his shoulder two or three times,

and Andrew Jackson—which was the name of the pup—Andrew Jackson would never let on but what *he* was satisfied, and hadn't expected nothing else—and the bets being doubled and doubled on the other side all the time, till the money was all up; and then all of a sudden he would grab that other dog jest by the j'int of his hind leg and freeze to it—not chaw, you understand, but only jest grip and hang on till they throwed up the sponge, if it was a year. Smiley always come out winner on that pup, till he harnessed a dog once that didn't have no hind legs, because they'd been sawed off by a circular saw, and when the thing had gone along far enough, and the money was all up, and he come to make a snatch for his pet holt, he saw in a minute how hc'd been imposed on, and how the other dog had him in the door, so to speak, and he 'peared surprised, and then he looked sorter discouraged-like, and didn't try no more to win the fight, and so he got shucked out bad. He give Smiley a look, as much as to say his heart was broke, and it was *his* fault, for putting up a dog that hadn't no hind legs for him to take holt of, which was his main dependence in a fight, and then he limped off a piece and laid down and died. It was a good pup, was that Andrew Jackson, and would have made a name for hisself if he'd lived, for the stuff was in him, and he had genius—I know it, because he hadn't had no opportunity to speak of, and it don't stand to reason that a dog could make such a fight as he could under them circumstances, if he hadn't no talent. It always makes me feel sorry when I think of that last fight of his'n, and the way it turned out.

Well, this-yer Smiley had rat-tarriers, and chicken cocks, and tom-cats, and all them kind of things, till you couldn't rest, and you couldn't fetch nothing for him to bet on but he'd match you. He ketched a frog one day, and took him home, and said he cal'klated to edercate him; and so he never done nothing for three months but set in his back yard and learn that frog to jump. And you bet he *did* learn him, too. He'd give him a little punch behind, and the next minute you'd see that frog whirling in the air like a doughnut—see him turn one summerset, or may be a couple, if he got a good start, and come down flat-footed and all right, like a cat. He got him up so in the matter of catching flies, and kept him in practice so constant, that he'd nail a fly every time as far as he could see him. Smiley said all a frog wanted was education, and he could do most anything—and I believe him. Why, I've seen him set Dan'l Webster down here on this floor—Dan'l Webster was the name of the frog—and sing out, 'Flies, Dan'l, flies!' and quicker'n you could wink, he'd spring straight up, and snake a fly off'n the counter there, and flop down on the floor again as solid as a gob of mud, and fall to scratching the side of his head with his hind foot as indifferent as if he hadn't no idea he'd been doin' any more'n any frog might do. You never see a frog so modest and straightfor'ard as he was, for all he was so gifted. And when it come to fair and square jumping on a dead level, he could get over more ground at one straddle than any animal of his breed you ever see. Jumping on a dead level was his strong suit, you understand; and when it come to that, Smiley would ante up money on him as long as he had a red. Smiley was monstrous proud of his frog, and well he might be, for fellers that had traveled and been everywheres, all said he laid over any frog that ever *they* see.

Well, Smiley kept the beast in a little lattice box, and he used to fetch him down town sometimes and lay for a bet. One day a feller—a stranger in the camp, he was—come across him with his box, and says:

'What might it be that you've got in the box?'

And Smiley says, sorter indifferent like, 'It might be a parrot, or it might be a canary, may be, but it ain't—it's only just a frog.'

And the feller took it, and looked at it careful, and turned it round this way and that, and says, 'H'm—so 'tis. Well, what's *he* good for?'

'Well,' Smiley says, easy and careless, 'He's good enough for *one* thing, I should judge—he can outjump ary frog in Calaveras county.'

The feller took the box again, and took another long, particular look, and give it back to Smiley, and says, very deliberate, 'Well, I don't see no p'ints about that frog that's any better'n any other frog.'

'May be you don't,' Smiley says. 'May be you understand frogs, and may be you

don't understand 'em; may be you've had experience, and may be you an't only a amature, as it were. Anyways, I've got *my* opinion, and I'll risk forty dollars he can outjump any frog in Calaveras county.'

And the feller studied a minute, and then says, kinder sad like, 'Well, I'm only a stranger here, and I an't got no frog, but if I had a frog, I'd bet you.'

And then Smiley says, 'That's all right—that's all right—if you'll hold my box a minute, I'll go and get you a frog.' And so the feller took the box, and put up his forty dollars along with Smiley's, and set down to wait.

So he set there a good while thinking and thinking to hisself, and then he got the frog out and prized his mouth open and took a teaspoon and filled him full of quail shot—filled him pretty near up to his chin—and set him on the floor. Smiley he went to the swamp and slopped around in the mud for a long time, and finally he ketched a frog, and fetched him in, and give him to this feller, and says:

'Now, if you're ready, set him alongside of Dan'l, with his fore-paws just even with Dan'l, and I'll give the word.' Then he says, 'One—two—three—jump!' and him and the feller touched up the frogs from behind, and the new frog hopped off, but Dan'l give a heave, and hysted up his shoulders—so—like a Frenchman, but it wa'n't no use—couldn't budge; he was planted as solid as an anvil, and he couldn't no more stir than if he was anchored out. Smiley was a good deal surprised, and he was disgusted too, but he didn't have no idea what the matter was, of course.

The feller took the money and started away; and when he was going out of the door, he sorter jerked his thumb over his shoulders—this way—at Dan'l, and says again, very deliberate, 'Well, *I* don' see no p'ints about that frog that's any better'n any other frog.'

Smiley he stood scratching his head and looking down at Dan'l a long time, and at last he says, 'I do wonder what in the nation that frog throw'd off for—I wonder if there ain't something the matter with him—he 'pears to look might baggy, somehow.' And he ketched Dan'l by the nap of the neck, and lifted him up and says, 'Why, blame my cats, if he don't weigh five pound!' and turned him upside down, and he belched out a double handful of shot. And then he sees how it was, and he was the maddest man—he set the frog down and took out after that feller, but he never ketched him. And—

(Here Simon Wheeler heard his name called from the front yard, and got up to see what was wanted.) And turning to me as he moved away, he said: 'Just set where you are, stranger, and rest easy—I an't going to be gone a second.'

But, by your leave, I did not think that a continuation of the history of the enterprising vagabond *Jim* Smiley would be likely to afford me much information concerning the Rev. *Leonidas W.* Smiley, and so I started away.

At the door I met the sociable Wheeler returning, and he buttonholed me and recommenced:

'Well, thish-yer Smiley had a yaller one-eyed cow that didn't have no tail, only jest a short stump like a bannanner, and—'

'Oh! hang Smiley and his afflicted cow!' I muttered, good-naturedly, and bidding the old gentleman good-day, I departed.

New York *Saturday Press*, 18 Nov. 1865
1865   1867

FROM LIFE ON THE MISSISSIPPI

HUCK FINN ON THE RAFT [1]

BY *way of illustrating keelboat talk and manners, and that now departed and hardly remembered raft life, I will throw in, in this place, a chapter from a book which I have been working at, by fits and starts, during the past five or six years, and may possibly finish in the course of five or six more. The book is a story which details some passages in the life of an ignorant village boy, Huck Finn, son of the town drunkard of my time out West, there. He has run away from his persecuting father, and from a persecuting good widow who wishes to make a nice, truth-telling, respectable boy of him; and with him a slave of the widow's has also escaped. They have found a fragment of a lumber-raft (it is high water and dead summer-time), and are floating down the river by night, and hiding in the willows by day—bound for Cairo, whence the Negro will seek freedom in the heart of the free states. But, in a fog, they pass Cairo without knowing it. By and by they begin to suspect the truth, and Huck Finn is persuaded to end the dismal suspense by swimming down to a huge raft which they have seen in the distance ahead of them, creeping aboard under cover of the darkness, and gathering the needed information by eavesdropping:*

But you know a young person can't wait very well when he is impatient to find a thing out. We talked it over, and by and by Jim said it was such a black night, now, that it wouldn't be no risk to swim down to the big raft and crawl aboard and listen—they would talk about Cairo, because they would be calculating to go ashore there for a spree, maybe; or anyway they would send boats ashore to buy whisky or fresh meat or something. Jim had a wonderful level head, for a nigger: he could most always start a good plan when you wanted one.

I stood up and shook my rags off and jumped into the river, and struck out for the raft's light. By and by, when I got down nearly to her, I eased up and went slow and cautious. But everything was all right—nobody at the sweeps. So I swum down along the raft till I was most abreast the camp-fire in the middle, then I crawled aboard and inched along and got in among some bundles of shingles on the weather side of the fire. There was thirteen men there—they was the watch on deck of course. And a mighty rough-looking lot, too. They had a jug, and tin cups, and they kept the jug moving. One man was singing—roaring, you may say; and it wasn't a nice song—for a parlor, anyway. He roared through his nose, and strung out the last word of every line very long. When he was done they all fetched a kind of Injun war-whoop, and then another was sung. It begun:

'There was a woman in our towdn,
    In our towdn did dwed'l [dwell],
She loved her husband dear-i-lee,
    But another man twyste as wed'L

'Singing too, riloo, riloo, riloo,
    Ri-too, riloo, rilay - - - e,
She loved her husband dear-i-lee,
    But another man twyste as wed'l.'

1   The selection, to which the title has been given by the editors, is from *Life on the Mississippi*(N.Y., 1931), 19–31.

And so on—fourteen verses. It was kind of poor, and when he was going to start on the next verse one of them said it was the tune the old cow died on; and another one said: 'Oh, give us a rest!' And another one told him to take a walk. They made fun of him till he got mad and jumped up and begun to cuss the crowd, and said he could lam any thief in the lot.

They was all about to make a break for him, but the biggest man there jumped up and says:

'Set whar you are, gentlemen. Leave him to me; he's my meat.'

Then he jumped up in the air three times, and cracked his heels together every time. He flung off a buckskin coat that was all hung with fringes, and says, 'You lay thar tell the chawin-up's done;' and flung his hat down, which was all over ribbons, and says, 'You lay thar tell his sufferin's is over.'

Then he jumped up in the air and cracked his heels together again, and shouted out:

'Whoo-oop! I'm the old original iron-jawed, brass-mounted, copper-bellied corpse-maker from the wilds of Arkansaw! Look at me! I'm the man they call Sudden Death and General Desolation! Sired by a hurricane, dam'd by an earthquake, half-brother to the cholera, nearly related to the smallpox on the mother's side! Look at me! I take nineteen alligators and a bar'l of whisky for breakfast when I'm in robust health, and a bushel of rattlesnakes and a dead body when I'm ailing. I split the everlasting rocks with my glance, and I squench the thunder when I speak! Whoo-oop! Stand back and give me room according to my strength! Blood's my natural drink, and the wails of the dying is music to my ear! Cast your eye on me, gentlemen! and lay low and hold your breath, for I'm 'bout to turn myself loose!'

All the time he was getting this off, he was shaking his head and looking fierce, and kind of swelling around in a little circle, tucking up his wristbands, and now and then straightening up and beating his breast with his fist, saying, 'Look at me, gentlemen!' When he got through, he jumped up and cracked his heels together three times, and let off a roaring 'Whoo-oop! I'm the bloodiest son of a wildcat that lives!'

Then the man that had started the row tilted his old slouch hat down over his right eye; then he bent stooping forward, with his back sagged and his south end sticking out far, and his fists a-shoving out and drawing in in front of him, and so went around in a little circle about three times, swelling himself up and breathing hard. Then he straightened, and jumped up and cracked his heels together three times before he lit again (that made them cheer), and he began to shout like this:

'Whoo-oop! bow your neck and spread, for the kingdom of sorrow's a-coming! Hold me down to the earth, for I feel my powers a-working! whoo-oop! I'm a child of sin, *don't* let me get a start! Smoked glass, here, for all! Don't attempt to look at me with the naked eye, gentlemen! When I'm playful I use the meridians of longitude and parallels of latitude for a seine, and drag the Atlantic Ocean for whales! I scratch my head with the lightning and purr myself to sleep with the thunder! When I'm cold, I bile the Gulf of Mexico and bathe in it; when I'm hot I fan myself with an equinoctial storm; when I'm thirsty I reach up and suck a cloud dry like a sponge; when I range the earth hungry, famine follows in my tracks! Whoo-oop! Bow your neck and spread! I put my hand on the sun's face and make it night in the earth; I bite a piece out of the moon and hurry the seasons; I shake myself and crumble the mountains! Contemplate me through leather—*don't* use the naked eye! I'm the man with a petrified heart and biler-iron bowels! The massacre of isolated communities is the pastime of my idle moments, the destruction of nationalities the serious business of my life! The boundless vastness of the great American desert is my inclosed property, and I bury my dead on my own premises!' He jumped up and cracked his heels together three times before he lit (they cheered him again), and as he come down he shouted out: 'Whoo-oop! bow your neck and spread, for the Pet Child of Calamity's a-coming!'

Then the other one went to swelling around and blowing again—the first one—the one they called Bob; next, the Child of Calamity chipped in again, bigger than ever; then they both got at it at the same time, swelling round and round each other and punching their fists most into each other's faces, and whooping and jawing like Injuns;

then Bob called the Child names, and the Child called him names back again; next, Bob called him a heap rougher names, and the Child come back at him with the very worst kind of language; next, Bob knocked the Child's hat off, and the Child picked it up and kicked Bob's ribbony hat about six foot; Bob went and got it and said never mind, this warn't going to be the last of this thing, because he was a man that never forgot and never forgive, and so the Child better look out, for there was a time a-coming, just as sure as he was a living man, that he would have to answer to him with the best blood in his body. The Child said no man was willinger than he for that time to come, and he would give Bob fair warning, *now*, never to cross his path again, for he could never rest till he had waded in his blood, for such was his nature, though he was sparing him now on account of his family, if he had one.

Both of them was edging away in different directions, growling and shaking their heads and going on about what they was going to do; but a little black-whiskered chap skipped up and says:

'Come back here, you couple of chicken-livered cowards, and I'll thrash the two of ye!'

And he done it, too. He snatched them, he jerked them this way and that, he booted them around, he knocked them sprawling faster than they could get up. Why, it warn't two minutes till they begged like dogs—and how the other lot did yell and laugh and clap their hands all the way through, and shout, 'Sail in, Corpse-Maker!' 'Hi! at him again, Child of Calamity!' 'Bully for you, little Davy!' Well, it was a perfect pow-wow for a while. Bob and the Child had red noses and black eyes when they got through. Little Davy made them own up that they was sneaks and cowards and not fit to eat with a dog or drink with a nigger; then Bob and the Child shook hands with each other, very solemn, and said they had always respected each other and was willing to let bygones be bygones. So then they washed their faces in the river; and just then there was a loud order to stand by for a crossing, and some of them went forward to man the sweeps there, and the rest went aft to handle the after sweeps.

I lay still and waited for fifteen minutes, and had a smoke out of a pipe that one of them left in reach; then the crossing was finished, and they stumped back and had a drink around and went to talking and singing again. Next they got out an old fiddle, and one played, and another patted juba, and the rest turned themselves loose on a regular old-fashioned keelboat breakdown. They couldn't keep that up very long without getting winded, so by and by they settled around the jug again.

They sung 'Jolly, Jolly Raftsman's the Life for Me,' with a rousing chorus, and then they got to talking about differences betwixt hogs, and their different kind of habits; and next about women and their different ways; and next about the best ways to put out houses that was afire; and next about what ought to be done with the Injuns; and next about what a king had to do, and how much he got; and next about how to make cats fight; and next about what to do when a man has fits; and next about differences betwixt clear-water rivers and muddy-water ones. The man they called Ed said the muddy Mississippi water was wholesomer to drink than the clear water of the Ohio; he said if you let a pint of this yaller Mississippi water settle, you would have about a half to three-quarters of an inch of mud in the bottom, according to the stage of the river, and then it warn't no better than Ohio water—what you wanted to do was to keep it stirred up—and when the river was low, keep mud on hand to put in and thicken the water up the way it ought to be.

The Child of Calamity said that was so; he said there was nutritiousness in the mud, and a man that drunk Mississippi water could grow corn in his stomach if he wanted to. He says:

'You look at the graveyards; that tells the tale. Trees won't grow worth shucks in a Cincinnati graveyard, but in a Sent Louis graveyard they grow upwards of eight hundred foot high. It's all on account of the water the people drunk before they laid up. A Cincinnati corpse don't richen a soil any.'

And they talked about how Ohio water didn't like to mix with Mississippi water. Ed said if you take the Mississippi on a rise when the Ohio is low, you'll find a wide band of clear water all the way down the east side of the Mississippi for a hundred mile or more, and the minute you get out a quarter of a mile from shore and pass the line, it is all thick and yaller the rest of the way across. Then they talked about how to keep tobacco from getting mouldy, and from that they went into ghosts and told about a lot that other folks had seen; but Ed says:

'Why don't you tell something that you've seen yourselves? Now let me have a say. Five years ago I was on a raft as big as this, and right along here it was a bright moonshiny night, and I was on watch and boss of the stabboard oar forrard, and one of my pards was a man named Dick Allbright, and he come along to where I was sitting, forrard—gaping and stretching, he was—and stooped down on the edge of the raft and washed his face in the river, and come and set down by me and got out his pipe, and had just got it filled, when he looks up and says:

' "Why looky-here," he says, "ain't that Buck Miller's place, over yander in the bend?"

' "Yes," says I, "it is—why?" He laid his pipe down and leant his head on his hand, and says:

' "I thought we'd be furder down." I says:

' "I thought it, too, when I went off watch"—we was standing six hours on and six off—"but the boys told me," I says, "that the raft didn't seem to hardly move, for the last hour," says I, "though she's a-slipping along all right now," says I. He give a kind of a groan, and says:

' "I've seed a raft act so before, along here," he says, " 'pears to me the current has most quit above the head of this bend durin' the last two years," he says.

'Well, he raised up two or three times, and looked away off and around on the water. That started me at it, too. A body is always doing what he sees somebody else doing, though there mayn't be no sense in it. Pretty soon I see a black something floating on the water away off to stabboard and quartering behind us. I see he was looking at it, too. I says:

' "What's that?" He says, sort of pettish:

' " 'Tain't nothing but an old empty bar'l."

' " 'An empty bar'l!" says I, "why," says

I, "a spy-glass is a fool to *your* eyes. How can you tell it's an empty bar'l?" He says:

' "I don't know; I reckon it ain't a bar'l, but I thought it might be," says he.

' "Yes," I says, "so it might be, and it might be anything else, too; a body can't tell nothing about it, such a distance as that," I says.

'We hadn't nothing else to do, so we kept on watching it. By and by I says:

' "Why looky-here, Dick Allbright, that thing's a-gaining on us, I believe."

'He never said nothing. The thing gained and gained, and I judged it must be a dog that was about tired out. Well, we swung down into the crossing, and the thing floated across the bright streak of the moonshine, and by George, it *was* a bar'l. Says I:

' "Dick Allbright, what made you think that thing was a bar'l, when it was half a mile off?" says I. Says he:

' "I don't know." Says I:

' "You tell me, Dick Allbright." Says he:

' "Well, I knowed it was a bar'l; I've seen it before; lots has seen it; they says it's a ha'nted bar'l."

'I called the rest of the watch, and they come and stood there, and I told them what Dick said. It floated right along abreast, now, and didn't gain any more. It was about twenty foot off. Some was for having it aboard, but the rest didn't want to. Dick Allbright said rafts that had fooled with it had got bad luck by it. The captain of the watch said he didn't believe in it. He said he reckoned the bar'l gained on us because it was in a little better current than what we was. He said it would leave by and by.

'So then we went to talking about other things, and we had a song, and then a breakdown; and after that the captain of the watch called for another song; but it was clouding up now, and the bar'l stuck right thar in the same place, and the song didn't seem to have much warm-up to it, somehow, and so they didn't finish it, and there warn't any cheers, but it sort of dropped flat, and nobody said anything for a minute. Then everybody tried to talk at once, and one chap got off a joke, but it warn't no use, they didn't laugh, and even the chap that made the joke didn't laugh at it, which ain't usual. We all just settled down glum, and watched the bar'l, and was oneasy and oncomfortable. Well, sir, it shut down black and still, and then the wind began to moan around, and next the lightning began to play and the thunder to grumble. And pretty soon there was a regular storm, and in the middle of it a man that was running aft stumbled and fell and sprained his ankle so that he had to lay up. This made the boys shake their heads. And every time the lightning come, there was that bar'l, with the blue lights winking around it. We was always on the lookout for it. But by and by, toward dawn, she was gone. When the day come we couldn't see her anywhere, and we warn't sorry, either.

'But next night about half past nine, when there was songs and high jinks going on, here she comes again, and took her old roost on the stabboard side. There warn't no more high jinks. Everybody got solemn; nobody talked; you couldn't get anybody to do anything but set around moody and look at the bar'l. It begun to cloud up again. When the watch changed, the off watch stayed up, 'stead of turning in. The storm ripped and roared around all night, and in the middle of it another man tripped and sprained his ankle, and had to knock off. The bar'l left toward day, and nobody see it go.

'Everybody was sober and down in the mouth all day. I don't mean the kind of sober that comes of leaving liquor alone— not that. They was quiet, but they all drunk more than usual—not together, but each man sidled off and took it private, by himself.

'After dark the off watch didn't turn in; nobody sung, nobody talked; the boys didn't scatter around, neither; they sort of huddled together, forrard; and for two hours they set there, perfectly still, looking steady in the one direction, and heaving a sigh once in a while. And then, here comes the bar'l again. She took up her old place. She stayed there all night; nobody turned in. The storm come on again, after midnight. It got awful dark; the rain poured down; hail, too; the thunder boomed and roared and bellowed; the wind blowed a hurricane; and the lightning spread over everything in big sheets of glare, and showed the whole raft as plain as day; and the river lashed up white as milk as far as you could see for miles, and there was that bar'l jiggering along, same as ever. The

captain ordered the watch to man the after sweeps for a crossing, and nobody would go—no more sprained ankles for them, they said. They wouldn't even *walk* aft. Well, then, just then the sky split wide open, with a crash, and the lightning killed two men of the after watch, and crippled two more. Crippled them how, say you? Why, *sprained their ankles!*

'The bar'l left in the dark betwixt lightnings, toward dawn. Well, not a body eat a bite at breakfast that morning. After that the men loafed around, in twos and threes, and talked low together. But none of them herded with Dick Allbright. They all give him the cold shake. If he come around where any of the men was, they split up and sidled away. They wouldn't man the sweeps with him. The captain had all the skiffs hauled up on the raft, alongside of his wigwam, and wouldn't let the dead men be took ashore to be planted; he didn't believe a man that got ashore would come back; and he was right.

'After night come, you could see pretty plain that there was going to be trouble if that bar'l come again; there was such a muttering going on. A good many wanted to kill Dick Allbright, because he'd seen the bar'l on other trips, and that had an ugly look. Some wanted to put him ashore. Some said: "Let's all go ashore in a pile, if the bar'l comes again."

'This kind of whispers was still going on, the men being bunched together forrard watching for the bar'l, when lo and behold you! here she comes again. Down she comes, slow and steady, and settles into her old tracks. You could 'a' heard a pin drop. Then up comes the captain, and says:

' "Boys, don't be a pack of children and fools; I don't want this bar'l to be dogging us all the way to Orleans, and *you* don't: Well, then, how's the best way to stop it? Burn it up—that's the way. I'm going to fetch it aboard," he says. And before anybody could say a word, in he went.

'He swum to it, and as he come pushing it to the raft, the men spread to one side. But the old man got it aboard and busted in the head, and there was a baby in it! Yes, sir; a stark-naked baby. It was Dick Allbright's baby; he owned up and said so.

' "Yes," he says, a-leaning over it, "yes, it is my own lamented darling, my poor lost

Charles William Allbright deceased," says he—for he could curl his tongue around the bulliest words in the language when he was a mind to, and lay them before you without a jint started anywheres. Yes, he said, he used to live up at the head of this bend, and one night he choked his child, which was crying, not intending to kill it—which was prob'ly a lie—and then he was scared, and buried it in a bar'l, before his wife got home, and off he went, and struck the northern trail and went to rafting; and this was the third year that the bar'l had chased him. He said the bad luck always begun light, and lasted till four men was killed, and then the bar'l didn't come any more after that. He said if the men would stand it one more night—and was a-going on like that—but the men had got enough. They started to get out a boat to take him ashore and lynch him, but he grabbed the little child all of a sudden and jumped overboard with it, hugged up to his breast and shedding tears, and we never see him again in this life, poor old suffering soul, nor Charles William neither.'

'*Who* was shedding tears?' says Bob; 'was it Allbright or the baby?'

'Why, Allbright, of course; didn't I tell you the baby was dead? Been dead three years—how could it cry?'

'Well, never mind how it could cry—how could it *keep* all that time?' says Davy. 'You answer me that.'

'I don't know how it done it,' says Ed. 'It done it, though—that's all I know about it.'

'Say—what did they do with the bar'l?' says the Child of Calamity.

'Why, they hove it overboard, and it sunk like a chunk of lead.'

'Edward, did the child look like it was choked?' says one.

'Did it have its hair parted?' says another.

'What was the brand on that bar'l, Eddy?' says a fellow they called Bill.

'Have you got the papers for them statistics, Edmund?' says Jimmy.

'Say, Edwin, was you one of the men that was killed by the lightning?' says Davy.

'Him? Oh, no! he was both of 'em,' says Bob. Then they all haw-hawed.

'Say, Edward, don't you reckon you'd better take a pill? You look bad—don't you feel pale?' says the Child of Calamity.

'Oh, come, now, Eddy,' says Jimmy, 'show up; you must 'a' kept part of that bar'l to prove the thing by. Show us the bung-hole—*do*—and we'll all believe you.'

'Say, boys,' says Bill, 'less divide it up. Thar's thirteen of us. I can swaller a thirteenth of the yarn, if you can worry down the rest.'

Ed got up mad and said they could all go to some place which he ripped out pretty savage, and then walked off aft, cussing to himself, and they yelling and jeering at him, and roaring and laughing so you could hear them a mile.

'Boys, we'll split a watermelon on that,' says the Child of Calamity; and he came rummaging around in the dark amongst the shingle bundles where I was, and put his hand on me. I was warm and soft and naked; so he says 'Ouch!' and jumped back.

'Fetch a lantern or a chunk of fire here, boys—there's a snake here as big as a cow!'

So they run there with a lantern, and crowded up and looked in on me.

'Come out of that, you beggar!' says one.

'Who are you?' says another.

'What are you after here? Speak up prompt, or overboard you go.'

'Snake him out, boys. Snatch him out by the heels.'

I began to beg, and crept out amongst them trembling. They looked me over, wondering, and the Child of Calamity says:

'A cussed thief! Lend a hand and less heave him overboard!'

'No,' says Big Bob, 'less get out the paint-pot and paint him a sky-blue all over from head to heel, and *then* heave him over.'

'Good! that's it. Go for the paint, Jimmy.'

When the paint come, and Bob took the brush and was just going to begin, the others laughing and rubbing their hands, I begun to cry, and that sort of worked on Davy, and he says:

' 'Vast there. He's nothing but a cub. I'll paint the man that teches him!'

So I looked around on them, and some of them grumbled and growled, and Bob put down the paint, and the others didn't take it up.

'Come here to the fire, and less see what you're up to here,' says Davy. 'Now set down there and give an account of yourself. How long have you been aboard here?'

'Not over a quarter of a minute, sir,' says I.

'How did you get dry so quick?'

'I don't know, sir. I'm always that way, mostly.'

'Oh, you are, are you? What's your name?'

I warn't going to tell my name. I didn't 10 know what to say, so I just says:

'Charles William Allbright, sir.'

Then they roared—the whole crowd; and I was mighty glad I said that, because, maybe, laughing would get them in a better humor.

When they got done laughing, Davy says: 'It won't hardly do, Charles William. You couldn't have growed this much in five year, and you was a baby when you come 20 out of the bar'l, you know, and dead at that. Come, now, tell a straight story, and nobody'll hurt you, if you ain't up to anything wrong. What *is* your name?'

'Aleck Hopkins, sir. Aleck James Hopkins.'

'Well, Aleck, where did you come from, here?'

'From a trading scow. She lays up the bend yonder. I was born on her. Pap has 30 traded up and down here all his life; and he told me to swim off here, because when you went by he said he would like to get some of you to speak to a Mr. Jonas Turner, in Cairo, and tell him—'

'Oh, come!'

'Yes, sir, it's as true as the world. Pap he says—'

'Oh, your grandmother!'

They all laughed, and I tried again to 40 talk, but they broke in on me and stopped me.

'Now, looky-here,' says Davy; 'you're scared, and so you talk wild. Honest, now, do you live in a scow, or is it a lie?'

'Yes, sir, in a trading scow. She lays up at the head of the bend. But I warn't born in her. It's our first trip.'

'Now you're talking! What did you come aboard here for? To steal?' 50

'No, sir, I didn't. It was only to get a ride on the raft. All boys does that.'

'Well, I know that. But what did you hide for?'

'Sometimes they drive the boys off.'

'So they do. They might steal. Looky-here; if we let you off this time, will you keep out of these kind of scrapes hereafter?'

' 'Deed I will, boss. You try me.'

'All right, then. You ain't but little ways from shore. Overboard with you, and don't you make a fool of yourself another time this way. Blast it, boy, some raftsmen would rawhide you till you were black and blue!'

I didn't wait to kiss good-by, but went overboard and broke for shore. When Jim come along by and by, the big raft was away out of sight around the point. I swum out and got aboard, and was mighty glad to see home again.

The boy did not get the information he was after, but his adventure has furnished the glimpse of the departed raftsman and keelboatman which I desire to offer in this place.

1883

THE MAN THAT CORRUPTED HADLEYBURG

I

IT was many years ago. Hadleyburg was the most honest and upright town in all the region around about. It had kept that reputation unsmirched during three generations, and was prouder of it than of any other of its possessions. It was so proud of it, and so anxious to insure its perpetuation, that it began to teach the principles of honest dealing to its babies in the cradle, and made the like teachings the staple of their culture thenceforward through all the years devoted to their education. Also, throughout the formative years temptations were kept out of the way of the young people, so that their honesty could have every chance to harden and solidify, and become a part of their very bone. The neighboring towns were jealous of this honorable supremacy, and affected to sneer at Hadleyburg's pride in it and call it vanity; but all the same they were obliged to acknowledge that Hadleyburg was in reality an incorruptible town; and if pressed they would also acknowledge that the mere fact that a young man hailed from Hadleyburg was all the recommendation he needed when he went forth from his natal town to seek for responsible employment.

But at last, in the drift of time, Hadleyburg had the ill luck to offend a passing stranger—possibly without knowing it, certainly without caring, for Hadleyburg was sufficient unto itself, and cared not a rap for strangers or their opinions. Still, it would have been well to make an exception in this one's case, for he was a bitter man and revengeful. All through his wanderings during a whole year he kept his injury in mind, and gave all his leisure moments to trying to invent a compensating satisfaction for it. He contrived many plans, and all of them were good, but none of them was quite sweeping enough; the poorest of them would hurt a great many individuals, but what he wanted was a plan which would comprehend the entire town, and not let so much as one person escape unhurt. At last he had a fortunate idea, and when it fell into his brain it lit up his whole head with an evil joy. He began to form a plan at once, saying to himself, 'That is the thing to do— I will corrupt the town.'

Six months later he went to Hadleyburg, and arrived in a buggy at the house of the old cashier of the bank about ten at night. He got a sack out of the buggy, shouldered it, and staggered with it through the cottage yard, and knocked at the door. A woman's voice said 'Come in,' and he entered, and set his sack behind the stove in the parlor, saying politely to the old lady who sat reading the *Missionary Herald* by the lamp:

'Pray keep your seat, madam, I will not disturb you. There—now it is pretty well concealed; one would hardly know it was there. Can I see your husband a moment, madam?'

No, he was gone to Brixton, and might not return before morning.

'Very well, madam, it is no matter. I merely wanted to leave that sack in his care, to be delivered to the rightful owner when he shall be found. I am a stranger; he does not know me; I am merely passing through the town to-night to discharge a matter which has been long in my mind. My errand is now completed, and I go pleased and a little proud, and you will never see me again. There is a paper attached to the sack which will explain everything. Good night, madam.'

The old lady was afraid of the mysterious big stranger, and was glad to see him go. But her curiosity was roused, and she went straight to the sack and brought away the paper. It began as follows:

TO BE PUBLISHED; or, the right man sought out by private inquiry—either will answer. This sack contains gold coin weighing a hundred and sixty pounds four ounces—

'Mercy on us, and the door not locked!'

Mrs. Richards flew to it all in a tremble and locked it, then pulled down the window-shades and stood frightened, worried, and wondering if there was anything else she could do toward making herself and the money more safe. She listened awhile for burglars, then surrendered to curiosity and went back to the lamp and finished reading the paper:

I am a foreigner, and am presently going back to my own country, to remain there permanently. I am grateful to America for what I have received at her hands during my long stay under her flag; and to one of her citizens —a citizen of Hadleyburg—I am especially grateful for a great kindness done me a year or two ago. Two great kindnesses, in fact. I will explain. I was a gambler. I say I WAS. I was a ruined gambler. I arrived in this village at night, hungry and without a penny. I asked for help—in the dark; I was ashamed to beg in the light. I begged of the right man. He gave me twenty dollars—that is to say, he gave me life, as I considered it. He also gave me fortune; for out of that money I have made myself rich at the gaming-table. And finally, a remark which he made to me has remained with me to this day, and has at last conquered me; and in conquering has saved the remnant of my morals; I shall gamble no more. Now I have no idea who that man was, but I want him found, and I want him to have this money, to give away, throw away, or keep, as he pleases. It is merely my way of testifying my gratitude to him. If I could stay, I would find him myself; but no matter, he will be found. This is an honest town, an incorruptible town, and I know I can trust it without fear. This man can be identified by the remark which he made to me; I feel persuaded that he will remember it.

And now my plan is this: If you prefer to conduct the inquiry privately, do so. Tell the contents of this present writing to any one who is likely to be the right man. If he shall an-

swer, '*I am the man; the remark I made was so-and-so,*' *apply the test—to wit: open the sack, and in it you will find a sealed envelope containing that remark. If the remark mentioned by the candidate tallies with it, give him the money, and ask no further questions, for he is certainly the right man.*

But if you shall prefer a public inquiry, then publish this present writing in the local paper—with these instructions added, to wit: Thirty days from now, let the candidate appear at the town-hall at eight in the evening (Friday), and hand his remark, in a sealed envelope, to the Rev. Mr. Burgess (if he will be kind enough to act); and let Mr. Burgess there and then destroy the seals of the sack, open it, and see if the remark is correct; if correct, let the money be delivered, with my sincere gratitude, to my benefactor thus identified.

Mrs. Richards sat down, gently quivering with excitement, and was soon lost in thinkings—after this pattern: 'What a strange thing it is! . . . And what a fortune for that kind man who set his bread afloat upon the waters! . . . If it had only been my husband that did it!—for we are so poor, so old and poor! . . .' Then, with a sigh—'But it was not my Edward; no, it was not he that gave a stranger twenty dollars. It is a pity, too; I see it now. . . .' Then, with a shudder—'But it is *gambler's* money! the wages of sin: we couldn't take it; we couldn't touch it. I don't like to be near it; it seems a defilement.' She moved to a farther chair. . . . 'I wish Edward would come and take it to the bank; a burglar might come at any moment; it is dreadful to be here all alone with it.'

At eleven Mr. Richards arrived, and while his wife was saying, 'I am *so* glad you've come!' he was saying, 'I'm so tired—tired clear out; it is dreadful to be poor, and have to make these dismal journeys at my time of life. Always at the grind, grind, grind, on a salary—another man's slave, and he sitting at home in his slippers, rich and comfortable.'

'I am so sorry for you, Edward, you know that; but be comforted: we have our livelihood; we have our good name—'

'Yes, Mary, and that is everything. Don't mind my talk—it's just a moment's irritation and doesn't mean anything. Kiss me—there, it's all gone now, and I am not complaining any more. What have you been getting? What's in the sack?'

Then his wife told him the great secret. It dazed him for a moment; then he said:

'It weighs a hundred and sixty pounds? Why, Mary, it's for-ty thou-sand dollars—think of it—a whole fortune! Not ten men in this village are worth that much. Give me the paper.'

He skimmed through it and said:

'Isn't it an adventure! Why, it's a romance; it's like the impossible things one reads about in books, and never sees in life.' He was well stirred up now; cheerful, even gleeful. He tapped his old wife on the cheek, and said, humorously, 'Why, we're rich, Mary, rich; all we've got to do is to bury the money and burn the papers. If the gambler ever comes to inquire, we'll merely look coldly upon him and say: "What is this nonsense you are talking? We have never heard of you and your sack of gold before;" and then he would look foolish, and—'

'And in the mean time, while you are running on with your jokes, the money is still here, and it is fast getting along toward burglar-time.'

'True. Very well, what shall we do—make the inquiry private? No, not that: it would spoil the romance. The public method is better. Think what a noise it will make! And it will make all the other towns jealous; for no stranger would trust such a thing to any town but Hadleyburg, and they know it. It's a great card for us. I must get to the printing-office now, or I shall be too late.'

'But stop—stop—don't leave me here alone with it, Edward!'

But he was gone. For only a little while, however. Not far from his own house he met the editor-proprietor of the paper, and gave him the document, and said, 'Here is a good thing for you, Cox—put it in.'

'It may be too late, Mr. Richards, but I'll see.'

At home again he and his wife sat down to talk the charming mystery over; they were in no condition for sleep. The first question was, Who could the citizen have been who gave the stranger the twenty dollars? It seemed a simple one; both answered it in the same breath:

'Barclay Goodson.'

'Yes,' said Richards, 'he could have done it, and it would have been like him, but there's not another in the town.'

'Everybody will grant that, Edward—grant it privately, anyway. For six months, now, the village has been its own proper self once more—honest, narrow, self-righteous, and stingy.'

'It is what he always called it, to the day of his death—said it right out publicly, too.'

'Yes, and he was hated for it.'

'Oh, of course; but he didn't care. I reckon he was the best-hated man among us, except the Reverend Burgess.'

'Well, Burgess deserves it—he will never get another congregation here. Mean as the town is, it knows how to estimate *him*. Edward, doesn't it seem odd that the stranger should appoint Burgess to deliver the money?'

'Well, yes—it does. That is—that is—'

'Why so much that-*is*-ing? Would *you* select him?'

'Mary, maybe the stranger knows him better than this village does.'

'Much *that* would help Burgess!'

The husband seemed perplexed for an answer; the wife kept a steady eye upon him, and waited. Finally Richards said, with the hesitancy of one who is making a statement which is likely to encounter doubt:

'Mary, Burgess is not a bad man.'

His wife was certainly surprised.

'Nonsense!' she exclaimed.

'He is not a bad man. I know. The whole of his unpopularity had its foundation in that one thing—the thing that made so much noise.'

'That "one thing," indeed! As if that "one thing" wasn't enough, all by itself.'

'Plenty. Plenty. Only he wasn't guilty of it.'

'How you talk! Not guilty of it! Everybody knows he *was* guilty.'

'Mary, I give you my word—he was innocent.'

'I can't believe it, and I don't. How do you know?'

'It is a confession. I am ashamed, but I will make it. I was the only man who knew he was innocent. I could have saved him, nd—and—well, you know how the town

was wrought up—I hadn't the pluck to do it. It would have turned everybody against me. I felt mean, ever so mean; but I didn't dare; I hadn't the manliness to face that.'

Mary looked troubled, and for a while was silent. Then she said, stammeringly:

'I—I don't think it would have done for you to—to—One mustn't—er—public opinion—one has to be so careful—so—' It was a difficult road, and she got mired; but after a little she got started again. 'It was a great pity, but—Why, we couldn't afford it, Edward—we couldn't indeed. Oh, I wouldn't have had you do it for anything!'

'It would have lost us the good will of so many people, Mary; and then—and then—'

'What troubles me now is, what *he* thinks of us, Edward.'

'He? *He* doesn't suspect that I could have saved him.'

'Oh,' exclaimed the wife, in a tone of relief, 'I am glad of that! As long as he doesn't know that you could have saved him, he—he—well, that makes it a great deal better. Why, I might have known he didn't know, because he is always trying to be friendly with us, as little encouragement as we give him. More than once people have twitted me with it. There's the Wilsons, and the Wilcoxes, and the Harknesses, they take a mean pleasure in saying, "*Your friend* Burgess," because they know it pesters me. I wish he wouldn't persist in liking us so; I can't think why he keeps it up.'

'I can explain it. It's another confession. When the thing was new and hot, and the town made a plan to ride him on a rail, my conscience hurt me so that I couldn't stand it, and I went privately and gave him notice, and he got out of the town and staid out till it was safe to come back.'

'Edward! If the town had found it out—'

'*Don't!* It scares me yet, to think of it. I repented of it the minute it was done; and I was even afraid to tell you, lest your face might betray it to somebody. I didn't sleep any that night, for worrying. But after a few days I saw that no one was going to suspect me, and after that I got to feeling glad I did it. And I feel glad yet, Mary—glad through and through.'

'So do I, now, for it would have been a dreadful way to treat him. Yes, I'm glad; for really you did owe him that, you know.

But, Edward, suppose it should come out yet, some day!'

'It won't.'

'Why?'

'Because everybody thinks it was Goodson.'

'Of course they would!'

'Certainly. And of course *he* didn't care. They persuaded poor old Sawlsberry to go and charge it on him, and he went blustering over there and did it. Goodson looked him over, like as if he was hunting for a place on him that he could despise the most, then he says, "So you are the Committee of Inquiry, are you?" Sawlsberry said that was about what he was. "Hm. Do they require particulars, or do you reckon a kind of a *general* answer will do?" "If they require particulars, I will come back, Mr. Goodson; I will take the general answer first." "Very well, then, tell them to go to hell—I reckon that's general enough. And I'll give you some advice, Sawlsberry; when you come back for the particulars, fetch a basket to carry the relics of yourself home in." '

'Just like Goodson; it's got all the marks. He had only one vanity: he thought he could give advice better than any other person.'

'It settled the business, and saved us, Mary. The subject was dropped.'

'Bless you, I'm not doubting *that*.'

Then they took up the gold-sack mystery again, with strong interest. Soon the conversation began to suffer breaks—interruptions caused by absorbed thinkings. The breaks grew more and more frequent. At last Richards lost himself wholly in thought. He sat long, gazing vacantly at the floor, and by and by he began to punctuate his thoughts with little nervous movements of his hands that seemed to indicate vexation. Meantime his wife too had relapsed into a thoughtful silence, and her movements were beginning to show a troubled discomfort. Finally Richards got up and strode aimlessly about the room, plowing his hands through his hair, much as a somnambulist might do who was having a bad dream. Then he seemed to arrive at a definite purpose; and without a word he put on his hat and passed quickly out of the house. His wife sat brooding, with a drawn face, and did not seem to be aware that she was

alone. Now and then she murmured, 'Lead us not into t— . . . but—but—we are so poor, so poor! . . . Lead us not into . . . Ah, who would be hurt by it?—and no one would ever know. . . . Lead us . . .' The voice died out in mumblings. After a little she glanced up and muttered in a half-frightened, half-glad way:

'He is gone! But, oh dear, he may be too late—too late. . . . Maybe not—maybe there is still time.' She rose and stood thinking, nervously clasping and unclasping her hands. A slight shudder shook her frame, and she said, out of a dry throat, 'God forgive me—it's awful to think such things—but . . . Lord, how we are made —how strangely we are made!'

She turned the light low, and slipped stealthily over and kneeled down by the sack and felt of its ridgy sides with her hands, and fondled them lovingly; and there was a gloating light in her poor old eyes. She fell into fits of absence; and came half out of them at times to mutter, 'If we had only waited!—oh, if we had only waited a little, and not been in such a hurry!'

Meantime Cox had gone home from his office and told his wife all about the strange thing that had happened, and they had talked it over eagerly, and guessed that the late Goodson was the only man in the town who could have helped a suffering stranger with so noble a sum as twenty dollars. Then there was a pause, and the two became thoughtful and silent. And by and by nervous and fidgety. At last the wife said, as if to herself:

'Nobody knows this secret but the Richardses . . . and us . . . nobody.'

The husband came out of his thinkings with a slight start, and gazed wistfully at his wife, whose face was become very pale; then he hesitatingly rose, and glanced furtively at his hat, then at his wife—a sort of mute inquiry. Mrs. Cox swallowed once or twice, with her hand at her throat, then in place of speech she nodded her head. In a moment she was alone, and mumbling to herself.

And now Richards and Cox were hurrying through the deserted streets, from opposite directions. They met, panting, at the foot of the printing-office stairs; by the night light there they read each other's face. Cox whispered:

'Nobody knows about this but us?'

The whispered answer was,

'Not a soul—on honor, not a soul!'

'If it isn't too late to—'

The men were starting up-stairs; at this moment they were overtaken by a boy, and Cox asked:

'Is that you, Johnny?'

'Yes, sir.'

'You needn't ship the early mail—nor any mail; wait till I tell you.'

'It's already gone, sir.'

'*Gone?*' It had the sound of an unspeakable disappointment in it.

'Yes, sir. Time-table for Brixton and all the towns beyond changed to-day, sir—had to get the papers in twenty minutes earlier than common. I had to rush; if I had been two minutes later—'

The men turned and walked slowly away, not waiting to hear the rest. Neither of them spoke during ten minutes; then Cox said, in a vexed tone:

'What possessed you to be in such a hurry, *I* can't make out.'

The answer was humble enough:

'I see it now, but somehow I never thought, you know, until it was too late. But the next time—'

'Next time be hanged! It won't come in a thousand years.'

Then the friends separated without a good night, and dragged themselves home with the gait of mortally stricken men. At their homes their wives sprang up with an eager 'Well?'—then saw the answer with their eyes and sank down sorrowing, without waiting for it to come in words. In both houses a discussion followed of a heated sort—a new thing; there had been discussions before, but not heated ones, not ungentle ones. The discussions to-night were a sort of seeming plagiarisms of each other. Mrs. Richards said,

'If you had only waited, Edward—if you had only stopped to think; but no, you must run straight to the printing-office and spread it all over the world.'

'It *said* publish it.'

'That is nothing; it also said do it privately, if you liked. There, now—is that true, or not?'

'Why, yes—yes, it is true; but when I thought what a stir it would make, and what a compliment it was to Hadleyburg that a stranger should trust it so—'

'Oh, certainly, I know all that; but if you had only stopped to think, you would have seen that you *couldn't* find the right man, because he is in his grave, and hasn't left chick nor child nor relation behind him; and as long as the money went to somebody that awfully needed it, and nobody would be hurt by it, and—and—'

She broke down, crying. Her husband tried to think of some comforting thing to say, and presently came out with this:

'But after all, Mary, it must be for the best—it *must* be; we know that. And we must remember that it was so ordered—'

'Ordered! Oh, everything's *ordered*, when a person has to find some way out when he has been stupid. Just the same, it was *ordered* that the money should come to us in this special way, and it was you that must take it on yourself to go meddling with the designs of Providence—and who gave you the right? It was wicked, that is what it was —just blasphemous presumption, and no more becoming to a meek and humble professor of—'

'But, Mary, you know how we have been trained all our lives long, like the whole village, till it is absolutely second nature to us to stop not a single moment to think when there's an honest thing to be done—'

'Oh, I know it, I know it—it's been one everlasting training and training and training in honesty—honesty shielded, from the very cradle, against every possible temptation, and so it's *artificial* honesty, and weak as water when temptation comes, as we have seen this night. God knows I never had shade nor shadow of a doubt of my petrified and indestructible honesty until now—and now, under the very first big and real temptation, I—Edward, it is my belief that this town's honesty is as rotten as mine is; as rotten as yours is. It is a mean town, a hard, stingy town, and hasn't a virtue in the world but this honesty it is so celebrated for and so conceited about; and so help me, I do believe that if ever the day comes that its honesty falls under great temptation, its grand reputation will go to ruin like a house of cards. There, now I've made confession, and I feel better; I am a humbug, and I've been one all my life, without knowing it. Let no man call me honest again—I will not have it.'

'I—well, Mary, I feel a good deal as you

do; I certainly do. It seems strange, too, so strange. I never could have believed it—never.'

A long silence followed; both were sunk in thought. At last the wife looked up and said:

'I know what you are thinking, Edward.'

Richards had the embarrassed look of a person who is caught.

'I am ashamed to confess it, Mary, but—'

'It's no matter, Edward, I was thinking the same question myself.'

'I hope so. State it.'

'You were thinking, if a body could only guess out *what the remark was* that Goodson made to the stranger.'

'It's perfectly true. I feel guilty and ashamed. And you?'

'I'm past it. Let us make a pallet here; we've got to stand watch till the bank vault opens in the morning and admits the sack. . . . Oh dear, oh dear—if we hadn't made the mistake!'

The pallet was made, and Mary said:

'The open sesame—what could it have been? I do wonder what that remark could have been? But come; we will get to bed now.'

'And sleep?'

'No: think.'

'Yes, think.'

By this time the Coxes too had completed their spat and their reconciliation, and were turning in—to think, to think, and toss, and fret, and worry over what the remark could possibly have been which Goodson made to the stranded derelict; that golden remark; that remark worth forty thousand dollars, cash.

The reason that the village telegraph-office was open later than usual that night was this: The foreman of Cox's paper was the local representative of the Associated Press. One might say its honorary representative, for it wasn't four times a year that he could furnish thirty words that would be accepted. But this time it was different. His despatch stating what he had caught got an instant answer:

Send the whole thing—all the details—twelve hundred words.

A colossal order! The foreman filled the bill; and he was the proudest man in the State. By breakfast-time the next morning the name of Hadleyburg the Incorruptible was on every lip in America, from Montreal to the Gulf, from the glaciers of Alaska to the orange-groves of Florida; and millions and millions of people were discussing the stranger and his money-sack, and wondering if the right man would be found, and hoping some more news about the matter would come soon—right away.

II

Hadleyburg village woke up world-celebrated—astonished—happy—vain. Vain beyond imagination. Its nineteen principal citizens and their wives went about shaking hands with each other, and beaming, and smiling, and congratulating, and saying *this* thing adds a new word to the dictionary—*Hadleyburg*, synonym for *incorruptible*—destined to live in dictionaries forever! And the minor and unimportant citizens and their wives went around acting in much the same way. Everybody ran to the bank to see the gold-sack; and before noon grieved and envious crowds began to flock in from Brixton and all neighboring towns; and that afternoon and next day reporters began to arrive from everywhere to verify the sack and its history and write the whole thing up anew, and make dashing free-hand pictures of the sack, and of Richards's house, and the bank, and the Presbyterian church, and the Baptist church, and the public square, and the town-hall where the test would be applied and the money delivered; and damnable portraits of the Richardses, and Pinkerton the banker, and Cox, and the foreman, and Reverend Burgess, and the postmaster—and even of Jack Halliday, who was the loafing, good-natured, no-account, irreverent fisherman, hunter, boys' friend, stray-dogs' friend, typical 'Sam Lawson' of the town. The little mean, smirking, oily Pinkerton showed the sack to all comers, and rubbed his sleek palms together pleasantly, and enlarged upon the town's fine old reputation for honesty and upon this wonderful indorsement of it, and hoped and believed that the example would now spread far and wide over the American world, and be epoch-making in the matter of moral regeneration. And so on, and so on.

By the end of a week things had quieted

down again; the wild intoxication of pride and joy had sobered to a soft, sweet, silent delight—a sort of deep, nameless, unutterable content. All faces bore a look of peaceful, holy happiness.

Then a change came. It was a gradual change: so gradual that its beginnings were hardly noticed; maybe were not noticed at all, except by Jack Halliday, who always noticed everything; and always made fun of it, too, no matter what it was. He began to throw out chaffing remarks about people not looking quite so happy as they did a day or two ago; and next he claimed that the new aspect was deepening to positive sadness; next, that it was taking on a sick look; and finally he said that everybody was become so moody, thoughtful, and absent-minded that he could rob the meanest man in town of a cent out of the bottom of his breeches pocket and not disturb his revery.

At this stage—or at about this stage—a saying like this was dropped at bedtime—with a sigh, usually—by the head of each of the nineteen principal households: 'Ah, what *could* have been the remark that Goodson made?'

And straightway—with a shudder—came this, from the man's wife:

'Oh, *don't*! What horrible thing are you mulling in your mind? Put it away from you, for God's sake!'

But that question was wrung from those men again the next night—and got the same retort. But weaker.

And the third night the men uttered the question yet again—with anguish, and absently. This time—and the following night—the wives fidgeted feebly, and tried to say something. But didn't.

And the night after that they found their tongues and responded—longingly:

'Oh, if we *could* only guess!'

Halliday's comments grew daily more and more sparklingly disagreeable and disparaging. He went diligently about, laughing at the town, individually and in mass. But his laugh was the only one left in the village: it fell upon a hollow and mournful vacancy and emptiness. Not even a smile was findable anywhere. Halliday carried a cigar-box around on a tripod, playing that it was a camera, and halted all passers and aimed the thing and said, 'Ready!—now look pleasant, please,' but not even this capital joke could surprise the dreary faces into any softening.

So three weeks passed—one week was left. It was Saturday evening—after supper. Instead of the aforetime Saturday-evening flutter and bustle and shopping and larking, the streets were empty and desolate. Richards and his old wife sat apart in their little parlor—miserable and thinking. This was become their evening habit now: the lifelong habit which had preceded it, of reading, knitting, and contented chat, or receiving or paying neighborly calls, was dead and gone and forgotten, ages ago—two or three weeks ago; nobody talked now, nobody read, nobody visited—the whole village sat at home, sighing, worrying, silent. Trying to guess out that remark.

The postman left a letter. Richards glanced listlessly at the superscription and the postmark—unfamiliar, both—and tossed the letter on the table and resumed his might-have-beens and his hopeless dull miseries where he had left them off. Two or three hours later his wife got wearily up and was going away to bed without a good night—custom now—but she stopped near the letter and eyed it awhile with a dead interest, then broke it open, and began to skim it over. Richards, sitting there with his chair tilted back against the wall and his chin between his knees, heard something fall. It was his wife. He sprang to her side, but she cried out:

'Leave me alone, I am too happy. Read the letter—read it!'

He did. He devoured it, his brain reeling. The letter was from a distant state, and it said:

I am a stranger to you, but no matter: I have something to tell. I have just arrived home from Mexico, and learned about that episode. Of course you do not know who made that remark, but I know, and I am the only person living who does know. It was GOOD-SON. I knew him well, many years ago. I passed through your village that very night, and was his guest till the midnight train came along. I overheard him make that remark to the stranger in the dark—it was in Hale Alley. He and I talked of it the rest of the way home, and while smoking in his house. He mentioned many of your villagers in the course of his talk—most of them in a very un-

complimentary way, but two or three favor-ably; among these latter yourself. I say 'fa-vorably'—nothing stronger. I remember his saying he did not actually LIKE *any person in the town—not one; but that you—I* THINK *he said you—am almost sure—had done him a very great service once, possibly without knowing the full value of it, and he wished he had a fortune, he would leave it to you when* 10 *he died, and a curse apiece for the rest of the citizens. Now, then, if it was you that did him that service, you are his legitimate heir, and entitled to the sack of gold. I know that I can trust to your honor and honesty, for in a citizen of Hadleyburg these virtues are an unfailing inheritance, and so I am going to reveal to you the remark, well satisfied that if you are not the right man you will seek and find the right one and see that poor Goodson's debt of gratitude for the service referred to is* 20 *paid. This is the remark:* 'YOU ARE FAR FROM BEING A BAD MAN: GO, AND REFORM.'

HOWARD L. STEPHENSON

'Oh, Edward, the money is ours, and I am so grateful, *oh*, so grateful—kiss me, dear, it's forever since we kissed—and we needed it so—the money—and now you are free of Pinkerton and his bank, and no-body's slave any more; it seems to me I 30 could fly for joy.'

It was a happy half-hour that the couple spent there on the settee caressing each other; it was the old days come again—days that had begun with their courtship and lasted without a break till the stranger brought the deadly money. By and by the wife said:

'Oh, Edward, how lucky it was you did him that grand service, poor Goodson! I 40 never liked him, but I love him now. And it was fine and beautiful of you never to mention it or brag about it.' Then, with a touch of reproach, 'But you ought to have told *me*, Edward, you ought to have told your wife, you know.'

'Well, I—er—well, Mary, you see—'

'Now stop hemming and hawing, and tell me about it, Edward. I always loved you, and now I'm proud of you. Everybody 50 believes there was only one good generous soul in this village, and now it turns out that you—Edward, why don't you tell me?'

'Well—er—er—Why, Mary, I can't!'

'You *can't*? *Why* can't you?'

'You see, he—well, he— he made me promise I wouldn't.'

The wife looked him over, and said, very slowly:

'Made—you—promise? Edward, what do you tell me that for?'

'Mary, do you think I would lie?'

She was troubled and silent for a mo-ment, then she laid her hand within his and said:

'No . . . no. We have wandered far enough from our bearings—God spare us that! In all your life you have never uttered a lie. But now—now that the foundations of things seem to be crumbling from under us, we—we—' She lost her voice for a mo-ment, then said, brokenly, 'Lead us not into temptation. . . . I think you made the promise, Edward. Let it rest so. Let us keep 20 away from that ground. Now—that is all gone by; let us be happy again; it is no time for clouds.'

Edward found it something of an effort to comply, for his mind kept wandering—trying to remember what the service was that he had done Goodson.

The couple lay awake the most of the night, Mary happy and busy, Edward busy but not so happy. Mary was planning what 30 she would do with the money. Edward was trying to recall that service. At first his con-science was sore on account of the lie he had told Mary—if it was a lie. After much reflection—suppose it *was* a lie? What then? Was it such a great matter? Aren't we al-ways *acting* lies? Then why not *tell* them? Look at Mary—look what she had done. While he was hurrying off on his honest errand, what was she doing? Lamenting 40 because the papers hadn't been destroyed and the money kept! Is theft better than lying?

That point lost its sting—the lie dropped into the background and left comfort be-hind it. The next point came to the front: *Had* he rendered that service? Well, here was Goodson's own evidence as reported in Stephenson's letter; there could be no bet-ter evidence than that—it was even *proof* 50 that he had rendered it. Of course. So that point was settled. . . . No, not quite. He recalled with a wince that this unknown Mr. Stephenson was just a trifle unsure as to whether the performer of it was Richards or some other—and, oh dear, he had put

Richards on his honor! He must himself decide whither that money must go—and Mr. Stephenson was not doubting that if he was the wrong man he would go honorably and find the right one. Oh, it was odious to put a man in such a situation—ah, why couldn't Stephenson have left out that doubt! What did he want to intrude that for?

Further reflection. How did it happen that *Richards's* name remained in Stephenson's mind as indicating the right man, and not some other man's name? That looked good. Yes, that looked very good. In fact, it went on looking better and better, straight along—until by and by it grew into positive *proof*. And then Richards put the matter at once out of his mind, for he had a private instinct that a proof once established is better left so.

He was feeling reasonably comfortable now, but there was still one other detail that kept pushing itself on his notice: of course he had done that service—that was settled; but what *was* that service? He must recall it—he would not go to sleep till he had recalled it; it would make his peace of mind perfect. And so he thought and thought. He thought of a dozen things—possible services, even probable services—but none of them seemed adequate, none of them seemed large enough, none of them seemed worth the money—worth the fortune Goodson had wished he could leave in his will. And besides, he couldn't remember having done them, anyway. Now, then—now, then—what *kind* of a service would it be that would make a man so inordinately grateful? Ah—the saving of his soul! That must be it. Yes, he could remember, now, how he once set himself the task of converting Goodson, and labored at it as much as —he was going to say three months; but upon closer examination it shrunk to a month, then to a week, then to a day, then to nothing. Yes, he remembered now, and with unwelcome vividness, that Goodson had told him to go to thunder and mind his own business—*he* wasn't hankering to follow Hadleyburg to heaven!

So that solution was a failure—he hadn't saved Goodson's soul. Richards was discouraged. Then after a little came another idea: had he saved Goodson's property? No, that wouldn't do—he hadn't any. His life? That is it! Of course. Why, he might have thought of it before. This time he was on the right track, sure. His imagination-mill was hard at work in a minute, now.

Thereafter during a stretch of two exhausting hours he was busy saving Goodson's life. He saved it in all kinds of difficult and perilous ways. In every case he got it saved satisfactorily up to a certain point; then, just as he was beginning to get well persuaded that it had really happened, a troublesome detail would turn up which made the whole thing impossible. As in the matter of drowning, for instance. In that case he had swum out and tugged Goodson ashore in an unconscious state with a great crowd looking on and applauding, but when he had got it all thought out and was just beginning to remember all about it, a whole swarm of disqualifying details arrived on the ground: the town would have known of the circumstance, Mary would have known of it, it would glare like a limelight in his own memory instead of being an inconspicuous service which he had possibly rendered 'without knowing its full value.' And at this point he remembered that he couldn't swim, anyway.

Ah—*there* was a point which he had been overlooking from the start: it had to be a service which he had rendered 'possibly without knowing the full value of it.' Why, really, that ought to be an easy hunt—much easier than those others. And sure enough, by and by he found it. Goodson, years and years ago, came near marrying a very sweet and pretty girl, named Nancy Hewitt, but in some way or other the match had been broken off; the girl died, Goodson remained a bachelor, and by and by became a soured one and a frank despiser of the human species. Soon after the girl's death the village found out, or thought it had found out, that she carried a spoonful of Negro blood in her veins. Richards worked at these details a good while, and in the end he thought he remembered things concerning them which must have gotten mislaid in his memory through long neglect. He seemed to dimly remember that it was *he* that found out about the Negro blood; that it was he that told the village; that the village told Goodson where they got it; that he thus saved Goodson from marrying the tainted girl; that he had done him this great service 'without knowing the full value of it,' in fact without knowing that he *was* doing it; but that Goodson knew the value of it, and what a narrow escape he had had, and so went to his grave grateful to his benefactor and wishing he had a fortune to leave him. It was all clear and simple now, and the more he went over it the more luminous and certain it grew; and at last, when he nestled to sleep satisfied and happy, he remembered the whole thing just as if it had been yesterday. In fact, he dimly remembered Goodson's *telling* him his gratitude once. Meantime Mary had spent six thousand dollars on a new house for herself and a pair of slippers for her pastor, and then had fallen peacefully to rest.

That same Saturday evening the postman had delivered a letter to each of the other principal citizens—nineteen letters in all. No two of the envelopes were alike, and no two of the superscriptions were in the same hand, but the letters inside were just like each other in every detail but one. They were exact copies of the letter received by Richards—handwriting and all—and were all signed by Stephenson, but in place of Richards's name each receiver's own name appeared.

All night long eighteen principal citizens did what their caste-brother Richards was doing at the same time—they put in their energies trying to remember what notable service it was that they had unconsciously done Barclay Goodson. In no case was it a holiday job; still they succeeded.

And while they were at this work, which was difficult, their wives put in the night spending the money, which was easy. During that one night the nineteen wives spent an average of seven thousand dollars each out of the forty thousand in the sack—a hundred and thirty-three thousand altogether.

Next day there was a surprise for Jack Halliday. He noticed that the faces of the nineteen chief citizens and their wives bore that expression of peaceful and holy happiness again. He could not understand it, neither was he able to invent any remarks about it that could damage it or disturb it. And so it was his turn to be dissatisfied with life. His private guesses at the reasons for the happiness failed in all instances, upon examination. When he met Mrs. Wilcox and noticed the placid ecstasy in her face, he said to himself, 'Her cat has had kittens'— and went and asked the cook: it was not so; the cook had detected the happiness, but did not know the cause. When Halliday found the duplicate ecstasy in the face of 'Shadbelly' Billson (village nickname), he was sure some neighbor of Billson's had broken his leg, but inquiry showed that this had not happened. The subdued ecstasy in Gregory Yates's face could mean but one thing—he was a mother-in-law short: it was another mistake. 'And Pinkerton— Pinkerton—he has collected ten cents that he thought he was going to lose.' And so on, and so on. In some cases the guesses had to remain in doubt, in the others they proved distinct errors. In the end Halliday said to himself, 'Anyway it foots up that there's nineteen Hadleyburg families temporarily in heaven: I don't know how it happened; I only know Providence is off duty to-day.'

An architect and builder from the next state had lately ventured to set up a small business in this unpromising village, and his sign had now been hanging out a week. Not a customer yet; he was a discouraged man, and sorry he had come. But his weather changed suddenly now. First one and then another chief citizen's wife said to him privately:

'Come to my house Monday week—but say nothing about it for the present. We think of building.'

He got eleven invitations that day. That night he wrote his daughter and broke off her match with her student. He said she could marry a mile higher than that.

Pinkerton the banker and two or three other well-to-do men planned country-seats —but waited. That kind don't count their chickens until they are hatched.

The Wilsons devised a grand new thing —a fancy-dress ball. They made no actual promises, but told all their acquaintanceship in confidence that they were thinking the matter over and thought they should give it—'and if we do, you will be invited, of course.' People were surprised, and said, one to another, 'Why, they are crazy, those poor Wilsons, they can't afford it.' Several among the nineteen said privately to their husbands, 'It is a good idea: we will keep still till their cheap thing is over, then *we* will give one that will make it sick.'

The days drifted along, and the bill of future squanderings rose higher and higher, wilder and wilder, more and more foolish and reckless. It began to look as if every member of the nineteen would not only spend his whole forty thousand dollars before receiving-day, but be actually in debt by the time he got the money. In some cases light-headed people did not stop with planning to spend, they really spent—on credit. They bought land, mortgages, farms, speculative stocks, fine clothes, horses, and various other things, paid down the bonus, and made themselves liable for the rest—at ten days. Presently the sober second thought came, and Halliday noticed that a ghastly anxiety was beginning to show up in a good many faces. Again he was puzzled, and didn't know what to make of it. 'The Wilcox kittens aren't dead, for they weren't born; nobody's broken a leg; there's no shrinkage in mother-in-laws; *nothing* has happened—it is an unsolvable mystery.'

There was another puzzled man, too— the Rev. Mr. Burgess. For days, wherever he went, people seemed to follow him or to be watching out for him; and if he ever found himself in a retired spot, a member of the nineteen would be sure to appear, thrust an envelope privately into his hand, whisper 'To be opened at the town-hall Friday evening,' then vanish away like a guilty thing. He was expecting that there might be one claimant for the sack—doubtful, however, Goodson being dead—but it never occurred to him that all this crowd might be claimants. When the great Friday came at last, he found that he had nineteen envelopes.

III

The town hall had never looked finer. The platform at the end of it was backed by a showy draping of flags; at intervals along the walls were festoons of flags; the gallery fronts were clothed in flags; the supporting columns were swathed in flags; all this was to impress the stranger, for he would be there in considerable force, and in a large degree he would be connected with the press. The house was full. The 412 fixed seats were occupied; also the 68 extra

chairs which had been packed into the aisles; the steps of the platform were occupied; some distinguished strangers were given seats on the platform; at the horseshoe of tables which fenced the front and sides of the platform sat a strong force of special correspondents who had come from everywhere. It was the best-dressed house the town had ever produced. There were some tolerably expensive toilets there, and in several cases the ladies who wore them had the look of being unfamiliar with that kind of clothes. At least the town thought they had that look, but the notion could have arisen from the town's knowledge of the fact that these ladies had never inhabited such clothes before.

The gold-sack stood on a little table at the front of the platform where all the house could see it. The bulk of the house gazed at it with a burning interest, a mouth-watering interest, a wistful and pathetic interest; a minority of nineteen couples gazed at it tenderly, lovingly, proprietarily, and the male half of this minority kept saying over to themselves the moving little impromptu speeches of thankfulness for the audience's applause and congratulations which they were presently going to get up and deliver. Every now and then one of these got a piece of paper out of his vest pocket and privately glanced at it to refresh his memory.

Of course there was a buzz of conversation going on—there always is; but at last when the Rev. Mr. Burgess rose and laid his hand on the sack he could hear his microbes gnaw, the place was so still. He related the curious history of the sack, then went on to speak in warm terms of Hadleyburg's old and well-earned reputation for spotless honesty, and of the town's just pride in this reputation. He said that this reputation was a treasure of priceless value; that under Providence its value had now become inestimably enhanced, for the recent episode had spread this fame far and wide, and thus had focused the eyes of the American world upon this village, and made its name for all time, as he hoped and believed, a synonym for commercial incorruptibility. [*Applause.*] 'And who is to be the guardian of this noble treasure—the community as a whole? No! The responsibility is individual, not communal. From this day forth each and every one of you is in his own person its special guardian, and individually responsible that no harm shall come to it. Do you—does each of you—accept this great trust? [*Tumultuous assent.*] Then all is well. Transmit it to your children and to your children's children. To-day your purity is beyond reproach—see to it that it shall remain so. To-day there is not a person in your community who could be beguiled to touch a penny not his own—see to it that you abide in this grace. ['*We will! we will!*'] This is not the place to make comparisons between ourselves and other communities—some of them ungracious toward us; they have their ways, we have ours; let us be content. [*Applause.*] I am done. Under my hand, my friends, rests a stranger's eloquent recognition of what we are; through him the world will always henceforth know what we are. We do not know who he is, but in your name I utter your gratitude, and ask you to raise your voices in indorsement.'

The house rose in a body and made the walls quake with the thunders of its thankfulness for the space of a long minute. Then it sat down, and Mr. Burgess took an envelope out of his pocket. The house held its breath while he slit the envelope open and took from it a slip of paper. He read its contents—slowly and impressively—the audience listening with tranced attention to this magic document, each of whose words stood for an ingot of gold:

'"*The remark which I made to the distressed stranger was this: 'You are very far from being a bad man: go, and reform.'*"' Then he continued:

'We shall know in a moment now whether the remark here quoted corresponds with the one concealed in the sack; and if that shall prove to be so—and it undoubtedly will—this sack of gold belongs to a fellow-citizen who will henceforth stand before the nation as the symbol of the special virtue which has made our town famous throughout the land—Mr. Billson!'

The house had gotten itself all ready to burst into the proper tornado of applause; but instead of doing it, it seemed stricken with a paralysis; there was a deep hush for a moment or two, then a wave of whispered murmurs swept the place—of about this tenor: '*Billson!* oh, come, this is *too* thin! Twenty dollars to a stranger—or *anybody*—

Billson! tell it to the marines!' And now at this point the house caught its breath all of a sudden in a new access of astonishment, for it discovered that whereas in one part of the hall Deacon Billson was standing up with his head meekly bowed, in another part of it Lawyer Wilson was doing the same. There was a wondering silence now for a while.

Everybody was puzzled, and nineteen couples were surprised and indignant.

Billson and Wilson turned and stared at each other. Billson asked, bitingly:

'Why do *you* rise, Mr. Wilson?'

'Because I have a right to. Perhaps you will be good enough to explain to the house why *you* rise?'

'With great pleasure. Because I wrote that paper.'

'It is an impudent falsity! I wrote it myself.'

It was Burgess's turn to be paralyzed. He stood looking vacantly at first one of the men and then the other, and did not seem to know what to do. The house was stupefied. Lawyer Wilson spoke up, now, and said,

'I ask the Chair to read the name signed to that paper.'

That brought the Chair to itself, and it read out the name:

' "John Wharton *Billson*." '

'There!' shouted Billson, 'what have you got to say for yourself, now? And what kind of apology are you going to make to me and to this insulted house for the imposture which you have attempted to play here?'

'No apologies are due, sir; and as for the rest of it, I publicly charge you with pilfering my note from Mr. Burgess and substituting a copy of it signed with your own name. There is no other way by which you could have gotten hold of the test-remark; I alone, of living men, possessed the secret of its wording.'

There was likely to be a scandalous state of things if this went on; everybody noticed with distress that the short-hand scribes were scribbling like mad; many people were crying 'Chair, Chair! Order! order!' Burgess rapped with his gavel, and said:

'Let us not forget the proprieties due. There has evidently been a mistake somewhere, but surely that is all. If Mr. Wilson gave me an envelope—and I remember now that he did—I still have it.'

He took one out of his pocket, opened it, glanced at it, looked surprised and worried, and stood silent a few moments. Then he waved his hand in a wandering and mechanical way, and made an effort or two to say something, then gave it up, despondently. Several voices cried out:

'Read it! read it! What is it?'

So he began in a dazed and sleep-walker fashion:

' "*The remark which I made to the unhappy stranger was this: 'You are far from being a bad man.* [The house gazed at him, marveling.] *Go, and reform.*' " [*Murmurs:* 'Amazing! what can this mean?'] This one,' said the Chair, 'is signed Thurlow G. Wilson.'

'There!' cried Wilson. 'I reckon that settles it! I knew perfectly well my note was purloined.'

'Purloined!' retorted Billson. 'I'll let you know that neither you nor any man of your kidney must venture to—'

The Chair. 'Order, gentlemen, order! Take your seats, both of you, please.'

They obeyed, shaking their heads and grumbling angrily. The house was profoundly puzzled; it did not know what to do with this curious emergency. Presently Thompson got up. Thompson was the hatter. He would have liked to be a Nineteener; but such was not for him: his stock of hats was not considerable enough for the position. He said:

'Mr. Chairman, if I may be permitted to make a suggestion, can both of these gentlemen be right? I put it to you, sir, can both have happened to say the very same words to the stranger? It seems to me—'

The tanner got up and interrupted him. The tanner was a disgruntled man; he believed himself entitled to be a Nineteener, but he couldn't get recognition. It made him a little unpleasant in his ways and speech. Said he:

'Sho, *that's* not the point! *That* could happen—twice in a hundred years—but not the other thing. *Neither* of them gave the twenty dollars!'

[*A ripple of applause.*]

Billson. 'I did!'

Wilson. 'I did!'

Then each accused the other of pilfering.

The Chair. 'Order! Sit down, if you please—both of you. Neither of the notes has been out of my possession at any moment.'

A Voice. 'Good—that settles *that!*'

The Tanner. 'Mr. Chairman, one thing is now plain: one of these men has been eavesdropping under the other one's bed, and filching family secrets. If it is not unparliamentary to suggest it, I will remark that both are equal to it. [*The Chair.* 'Order! order!'] I withdraw the remark, sir, and will confine myself to suggesting that *if* one of them has overheard the other reveal the test-remark to his wife, we shall catch him now.'

A Voice. 'How?'

The Tanner. 'Easily. The two have not quoted the remark in exactly the same words. You would have noticed that, if there hadn't been a considerable stretch of time and an exciting quarrel inserted between the two readings.'

A Voice. 'Name the difference.'

The Tanner. 'The word *very* is in Billson's note, and not in the other.'

Many Voices. 'That's so—he's right!'

The Tanner. 'And so, if the Chair will examine the test-remark in the sack, we shall know which of these two frauds—[*The Chair.* 'Order!']—which of these two adventurers—[*The Chair.* 'Order! order!']—which of these two gentlemen—[*laughter and applause*]—is entitled to wear the belt as being the first dishonest blatherskite ever bred in this town—which he has dishonored, and which will be a sultry place for him from now out!' [*Vigorous applause.*]

Many Voices. 'Open it!—open the sack!'

Mr. Burgess made a slit in the sack, slid his hand in and brought out an envelope. In it were a couple of folded notes. He said:

'One of these is marked, "Not to be examined until all written communications which have been addressed to the Chair—if any—shall have been read." The other is marked "The Test." Allow me. It is worded —to wit:

' "I do not require that the first half of the remark which was made to me by my benefactor shall be quoted with exactness, for it was not striking, and could be forgotten; but its closing fifteen words are quite striking, and I think easily rememberable; unless *these* shall be accurately reproduced, let the applicant be regarded as an impostor. My benefactor began by saying he seldom gave advice to any one, but that it always bore the hall-mark of high value when he did give it. Then he said this—and it has never faded from my memory: '*You are far from being a bad man—*' " '

Fifty Voices. 'That settles it—the money's Wilson's! Wilson! Wilson! Speech! Speech!'

People jumped up and crowded around Wilson, wringing his hand and congratulating fervently—meantime the Chair was hammering with the gavel and shouting:

'Order, gentlemen! Order! Order! Let me finish reading, please.' When quiet was restored, the reading was resumed—as follows:

' " '*Go, and reform—or, mark my words—some day, for your sins, you will die and go to hell or Hadleyburg*—TRY AND MAKE IT THE FORMER.' " '

A ghastly silence followed. First an angry cloud began to settle darkly upon the faces of the citizenship; after a pause the cloud began to rise, and a tickled expression tried to take its place; tried so hard that it was only kept under with great and painful difficulty; the reporters, the Brixtonites, and other strangers bent their heads down and shielded their faces with their hands, and managed to hold in by main strength and heroic courtesy. At this most inopportune time burst upon the stillness the roar of a solitary voice—Jack Halliday's:

'*That's* got the hall-mark on it!'

Then the house let go, strangers and all. Even Mr. Burgess's gravity broke down presently, then the audience considered itself officially absolved from all restraint, and it made the most of its privilege. It was a good long laugh, and a tempestuously whole-hearted one, but it ceased at last—long enough for Mr. Burgess to try to resume, and for the people to get their eyes partially wiped; then it broke out again; and afterward yet again; then at last Burgess was able to get out these serious words:

'It is useless to try to disguise the fact—we find ourselves in the presence of a matter of grave import. It involves the honor of your town, it strikes at the town's good name. The difference of a single word between the test-remarks offered by Mr. Wilson and Mr. Billson was itself a serious

thing, since it indicated that one or the other of these gentlemen had committed a theft—'

The two men were sitting limp, nerveless, crushed; but at these words both were electrified into movement, and started to get up—

'Sit down!' said the Chair, sharply, and they obeyed. 'That, as I have said, was a serious thing. And it was—but for only one of them. But the matter has become graver; for the honor of *both* is now in formidable peril. Shall I go even further, and say in inextricable peril? *Both* left out the crucial fifteen words.' He paused. During several moments he allowed the pervading stillness to gather and deepen its impressive effects, then added: 'There would seem to be but one way whereby this could happen. I ask these gentlemen—Was there *collusion?—agreement?*'

A low murmur sifted through the house; its import was, 'He's got them both.'

Billson was not used to emergencies; he sat in a helpless collapse. But Wilson was a lawyer. He struggled to his feet, pale and worried, and said:

'I ask the indulgence of the house while I explain this most painful matter. I am sorry to say what I am about to say, since it must inflict irreparable injury upon Mr. Billson, whom I have always esteemed and respected until now, and in whose invulnerability to temptation I entirely believed—as did you all. But for the preservation of my own honor I must speak—and with frankness. I confess with shame—and I now beseech your pardon for it—that I said to the ruined stranger all of the words contained in the test-remark, including the disparaging fifteen. [*Sensation.*] When the late publication was made I recalled them, and I resolved to claim the sack of coin, for by every right I was entitled to it. Now I will ask you to consider this point, and weigh it well: that stranger's gratitude to me that night knew no bounds; he said himself that he could find no words for it that were adequate, and that if he should ever be able he would repay me a thousand-fold. Now, then, I ask you this: Could I expect—could I believe—could I even remotely imagine—that, feeling as he did, he would do so ungrateful a thing as to add those quite unnecessary fifteen words to his test?—set a trap for me?—expose me as a slanderer of my own town before my own people assembled in a public hall? It was preposterous; it was impossible. His test would contain only the kindly opening clause of my remark. Of that I had no shadow of doubt. You would have thought as I did. You would not have expected a base betrayal from one whom you had befriended and against whom you had committed no offense. And so, with perfect confidence, perfect trust, I wrote on a piece of paper the opening words—ending with "Go, and reform,"—and signed it. When I was about to put it in an envelope I was called into my back office, and without thinking I left the paper lying open on my desk.' He stopped, turned his head slowly toward Billson, waited a moment, then added: 'I ask you to note this: when I returned, a little later, Mr. Billson was retiring by my street door.' [*Sensation.*]

In a moment Billson was on his feet and shouting:

'It's a lie! It's an infamous lie!'

The Chair. 'Be seated, sir! Mr. Wilson has the floor.'

Billson's friends pulled him into his seat and quieted him, and Wilson went on:

'Those are the simple facts. My note was now lying in a different place on the table from where I had left it. I noticed that, but attached no importance to it, thinking a draught had blown it there. That Mr. Billson would read a private paper was a thing which could not occur to me; he was an honorable man, and he would be above that. If you will allow me to say it, I think his extra word "*very*" stands explained; it is attributable to a defect of memory. I was the only man in the world who could furnish here any detail of the test-remark—by *honorable* means. I have finished.'

There is nothing in the world like a persuasive speech to fuddle the mental apparatus and upset the convictions and debauch the emotions of an audience not practised in the tricks and delusions of oratory. Wilson sat down victorious. The house submerged him in tides of approving applause; friends swarmed to him and shook him by the hand and congratulated him, and Billson was shouted down and not allowed to say a word. The Chair hammered and hammered with its gavel, and kept shouting:

'But let us proceed, gentlemen, let us proceed!'

At last there was a measurable degree of quiet, and the hatter said:

'But what is there to proceed with, sir, but to deliver the money?'

Voices. 'That's it! That's it! Come forward, Wilson!'

The Hatter. 'I move three cheers for Mr. Wilson, Symbol of the special virtue which—'

The cheers burst forth before he could finish; and in the midst of them—and in the midst of the clamor of the gavel also—some enthusiasts mounted Wilson on a big friend's shoulder and were going to fetch him in triumph to the platform. The Chair's voice now rose above the noise—

'Order! To your places! You forget that there is still a document to be read.' When quiet had been restored he took up the document, and was going to read it, but laid it down again, saying, 'I forgot; this is not to be read until all written communications received by me have first been read.' He took an envelope out of his pocket, removed its inclosure, glanced at it—seemed astonished—held it out and gazed at it—stared at it.

Twenty or thirty voices cried out:

'What is it? Read it! read it!'

And he did—slowly, and wondering:

' "The remark which I made to the stranger—[*Voices.* 'Hello! how's this?']—was this: 'You are far from being a bad man. [*Voices.* 'Great Scott!'] Go, and reform.' " [*Voice.* 'Oh, saw my leg off!'] Signed by Mr. Pinkerton, the banker.'

The pandemonium of delight which turned itself loose now was of a sort to make the judicious weep. Those whose withers were unwrung laughed till the tears ran down; the reporters, in throes of laughter, set down disordered pot-hooks which would never in the world be decipherable; and a sleeping dog jumped up, scared out of its wits, and barked itself crazy at the turmoil. All manner of cries were scattered through the din: 'We're getting rich—*two* Symbols of Incorruptibility!—without counting Billson!' '*Three!*—count Shadbelly in—we can't have too many!' 'All right —Billson's elected!' 'Alas, poor Wilson— victim of *two* thieves!'

A Powerful Voice. 'Silence! The Chair's fished up something more out of its pocket.'

Voices. 'Hurrah! Is it something fresh? Read it! read! read!'

The Chair [*reading*]. ' "The remark which I made," etc.: " 'You are far from being a bad man. Go,' " etc. Signed, "Gregory Yates." '

Tornado of Voices. 'Four Symbols!' ' 'Rah for Yates!' 'Fish again!'

The house was in a roaring humor now, and ready to get all the fun out of the occasion that might be in it. Several Nineteeners, looking pale and distressed, got up and began to work their way toward the aisles, but a score of shouts went up:

'The doors, the doors—close the doors; no Incorruptible shall leave this place! Sit down, everybody!'

The mandate was obeyed.

'Fish again! Read! read!'

The Chair fished again, and once more the familiar words began to fall from its lips —' "You are far from being a bad man." '

'Name! name! What's his name?'

' "L. Ingoldsby Sargent." '

'Five elected! Pile up the Symbols! Go on, go on!'

' "You are far from being a bad—" '

'Name! name!'

' "Nicholas Whitworth." '

'Hooray! hooray! it's a symbolical day!'

Somebody wailed in, and began to sing this rhyme (leaving out 'it's') to the lovely 'Mikado' tune of 'When a man's afraid, a beautiful maid—'; the audience joined in, with joy; then, just in time, somebody contributed another line—

'And don't you this forget—'

The house roared it out. A third line was at once furnished—

'Corruptibles far from Hadleyburg are—'

The house roared that one too. As the last note died, Jack Halliday's voice rose high and clear, freighted with a final line—

'But the Symbols are here, you bet!'

That was sung, with booming enthusiasm. Then the happy house started in at the beginning and sang the four lines through twice, with immense swing and dash, and finished up with a crashing three-times-three and a tiger for 'Hadleyburg the Incorruptible and all Symbols of it which we shall find worthy to receive the hall-mark to-night.'

Then the shoutings at the Chair began again, all over the place:

'Go on! go on! Read! read some more! Read all you've got!'

'That's it—go on! We are winning eternal celebrity!'

A dozen men got up now and began to protest. They said that this farce was the work of some abandoned joker, and was an insult to the whole community. Without a doubt these signatures were all forgeries—

'Sit down! sit down! Shut up! You are confessing. We'll find *your* names in the lot.'

'Mr. Chairman, how many of those envelopes have you got?'

The Chair counted.

'Together with those that have been already examined, there are nineteen.'

A storm of derisive applause broke out.

'Perhaps they all contain the secret. I move that you open them all and read every signature that is attached to a note of that sort—and read also the first eight words of the note.'

'Second the motion!'

It was put and carried—uproariously. Then poor old Richards got up, and his wife rose and stood at his side. Her head was bent down, so that none might see that she was crying. Her husband gave her his arm, and so supporting her, he began to speak in a quavering voice:

'My friends, you have known us two—Mary and me—all our lives, and I think you have liked us and respected us—'

The Chair interrupted him:

'Allow me. It is quite true—that which you are saying, Mr. Richards: this town *does* know you two; it *does* like you; it *does* respect you; more—it honors you and *loves* you—'

Halliday's voice rang out:

'That's the hall-marked truth, too! If the Chair is right, let the house speak up and say it. Rise! Now, then—hip! hip! hip!—all together!'

The house rose in mass, faced toward the old couple eagerly, filled the air with a snow-storm of waving handkerchiefs, and delivered the cheers with all its affectionate heart.

The Chair then continued:

'What I was going to say is this: We know your good heart, Mr. Richards, but this is not a time for the exercise of charity toward offenders. [*Shouts of 'Right! right!'*] I see your generous purpose in your face, but I cannot allow you to plead for these men—'

'But I was going to—'

'Please take your seat, Mr. Richards. We must examine the rest of these notes—simple fairness to the men who have already been exposed requires this. As soon as that has been done—I give you my word for this —you shall be heard.'

Many Voices. 'Right!—the Chair is right —no interruption can be permitted at this stage! Go on!—the names! the names!—according to the terms of the motion!'

The old couple sat reluctantly down, and the husband whispered to the wife, 'It is pitifully hard to have to wait; the shame will be greater than ever when they find we were only going to plead for *ourselves*.'

Straightway the jollity broke loose again with the reading of the names.

' "You are far from being a bad man—" Signature, "Robert J. Titmarsh." '

' "You are far from being a bad man—" Signature, "Eliphalet Weeks." '

' "You are far from being a bad man—" Signature, "Oscar B. Wilder." ' '

At this point the house lit upon the idea of taking the eight words out of the Chairman's hands. He was not unthankful for that. Thenceforward he held up each note in its turn, and waited. The house droned out the eight words in a massed and measured and musical deep volume of sound (with a daringly close resemblance to a well-known church chant)—' "You are f-a-r from being a b-a-a-a-d man." ' Then the Chair said, 'Signature, "Archibald Wilcox." ' And so on, and so on, name after name, and everybody had an increasingly and gloriously good time except the wretched Nineteen. Now and then, when a particularly shining name was called, the house made the Chair wait while it chanted the whole of the test-remark from the beginning to the closing words, 'And go to hell or Hadleyburg—try and make it the for-or-m-e-r!' and in these special cases they added a grand and agonized and imposing 'A-a-a-a-*men*!'

The list dwindled, dwindled, dwindled, poor old Richards keeping tally of the count, wincing when a name resembling his own was pronounced, and waiting in miserable suspense for the time to come when it would be his humiliating privilege to rise with Mary and finish his plea, which he was intending to word thus: '. . . for until now we have never done any wrong thing, but have gone our humble way unreproached. We are very poor, we are old, and have no chick nor child to help us; we were sorely tempted, and we fell. It was my purpose when I got up before to make confession and beg that my name might not be read out in this public place, for it seemed to us that we could not bear it; but I was prevented. It was just; it was our place to suffer with the rest. It has been hard for us. It is the first time we have ever heard our name fall from any one's lips—sullied. Be merciful—for the sake of the better days; make our shame as light to bear as in your charity you can.' At this point in his revery Mary nudged him, perceiving that his mind was absent. The house was chanting, 'You are f-a-r,' etc.

'Be ready,' Mary whispered. 'Your name comes now; he has read eighteen.'

The chant ended.

'Next! next! next!' came volleying from all over the house.

Burgess put his hand into his pocket. The old couple, trembling, began to rise. Burgess fumbled a moment, then said,

'I find I have read them all.'

Faint with joy and surprise, the couple sank into their seats, and Mary whispered:

'Oh, bless God, we are saved!—he has lost ours—I wouldn't give this for a hundred of those sacks!'

The house burst out with its 'Mikado' travesty, and sang it three times with ever-increasing enthusiasm, rising to its feet when it reached for the third time the closing line—

'But the Symbols are here, you bet!'

and finishing up with cheers and a tiger for 'Hadleyburg purity and our eighteen immortal representatives of it.'

Then Wingate, the saddler, got up and proposed cheers 'for the cleanest man in town, the one solitary important citizen in it who didn't try to steal that money—Edward Richards.'

They were given with great and moving heartiness; then somebody proposed that Richards be elected sole guardian and Symbol of the now Sacred Hadleyburg Tradition, with power and right to stand up and look the whole sarcastic world in the face.

Passed, by acclamation; then they sang the 'Mikado' again, and ended it with:

'And there's *one* Symbol left, you bet!'

There was a pause; then—

A Voice. 'Now, then, who's to get the sack?'

The Tanner (with bitter sarcasm). 'That's easy. The money has to be divided among the eighteen Incorruptibles. They gave the suffering stranger twenty dollars apiece— and that remark—each in his turn—it took twenty-two minutes for the procession to move past. Staked the stranger—total contribution, $360. All they want is just the loan back—and interest—forty thousand dollars altogether.'

Many Voices [derisively]. 'That's it! Divvy! divvy! Be kind to the poor—don't keep them waiting!'

The Chair. 'Order! I now offer the stranger's remaining document. It says "If no claimant shall appear [*grand chorus of groans*] I desire that you open the sack and count out the money to the principal citizens of your town, they to take it in trust [*cries of 'Oh! Oh! Oh!'*], and use it in such ways as to them shall seem best for the propagation and preservation of your community's noble reputation for incorruptible honesty [*more cries*]—a reputation to which their names and their efforts will add a new and far-reaching luster." [*Enthusiastic outburst of sarcastic applause.*] That seems to be all. No—here is a postscript:

' "P. S.—CITIZENS OF HADLEYBURG: There *is* no test-remark—nobody made one. [*Great sensation.*] There wasn't any pauper stranger, nor any twenty-dollar contribution, nor any accompanying benediction and compliment—these are all inventions. [*General buzz and hum of astonishment and delight.*] Allow me to tell my story—it will take but a word or two. I passed through your town at a certain time, and received a deep offense which I had not earned. Any other man would have been content to kill one or two of you and call it square, but to me that would have been a trivial revenge, and inadequate; for the dead do not *suffer*. Besides, I could not kill you all—and, anyway, made as I am, even that would not have satisfied me. I wanted to damage every man in the place, and every woman—and not in their bodies or in their estate, but in their vanity—the place where feeble and foolish people are most vulnerable. So I disguised myself and came back and studied you. You were easy game. You had an old and lofty reputation for honesty, and naturally you were proud of it—it was your treasure of treasures, the very apple of your eye. As soon as I found out that you carefully and vigilantly kept yourselves and your children *out of temptation*, I knew how to proceed. Why, you simple creatures, the weakest of all weak things is a virtue which has not been tested in the fire. I laid a plan, and gathered a list of names. My project was to corrupt Hadleyburg the Incorruptible. My idea was to make liars and thieves of nearly half a hundred smirchless men and women who had never in their lives uttered a lie or stolen a penny. I was afraid of Goodson. He was neither born nor reared in Hadleyburg. I was afraid that if I started to operate my scheme by getting my letter laid before you, you would say to yourselves, 'Goodson is the only man among us who would give away twenty dollars to a poor devil'—and then you might not bite at my bait. But Heaven took Goodson; then I knew I was safe, and I set my trap and baited it. It may be that I shall not catch all the men to whom I mailed the pretended test secret, but I shall catch the most of them, if I know Hadleyburg nature. [*Voices.* 'Right—he got every last one of them.'] I believe they will even steal ostensible *gamble*-money, rather than miss, poor, tempted, and mistrained fellows. I am hoping to eternally and everlastingly squelch your vanity and give Hadleyburg a new renown—one that will *stick*—and spread far. If I have succeeded, open the sack and summon the Committee on Propagation and Preservation of the Hadleyburg Reputation." '

A Cyclone of Voices. 'Open it! Open it! The Eighteen to the front! Committee on Propagation of the Tradition! Forward— the Incorruptibles!'

The Chair ripped the sack wide, and gathered up a handful of bright, broad, yellow coins, shook them together, then examined them—

'Friends, they are only gilded disks of lead!'

There was a crashing outbreak of delight over this news, and when the noise had subsided, the tanner called out:

'By right of apparent seniority in this business, Mr. Wilson is Chairman of the Committee on Propagation of the Tradition. I suggest that he step forward on behalf of his pals, and receive in trust the money.'

A Hundred Voices. 'Wilson! Wilson! Wilson! Speech! Speech!'

Wilson [*in a voice trembling with anger*]. 'You will allow me to say, and without apologies for my language, *damn* the money!'

A Voice. 'Oh, and him a Baptist!'

A Voice. 'Seventeen Symbols left! Step up, gentlemen, and assume your trust!'

There was a pause—no response.

The Saddler. 'Mr. Chairman, we've got *one* clean man left, anyway, out of the late aristocracy; and he needs money, and deserves it. I move that you appoint Jack Halliday to get up there and auction off that sack of gilt twenty-dollar pieces, and give the result to the right man—the man whom Hadleyburg delights to honor—Edward Richards.'

This was received with great enthusiasm, the dog taking a hand again; the saddler started the bids at a dollar, the Brixton folk and Barnum's representative fought hard for it, the people cheered every jump that the bids made, the excitement climbed moment by moment higher and higher, the bidders got on their mettle and grew steadily more and more daring, more and more determined, the jumps went from a dollar up to five, then to ten, then to twenty, then fifty, then to a hundred, then—

At the beginning of the auction Richards whispered in distress to his wife: 'O Mary, can we allow it? It—it—you see, it is an honor-reward, a testimonial to purity of character, and—and—can we allow it? Hadn't I better get up and—O Mary, what ought we to do?—what do you think we— [*Halliday's voice. 'Fifteen I'm bid!—fifteen for the sack!—twenty!—ah, thanks!—thirty —thanks again! Thirty, thirty, thirty!—do I*

hear forty?—forty it is! Keep the ball rolling, gentlemen, keep it rolling!—fifty! thanks, noble Roman! going at fifty, fifty, fifty!— seventy!—ninety!—splendid!—a hundred!— pile it up, pile it up!—hundred and twenty— forty!—just in time!—hundred and fifty!— TWO *hundred!—superb! Do I hear two h— thanks!—two hundred and fifty!—'*]

'It is another temptation, Edward—I'm all in a tremble—but, oh, we've escaped *one* temptation, and that ought to warn us to— [*'Six did I hear?—thanks!—six-fifty, six-f—* SEVEN *hundred!'*] And yet, Edward, when you think—nobody susp— [*'Eight hundred dollars!—hurrah!—make it nine!—Mr. Parsons, did I hear you say—thanks—nine!—this noble sack of virgin lead going at only nine hundred dollars, gilding and all—come! do I hear—a thousand!—gratefully yours!—did some one say eleven?—a sack which is going to be the most celebrated in the whole Uni—'*] O Edward' (beginning to sob), 'we are *so* poor! —but—but—do as you think best—do as you think best.'

Edward fell—that is, he sat still; sat with a conscience which was not satisfied, but which was overpowered by circumstances.

Meantime a stranger, who looked like an amateur detective gotten up as an impossible English earl, had been watching the evening's proceedings with manifest interest, and with a contented expression in his face; and he had been privately commenting to himself. He was now soliloquizing somewhat like this: 'None of the Eighteen are bidding; that is not satisfactory; I must change that—the dramatic unities require it; they must buy the sack they tried to steal; they must pay a heavy price, too—some of them are rich. And another thing, when I make a mistake in Hadleyburg nature the man that puts that error upon me is entitled to a high honorarium, and some one must pay it. This poor old Richards has brought my judgment to shame; he is an honest man:—I don't understand it, but I acknowledge it. Yes, he saw my deuces *and* with a straight flush, and by rights the pot is his. And it shall be a jack-pot, too, if I can manage it. He disappointed me, but let that pass.'

He was watching the bidding. At a thousand, the market broke; the prices tumbled swiftly. He waited—and still watched. One competitor dropped out; then another, and another. He put in a bid or two, now. When the bids had sunk to ten dollars, he added a five; some one raised him a three; he waited a moment, then flung in a fifty-dollar jump, and the sack was his—at $1,282. The house broke out in cheers—then stopped; for he was on his feet, and had lifted his hand. He began to speak.

'I desire to say a word, and ask a favor. I am a speculator in rarities, and I have dealings with persons interested in numismatics all over the world. I can make a profit on this purchase, just as it stands; but there is a way, if I can get your approval, whereby I can make every one of these leaden twenty-dollar pieces worth its face in gold, and perhaps more. Grant me that approval, and I will give part of my gains to your Mr. Richards, whose invulnerable probity you have so justly and so cordially recognized to-night; his share shall be ten thousand dollars, and I will hand him the money to-morrow. [*Great applause from the house.* But the 'invulnerable probity' made the Richardses blush prettily; however, it went for modesty, and did no harm.] If you will pass my proposition by a good majority—I would like a two-thirds vote—I will regard that as the town's consent, and that is all I ask. Rarities are always helped by any device which will rouse curiosity and compel remark. Now if I may have your permission to stamp upon the faces of each of these ostensible coins the names of the eighteen gentlemen who—'

Nine-tenths of the audience were on their feet in a moment—dog and all—and the proposition was carried with a whirlwind of approving applause and laughter.

They sat down, and all the Symbols except 'Dr.' Clay Harkness got up, violently protesting against the proposed outrage, and threatening to—

'I beg you not to threaten me,' said the stranger, calmly. 'I know my legal rights, and am not accustomed to being frightened at bluster.' [*Applause.*] He sat down. 'Dr.' Harkness saw an opportunity here. He was one of the two very rich men of the place, and Pinkerton was the other. Harkness was proprietor of a mint; that is to say, a popular patent medicine. He was running for the legislature on one ticket, and Pinkerton on the other. It was a close race and a hot one, and getting hotter every day. Both had strong appetites for money; each had bought a great tract of land, with a purpose; there was going to be a new railway, and each wanted to be in the legislature and help locate the route to his own advantage; a single vote might make the decision, and with it two or three fortunes. The stake was large, and Harkness was a daring speculator. He was sitting close to the stranger. He leaned over while one or another of the other Symbols was entertaining the house with protests and appeals, and asked, in a whisper.

'What is your price for the sack?'

'Forty thousand dollars.'

'I'll give you twenty.'

'No.'

'Twenty-five.'

'No.'

'Say thirty.'

'The price is forty thousand dollars; not a penny less.'

'All right, I'll give it. I will come to the hotel at ten in the morning. I don't want it known: will see you privately.'

'Very good.' Then the stranger got up and said to the house:

'I find it late. The speeches of these gentlemen are not without merit, not without interest, not without grace; yet if I may be excused I will take my leave. I thank you for the great favor which you have shown me in granting my petition. I ask the Chair to keep the sack for me until to-morrow, and to hand these three five-hundred-dollar notes to Mr. Richards.' They were passed up to the Chair. 'At nine I will call for the sack, and at eleven will deliver the rest of the ten thousand to Mr. Richards in person, at his home. Good night.'

Then he slipped out, and left the audience making a vast noise, which was composed of a mixture of cheers, the 'Mikado' song, dog-disapproval, and the chant, 'You are f-a-r from being a b-a-a-d man—a-a-a-men!'

IV

AT home the Richardses had to endure congratulations and compliments until midnight. Then they were left to themselves. They looked a little sad, and they sat silent and thinking. Finally Mary sighed and said,

'Do you think we are to blame, Edward—*much* to blame?' and her eyes wandered to the accusing triplet of big bank-notes lying on the table, where the congratulators had been gloating over them and reverently fingering them. Edward did not answer at once; then he brought out a sigh and said, hesitatingly:

'We—we couldn't help it, Mary. It—well, it was ordered. *All* things are.'

Mary glanced up and looked at him steadily, but he didn't return the look. Presently she said:

'I thought congratulations and praises always tasted good. But—it seems to me, now —Edward?'

'Well?'

'Are you going to stay in the bank?'

'N-no.'

'Resign?'

'In the morning—by note.'

'It does seem best.'

Richards bowed his head in his hands and muttered:

'Before, I was not afraid to let oceans of people's money pour through my hands, but—Mary, I am so tired, so tired—'

'We will go to bed.'

At nine in the morning the stranger called for the sack and took it to the hotel in a cab. At ten Harkness had a talk with him privately. The stranger asked for and got five checks on a metropolitan bank—drawn to 'Bearer'—four for $1,500 each, and one for $34,000. He put one of the former in his pocketbook, and the remainder, representing $38,500, he put in an envelope, and with these he added a note, which he wrote after Harkness was gone. At eleven he called at the Richards house and knocked. Mrs. Richards peeped through the shutters, then went and received the envelope, and the stranger disappeared without a word. She came back flushed and a little unsteady on her legs, and gasped out:

'I am sure I recognized him! Last night it seemed to me that maybe I had seen him somewhere before.'

'He is the man that brought the sack here?'

'I am almost sure of it.'

'Then he is the ostensible Stephenson, too, and sold every important citizen in this town with his bogus secret. Now if he has sent checks instead of money, we are sold, too, after we thought we had escaped. I was beginning to feel fairly comfortable once more, after my night's rest, but the look of that envelope makes me sick. It isn't fat enough; $8,500 in even the largest banknotes makes more bulk than that.'

'Edward, why do you object to checks?'

'Checks signed by Stephenson! I am resigned to take the $8,500 if it could come in bank-notes—for it does seem that it was so ordered, Mary—but I have never had much courage, and I have not the pluck to try to market a check signed with that disastrous name. It would be a trap. That man tried to catch me; we escaped somehow or other; and now he is trying a new way. If it is checks—'

'Oh, Edward, it is *too* bad!' and she held up the checks and began to cry.

'Put them in the fire! quick! we mustn't be tempted. It is a trick to make the world laugh at *us*, along with the rest, and—Give them to *me*, since you can't do it!' He snatched them and tried to hold his grip till he could get to the stove; but he was human, he was a cashier, and he stopped a moment to make sure of the signature. Then he came near to fainting.

'Fan me, Mary, fan me! They are the same as gold!'

'Oh, how lovely, Edward! Why?'

'Signed by Harkness. What can the mystery of that be, Mary?'

'Edward, do you think—'

'Look here—look at this! Fifteen—fifteen—fifteen—thirty-four. Thirty-eight thousand five hundred! Mary, the sack isn't worth twelve dollars, and Harkness—apparently—has paid about par for it.'

'And does it all come to us, do you think —instead of the ten thousand?'

'Why, it looks like it. And the checks are made to "Bearer," too.'

'Is that good, Edward? What is it for?'

'A hint to collect them at some distant bank, I reckon. Perhaps Harkness doesn't want the matter known. What is that—a note?'

'Yes. It was with the checks.'

It was in the 'Stephenson' handwriting, but there was no signature. It said:

'I am a disappointed man. Your honesty is beyond the reach of temptation. I had a different idea about it, but I wronged you in that, and I beg pardon, and do it sincerely. I honor you—and that is sincere too. This town is not worthy to kiss the hem of your garment. Dear

sir, I made a square bet with myself that there were nineteen debauchable men in your self-righteous community. I have lost. Take the whole pot, you are entitled to it.'

Richards drew a deep sigh, and said:

'It seems written with fire—it burns so. Mary—I am miserable again.'

'I, too. Ah, dear, I wish—'

'To think, Mary—he *believes* in me.'

'Oh, don't, Edward—I can't bear it.'

'If those beautiful words were deserved, Mary—and God knows I believed I deserved them once—I think I could give the forty thousand dollars for them. And I would put that paper away, as representing more than gold and jewels, and keep it always. But now—We could not live in the shadow of its accusing presence, Mary.'

He put it in the fire.

A messenger arrived and delivered an envelope.

Richards took from it a note and read it; it was from Burgess.

'You saved me, in a difficult time. I saved you last night. It was at cost of a lie, but I made the sacrifice freely, and out of a grateful heart. None in this village knows so well as I know how brave and good and noble you are. At bottom you cannot respect me, knowing as you do of that matter of which I am accused, and by the general voice condemned; but I beg that you will at least believe that I am a grateful man; it will help me to bear my burden.

[*Signed*]

BURGESS'

'Saved, once more. And on such terms!' He put the note in the fire. 'I—I wish I were dead, Mary, I wish I were out of it all.'

'Oh, these are bitter, bitter days, Edward. The stabs, through their very generosity, are so deep—and they come so fast!'

Three days before the election each of two thousand voters suddenly found himself in possession of a prized memento—one of the renowned bogus double-eagles. Around one of its faces was stamped these words: 'THE REMARK I MADE TO THE POOR STRANGER WAS—' Around the other face was stamped these: 'GO, AND REFORM. [SIGNED] PINKERTON.' Thus the entire remaining

refuse of the renowned joke was emptied upon a single head, and with calamitous effect. It revived the recent vast laugh and concentrated it upon Pinkerton; and Harkness's election was a walkover.

Within twenty-four hours after the Richardses had received their checks their consciences were quieting down, discouraged; the old couple were learning to reconcile themselves to the sin which they had committed. But they were to learn, now, that a sin takes on new and real terrors when there seems a chance that it is going to be found out. This gives it a fresh and most substantial and important aspect. At church the morning sermon was of the usual pattern; it was the same old things said in the same old way; they had heard them a thousand times and found them innocuous, next to meaningless, and easy to sleep under; but now it was different: the sermon seemed to bristle with accusations; it seemed aimed straight and specially at people who were concealing deadly sins. After church they got away from the mob of congratulators as soon as they could, and hurried homeward, chilled to the bone at they did not know what—vague, shadowy, indefinite fears. And by chance they caught a glimpse of Mr. Burgess as he turned a corner. He paid no attention to their nod of recognition! He hadn't seen it; but they did not know that. What could his conduct mean? It might mean—it might mean—oh, a dozen dreadful things. Was it possible that he knew that Richards could have cleared him of guilt in that bygone time, and had been silently waiting for a chance to even up accounts? At home, in their distress they got to imagining that their servant might have been in the next room listening when Richards revealed the secret to his wife that he knew of Burgess's innocence; next, Richards began to imagine that he had heard the swish of a gown in there at that time; next, he was sure he *had* heard it. They would call Sarah in, on a pretext, and watch her face: if she had been betraying them to Mr. Burgess, it would show in her manner. They asked her some questions—questions which were so random and incoherent and seemingly purposeless that the girl felt sure that the old people's minds had been affected by their sudden good fortune; the sharp and watchful gaze which they bent upon her frightened her, and that completed the business. She blushed, she became nervous and confused, and to the old people these were plain signs of guilt—guilt of some fearful sort or other—without doubt she was a spy and a traitor. When they were alone again they began to piece many unrelated things together and get horrible results out of the combination. When things had got about to the worst, Richards was delivered of a sudden gasp, and his wife asked:

'Oh, what is it?—what is it?'

'The note—Burgess's note! Its language was sarcastic, I see it now.' He quoted: ' "At bottom you cannot respect me, *knowing*, as you do, of *that matter* of which I am accused"—oh, it is perfectly plain, now, God help me! He knows that I know! You see the ingenuity of the phrasing. It was a trap—and like a fool, I walked into it. And Mary—?'

'Oh, it is dreadful—I know what you are going to say—he didn't return your transcript of the pretended test-remark.'

'No—kept it to destroy us with. Mary, he has exposed us to some already. I know it—I know it well. I saw it in a dozen faces after church. Ah, he wouldn't answer our nod of recognition—*he* knew what he had been doing!'

In the night the doctor was called. The news went around in the morning that the old couple were rather seriously ill—prostrated by the exhausting excitement growing out of their great windfall, the congratulations, and the late hours, the doctor said. The town was sincerely distressed; for these old people were about all it had left to be proud of, now.

Two days later the news was worse. The old couple were delirious, and were doing strange things. By witness of the nurses, Richards had exhibited checks—for $8,500? No—for an amazing sum—$38,500! What could be the explanation of this gigantic piece of luck?

The following day the nurses had more news—and wonderful. They had concluded to hide the checks, lest harm come to them; but when they searched they were gone from under the patient's pillow—vanished away. The patient said:

'Let the pillow alone; what do you want?'

'We thought it best that the checks—'

'You will never see them again—they are destroyed. They came from Satan. I saw the hell-brand on them, and I knew they were sent to betray me to sin.' Then he fell to gabbling strange and dreadful things which were not clearly understandable, and which the doctor admonished them to keep to themselves.

Richards was right; the checks were never seen again.

A nurse must have talked in her sleep, for within two days the forbidden gabblings were the property of the town; and they were of a surprising sort. They seemed to indicate that Richards had been a claimant for the sack himself, and that Burgess had concealed that fact and then maliciously betrayed it.

Burgess was taxed with this and stoutly denied it. And he said it was not fair to attach weight to the chatter of a sick old man who was out of his mind. Still, suspicion was in the air, and there was much talk.

After a day or two it was reported that Mrs. Richards's delirious deliveries were getting to be duplicates of her husband's. Suspicion flamed up into conviction, now, and the town's pride in the purity of its one undiscredited important citizen began to dim down and flicker toward extinction.

Six days passed, then came more news. The old couple were dying. Richards's mind cleared in his latest hour, and he sent for Burgess. Burgess said:

'Let the room be cleared. I think he wishes to say something in privacy.'

'No!' said Richards: 'I want witnesses. I want you all to hear my confession, so that I may die a man, and not a dog. I was clean—artificially—like the rest; and like the rest I fell when temptation came. I signed a lie, and claimed the miserable sack. Mr. Burgess remembered that I had done him a service, and in gratitude (and ignorance) he suppressed my claim and saved me. You know the thing that was charged against Burgess years ago. My testimony, and mine alone, could have cleared him, and I was a coward, and left him to suffer disgrace—'

'No—no—Mr. Richards, you—'

'My servant betrayed my secret to him—'

'No one has betrayed anything to me—'

—'and then he did a natural and justifiable thing, he repented of the saving kindness which he had done me, and he *exposed* me—as I deserved—'

'Never!—I make oath—'

'Out of my heart I forgive him.'

Burgess's impassioned protestations fell upon deaf ears; the dying man passed away without knowing that once more he had done poor Burgess a wrong. The old wife died that night.

The last of the sacred Nineteen had fallen a prey to the fiendish sack; the town was stripped of the last rag of its ancient glory. Its mourning was not showy, but it was deep.

By act of the Legislature—upon prayer and petition—Hadleyburg was allowed to change its name to (never mind what—I will not give it away), and leave one word out of the motto that for many generations had graced the town's official seal.

It is an honest town once more, and the man will have to rise early that catches it napping again.

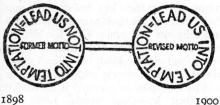

1898   1900

LITTLE BESSIE WOULD ASSIST PROVIDENCE [1]

[IT is dull, and I need wholesome excitements and distractions; so I will go lightly excursioning along the primrose path of theology.]

Little Bessie was nearly three years old. She was a good child, and not shallow, not frivolous, but meditative and thoughtful, and much given to thinking out the reasons of things and trying to make them harmonize with results. One day she said:

'Mama, why is there so much pain and sorrow and suffering? What is it all for?'

It was an easy question, and mama had no difficulty in answering it:

[1] Clemens 'often busied himself working out more extensively some of the ideas that came to him—moral ideas, he called them. One fancy which he followed in several forms (some of them not within the privilege of print) was that of an inquisitive little girl, Bessie, who pursues her mother with difficult questionings. He read these aloud as he finished them . . .' Paine, *Mark Twain*(N.Y., 1912),III,1515. The above selection was first published, ibid.,III,1671–73.

'It is for our good, my child. In His wisdom and mercy the Lord sends us these afflictions to discipline us and make us better.'

'Is it *He* that sends them?'

'Yes.'

'Does He send *all* of them, mama?'

'Yes, dear, all of them. None of them comes by accident; He alone sends them, and always out of love for us, and to make us better.'

'Isn't it strange?'

'Strange? Why, no, I have never thought of it in that way. I have not heard any one call it strange before. It has always seemed natural and right to me, and wise and most kindly and merciful.'

'Who first thought of it like that, mama? Was it you?'

'Oh no, child, I was taught it.'

'Who taught you so, mama?'

'Why, really, I don't know—I can't remember. My mother, I suppose; or the preacher. But it's a thing that everybody knows.'

'Well, anyway, it does seem strange. Did He give Billy Norris the typhus?'

'Yes.'

'What for?'

'Why, to discipline him and make him good.'

'But he died, mama, and so it *couldn't* make him good.'

'Well, then, I suppose it was for some other reason. We know it was a *good* reason, whatever it was.'

'What do you think it was, mama?'

'Oh, you ask so many questions! I think it was to discipline his parents.'

'Well, then, it wasn't fair, mama. Why should *his* life be taken away for their sake, when he wasn't doing anything?'

'Oh, *I* don't know! I only know it was for a good and wise and merciful reason.'

'What reason, mama?'

'I think—I think—well, it was a judgment; it was to punish them for some sin they had committed.'

'But *he* was the one that was punished, mama. Was that right?'

'Certainly, certainly. He does nothing that isn't right and wise and merciful. You can't understand these things now, dear, but when you are grown up you will understand them, and then you will see that they are just and wise.'

After a pause:

'Did He make the roof fall in on the stranger that was trying to save the crippled old woman from the fire, mama?'

'Yes, my child. *Wait!* Don't ask me why, because I don't know. I only know it was to discipline some one, or be a judgment upon somebody, or to show His power.'

'That drunken man that stuck a pitch-fork into Mrs. Welch's baby when—'

'Never mind about it, you needn't go into particulars; it was to discipline the child—*that* much is certain, anyway.'

'Mama, Mr. Burgess said in his sermon that billions of little creatures are sent into us to give us cholera, and typhoid, and lockjaw, and more than a thousand other sicknesses and—mama, does He send them?'

'Oh, certainly, child, certainly. Of course.'

'What for?'

'Oh, to *dis*cipline us! Haven't I told you so, over and over again?'

'It's awful cruel, mama! And silly! and if I—'

'Hush, oh *hush!* Do you want to bring the lightning?'

'You know the lightning *did* come last week, mama, and struck the new church, and burnt it down. Was it to discipline the church?'

(Wearily.) 'Oh, I suppose so.'

'But it killed a hog that wasn't doing anything. Was it to discipline the hog, mama?'

'Dear child, don't you want to run out and play a while? If you would like to—'

'Mama, only think! Mr. Hollister says there isn't a bird, or fish, or reptile, or any other animal that hasn't got an enemy that Providence has sent to bite it and chase it and pester it and kill it and suck its blood and discipline it and make it good and religious. Is that true, mother—because if it is true why did Mr. Hollister laugh at it?'

'That Hollister is a scandalous person, and I don't want you to listen to anything he says.'

'Why, mama, he is very interesting, and *I* think he tries to be good. He says the wasps catch spiders and cram them down into their nests in the ground—*alive*, mama!—and there they live and suffer days and days and days, and the hungry little wasps chewing their legs and gnawing into their bellies all the time, to make them good and religious and praise God for His infinite mercies. *I* think Mr. Hollister is just lovely, and ever so kind; for when I asked him if *he* would treat a spider like that he said he hoped to be damned if he would; and then he—*Dear* mama, have you fainted! I will run and bring help! Now *this* comes of staying in town this hot weather.'

1909   1912

HENRY TIMROD

1828–1867

THE COTTON BOLL

WHILE I recline
At ease beneath
This immemorial pine,
Small sphere!
(By dusky fingers brought this morning
    here
And shown with boastful smiles),
I turn thy cloven sheath,
Through which the soft white fibres peer,
That, with their gossamer bands,
Unite, like love, the sea-divided lands,   10
And slowly, thread by thread,
Draw forth the folded strands,

Than which the trembling line,
By whose frail help yon startled spider fled
Down the tall spear-grass from his swinging
    bed,
Is scarce more fine;
And as the tangled skein
Unravels in my hands,
Betwixt me and the noonday light,
A veil seems lifted, and for miles and miles
The landscape broadens on my sight,   21
As, in the little boll, there lurked a spell
Like that which, in the ocean shell,
With mystic sound,
Breaks down the narrow walls that hem us
    round,

And turns some city lane
Into the restless main,
With all his capes and isles!

Yonder bird,
Which floats, as if at rest,   30
In those blue tracts above the thunder,
        where
No vapors cloud the stainless air,
And never sound is heard,
Unless at such rare time
When, from the City of the Blest,
Rings down some golden chime,
Sees not from his high place
So vast a cirque of summer space
As widens round me in one mighty field,
Which, rimmed by seas and sands,   40
Doth hail its earliest daylight in the beams
Of gray Atlantic dawns;
And, broad as realms made up of many
        lands,
Is lost afar
Behind the crimson hills and purple lawns
Of sunset, among plains which roll their
        streams
Against the Evening Star!
And lo!
To the remotest point of sight,
Although I gaze upon no waste of snow,   50
The endless field is white;
And the whole landscape glows,
For many a shining league away,
With such accumulated light
As Polar lands would flash beneath a tropic
        day!
Nor lack there (for the vision grows,
And the small charm within my hands—
More potent even than the fabled one,
Which oped whatever golden mystery
Lay hid in fairy wood or magic vale,   60
The curious ointment of the Arabian tale—
Beyond all mortal sense
Doth stretch my sight's horizon, and I see,
Beneath its simple influence,
As if, with Uriel's crown,
I stood in some great temple of the Sun,
And looked, as Uriel, down!)
Nor lack there pastures rich and fields all
        green
With all the common gifts of God,
For temperate airs and torrid sheen   70
Weave Edens of the sod;
Through lands which look one sea of
        billowy gold
Broad rivers wind their devious ways;

A hundred isles in their embraces fold
A hundred luminous bays;
And through yon purple haze
Vast mountains lift their plumed peaks
        cloud-crowned;
And, save where up their sides the plowman
        creeps,
An unhewn forest girds them grandly
        round,
In whose dark shades a future navy sleeps!
Ye Stars, which, though unseen, yet with
        me gaze   81
Upon this loveliest fragment of the earth!
Thou Sun, that kindlest all thy gentlest rays
Above it, as to light a favorite hearth!
Ye Clouds, that in your temples in the West
See nothing brighter than its humblest
        flowers!
And you, ye Winds, that on the ocean's
        breast
Are kissed to coolness ere ye reach its
        bowers!
Bear witness with me in my song of praise,
And tell the world that, since the world
        began,   90
No fairer land hath fired a poet's lays,
Or given a home to man!

But these are charms already widely blown!
His be the meed whose pencil's trace
Hath touched our very swamps with grace,
And round whose tuneful way
All Southern laurels bloom;
The Poet of 'The Woodlands,' unto whom
Alike are known
The flute's low breathing and the trumpets'
        tone,   100
And the soft west wind's sighs;
But who shall utter all the debt,
O Land wherein all powers are met
That bind a people's heart,
The world doth owe thee at this day,
And which it never can repay,
Yet scarcely deigns to own!
Where sleeps the poet who shall fitly sing
The source wherefrom doth spring
That mighty commerce which, confined 110
To the mean channels of no selfish mart,
Goes out to every shore
Of this broad earth, and throngs the sea
        with ships
That bear no thunders; hushes hungry lips
In alien lands;
Joins with a delicate web remotest strands;
And gladdening rich and poor,

Doth gild Parisian domes,
Or feed the cottage-smoke of English
    homes,
And only bounds its blessings by mankind!
In offices like these, thy mission lies,   121
My Country! and it shall not end
As long as rain shall fall and heaven bend
In blue above thee; though thy foes be hard
And cruel as their weapons, it shall guard
Thy hearth-stones as a bulwark; make thee
    great
In white and bloodless state;
And haply, as the years increase—
Still working through its humbler reach
With that large wisdom which the ages
    teach—   130
Revive the half-dead dream of universal
    peace!
As men who labor in that mine
Of Cornwall, hollowed out beneath the bed
Of ocean, when a storm rolls overhead,
Hear the dull booming of the world of
    brine
Above them, and a mighty muffled roar
Of winds and waters, yet toil calmly on,
And split the rock, and pile the massive ore,
Or carve a niche, or shape the archèd roof;
So I, as calmly, weave my woof   140
Of song, chanting the days to come,
Unsilenced, though the quiet summer air
Stirs with the bruit of battles, and each
    dawn
Wakes from its starry silence to the hum
Of many gathering armies. Still,
In that we sometimes hear,
Upon the Northern winds, the voice of woe
Not wholly drowned in triumph, though I
    know
The end must crown us, and a few brief
    years
Dry all our tears,   150
I may not sing too gladly. To Thy will
Resigned, O Lord! we cannot all forget
That there is much even Victory must
    regret.
And, therefore, not too long
From the great burthen of our country's
    wrong
Delay our just release!
And, if it may be, save
These sacred fields of peace
From stain of patriot or of hostile blood!
Oh, help us, Lord! to roll the crimson flood
Back on its course, and, while our banners
    wing   161

Northward, strike with us! till the Goth
    shall cling
To his own blasted altar-stones, and crave
Mercy; and we shall grant it, and dictate
The lenient future of his fate
There, where some rotting ships and
    crumbling quays
Shall one day mark the Port which ruled the
    Western seas.
c.1862   1873

CHARLESTON

CALM as that second summer which
    precedes
    The first fall of the snow,
In the broad sunlight of heroic deeds,
    The city bides the foe.

As yet, behind their ramparts stern and
    proud,
    Her bolted thunders sleep—
Dark Sumter, like a battlemented cloud,
    Looms o'er the solemn deep.

No Calpe frowns from lofty cliff or scar
    To guard the holy strand;   10
But Moultrie holds in leash her dogs of war
    Above the level sand.

And down the dunes a thousand guns lie
    couched,
    Unseen, beside the flood—
Like tigers in some Orient jungle crouched,
    That wait and watch for blood.

Meanwhile, through streets still echoing
    with trade,
    Walk grave and thoughtful men,
Whose hands may one day wield the
    patriot's blade
    As lightly as the pen.   20

And maidens, with such eyes as would grow
    dim
    Over a bleeding hound,
Seem each one to have caught the strength
    of him
    Whose sword she sadly bound.

Thus girt without and garrisoned at home,
    Day patient following day,
Old Charleston looks from roof and spire
    and dome,
    Across her tranquil bay.

Ships, through a hundred foes, from Saxon
    lands
  And spicy Indian ports,   30
Bring Saxon steel and iron to her hands,
  And Summer to her courts.

But still, along yon dim Atlantic line,
  The only hostile smoke
Creeps like a harmless mist above the
    brine,
  From some frail floating oak.

Shall the Spring dawn, and she, still clad in
    smiles,
  And with an unscathed brow,
Rest in the strong arms of her palm-
    crowned isles,
  As fair and free as now?   40

We know not; in the temple of the Fates
  God has inscribed her doom;
And, all untroubled in her faith, she waits
  The triumph of the tomb.
    c.1861   1873

PAUL HAMILTON HAYNE

1830–1886

ASPECTS OF THE PINES

TALL, sombre, grim, against the morning
    sky
  They rise, scarce touched by melancholy
    airs,
Which stir the fadeless foliage dreamfully,
  As if from realms of mystical despairs.

Tall, sombre, grim, they stand with dusky
    gleams
  Brightening to gold within the wood-
    land's core,
Beneath the gracious noontide's tranquil
    beams—
  But the weird winds of morning sigh no
    more.

A stillness, strange, divine, ineffable,
  Broods round and o'er them in the wind's
    surcease,   10
And on each tinted copse and shimmering
    dell
  Rests the mute rapture of deep-hearted
    peace.

Last, sunset comes—the solemn joy and
    might
  Borne from the West when cloudless day
    declines—
Low, flutelike breezes sweep the waves of
    light,
  And lifting dark green tresses of the
    pines,

Till every lock is luminous--gently float,
  Fraught with hale odors up the heavens
    afar

To faint when twilight on her virginal
    throat
  Wears for a gem the tremulous vesper
    star.   20
          1875

THE MOCKING-BIRD

(AT NIGHT)

A GOLDEN pallor of voluptuous light
Filled the warm southern night:
The moon, clear orbed, above the sylvan
    scene
Moved like a stately queen,
So rife with conscious beauty all the while,
What could she do but smile
At her own perfect loveliness below,
Glassed in the tranquil flow
Of crystal fountains and unruffled streams?
Half lost in waking dreams,   10
As down the loneliest forest dell I strayed,
Lo! from a neighboring glade,
Flashed through the drifts of moonshine,
    swiftly came
A fairy shape of flame.
It rose in dazzling spirals overhead,
Whence to wild sweetness wed,
Poured marvellous melodies, silvery trill on
    trill;
The very leaves grew still
On the charmed trees to hearken; while for
    me,
Heart-trilled to ecstasy,   20
I followed—followed the bright shape that
    flew,
Still circling up the blue,
Till as a fountain that has reached its
    height,

Falls back in sprays of light
Slowly dissolved, so that enrapturing lay,
Divinely melts away
Through tremulous spaces to a music-mist,

Soon by the fitful breeze
  How gently kissed
Into remote and tender silences.   30

1882

SIDNEY LANIER

1842–1881

FROM TIGER LILIES

THE STORY OF CAIN AND GORM SMALLIN [1]

'Russet yeas and honest kersey noes.'
LOVE'S LABOR'S LOST

CAIN SMALLIN was the most indefatigable of scouts. He was always moving; the whole country side knew him. His good-natured face and communicated habits procured for him a cordial welcome at every house in that quiet country, where as yet only the distant roar of the war had been heard, where all was still and sunny and lonesome, where the house-hold talk was that of old men and women, of girls and children, whose sons and brothers were all away in the midst of that dimly-heard roaring. In this serene land a soldier's face that had been in front of cannon and bullets was a thing to be looked at twice, and a soldier's talk was the rare treasure of a fireside. The gunboats in the river, upon which these neighbors looked whenever they walked the river bank, had ceased to be objects of alarm, or even of curiosity. They lay there quietly and lazily, day after day, making no hostile sign; and had lain so since Norfolk fell. And as for the evening-gun at Fortress Monroe—that had boomed every sunset for many a year before the war.

On his way to the Point which terminates between Burwell's Bay and Smithfield Creek, and which afforded store of succulent grass and clover for the horses, Cain Smallin passed the house of a neighbor who had particularly distinguished himself in kindness to our little party of scouts. The old gentleman was seated in the open doorway, in midst of a pile of newspapers.

'Good mornin'! Mr. Smallin. Couldn't stand it any longer, you see, so I sent Dick away up to Ivor yesterday to try and get some papers. Here's another stinger in the *Examiner.* Sit down here; I want you to read it.'

'Thank'ee, sir, don't care if I do rest a leetle; toll!uble warm walkin' this mornin',' replied the mountaineer, and fell to reading —a slow operation for him whose eye was far more accustomed to sighting a rifle than deciphering letters.

'Massy me!' said he, after some silence, 'our men's desertin' mighty fast, up yan, f'om the army. Here's nigh to a whole column full of "Thirty Dollars Rewards" for each deserter. Let's see if I know any of 'em.'

Cain's lip moved busily, in what might well have been called a spell of silence. Suddenly he dropped the paper and looked piteously upward.

'May be I spelt it wrong, le'm me look again,' muttered he, and snatched the paper up to gaze again upon their dreadful Thirty Dollar column.

It was there.

THIRTY–DOLLARS REWARD.
'Deserted from the — Regiment, — Volunteers, GORM SMALLIN, *who enlisted,' &c., &c.*

Cain Smallin dropped his newspaper and strode hastily out of the door, unheeding the surprise of his host.

He walked rapidly, and aimlessly. The cruel torture would not permit him to rest; his grief drove him about; it lashed him with sharp thongs. Across fields and marshes, through creeks and woods, with bent head, with hands idly hanging, with unsteady step, he circled. A tear emerged from his eye. It stopped in a furrow, and glistened. Occasionally he muttered to himself,—

'We was poor. We aint never had much

---

[1] The selection, to which the title has been given by the editors, is Chapter 6 from Book II of *Tiger Lilies*(N.Y., 1876).

to live on but our name, which it was good as gold. An' now it aint no better'n rusty copper; hit'll be green an' pisenous. An' who's done it? Gorm Smallin! Nobody but Gorm Smallin! My own brother, Gorm Smallin! Gorm,—Gorm.' He repeated this name a hundred times, as if his mind wandered and he wished to fix it.

The hours passed on and still the mountaineer walked. His simple mountain-life had known few griefs. This was worse than any sorrow. It was disgrace. He knew no sophistries to retire into, in the ostrich-fashion wherewith men avoid dishonor. He had lost all. Not only he, but all whom he loved, would suffer.

'What will the Sterlin's say? Old John Sterlin'; him that stuck by us when corn was so scurce in the Cove? an' Philip! him that I've hunted with an' fished with an' camped with, by ourselves, in yan mountains? And Miss Felix! Miss Felix!'

The man dwelt on this name. His mind became a blank, except two luminous spots which were rather feelings than thoughts. These were, a sensation of disgrace and a sensation of loveliness: the one embodied in the name Gorm, the other in the name Felix. He recoiled from one; he felt as if religion demanded that he should also recoil from the other. He suffered more than if he had committed the crime himself. For he was innocence, and that is highly tender and sensitive, being unseared.

At length the gathering twilight attracted his attention. He looked around, to discover his locality. Leaping a fence he found himself in the main road, and a short walk brought him to a low house that stood in a field on the right. He opened the gate, and knocked at the door. 'Here's whar he said he'd stay,' he muttered. Gorm himself came to the door.

'Put on your hat, Gorm!'

The stern tone of his voice excited his brother's surprise.

'What fur, Cain?'

'I want you to walk with me, a little piece. Hurry!'

Gorm took down his hat and came out.

'Whar to, brother Cain?'

'Follow me,' replied Cain, with a motion of displeasure at the wheedling tone of his brother.

Leaving the road, he struck into a path leading to the Point from which he had wandered. As he walked his pace increased, until it required the most strenuous exertions on the part of his companion to keep up with his long and rapid strides.

'Whar the devil air you gwine to, Cain? Don't walk so fast, anyhow; I'm a'most out o' breath a'ready!'

The mountaineer made no reply, but slackened his pace. He only muttered to himself: 'Hits eight mile across; ye'll need your strength to git thar, may be.'

The path wound now amongst gloomy pines, for some distance, until suddenly they emerged upon the open beach. They were upon the extreme end of the lonely Point. The night was dark; but the sand-beach glimmered ghastly white through the darkness. Save the mournful hooting of an owl from his obscure cell in the woods, the place was silent. Hundreds of huge tree-stumps, with their roots upturned in the air, lay in all fantastic positions upon the white sand, as the tide had deposited them. These straggling clumps had been polished white by salt air and waves. They seemed like an agitated convention of skeletons, discussing the propriety of flesh. A small boat rested on the beach, with one end secured by a 'painter' to a stake driven in the sand.

'Little did I think, when I found it in the marsh this mornin' an' brought it thar, thinkin' to git it round to camp to-night, what use I was gwine put it to,' said Cain Smallin to himself.

As he led the way to the boat, suddenly he stopped and turned face to face with his recreant brother. His eyes glared into Gorm's. His right hand was raised, and a pistol-barrel protruded from the long fingers.

'Gorm Smallin,' he said, with grating voice, 'have ye ever know'd me to say I'd do anything an' then not to do it?'

'I—I—no, I haven't, Cain,' stuttered the deserter, cowering with terror and surprise.

'Remember them words. Now answer my questions, and don't say nothin' outside o' them. Gorm Smallin, whar was you born?'

'What makes you ax me sich foolish questions, Cain? I was born in Tennessy, an' you know it!'

'Answer my questions, Gorm Smallin! Who raised you, f'om a little un?'

'Mother an' father, o' course.'

'Who's your mother and father? what's ther name?'

'Cain, air you crazy? ther name's Smallin.'

'Gorm Smallin, did you ever know any o' the Smallins to cheat a man in a trade?'

'No, Cain; we've always been honest.'

'Did ye ever know a Smallin to swar to a lie afore the Jestis?'

'No.'

'Did ye ever know one to steal another man's horse, or his rifle, or anything?'

'No.'

'Did ye ever know one to sneak out f'om a rightful fight?'

'No.'

'Did ye ever know one to'—the words came like lightning with a zigzag jerk—'to desert f'om his rigiment?'

The flash struck Gorm Smallin. He visibly sank into himself like a jointed cane. He trembled, and gazed apprehensively at the pistol in his brother's right hand which still towered threateningly aloft. He made no reply.

'Ye don't like to say yes this time!' continued Cain. 'Gorm Smallin, altho' I say it which I'm your brother,—ye lied every time ye said no, afore. *You* has cheated in a dirty trade; *you* has swore to a lie afore God that's better than the Jestis; *you* has stole what's better'n any rifle or horse; *you* has sneaked out f'om the rightfullest fight ye ever was in; *you* has deserted f'om your rigiment, an' that when yer own brother an' every friend ye had in the world was fightin' along with ye.

'Gorm Smallin, you has cheated me, an' ole father an' mother an' all, out of our name which it was all we had; you has swore to a lie, for you swore to me 'at the colonel sent you down here to go a-scoutin' amongst the Yankees; you has stole our honest name, which it is more than ye can ever make to give to your wife's baby; you has sneaked out f'om a fight that we was fightin' to keep what was our'n an' to pertect them that has been kind to us an' them that raised us; you has deserted f'om your rigiment which it has fought now gwine on four years an' fought manful, too, an' never run a inch.

'Gorm Smallin, you has got your name in the paper 'ith thirty dollars reward over it, in big letters; big letters, so 'at father's ole eyes can read it 'ithout callin' sister Ginny to make it out for him. Thar it is, for every man, woman, *and* child in the whole Confederacy to read it, an' by this time they *has* read it, may be, an' every man in the rigiment has cussed you for a sneak an' a scoundrel, an' wonderin' whether Cain Smallin will do like his brother!

'Gorm Smallin, you has brung me to that, that I haint no sperrit to fight hearty an' cheerful. Ef ye had been killed in a fa'r battle, I mought ha' been able to fight hard enough for both of us, for every time I cried a-thinkin' of you, I'd ha' been twice as strong an' twice as clear-sighted as I was buffore. But—such things as these'—the mountaineer wiped off a tear with his coatsleeve—'burns me an' weakens me an' hurts my eyes that bad that I kin scarcely look a man straight forrard in the face. Hit don't make much diff'ence to me now, whether we whips the Yanks or they whips us. What good'll it do ef we conquer 'em? Everybody'll be a-shoutin' an' a-hurrahin' an' they'll leave *us* out o' the frolic, for we is kin to a deserter! An' the women'll be a-smilin' on them that has lived to git home, one minute, an' the next they'll be a-weepin' for them that's left dead in Virginy an' Pennsylvany an' Tennessy,—but *you* won't git home, an' *you* won't be left dead nowher; they cain't neither smile at you nor cry for you; what'll they do ef anybody speaks yer name? Gorm Smallin, they'll lift their heads high an' we'll hang our'n low. They'll scorn ye an' we'll blush for ye.

'Hadn't ye better be dead? Hadn't I better kill ye right here an' bury ye whar ye cain't do no more harm to the fambly name

'But I cain't shoot ye, hardly. The same uns raised us an' fed us. I cain't do it; an' I'm sorry I cain't!

'You air 'most on yer knees, anyhow; git down on 'em all the way. Listen to me. God A'mighty's a-lookin' at you out o' the star yan, an' he's a-listenin' at you out o' the sand here, an' he won't git tired by mornin' bu he'll keep a-listenin' an' a-lookin' at ye tomorrow all day. Now mind ye. I'm gwine to put ye in this boat here, an' you can paddle across to yan side the river, easy. E ye'll keep yer eye on yan bright star that's jest a-risin' over Bullitt Pint, ye'll strike t'other shore about the right place. Ef ye paddle out o' the way, the guard on yan gunboat'll be apt to fire into ye; keep yer eye on the star. Ye'll git to the beach on t'other side, an' lay down under a tree an' sleep till mornin'—ef ye *can* sleep. In the mornin' ye'll walk down the road, an' the Yankee pickets'll see yer gray coat an' take ye to Head-quarters. The officer at Head-quarters'll examine ye, an' when you tell him you air a deserter he'll make ye take the oath, an' ef he know'd how many oaths ye've already broke I think he would'n' take the trouble! Howsumdever, I'm gwine to do the same foolishness, for it's all I kin do. Now when ye take the oath the officer'll likely make ye sign yer name to it, or write yer name somewhar. Gorm Smallin, when ye write that name ye *shall* not write your own name; ye must write some other name. Swar to it, now, while ye air kneelin' buffore God A'mighty! Raise up yer hands, both of 'em; swar to it, that ye'll write some other name in the Yankee deserter-book, or I'll shoot ye, thar, right down!'

Cain had placed the muzzle of his pistol against his brother's forehead.

The oath was taken.

'Don't git up yet; kneel thar. Hit would'n' be right to put any other man's name in the deserter-book in place o' yourn, for ye mought be robbin' some other decent fambly of ther good name. Le'ss see. We must git some name that nobody ever was named afore. Take a stick thar an' write it in the sand, so you won't forgit it. The fust name don't make no diff'ence. Write Sam'l.'

It was written in great scrawling letters.

'Now write J, an' call out as you write, so you won't forgit it. For I'm gwine to captur' that deserter-book on' see ef your name's in it. Write J, an' call out.'

'J.'
'O.'
'O.'
'X.'
'X.'
'O.'
'O.'
'B.'
'B.'
'B, agin.'
'B, agin.'
'le,-bul!'
'le,-bul!'

'Sam'l Joxo—Joxy—I cain't call it, but you can write it—hit'll do. Git it by heart.'

Cain paused a moment.

'Now git up. Git in the boat. Gorm Smallin, don't never come back home, don't never come whar I may be! I cain't shake hands with ye; but I'll shove ye off.'

Cain loosened the head of the boat from the sand, turned her round, and gave a mighty push, running with her till he was waist deep in the water. He came out dripping, folded his arms, and stood still, watching the dusky form in the receding boat.

Gorm Smallin was a half-mile from shore. Suddenly he heard his brother's voice, across the water.

'Gorm!'

'Hello!'

'Joxo—Joxobabbul!' cried Cain Smallin at the top of his voice bending down to read the inscription on the sand.

1867

FROM THE SCIENCE OF ENGLISH VERSE

VERSE A PHENOMENON OF SOUND [1]

PERHAPS no one will find difficulty in accepting the assertion that when formal poetry, or verse,—two terms which will be always used here as convertible,—is repeated aloud, it impresses itself upon the ear as verse only by means of certain relations existing among its component words considered purely as sounds, without reference to their associated ideas. If the least doubt upon this point should be entertained, it may be dispelled by observing that all ideas may be abolished out of a poem without disturbing its effect upon the ear as verse. This may be practically demonstrated by the simple experiment of substituting for the words of a formal poem any other words which preserve the accentuation, alliteration, and rhyme, but which convey no ideas to the mind,—words of some foreign language not understood by the experimenter being the most effective for this purpose. Upon repeating aloud the poem thus treated it will be found that the verse-structure has not been impaired. If, therefore, the ear accepts as perfect verse a series

[1] The selection is from *The Science of English Verse* (N.Y., 1909),21–24,39–40,46–48,57–58.

of words from which ideas are wholly absent,—that is to say, a series of sounds,—it is clear that what we call 'verse' is a set of specially related sounds, at least in the case of a formal poem repeated aloud.

But a much more sweeping proposition is true. If we advance from the case of formal poetry repeated aloud to that of formal poetry silently perused by the eye of a reader, a slight examination will show the proposition good that here, as before, verse is still a set of specially related sounds. For, in this instance, the characters of print or writing in which the words are embodied are simply signs of sounds; and although originally received by the eye, they are handed over to the ear, are interpreted by the auditory sense, and take their final lodgement, not at all as conceptions of sight, but as conceptions of hearing. The function of the eye is now purely ministerial: it merely purveys for the ear. An analogous process is indicated in the Arabian saw which affirms that 'that is the best description which makes the ear and eye.' In general, the reader will do well to recall that each sense has not only what is ordinarily called its physical province, but also its corresponding imaginative province; the eye has its imagination, the ear its imagination; and when the term 'imagination of the ear' is hereinafter used it must be understood to suggest those perceptions of sound which come to exist in the mind, not by virtue of actual vibratory impact upon the tympanum immediately preceding the perception, but by virtue of indirect causes (such as the characters of print and of writing) which in any way amount to practical equivalents of such impact. Now these signs convey, along with their corresponding sounds, the same relations between those sounds which are suggested to the ear when the sounds themselves fall upon the tympanum. It is therefore strictly true that, although the great majority of formal poems in modern times are perceived by the mind through the original agency of the eye, the relations indicated by the term 'verse' are still relations between sounds.

Nor—to call the briefest attention to the only other case in which this fundamental proposition could seem at all doubtful—is this connection of verse with sound less essential when the formal poem is merely conceived in the thought of its author without ever reaching either visible or audible embodiment. For the formal poem is necessarily conceived in words, and in the imagination of the sounds (words) is necessarily involved the imagination of the relations between the sounds, that is, of verse.

In short, when we hear verse, we *hear* a set of relations between sounds; when we silently read verse, we *see* that which brings to us a set of relations between sounds; when we imagine verse, we *imagine* a set of relations between sounds.

Approached in this way, the proposition given below will probably not seem difficult of acceptance; indeed it is possible many will be surprised that the ideas leading to it have been dwelt upon so long. In point of fact, however, it is the very failure to recognize verse as in all respects a phenomenon of sound and to appreciate the necessary consequences thereof which has caused the non-existence of a science of formal poetry. Occasion will presently arise to show how this has happened, with some detail; meantime, we are now prepared to formulate a proposition which will serve as the basis of a science of verse.

The term 'verse' denotes a set of specially related sounds. . . .

Since an art of sound must depend primarily upon exact co-ordinations by the ear, and since these exact co-ordinations are, as just shown, possible only in respect of duration, pitch, and tone-color, it is evident that these three sound-relations constitute three distinct principles to one or the other of which all the primary phenomena of this art must be referred. They thus afford us three fundamental principles of classification for the effects of sound in art. The effects ordinarily known as 'rhythm' depend primarily upon duration; those known as 'tune' depend upon pitch; those known as 'colors' in music, and as 'rhymes' and 'alliterations' in verse,—besides many allied effects of verse which have never been named,—depend upon tone-color. Stated in other terms:—

I

When the ear exactly co-ordinates a series of sounds and silences with primary reference to their duration, the result is a conception of . . . . RHYTHM.

II

When the ear exactly co-ordinates a series of sounds with primary reference to their pitch, the result is a conception of . . . TUNE.

III

When the ear exactly co-ordinates a series of sounds with primary reference to their tone-color, the result is a conception of (in music, 10 *flute-tone as distinct from violin-tone, and the like; in verse, rhyme as opposed to rhyme, vowel varied with vowel, phonetic syzygy, and the like), in general* . . . . . TONE-COLOR.

. . .We have now reached a point where we can profitably inquire as to the precise differentiation between the two species of the art of sound—music and verse. We have found that the art of sound, in general, em- 20 braces phenomena of rhythm, of tune, and of tone-color. Many will be disposed to think that the second class of these phenomena just named—tune—is not found in verse, and that the absence of it should be one of the first differences to be noted as between music and verse. Tune is, however, quite as essential a constituent of verse as of music; and the disposition to believe otherwise is due only to the complete 30 unconsciousness with which we come to use these tunes after the myriad repetitions of them which occur in all our daily intercourse by words. We will presently find, from numerous proofs and illustrations which are submitted in Part II., on the Tunes of Verse, that our modern speech is made up quite as much of tunes as of words, and that our ability to convey our thoughts depends upon the existence of a 40 great number of curious melodies of speech which have somehow acquired form and significance. These 'tunes' are not mere vague variations of pitch in successive words,—which would deserve the name of tune only in the most general sense of that term,—but they are perfectly definite and organized melodies of the speaking-voice, composed of exact variations of pitch so well marked as to be instantly recognized 50 by every ear. If they were *not* thus recognized a large portion of the ideas which we now convey with ease would be wholly inexpressible. Reserving, then, all details upon this matter until their appropriate

place under the head of the Tunes of Verse, in Part II. above cited, it will be sufficient here if the reader is asked to realize them in a practical way by first attempting to utter any significant sentences of prose or verse in an absolutely unchanging voice from beginning to end. This will be found quite difficult, and when successfully executed produces an impression of strangeness which all the more clearly illustrates how habitually and how unconsciously the tunes of speech are used. If, having uttered the sentences in a rigidly unvarying tone, the reader will then utter them in the tunes which we feel—by some inward perceptions too subtle for treatment here—to be appropriate to them, it will be easily seen that definite successions of tones are being used,—so definite that they are kept in mind for their appropriate occasions just as words are, and so regular in their organizations as to be in all respects worthy the name of 'tunes,' instead of the vague terms 'intonation,' or 'inflection,' which have so long concealed the real function of these wonderful melodies of the speaking-voice.

The art of verse, then, as well as the art of music,—the two species of the genus art of sound,—includes all the three great classes of phenomena summed up under the terms rhythm, tune, and tone-color. We will presently find many problems solved by the full recognition of this fact that there is absolutely no difference between the sound-relations used in music and those used in verse.

If this be true,—if the sound-relations of music and verse are the same,—we are necessarily forced to look for the difference between the two arts in the nature of the *sounds* themselves with which they deal. Here, indeed, the difference lies. Expressed, as far as possible, in popular terms, it is as follows:—

When those exact co-ordinations which the ear perceives as rhythm, tune, and tone-color, are suggested to the ear by a series of 'musical sounds,' the result is . . . MUSIC.

When those exact co-ordinations which the ear perceives as rhythm, tune, and tone-color, are suggested to the ear by a series of 'spoken words,' the result is . . . . . . VERSE.

. . .The foregoing proposition aims only to state the distinctions between music and verse: it will not be found complete for other purposes. For example, it would not serve to discriminate verse and prose. Prose has its rhythms, its tunes, and its tone-colors, like verse; and, while the extreme forms of prose and verse are sufficiently unlike each other, there are such near grades of intermediate forms that they may be said to run into each other, and any line claiming to be distinctive must necessarily be more or less arbitrary. The art of sound must always be regarded the genus, and music and verse its two species. Prose, scientifically considered, is a wild variety of verse.

The science of verse, then, observes and classifies all the phenomena of rhythm, of tune, and of tone-color, so far as they can be exhibited to the ear directly by spoken words,—or to the ear, through the eye, by written or printed signs of spoken words,—or to the mind by the conception of spoken words; and,

The science of *English* verse observes and classifies these phenomena so far as they can be indicated through the medium of spoken English words. . . .

1880

THE SYMPHONY [1]

'O TRADE! O Trade! would thou wert dead!
The Time needs heart—'tis tired of head:
We're all for love,' the violins said.

[1] Lanier wrote, 12 Feb. 1876, to a friend: 'I met with a line in one of Shakspeare's sonnets some time ago which seems to me so completely a nutshell judgment on my side as regards the possibilities of interpreting—within limits—one sense by another through the forms of art that I cannot help sending it to you. It is: "To hear with eyes belongs to Love's fine wit." In my "Symphony" Love's fine wit—the love of one's fellowmen—attempts (not to hear with eyes, but precisely the reverse) to see with ears.' Starke, *Sidney Lanier* (Chapel Hill,N.C., 1933),205–06.

To Simms, 17 April 1872, Lanier wrote: 'Trade, Trade,Trade: pah, are we not all sick? A man cannot walk down a green alley of woods, in these days, without unawares getting his mouth and nose and eyes covered with some web or other that Trade has stretched across, to catch some gain or other. . . . You know what the commercial spirit is: you remember that Trade killed Chivalry and now sits in the throne. It was Trade that hatched the Jacquerie in the 14th Century: it was Trade that hatched John Brown, and broke the saintly heart of Robert Lee in the 19th.' Ibid.,201.

'Of what avail the rigorous tale
Of bill for coin and box for bale?
Grant thee, O Trade! thine uttermost hope:
Level red gold with blue sky-slope,
And base it deep as devils grope:
When all's done, what hast thou won
Of the only sweet that's under the sun?   10
Ay, canst thou buy a single sigh
Of true love's least, least ecstasy?'
Then, with a bridegroom's heart-beats trembling,
All the mightier strings assembling
Ranged them on the violins' side
As when the bridegroom leads the bride,
And, heart in voice, together cried:
'Yea, what avail the endless tale
Of gain by cunning and plus by sale?
Look up the land, look down the land   20
The poor, the poor, the poor, they stand
Wedged by the pressing of Trade's hand
Against an inward-opening door
That pressure tightens ever more:
They sigh a monstrous foul-air sigh
For the outside leagues of liberty,
Where Art, sweet lark, translates the sky
Into a heavenly melody.
"Each day, all day" (these poor folks say),
"In the same old year-long, drear-long way,   30
We weave in the mills and heave in the kilns,
We sieve mine-meshes under the hills,
And thieve much gold from the Devil's bank tills,
To relieve, O God, what manner of ills?—
The beasts, they hunger, and eat, and die;
And so do we, and the world's a sty;
Hush, fellow-swine: why nuzzle and cry?
Swinehood hath no remedy
Say many men, and hasten by,
Clamping the nose and blinking the eye   40
But who said once, in the lordly tone,
Man shall not live by bread alone
But all that cometh from the Throne?
     Hath God said so?
     But Trade saith No:
And the kilns and the curt-tongued mills say Go:
There's plenty that can, if you can't: we know.
Move out, if you think you're underpaid.
The poor are prolific; we're not afraid;
     Trade is trade." '   50
Thereat this passionate protesting
Meekly changed, and softened till

It sank to sad requesting
And suggesting sadder still:
And oh, if men might some time see
How piteous-false the poor decree
That trade no more than trade must be!
Does business mean, *Die, you—live, I?*
Then "Trade is trade" but sings a lie:
'Tis only war grown miserly.   60
If business is battle, name it so:
War-crimes less will shame it so,
And widows less will blame it so.
Alas, for the poor to have some part
In yon sweet living lands of Art,
Makes problem not for head, but heart.
Vainly might Plato's brain revolve it:
Plainly the heart of a child could solve it.'

And then, as when from words that seem
    but rude
We pass to silent pain that sits abroad   70
Back in our heart's great dark and solitude,
So sank the strings to gentle throbbing
Of long chords change-marked with
    sobbing—
Motherly sobbing, not distinctlier heard
Than half wing-openings of the sleeping
    bird,
Some dream of danger to her young hath
    stirred.
Then stirring and demurring ceased, and
    lo!
Every least ripple of the strings' song-flow
Died to a level with each level bow
And made a great chord tranquil-surfaced
    so,   80
As a brook beneath his curving bank doth
    go
To linger in the sacred dark and green
Where many boughs the still pool overlean
And many leaves make shadow with their
    sheen.
    But presently
A velvet flute-note fell down pleasantly
Upon the bosom of that harmony,
And sailed and sailed incessantly,
As if a petal from a wild-rose blown   89
Had fluttered down upon that pool of tone
And boatwise dropped o' the convex side
And floated down the glassy tide
And clarified and glorified
The solemn spaces where the shadows bide.
From the warm concave of that fluted note
Somewhat, half song, half odor, forth did
    float,
As if a rose might somehow be a throat:

'When Nature from her far-off glen
Flutes her soft messages to men,
    The flute can say them o'er again;   100
    Yea, Nature, singing sweet and lone,
Breathes through life's strident polyphone
The flute-voice in the world of tone.
    Sweet friends,
    Man's love ascends
To finer and diviner ends
Than man's mere thought e'er
    comprehends.
For I, e'en I,
As here I lie,
A petal on a harmony,   110
Demand of Science whence and why
Man's tender pain, man's inward cry,
When he doth gaze on earth and sky?
I am not overbold:
    I hold
Full powers from Nature manifold.
I speak for each no-tongued tree
That, spring by spring, doth nobler be,
And dumbly and most wistfully
His mighty prayerful arms outspreads   120
Above men's oft-unheeding heads,
And his big blessing downward sheds.
I speak for all-shaped blooms and leaves,
Lichens on stones and moss on eaves,
Grasses and grains in ranks and sheaves;
Broad-fronded ferns and keen-leaved canes,
And briery mazes bounding lanes,
And marsh-plants, thirsty-cupped for
    rains,
And milky stems and sugary veins;
For every long-armed woman-vine   130
That round a piteous tree doth twine;
For passionate odors, and divine
Pistils, and petals crystalline;
All purities of shady springs,
All shynesses of film-winged things
That fly from tree-trunks and bark-rings;
All modesties of mountain-fawns
That leap to covert from wild lawns,
And tremble if the day but dawns;
All sparklings of small beady eyes   140
Of birds, and sidelong glances wise
Wherewith the jay hints tragedies;
All piquancies of prickly burs,
And smoothnesses of downs and furs
Of eiders and of minevers;
All limpid honeys that do lie
At stamen-bases, nor deny
The humming-birds' fine roguery,
Bee-thighs, nor any butterfly;
All gracious curves of slender wings,   150

Bark-mottlings, fibre-spiralings,
Fern-wavings and leaf-flickerings;
Each dial-marked leaf and flower-bell
Wherewith in every lonesome dell
Time to himself his hours doth tell;
All tree-sounds, rustlings of pine cones,
Wind-sighings, doves' melodious moans,
And night's unearthly under-tones;
All placid lakes and waveless deeps,
All cool reposing mountain-steeps,   160
Vale-calms and tranquil lotos-sleeps;—
Yea, all fair forms, and sounds, and lights,
And warmths, and mysteries, and mights,
Of Nature's utmost depths and heights,
—These doth my timid tongue present,
Their mouthpiece and leal instrument
And servant, all love-eloquent.
I heard, when *All for love* the violins
     cried:
So, Nature calls through all her system
     wide,
Give me thy love, O man, so long denied.   170
Much time is run, and man hath changed
     his ways,
Since Nature, in the antique fable-days,
Was hid from man's true love by proxy
     fays,
False fauns and rascal gods that stole her
     praise.
The nymphs, cold creatures of man's colder
     brain,
Chilled Nature's streams till man's warm
     heart was fain
Never to lave its love in them again.
Later, a sweet Voice *Love thy neighbor* said;
Then first the bounds of neighborhood
     outspread
Beyond all confines of old ethnic dread. 180
Vainly the Jew might wag his covenant
     head:
All men are neighbors, so the sweet Voice
     said.
So, when man's arms had circled all man's
     race,
The liberal compass of his warm embrace
Stretched bigger yet in the dark bounds of
     space;
With hands a-grope he felt smooth Nature's
     grace,
Drew her to breast and kissed her sweet-
     heart face:
Yea, man found neighbors in great hills and
     trees
And streams and clouds and suns and birds
     and bees,

And throbbed with neighbor-loves in
     loving these.   100
But oh, the poor! the poor! the poor!
That stand by the inward-opening door
Trade's hand doth tighten ever more,
And sigh their monstrous foul-air sigh
For the outside hills of liberty,
Where Nature spreads her wild blue sky
For Art to make into melody!
Thou Trade! thou king of the modern
     days!
     Change thy ways,
     Change thy ways;   200
Let the sweaty laborers file
     A little while,
     A little while,
Where Art and Nature sing and smile.
Trade! is thy heart all dead, all dead?
And hast thou nothing but a head?
I'm all for heart,' the flute-voice said,
And into sudden silence fled,
Like as a blush that while 'tis red
Dies to a still, still white instead.   210

     Thereto a thrilling calm succeeds,
Till presently the silence breeds
A little breeze among the reeds
That seems to blow by sea-marsh weeds:
Then from the gentle stir and fret
Sings out the melting clarionet,
Like as a lady sings while yet
Her eyes with salty tears are wet.
'O Trade! O Trade!' the Lady said,
'I too will wish thee utterly dead   220
If all thy heart is in thy head.
For O my God! and O my God!
What shameful ways have women trod
At beckoning of Trade's golden rod!
Alas when sighs are traders' lies,
And heart's-ease eyes and violet eyes
     Are merchandise!
O purchased lips that kiss with pain!
O cheeks coin-spotted with smirch and
     stain!
O trafficked hearts that break in twain! 230
—And yet what wonder at my sisters'
     crime?
So hath Trade withered up Love's sinewy
     prime,
Men love not women as in olden time.
Ah, not in these cold merchantable days
Deem men their life an opal gray, where
     plays
The one red Sweet of gracious ladies'-
     praise.

Now, comes a suitor with sharp prying
    eye—
Says, *Here, you Lady, if you'll sell, I'll buy:*
Come, heart for heart—a trade? What!
    weeping? why?
Shame on such wooers' dapper mercery! 240
I would my lover kneeling at my feet
In humble manliness should cry, *O sweet!*
I know not if thy heart my heart will greet:
I ask not if thy love my love can meet:
Whate'er thy worshipful soft tongue shall
    say,
I'll kiss thine answer, be it yea or nay:
I do but know I love thee, and I pray
To be thy knight until my dying day.
Woe him that cunning trades in hearts
    contrives!   249
Base love good women to base loving drives
If men loved larger, larger were our lives;
And wooed they nobler, won they nobler
    wives.'

There thrust the bold straightforward horn
To battle for that lady lorn,
With heartsome voice of mellow scorn,
Like any knight in knighthood's morn.
    'Now comfort thee,' said he,
        'Fair Lady.
For God shall right thy grievous wrong,
And man shall sing thee a true-love song,
Voiced in act his whole life long,   261
    Yea, all thy sweet life long,
        Fair Lady.
Where's he that craftily hath said,
The day of chivalry is dead?
I'll prove that lie upon his head,
    Or I will die instead,
        Fair Lady.
Is Honor gone into his grave?
Hath Faith become a caitiff knave,   270
And Selfhood turned into a slave
    To work in Mammon's cave,
        Fair Lady?
Will Truth's long blade ne'er gleam again?
Hath Giant Trade in dungeons slain
All great contempts of mean-got gain
    And hates of inward stain,
        Fair Lady?
For aye shall name and fame be sold,
And place be hugged for the sake of gold,
And smirch-robed Justice feebly scold   281
    At Crime all money-bold,
        Fair Lady?
Shall self-wrapt husbands aye forget
Kiss-pardons for the daily fret

Wherewith sweet wifely eyes are wet—
    Blind to lips kiss-wise set—
        Fair Lady?
Shall lovers higgle, heart for heart,
Till wooing grows a trading mart   290
Where much for little, and all for part,
    Make love a cheapening art,
        Fair Lady?
Shall woman scorch for a single sin
That her betrayer may revel in,
And she be burnt, and he but grin
    When that the flames begin,
        Fair Lady?
Shall ne'er prevail the woman's plea,
We maids would far, far whiter be   300
If that our eyes might sometimes see
    Men maids in purity,
        Fair Lady?
Shall Trade aye salve his conscience-aches
With jibes at Chivalry's old mistakes—
The wars that o'erhot knighthood makes
    For Christ's and ladies' sakes,
        Fair Lady?
Now by each knight that e'er hath prayed
To fight like a man and love like a maid, 310
Since Pembroke's life, as Pembroke's
    blade,
    I' the scabbard, death, was laid,
        Fair Lady,
I dare avouch my faith is bright
That God doth right and God hath might.
Nor time hath changed His hair to white,
    Nor His dear love to spite,
        Fair Lady.
I doubt no doubts: I strive, and shrive my
    clay,
And fight my fight in the patient modern
    way   320
For true love and for thee—ah me! and
    pray
    To be thy knight until my dying day,
        Fair Lady.'
Made end that knightly horn, and spurred
    away
Into the thick of the melodious fray.

And then the hautboy played and smiled,
And sang like any large-eyed child,
Cool-hearted and all undefiled.
    'Huge Trade!' he said,
'Would thou wouldst lift me on thy head
And run where'er my finger led!   331
Once said a Man—and wise was He—
Never shalt thou the heavens see,
Save as a little child thou be.'

Then o'er sea-lashings of commingling
        tunes
The ancient wise bassoons,
    Like weird
    Gray-beard
Old harpers sitting on the high sea-dunes,
    Chanted runes: 340
'Bright-waved gain, gray waved loss,
The sea of all doth lash and toss,
One wave forward and one across:
But now 'twas trough, now 'tis crest,
And worst doth foam and flash to best,
    And curst to blest.

Life! Life! thou sea-fugue, writ from east
      to west,
    Love, Love alone can pore
    On thy dissolving score
    Of harsh half-phrasings,   350
      Blotted ere writ,
    And double erasings
    Of chords most fit.
Yea, Love, sole music master blest,
May read thy weltering palimpsest.
To follow Time's dying melodies through,
And never to lose the old in the new,
And ever to solve the discords true—
    Love alone can do.   359
And ever Love hears the poor-folks' crying,
And ever Love hears the women's sighing,
And ever sweet knighthood's death-defying,
And ever wise childhood's deep implying,
But never a trader's glozing and lying.

'And yet shall Love himself be heard,
Though long deferred, though long
      deferred:
O'er the modern waste a dove hath
      whirred:
Music is Love in search of a word.'
1875   1877

EVENING SONG

Look off, dear Love, across the sallow
      sands,
    And mark yon meeting of the sun and
      sea,
How long they kiss in sight of all the lands.
    Ah! longer, longer, we.

Now in the sea's red vintage melts the sun,
    As Egypt's pearl dissolved in rosy wine,
And Cleopatra night drinks all. 'Tis done,
    Love, lay thine hand in mine.

Come forth, sweet stars, and comfort
      heaven's heart;
    Glimmer, ye waves, round else unlighted
      sands.   10
O night! divorce our sun and sky apart
      Never our lips, our hands.
1876   1884

SONG OF THE CHATTAHOOCHEE

    Out of the hills of Habersham,
      Down the valleys of Hall,
I hurry amain to reach the plain,
Run the rapid and leap the fall,
Split at the rock and together again,
Accept my bed, or narrow or wide,
And flee from folly on every side
With a lover's pain to attain the plain
    Far from the hills of Habersham,
    Far from the valleys of Hall.   10

    All down the hills of Habersham,
      All through the valleys of Hall,
The rushes cried *Abide, abide,*
The willful waterweeds held me thrall,
The laving laurel turned my tide,
The ferns and the fondling grass said *Stay,*
The dewberry dipped for to work delay,
And the little reeds sighed *Abide, abide,*
    Here in the hills of Habersham,
    Here in the valleys of Hall.   20

    High o'er the hills of Habersham,
      Veiling the valleys of Hall,
The hickory told me manifold
Fair tales of shade, the poplar tall
Wrought me her shadowy self to hold,
The chestnut, the oak, the walnut, the pine,
Overleaning, with flickering meaning and
      sign,
Said, *Pass not, so cold, these manifold*
    Deep shades of the hills of Habersham,
    These glades in the valleys of Hall.   30

    And oft in the hills of Habersham,
      And oft in the valleys of Hall,
The white quartz shone, and the smooth
      brook-stone
Did bar me of passage with friendly brawl,
And many a luminous jewel lone
—Crystals clear or a-cloud with mist,
Ruby, garnet and amethyst—
Made lures with the lights of streaming
      stone

In the clefts of the hills of Habersham,
In the beds of the valleys of Hall.   40

But oh, not the hills of Habersham,
And oh, not the valleys of Hall
Avail: I am fain for to water the plain.
Downward the voices of Duty call—
Downward, to toil and be mixed with the
      main,
The dry fields burn, and the mills are to
      turn,
And a myriad flowers mortally yearn,
And the lordly main from beyond the plain
      Calls o'er the hills of Habersham,
      Calls through the valleys of Hall.   50
1877   1884

THE REVENGE OF HAMISH [1]

It was three slim does and a ten-tined buck
      in the bracken lay;
   And all of a sudden the sinister smell of a
      man,
   Awaft on a wind-shift, wavered and ran
Down the hill-side and sifted along through
      the bracken and passed that way.

Then Nan got a-tremble at nostril; she was
      the daintiest doe;
   In the print of her velvet flank on the
      velvet fern
   She reared, and rounded her ears in turn.
Then the buck leapt up, and his head as a
      king's to a crown did go

Full high in the breeze, and he stood as if
      Death had the form of a deer;
   And the two slim does long lazily stretch-
      ing arose,   10
   For their day-dream slowlier came to a
      close,
Till they woke and were still, breath-bound
      with waiting and wonder and fear.

[1] '. . . While alliteration was used among the Anglo-
Saxon poets to establish and fortify the main rhythm
of the verse, its effect in modern verse is to vary the
main rhythm by irregular and unlooked-for groups
which break the monotony of the set rhythmic movement.
. . . All alliteration for the sake of alliteration is
trifling, and . . . in modern English verse it is to be
used with such delicate art that the ear will unconsciously feel its indefinite presence, varying the verse
as brief irregular bird-calls, heard in the wood here
and there, seem to add a delight to the mass of green.'
Lanier, The Science of English Verse (N.Y., 1909), 310-
14.

Then Alan the huntsman sprang over the
      hillock, the hounds shot by,
   The does and the ten-tined buck made a
      marvellous bound,
   The hounds swept after with never a
      sound,
But Alan loud winded his horn in sign that
      the quarry was nigh.

For at dawn of that day proud Maclean of
      Lochbuy to the hunt had waxed
      wild,
   And he cursed at old Alan till Alan fared
      off with the hounds
   For to drive him the deer to the lower
      glen-grounds:
'I will kill a red deer,' quoth Maclean, 'in
      the sight of the wife and the child.'

So gayly he paced with the wife and the
      child to his chosen stand;   21
   But he hurried tall Hamish the hench-
      man ahead: 'Go turn,'—
   Cried Maclean—'if the deer seek to cross
      to the burn,
Do thou turn them to me: nor fail, lest thy
      back be red as thy hand.'

Now hard-fortuned Hamish, half blown of
      his breath with the height of the
      hill,
   Was white in the face when the ten-tined
      buck and the does
   Drew leaping to burn-ward; huskily rose
His shouts, and his nether lip twitched,
      and his legs were o'er-weak for
      his will.

So the deer darted lightly by Hamish and
      bounded away to the burn.
   But Maclean never bating his watch tar-
      ried waiting below.   30
   Still Hamish hung heavy with fear for to
      go
All the space of an hour; then he went, and
      his face was greenish and stern,

And his eye sat back in the socket, and
      shrunken the eyeballs shone,
   As withdrawn from a vision of deeds it
      were shame to see.
   'Now, now, grim henchman, what is't
      with thee?'
Brake Maclean, and his wrath rose red as a
      beacon the wind hath upblown.

'Three does and a ten-tined buck made out,'
    spoke Hamish, full mild,
    'And I ran for to turn, but my breath it
        was blown, and they passed;
I was weak, for ye called ere I broke me
    my fast.'
Cried Maclean: 'Now a ten-tined buck in
    the sight of the wife and the child 40

I had killed if the gluttonous kern had not
    wrought me a snail's own wrong!'
    Then he sounded, and down came kins-
        men and clansmen all:
    'Ten blows, for ten tine, on his back let
        fall,
And reckon no stroke if the blood follow
    not at the bite of thong!'

So Hamish made bare, and took him his
    strokes; at the last he smiled.
    'Now I'll to the burn,' quoth Maclean,
        'for it still may be,
If a slimmer-paunched henchman will
    hurry with me,
I shall kill me the ten-tined buck for a gift
    to the wife and the child!'

Then the clansmen departed, by this path
    and that; and over the hill
    Sped Maclean with an outward wrath for
        an inward shame; 50
    And that place of the lashing full quiet
        became;
And the wife and the child stood sad; and
    bloody-backed Hamish sat still.

But look! red Hamish has risen; quick about
    and about turns he.
    'There is none betwixt me and the crag-
        top!' he screams under breath.
    Then, livid as Lazarus lately from death,
He snatches the child from the mother, and
    clambers the crag toward the sea.

Now the mother drops breath; she is dumb,
    and her heart goes dead for a space,
    Till the motherhood, mistress of death,
        shrieks, shrieks through the glen,
    And that place of the lashing is live with
        men,
And Maclean, and the gillie that told him,
    dash up in a desperate race. 60

Not a breath's time for asking; an eye-
    glance reveals all the tale untold.

They follow mad Hamish afar up the
    crag toward the sea,
    And the lady cries: 'Clansmen, run for a
        fee!—
Yon castle and lands to the two first hands
    that shall hook him and hold

Fast Hamish back from the brink!'—and
    ever she flies up the steep,
    And the clansmen pant, and they sweat,
        and they jostle and strain.
    But, mother, 'tis vain; but, father, 'tis
        vain;
Stern Hamish stands bold on the brink, and
    dangles the child o'er the deep.

Now a faintness falls on the men that run,
    and they all stand still.
    And the wife prays Hamish as if he were
        God, on her knees, 70
    Crying: 'Hamish! O Hamish! but please,
        but please
For to spare him!' and Hamish still dangles
    the child, with a wavering will.

On a sudden he turns; with a sea-hawk
    scream, and a gibe, and a song,
    Cries: 'So; I will spare ye the child if, in
        sight of ye all,
    Ten blows on Maclean's bare back shall
        fall,
And ye reckon no stroke if the blood follow
    not at the bite of the thong!'

Then Maclean he set hardly his tooth to
    his lip that his tooth was red,
    Breathed short for a space, said: 'Nay,
        but it never shall be!
    Let me hurl off the damnable hound in
        the sea!'
But the wife: 'Can Hamish go fish us the
    child from the sea, if dead? 80

Say yea!—Let them lash *me*, Hamish?'—
    'Nay!' —'Husband, the lashing will
        heal;
    But, oh, who will heal me the bonny
        sweet bairn in his grave?
    Could ye cure me my heart with the
        death of a knave?
Quick! Love! I will bare thee—so—kneel!'
    Then Maclean 'gan slowly to kneel

With never a word, till presently downward
    he jerked to the earth.

Then the henchman—he that smote
    Hamish—would tremble and lag;
'Strike, hard!' quoth Hamish, full stern,
    from the crag;
Then he struck him, and 'One!' sang
    Hamish, and danced with the child
    in his mirth.

And no man spake beside Hamish; he
    counted each stroke with a song.
    When the last stroke fell, then he moved
    him a pace down the height,   90
And he held forth the child in the heart-
    aching sight
Of the mother, and looked all pitiful grave,
    as repenting a wrong.

And there as the motherly arms stretched
    out with the thanksgiving prayer—
    And there as the mother crept up with a
    fearful swift pace,
Till her finger nigh felt of the bairnie's
    face—
In a flash fierce Hamish turned round and
    lifted the child in the air,

And sprang with the child in his arms from
    the horrible height in the sea,
    Shrill screeching, 'Revenge!' in the wind-
    rush; and pallid Maclean,
Age-feeble with anger and impotent pain,
Crawled up on the crag, and lay flat, and
    'locked hold of dead roots of a tree—

And gazed hungrily o'er, and the blood from
    his back drip-dripped in the brine,
    And a sea-hawk flung down a skeleton
    fish as he flew,   102
And the mother stared white on the
    waste of blue,
And the wind drove a cloud to seaward, and
    the sun began to shine.
1878   1884

OPPOSITION

OF fret, of dark, of thorn, of chill,
    Complain no more; for these, O heart,
Direct the random of the will
    As rhymes direct the rage of art.

The lute's fixt fret, that runs athwart
    The strain and purpose of the string,
For governance and nice consort
    Doth bar his wilful wavering.

The dark hath many dear avails;
    The dark distils divinest dews;   10
The dark is rich with nightingales,
    With dreams, and with the heavenly Muse.

Bleeding with thorns of petty strife,
    I'll ease (as lovers do) my smart
With sonnets to my lady Life
    Writ red in issues from the heart.

What grace may lie within the chill
    Of favor frozen fast in scorn!
When Good's a-freeze, we call it Ill!
    This rosy Time is glacier-born.   20

Of fret, of dark, of thorn, of chill,
    Complain thou not, O heart; for these
Bank-in the current of the will
    To uses, arts, and charities.
1879–1880   1884

A BALLAD OF TREES
AND THE MASTER [1]

INTO the woods my Master went,
Clean forspent, forspent.
Into the woods my Master came,
Forspent with love and shame.
But the olives they were not blind to Him,
The little gray leaves were kind to Him:
The thorn-tree had a mind to Him
When into the woods He came.

Out of the woods my Master went,
And He was well content.   10
Out of the woods my Master came,
Content with death and shame.
When Death and Shame would woo Him
    last,
From under the trees they drew Him last:
'Twas on a tree they slew Him—last
When out of the woods He came.
1880   1884

THE CRYSTAL

AT midnight, death's and truth's unlocking
    time,
When far within the spirit's hearing rolls

1 ' "A Ballad of Trees and the Master" was conceived as
an interlude of the latest "Hymn of the Marshes,"
"Sunrise," although written earlier. . . . In Mr. Lanier's final copy the "Ballad" is omitted. It was one of
several interludes which he at first designed, but, for
some reason, afterwards abandoned.' Mrs. Lanier's
note, Poems of Sidney Lanier (N.Y., 1929), 255.

The great soft rumble of the course of
    things—
A bulk of silence in a mask of sound,—
When darkness clears our vision that by
    day
Is sun-blind, and the soul's a ravening owl
For truth and flitteth here and there about
Low-lying woody tracts of time and oft
Is minded for to sit upon a bough,
Dry-dead and sharp, of some long-stricken
    tree   10
And muse in that gaunt place,—'twas then
    my heart,
Deep in the meditative dark, cried out:

'Ye companies of governor-spirits grave,
Bards, and old bringers-down of flaming
    news
From steep-wall'd heavens, holy
    malcontents,
Sweet seers, and stellar visionaries, all
That brood about the skies of poesy,
Full bright ye shine, insuperable stars;
Yet, if a man look hard upon you, none
With total lustre blazeth, no, not one   20
But hath some heinous freckle of the flesh
Upon his shining cheek, not one but
    winks
His ray, opaqued with intermittent mist
Of defect; yea, you masters all must ask
Some sweet forgiveness, which we leap to
    give,
We lovers of you, heavenly-glad to meet
Your largesse so with love, and interplight
Your geniuses with our mortalities.

    Thus unto thee, O sweetest Shakspere
    sole,
A hundred hurts a day I do forgive   30
('Tis little, but, enchantment! 'tis for thee):
Small curious quibble; Juliet's prurient
    pun
In the poor, pale face of Romeo's fancied
    death;
Cold rant of Richard; Henry's fustian roar
Which frights away that sleep he invocates;
Wronged Valentine's unnatural haste to
    yield:
Too-silly shifts of maids that mask as men
In faint disguises that could ne'er
    disguise —
Viola, Julia, Portia, Rosalind;   39
Fatigues most drear, and needless overtax
Of speech obscure that had as lief be plain;
Last I forgive (with more delight, because

'Tis more to do) the labored-lewd discourse
That e'en thy young invention's youngest
    heir
Besmirched the world with.

                  Father Homer, thee,
Thee also I forgive thy sandy wastes
Of prose and catalogue, thy drear harangues
That tease the patience of the centuries,
Thy sleazy scrap of story,—but a rogue's 50
Rape of a light-o'-love,—too soiled a patch
To broider with the gods.

                  Thee, Socrates,
Thou dear and very strong one, I forgive
Thy year-worn cloak, thine iron
    stringencies
That were but dandy upside-down, thy
    words
Of truth that, mildlier spoke had mainlier
    wrought.

So, Buddha, beautiful! I pardon thee
That all the All thou hadst for needy
    man
Was Nothing, and thy Best of being was 60
But not to be.

                Worn Dante, I forgive
The implacable hates that in thy horrid
    hells
Or burn or freeze thy fellows, never loosed
By death, nor time, nor love.

                   And I forgive
Thee, Milton, those thy comic-dreadful
    wars
Where, armed with gross and inconclusive
    steel,
Immortals smite immortals mortalwise
And fill all heaven with folly.   70

                 Also thee,
Brave Æschylus, thee I forgive, for that
Thine eye, by bare bright justice basilisked,
Turned not, nor ever learned to look where
    Love
Stands shining.

            So, unto thee, Lucretius mine
(For oh, what heart hath loved thee like to
    this
That's now complaining?), freely I forgive
Thy logic poor, thine error rich, thine earth
Whose graves eat souls and all.   80

Yea, all you hearts
Of beauty, and sweet righteous lovers large:
Aurelius fine, oft superfine; mild Saint
A Kempis, overmild; Epictetus,
Whiles low in thought, still with old
    slavery tinct;
Rapt Behmen, rapt too far; high
    Swedenborg,
O'ertoppling; Langley, that with but a
    touch
Of art hadst sung Piers Plowman to the top
Of English songs, whereof 'tis dearest,
    now,
And most adorable; Cædmon, in the morn,
A-calling angels with the cow-herd's call 91
That late brought up the cattle; Emerson,
Most wise, that yet, in finding Wisdom,
    lost
Thy Self, sometimes; tense Keats, with
    angels' nerves
Where men's were better; Tennyson,
    largest voice
Since Milton, yet some register of wit
Wanting;—all, all, I pardon, ere 'tis asked,
Your more or less, your little mole that
    marks
You brother and your kinship seals to man.

But Thee, but Thee, O sovereign Seer of
    time,   100
But Thee, O poets' Poet, Wisdom's
    Tongue,
But Thee, O man's best Man, O love's best
    Love,
O perfect life in perfect labor writ,
O all men's Comrade, Servant, King, or
    Priest,—
What *if* or *yet*, what mole, what flaw, what
    lapse,
What least defect or shadow of defect,
What rumor, tattled by an enemy,
Of inference loose, what lack of grace
Even in torture's grasp, or sleep's, or ·
    death's—
Oh, what amiss may I forgive in Thee, 110
Jesus, good Paragon, thou Crystal Christ?'
1880   1884

FROM HYMNS OF THE MARSHES

I. SUNRISE

IN my sleep I was fain of their fellowship,
    fain
  Of the live-oak, the marsh, and the main.

The little green leaves would not let me
    alone in my sleep;
Up-breathed from the marshes, a message
    of range and of sweep,
Interwoven with waftures of wild sea-
    liberties, drifting,
  Came through the lapped leaves sifting,
    sifting,
    Came to the gates of sleep.
Then my thoughts, in the dark of the
    dungeon-keep
Of the Castle of Captives hid in the City of
    Sleep,
Upstarted, by twos and by threes
    assembling: 10
  The gates of sleep fell a-trembling
Like as the lips of a lady that forth falter
    yes,
    Shaken with happiness:
    The gates of sleep stood wide.

I have waked, I have come, my beloved! I
    might not abide:
I have come ere the dawn, O beloved, my
    live-oaks, to hide
    In your gospelling glooms,—to be
As a lover in heaven, the marsh my marsh
    and the sea my sea.

Tell me, sweet burly-bark'd, man-bodied
    Tree
That mine arms in the dark are em-
    bracing, dost know   20
From what fount are these tears at thy feet
    which flow?
They rise not from reason, but deeper
    inconsequent deeps.
    Reason's not one that weeps.
    What logic of greeting lies
. Betwixt dear over-beautiful trees and the
    rain of the eyes?

O cunning green leaves, little masters! like
    as ye gloss
All the dull-tissued dark with your luminous
    darks that emboss
The vague blackness of night into pattern
    and plan,
        So,
  (But would I could know, but would I
    could know,)   30
With your question embroid'ring the dark
    of the question of man,—
So, with your silences purfling this silence
    of man

While his cry to the dead for some knowl-
 edge is under the ban,
    Under the ban,—
 So, ye have wrought me
Designs on the night of our knowledge,—
 yea, ye have taught me,
   So,
 That haply we know somewhat more
  than we know.

  Ye lispers, whisperers, singers in
   storms,
  Ye consciences murmuring faiths
   under forms,   40
  Ye ministers meet for each passion
   that grieves,
  Friendly, sisterly, sweetheart leaves,
Oh, rain me down from your darks that contain me
Wisdoms ye winnow from winds that pain
 me,—
Sift down tremors of sweet-within-
 sweet
That advise me of more than they bring,—
 repeat
Me the woods-smell that swiftly but now
 brought breath
From the heaven-side bank of the river of
 death,—
 Teach me the terms of silence,—preach
 me
 The passion of patience,—sift me,—im-
 peach me,—   50
    And there, oh there
As ye hang with your myriad palms up-
 turned in the air,
    Pray me a myriad prayer.

  My gossip, the owl,—is it thou
That out of the leaves of the low-hanging
 bough,
  As I pass to the beach, art stirred?
  Dumb woods, have ye uttered a bird?

  . . . . . .

Reverend Marsh, low-couched along the
 sea,
 Old chemist, rapt in alchemy,
  Distilling silence,—lo,   60
That which our father-age had died to
 know—
 The menstruum that dissolves all matter
 —thou
Hast found it: for this silence, filling now
The globèd charity of receiving space,

This solves us all: man, matter, doubt,
 disgrace,
Death, love, sin, sanity,
Must in yon silence, clear solution lie.
Too clear! That crystal nothing who'll
 peruse?
The blackest night could bring us brighter
 news.
Yet precious qualities of silence haunt 70
Round these vast margins, ministrant.
Oh, if thy soul's at latter gasp for space,
With trying to breathe no bigger than thy
 race
Just to be fellow'd, when that thou hast
 found
No man with room, or grace enough of
 bound
To entertain that New thou tell'st, thou
 art,—
'Tis here, 'tis here, thou canst unhand thy
 heart
And breathe it free, and breathe it free,
By rangy marsh, in lone sea-liberty.

The tide's at full: the marsh with flooded
 streams   80
Glimmers, a limpid labyrinth of dreams.
Each winding creek in grave entrancement
 lies
A rhapsody of morning-stars. The
 skies
Shine scant with one forked galaxy,—
The marsh brags ten: looped on his
 breast they lie.

Oh, what if a sound should be made!
Oh, what if a bound should be laid
To this bow-and-string tension of beauty
 and silence a-spring,—
To the bend of beauty the bow, or the hold
 of silence the string!
I fear me. I fear me yon dome of diapha-
 nous gleam   90
Will break as a bubble o'er-blown in a
 dream,—
Yon dome of too-tenuous tissues of space
 and of night,
Over-weighted with stars, over-freighted
 with light,
Over-sated with beauty and silence, will
 seem
 But a bubble that broke in a dream,
If a bound of degree to this grace be
 laid,
   Or a sound or a motion made.

But no: it is made: list! somewhere,—
    mystery, where?
           In the leaves? in the air?
In my heart? is a motion made: 100
'Tis a motion of dawn, like a flicker of
    shade on shade.
In the leaves 'tis palpable: low multitudi-
    nous stirring
Upwinds through the woods; the little ones,
    softly conferring,
Have settled my lord's to be looked for; so;
    they are still;
But the air and my heart and the earth are
    a-thrill,—
And look where the wild duck sails round
    the bend of the river,—
    And look where a passionate shiver
    Expectant is bending the blades
Of the marsh-grass in serial shimmers and
    shades,—
And invisible wings, fast fleeting, fast
    fleeting,   110
           Are beating

The dark overhead as my heart beats,—
    and steady and free
Is the ebb-tide flowing from marsh to sea—
    (Run home, little streams,
    With your lapfulls of stars and
    dreams),—
And a sailor unseen is hoisting a-peak,
For list, down the inshore curve of the
    creek
    How merrily flutters the sail,—
And lo, in the East! Will the East unveil?
The East is unveiled, the East hath
    confessed   120
A flush: 'tis dead; 'tis alive: 'tis dead, ere
    the West
Was aware of it: nay, 'tis abiding, 'tis
    unwithdrawn:
    Have a care, sweet Heaven! 'Tis Dawn.

Now a dream of a flame through that dream
    of a flush is uprolled:
    To the zenith ascending, a dome of un-
    dazzling gold
Is builded, in shape as a bee-hive, from out
    of the sea:
The hive is of gold undazzling, but oh, the
    Bee,
    The star-fed Bee, the build-fire Bee,
    Of dazzling gold is the great Sun-Bee
That shall flash from the hive-hole over the
    sea.   130

Yet now the dew-drop, now the morn-
    ing gray,
    Shall live their little lucid sober day
    Ere with the sun their souls exhale
    away.
Now in each pettiest personal sphere of dew
The summ'd moon shines complete as in
    the blue
Big dew-drop of all heaven: with these lit
    shrines
O'er-silvered to the farthest sea-confines,
The sacramental marsh one pious plain
Of worship lies. Peace to the ante-reign
Of Mary Morning, blissful mother mild,
Minded of nought but peace, and of a
    child.   141

Not slower than Majesty moves, for a mean
    and a measure
Of motion,—not faster than dateless
    Olympian leisure
Might pace with unblown ample garments
    from pleasure to pleasure,—
The wave-serrate sea-rim sinks unjarring,
    unreeling,
    Forever revealing, revealing, revealing,
Edgewise, bladewise, halfwise, wholewise,
    —'tis done!
           'Good-morrow, lord Sun!
With several voice, with ascription one,
The woods and the marsh and the sea and
    my soul   150
Unto thee, whence the glittering stream of
    all morrows doth roll,
Cry good and past-good and most heavenly
    morrow, lord Sun.

O Artisan born in the purple,—Workman
    Heat,—
Parter of passionate atoms that travail to
    meet,
And be mixed in the death-cold oneness,—
    innermost Guest
At the marriage of elements,—fellow of
    publicans,—blest
King in the blouse of flame, that loiterest
    o'er
The idle skies yet laborest fast ever-
    more,—
Thou, in the fine forge-thunder, thou, in
    the beat
Of the heart of a man, thou Motive,—
    Laborer Heat: 160
Yea, Artist, thou, of whose art yon sea's all
    news,

With his inshore greens and manifold mid-
    sea blues,
Pearl-glint, shell-tint, ancientest perfectest
    hues
Ever shaming the maidens,—lily ahd rose
Confess thee, and each mild flame that
    glows
In the clarified virginal bosoms of stones
    that shine,
              It is thine, it is thine:

Thou chemist of storms, whether driving
    the winds a-swirl
Or a-flicker the subtiler essences polar that
    whirl
In the magnet earth,—yea, thou with a
    storm for a heart,   170
Rent with debate, many-spotted with ques-
    tion, part
From part oft sundered, yet ever a globèd
    light,
Yet ever the artist, ever more large and
    bright
Than the eye of a man may avail of:—mani-
    fold One,
I must pass from the face, I must pass from
    the face of the Sun:
Old Want is awake and agog, every wrinkle
    a-frown;
The worker must pass to his work in the
    terrible town:
But I fear not, nay, and I fear not the thing
    to be done;
    I am strong with the strength of my lord
        the Sun:
How dark, how dark soever the race that
    must needs be run,   180
              I am lit with the Sun.

Oh, never the mast-high run of the seas
    Of traffic shall hide thee,
Never the hell-colored smoke of the
    factories
              Hide thee,
Never the reek of the time's fen-politics
              Hide thee,
And ever my heart through the night shall
    with knowledge abide thee,
And ever by day shall my spirit, as one that
    hath tried thee,
    Labor, at leisure, in art,—till yonder be-
        side thee   190
    My soul shall float, friend Sun,
        The day being done.

1880   1884

IV. THE MARSHES OF GLYNN

GLOOMS of the live-oaks, beautiful-braided
    and woven
With intricate shades of the vines that
    myriad-cloven
    Clamber the forks of the multiform
        boughs,—
             Emerald twilights,—
             Virginal shy lights,
Wrought of the leaves to allure to the whis-
    per of vows,
When lovers pace timidly down through the
    green colonnades
Of the dim sweet woods, of the dear dark
    woods,
    Of the heavenly woods and glades,
That run to the radiant marginal sand-
    beach within   10
    The wide sea-marshes of Glynn;—

Beautiful glooms, soft dusks in the noon-
    day fire,—
Wildwood privacies, closets of lone desire,
Chamber from chamber parted with waver-
    ing arras of leaves,—
Cells for the passionate pleasure of prayer
    to the soul that grieves,
Pure with a sense of the passing of saints
    through the wood,
Cool for the dutiful weighing of ill with
    good;—

O braided dusks of the oak and woven
    shades of the vine,
While the riotous noon-day sun of the June-
    day long did shine
Ye held me fast in your heart and I held you
    fast in mine;   20
But now when the noon is no more, and
    riot is rest,
And the sun is a-wait at the ponderous gate
    of the West,
And the slant yellow beam down the wood-
    aisle doth seem
Like a lane into heaven that leads from a
    dream,—
Ay, now, when my soul all day hath
    drunken the soul of the oak,
And my heart is at ease from men, and the
    wearisome sound of the stroke
    Of the scythe of time and the trowel of
        trade is low,
    And belief overmasters doubt, and I
        know that I know,

And my spirit is grown to a lordly great
   compass within,
That the length and the breadth and the
   sweep of the marshes of Glynn   30
Will work me no fear like the fear they have
   wrought me of yore
When length was fatigue, and when breadth
   was but bitterness sore,
And when terror and shrinking and dreary
   unnamable pain
Drew over me out of the merciless miles of
   the plain,—

Oh, now, unafraid, I am fain to face
   The vast sweet visage of space.
To the edge of the wood I am drawn, I am
   drawn,
Where the gray beach glimmering runs, as
   a belt of the dawn,
   For a mete and a mark
     To the forest-dark:—   40
       So:
Affable live-oak, leaning low,—
Thus—with your favor—soft, with a
   reverent hand,
(Not lightly touching your person, Lord of
   the land!)
Bending your beauty aside, with a step I
   stand
On the firm-packed sand,
       Free
By a world of marsh that borders a world of
   sea.
   Sinuous southward and sinuous north-
    ward the shimmering band
Of the sand-beach fastens the fringe of the
   marsh to the folds of the land.   50
Inward and outward to northward and
   southward the beach-lines linger and
   curl
As a silver-wrought garment that clings to
   and follows the firm sweet limbs of
   a girl.
Vanishing, swerving, evermore curving
   again into sight,
Softly the sand-beach wavers away to a dim
   gray looping of light.
And what if behind me to westward the
   wall of the woods stands high?
The world lies east: how ample, the marsh
   and the sea and the sky!
A league and a league of marsh-grass,
   waist-high, broad in the blade,
Green, and all of a height, and unflecked
   with a light or a shade,

Stretch leisurely off, in a pleasant plain,
To the terminal blue of the main.   60

Oh, what is abroad in the marsh and the
   terminal sea?
   Somehow my soul seems suddenly
   free
From the weighing of fate and the sad discussion of sin,
By the length and the breadth and the
   sweep of the marshes of Glynn.

Ye marshes, how candid and simple and
   nothing-withholding and free
Ye publish yourselves to the sky and offer
   yourselves to the sea!
Tolerant plains, that suffer the sea and the
   rains and the sun,
Ye spread and span like the catholic man
   who hath mightily won
God out of knowledge and good out of infinite pain
And sight out of blindness and purity out
   of a stain.   70

As the marsh-hen secretly builds on the
   watery sod,
Behold I will build me a nest on the greatness of God:
I will fly in the greatness of God as the
   marsh-hen flies
In the freedom that fills all the space 'twixt
   the marsh and the skies:
By so many roots as the marsh-grass sends
   in the sod
I will heartily lay me a-hold on the greatness of God:
Oh, like to the greatness of God is the greatness within
The range of the marshes, the liberal
   marshes of Glynn.

And the sea lends large, as the marsh: lo,
   out of his plenty the sea
Pours fast: full soon the time of the flood-
   tide must be: 80
Look how the grace of the sea doth go
About and about through the intricate
   channels that flow
    Here and there,
       Everywhere,
Till his waters have flooded the uttermost
   creeks and the low-lying lanes,
And the marsh is meshed with a million
   veins,

That like as with rosy and silvery essences
flow
In the rose-and-silver evening glow.
      Farewell, my lord Sun! 89
The creeks overflow: a thousand rivulets run
'Twixt the roots of the sod; the blades of the
marsh-grass stir;
Passeth a hurrying sound of wings that
westward whirr;
Passeth, and all is still; and the currents
cease to run;
And the sea and the marsh are one.

How still the plains of the waters be!
The tide is in his ecstasy;

The tide is at his highest height:
      And it is night.

And now from the Vast of the Lord will the
waters of sleep
Roll in on the souls of men, 100
But who will reveal to our waking ken
The forms that swim and the shapes that
creep
      Under the waters of sleep?
And I would I could know what swimmeth
below when the tide comes in
On the length and the breadth of the
marvelous marshes of Glynn.
1878   1884

GEORGE WASHINGTON CABLE

1844–1925

BELLES DEMOISELLES PLANTATION

THE original grantee was Count——, assume the name to be De Charleu; the old Creoles never forgive a public mention. He was the French king's commissary. One day, called to France to explain the lucky accident of the commissariat having burned down with his account-books inside, he left his wife, a Choctaw Comptesse, behind.

Arrived at court, his excuses were accepted, and that tract granted him where afterwards stood Belles Demoiselles Plantation. A man cannot remember every thing! In a fit of forgetfulness he married a French gentlewoman, rich and beautiful, and 'brought her out.' However, 'All's well that ends well'; a famine had been in the colony, and the Choctaw Comptesse had starved, leaving nought but a half-caste orphan family lurking on the edge of the settlement, bearing our French gentle-woman's own new name, and being mentioned in Monsieur's will.

And the new Comptesse—she tarried but a twelve-month, left Monsieur a lovely son, and departed, led out of this vain world by the swamp-fever.

From this son sprang the proud Creole family of De Charleu. It rose straight up, up, up, generation after generation, tall, branchless, slender, palm-like; and finally, in the time of which I am to tell, flowered

with all the rare beauty of a century-plant, in Artemise, Innocente, Felicité, the twins Marie and Martha, Leontine and little Septima; the seven beautiful daughters for whom their home had been fitly named Belles Demoiselles.

The Count's grant had once been a long Pointe, round which the Mississippi used to whirl, and seethe, and foam, that it was horrid to behold. Big whirlpools would open and wheel about in the savage eddies under the low bank, and close up again, and others open, and spin, and disappear. Great circles of muddy surface would boil up from hundreds of feet below, and gloss over, and seem to float away,—sink, come back again under water, and with only a soft hiss surge up again, and again drift off, and vanish. Every few minutes the loamy bank would tip down a great load of earth upon its besieger, and fall back a foot,—sometimes a yard,—and the writhing river would press after, until at last the Pointe was quite swallowed up, and the great river glided by in a majestic curve, and asked no more; the bank stood fast, the 'caving' became a forgotten misfortune, and the diminished grant was a long, sweeping, willowy bend, rustling with miles of sugar-cane.

Coming up the Mississippi in the sailing craft of those early days, about the time one first could descry the white spires of the old St. Louis Cathedral, you would be pretty sure to spy, just over to your right under the levee, Belles Demoiselles Mansion, with its broad veranda and red painted cypress roof, peering over the embankment, like a bird in the nest, half hid by the avenue of willows which one of the departed De Charleus,—he that married a Marot,—had planted on the levee's crown.

The house stood unusually near the river, facing eastward, and standing four-square, with an immense veranda about its sides, and a flight of steps in front spreading broadly downward, as we open arms to a child. From the veranda nine miles of river were seen; and in their compass, near at hand, the shady garden full of rare and beautiful flowers; farther away broad fields of cane and rice, and the distant quarters of the slaves, and on the horizon everywhere a dark belt of cypress forest.

The master was old Colonel De Charleu, —Jean Albert Henri Joseph De Charleu-Marot, and 'Colonel' by the grace of the first American governor. Monsieur,—he would not speak to any one who called him 'Colonel,'—was a hoary-headed patriarch. His step was firm, his form erect, his intellect strong and clear, his countenance classic, serene, dignified, commanding, his manners courtly, his voice musical,—fascinating. He had had his vices,—all his life; but had borne them, as his race do, with a serenity of conscience and a cleanness of mouth that left no outward blemish on the surface of the gentleman. He had gambled in Royal Street, drunk hard in Orleans Street, run his adversary through in the duelling-ground at Slaughter-house Point, and danced and quarrelled at the St. Philippe-street-theatre quadroon balls. Even now, with all his courtesy and bounty, and a hospitality which seemed to be entertaining angels, he was bitter-proud and penurious, and deep down in his hard-finished heart loved nothing but himself, his name, and his motherless children. But these!— their ravishing beauty was all but excuse enough for the unbounded idolatry of their father. Against these seven goddesses he never rebelled. Had they even required him to defraud old De Carlos—

I can hardly say.

Old De Carlos was his extremely distant relative on the Choctaw side. With this single exception, the narrow thread-like line of descent from the Indian wife, diminished to a mere strand by injudicious alliances, and deaths in the gutters of old New Orleans, was extinct. The name, by Spanish contact, had become De Carlos; but this one surviving bearer of it was known to all, and known only, as Injin Charlie.

One thing I never knew a Creole to do. He will not utterly go back on the ties of blood, no matter what sort of knots those ties may be. For one reason, he is never ashamed of his or his father's sins; and for another,—he will tell you—he is 'all heart!'

So the different heirs of the De Charleu estate had always strictly regarded the rights and interests of the De Carloses, especially their ownership of a block of dilapidated buildings in a part of the city, which had once been very poor property, but was beginning to be valuable. This block had much more than maintained the last De Carlos through a long and lazy lifetime, and, as his household consisted only of himself, and an aged and crippled negress, the inference was irresistible that he 'had money.' Old Charlie, though by alias an 'Injin,' was plainly a dark white man, about as old as Colonel De Charleu, sunk in the bliss of deep ignorance, shrewd, deaf, and, by repute at least, unmerciful.

The Colonel and he always conversed in English. This rare accomplishment, which the former had learned from his Scotch wife,—the latter from up-river traders,— they found an admirable medium of communication, answering, better than French could, a similar purpose to that of the stick which we fasten to the bit of one horse and breast-gear of another, whereby each keeps his distance. Once in a while, too, by way of jest, English found its way among the ladies of Belles Demoiselles, always signifying that their sire was about to have business with old Charlie.

Now a long-standing wish to buy out Charlie troubled the Colonel. He had no desire to oust him unfairly; he was proud of being always fair; yet he did long to engross the whole estate under one title. Out of his luxurious idleness he had conceived this desire, and thought little of so slight an obstacle as being already somewhat in debt to old Charlie for money borrowed, and for which Belles Demoiselles was, of course, good, ten times over. Lots, buildings, rents, all, might as well be his, he thought, to give, keep, or destroy. 'Had he but the old man's heritage. Ah! he might bring that into existence which his *belles demoiselles* had been begging for, "since many years;" a home,—and such a home,—in the gay city. Here he should tear down this row of cottages, and make his garden wall; there that long rope-walk should give place to vine-covered arbors; the bakery yonder should make way for a costly conservatory; that wine warehouse should come down, and the mansion go up. It should be the finest in the state. Men should never pass it, but they should say—"the palace of the De Charleus; a family of grand descent, a people of elegance and bounty, a line as old as France, a fine old man, and seven daughters as beautiful as happy; whoever dare attempt to marry there must leave his own name behind him!"

'The house should be of stones fitly set, brought down in ships from the land of "les Yankees," and it should have an airy belvedere, with a gilded image tip-toeing and shining on its peak, and from it you should see, far across the gleaming folds of the river, the red roof of Belles Demoiselles, the country-seat. At the big stone gate there should be a porter's lodge, and it should be a privilege even to see the ground.'

Truly they were a family fine enough, and fancy-free enough to have fine wishes, yet happy enough where they were, to have had no wish but to live there always.

To those, who, by whatever fortune, wandered into the garden of Belles Demoiselles some summer afternoon as the sky was reddening towards evening, it was lovely to see the family gathered out upon the tiled pavement at the foot of the broad front steps, gayly chatting and jesting, with that ripple of laughter that comes so pleasingly from a bevy of girls. The father would be found seated in their midst, the centre of attention and compliment, witness, arbiter, umpire, critic, by his beautiful children's unanimous appointment, but the single vassal, too, of seven absolute sovereigns.

Now they would draw their chairs near together in eager discussion of some new step in the dance, or the adjustment of some rich adornment. Now they would start about him with excited comments to see the eldest fix a bunch of violets in his button-hole. Now the twins would move down a walk after some unusual flower, and be greeted on their return with the high-pitched notes of delighted feminine surprise.

As evening came on they would draw more quietly about their paternal centre. Often their chairs were forsaken, and they grouped themselves on the lower steps, one above another, and surrendered themselves to the tender influences of the approaching night. At such an hour the passer on the river, already attracted by the dark figures of the broad-roofed mansion, and its woody garden standing against the glowing sunset, would hear the voices of the hidden group rise from the spot in the soft harmonies of an evening song; swelling clearer and clearer as the thrill of music warmed them into feeling, and presently joined by the deeper tones of the father's voice; then, as the daylight passed quite away, all would be still, and he would know that the beautiful home had gathered its nestlings under its wings.

And yet, for mere vagary, it pleased them not to be pleased.

'Arti!' called one sister to another in the broad hall, one morning,—mock amazement in her distended eyes,—'something is goin' to took place!'

'*Comm-e-n-t?*'—long-drawn perplexity.

'Papa is goin' to town!'

The news passed up stairs.

'Inno!'—one to another meeting in a doorway,—'something is goin' to took place!'

'*Qu'est-ce-que c'est!*'—vain attempt at gruffness.

'Papa is goin' to town!'

The unusual tidings were true. It was afternoon of the same day that the Colonel tossed his horse's bridle to his groom, and stepped up to old Charlie, who was sitting on his bench under a China-tree, his head as was his fashion, bound in a Madras handkerchief. The 'old man' was plainly under the effect of spirits, and smiled a deferential salutation without trusting himself to his feet.

'Eh, well Charlie!'—the Colonel raised his voice to suit his kinsman's deafness,—'how is those times with my friend Charlie?'

'Eh?' said Charlie, distractedly.

'Is that goin' well with my friend Charlie?'

'In de house,—call her,'—making a pretence of rising.

'Non, non! I don't want,' the speaker paused to breathe—' 'ow is collection?'

'Oh!' said Charlie, 'every day he make me more poorer!'

'What do you hask for it?' asked the planter indifferently, designating the house by a wave of his whip.

'Ask for w'at?' said Injin Charlie.

'De house! What you ask for it?'

'I don't believe,' said Charlie.

'What you would take for it!' cried the planter.

'Wait for w'at?'

'What you would take for the whole block?'

'I don't want to sell him!'

'I'll give you ten thousand dollah for it.'

'Ten t'ousand dollah for dis house? Oh, no, dat is no price. He is blame good old house,—dat old house.' (Old Charlie and the Colonel never swore in presence of each other.) 'Forty year dat old house didn't had to be paint! I easy can get fifty t'ousand dollah for dat old house.'

'Fifty thousand picayunes; yes,' said the Colonel.

'She's a good house. Can make plenty money,' pursued the deaf man.

'That's what make you so rich, eh, Charlie?'

'Non, I don't make nothing. Too blame clever, me, dat's de troub'. She's a good house,—make money fast like a steamboat, —make a barrel full in a week! Me, I lose money all de days. Too blame clever.'

'Charlie!'

'Eh?'

'Tell me what you'll take.'

'Make? I don't make nothing. Too blame clever.'

'What will you take?'

'Oh! I got enough already,—half drunk now.'

'What will you take for the 'ouse?'

'You want to buy her?'

'I don't know,'—(shrug),—'maybe,—if you sell it cheap.'

'She's a bully old house.'

There was a long silence. By and by old Charlie commenced—

'Old Injin Charlie is a low-down dog.'

'C'est vrai, oui!' retorted the Colonel in an undertone.

'He's got Injin blood in him.'

The Colonel nodded assent.

'But he's got some blame good blood, too, ain't it?'

The Colonel nodded impatiently.

'Bien! Old Charlie's Injin blood says, "sell de house, Charlie, you blame old fool!" Mais, old Charlie's good blood says, "Charlie! if you sell dat old house, Charlie, you low-down old dog, Charlie, what de Compte De Charleu make for you grace-granmuzzer, de dev' can eat you, Charlie, I don't care." '

'But you'll sell it anyhow, won't you, old man?'

'No!' And the no rumbled off in muttered oaths like thunder out on the Gulf. The incensed old Colonel wheeled and started off.

'Curl!' (Colonel) said Charlie, standing up unsteadily.

The planter turned with an inquiring frown.

'I'll trade with you!' said Charlie.

The Colonel was tempted. ' 'Ow'l you trade?' he asked.

'My house for yours!'

The old Colonel turned pale with anger. He walked very quickly back, and came close up to his kinsman.

'Charlie!' he said.

'Injin Charlie,'—with a tipsy nod.

But by this time self-control was returning. 'Sell Belles Demoiselles to you?' he said in a high key, and then laughed 'Ho, ho, ho!' and rode away.

A cloud, but not a dark one, overshadowed the spirits of Belles Demoiselles' plantation. The old master, whose beaming presence had always made him a shining Saturn, spinning and sparkling within the bright circle of his daughters, fell into musing fits, started out of frowning reveries, walked often by himself, and heard business from his overseer fretfully.

No wonder. The daughters knew his closeness in trade, and attributed to it his failure to negotiate for the Old Charlie buildings,—so to call them. They began to depreciate Belles Demoiselles. If a north wind blew, it was too cold to ride. If a shower had fallen, it was too muddy to drive. In the morning the garden was wet.

In the evening the grasshopper was a burden. *Ennui* was turned into capital; every
headache was interpreted a premonition of
ague; and when the native exuberance of a
flock of ladies without a want or a care burst
out in laughter in the father's face, they
spread their French eyes, rolled up their
little hands, and with rigid wrists and mock
vehemence vowed and vowed again that
they only laughed at their misery, and
should pine to death unless they could
move to the sweet city. 'Oh! the theatre!
Oh! Orleans Street! Oh! the masquerade!
the Place d'Armes! the ball!' and they would
call upon Heaven with French irreverence,
and fall into each other's arms, and whirl
down the hall singing a waltz, end with a
grand collision and fall, and, their eyes
streaming merriment, lay the blame on the
slippery floor, that would some day be the
death of the whole seven.

Three times more the fond father, thus
goaded, managed, by accident,—business
accident,—to see old Charlie and increase
his offer; but in vain. He finally went to him
formally.

'Eh?' said the deaf and distant relative.
'For what you want him, eh? Why you don't
stay where you halways be 'appy? Dis is a
blame old rat-hole,—good for old Injin
Charlie,—da's all. Why you don't stay
where you be halways 'appy? Why you
don't buy somewheres else?'

'That's none of your business,' snapped
the planter. Truth was, his reasons were
unsatisfactory even to himself.

A sullen silence followed. Then Charlie
spoke:

'Well, now, look here; I sell you old Charlie's house.'

'*Bien!* and the whole block,' said the
Colonel.

'Hold on,' said Charlie. 'I sell you de
'ouse and de block. Den I go and git drunk,
and go to sleep; de dev' comes along and
says, "Charlie! old Charlie, you blame low-
down old dog, wake up! What you doin'
here? Where's de 'ouse what Monsieur le
Compte give your grace-gran-muzzer?
Don't you see dat fine gentyman, De Charleu, done gone and tore him down and make
him over new, you blame old fool, Charlie,
you low-down old Injin dog!" '

'I'll give you forty thousand dollars,' said
the Colonel.

'For de 'ouse?'

'For all.'

The deaf man shook his head.

'Forty-five!' said the Colonel.

'What a lie? For what you tell me "What
a lie?" I don't tell you no lie.'

'*Non, non!* I give you *forty-five!*' shouted
the Colonel.

Charlie shook his head again.

'Fifty!'

He shook it again.

The figures rose and rose to—

'Seventy-five!'

The answer was an invitation to go away
and let the owner alone, as he was, in certain specified respects, the vilest of living
creatures, and no company for a fine gentyman.

The 'fine gentyman' longed to blas-
pheme,—but before old Charlie!—in the
name of pride, how could he? He mounted
and started away.

'Tell you what I'll make wid you,' said
Charlie.

The other, guessing aright, turned back
without dismounting, smiling.

'How much Belles Demoiselles hoes me
now?' asked the deaf one.

'One hundred and eighty thousand dollars,' said the Colonel, firmly.

'Yass,' said Charlie. 'I don't want Belles
Demoiselles.'

The old Colonel's quiet laugh intimated
it made no difference either way.

'But me,' continued Charlie, 'me,—I'm
got le Compte De Charleu's blood in me,
any'ow,—a litt' bit, any'ow, ain't it?'

The Colonel nodded that it was.

'*Bien!* If I go out of dis place and don't
go to Belles Demoiselles, de peoples will
say,—dey will say, "Old Charlie he been
all doze time tell a blame *lie!* He ain't no
kin to his old grace-gran-muzzer, not a
blame bit! He don't got nary drop of De
Charleu blood to save his blame low-down
old Injin soul!" No, sare! What I want
wid money, den? No, sare! My place for
yours!'

He turned to go into the house, just too
soon to see the Colonel make an ugly whisk
at him with his riding-whip. Then the
Colonel, too, moved off.

Two or three times over, as he ambled
homeward, laughter broke through his annoyance, as he recalled old Charlie's family

pride and the presumption of his offer. Yet each time he could but think better of—not the offer to swap, but the preposterous ancestral loyalty. It was so much better than he could have expected from his 'low-down' relative, and not unlike his own whim withal—the proposition which went with it was forgiven.

This last defeat bore so harshly on the master of Belles Demoiselles, that the daughters, reading chagrin in his face, began to repent. They loved their father as daughters can, and when they saw their pretended dejection harassing him seriously they restrained their complaints, displayed more than ordinary tenderness, and heroically and ostentatiously concluded there was no place like Belles Demoiselles. But the new mood touched him more than the old, and only refined his discontent. Here was a man, rich without the care of riches, free from any real trouble, happiness as native to his house as perfume to his garden, deliberately, as it were with premeditated malice, taking joy by the shoulder and bidding her be gone to town, whither he might easily have followed, only that the very same ancestral nonsense that kept Injin Charlie from selling the old place for twice its value prevented him from choosing any other spot for a city home.

But by and by the charm of nature and the merry hearts around him prevailed; the fit of exalted sulks passed off, and after a while the year flared up at Christmas, flickered, and went out.

New Year came and passed; the beautiful garden of Belles Demoiselles put on its spring attire; the seven fair sisters moved from rose to rose; the cloud of discontent had warmed into invisible vapor in the rich sunlight of family affection, and on the common memory the only scar of last year's wound was old Charlie's sheer impertinence in crossing the caprice of the De Charleus. The cup of gladness seemed to fill with the filling of the river.

How high that river was! Its tremendous current rolled and tumbled and spun along, hustling the long funeral flotillas of drift,— and how near shore it came! Men were out day and night, watching the levee. On windy nights even the old Colonel took part, and grew light-hearted with occupation and excitement, as every minute the river threw a white arm over the levee's top, as though it would vault over. But all held fast, and, as the summer drifted in, the water sunk down into its banks and looked quite incapable of harm.

On a summer afternoon of uncommon mildness, old Colonel Jean Albert Henri Joseph De Charleu-Marot, being in a mood for revery, slipped the custody of his feminine rulers and sought the crown of the levee, where it was his wont to promenade. Presently he sat upon a stone bench,—a favorite seat. Before him lay his broad-spread fields; near by, his lordly mansion; and being still,—perhaps by female contact,—somewhat sentimental, he fell to musing on his past. It was hardly worthy to be proud of. All its morning was reddened with mad frolic, and far toward the meridian it was marred with elegant rioting. Pride had kept him well-nigh useless, and despised the honors won by valor; gaming had dimmed prosperity; death had taken his heavenly wife; voluptuous ease had mortgaged his lands; and yet his house still stood, his sweet-smelling fields were still fruitful, his name was fame enough; and yonder and yonder, among the trees and flowers, like angels walking in Eden, were the seven goddesses of his only worship.

Just then a slight sound behind him brought him to his feet. He cast his eyes anxiously to the outer edge of the little strip of bank between the levee's base and the river. There was nothing visible. He paused, with his ear toward the water, his face full of frightened expectation. Ha! There came a single plashing sound, like some great beast slipping into the river, and little waves in a wide semi-circle came out from under the bank and spread over the water!

'My God!'

He plunged down the levee and bounded through the low weeds to the edge of the bank. It was sheer, and the water about four feet below. He did not stand quite on the edge, but fell upon his knees a couple of yards away, wringing his hands, moaning and weeping, and staring through his watery eyes at a fine, long crevice just discernible under the matted grass, and curving outward on either hand toward the river.

'My God!' he sobbed aloud; 'my God!' and even while he called, his God answered: the tough Bermuda grass stretched and snapped, the crevice slowly became a gape, and softly, gradually, with no sound but the closing of the water at last, a ton or more of earth settled into the boiling eddy and disappeared.

At the same instant a pulse of the breeze brought from the garden behind, the joyous, thoughtless laughter of the fair mistresses of Belles Demoiselles.

The old Colonel sprang up and clambered over the levee. Then forcing himself to a more composed movement, he hastened into the house and ordered his horse.

'Tell my children to make merry while I am gone,' he left word. 'I shall be back to-night,' and the horse's hoofs clattered down a by-road leading to the city.

'Charlie,' said the planter, riding up to a window, from which the old man's nightcap was thrust out, 'what you say, Charlie, —my house for yours, eh, Charlie—what you say?'

'Ello!' said Charlie; 'from where you come from dis time of to-night?'

'I come from the Exchange in St. Louis Street.' (A small fraction of the truth.)

'What you want?' said matter-of-fact Charlie.

'I come to trade.'

The low-down relative drew the worsted off his ears. 'Oh! yass,' he said with an uncertain air.

'Well, old man Charlie, what you say: my house for yours,—like you said,—eh, Charlie?'

'I dunno,' said Charlie; 'it's nearly mine now. Why you don't stay dare youse'f?'

'Because I don't want!' said the Colonel savagely. 'Is dat reason enough for you? You better take me in de notion, old man, I tell you,—yes!'

Charlie never winced; but how his answer delighted the Colonel! Quoth Charlie:

'I don't care—I take him!—mais, possession give right off.'

'Not the whole plantation, Charlie; only'—

'I don't care,' said Charlie; 'we easy can fix dat. Mais, what for you don't want to keep him? I don't want him. You better keep him.'

'Don't you try to make no fool of me, old man,' cried the planter.

'Oh, no!' said the other. 'Oh, no! but you make a fool of yourself, ain't it?'

The dumbfounded Colonel stared; Charlie went on:

'Yass! Belles Demoiselles is more wort' dan tree block like dis one. I pass by dare since two weeks. Oh, pritty Belles Demoiselles! De cane was wave in de wind, de garden smell like a bouquet, de white-cap was jump up and down on de river; seven belles demoiselles was ridin' on horses. "Pritty, pritty, pritty!" says old Charlie. Ah! Monsieur le père, 'ow 'appy, 'appy, 'appy!

'Yass!' he continued—the Colonel still staring—'le Compte De Charleu have two familie. One was low-down Choctaw, one was high up noblesse. He gave the low-down Choctaw dis old rat-hole; he give Belles Demoiselles to you gran-fozzer; and now you don't be satisfait. What I'll do wid Belles Demoiselles? She'll break me in two years, yass. And what you'll do wid old Charlie's house, eh? You'll tear her down and make you'se'f a blame old fool. I rather wouldn't trade!'

The planter caught a big breathful of anger, but Charlie went straight on:

'I rather wouldn't, mais I will do it for you;—just the same, like Monsieur le Compte would say, "Charlie, you old fool, I want to shange houses wid you."'

So long as the Colonel suspected irony he was angry, but as Charlie seemed, after all, to be certainly in earnest, he began to feel conscience-stricken. He was by no means a tender man, but his lately-discovered misfortune had unhinged him, and this strange, undeserved, disinterested family fealty on the part of Charlie touched his heart. And should he still try to lead him into the pitfall he had dug? He hesitated;—no, he would show him the place by broad daylight, and if he chose to overlook the 'caving bank,' it would be his own fault;—a trade's a trade.

'Come,' said the planter, 'come at my house to-night; to-morrow we look at the place before breakfast, and finish the trade.'

'For what?' said Charlie.

'Oh, because I got to come in town in the morning.'

'I don't want,' said Charlie. 'How I'm goin' to come dere?'

'I git you a horse at the liberty stable.'

'Well—anyhow—I don't care—I'll go.'
And they went.

When they had ridden a long time, and were on the road darkened by hedges of Cherokee rose, the Colonel called behind him to the 'low-down' scion:

'Keep the road, old man.'

'Eh?'

'Keep the road.'

'Oh, yes; all right; I keep my word; we don't goin' to play no tricks, eh?'

But the Colonel seemed not to hear. His ungenerous design was beginning to be hateful to him. Not only old Charlie's unprovoked goodness was prevailing; the eulogy on Belles Demoiselles had stirred the depths of an intense love for his beautiful home. True, if he held to it, the caving of the bank, at its present fearful speed, would let the house into the river within three months; but were it not better to lose it so, than sell his birthright? Again,—coming back to the first thought,—to betray his own blood! It was only Injin Charlie; but had not the De Charleu blood just spoken out in him? Unconsciously he groaned.

After a time they struck a path approaching the plantation in the rear, and a little after, passing from behind a clump of live-oaks, they came in sight of the villa. It looked so like a gem, shining through its dark grove, so like a great glow-worm in the dense foliage, so significant of luxury and gayety, that the poor master, from an overflowing heart, groaned again.

'What?' asked Charlie.

The Colonel only drew his rein, and, dismounting mechanically, contemplated the sight before him. The high, arched doors and windows were thrown wide to the summer air; from every opening the bright light of numerous candelabra darted out upon the sparkling foliage of magnolia and bay, and here and there in the spacious verandas a colored lantern swayed in the gentle breeze. A sound of revel fell on the ear, the music of harps; and across one window, brighter than the rest, flitted, once or twice, the shadows of dancers. But oh! the shadows flitting across the heart of the fair mansion's master!

'Old Charlie,' said he, gazing fondly at his house, 'You and me is both old, eh?'

'Yaas,' said the stolid Charlie.

'And we has both been bad enough in our time, eh, Charlie?'

Charlie, surprised at the tender tone, repeated 'Yaas.'

'And you and me is mighty close?'

'Blame close, yaas.'

'But you never know me to cheat, old man!'

'No,'—impassively.

'And do you think I would cheat you now?'

'I dunno,' said Charlie. 'I don't believe.'

'Well, old man, old man,'—his voice began to quiver,—'I sha'n't cheat you now.. My God!—old man, I tell you—you better not make the trade!'

'Because for what?' asked Charlie in plain anger; but both looked quickly toward the house! The Colonel tossed his hands wildly in the air, rushed forward a step or two, and giving one fearful scream of agony and fright, fell forward on his face in the path. Old Charlie stood transfixed with horror. Belles Demoiselles, the realm of maiden beauty, the home of merriment, the house of dancing, all in the tremor and glow of pleasure, suddenly sunk, with one short, wild wail of terror—sunk, sunk, down, down, down, into the merciless, unfathomable flood of the Mississippi.

Twelve long months were midnight to the mind of the childless father; when they were only half gone, he took his bed; and every day, and every night, old Charlie, the 'low-down,' the 'fool,' watched him tenderly, tended him lovingly, for the sake of his name, his misfortunes, and his broken heart. No woman's step crossed the floor of the sick-chamber, whose western dormer-windows overpeered the dingy architecture of old Charlie's block; Charlie and a skilled physician, the one all interest, the other all gentleness, hope, and patience—these only entered by the door; but by the window came in a sweet-scented evergreen vine, transplanted from the caving bank of Belles Demoiselles. It caught the rays of sunset in its flowery net and let them softly in upon the sick man's bed; gathered the glancing beams of the moon at midnight, and often wakened the sleeper to look, with his mindless eyes, upon their pretty silver fragments strewn upon the floor.

By and by there seemed—there was—a

twinkling dawn of returning reason. Slowly, peacefully, with an increase unseen from day to day, the light of reason came into the eyes, and speech became coherent; but withal there came a failing of the wrecked body, and the doctor said that monsieur was both better and worse.

One evening, as Charlie sat by the vine-clad window with his fireless pipe in his hand, the old Colonel's eyes fell full upon his own, and rested there.

'Charl—,' he said with an effort, and his delighted nurse hastened to the bedside and bowed his best ear. There was an unsuccessful effort or two, and then he whispered, smiling with sweet sadness,—

'We didn't trade.'

The truth, in this case, was a secondary matter to Charlie; the main point was to give a pleasing answer. So he nodded his head decidedly, as who should say—'Oh yes, we did, it was a bona-fide swap!' but when he saw the smile vanish, he tried the other expedient and shook his head with still more vigor, to signify that they had not so much as approached a bargain; and the smile returned.

Charlie wanted to see the vine recognized. He stepped backward to the window

with a broad smile, shook the foliage, nodded and looked smart.

'I know,' said the Colonel, with beaming eyes, '—many weeks.'

The next day—

'Charl—'

The best ear went down.

'Send for a priest.'

The priest came, and was alone with him a whole afternoon. When he left, the patient was very haggard and exhausted, but smiled and would not suffer the crucifix to be removed from his breast.

One more morning came. Just before dawn Charlie, lying on a pallet in the room, thought he was called, and came to the bedside.

'Old man,' whispered the failing invalid, 'is it caving yet?'

Charlie nodded.

'It won't pay you out.'

'Oh, dat makes not'ing,' said Charlie. Two big tears rolled down his brown face. 'Dat makes not'in'.'

The Colonel whispered once more:

Mes belles demoiselles! in paradise;—in the garden—I shall be with them at sunrise;' and so it was.

1879

JOEL CHANDLER HARRIS

1848–1908

FROM UNCLE REMUS

UNCLE REMUS INITIATES THE LITTLE BOY[1]

ONE evening recently, the lady whom Uncle Remus calls 'Miss Sally' missed her little seven-year-old. Making search for him through the house and through the yard, she heard the sound of voices in the old man's cabin, and, looking through the win-

dow, saw the child sitting by Uncle Remus. His head rested against the old man's arm, and he was gazing with an expression of the most intense interest into the rough, weather-beaten face, that beamed so kindly upon him. This is what 'Miss Sally' heard:

'Bimeby, one day, arter Brer Fox bin doin' all dat he could fer ter ketch Brer Rabbit, en Brer Rabbit bin doin' all he could fer to keep 'im fum it, Brer Fox say to hisse'f dat he'd put up a game on Brer

[1] The selections are Chapters 1, 2, and 4 from the revised version of *Uncle Remus: His Songs and Sayings* (N.Y., 1925). In his introduction to the collection, Harris wrote: 'I am advised by my publishers that this book is to be included in their catalogue of humorous publications, and this friendly warning gives me an opportunity to say that however humorous it may be in effect, its intention is perfectly serious; and, even if it were otherwise, it seems to me that a volume written wholly in dialect must have its solemn, not to say melancholy, features. With respect to the Folk-Lore series, my purpose has been to preserve the legends

themselves in their original simplicity, and to wed them permanently to the quaint dialect—if, indeed, it can be called a dialect—through the medium of which they have become a part of the domestic history of every Southern family; and I have endeavored to give to the whole a genuine flavor of the old plantation.

'Each legend has its variants, but in every instance I have retained that particular version which seemed to me to be the most characteristic, and have given it without embellishment and without exaggeration.' Ibid., vii.

Rabbit, en' he ain't mo'n got de wuds out'n his mouf twel Brer Rabbit come a lopin' up de big road, lookin' des ez plump, en ez fat, en ez sassy ez a Moggin hoss in a barley-patch.

' "Hol' on dar, Brer Rabbit," sez Brer Fox, sezee.

' "I ain't got time, Brer Fox," sez Brer Rabbit, sezee, sorter mendin' his licks.

' "I wanter have some confab wid you, Brer Rabbit," sez Brer Fox, sezee.

' "All right, Brer Fox, but you better holler fum whar you stan'. I'm monstus full er fleas dis mawnin'," sez Brer Rabbit, sezee.

' "I seed Brer B'ar yistiddy," sez Brer Fox, sezee, "en he sorter rake me over de coals kaze you en me ain't make frens en live naberly, en I told 'im dat I'd see you."

'Den Brer Rabbit scratch one year wid his off hinefoot sorter jub'usly, en den he ups en sez, sezee:

' "All a settin', Brer Fox. Spose'n you drap roun' ter-morrer en take dinner wid me. We ain't got no great doin's at our house, but I speck de old 'oman en de chilluns kin sorter scramble roun' en git up sump'n fer ter stay yo' stummuck."

' "I'm 'gree'ble, Brer Rabbit," sez Brer Fox, sezee.

' "Den I'll 'pen' on you," sez Brer Rabbit, sezee.

'Nex' day, Mr. Rabbit an' Miss Rabbit got up soon, 'fo' day, en raided on a gyarden like Miss Sally's out dar, en got some cabbiges, en some roas'n years, en some sparrer-grass, en dey fixed up a smashin' dinner. Bimeby one er de little Rabbits, playin' out in de backyard, come runnin' in hollerin', "Oh, ma! oh, ma! I seed Mr. Fox a comin'!" En den Brer Rabbit he tuck de chilluns by der years en made um set down, en den him and Miss Rabbit sorter dally roun' waitin' for Brer Fox. En dey keep on waitin', but no Brer Fox ain't come. Atter 'while Brer Rabbit goes to de do', easy like, en peep out, en dar, stickin' fum behime de cornder, wuz de tip-een' er Brer Fox tail. Den Brer Rabbit shot de do' en sot down, en put his paws behime his years en begin fer ter sing:

' "De place wharbouts you spill de grease,
Right dar youer boun' ter slide,
An' whar you fine a bunch er ha'r,
You'll shoiy fine de hide."

'Nex' day, Brer Fox sont word by Mr. Mink an' skuze hisse'f kaze he wuz too sick fer ter come, en he ax Brer Rabbit fer to come en take dinner wid him, en Brer Rabbit say he wuz 'gree'ble.

'Bimeby, w'en de shadders wuz at der shortes', Brer Rabbit he sorter brush up en santer down ter Brer Fox's house, en w'en he got dar, he hear somebody groanin', en he look in de do' en dar he see Brer Fox settin' up in a rockin' cheer all wrop up wid flannil, en he look mighty weak. Brer Rabbit look all 'roun', he did, but he ain't see no dinner. De dish-pan wuz settin' on de table, en close by wuz a kyarvin' knife.

' "Look like you gwineter have chicken fer dinner, Brer Fox," sez Brer Rabbit, sezee.

' "Yes, Brer Rabbit, deyer nice, en fresh, en tender," sez Brer Fox, sezee.

'Den Brer Rabbit sorter pull his mustarsh, en say: "You ain't got no calamus root, is you, Brer Fox? I done got so now dat I can't eat no chicken 'ceppin she's seasoned up wid calamus root." En wid dat Brer Rabbit lipt out er de do' and dodge 'mong de bushes, en sot dar watchin' fer Brer Fox; en he ain't watch long, nudder, kaze Brer Fox flung off de flannil en crope out er de house en got whar he could cloze in on Brer Rabbit, en bimeby Brer Rabbit holler out: "Oh, Brer Fox! I'll des put yo' calamus root out yer on dis yer stump. Better come git it while hit's fresh," and wid dat Brer Rabbit gallop off home. En Brer Fox ain't never kotch 'im yit, en w'at's mo', honey, he ain't gwineter.'

THE WONDERFUL TAR-BABY STORY

'DIDN'T the fox *never* catch the rabbit, Uncle Remus?' asked the little boy the next evening.

'He come mighty nigh it, honey, sho's you born—Brer Fox did. One day atter Brer Rabbit fool 'im wid dat calamus root, Brer Fox went ter wuk en got 'im some tar, en mix it wid some turkentime, en fix up a contrapshun wat he call a Tar-Baby, en he tuck dish yer Tar-Baby en he sot 'er in de big road, en den he lay off in de bushes fer to see wat de news wuz gwineter be. En he didn't hatter wait long, nudder, kaze bimeby here come Brer Rabbit pacin' down

de road—lippity-clippity, clippity-lippity—
dez ez sassy ez a jay-bird. Brer Fox, he
lay low. Brer Rabbit come prancin' 'long
twel he spy de Tar-Baby, en den he fotch
up on his behime legs like he wuz 'ston-
ished. De Tar-Baby, she sot dar, she did, en
Brer Fox, he lay low.

' "Mawnin'!" sez Brer Rabbit, sezee.
"Nice wedder dis mawnin'," sezee.

'Tar-Baby ,ain't sayin' nothin', en Brer
Fox, he lay low.

' "How duz yo' sym'tums seem ter
segashuate?" sez Brer Rabbit, sezee.

'Brer Fox, he wink his eye slow, en lay
low, en de Tar-Baby, she ain't saying
nothin'.

' "How you come on, den? Is you deaf?"
sez Brer Rabbit, sezee. "Kaze if you is, I
kin holler louder," sezee.

'Tar-Baby stay still, en Brer Fox, he lay
low.

' "Youer stuck up, dat's w'at you is,"
says Brer Rabbit, sezee, "en I'm gwineter
kyore you, dat's w'at I'm a gwineter do,"
sezee.

'Brer Fox, he sorter chuckle in his stummuck, he did, but Tar-Baby ain't sayin'
nothin'.

' "I'm gwineter larn you howter talk ter
'specttubble fokes ef hit's de las' ack," sez
Brer Rabbit, sezee. "Ef you don't take off
dat hat en tell me howdy, I'm gwineter bus'
you wide open," sezee.

'Tar-Baby stay still, en Brer Fox, he lay
low.

'Brer Rabbit keep on axin' 'im, en de
Tar-Baby she keep on sayin' nothin', twel
present'y Brer Rabbit draw back wid his
fis', he did, en blip he tuck 'er side er de
head. Right dar's whar he broke his mer-
lasses jug. His fis' stuck, en he can't pull
loose. De tar hilt 'im. But Tar-Baby, she
stay still, en Brer Fox, he lay low.

' "Ef you don't lemme loose, I'll knock
you agin," sez Brer Rabbit, sezee, en wid
dat he fotch 'er a wipe wid de udder han',
en dat stuck. Tar-Baby, she ain't sayin'
nothin', en Brer Fox, he lay low.

' "Tu'n me loose, fo' I kick de natal
stuffin' outen you," sez Brer Rabbit, sezee,
but de Tar-Baby, she ain't sayin' nothin'.
She des hilt on, en den Brer Rabbit lose de
use er his feet in de same way. Brer Fox, he
lay low. Den Brer Rabbit squall out dat ef
de Tar-Baby don't tu'n 'im loose he butt

'er cranksided. En den he butted, en his head
got stuck. Den Brer Fox, he sa'ntered fort',
lookin' des ez innercent ez one er yo'
mammy's mockin' birds.

' "Howdy, Brer Rabbit," sez Brer Fox,
sezee. "You look sorter stuck up dis
mawnin'," sezee, en den he rolled on de
groun', en laughed en laughed twel he
couldn't laugh no mo'. "I speck you'll take
dinner wid me dis time, Brer Rabbit. I done
laid in some calamus root, en I ain't gwineter take no skuse," sez Brer Fox, sezee.'

Here Uncle Remus paused, and drew a
two-pound yam out of the ashes.

'Did the fox eat the rabbit?' asked the
little boy to whom the story had been
told.

'Dat's all de fur de tale goes,' replied the
old man. 'He mout, en den agin he mout-
ent. Some say Jedge B'ar come 'long en
loosed 'im—some say he didn't. I hear
Miss Sally callin'. You better run 'long.'

HOW MR. RABBIT WAS TOO SHARP FOR MR. FOX

'UNCLE REMUS,' said the little boy one evening, when he had found the old man with
little or nothing to do, 'did the fox kill and
eat the rabbit when he caught him with the
Tar-Baby?'

'Law, honey, ain't I tell you 'bout dat?'
replied the old darkey, chuckling slyly. 'I
'clar ter grashus I ought er tole you dat, but
old man Nod wuz ridin' on my eyeleds
'twel a leetle mo'n I'd a dis'member'd my
own name, en den on to dat here come yo'
mammy hollerin' atter you.

'W'at I tell you w'en I fus' begin? I tole
you Brer Rabbit wuz a monstus soon
creetur; leas'ways dat's w'at I laid out fer
ter tell you. Well, den, honey, don't you go
en make no udder calkalashuns, kaze in dem
days Brer Rabbit en his fambly wuz at de
head er de gang w'en enny racket wuz on
han', en dar dey stayed. 'Fo' you begins fer
ter wipe yo' eyes 'bout Brer Rabbit, you
wait en see whar'bouts Brer Rabbit gwineter fetch up at. But dat's needer yer ner dar.

'W'en Brer Fox fine Brer Rabbit mixt up
wid de Tar-Baby, he feel mighty good, en
he roll on de groun' en laff. Bimeby he up'n
say, sezee:

' "Well, I speck I got you dis time, Brer

Rabbit," sezee; "maybe I ain't, but I speck I is. You been runnin' roun' here sassin' atter me a mighty long time, but I speck you done come ter de een' er de row. You bin cuttin' up yo' capers en bouncin' 'roun' in dis neighberhood ontwel you come ter b'leeve yo'se'f de boss er de whole gang. En den youer allers some'rs whar you got no bizness," sez Brer Fox, sezee. "Who ax you fer ter come en strike up a 'quaintance wid dish yer Tar-Baby? En who stuck you up dar whar you iz? Nobody in de roun' worril. You des tuck en jam yo'se'f on dat Tar-Baby widout waitin' fer enny invite," sez Brer Fox, sezee, "en dar you is, en dar you'll stay twel I fixes up a bresh-pile and fires her up, kaze I'm gwineter bobbycue you dis day, sho'," sez Brer Fox, sezee.

'Den Brer Rabbit talk mighty 'umble.

' "I don't keer w'at you do wid me, Brer Fox," sezee, "so you don't fling me in dat brier-patch. Roas' me, Brer Fox," sezee, "but don't fling me in dat brier-patch," sezee.

' "Hit's so much trouble fer ter kindle a fier," sez Brer Fox, sezee, "dat I speck I'll hatter hang you," sezee.

' "Hang me des ez high as you please, Brer Fox," sez Brer Rabbit, sezee, "but do fer de Lord's sake don't fling me in dat brier-patch," sezee.

' "I ain't got no string," sez Brer Fox, sezee, "en now I speck I'll hatter drown you," sezee.

' "Drown me des ez deep ez you please, Brer Fox," sez Brer Rabbit, sezee, "but do don't fling me in dat brier-patch," sezee.

' "Dey ain't no water nigh," sez Brer Fox, sezee, "en now I speck I'll hatter skin you," sezee.

' "Skin me, Brer Fox," sez Brer Rabbit, sezee, "snatch out my eyeballs, t'ar out my years by de roots, en cut off my legs," sezee, "but do please, Brer Fox, don't fling me in dat brier-patch," sezee.

'Co'se Brer Fox wanter hurt Brer Rabbit bad ez he kin, so he cotch 'im by de behime legs en slung 'im right in de middle er de brier-patch. Dar wuz a considerbul flutter whar Brer Rabbit struck de bushes, en Brer Fox sorter hang 'roun' fer ter see w'at wuz gwineter happen. Bimeby he hear somebody call 'im, en way up de hill he see Brer Rabbit settin' cross-legged on a chinkapin log koamin' de pitch outen his har wid a chip. Den Brer Fox know dat he bin swop off mighty bad. Brer Rabbit wuz bleedzed fer ter fling back some er his sass, en he holler out:

' "Bred en bawn in a brier-patch, Brer Fox—bred en bawn in a brier-patch!" en wid dat he skip out des ez lively ez a cricket in de embers.'

1881

LAFCADIO HEARN [1]

1850–1904

FROM CHITA

THE LEGEND OF L'ÎLE DERNIÈRE [1]

I

TRAVELLING south from New Orleans to the Islands, you pass through a strange land into a strange sea, by various winding waterways. You can journey to the Gulf by lugger if you please; but the trip may be made much more rapidly and agreeably on some one of those light, narrow steamers, built especially for bayou-travel, which usually receive passengers at a point not far from the foot of old Saint-Louis Street, hard by the sugar-landing, where there is ever a pushing and flocking of steam-craft —all striving for place to rest their white breasts against the levée, side by side,—like great weary swans. But the miniature steamboat on which you engage passage to the Gulf never lingers long in the Mississippi: she crosses the river, slips into some canal-mouth, labors along the artificial channel awhile, and then leaves it with a scream of joy, to puff her free way down many a league of heavily shadowed bayou. Perhaps thereafter she may bear you through the immense silence of drenched ricefields, where the yellow-green level is broken at long intervals by the black silhouette of some irrigating machine;—but, whichever of the five different routes be

1 The selection is the first section of *Chita: A Memory of Last Island* (N.Y., 1889), 3–59.

pursued, you will find yourself more than once floating through sombre mazes of swamp-forest,—past assemblages of cypresses all hoary with the parasitic tillandsia, and grotesque as gatherings of fetich-gods. Ever from river or from lakelet the steamer glides again into canal or bayou,—from bayou or canal once more into lake or bay; and sometimes the swamp-forest visibly thins away from these shores into wastes of reedy morass where, even of breathless nights, the quaggy soil trembles to a sound like thunder of breakers on a coast: the storm-roar of billions of reptile voices chanting in cadence,—rhythmically surging in stupendous *crescendo* and *diminuendo*,—a monstrous and appalling chorus of frogs! . . . .

Panting, screaming, scraping her bottom ·over the sand-bars,—all day the little steamer strives to reach the grand blaze of blue open water below the marsh-lands; and perhaps she may be fortunate enough to enter the Gulf about the time of sunset. For the sake of passengers, she travels by day only; but there are other vessels which make the journey also by night—threading the bayou-labyrinths winter and summer: sometimes steering by the North Star,—sometimes feeling the way with poles in the white season of fogs,—sometimes, again, steering by that Star of Evening which in ·our sky glows like another moon, and drops over the silent lakes as she passes a quivering trail of silver fire.

Shadows lengthen; and at last the woods dwindle away behind you into thin bluish lines;—land and water alike take more luminous color;—bayous open into broad passes;—lakes link themselves with sea-bays;—and the ocean-wind bursts upon you, —keen, cool, and full of light. For the first time ·the vessel begins to swing,—rocking to the great living pulse of the tides. And gazing from the deck around you, with no forest walls to break the view, it will seem to you that the low land must have once been rent asunder by the sea, and strewn about the Gulf in fantastic tatters. . . .

Sometimes above a waste of wind-blown prairie-cane you see an oasis emerging,—a ridge or hillock heavily umbraged with the rounded foliage of evergreen oaks:—a *chénière*. And from the shining flood also kindred green knolls arise,—pretty islets, each with its beach-girdle of dazzling sand

and shells, yellow-white,—and all radiant with semi-tropical foliage, myrtle and palmetto, orange and magnolia. Under their emerald shadows curious little villages of palmetto huts are drowsing, where dwell a swarthy population of Orientals,—Malay fishermen, who speak the Spanish-Creole of the Philippines as well as their own Tagal, and perpetuate in Louisiana the Catholic traditions of the Indies. There are girls in those unfamiliar villages worthy to inspire any statuary,—beautiful with the beauty of ruddy bronze,—gracile as the palmettoes that sway above them. . . . Further seaward you may also pass a Chinese settlement: some queer camp of wooden dwellings clustering around a vast platform that stands above the water upon a thousand piles;—over the miniature wharf you can scarcely fail to observe a white sign-board painted with crimson ideographs. The great platform is used for drying fish in the sun; and the fantastic characters of the sign, literally translated, mean: '*Heap—Shrimp—Plenty*.' . . . And finally all the land melts down into desolations of sea-marsh, whose stillness is seldom broken, except by the melancholy cry of long-legged birds, and in wild seasons by that sound which shakes all shores when the weird Musician of the Sea touches the bass keys of his mighty organ. . . .

II

Beyond the sea-marshes a curious archipelago lies. If you travel by steamer to the sea-islands to-day, you are tolerably certain to enter the Gulf by Grande Pass—skirting Grande Terre, the most familiar island of all, not so much because of its proximity as because of its great crumbling fort and its graceful pharos: the stationary White-Light of Barataria. Otherwise the place is bleakly uninteresting: a wilderness of wind-swept grasses and sinewy weeds waving away from a thin beach ever speckled with drift and decaying things,—worm-riddled timbers, dead porpoises. Eastward the russet level is broken by the columnar silhouette of the light-house, and again, beyond it, by some puny scrub timber, above which rises the angular ruddy mass of the old brick fort, whose ditches swarm with crabs, and whose sluiceways are half choked by obsolete cannon-shot, now thickly covered

with incrustation of oyster shells. . . .
Around all the gray circling of a shark-
haunted sea. . . .

Sometimes of autumn evenings there,
when the hollow of heaven flames like the
interior of a chalice, and waves and clouds
are flying in one wild rout of broken gold,
—you may see the tawny grasses all covered with something like husks,—wheat-
colored husks,—large, flat, and disposed   10
evenly along the lee-side of each swaying
stalk, so as to present only their edges to
the wind. But, if you approach, those pale
husks all break open to display strange
splendors of scarlet and seal-brown, with
arabesque mottlings in white and black:
they change into wondrous living blossoms,
which detach themselves before your eyes
and rise in air, and flutter away by thousands to settle down farther off, and turn   20
into wheat-colored husks once more . . .
a whirling flower-drift of sleepy butterflies!

Southwest, across the pass, gleams beautiful Grande Isle: primitively a wilderness of palmetto (latanier);—then drained,
diked, and cultivated by Spanish sugar-
planters; and now familiar chiefly as a
bathing-resort. Since the war the ocean re-
claimed its own;—the cane-fields have degenerated into sandy plains, over which
tramways wind to the smooth beach;—the
plantation-residences have been converted
into rustic hotels, and the negro-quarters
remodelled into villages of cozy cottages
for the reception of guests. But with its imposing groves of oak, its golden wealth of
orange-trees, its odorous lanes of oleander,
its broad grazing-meadows yellow-starred   40
with wild camomile, Grande Isle remains
the prettiest island of the Gulf; and its
loveliness is exceptional. For the bleakness
of Grande Terre is reiterated by most of the
other islands,—Caillou, Cassetête, Calu-
met, Wine Island, the twin Timbaliers,
Gull Island, and the many islets haunted
by the gray pelican,—all of which are little
more than sand-bars covered with wiry
grasses, prairie-cane, and scrub-timber.   50
Last Island (L'Île Dernière),—well worthy
a long visit in other years, in spite of its
remoteness, is now a ghastly desolation
twenty-five miles long. Lying nearly forty
miles west of Grande Isle, it was neverthe-

less far more populated a generation ago:
it was not only the most celebrated island
of the group, but also the most fashionable
watering-place of the aristocratic South;—
to-day it is visited by fishermen only, at long
intervals. Its admirable beach in many respects resembled that of Grande Isle to-day;
the accommodations also were much similar, although finer: a charming village of
cottages facing the Gulf near the western
end. The hotel itself was a massive two-
story construction of timber, containing
many apartments, together with a large dining-room and dancing-hall. In the rear of
the hotel was a bayou, where passengers
landed—'Village Bayou' it is still called by
seamen;—but the deep channel which now
cuts the island in two a little eastwardly did
not exist while the village remained. The
sea tore it out in one night—the same night
when trees, fields, dwellings, all vanished
into the Gulf, leaving no vestige of former
human habitation except a few of those
strong brick props and foundations upon
which the frame houses and cisterns had
been raised. One living creature was found
there after the cataclysm—a cow! But how
that solitary cow survived the fury of a
storm-flood that actually rent the island in
twain has ever remained a mystery. . . .   30

III

On the Gulf side of these islands you may
observe that the trees—when there are any
trees—all bend away from the sea; and,
even of bright, hot days when the wind
sleeps, there is something grotesquely pathetic in their look of agonized terror. A
group of oaks at Grande Isle I remember as
especially suggestive: five stooping silhou-
ettes in line against the horizon, like fleeing
women with streaming garments and wind-
blown hair,—bowing grievously and thrusting out arms desperately northward as to
save themselves from falling. And they are
being pursued indeed;—for the sea is devouring the land. Many and many a mile of
ground has yielded to the tireless charging
of Ocean's cavalry: far out you can see,
through a good glass, the porpoises at play   50
where of old the sugar-cane shook out its
million bannerets; and shark-fins now seam
deep water above a site where pigeons used
to coo. Men build dikes; but the besieging
tides bring up their battering-rams—whole

forests of drift—huge trunks of water-oak and weighty cypress. Forever the yellow Mississippi strives to build; forever the sea struggles to destroy;—and amid their eternal strife the islands and the promontories change shape, more slowly, but not less fantastically, than the clouds of heaven.

And worthy of study are those wan battle-grounds where the woods made their last brave stand against the irresistible invasion,—usually at some long point of sea-marsh, widely fringed with billowing sand. Just where the waves curl beyond such a point you may discern a multitude of blackened, snaggy shapes protruding above the water,—some high enough to resemble ruined chimneys, others bearing a startling likeness to enormous skeleton-feet and skeleton-hands,—with crustaceous white growths clinging to them here and there like remnants of integument. These are bodies and limbs of drowned oaks,—so long drowned that the shell-scurf is inch-thick upon parts of them. Farther in upon the beach immense trunks lie overthrown. Some look like vast broken columns; some suggest colossal torsos imbedded, and seem to reach out mutilated stumps in despair from their deepening graves;—and beside these are others which have kept their feet with astounding obstinacy, although the barbarian tides have been charging them for twenty years, and gradually torn away the soil above and beneath their roots. The sand around,—soft beneath and thinly crusted upon the surface,—is everywhere pierced with holes made by a beautifully mottled and semi-diaphanous crab, with hairy legs, big staring eyes, and milk-white claws;—while in the green sedges beyond there is a perpetual rustling, as of some strong wind beating among reeds: a marvellous creeping of 'fiddlers,' which the inexperienced visitor might at first mistake for so many peculiar beetles, as they run about sideways, each with his huge single claw folded upon his body like a wing-case. Year by year that rustling strip of green land grows narrower; the sand spreads and sinks, shuddering and wrinkling like a living brown skin; and the last standing corpses of the oaks, ever clinging with naked, dead feet to the sliding beach, lean more and more out of the perpendicular. As the sands subside, the stumps appear to

creep; their intertwisted masses of snakish roots seem to crawl, to writhe,—like the reaching arms of cephalopods. . . .

. . . Grande Terre is going: the sea mines her fort, and will before many years carry the ramparts by storm. Grande Isle is going,—slowly but surely: the Gulf has eaten three miles into her meadowed land. Last Island has gone! How it went I first heard from the lips of a veteran pilot, while we sat one evening together on the trunk of a drifted cypress which some high tide had pressed deeply into the Grande Isle beach. The day had been tropically warm; we had sought the shore for a breath of living air. Sunset came, and with it the ponderous heat lifted,—a sudden breeze blew,—lightnings flickered in the darkening horizon,—wind and water began to strive together,—and soon all the low coast boomed. Then my companion began his story; perhaps the coming of the storm inspired him to speak! And as I listened to him, listening also to the clamoring of the coast, there flashed back to me recollection of a singular Breton fancy: that the Voice of the Sea is never one voice, but a tumult of many voices—voices of drowned men,—the muttering of multitudinous dead,—the moaning of innumerable ghosts, all rising, to rage against the living, at the great Witch-call of storms. . . .

IV

The charm of a single summer day on these island shores is something impossible to express, never to be forgotten. Rarely, in the paler zones, do earth and heaven take such luminosity: those will best understand me who have seen the splendor of a West Indian sky. And yet there is a tenderness of tint, a caress of color, in these Gulf-days which is not of the Antilles,—a spirituality, as of eternal tropical spring. It must have been to even such a sky that Xenophanes lifted up his eyes of old when he vowed the Infinite Blue was God;—it was indeed under such a sky that De Soto named the vastest and grandest of Southern havens Espiritu Santo,—the Bay of the Holy Ghost. There is a something unutterable in this bright Gulf-air that compels awe,—something vital, something holy, something pantheistic: and reverentially the mind asks itself if what the eye beholds is not the Πνεῦμα indeed, the Infinite Breath, the

Divine Ghost, the great Blue Soul of the Unknown. All, all is blue in the calm,—save the low land under your feet, which you almost forget, since it seems only as a tiny green flake afloat in the liquid eternity of day. Then slowly, caressingly, irresistibly, the witchery of the Infinite grows upon you: out of Time and Space you begin to dream with open eyes,—to drift into delicious oblivion of facts,—to forget the past, the present, the substantial,—to comprehend nothing but the existence of that infinite Blue Ghost as something into which you would wish to melt utterly away forever. . . .

And this day-magic of azure endures sometimes for months together. Cloudlessly the dawn reddens up through a violet east: there is no speck upon the blossoming of its Mystical Rose,—unless it be the silhouette of some passing gull, whirling his sickle-wings against the crimsoning. Ever, as the sun floats higher, the flood shifts its color. Sometimes smooth and gray, yet flickering with the morning gold, it is the vision of John,—the apocalyptic Sea of Glass mixed with fire;—again, with the growing breeze, it takes that incredible purple tint familiar mostly to painters of West Indian scenery;—once more, under the blaze of noon, it changes to a waste of broken emerald. With evening, the horizon assumes tints of inexpressible sweetness,—pearl-lights, opaline colors of milk and fire; and in the west are topaz-glowings and wondrous flushings as of nacre. Then, if the sea sleeps, it dreams of all these,—faintly, weirdly,—shadowing them even to the verge of heaven.

Beautiful, too, are those white phantasmagoria which, at the approach of equinoctial days, mark the coming of the winds. Over the rim of the sea a bright cloud gently pushes up its head. It rises; and others rise with it, to right and left—slowly at first; then more swiftly. All are brilliantly white and flocculent, like loose new cotton. Gradually they mount in enormous line high above the Gulf, rolling and wreathing into an arch that expands and advances,—bending from horizon to horizon. A clear, cold breath accompanies its coming. Reaching the zenith, it seems there to hang poised awhile,—a ghostly bridge arching the empyrean,—upreaching its measureless span

from either underside of the world. Then the colossal phantom begins to turn, as on a pivot of air,—always preserving its curvilinear symmetry, but moving its unseen ends beyond and below the sky-circle. And at last it floats away unbroken beyond the blue sweep of the world, with a wind following after. Day after day, almost at the same hour, the white arc rises, wheels, and passes. . . .

. . . Never a glimpse of rock on these low shores;—only long sloping beaches and bars of smooth tawny sand. Sand and sea teem with vitality;—over all the dunes there is a constant susurration, a blattering and swarming of crustacea;—through all the sea there is a ceaseless play of silver lightning,—flashing of myriad fish. Sometimes the shallows are thickened with minute, transparent, crab-like organisms,—all colorless as gelatine. There are days also when countless medusæ drift in—beautiful veined creatures that throb like hearts, with perpetual systole and diastole of their diaphanous envelops: some, of translucent azure or rose, seem in the flood the shadows or ghosts of huge campanulate flowers;—others have the semblance of strange living vegetables,—great milky tubers, just beginning to sprout. But woe to the human skin grazed by those shadowy sproutings and spectral stamens!—the touch of glowing iron is not more painful. . . . Within an hour or two after their appearance all these tremulous jellies vanish mysteriously as they came.

Perhaps, if a bold swimmer, you may venture out alone a long way—once! Not twice!—even in company. As the water deepens beneath you, and you feel those ascending wave-currents of coldness arising which bespeak profundity, you will also begin to feel innumerable touches, as of groping fingers—touches of the bodies of fish, innumerable fish, fleeing towards shore. The farther you advance, the more thickly you will feel them come; and above you and around you, to right and left, others will leap and fall so swiftly as to daze the sight, like intercrossing fountain-jets of fluid silver. The gulls fly lower about you, circling with sinister squeaking cries;—perhaps for an instant your feet touch in the deep something heavy, swift, lithe, that rushes past with a swirling shock. Then the fear of the

Abyss, the vast and voiceless Nightmare of the Sea, will come upon you; the silent panic of all those opaline millions that flee glimmering by will enter into you also. . . .

From what do they flee thus perpetually? Is it from the giant sawfish or the ravening shark?—from the herds of the porpoises, or from the *grande-écaille*,—that splendid monster whom no net may hold,—all ·helmed and armored in argent plate-mail? —or from the hideous devil-fish of the Gulf,—gigantic, flat-bodied, black, with immense side-fins ever outspread like the pinions of a bat,—the terror of luggermen, the uprooter of anchors? From all these, perhaps, and from other monsters likewise —goblin shapes evolved by Nature as destroyers, as equilibrists, as counterchecks to that prodigious fecundity, which, unhindered, would thicken the deep into one measureless and waveless ferment of being. . . . But when there are many bathers these perils are forgotten,—numbers give courage,—one can abandon one's self, without fear of the invisible, to the long, quivering, electrical caresses of the sea. . . .

V

Thirty years ago, Last Island lay steeped in the enormous light of even such magical days. July was dying;—for weeks no fleck of cloud had broken the heaven's blue dream of eternity; winds held their breath; slow wavelets caressed the bland brown beach with a sound as of kisses and whispers. To one who found himself alone, beyond the limits of the village and beyond the hearing of its voices,—the vast silence, the vast light, seemed full of weirdness. And these hushes, these transparencies, do not always inspire a causeless apprehension: they are omens sometimes—omens of coming tempest. Nature,—incomprehensible Sphinx! —before her mightiest bursts of rage, ever puts forth her divinest witchery, makes more manifest her awful beauty. . . .

But in that forgotten summer the witchery lasted many long days,—days born in rose-light, buried in gold. It was the height of the season. The long myrtle-shadowed village was thronged with its summer population;—the big hotel could hardly accommodate all its guests;—the bathing-houses were too few for the crowds who flocked to the water morning and evening.

There were diversions for all,—hunting and fishing parties, yachting excursions, rides, music, games, promenades. Carriage wheels whirled flickering along the beach, seaming its smoothness noiselessly, as if muffled. Love wrote its dreams upon the sand. . . .

. . . Then one great noon, when the blue abyss of day seemed to yawn over the world more deeply than ever before, a sudden change touched the quicksilver smoothness of the waters—the swaying shadow of a vast motion. First the whole sea-circle appeared to rise up bodily at the sky; the horizon-curve lifted to a straight line; the line darkened and approached,—a monstrous wrinkle, an immeasurable fold of green water, moving swift as a cloud-shadow pursued by sunlight. But it had looked formidable only by startling contrast with the previous placidity of the open: it was scarcely two feet high;—it curled slowly as it neared the beach, and combed itself out in sheets of woolly foam with a low, rich roll of whispered thunder. Swift in pursuit another followed—a third —a feebler fourth; then the sea only swayed a little, and stilled again. Minutes passed, and the immeasurable heaving recommenced—one, two, three, four . . . seven long swells this time;—and the Gulf smoothed itself once more. Irregularly the phenomenon continued to repeat itself, each time with heavier billowing and briefer intervals of quiet—until at last the whole sea grew restless and shifted color and flickered green;—the swells became shorter and changed form. Then from horizon to shore ran one uninterrupted heaving—one vast green swarming of snaky shapes, rolling in to hiss and flatten upon the sand. Yet no single cirrus-speck revealed itself through all the violet heights: there was no wind!—you might have fancied the sea had been upheaved from beneath. . . .

And indeed the fancy of a seismic origin for a windless surge would not appear in these latitudes to be utterly without foundation. On the fairest days a southeast breeze may bear you an odor singular enough to startle you from sleep,—a strong, sharp smell as of fish-oil; and gazing at the sea you might be still more startled at the sudden apparition of great oleaginous patches spreading over the water, sheeting over the swells. That is, if you had never heard of the mysterious submarine oil-wells, the volcanic fountains, unexplored, that well up with the eternal pulsing of the Gulf-Stream. . . .

But the pleasure-seekers of Last Island knew there must have been a 'great blow' somewhere that day. Still the sea swelled; and a splendid surf made the evening bath delightful. Then, just at sundown, a beautiful cloud-bridge grew up and arched the sky with a single span of cottony pink vapor, that changed and deepened color with the dying of the iridescent day. And the cloud-bridge approached, stretched, strained, and swung round at last to make way for the coming of the gale,—even as the light bridges that traverse the dreamy Têche swing open when luggermen sound through their conch-shells the long, bellowing signal of approach.

Then the wind began to blow, with the passing of July. It blew from the northeast, clear, cool. It blew in enormous sighs, dying away at regular intervals, as if pausing to draw breath. All night it blew; and in each pause could be heard the answering moan of the rising surf,—as if the rhythm of the sea moulded itself after the rhythm of the air,—as if the waving of the water responded precisely to the waving of the wind,—a billow for every puff, a surge for every sigh.

The August morning broke in a bright sky;—the breeze still came cool and clear from the northeast. The waves were running now at a sharp angle to the shore: they began to carry fleeces, an innumerable flock of vague green shapes, wind-driven to be despoiled of their ghostly wool. Far as the eye could follow the line of the beach, all the slope was white with the great shearing of them. Clouds came, flew as in a panic against the face of the sun, and passed. All that day and through the night and into the morning again the breeze continued from the northeast, blowing like an equinoctial gale. . . .

Then day by day the vast breath freshened steadily, and the waters heightened. A week later sea-bathing had become perilous: colossal breakers were herding in, like moving leviathan-backs, twice the height of a man. Still the gale grew, and the billowing waxed mightier, and faster and faster overhead flew the tatters of torn cloud. The

gray morning of the 9th wanly lighted a surf that appalled the best swimmers: the sea was one wild agony of foam, the gale was rending off the heads of the waves and veiling the horizon with a fog of salt spray. Shadowless and gray the day remained; there were mad bursts of lashing rain. Evening brought with it a sinister apparition, looming through a cloud-rent in the west—a scarlet sun in a green sky. His sanguine disk, enormously magnified, seemed barred like the body of a belted planet. A moment, and the crimson spectre vanished; and the moonless night came.

Then the Wind grew weird. It ceased being a breath; it became a Voice moaning across the world,—hooting,—uttering nightmare sounds,—*Whoo!—whoo!—whoo!* —and with each stupendous owl-cry the mooing of the waters seemed to deepen, more and more abysmally, through all the hours of darkness. From the northwest the breakers of the bay began to roll high over the sandy slope, into the salines;—the village bayou broadened to a bellowing flood. . . . So the tumult swelled and the turmoil heightened until morning,—a morning of gray gloom and whistling rain. Rain of bursting clouds and rain of wind-blown brine from the great spuming agony of the sea.

The steamer *Star* was due from St. Mary's that fearful morning. Could she come? No one really believed it,—no one. And nevertheless men struggled to the roaring beach to look for her, because hope is stronger than reason. . . .

Even to-day, in these Creole islands, the advent of the steamer is the great event of the week. There are no telegraph lines, no telephones: the mailpacket is the only trustworthy medium of communication with the outer world, bringing friends, news, letters. The magic of steam has placed New Orleans nearer to New York than to the Timbaliers, nearer to Washington than to Wine Island, nearer to Chicago than to Barataria Bay. And even during the deepest sleep of waves and winds there will come betimes to sojourners in this unfamiliar archipelago a feeling of lonesomeness that is a fear, a feeling of isolation from the world of men, —totally unlike that sense of solitude which haunts one in the silence of mountain-heights, or amid the eternal tumult of lofty granitic coasts: a sense of helpless insecurity. The land seems but an undulation of the sea-bed: its highest ridges do not rise more than the height of a man above the salines on either side;—the salines themselves lie almost level with the level of the flood-tides;—the tides are variable, treacherous, mysterious. But when all around and above these ever-changing shores the twin vastnesses of heaven and sea begin to utter the tremendous revelation of themselves as infinite forces in contention, then indeed this sense of separation from humanity appals. . . . Perhaps it was such a feeling which forced men, on the tenth day of August, eighteen hundred and fifty-six, to hope against hope for the coming of the *Star*, and to strain their eyes towards far-off Terrebonne. 'It was a wind you could lie down on,' said my friend the pilot.

. . . 'Great God!' shrieked a voice above the shouting of the storm,—'*she is coming!*' . . . It was true. Down the Atchafalaya, and thence through strange mazes of bayou, lakelet, and pass, by a rear route familiar only to the best of pilots, the frail river-craft had toiled into Caillou Bay, running close to the main shore;—and now she was heading right for the island, with the wind aft, over the monstrous sea. On she came, swaying, rocking, plunging,—with a great whiteness wrapping her about like a cloud, and moving with her moving,—a tempest-whirl of spray;—ghost-white and like a ghost she came, for her smoke-stacks exhaled no visible smoke—the wind devoured it! The excitement on shore became wild;—men shouted themselves hoarse; women laughed and cried. Every telescope and opera-glass was directed upon the coming apparition; all wondered how the pilot kept his feet; all marvelled at the madness of the captain.

But Captain Abraham Smith was not mad. A veteran American sailor, he had learned to know the great Gulf as scholars know deep books by heart: he knew the birthplace of its tempests, the mystery of its tides, the omens of its hurricanes. While lying at Brashear City he felt the storm had not yet reached its highest, vaguely foresaw a mighty peril, and resolved to wait no longer for a lull. 'Boys,' he said, 'we've got to take her out in spite of Hell!' And they 'took her out.' Through all the peril, his men stayed by him and obeyed him. By mid-morning the wind had deepened to a roar,—lowering sometimes to a rumble, sometimes bursting upon the ears like a measureless and deafening crash. Then the captain knew the *Star* was running a race with Death. 'She'll win it,' he muttered;—'she'll stand it. . . . Perhaps they'll have need of me to-night.'

She won! With a sonorous steamchant of triumph the brave little vessel rode at last into the bayou, and anchored hard by her accustomed resting-place, in full view of the hotel, though not near enough to shore to lower her gang-plank. . . . But she had sung her swan-song. Gathering in from the northeast, the waters of the bay were already marbling over the salines and half across the island; and still the wind increased its paroxysmal power.

Cottages began to rock. Some slid away from the solid props upon which they rested. A chimney tumbled. Shutters were wrenched off; verandas demolished. Light roofs lifted, dropped again, and flapped into ruin. Trees bent their heads to the earth. And still the storm grew louder and blacker with every passing hour.

The *Star* rose with the rising of the waters, dragging her anchor. Two more anchors were put out, and still she dragged —dragged in with the flood,—twisting, shuddering, careening in her agony. Evening fell; the sand began to move with the wind, stinging faces like a continuous fire of fine shot; and frenzied blasts came to buffet the steamer forward, sideward. Then one of her hog-chains parted with a clang like the boom of a big bell. Then another! . . . Then the captain bade his men to cut away all her upper works, clean to the deck. Overboard into the seething went her stacks, her pilot-house, her cabins,—and whirled away. And the naked hull of the *Star*, still dragging her three anchors, labored on through the darkness, nearer and nearer to the immense silhouette of the hotel, whose hundred windows were now all aflame. The vast timber building seemed to defy the storm. The wind, roaring round its broad verandas,—hissing through every crevice with the sound and force of steam,— appeared to waste its rage. And in the half-lull between two terrible gusts there came to the captain's ears a sound that seemed strange in that night of multitudinous terrors . . . a sound of music!

VI

. . . Almost every evening throughout the season there had been dancing in the great hall;—there was dancing that night also. The population of the hotel had been augmented by the advent of families from other parts of the island, who found their summer cottages insecure places of shelter: there were nearly four hundred guests assembled. Perhaps it was for this reason that the entertainment had been prepared upon a grander plan than usual, that it assumed the form of a fashionable ball. And all those pleasure-seekers,—representing the wealth and beauty of the Creole parishes,— whether from Ascension or Assumption, St. Mary's or St. Landry's, Iberville or Terrebonne, whether inhabitants of the multi-colored and many-balconied Creole quarter of the quaint metropolis, or dwellers in the dreamy paradises of the Têche, —mingled joyously, knowing each other, feeling in some sort akin—whether affiliated by blood, connaturalized by caste, or simply interassociated by traditional sympathies of class sentiment and class interest. Perhaps in the more than ordinary merriment of that evening something of nervous exaltation might have been discerned,— something like a feverish resolve to oppose apprehension with gayety, to combat uneasiness by diversion. But the hours passed in mirthfulness; the first general feeling of depression began to weigh less and less upon the guests; they had found reason to confide in the solidity of the massive building; there were no positive terrors, no outspoken fears; and the new conviction of all had found expression in the words of the host himself,—'*Il n'y a rien de mieux à faire que de s'amuser!*' Of what avail to lament the prospective devastation of cane-fields,—to discuss the possible ruin of crops? Better to seek solace in choregraphic harmonies, in the rhythm of gracious motion and of perfect melody, than hearken to the discords of the wild orchestra of storms;—wiser to admire the grace of Parisian toilets, the eddy of trailing robes with its fairy-foam of lace, the ivorine loveliness of glossy shoulders and jewelled throats, the glimmering of satin-slippered feet,—than to watch the raging of the flood without, or the flying of the wrack. . . .

So the music and the mirth went on: they made joy for themselves—those elegant guests;—they jested and sipped rich wines;—they pledged, and hoped, and loved, and promised, with never a thought of the morrow, on the night of the tenth of August, eighteen hundred and fifty-six. Observant parents were there, planning for the future bliss of their nearest and dearest;—mothers and fathers of handsome lads, lithe and elegant as young pines, and fresh from the polish of foreign university training;—mothers and fathers of splendid girls whose simplest attitudes were witcheries. Young cheeks flushed, young hearts fluttered with an emotion more puissant than the excitement of the dance;—young eyes betrayed the happy secret discreeter lips would have preserved. Slave-servants circled through the aristocratic press, bearing dainties and wines, praying permission to pass in terms at once humble and officious,—always in the excellent French which well-trained house-servants were taught to use on such occasions.

. . . Night wore on: still the shining floor palpitated to the feet of the dancers; still the piano-forte pealed, and still the violins sang,—and the sound of their singing shrilled through the darkness, in gasps of the gale, to the ears of Captain Smith, as he strove to keep his footing on the spray-drenched deck of the *Star*.

—'Christ!' he muttered,—'a dance! If that wind whips round south, there'll be another dance! . . . But I guess the *Star* will stay.' . . .

Half an hour might have passed; still the lights flamed calmly, and the violins trilled, and the perfumed whirl went on. . . . And suddenly the wind veered!

Again the *Star* reeled, and shuddered, and turned, and began to drag all her anchors. But she now dragged away from the great building and its lights,—away from the voluptuous thunder of the grand piano, —even at that moment outpouring the great joy of Weber's melody orchestrated by Berlioz: *l'Invitation à la Valse*,—with its marvellous musical swing!

—'Waltzing!' cried the captain. 'God help them!—God help us all now! . . .

The Wind waltzes to-night, with the Sea for
his partner!' . . .

O the stupendous Valse-Tourbillon! O
the mighty Dancer! One—two—three!
From northeast to east, from east to southeast, from southeast to south: then from the
south he came, whirling the Sea in his
arms. . . .

. . . Some one shrieked in the midst of
the revels;—some girl who found her pretty
slippers wet. What could it be? Thin
streams of water were spreading over the
level planking,—curling about the feet of
the dancers. . . . What could it be? All
the land had begun to quake, even as, but a
moment before, the polished floor was
trembling to the pressure of circling
steps;—all the building shook now; every
beam uttered its groan. What could it
be? . . .

There was a clamor, a panic, a rush to
the windy night. Infinite darkness above
and beyond; but the lantern-beams danced
far out over an unbroken circle of heaving
and swirling black water. Stealthily,
swiftly, the measureless sea-flood was rising.

—'*Messieurs—mesdames, ce n'est rien.*
Nothing serious, ladies, I assure you. . . .
Mais nous en avons vu bien souvent, les inon-
dations comme celle-ci; ça passe vite! The
water will go down in a few hours, ladies;—
it never rises higher than this; *il n'y a pas le*
moindre danger, je vous dis! Allons! il n'y a—
My God! what is that?' . . .

For a moment there was a ghastly hush
of voices. And through that hush there
burst upon the ears of all a fearful and unfamiliar sound, as of a colossal cannonade—
rolling up from the south, with volleying
lightnings. Vastly and swiftly, nearer and
nearer it came,—a ponderous and unbroken
thunder-roll, terrible as the long muttering
of an earthquake.

The nearest mainland,—across mad Caillou Bay to the sea-marshes,—lay twelve
miles north; west, by the Gulf, the nearest
solid ground was twenty miles distant.
There were boats, yes!—but the stoutest
swimmer might never reach them now!

Then rose a frightful cry,—the hoarse,
hideous, indescribable cry of hopeless fear,

—the despairing animal-cry man utters
when suddenly brought face to face with
Nothingness, without preparation, without
consolation, without possibility of respite.
. . . *Sauve qui peut!* Some wrenched down
the doors; some clung to the heavy ban-
quet-tables, to the sofas, to the billiard-
tables:—during one terrible instant,—
against fruitless heroisms, against futile
generosities,—raged all the frenzy of self-
ishness, all the brutalities of panic. And
then—then came, thundering through the
blackness, the giant swells, boom on boom!
. . . One crash!—the huge frame building
rocks like a cradle, seesaws, crackles. What
are human shrieks now?—the tornado is
shrieking! Another!—chandeliers splinter;
lights are dashed out; a sweeping cataract
hurls in: the immense hall rises,—oscillates,
—twirls as upon a pivot,—crepitates,—
crumbles into ruin. Crash again!—the
swirling wreck dissolves into the wallowing
of another monster billow; and a hundred
cottages overturn, spin in sudden eddies,
quiver, disjoint, and melt into the seething.

. . . So the hurricane passed,—tearing
off the heads of the prodigious waves, to
hurl them a hundred feet in air,—heaping
up the ocean against the land,—upturning
the woods. Bays and passes were swollen to
abysses; rivers regorged; the sea-marshes
were changed to raging wastes of water.
Before New Orleans the flood of the mile-
broad Mississippi rose six feet above highest water-mark. One hundred and ten miles
away, Donaldsonville trembled at the towering tide of the Lafourche. Lakes strove to
burst their boundaries. Far-off river steamers tugged wildly at their cables,—shivering like tethered creatures that hear by
night the approaching howl of destroyers.
Smoke-stacks were hurled overboard, pilot-
houses torn away, cabins blown to fragments.

And over roaring Kaimbuck Pass,—over
the agony of Caillou Bay,—the billowing
tide rushed unresisted from the Gulf,—
tearing and swallowing the land in its
course,—ploughing out deep-sea channels
where sleek herds had been grazing but a
few hours before,—rending islands in
twain,—and ever bearing with it, through
the night, enormous vortex of wreck and
vast wan drift of corpses. . . .

But the *Star* remained. And Captain Abraham Smith, with a long, good rope about his waist, dashed again and again into that awful surging to snatch victims from death,—clutching at passing hands, heads, garments, in the cataract-sweep of the seas, —saving, aiding, cheering, though blinded by spray and battered by drifting wreck, until his strength failed in the unequal struggle at last, and his men drew him aboard senseless, with some beautiful half-drowned girl safe in his arms. But well-nigh twoscore souls had been rescued by him; and the *Star* stayed on through it all.

Long years after, the weed-grown ribs of her graceful skeleton could still be seen, curving up from the sand-dunes of Last Island, in valiant witness of how well she stayed.

VII

Day breaks through the flying wrack, over the infinite heaving of the sea, over the low land made vast with desolation. It is a spectral dawn: a wan light, like the light of a dying sun.

The wind has waned and veered; the flood sinks slowly back to its abysses— abandoning its plunder,—scattering its piteous waifs over bar and dune, over shoal and marsh, among the silences of the mango-swamps, over the long low reaches of sand-grasses and drowned weeds, for more than a hundred miles. From the shell-reefs of Pointe-au-Fer to the shallows of Pelto Bay the dead lie mingled with the high-heaped drift;—from their cypress groves the vultures rise to dispute a share of the feast with the shrieking frigate-birds and squeaking gulls. And as the tremendous tide withdraws its plunging waters, all the pirates of air follow the great white-gleaming retreat: a storm of billowing wings and screaming throats.

And swift in the wake of gull and frigate-bird the Wreckers come, the Spoilers of the dead,—savage skimmers of the sea,—hurricane-riders wont to spread their canvas-pinions in the face of storms; Sicilian and Corsican outlaws, Manila-men from the marshes, deserters from many navies, Lascars, marooners, refugees of a hundred nationalities,—fishers and shrimpers by name, smugglers by opportunity,—wild channel-finders from obscure bayous and unfamiliar *chénières*, all skilled in the mysteries of these mysterious waters beyond the comprehension of the oldest licensed pilot. . . .

There is plunder for all—birds and men. There are drowned sheep in multitude, heaped carcasses of kine. There are casks of claret and kegs of brandy and legions of bottles bobbing in the surf. There are billiard-tables overturned upon the sand;— there are sofas, pianos, footstools and music-stools, luxurious chairs, lounges of bamboo. There are chests of cedar, and toilet-tables of rosewood, and trunks of fine stamped leather stored with precious apparel. There are *objets de luxe* innumerable. There are children's playthings: French dolls in marvellous toilets, and toy carts, and wooden horses, and wooden spades, and brave little wooden ships that rode out the gale in which the great *Nautilus* went down. There is money in notes and in coin—in purses, in pocket-books, and in pockets: plenty of it! There are silks, satins, laces, and fine linen to be stripped from the bodies of the drowned,— and necklaces, bracelets, watches, finger-rings and fine chains, brooches and trinkets. . . . *'Chi bidizza!—Oh! chi bedda mughieri! Eccu, la bidizza!'* [1] That ball-dress was made in Paris by—But you never heard of him, Sicilian Vicenzu. . . . *'Che bella sposina!'* [2] Her betrothal ring will not come off, Giuseppe; but the delicate bone snaps easily: your oyster-knife can sever the tendon. . . . *'Guardate! chi bedda picciota!'* [3] Over her heart you will find it, Valentino—the locket held by that fine Swiss chain of woven hair—*'Caya man-an!'* [4] And it is not your quadroon bonds-maid, sweet lady, who now disrobes you so roughly; those Malay hands are less deft than hers,—but she slumbers very far away from you, and may not be aroused from her sleep. *'No quita mo! dalaga!—na quita maganda!'* [5] . . . Juan, the fastenings of those diamond ear-drops are much too complicated for your peon fingers: tear them out!—*'Dispense, chulita!'* [6] . . .

1 'What a beauty!—Oh, what a beautiful woman! Look at the beauty!'
2 'What a lovely little bride!'
3 'Look! What a beautiful girl!'
4 'The wealth!'
5 'Have you seen it, lady? Have you seen the beauty?'
6 'Excuse me, my love!'

. . . Suddenly a long, mighty silver trilling fills the ears of all: there is a wild hurrying and scurrying; swiftly, one after another, the overburdened luggers spread wings and flutter away.

Thrice the great cry rings rippling through the gray air, and over the green sea, and over the far-flooded shell-reefs, where the huge white flashes are,—sheet-lightning of breakers,—and over the weird wash of corpses coming in.

It is the steam-call of the relief-boat, hastening to rescue the living, to gather in the dead.

The tremendous tragedy is over!

1889

SARAH ORNE JEWETT

1849–1909

FROM THE COUNTRY OF THE POINTED FIRS

GREEN ISLAND [1]

I

WE were standing where there was a fine view of the harbor and its long stretches of shore all covered by the great army of the pointed firs, darkly cloaked and standing as if they waited to embark. As we looked far seaward among the outer islands, the trees seemed to march seaward still, going steadily over the heights and down to the water's edge.

It had been growing gray and cloudy, like the first evening of autumn, and a shadow had fallen on the darkening shore. Suddenly, as we looked, a gleam of golden sunshine struck the outer islands, and one of them shone out clear in the light, and revealed itself in a compelling way to our eyes. Mrs. Todd was looking off across the bay with a face full of affection and interest. The sunburst upon that outermost island made it seem like a sudden revelation of the world beyond this which some believe to be so near.

'That's where mother lives,' said Mrs. Todd. 'Can't we see it plain? I was brought up out there on Green Island. I know every rock an' bush on it.'

'Your mother!' I exclaimed, with great interest.

'Yes, dear, cert'in; I've got her yet, old's I be. She's one of them spry, light-footed little women; always was, an' lighthearted, too,' answered Mrs. Todd, with satisfaction. 'She's seen all the trouble folks can see, without it's her last sickness; an' she's got a word of courage for everybody. Life ain't spoilt her a mite. She's eighty-six an' I'm sixty-seven, and I've seen the time I've felt a good sight the oldest. "Land sakes alive!" says she, last time I was out to see her. "How you do lurch about steppin' into a bo't!" I laughed so I liked to have gone right over into the water; an' we pushed off, an' left her laughin' there on the shore.'

The light had faded as we watched. Mrs. Todd had mounted a gray rock, and stood there grand and architectural, like a *carya-tide*. Presently she stepped down, and we continued our way homeward.

'You an' me, we'll take a bo't an' go out some day and see mother,' she promised me. ' 'Twould please her very much, an' there's one or two sca'ce herbs grows better on the island than anywheres else. I ain't seen their like nowheres here on the main.'

'Now I'm goin' right down to get us each a mug o' my beer,' she announced as we entered the house, 'an' I believe I'll sneak in a little mite o' camomile. Goin' to the funeral an' all, I feel to have had a very wearin' afternoon.'

I heard her going down into the cool little cellar, and then there was considerable delay. When she returned, mug in hand, I noticed the taste of camomile, in spite of my protest; but its flavor was disguised by some other herb that I did not know, and she stood over me until I drank it all and said that I liked it.

'I don't give that to everybody,' said Mrs. Todd kindly; and I felt for a moment as if it were part of a spell and incantation, and as if my enchantress would now begin to look like the cobweb shapes of the arctic town. Nothing happened but a quiet eve-

1 The selection is from *The Country of the Pointed Firs* (Boston, 1896),44–85.

ning and some delightful plans that we made about going to Green Island, and on the morrow there was the clear sunshine and blue sky of another day.

II

One morning, very early, I heard Mrs. Todd in the garden outside my window. By the unusual loudness of her remarks to a passer-by, and the notes of a familiar hymn which she sang as she worked among the herbs, and which came as if directed purposely to the sleepy ears of my consciousness, I knew that she wished I would wake up and come and speak to her.

In a few minutes she responded to a morning voice from behind the blinds. 'I expect you're goin' up to your schoolhouse to pass all this pleasant day; yes, I expect you're goin' to be dreadful busy,' she said despairingly.

'Perhaps not,' said I. 'Why, what's going to be the matter with you, Mrs. Todd?' For I supposed that she was tempted by the fine weather to take one of her favorite expeditions along the shore pastures to gather herbs and simples, and would like to have me keep the house.

'No, I don't want to go nowhere by land,' she answered gayly,—'no, not by land; but I don't know's we shall have a better day all the rest of the summer to go out to Green Island an' see mother. I waked up early thinkin' of her. The wind's light northeast, —'twill take us right straight out; an' this time o' year it's liable to change round southwest an' fetch us home pretty, 'long late in the afternoon. Yes, it's goin' to be a good day.'

'Speak to the captain and the Bowden boy, if you see anybody going by toward the landing,' said I. 'We'll take the big boat.'

'Oh, my sakes! now you let me do things my way,' said Mrs. Todd scornfully. 'No, dear, we won't take no big bo't. I'll just git a handy dory, an' Johnny Bowden an' me, we'll man her ourselves. I don't want no abler bo't than a good dory, an' a nice light breeze ain't goin' to make no sea; an' Johnny's my cousin's son,—mother'll like to have him come; an' he'll be down to the herrin' weirs all the time we're there, anyway; we don't want to carry no men folks havin' to be considered every minute an' takin' up all our time. No, you let me do; we'll just slip out an' see mother by ourselves. I guess what breakfast you'll want's about ready now.'

I had become well acquainted with Mrs. Todd as landlady, herb-gatherer, and rustic philosopher; we had been discreet fellow-passengers once or twice when I had sailed up the coast to a larger town than Dunnet Landing to do some shopping; but I was yet to become acquainted with her as a mariner. An hour later we pushed off from the landing in the desired dory. The tide was just on the turn, beginning to fall, and several friends and acquaintances stood along the side of the dilapidated wharf and cheered us by their words and evident interest. Johnny Bowden and I were both rowing in haste to get out where we could catch the breeze and put up the small sail which lay clumsily furled along the gunwale. Mrs. Todd sat aft, a stern and unbending lawgiver.

'You better let her drift; we'll get there 'bout as quick; the tide'll take her right out from under these old buildin's; there's plenty wind outside.'

'Your bo't ain't trimmed proper, Mis' Todd!' exclaimed a voice from shore. 'You're lo'ded so the bo't'll drag; you can't git her before the wind, ma'am. You set 'midships, Mis' Todd, an' let the boy hold the sheet 'n' steer after he gits the sail up; you won't never git out to Green Island that way. She's lo'ded bad, your bo't is,— she's heavy behind's she is now!'

Mrs. Todd turned with some difficulty and regarded the anxious adviser, my right oar flew out of water, and we seemed about to capsize. 'That you, Asa? Good-mornin',' she said politely. 'I al'ays liked the starn seat best. When'd you git back from up country?'

This allusion to Asa's origin was not lost upon the rest of the company. We were some little distance from shore, but we could hear a chuckle of laughter, and Asa, a person who was too ready with his criticism and advice on every possible subject, turned and walked indignantly away.

When we caught the wind we were soon on our seaward course, and only stopped to underrun a trawl, for the floats of which Mrs. Todd looked earnestly, explaining that her mother might not be prepared for three extra to dinner; it was her brother's trawl, and she meant to just run her eye along for the right sort of a little haddock. I leaned over the boat's side with great interest and excitement, while she skillfully handled the long line of hooks, and made scornful remarks upon worthless, bait-consuming creatures of the sea as she reviewed them and left them on the trawl or shook them off into the waves. At last we came to what she pronounced a proper haddock, 10 and having taken him on board and ended his life resolutely, we went our way.

As we sailed along I listened to an increasingly delightful commentary upon the islands, some of them barren rocks, or at best giving sparse pasturage for sheep in the early summer. On one of these an eager little flock ran to the water's edge and bleated at us so affectingly that I would willingly have stopped; but Mrs. Todd 20 steered away from the rocks, and scolded at the sheep's mean owner, an acquaintance of hers, who grudged the little salt and still less care which the patient creatures needed. The hot midsummer sun makes prisons of these small islands that are a paradise in early June, with their cool springs and short thick-growing grass. On a larger island, farther out to sea, my entertaining companion showed me with glee the small 30 houses of two farmers who shared the island between them, and declared that for three generations the people had not spoken to each other even in times of sickness or death or birth. 'When the news come that the war was over, one of 'em knew it a week, and never stepped across his wall to tell the others,' she said. 'There, they enjoy it: they've got to have somethin' to interest 'em in such a place; 'tis a good deal more tryin' 40 to be tied to folks you don't like than 'tis to be alone. Each of 'em tells the neighbors their wrongs; plenty likes to hear and tell again; them as fetch a bone'll carry one, an' so they keep the fight a-goin'. I must say I like variety myself; some folks washes Monday an' irons Tuesday the whole year round, even if the circus is goin' by!'

A long time before we landed at Green Island we could see the small white house, 50 standing high like a beacon, where Mrs. Todd was born and where her mother lived, on a green slope above the water, with dark spruce woods still higher. There were crops in the fields, which we presently distin-

guished from one another. Mrs. Todd examined them while we were still far at sea. 'Mother's late potatoes looks backward; ain't had rain enough so far,' she pronounced her opinion. 'They look weedier than what they call Front Street down to Cowper Centre. I expect brother William is so occupied with his herrin' weirs an' servin' out bait to the schooners that he don't think once a day of the land.'

'What's the flag for, up above the spruces there behind the house?' I inquired, with eagerness.

'Oh, that's the sign for herrin',' she explained kindly, while Johnny Bowden regarded me with contemptuous surprise. 'When they get enough for schooners they raise that flag; an' when 'tis a poor catch in the weir pocket they just fly a little signal down by the shore, an' then the small bo'ts comes and get enough an' over for their trawls. There, look! there she is: mother sees us; she's wavin' somethin' out o' the fore door! She'll be to the landin'-place quick's we are.'

I looked, and could see a tiny flutter in the doorway, but a quicker signal had made its way from the heart on shore to the heart on the sea.

'How do you suppose she knows it's me?' said Mrs. Todd, with a tender smile on her broad face. 'There, you never get over bein' a child long's you have a mother to go to. Look at the chimney, now; she's gone right in an' brightened up the fire. Well, there, I'm glad mother's well; you'll enjoy seein' her very much.'

Mrs. Todd leaned back into her proper position, and the boat trimmed again. She took a firmer grasp of the sheet, and gave an impatient look up at the gaff and the leech of the little sail, and twitched the sheet as if she urged the wind like a horse. There came at once a fresh gust, and we seemed to have doubled our speed. Soon we were near enough to see a tiny figure with handkerchiefed head come down across the field and stand waiting for us at the cove above a curve of pebble beach.

Presently the dory grated on the pebbles, and Johnny Bowden, who had been kept in abeyance during the voyage, sprang out and used manful exertions to haul us up with the next wave, so that Mrs. Todd could make a dry landing.

'You done that very well,' she said, mounting to her feet, and coming ashore somewhat stiffly, but with great dignity, refusing our outstretched hands, and returning to possess herself of a bag which had lain at her feet.

'Well, mother, here I be!' she announced with indifference; but they stood and beamed in each other's faces.

'Lookin' pretty well for an old lady, ain't she?' said Mrs. Todd's mother, turning away from her daughter to speak to me. She was a delightful little person herself, with bright eyes and an affectionate air of expectation like a child on a holiday. You felt as if Mrs. Blackett were an old and dear friend before you let go her cordial hand. We all started together up the hill.

'Now don't you haste too fast, mother,' said Mrs. Todd warningly; ' 'tis a far reach o' risin' ground to the fore door, and you won't set an' get your breath when you're once there, but go trotting about. Now don't you go a mite faster than we proceed with this bag an' basket. Johnny, there, 'll fetch up the haddock. I just made one stop to underrun William's trawl till I come to jes' such a fish's I thought you'd want to make one o' your nice chowders of. I've brought an onion with me that was layin' about on the window-sill at home.'

'That's just what I was wantin',' said the hostess. 'I give a sigh when you spoke o' chowder, knowin' my onions was out. William forgot to replenish us last time he was to the Landin'. Don't you haste so yourself, Almiry, up this risin' ground. I hear you commencin' to wheeze a'ready.'

This mild revenge seemed to afford great pleasure to both giver and receiver. They laughed a little, and looked at each other affectionately, and then at me. Mrs. Todd considerately paused, and faced about to regard the wide sea view. I was glad to stop, being more out of breath than either of my companions, and I prolonged the halt by asking the names of the neighboring islands. There was a fine breeze blowing, which we felt more there on the high land than when we were running before it in the dory.

'Why, this ain't that kitten I saw when I was out last, the one that I said didn't appear likely?' exclaimed Mrs. Todd as we went our way.

'That's the one, Almiry,' said her mother.

'She always had a likely look to me, an' she's right after her business. I never see such a mouser for one of her age. If 't wan't for William, I never should have housed that other dronin' old thing so long; but he sets by her on account of her havin' a bob tail. I don't deem it advisable to maintain cats just on account of their havin' bob tails; they're like all other curiosities, good for them that wants to see 'em twice. This kitten catches mice for both, an' keeps me respectable as I ain't been for a year. She's a real understandin' little help, this kitten is. I picked her from among five Miss Augusta Pennell had over to Burnt Island,' said the old woman, trudging along with the kitten close at her skirts. 'Augusta, she says to me, "Why, Mis' Blackett, you've took the homeliest;" an' says I, "I've got the smartest; I'm satisfied." '

'I'd trust nobody sooner 'n you to pick out a kitten, mother,' said the daughter handsomely, and we went on in peace and harmony.

The house was just before us now, on a green level that looked as if a huge hand had scooped it out of the long green field we had been ascending. A little way above, the dark spruce woods began to climb the top of the hill and cover the seaward slopes of the island. There was just room for the small farm and the forest; we looked down at the fish-house and its rough sheds, and the weirs stretching far out into the water. As we looked upward, the tops of the firs came sharp against the blue sky. There was a great stretch of rough pasture-land round the shoulder of the island to the eastward, and here were all the thick-scattered gray rocks that kept their places, and the gray backs of many sheep that forever wandered and fed on the thin sweet pasturage that fringed the ledges and made soft hollows and strips of green turf like growing velvet. I could see the rich green of bayberry bushes here and there, where the rocks made room. The air was very sweet; one could not help wishing to be a citizen of such a complete and tiny continent and home of fisherfolk.

The house was broad and clean, with a roof that looked heavy on its low walls. It was one of the houses that seem firm-rooted in the ground, as if they were two-thirds below the surface, like icebergs. The front door stood hospitably open in expectation of company, and an orderly vine grew at each side; but our path led to the kitchen door at the house-end, and there grew a mass of gay flowers and greenery, as if they had been swept together by some diligent garden broom into a tangled heap: there were portulacas all along under the lower step and straggling off into the grass, and clustering mallows that crept as near as they dared, like poor relations. I saw the bright eyes and brainless little heads of two half-grown chickens who were snuggled down among the mallows as if they had been chased away from the door more than once, and expected to be again.

'It seems kind o' formal comin' in this way,' said Mrs. Todd impulsively, as we passed the flowers and came to the front doorstep; but she was mindful of the proprieties, and walked before us into the best room on the left.

'Why, mother, if you haven't gone an' turned the carpet!' she exclaimed, with something in her voice that spoke of awe and admiration. 'When'd you get to it? I s'pose Mis' Addicks come over an' helped you, from White Island Landing?'

'No, she didn't,' answered the old woman, standing proudly erect, and making the most of a great moment. 'I done it all myself with William's help. He had a spare day, an' took right holt with me; an' 'twas all well beat on the grass, an' turned, an' put down again afore we went to bed. I ripped an' sewed over two o' them long breadths. I ain't had such a good night's sleep for two years.'

'There, what do you think o' havin' such a mother as that for eighty-six year old?' said Mrs. Todd, standing before us like a large figure of Victory.

As for the mother, she took on a sudden look of youth; you felt as if she promised a great future, and was beginning, not ending, her summers and their happy toils.

'My, my!' exclaimed Mrs. Todd. 'I couldn't ha' done it myself, I've got to own it.'

'I was much pleased to have it off my mind,' said Mrs. Blackett, humbly; 'the more so because along at the first of the next week I wasn't very well. I suppose it may have been the change of weather.'

Mrs. Todd could not resist a significant glance at me, but, with charming sympathy,

she forbore to point the lesson or to connect this illness with its apparent cause. She loomed larger than ever in the little old-fashioned best room, with its few pieces of good furniture and pictures of national interest. The green paper curtains were stamped with conventional landscapes of a foreign order,—castles on inaccessible crags, and lovely lakes with steep wooded shores; under-foot the treasured carpet was covered thick with home-made rugs. There were empty glass lamps and crystallized bouquets of grass and some fine shells on the narrow mantelpiece.

'I was married in this room,' said Mrs. Todd unexpectedly; and I heard her give a sigh after she had spoken, as if she could not help the touch of regret that would forever come with all her thoughts of happiness.

'We stood right there between the windows,' she added, 'and the minister stood here. William wouldn't come in. He was always odd about seein' folks, just's he is now. I run to meet 'em from a child, an' William, he'd take an' run away.'

'I've been the gainer,' said the old mother cheerfully. 'William has been son an' daughter both since you was married off the island. He's been 'most too satisfied to stop at home 'long o' his old mother, but I always tell 'em I'm the gainer.'

We were all moving toward the kitchen as if by common instinct. The best room was too suggestive of serious occasions, and the shades were all pulled down to shut out the summer light and air. It was indeed a tribute to Society to find a room set apart for her behests out there on so apparently neighborless and remote an island. Afternoon visits and evening festivals must be few in such a bleak situation at certain seasons of the year, but Mrs. Blackett was of those who do not live to themselves, and who have long since passed the line that divides mere self-concern from a valued share in whatever Society can give and take. There were those of her neighbors who never had taken the trouble to furnish a best room, but Mrs. Blackett was one who knew the uses of a parlor.

'Yes, do come right out into the old kitchen; I shan't make any stranger of you,' she invited us pleasantly, after we had been properly received in the room appointed to formality. 'I expect Almiry, here, 'll be driftin' out 'mongst the pasture-weeds quick's she can find a good excuse. 'Tis hot now. You'd better content yourselves till you get nice an' rested, an' 'long after dinner the sea-breeze'll spring up, an' then you can take your walks, an' go up an' see the prospect from the big ledge. Almiry'll want to show off everything there is. Then I'll get you a good cup o' tea before you start to go home. The days are plenty long now.'

While we were talking in the best room the selected fish had been mysteriously brought up from the shore, and lay all cleaned and ready in an earthen crock on the table.

'I think William might have just stopped an' said a word,' remarked Mrs. Todd, pouting with high affront as she caught sight of it. 'He's friendly enough when he comes ashore, an' was remarkable social the last time, for him.'

'He ain't disposed to be very social with the ladies,' explained William's mother, with a delightful glance at me, as if she counted upon my friendship and tolerance. 'He's very particular, and he's all in his old fishin'-clothes to-day. He'll want me to tell him everything you said and done, after you've gone. William has very deep affections. He'll want to see you, Almiry. Yes, I guess he'll be in by an' by.'

'I'll search for him by 'n' by, if he don't,' proclaimed Mrs. Todd, with an air of unalterable resolution. 'I know all of his burrows down 'long the shore. I'll catch him by hand 'fore he knows it. I've got some business with William, anyway. I brought forty-two cents with me that was due him for them last lobsters he brought in.'

'You can leave it with me,' suggested the little old mother, who was already stepping about among her pots and pans in the pantry, and preparing to make the chowder.

I became possessed of a sudden unwonted curiosity in regard to William, and felt that half the pleasure of my visit would be lost if I could not make his interesting acquaintance.

III

Mrs. Todd had taken the onion out of her basket and laid it down upon the kitchen table. 'There's Johnny Bowden come with us, you know,' she reminded her mother. 'He'll be hungry enough to eat his size.'

'I've got new doughnuts, dear,' said the little old lady. 'You don't often catch William 'n' me out o' provisions. I expect you might have chose a somewhat larger fish, but I'll try an' make it do. I shall have to have a few extra potatoes, but there's a field full out there, an' the hoe's leanin' against the well-house, in 'mongst the climbin'-beans.' She smiled, and gave her daughter a commanding nod.

'Land sakes alive! Le' 's blow the horn for William,' insisted Mrs. Todd, with some excitement. 'He needn't break his spirit so far's to come in. He'll know you need him for something particular, an' then we can call to him as he comes up the path. I won't put him to no pain.'

Mrs. Blackett's old face, for the first time, wore a look of trouble, and I found it necessary to counteract the teasing spirit of Almira. It was too pleasant to stay indoors altogether, even in such rewarding companionship; besides, I might meet William; and straying out presently, I found the hoe by the well-house and an old splint basket at the woodshed door, and also found my way down to the field where there was a great square patch of rough, weedy potato-tops and tall ragweed. One corner was already dug, and I chose a fat-looking hill where the tops were well withered. There is all the pleasure that one can have in gold-digging in finding one's hopes satisfied in the riches of a good hill of potatoes. I longed to go on; but it did not seem frugal to dig any longer after my basket was full, and at last I took my hoe by the middle and lifted the basket to go back up the hill. I was sure that Mrs. Blackett must be waiting impatiently to slice the potatoes into the chowder, layer after layer, with the fish.

'You let me take holt o' that basket, ma'am,' said a pleasant, anxious voice behind me.

I turned, startled in the silence of the wide field, and saw an elderly man, bent in the shoulders as fishermen often are, gray-headed and clean-shaven, and with a timid air. It was William. He looked just like his mother, and I had been imagining that he was large and stout like his sister, Almira Todd; and, strange to say, my fancy had led me to picture him not far from thirty and a little loutish. It was necessary instead to pay William the respect due to age.

I accustomed myself to plain facts on the instant, and we said good-morning like old friends. The basket was really heavy, and I put the hoe through its handle and offered him one end; then we moved easily toward the house together, speaking of the fine weather and of mackerel which were reported to be striking in all about the bay. William had been out since three o'clock, and had taken an extra fare of fish. I could feel that Mrs. Todd's eyes were upon us as we approached the house, and although I fell behind in the narrow path, and let William take the basket alone and precede me at some little distance the rest of the way, I could plainly hear her greet him.

'Got round to comin' in, didn't you?' she inquired, with amusement. 'Well, now, that's clever. Didn't know's I should see you to-day, William, an' I wanted to settle an account.'

I felt somewhat disturbed and responsible, but when I joined them they were on the most simple and friendly terms. It became evident that, with William, it was the first step that cost, and that, having once joined in social interests, he was able to pursue them with more or less pleasure. He was about sixty, and not young-looking for his years, yet so undying is the spirit of youth, and bashfulness has such a power of survival, that I felt all the time as if one must try to make the occasion easy for some one who was young and new to the affairs of social life. He asked politely if I would like to go up to the great ledge while dinner was getting ready; so, not without a deep sense of pleasure, and a delighted look of surprise from the two hostesses, we started, William and I, as if both of us felt much younger than we looked. Such was the innocence and simplicity of the moment that when I heard Mrs. Todd laughing behind us in the kitchen I laughed too, but William did not even blush. I think he was a little deaf, and he stepped along before me most businesslike and intent upon his errand.

We went from the upper edge of the field above the house into a smooth, brown path among the dark spruces. The hot sun brought out the fragrance of the pitchy bark, and the shade was pleasant as we climbed the hill. William stopped once or twice to show me a great wasps-nest close by, or some fishhawks'-nest below in a bit of swamp. He picked a few sprigs of late-blooming linnæa as we came out upon an open bit of pasture at the top of the island, and gave them to me without speaking, but he knew as well as I that one could not say half he wished about linnæa. Through this piece of rough pasture ran a huge shape of stone like the great backbone of an enormous creature. At the end, near the woods, we could climb up on it and walk along to the highest point; there above the circle of pointed firs we could look down over all the island, and could see the ocean that circled this and a hundred other bits of island-ground, the mainland shore and all the far horizons. It gave a sudden sense of space, for nothing stopped the eye or hedged one in,—that sense of liberty in space and time which great prospects always give.

'There ain't no such view in the world, I expect,' said William proudly, and I hastened to speak my heartfelt tribute of praise; it was impossible not to feel as if an untraveled boy had spoken, and yet one loved to have him value his native heath.

IV

We were a little late to dinner, but Mrs. Blackett and Mrs. Todd were lenient, and we all took our places after William had paused to wash his hands, like a pious Brahmin, at the well, and put on a neat blue coat which he took from a peg behind the kitchen door. Then he resolutely asked a blessing in words that I could not hear, and we ate the chowder and were thankful. The kitten went round and round the table, quite erect, and, holding on by her fierce young claws, she stopped to mew with pathos at each elbow, or darted off to the open door when a song sparrow forgot himself and lit in the grass too near. William did not talk much, but his sister Todd occupied the time and told all the news there was to tell of Dunnet Landing and its coasts, while the old mother listened with delight. Her hospitality was something exquisite; she had the gift which so many women lack, of being able to make themselves and their houses belong entirely to a guest's pleasure,—that charming surrender for the moment of themselves and whatever belongs to them, so that they make a part of one's own life that can never be forgotten. Tact is after all a kind of mind-reading, and my hostess held the golden gift. Sympathy is of the mind as well as the heart, and Mrs. Blackett's world and mine were one from the moment we met. Besides, she had that final, that highest gift of heaven, a perfect self-forgetfulness. Sometimes, as I watched her eager, sweet old face, I wondered why she had been set to shine on this lonely island of the northern coast. It must have been to keep the balance true, and make up to all her scattered and depending neighbors for other things which they may have lacked.

When we had finished clearing away the old blue plates, and the kitten had taken care of her share of the fresh haddock, just as we were putting back the kitchen chairs in their places, Mrs. Todd said briskly that she must go up into the pasture now to gather the desired herbs.

'You can stop here an' rest, or you can accompany me,' she announced. 'Mother ought to have her nap, and when we come back she an' William'll sing for you. She admires music,' said Mrs. Todd, turning to speak to her mother.

But Mrs. Blackett tried to say that she couldn't sing as she used, and perhaps William wouldn't feel like it. She looked tired, the good old soul, or I should have liked to sit in the peaceful little house while she slept; I had had much pleasant experience of pastures already in her daughter's company. But it seemed best to go with Mrs. Todd, and off we went.

Mrs. Todd carried the gingham bag which she had brought from home, and a small heavy burden in the bottom made it hang straight and slender from her hand. The way was steep, and she soon grew breathless, so that we sat down to rest awhile on a convenient large stone among the bayberry.

'There, I wanted you to see this,—'tis mother's picture,' said Mrs. Todd; ' 'twas taken once when she was up to Portland, soon after she was married. That's me,' she added, opening another worn case, and displaying the full face of the cheerful child she looked like still in spite of being past sixty. 'And here's William an' father together. I take after father, large and heavy, an' William is like mother's folks, short an'

thin. He ought to have made something o' himself, bein' a man an' so like mother; but though he's been very steady to work, an' kept up the farm, an' done his fishin' too right along, he never had mother's snap an' power o' seein' things just as they be. He's got excellent judgment, too,' meditated William's sister, but she could not arrive at any satisfactory decision upon what she evidently thought his failure in life. 'I think it is well to see any one so happy an' makin' the most of life just as it falls to hand,' she said as she began to put the daguerreotypes away again; but I reached out my hand to see her mother's once more, a most flowerlike face of a lovely young woman in quaint dress. There was in the eyes a look of anticipation and joy, a far-off look that sought the horizon; one often sees it in seafaring families, inherited by girls and boys alike from men who spend their lives at sea, and are always watching for distant sails or the first loom of the land. At sea there is nothing to be seen close by, and this has its counterpart in a sailor's character, in the large and brave and patient traits that are developed, the hopeful pleasantness that one loves so in a seafarer.

When the family pictures were wrapped again in a big handkerchief, we set forward in a narrow footpath and made our way to a lonely place that faced northward, where there was more pasturage and fewer bushes, and we went down to the edge of short grass above some rocky cliffs where the deep sea broke with a great noise, though the wind was down and the water looked quiet a little way from shore. Among the grass grew such pennyroyal as the rest of the world could not provide. There was a fine fragrance in the air as we gathered it sprig by sprig and stepped along carefully, and Mrs. Todd pressed her aromatic nosegay between her hands and offered it to me again and again.

'There's nothin' like it,' she said; 'oh no, there's no such pennyr'yal as this in the State of Maine. It's the right pattern of the plant, and all the rest I ever see is but an imitation. Don't it do you good?' And I answered with enthusiasm.

'There, dear, I never showed nobody else but mother where to find this place; 'tis kind of sainted to me. Nathan, my husband, an' I used to love this place when we was courtin', and'—she hesitated, and then spoke softly— 'when he was lost, 'twas just off shore tryin' to get in by the short channel out there between Squaw Islands, right in sight o' this headland where we'd set an' made our plans all summer long.'

I had never heard her speak of her husband before, but I felt that we were friends now since she had brought me to this place.

' 'Twas but a dream with us,' Mrs. Todd said. 'I knew it when he was gone. I knew it'—and she whispered as if she were at confession—'I knew it afore he started to go to sea. My heart was gone out o' my keepin' before I ever saw Nathan; but he loved me well, and he made me real happy, and he died before he ever knew what he'd had to know if we'd lived long together. 'Tis very strange about love. No, Nathan never found out, but my heart was troubled when I knew him first. There's more women likes to be loved than there is of those that loves. I spent some happy hours right here. I always liked Nathan, and he never knew. But this pennyr'yal always reminded me, as I'd sit and gather it and hear him talkin' —it always would remind me of—the other one.'

She looked away from me, and presently rose and went on by herself. There was something lonely and solitary about her great determined shape. She might have been Antigone alone on the Theban plain. It is not often given in a noisy world to come to the places of great grief and silence. An absolute, archaic grief possessed this country-woman; she seemed like a renewal of some historic soul, with her sorrows and the remoteness of a daily life busied with rustic simplicities and the scents of primeval herbs.

I was not incompetent at herb-gathering, and after a while, when I had sat long enough waking myself to new thoughts, and reading a page of remembrance with new pleasure, I gathered some bunches, as I was bound to do, and at last we met again higher up the shore, in the plain every-day world we had left behind when we went down to the pennyroyal plot. As we walked together along the high edge of the field we saw a hundred sails about the bay and farther seaward; it was mid-afternoon or after, and the day was coming to an end.

'Yes, they're all makin' towards the shore,—the small craft an' the lobster smacks an' all,' said my companion. 'We must spend a little time with mother now, just to have our tea, an' then put for home.'

'No matter if we lose the wind at sundown; I can row in with Johnny,' said I; and Mrs. Todd nodded reassuringly and kept to her steady plod, not quickening her gait even when we saw William come round the corner of the house as if to look for us, and wave his hand and disappear.

'Why, William's right on deck; I didn't know's we should see any more of him!' exclaimed Mrs. Todd. 'Now mother'll put the kettle right on; she's got a good fire goin'.' I too could see the blue smoke thicken, and then we both walked a little faster, while Mrs. Todd groped in her full bag of herbs to find the daguerreotypes and be ready to put them in their places.

V

William was sitting on the side door step, and the old mother was busy making her tea; she gave into my hand an old flowered-glass tea-caddy.

'William thought you'd like to see this, when he was settin' the table. My father brought it to my mother from the island of Tobago; an' here's a pair of beautiful mugs that came with it.' She opened the glass door of a little cupboard beside the chimney. 'These I call my best things, dear,' she said. 'You'd laugh to see how we enjoy 'em Sunday nights in winter: we have a real company tea 'stead o' livin' right along just the same, an' I make somethin' good for a s'prise an' put on some o' my preserves, an' we get a-talkin' together an' have real pleasant times.'

Mrs. Todd laughed indulgently, and looked to see what I thought of such childishness.

'I wish I could be here some Sunday evening,' said I.

'William an' me'll be talkin' about you an' thinkin' o' this nice day,' said Mrs. Blackett affectionately, and she glanced at William, and he looked up bravely and nodded. I began to discover that he and his sister could not speak their deeper feelings before each other.

'Now I want you an' mother to sing,' said Mrs. Todd abruptly, with an air of command, and I gave William much sympathy in his evident distress.

'After I've had my cup o' tea, dear,' answered the old hostess cheerfully; and so we sat down and took our cups and made merry while they lasted. It was impossible not to wish to stay on forever at Green Island, and I could not help saying so.

'I'm very happy here, both winter an' summer,' said old Mrs. Blackett. 'William an' I never wish for any other home, do we, William? I'm glad you find it pleasant; I wish you'd come an' stay, dear, whenever you feel inclined. But here's Almiry; I always think Providence was kind to plot an' have her husband leave her a good house where she really belonged. She'd been very restless if she'd had to continue here on Green Island. You wanted more scope, didn't you, Almiry, an' to live in a large place where more things grew? Sometimes folks wonders that we don't live together; perhaps we shall some time,' and a shadow of sadness and apprehension flitted across her face. 'The time o' sickness an' failin' has got to come to all. But Almiry's got an herb that's good for everything.' She smiled as she spoke, and looked bright again.

'There's some herb that's good for everybody, except for them that thinks they're sick when they ain't,' announced Mrs. Todd, with a truly professional air of finality. 'Come, William, let's have Sweet Home, an' then mother'll sing Cupid an' the Bee for us.'

Then followed a most charming surprise. William mastered his timidity and began to sing. His voice was a little faint and frail, like the family daguerreotypes, but it was a tenor voice, and perfectly true and sweet. I have never heard Home, Sweet Home sung as touchingly and seriously as he sang it; he seemed to make it quite new; and when he paused for a moment at the end of the first line and began the next, the old mother joined him and they sang together, she missing only the higher notes, where he seemed to lend his voice to hers for the moment and carry on her very note and air. It was the silent man's real and only means of expression, and one could have listened forever, and have asked for more and more songs of old Scotch and English inheritance and the best that have lived from the ballad music of the war. Mrs. Todd kept time visibly, and sometimes audibly, with her ample foot. I saw the tears in her eyes sometimes, when I could see beyond the tears in mine. But at last the songs ended and the time came to say good-by; it was the end of a great pleasure.

Mrs. Blackett, the dear old lady, opened the door of her bedroom while Mrs. Todd was tying up the herb bag, and William had gone down to get the boat ready and to blow the horn for Johnny Bowden, who had joined a roving boat party who were off the shore lobstering.

I went to the door of the bedroom, and thought how pleasant it looked, with its pink-and-white patchwork quilt and the brown unpainted paneling of its woodwork. 'Come right in, dear,' she said. 'I want you to set down in my old quilted rockin'-chair there by the window; you'll say it's the prettiest view in the house. I set there a good deal to rest me and when I want to read.'

There was a worn red Bible on the lightstand, and Mrs. Blackett's heavy silver-bowed glasses; her thimble was on the narrow window-ledge, and folded carefully on the table was a thick striped-cotton shirt that she was making for her son. Those dear old fingers and their loving stitches, that heart which had made the most of everything that needed love! Here was the real home, the heart of the old house on Green Island! I sat in the rocking-chair, and felt that it was a place of peace, the little brown bedroom, and the quiet outlook upon field and sea and sky.

I looked up, and we understood each other without speaking. 'I shall like to think o' your settin' here to-day,' said Mrs. Blackett. 'I want you to come again. It has been so pleasant for William.'

The wind served us all the way home, and did not fall or let the sail slacken until we were close to the shore. We had a generous freight of lobsters in the boat, and new potatoes which William had put aboard, and what Mrs. Todd proudly called a full 'kag' of prime number one salted mackerel; and when we landed we had to make business arrangements to have these conveyed to her house in a wheelbarrow.

I never shall forget the day at Green Island. The town of Dunnet Landing seemed large and noisy and oppressive as we came ashore. Such is the power of contrast; for the village was so still that I could hear the shy whippoorwills singing that night as I lay awake in my downstairs bedroom, and the scent of Mrs. Todd's herb garden under the window blew in again and again with every gentle rising of the sea-breeze.

1896

WILLIAM DEAN HOWELLS

1837–1920

FROM CRITICISM AND FICTION

THE NOVEL [1]

I

IN General Grant's confession of novel-reading there is a sort of inference that he had wasted his time, or else the guilty conscience of the novelist in me imagines such an inference. But however this may be, there is certainly no question concerning the intention of a correspondent who once wrote to me after reading some rather bragging claims I had made for fiction as a mental and moral means. 'I have very grave doubts,' he said, 'as to the whole list of magnificent things that you seem to think novels have done for the race, and can witness in myself many evil things which they have done for me. Whatever in my mental make-up is wild and visionary, whatever is untrue, whatever is injurious, I can trace to the perusal of some work of fiction. Worse than that, they beget such high-strung and supersensitive ideas of life that plain industry and plodding perseverance are despised, and matter-of-fact poverty, or every-day, commonplace distress, meets with no sympathy, if indeed noticed at all, by one who has wept over the impossibly accumulated sufferings of some gaudy hero or heroine.'

I am not sure that I had the controversy with this correspondent that he seemed to suppose; but novels are now so fully accepted by every one pretending to cultivated taste—and they really form the whole intellectual life of such immense numbers of people, without question of their influence, good or bad, upon the mind—that it is refreshing to have them frankly denounced, and to be invited to revise one's ideas and feelings in regard to them. A little honesty, or a great deal of honesty, in this quest will do the novel, as we hope yet to have it, and as we have already begun to have it, no harm; and for my own part I will confess that I believe fiction in the past to have been largely injurious, as I believe the stage play to be still almost wholly injurious, through its falsehood, its folly, its wantonness, and its aimlessness. It may be safely assumed that most of the novel-reading which people fancy an intellectual pastime is the emptiest dissipation, hardly more related to thought or the wholesome exercise of the mental faculties than opium-eating; in either case the brain is drugged, and left weaker and crazier for the debauch. If this may be called the negative result of the fiction habit, the positive injury that most novels work is by no means so easily to be measured in the case of young men whose character they help so much to form or deform, and the women of all ages whom they keep so much in ignorance of the world they misrepresent. Grown men have little harm from them, but in the other cases, which are the vast majority, they hurt because they are not true—not because they are malevolent, but because they are idle lies about human nature and the social fabric, which it behooves us to know and to understand, that we may deal justly with ourselves and with one another. One need not go so far as our correspondent, and trace to the fiction habit 'whatever is wild and visionary, whatever is untrue, whatever is injurious,' in one's life; bad as the fiction habit is it is probably not responsible for the whole sum of evil in its victims, and I believe that if the reader will use care in choosing from this fungus-growth with which the fields of literature teem every day, he may nourish himself as with the true mushroom, at no risk from the poisonous species.

The tests are very plain and simple, and they are perfectly infallible. If a novel flat=

1 The selection, to which the title has been given by the editors, is Chapters 18–19, and 24 of *Criticism and Fiction*(N.Y., 1891).

ters the passions, and exalts them above the principles, it is poisonous; it may not kill, but it will certainly injure; and this test will alone exclude an entire class of fiction, of which eminent examples will occur to all. Then the whole spawn of so-called unmoral romances, which imagine a world where the sins of sense are unvisited by the penalties following, swift or slow, but inexorably sure, in the real world, are deadly poison: these do kill. The novels that merely tickle our prejudices and lull our judgment, or that coddle our sensibilities or pamper our gross appetite for the marvellous are not so fatal, but they are innutritious, and clog the soul with unwholesome vapors of all kinds. No doubt they too help to weaken the moral fibre, and make their readers indifferent to 'plodding perseverance and plain industry,' and to 'matter-of-fact poverty and commonplace distress.'

Without taking them too seriously, it still must be owned that the 'gaudy hero and heroine' are to blame for a great deal of harm in the world. That heroine long taught by example, if not precept, that Love, or the passion or fancy she mistook for it, was the chief interest of a life, which is really concerned with a great many other things; that it was lasting in the way she knew it; that it was worthy of every sacrifice, and was altogether a finer thing than prudence, obedience, reason; that love alone was glorious and beautiful, and these were mean and ugly in comparison with it. More lately she has begun to idolize and illustrate Duty, and she is hardly less mischievous in this new role, opposing duty, as she did love, to prudence, obedience, and reason. The stock hero, whom, if we met him, we could not fail to see was a most deplorable person, has undoubtedly imposed himself upon the victims of the fiction habit as admirable. With him, too, love was and is the great affair, whether in its old romantic phase of chivalrous achievement or manifold suffering for love's sake, or its more recent development of the 'virile,' the bullying, and the brutal, or its still more recent agonies of self-sacrifice, as idle and useless as the moral experiences of the insane asylums. With his vain posturings and his ridiculous splendor he is really a painted barbarian, the prey of his passions and his delusions, full of obsolete ideals, and the

motives and ethics of a savage, which the guilty author of his being does his best—or his worst—in spite of his own light and knowledge, to foist upon the reader as something generous and noble. I am not merely bringing this charge against that sort of fiction which is beneath literature and outside of it, 'the shoreless lakes of ditch-water,' whose miasms fill the air below the empyrean where the great ones sit; but I am accusing the work of some of the most famous, who have, in this instance or in that, sinned against the truth, which can alone exalt and purify men. I do not say that they have constantly done so, or even commonly done so; but that they have done so at all marks them as of the past, to be read with the due historical allowance for their epoch and their conditions. For I believe that, while inferior writers will and must continue to imitate them in their foibles and their errors, no one hereafter will be able to achieve greatness who is false to humanity, either in its facts or its duties. The light of civilization has already broken even upon the novel, and no conscientious man can now set about painting an image of life without perpetual question of the verity of his work, and without feeling bound to distinguish so clearly that no reader of his may be misled, between what is right and what is wrong, what is noble and what is base, what is health and what is perdition, in the actions and the characters he portrays.

The fiction that aims merely to entertain—the fiction that is to serious fiction as the opera-bouffe, the ballet, and the pantomime are to the true drama—need not feel the burden of this obligation so deeply; but even such fiction will not be gay or trivial to any reader's hurt, and criticism will hold it to account if it passes from painting to teaching folly.

More and more not only the criticism which prints its opinions, but the infinitely vaster and powerfuler criticism which thinks and feels them merely, will make this demand. I confess that I do not care to judge any work of the imagination without first of all applying this test to it. We must ask ourselves before we ask anything else, Is it true?—true to the motives, the impulses, the principles that shape the life of actual men and women? This truth, which necessarily includes the highest morality and the highest artistry—this truth given, the book cannot be wicked and cannot be weak; and without it all graces of style and feats of invention and cunning of construction are so many superfluities of naughtiness. It is well for the truth to have all these, and shine in them, but for falsehood they are merely meretricious, the bedizenment of the wanton; they atone for nothing, they count for nothing. But in fact they come naturally of truth, and grace it without solicitation; they are added unto it. In the whole range of fiction we know of no true picture of life—that is, of human nature—which is not also a masterpiece of literature, full of divine and natural beauty. It may have no touch or tint of this special civilization or of that; it had better have this local color well ascertained; but the truth is deeper and finer than aspects, and if the book is true to what men and women know of one another's souls it will be true enough, and it will be great and beautiful. It is the conception of literature as something apart from life, superfinely aloof, which makes it really unimportant to the great mass of mankind, without a message or a meaning for them; and it is the notion that a novel may be false in its portrayal of causes and effects that makes literary art contemptible even to those whom it amuses, that forbids them to regard the novelist as a serious or right-minded person. If they do not in some moment of indignation cry out against all novels, as my correspondent does, they remain besotted in the fume of the delusions purveyed to them, with no higher feeling for the author than such maudlin affection as the habitué of an opium-joint perhaps knows for the attendant who fills his pipe with the drug.

Or, as in the case of another correspondent who writes that in his youth he 'read a great many novels, but always regarded it as an amusement, like horse-racing and card-playing,' for which he had no time when he entered upon the serious business of life, it renders them merely contemptuous. His view of the matter may be commended to the brotherhood and sisterhood of novelists as full of wholesome if bitter suggestion; and we urge them not to dismiss it with high literary scorn as that of some Bœotian dull to the beauty of art. Refuse it as we may, it is still the feeling of the vast majority of people for whom life is earnest, and who find only a distorted and misleading likeness of it in our books. We may fold ourselves in our scholars' gowns, and close the doors of our studies, and affect to despise this rude voice; but we cannot shut it out. It comes to us from wherever men are at work, from wherever they are truly living, and accuses us of unfaithfulness, of triviality, of mere stage-play; and none of us can escape conviction except he prove himself worthy of his time —a time in which the great masters have brought literature back to life, and filled its ebbing veins with the red tides of reality. We cannot all equal them; we need not copy them; but we can all go to the sources of their inspiration and their power; and to draw from these no one need go far—no one need really go out of himself.

Fifty years ago, Carlyle, in whom the truth was always alive, but in whom it was then unperverted by suffering, by celebrity, and by despair, wrote in his study of Diderot: 'Were it not reasonable to prophesy that this exceeding great multitude of novel-writers and such like must, in a new generation, gradually do one of two things: either retire into the nurseries, and work for children, minors, and semi-fatuous persons of both sexes, or else, what were far better, sweep their novel-fabric into the dust-cart, and betake themselves with such faculty as they have to understand and record what is true, of which surely there is, and will forever be, a whole infinitude unknown to us of infinite importance to us? Poetry, it will more and more come to be understood, is nothing but higher knowledge; and the only genuine Romance (for grown persons), Reality.'

If, after half a century, fiction still mainly works for 'children, minors, and semi-fatuous persons of both sexes,' it is nevertheless one of the hopefulest signs of the world's progress that it has begun to work for 'grown persons,' and if not exactly in the way that Carlyle might have solely intended in urging its writers to compile memoirs instead of building the 'novel-fabric,' still it has, in the highest and widest sense, already made Reality its Romance. I cannot judge it, I do not even care for it, except as it has done this; and I can hardly conceive of a literary self-respect in these days compatible with the old trade of make-believe, with the production of the kind of fiction which is too much honored by classification with card-playing and horse-racing. But let fiction cease to lie about life; let it portray men and women as they are, actuated by the motives and the passions in the measure we all know; let it leave off painting dolls and working them by springs and wires; let it show the different interests in their true proportions; let it forbear to preach pride and revenge, folly and insanity, egotism and prejudice, but frankly own these for what they are, in whatever figures and occasions they appear; let it not put on fine literary airs; let it speak the dialect, the language, that most Americans know—the language of unaffected people everywhere—and there can be no doubt of an unlimited future, not only of delightfulness but of usefulness, for it.

II

This is what I say in my severer moods, but at other times I know that, of course, no one is going to hold all fiction to such strict account. There is a great deal of it which may be very well left to amuse us, if it can, when we are sick or when we are silly, and I am not inclined to despise it in the performance of this office. Or, if people find pleasure in having their blood curdled for the sake of having it uncurdled again at the end of the book, I would not interfere with their amusement, though I do not desire it. There is a certain demand in primitive natures for the kind of fiction that does this, and the author of it is usually very proud of it. The kind of novels he likes, and likes to write, are intended to take his reader's mind, or what that reader would probably call his mind, off himself; they make one forget life and all its cares and duties; they are not in the least like the novels which make you think of these, and shame you into at least wishing to be a helpfuler and wholesomer creature than you are. No sordid details of verity here, if you please; no wretched being humbly and weakly struggling to do right and to be true, suffering for his follies and his sins, tasting joy only through the mortification of self, and in the help of others; nothing of all this, but a great, whirling splendor of

peril and achievement, a wild scene of heroic adventure and of emotional ground and lofty tumbling, with a stage 'picture' at the fall of the curtain, and all the good characters in a row, their left hands pressed upon their hearts, and kissing their right hands to the audience, in the good old way that has always charmed and always will charm. Heaven bless it!

In a world which loves the spectacular drama and the practically bloodless sports of the modern amphitheatre the author of this sort of fiction has his place, and we must not seek to destroy him because he fancies it the first place. In fact, it is a condition of his doing well the kind of work he does that he should think it important, that he should believe in himself; and I would not take away this faith of his, even if I could. As I say, he has his place. The world often likes to forget itself, and he brings on his heroes, his goblins, his feats, his hair-breadth escapes, his imminent deadly breaches, and the poor, foolish, childish old world renews the excitements of its nonage. Perhaps this is a work of beneficence; and perhaps our brave conjurer in his cabalistic robe is a philanthropist in disguise.

Within the last four or five years there has been throughout the whole English-speaking world what Mr. Grant Allen happily calls the 'recrudescence' of taste in fiction. The effect is less noticeable in America than in England, where effete Philistinism, conscious of the dry-rot of its conventionality, is casting about for cure in anything that is wild and strange and unlike itself. But the recrudescence has been evident enough here, too; and a writer in one of our periodicals has put into convenient shape some common errors concerning popularity as a test of merit in a book. He seems to think, for instance, that the love of the marvellous and impossible in fiction, which is shown not only by 'the unthinking multitude clamoring about the book counters' for fiction of that sort, but by the 'literary elect' also, is proof of some principle in human nature which ought to be respected as well as tolerated. He seems to believe that the ebullition of this passion forms a sufficient answer to those who say that art should represent life, and that the art which misrepresents life is feeble art and false art. But it appears to me that a little carefuler reasoning from a little closer inspection of the facts would not have brought him to these conclusions. In the first place, I doubt very much whether the 'literary elect' have been fascinated in great numbers by the fiction in question; but if I supposed them to have really fallen under that spell, I should still be able to account for their fondness and that of the 'unthinking multitude' upon the same grounds, without honoring either very much. It is the habit of hasty casuists to regard civilization as inclusive of all the members of a civilized community; but this is a palpable error. Many persons in every civilized community live in a state of more or less evident savagery with respect to their habits, their morals, and their propensities; and they are held in check only by the law. Many more yet are savage in their tastes, as they show by the decoration of their houses and persons, and by their choice of books and pictures; and these are left to the restraints of public opinion. In fact, no man can be said to be thoroughly civilized or always civilized; the most refined, the most enlightened person has his moods, his moments of barbarism, in which the best, or even the second best, shall not please him. At these times the lettered and the unlettered are alike primitive and their gratifications are of the same simple sort; the highly cultivated person may then like melodrama, impossible fiction, and the trapeze as sincerely and thoroughly as a boy of thirteen or a barbarian of any age.

I do not blame him for these moods; I find something instructive and interesting in them; but if they lastingly established themselves in him, I could not help deploring the state of that person. No one can really think that the 'literary elect,' who are said to have joined the 'unthinking multitude' in clamoring about the book counters for the romances of no-man's land, take the same kind of pleasure in them as they do in a novel of Tolstoï, Tourguéneff, George Eliot, Thackeray, Balzac, Manzoni, Hawthorne, Henry James, Thomas Hardy, Palacio Valdés, or even Walter Scott. They have joined the 'unthinking multitude,' perhaps because they are tired of thinking, and expect to find relaxation in feeling—feeling crudely, grossly, merely. For once in a way there is no great harm in this; perhaps no harm at all. It is perfectly natural; let them have their innocent debauch. But let us distinguish, for our own sake and guidance, between the different kinds of things that please the same kind of people; between the things that please them habitually and those that please them occasionally; between the pleasures that edify them and those that amuse them. Otherwise we shall be in danger of becoming permanently part of the 'unthinking multitude,' and of remaining puerile, primitive, savage. We shall be so in moods and at moments; but let us not fancy that those are high moods or fortunate moments. If they are harmless, that is the most that can be said for them. They are lapses from which we can perhaps go forward more vigorously; but even this is not certain.

My own philosophy of the matter, however, would not bring me to prohibition of such literary amusements as the writer quoted seems to find significant of a growing indifference to truth and sanity in fiction. Once more, I say, these amusements have their place, as the circus has, and the burlesque and negro minstrelsy, and the ballet, and prestidigitation. No one of these is to be despised in its place; but we had better understand that it is not the highest place, and that it is hardly an intellectual delight. The lapse of all the 'literary elect' in the world could not dignify unreality; and their present mood, if it exists, is of no more weight against that beauty in literature which comes from truth alone, and never can come from anything else, than the permanent state of the 'unthinking multitude.'

Yet even as regards the 'unthinking multitude,' I believe I am not able to take the attitude of the writer I have quoted. I am afraid that I respect them more than he would like to have me, though I cannot always respect their taste, any more than that of the 'literary elect.' I respect them for their good sense in most practical matters; for their laborious, honest lives; for their kindness, their good-will; for that aspiration towards something better than themselves which seems to stir, however dumbly, in every human breast not abandoned to literary pride or other forms of self-righteousness. I find every man interesting, whether he thinks or unthinks, whether he is savage or civilized; for this reason I cannot thank the novelist who teaches us not to know but to unknow our kind. Yet I should by no means hold him to such strict account as Emerson, who felt the absence of the best motive, even in the greatest of the masters, when he said of Shakespeare that, after all, he was only master of the revels. The judgment is so severe, even with the praise which precedes it, that one winces under it; and if one is still young, with the world gay before him, and life full of joyous promise, one is apt to ask, defiantly, Well, what is better than being such a master of the revels as Shakespeare was? Let each judge for himself. To the heart again of serious youth uncontaminate and exigent of ideal good, it must always be a grief that the great masters seem so often to have been willing to amuse the leisure and vacancy of meaner men, and leave their mission to the soul but partially fulfilled. This, perhaps, was what Emerson had in mind; and if he had it in mind of Shakespeare, who gave us, with his histories and comedies and problems, such a searching homily as 'Macbeth,' one feels that he scarcely recognized the limitations of the dramatist's art. Few consciences, at times, seem so enlightened as that of this personally unknown person, so withdrawn into his work, and so lost to the intensest curiosity of after-time; at other times he seems merely Elizabethan in his coarseness, his courtliness, his imperfect sympathy.

III

One of the great newspapers the other day invited the prominent American authors to speak their minds upon a point in the theory and practice of fiction which had already vexed some of them. It was the question of how much or how little the American novel ought to deal with certain facts of life which are not usually talked of before young people, and especially young ladies. Of course the question was not decided, and I forget just how far the balance inclined in favor of a larger freedom in the matter. But it certainly inclined that way; one or two writers of the sex which is somehow supposed to have purity in its keeping (as if purity were a thing that did not practically concern the other sex, preoccupied with

serious affairs) gave it a rather vigorous tilt to that side. In view of this fact it would not be the part of prudence to make an effort to dress the balance; and indeed I do not know that I was going to make any such effort. But there are some things to say, around and about the subject, which I should like to have some one else say, and which I may myself possibly be safe in suggesting.

One of the first of these is the fact, generally lost sight of by those who censure the Anglo-Saxon novel for its prudishness, that it is really not such a prude after all; and that if it is sometimes apparently anxious to avoid those experiences of life not spoken of before young people, this may be an appearance only. Sometimes a novel which has this shuffling air, this effect of truckling to propriety, might defend itself, if it could speak for itself, by saying that such experiences happened not to come within its scheme, and that, so far from maiming or mutilating itself in ignoring them, it was all the more faithfully representative of the tone of modern life in dealing with love that was chaste, and with passion so honest that it could be openly spoken of before the tenderest society bud at dinner. It might say that the guilty intrigue, the betrayal, the extreme flirtation even, was the exceptional thing in life, and unless the scheme of the story necessarily involved it, that it would be bad art to lug it in, and as bad taste as to introduce such topics in a mixed company. It could say very justly that the novel in our civilization now always addresses a mixed company, and that the vast majority of the company are ladies, and that very many, if not most, of these ladies are young girls. If the novel were written for men and for married women alone, as in continental Europe, it might be altogether different. But the simple fact is that it is not written for them alone among us, and it is a question of writing, under cover of our universal acceptance, things for young girls to read which you would be put out-of-doors for saying to them, or frankly giving notice of your intention, and so cutting yourself off from the pleasure—and it is a very high and sweet one—of appealing to these vivid, responsive intelligences, which are none the less brilliant and admirable because they are innocent.

One day a novelist who liked, after the

manner of other men, to repine at his hard fate, complained to his friend, a critic, that he was tired of the restriction he had put upon himself in this regard; for it is a mistake, as can be readily shown, to suppose that others impose it. 'See how free those French fellows are!' he rebelled. 'Shall we always be shut up to our tradition of decency?'

'Do you think it's much worse than being shut up to their tradition of indecency?' said his friend.

Then that novelist began to reflect, and he remembered how sick the invariable motive of the French novel made him. He perceived finally that, convention for convention, ours was not only more tolerable, but on the whole was truer to life, not only to its complexion, but also to its texture. No one will pretend that there is not vicious love beneath the surface of our society; if he did, the fetid explosions of the divorce trials would refute him; but if he pretended that it was in any just sense characteristic of our society, he could be still more easily refuted. Yet it exists, and it is unquestionably the material of tragedy, the stuff from which intense effects are wrought. The question, after owning this fact, is whether these intense effects are not rather cheap effects. I incline to think they are, and I will try to say why I think so, if I may do so without offence. The material itself, the mere mention of it, has an instant fascination; it arrests, it detains, till the last word is said, and while there is anything to be hinted. This is what makes a love intrigue of some sort all but essential to the popularity of any fiction. Without such an intrigue the intellectual equipment of the author must be of the highest, and then he will succeed only with the highest class of readers. But any author who will deal with a guilty love intrigue holds all readers in his hand, the highest with the lowest, as long as he hints the slightest hope of the smallest potential naughtiness. He need not at all be a great author; he may be a very shabby wretch, if he has but the courage or the trick of that sort of thing. The critics will call him 'virile' and 'passionate;' decent people will be ashamed to have been limed by him; but the low average will only ask another chance of flocking into his net. If he happens to be an able writer, his really fine and costly

work will be unheeded, and the lure to the appetite will be chiefly remembered. There may be other qualities which make reputations for other men, but in his case they will count for nothing. He pays this penalty for his success in that kind; and every one pays some such penalty who deals with some such material. It attaches in like manner to the triumphs of the writers who now almost form a school among us, and who may be said to have established themselves in an easy popularity simply by the study of erotic shivers and fervors. They may find their account in the popularity, or they may not; there is no question of the popularity.

But I do not mean to imply that their case covers the whole ground. So far as it goes, though, it ought to stop the mouths of those who complain that fiction is enslaved to propriety among us. It appears that of a certain kind of impropriety it is free to give us all it will, and more. But this is not what serious men and women writing fiction mean when they rebel against the limitations of their art in our civilization. They have no desire to deal with nakedness, as painters and sculptors freely do in the worship of beauty; or with certain facts of life, as the stage does, in the service of sensation. But they ask why, when the conventions of the plastic and histrionic arts liberate their followers to the portrayal of almost any phase of the physical or of the emotional nature, an American novelist may not write a story on the lines of *Anna Karenina* or *Madame Bovary*. Sappho they put aside, and from Zola's work they avert their eyes. They do not condemn him or Daudet, necessarily, or accuse their motives; they leave them out of the question; they do not want to do that kind of thing. But they do sometimes wish to do another kind, to touch one of the most serious and sorrowful problems of life in the spirit of Tolstoï and Flaubert, and they ask why they may not. At one time, they remind us, the Anglo-Saxon novelist did deal with such problems—DeFoe in his spirit, Richardson in his, Goldsmith in his. At what moment did our fiction lose this privilege? In what fatal hour did the Young Girl arise and seal the lips of Fiction, with a touch of her finger, to some of the most vital interests of life?

Whether I wished to oppose them in their aspiration for greater freedom, or whether

I wished to encourage them, I should begin to answer them by saying that the Young Girl had never done anything of the kind. The manners of the novel have been improving with those of its readers; that is all. Gentlemen no longer swear or fall drunk under the table, or abduct young ladies and shut them up in lonely country-houses, or so habitually set about the ruin of their neighbors' wives, as they once did. Generally, people now call a spade an agricultural implement; they have not grown decent without having also grown a little squeamish, but they have grown comparatively decent; there is no doubt about that. They require of a novelist whom they respect unquestionable proof of his seriousness, if he proposes to deal with certain phases of life; they require a sort of scientific decorum. He can no longer expect to be received on the ground of entertainment only; he assumes a higher function, something like that of a physician or a priest, and they expect him to be bound by laws as sacred as those of such professions; they hold him solemnly pledged not to betray them or abuse their confidence. If he will accept the conditions, they give him their confidence, and he may then treat to his greater honor, and not at all to his disadvantage, of such experiences, such relations of men and women as George Eliot treats in *Adam Bede*, in *Daniel Deronda*, in *Romola*, in almost all her books; such as Hawthorne treats in *The Scarlet Letter*; such as Dickens treats in *David Copperfield*; such as Thackeray treats in *Pendennis*, and glances at in every one of his fictions; such as most of the masters of English fiction have at some time treated more or less openly. It is quite false or quite mistaken to suppose that our novels have left untouched these most important realities of life. They have only not made them their stock in trade; they have kept a true perspective in regard to them; they have relegated them in their pictures of life to the space and place they occupy in life itself, as we know it in England and America. They have kept a correct proportion, knowing perfectly well that unless the novel is to be a map, with everything scrupulously laid down in it, a faithful record of life in far the greater extent could be made to the exclusion of guilty love and all its circumstances and consequences.

I justify them in this view not only because I hate what is cheap and meretricious, and hold in peculiar loathing the cant of the critics who require 'passion' as something in itself admirable and desirable in a novel, but because I prize fidelity in the historian of feeling and character. Most of these critics who demand 'passion' would seem to have no conception of any passion but one. Yet there are several other passions: the passion of grief, the passion of avarice, the passion of pity, the passion of ambition, the passion of hate, the passion of envy, the passion of devotion, the passion of friendship; and all these have a greater part in the drama of life than the passion of love, and infinitely greater than the passion of guilty love. Wittingly or unwittingly, English fiction and American fiction have recognized this truth, not fully, not in the measure it merits, but in greater degree than most other fiction.

1891

FROM A MODERN INSTANCE

THE DEPARTURE FROM EQUITY [1]

THIS last drop of the local meanness filled Bartley's bitter cup. As he passed the house at the end of the street he seemed to drain it all. He knew that the old lawyer was there sitting by the office stove, drawing his hand across his chin, and Bartley hoped that he was still as miserable as he had looked when he last saw him; but he did not know that by the window in the house, which he would not even look at, Marcia sat self-prisoned in her room, with her eyes upon the road, famishing for the thousandth part of a chance to see him pass. She saw him now for the instant of his coming and going. With eyes trained to take in every point, she saw the preparation which seemed like final departure, and with a gasp of 'Bartley!' as if she were trying to call after him, she sank back into her chair and shut her eyes.

He drove on, plunging into the deep hollow beyond the house, and keeping for several miles the road they had taken on

[1] The selection, to which the title has been given by the editors, is Chapter 12 from *A Modern Instance* (Boston, 1882). Bartley Hubbard has hurriedly quitted Equity, where his first attempt at an ambitious career has failed. Marcia Gaylord, whose father had understood Hubbard's essential weakness and forbidden their marriage, follows after him.

that Sunday together; but he did not make the turn that brought them back to the village again. The pale sunset was slanting over the snow when he reached the Junction, for he had slackened his colt's pace after he had put ten miles behind him, not choosing to reach a prospective purchaser with his horse all blown and bathed with sweat. He wished to be able to say, 'Look at him! He's come fifteen miles since three o'clock, and he's as keen as when he started.'

This was true, when, having left his baggage at the Junction, he drove another mile into the country to see the farmer of the gentleman who had his summer-house here, and who had once bantered Bartley to sell him his colt. The farmer was away, and would not be at home till the up-train from Boston was in. Bartley looked at his watch, and saw that to wait would lose him the six o'clock down-train. There would be no other till eleven o'clock. But it was worth while: the gentleman had said, 'When you want the money for that colt, bring him over any time; my farmer will have it ready for you.' He waited for the up-train; but when the farmer arrived, he was full of all sorts of scruples and reluctances. He said he should not like to buy it till he had heard from Mr. Farnham; he ended by offering Bartley eighty dollars for the colt on his own account; he did not want the cutter.

'You write to Mr. Farnham,' said Bartley, 'that you tried that plan with me, and it wouldn't work; he's lost the colt.'

He made this brave show of indifference, but he was disheartened, and, having carried the farmer home from the Junction for the convenience of talking over the trade with him, he drove back again through the early night-fall in sullen desperation.

The weather had softened and was threatening rain or snow; the dark was closing in spiritlessly; the colt, shortening from a trot into a short, springy jolt, dropped into a walk at last as if he were tired, and gave Bartley time enough on his way back to the Junction for reflection upon the disaster into which his life had fallen. These passages of utter despair are commoner to the young than they are to those whom years have experienced in the impermanence of any fate, good, bad, or indifferent, unless, perhaps, the last may seem rather constant. Taken in reference to all that had been ten

days ago, the present ruin was incredible, and had nothing reasonable in proof of its existence. Then he was prosperously placed and in the way to better himself indefinitely. Now, he was here in the dark, with fifteen dollars in his pocket, and an unsalable horse on his hands; outcast, deserted, homeless, hopeless: and by whose fault? He owned even then that he had committed some follies; but in his sense of Marcia's all-giving love he had risen for once in his life to a conception of self-devotion, and in taking herself from him as she did, she had taken from him the highest incentive he had ever known, and had checked him in his first feeble impulse to do and be all in all for another. It was she who had ruined him.

As he jumped out of the cutter at the Junction the station-master stopped with a cluster of party-colored signal-lanterns in his hand and cast their light over the sorrel.

'Nice colt you got there.'

'Yes,' said Bartley, blanketing the horse, 'do you know anybody who wants to buy?'

'Whose is he?' asked the man.

'He's mine!' shouted Bartley. 'Do you think I stole him?'

'*I* don't know where you got him,' said the man, walking off, and making a soft play of red and green lights on the snow beyond the narrow platform.

Bartley went into the great ugly barn of a station, trembling, and sat down in one of the gouged and whittled arm-chairs near the stove. A pomp of timetables and luminous advertisements of Western railroads and their land-grants decorated the wooden walls of the gentlemen's waiting-room, which had been sanded to keep the gentlemen from writing and sketching upon them. This was the more judicious because the ladies' room, in the absence of tourist travel, was locked in winter, and they were obliged to share the gentlemen's. In summer, the Junction was a busy place, but after the snow fell, and until the snow thawed, it was a desolation relieved only by the arrival of the sparsely peopled through-trains from the north and east, and by such local travellers as wished to take trains not stopping at their own stations. These broke in upon the solitude of the joint station-master and baggage-man and switch-tender with just sufficient frequency to keep him in a state of uncharitable irritation and unrest.

To-night Bartley was the sole intruder, and he sat by the stove wrapped in a cloud of rebellious memories, when one side of a colloquy without made itself heard.

'What?'

Some question was repeated.

'No; it went down half an hour ago.'

An inaudible question followed.

'Next down-train at eleven.'

There was now a faintly audible lament or appeal.

'Guess you'll have to have come earlier next time. Most folks does that wants to take it.'

Bartley now heard the despairing moan of a woman: he had already divined the sex of the futile questioner whom the stationmaster was bullying; but he had divined it without compassion, and if he had not himself been a sufferer from the man's insolence he might even have felt a ferocious satisfaction in it. In a word, he was at his lowest and worst when the door opened and the woman came in, with a movement at once bewildered and daring, which gave him the impression of a despair as complete and final as his own. He doggedly kept his place; she did not seem to care for him, but in the uncertain light of the lamp above them she drew near the stove, and, putting one hand to her pocket as if to find her handkerchief, she flung aside her veil with her other, and showed her tear-stained face.

He was on his feet somehow. 'Marcia!'

'Oh! Bartley—'

He had seized her by the arm to make sure that she was there in verity of flesh and blood, and not by some trick of his own senses, as a cold chill running over him had made him afraid. At the touch their passion ignored all that they had made each other suffer; her head was on his breast, his embrace was round her; it was a moment of delirious bliss that intervened between the sorrows that had been and the reasons that must come.

'What—what are you doing here, Marcia?' he asked at last.

They sank on the benching that ran round the wall; he held her hands fast in one of his, and kept his other arm about her as they sat side by side.

'I don't know—I—' She seemed to rouse herself by an effort from her rapture. 'I was going to see Nettie Spaulding. And I saw you driving past our house; and I thought you were coming here; and I couldn't bear—I couldn't bear to let you go away without telling you that I was wrong; and asking—asking you to forgive me. I thought you would do it,—I thought you would know that I had behaved that way because I—I—cared so much for you. I thought—I was afraid you had gone on the other train—' She trembled and sank back in his embrace, from which she had lifted herself a little.

'How did you get here?' asked Bartley, as if willing to give himself all the proofs he could of the every-day reality of her presence.

'Andy Morrison brought me. Father sent him from the hotel. I didn't care what you would say to me. I wanted to tell you that I was wrong, and not let you go away feeling that—that—you were all to blame. I thought when I had done that you might drive me away,—or laugh at me, or anything you pleased, if only you would let me take back—'

'Yes,' he answered dreamily. All that wicked hardness was breaking up within him; he felt it melting drop by drop in his heart. This poor love-tossed soul, this frantic, unguided, reckless girl, was an angel of mercy to him, and in her folly and error a messenger of heavenly peace and hope. 'I am a bad fellow, Marcia,' he faltered. 'You ought to know that. You did right to give me up. I made love to Hannah Morrison; I never promised to marry her, but I made her think that I was fond of her.'

'I don't care for that,' replied the girl. 'I told you when we were first engaged that I would never think of anything that had gone before that; and then when I would not listen to a word from you, that day, I broke my promise.'

'When I struck Henry Bird because he was jealous of me, I was as guilty as if I had killed him.'

'If you had killed him, I was bound to you by my word. Your striking him was part of the same thing,—part of what I had promised I never would care for.' A gush of tears came into his eyes, and she saw them. 'Oh, poor Bartley! Poor Bartley!'

She took his head between her hands and pressed it hard against her heart, and then wrapped her arms tight about him, and softly bemoaned him.

They drew a little apart when the man came in with his lantern, and set it down to mend the fire. But as a railroad employee he was far too familiar with the love that vaunts itself on all railroad trains to feel that he was an intruder. He scarcely looked at them, and went out when he had mended the fire, and left it purring.

'Where is Andy Morrison?' asked Bartley. 'Has he gone back?'

'No; he is at the hotel over there. I told him to wait till I found out when the train went north.'

'So you inquired when it went to Boston,' said Bartley, with a touch of his old raillery. 'Come,' he added, taking her hand under his arm. He led her out of the room, to where his cutter stood outside. She was astonished to find the colt there.

'I wonder I didn't see it. But if I had, I should have thought that you had sold it and gone away; Andy told me you were coming here to sell the colt. When the man told me the express was gone, I knew you were on it.'

They found the boy stolidly waiting for Marcia on the veranda of the hotel, stamping first upon one foot and then the other, and hugging himself in his great-coat as the coming snow-fall blew its first flakes in his face.

'Is that you, Andy?' asked Bartley.

'Yes, sir,' answered the boy, without surprise at finding him with Marcia.

'Well, here! Just take hold of the colt's head a minute.'

As the boy obeyed, Bartley threw the reins on the dashboard, and leaped out of the cutter, and went within. He returned after a brief absence, followed by the landlord.

'Well, it ain't more'n a mile'n a half, if it's that. You just keep straight along this street, and take your first turn to the left, and you're right at the house; it's the first house on the left-hand side.'

'Thanks,' returned Bartley. 'Andy, you tell the Squire that you left Marcia with me, and I said I would see about her getting back. You needn't hurry.'

'All right,' said the boy, and he disappeared round the corner of the house to get his horse from the barn.

'Well, I'll be all ready by the time you're here,' said the landlord, still holding the hall-door ajar. 'Luck to you!' he shouted, shutting it.

Marcia locked both her hands through Bartley's arm, and leaned her head on his shoulder. Neither spoke for some minutes; then he asked, 'Marcia, do you know where you are?'

'With you,' she answered, in a voice of utter peace.

'Do you know where we are going?' he asked, leaning over to kiss her cold, pure cheek.

'No,' she answered in as perfect content as before.

'We are going to get married.'

He felt her grow tense in her clasp upon his arm, and hold there rigidly for a moment, while the swift thoughts whirled through her mind. Then, as if the struggle had ended, she silently relaxed, and leaned more heavily against him.

'There's still time to go back, Marcia,' he said, 'if you wish. That turn to the right, yonder, will take us to Equity, and you can be at home in two hours.' She quivered. 'I'm a poor man,—I suppose you know that; I've only got fifteen dollars in the world, and the colt here. I know I can get on; I'm not afraid for myself; but if you would rather wait,—if you're not perfectly certain of yourself,—remember, it's going to be a struggle; we're going to have some hard times—'

'You forgive me?' she huskily asked, for all answer, without moving her head from where it lay.

'Yes, Marcia.'

'Then—hurry.'

The minister was an old man, and he seemed quite dazed at the suddenness of their demand for his services. But he gathered himself together, and contrived to make them man and wife, and to give them his marriage certificate.

'It seems as if there were something else,' he said, absently, as he handed the paper to Bartley.

'Perhaps it's this,' said Bartley, giving him a five-dollar note in return.

'Ah, perhaps,' he replied, in unabated perplexity. He bade them serve God, and let them out into the snowy night, through which they drove back to the hotel.

The landlord had kindled a fire on the hearth of the Franklin stove in his parlor, and the blazing hickory snapped in electrical sympathy with the storm when they shut themselves into the bright room, and Bartley took Marcia fondly into his arms.

'Wife!'

'Husband!'

They sat down before the fire, hand in hand, and talked of the light things that swim to the top, and eddy round and round on the surface of our deepest moods. They made merry over the old minister's perturbation, which Bartley found endlessly amusing. Then he noticed that the dress Marcia had on was the one she had worn to the sociable in Lower Equity, and she said, yes, she had put it on because he once said he liked it. He asked her when, and she said, oh, she knew; but if he could not remember, she was not going to tell him. Then she wanted to know if he recognized her by the dress before she lifted her veil in the station.

'No,' he said, with a teasing laugh. 'I wasn't thinking of you.'

'Oh, Bartley!' she joyfully reproached him. 'You must have been!'

'Yes, I was! I was so mad at you, that I was glad to have that brute of a station-master bullying *some* woman!'

'Bartley!'

He sat holding her hand. 'Marcia,' he said, gravely, 'we must write to your father at once, and tell him. I want to begin life in the right way, and I think it's only fair to him.'

She was enraptured at his magnanimity. 'Bartley! That's *like* you! Poor father! I declare—Bartley, I'm afraid I had forgotten him! It's dreadful; but—*you* put everything else out of my head. I do believe I've died and come to life somewhere else!'

'Well, *I* haven't,' said Bartley, 'and I guess you'd better write to your father. *You'd* better write; at present, he and I are not on speaking terms. Here!' He took out his note-book, and gave her his stylographic pen after striking the fist that held it upon his other fist, in the fashion of the amateurs of that reluctant instrument, in order to bring down the ink.

'Oh, what's that?' she asked.

'It's a new kind of pen. I got it for a notice in the Free Press.'

'Is Henry Bird going to edit the paper?'

'I don't know, and I don't care,' answered Bartley. 'I'll go out and get an envelope, and ask the landlord what's the quickest way to get the letter to your father.'

He took up his hat, but she laid her hand on his arm. 'Oh, send for him!' she said.

'Are you afraid I sha'n't come back?' he demanded, with a laughing kiss. 'I want to see him about something else, too.'

'Well, don't be gone long.'

They parted with an embrace that would have fortified older married people for a year's separation. When Bartley came back, she handed him the leaf she had torn out of his book, and sat down beside him while he read it, with her arm over his shoulder.

'Dear father,' the letter ran, 'Bartley and I are married. We were married an hour ago, just across the New Hampshire line, by the Rev. Mr. Jessup. Bartley wants I should let you know the very first thing. I am going to Boston with Bartley to-night, and, as soon as we get settled there, I will write again. I want you should forgive us both; but if you won't forgive Bartley, you mustn't forgive me. You were mistaken about Bartley, and I was right. Bartley has told me everything, and I am perfectly satisfied. Love to mother.
                                        'MARCIA.'

'P.S.—I *did* intend to visit Netty Spaulding. But I saw Bartley driving past on his way to the Junction, and I determined to see him if I could before he started for Boston, and tell him I was all wrong, no matter what he said or did afterwards. I ought to have told you I meant to see Bartley; but then you would not have let me come, and if I had not come, I should have died.'

'There's a good deal of Bartley in it,' said the young man with a laugh.

'You don't like it!'

'Yes, I do; it's all right. Did you use to take the prize for composition at boarding-school?'

'Why, I think it's a very good letter for when I'm in such an excited state.'

'It's beautiful!' cried Bartley, laughing more and more. The tears started to her eyes.

'Marcia,' said her husband fondly, 'what a child you are! If ever I do anything to betray your trust in me—'

There came a shuffling of feet outside the door, a clinking of glass and crockery, and a jarring sort of blow, as if some one were trying to rap on the panel with the edge of a heavy-laden waiter. Bartley threw the door open and found the landlord there, red and smiling, with the waiter in his hand.

'I thought I'd bring your supper in here, you know,' he explained confidentially, 'so 's't you could have it a little more snug. And my wife she kind o' got wind o' what was going on,—women will, you know,' he said with a wink,—'and she's sent ye in some hot biscuit and a little jell, and some of her cake.' He set the waiter down on the table, and stood admiring its mystery of napkined dishes. 'She guessed you wouldn't object to some cold chicken, and she's put a little of that on. Sha'n't cost ye any more,' he hastened to assure them. 'Now this is your room till the train comes, and there ain't agoin' to anybody come in here. So you can make yourselves at home. And I hope you'll enjoy your supper as much as we did ourn the night we was married. There! I guess I'll let the lady fix the table; she looks as if she knowed how.'

He got himself out of the room again, and then Marcia, who had made him some embarrassed thanks, burst out in praise of his pleasantness.

'Well, he ought to be pleasant,' said Bartley, 'he's just beaten me on a horse-trade. I've sold him the colt.'

'Sold him the colt!' cried Marcia, tragically dropping the napkin she had lifted from the plate of cold chicken.

'Well, we couldn't very well have taken him to Boston with us. And we couldn't have got there without selling him. You know you haven't married a millionnaire, Marcia.'

'How much did you get for the colt?'

'Oh, I didn't do so badly. I got a hundred and fifty for him.'

'And you had fifteen besides.'

'That was before we were married. I gave the minister five for you,—I think you are worth it. I wanted to give fifteen.'

'Well, then, you have a hundred and sixty now. Isn't that a great deal?'

'An everlasting lot,' said Bartley, with an impatient laugh. 'Don't let the supper cool, Marcia!'

She silently set out the feast, but regarded it ruefully. 'You oughtn't to have ordered so much, Bartley,' she said. 'You couldn't afford it.'

'I can afford anything when I'm hungry. Besides, I only ordered the oysters and coffee; all the rest is conscience money—or sentiment—from the landlord. Come, come! cheer up, now! We sha'n't starve to-night, anyhow.'

'Well, I know father will help us.'

'We sha'n't count on him,' said Bartley. 'Now drop it!' He put his arm round her shoulders and pressed her against him, till she raised her face for his kiss.

'Well, I will!' she said, and the shadow lifted itself from their wedding feast, and they sat down and made merry as if they had all the money in the world to spend. They laughed and joked; they praised the things they liked, and made fun of the others.

'How strange! How perfectly impossible it all seems! Why, last night I was taking supper at Kinney's logging-camp, and hating you at every mouthful with all my might. Everything seemed against me, and I was feeling ugly, and flirting like mad with a fool from Montreal: she had come out there from Portland for a frolic with the owners' party. You made me do it, Marcia!' he cried jestingly. 'And remember that, if you want me to be good, you must be kind. The other thing seems to make me worse and worse.'

'I will,—I will, Bartley,' she said humbly. 'I will try to be kind and patient with you. I will indeed.'

He threw back his head, and laughed and laughed. 'Poor—poor old Kinney! He's the cook, you know, and he thought I'd been making fun of him to that woman, and he behaved so, after they were gone, that I started home in a rage; and he followed me out with his hands all covered with dough, and wanted to stop me, but he couldn't for fear of spoiling my clothes—' He lost himself in another paroxysm.

Marcia smiled a little. Then, 'What sort of a looking person was she?' she tremulously asked.

Bartley stopped abruptly. 'Not one ten-thousandth part as good-looking, nor one millionth part as bright, as Marcia Hubbard!' He caught her and smothered her against his breast.

'I don't care! I don't care!' she cried. ' was to blame more than you, if you flirted with her, and it serves me right. Yes, I will

...never say anything to you for anything that happened after I behaved so to you.'

'There wasn't anything else happened,' cried Bartley. 'And the Montreal woman snubbed me soundly before she was done with me.'

'Snubbed you!' exclaimed Marcia, with illogical indignation. This delighted Bartley so much that it was long before he left off laughing over her.

Then they sat down, and were silent till she said, 'And did you leave him in a temper?'

'Who? Kinney? In a perfect devil of a temper. I wouldn't even borrow some money he wanted to lend me.'

'Write to him, Bartley,' said his wife, seriously. 'I love you so I can't bear to have anybody bad friends with you.'

1882

FREDERICK GODDARD TUCKERMAN

1821–1873

SIX SONNETS [1]

I

As one turned round on some high moun-
    tain top
Views all things as they are, but out of
    place,
Reversing recognition, so I trace
Dimly those dreams of youth and love and
    stop
Kindly; for in such mood landmarks and
    ways
That we have trodden all our lives and know
We seem not to have known and cannot
    guess:
Like one who told his footsteps over to me
In the opposite world and where he wan-
    dered through
Whilst the hot wind blew from the sultry
    north—   10
Forests that give no shade and bottomless
Sands where the plummet sinks as in the
    sea,
Saw the sky struck by lightning from the
    earth,
Rain salt like blood, and flights of fiery
    snow.

1872   1931

2

LONG ISLAND! Yes! When first my vision
    swept
Thy far faint shores with inlet and lagoon
Or misty woodflats, where the senses swoon
As in that land where Christian sank and
    slept,
I thought of him; and then when in the
    rain
We reached the Inn; and when I heard them
    speak
Of Fire Place at hand and Devil's Neck
And Good Ground and Mount Sinai west
    away,
As in a dream I seemed to tread again
The Pilgrim's steps and trace the Heavenly
    Way.   10
But there sat Happy Jack, with dumb
    Rejoice,
Red Ike the hostler with his whistling
    voice,
And an old man I called Legality . . .
Craftily quaint the tale he told to me.

1872   1931

3

'YOUNG Silas Long, a carrier through these
    woods,
Drove home one night in not the best of
    moods,
Having just seen a drowned man flung
    ashore
With a strange feather cap. And once
    before,
When he was hauling seine in Southold
    Bay
About this time of year, a seaman's corse
Washed up, with such a cap and such a
    face,
And it had brought misfortune on the
    place.
Pondering he drove; when lo, across the
    way
He saw, too late, that there a body lay,   10

[1] The sonnets have been selected from sequences written in 1872, and not printed before their appearance in Bynner, ed., *The Sonnets of Frederick Goddard Tuckerman* (N.Y., 1931). They are, respectively, sonnets 8, 11, 12, and 13 from the third sequence; and sonnets 6 and 10 from the fourth.

Felt the wheels tilt but could not stop his
    horse
Or not at once, then—flinging with a
    slap
The old cloth cover down he called a cap—
Ran back, ten steps or more, and nothing
    found . . .'
1872   1931

4

'YES, the dead pines and deersfoot on the
    ground,—
So quick returned again in five or six.
His cap was gone and in its stead thrown
    down
The very loon-skin the twice-drowned had
    on,
With bits of seaweed sticking to the flix.
So Long rode home, of cap and sense
    bereft,
But still can show the dead man's that was
    left,
And the webs crawl, he says, when the sea
    rolls.'
Then he, having told his tale and said his
    say,
By way of emphasis or corollary   10
Spat a torpedo in the bed of coals.
'And what, what, what,' squealed Ike,
    'became of Long's?'
But the old man here rose and reached the
    tongs,
Laid fire to his pipe and phewed away.
1872   1931

5

AND two I knew, an old man and a boy,
Alternate helpers: for their day was spent
In gathering forest bark; and when they
    went
Late home, the elder did his time employ
To teach the other and tell him what he
    knew

Of history, myth, or mathematics hard,
In hours of night and, when the night was
    dark,
Showed him Job's Coffin, and the Golden
    Yard,
Showed the nine moonstars in the moonless
    blue,
And the great Circle of the Bestiary;   10
So that the child grew up to love the
    sky
And, in the woods beyond the hemlock
    bark,
To heed the intricate moss that o'er it
    grew,
The shadowy flower all wet with all-day
    dew.
1872   1931

6

HAST thou seen reversed the prophet's
    miracle—
The worm that, touched, a twig-like
    semblance takes?
Or hast thou mused what giveth the craft
    that makes
The twirling spider at once invisible,
And the spermal odour to the barberry
    flower,
Or heard the singing sand by the cold coast
    foam,
Or late—in inland autumn groves afar—
Hast thou ever plucked the little chick-
    wintergreen star
And tasted the sour of its leaf? Then come
With me betimes, and I will show thee
    more   10
Than these, of nature's secrecies the least:
In the first morning, overcast and chill,
And in the day's young sunshine, seeking
    still
For earliest flowers and gathering to the
    east.
1872   1931

EDWARD ROWLAND SILL

1841–1887

TRUTH AT LAST

DOES a man ever give up hope, I wonder,—
Face the grim fact, seeing it clear as day?
When Bennen saw the snow slip, heard its
    thunder

Low, louder, roaring round him, felt the
    speed
Grow swifter as the avalanche hurled
    downward,
Did he for just one heart-throb—did he
    indeed

Know with all certainty, as they swept
    onward,
There was the end, where the crag dropped
    away?
Or did he think, even till they plunged and
    fell,
Some miracle would stop them? Nay, they
    tell   10
That he turned round, face forward, calm
    and pale,
Stretching his arms out toward his native
    vale
As if in mute, unspeakable farewell,
And so went down.—'Tis something, if at
    last,
Though only for a flash, a man may see
Clear-eyed the future as he sees the past,
From doubt, or fear, or hope's illusion free.
    1883

FIVE LIVES

FIVE mites of monads dwelt in a round
    drop
That twinkled on a leaf by a pool in the sun.
To the naked eye they lived invisible;
Specks, for a world of whom the empty
    shell
Of a mustard-seed had been a hollow sky.

One was a meditative monad, called a
    sage;
And, shrinking all his mind within, he
    thought:
'Tradition, handed down for hours and
    hours,
Tells that our globe, this quivering crystal
    world,
Is slowly dying. What if, seconds hence,   10
When I am very old, yon shimmering
    dome
Come drawing down and down, till all
    things end?'
Then with a weazen smirk he proudly felt
No other mote of God had ever gained
Such giant grasp of universal truth.

One was a transcendental monad; thin
And long and slim in the mind; and thus he
    mused:
'Oh, vast, unfathomable monad-souls!
Made in the image'—a hoarse frog croaks
    from the pool—
'Hark! 'twas some god, voicing his glorious
    thought   20

In thunder music! Yea, we hear their voice,
And we may guess their minds from ours,
    their work.
Some taste they have like ours, some
    tendency
To wriggle about, and munch a trace of
    scum.'
He floated up on a pin-point bubble of
    gas
That burst, pricked by the air, and he was
    gone.

One was a barren-minded monad, called
A positivist; and he knew positively:
'There is no world beyond this certain
    drop.
Prove me another! Let the dreamers dream
Of their faint dreams, and noises from
    without,   31
And higher and lower; life is life enough.'
Then swaggering half a hair's breadth,
    hungrily
He seized upon an atom of bug, and fed.

One was a tattered monad, called a poet;
And with shrill voice ecstatic thus he
    sang:
'Oh, the little female monad's lips!
Oh, the little female monad's eyes:
Ah, the little, little, female, female monad!'

The last was a strong-minded monadess,
Who dashed amid the infusoria,   41
Danced high and low, and wildly spun and
    dove
Till the dizzy others held their breath to
    see.

But while they led their wondrous little
    lives
Æonian moments had gone wheeling by,
The burning drop had shrunk with fearful
    speed;
A glistening film—'twas gone; the leaf was
    dry.
The little ghost of an inaudible squeak
Was lost to the frog that goggled from his
    stone;
Who, at the huge, slow tread of a thoughtful
    ox   50
Coming to drink, stirred sideways fatly,
    plunged,
Launched backward twice, and all the pool
    was still.
    1883

THE FOOL'S PRAYER

THE royal feast was done; the King
  Sought some new sport to banish care,
And to his jester cried: 'Sir Fool,
  Kneel now, and make for us a prayer!'

The jester doffed his cap and bells,
  And stood the mocking court before;
They could not see the bitter smile
  Behind the painted grin he wore.

He bowed his head, and bent his knee
  Upon the monarch's silken stool;   10
His pleading voice arose: 'O Lord,
  Be merciful to me, a fool!

'No pity, Lord, could change the heart
  From red with wrong to white as wool;
The rod must heal the sin: but, Lord,
  Be merciful to me, a fool!

' 'Tis not by guilt the onward sweep
  Of truth and right, O Lord, we stay;
'Tis by our follies that so long
  We hold the earth from heaven away.   20

'These clumsy feet, still in the mire,
  Go crushing blossoms without end;
These hard, well-meaning hands we thrust
  Among the heart-strings of a friend.

'The ill-timed truth we might have kept—
  Who knows how sharp it pierced and
     stung?
The word we had not sense to say—
  Who knows how grandly it had rung?

'Our faults no tenderness should ask,
  The chastening stripes must cleanse them
     all;   30
But for our blunders—oh, in shame
  Before the eyes of heaven we fall.

'Earth bears no balsam for mistakes;
  Men crown the knave; and scourge the
     tool
That did his will; but Thou, O Lord,
  Be merciful to me, a fool!'

The room was hushed; in silence rose
  The King, and sought his gardens
     cool,
And walked apart, and murmured low,
  'Be merciful to me, a fool!'   40
          1883

OPPORTUNITY

THIS I beheld, or dreamed it in a dream:—
There spread a cloud of dust along a
    plain;
And underneath the cloud, or in it, raged
A furious battle, and men yelled, and
    swords
Shocked upon swords and shields. A
    prince's banner
Wavered, then staggered backward,
    hemmed by foes.
A craven hung along the battle's edge,
And thought, 'Had I a sword of keener
    steel—
That blue blade that the king's son bears,—
    but this
Blunt thing—!' he snapt and flung it from
    his hand,   10
And lowering crept away and left the field.
Then came the king's son, wounded, sore
    bestead,
And weaponless, and saw the broken
    sword,
Hilt-buried in the dry and trodden sand,
And ran and snatched it, and with battle-
    shout
Lifted afresh he hewed his enemy down,
And saved a great cause that heroic day.
          1887

JOHN BANISTER TABB

1845–1909

FATHER DAMIEN [1]

(DIED APRIL 10TH, 1889)

O GOD, the cleanest offering
Of tainted earth below,
Unblushing to thy feet we bring—
'*A leper white as snow!*'

1889   1894

EVOLUTION

OUT of the dusk a shadow,
    Then a spark;
Out of the cloud a silence,
    Then a lark;

Out of the heart a rapture,
    Then a pain;
Out of the dead, cold ashes,
    Life again.

1894

BLOSSOM

FOR this the fruit, for this the
        seed,
    For this the parent tree;
The least to man, the most to God—
    A fragrant mystery
Where love, with beauty glorified,
    Forgets utility.

1892   1894

THE PEAK

As on some solitary height
Abides, in summer's fierce despite,
Snow-blossom that no sun can
        blight,
    No frost can kill;
So, in my soul—all else below
To change succumbing—stands
        aglow
One wreath of immemorial snow,
    Unscattered still.

1892   1894

1 Father Damien, a Roman Catholic priest, was a missionary among the lepers at Molokai, Hawaii. He himself at last contracted the disease, and died of it.

PREJUDICE

A LEAF may hide the largest star
    From love's uplifted eye;
A mote of prejudice out-bar
    A world of charity.

1892   1894

FAME

THEIR noonday never knows
    What names immortal are;
'Tis night alone that shows
    How star surpasseth star.

1894   1897

EXPECTANCY

AN eagle on the summit—Hope and Fear,
    Alternate pinions, moving restlessly.
O Distance, doth the better part appear
    Doubt or fulfilment of the thing to be?

1923

SUNDERED

THOU sleepest sound, and I
Anear thee lie,
Yet worlds apart:
Thou in the light of dreams;
I, where the midnight seems—
An ashen sea—
From this my world and that wherein thou
        art
To blot out all but me.

1908   1910

GOING BLIND

BACK to the primal gloom
    Where life began,
As to my mother's womb
    Must I a man
        Return:
Not to be born again,
    But to remain;
And in the School of Darkness learn
        What mean
'The things unseen.'   1(

1908   1910

RICHARD HOVEY

1864–1900

THE WANDER-LOVERS

Down the world with Marna!
That's the life for me!
Wandering with the wandering wind,
Vagabond and unconfined!
Roving with the roving rain
Its unboundaried domain!
Kith and kin of wander-kind,
Children of the sea!

Petrels of the sea-drift!
Swallows of the lea!   10
Arabs of the whole wide girth
Of the wind-encircled earth!
In all climes we pitch our tents,
Cronies of the elements,
With the secret lords of birth
Intimate and free.

All the seaboard knows us
From Fundy to the Keys;
Every bend and every creek
Of abundant Chesapeake;   20
Ardise hills and Newport coves
And the far-off orange groves,
Where Floridian oceans break,
Tropic tiger seas.

Down the world with Marna,
Tarrying there and here!
Just as much at home in Spain
As in Tangier or Touraine!
Shakespeare's Avon knows us well,
And the crags of Neufchâtel;   30
And the ancient Nile is fain
Of our coming near.

Down the world with Marna,
Daughter of the air!
Marna of the subtle grace,
And the vision in her face!
Moving in the measures trod
By the angels before God!
With her sky-blue eyes amaze
And her sea-blue hair!   40

Marna with the trees' life
In her veins a-stir!
Marna of the aspen heart
Where the sudden quivers start!

Quick-responsive, subtle, wild!
Artless as an artless child,
Spite of all her reach of art!
Oh, to roam with her!

Marna with the wind's will,
Daughter of the sea!   50
Marna of the quick disdain,
Starting at the dream of stain!
At a smile with love aglow,
At a frown a statued woe,
Standing pinnacled in pain
Till a kiss sets free!

Down the world with Marna,
Daughter of the fire!
Marna of the deathless hope,
Still alert to win new scope   60
Where the wings of life may spread
For a flight unhazarded!
Dreaming of the speech to cope
With the heart's desire!

Marna of the far quest
After the divine!
Striving ever for some goal
Past the blunder-god's control!
Dreaming of potential years
When no day shall dawn in fears!   70
That's the Marna of my soul,
Wander-bride of mine!

                                                       1894

COMRADES

Comrades, pour the wine to-night
For the parting is with dawn!
Oh, the clink of cups together,
With the daylight coming on!
Greet the morn
With a double horn,
When strong men drink together!

Comrades, gird your swords to-
        night,
For the battle is with dawn!
Oh, the clash of shields together,   10
With the triumph coming on!
Greet the foe,
And lay him low,
When strong men fight together!

Comrades, watch the tides to-night,
For the sailing is with dawn!
Oh, to face the spray together,
With the tempest coming on!
Greet the sea
With a shout of glee,   20
When strong men roam together!

Comrades, give a cheer to-night,
For the dying is with dawn!
Oh, to meet the stars together,
With the silence coming on!
Greet the end
As a friend a friend,
When strong men die together!
                                                       1894

THE SEA GYPSY

I AM fevered with the sunset,
I am fretful with the bay,
For the wander-thirst is on me
And my soul is in Cathay.

There's a schooner in the offing,
With her topsails shot with fire,
And my heart has gone aboard her
For the Islands of Desire.

I must forth again to-morrow!
With the sunset I must be   10
Hull down on the trail of rapture
In the wonder of the sea.
                                                       1896

A STEIN SONG

GIVE a rouse, then, in the Maytime
For a life that knows no fear!
Turn night-time into day-time
With the sunlight of good cheer!
For it's always fair weather
When good fellows get together,
With a stein on the table and a good song
        ringing clear.

When the wind comes up from
        Cuba
And the birds are on the wing,
And our hearts are patting juba   10
To the banjo of the spring,
Then it's no wonder whether
The boys will get together,
With a stein on the table and a cheer for
        everything.

For we're all frank-and-twenty
When the spring is in the air;
And we've faith and hope a-plenty,
And we've life and love to spare;
And it's birds of a feather
When we all get together,   20
With a stein on the table and a heart with-
        out a care.

For we know the world is glorious,
And the goal a golden thing,
And that God is not censorious
When his children have their fling;
And life slips its tether
When the boys get together,
With a stein on the table in the fellowship
        of spring.
                                                       1896

UNMANIFEST DESTINY

To what new fates, my country, far
    And unforeseen of foe or friend,
Beneath what unexpected star,
    Compelled to what unchosen end,

Across the sea that knows no beach
    The Admiral of Nations guides
Thy blind obedient keels to reach
    The harbor where thy future rides!

The guns that spoke at Lexington
    Knew not that God was planning then   10
The trumpet word of Jefferson
    To bugle forth the rights of men.

To them that wept and cursed Bull Run,
    What was it but despair and shame?
Who saw behind the cloud the sun?
    Who knew that God was in the flame?

Had not defeat upon defeat,
    Disaster on disaster come,
The slave's emancipated feet
    Had never marched behind the drum. 20

There is a Hand that bends our deeds
    To mightier issues than we planned,
Each son that triumphs, each that bleeds,
    My country, serves Its dark command.

I do not know beneath what sky
    Nor on what seas shall be thy fate;
I only know it shall be high,
    I only know it shall be great.
1898   1898

AT THE CROSSROADS

You to the left and I to the right,
For the ways of men must sever—
And it well may be for a day and a night,
And it well may be forever.
But whether we meet or whether we part
(For our ways are past our knowing),
A pledge from the heart to its fellow heart
On the ways we all are going!
Here's luck!
For we know not where we are going.   10

We have striven fair in love and war,
But the wheel was always weighted;
We have lost the prize that we struggled
    for,
We have won the prize that was fated.
We have met our loss with a smile and a
    song,
And our gains with a wink and a whistle,—
For, whether we're right or whether we're
    wrong,
There's a rose for every thistle.
Here's luck—
And a drop to wet your whistle!   20

Whether we win or whether we lose
With the hands that life is dealing,
It is not we nor the ways we choose
But the fall of the cards that's sealing.

There's a fate in love and a fate in fight,
And the best of us all go under—
And whether we're wrong or whether we're
    right,
We win, sometimes, to our wonder.
Here's luck—
That we may not yet go under!   30

With a steady swing and an open brow
We have tramped the ways together,
But we're clasping hands at the crossroads
    now
In the Fiend's own night for weather;
And whether we bleed or whether we smile
In the leagues that lie before us,
The ways of life are many a mile
And the dark of Fate is o'er us.
Here's luck!
And a cheer for the dark before us!   40

You to the left and I to the right,
For the ways of men must sever,
And it well may be for a day and a night,
And it well may be forever!
But whether we live or whether we die
(For the end is past our knowing),
Here's two frank hearts and the open sky,
Be a fair or an ill wind blowing!
Here's luck!
In the teeth of all winds blowing.   50

                                    1900

LOUISE IMOGEN GUINEY

1861–1920

THE WILD RIDE

I HEAR in my heart, I hear in its ominous
    pulses
All day, on the road, the hoofs of invisible
    horses,
All night, from their stalls, the importunate
    pawing and neighing.

Let cowards and laggards fall back! but
    alert to the saddle
Weather-worn and abreast, go men of our
    galloping legion,
With a stirrup-cup each to the lily of women
    that loves him.

The trail is through dolour and dread, over
    crags and morasses;

There are shapes by the way, there are
    things that appal or entice us:
What odds? We are Knights of the Grail,
    we are vowed to the riding.

Thought's self is a vanishing wing, and joy
    is a cobweb,   10
And friendship a flower in the dust, and
    glory a sunbeam:
Not here is our prize, nor, alas! after these
    our pursuing.

A dipping of plumes, a tear, a shake of the
    bridle,
A passing salute to this world and
    her pitiful beauty:
We hurry with never a word in the track
    of our fathers.

(I hear in my heart, I hear in its ominous
    pulses
All day, on the road, the hoofs of invisible
    horses,
All night, from their stalls, the importunate
    pawing and neighing.)

We spur to a land of no name, out-racing
    the storm-wind;
We leap to the infinite dark like sparks from
    the anvil.   20
Thou leadest, O God! All's well with Thy
    troopers that follow.

                1887

A FRIEND'S SONG FOR SIMOISIUS [1]

THE breath of dew and twilight's grace
Be on the lonely battle-place,
And to so young, so kind a face,
The long protecting grasses cling!
(Alas, alas,
That one inexorable thing!)

In rocky hollows cool and deep,
The honey-bees unrifled sleep;
The early moon from Ida steep
Comes to the empty wrestling-ring;   10

Upon the widowed wind recede
No echoes of the shepherd's reed;
And children without laughter lead
The war-horse to the watering;

With footstep separate and slow
The father and the mother go,
Not now upon an urn they know
To mingle tears for comforting.

Thou stranger Ajax Telamon!
What to the lovely hast thou done,   26
That nevermore a maid may run
With him across the flowery Spring?

The world to me has nothing dear
Beyond the namesake river here:
Oh, Simois is wild and clear!
And to his brink my heart I bring;

My heart, if only this might be,
Would stay his waters from the
    sea,
To cover Troy, to cover me,
To haste the hour of perishing.   30
(Alas, alas,
That one inexorable thing!)

                1893

LIZETTE REESE
1856–1936

IMMORTALITY

BATTLES nor songs can from oblivion save,
    But Fame upon a white deed loves to
        build;
From out that cup of water Sidney gave,
    Not one drop has been spilled.

                1892

IN TIME OF GRIEF

DARK, thinned, beside the wall of
    stone,
The box dripped in the air;
Its odor through my house was blown
Into the chamber there.

Remote and yet distinct the scent,
The sole thing of the kind,
As though one spoke a word half meant
That left a sting behind.

I knew not Grief would go from me,
And naught of it be plain,   10
Except how keen the box can be
After a fall of rain.

                1896

1 'Having to do with *Iliad*,IV,473–489.' Author's note, Guiney, *Happy Ending*(Boston, 1937),191. 'Next Telamonian Aias smote Anthemion's son, the lusty stripling Simoeisios, whom erst his mother bare beside the banks of Simoeis on the way down from Ida whither she had followed with her parents to see their flocks. Therefore they called him Simoeisios, but he repaid not his dear parents the recompense of his nurture; scanty was his span of life by reason of the spear of great-hearted Aias that laid him low. For as he went he first was smitten on his right breast beside the pap; straight through his shoulder passed the spear of bronze, and he fell to the ground in the dust like a poplar-tree, that hath grown up smooth in the lowland of a great marsh, and its branches grow upon the top thereof; this hath a wainwright felled with gleaming steel, to bend him a felloe for a goodly chariot, and so it lies drying by a river's banks. In such fashion did heaven-sprung Aias slay Simoeisios son of Anthemion . . .' Lang, trans.

TEARS [1]

WHEN I consider Life and its few
    years—
A wisp of fog betwixt us and the
    sun;
A call to battle, and the battle done
Ere the last echo dies within our
    ears;
A rose choked in the grass; an hour of
    fears;
The gusts that past a darkening shore do
    beat;
The burst of music down an unlistening
    street—
I wonder at the idleness of tears.
Ye old, old dead, and ye of yester-
    night,
Chieftains, and bards, and keepers of the
    sheep,   10
By every cup of sorrow that you had,
Loose me from tears, and make me see
    aright
How each hath back what once he stayed to
    weep;
Homer his sight, David his little lad!

                                     1909

A PURITAN LADY

WILD Carthage held her, Rome,
    Sidon. She stared to tears
Tall, golden Helen, wearying
    Behind the Trojan spears.

Towered Antwerp knew her well;
    She wore her quiet gown
In some hushed house in Oxford grass,
    Or lane in Salem town.

Humble and high in one,
    Cool, certain, different,   10
She lasts; scarce saint, yet half a child,
    As hard, as innocent.

What grave, long afternoons,
    What caged airs round her blown,
Stripped her of humor, left her bare
    As cloud, or wayside stone?

Made her as clear a thing,
    In this slack world as plain
As a white flower on a grave,
    Or sleet sharp at a pane?   20

                                     1923

GEORGE STERLING

1869–1926

THE NIGHT OF GODS

THEIR mouths have drunken Death's eter-
    nal wine—
    The draught that Baal in oblivion sips.
    Unseen about their courts the adder
        slips,
Unheard the sucklings of the leopard
    whine;
The toad has found a resting-place divine,
    And bloats in stupor between Ammon's
        lips.

1 Miss Reese, with most of her public, thought 'Tears'
her best poem. 'What mood brought it into being?
Again I am ignorant. However, I will tell you all that I
remember. My father had been a semi-invalid for
years. Suddenly he died. The check for the poem came
the day the crepe was hung on the door to announce
his death. Now it may be that I had him in mind during the making of this poem. The scientists—who now
have us in their keeping—speak about the subcon-
scious: old-fashioned folks use the worn word "premonition." You may take your choice.' Benét,ed.,
Fifty Poets(N.Y , 1933),14.

O Carthage and the unreturning ships,
The fallen pinnacle, the shifting Sign!

Lo! when I hear from voiceless court and
    fane
    Time's adoration of Eternity—   10
    The cry of kingdoms past and gods
        undone—
I stand as one whose feet at noontide gain
    A lonely shore; who feels his soul set
        free,
    And hears the blind sea chanting to the
        sun.

                                     1909

ALDEBARAN AT DUSK

THOU art the star for which all evening
    waits—
O star of peace, come tenderly and soon,
Nor heed the drowsy and enchanted
    moon,

Who dreams in silver at the eastern gates
Ere yet she brim with light the blue estates
  Abandoned by the eagles of the noon.
  But shine thou swiftly on the darkling
    dune
And woodlands where the twilight
    hesitates.

Above that wide and ruby lake to-West,
  Wherein the sunset waits reluctantly, 10
    Stir silently the purple wings of Night.
She stands afar, upholding to her breast,
  As mighty murmurs reach her from the
    sea,
    Thy lone and everlasting rose of light.
                      1911

THE BLACK VULTURE

ALOOF within the day's enormous dome,
  He holds unshared the silence of the
    sky.
  Far down his bleak, relentless eyes descry
The eagle's empire and the falcon's home—
Far down, the galleons of sunset roam;
  His hazards on the sea of morning lie;
  Serene, he hears the broken tempest
    sigh
Where cold sierras gleam like scattered
    foam.

And least of all he holds the human
    swarm—
  Unwitting now that envious men
    prepare   10
    To make their dream and its fulfill-
    ment one,
When, poised above the caldrons of the
    storm,
  Their hearts, contemptuous of death,
    shall dare
    His roads between the thunder and the
    sun.
                    1911

THE YOUNG WITCH [1]

1698

(ELDER DAVENPORT SPEAKS)

CRY bravely, O town-crier,
  (And ye, young men, beware!)
How Yale Ratchford, the strong smith,
  Is gone God knoweth where.

[1] Printed in *The Century Magazine*,CVI,iv,588–91; and not included in any volume by Sterling.

Yea, the tall smith is gone,
  And comes not home again.
Though he had a shrewish wife,
  He was man among men.

He shall drink no more ale,
  Nor smoke at the tavern door,   10
Nor sing old songs at his forge,
  And wrestle young men no more.

This he got for being so strong,
  And this for being so bold
As to have in scorn the white witch
  Who slept in her hair of gold.

By the dark pond in the hills
  She lived when her dam died,
With a black cat which minded
    her,
  And a black dog at her side.   20

In pine-wood and marshy places
  Her low song was sung,
Where long moss is, and toadstools
  The hue of a goblin's tongue.

Where got she her sullen mouth
  And where her swaying form?
Would she live on eggs and apples
  When the blood of men is warm?

All the town people went shy of her
  When the Ratchford baby died.   30
Folk tell how she laughed that day,
  And no folk say she cried.

Yale Ratchford cut him a switch
  From a hickory at his door,
And he went up among the hills
  To see she laughed no more.

There were whispers of a hanging
  The day that he went forth,
As had been done by holy men
  At Salem in the north.   40

A bear was shot at Hadlyme
  With fur as soft as silk,
And Goodman Ames of Saybrook
  Found minnows in the milk.

That night the geese went over,
  A-belling for the pole.
Some say it was the dark hounds
  That bay a loosened soul.

But saved, or damned forever,
  He comes back home no more,   50
And we who searched at the witch's
    house
  Found grass against the door.

It was not wise to go hillward
  With hand shut on a switch;
It is not given to young men
  To rid the land of a witch—

Not with eyes so wide apart,
  And in a face so white.

Not if she wander naked
  By a shrunk moon's light.   60

What shall he do her of service,
  As the strong do for the fair?
Shall he forge her an iron marriage-ring,
  Or shoes for the devil's mare?

For they ha' gone forever—
  Vanished, as men say true,
In blue sky or blue water
  Or the wind between the two.

1923

AMBROSE BIERCE
1842–1914?

AN OCCURRENCE AT OWL CREEK BRIDGE

I

A MAN stood upon a railroad bridge in northern Alabama, looking down into the swift water twenty feet below. The man's hands were behind his back, the wrists bound with a cord. A rope closely encircled his neck. It was attached to a stout cross-timber above his head and the slack fell to the level of his knees. Some loose boards laid upon the sleepers supporting the metals of the railway supplied a footing for him and his executioners—two private soldiers of the Federal army, directed by a sergeant who in civil life may have been a deputy sheriff. At a short remove upon the same temporary platform was an officer in the uniform of his rank, armed. He was a captain. A sentinel at each end of the bridge stood with his rifle in the position known as 'support,' that is to say, vertical in front of the left shoulder, the hammer resting on the forearm thrown straight across the chest—a formal and unnatural position, enforcing an erect carriage of the body. It did not appear to be the duty of these two men to know what was occurring at the centre of the bridge; they merely blockaded the two ends of the foot planking that traversed it.

Beyond one of the sentinels nobody was in sight; the railroad ran straight away into a forest for a hundred yards, then, curving, was lost to view. Doubtless there was an outpost farther along. The other bank of the stream was open ground—a gentle acclivity topped with a stockade of vertical tree trunks, loop-holed for rifles, with a single embrasure through which protruded the muzzle of a brass cannon commanding the bridge. Midway of the slope between bridge and fort were the spectators—a single company of infantry in line, at 'parade rest,' the butts of the rifles on the ground, the barrels inclining slightly backward against the right shoulder, the hands crossed upon the stock. A lieutenant stood at the right of the line, the point of his sword upon the ground, his left hand resting upon his right. Excepting the group of four at the centre of the bridge, not a man moved. The company faced the bridge, staring stonily, motionless. The sentinels, facing the banks of the stream, might have been statues to adorn the bridge. The captain stood with folded arms, silent, observing the work of his subordinates, but making no sign. Death is a dignitary who when he comes announced is to be received with formal manifestations of respect, even by those most familiar with him. In the code of military etiquette silence and fixity are forms of deference.

The man who was engaged in being hanged was apparently about thirty-five years of age. He was a civilian, if one might judge from his habit, which was that of a planter. His features were good—a straight nose, firm mouth, broad forehead, from which his long, dark hair was combed straight back, falling behind his ears to the ollar of his well-fitting frock-coat. He wore mustache and pointed beard, but no whiskers; his eyes were large and dark gray, and had a kindly expression which one would hardly have expected in one whose neck was in the hemp. Evidently this was no vulgar assassin. The liberal military code makes provision for hanging many kinds of persons, and gentlemen are not excluded.

The preparations being complete, the two private soldiers stepped aside and each drew away the plank upon which he had been standing. The sergeant turned to the captain, saluted and placed himself immediately behind that officer, who in turn moved apart one pace. These movements left the condemned man and the sergeant standing on the two ends of the same plank, which spanned three of the cross-ties of the bridge. The end upon which the civilian stood almost, but not quite, reached a fourth. This plank had been held in place by the weight of the captain; it was now held by that of the sergeant. At a signal from the former the latter would step aside, the plank would tilt and the condemned man go down between two ties. The arrangement commended itself to his judgment as simple and effective. His face had not been covered nor his eyes bandaged. He looked a moment at his 'unsteadfast footing,' then let his gaze wander to the whirling water of the stream racing madly beneath his feet. A piece of dancing driftwood caught his attention and his eyes followed it down the current. How slowly it appeared to move! What a sluggish stream! He closed his eyes in order to fix his last thoughts upon his wife and children. The water, touched to gold by the early sun, the brooding mists under the banks at some distance down the stream, the fort, the soldiers, the piece of drift—all had distracted him. And now he became conscious of a new disturbance. Striking through the thought of his dear ones was a sound which he could neither ignore nor understand, a sharp, distinct, metallic percussion like the stroke of a blacksmith's hammer upon the anvil; it had the same ringing quality. He wondered what it was, and whether immeasurably distant or near by—it seemed both. Its recurrence was regular, but as slow as the tolling of a death knell. He awaited each stroke with impatience and—he knew not why—apprehension. The intervals of silence grew progressively longer; the delays became maddening. With their greater infrequency the sounds increased in strength and sharpness. They hurt his ear like the thrust of a knife; he feared he would shriek. What he heard was the ticking of his watch.

He unclosed his eyes and saw again the water below him. 'If I could free my hands,' he thought, 'I might throw off the noose and spring into the stream. By diving I could evade the bullets and, swimming vigorously, reach the bank, take to the woods and get away home. My home, thank God, is as yet outside their lines; my wife and little ones are still beyond the invader's farthest advance.'

As these thoughts, which have here to be set down in words, were flashed into the doomed man's brain rather than evolved from it, the captain nodded to the sergeant. The sergeant stepped aside.

II

Peyton Farquhar was a well-to-do planter, of an old and highly respected Alabama family. Being a slave owner and, like other slave owners, a politician he was naturally an original secessionist and ardently devoted to the Southern cause. Circumstances of an imperious nature, which it is unnecessary to relate here, had prevented him from taking service with the gallant army that had fought the disastrous campaigns ending with the fall of Corinth, and he chafed under the inglorious restraint, longing for the release of his energies, the larger life of the soldier, the opportunity for distinction. That opportunity, he felt, would come, as it comes to all in war time. Meanwhile he did what he could. No service was too humble for him to perform in aid of the South, no adventure too perilous for him to undertake if consistent with the character of a civilian who was at heart a soldier, and who in good faith and without too much qualification assented to at least a part of the frankly villainous dictum that all is fair in love and war.

One evening while Farquhar and his wife were sitting on a rustic bench near the entrance to his grounds, a gray-clad soldier rode up to the gate and asked for a drink of water. Mrs. Farquhar was only too happy to serve him with her own white hands. While she was fetching the water her husband approached the dusty horseman and inquired eagerly for news from the front.

'The Yanks are repairing the railroads,' said the man, 'and are getting ready for another advance. They have reached the Owl Creek bridge, put it in order and built a stockade on the north bank. The commandant has issued an order, which is posted everywhere, declaring that any civilian caught interfering with the railroad, its bridges, tunnels or trains will be summarily hanged. I saw the order.'

'How far is it to the Owl Creek bridge?' Farquhar asked.

'About thirty miles.'

'Is there no force on this side the creek?'

'Only a picket post half a mile out, on the railroad, and a single sentinel at this end of the bridge.'

'Suppose a man—a civilian and student of hanging—should elude the picket post and perhaps get the better of the sentinel,' said Farquhar, smiling, 'what could he accomplish?'

The soldier reflected. 'I was there a month ago,' he replied. 'I observed that the flood of last winter had lodged a great quantity of driftwood against the wooden pier at this end of the bridge. It is now dry and would burn like tow.'

The lady had now brought the water, which the soldier drank. He thanked her ceremoniously, bowed to her husband and rode away. An hour later, after nightfall, he repassed the plantation, going northward in the direction from which he had come. He was a Federal scout.

III

As Peyton Farquhar fell straight downward through the bridge he lost consciousness and was as one already dead. From this state he was awakened—ages later, it seemed to him—by the pain of a sharp pressure upon his throat, followed by a sense of suffocation. Keen, poignant agonies seemed to shoot from his neck downward through every fibre of his body and limbs. These pains appeared to flash along well-defined lines of ramification and to beat with an inconceivably rapid perio-

dicity. They seemed like streams of pulsating fire heating him to an intolerable temperature. As to his head, he was conscious of nothing but a feeling of fulness—of congestion. These sensations were unaccompanied by thought. The intellectual part of his nature was already effaced; he had power only to feel, and feeling was torment. He was conscious of motion. Encompassed in a luminous cloud, of which he was now merely the fiery heart, without material substance, he swung through unthinkable arcs of oscillation, like a vast pendulum.

Then all at once, with terrible suddenness, the light about him shot upward with the noise of a loud plash; a frightful roaring was in his ears, and all was cold and dark. The power of thought was restored; he knew that the rope had broken and he had fallen into the stream. There was no additional strangulation; the noose about his neck was already suffocating him and kept the water from his lungs. To die of hanging at the bottom of a river!—the idea seemed to him ludicrous. He opened his eyes in the darkness and saw above him a gleam of light, but how distant, how inaccessible! He was still sinking, for the light became fainter and fainter until it was a mere glimmer. Then it began to grow and brighten, and he knew that he was rising toward the surface—knew it with reluctance, for he was now very comfortable. 'To be hanged and drowned,' he thought, 'that is not so bad; but I do not wish to be shot. No; I will not be shot; that is not fair.'

He was not conscious of an effort, but a sharp pain in his wrist apprised him that he was trying to free his hands. He gave the struggle his attention, as an idler might observe the feat of a juggler, without interest in the outcome. What splendid effort! What magnificent, what superhuman strength! Ah, that was a fine endeavor! Bravo! The cord fell away; his arms parted and floated upward, the hands dimly seen on each side in the growing light. He watched them with a new interest as first one and then the other pounced upon the noose at his neck. They tore it away and thrust it fiercely aside, its undulations resembling those of a water-snake. 'Put it back, put it back!' He thought he shouted these words to his hands, for the undoing of the noose had been succeeded by the direst pang that he had yet experienced. His neck ached horribly; his brain was on fire; his heart, which had been fluttering faintly, gave a great leap, trying to force itself out at his mouth. His whole body was racked and wrenched with an insupportable anguish! But his disobedient hands gave no heed to the command. They beat the water vigorously with quick, downward strokes, forcing him to the surface. He felt his head emerge; his eyes were blinded by the sunlight; his chest expanded convulsively, and with a supreme and crowning agony his lungs engulfed a great draught of air, which instantly he expelled in a shriek!

He was now in full possession of his physical senses. They were, indeed, preternaturally keen and alert. Something in the awful disturbance of his organic system had so exalted and refined them that they made record of things never before perceived. He felt the ripples upon his face and heard their separate sounds as they struck. He looked at the forest on the bank of the stream, saw the individual trees, the leaves and the veining of each leaf—saw the very insects upon them: the locusts, the brilliant-bodied flies, the gray spiders stretching their webs from twig to twig. He noted the prismatic colors in all the dewdrops upon a million blades of grass. The humming of the gnats that danced above the eddies of the stream, the beating of the dragon-flies' wings, the strokes of the water-spiders' legs, like oars which had lifted their boat—all these made audible music. A fish slid along beneath his eyes and he heard the rush of its body parting the water.

He had come to the surface facing down the stream; in a moment the visible world seemed to wheel slowly round, himself the pivotal point, and he saw the bridge, the fort, the soldiers upon the bridge, the captain, the sergeant, the two privates, his executioners. They were in silhouette against the blue sky. They shouted and gesticulated, pointing at him. The captain had drawn his pistol, but did not fire; the others were unarmed. Their movements were grotesque and horrible, their forms gigantic.

Suddenly he heard a sharp report and something struck the water smartly within a few inches of his head, spattering his face with spray. He heard a second report, and

saw one of the sentinels with his rifle at his shoulder, a light cloud of blue smoke rising from the muzzle. The man in the water saw the eye of the man on the bridge gazing into his own through the sights of the rifle. He observed that it was a gray eye and remembered having read that gray eyes were keenest, and that all famous marksmen had them. Nevertheless, this one had missed.

A counter-swirl had caught Farquhar and turned him half round; he was again looking into the forest on the bank opposite the fort. The sound of a clear, high voice in a monotonous singsong now rang out behind him and came across the water with a distinctness that pierced and subdued all other sounds, even the beating of the ripples in his ears. Although no soldier, he had frequented camps enough to know the dread significance of that deliberate, drawling, aspirated chant; the lieutenant on shore was taking a part in the morning's work. How coldly and pitilessly—with what an even, calm intonation, presaging and enforcing tranquillity in the men—with what accurately measured intervals fell those cruel words:

'Attention, company! . . . Shoulder arms! . . . Ready! . . . Aim! . . . Fire!'

Farquhar dived—dived as deeply as he could. The water roared in his ears like the voice of Niagara, yet he heard the dulled thunder of the volley and, rising again toward the surface, met shining bits of metal, singularly flattened, oscillating slowly downward. Some of them touched him on the face and hands, then fell away, continuing their descent. One lodged between his collar and neck; it was uncomfortably warm and he snatched it out.

As he rose to the surface, gasping for breath, he saw that he had been a long time under water; he was perceptibly farther down stream—nearer to safety. The soldiers had almost finished reloading; the metal ramrods flashed all at once in the sunshine as they were drawn from the barrels, turned in the air, and thrust into their sockets. The two sentinels fired again, independently and ineffectually.

The hunted man saw all this over his shoulder; he was now swimming vigorously with the current. His brain was as energetic as his arms and legs; he thought with the rapidity of lightning.

'The officer,' he reasoned, 'will not make that martinet's error a second time. It is as easy to dodge a volley as a single shot. He has probably already given the command to fire at will. God help me, I cannot dodge them all!'

An appalling plash within two yards of him was followed by a loud, rushing sound, *diminuendo*, which seemed to travel back through the air to the fort and died in an explosion which stirred the very river to its deeps! A rising sheet of water curved over him, fell down upon him, blinded him, strangled him! The cannon had taken a hand in the game. As he shook his head free from the commotion of the smitten water he heard the deflected shot humming through the air ahead, and in an instant it was cracking and smashing the branches in the forest beyond.

'They will not do that again,' he thought, 'the next time they will use a charge of grape. I must keep my eye upon the gun; the smoke will apprise me—the report arrives too late; it lags behind the missile. That is a good gun.'

Suddenly he felt himself whirled round and round—spinning like a top. The water, the banks, the forests, the now distant bridge, fort and men—all were commingled and blurred. Objects were represented by their colors only; circular horizontal streaks of color—that was all he saw. He had been caught in a vortex and was being whirled on with a velocity of advance and gyration that made him giddy and sick. In a few moments he was flung upon the gravel at the foot of the left bank of the stream—the southern bank—and behind a projecting point which concealed him from his enemies. The sudden arrest of his motion, the abrasion of one of his hands on the gravel, restored him, and he wept with delight. He dug his fingers into the sand, threw it over himself in handfuls and audibly blessed it. It looked like diamonds, rubies, emeralds; he could think of nothing beautiful which it did not resemble. The trees upon the bank were giant garden plants; he noted a definite order in their arrangement, inhaled the fragrance of their blooms. A strange, roseate light shone through the spaces among their trunks and the wind made in their branches the music of æolian harps. He had no wish to perfect his escape—was content to remain in that enchanting spot until retaken.

A whiz and rattle of grapeshot among the branches high above his head roused him from his dream. The baffled cannoneer had fired him a random farewell. He sprang to his feet, rushed up the sloping bank, and plunged into the forest.

All that day he traveled, laying his course by the rounding sun. The forest seemed interminable; nowhere did he discover a break in it, not even a woodman's road. He had not known that he lived in so wild a region. There was something uncanny in the revelation.

By nightfall he was fatigued, footsore, famishing. The thought of his wife and children urged him on. At last he found a road which led him in what he knew to be the right direction. It was as wide and straight as a city street, yet it seemed untraveled. No fields bordered it, no dwelling anywhere. Not so much as the barking of a dog suggested human habitation. The black bodies of the trees formed a straight wall on both sides, terminating on the horizon in a point, like a diagram in a lesson in perspective. Overhead, as he looked up through this rift in the wood, shone great golden stars looking unfamiliar and grouped in strange constellations. He was sure they were arranged in some order which had a secret and malign significance. The wood on either side was full of singular noises, among which—once, twice, and again—he distinctly heard whispers in an unknown tongue.

His neck was in pain and lifting his hand to it he found it horribly swollen. He knew that it had a circle of black where the rope had bruised it. His eyes felt congested; he could no longer close them. His tongue was swollen with thirst; he relieved its fever by thrusting it forward from between his teeth into the cold air. How softly the turf had carpeted the untraveled avenue—he could no longer feel the roadway beneath his feet!

Doubtless, despite his suffering, he had fallen asleep while walking, for now he sees another scene—perhaps he has merely recovered from a delirium. He stands at the gate of his own home. All is as he left it, and all bright and beautiful in the morning sunshine. He must have traveled the entire night. As he pushes open the gate and passes up the wide white walk, he sees a flutter of female garments; his wife, looking fresh and cool and sweet, steps down from the veranda to meet him. At the bottom of the steps she stands waiting, with a smile of ineffable joy, an attitude of matchless grace and dignity. Ah, how beautiful she is! He springs forward with extended arms. As he is about to clasp her he feels a stunning blow upon the back of the neck; a blinding white light blazes all about him with a sound like the shock of a cannon—then all is darkness and silence!

Peyton Farquhar was dead; his body, with a broken neck, swung gently from side to side beneath the timbers of the Owl Creek bridge.

1891

PHILOSOPHERS THREE

A BEAR, a Fox and an Opossum were attacked by an inundation.

'Death loves a coward,' said the Bear, and went forward to fight the flood.

'What a fool!' said the Fox. 'I know a trick worth two of that.' And he slipped into a hollow stump.

'There are malevolent forces,' said the Opossum, 'which the wise will neither confront nor avoid. The thing is to know the nature of your antagonist.'

So saying the Opossum lay down and pretended to be dead.

1899

TWO SONS

A MAN had Two Sons. The elder was virtuous and dutiful, the younger wicked and crafty. When the father was about to die, he called them before him and said: 'I have only two things of value—my herd of camels and my blessing. How shall I allot them?'

'Give to me,' said the Younger Son, 'thy blessing, for it may reform me. The camels I should be sure to sell and squander the money.'

The Elder Son, disguising his joy, said that he would try to be content with the camels and a pious mind.

It was so arranged and the Man died. Then the wicked Younger Son went before the Cadi and said: 'Behold, my brother has defrauded me of my lawful heritage. He is so bad that our father, as is well known, denied him his blessing; is it likely that he gave him the camels?'

So the Elder Son was compelled to give up the herd and was soundly bastinadoed for his rapacity.

1899

THE ELIGIBLE SON-IN-LAW

A TRULY Clever Person who conducted a savings bank and lent money to his sisters and his cousins and his aunts was approached by a Tatterdemalion who applied for a loan of one hundred thousand dollars.

'What security have you to offer?' asked the Truly Clever Person.

'The best in the world,' the applicant replied, confidentially; 'I am about to become your son-in-law.'

'That would indeed be gilt-edged,' said the Banker, gravely; 'but what claim have you to the hand of my daughter?'

'One that cannot be lightly denied,' said the Tatterdemalion. 'I am about to become worth one hundred thousand dollars.'

Unable to detect a weak point in this scheme of mutual advantage, the Financier gave the Promoter in Disguise an order for the money and wrote a note to his wife directing her to count out the girl.

1899

MORAL PRINCIPLE AND MATERIAL INTEREST

A MORAL Principle met a Material Interest on a bridge wide enough for but one.

'Down, you base thing!' thundered the Moral Principle, 'and let me pass over you!'

The Material Interest merely looked in the other's eyes without saying anything.

'Ah,' said the Moral Principle, hesitatingly, 'let us draw lots to see which one of us shall retire till the other has crossed.'

The Material Interest maintained an unbroken silence and an unwavering stare.

'In order to avoid a conflict,' the Moral Principle resumed, somewhat uneasily, 'I shall myself lie down and let you walk over me.'

Then the Material Interest found his tongue. 'I don't think you are very good walking,' he said. 'I am a little particular about what I have underfoot. Suppose you get off into the water.'

It occurred that way.

1899

FROM THE CYNIC'S WORD BOOK
DEFINITIONS

ABSURDITY, *n.* A statement or belief manifestly inconsistent with one's own opinion.

AIR, *n.* A nutritious substance supplied by a bountiful Providence for the fattening of the poor.

CIRCUS, *n.* A place where horses, ponies and elephants are permitted to see men, women and children acting the fool.

COMFORT, *n.* A state of mind produced by contemplation of a neighbor's uneasiness.

CYNIC, *n.* A blackguard whose faulty vision sees things as they are, not as they ought to be. Hence the custom among the Scythians of plucking out a cynic's eyes to improve his vision.

DELUSION, *n.* The father of a most respectable family, comprising Enthusiasm, Affection, Self-denial, Faith, Hope, Charity and many other goodly sons and daughters.

All hail, Delusion! Were it not for thee
The world turned topsy-turvy we should
    see;
For Vice, respectable with cleanly fancies,
Would fly abandoned Virtue's gross
    advances.
                        Mumfrey Mappel.

DUTY, *n.* That which sternly impels us in the direction of profit, along the line of desire.

Sir Lavender Portwine, in favor at
    court,
Was wroth at his master, who'd kissed
    Lady Port.
His anger provoked him to take the king's
    head,
But duty prevailed, and he took the king's
    bread,
    Instead.
                        G.J.

ELEGY, *n.* A composition in verse, in which, without employing any of the methods of humor, the writer aims to produce in the reader's mind the dampest kind of dejection. The most famous English example begins somewhat like this:

The cur foretells the knell of parting day;
    The loafing herd winds slowly o'er the
        lea;
The wise man homeward plods; I only stay
    To fiddle-faddle in a minor key.

ERUDITION, *n.* Dust shaken out of a book into an empty skull.

So wide his erudition's mighty span,
He knew Creation's origin and plan
And only came by accident to grief—
He thought, poor man, 'twas right to be a
    thief.
                        Romach Pute.

FUTURE, *n.* That period of time in which our affairs prosper, our friends are true, and our happiness is assured.

HISTORIAN, *n.* A broad-gauge gossip.

I is the first letter of the alphabet, the first word of the language, the first thought of the mind, the first object of affection. In grammar it is a pronoun of the first person and singular number. Its plural is said to be *We,* but how there can be more than one myself is doubtless clearer to the grammarians than it is to the author of this incomparable dictionary. Conception of two myselves is difficult, but fine. The frank yet graceful use of 'I' distinguishes a good writer from a bad; the latter carries it with the manner of a thief trying to cloak his loot.

IMPUNITY, *n.* Wealth.

KLEPTOMANIAC, *n.* A rich thief.

NOVEL, *n.* A short story padded. A species of composition bearing the same relation to literature that the panorama bears to art. As it is too long to be read at a sitting the impressions made by its successive parts are successively effaced, as in the panorama. Unity, totality of effect, is impossible; for besides the few pages last read all that is carried in mind is the mere plot of what has gone before. To the romance the novel is what photography is to painting. Its distinguishing principle, probability, corresponds to the literal actuality of the photograph and puts it distinctly into the category of reporting; whereas the free wing of the romancer enables him to mount to such altitudes of imagination as he may be fitted to attain; and the first three essentials of the literary art are imagination, imagination and imagination. The art of writing novels, such as it was, is long dead everywhere except in Russia, where it is new. Peace to its ashes—some of which have a large sale.

OCEAN, *n.* A body of water occupying about two-thirds of a world made for man —who has no gills.

PAINTING, *n.* The art of protecting flat surfaces from the weather and exposing them to the critic.

Formerly, painting and sculpture were combined in the same work: the ancients painted their statues. The only present alliance between the two arts is that the modern painter chisels his patrons.

PLATITUDE, *n.* The fundamental element and special glory of popular literature. A thought that snores in words that smoke. The wisdom of a million fools in the diction of a dullard. A fossil sentiment in artificial rock. A moral without the fable. All that is mortal of a departed truth. A demi-tasse of milk-and-morality. The Pope's-nose of a featherless peacock. A jelly-fish withering on the shore of the sea of thought. The cackle surviving the egg. A desiccated epigram.

POSITIVE, *adj.* Mistaken at the top of one's voice.

PRAY, *v.* To ask that the laws of the universe be annulled in behalf of a single petitioner confessedly unworthy.

RADICALISM, *n.* The conservatism of to-morrow injected into the affairs of to-day.

REASON, *v.i.* To weigh probabilities in the scales of desire.

REFLECTION, *n.* An action of the mind whereby we obtain a clearer view of our relation to the things of yesterday and are able to avoid the perils that we shall not again encounter.

RESTITUTION, *n.* The founding or endowing of universities and public libraries by gift or bequest.

SAW, *n.* A trite popular saying, or proverb. (Figurative and colloquial.) So called because it makes its way into a wooden head. Following are examples of old saws fitted with new teeth.

A penny saved is a penny to squander.
A man is known by the company that he organizes.
A bad workman quarrels with the man who calls him that.
A bird in the hand is worth what it will bring.
Better late than before anybody has invited you.
Example is better than following it.
Half a loaf is better than a whole one if there is much else.
Think twice before you speak to a friend in need.
What is worth doing is worth the trouble of asking somebody to do it.
Least said is soonest disavowed.
He laughs best who laughs least.
Speak of the Devil and he will hear about it.
Of two evils choose to be the least.
Strike while your employer has a big contract.
Where there's a will there's a won't.

SELF–EVIDENT, *adj.* Evident to one's self and to nobody else.

SLANG, *n.* The grunt of the human hog (*Pignoramus intolerabilis*) with an audible memory. The speech of one who utters with his tongue what he thinks with his ear, and feels the pride of a creator in accomplishing the feat of a parrot. A means (under Providence) of setting up as a wit without a capital of sense.

ZIGZAG, *v.t.* To move forward uncertainly, from side to side, as one carrying the white man's burden. (From *zed*, z, and *jag*, an Icelandic word of unknown meaning.)

He zedjagged so uncomen wyde
Thet non coude pas on eyder syde;
So, to com saufly thruh, I been
Constreynet for to doodge betwene.
Munwele

STEPHEN CRANE

1871–1900

THE OPEN BOAT

A Tale intended to be after the Fact. Being the Experience of Four Men from the Sunk Steamer 'Commodore'

I

NONE of them knew the colour of the sky. Their eyes glanced level, and were fastened upon the waves that swept toward them. These waves were of the hue of slate, save for the tops, which were of foaming white, and all of the men knew the colours of the sea. The horizon narrowed and widened, and dipped and rose, and at all times its edge was jagged with waves that seemed thrust up in points like rocks.

Many a man ought to have a bath-tub larger than the boat which here rode upon the sea. These waves were most wrongfully and barbarously abrupt and tall, and each froth-top was a problem in small boat navigation.

The cook squatted in the bottom and looked with both eyes at the six inches of gunwale which separated him from the ocean. His sleeves were rolled over his fat forearms, and the two flaps of his unbuttoned vest dangled as he bent to bail out the boat. Often he said: 'Gawd! That was a narrow clip.' As he remarked it he invariably gazed eastward over the broken sea.

The oiler, steering with one of the two oars in the boat, sometimes raised himself suddenly to keep clear of water that swirled in over the stern. It was a thin little oar and it seemed often ready to snap.

The correspondent, pulling at the other oar, watched the waves and wondered why he was there.

The injured captain, lying in the bow, was at this time buried in that profound dejection and indifference which comes, temporarily at least, to even the bravest and most enduring when, willy nilly, the firm fails, the army loses, the ship goes down. The mind of the master of a vessel is rooted deep in the timbers of her, though he command for a day or a decade, and this captain had on him the stern impression of a scene in the greys of dawn of seven turned faces, and later a stump of a top-mast with a white ball on it that slashed to and fro at the waves, went low and lower, and down. Thereafter there was something strange in his voice. Although steady, it was deep with mourning, and of a quality beyond oration or tears.

'Keep 'er a little more south, Billie,' said he.

'A little more south, sir,' said the oiler in the stern.

A seat in this boat was not unlike a seat upon a bucking broncho, and, by the same token, a broncho is not much smaller. The craft pranced and reared, and plunged like an animal. As each wave came, and she rose for it, she seemed like a horse making at a fence outrageously high. The manner of her scramble over these walls of water is a mystic thing, and, moreover, at the top of them were ordinarily these problems in white water, the foam racing down from the summit of each wave, requiring a new leap, and a leap from the air. Then, after scornfully bumping a crest, she would slide, and race, and splash down a long incline, and arrive bobbing and nodding in front of the next menace.

A singular disadvantage of the sea lies in the fact that after successfully surmounting one wave you discover that there is another behind it just as important and just as nervously anxious to do something effective in the way of swamping boats. In a ten-foot dingey one can get an idea of the resources of the sea in the line of waves that is not probable to the average experience which is never at sea in a dingey. As each slaty wall of water approached, it shut all else from the view of the men in the boat, and it was not difficult to imagine that this particular wave was the final outburst of the ocean, the last effort of the grim water. There was a terrible grace in the move of the waves, and they came in silence, save for the snarling of the crests.

In the wan light, the faces of the men must have been grey. Their eyes must have glinted in strange ways as they gazed steadily astern. Viewed from a balcony, the whole thing would doubtlessly have been weirdly picturesque. But the men in the boat had no time to see it, and if they had had leisure there were other things to occupy their minds. The sun swung steadily up the sky, and they knew it was broad day because the colour of the sea changed from slate to emerald-green, streaked with amber lights, and the foam was like tumbling snow. The process of the breaking day was unknown to them. They were aware only of this effect upon the colour of the waves that rolled toward them.

In disjointed sentences the cook and the correspondent argued as to the difference between a life-saving station and a house of refuge. The cook had said: 'There's a house of refuge just north of the Mosquito Inlet Light, and as soon as they see us, they'll come off in their boat and pick us up.'

'As soon as who see us?' said the correspondent.

'The crew,' said the cook.

'Houses of refuge don't have crews,' said the correspondent. 'As I understand them, they are only places where clothes and grub are stored for the benefit of shipwrecked people. They don't carry crews.'

'Oh, yes, they do,' said the cook.

'No, they don't,' said the correspondent.

'Well, we're not there yet, anyhow,' said the oiler, in the stern.

'Well,' said the cook, 'perhaps it's not a house of refuge that I'm thinking of as being near Mosquito Inlet Light. Perhaps it's a life-saving station.'

'We're not there yet,' said the oiler, in the stern.

II

As the boat bounced from the top of each wave, the wind tore through the hair of the hatless men, and as the craft plopped her stern down again the spray slashed past them. The crest of each of these waves was a hill, from the top of which the men surveyed, for a moment, a broad tumultuous expanse, shining and wind-riven. It was probably splendid. It was probably glorious, this play of the free sea, wild with lights of emerald and white and amber.

'Bully good thing it's an on-shore wind,' said the cook. 'If not, where would we be? Wouldn't have a show.'

'That's right,' said the correspondent.

The busy oiler nodded his assent.

Then the captain, in the bow, chuckled in a way that expressed humour, contempt, tragedy, all in one. 'Do you think we've got much of a show now, boys?' said he.

Whereupon the three were silent, save for a trifle of hemming and hawing. To express any particular optimism at this time they felt to be childish and stupid, but they all doubtless possessed this sense of the situation in their mind. A young man thinks doggedly at such times. On the other hand, the ethics of their condition was decidedly against any open suggestion of hopelessness. So they were silent.

'Oh, well,' said the captain, soothing his children, 'we'll get ashore all right.'

But there was that in his tone which made them think, so the oiler quoth: 'Yes! If this wind holds!'

The cook was bailing: 'Yes! If we don't catch hell in the surf.'

Canton flannel gulls flew near and far. Sometimes they sat down on the sea, near patches of brown seaweed that rolled over the waves with a movement like carpets on a line in a gale. The birds sat comfortably in groups, and they were envied by some in the dingey, for the wrath of the sea was no more to them than it was to a covey of prairie chickens a thousand miles inland. Often they came very close and stared at the men with black bead-like eyes. At these times they were uncanny and sinister in their unblinking scrutiny, and the men hooted angrily at them, telling them to be gone. One came, and evidently decided to alight on the top of the captain's head. The bird flew parallel to the boat and did not circle, but made short sidelong jumps in the air in chicken-fashion. His black eyes were wistfully fixed upon the captain's head. 'Ugly brute,' said the oiler to the bird. 'You look as if you were made with a jack-knife.' The cook and the correspondent swore darkly at the creature. The captain naturally wished to knock it away with the end of the heavy painter; but he did not dare do it, because anything resembling an emphatic gesture would have capsized this freighted boat, and so with his open hand, the captain gently and carefully waved the gull away. After it had been discouraged from the pursuit the captain breathed easier on account of his hair, and others breathed easier because the bird struck their minds at this time as being somehow gruesome and ominous.

In the meantime the oiler and the correspondent rowed. And also they rowed.

They sat together in the same seat, and each rowed an oar. Then the oiler took both oars; then the correspondent took both oars; then the oiler; then the correspondent. They rowed and they rowed. The very ticklish part of the business was when the time came for the reclining one in the stern to take his turn at the oars. By the very last star of truth, it is easier to steal eggs from under a hen than it was to change seats in the dingey. First the man in the stern slid his hand along the thwart and moved with care, as if he were of Sèvres. Then the man in the rowing seat slid his hand along the other thwart. It was all done with the most extraordinary care. As the two sidled past each other, the whole party kept watchful eyes on the coming wave, and the captain cried: 'Look out now! Steady there!'

The brown mats of seaweed that appeared from time to time were like islands, bits of earth. They were travelling, apparently, neither one way nor the other. They were, to all intents, stationary. They informed the men in the boat that it was making progress slowly toward the land.

The captain, rearing cautiously in the bow, after the dingey soared on a great swell, said that he had seen the lighthouse at Mosquito Inlet. Presently the cook remarked that he had seen it. The correspondent was at the oars then, and for some reason he too wished to look at the lighthouse, but his back was toward the far shore and the waves were important, and for some time he could not seize an opportunity to turn his head. But at last there came a wave more gentle than the others, and when at the crest of it he swiftly scoured the western horizon.

'See it?' said the captain.

'No,' said the correspondent slowly, 'I didn't see anything.'

'Look again,' said the captain. He pointed. 'It's exactly in that direction.'

At the top of another wave, the correspondent did as he was bid, and this time his eyes chanced on a small still thing on the edge of the swaying horizon. It was precisely like the point of a pin. It took an anxious eye to find a lighthouse so tiny.

'Think we'll make it, captain?'

'If this wind holds and the boat don't swamp, we can't do much else,' said the captain.

The little boat, lifted by each towering sea, and splashed viciously by the crests, made progress that in the absence of seaweed was not apparent to those in her. She seemed just a wee thing wallowing, miraculously top up, at the mercy of five oceans. Occasionally, a great spread of water, like white flames, swarmed into her.

'Bail her, cook,' said the captain serenely.

'All right, captain,' said the cheerful cook.

III

It would be difficult to describe the subtle brotherhood of men that was here established on the seas. No one said that it was so. No one mentioned it. But it dwelt in the boat, and each man felt it warm him. They were a captain, an oiler, a cook, and a correspondent, and they were friends, friends in a more curiously iron-bound degree than may be common. The hurt captain, lying against the water-jar in the bow, spoke always in a low voice and calmly, but he could never command a more ready and swiftly obedient crew than the motley three of the dingey. It was more than a mere recognition of what was best for the common safety. There was surely in it a quality that was personal and heartfelt. And after this devotion to the commander of the boat there was this comradeship that the correspondent, for instance, who had been taught to be cynical of men, knew even at the time was the best experience of his life. But no one said that it was so. No one mentioned it.

'I wish we had a sail,' remarked the captain. 'We might try my overcoat on the end of an oar and give you two boys a chance to rest.' So the cook and the correspondent held the mast and spread wide the overcoat. The oiler steered, and the little boat made good way with her new rig. Sometimes the oiler had to scull sharply to keep a sea from breaking into the boat, but otherwise sailing was a success.

Meanwhile the lighthouse had been growing slowly larger. It had now almost assumed colour, and appeared like a little grey shadow on the sky. The man at the oars could not be prevented from turning his head rather often to try for a glimpse of this little grey shadow.

At last, from the top of each wave the men in the tossing boat could see land. Even as the lighthouse was an upright shadow on the sky, this land seemed but a long black shadow on the sea. It certainly was thinner than paper. 'We must be about opposite New Smyrna,' said the cook, who had coasted this shore often in schooners. 'Captain, by the way, I believe they abandoned that life-saving station there about a year ago.'

'Did they?' said the captain.

The wind slowly died away. The cook and the correspondent were not now obliged to slave in order to hold high the oar. But the waves continued their old impetuous swooping at the dingey, and the little craft, no longer under way, struggled woundily over them. The oiler or the correspondent took the oars again.

Shipwrecks are apropos of nothing. If men could only train for them and have them occur when the men had reached pink condition, there would be less drowning at sea. Of the four in the dingey none had slept any time worth mentioning for two days and two nights previous to embarking in the dingey, and in the excitement of clambering about the deck of a foundering ship they had also forgotten to eat heartily.

For these reasons, and for others, neither the oiler nor the correspondent was fond of rowing at this time. The correspondent wondered ingenuously how in the name of all that was sane could there be people who thought it amusing to row a boat. It was not an amusement; it was a diabolical punishment, and even a genius of mental aberrations could never conclude that it was anything but a horror to the muscles and a crime against the back. He mentioned to the boat in general how the amusement of rowing struck him, and the weary-faced oiler smiled in full sympathy. Previously to the foundering, by the way, the oiler had worked double-watch in the engine-room of the ship.

'Take her easy, now, boys,' said the captain. 'Don't spend yourselves. If we have to run a surf you'll need all your strength, because we'll sure have to swim for it. Take your time.'

Slowly the land arose from the sea. From a black line it became a line of black and a line of white, trees and sand. Finally, the captain said that he could make out a house on the shore. 'That's the house of refuge, sure,' said the cook. 'They'll see us before long, and come out after us.'

The distant lighthouse reared high. 'The keeper ought to be able to make us out now, if he's looking through a glass,' said the captain. 'He'll notify the life-saving people.'

'None of those other boats could have got ashore to give word of the wreck,' said the oiler, in a low voice. 'Else the lifeboat would be out hunting us.'

Slowly and beautifully the land loomed out of the sea. The wind came again. It had veered from the north-east to the southeast. Finally, a new sound struck the ears of the men in the boat. It was the low thunder of the surf on the shore. 'We'll never be able to make the lighthouse now,' said the captain. 'Swing her head a little more north, Billie.'

'A little more north, sir,' said the oiler.

Whereupon the little boat turned her nose once more down the wind, and all but the oarsmen watched the shore grow. Under the influence of this expansion doubt and direful apprehension was leaving the minds of the men. The management of the boat was still most absorbing, but it could not prevent a quiet cheerfulness. In an hour, perhaps, they would be ashore.

Their backbones had become thoroughly used to balancing in the boat, and they now rode this wild colt of a dingey like circus men. The correspondent thought that he had been drenched to the skin, but happening to feel in the top pocket of his coat, he found therein eight cigars. Four of them were soaked with sea-water; four were perfectly scatheless. After a search, somebody produced three dry matches, and thereupon the four waifs rode impudently in their little boat, and with an assurance of an impending rescue shining in their eyes, puffed at the big cigars and judged well and ill of all men. Everybody took a drink of water.

IV

'Cook,' remarked the captain, 'there don't seem to be any signs of life about your house of refuge.'

'No,' replied the cook. 'Funny they don't see us!'

A broad stretch of lowly coast lay before the eyes of the men. It was of low dunes topped with dark vegetation. The roar of the surf was plain, and sometimes they could see the white lip of a wave as it spun up the beach. A tiny house was blocked out black upon the sky. Southward, the slim lighthouse lifted its little grey length.

Tide, wind, and waves were swinging the dingey northward. 'Funny they don't see us,' said the men.

The surf's roar was here dulled, but its tone was, nevertheless, thunderous and mighty. As the boat swam over the great rollers, the men sat listening to this roar. 'We'll swamp sure,' said everybody.

It is fair to say here that there was not a life-saving station within twenty miles in either direction, but the men did not know this fact, and in consequence they made dark and opprobrious remarks concerning the eyesight of the nation's life-savers. Four scowling men sat in the dingey and surpassed records in the invention of epithets.

'Funny they don't see us.'

The light-heartedness of a former time had completely faded. To their sharpened minds it was easy to conjure pictures of all kinds of incompetency and blindness and, indeed, cowardice. There was the shore of the populous land, and it was bitter and bitter to them that from it came no sign.

'Well,' said the captain, ultimately, 'I suppose we'll have to make a try for ourselves. If we stay out here too long, we'll none of us have strength left to swim after the boat swamps.'

And so the oiler, who was at the oars, turned the boat straight for the shore. There was a sudden tightening of muscles. There was some thinking.

'If we don't all get ashore—' said the captain. 'If we don't all get ashore, I suppose you fellows know where to send news of my finish?'

They then briefly exchanged some addresses and admonitions. As for the reflections of the men, there was a great deal of rage in them. Perchance they might be formulated thus: 'If I am going to be drowned —if I am going to be drowned—if I am going to be drowned, why, in the name of the seven mad gods who rule the sea, was I allowed to come thus far and contemplate sand and trees? Was I brought here merely to have my nose dragged away as I was about to nibble the sacred cheese of life? It is preposterous. If this old ninny-woman, Fate, cannot do better than this, she should be deprived of the management of men's fortunes. She is an old hen who knows not her intention. If she has decided to drown me, why did she not do it in the beginning and save me all this trouble? The whole affair is absurd. . . . But no, she cannot mean to drown me. She dare not drown me. She cannot drown me. Not after all this work.' Afterward the man might have had an impulse to shake his fist at the clouds: 'Just you drown me, now, and then hear what I call you!'

The billows that came at this time were more formidable. They seemed always just about to break and roll over the little boat in a turmoil of foam. There was a preparatory and long growl in the speech of them. No mind unused to the sea would have concluded that the dingey could ascend these sheer heights in time. The shore was still afar. The oiler was a wily surfman. 'Boys,' he said swiftly, 'she won't live three minutes more, and we're too far out to swim. Shall I take her to sea again, captain?'

'Yes! Go ahead!' said the captain.

This oiler, by a series of quick miracles, and fast and steady oarsmanship, turned the boat in the middle of the surf and took her safely to sea again.

There was a considerable silence as the boat bumped over the furrowed sea to deeper water. Then somebody in gloom spoke. 'Well, anyhow, they must have seen us from the shore by now.'

The gulls went in slanting flight up the wind toward the grey desolate east. A squall, marked by dingy clouds, and clouds brick-red, like smoke from a burning building, appeared from the south-east.

'What do you think of those life-saving people? Ain't they peaches?'

'Funny they haven't seen us.'

'Maybe they think we're out here for sport! Maybe they think we're fishin'. Maybe they think we're damned fools.'

It was a long afternoon. A changed tide tried to force them southward, but wind and wave said northward. Far ahead, where coastline, sea, and sky formed their mighty angle, there were little dots which seemed to indicate a city on the shore.

'St. Augustine?'

The captain shook his head. 'Too near Mosquito Inlet.'

And the oiler rowed, and then the correspondent rowed. Then the oiler rowed. It was a weary business. The human back can become the seat of more aches and pains than are registered in books for the composite anatomy of a regiment. It is a limited area, but it can become the theatre of innumerable muscular conflicts, tangles, wrenches, knots, and other comforts.

'Did you ever like to row, Billie?' asked the correspondent.

'No,' said the oiler. 'Hang it.'

When one exchanged the rowing-seat for a place in the bottom of the boat, he suffered a bodily depression that caused him to be careless of everything save an obligation to wiggle one finger. There was cold sea-water swashing to and fro in the boat, and he lay in it. His head, pillowed on a thwart, was within an inch of the swirl of a wave crest, and sometimes a particularly obstreperous sea came in-board and drenched him once more. But these matters did not annoy him. It is almost certain that if the boat had capsized he would have tumbled comfortably out upon the ocean as if he felt sure that it was a great soft mattress.

'Look! There's a man on the shore!'

'Where?'

'There! See 'im? See 'im?'

'Yes, sure! He's walking along.'

'Now he's stopped. Look! He's facing us!'

'He's waving at us!'

'So he is! By thunder!'

'Ah, now we're all right! Now we're all right! There'll be a boat out here for us in half an hour.'

'He's going on. He's running. He's going up to that house there.'

The remote beach seemed lower than the sea, and it required a searching glance to discern the little black figure. The captain saw a floating stick and they rowed to it. A bath-towel was by some weird chance in the boat, and, tying this on the stick, the captain waved it. The oarsman did not dare turn his head, so he was obliged to ask questions.

'What's he doing now?'

'He's standing still again. He's looking, I think. . . . There he goes again. Toward the house. . . . Now he's stopped again.'

'Is he waving at us?'

'No, not now! he was, though'

'Look! There comes another man!'

'He's running.'

'Look at him go, would you.'

'Why, he's on a bicycle. Now he's met the other man. They're both waving at us. Look!'

'There comes something up the beach.'

'What the devil is that thing?'

'Why, it looks like a boat.'

'Why, certainly it's a boat.'

'No, it's on wheels.'

'Yes, so it is. Well, that must be the life-boat. They drag them along shore on a wagon.'

'That's the life-boat, sure.'

'No, by—, it's—it's an omnibus.'

'I tell you it's a life-boat.'

'It is not! It's an omnibus. I can see it plain. See? One of these big hotel omnibuses.'

'By thunder, you're right. It's an omnibus, sure as fate. What do you suppose they are doing with an omnibus? Maybe they are going around collecting the life-crew, hey?'

'That's it, likely. Look! There's a fellow waving a little black flag. He's standing on the steps of the omnibus. There come those other two fellows. Now they're all talking together. Look at the fellow with the flag. Maybe he ain't waving it.'

'That ain't a flag, is it? That's his coat. Why, certainly, that's his coat.'

'So it is. It's his coat. He's taken it off and is waving it around his head. But would you look at him swing it.'

'Oh, say, there isn't any life-saving station there. That's just a winter resort hotel omnibus that has brought over some of the boarders to see us drown.'

'What's that idiot with the coat mean? What's he signaling, anyhow?'

'It looks as if he were trying to tell us to go north. There must be a life-saving station up there.'

'No! He thinks we're fishing. Just giving us a merry hand. See? Ah, there, Willie.'

'Well, I wish I could make something out of those signals. What do you suppose he means?'

'He don't mean anything. He's just playing.'

'Well, if he'd just signal us to try the surf again, or to go to sea and wait, or go north, or go south, or go to hell—there would be some reason in it. But look at him. He just stands there and keeps his coat revolving like a wheel. The ass!'

'There come more people.'

'Now there's quite a mob. Look! Isn't that a boat?'

'Where? Oh, I see where you mean. No, that's no boat.'

'That fellow is still waving his coat.'

'He must think we like to see him do that. Why don't he quit it? It don't mean anything.'

'I don't know. I think he is trying to make us go north. It must be that there's a life-saving station there somewhere.'

'Say, he ain't tired yet. Look at 'im wave.'

'Wonder how long he can keep that up. He's been revolving his coat ever since he caught sight of us. He's an idiot. Why aren't they getting men to bring a boat out? A fishing boat—one of those big yawls—could come out here all right. Why don't he do something?'

'Oh, it's all right, now.'

'They'll have a boat out here for us in less than no time, now that they've seen us.'

A faint yellow tone came into the sky over the low land. The shadows on the sea slowly deepened. The wind bore coldness with it, and the men began to shiver.

'Holy smoke!' said one, allowing his voice to express his impious mood, 'if we keep on monkeying out here! If we've got to flounder out here all night!'

'Oh, we'll never have to stay here all night! Don't you worry. They've seen us now, and it won't be long before they'll come chasing out after us.'

The shore grew dusky. The man waving a coat blended gradually into this gloom, and it swallowed in the same manner the omnibus and the group of people. The spray, when it dashed uproariously over the side, made the voyagers shrink and swear like men who were being branded.

'I'd like to catch the chump who waved the coat. I feel like soaking him one, just for luck.'

'Why? What did he do?'

'Oh, nothing, but then he seemed so damned cheerful.'

In the meantime the oiler rowed, and then the correspondent rowed, and then the oiler rowed. Grey-faced and bowed forward, they mechanically, turn by turn, plied the leaden oars. The form of the light-house had vanished from the southern horizon, but finally a pale star appeared, just lifting from the sea. The streaked saffron in the west passed before the all-merging darkness, and the sea to the east was black. The land had vanished, and was expressed only by the low and drear thunder of the surf.

'If I am going to be drowned—if I am going to be drowned—if I am going to be drowned, why, in the name of the seven mad gods who rule the sea, was I allowed to come thus far and contemplate sand and trees? Was I brought here merely to have my nose dragged away as I was about to nibble the sacred cheese of life?'

The patient captain, drooped over the water-jar, was sometimes obliged to speak to the oarsman.

'Keep her head up! Keep her head up!'

' "Keep her head up," sir.' The voices were weary and low.

This was surely a quiet evening. All save the oarsman lay heavily and listlessly in the boat's bottom. As for him, his eyes were just capable of noting the tall black waves that swept forward in a most sinister silence, save for an occasional subdued growl of a crest.

The cook's head was on a thwart, and he looked without interest at the water under his nose. He was deep in other scenes. Finally he spoke. 'Billie,' he murmured, dreamfully, 'what kind of pie do you like best?'

V

'Pie,' said the oiler and the correspondent, agitatedly. 'Don't talk about those things, blast you!'

'Well,' said the cook, 'I was just thinking about ham sandwiches, and—'

A night on the sea in an open boat is a long night. As darkness settled finally, the shine of the light, lifting from the sea in the south, changed to full gold. On the northern horizon a new light appeared, a small bluish gleam on the edge of the waters. These two lights were the furniture of the world. Otherwise there was nothing but waves.

Two men huddled in the stern, and distances were so magnificent in the dingey that the rower was enabled to keep his feet partly warmed by thrusting them under his companions. Their legs indeed extended far under the rowing-seat until they touched the feet of the captain forward. Sometimes, despite the efforts of the tired oarsman, a wave came piling into the boat, an icy wave of the night, and the chilling water soaked them anew. They would twist their bodies for a moment and groan, and sleep the dead sleep once more, while the water in the boat gurgled about them as the craft rocked.

The plan of the oiler and the correspondent was for one to row until he lost the ability, and then arouse the other from his sea-water couch in the bottom of the boat.

The oiler plied the oars until his head drooped forward, and the overpowering sleep blinded him. And he rowed yet afterward. Then he touched a man in the bottom of the boat, and called his name. 'Will you spell me for a little while?' he said, meekly.

'Sure, Billie,' said the correspondent, awakening and dragging himself to a sitting position. They exchanged places carefully, and the oiler, cuddling down in the sea-water at the cook's side, seemed to go to sleep instantly.

The particular violence of the sea had ceased. The waves came without snarling. The obligation of the man at the oars was to keep the boat headed so that the tilt of the rollers would not capsize her, and to preserve her from filling when the crests rushed past. The black waves were silent and hard to be seen in the darkness. Often one was almost upon the boat before the oarsman was aware.

In a low voice the correspondent addressed the captain. He was not sure that the captain was awake, although this iron man seemed to be always awake. 'Captain, shall I keep her making for that light north, sir?'

The same steady voice answered him. 'Yes. Keep it about two points off the port bow.'

The cook had tied a life-belt around himself in order to get even the warmth which this clumsy cork contrivance could donate, and he seemed almost stove-like when a rower, whose teeth invariably chattered wildly as soon as he ceased his labour, dropped down to sleep.

The correspondent, as he rowed, looked down at the two men sleeping underfoot. The cook's arm was around the oiler's shoulders, and, with their fragmentary clothing and haggard faces, they were the babes of the sea, a grotesque rendering of the old babes in the wood.

Later he must have grown stupid at his work, for suddenly there was a growling of water, and a crest came with a roar and a swash into the boat, and it was a wonder that it did not set the cook afloat in his life-belt. The cook continued to sleep, but the oiler sat up, blinking his eyes and shaking with the new cold.

'Oh, I'm awful sorry, Billie,' said the correspondent, contritely.

'That's all right, old boy,' said the oiler, and lay down again and was asleep.

Presently it seemed that even the captain dozed, and the correspondent thought that he was the one man afloat on all the oceans. The wind had a voice as it came over the waves, and it was sadder than the end.

There was a long, loud swishing astern of the boat, and a gleaming trail of phosphorescence, like blue flame, was furrowed on the black waters. It might have been made by a monstrous knife.

Then there came a stillness, while the correspondent breathed with the open mouth and looked at the sea.

Suddenly there was another swish and another long flash of bluish light, and this time it was alongside the boat, and might almost have been reached with an oar. The correspondent saw an enormous fin speed like a shadow through the water, hurling the crystalline spray and leaving the long glowing trail.

The correspondent looked over his shoulder at the captain. His face was hidden, and he seemed to be asleep. He looked at the babes of the sea. They certainly were asleep. So, being bereft of sympathy, he leaned a little way to one side and swore softly into the sea.

But the thing did not then leave the vicinity of the boat. Ahead or astern, on one side or the other, at intervals long or short, fled the long sparkling streak, and there was to be heard the whiroo of the dark fin. The speed and power of the thing was greatly to be admired. It cut the water like a gigantic and keen projectile.

The presence of this biding thing did not affect the man with the same horror that it would if he had been a picnicker. He simply looked at the sea dully and swore in an undertone.

Nevertheless, it is true that he did not wish to be alone with the thing. He wished one of his companions to awaken by chance and keep him company with it. But the captain hung motionless over the water-jar, and the oiler and the cook in the bottom of the boat were plunged in slumber.

VI

'If I am going to be drowned—if I am going to be drowned—if I am going to be drowned, why, in the name of the seven mad gods who rule the sea, was I allowed to come thus far and contemplate sand and trees?'

During this dismal night, it may be remarked that a man would conclude that it was really the intention of the seven mad gods to drown him, despite the abominable injustice of it. For it was certainly an abominable injustice to drown a man who had worked so hard, so hard. The man felt it would be a crime most unnatural. Other people had drowned at sea since galleys swarmed with painted sails, but still—

When it occurs to a man that nature does not regard him as important, and that she feels she would not maim the universe by disposing of him, he at first wishes to throw bricks at the temple, and he hates deeply the fact that there are no bricks and no temples. Any visible expression of nature would surely be pelleted with his jeers.

Then, if there be no tangible thing to hoot he feels, perhaps, the desire to confront a personification and indulge in pleas, bowed to one knee, and with hands supplicant, saying: 'Yes, but I love myself.'

A high cold star on a winter's night is the word he feels that she says to him. Thereafter he knows the pathos of his situation.

The men in the dingey had not discussed these matters, but each had, no doubt, reflected upon them in silence and according to his mind. There was seldom any expression upon their faces save the general one of complete weariness. Speech was devoted to the business of the boat.

To chime the notes of his emotion, a verse mysteriously entered the correspondent's head. He had even forgotten that he had forgotten this verse, but it suddenly was in his mind.

> 'A soldier of the Legion lay dying in Algiers,
> There was lack of woman's nursing, there was dearth of woman's tears;
> But a comrade stood beside him, and he took that comrade's hand,
> And he said: "I shall never see my own, my native land."'

In his childhood, the correspondent had been made acquainted with the fact that a soldier of the Legion lay dying in Algiers, but he had never regarded the fact as important. Myriads of his school-fellows had informed him of the soldier's plight, but the dinning had naturally ended by making him perfectly indifferent. He had never considered it his affair that a soldier of the Legion lay dying in Algiers, nor had it appeared to him as a matter for sorrow. It was less to him than the breaking of a pencil's point.

Now, however, it quaintly came to him, as a human, living thing. It was no longer merely a picture of a few throes in the breast of a poet, meanwhile drinking tea and warming his feet at the grate; it was an actuality—stern, mournful, and fine.

The correspondent plainly saw the soldier. He lay on the sand with his feet out straight and still. While his pale left hand was upon his chest in an attempt to thwart the going of his life, the blood came between his fingers. In the far Algerian distance, a city of low square forms was set against a sky that was faint with the last sunset hues. The correspondent, plying the oars and dreaming of the slow and slower movements of the lips of the soldier, was moved by a profound and perfectly impersonal comprehension. He was sorry for the soldier of the Legion who lay dying in Algiers.

The thing which had followed the boat and waited had evidently grown bored at the delay. There was no longer to be heard the slash of the cut-water, and there was no longer the flame of the long trail. The light in the north still glimmered, but it was apparently no nearer to the boat. Sometimes the boom of the surf rang in the correspondent's ears, and he turned the craft seaward then and rowed harder. Southward, someone had evidently built a watch-fire on the beach. It was too low and too far to be seen, but it made a shimmering, roseate reflection upon the bluff back of it, and this could be discerned from the boat. The wind came stronger, and sometimes a wave suddenly raged out like a mountain-cat, and there was to be seen the sheen and sparkle of a broken crest.

The captain, in the bow, moved on his water-jar and sat erect. 'Pretty long night,' he observed to the correspondent. He looked at the shore. 'Those life-saving people take their time.'

'Did you see that shark playing around?'

'Yes, I saw him. He was a big fellow, all right.'

'Wish I had known you were awake.'

Later the correspondent spoke into the bottom of the boat.

'Billie!' There was a slow and gradual disentanglement. 'Billie, will you spell me?'

'Sure,' said the oiler.

As soon as the correspondent touched the cold comfortable sea-water in the bottom of the boat, and had huddled close to the cook's life-belt he was deep in sleep, despite the fact that his teeth played all the popular airs. This sleep was so good to him that it was but a moment before he heard a voice call his name in a tone that demonstrated the last stages of exhaustion. 'Will you spell me?'

'Sure, Billie.'

The light in the north had mysteriously vanished, but the correspondent took his course from the wide-awake captain.

Later in the night they took the boat farther out to sea, and the captain directed the cook to take one oar at the stern and keep the boat facing the seas. He was to call out if he should hear the thunder of the surf. This plan enabled the oiler and the correspondent to get respite together. 'We'll give those boys a chance to get into shape again,' said the captain. They curled down and, after a few preliminary chatterings and trembles, slept once more the dead sleep. Neither knew they had bequeathed to the cook the company of another shark, or perhaps the same shark.

As the boat caroused on the waves, spray occasionally bumped over the side and gave them a fresh soaking, but this had no power to break their repose. The ominous slash of the wind and the water affected them as it would have affected mummies.

'Boys,' said the cook, with the notes of every reluctance in his voice, 'she's drifted in pretty close. I guess one of you had better take her to sea again.' The correspondent, aroused, heard the crash of the toppled crests.

As he was rowing, the captain gave him some whisky-and-water, and this steadied the chills out of him. 'If I ever get ashore and anybody shows me even a photograph of an oar—'

At last there was a short conversation.

'Billie. . . . Billie, will you spell me?'

'Sure,' said the oiler.

VII

When the correspondent again opened his eyes, the sea and the sky were each of the grey hue of the dawning. Later, carmine and gold was painted upon the waters. The morning appeared finally, in its splendour, with a sky of pure blue, and the sunlight flamed on the tips of the waves.

On the distant dunes were set many little black cottages, and a tall white windmill reared above them. No man, nor dog, nor bicycle appeared on the beach. The cottages might have formed a deserted village.

The voyagers scanned the shore. A conference was held in the boat. 'Well,' said the captain, 'if no help is coming, we might better try a run through the surf right away. If we stay out here much longer we will be too weak to do anything for ourselves at all.' The others silently acquiesced in this reasoning. The boat was headed for the beach. The correspondent wondered if none ever ascended the tall wind-tower, and if then they never looked seaward. This tower was a giant, standing with its back to the plight of the ants. It represented in a degree, to the correspondent, the serenity of nature amid the struggles of the individual—nature in the wind, and nature in the vision of men. She did not seem cruel to him then, nor beneficent, nor treacherous, nor wise. But she was indifferent, flatly indifferent. It is, perhaps, plausible that a man in this situation, impressed with the unconcern of the universe, should see the innumerable flaws of his life, and have them taste wickedly in his mind and wish for another chance. A distinction between right and wrong seems absurdly clear to him, then, in this new ignorance of the grave-edge, and he understands that if he were given another opportunity he would mend his conduct and his words, and be better and brighter during an introduction or at a tea.

'Now, boys,' said the captain, 'she is going to swamp sure. All we can do is to work her in as far as possible, and then when she swamps, pile out and scramble for the beach. Keep cool now, and don't jump until she swamps sure.'

The oiler took the oars. Over his shoulders he scanned the surf. 'Captain,' he said, 'I think I'd better bring her about, and keep her head-on to the seas and back her in.'

'All right, Billie,' said the captain. 'Back her in.' The oiler swung the boat then and, seated in the stern, the cook and the correspondent were obliged to look over their shoulders to contemplate the lonely and indifferent shore.

The monstrous in-shore rollers heaved the boat high until the men were again enabled to see the white sheets of water scudding up the slanted beach. 'We won't get in very close,' said the captain. Each time a man could wrest his attention from the rollers, he turned his glance toward the shore, and in the expression of the eyes during this contemplation there was a singular quality. The correspondent, observing the others, knew that they were not afraid, but the full meaning of their glances was shrouded.

As for himself, he was too tired to grapple fundamentally with the fact. He tried to coerce his mind into thinking of it, but the mind was dominated at this time by the muscles, and the muscles said they did not care. It merely occurred to him that if he should drown it would be a shame.

There were no hurried words, no pallor, no plain agitation. The men simply looked at the shore. 'Now, remember to get well clear of the boat when you jump,' said the captain.

Seaward the crest of a roller suddenly fell with a thunderous crash, and the long white comber came roaring down upon the boat.

'Steady now,' said the captain. The men were silent. They turned their eyes from the shore to the comber and waited. The boat slid up the incline, leaped at the furious top, bounced over it, and swung down the long back of the waves. Some water had been shipped and the cook bailed it out.

But the next crest crashed also. The tumbling boiling flood of white water caught the boat and whirled it almost perpendicular. Water swarmed in from all sides. The correspondent had his hands on the gunwale at this time, and when the water entered at that place he swiftly withdrew his fingers, as if he objected to wetting them.

The little boat, drunken with this weight of water, reeled and snuggled deeper into the sea.

'Bail her out, cook! Bail her out,' said the captain.

'All right, captain,' said the cook.

'Now, boys, the next one will do for us, sure,' said the oiler. 'Mind to jump clear of the boat.'

The third wave moved forward, huge, furious, implacable. It fairly swallowed the dingey, and almost simultaneously the men tumbled into the sea. A piece of life-belt had lain in the bottom of the boat, and as the correspondent went overboard he held this to his chest with his left hand.

The January water was icy, and he reflected immediately that it was colder than he had expected to find it off the coast of Florida. This appeared to his dazed mind as a fact important enough to be noted at the time. The coldness of the water was sad; it was tragic. This fact was somehow mixed and confused with his opinion of his own situation that it seemed almost a proper reason for tears. The water was cold.

When he came to the surface he was conscious of little but the noisy water. Afterward he saw his companions in the sea. The oiler was ahead in the race. He was swimming strongly and rapidly. Off to the correspondent's left, the cook's great white and corked back bulged out of the water, and in the rear the captain was hanging with his one good hand to the keel of the overturned dingey.

There is a certain immovable quality to a shore, and the correspondent wondered at it amid the confusion of the sea.

It seemed also very attractive, but the correspondent knew that it was a long journey, and he paddled leisurely. The piece of life-preserver lay under him, and sometimes he whirled down the incline of a wave as if he were on a hand-sled.

But finally he arrived at a place in the sea where travel was beset with difficulty. He did not pause swimming to inquire what manner of current had caught him, but there his progress ceased. The shore was set before him like a bit of scenery on a stage, and he looked at it and understood with his eyes each detail of it.

As the cook passed, much farther to the left, the captain was calling to him, 'Turn over on your back, cook! Turn over on your back and use the oar.'

'All right, sir.' The cook turned on his back, and, paddling with an oar, went ahead as if he were a canoe.

Presently the boat also passed to the left of the correspondent with the captain clinging with one hand to the keel. He would have appeared like a man raising himself to look over a board fence, if it were not for the extraordinary gymnastics of the boat. The correspondent marvelled that the captain could still hold to it.

They passed on, nearer to shore—the oiler, the cook, the captain—and following them went the water-jar, bouncing gaily over the seas.

The correspondent remained in the grip of this strange new enemy—a current. The shore, with its white slope of sand and its green bluff, topped with little silent cottages, was spread like a picture before him. It was very near to him then, but he was impressed as one who in a gallery looks at a scene from Brittany or Algiers.

He thought: 'I am going to drown? Can it be possible? Can it be possible? Can it be possible?' Perhaps an individual must consider his own death to be the final phenomenon of nature.

But later a wave perhaps whirled him out of this small deadly current, for he found suddenly that he could again make progress toward the shore. Later still, he was aware that the captain, clinging with one hand to the keel of the dingey, had his face turned away from the shore and toward him, and was calling his name. 'Come to the boat! Come to the boat!'

In his struggle to reach the captain and the boat, he reflected that when one gets properly wearied, drowning must really be a comfortable arrangement, a cessation of hostilities accompanied by a large degree of relief, and he was glad of it, for the main thing in his mind for some moments had been horror of the temporary agony. He did not wish to be hurt.

Presently he saw a man running along the shore. He was undressing with most remarkable speed. Coat, trousers, shirt, everything flew magically off him.

'Come to the boat,' called the captain.

'All right, captain.' As the correspondent paddled, he saw the captain let himself down to bottom and leave the boat. Then the correspondent performed his one little marvel of the voyage. A large wave caught him and flung him with ease and supreme speed completely over the boat and far beyond it. It struck him even then as an event in gymnastics, and a true miracle of the sea. An overturned boat in the surf is not a plaything to a swimming man.

The correspondent arrived in water that reached only to his waist, but his condition did not enable him to stand for more than a moment. Each wave knocked him into a heap, and the under-tow pulled at him.

Then he saw the man who had been running and undressing, and undressing and running, come bounding into the water. He dragged ashore the cook, and then waded toward the captain, but the captain waved him away, and sent him to the correspondent. He was naked, naked as a tree in winter, but a halo was about his head, and he shone like a saint. He gave a strong pull, and a long drag, and a bully heave at the correspondent's hand. The correspondent, schooled in the minor formulæ, said: 'Thanks, old man.' But suddenly the man cried: 'What's that?' He pointed a swift finger. The correspondent said: 'Go.'

In the shallows, face downward, lay the oiler. His forehead touched sand that was periodically, between each wave, clear of the sea.

The correspondent did not know all that transpired afterward. When he achieved safe ground he fell, striking the sand with each particular part of his body. It was as if he had dropped from a roof, but the thud was grateful to him.

It seems that instantly the beach was populated with men with blankets, clothes, and flasks, and women with coffee-pots and all the remedies sacred to their minds. The welcome of the land to the men from the sea was warm and generous, but a still and dripping shape was carried slowly up the beach, and the land's welcome for it could only be the different and sinister hospitality of the grave.

When it came night, the white waves paced to and fro in the moonlight, and the wind brought the sound of the great sea's voice to the men on shore, and they felt that they could then be interpreters.

1898

THE UPTURNED FACE

'WHAT will we do now?' said the adjutant, troubled and excited.

'Bury him,' said Timothy Lean.

The two officers looked down close to their toes where lay the body of their comrade. The face was chalk-blue; gleaming eyes stared at the sky. Over the two upright figures was a windy sound of bullets, and on the top of the hill Lean's prostrate company of Spitzbergen infantry was firing measured volleys.

'Don't you think it would be better—' began the adjutant. 'We might leave him until to-morrow.'

'No,' said Lean. 'I can't hold that post an hour longer. I've got to fall back, and we've got to bury old Bill.'

'Of course,' said the adjutant, at once. 'Your men got intrenching tools?'

Lean shouted back to his little line, and two men came slowly, one with a pick, one with a shovel. They started in the direction of the Rostina sharpshooters. Bullets cracked near their ears. 'Dig here,' said Lean gruffly. The men, thus caused to lower their glances to the turf, became hurried and frightened, merely because they could not look to see whence the bullets came. The dull beat of the pick striking the earth sounded amid the swift snap of close bullets. Presently the other private began to shovel.

'I suppose,' said the adjutant, slowly, 'we'd better search his clothes for—things.'

Lean nodded. Together in curious abstraction they looked at the body. Then Lean stirred his shoulders suddenly, arousing himself.

'Yes,' he said, 'we'd better see what he's got.' He dropped to his knees, and his hands approached the body of the dead officer. But his hands wavered over the buttons of the tunic. The first button was brick-red with drying blood, and he did not seem to dare touch it.

'Go on,' said the adjutant, hoarsely.

Lean stretched his wooden hand, and his fingers fumbled the blood-stained buttons. At last he rose with ghastly face. He had gathered a watch, a whistle, a pipe, a tobacco-pouch, a handkerchief, a little case of cards and papers. He looked at the adjutant. There was a silence. The adjutant was feeling that he had been a coward to make Lean do all the grisly business.

'Well,' said Lean, 'that's all, I think. You have his sword and revolver?'

'Yes,' said the adjutant, his face working, and then he burst out in a sudden strange fury at the two privates. 'Why don't you hurry up with that grave? What are you doing, anyhow? Hurry, do you hear? I never saw such stupid—'

Even as he cried out in his passion the two men were labouring for their lives. Ever overhead the bullets were spitting.

The grave was finished. It was not a masterpiece—a poor little shallow thing. Lean and the adjutant again looked at each other in a curious silent communication.

Suddenly the adjutant croaked out a weird laugh. It was a terrible laugh, which had its origin in that part of the mind which is first moved by the singing of the nerves. 'Well,' he said, humorously to Lean, 'I suppose we had best tumble him in.'

'Yes,' said Lean. The two privates stood waiting, bent over their implements. 'I suppose,' said Lean, 'it would be better if we laid him in ourselves.'

'Yes,' said the adjutant. Then, apparently remembering that he had made Lean search the body, he stooped with great fortitude and took hold of the dead officer's clothing. Lean joined him. Both were particular that their fingers should not feel the corpse. They tugged away; the corpse lifted, heaved, toppled, flopped into the grave, and the two officers, straightening, looked again at each other—they were always looking at each other. They sighed with relief.

The adjutant said, 'I suppose we should —we should say something. Do you know the service, Tim?'

'They don't read the service until the

grave is filled in,' said Lean, pressing his lips to an academic expression.

'Don't they?' said the adjutant, shocked that he had made the mistake.

'Oh, well,' he cried, suddenly, 'let us—let us say something—while he can hear us.'

'All right,' said Lean. 'Do you know the service?'

'I can't remember a line of it,' said the adjutant.

Lean was extremely dubious. 'I can repeat two lines, but—'

'Well, do it,' said the adjutant. 'Go as far as you can. That's better than nothing. And the beasts have got our range exactly.'

Lean looked at his two men. 'Attention,' he barked. The privates came to attention with a click, looking much aggrieved. The adjutant lowered his helmet to his knee. Lean, bareheaded, stood over the grave. The Rostina sharpshooters fired briskly.

'O Father, our friend has sunk in the deep waters of death, but his spirit has leaped toward Thee as the bubble arises from the lips of the drowning. Perceive, we beseech, O Father, the little flying bubble, and—'

Lean, although husky and ashamed, had suffered no hesitation up to this point, but he stopped with a hopeless feeling and looked at the corpse.

The adjutant moved uneasily. 'And from Thy superb heights—' he began, and then he too came to an end.

'And from Thy superb heights,' said Lean.

The adjutant suddenly remembered a phrase in the back part of the Spitzbergen burial service, and he exploited it with the triumphant manner of a man who has recalled everything, and can go on.

'O God, have mercy—'

'O God, have mercy—' said Lean.

'Mercy,' repeated the adjutant, in quick failure.

'Mercy,' said Lean. And then he was moved by some violence of feeling, for he turned suddenly upon his two men and tigerishly said, 'Throw the dirt in.'

The fire of the Rostina sharpshooters was accurate and continuous.

One of the aggrieved privates came forward with his shovel. He lifted his first shovel-load of earth, and for a moment of inexplicable hesitation it was held poised above this corpse, which from its chalk-blue face looked keenly out from the grave. Then the soldier emptied his shovel on—on the feet.

Timothy Lean felt as if tons had been swiftly lifted from off his forehead. He had felt that perhaps the private might empty the shovel on—on the face. It had been emptied on the feet. There was a great point gained there—ha, ha!—the first shovelful had been emptied on the feet. How satisfactory!

The adjutant began to babble. 'Well, of course—a man we've messed with all these years—impossible—you can't, you know, leave your intimate friends rotting on the field. Go on, for God's sake, and shovel, you!'

The man with the shovel suddenly ducked, grabbed his left arm with his right hand, and looked at his officer for orders. Lean picked the shovel from the ground. 'Go to the rear,' he said to the wounded man. He also addressed the other private. 'You get under cover, too; I'll finish this business.'

The wounded man scrambled hard still for the top of the ridge without devoting any glances to the direction from whence the bullets came, and the other man followed at an equal pace; but he was different, in that he looked back anxiously three times.

This is merely the way—often—of the hit and unhit.

Timothy Lean filled the shovel, hesitated, and then, in a movement which was like a gesture of abhorrence, he flung the dirt into the grave, and as it landed it made a sound—plop! Lean suddenly stopped and mopped his brow—a tired labourer.

'Perhaps we have been wrong,' said the adjutant. His glance wavered stupidly. 'It might have been better if we hadn't buried him just at this time. Of course, if we advance to-morrow the body would have been—'

'Damn you,' said Lean, 'shut your mouth!' He was not the senior officer.

He again filled the shovel and flung the earth. Always the earth made that sound—plop! For a space Lean worked frantically, like a man digging himself out of danger.

Soon there was nothing to be seen but

the chalk-blue face. Lean filled the shovel.
'Good God,' he cried to the adjutant. 'Why
didn't you turn him somehow when you
put him in? This—' Then Lean began to
stutter.

The adjutant understood. He was pale to
the lips. 'Go on, man,' he cried, beseechingly, almost in a shout. Lean swung back
the shovel. It went forward in a pendulum
curve. When the earth landed it made a   10
sound—plop!

                                         1902

TEN POEMS

I

IN heaven,
Some little blades of grass
Stood before God.
'What did you do?'
Then all save one of the little blades
Began eagerly to relate
The merits of their lives.
This one stayed a small way behind,
Ashamed.
Presently, God said,   10
'And what did you do?'
The little blade answered, 'O my lord,
Memory is bitter to me,
For, if I did good deeds,
I know not of them.'
Then God, in all His splendour,
Arose from His throne.
'O best little blade of grass!' He said.
                                         1895

2

PLACES among the stars,
Soft gardens near the sun,
Keep your distant beauty;
Shed no beams upon my weak heart.
Since she is here
In a place of blackness,
Not your golden days
Nor your silver nights
Can call me to you.
Since she is here   10
In a place of blackness,
Here I stay and wait.   1895

3

A YOUTH in apparel that glittered
Went to walk in a grim forest.
There he met an assassin
Attired all in garb of old days;

He, scowling through the thickets,
And dagger poised quivering,
Rushed upon the youth.
'Sir,' said this latter,
'I am enchanted, believe me,
To die, thus,   10
In this mediæval fashion,
According to the best legends;
Ah, what joy!'
Then took he the wound, smiling,
And died, content.
                                         1895

4

Do not weep, maiden, for war is kind.
Because your lover threw wild hands
        toward the sky
And the affrighted steed ran on alone,
Do not weep.
War is kind.

        Hoarse, booming drums of the
            regiment,
        Little souls who thirst for fight,
        These men were born to drill and
            die.
        The unexplained glory flies above
            them,
        Great is the battle-god, great, and his
            kingdom—   10
        A field where a thousand corpses lie.

Do not weep, babe, for war is kind.
Because your father tumbled in the yellow
        trenches,
Raged at his breast, gulped and died,
Do not weep.
War is kind.

        Swift blazing flag of the regiment,
        Eagle with crest of red and gold,
        These men were born to drill and
            die.
        Point for them the virtue of slaughter,
        Make plain to them the excellence of
            killing   21
        And a field where a thousand corpses
            lie.

Mother whose heart hung humble as a
        button
On the bright splendid shroud of your son,
Do not weep.
War is kind.
                                         1899

5

A NEWSPAPER is a collection of half-
    injustices
Which, bawled by boys from mile to mile,
Spreads its curious opinion
To a million merciful and sneering men,
While families cuddle the joys of the
    fireside
When spurred by tale of dire lone agony.
A newspaper is a court
Where everyone is kindly and unfairly
    tried
By a squalor of honest men.
A newspaper is a market   10
Where wisdom sells its freedom
And melons are crowned by the crowd.
A newspaper is a game
Where his error scores the player victory
While another's skill wins death.
A newspaper is a symbol;
It is feckless life's chronicle,
A collection of loud tales
Concentrating eternal stupidities,
That in remote ages lived unhaltered,   20
Roaming through a fenceless world.
                       1899

6

The wayfarer,
Perceiving the pathway to truth,
Was struck by astonishment.
It was thickly grown with weeds.
'Ha,' he said,
'I see that none has passed here
In a long time.'
Later he saw that each weed
Was a singular knife.
'Well,' he mumbled at last,   10
'Doubtless there are other roads.'
                       1899

7

A SLANT of sun on dull brown walls,
A forgotten sky of bashful blue.

Toward God a mighty hymn,
A song of collisions and cries,
Rumbling wheels, hoof-beats, bells,
Welcomes, farewells, love-calls, final
    moans,
Voices of joy, idiocy, warning, despair,
The unknown appeals of brutes,
The chanting of flowers,
The screams of cut trees.   10

The senseless babble of hens and wise
    men—
A cluttered incoherency that says at the
    stars:
'O God, save us!'
                       1899

8

In the night
Grey heavy clouds muffled the valleys,
And the peaks looked toward God
    alone.
  'O Master, that movest the wind with
    a finger,
  Humble, idle, futile peaks are we.
  Grant that we may run swiftly across
    the world
  To huddle in worship at Thy feet.'

In the morning
A noise of men at work came the clear blue
    miles,
And the little black cities were apparent. 10
  'O Master, that knowest the meaning
    of raindrops,
  Humble, idle, futile peaks are we.
  Give voice to us, we pray, O Lord,
  That we may sing Thy goodness to the
    sun.'

In the evening
The far valleys were sprinkled with tiny
    lights.
  'O Master,
  Thou that knowest the value of kings
    and birds,
  Thou hast made us humble, idle, futile
    peaks.
  Thou only needst eternal patience;   20
  We bow to Thy wisdom, O Lord—
  Humble, idle, futile peaks.'

In the night
Grey heavy clouds muffled the valleys,
And the peaks looked toward God
    alone.
                       1899

9

A MAN said to the universe:
'Sir, I exist!'
'However,' replied the universe,
'The fact has not created in me
A sense of obligation.'
                       1899

10

THE trees in the garden rained flowers.
Children ran there joyously.
They gathered the flowers
Each to himself.
Now there were some
Who gathered great heaps—
Having opportunity and skill—
Until, behold, only chance blossoms
Remained for the feeble.
Then a little spindling tutor   10
Ran importantly to the father, crying:
'Pray, come hither!
See this unjust thing in your garden!'
But when the father had surveyed,

He admonished the tutor:
'Not so, small sage!
This thing is just.
For, look you,
Are not they who possess the flowers
Stronger, bolder, shrewder   20
Than they who have none?
Why should the strong—
The beautiful strong—
Why should they not have the flowers?'
Upon reflection, the tutor bowed to the
        ground,
'My lord,' he said,
'The stars are displaced
By this towering wisdom.'

                                                          1899

FRANK NORRIS

1870–1902

FROM THE OCTOPUS AND THE PIT

WHEAT [1]

I

THE evening before, when the foreman had
blown his whistle at six o'clock, the long
line of ploughs had halted upon the instant, and the drivers, unharnessing their
teams, had taken them back to the division
barns—leaving the ploughs as they were in   10
the furrows. But an hour after daylight the
next morning the work was resumed. After
breakfast, Vanamee, riding one horse and
leading the others, had returned to the line
of ploughs together with the other drivers.
Now he was busy harnessing the team. At
the division blacksmith shop—temporarily

[1] These selections, to which the title has been given by
    the editors, are, respectively, from *The Octopus*(N.Y.,
    1901),126–33; and *The Pit*(N.Y., 1903),380–96. They   20
    are keystones from Norris' trilogy on wheat, which, in
    his brother's words, 'stood to him as a great world-
    force.' Of Norris' projected conclusion to the trilogy,
    his brother wrote: '. . . He told me of the last novel of
    the trilogy of "The Wheat," to which *The Octopus*
    and *The Pit* belonged. Not one word of this was ever
    written. It was not to be called *The Wolf*, however, as
    was announced. Its pivotal episode was to deal with a
    famine-stricken country of Europe, and the timely
    appearance, from across the sea, of three huge Amer-
    ican schooners,—wheat-ships,—loaded to their capac-
    ity with the great crop that, in spite of the quarrels of   30
    farmers and railroads, and in spite of the manipula-
    tions of the bulls and bears on the stock market, was to
    fulfill its destiny as "the nourisher of nations." '
    Charles Norris, *Frank Norris*(N.Y , 1916),14.

put up—he had been obliged to wait while
one of his lead horses was shod, and he
had thus been delayed quite five minutes.
Nearly all the other teams were harnessed,
the drivers on their seats, waiting for the
foreman's signal.

'All ready here?' inquired the foreman,
driving up to Vanamee's team in his buggy.

'All ready, sir,' answered Vanamee, buck-
ling the last strap.

He climbed to his seat, shaking out the
reins, and turning about, looked back along
the line, then all around him at the landscape inundated with the brilliant glow of
the early morning.

The day was fine. Since the first rain of
the season, there had been no other. Now
the sky was without a cloud, pale blue, delicate, luminous, scintillating with morning.
The great brown earth turned a huge flank
to it, exhaling the moisture of the early dew.
The atmosphere, washed clean of dust and
mist, was translucent as crystal. Far off to
the east, the hills on the other side of
Broderson Creek stood out against the pallid saffron of the horizon as flat and as
sharply outlined as if pasted on the sky. The
campanile of the ancient Mission of San
Juan seemed as fine as frost work. All
about between the horizons, the carpet of
the land unrolled itself to infinity. But now
it was no longer parched with heat, cracked
and warped by a merciless sun, powdered

with dust. The rain had done its work; not a clod that was not swollen with fertility, not a fissure that did not exhale the sense of fecundity. One could not take a dozen steps upon the ranches without the brusque sensation tnat underfoot the land was alive; aroused at last from its sleep, palpitating with the desire of reproduction. Deep down there in the recesses of the soil, the great heart throbbed once more, thrilling with passion, vibrating with desire, offering itself to the caress of the plough, insistent, eager, imperious. Dimly one felt the deep-seated trouble of the earth, the uneasy agitation of its members, the hidden tumult of its womb, demanding to be made fruitful, to reproduce, to disengage the eternal renascent germ of Life that stirred and struggled in its loins.

The ploughs, thirty-five in number, each drawn by its team of ten, stretched in an interminable line, nearly a quarter of a mile in length, behind and ahead of Vanamee. They were arranged, as it were, *en échelon*, not in file—not one directly behind the other, but each succeeding plough its own width farther in the field than the one in front of it. Each of these ploughs held five shears, so that when the entire company was in motion, one hundred and seventy-five furrows were made at the same instant. At a distance, the ploughs resembled a great column of field artillery. Each driver was in his place, his glance alternating between his horses and the foreman nearest at hand. Other foremen, in their buggies or buckboards, were at intervals along the line, like battery lieutenants. Annixter himself, on horseback, in boots and campaign hat, a cigar in his teeth, overlooked the scene.

The division superintendent, on the opposite side of the line, galloped past to a position at the head. For a long moment there was a silence. A sense of preparedness ran from end to end of the column. All things were ready, each man in his place. The day's work was about to begin.

Suddenly, from a distance at the head of the line came the shrill trilling of a whistle. At once the foreman nearest Vanamee repeated it, at the same time turning down the line, and waving one arm. The signal was repeated, whistle answering whistle, till the sounds lost themselves in the dis-

tance. At once the line of ploughs lost its immobility, moving forward, getting slowly under way, the horses straining in the traces. A prolonged movement rippled from team to team, disengaging in its passage a multitude of sounds—the click of buckles, the creak of straining leather, the subdued clash of machinery, the cracking of whips, the deep breathing of nearly four hundred horses, the abrupt commands and cries of the drivers, and, last of all, the prolonged, soothing murmur of the thick brown earth turning steadily from the multitude of advancing shears.

The ploughing thus commenced, continued. The sun rose higher. Steadily the hundred iron hands kneaded and furrowed and stroked the brown, humid earth, the hundred iron teeth bit deep into the Titan's flesh. Perched on his seat, the moist living reins slipping and tugging in his hands, Vanamee, in the midst of this steady confusion of constantly varying sensation, sight interrupted by sound, sound mingling with sight, on this swaying, vibrating seat, quivering with the prolonged thrill of the earth, lapsed to a sort of pleasing numbness, in a sense, hypnotised by the weaving maze of things in which he found himself involved. To keep his team at an even, regular gait, maintaining the precise interval, to run his furrows as closely as possible to those already made by the plough in front —this for the moment was the entire sum of his duties. But while one part of his brain, alert and watchful, took cognisance of these matters, all the greater part was lulled and stupefied with the long monotony of the affair.

The ploughing, now in full swing, enveloped him in a vague, slow-moving whirl of things. Underneath him was the jarring, jolting, trembling machine; not a clod was turned, not an obstacle encountered, that he did not receive the swift impression of it through all his body, the very friction of the damp soil, sliding incessantly from the shiny surface of the shears, seemed to reproduce itself in his finger-tips and along the back of his head. He heard the horse-hoofs by the myriads crushing down easily, deeply, into the loam, the prolonged clinking of trace-chains, the working of the smooth brown flanks in the harness, the clatter of wooden hames, the champing of bits, the click of iron shoes against pebbles, the brittle stubble of the surface ground crackling and snapping as the furrows turned, the sonorous, steady breaths wrenched from the deep, labouring chests, strap-bound, shining with sweat, and all along the line the voices of the men talking to the horses. Everywhere there were visions of glossy brown backs, straining, heaving, swollen with muscle; harness streaked with specks of froth, broad, cup-shaped hoofs, heavy with brown loam, men's faces red with tan, blue overalls spotted with axle-grease; muscled hands, the knuckles whitened in their grip on the reins, and through it all the ammoniacal smell of the horses, the bitter reek of perspiration of beasts and men, the aroma of warm leather, the scent of dead stubble— and stronger and more penetrating than everything else, the heavy, enervating odour of the upturned, living earth.

At intervals, from the tops of one of the rare, low swells of the land, Vanamee overlooked a wider horizon. On the other divisions of Quien Sabe the same work was in progress. Occasionally he could see another column of ploughs in the adjoining division—sometimes so close at hand that the subdued murmur of its movements reached his ear; sometimes so distant that it resolved itself into a long, brown streak upon the grey of the ground. Farther off to the west on the Osterman ranch other columns came and went, and, once, from the crest of the highest swell on his division, Vanamee caught a distant glimpse of the Broderson ranch. There, too, moving specks indicated that the ploughing was under way. And farther away still, far off there beyond the fine line of the horizons, over the curve of the globe, the shoulder of the earth, he knew were other ranches, and beyond these others, and beyond these still others, the immensities multiplying to infinity.

Everywhere throughout the great San Joaquin, unseen and unheard, a thousand ploughs up-stirred the land, tens of thousands of shears clutched deep into the warm, moist soil.

It was the long stroking caress, vigorous, male, powerful, for which the Earth seemed panting. The heroic embrace of a multitude of iron hands, gripping deep into the brown, warm flesh of the land that quivered responsive and passionate under this rude advance, so robust as to be almost an assault, so violent as to be veritably brutal. There, under the sun and under the speckless sheen of the sky, the wooing of the Titan began, the vast primal passion, the two world-forces, the elemental Male and Female, locked in a colossal embrace, at grapples in the throes of an infinite desire, at once terrible and divine, knowing no law, untamed, savage, natural, sublime.

From time to time the gang in which Vanamee worked halted on the signal from foreman or overseer. The horses came to a standstill, the vague clamour of the work lapsed away. Then the minutes passed. The whole work hung suspended. All up and down the line one demanded what had happened. The division superintendent galloped past, perplexed and anxious. For the moment, one of the ploughs was out of order, a bolt had slipped, a lever refused to work, or a machine had become immobilised in heavy ground, or a horse had lamed himself. Once, even, toward noon, an entire plough was taken out of the line, so out of gear that a messenger had to be sent to the division forge to summon the machinist.

Annixter had disappeared. He had ridden farther on to the other divisions of his ranch, to watch the work in progress there. At twelve o'clock, according to his orders, all the division superintendents put themselves in communication with him by means of the telephone wires that connected each of the division houses, reporting the condition of the work, the number of acres covered, the prospects of each plough traversing its daily average of twenty miles.

At half-past twelve, Vanamee and the rest of the drivers ate their lunch in the field, the tin buckets having been distributed to them that morning after breakfast. But in the evening, the routine of the previous day was repeated, and Vanamee, unharnessing his team, riding one horse and leading the others, returned to the division barns and bunk-house.

It was between six and seven o'clock. The half hundred men of the gang threw themselves upon the supper the Chinese cooks had set out in the shed of the eating-ouse, long as a bowling alley, unpainted, rude, the seats benches, the table covered with oil cloth. Overhead a half-dozen kerosene lamps flared and smoked.

The table was taken as if by assault; the latter of iron knives upon the tin plates was as the reverberation of hail upon a metal roof. The ploughmen rinsed their throats with great draughts of wine, and, their elbows wide, their foreheads flushed, resumed the attack upon the beef and bread, eating as though they would never have enough. All up and down the long table, where the kerosene lamps reflected themselves deep in the oil cloth cover, one heard the incessant sounds of mastication, and saw the uninterrupted movement of great jaws. At every moment one or another of the men demanded a fresh portion of beef, another pint of wine, another half-loaf of bread. For upwards of an hour the gang ate. It was no longer a supper. It was a veritable barbecue, a crude and primitive feasting, barbaric, homeric.

But in all this scene Vanamee saw nothing repulsive. Presley would have abhorred it—this feeding of the People, this gorging of the human animal, eager for its meat. Vanamee, simple, uncomplicated, living so close to nature and the rudimentary life, understood its significance. He knew very well that within a short half-hour after this meal the men would throw themselves down in their bunks to sleep without moving, inert and stupefied with fatigue, till the morning. Work, food, and sleep, all life reduced to its bare essentials, uncomplex, honest, healthy. They were strong, these men, with the strength of the soil they worked, in touch with the essential things, back again to the starting point of civilisation, coarse, vital, real, and sane.

For a brief moment immediately after the meal, pipes were lit, and the air grew thick with fragrant tobacco smoke. On a corner of the dining-room table, a game of poker was begun. One of the drivers, a Swede, produced an accordion; a group on the steps of the bunk-house listened, with alternate gravity and shouts of laughter, to the acknowledged story-teller of the gang. But soon the men began to turn in, stretching themselves at full length on the horse blankets in the racklike bunks. The sounds of heavy breathing increased steadily, lights

were put out, and before the afterglow had faded from the sky, the gang was asleep.

1901

II

For on this morning of the thirteenth of June, the Board of Trade, its halls, corridors, offices, and stairways were already thrilling with a vague and terrible sound. It was only a little after nine o'clock. The trading would not begin for another half hour, but, even now, the mutter of the whirlpool, the growl of the Pit was making itself felt. The eddies were gathering; the thousands of subsidiary torrents that fed the cloaca were moving. From all over the immediate neighbourhood they came, from the offices of hundreds of commission houses, from brokers' offices, from banks, from the tall, grey buildings of LaSalle Street, from the street itself. And even from greater distances they came; auxiliary currents set in from all the reach of the Great Northwest, from Minneapolis, Duluth, and Milwaukee. From the Southwest, St. Louis, Omaha, and Kansas City contributed to the volume. The Atlantic Seaboard, New York, and Boston and Philadelphia sent out their tributary streams; London, Liverpool, Paris, and Odessa merged their influences with the vast world-wide flowing that bore down upon Chicago, and that now began slowly, slowly to centre and circle about the Wheat Pit of the Board of Trade.

Small wonder that the building to Page's ears vibrated to a strange and ominous humming. She heard it in the distant clicking of telegraph keys, in the echo of hurried whispered conversations held in dark corners, in the noise of rapid footsteps, in the trilling of telephone bells. These sounds came from all around her; they issued from the offices of the building below her, above her, and on either side. She was surrounded with them, and they mingled together to form one prolonged and muffled roar, that from moment to moment increased in volume.

The Pit was getting under way; the whirlpool was forming, and the sound of its courses was like the sound of the ocean in storm, heard at a distance.

Page and Landry were still halfway up the last stairway. Above and below, the throng was packed dense and immobilised.

But, little by little, Landry wormed a way for them, winning one step at a time. But he was very anxious; again and again he looked at his watch. At last he said:

'I've *got* to go. It's just madness for me to stay another minute. I'll give you my card.'

'Well, leave me here,' Page urged. 'It can't be helped. I'm all right. Give me your card. I'll tell the guide in the gallery that you kept the seat for me—if I ever can get there. You must go. Don't stay another minute. If you can, come for me here in the gallery, when it's over. I'll wait for you. But if you can't come, all right. I can take care of myself.'

He could but assent to this. This was no time to think of small things. He left her and bore back with all his might through the crowd, gained the landing at the turn of the balustrade, waved his hat to her and disappeared.

A quarter of an hour went by. Page, caught in the crowd, could neither advance nor retreat. Ahead of her, some twenty steps away, she could see the back rows of seats in the gallery. But they were already occupied. It seemed hopeless to expect to see anything of the floor that day. But she could no longer extricate herself from the press; there was nothing to do but stay where she was.

On every side of her she caught odds and ends of dialogues and scraps of discussions, and while she waited she found an interest in listening to these, as they reached her from time to time.

'Well,' observed the man in the tall white hat, who had discouraged Landry from attempting to reach the gallery, 'well, he's shaken 'em up pretty well. Whether he downs 'em or they down him, he's made a good fight.'

His companion, a young man with eyeglasses, who wore a wonderful white waistcoat with queer glass buttons, assented, and Page heard him add:

'Big operator, that Jadwin.'

'They're doing for him now, though.'

'I ain't so sure. He's got another fight in him. You'll see.'

'Ever see him?'

'No, no, he don't come into the Pit—these big men never do.'

Directly in front of Page two women kept up an interminable discourse.

'Well,' said the one, 'that's all very well but Mr. Jadwin made my sister-in-law—she lives in Dubuque, you know—a rich woman. She bought some wheat, just for fun, you know, a long time ago, and held on till Mr. Jadwin put the price up to four times what she paid for it. Then she sold out. My, you ought to see the lovely house she's building, and her son's gone to Europe, to study art, if you please, and a year ago, my dear, they didn't have a cent, not a cent, but her husband's salary.'

'There's the other side, too, though,' answered her companion, adding in a hoarse whisper: 'If Mr. Jadwin fails to-day—well, honestly, Julia, I don't know what Philip will do.'

But, from another group at Page's elbow, a man's bass voice cut across the subdued chatter of the two women.

'Guess we'll pull through, somehow. Burbank & Co., though—by George! I'm not sure about them. They are pretty well involved in this thing, and there's two or three smaller firms that are dependent on them. If Gretry-Converse & Co. should suspend, Burbank would go with a crash sure. And there's that bank in Keokuk; they can't stand much more. Their depositors would run 'em quick as how-do-you-do, if there was a smash here in Chicago.'

'Oh, Jadwin will pull through.'

'Well, I hope so—by Jingo! I hope so. Say, by the way, how did you come out?'

'Me! Hoh! Say my boy, the next time I get into a wheat trade you'll know it. I was one of the merry paretics who believed that Crookes was the Great Lumtum. I tailed on to his clique. Lord love you! Jadwin put the knife into me to the tune of twelve thousand dollars. But, say, look here; aren't we ever going to get up to that blame gallery? We ain't going to see any of this, and I—*hark!* —by God! there goes the gong. They've begun. Say, say, *hear 'em, will you!* Holy Moses! say—listen to that! Did you ever hear—Lord! I wish we could see—could get somewhere where we could see something.'

His friend turned to him and spoke a sentence that was drowned in the sudden vast volume of sound that all at once shook the building.

'Hey—what?'

The other shouted into his ear. But even

then his friend could not hear. Nor did he listen. The crowd upon the staircases had surged irresistibly forward and upward. There was a sudden outburst of cries. Women's voices were raised in expostulation, and even fear.

'Oh, oh—don't push so!'

'My arm! oh!—oh, I shall faint . . . please.'

But the men, their escorts, held back furiously; their faces purple, they shouted imprecations over their shoulders.

'Here, here, you damn fools, what you doing?'

'Don't crowd so!'

'Get back, back!'

'There's a lady fainted here. Get back you! We'll all have a chance to see. Good Lord! ain't there a policeman anywheres?'

'Say, say! It's going down—the price. It broke three cents, just then, at the opening, they say.'

'This is the worst I ever saw or heard of.'

'My God! if Jadwin can only *hold* 'em.'

'You bet he'll hold 'em.'

'Hold nothing!—Oh! say my friend, it don't do you any good to crowd like that.'

'It's the people behind: I'm not doing it. Say, do you know where they're at on the floor? The wheat, I mean, is it going up or down?'

'Up, they tell me. There was a rally; I don't know. How can we tell here? We— Hi! there they go again. Lord! that must have been a smash. I guess the Board of Trade won't forget this day in a hurry. Heavens, you can't hear yourself think!'

'Glad I ain't down there in the Pit.'

But, at last, a group of policemen appeared. By main strength they shouldered their way to the top of the stairs, and then began pushing the crowd back. At every instant they shouted:

'Move on now, clear the stairway. No seats left!'

But at this Page, who, by the rush of the crowd, had been carried almost to the top of the stairs, managed to extricate an arm from the press, and hold Landry's card in the air. She even hazarded a little deception:

'I have a pass. Will you let me through, please?'

Luckily one of the officers heard her. He bore down heavily with all the mass of his two hundred pounds and the majesty of the law he represented, to the rescue and succour of this very pretty girl.

'Let the lady through,' he roared, forcing a passage with both elbows. 'Come right along, Miss. Stand back you, now. Can't you see the lady has a pass? Now then, Miss, and be quick about it, I can't keep 'em back forever.'

Jostled and hustled, her dress crumpled, her hat awry, Page made her way forward, till the officer caught her by the arm, and pulled her out of the press. With a long breath she gained the landing of the gallery.

The guide, an old fellow in a uniform of blue, with brass buttons and a visored cap, stood near by, and to him she presented Landry's card.

'Oh, yes, oh, yes,' he shouted in her ear, after he had glanced it over. 'You are the party Mr. Court spoke about. You just came in time. I wouldn't 'a dared hold your seat a minute longer.'

He led her down the crowded aisle between rows of theatre chairs, all of which were occupied, to one vacant seat in the very front row.

'You can see everything now,' he cried, making a trumpet of his palm. 'You're Mister Jadwin's niece. I know, I know. Ah, it's a wild day, Miss. They ain't done much yet, and Mr. Jadwin's holding his own, just now. But I thought for a moment they had him on the run. You see that—my, my, there was a sharp rally. But he's holding on strong yet.'

Page took her seat, and leaning forward looked down into the Wheat Pit.

Once free of the crowd after leaving Page, Landry ran with all the swiftness of his long legs down the stair, and through the corridors till, all out of breath, he gained Gretry's private office. The other Pit traders for the house, some eight or ten men, were already assembled, and just as Landry entered by one door, the broker himself came in from the customers' room. Jadwin was nowhere to be seen.

'What are the orders for to-day, sir?'

Gretry was very pale. Despite his long experience on the Board of Trade, Landry could see anxiety in every change of his expression, in every motion of his hands. The broker before answering the question crossed the room to the water cooler and drank a brief swallow. Then emptying the glass he refilled it, moistened his lips again, and again emptied and filled the goblet. He put it down, caught it up once more, filled it, emptied it, drinking now in long draughts, now in little sips. He was quite unconscious of his actions, and Landry as he watched, felt his heart sink. Things must, indeed, be at a desperate pass when Gretry, the calm, the clear-headed, the placid, was thus upset.

'Your orders?' said the broker, at last. 'The same as yesterday; keep the market up—that's all. It must not go below a dollar fifteen. But act on the defensive. Don't be aggressive, unless I send word. There will probably be very heavy selling the first few moments. You can buy, each of you, up to half a million bushels apiece. If that don't keep the price up, if they still are selling after that . . . well'; Gretry paused a moment, irresolutely, 'well,' he added suddenly, 'if they are still selling freely after you've each bought half a million, I'll let you know what to do. And, look here,' he continued, facing the group, 'look here —keep your heads cool . . . I guess today will decide things. Watch the Crookes crowd pretty closely. I understand they're up to something again. That's all, I guess.'

Landry and the other Gretry traders hurried from the office up to the floor. Landry's heart was beating thick and slow and hard, his teeth were shut tight. Every nerve, every fibre of him braced itself with the rigidity of drawn wire, to meet the issue of the impending hours. Now was to come the last grapple. He had never lived through a crisis such as this before. Would he prevail, would he keep his head? Would he avoid or balk the thousand and one little subterfuges, tricks, and traps that the hostile traders would prepare for him—prepare with a quickness, a suddenness that all but defied the sharpest, keenest watchfulness?

Was the gong never going to strike? He found himself, all at once, on the edge of the Wheat Pit. It was jammed tight with the crowd of traders, and the excitement that disengaged itself from that tense, vehement crowd of white faces and glittering eyes was veritably sickening, veritably weakening. Men on either side of him were shouting mere incoherencies, to which nobody, not even themselves, were listening. Others, silent, gnawed their nails to the quick, breathing rapidly, audibly even, their nostrils expanding and contracting. All around roared the vague thunder that since early morning had shaken the building. In the Pit the bids leaped to and fro, though the time of opening had not yet come; the very planks under foot seemed spinning about in the first huge warning swirl of the Pit's centripetal convulsion. There was dizziness in the air. Something, some infinite immeasurable power, onrushing in its eternal courses, shook the Pit in its grasp. Something deafened the ears, blinded the eyes, dulled and numbed the mind, with its roar, with the chaff and dust of its whirlwind passage, with the stupefying sense of its power, coeval with the earthquake and glacier, merciless, allpowerful, a primal basic throe of creation itself, unassailable, inviolate, and untamed.

Had the trading begun? Had the gong struck? Landry never knew, never so much as heard the clang of the great bell. All at once he was fighting; all at once he was caught, as it were, from off the stable earth, and flung headlong into the heart and centre of the Pit. What he did, he could not say; what went on about him, he could not distinguish. He only knew that roar was succeeding roar, that there was crashing through his ears, through his very brain, the combined bellow of a hundred Niagaras. Hands clutched and tore at him, his own tore and clutched in turn. The Pit was mad, was drunk and frenzied; not a man of all those who fought and scrambled and shouted who knew what he or his neighbour did. They only knew that a support long thought to be secure was giving way, not gradually, not evenly, but by horrible collapses, and equally horrible upward leaps. Now it held, now it broke, now it reformed again, rose again, then again in hideous cataclysms fell from beneath their feet to lower depths than before. The official reporter leaned back in his place, helpless. On the wall overhead, the indicator on the dial was rocking back and forth, like the mast of a ship caught in a monsoon. The price of July wheat no man could so much as approximate. The fluctuations were no longer by fractions of a cent, but by ten cents, fifteen cents, twenty-five cents at a time. On one side of the Pit wheat sold at ninety cents, on the other at a dollar and a quarter.

And all the while above the din upon the floor, above the tramplings and the shoutings in the Pit, there seemed to thrill and swell that appalling roar of the Wheat itself coming in, coming on like a tidal wave, bursting through, dashing barriers aside, rolling like a measureless, almighty river, from the farms of Iowa and the ranches of California, on to the East—to the bakeshops and hungry mouths of Europe.

Landry caught one of the Gretry traders by the arm.

'What shall we do?' he shouted. 'I've bought up to my limit. No more orders have come in. The market has gone from under us. What's to be done?'

'I don't know,' the other shouted back. 'I don't know. We're all gone to hell; looks like the last smash. There are no more supporting orders—something's gone wrong. Gretry hasn't sent any word.'

Then, Landry, beside himself with excitement and with actual terror, hardly knowing even yet what he did, turned sharply about. He fought his way out of the Pit; he ran hatless and panting across the floor, in and out between the groups of spectators, down the stairs to the corridor below, and into the Gretry-Converse offices.

In the outer office a group of reporters and the representatives of a great commercial agency were besieging one of the heads of the firm. They assaulted him with questions.

'Just tell us where you are at—that's all we want to know.'

'Just what is the price of July wheat?'

'Is Jadwin winning or losing?'

But the other threw out an arm in a wild gesture of helplessness.

'We don't know, ourselves,' he cried. 'The market has run clean away from everybody. You know as much about it as I do. It's simply hell broken loose, that's all. We can't tell where we are at for days to come.'

Landry rushed on. He swung open the door of the private office and entered, slamming it behind him and crying out:

'Mr. Gretry, what are we to do? We've had no orders.'

But no one listened to him. Of the group that gathered around Gretry's desk, no one so much as turned a head.

Jadwin stood there in the centre of the others, hatless, his face pale, his eyes congested with blood. Gretry fronted him, one hand upon his arm. In the remainder of the group Landry recognised the senior clerk of the office, one of the heads of a great banking house, and a couple of other men —confidential agents, who had helped to manipulate the great corner.

'But you can't,' Gretry was exclaiming. 'You can't; don't you see we can't meet our margin calls? It's the end of the game. You've got no more money.'

'It's a lie!' Never so long as he lived did Landry forget the voice in which Jadwin cried the words: 'It's a lie! Keep on buying, I tell you. Take all they'll offer. I tell you we'll touch the two-dollar mark before noon.'

'Not another order goes up to that floor,' retorted Gretry. 'Why, J., ask any of these gentlemen here. They'll tell you.'

'It's useless, Mr. Jadwin,' said the banker, quietly. 'You were practically beaten two days ago.'

'Mr. Jadwin,' pleaded the senior clerk, 'for God's sake listen to reason. Our firm—'

But Jadwin was beyond all appeal. He threw off Gretry's hand.

'Your firm, your firm—you've been cowards from the start. I know you, I know you. You have sold me out. Crookes has bought you. Get out of my way!' he shouted. 'Get out of my way! Do you hear? I'll play my hand alone from now on.'

'J., old man—why—see here, man,' Gretry implored, still holding him by the arm; 'here, where are you going?'

Jadwin's voice rang like a trumpet call:

'*Into the Pit.*'

'Look here—wait—here. Hold him back, gentlemen. He don't know what he's about.'

'If you won't execute my orders, I'll act myself. I'm going into the Pit, I tell you.'

'J., you're mad, old fellow. You're ruined—don't you understand?—you're ruined.'

'Then God curse you, Sam Gretry, for the man who failed me in a crisis.' And as he spoke Curtis Jadwin struck the broker full in the face.

Gretry staggered back from the blow, catching at the edge of his desk. His pale face flashed to crimson for an instant, his fists clinched; then his hands fell to his sides.

'No,' he said, 'let him go, let him go. The man is merely mad.'

But Jadwin, struggling for a second in the midst of the group that tried to hold him, suddenly flung off the restraining clasps, thrust the men to one side, and rushed from the room.

Gretry dropped into his chair before his desk.

'It's the end,' he said, simply.

He drew a sheet of note paper to him, and in a shaking hand wrote a couple of lines.

'Take that,' he said, handing the note to the senior clerk, 'take that to the secretary of the Board at once.'

And straight into the turmoil and confusion of the Pit, to the scene of so many of his victories, the battleground whereon again and again, his enemies routed, he had remained the victor undisputed, undismayed came the 'Great Bull.' No sooner had he set foot within the entrance to the Floor, than the news went flashing and flying from lip to lip. The galleries knew it, the public room and the Western Union knew it, the telephone booths knew it, and lastly even the Wheat Pit, torn and tossed and rent asunder by the force this man himself had unchained, knew it, and knowing, stood dismayed.

For even then, so great had been his power, so complete his dominion, and so well-rooted the fear which he had inspired, that this last move in the great game he had been playing, this unexpected, direct, personal assumption of control struck a sense of consternation into the heart of the hardiest of his enemies.

Jadwin himself, the great man, the 'Great Bull,' in the Pit! What was about to happen? Had they been too premature in their hope of his defeat? Had he been preparing some secret, unexpected manœuvre? For a second they hesitated, then moved by a common impulse, feeling the push of the wonderful new harvest behind them, they gathered themselves together for the final assault, and again offered the wheat for sale; offered it by thousands upon thousands of bushels; poured, as it were, the reapings of entire principalities out upon the floor of the Board of Trade.

Jadwin was in the thick of the confusion by now. And the avalanche, the undiked Ocean of the Wheat, leaping to the lash of the hurricane, struck him fairly in the face.

He heard it now, he heard nothing else. The Wheat had broken from his control. For months, he had, by the might of his single arm, held it back; but now it rose like the upbuilding of a colossal billow. It towered, towered, hung poised for an instant, and then, with a thunder as of the grind and crash of chaotic worlds, broke upon him, burst through the Pit and raced past him, on and on to the eastward and to the hungry nations.

And then, under the stress and violence of the hour, something snapped in his brain. The murk behind his eyes had been suddenly pierced by a white flash. The strange qualms and tiny nervous paroxysms of the last few months all at once culminated in some indefinite, indefinable crisis, and the wheels and cogs of all activities save one lapsed away and ceased. Only one function of the complicated machine persisted; but it moved with a rapidity of vibration that seemed to be tearing the tissues of being to shreds, while its rhythm beat out the old and terrible cadence:

'Wheat—wheat—wheat, wheat—wheat—wheat.'

Blind and insensate, Jadwin strove against the torrent of the Wheat. There in the middle of the Pit, surrounded and assaulted by herd after herd of wolves yelping for his destruction, he stood braced, rigid upon his feet, his head up, his hand, the great bony hand that once had held the whole Pit in its grip, flung high in the air in a gesture of defiance, while his voice like the clangour of bugles sounding to the charge of the forlorn hope, rang out again and again, over the din of his enemies:

'Give a dollar for July—give a dollar for July!'

With one accord they leaped upon him. The little group of his traders was swept aside. Landry alone, Landry who had never left his side since his rush from out Gretry's office, Landry Court, loyal to the last, his one remaining soldier, white, shaking, the sobs strangling in his throat, clung to him desperately. Another billow of wheat was preparing. They two—the beaten general and his young armour bearer—heard it coming; hissing, raging, bellowing, it swept down upon them. Landry uttered a cry. Flesh and blood could not stand this strain. He cowered at his chief's side, his shoulders bent, one arm above his head, as if to ward off an actual physical force.

But Jadwin, iron to the end, stood erect. All unknowing what he did, he had taken Landry's hand in his and the boy felt the grip on his fingers like the contracting of a vise of steel. The other hand, as though holding up a standard, was still in the air, and his great deep-toned voice went out across the tumult, proclaiming to the end his battle cry:

'Give a dollar for July—give a dollar for July!'

But, little by little, Landry became aware that the tumult of the Pit was intermitting. There were sudden lapses in the shouting, and in these lapses he could hear from somewhere out upon the floor voices that were crying: 'Order—order, order, gentlemen.'

But again and again the clamour broke out. It would die down for an instant, in response to these appeals, only to burst out afresh as certain groups of traders started the pandemonium again, by the wild outcrying of their offers. At last, however, the older men in the Pit, regaining some measure of self-control, took up the word, going to and fro in the press, repeating 'Order, order.'

And then, all at once, the Pit, the entire floor of the Board of Trade was struck dumb. All at once the tension was relaxed, the furious struggling and stamping was stilled. Landry, bewildered, still holding his chief by the hand, looked about him. On the floor, near at hand, stood the President of the Board of Trade himself, and with him the vice-president and a group of the directors. Evidently it had been these who had called the traders to order. But it was not toward them now that the hundreds of men in the Pit and on the floor were looking.

In the little balcony on the south wall opposite the visitors' gallery a figure had appeared, a tall grave man, in a long black coat—the secretary of the Board of Trade.

Landry with the others saw him, saw him advance to the edge of the railing, and fix his glance upon the Wheat Pit. In his hand he carried a slip of paper.

And then in the midst of that profound silence the secretary announced:

'All trades with Gretry, Converse & Co. must be closed at once.'

The words had not ceased to echo in the high vaultings of the roof before they were greeted with a wild, shrill yell of exultation and triumph, that burst from the crowding masses in the Wheat Pit.

Beaten; beaten at last, the 'Great Bull!' Smashed! The great corner smashed! Jadwin busted! They themselves saved, saved, saved! Cheer followed upon cheer, yell after yell. Hats went into the air. In a frenzy of delight men danced and leaped and capered upon the edge of the Pit, clasping their arms about each other, shaking each others' hands, cheering and hurrahing till their strained voices became hoarse and faint.

Some few of the older men protested. There were cries of:

'Shame, shame!'

'Order—let him alone.'

'Let him be; he's down now. Shame, shame!'

But the jubilee was irrepressible, they had been too cruelly pressed, these others; they had felt the weight of the Bull's hoof, the rip of his horn. Now they had beaten him, had pulled him down.

'Yah-h-h, whoop, yi, yi, yi. Busted, busted, busted. Hip, hip, hip, and a tiger!'

'Come away, sir. For God's sake, Mr. Jadwin, come away.'

Landry was pleading with Jadwin, clutching his arm in both his hands, his lips to his chief's ear to make himself heard above the yelping of the mob.

Jadwin was silent now. He seemed no longer to see or hear; heavily, painfully he leaned upon the young man's shoulder.

'Come away, sir—for God's sake!'

The group of traders parted before them, cheering even while they gave place, cheering with eyes averted, unwilling to see the ruin that meant for them salvation.

'Yah-h-h. Yah-h-h, busted, busted!'

Landry had put his arm about Jadwin, and gripped him close as he led him from the Pit. The sobs were in his throat again, and tears of excitement, of grief, of anger and impotence were running down his face.

'Yah-h-h. Yah-h-h, he's done for, busted, busted!'

'Damn you all,' cried Landry, throwing out a furious fist, 'damn you all; you brutes, you beasts! If he'd so much as raised a finger a week ago, you'd have run for your lives.'

But the cheering drowned his voice; and as the two passed out of the Pit upon the floor, the gong that closed the trading struck and, as it seemed, put a period, definite and final to the conclusion of Curtis Jadwin's career as speculator.

Across the floor towards the doorway Landry led his defeated captain. Jadwin was in a daze, he saw nothing, heard nothing. Quietly he submitted to Landry's guiding arm. The visitors in the galleries bent far over to see him pass, and from all over the floor, spectators, hangers-on, corn-and-provision traders, messenger boys, clerks and reporters came hurrying to watch the final exit of the 'Great Bull,' from the scene of his many victories and his one overwhelming defeat.

In silence they watched him go by. Only in the distance from the direction of the Pit itself came the sound of dying cheers. But at the doorway stood a figure that Landry recognised at once—a small man, lean-faced, trimly dressed, his clean-shaven lips pursed like the mouth of a shut money bag, imperturbable as ever, cold, unexcited —Calvin Crookes himself.

And as Jadwin passed, Landry heard the Bear leader say:

'They can cheer now, all they want. *They* didn't do it. It was the wheat itself that beat him; no combination of men could have done it—go on, cheer, you damn fools! He was a bigger man than the best of us.'

1903

EDWIN MARKHAM

1852–1940

THE MAN WITH THE HOE [1]

WRITTEN AFTER SEEING MILLET'S WORLD-FAMOUS PAINTING

God made man in His own image,
in the image of God made He him.
                    GENESIS.

BOWED by the weight of centuries he leans
Upon his hoe and gazes on the ground,
The emptiness of ages in his face,
And on his back the burden of the world.
Who made him dead to rapture and despair,
A thing that grieves not and that never
        hopes,
Stolid and stunned, a brother to the ox?
Who loosened and let down this brutal
        jaw?

[1] Markham wrote: 'The theme of the Hoe-Man is as old as the world and as deep as the world's injustice. The tragic plight has toucht my heart from earliest boyhood. I have cried his cause in many of my poems. . . . The Hoe-Man, of course, is not the intelligent working man. He is not the savage of the wilderness, who has at times a step of dignity and a tongue of eloquence. The Hoe-Man is the savage of civilization.' Benét, ed., *Fifty Poets*(N.Y., 1933),4.

Whose was the hand that slanted back this
        brow?
Whose breath blew out the light within this
        brain?   10

Is this the Thing the Lord God made and
        gave
To have dominion over sea and land;
To trace the stars and search the heavens
        for power;
To feel the passion of Eternity?
Is this the Dream He dreamed who shaped
        the suns
And pillared the blue firmament with light?
Down all the stretch of Hell to its last gulf
There is no shape more terrible than this—
More tongued with censure of the world's
        blind greed—
More filled with signs and portents for the
        soul—   20
More fraught with menace to the universe.

What gulfs between him and the seraphim!
Slave of the wheel of labor, what to him
Are Plato and the swing of Pleiades?
What the long reaches of the peaks of song,

The rift of dawn, the reddening of the rose?
Through this dread shape the suffering ages
      look;
Time's tragedy is in that aching stoop;
Through this dread shape humanity
      betrayed,
Plundered, profaned and disinherited,   30
Cries protest to the Judges of the World,
A protest that is also prophecy.

O masters, lords and rulers in all lands,
Is this the handiwork you give to God,
This monstrous thing distorted and soul-
      quenched?
How will you ever straighten up this shape;
Touch it again with immortality;
Give back the upward looking and the light;

Rebuild in it the music and the dream;
Make right the immemorial infamies,   40
Perfidious wrongs, immedicable woes?

O masters, lords and rulers in all lands,
How will the Future reckon with this Man?
How answer his brute question in that
      hour
When whirlwinds of rebellion shake the
      world?
How will it be with kingdoms and with
      kings—
With those who shaped him to the thing he
      is—
When this dumb Terror shall reply to God,
After the silence of the centuries?
1886–1898   1899

CHARLES ERSKINE SCOTT WOOD

1852–1944

FIRST SNOW

THE cows are bawling in the mountains;
The snowflakes fall.
They are leaving the pools and pebbled
      fountains;
Troubled they bawl.
They are winding down the mountains'
      shoulders
Through the open pines,
The wild rose thickets and the granite
      boulders,
In broken lines.
Each calf trots close beside its mother;
And so they go,   10
Bawling and calling to one another
About the snow.
1916   1929

FROM THE POET IN THE DESERT [1]

15

BEHOLD silver-kirtled Dawn, the life-
      renewer,
The comforter, bringer of a new hope.
The skies are listening to Earth's silence.
The Desert is asleep, cool, grey, silent.

A shy little breeze runs across her face
And presently her fretful babies stir upon
      her bosom.
The comforter casts abroad her gossamer
      mantle.
A lean coyote, prowler of the night,
Slips to his rocky fastness
And noiselessly, through the grey sage,   10
Jack-rabbits shuttle.
From castellated cliffs rock ravens launch

deliberately selected with the purpose aforethought,
but was rather compelled little by little by the desert
itself, that brooding place of the soul, with its vivid
concrete evidence of Nature's universal beauty. Under
its influence the vast inequality between Nature's
ways and Man's are inventoried and defined, and the
way of Freedom (Nature's way) through revolution indicated as man's only salvation.

   'The particular problem arising from the expression
of such a theme was the transmutation of the propa-
gandistic, didactic and statistical elements involved
into what is *felt* to be poetry; and, where this was not
entirely possible, an effort was made to produce a
poetic effect through deliberate contrast, after the
manner of the Bible, with passages of pure poetry
thrown into high light by contrast with the shadow-
content of less poetic lines.

   'The first version of *The Poet in the Desert* was composed between the years 1911 and 1915, and was published in 1915. The first revised edition was being
written off and on, as the opportunity in a busy lawyer's life came, during the years 1916 to 1918, and
was published in 1918. The edition of 1929 contains
revisions made in that year.' Author's note.

   The version used here is, with the exception of section 52, that of 1929. Section 52 is as printed in Benét,
ed., *Fifty Poets* (N.Y., 1933).

[1] 'The Poet in the Desert had its origin in the experience
of my life as a young army officer, lying down amid the
majesty of the desert and looking up into the eternity
above; contrasting the inexorable justice, beauty and
wisdom of Nature with the relentless injustice, ugliness and folly of Man. The theme, as a whole, was not

On broad black sails.
Wild horses, neighing and tossing their
    manes,
Having drunk their fill, troop back to
    pasture;
A sage-brush thrasher warbles a varied
    ecstasy:
And the waking Desert watches breathlessly
The thin, white skirts of Dawn, Dancer of
    the sky,
Tripping daintily down the sunrise-molten
    mountain,
Emptying a golden basin, filled with roses.
Now along the irrigation ditch, from   21
    cottonwoods,
Tremulous with caress of unseen fingers,
Orioles begin a rivalry of joy,
And from a pointed poplar top
A red bird, dipped in sunrise,
Cracks an exultant whip above a silver
    world.

29

THIS is the pedigree of degradation:
Authority, father of laws made by the
    masters,
Laws, father of Privilege, snatched by the
    masters;
Privilege for the few, father of Poverty, to
    the many;
Poverty, the black bitch spawning—igno-
    rance—crime—degradation.
I am a reaper in disordered fields
And the sheaves which I gather are
Drunkenness, crime, hate, ugliness,
    despair.
Palaces of the idle rich
And filthy nest of the debased poor;   10
Jails and churches hugging each other in a
    filthy incest.
A killing hunger of the body;
The hunger of the soul denied.

Shall I pity the debased ones and not pity
Those who have wrought the debasement?
Shall I forgive the criminals, haughtily,
And go my way and forget their fashioners?
What trick of the great wheel, invisible,
Gave to them their places, and to me mine?
I have not wrought myself in any part,   20
Nor have they wrought themselves in any
    part.
We are thrown off, as bubbles of the sea.
We are thistledown which voyages upon
The unseen air,

Or the globed gossamer of the dandelion
Which the wind seedeth.
There is not one who would not rather
    rejoice
To walk erect, knowing man's nobility,
Leading his soul up to tranquil heights,
To sit a little while beyond the clouds.   30
There is none who does not prefer
To walk in the fields, psalm with the birds,
And in the vastness of the morning
Drink the air of grandeur.
Even the makers of poverty shrink from its
    ugliness,
But they have not the courage to set aside
    the lesser law for the greater.
They do not know they, too, will be happier
    when all are happy.

38

THE desert murmurs to the sun a strange
    murmur
As a whisper of a bride to the bridegroom.
Larks are telling a triumph;
Magpies are screaming their summons,
And finches in wild-rose thicket recite
    delicate poems.
Brooks commune with their pebbled floors,
Tricking the May-flies to a gauzy dance,
And warbling to mouth-dripping kine
Music of pastures,
Of minty beds and purple bergamot.   10
I will go where the little rivers
Are calling almost impatiently,
'Lie down by our hurrying.
'Rest ye beside us.
'Let us whisper to you of our eternity,
'Soothing your ears with our legends.
'You are for a moment, but we are forever.
'Chattering, laughing, brawling,
'Intoning our invocation.
'We are of the Past and of the Future.   20
'You creep back into Earth and are gone;
'But we will soothe the ears of your children
    forever.'

My ears are awake to the music of the
    morning.
I hear the pied yellow hammer beating on
    the barn gable;
Drumming to drowsy Summer.
Hid marsh-wrens trill restlessly in the tules;
Making a gay noise, chirping and twittering.
From somewhere the voice of a white-
    crowned sparrow.
And, further off, near the irrigation-ditch,

Where the top of a poplar is lighted as a
    candle,   30
An oriole empties his heart, lest it break.

52

FROM my minaret the level desert widened
To the far pale mountains: a sheet of
    burnished gold;
Beaten by the hammers of the Sun.
Cattle grazed: emblems of contented peace.
    I saw
Far off against the distant mountains,
A storm marching across the Desert: an
    army of
Titans flaunting dark banners, rolling
    reverberant drums
And flailing the back of the Desert with
    flails of lightning
So she trembled and drew the sky about her.
Steadily marched the Storm, walking on
    water-spouts,   10
And slowly drawing away to its purple tents
    in the mountains.
The drums muttered—a sleepy child—
    fretful—
The mountains came forth as gladiators
    and the Sun threw them
Their shields of gold.
The thunder-throated bull called his people
    and led
Them to drink at the small river which,
    impatient as
A schoolboy, released, burst from under
    my lava citadel.
Dreamy-eyed with motherhood, the cows
    submitted to
The plundering calves, and the bull lifted
    his massive head,
Dripping with crystal water, and gazed
    upon his flock,   20
Well-satisfied. He did not know that they
    were by the Masters
Bred for beef: he and the mothers and their
    little ones,
All bred for slaughter. Their brains only
    bits of pulp
Quickened for procreation.
Sunset dipped the world in amethyst, and
    as the purple tide
Welled slowly up, the lordly bull, the
    patient cows,
The querulous and greedy calves, intoned a
    deep recessional.
Suddenly Night flung wide the sapphire
    gate, and the breastplate

Of the Infinite leaped forth ablaze, so I
    covered my eyes
That I be not made blind. Worlds on
    worlds—   30
Universe on universe, infinity upon
    infinity.
Among the golden swarm, I saw a bit of
    luminous mist, a mote:
The necklace of Andromeda—three
    hundred million billion miles
Its span. A wanderer in that same dark
    where we too are lost,
Questioning, questioning—never a question
    answered.
And we enter the narrow corridor
To forget all—nor ever know we have found
    peace.
I looked into the jeweled cup which I shall
    never drink.
I looked toward my cold bedfellows of the
    sky whom I
Shall never know nor one of them shall
    know another and   40
I whispered to Andromeda—'Yet Man
    makes War.'
O heavenly solitudes, you are not more
    unguessed
Than the vast and lonely spaces of Man's
    soul.
We know Canopus, giant of the sky, could
    swallow our
Whole universe as would a goat a thistle,
    and the feet
Of Light grow weary in their race to us,
    but who
Has ever caught his neighbor's soul within
    his own?
Or the soul of one, the best-beloved, or who
Shall ever know that soul which is
    himself—
A lone bird, lost in night: a weary wanderer,
Hopeless of rest until the Dark Hunter
    casts his net.   51
O who can know the Soul of Man?—Part of
The Primal Harmony, that has put on
    wings
And refusing all arbitraments of force
Soars high above the jungle—more, above
    all peaks
Terrestrial, and more, beyond the lantern
    of the Lyre,
Arcturus or Orion, on, forever endless—
Knowing itself to be part of the Whole as
    these are part:
Part of the Creator; itself a creator

Which has brought down from the skies the
    Primal Harmony: 60
Love—from which all else immortal
    comes—
The Soul continually whispering eternal
    verities,
And Thought, the Gleaner, continually
    listening;
Carefully selecting the immortal forces of
    the Soul,
Justice, Equality, Freedom, Mercy,
Stronger than armies or armored fleets;
    stronger than

Navies of the air which strangle cities in
    their claws,
As a hawk a sparrow—stronger than every
    force or power
The body can possess: the Soul of Man;
Which flies above this shadowy world as a
    wild swan   70
Flies through the night above a darkened
    Earth
Until at dawn, high in the coming blue
The heavenly breast is lighted by the
    sunrise.

1911–1933   1915–1933

TRUMBULL STICKNEY

1874–1904

FROM A DRAMATIC SCENE [1]

In Campo Santo is a grave
Where I and the moon together
Go linger oft and cannot leave
    Tho' dawn be in the weather.
Oh, let me hold her in my arms.
Cold tho' she be, there let her languish.
Only her kiss of death can warm
    The snow-fields of my anguish.

1903–1904   1905

MT. LYKAION

Alone on Lykaion since man hath been
Stand on the height two columns, where at
    rest
Two eagles hewn of gold sit looking East
Forever; and the sun goes up between.
Far down around the mountain's oval green
And order keeps the falling stones abreast.
Below within the chaos last and least
A river like a curl of light is seen.
Beyond the river lies the even sea,
Beyond the sea another ghost of sky,—   10
O God, support the sickness of my eye
Lest the far space and long antiquity
Suck out my heart, and on this awful
    ground
The great wind kill my little shell with
    sound.

1903   1905

1 The selection is one of the snatches of song from a
drama on Benvenuto Cellini, and is sung by him.

THE SOUL OF TIME

Time's a circumference
Whereof the segment of our station
    seems
A long straight line from nothing into
    naught.
Therefore we say 'progress,' 'infinity'—
Dull words whose object
Hangs in the air of error and delights
Our boyish minds ahunt for butterflies.
For aspiration studies not the sky
But looks for stars; the victories of faith
Are soldiered none the less with
    certainties,   10
And all the multitudinous armies decked
With banners blown ahead and flute
    before
March not to the desert or th' Elysian
    fields,
But in the track of some discovery,
The grip and cognizance of something
    true,
Which won resolves a better distribution
Between the dreaming mind and real
    truth.

I cannot understand you.

                  'Tis because
You lean over my meaning's edge and
    feel
A dizziness of the things I have not said. 20

1904   1905

WILLIAM VAUGHN MOODY

1869–1910

GLOUCESTER MOORS

A MILE behind is Gloucester town
Where the fishing fleets put in,
A mile ahead the land dips down
And the woods and farms begin.
Here, where the moors stretch free
In the high blue afternoon,
Are the marching sun and talking sea,
And the racing winds that wheel and
    flee
On the flying heels of June.

Jill-o'er-the-ground is purple blue,   10
Blue is the quaker-maid,
The wild geranium holds its dew
Long in the boulder's shade.
Wax-red hangs the cup
From the huckleberry boughs,
In barberry bells the grey moths sup,
Or where the choke-cherry lifts high up
Sweet bowls for their carouse.

Over the shelf of the sandy cove
Beach-peas blossom late.   20
By copse and cliff the swallows rove
Each calling to his mate.
Seaward the sea-gulls go,
And the land-birds all are here;
That green-gold flash was a vireo,
And yonder flame where the marsh-flags
    grow
Was a scarlet tanager.

This earth is not the steadfast place
we landsmen build upon;
From deep to deep she varies pace,   30
And while she comes is gone.
Beneath my feet I feel
Her smooth bulk heave and dip;
With velvet plunge and soft upreel
She swings and steadies to her keel
Like a gallant, gallant ship.

These summer clouds she sets for sail,
The sun is her masthead light,
She tows the moon like a pinnace frail
Where her phosphor wake churns bright.   40
Now hid, now looming clear,
On the face of the dangerous blue
The star fleets tack and wheel and veer,

But on, but on does the old earth steer
As if her port she knew.

God, dear God! Does she know her port,
Though she goes so far about?
Or blind astray, does she make her sport
To brazen and chance it out?
I watched when her captains passed: 50
She were better captainless.
Men in the cabin, before the mast,
But some were reckless and some aghast,
And some sat gorged at mess.

By her battened hatch I leaned and caught
Sounds from the noisome hold,—
Cursing and sighing of souls distraught
And cries too sad to be told.
Then I strove to go down and see;
But they said, 'Thou art not of us!'   60
I turned to those on the deck with me
And cried, 'Give help!' But they said,
      'Let be:
Our ship sails faster thus.'

Jill-o'er-the-ground is purple blue,
Blue is the quaker-maid,
The alder-clump where the brook **comes**
    through
Breeds cresses in its shade.
To be out of the moiling street
With its swelter and its sin!
Who has given to me this sweet,   70
And given my brother dust to eat?
And when will his wage come in?

Scattering wide or blown in ranks,
Yellow and white and brown,
Boats and boats from the fishing banks
Come home to Gloucester town.
There is cash to purse and spend,
There are wives to be embraced,
Hearts to borrow and hearts to lend,
And hearts to take and keep to the end,— 80
O little sails, make haste!

But thou, vast outbound ship of souls,
What harbor town for thee?
What shapes, when thy arriving tolls,
Shall crowd the banks to see?
Shall all the happy shipmates then
Stand singing brotherly?

Or shall a haggard ruthless few
Warp her over and bring her to,
While the many broken souls of men   90
Fester down in the slaver's pen,
And nothing to say or do?
1900   1902

THE MENAGERIE

THANK God my brain is not inclined to cut
Such capers every day! I'm just about
Mellow, but then—There goes the tent-
    flap shut.
Rain's in the wind. I thought so: every
    snout
Was twitching when the keeper turned me
    out.

That screaming parrot makes my blood run
    cold.
Gabriel's trump! the big bull elephant
Squeals 'Rain!' to the parched herd. The
    monkeys scold,
And jabber that it's rain water they want.
(It makes me sick to see a monkey pant.)   10

I'll foot it home, to try and make believe
I'm sober. After this I stick to beer,
And drop the circus when the sane folks
    leave.
A man's a fool to look at things too near:
They look back, and begin to cut up queer.

Beasts do, at any rate; especially
Wild devils caged. They have the coolest
    way
Of being something else than what you see:
You pass a sleek young zebra nosing hay,   19
A nylghau looking bored and distingué,—

And think you've seen a donkey and a
    bird.
Not on your life! Just glance back, if you
    dare.
The zebra chews, the nylghau hasn't stirred;
But something's happened, Heaven knows
    what or where
To freeze your scalp and pompadour your
    hair.

I'm not precisely an æolian lute
Hung in the wandering winds of sentiment,
But drown me if the ugliest, meanest brute
Grunting and fretting in that sultry tent
Didn't just floor me with embarrassment!

'Twas like a thunder-clap from out the
    clear,—   31
One minute they were circus beasts, some
    grand,
Some ugly, some amusing, and some queer:
Rival attractions to the hobo band,
The flying jenny, and the peanut stand.

Next minute they were old hearth-mates of
    mine!
Lost people, eyeing me with such a stare!
Patient, satiric, devilish, divine;
A gaze of hopeless envy, squalid care,
Hatred, and thwarted love, and dim
    despair.

Within my blood my ancient kindred
    spoke,—   41
Grotesque and monstrous voices, heard
    afar
Down ocean caves when behemoth awoke,
Or through fern forests roared the
    plesiosaur
Locked with the giant-bat in ghastly war.

And suddenly, as in a flash of light,
I saw great Nature working out her plan;
Through all her shapes from mastodon to
    mite
Forever groping, testing, passing on
To find at last the shape and soul of Man. 50

Till in the fullness of accomplished time,
Comes brother Forepaugh,[1] upon business
    bent,
Tracks her through frozen and through
    torrid clime,
And shows us, neatly labeled in a tent,
The stages of her huge experiment;

Blabbing aloud her shy and reticent hours;
Dragging to light her blinking, slothful
    moods;
Publishing fretful seasons when her powers
Worked wild and sullen in her solitudes,
Or when her mordant laughter shook the
    woods.   60

Here, round about me, were her vagrant
    births;
Sick dreams she had, fierce projects she
    essayed;
Her qualms, her fiery prides, her crazy
    mirths;

1 A famous circus owner.

The troublings of her spirit as she strayed,
Cringed, gloated, mocked, was lordly, was
    afraid,

On that long road she went to seek
    mankind;
Here were the darkling coverts that she beat
To find the Hider she was sent to find;
Here the distracted footprints of her feet
Whereby her soul's Desire she came to
    greet.   70

But why should they, her botch-work, turn
    about
And stare disdain at me, her finished job?
Why was the place one vast suspended
    shout
Of laughter? Why did all the daylight throb
With soundless guffaw and dumb-stricken
    sob?

Helpless I stood among those awful cages;
The beasts were walking loose, and I was
    bagged!
I, I, last product of the toiling ages,
Goal of heroic feet that never lagged,—
A little man in trousers, slightly jagged.   80

Deliver me from such another jury!
The Judgment Day will be a picnic to't.
Their satire was more dreadful than their
    fury,
And worst of all was just a kind of brute
Disgust, and giving up, and sinking mute.

Survival of the fittest, adaptation,
And all their other evolution terms,
Seem to omit one small consideration,
To wit, that tumblebugs and angleworms
Have souls: there's soul in everything that
    squirms.   90

And souls are restless, plagued, impatient
    things,
All dream and unaccountable desire;
Crawling, but pestered with the thought of
    wings;
Spreading through every inch of earth's old
    mire
Mystical hanker after something higher.

Wishes *are* horses, as I understand.
I guess a wistful polyp that has strokes
Of feeling faint to gallivant on land
Will come to be a scandal to his folks;

Legs he will sprout, in spite of threats and
    jokes.   100

And at the core of every life that crawls,
Or runs or flies or swims or vegetates—
Churning the mammoth's heart-blood, in
    the galls
Of shark and tiger planting gorgeous hates,
Lighting the love of eagles for their mates;

Yes, in the dim brain of the jellied fish
That is and is not living—moved and stirred
From the beginning a mysterious wish,
A vision, a command, a fatal Word:
The name of Man was uttered, and they
    heard.   110

Upward along the æons of old war
They sought him: wing and shank-bone,
    claw and bill
Were fashioned and rejected; wide and far
They roamed the twilight jungles of their
    will;
But still they sought him, and desired him
    still.

Man they desired, but mind you, Perfect
    Man,
The radiant and the loving, yet to be!
I hardly wonder, when they came to scan
The upshot of their strenuosity,
They gazed with mixed emotions upon *me*.

Well, my advice to you is, Face the
    creatures,   121
Or spot them sideways with your weather
    eye,
Just to keep tab on their expansive features;
It isn't pleasant when you're stepping high
To catch a giraffe smiling on the sly.

If nature made you graceful, don't get gay
Back-to before the hippopotamus;
If meek and godly, find some place to play
Besides right where three mad hyenas fuss:
You may hear language that we won't
    discuss.   130

If you're a sweet thing in a flower-bed hat,
Or her best fellow with your tie tucked in,
Don't squander love's bright springtime
    girding at
An old chimpanzee with an Irish chin:
There may be hidden meaning in his grin.
1900   1902

HENRY ADAMS

1838-1918

FROM THE EDUCATION OF
HENRY ADAMS

QUINCY (1838–1848) [1]

UNDER the shadow of Boston State House,
turning its back on the house of John Hancock, the little passage called Hancock Avenue runs, or ran, from Beacon Street, skirting the State House grounds, to Mount
Vernon Street, on the summit of Beacon
Hill; and there, in the third house below
Mount Vernon Place, February 16, 1838, a
a child was born, and christened later by
his uncle, the minister of the First Church
after the tenets of Boston Unitarianism, as
Henry Brooks Adams.

Had he been born in Jerusalem under the
shadow of the Temple and circumcised in
the Synagogue by his uncle the high priest,
under the name of Israel Cohen, he would
scarcely have been more distinctly branded,
and not much more heavily handicapped in
the races of the coming century, in running
for such stakes as the century was to offer;
but, on the other hand, the ordinary traveller, who does not enter the field of racing,
finds advantage in being, so to speak,
ticketed through life, with the safeguards of
an old, established traffic. Safeguards are
often irksome, but sometimes convenient,
and if one needs them at all, one is apt to
need them badly. A hundred years earlier,
such safeguards as his would have secured
any young man's success; and although in
1838 their value was not very great compared with what they would have had in
1738, yet the mere accident of starting a
twentieth-century career from a nest of associations so colonial—so troglodytic—as
the First Church, the Boston State House,
Beacon Hill, John Hancock and John
Adams, Mount Vernon Street and Quincy,
all crowding on ten pounds of unconscious
babyhood, was so queer as to offer a subject of curious speculation to the baby long
after he had witnessed the solution. What
could become of such a child of the seventeenth and eighteenth centuries, when he

should wake up to find himself required to
play the game of the twentieth? Had he been
consulted, would he have cared to play the
game at all, holding such cards as he held,
and suspecting that the game was to be one
of which neither he nor any one else back to
the beginning of time knew the rules or the
risks or the stakes? He was not consulted
and was not responsible, but had he been
taken into the confidence of his parents, he
would certainly have told them to change
nothing as far as concerned him. He would
have been astounded by his own luck. Probably no child, born in the year, held better
cards than he. Whether life was an honest
game of chance, or whether the cards were
marked and forced, he could not refuse to
play his excellent hand. He could never
make the usual plea of irresponsibility. He
accepted the situation as though he had
been a party to it, and under the same circumstances would do it again, the more
readily for knowing the exact values. To his
life as a whole he was a consenting, contracting party and partner from the moment he
was born to the moment he died. Only with
that understanding—as a consciously as-
senting member in full partnership with the
society of his age—had his education an interest to himself or to others.

As it happened, he never got to the point
of playing the game at all; he lost himself in
the study of it, watching the errors of the
players; but this is the only interest in the
story, which otherwise has no moral and
little incident. A story of education—seventy years of it—the practical value remains
to the end in doubt, like other values about
which men have disputed since the birth of
Cain and Abel; but the practical value of
the universe has never been stated in dollars. Although every one cannot be a Gar-
gantua-Napoleon-Bismarck and walk off
with the great bells of Notre Dame, every
one must bear his own universe, and most
persons are moderately interested in learning how their neighbors have managed to
carry theirs.

This problem of education, started in
1838, went on for three years, while the
baby grew, like other babies, unconsciously,

---

1 The two selections are Chapters 1 and 15 from *The
Education of Henry Adams*(Boston, 1918). The book was
privately printed in 1907.

as a vegetable, the outside world working as it never had worked before, to get his new universe ready for him. Often in old age he puzzled over the question whether, on the doctrine of chances, he was at liberty to accept himself or his world as an accident. No such accident had ever happened before in human experience. For him, alone, the old universe was thrown into the ash-heap and a new one created. He and his eighteenth-century, troglodytic Boston were suddenly cut apart—separated forever—in act if not in sentiment, by the opening of the Boston and Albany Railroad; the appearance of the first Cunard steamers in the bay; and the telegraphic messages which carried from Baltimore to Washington the news that Henry Clay and James K. Polk were nominated for the Presidency. This was in May, 1844; he was six years old; his new world was ready for use, and only fragments of the old met his eyes.

Of all this that was being done to complicate his education, he knew only the color of yellow. He first found himself sitting on a yellow kitchen floor in strong sunlight. He was three years old when he took this earliest step in education; a lesson of color. The second followed soon; a lesson of taste. On December 3, 1841, he developed scarlet fever. For several days he was as good as dead, reviving only under the careful nursing of his family. When he began to recover strength, about January 1, 1842, his hunger must have been stronger than any other pleasure or pain, for while in after life he retained not the faintest recollection of his illness, he remembered quite clearly his aunt entering the sick-room bearing in her hand a saucer with a baked apple.

The order of impressions retained by memory might naturally be that of color and taste, although one would rather suppose that the sense of pain would be first to educate. In fact, the third recollection of the child was that of discomfort. The moment he could be removed, he was bundled up in blankets and carried from the little house in Hancock Avenue to a larger one which his parents were to occupy for the rest of their lives in the neighboring Mount Vernon Street. The season was midwinter, January 10, 1842, and he never forgot his acute distress for want of air under his blankets, or the noises of moving furniture.

As a means of variation from a normal type, sickness in childhood ought to have a certain value not to be classed under any fitness or unfitness of natural selection; and especially scarlet fever affected boys seriously, both physically and in character, though they might through life puzzle themselves to decide whether it had fitted or unfitted them for success; but this fever of Henry Adams took greater and greater importance in his eyes, from the point of view of education, the longer he lived. At first, the effect was physical. He fell behind his brothers two or three inches in height, and proportionally in bone and weight. His character and processes of mind seemed to share in this fining-down process of scale. He was not good in a fight, and his nerves were more delicate than boys' nerves ought to be. He exaggerated these weaknesses as he grew older. The habit of doubt; of distrusting his own judgment and of totally rejecting the judgment of the world; the tendency to regard every question as open; the hesitation to act except as a choice of evils; the shirking of responsibility; the love of line, form, quality; the horror of ennui; the passion for companionship and the antipathy to society—all these are well-known qualities of New England character in no way peculiar to individuals but in this instance they seemed to be stimulated by the fever, and Henry Adams could never make up his mind whether, on the whole, the change of character was morbid or healthy, good or bad for his purpose. His brothers were the type; he was the variation.

As far as the boy knew, the sickness did not affect him at all, and he grew up in excellent health, bodily and mental, taking life as it was given; accepting its local standards without a difficulty, and enjoying much of it as keenly as any other boy of his age. He seemed to himself quite normal, and his companions seemed always to think him so. Whatever was peculiar about him was education, not character, and came to him, directly and indirectly, as the result of that eighteenth-century inheritance which he took with his name.

The atmosphere of education in which he lived was colonial, revolutionary, almost Cromwellian, as though he were steeped, from his greatest grandmother's birth, in the odor of political crime. Resistance to something was the law of New England nature; the boy looked out on the world with the instinct of resistance; for numberless generations his predecessors had viewed the world chiefly as a thing to be reformed, filled with evil forces to be abolished, and they saw no reason to suppose that they had wholly succeeded in the abolition; the duty was unchanged. That duty implied not only resistance to evil, but hatred of it. Boys naturally look on all force as an enemy, and generally find it so, but the New Englander, whether boy or man, in his long struggle with a stingy or hostile universe, had learned also to love the pleasure of hating; his joys were few.

Politics, as a practice, whatever its professions, had always been the systematic organization of hatreds, and Massachusetts politics had been as harsh as the climate. The chief charm of New England was harshness of contrasts and extremes of sensibility—a cold that froze the blood, and a heat that boiled it—so that the pleasure of hating—one's self if no better victim offered—was not its rarest amusement; but the charm was a true and natural child of the soil, not a cultivated weed of the ancients. The violence of the contrast was real and made the strongest motive of education. The double exterior nature gave life its relative values. Winter and summer, cold and heat, town and country, force and freedom, marked two modes of life and thought, balanced like lobes of the brain. Town was winter confinement, school, rule, discipline; straight, gloomy streets, piled with six feet of snow in the middle; frosts that made the snow sing under wheels or runners; thaws when the streets became dangerous to cross; society of uncles, aunts, and cousins who expected children to behave themselves, and who were not always gratified; above all else, winter represented the desire to escape and go free. Town was restraint, law, unity. Country, only seven miles away, was liberty, diversity, outlawry, the endless delight of mere sense impressions given by nature for nothing, and breathed by boys without knowing it.

Boys are wild animals, rich in the treasures of sense, but the New England boy had a wider range of emotions than boys of more equable climates. He felt his nature crudely, as it was meant. To the boy Henry Adams,

summer was drunken. Among senses, smell was the strongest—smell of hot pine-woods and sweet-fern in the scorching summer noon; of new-mown hay; of ploughed earth; of box hedges; of peaches, lilacs, syringas; of stables, barns, cow-yards; of salt water and low tide on the marshes; nothing came amiss. Next to smell came taste, and the children knew the taste of everything they saw or touched, from pennyroyal and flagroot to the shell of a pignut and the letters of a spelling-book—the taste of A–B, AB, suddenly revived on the boy's tongue sixty years afterwards. Light, line, and color as sensual pleasures, came later and were as crude as the rest. The New England light is glare, and the atmosphere harshens color. The boy was a full man before he ever knew what was meant by atmosphere; his idea of pleasure in light was the blaze of a New England sun. His idea of color was a peony, with the dew of early morning on its petals. The intense blue of the sea, as he saw it a mile or two away, from the Quincy hills; the cumuli in a June afternoon sky; the strong reds and greens and purples of colored prints and children's picture-books, as the American colors then ran; these were ideals. The opposites or antipathies were the cold grays of November evenings, and the thick, muddy thaws of Boston winter. With such standards, the Bostonian could not but develop a double nature. Life was a double thing. After a January blizzard, the boy who could look with pleasure into the violent snow-glare of the cold white sunshine, with its intense light and shade, scarcely knew what was meant by tone. He could reach it only by education.

Winter and summer, then, were two hostile lives, and bred two separate natures. Winter was always the effort to live; summer was tropical license. Whether the children rolled in the grass, or waded in the brook, or swam in the salt ocean, or sailed in the bay, or fished for smelts in the creeks, or netted minnows in the salt-marshes, or took to the pine-woods and the granite quarries, or chased muskrats and hunted snapping-turtles in the swamps, or mushrooms or nuts on the autumn hills, summer and country were always sensual living, while winter was always compulsory learning. Summer was the multiplicity of nature; winter was school.

The bearing of the two seasons on the education of Henry Adams was no fancy; it was the most decisive force he ever knew; it ran through life, and made the division between its perplexing, warring, irreconcilable problems, irreducible opposites, with growing emphasis to the last year of study. From earliest childhood the boy was accustomed to feel that, for him, life was double. Winter and summer, town and country, law and liberty, were hostile, and the man who pretended they were not, was in his eyes a schoolmaster—that is, a man employed to tell lies to little boys. Though Quincy was but two hours' walk from Beacon Hill, it belonged in a different world. For two hundred years, every Adams, from father to son, had lived within sight of State Street, and sometimes had lived in it, yet none had ever taken kindly to the town, or been taken kindly by it. The boy inherited his double nature. He knew as yet nothing about his great-grandfather, who had died a dozen years before his own birth: he took for granted that any great-grandfather of his must have always been good, and his enemies wicked; but he divined his great-grandfather's character from his own. Never for a moment did he connect the two ideas of Boston and John Adams; they were separate and antagonistic; the idea of John Adams went with Quincy. He knew his grandfather John Quincy Adams only as an old man of seventy-five or eighty who was friendly and gentle with him, but except that he heard his grandfather always called 'the President,' and his grandmother 'the Madam,' he had no reason to suppose that his Adams grandfather differed in character from his Brooks grandfather who was equally kind and benevolent. He liked the Adams side best, but for no other reason than that it reminded him of the country, the summer, and the absence of restraint. Yet he felt also that Quincy was in a way inferior to Boston, and that socially Boston looked down on Quincy. The reason was clear enough even to a five-year old child. Quincy had no Boston style. Little enough style had either; a simpler manner of life and thought could hardly exist, short of cave-dwelling. The flint-and-steel with which his grandfather Adams used to light his own fires in the early morning was still on the mantelpiece of his study. The idea of a livery or even a dress for servants, or of an evening toilette, was next to blasphemy. Bathrooms, water-supplies, lighting, heating, and the whole array of domestic comforts, were unknown at Quincy. Boston had already a bathroom, a water-supply, a furnace, and gas. The superiority of Boston was evident, but a child liked it no better for that.

The magnificence of his grandfather Brooks's house in Pearl Street or South Street has long ago disappeared, but perhaps his country house at Medford may still remain to show what impressed the mind of a boy in 1845 with the idea of city splendor. The President's place at Quincy was the larger and older and far the more interesting of the two; but a boy felt at once its inferiority in fashion. It showed plainly enough its want of wealth. It smacked of colonial age, but not of Boston style or plush curtains. To the end of his life he never quite overcame the prejudice thus drawn in with his childish breath. He never could compel himself to care for nineteenth-century style. He was never able to adopt it, any more than his father or grandfather or great-grandfather had done. Not that he felt it as particularly hostile, for he reconciled himself to much that was worse; but because, for some remote reason, he was born an eighteenth-century child. The old house at Quincy was eighteenth century. What style it had was in its Queen Anne mahogany panels and its Louis Seize chairs and sofas. The panels belonged to an old colonial Vassall who built the house; the furniture had been brought back from Paris in 1789 or 1801 or 1817, along with porcelain and books and much else of old diplomatic remnants; and neither of the two eighteenth-century styles—neither English Queen Anne nor French Louis Seize—was comfortable for a boy, or for any one else. The dark mahogany had been painted white to suit daily life in winter gloom. Nothing seemed to favor, for a child's objects, the older forms. On the contrary, most boys, as well as grown-up people, preferred the new, with good reason, and the child felt himself distinctly at a disadvantage for the taste.

Nor had personal preference any share in his bias. The Brooks grandfather was as amiable and as sympathetic as the Adams grandfather. Both were born in 1767, and both died in 1848. Both were kind to children, and both belonged rather to the eighteenth than to the nineteenth centuries. The child knew no difference between them except that one was associated with winter and the other with summer; one with Boston, the other with Quincy. Even with Medford, the association was hardly easier. Once as a very young boy he was taken to pass a few days with his grandfather Brooks under charge of his aunt, but became so violently homesick that within twenty-four hours he was brought back in disgrace. Yet he could not remember ever being seriously homesick again.

The attachment to Quincy was not altogether sentimental or wholly sympathetic. Quincy was not a bed of thornless roses. Even there the curse of Cain set its mark. There as elsewhere a cruel universe combined to crush a child. As though three or four vigorous brothers and sisters, with the best will, were not enough to crush any child, every one else conspired towards an education which he hated. From cradle to grave this problem of running order through chaos, direction through space, discipline through freedom, unity through multiplicity, has always been, and must always be, the task of education, as it is the moral of religion, philosophy, science, art, politics, and economy; but a boy's will is his life, and he dies when it is broken, as the colt dies in harness, taking a new nature in becoming tame. Rarely has the boy felt kindly towards his tamers. Between him and his master has always been war. Henry Adams never knew a boy of his generation to like a master, and the task of remaining on friendly terms with one's own family, in such a relation, was never easy.

All the more singular it seemed afterwards to him that his first serious contact with the President should have been a struggle of will, in which the old man almost necessarily defeated the boy, but instead of leaving, as usual in such defeats, a lifelong sting, left rather an impression of as fair treatment as could be expected from a natural enemy. The boy met seldom with such restraint. He could not have been much more than six years old at the time— seven at the utmost—and his mother had taken him to Quincy for a long stay with the President during the summer. What became of the rest of the family he quite forgot; but he distinctly remembered standing at the house door one summer morning in a passionate outburst of rebellion against going to school. Naturally his mother was the immediate victim of his rage; that is what mothers are for, and boys also; but in this case the boy had his mother at unfair disadvantage, for she was a guest, and had no means of enforcing obedience. Henry showed a certain tactical ability by refusing to start, and he met all efforts at compulsion by successful, though too vehement protest. He was in fair way to win, and was holding his own, with sufficient energy, at the bottom of the long staircase which led up to the door of the President's library, when the door opened, and the old man slowly came down. Putting on his hat, he took the boy's hand without a word, and walked with him, paralyzed by awe, up the road to the town. After the first moments of consternation at this interference in a domestic dispute, the boy reflected that an old gentleman close on eighty would never trouble himself to walk near a mile on a hot summer morning over a shadeless road to take a boy to school, and that it would be strange if a lad imbued with the passion of freedom could not find a corner to dodge around, somewhere before reaching the school door. Then and always, the boy insisted that this reasoning justified his apparent submission; but the old man did not stop, and the boy saw all his strategical points turned, one after another, until he found himself seated inside the school, and obviously the centre of curious if not malevolent criticism. Not till then did the President release his hand and depart.

The point was that this act, contrary to the inalienable rights of boys, and nullifying the social compact, ought to have made him dislike his grandfather for life. He could not recall that it had this effect even for a moment. With a certain maturity of mind, the child must have recognized that the President, though a tool of tyranny, had done his disreputable work with a certain intelligence. He had shown no temper, no irritation, no personal feeling, and had made no display of force. Above all, he had held his tongue. During their long walk he had said nothing; he had uttered no syllable of revolting cant about the duty of obedience and the wickedness of resistance to law; he had shown no concern in the matter; hardly even a consciousness of the boy's existence. Probably his mind at that moment was actually troubling itself little about his grandson's iniquities, and much about the iniquities of President Polk, but the boy could scarcely at that age feel the whole satisfaction of thinking that President Polk was to be the vicarious victim of his own sins, and he gave his grandfather credit for intelligent silence. For this forbearance he felt instinctive respect. He admitted force as a form of right; he admitted even temper, under protest; but the seeds of a moral education would at that moment have fallen on the stoniest soil in Quincy, which is, as every one knows, the stoniest glacial and tidal drift known in any Puritan land.

Neither party to this momentary disagreement can have felt rancor, for during these three or four summers the old President's relations with the boy were friendly and almost intimate. Whether his older brothers and sisters were still more favored he failed to remember, but he was himself admitted to a sort of familiarity which, when in his turn he had reached old age, rather shocked him, for it must have sometimes tried the President's patience. He hung about the library; handled the books; deranged the papers; ransacked the drawers; searched the old purses and pocket-books for foreign coins; drew the sword-cane; snapped the travelling-pistols; upset everything in the corners, and penetrated the President's dressing-closet where a row of tumblers, inverted on the shelf, covered caterpillars which were supposed to become moths or butterflies, but never did. The Madam bore with fortitude the loss of the tumblers which her husband purloined for these hatcheries; but she made protest when he carried off her best cut-glass bowls to plant with acorns or peachstones that he might see the roots grow, but which, she said, he commonly forgot like the caterpillars.

At that time the President rode the hobby of tree-culture, and some fine old trees should still remain to witness it, unless they have been improved off the ground; but his was a restless mind, and although he took his hobbies seriously and would have been annoyed had his grandchild asked whether he was bored like an English duke, he probably cared more for the processes than for the results, so that his grandson was saddened by the sight and smell of peaches and pears, the best of their kind, which he brought up from the garden to rot on his shelves for seed. With the inherited virtues of his Puritan ancestors, the little boy Henry conscientiously brought up to him in his study the finest peaches he found in the garden, and ate only the less perfect. Naturally he ate more by way of compensation, but the act showed that he bore no grudge. As for his grandfather, it is even possible that he may have felt a certain self-reproach for his temporary rôle of schoolmaster—seeing that his own career did not offer proof of the worldly advantages of docile obedience—for there still exists somewhere a little volume of critically edited Nursery Rhymes with the boy's name in full written in the President's trembling hand on the fly-leaf. Of course there was also the Bible, given to each child at birth, with the proper inscription in the President's hand on the fly-leaf; while their grandfather Brooks supplied the silver mugs.

So many Bibles and silver mugs had to be supplied, that a new house, or cottage, was built to hold them. It was 'on the hill,' five minutes' walk above 'the old house,' with a far view eastward over Quincy Bay, and northward over Boston. Till his twelfth year, the child passed his summers there, and his pleasures of childhood mostly centered in it. Of education he had as yet little to complain. Country schools were not very serious. Nothing stuck to the mind except home impressions, and the sharpest were those of kindred children; but as influences that warped a mind, none compared with the mere effect of the back of the President's bald head, as he sat in his pew on Sundays, in line with that of President Quincy, who, though some ten years younger, seemed to children about the same age. Before railways entered the New England town, every parish church showed half-a-dozen of these leading citizens, with gray hair, who sat on the main aisle in the best pews, and had sat there, or in some equivalent dignity, since the time of St. Augustine, if not since the glacial epoch. It was unusual for boys to sit behind a President grandfather, and to read over his head the tablet in memory of a President great-grandfather, who had 'pledged his life, his fortune, and his sacred honor' to secure the independence of his country and so forth; but boys naturally supposed, without much reasoning, that other boys had the equivalent of President grandfathers, and that churches would always go on, with the bald-headed leading citizens on the main aisle, and Presidents or their equivalents on the walls. The Irish gardener once said to the child: 'You'll be thinkin' you'll be President too!' The casualty of the remark made so strong an impression on his mind that he never forgot it. He could not remember ever to have thought on the subject; to him, that there should be a doubt of his being President was a new idea. What had been would continue to be. He doubted neither about Presidents nor about Churches, and no one suggested at that time a doubt whether a system of society which had lasted since Adam would outlast one Adams more.

The Madam was a little more remote than the President, but more decorative. She stayed much in her own room with the Dutch tiles, looking out on her garden with the box walks, and seemed a fragile creature to a boy who sometimes brought her a note or a message, and took distinct pleasure in looking at her delicate face under what seemed to him very becoming caps. He liked her refined figure; her gentle voice and manner; her vague effect of not belonging there, but to Washington or to Europe, like her furniture, and writing-desk with little glass doors above and little eighteenth-century volumes in old binding, labelled *Peregrine Pickle* or *Tom Jones* or Hannah More. Try as she might, the Madam could never be Bostonian, and it was her cross in life, but to the boy it was her charm. Even at that age, he felt drawn to it. The Madam's life had been in truth far from Boston. She was born in London in 1775, daughter of Joshua Johnson, an American merchant, brother of Governor Thomas Johnson of Maryland; and Catherine Nuth, of an English family in London. Driven from England by the Revolutionary War, Joshua Johnson took his family to Nantes, where they remained till the peace. The girl Louisa Catherine was nearly ten years old when brought back to London, and her sense of nationality must have been confused; but the influence of the Johnsons and the services of Joshua obtained for him from President Washington the appointment of Consul in London on the organization of the Government in 1790. In 1794 President Washington appointed John Quincy Adams Minister to The Hague. He was twenty-seven years old when he returned to London, and found the Consul's house a very agreeable haunt. Louisa was then twenty.

At that time, and long afterwards, the Consul's house, far more than the Minister's, was the centre of contact for travelling Americans, either official or other. The Legation was a shifting point, between 1785 and 1815; but the Consulate, far down in the City, near the Tower, was convenient and inviting; so inviting that it proved fatal to young Adams. Louisa was charming, like a Romney portrait, but among her many charms that of being a New England woman was not one. The defect was serious. Her future mother-in-law, Abigail, a famous New England woman whose authority over her turbulent husband, the second President, was hardly so great as that which she exercised over her son, the sixth to be, was troubled by the fear that Louisa might not be made of stuff stern enough, or brought up in conditions severe enough, to suit a New England climate, or to make an efficient wife for her paragon son, and Abigail was right on that point, as on most others where sound judgment was involved; but sound judgment is sometimes a source of weakness rather than of force, and John Quincy already had reason to think that his mother held sound judgments on the subject of daughters-in-law which human nature, since the fall of Eve, made Adams helpless to realize. Being three thousand miles away from his mother, and equally far in love, he married Louisa in London, July 26, 1797, and took her to Berlin to be the head of the United States Legation. During three or four exciting years, the young bride lived in Berlin; whether she was happy or not, whether she was content or not, whether she was socially successful or not, her descendants did not surely know; but in any case she could by no chance have become educated there for a life in Quincy or Boston. In 1801 the overthrow of the Federalist Party drove her and her husband to America, and she became at last a member of the Quincy household, but by that time her children needed all her attention, and she remained there with occasional winters in Boston and Washington, till 1809. Her husband was made Senator in 1803, and in 1809 was appointed Minister to Russia. She went with him to St. Petersburg, taking her baby, Charles Francis, born in 1807; but broken-hearted at having to leave her two older boys behind. The life at St. Petersburg was hardly gay for her; they were far too poor to shine in that extravagant society; but she survived it, though her little girl baby did not, and in the winter of 1814–15, alone with the boy of seven years old, crossed Europe from St. Petersburg to Paris, in her travelling-carriage, passing through the armies, and reaching Paris in the *Cent Jours* after Napoleon's return from Elba. Her husband next went to England as Minister, and she was for two years at the Court of the Regent. In 1817 her husband came home to be Secretary of State, and she lived for eight years in F Street, doing her work of entertainer for President Monroe's administration. Next she lived four miserable years in the White House. When that chapter was closed in 1829, she had earned the right to be tired and delicate, but she still had fifteen years to serve as wife of a Member of the House, after her husband went back to Congress in 1833. Then it was that the little Henry, her grandson, first remembered her, from 1843 to 1848, sitting in her panelled room, at breakfast, with her heavy silver teapot and sugar-bowl and cream-jug, which still exist somewhere as an heirloom of the modern safety-vault. By that time she was seventy years old or more, and thoroughly weary of being beaten about a stormy world. To the boy she seemed singularly peaceful, a vision of silver gray, presiding over her old President and her Queen Anne mahogany; an exotic, like her Sèvres china; an object of deference to every one, and of great affection to her son Charles; but hardly more Bostonian than she had been fifty years before, on her wedding-day, in the shadow of the Tower of London.

Such a figure was even less fitted than that of her old husband, the President, to impress on a boy's mind, the standards of the coming century. She was Louis Seize,

like the furniture. The boy knew nothing of her interior life, which had been, as the venerable Abigail, long since at peace, foresaw, one of severe stress and little pure satisfaction. He never dreamed that from her might come some of those doubts and self-questionings, those hesitations, those rebellions against law and discipline, which marked more than one of her descendants; but he might even then have felt some vague instinctive suspicion that he was to inherit from her the seeds of the primal sin, the fall from grace, the curse of Abel, that he was not of pure New England stock, but half exotic. As a child of Quincy he was not a true Bostonian, but even as a child of Quincy he inherited a quarter taint of Maryland blood. Charles Francis, half Marylander by birth, had hardly seen Boston till he was ten years old, when his parents left him there at school in 1817, and he never forgot the experience. He was to be nearly as old as his mother had been in 1845, before he quite accepted Boston, or Boston quite accepted him.

A boy who began his education in these surroundings, with physical strength inferior to that of his brothers, and with a certain delicacy of mind and bone, ought rightly to have felt at home in the eighteenth century and should, in proper self-respect, have rebelled against the standards of the nineteenth. The atmosphere of his first ten years must have been very like that of his grandfather at the same age, from 1767 till 1776, barring the battle of Bunker Hill, and even as late as 1846, the battle of Bunker Hill remained actual. The tone of Boston society was colonial. The true Bostonian always knelt in self-abasement before the majesty of English standards; far from concealing it as a weakness, he was proud of it as his strength. The eighteenth-century ruled society long after 1850. Perhaps the boy began to shake it off rather earlier than most of his mates.

Indeed this prehistoric stage of education ended rather abruptly with his tenth year. One winter morning he was conscious of a certain confusion in the house in Mount Vernon Street, and gathered, from such words as he could catch, that the President, who happened to be then staying there, on his way to Washington, had fallen and hurt himself. Then he heard the word paralysis.

After that day he came to associate the word with the figure of his grandfather, in a tall-backed, invalid armchair, on one side of the spare bedroom fireplace, and one of his old friends, Dr. Parkman or P. P. F. Degrand, on the other side, both dozing.

The end of this first, or ancestral and Revolutionary, chapter came on February 21, 1848—and the month of February brought life and death as a family habit—when the eighteenth century, as an actual and living companion, vanished. If the scene on the floor of the House, when the old President fell, struck the still simple-minded American public with a sensation unusually dramatic, its effect on a ten-year-old boy, whose boy-life was fading away with the life of his grandfather, could not be slight. One had to pay for Revolutionary patriots; grandfathers and grandmothers; Presidents; diplomats; Queen Anne mahogany and Louis Seize chairs, as well as for Stuart portraits. Such things warp young life. Americans commonly believed that they ruined it, and perhaps the practical common-sense of the American mind judged right. Many a boy might be ruined by much less than the emotions of the funeral service in the Quincy church, with its surroundings of national respect and family pride. By another dramatic chance it happened that the clergyman of the parish, Dr. Lunt, was an unusual pulpit orator, the ideal of a somewhat austere intellectual type, such as the school of Buckminster and Channing inherited from the old Congregational clergy. His extraordinarily refined appearance, his dignity of manner, his deeply cadenced voice, his remarkable English and his fine appreciation, gave to the funeral service a character that left an overwhelming impression on the boy's mind. He was to see many great functions—funerals and festivals—in after-life, till his only thought was to see no more, but he never again witnessed anything nearly so impressive to him as the last services at Quincy over the body of one President and the ashes of another.

The effect of the Quincy service was deepened by the official ceremony which afterwards took place in Faneuil Hall, when the boy was taken to hear his uncle, Edward Everett, deliver a Eulogy. Like all Mr. Everett's orations, it was an admirable piece of oratory, such as only an admirable orator and scholar could create; too good for a ten-year-old boy to appreciate at its value; but already the boy knew that the dead President could not be in it, and had even learned why he would have been out of place there; for knowledge was beginning to come fast. The shadow of the War of 1812 still hung over State Street; the shadow of the Civil War to come had already begun to darken Faneuil Hall. No rhetoric could have reconciled Mr. Everett's audience to his subject. How could he say there, to an assemblage of Bostonians in the heart of mercantile Boston, that the only distinctive mark of all the Adamses, since old Sam Adams's father a hundred and fifty years before, had been their inherited quarrel with State Street, which had again and again broken out into riot, bloodshed, personal feuds, foreign and civil war, wholesale banishments and confiscations, until the history of Florence was hardly more turbulent than that of Boston? How could he whisper the word Hartford Convention before the men who had made it? What would have been said had he suggested the chance of Secession and Civil War?

Thus already, at ten years old, the boy found himself standing face to face with a dilemma that might have puzzled an early Christian. What was he?—where was he going? Even then he felt that something was wrong, but he concluded that it must be Boston. Quincy had always been right, for Quincy represented a moral principle—the principle of resistance to Boston. His Adams ancestors must have been right, since they were always hostile to State Street. If State Street was wrong, Quincy must be right! Turn the dilemma as he pleased, he still came back on the eighteenth century and the law of Resistance; of Truth; of Duty, and of Freedom. He was a ten-year-old priest and politician. He could under no circumstances have guessed what the next fifty years had in store, and no one could teach him; but sometimes, in his old age, he wondered—and could never decide—whether the most clear and certain knowledge would have helped him. Supposing he had seen a New York stock-list of 1900, and had studied the statistics of railways, telegraphs, coal, and steel—would he have quitted his eighteenth-century, his ancestral prejudices, his abstract ideals, his semi-clerical training, and the rest, in order to perform an expiatory pilgrimage to State Street, and ask for the fatted calf of his grandfather Brooks and a clerkship in the Suffolk Bank?

Sixty years afterwards he was still unable to make up his mind. Each course had its advantages, but the material advantages, looking back, seemed to lie wholly in State Street.

The Dynamo and the Virgin (1900)

Until the Great Exposition of 1900 closed its doors in November, Adams haunted it, aching to absorb knowledge, and helpless to find it. He would have liked to know how much of it could have been grasped by the best-informed man in the world. While he was thus meditating chaos, Langley came by, and showed it to him. At Langley's behest, the Exhibition dropped its super-fluous rags and stripped itself to the skin, for Langley knew what to study, and why, and how; while Adams might as well have stood outside in the night, staring at the Milky Way. Yet Langley said nothing new, and taught nothing that one might not have learned from Lord Bacon, three hundred years before; but though one should have known the *Advancement of Science* as well as one knew the *Comedy of Errors*, the lit-erary knowledge counted for nothing until some teacher should show how to apply it. Bacon took a vast deal of trouble in teach-ing King James I and his subjects, Ameri-can or other, towards the year 1620, that true science was the development or econ-omy of forces; yet an elderly American in 1900 knew neither the formula nor the forces; or even so much as to say to himself that his historical business in the Exposition concerned only the economies or develop-ments of force since 1893, when he began the study at Chicago.

Nothing in education is so astonishing as the amount of ignorance it accumulates in the form of inert facts. Adams had looked at most of the accumulations of art in the storehouses called Art Museums; yet he did not know how to look at the art exhibits of 1900. He had studied Karl Marx and his doctrines of history with profound atten-tion, yet he could not apply them at Paris. Langley, with the ease of a great master of experiment, threw out of the field every exhibit that did not reveal a new application of force, and naturally threw out, to begin with, almost the whole art exhibit. Equally, he ignored almost the whole industrial ex-hibit. He led his pupil directly to the forces. His chief interest was in new motors to make his airship feasible, and he taught Adams the astonishing complexities of the Daimler motor, and of the automobile, which, since 1893, had become a nightmare at a hundred kilometres an hour, almost as destructive as the electric tram which was only ten years older; and threatening to be-come as terrible as the locomotive steam-engine itself, which was almost exactly Adams's own age.

Then he showed his scholar the great hall of dynamos, and explained how little he knew about electricity or force of any kind, even of his own special sun, which spouted heat in inconceivable volume, but which, as far as he knew, might spout less or more, at any time, for all the certainty he felt in it. To him, the dynamo itself was but an ingenious channel for conveying some-where the heat latent in a few tons of poor coal hidden in a dirty engine-house care-fully kept out of sight; but to Adams the dynamo became a symbol of infinity. As he grew accustomed to the great gallery of machines, he began to feel the forty-foot dynamos as a moral force, much as the early Christians felt the Cross. The planet itself seemed less impressive, in its old-fashioned, deliberate, annual or daily revo-lution, than this huge wheel, revolving within arm's-length at some vertiginous speed, and barely murmuring—scarcely humming an audible warning to stand a hair's-breadth further for respect of power—while it would not wake the baby lying close against its frame. Before the end, one began to pray to it; inherited instinct taught the natural expression of man before silent and infinite force. Among the thousand symbols of ultimate energy, the dynamo was not so human as some, but it was the most expressive.

Yet the dynamo, next to the steam-en-gine, was the most familiar of exhibits. For Adams's objects its value lay chiefly in its occult mechanism. Between the dynamo in the gallery of machines and the engine-house outside, the break of continuity amounted to abysmal fracture for a historian's objects. No more relation could he discover between the steam and the electric current than between the Cross and the cathedral. The forces were interchangeable if not reversible, but he could see only an absolute *fiat* in electricity as in faith. Langley could not help him. Indeed, Langley seemed to be worried by the same trouble, for he constantly repeated that the new forces were anarchical, and especially that he was not responsible for the new rays, that were little short of parricidal in their wicked spirit towards science. His own rays, with which he had doubled the solar spectrum, were altogether harmless and beneficent; but Radium denied its God—or, what was to Langley the same thing, denied the truths of his Science. The force was wholly new.

A historian who asked only to learn enough to be as futile as Langley or Kelvin, made rapid progress under this teaching, and mixed himself up in the tangle of ideas until he achieved a sort of Paradise of ignorance vastly consoling to his fatigued senses. He wrapped himself in vibrations and rays which were new, and he would have hugged Marconi and Branly had he met them, as he hugged the dynamo; while he lost his arithmetic in trying to figure out the equation between the discoveries and the economies of force. The economies, like the discoveries, were absolute, super-sensual, occult; incapable of expression in horse-power. What mathematical equivalent could he suggest as the value of a Branly coherer? Frozen air, or the electric furnace, had some scale of measurement, no doubt, if somebody could invent a thermometer adequate to the purpose; but X-rays had played no part whatever in man's consciousness, and the atom itself had figured only as a fiction of thought. In these seven years man had translated himself into a new universe which had no common scale of measurement with the old. He had entered a supersensual world, in which he could measure nothing except by chance collisions of movements imperceptible to his senses, perhaps even imperceptible to his instruments, but perceptible to each other, and so to some known ray at the end

of the scale. Langley seemed prepared for anything, even for an indeterminable number of universes interfused—physics stark mad in metaphysics.

Historians undertake to arrange sequences,—called stories, or histories—assuming in silence a relation of cause and effect. These assumptions, hidden in the depths of dusty libraries, have been astounding, but commonly unconscious and childlike; so much so, that if any captious critic were to drag them to light, historians would probably reply, with one voice, that they had never supposed themselves required to know what they were talking about. Adams, for one, had toiled in vain to find out what he meant. He had even published a dozen volumes of American history for no other purpose than to satisfy himself whether, by the severest process of stating, with the least possible comment, such facts as seemed sure, in such order as seemed rigorously consequent, he could fix for a familiar moment a necessary sequence of human movement. The result had satisfied him as little as at Harvard College. Where he saw sequence, other men saw something quite different, and no one saw the same unit of measure. He cared little about his experiments and less about his statesmen, who seemed to him quite as ignorant as himself and, as a rule, no more honest; but he insisted on a relation of sequence, and if he could not reach it by one method, he would try as many methods as science knew. Satisfied that the sequence of men led to nothing and that the sequence of their society could lead no further, while the mere sequence of time was artificial, and the sequence of thought was chaos, he turned at last to the sequence of force; and thus it happened that, after ten years' pursuit, he found himself lying in the Gallery of Machines at the Great Exposition of 1900, his historical neck broken by the sudden irruption of forces totally new.

Since no one else showed much concern, an elderly person without other cares had no need to betray alarm. The year 1900 was not the first to upset schoolmasters. Copernicus and Galileo had broken many professorial necks about 1600; Columbus had stood the world on its head towards 1500; but the nearest approach to the revolution of 1900 was that of 310, when Constantine set up the Cross. The rays that Langley disowned, as well as those which he fathered, were occult, supersensual, irrational; they were a revelation of mysterious energy like that of the Cross; they were what, in terms of mediæval science, were called immediate modes of the divine substance.

The historian was thus reduced to his last resources. Clearly if he was bound to reduce all these forces to a common value, this common value could have no measure but that of their attraction on his own mind. He must treat them as they had been felt; as convertible, reversible, interchangeable attractions on thought. He made up his mind to venture it; he would risk translating rays into faith. Such a reversible process would vastly amuse a chemist, but the chemist could not deny that he, or some of his fellow physicists, could feel the force of both. When Adams was a boy in Boston, the best chemist in the place had probably never heard of Venus except by way of scandal, or of the Virgin except as idolatry; neither had he heard of dynamos or automobiles or radium; yet his mind was ready to feel the force of all, though the rays were unborn and the women were dead.

Here opened another totally new education, which promised to be by far the most hazardous of all. The knife-edge along which he must crawl, like Sir Lancelot in the twelfth century, divided two kingdoms of force which had nothing in common but attraction. They were as different as a magnet is from gravitation, supposing one knew what a magnet was, or gravitation, or love. The force of the Virgin was still felt at Lourdes, and seemed to be as potent as X-rays; but in America neither Venus nor Virgin ever had value as force—at most as sentiment. No American had ever been truly afraid of either.

This problem in dynamics gravely perplexed an American historian. The Woman had once been supreme; in France she still seemed potent, not merely as a sentiment, but as a force. Why was she unknown in America? For evidently America was ashamed of her, and she was ashamed herself, otherwise they would not have strewn fig-leaves so profusely all over her. When she was a true force, she was ignorant of fig-leaves, but the monthly-magazine-made American female had not a feature

that would have been recognized by Adam. The trait was notorious, and often humorous, but any one brought up among Puritans knew that sex was sin. In any previous age, sex was strength. Neither art nor beauty was needed. Every one, even among Puritans, knew that neither Diana of the Ephesians nor any of the Oriental goddesses was worshipped for her beauty. She was goddess because of her force; she was the animated dynamo; she was reproduction—the greatest and most mysterious of all energies; all she needed was to be fecund. Singularly enough, not one of Adams's many schools of education had ever drawn his attention to the opening lines of Lucretius, though they were perhaps the finest in all Latin Literature, where the poet invoked Venus exactly as Dante invoked the Virgin:—

'Quæ quoniam rerum naturam *sola* gubernas.' [1]

The Venus of Epicurean philosophy survived in the Virgin of the Schools:

'Donna, sei tanto grande, e tanto vali,
Che qual vuol grazia, e a te non ricorre,
Sua disianza vuol volar senz' ali.' [2]

All this was to American thought as though it had never existed. The true American knew something of the facts, but nothing of the feelings; he read the letter, but he never felt the law. Before this historical chasm, a mind like that of Adams felt itself helpless; he turned from the Virgin to the Dynamo as though he were a Branly coherer. On one side, at the Louvre and at Chartres, as he knew by the record of work actually done and still before his eyes, was the highest energy ever known to man, the creator of four-fifths of his noblest art, exercising vastly more attraction over the human mind than all the steam-engines and dynamos ever dreamed of; and yet this energy was unknown to the American mind. An American Virgin would never dare command; an American Venus would never dare exist.

1 'Thou, since thou dost alone govern the nature of things.'
2 'Lady, thou so prevailest in all things
   That whoso would have grace, and seeks not thee,
   Would have his wish fly upward without wings.'
   —Dante, *Paradiso*, XXXIII, 13–15. Fletcher, trans.

The question, which to any plain American of the nineteenth century seemed as remote as it did to Adams, drew him almost violently to study, once it was posed; and on this point Langleys were as useless as though they were Herbert Spencers or dynamos. The idea survived only as art. There one turned as naturally as though the artist were himself a woman. Adams began to ponder, asking himself whether he knew of any American artist who had ever insisted on the power of sex, as every classic had always done; but he could think only of Walt Whitman; Bret Harte, as far as the magazines would let him venture; and one or two painters, for the flesh-tones. All the rest had used sex for sentiment, never for force; to them, Eve was a tender flower, and Herodias an unfeminine horror. American art, like the American language and American education, was as far as possible sexless. Society regarded this victory over sex as its greatest triumph, and the historian readily admitted it, since the moral issue, for the moment, did not concern one who was studying the relations of unmoral force. He cared nothing for the sex of the dynamo until he could measure its energy.

Vaguely seeking a clue, he wandered through the art exhibit, and, in his stroll, stopped almost every day before Saint-Gaudens's General Sherman, which had been given the central post of honor. Saint-Gaudens himself was in Paris, putting on the work his usual interminable last touches, and listening to the usual contradictory suggestions of brother sculptors. Of all the American artists who gave to American art whatever life it breathed in the seventies, Saint-Gaudens was perhaps the most sympathetic, but certainly the most inarticulate. General Grant or Don Cameron had scarcely less instinct of rhetoric than he. All the others—the Hunts, Richardson, John La Farge, Stanford White—were exuberant; only Saint-Gaudens could never discuss or dilate on an emotion, or suggest artistic arguments for giving to his work the forms that he felt. He never laid down the law, or affected the despot, or became brutalized like Whistler by the brutalities of his world. He required no incense; he was no egoist; his simplicity of thought was excessive; he could not imitate, or give any form but his own to the creations of his hand. No

one felt more strongly than he the strength of other men, but the idea that they could affect him never stirred an image in his mind.

This summer his health was poor and his spirits were low. For such a temper, Adams was not the best companion, since his own gaiety was not *folle*; but he risked going now and then to the studio on Mont Parnasse to draw him out for a stroll in the Bois de Boulogne, or dinner as pleased his moods, and in return Saint-Gaudens sometimes let Adams go about in his company.

Once Saint-Gaudens took him down to Amiens, with a party of Frenchmen, to see the cathedral. Not until they found themselves actually studying the sculpture of the western portal, did it dawn on Adams's mind that, for his purposes, Saint-Gaudens on that spot had more interest to him than the cathedral itself. Great men before great monuments express great truths, provided they are not taken too solemnly. Adams never tired of quoting the supreme phrase of his idol Gibbon, before the Gothic cathedrals: 'I darted a contemptuous look on the stately monuments of superstition.' Even in the footnotes of his history, Gibbon had never inserted a bit of humor more human than this, and one would have paid largely for a photograph of the fat little historian, on the background of Notre Dame of Amiens, trying to persuade his readers—perhaps himself—that he was darting a contemptuous look on the stately monument, for which he felt in fact the respect which every man of his vast study and active mind always feels before objects worthy of it; but besides the humor, one felt also the relation. Gibbon ignored the Virgin, because in 1789 religious monuments were out of fashion. In 1900 his remark sounded fresh and simple as the green fields to ears that had heard a hundred years of other remarks, mostly no more fresh and certainly less simple. Without malice, one might find it more instructive than a whole lecture of Ruskin. One sees what one brings, and at that moment Gibbon brought the French Revolution. Ruskin brought reaction against the Revolution. Saint-Gaudens had passed beyond all. He liked the stately monuments much more than he liked Gibbon or Ruskin; he loved their dignity; their unity; their scale; their lines; their lights and shadows; their decorative sculpture; but he was even less conscious than they of the force that created it all—the Virgin, the Woman—by whose genius 'the stately monuments of superstition' were built, through which she was expressed. He would have seen more meaning in Isis with the cow's horns, at Edfoo, who expressed the same thought. The art remained, but the energy was lost even upon the artist.

Yet in mind and person Saint-Gaudens was a survival of the 1500; he bore the stamp of the Renaissance, and should have carried an image of the Virgin round his neck, or stuck in his hat, like Louis XI. In mere time he was a lost soul that had strayed by chance into the twentieth century, and forgotten where it came from. He writhed and cursed at his ignorance, much as Adams did at his own, but in the opposite sense. Saint-Gaudens was a child of Benvenuto Cellini, smothered in an American cradle. Adams was a quintessence of Boston, devoured by curiosity to think like Benvenuto. Saint-Gaudens's art was starved from birth, and Adams's instinct was blighted from babyhood. Each had but half of a nature, and when they came together before the Virgin of Amiens they ought both to have felt in her the force that made them one; but it was not so. To Adams she became more than ever a channel of force; to Saint-Gaudens she remained as before a channel of taste.

For a symbol of power, Saint-Gaudens instinctively preferred the horse, as was plain in his horse and Victory of the Sherman monument. Doubtless Sherman also felt it so. The attitude was so American that, for at least forty years, Adams had never realized that any other could be in sound taste. How many years had he taken to admit a notion of what Michaelangelo and Rubens were driving at? He could not say; but he knew that only since 1895 had he begun to feel the Virgin or Venus as force, and not everywhere even so. At Chartres—perhaps at Lourdes—possibly at Cnidos if one could still find there the divinely naked Aphrodite of Praxiteles—but otherwise one must look for force to the goddesses of Indian mythology. The idea died out long ago in the German and English stock. Saint-Gaudens at Amiens was hardly less sensitive to the force of the female energy than Matthew Arnold at the Grande Chartreuse. Neither of them felt goddesses as power—only as reflected emotion, human expression, beauty, purity, taste, scarcely even as sympathy. They felt a railway train as power; yet they, and all other artists, constantly complained that the power embodied in a railway train could never be embodied in art. All the steam in the world could not, like the Virgin, build Chartres.

Yet in mechanics, whatever the mechanicians might think, both energies acted as interchangeable forces on man, and by action on man all known force may be measured. Indeed, few men of science measured force in any other way. After once admitting that a straight line was the shortest distance between two points, no serious mathematician cared to deny anything that suited his convenience, and rejected no symbol, unproved or unproveable, that helped him to accomplish work. The symbol was force, as a compass-needle or a triangle was force, as the mechanist might prove by losing it, and nothing could be gained by ignoring their value. Symbol or energy, the Virgin had acted as the greatest force the Western world ever felt, and had drawn man's activities to herself more strongly than any other power, natural or super-natural, had ever done; the historian's business was to follow the track of the energy; to find where it came from and where it went to; its complex source and shifting channels; its values, equivalents, conversions. It could scarcely be more complex than radium; it could hardly be deflected, diverted, polarized, absorbed more perplexingly than other radiant matter. Adams knew nothing about any of them, but as a mathematical problem of influence on human progress, though all were occult, all reacted on his mind, and he rather inclined to think the Virgin easiest to handle.

The pursuit turned out to be long and tortuous, leading at last into the vast forests of scholastic science. From Zeno to Descartes, hand in hand with Thomas Aquinas, Montaigne, and Pascal, one stumbled as stupidly as though one were still a German student of 1860. Only with the instinct of despair could one force one's self into this old thicket of ignorance after having been repulsed at a score of entrances more promising and more popular. Thus far, no path had led anywhere, unless perhaps to an exceedingly modest living. Forty-five years of study had proved to be quite futile for the pursuit of power; one controlled no more force in 1900 than in 1850, although the amount of force controlled by society had enormously increased. The secret of education still hid itself somewhere behind ignorance, and one fumbled over it as feebly as ever. In such labyrinths, the staff is a force almost more necessary than the legs; the pen becomes a sort of blind-man's dog, to keep him from falling into the gutters. The pen works for itself, and acts like a hand, modelling the plastic material over and over again to the form that suits it best. The form is never arbitrary, but is a sort of growth like crystallization, as any artist

knows too well; for often the pencil or pen runs into sidepaths and shapelessness, loses its relations, stops or is bogged. Then it has to return on its trail, and recover, if it can, its line of force. The result of a year's work depends more on what is struck out than on what is left in; on the sequence of the main lines of thought, than on their play or variety. Compelled once more to lean heavily on this support, Adams covered more thousands of pages with figures as formal as though they were algebra, laboriously striking out, altering, burning, experimenting, until the year had expired, the Exposition had long been closed, and winter drawing to its end, before he sailed from Cherbourg, on January 19, 1901, for home.

1907

WILLIAM SYDNEY PORTER

(O. HENRY)

1862–1910

A MUNICIPAL REPORT

The cities are full of pride,
Challenging each to each—
This from her mountainside,
That from her burthened beach.
R. KIPLING.

Fancy a novel about Chicago or Buffalo, let us say, or Nashville, Tennessee! There are just three big cities in the United States that are 'story cities'—New York, of course, New Orleans, and, best of the lot, San Francisco.

FRANK NORRIS.

EAST is East, and West is San Francisco, according to Californians. Californians are a race of people; they are not merely inhabitants of a State. They are the Southerners of the West. Now, Chicagoans are no less loyal to their city; but when you ask them why, they stammer and speak of lake fish and the new Odd Fellows Building. But Californians go into detail.

Of course they have, in the climate, an argument that is good for half an hour while you are thinking of your coal bills and heavy underwear. But as soon as they come

to mistake your silence for conviction, madness comes upon them, and they picture the city of the Golden Gate as the Bagdad of the New World. So far, as a matter of opinion, no refutation is necessary. But, dear cousins all (from Adam and Eve descended), it is a rash one who will lay his finger on the map and say: 'In this town there can be no romance—what could happen here?' Yes, it is a bold and a rash deed to challenge in one sentence history, romance, and Rand and McNally.

Nashville.—A city, port of delivery, and the capital of the State of Tennessee, is on the Cumberland River and on the N.C. & ST.L. and the L. & N. railroads. This city is regarded as the most important educational centre in the South.

I stepped off the train at 8 P.M. Having searched the thesaurus in vain for adjectives, I must, as a substitution, hie me to comparison in the form of a recipe.

Take of London fog 30 parts; malaria 10 parts; gas leaks 20 parts; dewdrops gathered in a brick yard at sunrise 25 parts; odor of honeysuckle 15 parts. Mix.

The mixture will give you an approximate conception of a Nashville drizzle. It is not so fragrant as a moth-ball nor as thick as pea-soup; but 'tis enough—'twill serve.

I went to a hotel in a tumbril. It required strong self-suppression for me to keep from climbing to the top of it and giving an imitation of Sidney Carton. The vehicle was drawn by beasts of a bygone era and driven by something dark and emancipated.

I was sleepy and tired, so when I got to the hotel I hurriedly paid it the fifty cents it demanded (with approximate lagniappe, I assure you). I knew its habits; and I did not want to hear it prate about its old 'marster' or anything that happened 'befo' de wah.'

The hotel was one of the kind described as 'renovated.' That means $30,000 worth of new marble pillars, tiling, electric lights and brass cuspidors in the lobby, and a new L. & N. time table and a lithograph of Lookout Mountain in each one of the great rooms above. The management was without reproach, the attention full of exquisite Southern courtesy, the service as slow as the progress of a snail and as good-humored as Rip Van Winkle. The food was worth traveling a thousand miles for. There is no other hotel in the world where you can get such chicken livers *en brochette*.

At dinner I asked a Negro waiter if there was anything doing in town. He pondered gravely for a minute, and then replied: 'Well, boss, I don't really reckon there's anything at all doin' after sundown.'

Sundown had been accomplished; it had been drowned in the drizzle long before. So that spectacle was denied me. But I went forth upon the streets in the drizzle to see what might be there.

It is built on undulating grounds; and the streets are lighted by electricity at a cost of $32,470 per annum.

As I left the hotel there was a race riot. Down upon me charged a company of freedmen, or Arabs, or Zulus, armed with —no, I saw with relief that they were not rifles, but whips. And I saw dimly a caravan of black, clumsy vehicles; and at the reassuring shouts, 'Kyar you anywhere in the town, boss, fuh fifty cents,' I reasoned that I was merely a 'fare' instead of a victim.

I walked through long streets, all leading uphill. I wondered how those streets ever came down again. Perhaps they didn't until they were 'graded.' On a few of the 'main streets' I saw lights in stores here and there; saw street cars go by conveying worthy burghers hither and yon; saw people pass engaged in the art of conversation, and heard a burst of semi-lively laughter issuing from a soda-water and ice-cream parlor. The streets other than 'main' seemed to have enticed upon their borders houses consecrated to peace and domesticity. In many of them lights shone behind discreetly drawn window shades; in a few pianos tinkled orderly and irreproachable music. There was, indeed, little 'doing.' I wished I had come before sundown. So I returned to my hotel.

In November, 1864, the Confederate General Hood advanced against Nashville, where he shut up a National force under General Thomas. The latter then sallied forth and defeated the Confederates in a terrible conflict.

All my life I have heard of, admired, and witnessed the fine marksmanship of the South in its peaceful conflicts in the tobacco-chewing regions. But in my hotel a surprise awaited me. There were twelve bright, new, imposing, capacious brass cuspidors in the great lobby, tall enough to be called urns and so wide-mouthed that the crack pitcher of a lady baseball team should have been able to throw a ball into one of them at five paces distant. But, although a terrible battle had raged and was still raging, the enemy had not suffered. Bright, new, imposing, capacious, untouched, they stood. But, shades of Jefferson Brick! the tile floor—the beautiful tile floor! I could not avoid thinking of the battle of Nashville, and trying to draw, as is my foolish habit, some deductions about hereditary marksmanship.

Here I first saw Major (by misplaced courtesy) Wentworth Caswell. I knew him for a type the moment my eyes suffered from the sight of him. A rat has no geographical habitat. My old friend, A. Tennyson, said, as he so well said almost everything:

Prophet, curse me the blabbing lip,
And curse me the British vermin, the rat.

Let us regard the word 'British' as interchangeable *ad lib*. A rat is a rat.

This man was hunting about the hotel lobby like a starved dog that had forgotten where he had buried a bone. He had a face of great acreage, red, pulpy, and with a kind of sleepy massiveness like that of Buddha. He possessed one single virtue—he was very smoothly shaven. The mark of the beast is not indelible upon a man until he goes about with a stubble. I think that if he had not used his razor that day I would have repulsed his advances, and the criminal calendar of the world would have been spared the addition of one murder.

I happened to be standing within five feet of a cuspidor when Major Caswell opened fire upon it. I had been observant enough to perceive that the attacking force was using Gatlings instead of squirrel rifles; so I side-stepped so promptly that the major seized the opportunity to apologize to a noncombatant. He had the blabbing lip. In four minutes he had become my friend and had dragged me to the bar.

I desire to interpolate here that I am a Southerner. But I am not one by profession or trade. I eschew the string tie, the slouch hat, the Prince Albert, the number of bales of cotton destroyed by Sherman, and plug chewing. When the orchestra plays Dixie I do not cheer. I slide a little lower on the leather-cornered seat and, well, order another Würzburger and wish that Longstreet had—but what's the use?

Major Caswell banged the bar with his fist, and the first gun at Fort Sumter reechoed. When he fired the last one at Appomattox I began to hope. But then he began on family trees, and demonstrated that Adam was only a third cousin of a collateral branch of the Caswell family. Genealogy disposed of, he took up, to my distaste, his private family matters. He spoke of his wife, traced her descent back to Eve, and profanely denied any possible rumor that she may have had relations in the land of Nod.

By this time I began to suspect that he was trying to obscure by noise the fact that he had ordered the drinks, on the chance that I would be bewildered into paying for them. But when they were down he crashed a silver dollar loudly upon the bar. Then, of course, another serving was obligatory.

And when I had paid for that I took leave of him brusquely; for I wanted no more of him. But before I had obtained my release he had prated loudly of an income that his wife received, and showed a handful of silver money.

When I got my key at the desk the clerk said to me courteously: 'If that man Caswell has annoyed you, and if you would like to make a complaint, we will have him ejected. He is a nuisance, a loafer, and without any known means of support, although he seems to have some money most of the time. But we don't seem to be able to hit upon any means of throwing him out legally.'

'Why, no,' said I, after some reflection; 'I don't see my way clear to making a complaint. But I would like to place myself on record as asserting that I do not care for his company. Your town,' I continued, 'seems to be a quiet one. What manner of entertainment, adventure, or excitement have you to offer to the stranger within your gates?'

'Well, sir,' said the clerk, 'there will be a show here next Thursday. It is—I'll look it up and have the announcement sent up to your room with the ice water. Good night.'

After I went up to my room I looked out the window. It was only about ten o'clock, but I looked upon a silent town. The drizzle continued, spangled with dim lights, as far apart as currants in a cake sold at the Ladies' Exchange.

'A quiet place,' I said to myself, as my first shoe struck the ceiling of the occupant of the room beneath mine. 'Nothing of the life here that gives color and variety to the cities in the East and West. Just a good, ordinary, humdrum, business town.'

Nashville occupies a foremost place among the manufacturing centres of the country. It is the fifth boot and shoe market in the United States, the largest candy and cracker manufacturing city in the South, and does an enormous wholesale drygoods, grocery, and drug business.

I must tell you how I came to be in Nashville, and I assure you the digression brings as much tedium to me as it does to you. I was traveling elsewhere on my own business, but I had a commission from a Northern literary magazine to stop over there and establish a personal connection between the publication and one of its contributors, Azalea Adair.

Adair (there was no clue to the personality except the handwriting) had sent in some essays (lost art!) and poems that had made the editors swear approvingly over their one o'clock luncheon. So they had commissioned me to round up said Adair and corner by contract his or her output at two cents a word before some other publisher offered her ten or twenty.

At nine o'clock the next morning, after my chicken livers *en brochette* (try them if you can find that hotel), I strayed out into the drizzle, which was still on for an unlimited run. At the first corner I came upon Uncle Cæsar. He was a stalwart Negro, older than the pyramids, with gray wool and a face that reminded me of Brutus, and a second afterwards of the late King Cettiwayo. He wore the most remarkable coat that I ever had seen or expect to see. It reached to his ankles and had once been a Confederate gray in colors. But rain and sun and age had so variegated it that Joseph's coat, beside it, would have faded to a pale monochrome. I must linger with that coat, for it has to do with the story—the story that is so long in coming, because you can hardly expect anything to happen in Nashville.

Once it must have been the military coat of an officer. The cape of it had vanished, but all adown its front it had been frogged and tasseled magnificently. But now the frogs and tassels were gone. In their stead had been patiently stitched (I surmised by some surviving 'black mammy') new frogs made of cunningly twisted common hempen twine. The twine was frayed and disheveled. It must have been added to the coat as a substitute for vanished splendors, with tasteless but painstaking devotion, for it followed faithfully the curves of the long-missing frogs. And, to complete the comedy and pathos of the garment, all its buttons were gone save one. The second button from the top alone remained. The coat was fastened by other twine strings tied through the buttonholes and other holes rudely pierced in the opposite side. There was never such a weird garment so fantastically bedecked and of so many mottled hues. The

lone button was the size of a half-dollar, made of yellow horn and sewed on with coarse twine.

This Negro stood by a carriage so old that Ham himself might have started a hack line with it after he left the ark with the two animals hitched to it. As I approached he threw open the door, drew out a feather duster, waved it without using it, and said in deep, rumbling tones:

'Step right in, suh; ain't a speck of dust in it—jus' got back from a funeral, suh.'

I inferred that on such gala occasions carriages were given an extra cleaning. I looked up and down the street and perceived that there was little choice among the vehicles for hire that lined the curb. I looked in my memorandum book for the address of Azalea Adair.

'I want to go to 861 Jessamine Street,' I said, and was about to step into the hack.

But for an instant the thick, long, gorilla-like arm of the old Negro barred me. On his massive and saturnine face a look of sudden suspicion and enmity flashed for a moment. Then, with quickly returning conviction, he asked blandishingly: 'What are you gwine there for, boss?'

'What is that to you?' I asked, a little sharply.

'Nothin', suh, jus' nothin'. Only it's a lonesome kind of part of town and few folks ever has business out there. Step right in. The seats is clean—jes' got back from a funeral, suh.'

A mile and a half it must have been to our journey's end. I could hear nothing but the fearful rattle of the ancient hack over the uneven brick paving; I could smell nothing but the drizzle, now further flavored with coal smoke and something like a mixture of tar and oleander blossoms. All I could see through the streaming windows were two rows of dim houses.

The city has an area of 10 square miles; 181 miles of streets, of which 137 miles are paved; a system of waterworks that cost $2,000,000, with 77 miles of mains.

861 Jessamine Street was a decayed mansion. Thirty yards back from the street it stood, outmerged in a splendid grove of trees and untrimmed shrubbery. A row of box bushes overflowed and almost hid the

paling fence from sight; the gate was kept closed by a rope noose that encircled the gatepost and the first paling of the gate. But when you got inside you saw that 861 was a shell, a shadow, a ghost of former grandeur and excellence. But in the story, I have not yet got inside.

When the hack had ceased from rattling and the weary quadrupeds came to a rest I handed my jehu his fifty cents with an additional quarter, feeling a glow of conscious generosity, as I did so. He refused it.

'It's two dollars, suh,' he said.

'How's that?' I asked. 'I plainly heard you call out at the hotel: "Fifty cents to any part of the town." '

'It's two dollars, suh,' he repeated obstinately. 'It's a long ways from the hotel.'

'It is within the city limits and well within them,' I argued. 'Don't think that you have picked up a greenhorn Yankee. Do you see those hills over there?' I went on, pointing toward the east (I could not see them, myself, for the drizzle); 'well, I was born and raised on their other side. You old fool nigger, can't you tell people from other people when you see 'em?'

The grim face of King Cettiwayo softened. 'Is you from the South, suh? I reckon it was them shoes of yourn fooled me. They is somethin' sharp in the toes for a Southern gen'l'man to wear.'

'Then the charge is fifty cents, I suppose?' said I inexorably.

His former expression, a mingling of cupidity and hostility, returned, remained ten seconds, and vanished.

'Boss,' he said, 'fifty cents is right; but I *needs* two dollars, suh; I'm *obleeged* to have two dollars. I ain't *demandin'* it now, suh; after I knows whar you's from; I'm jus' sayin' that I *has* to have two dollars tonight, and business is mighty po'.'

Peace and confidence settled upon his heavy features. He had been luckier than he had hoped. Instead of having picked up a greenhorn, ignorant of rates, he had come upon an inheritance.

'You confounded old rascal,' I said, reaching down to my pocket, 'you ought to be turned over to the police.'

For the first time I saw him smile. He knew; *he knew; HE KNEW.*

I gave him two one-dollar bills. As I handed them over I noticed that one of them had seen parlous times. Its upper right-hand corner was missing, and it had been torn through in the middle, but joined again. A strip of blue tissue paper, pasted over the split, preserved its negotiability.

Enough of the African bandit for the present: I left him happy, lifted the rope and opened the creaky gate.

The house, as I said, was a shell. A paint brush had not touched it in twenty years. I could not see why a strong wind should not have bowled it over like a house of cards until I looked again at the trees that hugged it close—the trees that saw the battle of Nashville and still drew their protecting branches around it against storm and enemy and cold.

Azalea Adair, fifty years old, white-haired, a descendant of the cavaliers, as thin and frail as the house she lived in, robed in the cheapest and cleanest dress I ever saw, with an air as simple as a queen's, received me.

The reception room seemed a mile square, because there was nothing in it except some rows of books, on unpainted white-pine bookshelves, a cracked marble-top table, a rag rug, a hairless horsehair sofa and two or three chairs. Yes, there was a picture on the wall, a colored crayon drawing of a cluster of pansies. I looked around for the portrait of Andrew Jackson and the pine-cone hanging basket but they were not there.

Azalea Adair and I had conversation, a little of which will be repeated to you. She was a product of the old South, gently nurtured in the sheltered life. Her learning was not broad, but was deep and of splendid originality in its somewhat narrow scope. She had been educated at home, and her knowledge of the world was derived from inference and by inspiration. Of such is the precious, small group of essayists made. While she talked to me I kept brushing my fingers, trying, unconsciously, to rid them guiltily of the absent dust from the half-calf backs of Lamb, Chaucer, Hazlitt, Marcus Aurelius, Montaigne and Hood. She was exquisite, she was a valuable discovery. Nearly everybody nowadays knows too much—oh, so much too much—of real life.

I could perceive clearly that Azalea Adair was very poor. A house and a dress she had, not much else, I fancied. So, divided between my duty to the magazine and my loyalty to the poets and essayists who fought Thomas in the valley of the Cumberland, I listened to her voice, which was like a harpsichord's, and found that I could not speak of contracts. In the presence of the nine Muses and the three Graces one hesitated to lower the topic to two cents. There would have to be another colloquy after I had regained my commercialism. But I spoke of my mission, and three o'clock of the next afternoon was set for the discussion of the business proposition.

'Your town,' I said, as I began to make ready to depart (which is the time for smooth generalities), 'seems to be a quiet, sedate place. A home town, I should say, where few things out of the ordinary ever happen.'

It carries on an extensive trade in stoves and hollow ware with the West and South, and its flouring mills have a daily capacity of more than 2,000 barrels.

Azalea Adair seemed to reflect.

'I have never thought of it that way,' she said, with a kind of sincere intensity that seemed to belong to her. 'Isn't it in the still, quiet places that things do happen? I fancy that when God began to create the earth on the first Monday morning one could have leaned out one's window and heard the drops of mud splashing from His trowel as He built up the everlasting hills. What did the noisiest project in the world—I mean the building of the tower of Babel—result in finally? A page and a half of Esperanto in the *North American Review*.'

'Of course,' said I platitudinously, 'human nature is the same everywhere; but there is more color—er—more drama and movement and—er—romance in some cities than in others.'

'On the surface,' said Azalea Adair. 'I have traveled many times around the world in a golden airship wafted on two wings—print and dreams. I have seen (on one of my imaginary tours) the Sultan of Turkey bowstring with his own hands one of his wives who had uncovered her face in public. I have seen a man in Nashville tear up his theatre tickets because his wife was going out with her face covered—with rice powder. In San Francisco's Chinatown I saw the slave girl Sing Yee dipped slowly, inch by inch, in boiling almond oil to make her swear she would never see her American lover again. She gave in when the boiling oil had reached three inches above her knee. At a euchre party in East Nashville the other night I saw Kitty Morgan cut dead by seven of her schoolmates and lifelong friends because she had married a house painter. The boiling oil was sizzling as high as her heart; but I wish you could have seen the fine little smile that she carried from table to table. Oh, yes, it is a humdrum town. Just a few miles of red brick houses and mud and stores and lumber yards.'

Some one knocked hollowly at the back of the house. Azalea Adair breathed a soft apology and went to investigate the sound. She came back in three minutes with brightened eyes, a faint flush on her cheeks, and ten years lifted from her shoulders.

'You must have a cup of tea before you go,' she said, 'and a sugar cake.'

She reached and shook a little iron bell. In shuffled a small Negro girl about twelve, barefoot, not very tidy, glowering at me with thumb in mouth and bulging eyes.

Azalea Adair opened a tiny, worn purse and drew out a dollar bill, a dollar bill with the upper right-hand corner missing, torn in two pieces and pasted together again with a strip of blue tissue paper. It was one of the bills I had given the piratical Negro—there was no doubt of it.

'Go up to Mr. Baker's store on the corner, Impy,' she said, handing the girl the dollar bill, 'and get a quarter of a pound of tea—the kind he always sends me—and ten cents worth of sugar cakes. Now, hurry. The supply of tea in the house happens to be exhausted,' she explained to me.

Impy left by the back way. Before the scrape of her hard, bare feet had died away on the back porch, a wild shriek—I was sure it was hers—filled the hollow house. Then the deep, gruff tones of an angry man's voice mingled with the girl's further squeals and unintelligible words.

Azalea Adair rose without surprise or emotion and disappeared. For two minutes I heard the hoarse rumble of the man's voice; then something like an oath and a slight scuffle, and she returned calmly to her chair.

'This is a roomy house,' she said, 'and I

have a tenant for part of it. I am sorry to have to rescind my invitation to tea. It was impossible to get the kind I always use at the store. Perhaps to-morrow Mr. Baker will be able to supply me.'

I was sure that Impy had not had time to leave the house. I inquired concerning street-car lines and took my leave. After I was well on my way I remembered that I had not learned Azalea Adair's name. But to-morrow would do.

That same day I started in on the course of iniquity that this uneventful city forced upon me. I was in the town only two days, but in that time I managed to lie shamelessly by telegraph, and to be an accomplice —after the fact, if that is the correct legal term—to a murder.

As I rounded the corner nearest my hotel the Afrite coachman of the polychromatic, nonpareil coat seized me, swung open the dungeony door of his peripatetic sarcophagus, flirted his feather duster and began his ritual: 'Step right in, boss. Carriage is clean—jus' got back from a funeral. Fifty cents to any—'

And then he knew me and grinned broadly. ' 'Scuse me, boss; you is de gen'l'-man what rid out with me dis mawnin'. Thank you kindly, suh.'

'I am going out to 861 again to-morrow afternoon at three,' said I, 'and if you will be here, I'll let you drive me. So you know Miss Adair?' I concluded, thinking of my dollar bill.

'I belonged to her father, Judge Adair, suh,' he replied.

'I judge that she is pretty poor,' I said. 'She hasn't much money to speak of, has she?'

For an instant I looked again at the fierce countenance of King Cettiwayo, and then he changed back to an extortionate old Negro hack driver.

'She ain't gwine to starve, suh,' he said slowly. 'She has reso'ces, suh; she has re-so'ces.'

'I shall pay you fifty cents for the trip,' said I.

'Dat is puffeckly correct, suh,' he an-swered humbly. 'I jus' had to have dat two dollars dis mawnin', boss.'

I went to the hotel and lied by electricity. I wired the magazine: 'A. Adair holds out for eight cents a word.'

The answer that came back was: 'Give it to her quick, you duffer.'

Just before dinner 'Major' Wentworth Caswell bore down upon me with the greetings of a long-lost friend. I have seen few men whom I have so instantaneously hated, and of whom it was so difficult to be rid. I was standing at the bar when he invaded me; therefore I could not wave the white ribbon in his face. I would have paid gladly for the drinks, hoping, thereby, to escape another; but he was one of those despicable, roaring, advertising bibbers who must have brass bands and fireworks attend upon every cent that they waste in their follies.

With an air of producing millions he drew two one-dollar bills from a pocket and dashed one of them upon the bar. I looked once more at the dollar bill with the upper right-hand corner missing, torn through the middle, and patched with a strip of blue tissue paper. It was my dollar bill again. It could have been no other.

I went up to my room. The drizzle and the monotony of a dreary, eventless Southern town had made me tired and listless. I remember that just before I went to bed I mentally disposed of the mysterious dollar bill (which might have formed the clew to a tremendously fine detective story of San Francisco) by saying to myself sleepily: 'Seems as if a lot of people here own stock in the Hack-Driver's Trust. Pays dividends promptly, too. Wonder if—' Then I fell asleep.

King Cettiwayo was at his post the next day, and rattled my bones over the stones out to 861. He was to wait and rattle me back again when I was ready.

Azalea Adair looked paler and cleaner and frailer than she had looked on the day before. After she had signed the contract at eight cents per word she grew still paler and began to slip out of her chair. Without much trouble I managed to get her up on the antediluvian horsehair sofa and then I ran out to the sidewalk and yelled to the coffee-colored Pirate to bring a doctor. With a wisdom that I had not suspected in him, he abandoned his team and struck off up the street afoot, realizing the value of speed. In ten minutes he returned with a grave, gray-haired and capable man of medicine. In a few words (worth much less than eight cents each) I explained to him my presence in the hollow house of mystery. He bowed with stately understanding, and turned to the old Negro.

'Uncle Cæsar,' he said calmly, 'run up to my house and ask Miss Lucy to give you a cream pitcher full of fresh milk and half a tumbler of port wine. And hurry back. Don't drive—run. I want you to get back sometime this week.'

It occurred to me that Dr. Merriman also felt a distrust as to the speeding powers of the land-pirate's steeds. After Uncle Cæsar was gone, lumberingly, but swiftly, up the street, the doctor looked me over with great politeness and as much careful calculation until he had decided that I might do.

'It is only a case of insufficient nutrition,' he said. 'In other words, the result of poverty, pride, and starvation. Mrs. Caswell has many devoted friends who would be glad to aid her, but she will accept nothing except from that old Negro, Uncle Cæsar, who was once owned by her family.'

'Mrs. Caswell!' said I, in surprise. And then I looked at the contract and saw that she had signed it 'Azalea Adair Caswell.'

'I thought she was Miss Adair,' I said.

'Married to a drunken, worthless loafer, sir,' said the doctor. 'It is said that he robs her even of the small sums that her old servant contributes toward her support.'

When the milk and wine had been brought the doctor soon revived Azalea Adair. She sat up and talked of the beauty of the autumn leaves that were then in season, and their height of color. She referred lightly to her fainting seizure as the outcome of an old palpitation of the heart. Impy fanned her as she lay on the sofa. The doctor was due elsewhere, and I followed him to the door. I told him that it was within my power and intentions to make a reasonable advance of money to Azalea Adair on future contributions to the magazine, and he seemed pleased.

'By the way,' he said, 'perhaps you would like to know that you have had royalty for a coachman. Old Cæsar's grandfather was a king in Congo. Cæsar himself has royal ways, as you may have observed.'

As the doctor was moving off I heard Uncle Cæsar's voice inside: 'Did he git bofe of dem two dollars from you, Mis' Zalea?'

'Yes, Cæsar,' I heard Azalea Adair answer weakly.

And then I went in and concluded business negotiations with our contributor. I assumed the responsibility of advancing fifty dollars, putting it as a necessary formality in binding our bargain. And then Uncle Cæsar drove me back to the hotel.

Here ends all of the story as far as I can testify as a witness. The rest must be only bare statements of facts.

At about six o'clock I went out for a stroll. Uncle Cæsar was at his corner. He threw open the door of his carriage, flourished his duster, and began his depressing formula: 'Step right in, suh. Fifty cents to anywhere in the city—hack's puffickly clean, suh—jus' got back from a funeral—'

And then he recognized me. I think his eyesight was getting bad. His coat had taken on a few more faded shades of color, the twine strings were more frayed and ragged, the last remaining button—the button of yellow horn—was gone. A motley descendant of kings was Uncle Cæsar!

About two hours later I saw an excited crowd besieging the front of a drug store. In a desert where nothing happens this was manna; so I edged my way inside. On an extemporized couch of empty boxes and chairs was stretched the mortal corporeality of Major Wentworth Caswell. A doctor was testing him for the immortal ingredient. His decision was that it was conspicuous by its absence.

The erstwhile Major had been found dead on a dark street and brought by curious and ennuied citizens to the drug store. The late human being had been engaged in terrific battle—the details showed that. Loafer and reprobate though he had been, he had been also a warrior. But he had lost. His hands were yet clinched so tightly that his fingers would not be opened. The gentle citizens who had known him stood about and searched their vocabularies to find some good words, if it were possible, to speak of him. One kind-looking man said, after much thought: 'When "Cas" was about fo'teen he was one of the best spellers in school.'

While I stood there the fingers of the right hand of 'the man that was,' which hung down the side of a white pine box, relaxed, and dropped something at my feet. I covered it with one foot quietly, and a little later on I picked it up and pocketed it.

I reasoned that in his last struggle his hand must have seized that object unwittingly and held it in a death grip.

At the hotel that night the main topic of conversation, with the possible exceptions of politics and prohibition, was the demise of Major Caswell. I heard one man say to a group of listeners:

'In my opinion, gentlemen, Caswell was murdered by some of these no-account niggers for his money. He had fifty dollars this afternoon which he showed to several gen-tlemen in the hotel. When he was found the money was not on his person.'

I left the city the next morning at nine, and as the train was crossing the bridge over the Cumberland River I took out of my pocket a yellow horn overcoat button the size of a fifty-cent piece, with frayed ends of coarse twine hanging from it, and cast it out of the window into the slow muddy waters below.

I wonder what's doing in Buffalo!

1910

HENRY JAMES

1843-1916

THE ART OF FICTION

I SHOULD not have affixed so comprehensive a title to these few remarks, necessarily wanting in any completeness upon a subject the full consideration of which would carry us far, did I not seem to discover a pretext for my temerity in the interesting pamphlet lately published under this name by Mr. Walter Besant. Mr. Besant's lecture at the Royal Institution—the original form of his pamphlet—appears to indicate that many persons are interested in the art of fiction, and are not indifferent to such remarks, as those who practise it may attempt to make about it. I am therefore anxious not to lose the benefit of this favourable association, and to edge in a few words under cover of the attention which Mr. Besant is sure to have excited. There is something very encouraging in his having put into form certain of his ideas on the mystery of story-telling.

It is a proof of life and curiosity—curiosity on the part of the brotherhood of novelists as well as on the part of their readers. Only a short time ago it might have been supposed that the English novel was not what the French call *discutable*. It had no air of having a theory, a conviction, a consciousness of itself behind it—of being the expression of an artistic faith, the result of choice and comparison. I do not say it was necessarily the worse for that: it would take much more courage than I possess to intimate that the form of the novel as Dickens and Thackeray (for instance) saw it had any taint of incompleteness. It was, however, *naïf* (if I may help myself out with another French word); and evidently if it be destined to suffer in any way for having lost its *naïveté* it has now an idea of making sure of the corresponding advantages. During the period I have alluded to there was a comfortable, good-humoured feeling abroad that a novel is a novel, as a pudding is a pudding, and that our only business with it could be to swallow it. But within a year or two, for some reason or other, there have been signs of returning animation—the era of discussion would appear to have been to a certain extent opened. Art lives upon discussion, upon experiment, upon curiosity, upon variety of attempt, upon the exchange of views and the comparison of standpoints; and there is a presumption that those times when no one has anything particular to say about it, and has no reason to give for practice or preference, though they may be times of honour, are not times of development—are times, possibly even, a little of dulness. The successful application of any art is a delightful spectacle, but the theory too is interesting; and though there is a great deal of the latter without the former I suspect there has never been a genuine success that has not had a latent core of conviction. Discussion, suggestion, formulation, these things are fertilising when they are frank and sincere. Mr. Besant has set an excellent example in saying what he thinks, for his part, about the way in which fiction should be written, as well as about the way in which it should be published; for his view

f the 'art,' carried on into an appendix,
covers that too. Other labourers in the same
field will doubtless take up the argument,
they will give it the light of their experience,
and the effect will surely be to make our interest in the novel a little more what it had
for some time threatened to fail to be—a
serious, active, inquiring interest, under
protection of which this delightful study
may, in moments of confidence, venture to
say a little more what it thinks of itself.

It must take itself seriously for the public
to take it so. The old superstition about
fiction being 'wicked' has doubtless died
out in England; but the spirit of it lingers in
certain oblique regard directed toward
any story which does not more or less admit
that it is only a joke. Even the most jocular
novel feels in some degree the weight of the
proscription that was formerly directed
against literary levity: the jocularity does
not always succeed in passing for ortho-
doxy. It is still expected, though perhaps
people are ashamed to say it, that a production which is after all only a 'make-believe'
(for what else is a 'story'?) shall be in some
degree apologetic—shall renounce the pretension of attempting really to represent
life. This, of course, any sensible, wide-
awake story declines to do, for it quickly
perceives that the tolerance granted to it on
such a condition is only an attempt to stifle
it disguised in the form of generosity. The
old evangelical hostility to the novel, which
was as explicit as it was narrow, and which
regarded it as little less favourable to our
immortal part than a stage-play, was in
reality far less insulting. The only reason
for the existence of a novel is that it does attempt to represent life. When it relinquishes
this attempt, the same attempt that we see
in the canvas of the painter, it will have arrived at a very strange pass. It is not expected of the picture that it will make itself
humble in order to be forgiven; and the
analogy between the art of the painter and
the art of the novelist is, so far as I am able
to see, complete. Their inspiration is the
same, their process (allowing for the different quality of the vehicle) is the same, their
success is the same. They may learn from
each other, they may explain and sustain
each other. Their cause is the same, and the
honour of one is the honour of another. The
Mahometans think a picture an unholy

thing, but it is a long time since any Christian did, and it is therefore the more odd
that in the Christian mind the traces (dissimulated though they may be) of a suspicion of the sister art should linger to this
day. The only effectual way to lay it to rest
is to emphasise the analogy to which I just
alluded—to insist on the fact that as the picture is reality, so the novel is history. That
is the only general description (which does
it justice) that we may give of the novel.
But history also is allowed to represent life;
it is not, any more than painting, expected
to apologise. The subject-matter of fiction
is stored up likewise in documents and records, and if it will not give itself away, as
they say in California, it must speak with
assurance, with the tone of the historian.
Certain accomplished novelists have a habit
of giving themselves away which must often
bring tears to the eyes of people who take
their fiction seriously. I was lately struck, in
reading over many pages of Anthony Trollope, with his want of discretion in this
particular. In a digression, a parenthesis or
an aside, he concedes to the reader that he
and this trusting friend are only 'making believe.' He admits that the events he narrates
have not really happened, and that he can
give his narrative any turn the reader may
like best. Such a betrayal of a sacred office
seems to me, I confess, a terrible crime; it is
what I mean by the attitude of apology, and
it shocks me every whit as much in Trollope
as it would have shocked me in Gibbon or
Macaulay. It implies that the novelist is less
occupied in looking for the truth (the truth,
of course I mean, that he assumes, the
premises that we must grant him, whatever
they may be), than the historian, and in
doing so it deprives him at a stroke of all his
standing-room. To represent and illustrate
the past, the actions of men, is the task of
either writer, and the only difference that I
can see is, in proportion as he succeeds, to
the honour of the novelist, consisting as it
does in his having more difficulty in collecting his evidence, which is so far from being
purely literary. It seems to me to give him a
great character, the fact that he has at once
so much in common with the philosopher
and the painter; this double analogy is a
magnificent heritage.

It is of all this evidently that Mr. Besant
is full when he insists upon the fact that

fiction is one of the *fine* arts, deserving in its turn of all the honours and emoluments that have hitherto been reserved for the successful profession of music, poetry, painting, architecture. It is impossible to insist too much on so important a truth, and the place that Mr. Besant demands for the work of the novelist may be represented, a trifle less abstractly, by saying that he demands not only that it shall be reputed artistic, but that it shall be reputed very artistic indeed. It is excellent that he should have struck this note, for his doing so indicates that there was need of it, that his proposition may be to many people a novelty. One rubs one's eyes at the thought; but the rest of Mr. Besant's essay confirms the revelation. I suspect in truth that it would be possible to confirm it still further, and that one would not be far wrong in saying that in addition to the people to whom it has never occurred that a novel ought to be artistic, there are a great many others who, if this principle were urged upon them, would be filled with an indefinable mistrust. They would find it difficult to explain their repugnance, but it would operate strongly to put them on their guard. 'Art,' in our Protestant communities, where so many things have got so strangely twisted about, is supposed in certain circles to have some vaguely injurious effect upon those who make it an important consideration, who let it weigh in the balance. It is assumed to be opposed in some mysterious manner to morality, to amusement, to instruction. When it is embodied in the work of the painter (the sculptor is another affair!) you know what it is: it stands there before you, in the honesty of pink and green and a gilt frame; you can see the worst of it at a glance, and you can be on your guard. But when it is introduced into literature it becomes more insidious—there is danger of its hurting you before you know it. Literature should be either instructive or amusing, and there is in many minds an impression that these artistic preoccupations, the search for form, contribute to neither end, interfere indeed with both. They are too frivolous to be edifying, and too serious to be diverting; and they are moreover priggish and paradoxical and superfluous. That, I think, represents the manner in which the latent thought of many people who read novels as

an exercise in skipping would explain itself if it were to become articulate. They would argue, of course, that a novel ought to be 'good,' but they would interpret this term in a fashion of their own, which indeed would vary considerably from one critic to another. One would say that being good means representing virtuous and aspiring characters, placed in prominent positions; another would say that it depends on a 'happy ending,' on a distribution at the last of prizes, pensions, husbands, wives, babies, millions, appended paragraphs, and cheerful remarks. Another still would say that it means being full of incident and movement, so that we shall wish to jump ahead, to see who was the mysterious stranger, and if the stolen will was ever found, and shall not be distracted from this pleasure by any tiresome analysis or 'description.' But they would all agree that the 'artistic' idea would spoil some of their fun. One would hold it accountable for all the description, another would see it revealed in the absence of sympathy. Its hostility to a happy ending would be evident, and it might even in some cases render any ending at all impossible. The 'ending' of a novel is, for many persons, like that of a good dinner, a course of desert and ices, and the artist in fiction is regarded as a sort of meddlesome doctor who forbids agreeable aftertastes. It is therefore true that this conception of Mr. Besant's of the novel as a superior form encounters not only a negative but a positive indifference. It matters little that as a work of art it should really be as little or as much of its essence to supply happy endings, sympathetic characters, and an objective tone, as if it were a work of mechanics: the association of ideas, however incongruous, might easily be too much for it if an eloquent voice were not sometimes raised to call attention to the fact that it is at once as free and as serious a branch of literature as any other.

Certainly this might sometimes be doubted in presence of the enormous number of works of fiction that appeal to the credulity of our generation, for it might easily seem that there could be no great character in a commodity so quickly and easily produced. It must be admitted that good novels are much compromised by bad ones, and that the field at large suffers discredit from overcrowding. I think, however that this injury is only superficial, and that the superabundance of written fiction proves nothing against the principle itself. It has been vulgarised, like all other kinds of literature, like everything else to-day, and it has proved more than some kinds accessible to vulgarisation. But there is as much difference as there ever was between a good novel and a bad one: the bad is swept with all the daubed canvases and spoiled marble into some unvisited limbo, or infinite rubbish-yard beneath the back-windows of the world, and the good subsists and emits its light and stimulates our desire for perfection. As I shall take the liberty of making but a single criticism of Mr. Besant, whose tone is so full of the love of his art, I may as well have done with it at once. He seems to me to mistake in attempting to say so definitely beforehand what sort of an affair the good novel will be. To indicate the danger of such an error as that has been the purpose of these few pages; to suggest that certain traditions on the subject, applied *a priori*, have already had much to answer for, and that the good health of an art which undertakes so immediately to reproduce life must demand that it be perfectly free. It lives upon exercise, and the very meaning of exercise is freedom. The only obligation to which in advance we may hold a novel, without incurring the accusation of being arbitrary, is that it be interesting. That general responsibility rests upon it, but it is the only one I can think of. The ways in which it is at liberty to accomplish this result (of interesting us) strike me as innumerable, and such as can only suffer from being marked out or fenced in by prescription. They are as various as the temperament of man, and they are successful in proportion as they reveal a particular mind, different from others. A novel is in its broadest definition a personal, a direct impression of life: that, to begin with, constitutes its value, which is greater or less according to the intensity of the impression. But there will be no intensity at all, and therefore no value, unless there is freedom to feel and say. The tracing of a line to be followed, of a tone to be taken, of a form to be filled out, is a limitation of that freedom and a suppression of the very thing that we are most curious about. The form, it seems to me, is to be appreciated after the fact:

then the author's choice has been made, his standard has been indicated; then we can follow lines and directions and compare tones and resemblances. Then in a word we can enjoy one of the most charming of pleasures, we can estimate quality, we can apply the test of execution. The execution belongs to the author alone; it is what is most personal to him, and we measure him by that. The advantage, the luxury, as well as the torment and responsibility of the novelist, is that there is no limit to what he may attempt as an executant—no limit to his possible experiments, efforts, discoveries, successes. Here it is especially that he works, step by step, like his brother of the brush, of whom we may always say that he has painted his picture in a manner best known to himself. His manner is his secret, not necessarily a jealous one. He cannot disclose it as a general thing if he would; he would be at a loss to teach it to others. I say this with a due recollection of having insisted on the community of method of the artist who paints a picture and the artist who writes a novel. The painter *is* able to teach the rudiments of his practice, and it is possible, from the study of good work (granted the aptitude), both to learn how to paint and to learn how to write. Yet it remains true, without injury to the *rapprochement*, that the literary artist would be obliged to say to his pupil much more than the other, 'Ah, well, you must do it as you can!' It is a question of degree, a matter of delicacy. If there are exact sciences, there are also exact arts, and the grammar of painting is so much more definite that it makes the difference.

I ought to add, however, that if Mr. Besant says at the beginning of his essay that the 'laws of fiction may be laid down and taught with as much precision and exactness as the laws of harmony, perspective, and proportion,' he mitigates what might appear to be an extravagance by applying his remark to 'general' laws, and by expressing most of these rules in a manner with which it would certainly be unaccommodating to disagree. That the novelist must write from his experience, that his 'characters must be real and such as might be met with in actual life;' that 'a young lady brought up in a quiet country village should avoid descriptions of garrison life,' and 'a writer whose friends and personal experiences belong to the lower middle-class should carefully avoid introducing his characters into society'; that one should enter one's notes in a common-place book; that one's figures should be clear in outline; that making them clear by some trick of speech or of carriage is a bad method, and 'describing them at length' is a worse one; that English Fiction should have a 'conscious moral purpose'; that 'it is almost impossible to estimate too highly the value of careful workmanship—that is, of style'; that 'the most important point of all is the story,' that 'the story is everything': these are principles with most of which it is surely impossible not to sympathise. That remark about the lower middle-class writer and his knowing his place is perhaps rather chilling; but for the rest I should find it difficult to dissent from any one of these recommendations. At the same time, I should find it difficult positively to assent to them, with the exception, perhaps, of the injunction as to entering one's notes in a common-place book. They scarcely seem to me to have the quality that Mr. Besant attributes to the rules of the novelist —the 'precision and exactness' of 'the laws of harmony, perspective, and proportion.' They are suggestive, they are even inspiring, but they are not exact, though they are doubtless as much so as the case admits of: which is a proof of that liberty of interpretation for which I just contended. For the value of these different injunctions—so beautiful and so vague—is wholly in the meaning one attaches to them. The characters, the situation, which strike one as real will be those that touch and interest one most, but the measure of reality is very difficult to fix. The reality of Don Quixote or of Mr. Micawber is a very delicate shade; it is a reality so coloured by the author's vision that, vivid as it may be, one would hesitate to propose it as a model: one would expose one's self to some very embarrassing questions on the part of a pupil. It goes without saying that you will not write a good novel unless you possess the sense of reality; but it will be difficult to give you a recipe for calling that sense into being. Humanity is immense, and reality has a myriad forms; the most one can affirm is that some of the flowers of fiction have the odour of

it, and others have not; as for telling you in advance how your nosegay should be composed, that is another affair. It is equally excellent and inconclusive to say that one must write from experience; to our supposititious aspirant such a declaration might savour of mockery. What kind of experience is intended, and where does it begin and end? Experience is never limited, and it is never complete; it is an immense sensibility, a kind of huge spiderweb of the finest silken threads suspended in the chamber of consciousness, and catching every air-borne particle in its tissue. It is the very atmosphere of the mind; and when the mind is imaginative—much more when it happens to be that of a man of genius—it takes to itself the faintest hints of life, it converts the very pulses of the air into revelations. The young lady living in a village has only to be a damsel upon whom nothing is lost to make it quite unfair (as it seems to me) to declare to her that she shall have nothing to say about the military. Greater miracles have been seen than that, imagination assisting, she should speak the truth about some of these gentlemen. I remember an English novelist, a woman of genius, telling me that she was much commended for the impression she had managed to give in one of her tales of the nature and way of life of the French Protestant youth. She had been asked where she learned so much about this recondite being, she had been congratulated on her peculiar opportunities. These opportunities consisted in her having once, in Paris, as she ascended a staircase, passed an open door where, in the household of a *pasteur*, some of the young Protestants were seated at table round a finished meal. The glimpse made a picture; it lasted only a moment, but that moment was experience. She had got her direct personal impression, and she turned out her type. She knew what youth was, and what Protestantism; she also had the advantage of having seen what it was to be French, so that she converted these ideas into a concrete image and produced a reality. Above all, however, she was blessed with the faculty which when you give it an inch takes an ell, and which for the artist is a much greater source of strength than any accident of residence or of place in the social scale. The power to guess the unseen from the seen, to trace the implication of things, to judge the whole piece by the pattern, the condition of feeling life in general so completely that you are well on your way to knowing any particular corner of it—this cluster of gifts may almost be said to constitute experience, and they occur in country and in town, and in the most differing stages of education. If experience consists of impressions, it may be said that impressions *are* experience, just as (have we not seen it?) they are the very air we breathe. Therefore, if I should certainly say to a novice, 'Write from experience and experience only,' I should feel that this was rather a tantalising monition if I were not careful immediately to add, 'Try to be one of the people on whom nothing is lost!'

I am far from intending by this to minimise the importance of exactness—of truth of detail. One can speak best from one's own taste, and I may therefore venture to say that the air of reality (solidity of specification) seems to me to be the supreme virtue of a novel—the merit on which all its other merits (including that conscious moral purpose of which Mr. Besant speaks) helplessly and submissively depend. If it be not there they are all as nothing, and if these be there, they owe their effect to the success with which the author has produced the illusion of life. The cultivation of this success, the study of this exquisite process, form, to my taste, the beginning and the end of the art of the novelist. They are his inspiration, his despair, his reward, his torment, his delight. It is here in very truth that he competes with life; it is here that he competes with his brother the painter in *his* attempt to render the look of things, the look that conveys their meaning, to catch the colour, the relief, the expression, the surface, the substance of the human spectacle. It is in regard to this that Mr. Besant is well inspired when he bids him take notes. He cannot possibly take too many, he cannot possibly take enough. All life solicits him, and to 'render' the simplest surface, to produce the most momentary illusion, is a very complicated business. His case would be easier, and the rule would be more exact, if Mr. Besant had been able to tell him what notes to take. But this, I fear, he can never learn in any manual; it is the business of his life. He has to take a great many in order to select a few, he has to work them up as he

can, and even the guides and philosophers who might have most to say to him must leave him alone when it comes to the application of precepts, as we leave the painter in communion with his palette. That his characters 'must be clear in outline,' as Mr. Besant says—he feels that down to his boots; but how he shall make them so is a secret between his good angel and himself. It would be absurdly simple if he could be taught that a great deal of 'description' would make them so, or that on the contrary the absence of description and the cultivation of dialogue, or the absence of dialogue and the multiplication of 'incident,' would rescue him from his difficulties. Nothing, for instance, is more possible than that he be of a turn of mind for which this odd, literal opposition of description and dialogue, incident and description, has little meaning and light. People often talk of these things as if they had a kind of internecine distinctness, instead of melting into each other at every breath, and being intimately associated parts of one general effort of expression. I cannot imagine composition existing in a series of blocks, nor conceive, in any novel worth discussing at all, of a passage of description that is not in its intention narrative, a passage of dialogue that is not in its intention descriptive, a touch of truth of any sort that does not partake of the nature of incident, or an incident that derives its interest from any other source than the general and only source of the success of a work of art—that of being illustrative. A novel is a living thing, all one and continuous, like any other organism, and in proportion as it lives will it be found, I think, that in each of the parts there is something of each of the other parts. The critic who over the close texture of a finished work shall pretend to trace a geography of items will mark some frontiers as artificial, I fear, as any that have been known to history. There is an old-fashioned distinction between the novel of character and the novel of incident which must have cost many a smile to the intending fabulist who was keen about his work. It appears to me as little to the point as the equally celebrated distinction between the novel and the romance—to answer as little to any reality. There are bad novels and good novels, as there are bad pictures and good pictures;

but that is the only distinction in which I see any meaning, and I can as little imagine speaking of a novel of character as I can imagine speaking of a picture of character. When one says picture one says of character, when one says novel one says of incident, and the terms may be transposed at will. What is character but the determination of incident? What is incident but the illustration of character? What is either a picture or a novel that is *not* of character? What else do we seek in it and find in it? It is an incident for a woman to stand up with her hand resting on a table and look out at you in a certain way; or if it be not an incident I think it will be hard to say what it is. At the same time it is an expression of character. If you say you don't see it (character in *that* —*allons donc!*), this is exactly what the artist who has reasons of his own for thinking he *does* see it undertakes to show you. When a young man makes up his mind that he has not faith enough after all to enter the church as he intended, that is an incident, though you may not hurry to the end of the chapter to see whether perhaps he doesn't change once more. I do not say that these are extraordinary or startling incidents. I do not pretend to estimate the degree of interest proceeding from them, for this will depend upon the skill of the painter. It sounds almost puerile to say that some incidents are intrinsically much more important than others, and I need not take this precaution after having professed my sympathy for the major ones in remarking that the only classification of the novel that I can understand is into that which has life and that which has it not.

The novel and the romance, the novel of incident and that of character—these clumsy separations appear to me to have been made by critics and readers for their own convenience, and to help them out of some of their occasional queer predicaments, but to have little reality or interest for the producer, from whose point of view it is of course that we are attempting to consider the art of fiction. The case is the same with another shadowy category which Mr. Besant apparently is disposed to set up— that of the 'modern English novel'; unless indeed it be that in this matter he has fallen into an accidental confusion of standpoints. It is not quite clear whether he intends the remarks in which he alludes to it to be didactic or historical. It is as difficult to suppose a person intending to write a modern English as to suppose him writing an ancient English novel: that is a label which begs the question. One writes the novel, one paints the picture, of one's language and of one's time, and calling it modern English will not, alas! make the difficult task any easier. No more, unfortunately, will calling this or that work of one's fellow-artist a romance—unless it be, of course, simply for the pleasantness of the thing, as for instance when Hawthorne gave this heading to his story of *Blithedale*. The French, who have brought the theory of fiction to remarkable completeness, have but one name for the novel, and have not attempted smaller things in it, that I can see, for that. I can think of no obligation to which the 'romancer' would not be held equally with the novelist; the standard of execution is equally high for each. Of course it is of execution that we are talking—that being the only point of a novel that is open to contention. This is perhaps too often lost sight of, only to produce interminable confusions and cross-purposes. We must grant the artist his subject, his idea, his *donnée:* our criticism is applied only to what he makes of it. Naturally I do not mean that we are bound to like it or find it interesting: in case we do not our course is perfectly simple— to let it alone. We may believe that of a certain idea even the most sincere novelist can make nothing at all, and the event may perfectly justify our belief; but the failure will have been a failure to execute, and it is in the execution that the fatal weakness is recorded. If we pretend to respect the artist at all, we must allow him his freedom of choice, in the face, in particular cases, of innumerable presumptions that the choice will not fructify. Art derives a considerable part of its beneficial exercise from flying in the face of presumptions, and some of the most interesting experiments of which it is capable are hidden in the bosom of common things. Gustave Flaubert has written a story about the devotion of a servant-girl to a parrot, and the production, highly finished as it is, cannot on the whole be called a success. We are perfectly free to find it flat, but I think it might have been interesting; and I, for my part, am extremely glad

he should have written it; it is a contribution to our knowledge of what can be done
—or what cannot. Ivan Turgénieff has
written a tale about a deaf and dumb serf
and a lap-dog, and the thing is touching,
loving, a little masterpiece. He struck the
note of life where Gustave Flaubert missed
it—he flew in the face of a presumption and
achieved a victory.

Nothing, of course, will ever take the
place of the good old fashion of 'liking' a
work of art or not liking it: the most improved criticism will not abolish that primitive, that ultimate test. I mention this to
guard myself from the accusation of intimating that the idea, the subject, of a novel
or a picture, does not matter. It matters, to
my sense, in the highest degree, and if I
might put up a prayer it would be that artists should select none but the richest.
Some, as I have already hastened to admit,
are much more remunerative than others,
and it would be a world happily arranged
in which persons intending to treat them
should be exempt from confusions and mistakes. This fortunate condition will arrive
only, I fear, on the same day that critics become purged from error. Meanwhile, I repeat, we do not judge the artist with fairness
unless we say to him, 'Oh, I grant you your
starting-point, because if I did not I should
seem to prescribe to you, and heaven forbid
I should take that responsibility. If I pretend to tell you what you must not take,
you will call upon me to tell you then what
you must take; in which case I shall be
prettily caught. Moreover, it isn't till I
have accepted your data that I can begin to
measure you. I have the standard, the
pitch; I have no right to tamper with your
flute and then criticise your music. Of
course I may not care for your idea at all; I
may think it silly, or stale, or unclean; in
which case I wash my hands of you altogether. I may content myself with believing
that you will not have succeeded in being
interesting, but I shall, of course, not attempt to demonstrate it, and you will be as
indifferent to me as I am to you. I needn't
remind you that there are all sorts of tastes:
who can know it better? Some people, for
excellent reasons, don't like to read about
carpenters; others, for reasons even better,
don't like to read about courtesans. Many
object to Americans. Others (I believe they
are mainly editors and publishers) won't
look at Italians. Some readers don't like
quiet subjects; others don't like bustling
ones. Some enjoy a complete illusion, others
the consciousness of large concessions.
They choose their novels accordingly, and
if they don't care about your idea they
won't, *a fortiori*, care about your treatment.'

So that it comes back very quickly, as I
have said, to the liking: in spite of M. Zola,
who reasons less powerfully than he represents, and who will not reconcile himself to
this absoluteness of taste, thinking that
there are certain things that people ought to
like, and that they can be made to like. I am
quite at a loss to imagine anything (at any
rate in this matter of fiction) that people
ought to like or to dislike. Selection will be
sure to take care of itself, for it has a constant motive behind it. That motive is simply experience. As people feel life, so they
will feel the art that is most closely related
to it. This closeness of relation is what we
should never forget in talking of the effort
of the novel. Many people speak of it as a
factitious, artificial form, a product of ingenuity, the business of which is to alter
and arrange the things that surround us, to
translate them into conventional, traditional
moulds. This, however, is a view of the
matter which carries us but a very short
way, condemns the art to an eternal repetition of a few familiar *clichés*, cuts short its
development, and leads us straight up to a
dead wall. Catching the very note and trick,
the strange irregular rhythm of life, that is
the attempt whose strenuous force keeps
Fiction upon her feet. In proportion as in
what she offers us we see life *without* rearrangement do we feel that we are touching the truth; in proportion as we see it *with*
rearrangement do we feel that we are being
put off with a substitute, a compromise and
convention. It is not uncommon to hear an
extraordinary assurance of remark in regard
to this matter of rearranging, which is often
spoken of as if it were the last word of art.
Mr. Besant seems to me in danger of falling
into the great error with his rather unguarded talk about 'selection.' Art is essentially selection, but it is a selection whose
main care is to be typical, to be inclusive.
For many people art means rose-coloured
window-panes, and selection means picking
a bouquet for Mrs. Grundy. They will tell

you glibly that artistic considerations have nothing to do with the disagreeable, with the ugly; they will rattle off shallow commonplaces about the province of art and the limits of art till you are moved to some wonder in return as to the province and the limits of ignorance. It appears to me that no one can ever have made a seriously artistic attempt without becoming conscious of an immense increase—a kind of revelation—of freedom. One perceives in that case—by the light of a heavenly ray—that the province of art is all life, all feeling, all observation, all vision. As Mr. Besant so justly intimates, it is all experience. That is a sufficient answer to those who maintain that it must not touch the sad things of life, who stick into its divine unconscious bosom little prohibitory inscriptions on the end of sticks such as we see in public gardens—'It is forbidden to walk on the grass; it is forbidden to touch the flowers; it is not allowed to introduce dogs or to remain after dark; it is requested to keep to the right.' The young aspirant in the line of fiction whom we continue to imagine will do nothing without taste, for in that case his freedom would be of little use to him; but the first advantage of his taste will be to reveal to him the absurdity of the little sticks and tickets. If he have taste, I must add, of course he will have ingenuity, and my disrespectful reference to that quality just now was not meant to imply that it is useless in fiction. But it is only a secondary aid; the first is a capacity for receiving straight impressions.

Mr. Besant has some remarks on the question of 'the story' which I shall not attempt to criticise, though they seem to me to contain a singular ambiguity, because I do not think I understand them. I cannot see what is meant by talking as if there were a part of a novel which is the story and part of it which for mystical reasons is not—unless indeed the distinction be made in a sense in which it is difficult to suppose that any one should attempt to convey anything. 'The story,' if it represents anything, represents the subject, the idea, the *donnée* of the novel; and there is surely no 'school'—Mr. Besant speaks of a school—which urges that a novel should be all treatment and no subject. There must assuredly be something to treat; every school is intimately conscious of that. This sense of the story being the idea, the starting-point, of the novel, is the only one that I see in which it can be spoken of as something different from its organic whole; and since in proportion as the work is successful the idea permeates and penetrates it, informs and animates it, so that every word and every punctuation-point contribute directly to the expression, in that proportion do we lose our sense of the story being a blade which may be drawn more or less out of its sheath. The story and the novel, the idea and the form, are the needle and thread, and I never heard of a guild of tailors who recommended the use of the thread without the needle, or the needle without the thread. Mr. Besant is not the only critic who may be observed to have spoken as if there were certain things in life which constitute stories, and certain others which do not. I find the same odd implication in an entertaining article in the *Pall Mall Gazette*, devoted, as it happens, to Mr. Besant's lecture. 'The story is the thing!' says this graceful writer, as if with a tone of opposition to some other idea. I should think it was, as every painter who, as the time for 'sending in' his picture looms in the distance, finds himself still in quest of a subject—as every belated artist not fixed about his theme will heartily agree. There are some subjects which speak to us and others which do not, but he would be a clever man who should undertake to give a rule—an index expurgatorius—by which the story and the no-story should be known apart. It is impossible (to me at least) to imagine any such rule which shall not be altogether arbitrary. The writer in the *Pall Mall* opposes the delightful (as I suppose) novel of *Margot la Balafrée* to certain tales in which 'Bostonian nymphs' appear to have 'rejected English dukes for psychological reasons.' I am not acquainted with the romance just designated, and can scarcely forgive the *Pall Mall* critic for not mentioning the name of the author, but the title appears to refer to a lady who may have received a scar in some heroic adventure. I am inconsolable at not being acquainted with this episode, but am utterly at a loss to see why it is a story when the rejection (or acceptance) of a duke is not, and why a reason, psychological or other, is not a subject when a cicatrix is. They are all particles of the multitudinous life with which the novel deals, and surely no dogma which pretends to make it lawful to touch the one and unlawful to touch the other will stand for a moment on its feet. It is the special picture that must stand or fall, according as it seem to possess truth or to lack it. Mr. Besant does not, to my sense, light up the subject by intimating that a story must, under penalty of not being a story, consist of 'adventures.' Why of adventures more than of green spectacles? He mentions a category of impossible things, and among them he places 'fiction without adventure.' Why without adventure, more than without matrimony, or celibacy, or parturition, or cholera, or hydropathy, or Jansenism? This seems to me to bring the novel back to the hapless little *rôle* of being an artificial, ingenious thing—bring it down from its large, free character of an immense and exquisite correspondence with life. And what *is* adventure, when it comes to that, and by what sign is the listening pupil to recognise it? It is an adventure—an immense one— for me to write this little article; and for a Bostonian nymph to reject an English duke is an adventure only less stirring, I should say, than for an English duke to be rejected by a Bostonian nymph. I see dramas within dramas in that, and innumerable points of view. A psychological reason is, to my imagination, an object adorably pictorial; to catch the tint of its complexion—I feel as if that idea might inspire one to Titianesque efforts. There are few things more exciting to me, in short, than a psychological reason, and yet, I protest, the novel seems to me the most magnificent form of art. I have just been reading, at the same time, the delightful story of *Treasure Island*, by Mr. Robert Louis Stevenson and, in a manner less consecutive, the last tale from M. Edmond de Goncourt, which is entitled *Chérie*. One of these works treats of murders, mysteries, islands of dreadful renown, hairbreadth escapes, miraculous coincidences and buried doubloons. The other treats of a little French girl who lived in a fine house in Paris, and died of wounded sensibility because no one would marry her. I call *Treasure Island* delightful, because it appears to me to have succeeded wonderfully in what it attempts; and I venture to bestow no epithet upon *Chérie*, which strikes me as having failed deplorably in what it attempts—

that is in tracing the development of the moral consciousness of a child. But one of these productions strikes me as exactly as much of a novel as the other, and as having a 'story' quite as much. The moral consciousness of a child is as much a part of life as the islands of the Spanish Main, and the one sort of geography seems to me to have those 'surprises' of which Mr. Besant speaks quite as much as the other. For myself (since it comes back in the last resort, as I say, to the preference of the individual), the picture of the child's experience has the advantage that I can at successive steps (an immense luxury, near to the 'sensual pleasure' of which Mr. Besant's critic in the *Pall Mall* speaks) say Yes or No, as it may be, to what the artist puts before me. I have been a child in fact, but I have been on a quest for a buried treasure only in supposition, and it is a simple accident that with M. de Goncourt I should have for the most part to say No. With George Eliot, when she painted that country with a far other intelligence, I always said Yes.

The most interesting part of Mr. Besant's lecture is unfortunately the briefest passage —his very cursory allusion to the 'conscious moral purpose' of the novel. Here again it is not very clear whether he be recording a fact or laying down a principle; it is a great pity that in the latter case he should not have developed his idea. This branch of the subject is of immense importance, and Mr. Besant's few words point to considerations of the widest reach, not to be lightly disposed of. He will have treated the art of fiction but superficially who is not prepared to go every inch of the way that these considerations will carry him. It is for this reason that at the beginning of these remarks I was careful to notify the reader that my reflections on so large a theme have no pretension to be exhaustive. Like Mr. Besant, I have left the question of the morality of the novel till the last, and at the last I find I have used up my space. It is a question surrounded with difficulties, as witness the very first that meets us, in the form of a definite question, on the threshold. Vagueness, in such a discussion, is fatal, and what is the meaning of your morality and your conscious moral purpose? Will you not define your terms and explain how (a novel being a picture) a picture can be either moral or immoral? You wish to paint a moral picture or carve a moral statue: will you not tell us how you would set about it? We are discussing the Art of Fiction; questions of art are questions (in the widest sense) of execution; questions of morality are quite another affair, and will you not let us see how it is that you find it so easy to mix them up? These things are so clear to Mr. Besant that he has deduced from them a law which he sees embodied in English Fiction, and which is 'a truly admirable thing and a great cause for congratulation.' It is a great cause for congratulation indeed when such thorny problems become as smooth as silk. I may add that in so far as Mr. Besant perceives that in point of fact English Fiction has addressed itself preponderantly to these delicate questions he will appear to many people to have made a vain discovery. They will have been positively struck, on the contrary, with the moral timidity of the usual English novelist; with his (or with her) aversion to face the difficulties with which on every side the treatment of reality bristles. He is apt to be extremely shy (whereas the picture that Mr. Besant draws is a picture of boldness), and the sign of his work, for the most part, is a cautious silence on certain subjects. In the English novel (by which of course I mean the American as well), more than in any other, there is a traditional difference between that which people know and that which they agree to admit that they know, that which they see and that which they speak of, that which they feel to a part of life and that which they allow to enter into literature. There is the great difference, in short, between what they talk of in conversation and what they talk of in print. The essence of moral energy is to survey the whole field, and I should directly reverse Mr. Besant's remark and say not that the English novel has a purpose, but that it has a diffidence. To what degree a purpose in a work of art is a source of corruption I shall not attempt to inquire; the one that seems to me least dangerous is the purpose of making a perfect work. As for our novel, I may say lastly on this score that as we find it in England to-day it strikes me as addressed in a large degree to 'young people,' and that this in itself constitutes a presumption that it will be rather shy. There are certain things which it is generally agreed not to

discuss, not even to mention, before young people. That is very well, but the absence of discussion is not a symptom of the moral passion. The purpose of the English novel —'a truly admirable thing, and a great cause for congratulation'—strikes me therefore as rather negative.

There is one point at which the moral sense and the artistic sense lie very near together; that is in the light of the very obvious truth that the deepest quality of a work of art will always be the quality of the mind of the producer. In proportion as that intelligence is fine will the novel, the picture, the statue partake of the substance of beauty and truth. To be constituted of such elements is, to my vision, to have purpose enough. No good novel will ever proceed from a superficial mind; that seems to me an axiom which, for the artist in fiction, will cover all needful moral ground: if the youthful aspirant take it to heart it will illuminate for him many of the mysteries of 'purpose.' There are many other useful things that might be said to him, but I have come to the end of my article, and can only touch them as I pass. The critic in the *Pall Mall Gazette*, whom I have already quoted, draws attention to the danger, in speaking of the art of fiction, of generalising. The danger that he has in mind is rather, I imagine, that of particularising, for there are some comprehensive remarks which, in addition to those embodied in Mr. Besant's suggestive lecture, might without fear of misleading him be addressed to the ingenuous student. I should remind him first of the magnificence of the form that is open to him, which offers to sight so few restrictions and such innumerable opportunities. The other arts, in comparison, appear confined and hampered; the various conditions under which they are exercised are so rigid and definite. But the only condition that I can think of attaching to the composition of the novel is, as I have already said, that it be sincere. This freedom is a splendid privilege, and the first lesson of the young novelist is to learn to be worthy of it. 'Enjoy it as it deserves,' I should say to him; 'take possession of it, explore it to its utmost extent, publish it, rejoice in it. All life belongs to you, and do not listen either to those who would shut you up into corners of it and tell you that it is only here and there that art inhabits, or to those who would persuade you that this heavenly messenger wings her way outside of life altogether, breathing a super-fine air, and turning away her head from the truth of things. There is no impression of life, no manner of seeing it and feeling it, to which the plan of the novelist may not offer a place; you have only to remember that talents so dissimilar as those of Alexandre Dumas and Jane Austen, Charles Dickens and Gustave Flaubert have worked in this field with equal glory. Do not think too much about optimism and pessimism; try and catch the colour of life itself. In France to-day we see a prodigious effort (that of Emile Zola, to whose solid and serious work no explorer of the capacity of the novel can allude without respect), we see an ex-traordinary effort, vitiated by a spirit of pessimism on a narrow basis. M. Zola is magnificent, but he strikes an English reader as ignorant; he has an air of working in the dark; if he had as much light as energy, his results would be of the highest value. As for the aberrations of a shallow optimism, the ground (of English fiction especially) is strewn with their brittle particles as with broken glass. If you must indulge in conclusions, let them have the taste of a wide knowledge. Remember that your first duty is to be as complete as pos-sible—to make as perfect a work. Be gen-erous and delicate and pursue the prize.'

1884

CRAPY CORNELIA

THREE times within a quarter of an hour—shifting the while his posture on his chair of contemplation—had he looked at his watch as for its final sharp hint that he should de-cide, that he should get up. His seat was one of a group fairly sequestered, unoccupied save for his own presence, and from where he lingered he looked off at a stretch of lawn freshened by recent April showers and on which sundry small children were at play. The trees, the shrubs, the plants, every stem and twig just ruffled as by the first touch of the light finger of the relenting year, struck him as standing still in the blest hope of more of the same caress; the quarter about him held its breath after the fashion of the child who waits with the rigour of an open mouth and shut eyes for the promised

sensible effect of his having been good. So, in the windless, sun-warmed air of the beautiful afternoon, the Park of the winter's end had struck White-Mason as waiting; even New York, under such an impression, was 'good,' good enough—for *him*; its very sounds were faint, were almost sweet, as they reached him from so seemingly far be-yond the wooded horizon that formed the remoter limit of his large shallow glade. The tones of the frolic infants ceased to be non-descript and harsh—were in fact almost as fresh and decent as the frilled and puckered and ribboned garb of the little girls, which had always a way, in those parts, of so por-tentously flaunting the daughters of the strange native—that is of the overwhelm-ingly alien—populace at him.

Not that these things in particular were his matter of meditation now; he had wanted, at the end of his walk, to sit apart a little and think—and had been doing that for twenty minutes, even though as yet to no break in the charm of procrastination. But he had looked without seeing and lis-tened without hearing: all that had been positive for him was that he hadn't failed vaguely to feel. He had felt in the first place, and he continued to feel—yes, at forty-eight quite as much as at any point of the supposed reign of younger intensities—the great spirit of the air, the fine sense of the season, the supreme appeal of Nature, he might have said, to his time of life; quite as if she, easy, indulgent, indifferent, cyni-cal Power, were offering him the last chance it would rest with his wit or his blood to embrace. Then with that he had been en-tertaining, to the point and with the pro-longed consequence of accepted immobili-zation, the certitude that if he did call on Mrs. Worthingham and find her at home he couldn't in justice to himself not put to her the question that had lapsed the other time, the last time, through the irritating and persistent, even if accidental, presence of others. What friends she had—the people who so stupidly, so wantonly stuck! If they *should*, he and she, come to an un-derstanding, that would presumably have to include certain members of her singu-larly ill-composed circle, in whom it was incredible to him that he should ever take an interest. This defeat, to do himself justice—he had bent rather predominantly on *that*, you see; ideal justice to *her*, with her possible conception of what it should consist of, being another and quite a different matter—he had had the fact of the Sunday afternoon to thank for; she didn't 'keep' that day for him, since they hadn't, up to now, quite begun to cultivate the appointment or assignation founded on explicit sacrifices. He might at any rate look to find this pleasant practical Wednesday— should he indeed, at his actual rate, stay it before it ebbed—more liberally and intendingly given him.

The sound he at last most wittingly distinguished in his nook was the single deep note of half-past five borne to him from some high-perched public clock. He finally got up with the sense that the time from then on *ought* at least to be felt as sacred to him. At this juncture it was—while he stood there shaking his garments, settling his hat, his necktie, his shirt-cuffs, fixing the high polish of his fine shoes as if for some reflection in it of his straight and spare and grizzled, his refined and trimmed and dressed, his altogether distinguished person, that of a gentleman abundantly settled, but of a bachelor markedly nervous—at this crisis it was, doubtless, that he at once most measured and least resented his predicament. If he should go he would almost to a certainty find her, and if he should find her he would almost to a certainty come to the point. He wouldn't put it off again—there was that high consideration for him of justice at least to himself. He had never yet denied himself anything so apparently fraught with possibilities as the idea of proposing to Mrs. Worthingham—never yet, in other words, denied himself anything he had so distinctly wanted to do; and the results of that wisdom had remained for him precisely the precious parts of experience. Counting only the offers of his honourable hand, these had been on three remembered occasions at least the consequence of an impulse as sharp and a self-respect as reasoned; a self-respect that hadn't in the least suffered, moreover, from the failure of each appeal. He had been met in the three cases—the only one she at all compared with his present case—by the frank confession that he didn't somehow, charming as he was, cause himself to be superstitiously believed in; and the lapse of life, afterward, had cleared up many doubts.

It *wouldn't* have done, he eventually, he lucidly saw, each time he had been refused; and the candour of his nature was such that he could live to think of these very passages as a proof of how right he had been—right, that is, to have put himself forward always, by the happiest instinct, only in impossible conditions. He had the happy consciousness of having exposed the important question to the crucial test, and of having escaped, by that persistent logic, a grave mistake. What better proof of his escape than the fact that he was now free to renew the all-interesting inquiry, and should be exactly, about to do so in different and better conditions? The conditions were better by as much more—as much more of his career and character, of his situation, his reputation he could even have called it, of his knowledge of life, of his somewhat extended means, of his possibly augmented charm, of his certainly improved mind and temper—as was involved in the actual impending settlement. Once he had got into motion, once he had crossed the Park and passed out of it, entering, with very little space to traverse, one of the short new streets that abutted on its east side, his step became that of a man young enough to find confidence, quite to find felicity, in the sense, in almost any sense, of action. He could still enjoy almost anything, absolutely an unpleasant thing, in default of a better, that might still remind him he wasn't so old. The standing newness of everything about him would, it was true, have weakened this cheer by too much presuming on it; Mrs. Worthingham's house, before which he stopped, had that gloss of new money, that glare of a piece fresh from the mint and ringing for the first time on any counter, which seems to claim for it, in any transaction, something more than the 'face' value.

This could but be yet more the case for the impression of the observer introduced and committed. On our friend's part I mean, after his admission and while still in the hall, the sense of the general shining immediacy, of the still unhushed clamour of the shock, was perhaps stronger than he had ever known it. That broke out from every corner as the high pitch of interest, and with a candour that—no, certainly—he had never seen equalled; every particular

pensive object shrieking at him in its art-
ss pride that it had just 'come home.' He
et the whole vision with something of the
imace produced on persons without gog-
es by the passage from a shelter to a
inding light; and if he had—by a perfectly
ossible chance—been 'snap-shotted' on
e spot, would have struck you as showing
r his first tribute to the temple of Mrs.
orthingham's charming presence a scowl
most of anguish. He wasn't constitution-
ly, it may at once be explained for him, a
ggled person; and he was condemned, in
ew York, to this frequent violence of
ansition—having to reckon with it when-
er he went out, as who should say, from
mself. The high pitch of interest, to his
ste, was the pitch of history, the pitch of
quired and earned suggestion, the pitch
association, in a word; so that he lived by
eference, incontestably, if not in a rich
oom, which would have been beyond his
eans and spirits, at least amid objects and
ages that confessed to the tone of time.
He had ever felt that an indispensable
esence—with a need of it moreover that
terfered at no point with his gentle habit,
t to say his subtle art, of drawing out
nat was left him of his youth, of thinly
d thriftily spreading the rest of that
oicest jam-pot of the cupboard of con-
iousness over the remainder of a slice of
e still possibly thick enough to bear it; or
other words of moving the melancholy
nits, the significant signs, constantly a lit-
e further on, very much as property-
arks or staked boundaries are sometimes
althily shifted at night. He positively
erished in fact, as against the too invet-
ate gesture of distressfully guarding his
eballs—so many New York aspects
emed to keep him at it—an ideal of ad-
sted appreciation, of courageous curios-
, of fairly letting the world about him, a
orld of constant breathless renewals and
erciless substitutions, make its flaring as-
ult on its own inordinate terms. Newness
s value in the piece—for the acquisitor,
at least sometimes might be, even though
e act of 'blowing' hard, the act marking a
ated freshness of arrival, or other form of
uption, could never minister to the peace
those already and long on the field; and
is if only because maturer tone was after
most appreciable and most consoling

when one staggered back to it, wounded,
bleeding, blinded, from the riot of the raw
—or, to put the whole experience more
prettily, no doubt, from excesses of light.

II

If he went in, however, with something
of his more or less inevitable scowl, there
were really, at the moment, two rather
valid reasons for screened observation; the
first of these being that the whole place
seemed to reflect as never before the lustre
of Mrs. Worthingham's own polished and
prosperous little person—to smile, it struck
him, with her smile, to twinkle not only
with the gleam of her lovely teeth, but with
that of all her rings and brooches and ban-
gles and other gewgaws, to curl and spas-
modically cluster as in emulation of her
charming complicated yellow tresses, to
surround the most animated of pink-and-
white, of ruffled and ribboned, of frilled
and festooned Dresden china shepherdesses
with exactly the right system of rococo
curves and convolutions and other flour-
ishes, a perfect bower of painted and gilded
and moulded conceits. The second ground
of this immediate impression of scenic extravagance, almost as if the curtain rose for
him to the first act of some small and ex-
pensively mounted comic opera, was that
she hadn't, after all, awaited him in fond
singleness, but had again just a trifle incon-
siderately exposed him to the drawback of
having to reckon, for whatever design he
might amiably entertain, with the presence
of a third and quite superfluous person, a
small black insignificant but none the less
oppressive stranger. It was odd how, on the
instant, the little lady engaged with her did
affect him as comparatively black—very
much as if that had absolutely, in such a
medium, to be the graceless appearance of
any item not positively of some fresh shade
of a light colour or of some pretty pretension to a charming twist. Any witness of
their meeting, his hostess should surely
have felt, would have been a false note in
the whole rosy glow; but what note so false
as that of the dingy little presence that she
might actually, by a refinement of her perhaps always too visible study of effect, have
provided as a positive contrast or foil?
whose name and intervention, moreover,
she appeared to be no more moved to men-

tion and account for than she might have been to 'present'—whether as stretched at her feet or erect upon disciplined haunches —some shaggy old domesticated terrier or poodle.

Extraordinarily, after he had been in the room five minutes—a space of time during which his fellow-visitor had neither budged nor uttered a sound—he had made Mrs. Worthingham out as all at once perfectly pleased to see him, completely aware of what he had most in mind, and singularly serene in face of his sense of their impediment. It was as if for all the world she didn't take it for one, the immobility, to say nothing of the seeming equanimity, of their tactless companion; at whom meanwhile indeed our friend himself, after his first ruffled perception, no more adventured a look than if advised by his constitutional kindness that to notice her in any degree would perforce be ungraciously to glower. He talked after a fashion with the woman as to whose power to please and amuse and serve him, as to whose really quite organised and indicated fitness for lighting up his autumn afternoon of life his conviction had lately strained itself so clear; but he was all the while carrying on an intenser exchange with his own spirit and trying to read into the charming creature's behaviour, as he could only call it, some confirmation of his theory that she also had her inward flutter and anxiously counted on him. He found support, happily for the conviction just named, in the idea, at no moment as yet really repugnant to him, the idea bound up in fact with the finer essence of her appeal, that she had her own vision too of her quality and her price, and that the last appearance she would have liked to bristle with was that of being forewarned and eager.

He had, if he came to think of it, scarce definitely warned her, and he probably wouldn't have taken to her so consciously in the first instance without an appreciative sense that, as she was a little person of twenty superficial graces, so she was also a little person with her secret pride. She might just have planted her mangy lion— not to say her muzzled house-dog—there in his path as a symbol that she wasn't cheap and easy; which would be a thing he couldn't possibly wish his future wife to have shown herself in advance, even if to

him alone. That she could make him put himself such questions was precisely part of the attaching play of her iridescent surface, the shimmering interfusion of her various aspects; that of her youth with her independence—her pecuniary perhaps in particular, that of her vivacity with her beauty, that of her facility above all with her odd novelty; the high modernity, as people appeared to have come to call it, that made her so much more 'knowing' in some directions than even he, man of the world as he certainly was, could pretend to be, though all on a basis of the most unconscious and instinctive and luxurious assumption. She was 'up' to everything, aware of everything—if one counted from a short enough time back (from week before last, say, and as if quantities of history had burst upon the world within the fortnight), she was likewise surprised at nothing, and in that direction one might reckon as far ahead as the rest of her lifetime, or at any rate as the rest of his, which was all that would concern him: it was as if the suitability of the future to her personal and rather pampered tastes was what she most took for granted, so that he could see her for all her Dresden-china shoes and her flutter of wondrous befrilled contemporary skirts, skip by the side of the coming age and over the floor of a ball-room, keeping step with its monstrous stride and prepared for every figure of the dance.

Her outlook took form to him suddenly as a great square sunny window that hung in assured fashion over the immensity of life. There rose toward it as from a vast swarming *plaza* a high tide of emotion and sound; yet it was at the same time as if even while he looked her light gemmed hand flashing on him in addition to those other things the perfect polish of the prettiest pink finger-nails in the world, had touched a spring, the most ingenious of recent devices for instant ease, which dropped half across the scene a soft-coloured mechanical blind, a fluttered, fringed awning of charmingly toned silk, such as would make a bath of cool shade for the favoured friend leaning with her there—that is for the happy couple itself—on the balcony. The great view would be the prospect and privilege of the very state he coveted—since didn't he covet it?—the state of being so securely at he side; while the wash of privacy, as one might count it, the broad fine brush dipped into clear umber and passed, full and wet, straight across the strong scheme of colour, would represent the security itself, all the uplifted inner elegance, the condition, so ideal, of being shut out from nothing and yet of having, so gaily and breezily aloft, none of the burden or worry of anything. Thus, as I say, for our friend, the place itself, while his vivid impression lasted, portentously opened and spread, and what was before him took, to his vision, though indeed at so other a crisis, the form of the 'glimmering square' of the poet; yet, for a still more remarkable fact, with an incongruous object usurping at a given instant the privilege of the frame and seeming, even as he looked, to block the view.

The incongruous object was a woman's head, crowned with a little sparsely feathered black hat, an ornament quite unlike those the women mostly noticed by White-Mason were now 'wearing,' and that grew and grew, that came nearer and nearer, while it met his eyes, after the manner of images in the kinematograph. It had presently loomed so large that he saw nothing else—not only among the things at a considerable distance, the things Mrs. Worthingham would eventually, yet unmistakably, introduce him to, but among those of this lady's various attributes and appurtenances as to which he had been in the very act of cultivating his consciousness. It was in the course of another minute the most extraordinary thing in the world: everything had altered, dropped, darkened, disappeared; his imagination had spread its wings only to feel them flop all grotesquely at its sides as he recognised in his hostess's quiet companion, the oppressive alien who hadn't indeed interfered with his fanciful flight, though she had prevented his immediate declaration and brought about the thud, not to say the felt violent shock, of his fall to earth, the perfectly plain identity of Cornelia Rasch. It was she who had remained there at attention; it was she their companion hadn't introduced; it was she he had forborne to face with his fear of incivility. He stared at her—everything else went.

'Why it has been *you* all this time?'

Miss Rasch fairly turned pale. 'I was waiting to see if you'd know me.'

'Ah, my dear Cornelia'—he came straight out with it—'rather!'

'Well, it isn't,' she returned with a quick change to red now, 'from having taken much time to look at me!'

She smiled, she even laughed, but he could see how she had felt his unconsciousness, poor thing; the acquaintance, quite the friend of his youth, as she had been, the associate of his childhood, of his early manhood, of his middle age in fact, up to a few years back, not more than ten at the most; the associate too of so many of his associates and of almost all of his relations, those of the other time, those who had mainly gone for ever; the person in short whose noted disappearance, though it might have seemed final, had been only of recent seasons. She was present again now, all unexpectedly— he had heard of her having at last, left alone after successive deaths and with scant resources, sought economic salvation in Europe, the promised land of American thrift —she was present as this almost ancient and this oddly unassertive little rotund figure whom one seemed no more obliged to address than if she had been a black satin ottoman 'treated' with buttons and gimp; a class of object as to which the policy of blindness was imperative. He felt the need of some explanatory plea, and before he could think had uttered one at Mrs. Worthingham's expense. 'Why, you see we weren't introduced—!'

'No—but I didn't suppose I should have to be named to you.'

'Well, my dear woman, you haven't—do me that justice!' He could at least make this point. 'I felt all the while—!' However, it would have taken him long to say what he had been feeling; and he was aware now of the pretty projected light of Mrs. Worthingham's wonder. She looked as if, out for a walk with her, he had put her to the inconvenience of his stopping to speak to a strange woman in the street.

'I never supposed you knew her!'—it was to him his hostess excused herself.

This made Miss Rasch spring up, distinctly flushed, distinctly strange to behold, but not vulgarly nettled—Cornelia was incapable of that; only rather funnily bridling and laughing, only showing that this was all she had waited for, only saying just the right thing, the thing she could make so clearly a jest. 'Of course if you *had* you'd have presented him.'

Mrs. Worthingham looked while answering at White-Mason. 'I didn't want you to go—which you see you do as soon as he speaks to you. But I never dreamed—!'

'That there was anything between us? Ah, there are no end of things!' He, on his side, though addressing the younger and prettier woman, looked at his fellow-guest; to whom he even continued: 'When did you get back? May I come and see you the very first thing?'

Cornelia gasped and wriggled—she practically giggled; she had lost every atom of her little old, her little young, though always unaccountable prettiness, which used to peep so, on the bare chance of a shot, from behind indefensible features, that it almost made watching her a form of sport. He had heard vaguely of her, it came back to him (for there had been no letters; their later acquaintance, thank goodness, hadn't involved that) as experimenting, for economy, and then as settling, to the same rather dismal end, somewhere in England, at one of those intensely English places, St. Leonards, Cheltenham, Bognor, Dawlish—which, awfully, *was* it?—and she now affected him for all the world as some small squirming, exclaiming, genteelly conversing old maid of a type vaguely associated with the three-volume novels he used to feed on (besides his so often encountering it in 'real life,') during a far-away stay of his own at Brighton. Odder than any element of his ex-gossip's identity itself, however, was the fact that she somehow, with it all, rejoiced his sight. Indeed the supreme oddity was that the manner of her reply to his request for leave to call should have absolutely charmed his attention. She didn't look at him; she only, from under her frumpy, crapy, curiously exotic hat, and with her good little near-sighted insinuating glare, expressed to Mrs. Worthingham, while she answered him, wonderful arch things, the overdone things of a shy woman. 'Yes, you may call—but only when this dear lovely lady has done with you!' The moment after which she had gone.

III

Forty minutes later he was taking his way back from the queer miscarriage of his adventure; taking it, with no conscious positive felicity, through the very spaces that had witnessed shortly before the considerable serenity of his assurance. He had said to himself then, or had as good as said it, that, since he might do perfectly as he liked, it couldn't fail for him that he must soon retrace those steps, humming, to all intents, the first bars of a wedding-march; so beautifully had it cleared up that he was 'going to like' letting Mrs. Worthingham accept him. He was to have hummed no wedding-march, as it seemed to be turning out—he had none, up to now, to hum; and yet, extraordinarily, it wasn't in the least because she had refused him. Why then hadn't he liked as much as he had intended to like it putting the pleasant act, the act of not refusing him, in her power? Could it all have come from the awkward minute of his failure to decide sharply, on Cornelia's departure, whether or no he would attend her to the door? He hadn't decided at all—what the deuce had been in him?—but had danced to and fro in the room, thinking better of each impulse and then thinking worse. He had hesitated like an ass erect on absurd hind legs between two bundles of hay; the upshot of which must have been his giving the falsest impression. In what way that was to be for an instant considered had their common past committed him to crapy Cornelia? He repudiated with a whack on the gravel any ghost of an obligation.

What he could get rid of with scanter success, unfortunately, was the peculiar sharpness of his sense that, though mystified by his visible flurry—and yet not mystified enough for a sympathetic question either—his hostess had been, on the whole, even more frankly diverted: which was precisely an example of that newest, freshest, finest freedom in her, the air and the candour of assuming, not 'heartlessly,' not viciously, not even very consciously, but with a bright pampered confidence which would probably end by affecting one's nerves as the most impertinent stroke in the world, that every blest thing coming up for her in any connection was somehow matter for her general recreation. There she was again with the innocent egotism, the gilded and overflowing anarchism, really, of her doubtless quite unwitting but none the less rabid

modern note. Her grace of ease was perfect, but it was all grace of ease, not a single
shred of it grace of uncertainty or of difficulty—which meant, when you came to see,
that, for its happy working, not a grain of
provision was left by it to mere manners.
This was clearly going to be the music of
the future—that if people were but rich
enough and furnished enough and fed
enough, exercised and sanitated and mani-
cured and generally advised and advertised
and made 'knowing' enough, *avertis*
enough, as the term appeared to be nowadays in Paris, all they had to do for civility
was to take the amused ironic view of those
who might be less initiated. In *his* time,
when he was young or even when he was
only but a little less middle-aged, the best
manners had been the best kindness, and
the best kindness had mostly been some art
of not insisting on one's luxurious differences, of concealing rather, for common humanity, if not for common decency, a part
at least of the intensity or the ferocity with
which one might be 'in the know.'
   Oh, the 'know'—Mrs. Worthingham was
in it, all instinctively, inevitably, and as a
matter of course, up to her eyes; which
didn't, however, the least little bit prevent
her being as ignorant as a fish of everything
that really and intimately and fundamentally concerned *him*, poor dear old White-
Mason. She didn't, in the first place, so
much as know who he was—by which he
meant know who and what it was to *be* a
White-Mason, even a poor and a dear and
old one, 'anyway.' That indeed—he did her
perfect justice—was of the very essence of
the newness and freshness and beautiful,
brave, social irresponsibility by which she
had originally dazzled him: just exactly that
circumstance of her having no instinct for
any old quality or quantity or identity, a
single historic or social value, as he might
say, of the New York of his already almost
legendary past; and that additional one of
his, on his side, having, so far as this went,
cultivated blankness, cultivated positive
prudence, as to her own personal background—the vagueness, at the best, with
which all honest gentlefolk, the New
Yorkers of his approved stock and conservative generation, were content, as for the
most part they were indubitably wise, to
surround the origins and antecedents and

queer unimaginable early influences of persons swimming into their ken from those
parts of the country that quite necessarily
and naturally figured to their view as 'God-
forsaken' and generally impossible.
   The few scattered surviving representatives of a society once 'good'—*rari nantes in
gurgite vasto*[1]—were liable, at the pass
things had come to, to meet, and even amid
old shades once sacred, or what was left of
such, every form of social impossibility,
and, more irresistibly still, to find these apparitions often carry themselves (often at
least in the case of the women) with a wondrous wild gallantry, equally imperturbable
and inimitable, the sort of thing that
reached its maximum in Mrs. Worthingham. Beyond that who ever wanted to look
up their annals, to reconstruct their steps
and stages, to dot their i's in fine, or to 'go
behind' anything that was theirs? One
wouldn't do that for the world—a rudimentary discretion forbade it; and yet this check
from elementary undiscussable taste quite
consorted with a due respect for them, or at
any rate with a due respect for oneself in
connection with them; as was just exemplified in what would be his own, what would
be poor dear old White-Mason's, insur-
mountable aversion to having, on any pretext, the doubtless very queer spectre of the
late Mr. Worthingham presented to him.
No question had he asked, or would he ever
ask, should his life—that is should the success of his courtship—even intimately depend on it, either about that obscure agent
of his mistress's actual affluence or about
the happy head-spring itself, and the apparently copious tributaries, of the golden
stream.
   From all which marked anomalies, at any
rate, what was the moral to draw? He
dropped into a Park chair again with that
question, he lost himself in the wonder of
why he had come away with his homage so
very much unpaid. Yet it didn't seem at all,
actually, as if he could say or conclude, as if
he could do anything but keep on worrying
—just in conformity with his being a person
who, whether or no familiar with the need
to make his conduct square with his conscience and his taste, was never wholly exempt from that of making his taste and his
conscience square with his conduct. To this

[1] 'A few scattered men swimming in the deep.'

latter occupation he further abandoned himself, and it didn't release him from his second brooding session till the sweet spring sunset had begun to gather and he had more or less cleared up, in the deepening dusk, the effective relation between the various parts of his ridiculously agitating experience. There were vital facts he seemed thus to catch, to seize, with a nervous hand, and the twilight helping, by their vaguely whisked tails; unquiet truths that swarmed out after the fashion of creatures bold only at eventide, creatures that hovered and circled, that verily brushed his nose, in spite of their shyness. Yes, he had practically just sat on with his 'mistress'—heaven save the mark!—as if *not* to come to the point; as if it had absolutely come up that there would be something rather vulgar and awful in doing so. The whole stretch of his stay after Cornelia's withdrawal had been consumed by his almost ostentatiously treating himself to the opportunity of which he was to make nothing. It was as if he had sat and watched himself—that came back to him: Shall I now or sha'n't I? Will I now or won't I? 'Say within the next three minutes, say by a quarter past six, or by twenty minutes past, at the furthest—always if nothing more comes up to prevent.'

What had already come up to prevent was, in the strangest and drollest, or at least in the most preposterous, way in the world, that not Cornelia's presence, but her very absence, with its distraction of his thoughts, the thoughts that lumbered after her, had made the difference; and without his being the least able to tell why and how. He put it to himself after a fashion by the image that, this distraction once created, his working round to his hostess again, his reverting to the matter of his errand, began suddenly to represent a return from so far. That was simply all—or rather a little less than all; for something else had contributed. 'I never dreamed you knew her,' and 'I never dreamed *you* did,' were inevitably what had been exchanged between them—supplemented by Mrs. Worthingham's mere scrap of an explanation: 'Oh yes—to the small extent you see. Two years ago in Switzerland when I was at a high place for an "aftercure," during twenty days of incessant rain, she was the only person in an

hotel full of roaring, gorging, smoking Germans with whom I could have a word of talk. She and I were the only speakers of English, and were thrown together like castaways on a desert island and in a raging storm. She was ill besides, and she had no maid, and mine looked after her, and she was very grateful—writing to me later on and saying she should certainly come to see me if she ever returned to New York. She *has* returned, you see—and there she was, poor little creature!' Such was Mrs. Worthingham's tribute—to which even his asking her if Miss Rasch had ever happened to speak of him caused her practically to add nothing. Visibly she had never thought again of any one Miss Rasch had spoken of or anything Miss Rasch had said; right as she was, naturally, about her being a little clever queer creature. This was perfectly true, and yet it was probably—by being *all* she could dream of about her—what had paralysed his proper gallantry. Its effect had been not in what it simply stated, but in what, under his secretly disintegrating criticism, it almost luridly symbolised.

He had quitted his seat in the Louis Quinze drawing-room without having, as he would have described it, done anything but give the lady of the scene a superior chance not to betray a defeated hope—not, that is, to fail of the famous 'pride' mostly supposed to prop even the most infatuated women at such junctures; by which chance, to do her justice, she had thoroughly seemed to profit. But he finally rose from his later station with a feeling of better success. He had by a happy turn of his hand got hold of the most precious, the least obscure of the flitting, circling things that brushed his ears. What he wanted—as justifying for him a little further consideration—was there before him from the moment he could put it that Mrs. Worthingham had no data. He almost hugged that word—it suddenly came to mean so much to him. No data, he felt, for a conception of the sort of thing the New York of 'his time' had been in his personal life—the New York so unexpectedly, so vividly and, as he might say, so perversely called back to all his senses by its identity with that of poor Cornelia's time: since even she had had a time, small show as it was likely to make now, and his time and hers had been the same. Cornelia figured to him while he walked away as, by contrast and opposition, a massive little bundle of data; his impatience to go to see her sharpened as he thought of this: so certainly should he find out that wherever he might touch her, with a gentle though firm pressure, he would, as the fond visitor of old houses taps and fingers a disfeatured, overpapered wall with the conviction of a wainscot-edge beneath, recognise some small extrusion of history.

IV

There would have been a wonder for us meanwhile in his continued use, as it were, of his happy formula—brought out to Cornelia Rasch within ten minutes, or perhaps only within twenty, of his having settled into the quite comfortable chair that, two days later, she indicated to him by her fireside. He had arrived at her address through the fortunate chance of his having noticed her card, as he went out, deposited, in the good old New York fashion, on one of the rococo tables of Mrs. Worthingham's hall. His eye had been caught by the pencilled indication that was to affect him, the next instant, as fairly placed there for his sake. This had really been his luck, for he shouldn't have liked to write to Mrs. Worthingham for guidance—*that* he felt, though too impatient just now to analyse the reluctance. There was nobody else he could have approached for a clue, and with this reflection he was already aware of how it testified to their rare little position, his and Cornelia's—position as conscious, ironic, pathetic survivors together of a dead and buried society—that there would have been, in all the town, under such stress, not a member of their old circle left to turn to. Mrs. Worthingham had practically, even if accidentally, helped him to knowledge; the last nail in the coffin of the poor dear extinct past had been planted for him by his having thus to reach his antique contemporary through perforation of the newest newness. The note of this particular recognition was in fact the more prescribed to him that the ground of Cornelia's return to a scene swept so bare of the associational charm was certainly inconspicuous. What had she then come back for?—he had asked himself that; with the effect of deciding that it probably would have been, a little, to

'look after' her remnant of property. Perhaps she had come to save what little might still remain of that shrivelled interest; perhaps she had been, by those who took care of it for her, further swindled and despoiled, so that she wished to get at the facts. Perhaps on the other hand—it was a more cheerful chance—her investments, decently administered, were making larger returns, so that the rigorous thrift of Bognor could be finally relaxed.

He had little to learn about the attraction of Europe, and rather expected that in the event of his union with Mrs. Worthingham he should find himself pleading for it with the competence of one more in the 'know' about Paris and Rome, about Venice and Florence, than even she could be. He could have lived on in *his* New York, that is in the sentimental, the spiritual, the more or less romantic visitation of it; but had it been positive for him· that he could live on in hers?—unless indeed the possibility of this had been just (like the famous *vertige de l'abîme*, like the solicitation of danger, or otherwise of the dreadful) the very hinge of his whole dream. However that might be, his curiosity was occupied rather with the conceivable hinge of poor Cornelia's: it was perhaps thinkable that even Mrs. Worthingham's New York, once it should have become possible again at all, might have put forth to this lone exile a plea that wouldn't be in the chords of Bognor. For himself, after all, too, the attraction had been much more of the Europe over which one might move at one's ease, and which therefore could but cost, and cost much, right and left, than of the Europe adapted to scrimping. He saw himself on the whole scrimping with more zest even in Mrs. Worthingham's New York than under the inspiration of Bognor. Apart from which it was yet again odd, not to say perceptibly pleasing to him, to note where the emphasis of his interest fell in this fumble of fancy over such felt oppositions as the new, the latest, the luridest power of money and the ancient reserves and moderations and mediocrities. These last struck him as showing by contrast the old brown surface and tone as of velvet rubbed and worn, shabby, and even a bit dingy, but all soft and subtle and still velvety—which meant still dignified; whereas the angular facts of current finance were as harsh and metallic and bewildering as some stacked 'exhibit' of ugly patented inventions, things his mediæval mind forbade his taking in. He had for instance the sense of knowing the pleasant little old Rasch fortune—pleasant as far as it went; blurred memories and impressions of what it had been and what it hadn't, of how it had grown and how languished and how melted; they came back to him and put on such vividness that he could almost have figured himself testify for them before a bland and encouraging Board. The idea of taking the field in any manner on the subject of Mrs. Worthingham's resources would have affected him on the other hand as an odious ordeal, some glare of embarrassment and exposure in a circle of hard unhelpful attention, of converging, derisive, unsuggestive eyes.

In Cornelia's small and quite cynically modern flat—the house had a grotesque name, 'The Gainsborough,' but at least wasn't an awful boarding-house, as he had feared, and she could receive him quite honourably, which was so much to the good—he would have been ready to use at once to her the greatest freedom of friendly allusion: 'Have you still your old "family interest" in those two houses in Seventh Avenue?—one of which was next to a corner grocery, don't you know? and was occupied as to its lower part by a candy-shop where the proportion of the stock of suspectedly stale popcorn to that of rarer and stickier joys betrayed perhaps a modest capital on the part of your father's, your grandfather's, or whoever's tenant, but out of which I nevertheless remember once to have come as out of a bath of sweets, with my very garments, and even the separate hairs of my head, glued together. The other of the pair, a tobacconist's, further down, had before it a wonderful huge Indian who thrust out wooden cigars at an indifferent world—you could buy candy cigars too, at the popcorn shop, and I greatly preferred them to the wooden; I remember well how I used to gape in fascination at the Indian and wonder if the last of the Mohicans was like him; besides admiring so the resources of a family whose "property" was in such forms. I haven't been round there lately—we must go round together; but don't tell me the forms have utterly perished!' It was

after *that* fashion he might easily have been moved, and with almost no transition, to break out to Cornelia—quite as if taking up some old talk, some old community of gossip, just where they had left it; even with the consciousness perhaps of overdoing a little, of putting at its maximum, for the present harmony, recovery, recapture (what should he call it?) the pitch and quantity of what the past had held for them.

He didn't in fact, no doubt, dart straight off to Seventh Avenue, there being too many other old things and much nearer and long subsequent; the point was only that for everything they spoke of after he had fairly begun to lean back and stretch his legs, and after she had let him, above all, light the first of a succession of cigarettes—for everything they spoke of he positively cultivated extravagance and excess, piling up the crackling twigs as on the very altar of memory; and that by the end of half an hour she had lent herself, all gallantly, to their game. It was the game of feeding the beautiful iridescent flame, ruddy and green and gold, blue and pink and amber and silver, with anything they could pick up, anything that would burn and flicker. Thickstrown with such gleanings the occasion seemed indeed, in spite of the truth that they perhaps wouldn't have proved, under cross-examination, to have rubbed shoulders in the other life so very hard. Casual contacts, qualified communities enough, there had doubtless been, but not particular 'passages,' nothing that counted, as he might think of it, for their 'very own' together, for nobody's else at all. These shades of historic exactitude didn't signify; the more and the less that there had been made perfect terms—and just by his being there and by her rejoicing in it—with their present need to have *had* all their past could be made to appear to have given them. It was to this tune they proceeded, the least little bit as if they knowingly pretended—he giving her the example and setting her the pace of it, and she, poor dear, after a first inevitable shyness, an uncertainty of wonder, a breathlessness of courage, falling into step and going whatever length he would.

She showed herself ready for it, grasping gladly at the perception of what he must mean; and if she didn't immediately and completely fall in—not in the first half-hour, not even in the three or four others that his visit, even whenever he consulted his watch, still made nothing of—she yet understood enough as soon as she understood that, if their finer economy hadn't so beautifully served, he might have been conveying this, that, and the other incoherent and easy thing by the comparatively clumsy method of sound and statement. 'No, I never made love to you; it would in fact have been absurd, and I don't care—though I almost know, in the sense of almost remembering!—who did and who didn't; but you were always about, and so was I, and, little as you may yourself care who *I* did it to, I dare say you remember (in the sense of having known of it!) any old appearances that told. But we can't afford at this time of day not to help each other to have had—well, everything there was, since there's no more of it now, nor any way of coming by it *except so*; and therefore let us make together, let us make over and recreate, our lost world; for which we have after all and at the worst such a lot of material. You were in particular my poor dear sisters' friend—they thought you the funniest little brown thing possible; so isn't that again to the good? You were mine only to the extent that you were so much in and out of the house—as how much, if we come to that, wasn't one in and out, south of Thirtieth Street and north of Washington Square, in those days, those spacious, sociable, Arcadian days, that we flattered ourselves we filled with the modern fever, but that were so different from any of these arrangements of pretended hourly Time that dash themselves forever to pieces as from the fiftieth floors of sky-scrapers.'

This was the kind of thing that was in the air, whether he said it or not, and that could hang there even with such quite other things as more crudely came out; came in spite of its being perhaps calculated to strike us that these last would have been rather and most the unspoken and the indirect. They were Cornelia's contribution, and as soon as she had begun to talk of Mrs. Worthingham—*he* didn't begin it!—they had taken their place bravely in the centre of the circle. There they made, the while, their considerable little figure, but all within the ring formed by fifty other allusions, fitful but really intenser irruptions that hovered and wavered and came and went, joining hands at moments and whirling round as in chorus, only then again to dash at the slightly huddled centre with a free twitch or peck or push or other taken liberty, after the fashion of irregular frolic motions in a country dance or a Christmas game.

'You're so in love with her and want to marry her!'—she said it all sympathetically and yearningly, poor crapy Cornelia; as if it were to be quite taken for granted that she knew all about it. And then when he had asked how she knew—why she took so informed a tone about it; all on the wonder of her seeming so much more 'in' it just at that hour than he himself quite felt he could figure for: 'Ah, how but from the dear lovely thing herself? Don't you suppose *she* knows it?'

'Oh, she absolutely "knows" it, does she?'—he fairly heard himself ask that; and with the oddest sense at once of sharply wanting the certitude and yet of seeing the question, of hearing himself say the words, through several thicknesses of some wrong medium. He came back to it from a distance; as he would have had to come back (this was again vivid to him) should he have got round again to his ripe intention three days before—after his now present but then absent friend, that is, had left him planted before his now absent but then present one for the purpose. 'Do you mean she—at all confidently!—expects?' he went on, not much minding if it couldn't but sound foolish; the time being given it for him meanwhile by the sigh, the wondering gasp, all charged with the unutterable, that the tone of his appeal set in motion. He saw his companion look at him, but it might have been with the eyes of thirty years ago; when—very likely!—he had put her some such question about some girl long since dead. Dimly at first, then more distinctly, didn't it surge back on him for the very strangeness that there had been some such passage as this between them—yes, about Mary Cardew!—in the autumn of '68?

'Why, don't you realise your situation?' Miss Rasch struck him as quite beautifully wailing—above all to such an effect of deep interest, that is, on her own part and in him.

'My situation?'—he echoed, he considered; but reminded afresh, by the note of the detached, the far-projected in it, of what he had last remembered of his sentient state on his once taking ether at the dentist's.

'Yours and hers—the situation of her adoring you. I suppose you at least know it,' Cornelia smiled.

Yes, it was like the other time and yet it wasn't. *She* was like—poor Cornelia was—everything that used to be; that somehow was most definite to him. Still he could quite reply 'Do you call it—her adoring me —*my* situation?'

'Well, it's a part of yours, surely—if you're in love with her.'

'Am I, ridiculous old person! in love with her?' White-Mason asked.

'I may be a ridiculous old person,' Cornelia returned—'and, for that matter, of course I am! But she's young and lovely and rich and clever: so what could be more natural?'

'Oh, I was applying that opprobrious epithet—!' He didn't finish, though he meant he had applied it to himself. He had got up from his seat; he turned about and, taking in, as his eyes also roamed, several objects in the room, serene and sturdy, not a bit cheap-looking, little old New York objects of '68, he made, with an inner art, as if to recognise them—made so, that is, for himself; had quite the sense for the moment of asking them, of imploring them, to recognise *him*, to be for him things of his own past. Which they truly were, he could have the next instant cried out; for it meant that if three or four of them, small sallow carte-de-visite photographs, faithfully framed but spectrally faded, hadn't in every particular, frames and balloon skirts and false 'property' balustrades of unimaginable terraces and all, the tone of time, the secret for warding and easing off the perpetual imminent ache of one's protective scowl, one would verily but have to let the scowl stiffen, or to take up seriously the question of blue goggles, during what might remain of life.

V

What he actually took up from a little old Twelfth-Street table that piously preserved the plain mahogany circle, with never a curl nor a crook nor a hint of a brazen flourish, what he paused there a moment for commerce with, his back presented to crapy Cornelia, who sat taking that view of him, during this opportunity, very protrusively and frankly and fondly, was one of the wasted mementos just mentioned, over which he both uttered and suppressed a small comprehensive cry. He stood there another minute to look at it, and when he turned about and still kept it in his hand, only holding it now a little behind him. 'You *must* have come back to stay—with all your beautiful things. What else does it mean?'

' "Beautiful?" ' his old friend commented with her brow all wrinkled and her lips thrust out in expressive dispraise. They might at that rate have been scarce more beautiful than she herself. 'Oh, don't talk so —after Mrs. Worthingham's! *They're* wonderful, if you will: such things, such things! But one's own poor relics and odds and ends are one's own at least; and one *has*—yes —come back to them. They're all I have in the world to come back to. They were stored, and what I was paying—!' Miss Rasch woefully added.

He had possession of the small old picture; he hovered there; he put his eyes again to it intently; then again held it a little behind him as if it might have been snatched away or the very feel of it, pressed against him, was good to his palm. 'Mrs. Worthingham's things? You think them beautiful?'

Cornelia did now, if ever, show an odd face. 'Why certainly prodigious, or whatever. Isn't that conceded?'

'No doubt every horror, at the pass we've come to, is conceded. That's just what I complain of.'

'Do you *complain*?'—she drew it out as for surprise: she couldn't have imagined such a thing.

'To me her things are awful. They're the newest of the new.'

'Ah, but the old forms!'

'Those are the most blatant. I mean the swaggering reproductions.'

'Oh but,' she pleaded, 'we can't all be *really* old.'

'No, we can't, Cornelia. But *you* can—!' said White-Mason with the frankest appreciation.

She looked up at him from where she sat as he could imagine her looking up at the curate at Bognor. 'Thank you, sir! If that's all you want—!'

'It *is*,' he said, 'all I want—or almost.'

'Then no wonder such a creature as that,' he lightly moralised, 'won't suit you!'

He bent upon her, for all the weight of his question, his smoothest stare. 'You hold he certainly won't suit me?'

'Why, what can I tell about it? Haven't you by this time found out?'

'No, but I think I'm finding.' With which he began again to explore.

Miss Rasch immensely wondered. 'You mean you don't expect to come to an understanding with her?' And then as even to this straight challenge he made at first no answer: 'Do you mean you give it up?'

He waited some instants more, but not meeting her eyes—only looking again about the room. 'What do you think of my chance?'

'Oh,' his companion cried, 'what has what I think to do with it? How can I think anything but that she must like you?'

'Yes—of course. But how much?'

'Then don't you really know?' Cornelia asked.

He kept up his walk, oddly preoccupied and still not looking at her. 'Do you, my dear?'

She waited a little. 'If you haven't really put it to her I don't suppose she knows.'

This at last arrested him again. 'My dear Cornelia, she doesn't know—!'

He had paused as for the desperate tone, or at least the large emphasis of it, so that she took him up. 'The more reason then to help her to find it out.'

'I mean,' he explained, 'that she doesn't know anything.'

'Anything?'

'Anything else, I mean—even if she does know *that*.'

Cornelia considered of it. 'But what else need she—in particular—know? Isn't that the principal thing?'

'Well'—and he resumed his circuit—'she doesn't know anything that *we* know. But nothing,' he re-emphasised—'nothing whatever!'

'Well, can't she do without that?'

'Evidently she can—and evidently she does, beautifully. But the question is whether *I* can!'

He had paused once more with his point —but she glared, poor Cornelia, with her wonder. 'Surely if you know for yourself—!'

'Ah, it doesn't seem enough for me to know for myself! One wants a woman,' he argued—but still, in his prolonged tour, quite without his scowl—'to know *for* one, to know *with* one. That's what you do now,' he candidly put to her.

It made her again gape. 'Do you mean you want to marry *me*?'

He was so full of what he did mean, however, that he failed even to notice it. 'She doesn't in the least know, for instance, how old I am.'

'That's because you're so young!'

'Ah, there you are!'—and he turned off afresh and as if almost in disgust. It left her visibly perplexed—though even the perplexed Cornelia was still the exceedingly pointed; but he had come to her aid after another turn. 'Remember, please, that I'm pretty well as old as you.'

She had all her point at least, while she bridled and blinked, for this. 'You're exactly a year and ten months older.'

It checked him there for delight. 'You remember my birthday?'

She twinkled indeed like some far-off light of home. 'I remember every one's. It's a little way I've always had—and that I've never lost.'

He looked at her accomplishment, across the room, as at some striking, some charming phenomenon. 'Well, *that's* the sort of thing I want!' All the ripe candour of his eyes confirmed it.

What could she do therefore, she seemed to ask him, but repeat her question of a moment before?—which indeed presently she made up her mind to. 'Do you want to marry *me*?'

It had this time better success—if the term may be felt in any degree to apply. All his candour, or more of it at least, was in his slow, mild, kind, considering head-shake. 'No, Cornelia—not to *marry* you.'

His discrimination was a wonder; but since she was clearly treating him now as if everything about him was, so she could as exquisitely meet it. 'Not at least,' she convulsively smiled, 'until you've honourably tried Mrs. Worthingham. Don't you really *mean* to?' she gallantly insisted.

He waited again a little; then he brought out: 'I'll tell you presently.' He came back, and as by still another mere glance over the room, to what seemed to him so much nearer. 'That table *was* old Twelfth-Street?'

'Everything here was.'

'Oh, the pure blessings! With you, ah, with you, I haven't to wear a green shade.' And he had retained meanwhile his small photograph, which he again showed himself. 'Didn't we talk of Mary Cardew?'

'Why, do you remember it?' she marvelled to extravagance.

'You make me. You connect me with it. You connect it with *me*.' He liked to display to her this excellent use she thus had, the service she rendered. 'There are so many connections—there will *be* so many. I feel how, with you, they must all come up again for me: in fact you're bringing them out already, just while I look at you, as fast as ever you can. The fact that you knew every one—!' he went on; yet as if there were more in that too than he could quite trust himself about.

'Yes, I knew every one,' said Cornelia Rasch; but this time with perfect simplicity. 'I knew, I imagine, more than you do —or more than you did.'

It kept him there, it made him wonder with his eyes on her. 'Things about *them*—our people?'

'Our people. Ours only now.'

Ah, such an interest as he felt in this—taking from her while, so far from scowling, he almost gaped, all it might mean! 'Ours indeed—and it's awfully good they are; or that we're still here for them! Nobody else is—nobody but you: not a cat!'

'Well, I *am* a cat!' Cornelia grinned.

'Do you mean you can tell me things—?' It was too beautiful to believe.

'About what really *was*?' she artfully considered, holding him immensely now. 'Well, unless they've come to you with time; unless you've learned—or found out.'

'Oh,' he reassuringly cried—reassuringly, it most seemed, for himself—'nothing has come to me with time, everything has gone from me. How can I find out now! What creature has an idea—?'

She threw up her hands with the shrug of old days—the sharp little shrug his sisters used to imitate and that she hadn't had to go to Europe for. The only thing was that he blessed her for bringing it back. 'Ah, the ideas of people now—!'

'Yes, their ideas are certainly not about

us.' But he ruefully faced it. 'We've non the less, however, to live with them.'

'With their ideas—?' Cornelia questioned.

'With *them*—these modern wonder such as they are!' Then he went on: ' must have been to help me you've com back.'

She said nothing for an instant about tha only nodding instead at his photograph 'What has become of yours? I mean of *her*

This time it made him turn pale. 'Yo remember I *have* one?'

She kept her eyes on him. 'In a "pork pie" hat, with her hair in a long net. Tha was so "smart" then; especially with one skirt looped up, over one's hooped magent petticoat, in little festoons, and a row c very big onyx beads over one's braided vel veteen sack—braided quite plain and ver broad, don't you know?'

He smiled for her extraordinary posses sion of these things—she was as prompt a if she had had them before her. 'Oh, rathe —"don't I know?" You wore brown vel veteen, and, on those remarkably smal hands, funny gauntlets—like mine.'

'Oh, do *you* remember? But like yours: she wondered.

'I mean like hers in my photograph.' Bu he came back to the present picture. 'Thi is better, however, for really showing he lovely head.'

'Mary's head was a perfection!' Corneli testified.

'Yes—it was better than her heart.'

'Ah, don't say that!' she pleaded. 'Yo weren't fair.'

'Don't you think I was fair?' It intereste him immensely—and the more that he in deed mightn't have been; which he seemed somehow almost to hope.

'She didn't think so—to the very end.'

'She didn't?'—ah the right things Cor nelia said to him! But before she could an swer he was studying again closely the smal faded face. 'No, she doesn't, she doesn't Oh, her charming sad eyes and the way the; *say* that, across the years, straight int mine! But I don't know, I don't know! White-Mason quite comfortably sighed.

His companion appeared to appreciat this effect. 'That's just the way you used t flirt with her, poor thing. Wouldn't you lik to have it?' she asked.

'This—for my very own?' He looked up delighted. 'I really may?'

'Well, if you'll give me yours. We'll exchange.'

'That's a charming idea. We'll exchange. But you must come and get it at my rooms —where you'll see my things.'

For a little she made no answer—as if for some feeling. Then she said: 'You asked me just now why I've come back.'

He stared as for the connection; after which with a smile: 'Not to do *that*—?'

She waited briefly again, but with a queer little look. 'I can do those things now; and—yes!—that's in a manner why. I came,' she then said, 'because I knew of a sudden one day—knew as never before—that I was old.'

'I see. I see.' He quite understood—she had notes that so struck him. 'And how did you like it?'

She hesitated—she decided. 'Well, if I liked it, it was on the principle perhaps on which some people like high game!'

'High game—that's good!' he laughed. 'Ah, my dear, we're "high"!'

She shook her head. 'No, not you—yet. I at any rate didn't want any more adventures,' Cornelia said.

He showed their small relic again with assurance. 'You wanted *us*. Then here we are. Oh how we can talk!—with all those things you know! You *are* an invention. And you'll see there are things *I* know. I shall turn up here—well, daily.'

She took it in, but only after a moment answered. 'There was something you said just now you'd tell me. Don't you mean to try—?'

'Mrs. Worthingham?' He drew from within his coat his pocket-book and carefully found a place in it for Mary Cardew's carte-de-visite, folding it together with deliberation over which he put it back. Finally he spoke. 'No—I've decided. I can't —I don't want to.'

Cornelia marvelled—or looked as if she did. 'Not for all she has?'

'Yes—I know all she has. But I also know all she hasn't. And, as I told you, she herself doesn't—hasn't a glimmer of a suspicion of it; and never will have.'

Cornelia magnanimously thought. 'No— but she knows other things.'

He shook his head as at the portentous heap of them. 'Too many—too many. And other indeed—*so* other! Do you know,' he went on, 'that it's as if *you*—by turning up for me—had brought that home to me?'

' "For you," ' she candidly considered. 'But what—since you can't marry me!—can you do with me?'

Well, he seemed to have it all. 'Everything. I can live with you—just this way.' To illustrate which he dropped into the other chair by her fire; where, leaning back, he gazed at the flame. 'I can't give you up. It's very curious. It has come over me as it did over you when you renounced Bognor. That's it—I know it at last, and I see one can like it. I'm "high." You needn't deny it. That's my taste. I'm old.' And in spite of the considerable glow there of her little household altar he said it without the scowl.

1910

THE SENSE OF NEWPORT [1]

NEWPORT, on my finding myself back there, threatened me sharply, quite at first, with that predicament at which I have glanced in another connection or two—the felt condition of having known it too well and loved it too much for description or definition. What was one to say about it except that one *had* been so affected, so distraught, and that discriminations and reasons were buried under the dust of use? There was a chance indeed that the breath of the long years (of the interval of absence, I mean) would have blown away this dust—and that, precisely, was what one was eager to see. To go out, to look about, to recover the

1 In his preface to *The American Scene*, from which this sketch is taken, James wrote: 'There are features of the human scene, there are properties of the social air, that the newspapers, reports, surveys and blue-books would seem to confess themselves powerless to "handle," and that yet represented to me a greater array of items, a heavier expression of character, than my own pair of scales would ever weigh, keep them as clear for it as I might. I became aware soon enough, on the spot, that these elements of the human subject, the results of these attempted appreciations of life itself, would prove much too numerous even for a capacity all given to them for some ten months; but at least therefore, artistically concerned as I had been all my days with the human subject, with the appreciation of life itself, and with the consequent question of literary representation, I should not find such matters scant or simple. I was not in fact to do so, and they but led me on and on. How far this might have been my several chapters show; and yet even here I fall short.' James, *The American Scene* (N.Y., 1907), vi.

sense, was accordingly to put the question, without delay, to the proof—and with the happy consequence, I think, of an escape from a grave discomfiture. The charm was there again, unmistakably, the little old strange, very simple charm—to be expressed, as a fine proposition, or to be given up; but the answer came in the fact that to have walked about for half an hour was to have felt the question clear away. It cleared away so conveniently, so blissfully, in the light of the benign little truth, that nothing had been less possible, even in the early, ingenuous, infatuated days, than to describe or define Newport. It had clearly had nothing about it *to* describe or define, so that one's fondness had fairly rested on this sweet oddity in it. One had only to look back to recognise that it had never condescended to give a scrap of reasoned account of itself (as a favourite of fortune and the haunt of the *raffiné*); it had simply lain there like a little bare, white, open hand, with slightly-parted fingers, for the observer with a presumed sense for hands to take or to leave. The observer with a real sense never failed to pay this image the tribute of quite tenderly grasping the hand, and even of raising it, delicately, to his lips; having no less, at the same time, the instinct of not shaking it too hard, and that above all of never putting it to any rough work.

Such had been from the first, under a chastened light and in a purple sea, the dainty isle of Aquidneck; which might have avoided the weak mistake of giving up its pretty native name and of becoming thereby as good as nameless—with an existence as Rhode Island practically monopolised by the State and a Newport identity borrowed at the best and applicable but to a corner. Does not this vagueness of condition, however, fitly symbolise the small virtual promontory, of which, superficially, nothing could be predicated but its sky and its sea and its sunsets? One views it as placed there, by some refinement in the scheme of nature, just as a touchstone of taste—with a beautiful little sense to be read into it by a few persons, and nothing at all to be made of it, as to its essence, by most others. I come back, for its essence, to that figure of the little white hand, with the gracefully-spread fingers and the fine grain of skin, even the dimples at the joints and the shell-like delicacy of the pink nails—all the charms in short that a little white hand may have. I see all the applications of the image —I see a special truth in each. It is the back of the hand, rising to the swell of the wrist, that is exposed—which is the way, I think, the true lover takes and admires it. He makes out in it, bending over it—or he used to in the old days—innumerable shy and subtle beauties, almost requiring, for justice, a magnifying-glass; and he winces at the sight of certain other obtruded ways of dealing with it. The touchstone of taste was indeed to operate, for the critical, the tender spirit, from the moment the pink palm was turned up on the chance of what might be 'in' it. For nine persons out of ten, among its visitors, its purchasers of sites and builders of (in the old parlance) cottages, there had never been anything in it at all— except of course an opportunity: an opportunity for escaping the summer heat of other places, for bathing, for boating, for riding and driving, and for many sorts of more or less expensive riot. The pink palm being empty, in other words, to their vision, they had begun, from far back, to put things into it, things of their own, and of all sorts, and of many ugly, and of more and more expensive, sorts; to fill it substantially, that is, with gold, the gold that they have ended by heaping up there to an amount so oddly out of proportion to the scale of nature and of space.

This process, one was immediately to perceive with that renewal of impression, this process of injection and elaboration, of creating the palpable pile, had been going on for years to such a tune that the face of nature was now as much obliterated as possible, and the original shy sweetness as much as possible bedizened and bedevilled: all of which, moreover, might also at present be taken as having led, in turn, to the most unexpected climax, a matter of which I shall presently speak. The original shy sweetness, however, that range of effect which I have referred to as practically too latent and too modest for notation, had meanwhile had its votaries, the fond pedestrian minority, for whom the little white hand (to return for an instant to my figure with which, as you see, I am charmed) had always been so full of treasures of its own as to discredit, from the point of view of taste, any attempt, from without, to stuff it fuller. Such attempts had, in the nature of the case, and from far back, been condemned to show for violations; violations of taste and discretion, to begin with—violations, more intimately, as the whole business became brisker, of a thousand delicate secret places, dear to the disinterested rambler, small, mild 'points' and promontories, far away little lonely, sandy coves, rock-set, lily-sheeted ponds, almost hidden, and shallow Arcadian summer-haunted valleys, with the sea just over some stony shoulder: a whole world that called out to the long afternoons of youth, a world with its scale so measured and intended and happy, its detail so finished and pencilled and stippled (certainly for American detail!) that there comes back to me, across the many years, no better analogy for it than that of some fine foreground in an old 'line' engraving. There remained always a sense, of course, in which the superimpositions, the multiplied excrescences, were a tribute to the value of the place; where no such liberty was ever taken save exactly *because* (as even the most blundering builder would have claimed) it was all so beautiful, so solitary and so 'sympathetic.' And that indeed has been, thanks to the 'pilers-on' of gold, the fortune, the history of its beauty: that it now bristles with the villas and palaces into which the cottages have all turned, and that these monuments of pecuniary power rise thick and close, precisely, in order that their occupants may constantly remark to each other, from the windows to the 'grounds,' and from house to house, that it *is* beautiful, it *is* solitary and sympathetic. The thing has been done, it is impossible not to perceive, with the best faith in the world—though not altogether with the best light, which is always so different a matter; and it is with the general consequence only, at the end of the story, that I find myself to-day concerned.

So much concerned I found myself, I profess, after I had taken in this fact of a very distinct general consequence, that the whole interest of the vision was quickened by it; and that when, in particular, on one of the last days of June, among the densely-arrayed villas, I had followed the beautiful 'ocean drive' to its uttermost reach and back without meeting either another vehicle or a single rider, let alone a single pedes-

trian, I recognised matter for the intellectual thrill that attests a social revolution foreseen and completed. The term I use may appear extravagant, but it was a fact, none the less, that I seemed to take full in my face, on this occasion, the cold stir of air produced when the whirligig of time has made one of its liveliest turns. It is always going, the whirligig, but its effect is so to blow up the dust that we must wait for it to stop a moment, as it now and then does with a pant of triumph, in order to see what it has been at. I saw, beyond all doubt, on the spot—and *there* came in, exactly, the thrill; I could remember far back enough to have seen it begin to blow all the artless buyers and builders and blunderers into their places, leaving them there for half a century or so of fond security, and then to see it, of a sudden, blow them quite out again, as with the happy consciousness of some new amusing use for them, some other game still to play with them. This acquaintance, as it practically had been, with the whole rounding of the circle (even though much of it from a distance), was tantamount to the sense of having sat out the drama, the social, the local, that of a real American period, from the rise to the fall of the curtain—always assuming that truth of the reached catastrophe or *dénouement. How* this climax or solution had been arrived at—that, clearly, for the spectator, would have been worth taking note of; but what he made of it I shall not glance at till I have shown him as first of all, on the spot, quite modestly giving in to mere primary beguilement. It had been certain in advance that he would find the whole picture overpainted, and the question could only be, at the best, of how much of the ancient surface would here and there glimmer through. The ancient surface had been the concern, as I have hinted, of the small fond minority, the comparatively few people for whom the lurking shy charm, all there, but all to be felt rather than published, did in fact constitute a surface. The question, as soon as one arrived, was of whether some ghost of that were recoverable.

There was always, to begin with, the Old Town—we used, before we had become

Old ourselves, to speak of it that way, in the manner of an allusion to Nuremberg or to Carcassonne, since it had been leading its little historic life for centuries (as we implied) before 'cottages' and house-agents were dreamed of. It was not that we had great illusions about it or great pretensions for it; we only thought it, without interference, very 'good of its kind,' and we had as to its *being* of that kind no doubt whatever. Would it still be of that kind, and what had the kind itself been?—these questions made one's heart beat faster as one went forth in search of it. Distinctly, if it had been of a kind it *would* still be of it; for the kind wouldn't at the worst or at the best (one scarce knew how to put it) have been worth changing: so that the question for the restored absentee, who so palpitated with the sense of it, all hung, absolutely, on the validity of the past. One might well hold one's breath if the past, with the dear little blue distances in it, were in danger now of being given away. One might well pause before the possible indication that a cherished impression of youth had been but a figment of the mind. Fortunately, however, at Newport, and especially where the antiquities cluster, distances are short, and the note of reassurance awaited me almost round the first corner. One had been a hundred times right—for how *was* one to think of it all, as one went on, if one didn't think of it as Old? There played before one's eyes again, in fine, in that unmistakable silvery shimmer, a particular property of the local air, the exquisite law of the relative—the application of which, on the spot, is required to make even such places as Viterbo and Bagdad not seem new. One may sometimes be tired of the word, but anything that has succeeded in living long enough to become conscious of its *note*, is capable on occasion of making that note effectively sound. It *will* sound, we gather, if we listen for it, and the small silver whistle of the past, with its charming quaver of weak gayety, quite played the tune I asked of it up and down the tiny, sunny, empty Newport vistas, perspectives coming to a stop like the very short walks of very old ladies. What indeed but little very old ladies did they resemble, the little very old streets? with the same suggestion of present timidity and frugality of life, the same implication in their few folds

of drab, of mourning, of muslin still mysteriously starched, the implication of no adventure at any time, however far back, that mightn't have been suitable to a lady.

The whole low promontory, in its wider and remoter measurements, is a region of jutting, tide-troubled 'points,' but we had admired the Old Town too for the emphasis of its peculiar point, *the* Point; a quarter distinguished, we considered, by a really refined interest. Here would have been my misadventure, if I was to have any—that of missing, on the grey page of to-day, the suggestive passages I remembered; but I was to find, to my satisfaction, that there was still no more mistaking their pleasant sense than there had ever been: a quiet, mild waterside sense, not that of the bold, bluff outer sea, but one in which shores and strands and small coast things played the greater part; with overhanging back verandas, with little private wooden piers, with painted boat-houses and boats laid up, with still-water bathing (the very words, with their old, slightly prim discrimination, as of ladies and children jumping up and down, reach me across the years), with a wide-curving Bay and dim landward distances that melted into a mysterious, rich, superior, but quite disconnected and not at all permittedly patronising Providence. There were stories, anciently, for the Point—so prescribed a feature of it that one made them up, freely and handsomely, when they were not otherwise to be come by; though one was never quite sure if they ought most to apply to the rather blankly and grimly Colonial houses, fadedly drab at their richest and mainly, as the legend ran, appurtenant to that Quaker race whom Massachusetts and Connecticut had prehistorically cast forth and the great Roger Williams had handsomely welcomed, or to the other habitations, the felicitous cottages, with their galleries on the Bay and towards the sunset, their pleasure-boats at their little wharves, and the supposition, that clung to them, of their harbouring the less fashionable of the outer Great, but also the more cultivated and the more artistic. Everything was there still, as I say, and quite as much as anything the prolonged echo of that ingenuous old-time distinction. It was a marvel, no doubt, that the handful of light elements I have named should add up to any total deserving the name of *picture*, and if I must produce an explanation I seek it with a certain confidence in the sense of the secret enjoyed by that air for bathing or, as one figures, for dipping, the objects it deals with. It takes them uninteresting, but feels immediately what submersion can do for them; tips them in, keeps them down, holds them under, just for the proper length of time: after which they come up, as I say, irradiating vague silver—the reflection of which I have perhaps here been trying to catch even to extravagance.

I did nothing, at any rate, all an autumn morning, but discover again how 'good' everything had been—positively better than one had ventured to suppose in one's care to make the allowance for one's young simplicity. Some things indeed, clearly, had been better than one knew, and now seemed to surpass any fair probability: else why, for instance, should I have been quite awe-struck by the ancient State House that overlooks the ancient Parade?—an edifice ample, majestic, archaic, of the finest proportions and full of a certain public Dutch dignity, having brave, broad, high windows, in especial, the distinctness of whose innumerable square white-framed panes is the recall of some street view of Haarlem or Leyden. Here was the charming impression of a treasure of antiquity to the vague image of which, through the years, one hadn't done justice—any more than one had done it, positively, to three or four of the other old-time ornaments of the Parade (which, with its wide, cobbly, sleepy space, of those years, in the shadow of the State House, must have been much more of a Van der Heyden, or somebody of that sort, than one could have dreamed). There was a treasure of modernity to reckon with, in the form of one of the Commodores Perry (they are somehow much multiplied at Newport, and quite monumentally ubiquitous) engaged in his great naval act; but this was swept away in the general flood of justice to be done. I continued to do it all over the place, and I remember doing it next at a certain ample old-time house which used to unite with the still prettier and archaic Vernon, near it, to form an honourable pair. In this mild town-corner, where it was so indicated that the grass should be growing between the primitive paving-stones, and where indeed I honestly think it mainly is, amid whatever remains of them, ancient peace had appeared formerly to reign—though attended by the ghost of ancient war, inasmuch as these had indubitably been the haunts of our auxiliary French officers during the Revolution, and no self-respecting legend could fail to report that it was in the Vernon house Washington would have visited Rochambeau. There had hung about this structure, which is, architecturally speaking, all 'rusticated' and indefinable decency, the implication of an inward charm that refined even on its outward, and this was the tantalising message its clean, serious windows, never yet debased, struck me as still giving. But it was still (something told me) a question of not putting, anywhere, too many presumptions to the touch; so that my hand quitted the knocker when I was on the point of a tentative tap, and I fell back on the neighbour and mate, as to which there was unforgotten acquaintance to teach me certainty. Here, alas, cold change was installed; the place had become a public office—none of the 'artistic' super-civilised, no *raffiné* of them all, among the passing fanciers or collectors, having, strangely enough, marked it for his own. This mental appropriation it is, or it was a few months ago, really impossible not to make, at sight of its delightful hall and almost 'grand' staircase, its charming recessed, cupboarded, window-seated parlours, of its general panelled amplitude and dignity: the due taster of such things putting himself straight into possession on the spot, and, though wondering at the indifference and neglect, breathing thanks for the absence of positive ravage. For me there were special ghosts on the staircase, known voices in the brown old rooms—presences that one would have liked, however, to call a little to account. 'People don't do those things'; people didn't let so clear a case—clear for sound curiosity—go like that; they didn't, somehow, even if they were only ghosts. But I thought too, as I turned away, of all the others of the foolish, or at least of the responsible, those who for so long have swarmed in the modern quarter and who make profession of the finer sense.

This impression had been disturbing, but it had served its purpose in reconstituting, with a touch, a link—in laying down again it had served its purpose in reconstituting, every inch of the train of association with the human, the social, personal Newport of what I may call the middle years. To go farther afield, to measure the length of the little old Avenue and tread again the little old cliff-walk, to hang over, from above, the little old white crescent of the principal bathing-sands, with the big pond, behind them, set in its stone-walled featureless fields; to do these things and many others, every one of them thus accompanied by the admission that all that *had* been had been little, was to feel dead and buried generations push off even the transparence of their shroud and get into motion for the peopling of a scene that a present posterity has outgrown. The company of the middle years, the so considerably prolonged formative, tentative, imaginative Newport time, hadn't outgrown it—this catastrophe was still to come, as it constitutes, precisely, the striking dramatic *dénouement* I have already referred to. American society—so far as that free mixture was to have arrived at cohesion—had for half a century taken its whole relation with the place seriously (which was by intention very gayly); it long remained, for its happiness, quite at one with this most favoured resort of its comparative innocence. In the attesting presence of all the constant elements, of natural conditions that have, after all, persisted more than changed, a hundred far-away passages of the extinct life and joy, and of the comparative innocence, came back to me with an inevitable grace. A glamour as of the flushed ends of beautiful old summers, making a quite rich medium, a red sunset haze, as it were, for a processional throng of charioteers and riders, fortunate folk, fortunate above all in their untouched good faith, adjourning from the pleasures of the day to those of the evening—this benignity in particular overspread the picture, hanging it there as the Newport aspect that most lived again. Those good people all could make discoveries within the frame itself—beginning of course to push it out, in all directions, so as sufficiently to enlarge it, as they fondly fancied, even for the experience of a sophisticated world. They danced and they drove and they rode, they dined and wined and dressed and flirted and yachted and polo'd and Casino'd, responding to the subtlest inventions of their age; on the old lawns and verandas I saw them gather, on the old shining sands I saw them gallop, past the low headlands I saw their white sails verily flash, and through the dusky old shrubberies came the light and sound of their feasts.

It had all been in truth a history—for the imagination that could take it so; and when once that kindly stage was offered them it was a wonder how many figures and faces, how many names and voices, images and embodiments of youth mainly, and often of Beauty, and of felicity and fortune almost always, or of what then passed for such, pushed, under my eyes, in blurred gayety, to the front. Hadn't it been above all, in its good faith, the Age of Beauties—the blessed age when it was so easy to *be*, 'on the Avenue,' a Beauty, and when it was so easy, not less, not to doubt of the unsurpassability of such as appeared there? It was through the fact that the whole scheme and opportunity satisfied them, the fact that the place was, as I say, good enough for them—it was through this that, with ingenuities and audacities and refinements of their own (some of the more primitive of which are still touching to think of) they extended the boundaries of civilisation, and fairly taught themselves to believe they were doing it in the interest of nature. Beautiful the time when the Ocean Drive had been hailed at once as a triumph of civilisation and as a proof of the possible appeal of Scenery even to the dissipated. It was spoken of as of almost boundless extent—as one of the wonders of the world; as indeed it does turn often, in the gloaming, to purple and gold, and as the small sea-coves then gleam on its edge like barbaric gems on a mantle. Yet if it was a question of waving the wand and of breathing again, till it stirred, on the quaintness of the old manners—I refer to those of the fifties, sixties, seventies, and don't exclude those of the eighties—it was most touching of all to go back to dimmest days, days, such as now appear antediluvian, when ocean-drives, engineered by landscape artists and literally macadamized all the way, were still in the lap of time; when there was only an afternoon for the Fort, and another for the Beach, and another for

the 'Boathouse'—inconceivable innocence!
—and even the shortness of the Avenue
seemed very long, and even its narrowness
very wide, and even its shabbiness very
promising for the future, and when, in fine,
chariots and cavaliers took their course,
across country, to Bateman's, by inelegant
precarious tracts and returned, through the
darkling void, with a sense of adventure and
fatigue. That, I can't but think, was the
pure Newport time, the most perfectly
guarded by a sense of margin and of mystery.

It was the time of settled possession, and
yet furthest removed from these blank days
in which margin has been consumed and
the palaces, on the sites but the other day
beyond price, stare silently seaward, monuments to the *blasé* state of their absent proprietors. Purer still, however, I remind myself, was that stretch of years which I have
reasons for thinking sacred, when the custom of seeking hibernation on the spot
partly prevailed, when the local winter inherited something of the best social grace
(as it liked at least to think) of the splendid
summer, and when the strange sight might
be seen of a considerable company of
Americans, not gathered at a mere rest-
cure, who confessed brazenly to not being
in business. Do I grossly exaggerate in saying that this company, candidly, quite excitedly self-conscious, as all companies not
commercial, in America, may be pleasantly
noted as being, formed, for the time of its
persistence, an almost unprecedented small
body—unprecedented in American conditions; a collection of the detached, the
slightly disenchanted and casually dis-
qualified, and yet of the resigned and contented, of the socially orthodox: a handful
of mild, oh delightfully mild, cosmopolites,
united by three common circumstances,
that of their having for the most part more
or less lived in Europe, that of their sacri-
ficing openly to the ivory idol whose name
is leisure, and that, not least, of a formed
critical habit. These things had been felt as
making them excrescences on the American
surface, where nobody ever criticised, especially after the grand tour, and where the
great black ebony god of business was the
only one recognised. So I see them, at all
events, in fond memory, lasting as long as
they could and finding no successors; and

they are most embalmed for me, I confess,
in that scented, somewhat tattered, but
faintly spiced, wrapper of their various
'European' antecedents. I see them move
about in the light of these, and I understand
how it was this that made them ask what
would have become of them, and where in
the world, the hard American world, they
could have hibernated, how they could even,
in the Season, have bowed their economic
heads and lurked, if it hadn't been for Newport. I think of that question as, in their reduced establishments, over their winter
whist, under their private theatricals, and
pending, constantly, their loan and their
return of the *Revue des Deux-Mondes*,
their main conversational note. I find myself in fact tenderly evoking them as special instances of the great—or perhaps I
have a right only to say of the small—
American complication; the state of one's
having been so pierced, betimes, by the
sharp outland dart as to be able ever afterwards but to move about, vaguely and
helplessly, with the shaft still in one's
side.

Their nostalgia, however exquisite, was,
I none the less gather, sterile, for they appear to have left no seed. They must have
died, some of them, in order to 'go back'—
to go back, that is, to Paris. If I make, at all
events, too much of them, it is for their propriety as a delicate subjective value matching with the intrinsic Newport delicacy.
They must have felt that they, obviously,
notably, notoriously, did match—the proof
of which was in the fact that to them alone,
of the customary thousands, was the beauty
of the good walk, over the lovely little land,
revealed. The customary thousands here,
as throughout the United States, never set
foot to earth—yet this had happened so, of
old, to be the particular corner of *their*
earth that made that adventure most possible. At Newport, as the phrase was, in autumnal, in vernal hibernation, you *could*
walk—failing which, in fact, you failed of
impressions the most consolatory; and it is
mainly to the far ends of the low, densely
shrubbed and perfectly finished little headlands that I see our friends ramble as if to
stretch fond arms across the sea. There
used to be distant places beyond Bateman's,
or better still on the opposite isle of Conani-
cut, now blighted with ugly uses, where

nursing a nostalgia on the sun-warmed rocks was almost as good as having none at all. So it was not only not our friends who had overloaded and overcrowded, but it was they at last, I infer, who gave way before that grossness. How should they have wished to leave seed only to be trampled by the white elephants?

The white elephants, as one may best call them, all cry and no wool, all house and no garden, make now, for three or four miles, a barely interrupted chain, and I dare say I think of them best, and of the distressful, inevitable waste they represent, as I recall the impression of a divine little drive, roundabout them and pretty well everywhere, taken, for renewal of acquaintance, while November was still mild. I sought another renewal, as I have intimated, in the vacant splendour of June, but the interesting evidence then only refined on that already gathered. The place itself, as man—and often, no doubt, alas, as woman, with her love of the immediate and contiguous—had taken it over, was more than ever, to the fancy, like some dim, simplified ghost of a small Greek island, where the clear walls of some pillared portico or pavilion, perched afar, looked like those of temples of the gods, and where Nature, deprived of that ease in merely massing herself on which 'American scenery,' as we lump it together, is too apt to depend for its effect, might have shown a piping shepherd on any hillside or attached a mythic image to any point of rocks. What an idea, originally, to have seen this miniature spot of earth, where the sea-nymphs on the curved sands, at the worst, might have chanted back to the shepherds, as a mere breeding-ground for white elephants! They look queer and conscious and lumpish—some of them, as with an air of the brandished proboscis, really grotesque—while their averted owners, roused from a witless dream, wonder what in the world is to be done with them. The answer to which, I think, can only be that there is absolutely nothing to be done; nothing but to let them stand there always, vast and blank, for reminder to those concerned of the prohibited degrees of witlessness, and of the peculiarly awkward vengeances of affronted proportion and discretion.

1906   1907

THREE FRAGMENTS[1]
FROM THE WINGS OF THE DOVE
Sir Luke Strett

WHAT it really came to, on the morrow this first time—the time Kate went with her—was that the great man had, a little, to excuse himself; had, by a rare accident—for he kept his consulting-hours in general rigorously free—but ten minutes to give her; ten mere minutes which he yet placed at her service in a manner that she admired still more than she could meet it: so crystal-clean the great empty cup of attention that he set between them on the table. He was presently to jump into his carriage, but he promptly made the point that he must see her again, see her within a day or two; and he named for her at once another hour—easing her off beautifully too even then in respect to her possibly failing of justice to her errand. The minutes affected her in fact as ebbing more swiftly than her little army of items could muster, and they would probably have gone without her doing much more than secure another hearing, hadn't it been for her sense, at the last, that she had gained above all an impression. The impression—all the sharp growth of the final few moments—was neither more nor less than that she might make, of a sudden, in quite another world, another straight friend, and a friend who would moreover be, wonderfully, the most appointed, the most thoroughly adjusted of the whole collection, inasmuch as he would somehow wear the character scientifically, ponderably, proveably—not just loosely and sociably. Literally, furthermore, it wouldn't really depend on herself, Sir Luke Strett's friendship, in the least: perhaps what made her most stammer and pant was its thus queerly coming over her that she might find she had interested him even beyond her intention, find she was in fact launched in some current that would lose itself in the sea of science. At the same time that she struggled, however, she also surrendered; there was a moment at which she almost dropped the form of stating, of explaining, and threw herself, without violence, only

[1] These fragments, illustrative of James' highly developed use of the simile, are, consecutively, from *The Novels and Tales of Henry James*(N.Y., 1909),XIX, 230–31;XX,138–40;XXIV,3–4.

with a supreme pointless quaver that had turned the next instant to an intensity of interrogative stillness, upon his general good will. His large settled face, though firm, was not, as she had thought at first, hard; he looked, in the oddest manner, to her fancy, half like a general and half like a bishop, and she was soon sure that, within some such handsome range, what it would show her would be what was good, what was best for her. She had established, in other words, in this time-saving way, a relation with it; and the relation was the special trophy that, for the hour, she bore off. It was like an absolute possession, a new resource altogether, something done up in the softest silk and tucked away under the arm of memory. She hadn't had it when she went in, and she had it when she came out; she had it there under her cloak, but dissimulated, invisibly carried, when smiling, smiling, she again faced Kate Croy.

1902

The Play of Friendship

THESE puttings-off of the mask had finally quite become the form taken by their moments together, moments indeed not increasingly frequent and not prolonged, thanks to the consciousness of fatigue on Milly's side whenever, as she herself expressed it, she got out of harness. They flourished their masks, the independent pair, as they might have flourished Spanish fans; they smiled and sighed on removing them; but the gesture, the smiles, the sighs, strangely enough, might have been suspected the greatest reality in the business. Strangely enough, we say, for the volume of effusion in general would have been found by either on measurement to be scarce proportional to the paraphernalia of relief. It was when they called each other's attention to their ceasing to pretend, it was then that what they were keeping back was most in the air. There was a difference, no doubt, and mainly to Kate's advantage: Milly didn't quite see what her friend could keep back, was possessed of, in fine, that would be so subject to retention; whereas it was comparatively plain sailing for Kate that poor Milly had a treasure to hide. This was not the treasure of a shy, an abject affection—concealment, on that head, belonging to

quite another phase of such states; it was much rather a principle of pride relatively bold and hard, a principle that played up like a fine steel spring at the lightest pressure of too near a footfall. Thus insuperably guarded was the truth about the girl's own conception of her validity; thus was a wondering pitying sister condemned wistfully to look at her from the far side of the moat she had dug round her tower. Certain aspects of the connexion of these young women show for us, such is the twilight that gathers about them, in the likeness of some dim scene in a Maeterlinck play; we have positively the image, in the delicate dusk, of the figures so associated and yet so opposed, so mutually watchful: that of the angular pale princess, ostrich-plumed, black-robed, hung about with amulets, reminders, relics, mainly seated, mainly still, and that of the upright restless slow-circling lady of her court who exchanges with her, across the black water streaked with evening gleams, fitful questions and answers. The upright lady, with thick dark braids down her back, drawing over the grass a more embroidered train, makes the whole circuit, and makes it again, and the broken talk, brief and sparingly allusive, seems more to cover than to free their sense. This is because, when it fairly comes to not having others to consider, they meet in an air that appears rather anxiously to wait for their words. Such an impression as that was in fact grave, and might be tragic; so that, plainly enough, systematically at last, they settled to a care of what they said.

1902

FROM THE GOLDEN BOWL
The Pagoda Arrangement

IT wasn't till many days had passed that the Princess began to accept the idea of having done, a little, something she was not always doing, or indeed that of having listened to any inward voice that spoke in a new tone. Yet these instinctive postponements of reflexion were the fruit, positively, of recognitions and perceptions already active; of the sense above all that she had made at a particular hour, made by the mere touch of her hand, a difference in the situation so long present to her as practically unattackable. This situation had been occupying for months and months the very centre of the garden of her life, but it had reared itself there like some strange tall tower of ivory, or perhaps rather some wonderful beautiful but outlandish pagoda, a structure plated with hard bright porcelain, coloured and figured and adorned at the overhanging eaves with silver bells that tinkled ever so charmingly when stirred by chance airs. She had walked round and round it—that was what she felt; she had carried on her existence in the space left her for circulation, a space that sometimes seemed ample and sometimes narrow: looking up all the while at the fair structure that spread itself so amply and rose so high, but never quite making out as yet where she might have entered had she wished. She hadn't wished till now—such was the odd case; and what was doubtless equally odd besides was that though her raised eyes seemed to distinguish places that must serve from within, and especially far aloft, as apertures and outlooks, no door appeared to give access from her convenient garden level. The great decorated surface had remained consistently impenetrable and inscrutable. At present however, to her considering mind, it was as if she had ceased merely to circle and to scan the elevation, ceased so vaguely, so quite helplessly to stare and wonder: she had caught herself distinctly in the act of pausing, then in that of lingering, and finally in that of stepping unprecedentedly near. The thing might have been, by the distance at which it kept her, a Mahometan mosque, with which no base heretic could take a liberty; there so hung about it the vision of putting off one's shoes to enter and even verily of one's paying with one's life if found there as an interloper. She hadn't certainly arrived at the conception of paying with her life for anything she might do; but it was nevertheless quite as if she had sounded with a tap or two one of the rare porcelain plates. She had knocked in short —though she could scarce have said whether for admission or for what; she had applied her hand to a cool smooth spot and had waited to see what would happen. Something *had* happened; it was as if a sound, at her touch, after a little, had come back to her from within; a sound sufficiently suggesting that her approach had been noted.

1904

EDITH WHARTON

1862–1937

THE OTHER TWO

I

WAYTHORN, on the drawing-room hearth, waited for his wife to come down to dinner.

It was their first night under his own roof, and he was surprised at his thrill of boyish agitation. He was not so old, to be sure—his glass gave him little more than the five-and-thirty years to which his wife confessed—but he had fancied himself already in the temperate zone; yet here he was listening for her step with a tender sense of all it symbolised, with some old trail of verse about the garlanded nuptial door-posts floating through his enjoyment of the pleasant room and the good dinner just beyond it.

They had been hastily recalled from their honeymoon by the illness of Lily Haskett, the child of Mrs. Waythorn's first marriage. The little girl, at Waythorn's desire, had been transferred to his house on the day of her mother's wedding, and the doctor, on their arrival, broke the news that she was ill with typhoid, but declared that all the symptoms were favourable. Lily could show twelve years of unblemished health, and the case promised to be a light one. The nurse spoke as reassuringly, and after a moment of alarm Mrs. Waythorn had adjusted herself to the situation. She was very fond of Lily—her affection for the child had perhaps been her decisive charm in Waythorn's eyes—but she had the perfectly balanced nerves which her little girl had inherited, and no woman ever wasted less tissue in unproductive worry. Waythorn was therefore quite prepared to see her come in presently, a little late because of a last look at Lily, but as serene and well-appointed as if her good-night kiss had been laid on the brow of health. Her composure was restful to him; it acted as ballast to his somewhat unstable sensibilities. As he pictured her bending over the child's bed he thought how soothing her presence must be in illness: her very step would prognosticate recovery.

His own life had been a gray one, from temperament rather than circumstance, and he had been drawn to her by the unperturbed gaiety which kept her fresh and elastic at an age when most women's activities are growing either slack or febrile. He knew what was said about her; for, popular as she was, there had always been a faint undercurrent of detraction. When she had appeared in New York, nine or ten years earlier, as the pretty Mrs. Haskett whom Gus Varick had unearthed somewhere—was it in Pittsburgh or Utica?—society, while promptly accepting her, had reserved the right to cast a doubt on its own indiscrimination. Enquiry, however, established her undoubted connection with a socially reigning family, and explained her recent divorce as the natural result of a runaway match at seventeen; and as nothing was known of Mr. Haskett it was easy to believe the worst of him.

Alice Haskett's remarriage with Gus Varick was a passport to the set whose recognition she coveted, and for a few years the Varicks were the most popular couple in town. Unfortunately the alliance was brief and stormy, and this time the husband had his champions. Still, even Varick's stanchest supporters admitted that he was not meant for matrimony, and Mrs. Varick's grievances were of a nature to bear the inspection of the New York courts. A New York divorce is in itself a diploma of virtue, and in the semi-widowhood of this second separation Mrs. Varick took on an air of sanctity, and was allowed to confide her wrongs to some of the most scrupulous ears in town. But when it was known that she was to marry Waythorn there was a momentary reaction. Her best friends would have preferred to see her remain in the rôle of the injured wife, which was as becoming to her as crape to a rosy complexion. True, a decent time had elapsed, and it was not even suggested that Waythorn had supplanted his predecessor. People shook their heads over him, however, and one grudging friend, to whom he affirmed that he took the step with his eyes open, replied oracularly: 'Yes—and with your ears shut.'

Waythorn could afford to smile at these innuendoes. In the Wall Street phrase, he had 'discounted' them. He knew that society has not yet adapted itself to the consequences of divorce, and that till the adaptation takes place every woman who uses the freedom the law accords her must be her own social justification. Waythorn had an amused confidence in his wife's ability to justify herself. His expectations were fulfilled, and before the wedding took place Alice Varick's group had rallied openly to her support. She took it all imperturbably: she had a way of surmounting obstacles without seeming to be aware of them, and Waythorn looked back with wonder at the trivialities over which he had worn his nerves thin. He had the sense of having found refuge in a richer, warmer nature than his own, and his satisfaction, at the moment, was humourously summed up in the thought that his wife, when she had done all she could for Lily, would not be ashamed to come down and enjoy a good dinner.

The anticipation of such enjoyment was not, however, the sentiment expressed by Mrs. Waythorn's charming face when she presently joined him. Though she had put on her most engaging teagown she had neglected to assume the smile that went with it, and Waythorn thought he had never seen her look so nearly worried.

'What is it?' he asked. 'Is anything wrong with Lily?'

'No; I've just been in and she's still sleeping.' Mrs. Waythorn hesitated. 'But something tiresome has happened.'

He had taken her two hands, and now perceived that he was crushing a paper between them.

'This letter?'

'Yes—Mr. Haskett has written—I mean his lawyer has written.'

Waythorn felt himself flush uncomfortably. He dropped his wife's hands.

'What about?'

'About seeing Lily. You know the courts —'

'Yes, yes,' he interrupted nervously.

Nothing was known about Haskett in New York. He was vaguely supposed to have remained in the outer darkness from which his wife had been rescued, and Waythorn was one of the few who were aware that he had given up his business in Utica and followed her to New York in order to be near his little girl. In the days of his wooing, Waythorn had often met Lily on the doorstep, rosy and smiling, on her way 'to see papa.'

'I am so sorry,' Mrs. Waythorn murmured.

He roused himself. 'What does he want?'

'He wants to see her. You know she goes to him once a week.'

'Well—he doesn't expect her to go to him now, does he?'

'No—he has heard of her illness; but he expects to come here.'

'*Here?*'

Mrs. Waythorn reddened under his gaze. They looked away from each other.

'I'm afraid he has the right. . . . You'll see. . . .' She made a proffer of the letter.

Waythorn moved away with a gesture of refusal. He stood staring about the softly lighted room, which a moment before had seemed so full of bridal intimacy.

'I'm so sorry,' she repeated. 'If Lily could have been moved—'

'That's out of the question,' he returned impatiently.

'I suppose so.'

Her lip was beginning to tremble, and he felt himself a brute.

'He must come, of course,' he said. 'When is—his day?'

'I'm afraid—to-morrow.'

'Very well. Send a note in the morning.'

The butler entered to announce dinner.

Waythorn turned to his wife. 'Come—you must be tired. It's beastly, but try to forget about it,' he said, drawing her hand through his arm.

'You're so good, dear. I'll try,' she whispered back.

Her face cleared at once, and as she looked at him across the flowers, between the rosy candle-shades, he saw her lips waver back into a smile.

'How pretty everything is!' she sighed luxuriously.

He turned to the butler. 'The champagne at once, please. Mrs. Waythorn is tired.'

In a moment or two their eyes met above the sparkling glasses. Her own were quite clear and untroubled: he saw that she had obeyed his injunction and forgotten.

II

Waythorn, the next morning, went down town earlier than usual. Haskett was not likely to come till the afternoon, but the instinct of flight drove him forth. He meant to stay away all day—he had thoughts of dining at his club. As his door closed behind him he reflected that before he opened it again it would have admitted another man who had as much right to enter it as himself, and the thought filled him with a physical repugnance.

He caught the 'elevated' at the employés' hour, and found himself crushed between two layers of pendulous humanity. At Eighth Street the man facing him wriggled out, and another took his place. Waythorn glanced up and saw that it was Gus Varick. The men were so close together that it was impossible to ignore the smile of recognition on Varick's handsome overblown face. And after all—why not? They had always been on good terms, and Varick had been divorced before Waythorn's attentions to his wife began. The two exchanged a word on the perennial grievance of the congested trains, and when a seat at their side was miraculously left empty the instinct of self-preservation made Waythorn slip into it after Varick.

The latter drew the stout man's breath of relief. 'Lord—I was beginning to feel like a pressed flower.' He leaned back, looking unconcernedly at Waythorn. 'Sorry to hear that Sellers is knocked out again.'

'Sellers?' echoed Waythorn, starting at his partner's name.

Varick looked surprised. 'You didn't know he was laid up with the gout?'

'No, I've been away—I only got back last night.' Waythorn felt himself reddening in anticipation of the other's smile.

'Ah—yes; to be sure. And Sellers's attack came on two days ago. I'm afraid he's pretty bad. Very awkward for me, as it happens, because he was just putting through a rather important thing for me.'

'Ah?' Waythorn wondered vaguely since when Varick had been dealing in 'important things.' Hitherto he had dabbled only in the shallow pools of speculation, with which Waythorn's office did not usually concern itself.

It occurred to him that Varick might be talking at random, to relieve the strain of their propinquity. That strain was becoming momentarily more apparent to Waythorn, and when, at Cortlandt Street, he caught sight of an acquaintance and had a sudden vision of the picture he and Varick must present to an initiated eye, he jumped up with a muttered excuse.

'I hope you'll find Sellers better,' said Varick civilly, and he stammered back: 'If I can be of any use to you—' and let the departing crowd sweep him to the platform.

At his office he heard that Sellers was in fact ill with the gout, and would probably not be able to leave the house for some weeks.

'I'm sorry it should have happened so, Mr. Waythorn,' the senior clerk said with affable significance. 'Mr. Sellers was very much upset at the idea of giving you such a lot of extra work just now.'

'Oh, that's no matter,' said Waythorn hastily. He secretly welcomed the pressure of additional business, and was glad to think that, when the day's work was over, he would have to call at his partner's on the way home.

He was late for luncheon, and turned in at the nearest restaurant instead of going to his club. The place was full, and the waiter hurried him to the back of the room to capture the only vacant table. In the cloud of cigar-smoke Waythorn did not at once distinguish his neighbours; but presently, looking about him, he saw Varick seated a few feet off. This time, luckily, they were too far apart for conversation, and Varick, who faced another way, had probably not even seen him; but there was an irony in their renewed nearness.

Varick was said to be fond of good living, and as Waythorn sat despatching his hurried luncheon he looked across half enviously at the other's leisurely degustation of his meal. When Waythorn first saw him he had been helping himself with critical deliberation to a bit of Camembert at the ideal point of liquefaction, and now, the cheese removed, he was just pouring his *café double* from its little two-storied earthen pot. He poured slowly, his ruddy profile bent above the task, and one be-ringed white hand steadying the lid of the coffee-pot; then he stretched his other hand to the decanter of cognac at his elbow, filled a liqueur-glass, took a tentative sip, and poured the brandy into his coffee-cup.

Waythorn watched him in a kind of fascination. What was he thinking of—only of the flavour of the coffee and the liqueur? Had the morning's meeting left no more trace in his thoughts than on his face? Had his wife so completely passed out of his life that even this odd encounter with her present husband, within a week after her remarriage, was no more than an incident in his day? And as Waythorn mused, another idea struck him: had Haskett ever met Varick as Varick and he had just met? The recollection of Haskett perturbed him, and he rose and left the restaurant, taking a circuitous way out to escape the placid irony of Varick's nod.

It was after seven when Waythorn reached home. He thought the footman who opened the door looked at him oddly.

'How is Miss Lily?' he asked in haste.

'Doing very well, sir. A gentleman—'

'Tell Barlow to put off dinner for half an hour,' Waythorn cut him off, hurrying upstairs.

He went straight to his room and dressed without seeing his wife. When he reached the drawing-room she was there, fresh and radiant. Lily's day had been good; the doctor was not coming back that evening.

At dinner Waythorn told her of Sellers' illness and of the resulting complications. She listened sympathetically, adjuring him not to let himself be overworked, and asking vague feminine questions about the routine of the office. Then she gave him the chronicle of Lily's day; quoted the nurse and doctor, and told him who had called to inquire. He had never seen her more serene and unruffled. It struck him, with a curious pang, that she was very happy in being with him, so happy that she found a childish pleasure in rehearsing the trivial incidents of her day.

After dinner they went to the library, and the servant put the coffee and liqueurs on a low table before her and left the room. She looked singularly soft and girlish in her rosy pale dress, against the dark leather of one of his bachelor armchairs. A day earlier the contrast would have charmed him.

He turned away now, choosing a cigar with affected deliberation.

'Did Haskett come?' he asked, with his back to her.

'Oh, yes—he came.'

'You didn't see him, of course?'

She hesitated a moment. 'I let the nurse see him.'

That was all. There was nothing more to ask. He swung round toward her, applying a match to his cigar. Well, the thing was over for a week, at any rate. He would try not to think of it. She looked up at him, a trifle rosier than usual, with a smile in her eyes.

'Ready for your coffee, dear?'

He leaned against the mantelpiece, watching her as she lifted the coffee-pot. The lamplight struck a gleam from her bracelets and tipped her soft hair with brightness. How light and slender she was, and how each gesture flowed into the next! She seemed a creature all compact of harmonies. As the thought of Haskett receded, Waythorn felt himself yielding again to the joy of possessorship. They were his, those white hands with their flitting motions, his the light haze of hair, the lips and eyes. . . .

She set down the coffee-pot, and reaching for the decanter of cognac, measured off a liqueur-glass and poured it into his cup.

Waythorn uttered a sudden exclamation.

'What is the matter?' she said, startled.

'Nothing; only—I don't take cognac in my coffee.'

'Oh, how stupid of me,' she cried.

Their eyes met, and she blushed a sudden agonised red.

III

Ten days later, Mr. Sellers, still house-bound, asked Waythorn to call on his way down town.

The senior partner, with his swaddled foot propped up by the fire, greeted his associate with an air of embarrassment.

'I'm sorry, my dear fellow; I've got to ask you to do an awkward thing for me.'

Waythorn waited, and the other went on, after a pause apparently given to the arrangement of his phrases: 'The fact is, when I was knocked out I had just gone into a rather complicated piece of business for—Gus Varick.'

'Well?' said Waythorn, with an attempt to put him at his ease.

'Well—it's this way: Varick came to me the day before my attack. He had evidently had an inside tip from somebody, and had made about a hundred thousand. He came to me for advice, and I suggested his going in with Vanderlyn.'

'Oh, the deuce!' Waythorn exclaimed. He saw in a flash what had happened. The investment was an alluring one, but required negotiation. He listened quietly while Sellers put the case before him, and, the statement ended, he said: 'You think I ought to see Varick?'

'I'm afraid I can't as yet. The doctor is obdurate. And this thing can't wait. I hate to ask you, but no one else in the office knows the ins and outs of it.'

Waythorn stood silent. He did not care a farthing for the success of Varick's venture, but the honour of the office was to be considered, and he could hardly refuse to oblige his partner.

'Very well,' he said, 'I'll do it.'

That afternoon, apprised by telephone, Varick called at the office. Waythorn, waiting in his private room, wondered what the others thought of it. The newspapers, at the time of Mrs. Waythorn's marriage, had acquainted their readers with every detail of her previous matrimonial ventures, and Waythorn could fancy the clerks smiling behind Varick's back as he was ushered in.

Varick bore himself admirably. He was easy without being undignified, and Waythorn was conscious of cutting a much less impressive figure. Varick had no experience of business, and the talk prolonged itself for nearly an hour while Waythorn set forth with scrupulous precision the details of the proposed transaction.

'I'm awfully obliged to you,' Varick said as he rose. 'The fact is I'm not used to having much money to look after, and I don't want to make an ass of myself—' He smiled, and Waythorn could not help noticing that there was something pleasant about his smile. 'It feels uncommonly queer to have enough cash to pay one's bills. I'd have sold my soul for it a few years ago!'

Waythorn winced at the allusion. He had heard it rumoured that a lack of funds had been one of the determining causes of the Varick separation, but it did not occur to him that Varick's words were intentional. It seemed more likely that the desire to keep clear of embarrassing topics had fatally drawn him into one. Waythorn did not wish to be outdone in civility.

'We'll do the best we can for you,' he said. 'I think this is a good thing you're in.'

'Oh, I'm sure it's immense. It's awfully good of you—' Varick broke off, embarrassed. 'I suppose the thing's settled now—but if—'

'If anything happens before Sellers is about, I'll see you again,' said Waythorn quietly. He was glad, in the end, to appear the more self-possessed of the two.

The course of Lily's illness ran smooth, and as the days passed Waythorn grew used to the idea of Haskett's weekly visit. The first time the day came round, he stayed out late, and questioned his wife as to the visit on his return. She replied at once that Haskett had merely seen the nurse downstairs, as the doctor did not wish any one in the child's sick-room till after the crisis.

The following week Waythorn was again conscious of the recurrence of the day, but had forgotten it by the time he came home to dinner. The crisis of the disease came a few days later, with a rapid decline of fever, and the little girl was pronounced out of danger. In the rejoicing which ensued the thought of Haskett passed out of Waythorn's mind, and one afternoon, letting himself into the house with a latch-key, he went straight to his library without noticing a shabby hat and umbrella in the hall.

In the library he found a small effaced-looking man with a thinnish gray beard sitting on the edge of a chair. The stranger might have been a piano-tuner, or one of those mysteriously efficient persons who are summoned in emergencies to adjust some detail of the domestic machinery. He blinked at Waythorn through a pair of gold-rimmed spectacles and said mildly: 'Mr. Waythorn, I presume? I am Lily's father.'

Waythorn flushed. 'Oh—' he stammered uncomfortably. He broke off, disliking to appear rude. Inwardly he was trying to adjust the actual Haskett to the image of him projected by his wife's reminiscences. Waythorn had been allowed to infer that Alice's first husband was a brute.

'I am sorry to intrude,' said Haskett, with his over-the-counter politeness.

'Don't mention it,' returned Waythorn, collecting himself. 'I suppose the nurse has been told?'

'I presume so. I can wait,' said Haskett. He had a resigned way of speaking, as though life had worn down his natural powers of resistance.

Waythorn stood on the threshold, nervously pulling off his gloves.

'I'm sorry you've been detained. I will send for the nurse,' he said; and as he opened the door he added with an effort: 'I'm glad we can give you a good report of Lily.' He winced as the *we* slipped out, but Haskett seemed not to notice it.

'Thank you, Mr. Waythorn. It's been an anxious time for me.'

'Ah, well, that's past. Soon she'll be able to go to you.' Waythorn nodded and passed out.

In his own room he flung himself down with a groan. He hated the womanish sensibility which made him suffer so acutely from the grotesque chances of life. He had known when he married that his wife's former husbands were both living, and that amid the multiplied contacts of modern existence there were a thousand chances to one that he would run against one or the other, yet he found himself as much disturbed by his brief encounter with Haskett as though the law had not obligingly removed all difficulties in the way of their meeting.

Waythorn sprang up and began to pace the room nervously. He had not suffered half as much from his two meetings with Varick. It was Haskett's presence in his own house that made the situation so intolerable. He stood still, hearing steps in the passage.

'This way, please,' he heard the nurse say. Haskett was being taken upstairs, then: not a corner of the house but was open to him. Waythorn dropped into another chair, staring vaguely ahead of him. On his dressing-table stood a photograph of Alice, taken when he had first known her. She was Alice Varick then—how fine and exquisite he had thought her! Those were Varick's pearls about her neck. At Waythorn's instance they had been returned before her marriage. Had Haskett ever given her any trinkets—

and what had become of them, Waythorn wondered? He realised suddenly that he knew very little of Haskett's past or present situation; but from the man's appearance and manner of speech he could reconstruct with curious precision the surroundings of Alice's first marriage. And it startled him to think that she had, in the background of her life, a phase of existence so different from anything with which he had connected her. Varick, whatever his faults, was a gentleman, in the conventional, traditional sense of the term: the sense which at that moment seemed, oddly enough, to have most meaning to Waythorn. He and Varick had the same social habits, spoke the same language, understood the same allusions. But this other man . . . it was grotesquely uppermost in Waythorn's mind that Haskett had worn a made-up tie attached with an elastic. Why should that ridiculous detail symbolise the whole man? Waythorn was exasperated by his own paltriness, but the fact of the tie expanded, forced itself on him, became as it were the key to Alice's past. He could see her, as Mrs. Haskett, sitting in a 'front parlour' furnished in plush, with a pianola, and a copy of *Ben Hur* on the centre-table. He could see her going to the theatre with Haskett—or perhaps even to a 'Church Sociable'—she in a 'picture hat' and Haskett in a black frock-coat, a little creased, with the made-up tie on an elastic. On the way home they would stop and look at the illuminated shop-windows, lingering over the photographs of New York actresses. On Sunday afternoons Haskett would take her for a walk, pushing Lily ahead of them in a white enamelled perambulator, and Waythorn had a vision of the people they would stop and talk to. He could fancy how pretty Alice must have looked, in a dress adroitly constructed from the hints of a New York fashion-paper, and how she must have looked down on the other women chafing at her life, and secretly feeling that she belonged in a bigger place.

For the moment his foremost thought was one of wonder at the way in which she had shed the phase of existence which her marriage with Haskett implied. It was as if her whole aspect, every gesture, every inflection, every allusion, were a studied negation of that period of her life. If she had denied being married to Haskett she could hardly have stood more convicted of duplicity than in this obliteration of the self which had been his wife.

Waythorn started up, checking himself in the analysis of her motives. What right had he to create a fantastic effigy of her and then pass judgment on it? She had spoken vaguely of her first marriage as unhappy, had hinted, with becoming reticence, that Haskett had wrought havoc among her young illusions. . . . It was a pity for Waythorn's peace of mind that Haskett's very inoffensiveness shed a new light on the nature of those illusions. A man would rather think that his wife has been brutalised by her first husband than that the process has been reversed.

IV

'Mr. Waythorn, I don't like that French governess of Lily's.'

Haskett, subdued and apologetic, stood before Waythorn in the library, revolving his shabby hat in his hand.

Waythorn, surprised in his armchair over the evening paper, stared back perplexedly at his visitor.

'You'll excuse my asking to see you,' Haskett continued. 'But this is my last visit, and I thought if I could have a word with you it would be a better way than writing to Mrs. Waythorn's lawyer.'

Waythorn rose uneasily. He did not like the French governess either; but that was irrelevant.

'I am not so sure of that,' he returned stiffly; 'but since you wish it I will give your message to—my wife.' He always hesitated over the possessive pronoun in addressing Haskett.

The latter sighed. 'I don't know as that will help much. She didn't like it when I spoke to her.'

Waythorn turned red. 'When did you see her?' he asked.

'Not since the first day I came to see Lily—right after she was taken sick. I remarked to her then that I didn't like the governess.'

Waythorn made no answer. He remembered distinctly that, after that first visit, he had asked his wife if she had seen Haskett. She had lied to him then, but she had respected his wishes since; and the incident cast a curious light on her character. He was sure she would not have seen Haskett that first day if she had divined that Waythorn would object, and the fact that she did not divine it was almost as disagreeable to the latter as the discovery that she had lied to him.

'I don't like the woman,' Haskett was repeating with mild persistency. 'She ain't straight, Mr. Waythorn—she'll teach the child to be underhand. I've noticed a change in Lily—she's too anxious to please—and she don't always tell the truth. She used to be the straightest child, Mr. Waythorn—' He broke off, his voice a little thick. 'Not but what I want her to have a stylish education,' he ended.

Waythorn was touched. 'I'm sorry, Mr. Haskett; but frankly, I don't quite see what I can do.'

Haskett hesitated. Then he laid his hat on the table, and advanced to the hearth-rug, on which Waythorn was standing. There was nothing aggressive in his manner, but he had the solemnity of a timid man resolved on a decisive measure.

'There's just one thing you can do, Mr. Waythorn,' he said. 'You can remind Mrs. Waythorn that, by the decree of the courts, I am entitled to have a voice in Lily's bringing up.' He paused, and went on more deprecatingly: 'I'm not the kind to talk about enforcing my rights, Mr. Waythorn. I don't know as I think a man is entitled to rights he hasn't known how to hold on to; but this business of the child is different. I've never let go there—and I never mean to.'

The scene left Waythorn deeply shaken. Shamefacedly, in indirect ways, he had been finding out about Haskett; and all that he had learned was favourable. The little man, in order to be near his daughter, had sold out his share in a profitable business in Utica, and accepted a modest clerkship in a New York manufacturing house. He boarded in a shabby street and had few acquaintances. His passion for Lily filled his life. Waythorn felt that this exploration of Haskett was like groping about with a dark-lantern in his wife's past; but he saw now that there were recesses his lantern had not explored. He had never enquired into the exact circumstances of his wife's first matrimonial rupture. On the surface all had been fair. It was she who had obtained the divorce, and the court had given her the child. But Waythorn knew how many ambiguities such a verdict might cover. The mere fact that Haskett retained a right over his daughter implied an unsuspected compromise. Waythorn was an idealist. He always refused to recognise unpleasant contingencies till he found himself confronted with them, and then he saw them followed by a spectral train of consequences. His next days were thus haunted, and he determined to try to lay the ghosts by conjuring them up in his wife's presence.

When he repeated Haskett's request a flame of anger passed over her face; but she subdued it instantly and spoke with a slight quiver of outraged motherhood.

'It is very ungentlemanly of him,' she said.

The word grated on Waythorn. 'That is neither here nor there. It's a bare question of rights.'

She murmured: 'It's not as if he could ever be a help to Lily—'

Waythorn flushed. This was even less to his taste. 'The question is,' he repeated, 'what authority has he over her?'

She looked downward, twisting herself a little in her seat. 'I am willing to see him—I thought you objected,' she faltered.

In a flash he understood that she knew the extent of Haskett's claims. Perhaps it was not the first time she had resisted them.

'My objecting has nothing to do with it,' he said coldly; 'if Haskett has a right to be consulted you must consult him.'

She burst into tears, and he saw that she expected him to regard her as a victim.

Haskett did not abuse his rights. Waythorn had felt miserably sure that he would not. But the governess was dismissed, and from time to time the little man demanded an interview with Alice. After the first outburst she accepted the situation with her usual adaptability. Haskett had once reminded Waythorn of the piano-tuner, and Mrs. Waythorn, after a month or two, appeared to class him with that domestic familiar. Waythorn could not but respect the father's tenacity. At first he had tried to cultivate the suspicion that Haskett might be 'up to' something, that he had an object in securing a foothold in the house. But in his heart Waythorn was sure of Haskett's single-mindedness; he even guessed in the latter a mild contempt for such advantages as his relation with the Waythorns might offer. Haskett's sincerity of purpose made him invulnerable, and his successor had to accept him as a lien on the property.

Mr. Sellers was sent to Europe to recover from his gout, and Varick's affairs hung on Waythorn's hands. The negotiations were prolonged and complicated; they necessitated frequent conferences between the two men, and the interests of the firm forbade Waythorn's suggesting that his client should transfer his business to another office.

Varick appeared well in the transaction. In moments of relaxation his coarse streak appeared, and Waythorn dreaded his geniality; but in the office he was concise and clear-headed, with a flattering deference to Waythorn's judgment. Their business relations being so affably established, it would have been absurd for the two men to ignore each other in society. The first time they met in a drawing-room, Varick took up their intercourse in the same easy key, and his hostess's grateful glance obliged Waythorn to respond to it. After that they ran across each other frequently, and one evening at a ball Waythorn, wandering through the remoter rooms, came upon Varick seated beside his wife. She coloured a little, and faltered in what she was saying; but Varick nodded to Waythorn without rising, and the latter strolled on.

In the carriage, on the way home, he broke out nervously: 'I didn't know you spoke to Varick.'

Her voice trembled a little. 'It's the first time—he happened to be standing near me; I didn't know what to do. It's so awkward, meeting everywhere—and he said you had been very kind about some business.'

'That's different,' said Waythorn.

She paused a moment. 'I'll do just as you wish,' she returned pliantly. 'I thought it would be less awkward to speak to him when we meet.'

Her pliancy was beginning to sicken him. Had she really no will of her own—no theory about her relation to these men? She had accepted Haskett—did she mean to accept Varick? It was 'less awkward,' as she had said, and her instinct was to evade diffi-culties or to circumvent them. With sudden vividness Waythorn saw how the instinct had developed. She was 'as easy as an old shoe'—a shoe that too many feet had worn. Her elasticity was the result of tension in too many different directions. Alice Haskett—Alice Varick—Alice Waythorn—she had been each in turn, and had left hanging to each name a little of her privacy, a little of her personality, a little of the inmost self where the unknown god abides.

'Yes—it's better to speak to Varick,' said Waythorn wearily.

V

The winter wore on, and society took advantage of the Waythorns' acceptance of Varick. Harassed hostesses were grateful to them for bridging over a social difficulty, and Mrs. Waythorn was held up as a miracle of good taste. Some experimental spirits could not resist the diversion of throwing Varick and his former wife together, and there were those who thought he found a zest in the propinquity. But Mrs. Waythorn's conduct remained irreproachable. She neither avoided Varick nor sought him out. Even Waythorn could not but admit that she had discovered the solution of the newest social problem.

He had married her without giving much thought to that problem. He had fancied that a woman can shed her past like a man. But now he saw that Alice was bound to hers both by the circumstances which forced her into continued relation with it, and by the traces it had left on her nature. With grim irony Waythorn compared himself to a member of a syndicate. He held so many shares in his wife's personality and his predecessors were his partners in the business. If there had been any element of passion in the transaction he would have felt less deteriorated by it. The fact that Alice took her change of husbands like a change of weather reduced the situation to mediocrity. He could have forgiven her for blunders, for excesses; for resisting Haskett, for yielding to Varick; for anything but her acquiescence and her tact. She reminded him of a juggler tossing knives; but the knives were blunt and she knew they would never cut her.

And then, gradually, habit formed a protecting surface for his sensibilities. If he paid for each day's comfort with the small change of his illusions, he grew daily to value the comfort more and set less store upon the coin. He had drifted into a dulling propinquity with Haskett and Varick and he took refuge in the cheap revenge of satirising the situation. He even began to reckon up the advantages which accrued from it, to ask himself if it were not better to own a third of a wife who knew how to make a man happy than a whole one who had lacked opportunity to acquire the art. For it *was* an art, and made up, like all others, of concessions, eliminations and embellishments; of lights judiciously thrown and shadows skilfully softened. His wife knew exactly how to manage the lights, and he knew exactly to what training she owed her skill. He even tried to trace the source of his obligations, to discriminate between the influences which had combined to produce his domestic happiness: he perceived that Haskett's commonness had made Alice worship good breeding, while Varick's liberal construction of the marriage bond had taught her to value the conjugal virtues; so that he was directly indebted to his predecessors for the devotion which made his life easy if not inspiring.

From this phase he passed into that of complete acceptance. He ceased to satirise himself because time dulled the irony of the situation and the joke lost its humour with its sting. Even the sight of Haskett's hat on the hall table had ceased to touch the springs of epigram. The hat was often seen there now, for it had been decided that it was better for Lily's father to visit her than for the little girl to go to his boarding-house. Waythorn, having acquiesced in this arrangement, had been surprised to find how little difference it made. Haskett was never obtrusive, and the few visitors who met him on the stairs were unaware of his identity. Waythorn did not know how often he saw Alice, but with himself Haskett was seldom in contact.

One afternoon, however, he learned on entering that Lily's father was waiting to see him. In the library he found Haskett occupying a chair in his usual provisional way. Waythorn always felt grateful to him for not leaning back.

'I hope you'll excuse me, Mr. Waythorn,' he said rising. 'I wanted to see Mrs. Way-

thorn about Lily, and your man asked me to wait here till she came in.'

'Of course,' said Waythorn, remembering that a sudden leak had that morning given over the drawing-room to the plumbers.

He opened his cigar-case and held it out to his visitor, and Haskett's acceptance seemed to mark a fresh stage in their intercourse. The spring evening was chilly, and Waythorn invited his guest to draw up his chair to the fire. He meant to find an excuse to leave Haskett in a moment; but he was tired and cold, and after all the little man no longer jarred on him.

The two were enclosed in the intimacy of their blended cigar-smoke when the door opened and Varick walked into the room. Waythorn rose abruptly. It was the first time that Varick had come to the house, and the surprise of seeing him, combined with the singular inopportuneness of his arrival, gave a new edge to Waythorn's blunted sensibilities. He stared at his visitor without speaking.

Varick seemed too preoccupied to notice his host's embarrassment.

'My dear fellow,' he exclaimed in his most expansive tone, 'I must apologise for tumbling in on you in this way, but I was too late to catch you down town, and so I thought—'

He stopped short, catching sight of Haskett, and his sanguine colour deepened to a flush which spread vividly under his scant blond hair. But in a moment he recovered himself and nodded slightly. Haskett returned the bow in silence, and Waythorn was still groping for speech when the footman came in carrying a tea-table.

The intrusion offered a welcome vent to Waythorn's nerves. 'What the deuce are you bringing this here for?' he said sharply.

'I beg your pardon, sir, but the plumbers are still in the drawing-room, and Mrs. Waythorn said she would have tea in the library.' The footman's perfectly respectful tone implied a reflection on Waythorn's reasonableness.

'Oh, very well,' said the latter resignedly, and the footman proceeded to open the folding tea-table and set out its complicated appointments. While this interminable process continued the three men stood motionless, watching it with a fas-

OXFORD ANTHOLOGY OF AMERICAN LITERATURE

cinated stare, till Waythorn, to break the silence, said to Varick: 'Won't you have a cigar?'

He held out the case he had just tendered to Haskett, and Varick helped himself with a smile. Waythorn looked about for a match, and finding none, proffered a light from his own cigar. Haskett, in the background, held his ground mildly, examining his cigar-tip now and then, and stepping forward at the right moment to knock its ashes into the fire.

The footman at last withdrew, and Varick immediately began: 'If I could just say half a word to you about this business—'

'Certainly,' stammered Waythorn; 'in the dining-room—'

But as he placed his hand on the door it opened from without, and his wife appeared on the threshold.

She came in fresh and smiling, in her street dress and hat, shedding a fragrance from the boa which she loosened in advancing.

'Shall we have tea in here, dear?' she began; and then she caught sight of Varick. Her smile deepened, veiling a slight tremor of surprise.

'Why, how do you do?' she said with a distinct note of pleasure.

As she shook hands with Varick she saw Haskett standing behind him. Her smile faded for a moment, but she recalled it quickly, with a scarcely perceptible side-glance at Waythorn.

'How do you do, Mr. Haskett?' she said, and shook hands with him a shade less cordially.

The three men stood awkwardly before her, till Varick, always the most self-possessed, dashed into an explanatory phrase. 'We—I had to see Waythorn a moment on business,' he stammered, brick-red from chin to nape.

Haskett stepped forward with his air of mild obstinacy. 'I am sorry to intrude; but you appointed five o'clock—' he directed his resigned glance to the time-piece on the mantel.

She swept aside their embarrassment with a charming gesture of hospitality. 'I'm so sorry—I'm always late; but the afternoon was so lovely.' She stood drawing off her gloves, propitiatory and graceful, diffusing about her a sense of ease and familiarity in which the situation lost its grotesqueness. 'But before talking business,' she added brightly, 'I'm sure every one wants a cup of tea.'

She dropped into her low chair by the tea-table, and the two visitors, as if drawn by her smile, advanced to receive the cups she held out.

She glanced about for Waythorn, and he took the third cup with a laugh.

1904

PAUL ELMER MORE

1864–1937

CRITICISM [1]

Of all Matthew Arnold's books I sometimes think that not the least precious is the slender posthumous volume published by his daughter in 1902. It was long his habit to carry in his pocket a narrow diary in which he jotted down engagements for the day, mingled with short quotations from the books he was reading to serve as amulets, so to speak, against the importunities of business. The quotations for a selection of years printed by Mrs. Wodehouse from these *Notebooks* form what might be called the critic's breviary. Here, if anywhere, we seem to feel the very beating of the critic's heart, and to catch the inner voice of recollection and duty, corresponding to the poet's 'gleam,' which he followed so devoutly in his life. I do not know to what

[1] More, in his preface to his *Selected Essays*, in which this essay was included, wrote: 'As it is, what strikes me most forcibly is the fact that the essays here selected will appear very old fashioned to those caught by the present trend of ideas. For the one thing characteristic of modern criticism, as exemplified by so influential a writer as I.A.Richards, is the complete absence of any search for the meaning of life, and in place of that an

absorbing interest in what might be called the problem of æsthetic psychology,—which is indeed no more than a late-born offspring of the romantic heresy of art for art's sake. For this old-fashioned note I offer no apology; I am utterly convinced that literature divorced from life is an empty pursuit, and that an honest search for the meaning of life must lead to the simple faith of theism.' More, *Selected Essays* (N.Y., 1935), xii–xiii.

work in English to liken it unless it be the notebooks containing quotations from Marcus Aurelius and Epictetus written down by the author of the *Characteristics* with his comments, which Dr. Rand edited in 1900 as the *Philosophical Regimen of Anthony, Earl of Shaftesbury*.

Nor is it mere chance that Matthew Arnold and Shaftesbury should have left for posthumous publication these private memoranda, which with all their differences of form and substance are in their final impression upon the mind so curiously alike; for the two men themselves, in their outlook on life and in their relation to their respective ages, had much in common, and there is perhaps no better way to reach a dispassionate understanding of the virtue and limitations of criticism than by comparing Arnold with his great forerunner of the early eighteenth century. Both men were essentially critical in their mental habit, and both magnified the critic's office. 'I take upon me,' said Shaftesbury, 'absolutely to condemn the fashionable and prevailing custom of inveighing against critics as the common enemies, the pests and incendiaries of the commonwealth of Wit and Letters. I assert, on the contrary, that they are the props and pillars of this building; and that without the encouragement and propagation of such a race, we should remain as Gothic architects as ever.' And the purpose of Shaftesbury in upholding the function of criticism was much the same as Arnold's; he too was offended by the Gothic and barbarous self-complacency of his contemporaries—the Philistines, as he might have called them. As Arnold protested that the work of the English romantic revival was doomed 'to prove hardly more lasting than the productions of far less splendid epochs'; that Byron was 'empty of matter,' Shelley 'incoherent,' and Wordsworth 'wanting in completeness and variety,' just because they lacked critical background; so his predecessor censured the literature of his day. 'An English author would be all genius,' says Shaftesbury. 'He would reap the fruits of art, but without study, pains, or application. He thinks it necessary, indeed (lest his learning should be called in question), to show the world that he errs knowingly against the rules of art.'

Against this presumption of genius on the one hand and the self-complacency of Philistinism on the other, both critics took up the same weapons—the barbs of ridicule and irony. With Shaftesbury this method was an avowed creed. His essays are no more than sermons on two texts: that of Horace, '*Ridiculum acri Fortius et melius magnas plerumque secat res*—a jest often decides weighty matters better and more forcibly than can asperity'; and the saying of Gorgias Leontinus, which he misinterprets and expands for his own purpose, 'That humour was the only test of gravity; and gravity of humour. For a subject which would not bear raillery was suspicious; and a jest which would not bear a serious examination was certainly false wit.' With this touchstone of truth he proceeds to test the one-sided enthusiasm of his day, the smirking conceits, the pedantic pretensions, and the narrow dogmatisms whether of science or religion. 'There is a great difference,' he says, 'between seeking how to raise a laugh from everything, and seeking in everything what justly may be laughed at. For nothing is ridiculous except what is deformed; nor is anything proof against raillery except what is handsome and just.' The comic spirit is thus a kind of purgation of taste, and a way of return to nature. How deliberately Matthew Arnold used this weapon of ridicule in the service of sweet reasonableness, which is only his modern phrase, a little sentimentalised, for eighteenth-century nature; how magisterially he raised the laugh against his enemies, the bishops and the great austere toilers of the press and the mighty men of political Philistia, no one needs be told who has enjoyed the elaborate irony of *Culture and Anarchy* or of *Friendship's Garland*.

Sweet reasonableness, or 'sweetness and light,' to use the phrase as Arnold took it from Swift's *Battle of the Books*, is, I have suggested, little more than the modern turn for the deist's nature and reason; how nearly the two ideals approach each other you may see by comparing the 'good-breeding,' which is the aim of Shaftesbury's philosophy, with the 'culture' which is the end of Arnold's criticism. 'To philosophise,' said the former, 'in a just signification, is but to carry good-breeding a step higher. For the accomplishment of breeding is, to learn whatever is decent in company or beautiful in arts, and the sum of philosophy is, to learn what is just in society and beautiful in Nature and the order of the world.' I have wondered sometimes whether Matthew Arnold had these words in mind when he formulated his definition of culture; whether his famous command is really but another echo from the ancient quarrel of the deists. The whole scope of the essay on *Sweetness and Light* is, he avows, 'to recommend culture as the great help out of our present difficulties; culture being a pursuit of our total perfection by means of getting to know, on all the matters which most concern us, the best which has been thought and said in the world [Shaftesbury, too, like Arnold, is insistent on the *exemplaria Græca*]; and through this knowledge, turning a stream of fresh and free thought upon our stock notions and habits.'

There is, I trust, something more than a pedantic curiosity in such a parallel, which might yet be much prolonged, between the author of *Culture and Anarchy* and the author of the *Characteristics*. It proves, if proof be necessary, more clearly than would any amount of direct exposition, that Matthew Arnold's method of criticism was not an isolated product of the nineteenth century, but that he belongs to one of the great families of human intelligence, which begins with Cicero, the father of them all, and passes through Erasmus and Boileau and Shaftesbury and Sainte-Beuve. These are the exemplars—not complete individually, I need not say—of what may be called the critical spirit: discriminators between the false and the true, the deformed and the normal; preachers of harmony and proportion and order, prophets of the religion of taste. If they deal much with the criticism of literature, this is because in literature more manifestly than anywhere else life displays its infinitely varied motives and results; and their practice is always to render literature itself more consciously a criticism of life. The past is the field out of which they draw their examples of what is in conformity with nature and of what departs from that norm. In that field they balance and weigh and measure; they are by intellect hesitators, but at heart very much in earnest.

These critics are sometimes contrasted to their detriment with the so-called creative writers, yet they themselves stood each among the first writers of his day, and it is not plain that, for instance, Tennyson, in any true estimation, added more to the intellectual life of the world than Matthew Arnold, or Lucretius than Cicero, though their method and aim may have been different. The more significant comparison at least is not with the so-called creative writers, but with the great fulminators of new creeds—between Matthew Arnold and the Carlyles and Ruskins and Huxleys of his day; between Shaftesbury and, let us say, Rousseau; Boileau and Descartes; Erasmus and Luther; Cicero and St. Paul. Such a contrast might seem at first to lie as much in efficiency as in quality. In the very nature of things the man who seizes on one deep-reaching idea, whether newly found or rediscovered, and with single-hearted fervour forces it upon the world, might appear to have the advantage in power over the man of critical temper, who weighs and refines; who is for ever checking the enthusiasm of the living by the authority of the dead; and whose doctrine, even though in the end he may assert it with sovereign contempt of doubters, is still the command to follow the well-tried path of common-sense. Better the half-truth that makes for action and jostles the world out of its ruts, men cry, than such a timid search for the whole truth as paralyses the will, and may after all prove only an exchange of depth for breadth. That might appear to be the plain lesson of history; yet I am not so sure. Is there not a possibility that in our estimate of these powers we are a little betrayed by the tumult of the times, just as we are prone in other things to mistake bustle for movement? The critical spirit, as it has been exercised, may have its limitations and may justly be open to censure, but I doubt if its true reproach will turn out in the end to be a lack of efficiency in comparison with the more assertive force of the reformers. I am inclined to believe, for instance, that the balancing spirit of Erasmus is really more at work among us to-day than that of the dogmatic and reforming Luther; that Cicero's philosophy, though they would gape to hear it said, is really more in the hearts of the men you will meet in the street than is the theology of St. Paul. This may be in part because the representatives of the critical spirit, by their very lack of warping originality and by their endeavour to separate the true from the false, the complete from the one-sided, stand with the great conservative forces of human nature, having their fame certified by the things that endure amid all the betrayals of time and fashion.

I know the deductions that must be made from that kind of fame. Cicero, it will be said, when in his *De Finibus* he brought together the various experiences of antiquity in regard to the meaning and values of life, weighing the claims of Stoic and Epicurean and the others, may have stood for something more comprehensive and balanced than did St. Paul with his new dogma of justification by faith. Yet St. Paul's theory of justification by faith, though it may be losing for us its cogent veracity, was the immediate driving force of history and a power that remade the world, while Cicero's nice discussions remained a luxury of the learned few. In one sense that is indisputably true; and yet, imprudent as it may sound, I question whether it is the whole truth. When I consider the part played by Stoic and Epicurean philosophies in the Renaissance and the transcendent influence of Cicero's dissertations upon the men of that day; when I consider that the impulse of Deism in the eighteenth century, as seen in Shaftesbury and his successors, was at bottom little more than a revival of this same Stoicism, as it had been subdued to the emotions by Cicero and mixed with Epicureanism; that Shaftesbury was, in fact, despite his worship of Epictetus, almost a pure Ciceronian; and when I consider that out of Deism sprang the dominant religion and social philosophy of our present world—when I consider these and many other facts, I question whether Cicero, while he certainly represents what is more enduring, has not been also, actually and personally, as dynamic an influence in civilisation as St. Paul, though the noise, no doubt, and the tumult have been around the latter.

We are still too near Matthew Arnold's day to determine the resultant of all the forces then at work, yet it would not be very rash even now to assert that his critical essays will be found in the end a broader and more lasting, as they are a saner, influence than the exaggerated æstheticism of Ruskin or the shrill prophesying of Carlyle or the scientific dogmatism of Huxley. No, if there is any deduction to be made to the value of criticism, it is not on the side of efficiency. It is well to remember Matthew Arnold's own words. 'Violent indignation with the past,' he says, 'abstract systems of renovation applied wholesale, a new doctrine drawn up in black and white for elaborating down to the very smallest details a rational society for the future—these are the ways of Jacobinism. . . Culture [it is his word here for criticism] is always assigning to system-makers and systems a smaller share in the bent of human destiny than their friends like.'

Perhaps it is a secret inkling of this vanity of the critic in its widest bearing, besides a natural antagonism of temper, that leads so many to carp against him and his trade. The inveterate hostility of 'creative' writers to criticism is well known, and has been neatly summed up by E. S. Dallas in *The Gay Science*:

'Ben Jonson spoke of critics as tinkers, who make more faults than they mend; Samuel Butler, as the fierce inquisitors of wit, and as butchers who have no right to sit on a jury; Sir Richard Steele, as of all mortals the silliest; Swift, as dogs, rats, wasps, or, at best, drones of the learned world; Shenstone, as asses, which by gnawing vines first taught the advantage of pruning them; Burns, as cut-throat bandits in the path of fame; Walter Scott, humorously reflecting the general sentiment, as caterpillars.'

The droll thing about it is that every one of these critics of criticism was so ready to act himself as butcher or ass or caterpillar. It is a common trick of the guild. For a modern instance, turn to Mr. Horace Traubel, the shirt-sleeved Boswell of Walt Whitman, and you will find pages of conversation recorded in which the seer of Camden belabours the professors of criticism and in almost the same breath exercises the art upon his brother poets with delightful frankness and at times rare penetration. But this ancient feud of the gentlemen of the pen is a special form, due in part to special causes, of the hostility that so often manifests itself against the critical spirit in general. The man of system and the man of unhesitating action are likely to feel something like contempt for the mind that balances and waits. The imperial Mommsen felt this contempt, and showed it, in his treatment of Cicero; it is rife even yet in the current tone of condescension towards Erasmus as compared with Luther, to which Matthew Arnold replied by calling Luther 'a Philistine of genius'; Warburton showed it in his sneers at Shaftesbury as the man of taste, and Cardinal Newman has, with splendid politeness, echoed them; Matthew Arnold was equally feared and despised in his own lifetime, and it is an odd fact that you will to-day scarcely pick up a piece of third-rate criticism (in which there is likely to be anything at work rather than the critical spirit), but you will come upon some gratuitous fling against him. Most bitter of all was Henry Sidgwick's arraignment of 'The Prophet of Culture' in *Macmillan's Magazine* for August, 1867. There if anywhere the critical spirit was stabbed with its own weapon. You will recall the image of the pouncet-box:

'Mr. Arnold may say that he does not discourage action, but only asks for delay, in order that we may act with sufficient knowledge. This is the eternal excuse of indolence—insufficient knowledge. . . One cannot think on this subject without recalling the great man who recommended to philosophy a position very similar to that now claimed for culture. I wish to give Mr. Arnold the full benefit of his resemblance to Plato. But when we look closer at the two positions, the dissimilarity comes out: they have a very different effect on our feelings and imagination; and I confess I feel more sympathy with the melancholy philosopher looking out with hopeless placidity "from beneath the shelter of some wall" than with a cheerful modern liberal, tempered by renouncement, shuddering aloof from the rank exhalations of vulgar enthusiasm, and holding up the pouncet-box of culture betwixt the wind and his nobility.'

Such an onslaught on our prophet of culture as a languid and shrinking dilettante was fair enough in the heat of controversy and was at least justified by its own art, if not by certain affectations of its victim's style; but I protest against accepting it as essentially true. Any one might perceive that Matthew Arnold had beneath the irony and suavity of his manner a temper of determined seriousness; that, like the bride of Giacopone di Todi in his sonnet, his Muse might be young, gay, and radiant outside, but had

'a hidden ground
Of thought and of austerity within.'

It would be interesting in this respect to continue the comparison of Arnold and Shaftesbury, and to show how near together they stood in their attitude towards nature and society and in their religion, and how profound was their own enthusiasm beneath their hostility to the sham or undisciplined enthusiasms of the day. Lord Shaftesbury might say that we have 'in the main a witty and good-humoured religion,' as Matthew Arnold might ridicule the sourness of the Nonconformists and the bleakness of the reformers in whose assemblies any child of nature, if he shall stray thither, is smitten with lamentation and mourning and woe; but there was solemnity enough, however we may rate their insight, in their own search for the God that sits concealed at the centre. Shaftesbury's creed became the formula of the deists. 'Still ardent in its pursuit,' the soul, he says, 'rests not here, nor satisfies itself with the beauty of a part, but, extending further its communicative bounty, seeks the good of all, and affects the interest and prosperity of the whole. True to its native world and higher country, 'tis here it seeks order and perfection; wishing the best, and hoping still to find a just and wise administration. And since all hope of this were vain and idle if no universal mind presided; since without such a supreme intelligence and providential care the distracted universe must be condemned to suffer infinite calamities; 'tis here the generous mind labours to discover that healing cause by which the interest of the whole is securely established, the beauty of things and the universal order happily sustained.' Matthew Arnold condensed that rhetoric into a phrase: 'The stream of tendency, not ourselves, which makes for righteousness.'

But the strongest evidence of their austerity of purpose is seen in those private notebooks which led me to couple their names together in this study of the spirit of criticism. This is not the time to deal at length with that sober and anxious self-examination of the noble Lord, as Shaftesbury's enemies in the Church were so fond of calling him. It is one of the important documents to show how completely Deism was a revival of pagan morality. It is, in brief, no more than a translation of the great maxims of antiquity into modern purposes: the inner record of a man seeking character in the two elements of attention (προσοχή) and the harmony of life (veræ numerosque modosque vitæ), and of a man who thought that this pursuit must be maintained unrelentingly. Of the two books it may seem strange that Matthew Arnold's, which consists merely of brief quotations without comment, should really open to us more intimately the author's heart than does the direct self-questioning of Shaftesbury's. Yet a book more filled with sad sincerity, a more perfect confession of a life's purpose, will scarcely be found than these memoranda. 'I am glad to find,' he wrote once in a letter to his sister, 'that in the past year I have at least accomplished more than usual in the way of reading the books which at the beginning of the year I had put down to be read. . . The importance of reading, not slight stuff to get through the time, but the best that has been written, forces itself upon me more and more every year I live.' Now the *Notebooks* not only preserve some of these annual lists of books to be read, but show, in quintessential phrase, just what the books actually read meant to him. Some of the quotations are repeated a number of times, and if frequency of repetition can be taken as a criterion the maxim closest to Arnold's heart was the sentence, from what source I do not know: '*Semper aliquid certi proponendum est*—always some certain end must be kept in view.' It is but an expansion of the same idea that he expresses in the words set down more than once from some French author: 'A working life, a succession of labours which fill and moralise the days!' and in the beloved command of the *Imitation*: '*Cum multa legeris et cognoveris, ad unum semper oportet redire principium*—when you have read and learned many things, it is necessary always to return to one principle.' That principle he sets down in aphorisms and exhortations from a hun-

dred diverse sources—nowhere, perhaps, more succinctly than in the broken phrases of the stoic Lucan:

> 'servare modum, finemque tenere
> Naturamque sequi—
> Nec sibi, sed toti genitum se credere
> mundo—
> In commune bonus.'

'(To preserve measure, to hold fast to the end, and follow nature—To believe oneself born not for oneself alone but for all the world—good for the community of mankind.)'

He might well have applied to his own pursuit of culture the eulogy he quotes concerning another: 'Study, which for most men is only a frivolous amusement and often dangerous, was for Dom Rivet a serious occupation consecrated by religion.'

It was not a mere dilettante of sweetness and light who day by day laid such maxims as these upon his breast; it was not one who held up the pouncet-box of culture betwixt the wind and his nobility. Matthew Arnold, if any man in his generation, was by temperament a stoic for whom duty and submission and reverence made up the large part of life; and there is something of what we call the irony of fate in the thought that he who made σπουδαιότης, *high seriousness*, the test of great literature, should have suffered the reproach of levity. Yet, after all, fate is never quite blind in these things, and if criticism has thus drawn upon itself the censure of men like Sidgwick we may feel assured that in some way it has failed of the deeper truth. Those reproaches may in part be due to prejudice and revenge and the inevitable contrast of temperaments; they may err in ascribing to the critic a want of efficiency, as they may be wantonly perverse in denouncing him for frivolity; but they have a meaning and they cannot be overlooked. Now the future is often a strange revealer of secret things, and there is no surer way to detect the weak side of a leader than by studying the career of his disciples, or even of his successors.

You are familiar with the story of the concluding chapter of Pater's *Renaissance*—how it was withdrawn from the second edition of that book because the author 'conceived it might possibly mislead some of those young men into whose hands it might fall'; and how it was restored, with some slight changes, to the later editions where it now stands. And you know the moral of that essay: that life is but an uncertain interval before the universal judgment of death, a brief illusion of stability in the eternal flux, and that 'our one chance lies in expanding that interval, in getting as many pulsations as possible into the given time.' And 'of this wisdom,' he concludes, 'the poetic passion, the desire of beauty, the love of art for art's sake, has most; for art comes to you professing frankly to give nothing but the highest quality to your moments as they pass, and simply for those moments' sake.' That philosophy of the Oxonian Epicurus and its scandal in a very un-Epicurean land are familiar enough; but perhaps we do not always stop to think how plausibly this doctrine of crowning our moments with the highest sensations of art flows from Matthew Arnold's definition of criticism as the disinterested endeavour 'to know the best that is known and thought in the world, irrespectively of practice, politics, and everything of the kind.'

The next step from Pater's Epicureanism, and so by a further remove from Arnold's criticism, brings us to one whose name, unfortunately, must always be mentioned with regret, but who is more significant in the development of English letters than is sometimes allowed. At the time when Paterism, as a recent writer has said, was 'tripping indelicately along the Oxford High and by the banks of the Cherwell,' a young votary of the Muses from Dublin came upon the scene, and began to push the doctrine of Pater as far beyond what the master intended as Pater had gone beyond Matthew Arnold. This is the young man who 'would occasionally be seen walking the streets carrying a lily or a sunflower in his hand, at which he would gaze intently and admiringly.' He had fashioned himself deliberately to pose as the head of a new sect of 'æsthetes,' as they styled themselves, who expanded Arnold's excluded tribe of Philistines to embrace all the sober citizens of the world. The fate of Oscar Wilde is still like a fresh wound in the public memory. What I wish to call to your mind is the direct connection (strengthened no doubt by influences from across the Channel) between Pater's philosophy of the sensation-crowded moment and such a poem as that in which Wilde attempted to concentrate all the passionate moments of the past in his gloating revery upon *The Sphinx*. He was himself not unaware of the treachery of the path he had chosen; the sonnet which he prefixed to his book of poems is sincere with the pathos of conscious insincerity, and is a memorable comment on one of the tragic ambitions of a century:

'To drift with every passion till my soul
Is a stringed lute on which all winds can
    play,
Is it for this that I have given away
Mine ancient wisdom, and austere control?

. . . . . .

Surely there was a time I might have trod
The sunlit heights, and from life's
    dissonance
Struck one clear chord to reach the ears of
    God:
Is that time dead? lo! with a little rod
I did but touch the honey of romance—
And must I lose a soul's inheritance?'

The answer to the poet's query he was himself to write in *The Ballad of Reading Gaol*:

'Silently we went round and round,
    And through each hollow mind
The Memory of dreadful things
    Rushed like a dreadful wind,
And Horror stalked before each man,
    And Terror crept behind.'

This Memory of dreadful things is the too logical end, step by step, of the philosophy of the sensation-crowded moment; the concealed suspicion of it in Matthew Arnold's definition of criticism was the justification, if any there be, of the contempt hurled upon him by some of his contemporaries.

It is necessary to repeat that such a derivation from Matthew Arnold is essentially unfair because it leaves out of view the real purpose and heart of the man. If we could not read his great moral energy in his *Essays*, as I trust we all of us can, and if we did not know the profound influence of his critical philosophy upon the better life of our age, we could still dispel our doubts by looking into the *Notebooks*, in which memory is not turned to dreadful things for the soul's disgrace, but is the guide and impulse to strong resolution and beautiful forbearance. Yet withal it remains true that the Epicureanism of Pater and the hedonism of Oscar Wilde were able to connect themselves in a disquieting way with one side of Matthew Arnold's gospel of culture; and it behooves us who come upon the heels of this movement and who believe that the critical spirit is still to be one of the powers making in the world for right enjoyment, it behooves us to examine the first definition of culture or criticism—the words had about the same meaning as Arnold used them— and see whether something was not there forgotten. The fault lay not in any intrinsic want of efficiency in the critical spirit, nor in any want of moral earnestness in Matthew Arnold or Shaftesbury: that we have seen. But these men were lacking in another direction: they missed a philosophy which could bind together their moral and their æsthetic sense, a positive principle besides the negative force of ridicule and irony; and, missing this, they left criticism more easily subject to a one-sided and dangerous development.

To the nature of that omission, to the *porro unum necessarium,* we may be directed, I think, by the critical theory of the one who carried the practice, in other respects, to its lowest degradation. In Oscar Wilde's dialogue on *The Critic as Artist,* one of the most extraordinary mixtures ever compounded of truth flaunting in the robes of error and error assuming the gravity of truth, you will remember that the advocate of criticism at the height of his argument proclaims the true man of culture to be him who has learned 'the best that is known and thought in the world' (he uses Matthew Arnold's words), and who thus, as Matthew Arnold neglected to add, 'bears within himself the dreams, and ideas, and feelings of myriad generations.' The addition is important, how important, or at least how large, may be seen in the really splendid, if somewhat morbid, passage in which the idea is developed. Let me quote at some length:

'To know anything about oneself, one must know all about others. There must

be no mood with which one cannot sympathise, no dead mode of life that one cannot make alive. Is this impossible? I think not. By revealing to us the absolute mechanism of all action, and so freeing us from the self-imposed and trammelling burden of moral responsibility, the scientific principle of Heredity has become, as it were, the warrant for the contemplative life. It has shown us that we are never less free than when we try to act. It has hemmed us round with the nets of the hunter, and written upon the wall the prophecy of our doom. We may not watch it, for it is within us. We may not see it, save in a mirror that mirrors the soul. It is Nemesis without her mask. It is the last of the Fates, and the most terrible. It is the only one of the Gods whose real name we know.

'And yet, while in the sphere of practical and external life it has robbed energy of its freedom and activity of its choice, in the subjective sphere, where the soul is at work, it comes to us, this terrible shadow, with many gifts in its hands, gifts of strange temperaments and subtle susceptibilities, gifts of wild ardours and chill moods of indifference, complex multiform gifts of thoughts that are at variance with each other, and passions that war against themselves. And so, it is not our own life that we live, but the lives of the dead, and the soul that dwells within us is no single spiritual entity, making us personal and individual, created for our service, and entering into us for our joy. . . It can help us to leave the age in which we were born, and to pass into other ages, and find ourselves not exiled from their air. It can teach us how to escape from our experience, and to realise the experiences of those who are greater than we are. The pain of Leopardi crying out against life becomes our pain. Theocritus blows on his pipe, and we laugh with the lips of nymph and shepherd. In the wolfskin of Pierre Vidal we flee before the hounds, and in the armour of Lancelot we ride from the bower of the Queen. We have whispered the secret of our love beneath the cowl of Abelard, and in the stained raiment of Villon have put our shame into song. We can see the dawn through Shelley's eyes, and when we wander with Endymion the Moon grows amorous of our youth. Ours is the anguish of Atys, and ours the weak rage and noble sorrows of the Dane. Do you think that it is the imagination that enables us to live these countless lives? Yes: it is the imagination; and the imagination is the result of heredity. It is simply concentrated race-experience.'

Now, this theory of race-experience, as Oscar Wilde formulated it, lends itself, no doubt, to an easy fallacy. I am aware of the rebuke administered to one who was by the range of his knowledge and by his historic sense much more justified in such a presumption than was Oscar Wilde. 'Is it not the strangest illusion,' exclaimed the biographer of Renan, 'to believe that the mere reading of the Acts of the martyrs is sufficient to give us their soul, to transfer to us in its real intensity the ardour which ravished them amidst their tortures? . . . Those who have lost all the energy of living and acting may, if they choose, shut themselves up in this kingdom of shadows; that is their affair. But that they should proclaim theirs as the true life, is not to be conceded to them.' Séailles was right. These men, whether it be a paradox-monger like Oscar Wilde or a great scholar like Renan, should have laid to heart the favourite maxim of Matthew Arnold, *semper aliquid certi proponendum est*: true culture has always before its eyes a definite end and is for self-discipline, not for revery. Nor am I unaware that the theory as expressed by Oscar Wilde is mixed up with his own personal taint of decadence. One thing at least is certain: that the way of the true critical spirit is not to free us, as he boasts, from 'the self-imposed and trammelling burden of moral responsibility.' His avowal in the same dialogue that the sole aim of art is to produce the 'beautiful sterile emotions' so hateful to the world, his shameless vaunt that 'there is nothing sane about the worship of beauty,' his whole philosophy of the ego as above the laws of society, cannot be severed from the memory of dreadful things in which his own song ended: such a philosophy is in fact a denial of the validity of that very race-experience out of which he attempts to derive it. In this respect again he

should have remembered the maxim of Matthew Arnold: 'A working life, a succession of labours that fill and moralise the days.' The aim of culture is not to merge the present in a sterile dream of the past, but to hold the past as a living force in the present. In omitting these aspects of criticism Pater and, to a greater extent, Oscar Wilde fell into extravagance far more deleterious to culture than was any omission or incompleteness on the part of Matthew Arnold.

Nevertheless, with all its false emphasis and its admixture of personal error, that positive and emotional reassumption of the past, that association of the contemplative life (the βίος θεωρητικός) with the rapture of memory, contains the hint of a great truth which must be grasped and properly exercised if criticism is to confirm itself against such hostility as has hitherto kept it on the defensive. I would not say even that the mysticism, out of which Oscar Wilde's critical theory really springs, though expressed in the modish language of scientific evolution, is essentially perverse. For in a very true sense the past of mankind, by the larger race-memory and particularly by that form of it which we call literature, abides as a living reality in our present. We suffer not our individual destiny alone but the fates of humanity also. We are born into an inheritance of great emotions—into the unconquerable hopes and defeated fears of an immeasurable past, the tragedies and the comedies of love, the ardent aspirations of faith, the baffled questionings of evil, the huge laughter at facts, the deep-welling passion of peace. Without that common inheritance how inconceivably poor and shallow would be this life of the world and our life in it! These recorded emotions are, indeed, not for us what they were in actuality, nor by sitting at our own ease with memory can we enter into the exact emotions of the martyr at the stake and the hero in his triumph. These things are now transmuted into something the same and different, something less and greater. The intensity of the actual moment they cannot possess, but on the other hand with this loss of separate reality they are associated with life as a whole, and in that unity of experience obtain, what they lacked before, a significance and design. They bear in a way the same relation to practical life as that life bore to the ideal world out of which it arose and into which it is continually passing. And thus this larger memory, in its transmuting and unifying power, may not unmeaningly be regarded as the purpose of activity, and literature may not too presumptuously be cherished as the final end of existence. Some such mystery as this was hinted in the Greek and Gnostic doctrine of the *logos*, the Word, and in the Hindu name for the creator as *vâcas pati*, Lord of the Word. And if such a theory sounds too absurdly metaphysical for the ears of prudent common-sense, consider that Homer, no philosopher of empty phrases surely, meant nothing very different when he judged of actions by their fame in future story. To him the warring of armies for ten long years and the desolation of Troy were for no other purpose than that the inner life of the race might be enriched by memory:

'Thus the gods fated, and such ruin wove
That song might flourish for posterity.'

And in this theory of memory criticism has an important office. We are beginning to hear a good deal these days about the French metaphysician, M. Henri Bergson, of whom Prof. William James has avowed himself a willing disciple, and whose disquisitions on *Matière et mémoire* and *L'Évolution créatrice* are perhaps more talked of than any other recent books of philosophy. I do not pretend to pronounce on the full scope of his theories, but his conception of the function of memory is rich with applications to the matter we have in hand. Our consciousness, that is to say our very self, is not, he says, a thing born new with each moment, not a *mens momentanea*, but an uninterrupted stream of activity, and what we now feel is directly bound up with what we have felt before. Nor is this consciousness, on the other hand, a mere heaping together indiscriminately of perceptions and emotions, but it is an active faculty, or, I should prefer to say, the servant of some active faculty, that depresses this particular experience into the background and centres attention upon that other experience, thus by a process of criticism secreting the present, so to speak, out of the past. Such a philosophy finds a new and profound truth

in the saying of Pascal: '*La mémoire est nécessaire à toutes les opérations de l'esprit*—memory is necessary to all the operations of the mind.'

This notion of the active memory is, I am told by those who should know, mixed up in Bergson with a questionable metaphysic, yet in itself alone it should seem to be nothing more than the laborious expression of a very simple fact. We have all of us met now and then in our daily intercourse a man whose conversation impressed us immediately as possessing a certain ripeness of wisdom, a certain pertinency and depth of meaning. If we wished to characterise such a man in a single word, we should perhaps say that he was essentially educated. We feel that he has within him some central force which enables him to choose consistently amidst the innumerable conflicting impulses and attractions and dissipations of life, that he moves forward, not at haphazard, but by the direction of some principle of conduct, and that he can be depended upon for counsel and comfort. Well, if you stop to analyse this quality of mind, which we will call education, you will discover in every case, I believe, that the determining trait is just the force of a critical memory. I do not mean by this the mere facility of recalling the emotions and events and spectacles which have come to a man with the years; for such undisciplined reminiscence may be but a shabby wisdom to the man himself, as it may be the very contrary of joy to his hearer. I mean rather the faculty of selection as well as of retention, the weighing of cause and effect, the constant and active assumption of the past in the present, by which the events of life are no longer regarded as isolated and fortuitous moments, but are merged into a unity of experience. Those in whom this faculty rules are commonly the possessors of practical wisdom, but there are others, a few, who by its virtue are raised into another kind of wisdom. With these men the selective, reconciling memory is associated, more or less consciously, with the Platonic reminiscence in such a manner that not only are the past and present of passing time made one but our ephemeral life is fitted into that great ring of eternity which Henry Vaughan saw as in a dream. So it is that to them the things which others behold as sudden unrelated facts are made shadows and types of the everlasting ideas; and with the accumulation of knowledge they grow ripe in vision,

> 'Till old experience do attain
> To something like prophetic strain.'

And as our private memory is not a merely passive retention of sensations, so in literature the critical spirit is at work as a conscious energy of selection. The function of criticism, as thus understood, is far removed from the surrender to luxurious revery which the impressionists believed it to be; nor is the good critic, as Anatole France said, he who recounts the adventures of his soul amid masterpieces; he is rather one who has before him always the *aliquid certi*, the definite aim of a Matthew Arnold. He does not, like Oscar Wilde, seek by losing the present in the past to throw off 'the self-imposed and trammelling burden of moral responsibility'; he is rather one whose life is 'a succession of labours that fill and moralise the days'— not in the narrow didactic sense, it need scarcely be said, but in so far as his task is a continual weighing of values. But the critical spirit is also something deeper than Matthew Arnold perceived, or, at least, clearly expressed. The error of criticism in his hands, as in the hands of his predecessors, was that in the exercise of judgment it used the past too much as a dead storehouse of precepts for schoolmastering the present; it was not sufficiently aware of the relation of this faculty of judgment to the indwelling and ever-acting memory of things. Here is the one touch of insight needed, I think, to raise criticism, while not forgetting its special duty of discrimination and judgment, to a more independent and self-respecting *genre*. In its conscious creation of the field of the present out of the past it takes an honoured, if not equal, place by the side of those impulses, more commonly recognised as creative, which are continually adding new material for its selective energy. 'Valuing is creating,' said Nietzsche; 'to value is the treasure and jewel among all things valued.' The critical spirit is thus akin to that force of design or final cause in the Aristotelian sense, which we are beginning once more to divine as the guiding principle, itself unchanged, at work within the evolutionary changes of nature; and in so far as it becomes aware of this high office it introduces into our intellectual life an element outside of alteration and growth and decay, a principle to which time is the minister and not the master.

Literary criticism is, indeed, in this sense only the specific exercise of a faculty which works in many directions. All scholars, whether they deal with history or sociology or philosophy or language or, in the narrower use of the word, literature, are servants of the critical spirit, in so far as they transmit and interpret and mould the sum of experience from man to man and from generation to generation. Might not one even say that at a certain point criticism becomes almost identical with education, and that by this standard we may judge the value of any study as an instrument of education, and may estimate the merit of any special presentation of that study? It is at least, in the existing chaos of pedagogical theories, a question worthy of consideration.

1910

GEORGE SANTAYANA

1863–

JUSTIFICATION OF ART

IT is no longer the fashion among philosophers to decry art. Either its influence seems to them too slight to excite alarm, or their systems are too lax to subject anything to censure which has the least glamour or ideality about it. Tired, perhaps, of daily resolving the conflict between science and religion, they prefer to assume silently a harmony between morals and art. Moral harmonies, however, are not given; they have to be made. The curse of superstition is that it justifies and protracts their absence by proclaiming their invisible presence. Of course a rational religion could not conflict with a rational science; and similarly an art that was wholly admirable would necessarily play into the hand of progress. But as the real difficulty in the former case lies in saying what religion and what science would be truly rational, so here the problem is how far extant art is a benefit to mankind, and how far, perhaps, a vice or a burden.

That art is *prima facie* and in itself a good cannot be doubted. It is a spontaneous activity, and that settles the question. Yet the function of ethics is precisely to revise *prima facie* judgements of this kind and to fix the ultimate resultant of all given interests, in so far as they can be combined. In the actual disarray of human life and desire, wisdom consists in knowing what goods to sacrifice and what simples to pour into the supreme mixture. The extent to which æsthetic values are allowed to colour the resultant or highest good is a point of great theoretic importance, not only for art but for general philosophy. If art is excluded altogether or given only a trivial rôle, perhaps as a necessary relaxation, we feel at once that a philosophy so judging human arts is ascetic or post-rational. It pretends to guide life from above and from without; it has discredited human nature and mortal interests, and has thereby undermined itself, since it is at best but a partial expression of that humanity which it strives to transcend. If, on the contrary, art is prized as something supreme and irresponsible, if the poetic and mystic glow which it may bring seems its own complete justification, then philosophy is evidently still pre-rational or, rather, non-existent; for the beasts that listened to Orpheus belong to this school.

To be bewitched is not to be saved, though all the magicians and æsthetes in the world should pronounce it to be so. Intoxication is a sad business, at least for a philosopher; for you must either drown yourself altogether, or else when sober again you will feel somewhat fooled by yesterday's joys and somewhat lost in to-day's vacancy. The man who would emancipate art from discipline and reason is trying to elude rationality, not merely in art, but in all existence. He is vexed at conditions of excellence that make him conscious of his own incompetence and failure. Rather than consider his function, he proclaims his self-sufficiency. A way foolishness has of revenging itself is to excommunicate the world.

If a practice can point to its innocence, if it can absolve itself from concern for a world with which it does not interfere, it has justified itself to those who love it, though it may not yet have recommended itself to those who do not. Now art, more than any other considerable pursuit, more even than speculation, is abstract and inconsequential. Born of suspended attention, it ends in itself. It encourages sensuous abstraction, and nothing concerns it less than to influence the world. Nor does it really do so in a notable degree. Social changes do not reach artistic expression until after their momentum is acquired and their other collateral effects are fully predetermined. Scarcely is a school of art established, giving expression to prevailing sentiment, when this sentiment changes and makes that style seem empty and ridiculous. The expression has little or no power to maintain the movement it registers, as a waterfall has little or no power to bring more water down. Currents may indeed cut deep channels, but they cannot feed their own springs—at least not until the whole revolution of nature is taken into account.

In the individual, also, art registers passions without stimulating them; on the contrary, in stopping to depict them it steals away their life; and whatever interest and delight it transfers to their expression it subtracts from their vital energy. This appears unmistakably in erotic and in religious art. Though the artist's avowed purpose here be to arouse a practical impulse, he fails in so far as he is an artist in truth; for he then will seek to move the given passions only through beauty, but beauty is a rival object of passion in itself. Lascivious and pious works, when beauty has touched them, cease to give out what is wilful and disquieting in their subject and become altogether intellectual and sublime. There is a high breathlessness about beauty that cancels lust and superstition. The artist, in taking the latter for his theme, renders them innocent and interesting, because he looks at them from above, composes their attitudes and surroundings harmoniously, and makes them food for the mind. Accordingly it is only in a refined and secondary stage that active passions like to amuse themselves with their æsthetic expression. Unmitigated lustiness and raw fanaticism will snarl at pictures. Representations begin to interest when crude passions recede, and feel the need of conciliating liberal interests and adding some intellectual charm to their dumb attractions. Thus art, while by its subject it may betray the preoccupations among which it springs up, embodies a new and quite innocent interest.

This interest is more than innocent; it is liberal. Art has met, on the whole, with more success than science or morals. Beauty gives men the best hint of ultimate good which their experience as yet can offer; and the most lauded geniuses have been poets, as if people felt that those seers, rather than men of action or thought, had lived ideally and known what was worth knowing. That such should be the case, if the fact be admitted, would indeed prove the rudimentary state of human civilization. The truly comprehensive life should be the statesman's, for whom perception and theory might be expressed and rewarded in action. The ideal dignity of art is therefore merely symbolic and vicarious. As some people study character in novels, and travel by reading tales of adventure, because real life is not yet so interesting to them as fiction, or because they find it cheaper to make their experiments in their dreams, so art in general is a rehearsal of rational living, and recasts in idea a world which we have no present means of recasting in reality. Yet this rehearsal reveals the glories of a possible performance better than do the miserable experiments until now executed on the reality.

When we consider the present distracted state of government and religion, there is much relief in turning from them to almost any art, where what is good is altogether and finally good, and what is bad is at least not treacherous. When we consider further the senseless rivalries, the vanities, the ignominy that reign in the 'practical' world, how doubly blessed it becomes to find a sphere where limitation is an excellence, where diversity is a beauty, and where every man's ambition is consistent with every other man's and even favourable to it! It is indeed so in art; for we must not import into its blameless labours the bickerings and jealousies of criticism. Critics quarrel with other critics, and that is a part of philosophy. With an artist no sane man quarrels, any more than with the colour of a child's eyes. As nature, being full of seeds, rises into all sorts of crystallizations, each having its own ideal and potential life, each a nucleus of order and a habitation for the absolute self, so art, though in a medium poorer than pregnant matter, and incapable of intrinsic life, generates a semblance of all conceivable beings. What nature does with existence, art does with appearance; and while the achievement leaves us, unhappily, much where we were before in all our efficacious relations, it entirely renews our vision and breeds a fresh world in fancy, where all form has the same inner justification that all life has in the real world. As no insect is without its rights and every cripple has his dream of happiness, so no artistic fact, no child of imagination, is without its small birthright of beauty. In this freer element, competition does not exist and everything is Olympian. Hungry generations do not tread down the ideal but only its spokesmen or embodiments, that have cast in their lot with other material things. Art supplies constantly to contemplation what nature seldom affords in concrete experience—the union of life and peace.

1905

SOCIETY AND SOLITUDE

O solitudo, sola beatitudo,[1] Saint Bernard said; but might he not have said just as well, O societas, sola felicitas?[2] Just as truly, I think; because when a man says that the only happiness is this or that, he is like a lover saying that Mary Jane is the one woman in the world. She may be truly the one woman for him, though even that is not probable; but he cannot mean to assert that she is the only woman living, nor to deny that each of the others might be the one woman for somebody. Now, when a Hegelian philosopher, contradicting Saint Bernard, says that society is his be-all and end-all, that he himself is nothing but an invisible point at which relations cross, and that if you removed from him his connection with Hegel, with his university, his church, his wife, and his publishers, there

1 'O Solitude, sole felicity!'
2 'O Society, sole felicity!'

would be nothing left, or at best a name and a peg to hang a gown on, far be it from me to revise his own analysis of his nature; society may be the only felicity and the only reality for him. But that cannot annul the judgement of Saint Bernard. He had a great mind and a great heart, and he knew society well; at least, he accepted the verdict which antiquity had passed on society, after a very long, brilliant, and hearty experience of it; and he knew the religious life and solitude as well; and I can't help thinking that he, too, must have been right in his self-knowledge, and that solitude must have been the only happiness for him.

Nevertheless, the matter is not limited to this confronting of divers honest judgements, or confessions of moral experience. The natures expressed in these judgements have a long history, and are on different levels; the one may be derived from the other. Thus it is evident that the beatific solitude of Saint Bernard was filled with a kind of society; he devoted it to communion with the Trinity, or to composing fervent compliments to the Virgin Mary. It was only the society to be found in inns and hovels, in castles, sacristies, and refectories, that he thought it happiness to avoid. That the wilderness to which hermits flee must be peopled by their fancy, could have been foreseen by any observer of human nature. Tormenting demons or ministering angels must needs appear, because man is rooted in society and his instincts are addressed to it; for the first nine months, or even years, of his existence he is a parasite; and scarcely are these parental bonds a little relaxed, when he instinctively forms other ties, that turn him into a husband and father, and keep him such all his days. If ever he finds happiness in solitude, it can only be by lavishing on objects of his imagination the attentions which his social functions require that he should lavish on something. Without exercising these faculties somehow his nature would be paralysed; there would be no fuel to feed a spiritual flame. All Saint Bernard could mean, then, is that happiness lies in this substitution of an ideal for a natural society, in converse with thoughts rather than with things. Such a substitution is normal, and a mark of moral vigour; we must not be misled into comparing it with a love of dolls or of lap-dogs.

Dolls are not impersonal, and lap-dogs are not ideas: they are only less rebellious specimens of the genus thing; they are more portable idols. To substitute the society of ideas for that of things is simply to live in the mind; it is to survey the world of existences in its truth and beauty rather than in its personal perspectives, or with practical urgency. It is the sole path to happiness for the intellectual man, because the intellectual man cannot be satisfied with a world of perpetual change, defeat, and imperfection. It is the path trodden by ancient philosophers and modern saints or poets; not, of course, by modern writers on philosophy (except Spinoza), because these have not been philosophers in the vital sense; they have practised no spiritual discipline, suffered no change of heart, but lived on exactly like other professors, and exerted themselves to prove the existence of a God favourable to their own desires, instead of searching for the God that happens to exist. Certainly this path, in its beginnings, is arduous, and leaves the natural man somewhat spare and haggard; he seems to himself to have fasted for forty days and forty nights, and the world regards his way of living afterwards as rather ghostly and poor. But he usually congratulates himself upon it in the end; and of those who persevere some become saints and some poets and some philosophers.

Yet why, we may ask, should happiness be found exclusively in this ideal society where none intrudes? If the intellectual man cannot lay up his treasures in a world of change, the natural man can perfectly well satisfy his instincts within it; and why shouldn't the two live amicably together in a house of two stories? I can see no essential reason; but historically natural society long ago proved a moral failure. It could not harmonize nor decently satisfy even the instincts on which it rests. Hence the philosophers have felt bound not only to build themselves a superstructure but to quit the ground floor—materially, if possible, by leading a monastic life, religiously in any case by not expecting to find much except weeping and wailing in this vale of tears. We may tax this despair with being premature, and call such a flight into an imaginary world a desperate expedient; at any time the attempts of the natural man to live his comic life happily may be renewed, and may succeed. Solitude peopled with ideas might still remain to employ the mind; but it would not be the only beatitude.

Yet the insecurity of natural society runs deeper, for natural society itself is an expedient and a sort of refuge of despair. It, too, in its inception, seemed a sacrifice and a constraint. The primitive soul hates order and the happiness founded on order. The barbarous soul hates justice and peace. The belly is always rebelling against the members. The belly was once all in all; it was a single cell floating deliciously in a warm liquid; it had no outer organs; it thought it didn't need them. It vegetated in peace; no noises, no alarms, no lusts, no nonsense. Ah, veritably solitude was blessedness then! But it was a specious solitude and a precarious blessedness, resting on ignorance. The warm liquid might cool, or might dry up; it might breed all sorts of enemies; presently heaven might crack and the cell be cleft in two. Happy the hooded microbe that put forth feelers in time, and awoke to its social or unsocial environment! I am not sure that, beneath the love of ideal society, there was not in Saint Bernard a lingering love of primeval peace, of seminal slumber; that he did not yearn for the cell biological as well as for the cell monastic. Life, mere living, is a profound ideal, pregnant with the memory of a possible happiness, the happiness of protoplasm; and the advocate of moral society must not reckon without his host. He has a rebellious material in hand; his every atom is instinct with a life of its own which it may reassert, upsetting his calculations and destroying his organic systems. Only the physical failure of solitude drove the spirit at first into society, as the moral failure of society may drive it later into solitude again. If any one said, then, that happiness lies only in society, his maxim would be no less sincere and solid than Saint Bernard's, but it would not be so profound. For beneath natural society, in the heart of each of its members, there is always an intense and jealous solitude, the sleep of elemental life which can never be wholly broken; and above natural society there is always another solitude—a placid ethereal wilderness, the heaven of ideas—beckoning the mind.

1918–1921   1922

AT HEAVEN'S GATE

SKYLARKS, if they exist elsewhere, must be homesick for England. They need these kindly mists to hide and to sustain them. Their flexible throats would soon be parched, far from these vaporous meadows and hedgerows rich in berries and loam. How should they live in arid tablelands, or at merciless altitudes, where there is nothing but scorching heat or a freezing blizzard? What space could they find for solitude and freedom in the tangle of tropical forests, amongst the monkeys and parrots? What reserve, what tenderness, what inward springs of happiness could they treasure amid those gross harlot-like flowers? No, they are the hermits of this mild atmosphere, fled to its wilderness of gentle light. Well may they leave it to eagles to rush against the naked sun, as if its round eye challenged them to single combat: not theirs the stupid ferocity of passion against fact, anger against fact, swiftness against poise, beak and talons against intangible fire. Larks may not be very clever, but they are not so foolish as to be proud, or to scream hoarsely against the nature of things. Having wings and voluble throats they play with them for pure pleasure; they are little artists and little gentlemen; they disdain to employ their faculties for their mere utility, or only in order to pounce down to the earth, whenever they spy a dainty morsel, or to return to sulk shivering on some solitary crag, their voracity but half appeased, like eagles dreaming of their next victim. Of course, even the most playful songster must eat, and skylarks no doubt keep an eye open for worms, and their nest calls them back to terrene affections; but they are as forgetful of earth as they can be, and insatiable craving does not stamp itself on their bent necks, as if they were vultures, nor strain their feathers of iron. No more are they inspired by sentimental pangs and love-sick like the nightingale; they do not hide in the labyrinthine shade of ilex or cypress, from there to wail in the melancholy moonlight, as it were a seductive serenade addressed to mortal lovers. No, the trilling of larks is not for mankind. Like English poets they sing to themselves of nature, inarticulately happy in a bath of light and freedom, sporting for the sake of sport, turning what doubts they may have into sweetness, not asking to see or to know anything ulterior. They must needs drink the dew amongst these English fields, peeping into the dark little hearts and flushed petals of these daisies, like the heart and cheeks of an English child, or into these buttercups, yellow like his Saxon hair. They could hardly have built their nests far from this maze of little streams, or from these narrow dykes and ditches, arched with the scented tracery of limes and willows. They needed this long, dull, chilly winter in which to gather their un-suspected fund of yearning and readiness for joy; so that when high summer comes at last they may mount with virgin con-fidence and ardour through these sunlit spaces, to pour their souls out at heaven's gate.

At heaven's gate, but not in heaven. The sky, as these larks rise higher and higher, grows colder and thinner; if they could rise high enough, it would be a black void. All this fluid and dazzling atmosphere is but the drapery of earth; this cerulean vault is only a film round the oceans. As these chor-isters pass beyond the nether veils of air, the sun becomes fierce and comfortless; they freeze and are dazzled; they must hurry home again to earth if they would live. They must put fuel in their little engines: after all it was flesh and blood in them that were praising the Lord. And accordingly, down they drop to their nests and peck about, anxious and silent; but their song never comes down. Up there they leave it, in the glittering desert it once ravished, in what we call the past. They bore their glad offer-ing to the gate and returned empty; but the gladness of it, which in their palpitation and hurry they only half guessed, passed in and is a part of heaven. In the home of all good, from which their frail souls fetched it for a moment, it is still audible for any ear that ever again can attune itself to that measure. All that was loved or beautiful at any time, or that shall be so hereafter, all that never was but that ought to have been, lives in that paradise, in the brilliant treasure-house of the gods.

How many an English spirit, too modest to be heard here, has now committed its secret to that same heaven! Caught by the impulse of the hour, they rose like larks in the morning, cheerily, rashly, to meet the unforeseen, fatal, congenial adventure, the goal not seen, the air not measured, but the firm heart steady through the fog or blind-ing fire, making the best of what came, trembling but ready for what might come, with a simple courage which was half joy in living and half willingness to die. Their first flight was often their last. What fell to earth was only a poor dead body, one of a million; what remained above perhaps nothing to speak of, some boyish sally or wistful fancy, less than the song of a lark for God to treasure up in his omniscience and eternity. Yet these common brave fools knew as well as the lark the thing that they could do, and did it; and of other gifts and other adventures they were not envious. Boys and free men are always a little in-clined to flout what is not the goal of their present desires, or is beyond their present scope; spontaneity in them has its ebb-flow in mockery. Their tight little selves are too vigorous and too clearly determined to brood much upon distant things; but they are true to their own nature, they know and love the sources of their own strength. Like the larks, those English boys had drunk here the quintessence of many a sunlit morning; they had rambled through these same fields, fringed with hedges and peep-ing copse and downs purple with heather; these paths and streams had enticed them often; they had been vaguely happy in these quiet, habitable places. It was enough for them to live, as for nature to revolve; and fate, in draining in one draught the modest cup of their spirit, spared them the weary dilution and waste of it in the world. The length of things is vanity, only their height is joy.

Of myself also I would keep nothing but what God may keep of me—some lovely essence, mine for a moment in that I beheld it, some object of devout love enshrined where all other hearts that have a like intelli-gence of love in their day may worship it; but my loves themselves and my reason-ings are but a flutter of feathers weaker than a lark's, a prattle idler than his war-blings, happy enough if they too may fly with him and die with him at the gate of heaven.

1914–1918   1922

O WORLD, THOU CHOOSEST NOT THE BETTER PART !![1]

O WORLD, thou choosest not the better part!
It is not wisdom to be only wise,
And on the inward vision close the eyes,
But it is wisdom to believe the heart.
Columbus found a world, and had no chart,
Save one that faith deciphered in the skies;
To trust the soul's invincible surmise
Was all his science and his only art.
Our knowledge is a torch of smoky pine
That lights the pathway but one step ahead
Across a void of mystery and dread.   11
Bid, then, the tender light of faith to shine
By which alone the mortal heart is led
Unto the thinking of the thought divine.
1884   1894

ON THE DEATH OF A METAPHYSICIAN

UNHAPPY dreamer, who outwinged in flight
The pleasant region of the things I love,
And soared beyond the sunshine, and above
The golden cornfields and the dear and
      bright
Warmth of the hearth,—blasphemer of
      delight,
Was your proud bosom not at peace with
      Jove,
That you sought, thankless for his guarded
      grove,
The empty horror of abysmal night?
Ah, the thin air is cold above the moon!
I stood and saw you fall, befooled in death,
As, in your numbèd spirit's fatal swoon,   11
You cried you were a god, or were to be;
I heard with feeble moan your boastful
      breath
Bubble from depths of the Icarian sea.
c.1890   1923

1 Of his poetry, Santayana says: 'If their prosody is worn
and traditional, like a liturgy, it is because they represent the initiation of a mind into a world older and
larger than itself; not the chance experiences of a stray
individual, but his submission to what is not his chance
experience; to the truth of nature and the moral heritage of mankind. Here is the uncertain hand of an apprentice, but of an apprentice in a great school. Verse
is one of the traditions of literature. Like the orders of
Greek architecture, the sonnet or the couplet or the
quatrain are better than anything else that has been
devised to serve the same function; and the innate freedom of poets to hazard new forms does not abolish the
freedom of all men to adopt the old ones. . . . For as
to the subject of these poems, it is simply my philosophy in the making.' Santayana, *Poems* (N.Y., 1935),
ix–xii.

OF THEE THE NORTHMAN BY HIS BEACHÈD GALLEY [2]

OF thee the Northman by his beachèd
      galley
Dreamt, as he watched the never-setting
      Ursa
And longed for summer and thy light, O
      sacred
      Mediterranean.

Unseen he loved thee; for the heart within
      him
Knew earth had gardens where he might be
      blessed
Putting away long dreams and aimless,
      barbarous
      Hunger for battle.

The foretaste of thy languors thawed his
      bosom;
A great need drove him to thy caverned
      islands   10
From the gray, endless reaches of the outer
      Desert of ocean.

He saw thy pillars, saw thy sudden
      mountains
Wrinkled and stark, and in their crooked
      gorges,
'Neath peeping pine and cypress, guessed
      the torrent
      Smothered in flowers.

Thine incense to the sun, thy gathered
      vapours,
He saw suspended on the flanks of
      Taurus,
Or veiling the snowed bosom of the virgin
      Sister of Atlas.   20

He saw the luminous top of wide Olympus,
Fit for the happy gods; he saw the pilgrim
River, with rains of Ethiopia flooding
      Populous Egypt.

And having seen, he loved thee. His racked
      spirit,
By thy breath tempered and the light that
      clothes thee,

2 'All these "Odes" were written about the same time,
inspired not by Sappho (for they are not in true Sap-
phics) but by a translation of her poems in Spanish
which I had come upon among my father's books.'
Author's note.

Forgot the monstrous gods, and made of
    Nature
      Mistress and mother.

The more should I, O fatal sea, before thee
Of alien words make echoes to thy music; 30
For I was born where first the rills of Tagus
    Turn to the westward,

And wandering long, alas! have need of
    drinking
Deep of the patience of thy perfect sadness,
O thou that constant through the change of
    ages,
      Beautiful ever,

Never wast wholly young and void of
    sorrows,
Nor ever canst be old, while yet the
    morning
Kindles thy ripples, or the golden evening
    Dyes thee in purple.   40

Thee, willing to be tamed but still
    untamable,
The Roman called his own until he
    perished,
As now the busy English hover o'er thee,
    Stalwart and noble;

But all is naught to thee, while no harsh
    winter
Congeals thy fountains, and the blown
    Sahara
Chokes not with dreadful sand thy deep and
    placid
      Rock-guarded havens.

Thou carest not what men may tread thy
    margin;
Nor I, while from some heather-scented
    headland   50
I may behold thy beauty, the eternal
    Solace of mortals.
1887   1894

MY HEART REBELS AGAINST MY
GENERATION

My heart rebels against my generation,
That talks of freedom and is slave to
    riches,
And, toiling 'neath each day's ignoble
    burden,
      Boasts of the morrow.

No space for noonday rest or midnight
    watches,
No purest joy of breathing under heaven!
Wretched themselves, they heap, to make
    them happy,
      Many possessions.

But thou, O silent Mother, wise, immortal,
To whom our toil is laughter,—take, divine
    one,   10
This vanity away, and to thy lover
    Give what is needful:—

A staunch heart, nobly calm, averse to
    evil,
The windy sky for breath, the sea, the
    mountain,
A well-born, gentle friend, his spirit's
    brother,
      Ever beside him.

What would you gain, ye seekers, with your
    striving,
Or what vast Babel raise you on your
    shoulders?
You multiply distresses, and your children
    Surely will curse you.   20

O leave them rather friendlier gods, and
    fairer
Orchards and temples, and a freer bosom!
What better comfort have we, or what other
    Profit in living,

Than to feed, sobered by the truth of
    Nature,
Awhile upon her bounty and her beauty,
And hand her torch of gladness to the ages
    Following after?

She hath not made us, like her other
    children,
Merely for peopling of her spacious
    kingdoms,   30
Beasts of the wild, or insects of the summer,
    Breeding and dying,

But also that we might, half knowing,
    worship
The deathless beauty of her guiding
    vision,
And learn to love, in all things mortal,
    only
      What is eternal.
1890   1894

A MINUET

ON REACHING THE AGE OF FIFTY

I

OLD AGE, on tiptoe, lays her jewelled hand
Lightly in mine.—Come, tread a stately
      measure,
Most gracious partner, nobly poised and
      bland.
      Ours be no boisterous pleasure,
But smiling conversation, with quick glance
And memories dancing lightlier than we
      dance,
      Friends who a thousand joys
Divide and double, save one joy supreme
      Which many a pang alloys.
      Let wanton girls and boys   10
Cry over lovers' woes and broken toys.
Our waking life is sweeter than their dream.

II

Dame Nature, with unwitting hand,
Has sparsely strewn the black abyss with
      lights
Minute, remote, and numberless. We stand
      Measuring far depths and heights,
      Arched over by a laughing heaven,
Intangible and never to be scaled.
If we confess our sins, they are forgiven.
      We triumph, if we know we failed.   20

III

      Tears that in youth you shed,
Congealed to pearls, now deck your silvery
      hair;
      Sighs breathed for loves long dead

Frosted the glittering atoms of the air
      Into the veils you wear
Round your soft bosom and most queenly
      head;
      The shimmer of your gown
Catches all tints of autumn, and the
      dew
Of gardens where the damask roses blew;
The myriad tapers from these arches hung
      Play on your diamonded crown;   31
And stars, whose light angelical caressed
      Your virgin days,
Give back in your calm eyes their holier
      rays.
      The deep past living in your breast
      Heaves these half-merry sighs;
      And the soft accents of your tongue
      Breathe unrecorded charities.

IV

      Hasten not; the feast will wait.
This is a master-night without a morrow. 40
No chill and haggard dawn, with after-
      sorrow,
      Will snuff the spluttering candle
      out,
Or blanch the revellers homeward straggling
      late.
      Before the rout
Wearies or wanes, will come a calmer
      trance.
Lulled by the poppied fragrance of this
      bower,
      We'll cheat the lapsing hour,
And close our eyes, still smiling, on the
      dance.
1913   1923

EDWIN ARLINGTON ROBINSON

1869–1935

CLIFF KLINGENHAGEN

CLIFF KLINGENHAGEN had me in to dine
With him one day; and after soup and
      meat,
And all the other things there were to
      eat,
Cliff took two glasses and filled one with
      wine
And one with wormwood. Then, without a
      sign
For me to choose at all, he took the draught

Of bitterness himself, and lightly quaffed
It off, and said the other one was mine.

And when I asked him what the deuce he
      meant
By doing that, he only looked at me   10
And smiled, and said it was a way of his.
And though I know the fellow, I have
      spent
Long time a-wondering when I shall be
As happy as Cliff Klingenhagen is.
                                        1897

RICHARD CORY

WHENEVER Richard Cory went down town,
We people on the pavement looked at him:
He was a gentleman from sole to crown,
Clean favored, and imperially slim.

And he was always quietly arrayed,
And he was always human when he
     talked;
But still he fluttered pulses when he said,
'Good-morning,' and he glittered when
     he walked.

And he was rich—yes, richer than a king—
And admirably schooled in every grace: 10
In fine, we thought that he was everything
To make us wish that we were in his
     place.

So on we worked, and waited for the light,
And went without the meat, and cursed
     the bread;
And Richard Cory, one calm summer night,
Went home and put a bullet through his
     head.   1897

HOW ANNANDALE WENT OUT

'THEY called it Annandale—and I was there
To flourish, to find words, and to attend:
Liar, physician, hypocrite, and friend,
I watched him; and the sight was not so
     fair
As one or two that I have seen elsewhere:
An apparatus not for me to mend—
A wreck, with hell between him and the
     end,
Remained of Annandale; and I was there.

'I knew the ruin as I knew the man;
So put the two together, if you can,   10
Remembering the worst you know of me.
Now view yourself as I was, on the spot—
With a slight kind of engine. Do you see?
Like this. . . . You wouldn't hang me? I
     thought not.'   1910

MINIVER CHEEVY

MINIVER CHEEVY, child of scorn,
  Grew lean while he assailed the seasons;
He wept that he was ever born,
  And he had reasons.

Miniver loved the days of old
  When swords were bright and steeds
     were prancing;
The vision of a warrior bold
  Would set him dancing.

Miniver sighed for what was not,
  And dreamed, and rested from his
     labors;   10
He dreamed of Thebes and Camelot,
  And Priam's neighbors.

Miniver mourned the ripe renown
  That made so many a name so fragrant;
He mourned Romance, now on the town,
  And Art, a vagrant.

Miniver loved the Medici,
  Albeit he had never seen one;
He would have sinned incessantly
  Could he have been one.   20

Miniver cursed the commonplace
  And eyed a khaki suit with loathing;
He missed the mediæval grace
  Of iron clothing.

Miniver scorned the gold he sought,
  But sore annoyed was he without it;
Miniver thought, and thought, and thought,
  And thought about it.

Miniver Cheevy, born too late,
  Scratched his head and kept on thinking;
Miniver coughed and called it fate,   31
  And kept on drinking.   1910

FOR A DEAD LADY

No more with overflowing light
Shall fill the eyes that now are faded,
Nor shall another's fringe with night
Their woman-hidden world as they did.
No more shall quiver down the days
The flowing wonder of her ways,
Whereof no language may requite
The shifting and the many-shaded.

The grace, divine, definitive,
Clings only as a faint forestalling;   10
The laugh that love could not forgive
Is hushed, and answers to no calling;
The forehead and the little ears
Have gone where Saturn keeps the years;

The breast where roses could not live
Has done with rising and with falling.

The beauty, shattered by the laws
That have creation in their keeping,
No longer trembles at applause,
Or over children that are sleeping;　　20
And we who delve in beauty's lore
Know all that we have known before
Of what inexorable cause
Makes Time so vicious in his reaping.

　　　　　　　　　　　　1910

THE MASTER [1]

(LINCOLN)

A FLYING word from here and there
Had sown the name at which we sneered,
But soon the name was everywhere,
To be reviled and then revered:
A presence to be loved and feared,
We cannot hide it, or deny
That we, the gentlemen who jeered,
May be forgotten by and by.

He came when days were perilous
And hearts of men were sore beguiled;　　10
And having made his note of us,
He pondered and was reconciled.
Was ever master yet so mild
As he, and so untamable?
We doubted, even when he smiled,
Not knowing what he knew so well.

He knew that undeceiving fate
Would shame us whom he served un-
　　sought;
He knew that he must wince and wait—
The jest of those for whom he fought;　　20
He knew devoutly what he thought
Of us and of our ridicule;
He knew that we must all be taught
Like little children in a school.

We gave a glamour to the task
That he encountered and saw through,
But little of us did he ask,
And little did we ever do.
And what appears if we review
The season when we railed and chaffed?　　30
It is the face of one who knew
That we were learning while we laughed.

1 'Supposed to have been written not long after the Civil
　War.' Author's note, Collected Poems (N.Y., 1937), 317.

The face that in our vision feels
Again the venom that we flung,
Transfigured to the world reveals
The vigilance to which we clung.
Shrewd, hallowed, harassed, and among
The mysteries that are untold,
The face we see was never young
Nor could it wholly have been old.　　40

For he, to whom we had applied
Our shopman's test of age and worth,
Was elemental when he died,
As he was ancient at his birth:
The saddest among kings of earth,
Bowed with a galling crown, this man
Met rancor with a cryptic mirth,
Laconic—and Olympian.

The love, the grandeur, and the fame
Are bounded by the world alone;　　50
The calm, the smouldering, and the flame
Of awful patience were his own:
With him they are forever flown
Past all our fond self-shadowings,
Wherewith we cumber the Unknown
As with inept, Icarian wings.

For we were not as other men:
'Twas ours to soar and his to see;
But we are coming down again,
And we shall come down pleasantly;　　60
Nor shall we longer disagree
On what it is to be sublime,
But flourish in our perigee
And have one Titan at a time.

　　　　　　　　　　　　1910

BEN JONSON ENTERTAINS A MAN
FROM STRATFORD

YOU are a friend then, as I make it out,
Of our man Shakespeare, who alone of us
Will put an ass's head in Fairyland
As he would add a shilling to more shilling,
All most harmonious,—and out of his
Miraculous inviolable increase
Fills Ilion, Rome, or any town you like
Of olden time with timeless Englishmen;
And I must wonder what you think of
　　him—
All you down there where your small Avon
　　flows
By Stratford, and where you're an
　　Alderman.

Some, for a guess, would have him riding
      back
To be a farrier there, or say a dyer;
Or maybe one of your adept surveyors;
Or like enough the wizard of all tanners.
Not you—no fear of that; for I discern
In you a kindling of the flame that saves—
The nimble element, the true caloric;
I see it, and was told of it, moreover,
By our discriminate friend himself, no
      other.   20
Had you been one of the sad average,
As he would have it,—meaning, as I take it,
The sinew and the solvent of our Island,
You'd not be buying beer for this
      Terpander's
Approved and estimated friend Ben Jonson;
He'd never foist it as a part of his
Contingent entertainment of a townsman
While he goes off rehearsing, as he must,
If he shall ever be the Duke of Stratford.
And my words are no shadow on your
      town—   30
Far from it; for one town's as like another
As all are unlike London. Oh, he knows
      it,—
And there's the Stratford in him; he denies
      it,
And there's the Shakespeare in him. So,
      God help him!
I tell him he needs Greek; but neither God
Nor Greek will help him. Nothing will help
      that man.
You see the fates have given him so much,
He must have all or perish,—or look out
Of London, where he sees too many lords.
They're part of half what ails him: I
      suppose   40
There's nothing fouler down among the
      demons
Than what it is he feels when he remembers
The dust and sweat and ointment of his
      calling
With his lords looking on and laughing at
      him.
King as he is, he can't be king *de facto*,
And that's as well, because he wouldn't like
      it;
He'd frame a lower rating of men then
Than he has now; and after that would
      come
An abdication or an apoplexy.
He can't be king, not even king of
      Stratford,—   50
Though half the world, if not the whole of it,

May crown him with a crown that fits no
      king
Save Lord Apollo's homesick emissary:
Not there on Avon, or on any stream
Where Naiads and their white arms are no
      more,
Shall he find home again. It's all too bad.
But there's a comfort, for he'll have that
      House—
The best you ever saw; and he'll be there 58
Anon, as you're an Alderman. Good God!
He makes me lie awake o'nights and laugh.

And you have known him from his origin,
You tell me; and a most uncommon urchin
He must have been to the few seeing ones—
A trifle terrifying, I dare say,
Discovering a world with his man's eyes,
Quite as another lad might see some finches,
If he looked hard and had an eye for nature.
But this one had his eyes and their
      foretelling,
And he had you to fare with, and what
      else?
He must have had a father and a mother—
In fact I've heard him say so—and a dog, 71
As a boy should, I venture; and the dog,
Most likely, was the only man who knew
      him.
A dog, for all I know, is what he needs
As much as anything right here to-day,
To counsel him about his disillusions,
Old aches, and parturitions of what's
      coming,—
A dog of orders, an emeritus,
To wag his tail at him when he comes home,
And then to put his paws up on his knees 80
And say, 'For God's sake, what's it all
      about?'

I don't know whether he needs a dog or
      not—
Or what he needs. I tell him he needs Greek;
I'll talk of rules and Aristotle with him,
And if his tongue's at home he'll say to that,
'I have your word that Aristotle knows,
And you mine that I don't know Aristotle.'
He's all at odds with all the unities,
And what's yet worse, it doesn't seem to
      matter;
He treads along through Time's old
      wilderness   90
As if the tramp of all the centuries
Had left no roads—and there are none, for
      him;

He doesn't see them, even with those
                eyes,—
And that's a pity, or I say it is.
Accordingly we have him as we have him—
Going his way, the way that he goes best,
A pleasant animal with no great noise
Or nonsense anywhere to set him off—
Save only divers and inclement devils
Have made of late his heart their dwelling
                place.   100
A flame half ready to fly out sometimes
At some annoyance may be fanned up in
                him,
But soon it falls, and when it falls goes out;
He knows how little room there is in there
For crude and futile animosities,
And how much for the joy of being whole,
And how much for long sorrow and old
                pain.
On our side there are some who may be
                given
To grow old wondering what he thinks of
                us
And some above us, who are, in his eyes, 110
Above himself,—and that's quite right and
                English.
Yet here we smile, or disappoint the gods
Who made it so: the gods have always eyes
To see men scratch; and they see one down
                here
Who itches, manor-bitten to the bone,
Albeit he knows himself—yes, yes, he
                knows—
The lord of more than England and of more
Than all the seas of England in all time
Shall ever wash. D'ye wonder that I laugh?
He sees me, and he doesn't seem to care;
And why the devil should he? I can't tell
                you.   121

I'll meet him out alone of a bright Sunday,
Trim, rather spruce, and quite the
                gentleman.
'What ho, my lord!' say I. He doesn't hear
                me;
Wherefore I have to pause and look at him.
He's not enormous, but one looks at him.
A little on the round if you insist,
For now, God save the mark, he's growing
                old;
He's five and forty, and to hear him talk
These days you'd call him eighty; then
                you'd add   130
More years to that. He's old enough to be
The father of a world, and so he is.

'Ben, you're a scholar, what's the time of
                day?'
Says he; and there shines out of him again
An aged light that has no age or station—
The mystery that's his—a mischievous
Half-mad serenity that laughs at fame
For being won so easy, and at friends
Who laugh at him for what he wants the
                most,
And for his dukedom down in
                Warwickshire;—   140
By which you see we're all a little
                jealous. . . .
Poor Greene! I fear the color of his name
Was even as that of his ascending soul;
And he was one where there are many
                others,—
Some scrivening to the end against their
                fate,
Their puppets all in ink and all to die there;
And some with hands that once would shade
                an eye
That scanned Euripides and Æschylus
Will reach by this time for a pot-house mop
To slush their first and last of royalties. 150
Poor devils! and they all play to his hand;
For so it was in Athens and old Rome.
But that's not here or there; I've wandered
                off.
Greene does it, or I'm careful. Where's that
                boy?

Yes, he'll go back to Stratford. And we'll
                miss him?
Dear sir, there'll be no London here
                without him.
We'll all be riding, one of these fine days,
Down there to see him—and his wife won't
                like us;
And then we'll think of what he never said
Of women—which, if taken all in all   160
With what he did say, would buy many
                horses.
Though nowadays he's not so much for
                women.
'So few of them,' he says, 'are worth the
                guessing.'
But there's a worm at work when he says
                that,
And while he says it one feels in the air
A deal of circumambient hocus-pocus.
They've had him dancing till his toes were
                tender,
And he can feel 'em now, come chilly rains.
There's no long cry for going into it,

However, and we don't know much about
    it.   170
But you in Stratford, like most here in
    London,
Have more now in the *Sonnets* than you
    paid for;
He's put one there with all her poison on,
To make a singing fiction of a shadow
That's in his life a fact, and always will be.
But she's no care of ours, though Time, I
    fear,
Will have a more reverberant ado
About her than about another one
Who seems to have decoyed him, married
    him,
And sent him scuttling on his way to
    London,—   180
With much already learned, and more to
    learn,
And more to follow. Lord! how I see him
    now,
Pretending, maybe trying, to be like us.
Whatever he may have meant, we never had
    him;
He failed us, or escaped, or what you will,—
And there was that about him (God knows
    what,—
We'd flayed another had he tried it on us)
That made as many of us as had wits
More fond of all his easy distances
Than one another's noise and clap-your-
    shoulder.   190
But think you not, my friend, he'd never
    talk!
Talk? He was eldritch at it; and we
    listened—
Thereby acquiring much we knew before
About ourselves, and hitherto had held
Irrelevant, or not prime to the purpose.
And there were some, of course, and there
    be now,
Disordered and reduced amazedly
To resignation by the mystic seal
Of young finality the gods had laid
On everything that made him a young
    demon;   200
And one or two shot looks at him already
As he had been their executioner;
And once or twice he was, not knowing it,—
Or knowing, being sorry for poor clay
And saying nothing. . . . Yet, for all his
    engines,
You'll meet a thousand of an afternoon
Who strut and sun themselves and see
    around 'em

A world made out of more that has a reason
Than his, I swear, that he sees here to-day;
Though he may scarcely give a Fool an exit
But we mark how he sees in everything 211
A law that, given that we flout it once too
    often,
Brings fire and iron down on our naked
    heads.
To me it looks as if the power that made
    him,
For fear of giving all things to one creature,
Left out the first—faith, innocence, illusion,
Whatever 'tis that keeps us out o' Bedlam,—
And thereby, for his too consuming vision,
Empowered him out of nature; though to
    see him,
You'd never guess what's going on inside
    him.   220
He'll break out some day like a keg of ale
With too much independent frenzy in it;
And all for cellaring what he knows won't
    keep,
And what he'd best forget—but that he
    can't.
You'll have it, and have more than I'm
    foretelling;
And there'll be such a roaring at the Globe
As never stunned the bleeding gladiators.
He'll have to change the color of its hair
A bit, for now he calls it Cleopatra.
Black hair would never do for Cleopatra. 230
But you and I are not yet two old women,
And you're a man of office. What he does
Is more to you than how it is he does it,—
And that's what the Lord God has never
    told him.
They work together, and the Devil helps
    'em;
They do it of a morning, or if not,
They do it of a night; in which event
He's peevish of a morning. He seems old;
He's not the proper stomach or the sleep—
And they're two sovran agents to conserve
    him   240
Against the fiery art that has no mercy
But what's in that prodigious grand new
    House.
I gather something happening in his
    boyhood
Fulfilled him with a boy's determination
To make all Stratford 'ware of him. Well,
    well,
I hope at last he'll have his joy of it,
And all his pigs and sheep and bellowing
    beeves,

And frogs and owls and unicorns, moreover,
Be less than hell to his attendant ears.
Oh, past a doubt we'll all go down to see
    him.   250

He may be wise. With London two days off,
Down there some wind of heaven may yet
    revive him;
But there's no quickening breath from
    anywhere
Shall make of him again the poised young
    faun
From Warwickshire, who'd made, it seems,
    already
A legend of himself before I came
To blink before the last of his first lightning.
Whatever there be, there'll be no more of
    that;
The coming on of his old monster Time
Has made him a still man; and he has
    dreams   260
Were fair to think on once, and all found
    hollow.
He knows how much of what men paint
    themselves
Would blister in the light of what they are;
He sees how much of what was great now
    shares
An eminence transformed and ordinary;
He knows too much of what the world has
    hushed
In others, to be loud now for himself;
He knows now at what height low enemies
May reach his heart, and high friends let
    him fall;
But what not even such as he may know 270
Bedevils him the worst: his lark may sing
At heaven's gate how he will, and for as
    long
As joy may listen, but *he* sees no gate,
Save one whereat the spent clay waits a little
Before the churchyard has it, and the worm.
Not long ago, late in an afternoon,
I came on him unseen down Lambeth way,
And on my life I was afear'd of him:
He gloomed and mumbled like a soul from
    Tophet,
His hands behind him and his head bent
    solemn.   280
'What is it now,' said I, 'another woman?'
That made him sorry for me, and he smiled.
'No, Ben,' he mused; 'it's Nothing. It's all
    Nothing.
We come, we go; and when we're done,
    we're done;

Spiders and flies—we're mostly one or
    t'other—
We come, we go; and when we're done,
    we're done';
'By God, you sing that song as if you knew
    it!'
Said I, by way of cheering him; 'what ails
    ye?'
'I think I must have come down here to
    think,'
Says he to that, and pulls his little beard;
'Your fly will serve as well as anybody, 290
And what's his hour? He flies, and flies, and
    flies,
And in his fly's mind has a brave
    appearance;
And then your spider gets him in her net,
And eats him out, and hangs him up to dry
That's Nature, the kind mother of us all.
And then your slattern housemaid swings
    her broom,
And where's your spider? And that's
    Nature, also.
It's Nature, and it's Nothing. It's all
    Nothing.
It's all a world where bugs and emperors
Go singularly back to the same dust,   300
Each in his time; and the old, ordered stars
That sang together, Ben, will sing the same
Old stave to-morrow.'

            When he talks like that,
There's nothing for a human man to do
But lead him to some grateful nook like
    this
Where we be now, and there to make him
    drink.
He'll drink, for love of me, and then be sick;
A sad sign always in a man of parts,   310
And always very ominous. The great
Should be as large in liquor as in love,—
And our great friend is not so large in
    either:
One disaffects him, and the other fails him;
Whatso he drinks that has an antic in it,
He's wondering what's to pay in his insides;
And while his eyes are on the Cyprian
He's fribbling all the time with that damned
    House.
We laugh here at his thrift, but after all
It may be thrift that saves him from the
    devil;   320
God gave it, anyhow,—and we'll suppose
He knew the compound of his handiwork.
To-day the clouds are with him, but anon

He'll out of 'em enough to shake the tree
Of life itself and bring down fruit unheard-
of,—
And, throwing in the bruised and whole
together,
Prepare a wine to make us drunk with
wonder;
And if he live, there'll be a sunset spell
Thrown over him as over a glassed lake
That yesterday was all a black wild water.

God send he live to give us, if no more,   331
What now's a-rampage in him, and exhibit,
With a decent half-allegiance to the ages
An earnest of at least a casual eye
Turned once on what he owes to
Gutenberg,
And to the fealty of more centuries
Than are as yet a picture in our vision.
'There's time enough—I'll do it when I'm
old,
And we're immortal men,' he says to that;
And then he says to me, 'Ben, what's
"immortal?"   340
Think you by any force of ordination
It may be nothing of a sort more noisy
Than a small oblivion of component ashes
That of a dream-addicted world was once
A moving atomy much like your friend
here?'
Nothing will help that man. To make him
laugh,
I said then he was a mad mountebank,—
And by the Lord I nearer made him cry.
I could have eat an eft then, on my knees,
Tail, claws, and all of him; for I had stung
The king of men, who had no sting for
me,   351
And I had hurt him in his memories;
And I say now, as I shall say again,
I love the man this side idolatry.

He'll do it when he's old, he says. I wonder.
He may not be so ancient as all that.
For such as he, the thing that is to do
Will do itself,—but there's a reckoning;
The sessions that are now too much his
own,
The roiling inward of a still outside,   360
The churning out of all those blood-fed
lines,
The nights of many schemes and little
sleep,
The full brain hammered hot with too
much thinking,

The vexed heart over-worn with too much
aching,—
This weary jangling of conjoined affairs
Made out of elements that have no end,
And all confused at once, I understand,
Is not what makes a man to live forever.
O no, not now! He'll not be going now:
There'll be time yet for God knows what
explosions   370
Before he goes. He'll stay awhile. Just
wait:
Just wait a year or two for Cleopatra,
For she's to be a balsam and a comfort;
And that's not all a jape of mine now,
either.
For granted once the old way of Apollo
Sings in a man, he may then, if he's able,
Strike unafraid whatever strings he will
Upon the last and wildest of new lyres;
Nor out of his new magic, though it hymn
The shrieks of dungeoned hell, shall he
create   380
A madness or a gloom to shut quite out
A cleaving daylight, and a last great calm
Triumphant over shipwreck and all storms.
He might have given Aristotle creeps,
But surely would have given him his
katharsis.

He'll not be going yet. There's too much
yet
Unsung within the man. But when he
goes,
I'd stake ye coin o' the realm his only
care
For a phantom world he sounded and
found wanting
Will be a portion here, a portion there,   390
Of this or that thing or some other thing
That has a patent and intrinsical
Equivalence in those egregious shillings.
And yet he knows, God help him! Tell me,
now,
If ever there was anything let loose
On earth by gods or devils heretofore
Like this mad, careful, proud, indifferent
Shakespeare!
Where was it, if it ever was? By heaven,
'Twas never yet in Rhodes or Pergamon—
In Thebes or Nineveh, a thing like this!   400
No thing like this was ever out of England;
And this he knows. I wonder if he cares.
Perhaps he does. . . . O Lord, that House
in Stratford!

1916

FLAMMONDE

The man Flammonde, from God knows
    where,
With firm address and foreign air,
With news of nations in his talk
And something royal in his walk,
With glint of iron in his eyes,
But never doubt, nor yet surprise,
Appeared, and stayed, and held his
    head
As one by kings accredited.

Erect, with his alert repose
About him, and about his clothes,   10
He pictured all tradition hears
Of what we owe to fifty years.
His cleansing heritage of taste
Paraded neither want nor waste;
And what he needed for his fee
To live, he borrowed graciously.

He never told us what he was,
Or what mischance, or other cause,
Had banished him from better days
To play the Prince of Castaways.   20
Meanwhile he played surpassing well
A part, for most, unplayable;
In fine, one pauses, half afraid
To say for certain that he played.

For that, one may as well forego
Conviction as to yes or no;
Nor can I say just how intense
Would then have been the difference
To several, who, having striven
In vain to get what he was given,   30
Would see the stranger taken on
By friends not easy to be won.

Moreover, many a malcontent
He soothed and found munificent;
His courtesy beguiled and foiled
Suspicion that his years were soiled;
His mien distinguished any crowd,
His credit strengthened when he bowed;
And women, young and old, were fond
Of looking at the man Flammonde.   40

There was a woman in our town
On whom the fashion was to frown;
But while our talk renewed the tinge
Of a long-faded scarlet fringe,
The man Flammonde saw none of that,
And what he saw we wondered at—

That none of us, in her distress,
Could hide or find our littleness.

There was a boy that all agreed
Had shut within him the rare seed   50
Of learning. We could understand,
But none of us could lift a hand.
The man Flammonde appraised the youth,
And told a few of us the truth;
And thereby, for a little gold,
A flowered future was unrolled.

There were two citizens who fought
For years and years, and over nought;
They made life awkward for their friends,
And shortened their own dividends.   60
The man Flammonde said what was
    wrong
Should be made right; nor was it long
Before they were again in line,
And had each other in to dine.

And these I mention are but four
Of many out of many more.
So much for them. But what of him—
So firm in every look and limb?
What small satanic sort of kink
Was in his brain? What broken link   70
Withheld him from the destinies
That came so near to being his?

What was he, when we came to sift
His meaning, and to note the drift
Of incommunicable ways
That make us ponder while we praise?
Why was it that his charm revealed
Somehow the surface of a shield?
What was it that we never caught?
What was he, and what was he not?   80

How much it was of him we met
We cannot ever know; nor yet
Shall all he gave us quite atone
For what was his, and his alone;
Nor need we now, since he knew best,
Nourish an ethical unrest:
Rarely at once will nature give
The power to be Flammonde and live.

We cannot know how much we learn
From those who never will return,   90
Until a flash of unforeseen
Remembrance falls on what has been.
We've each a darkening hill to climb;
And this is why, from time to time

In Tilbury Town, we look beyond
Horizons for the man Flammonde.

                                        1910

THE MAN AGAINST THE SKY [1]

BETWEEN me and the sunset, like a dome
Against the glory of a world on fire,
Now burned a sudden hill,
Bleak, round, and high, by flame-lit height
        made higher,
With nothing on it for the flame to kill
Save one who moved and was alone up
        there
To loom before the chaos and the glare
As if he were the last god going home
Unto his last desire.

Dark, marvelous, and inscrutable he moved
        on   10
Till down the fiery distance he was gone,
Like one of those eternal, remote things
That range across a man's imaginings
When a sure music fills him and he knows
What he may say thereafter to few men,—
The touch of ages having wrought
An echo and a glimpse of what he thought
A phantom or a legend until then;
For whether lighted over ways that save,
Or lured from all repose,   20
If he go on too far to find a grave,
Mostly alone he goes.

Even he, who stood where I had found him,
On high with fire all round him,
Who moved along the molten west,
And over the round hill's crest
That seemed half ready with him to go
        down,
Flame-bitten and flame-cleft,
As if there were to be no last thing left
Of a nameless unimaginable town,—   30
Even he who climbed and vanished may
        have taken
Down to the perils of a depth not known,
From death defended though by men
        forsaken,
The bread that every man must eat alone;
He may have walked while others hardly
        dared

[1] Robinson wrote, 7 Jan. 1932, in answer to a query:
'Perhaps "The Man against the Sky" comes as near as
anything to representing my poetic vision—as you
are good enough to call it.' *Univ. of Colorado Studies*,
XIX,i, to face 318.

Look on to see him stand where many fell;
And upward out of that, as out of hell,
He may have sung and striven
To mount where more of him shall yet be
        given,
Bereft of all retreat,   40
To sevenfold heat,—
As on a day when three in Dura shared
The furnace, and were spared
For glory by that king of Babylon
Who made himself so great that God, who
        heard,
Covered him with long feathers, like a bird.

Again, he may have gone down easily,
By comfortable altitudes, and found,
As always, underneath him solid ground
Whereon to be sufficient and to stand   50
Possessed already of the promised land,
Far stretched and fair to see:
A good sight, verily,
And one to make the eyes of her who bore
        him
Shine glad with hidden tears.
Why question of his ease of who before
        him,
In one place or another where they left
Their names as far behind them as their
        bones,
And yet by dint of slaughter toil and theft,
And shrewdly sharpened stones,   60
Carved hard the way for his ascendency
Through deserts of lost years?
Why trouble him now who sees and hears
No more than what his innocence requires,
And therefore to no other height aspires
Than one at which he neither quails nor
        tires?
He may do more by seeing what he sees
Than others eager for iniquities;
He may, by seeing all things for the best,
Incite futurity to do the rest.   70

Or with an even likelihood,
He may have met with atrabilious eyes
The fires of time on equal terms and passed
Indifferently down, until at last
His only kind of grandeur would have been,
Apparently, in being seen.
He may have had for evil or for good
No argument; he may have had no care
For what without himself went anywhere
To failure or to glory, and least of all   80
For such a stale, flamboyant miracle;
He may have been the prophet of an art

Immovable to old idolatries;
He may have been a player without a part,
Annoyed that even the sun should have the
    skies
For such a flaming way to advertise;
He may have been a painter sick at heart
With Nature's toiling for a new surprise;
He may have been a cynic, who now, for all
Of anything divine that his effete   90
Negation may have tasted,
Saw truth in his own image, rather small,
Forbore to fever the ephemeral,
Found any barren height a good retreat
From any swarming street,
And in the sun saw power superbly wasted;
And when the primitive old-fashioned stars
Came out again to shine on joys and wars
More primitive, and all arrayed for doom,
He may have proved a world a sorry thing
In his imagining,   101
And life a lighted highway to the tomb.

Or, mounting with infirm unsearching
    tread,
His hopes to chaos led,
He may have stumbled up there from the
    past,
And with an aching strangeness viewed the
    last
Abysmal conflagration of his dreams,—
A flame where nothing seems
To burn but flame itself, by nothing fed;
And while it all went out,   110
Not even the faint anodyne of doubt
May then have eased a painful going down
From pictured heights of power and lost
    renown,
Revealed at length to his outlived endeavor
Remote and unapproachable forever;
And at his heart there may have gnawed
Sick memories of a dead faith foiled and
    flawed
And long dishonored by the living death
Assigned alike by chance
To brutes and hierophants;   120
And anguish fallen on those he loved around
    him
May once have dealt the last blow to
    confound him,
And so have left him as death leaves a
    child,
Who sees it all too near;
And he who knows no young way to forget
May struggle to the tomb unreconciled.
Whatever suns may rise or set

There may be nothing kinder for him here
Than shafts and agonies;
And under these   130
He may cry out and stay on horribly;
Or, seeing in death too small a thing to
    fear,
He may go forward like a stoic Roman
Where pangs and terrors in his pathway
    lie,—
Or, seizing the swift logic of a woman,
Curse God and die.

Or maybe there, like many another one
Who might have stood aloft and looked
    ahead,
Black-drawn against wild red,
He may have built, unawed by fiery gules   140
That in him no commotion stirred,
A living reason out of molecules
Why molecules occurred,
And one for smiling when he might have
    sighed
Had he seen far enough,
And in the same inevitable stuff
Discovered an odd reason too for pride
In being what he must have been by laws
Infrangible and for no kind of cause.
Deterred by no confusion or surprise   150
He may have seen with his mechanic eyes
A world without a meaning, and had room,
Alone amid magnificence and doom,
To build himself an airy monument
That should, or fail him in his vague intent,
Outlast an accidental universe—
To call it nothing worse—
Or, by the burrowing guile
Of Time disintegrated and effaced,
Like once-remembered mighty trees go
    down   160
To ruin, of which by man may now be
    traced
No part sufficient even to be rotten,
And in the book of things that are forgotten
Is entered as a thing not quite worth while.
He may have been so great
That satraps would have shivered at his
    frown,
And all he prized alive may rule a state
No larger than a grave that holds a clown;
He may have been a master of his fate,
And of his atoms,—ready as another   170
In his emergence to exonerate
His father and his mother;
He may have been a captain of a host,
Self-eloquent and ripe for prodigies,

Doomed here to swell by dangerous
    degrees,
And then give up the ghost.
Nahum's great grasshoppers were such as
    these,
Sun-scattered and soon lost.

Whatever the dark road he may have
    taken,
This man who stood on high   180
And faced alone the sky,
Whatever drove or lured or guided him,—
A vision answering a faith unshaken,
An easy trust assumed by easy trials,
A sick negation born of weak denials,
A crazed abhorrence of an old condition,
A blind attendance on a brief ambition,—
Whatever stayed him or derided him,
His way was even as ours;
And we, with all our wounds and all our
    powers,   190
Must each await alone at his own height
Another darkness or another light;
And there, of our poor self dominion reft,
If inference and reason shun
Hell, Heaven, and Oblivion,
May thwarted will (perforce precarious,
But for our conservation better thus)
Have no misgiving left
Of doing yet what here we leave undone?
Or if unto the last of these we cleave,   200
Believing or protesting we believe
In such an idle and ephemeral
Florescence of the diabolical,—
If, robbed of two fond old enormities,
Our being had no onward auguries,
What then were this great love of ours to
    say
For launching other lives to voyage again
A little farther into time and pain,
A little faster in a futile chase
For a kingdom and a power and a Race   210
That would have still in sight
A manifest end of ashes and eternal night?
Is this the music of the toys we shake
So loud,—as if there might be no mistake
Somewhere in our indomitable will?
Are we no greater than the noise we make
Along one blind atomic pilgrimage
Whereon by crass chance billeted we go
Because our brains and bones and cartilage
Will have it so?   220
If this we say, then let us all be still
About our share in it, and live and die
More quietly thereby.

Where was he going, this man against the
    sky?
You know not, nor do I.
But this we know, if we know anything:
That we may laugh and fight and sing
And of our transcience here make
    offering
To an orient Word that will not be erased,
Or, save in incommunicable gleams   230
Too permanent for dreams,
Be found or known.
No tonic and ambitious irritant
Of increase or of want
Has made an otherwise insensate waste
Of ages overthrown
A ruthless, veiled, implacable foretaste
Of other ages that are still to be
Depleted and rewarded variously
Because a few, by fate's economy,   240
Shall seem to move the world the way it
    goes;
No soft evangel of equality,
Safe-cradled in a communal repose
That huddles into death and may at last
Be covered well with equatorial snows—
And all for what, the devil only knows—
Will aggregate an inkling to confirm
The credit of a sage or of a worm,
Or tell us why one man in five
Should have a care to stay alive   250
While in his heart he feels no violence
Laid on his humor and intelligence
When infant Science makes a pleasant
    face
And waves again that hollow toy, the
    Race;
No planetary trap where souls are wrought
For nothing but the sake of being caught
And sent again to nothing will attune
Itself to any key of any reason
Why man should hunger through another
    season
To find out why 'twere better late than
    soon   260
To go away and let the sun and moon
And all the silly stars illuminate
A place for creeping things,
And those that root and trumpet and have
    wings,
And herd and ruminate,
Or dive and flash and poise in rivers and
    seas,
Or by their loyal tails in lofty trees
Hang screeching lewd victorious derision
Of man's immortal vision.

Shall we, because Eternity records   270
Too vast an answer for the time-born
    words
We spell, whereof so many are dead that
    once
In our capricious lexicons
Were so alive and final, hear no more
The Word itself, the living word
That none alive has ever heard
Or ever spelt,
And few have ever felt
Without the fears and old surrenderings
And terrors that began   280
When Death let fall a feather from his
    wings
And humbled the first man?
Because the weight of our humility,
Wherefrom we gain
A little wisdom and much pain,
Falls here too sore and there too tedious,
Are we in anguish or complacency,
Not looking far enough ahead
To see by what mad couriers we are led
Along the roads of the ridiculous,   290
To pity ourselves and laugh at faith
And while we curse life bear it?
And if we see the soul's dead end in death,
Are we to fear it?
What folly is here that has not yet a name
Unless we say outright that we are liars?
What have we seen beyond our sunset
    fires
That lights again the way by which we
    came?
Why pay we such a price, and one we
    give
So clamoringly, for each racked empty
    day   300
That leads one more last human hope
    away,
As quiet fiends would lead past our crazed
    eyes
Our children to an unseen sacrifice?
If after all that we have lived and thought,
All comes to Nought,—
If there be nothing after Now,
And we be nothing anyhow,
And we know that,—why live?
'Twere sure but weaklings' vain distress
To suffer dungeons where so many doors
Will open on the cold eternal shores   311
That look sheer down
To the dark tideless floods of Nothingness
Where all who know may drown.
                1916

JOHN GORHAM

'TELL me what you're doing over here,
    John Gorham,
Sighing hard and seeming to be sorry when
    you're not;
Make me laugh or let me go now, for long
    faces in the moonlight
Are a sign for me to say again a word that
    you forgot.'—

'I'm over here to tell you what the moon
    already
May have said or maybe shouted ever since
    a year ago;
I'm over here to tell you what you are Jane
    Wayland,
And to make you rather sorry, I should say,
    for being so.'—

'Tell me what you're saying to me now,
    John Gorham,
Or you'll never see as much of me as ribbons
    any more;   10
I'll vanish in as many ways as I have toes
    and fingers,
And you'll not follow far for one where
    flocks have been before.'—

'I'm sorry now you never saw the flocks,
    Jane Wayland,
But you're the one to make of them as many
    as you need.
And then about the vanishing. It's I who
    mean to vanish;
And when I'm here no longer you'll be
    done with me indeed.'—

'That's a way to tell me what I am, John
    Gorham!
How am I to know myself until I make you
    smile?
Try to look as if the moon were making
    faces at you,
And a little more as if you meant to stay a
    little while.'—   20

'You are what it is that over rose-blown
    gardens
Makes a pretty flutter for a season in the
    sun;
You are what it is that with a mouse, Jane
    Wayland,
Catches him and lets him go and eats him
    up for fun.'—

'Sure I never took you for a mouse, John
    Gorham;
All you say is easy, but so far from being
    true
That I wish you wouldn't ever be again the
    one to think so;
For it isn't cats and butterflies that I would
    be to you.'—

'All your little animals are in one picture—
One I've had before me since a year ago
    to-night;   30
And the picture where they live will be of
    you, Jane Wayland,
Till you find a way to kill them or to keep
    them out of sight.'—

'Won't you ever see me as I am, John
    Gorham,
Leaving out the foolishness and all I never
    meant?
Somewhere in me there's a woman, if you
    know the way to find her.
Will you like me any better if I prove it and
    repent?'—

'I doubt if I shall ever have the time, Jane
    Wayland;
And I dare say all this moonlight lying
    round us might as well
Fall for nothing on the shards of broken
    urns that are forgotten,
As on two that have no longer much of
    anything to tell.'   40
                1916

EROS TURANNOS

She fears him, and will always ask
    What fated her to choose him;
She meets in his engaging mask
    All reasons to refuse him;
But what she meets and what she fears
Are less than are the downward years,
Drawn slowly to the foamless weirs
    Of age, were she to lose him.

Between a blurred sagacity
    That once had power to sound him, 10
And Love, that will not let him be
    The Judas that she found him,
Her pride assuages her almost,
As if it were alone the cost.—
He sees that he will not be lost,
    And waits and looks around him.

A sense of ocean and old trees
    Envelops and allures him;
Tradition, touching all he sees,
    Beguiles and reassures him;   20
And all her doubts of what he says
Are dimmed with what she knows of days—
Till even prejudice delays
    And fades, and she secures him.

The falling leaf inaugurates
    The reign of her confusion;
The pounding wave reverberates
    The dirge of her illusion;
And home, where passion lived and died,
Becomes a place where she can hide,   30
While all the town and harbor side
    Vibrate with her seclusion.

We tell you, tapping on our brows,
    The story as it should be,—
As if the story of a house
    Were told, or ever could be;
We'll have no kindly veil between
Her visions and those we have seen,—
As if we guessed what hers have been,
    Or what they are or would be.   40

Meanwhile we do no harm; for they
    That with a god have striven,
Not hearing much of what we say,
    Take what the god has given;
Though like waves breaking it may be,
Or like a changed familiar tree,
Or like a stairway to the sea
    Where down the blind are driven.
                1916

THE GIFT OF GOD

Blessed with a joy that only she
Of all alive shall ever know,
She wears a proud humility
For what it was that willed it so,—
That her degree should be so great
Among the favored of the Lord
That she may scarcely bear the weight
Of her bewildering reward.

As one apart, immune, alone,
Or featured for the shining ones,   10
And like to none that she has known
Of other women's other sons,—
The firm fruition of her need,
He shines anointed; and he blurs
Her vision, till it seems indeed
A sacrilege to call him hers.

She fears a little for so much
Of what is best, and hardly dares
To think of him as one to touch
With aches, indignities, and cares;   20
She sees him rather at the goal,
Still shining; and her dream foretells
The proper shining of a soul
Where nothing ordinary dwells.

Perchance a canvass of the town
Would find him far from flags and shouts,
And leave him only the renown
Of many smiles and many doubts;
Perchance the crude and common tongue
Would havoc strangely with his worth;   30
But she, with innocence unwrung,
Would read his name around the earth.

And others, knowing how this youth
Would shine, if love could make him great,
When caught and tortured for the truth
Would only writhe and hesitate;
While she, arranging for his days
What centuries could not fulfill,
Transmutes him with her faith and praise,
And has him shining where she will.   40

She crowns him with her gratefulness,
And says again that life is good;
And should the gift of God be less
In him than in her motherhood,
His fame, though vague, will not be small,
As upward through her dream he fares,
Half clouded with a crimson fall
Of roses thrown on marble stairs.

                                    1916

THE DARK HILLS

DARK hills at evening in the west,
Where sunset hovers like a sound
Of golden horns that sang to rest
Old bones of warriors under ground,
Far now from all the bannered ways
Where flash the legions of the sun,
You fade—as if the last of days
Were fading, and all wars were done.

                                    1920

MR. FLOOD'S PARTY

OLD Eben Flood, climbing alone one night
Over the hill between the town below
And the forsaken upland hermitage
That held as much as he should ever know

On earth again of home, paused warily.
The road was his with not a native near;
And Eben, having leisure, said aloud,
For no man else in Tilbury Town to hear:

'Well, Mr. Flood, we have the harvest
        moon
Again, and we may not have many more;   10
The bird is on the wing, the poet says,
And you and I have said it here before.
Drink to the bird.' He raised up to the
        light
The jug that he had gone so far to fill,
And answered huskily: 'Well, Mr. Flood,
Since you propose it, I believe I will.'

Alone, as if enduring to the end
A valiant armor of scarred hopes outworn,
He stood there in the middle of the road
Like Roland's ghost winding a silent horn.
Below him, in the town among the trees,   20
Where friends of other days had honored
        him,
A phantom salutation of the dead
Rang thinly till old Eben's eyes were dim.

Then, as a mother lays her sleeping child
Down tenderly, fearing it may awake,
He set the jug down slowly at his feet
With trembling care, knowing that most
        things break;
And only when assured that on firm earth
It stood, as the uncertain lives of men   30
Assuredly did not, he paced away,
And with his hand extended paused again:

'Well, Mr. Flood, we have not met like this
In a long time; and many a change has come
To both of us, I fear, since last it was
We had a drop together. Welcome home!'
Convivially returning with himself,
Again he raised the jug up to the light;
And with an acquiescent quaver said:
'Well, Mr. Flood, if you insist, I might.   40

'Only a very little, Mr. Flood—
For auld lang syne. No more, sir; that will
        do.'
So, for the time, apparently it did,
And Eben evidently thought so too;
For soon amid the silver loneliness
Of night he lifted up his voice and sang,
Secure, with only two moons listening,
Until the whole harmonious landscape
        rang—

'For auld lang syne.' The weary throat gave
    out,
The last word wavered, and the song was
    done.   50
He raised again the jug regretfully
And shook his head, and was again alone.
There was not much that was ahead of
    him,
And there was nothing in the town below—
Where strangers would have shut the many
    doors
That many friends had opened long ago.
                              1921

THE SHEAVES

WHERE long the shadows of the wind had
    rolled,
Green wheat was yielding to the change
    assigned;
And as by some vast magic undivined
The world was turning slowly into gold.
Like nothing that was ever bought or sold
It waited there, the body and the mind;
And with a mighty meaning of a kind
That tells the more the more it is not told.

So in a land where all days are not fair,
Fair days went on till on another day   10
A thousand golden sheaves were lying there,
Shining and still, but not for long to stay—
As if a thousand girls with golden hair
Might rise from where they slept and go
    away.
                              1925

NEW ENGLAND[1]

HERE where the wind is always north-north-
    east
And children learn to walk on frozen toes,
Wonder begets an envy of all those
Who boil elsewhere with such a lyric yeast
Of love that you will hear them at a feast

[1] Concerning a misinterpretation of this sonnet in a correspondent's letter to *The Gardiner* [Me.] *Journal*,
Robinson wrote, 7 Feb. 1924, in answer: '. . . he will
see that the whole thing is a satirical attack not upon
New England, but upon the same patronizing pagans
whom he [the correspondent] flays with such vehemence in his own poem. As a matter of fact, I cannot
quite see how the first eight lines of my sonnet are to
be regarded as even intelligible if read in any other way
than as an oblique attack upon all those who are forever
throwing dead cats at New England for its alleged emotional and moral frigidity.' Quoted, Hogan, *A Bibliography of . . . Robinson*(New Haven, 1936),179–80.

Where demons would appeal for some
    repose,
Still clamoring where the chalice overflows
And crying wildest who have drunk the
    least.

Passion is here a soilure of the wits,
We're told, and Love a cross for them to
    bear;   10
Joy shivers in the corner where she knits
And Conscience always has the rocking-
    chair,
Cheerful as when she tortured into fits
The first cat that was ever killed by Care.
                              1925

FROM TRISTRAM

TRISTRAM AND ISOLT
OF IRELAND [2]

                  'GOD knows,' he said,
'How far a man may be from his deserving
And yet be fated for the undeserved.   470
I might, were I the lord of your
    misgivings,
Be worthier of them for destroying them;
And even without the mightiness in me
For that, I'll tell you, for your contem-
    plation,
Time is not life. For many, and many
    more,
Living is mostly for a time not dying—
But not for me. For me, a few more years
Of shows and slaughters, or the tinsel seat
Of a small throne, would not be life.
                    Whatever
It is that fills life high and full, till fate   480
Itself may do no more, it is not time.
Years are not life.'

                    'I have not come so far
To learn,' she said, and shook her head at
    him,
'What years are, for I know. Years are not
    life;
Years are the shells of life, and empty shells
When they hold only days, and days, and
    days.
God knows if I know that—so let it pass.
Let me forget; and let me ask you only
Not to forget that all your feats at arms,   490
Your glamour that is almost above envy,
Your strength and eminence and
    everything,

[2] The title is given by the editors.

Leave me a woman still—a one-love
    woman,
Meaning a sort of ravenous one-child
    mother,
Whose one-love pictures in her composition
Panthers and antelopes, children asleep,
And all sorts of engaging animals
That most resemble a much-disordered
    queen,
Her crown abandoned and her hair in peril,
And she herself a little deranged, no doubt,
With too much happiness. Whether he lives
Or dies for her, he tells her is no matter, 502
Wherefore she must obediently believe
    him.
All he would ask of her would be as easy
As hearing waves, washing the shore down
    there
For ever, and believing herself drowned.
In seeing so many of her, he might believe
    her
To be as many at once as drops of rain;
Perhaps a panther and a child asleep
At the same time.'   510

        He saw dark laughter sparkling
Out of her eyes, but only until her face
Found his, and on his mouth a moving fire

Told him why there was death, and what
    lost song
Ulysses heard, and would have given his
    hands
And friends to follow and to die for. Slowly,
At last, the power of helplessness there was
In all that beauty of hers that was for him,
Breathing and burning there alone with
    him,
Until it was almost a part of him,   520
Suffused his passion with a tenderness
Attesting a sealed certainty not his
To cozen or wrench from fate, and one
    withheld
In waiting mercy from oblivious eyes—
His eyes and hers, that over darker water,
Where darker things than shadows would
    be coming,
Saw now no more than more stars in the
    sky.
He felt her throbbing softly in his arms,
And held her closer still—with half a fear
Returning that she might not be Isolt,   530
And might yet vanish where she sat with
    him,
Leaving him there alone, with only devils
Of hell supplanting her.
                      1927

WILLIAM ELLERY LEONARD
1876–1944

TOM MOONEY

1

TOM MOONEY sits behind a grating,
Beside a corridor. (He's waiting.)
Long since he picked or peeled or bit away
The last white callous from his palms, they
    say.
The crick is gone from out his back;
And all the grease and grime
Gone from each finger-nail and every
    knuckle-crack.
(And that took time.)

2

Tom Mooney breathes behind a grating,
Beside a corridor. (He's waiting.)   10
The Gold-men from ten cities hear in
    sleep
Tom Mooney breathing—for he breathes
    so deep.

The Gold-men from ten cities rise from
    bed
To make a brass crown for Tom Mooney's
    head;
They gather round great oaken desks—
    each twists
Two copper bracelets for Tom Mooney's
    wrists.
And down sky-scraper basements (all their
    own)
They forge the spikes for his galvanic
    throne.
The Gold-men love the jests of old
    Misrule—
At ease at last, they'll laugh their fill;   20
They'll deck Tom Mooney king, they will—
King over knave and fool.
And from enameled doors of rearward
    office-vaults,
Lettered in gold with names that never
    crock,

They will draw back the triple iron bolts,
Then scatter from the ridges of their roofs
The affidavits of their paper-proofs
Of pallid Tomfool's low and lubber stock.

3

Tom Mooney thinks behind a grating,
Beside a corridor. (He's waiting.)   30
(Tom Mooney free was but a laboring man;
Tom Mooney jailed's the Thinker of
    Rodin.)
The Workers in ten nations now have caught
The roll and rhythm of Tom Mooney's
    thought—
By that earth-girdling S.O.S.,
The subtle and immortal wireless
Of Man's strong justice in distress.
The Workers in ten nations think and plan:
The pick-ax little Naples man,
The rice-swamp coolies in Japan   40
(No longer mere embroidery on a screen),
The crowds that swarm from factory gates,
At yellow dusks with all their hates,
In Ireland, Austria, Argentine,
In England, France, and Russia far
(That slew a Czar),—
Or where the Teutons lately rent
The Iron Cross (on finding what it meant);
At yellow dusks with all their hates
From fiery shops or gas-choked mines,   50
From round-house, mill, or lumber-pines,
In the broad belt of these United States.
The Workers, like the Gold-men, plan and
    wake,—
What bodes their waking?
The Workers, like the Gold-men,
    something make,—
What are they making?—
The Gold-men answer often—
'They make Tom Mooney's coffin.'

4

Tom Mooney talks behind a grating,
Beside a corridor. (He's waiting.)   60
You cannot get quite near
Against the bars to lay your ear;
You find the light too dim
To spell the lips of him.
But, like a beast's within a zoo
(That was of old a god to savage clans),
His body shakes at you—
A beast's, a god's, a man's!
And from its ponderous, ancient rhythmic
    shaking

Ye'll guess what 'tis the workers now are
    making.   70
They make for times to come
From times of old—how old!—
From sweat, from blood, from hunger, and
    from tears,
From scraps of hope (conserved through
    bitter years
Despite the might and mockery of gold),
They make, these haggard men, a bomb,—
These haggard men with shawl-wives
    dumb
And pinched-faced children cold,
Descendants of the oldest, earth-born
    stock,
Gnarled brothers of the surf, the ice, the
    fire, the rock,   80
Gray wolf and gaunt storm-bird.
They make a bomb more fierce than
    dynamite,—
They weld a Word.
And on the awful night
The Gold-men set Tom Mooney grinning
(If such an hour shall be in truth's despite)
They'll loose the places of much
    underpinning
In more than ten big cities, left and right.
c.1918   1920

from TWO LIVES [1]

I

viii

ONE night when early winter had begun
With gusty snows and frosty stars to keep
Our lives still closer, and our love more
    deep
Than even in autumn wanderings with the
    sun,

[1] 'The austere form itself, the sonnet (if in any organic creation, whether oak-tree or poem, one can separate "form" itself from essence, meaning, end) grew inevitably out of the need, an absolute need, of an especially austere control, masterful and unrelenting, over especially intense and fierce emotional experience, while a certain freedom resulted from variations within the norm (rime-arrangement, management of the "turn," etc.) and from linking sonnets as stanzas (both in narrative progress and in end-enjambements). *Two Lives* is *not* a "sonnet-sequence." I seemed to be speaking directly to a few friends. The reworking of the raw stuff of life was in part the impersonal urge of art—as in the simplifications of time and action, and in the college atmosphere conceived as a little more intimate than that of a latter-day State university. . . . The speech I used I had learned from my father's house, from schoolmates, from New England farmers, from Agatha

One night when we together, one-and-one,
Were sitting in the cushioned window-
          space,
Planning some purple flower-beds for the
          place
After our marriage, with new vines to run
About the basement wall; one night when
          time
Seemed all to come, and at its coming ours,
And we (as by an irony, sublime   11
In its gaunt mockery of human powers!)
Drifted at last backward to clime and clime
And years and years of uncompanioned
          hours,

From her own lips I learned the awful
          truth—
Which, like a child of hope with perfect
          smile,
She babbled, O so innocent of guile—
As some adventure of an alien youth,
Rescued by white sails from a midsea isle
Of shrieking beaks and fins and claws
          uncouth,   20
Or eery dream demanding never ruth
Because but dream and vanished the long
          while—
As something far and strange that I should
          hear. . . .
And why? Because she would conceal me
          naught,
As bound in honor? No. Because of fear
I'd learn of others some day? No.—She
          thought
Her lover would rejoice—rejoice to share
Her exaltation after *such* despair.

From her own lips—yes, even as they
          smiled—
I learned full truth: 'In France, five years
          ago   30

herself, and from some old acquaintances, like Shakspere, Byron, Wordsworth, and Emerson. For me one
organic complex of speech. This was in 1913, remember, before the Poetic Renascence. Hence, some reviewers in 1925, otherwise friendly, regretted an un-
emancipated diction and "helpless inversions." But
English diction in higher art is still for me more than
the usage of the twentieth century . . . *o'er* beside
over on occasion—if you have the instinct for the occasion. And English syntax and word order, in the
higher art, loses, not gains, by reduction of its old
plasticity to the rigidity of modern French. It is all a
question of means to ends—of sincerity too of ends.'
Leonard, *The Locomotive God* (N.Y., 1927), 339–41.

(When father was ambassador, you know),
I lived with a band of ladies wan and wild,—
Myself a shuddering maniac, exiled
With strange physicians, and behind locked
          door
Mumbling in bed, or tracing on the floor,
"The Lord is my shepherd, I . . ." '
          'Goodnight, my child'—
(That none had told me, seems, you fancy,
          odd?)—
And so I kissed and left her. Did I cry?—
I've never cried. Or did I moan 'My
          God'?—
Nor that. Or walk out under starry sky?—
I went upstairs, undressed, put out the
          light;   41
And shook with pity and terror all the
          night.

ix [1]

. . .   .

WE act in crises not as one who dons
A judge's robe and sits to praise or blame
With walnut gavel, before high window-
          frame,
Beside a Justice-and-her-scales in bronze;
We act in crises not by pros and cons
Of volumes in brown calfskin still the same;
But, like the birds and beasts from which
          we came,
By the long trend of character—the *fons*,
Fons et origo—fountainhead and source—
Of deeper conduct, whether in unleashed
          hound   10
That tears the fleeing stag unto the ground,
Or thrush in battle for its fledgeling's corse,
Or boy who sees the cracked dam, hears a
          sound,
And down the peopled valley spurs his
          horse.

xiii

MID-MORNING of mid-June: Her sudden
          whim
Among the guests (who chatted ill at ease):
'O let's be married out beneath the trees—
This mantel with its garlands is so prim.'

1 Of this sonnet Leonard has said: 'It seems to combine
my own authentic ethical bent with intellectual analysis, concentrated feeling, concrete symbolic pictures
from nature and human life, and homely honest phrasing—without the cant of sentiment or the worse cant
of "originality." ' Benét, ed., *Fifty Poets* (N.Y., 1933),
40.

As if she said, 'Let's row an hour or swim;'
As if she said, 'Let's pick the white sweet
    pease,
And leave the pink and purple for the bees;'
As if she said, 'Let's get the shears and trim
The lilac stems.' . . . Blue lake and bluer
    sky
Merged with the green of earth, of odorous
    earth,   10
A scarlet tanager went flashing by,
The unseen thrasher sang with all his
    mirth. . . .
The old dame neighbor said with happy
    tears:
'The sweetest wedding of my eighty years.'

. . . .

II

iii

. . . .

BUT I, grown fatuous in my love and lore—
Love that I thought was round her as a buoy
Lore that I thought was cunning to destroy
Disease and doom—toiled with her more
    and more:
My skill at mind should train the wild away,
The wild and eery, from that brow I kissed,
Till she should grow like girls of everyday
Through me (triumphant lover-alienist!),—
Thus to establish her in selfhood strong
Against disasters I was fearsome of—   10
Pain, slander, grief, and all gaunt broods of
    Life,—
Thus, also, to establish her as wife—
As apt in judgment as she was in song,
As fixed in purpose as she was in love.

. . . .

I FOUND a paper on her chiffonier—
Manila wrapping of a scarf or gloves,—
I read its penciling: 'He says, my love's
More than my tact . . . a child of fifteen
    year. . . .
He says he wishes I were more like
    sister. . . .
He says he needs'—and there I saw her
    stand

In the door, white-plume on head, her
    shopping in hand,
Smiles on her lips. She came to me. . . .
    I kissed her. . . .
She marked. . . . Her face fell on my
    shoulder; so
We clung together. 'I'm so sorry, friend,   10
You found my scrawl.'—'I love you,
    child.'—'I know.'—
'Forgive.'—' 'Twas for my good—and
    there's an end.'
The rest was silence—the embrace and kiss
Of love with love upon the precipice.

xi

. . . .

THAT afternoon the Postman brought,
    among
The notes of condolence for father dead,
Our monthly magazine. I opened, read,
And found at last, at last, the song I'd sung
(Two years before) in print for old and
    young,
In print at last for every clime and zone—
'Amor Triumphans—Love is on the
    Throne'—
And ran to her with news upon my
    tongue. . . .
Sitting in parlor, by the jardinière
Under the mother's portrait, with a book: 10
An instant flashed to life her olden look;
Her olden crimson glowed an instant there;
'Dear husband, thank you.'—But upon her
    knees
Lay the 'Alcestis' of Euripides.

Thereafter I found these Greek lines
    underscored:
κἄπειτα θάλαμον—and her chamber
    then— . . .
(. . . O? . . .) ἐσπεσοῦσα—hurrying,
    hurrying toward— . . .
(. . . So? . . .) καὶ λέχος —and couch—
    ἐνταῦθα δὴ—
Ah, there—'δάκρυσε—she did weep again—
(. . . Yes . . .) καὶ λέγει τάδε—and this did
    say—   20
Ὦ λέκτρον —O bed—ἔνθα παρθένει
ἔλυσ' ἐγὼ κορεύματ'—where I unbound
My virgin girdle—ἐκ τοῦδ' ἀνδρός—for
This man, my lover—οὗ θνῄσκω πέρι
For whose dear sake I die— . . . (And here
    I found

The margin with blurred letters scribbled
o'er—
Was it some final message meant for
me?) . . .
χαῖρ'—O farewell. . . .   (Dear, χαῖρε
evermore!)

. . . .

III

xxix

Indian Summer

(*O Earth-and-Autumn of the Setting Sun,
She is not by, to know my task is done!*)

In the brown grasses slanting with the
wind,
Lone as a lad whose dog's no longer near,
Lone as a mother whose only child has
sinned,
Lone on the loved hill . . . and below me
here
The thistle-down in tremulous atmosphere
Along red clusters of the sumach streams;
The shriveled stalks of goldenrod are sere,
And crisp and white their flashing old
racemes.   10
(. . . forever . . . forever . . . forever . . .)
This is the lonely season of the year,
This is the season of our lonely dreams.

(*O Earth-and-Autumn of the Setting Sun,
She is not by, to know my task is done!*)

The corn-shocks westward on the stubble
plain
Show like an Indian village of dead days;
The long smoke trails behind the crawling
train,
And floats atop the distant woods ablaze
With orange, crimson, purple. The low
haze   20
Dims the scarped bluffs above the inland
sea,

Whose wide and slaty waters in cold glaze
Await yon full-moon of the night-to-be.
(. . . far . . . and far . . . and far . . .)
These are the solemn horizons of man's
ways,
These the horizons of solemn thought to
me.

(*O Earth-and-Autumn of the Setting Sun,
She is not by to know my task is done!*)

And this the hill she visited, as friend;
And this the hill she lingered on, as bride—
Down in the yellow valley is the end: 31
They laid her . . . in no evening Autumn
tide. . . .
Under fresh flowers of that May morn,
beside
The queens and cave-women of ancient
earth. . . .

This is the hill . . . and over my city's
towers,
Across the world from sunset, yonder in
air,
Shines, through its scaffoldings, a civic
dome
Of pilèd masonry, which shall be ours
To give, completed, to our children
there. . . .
And yonder far roof of my abandoned
home   40
Shall house new laughter. . . . Yet I
tried. . . . I tried. . . .
And, ever wistful of the doom to come,
I built her many a fire for love . . . for
mirth. . . .
(When snows were falling on our oaks
outside,
Dear, many a winter fire upon the
hearth) . . .
(. . . farewell . . . farewell . . . farewell . . .)
We dare not think too long on those who
died,
While still so many yet must come to birth.
1913   1922

ROBERT FROST

1875-

MOWING

THERE was never a sound beside the wood
    but one,
And that was my long scythe whispering to
    the ground.
What was it it whispered? I knew not well
    myself;
Perhaps it was something about the heat of
    the sun,
Something, perhaps, about the lack of
    sound—
And that was why it whispered and did not
    speak.
It was no dream of the gift of idle hours,
Or easy gold at the hand of fay or elf:
Anything more than the truth would have
    seemed too weak
To the earnest love that laid the swale in
    rows,   10
Not without feeble-pointed spikes of
    flowers
(Pale orchises), and scared a bright green
    snake.
The fact is the sweetest dream that labor
    knows.
My long scythe whispered and left the hay
    to make.

1901   1913

THE TUFT OF FLOWERS

I WENT to turn the grass once after one
Who mowed it in the dew before the sun.

The dew was gone that made his blade so
    keen
Before I came to view the levelled scene.

I looked for him behind an isle of trees;
I listened for his whetstone on the breeze.

But he had gone his way, the grass all
    mown,
And I must be, as he had been,—alone,

'As all must be,' I said within my heart,
'Whether they work together or apart.'   10

But as I said it, swift there passed me by
On noiseless wing a bewildered butterfly,

Seeking with memories grown dim o'er
    night
Some resting flower of yesterday's delight.

And once I marked his flight go round and
    round,
As where some flower lay withering on the
    ground.

And then he flew as far as eye could see,
And then on tremulous wing came back to
    me.

I thought of questions that have no reply,
And would have turned to toss the grass to
    dry;   20

But he turned first, and led my eye to look
At a tall tuft of flowers beside a brook,

A leaping tongue of bloom the scythe had
    spared
Beside a reedy brook the scythe had bared.

I left my place to know them by their name,
Finding them butterfly weed when I came.

The mower in the dew had loved them
    thus,
By leaving them to flourish, not for us,

Nor yet to draw one thought of ours to
    him,
But from sheer morning gladness at the
    brim.   30

The butterfly and I had lit upon,
Nevertheless, a message from the dawn,

That made me hear the wakening birds
    around,
And hear his long scythe whispering to the
    ground,

And feel a spirit kindred to my own;
So that henceforth I worked no more alone;

But glad with him, I worked as with his
    aid,
And weary, sought at noon with him the
    shade;

And dreaming, as it were, held brotherly
    speech
With one whose thought I had not hoped to
    reach.   40

'Men work together,' I told him from the
    heart,
'Whether they work together or apart.'
1904   1913

MENDING WALL

SOMETHING there is that doesn't love a wall,
That sends the frozen-ground-swell under
    it,
And spills the upper boulders in the sun;
And makes gaps even two can pass abreast.
The work of hunters is another thing:
I have come after them and made repair
Where they have left not one stone on a
    stone,
But they would have the rabbit out of
    hiding,
To please the yelping dogs. The gaps I
    mean,
No one has seen them made or heard them
    made,   10
But at spring mending-time we find them
    there.
I let my neighbor know beyond the hill;
And on a day we meet to walk the line
And set the wall between us once again.
We keep the wall between us as we go.
To each the boulders that have fallen to
    each.
And some are loaves and some so nearly
    balls
We have to use a spell to make them
    balance:
'Stay where you are until our backs are
    turned!'
We wear our fingers rough with handling
    them.   20
Oh, just another kind of out-door game,
One on a side. It comes to little more:
There where it is we do not need the wall:
He is all pine and I am apple orchard.
My apple trees will never get across
And eat the cones under his pines, I tell
    him.
He only says, 'Good fences make good
    neighbors.'
Spring is the mischief in me, and I wonder
If I could put a notion in his head:
'*Why* do they make good neighbors? Isn't it

Where there are cows? But here there are no
    cows.   31
Before I built a wall I'd ask to know
What I was walling in or walling out,
And to whom I was like to give offence.
Something there is that doesn't love a wall,
That wants it down.' I could say 'Elves' to
    him,
But it's not elves exactly, and I'd rather
He said it for himself. I see him there
Bringing a stone grasped firmly by the top
In each hand, like an old-stone savage
    armed.   40
He moves in darkness as it seems to me,
Not of woods only and the shade of trees.
He will not go behind his father's saying,
And he likes having thought of it so well
He says again, 'Good fences make good
    neighbors.'
1913   1914

THE DEATH OF THE HIRED MAN

MARY sat musing on the lamp-flame at the
    table
Waiting for Warren. When she heard his
    step,
She ran on tip-toe down the darkened
    passage
To meet him in the doorway with the news
And put him on his guard. 'Silas is back.'
She pushed him outward with her through
    the door
And shut it after her. 'Be kind,' she said.
She took the market things from Warren's
    arms
And set them on the porch, then drew him
    down
To sit beside her on the wooden steps.   10

'When was I ever anything but kind to
    him?
But I'll not have the fellow back,' he said.
'I told him so last haying, didn't I?
"If he left then," I said, "that ended it."
What good is he? Who else will harbor
    him
At his age for the little he can do?
What help he is there's no depending on.
Off he goes always when I need him most.
"He thinks he ought to earn a little pay,
Enough at least to buy tobacco with,   20
So he won't have to beg and be beholden."
"All right," I say, "I can't afford to pay
Any fixed wages, though I wish I could."

"Someone else can." "Then someone else
    will have to."
I shouldn't mind his bettering himself
If that was what it was. You can be certain,
When he begins like that, there's someone
    at him
Trying to coax him off with pocket-
    money,—
In haying time, when any help is scarce.
In winter he comes back to us. I'm done.' 30

'Sh! not so loud: he'll hear you,' Mary said.

'I want him to: he'll have to soon or late.'

'He's worn out. He's asleep beside the
    stove.
When I came up from Rowe's I found him
    here,
Huddled against the barn-door fast asleep,
A miserable sight, and frightening, too—
You needn't smile—I didn't recognize
    him—
I wasn't looking for him—and he's
    changed.
Wait till you see.'

      'Where did you say he'd been?'   40

'He didn't say. I dragged him to the house,
And gave him tea and tried to make him
    smoke.
I tried to make him talk about his travels.
Nothing would do: he just kept nodding
    off.'

'What did he say? Did he say anything?'

'But little.'

      'Anything? Mary, confess
He said he'd come to ditch the meadow for
    me.'

'Warren!'

      'But did he? I just want to know.' 50

'Of course he did. What would you have
    him say?
Surely you wouldn't begrudge the poor old
    man
Some humble way to save his self-respect.
He added, if you really care to know,
He meant to clear the upper pasture, too.

That sounds like something you have heard
    before?
Warren, I wish you could have heard the
    way
He jumbled everything. I stopped to look
Two or three times—he made me feel so
    queer—
To see if he was talking in his sleep.   60
He ran on Harold Wilson—you
    remember—
The boy you had in haying four years since.
He's finished school, and teaching in his
    college.
Silas declares you'll have to get him back.
He says they two will make a team for work:
Between them they will lay this farm as
    smooth!
The way he mixed that in with other things.
He thinks young Wilson a likely lad, though
    daft
On education—you know how they fought
All through July under the blazing sun, 70
Silas up on the cart to build the load,
Harold along beside to pitch it on.'

'Yes, I took care to keep well out of earshot.'

'Well, those days trouble Silas like a dream.
You wouldn't think they would. How some
    things linger!
Harold's young college boy's assurance
    piqued him.
After so many years he still keeps finding
Good arguments he sees he might have
    used.
I sympathize. I know just how it feels
To think of the right thing to say too late. 80
Harold's associated in his mind with Latin.
He asked me what I thought of Harold's
    saying
He studied Latin like a violin
Because he liked it—that an argument!
He said he couldn't make the boy believe
He could find water with a hazel prong—
Which showed how much good school had
    ever done him.
He wanted to go over that. But most of all
He thinks if he could have another chance
To teach him how to build a load of hay—'

'I know, that's Silas' one accomplishment.
He bundles every forkful in its place, 92
And tags and numbers it for future
    reference,
So he can find and easily dislodge it

In the unloading. Silas does that well.
He takes it out in bunches like big birds'
      nests.
You never see him standing on the hay
He's trying to lift, straining to lift himself.'

'He thinks if he could teach him that, he'd
      be
Some good perhaps to someone in the
      world.   100
He hates to see a boy the fool of books.
Poor Silas, so concerned for other folk,
And nothing to look backward to with pride,
And nothing to look forward to with hope,
So now and never any different.'

Part of a moon was falling down the west,
Dragging the whole sky with it to the hills.
Its light poured softly in her lap. She saw
And spread her apron to it. She put out her
      hand   109
Among the harp-like morning-glory strings,
Taut with the dew from garden bed to eaves,
As if she played unheard some tenderness
That wrought on him beside her in the
      night.
'Warren,' she said, 'he has come home to
      die:
You needn't be afraid he'll leave you this
      time.'

'Home,' he mocked gently.

                'Yes, what else but home?
It all depends on what you mean by home
Of course he's nothing to us, any more
Than was the hound that came a stranger to
      us   120
Out of the woods, worn out upon the trail.'
'Home is the place where, when you have to
      go there,
They have to take you in.'

                'I should have called it
Something you somehow haven't to
      deserve.'

Warren leaned out and took a step or two,
Picked up a little stick, and brought it
      back
And broke it in his hand and tossed it by.
'Silas has better claim on us you think
Than on his brother? Thirteen little miles
As the road winds would bring him to his
      door.   131

Silas has walked that far no doubt to-day.
Why didn't he go there? His brother's
      rich,
A somebody—director in the bank.'

'He never told us that.'

                'We know it though.'

'I think his brother ought to help, of
      course.
I'll see to that if there is need. He ought of
      right
To take him in, and might be willing to—
He may be better than appearances.   140
But have some pity on Silas. Do you think
If he had any pride in claiming kin
Or anything he looked for from his brother,
He'd keep so still about him all this time?'

'I wonder what's between them.'

                        'I can tell you.
Silas is what he is—we wouldn't mind
      him—
But just the kind that kinsfolk can't abide.
He never did a thing so very bad.
He don't know why he isn't quite as good
As anybody. Worthless though he is,   151
He won't be made ashamed to please his
      brother.'

'I can't think Si ever hurt anyone.'

'No, but he hurt my heart the way he lay
And rolled his old head on that sharp-edged
      chair-back.
He wouldn't let me put him on the lounge.
You must go in and see what you can do.
I made the bed up for him there to-night.
You'll be surprised at him—how much he's
      broken.
His working days are done; I'm sure of it.'

'I'd not be in a hurry to say that.'   161

'I haven't been. Go, look, see for yourself.
But, Warren, please remember how it is:
He's come to help you ditch the meadow.
He has a plan. You mustn't laugh at
      him.
He may not speak of it, and then he may.
I'll sit and see if that small sailing cloud
Will hit or miss the moon.'

It hit the moon.
Then there were three there, making a dim
    row,   170
The moon, the little silver cloud, and she.

Warren returned—too soon, it seemed to
    her,
Slipped to her side, caught up her hand and
    waited.

'Warren?' she questioned.

        'Dead,' was all he answered.
1905   1914

HOME BURIAL

He saw her from the bottom of the stairs
Before she saw him. She was starting down,
Looking back over her shoulder at some
    fear.
She took a doubtful step and then undid it
To raise herself and look again. He spoke
Advancing toward her: 'What is it you see
From up there always—for I want to know.'
She turned and sank upon her skirts at
    that,
And her face changed from terrified to dull.
He said to gain time: 'What is it you see,' 10
Mounting until she cowered under him.
'I will find out now—you must tell me,
    dear.'
She, in her place, refused him any help
With the least stiffening of her neck and
    silence.
She let him look, sure that he wouldn't see,
Blind creature; and a while he didn't see.
But at last he murmured, 'Oh,' and again,
    'Oh.'

'What is it—what?' she said.

               'Just that I see.'

'You don't,' she challenged. 'Tell me what
    it is.'   20

'The wonder is I didn't see at once.
I never noticed it from here before.
I must be wonted to it—that's the reason.
The little graveyard where my people are!
So small the window frames the whole of it.
Not so much larger than a bedroom, is it?
There are three stones of slate and one of
    marble,

Broad-shouldered little slabs there in the
    sunlight
On the sidehill. We haven't to mind *those*.
But I understand: it is not the stones,   30
But the child's mound—'

    'Don't, don't, don't, don't,' she cried.

She withdrew shrinking from beneath his
    arm
That rested on the banister, and slid
    downstairs;
And turned on him with such a daunting
    look,
He said twice over before he knew himself:
'Can't a man speak of his own child he's
    lost?'

'Not you! Oh, where's my hat? Oh, I don't
    need it!
I must get out of here. I must get air.   39
I don't know rightly whether any man can.'

'Amy! Don't go to someone else this time.
Listen to me. I won't come down the stairs.'
He sat and fixed his chin between his fists.
'There's something I should like to ask you,
    dear.'

'You don't know how to ask it.'

                  'Help me, then.'

Her fingers moved the latch for all reply.

'My words are nearly always an offence.
I don't know how to speak of anything
So as to please you. But I might be taught 50
I should suppose. I can't say I see how.
A man must partly give up being a man
With women-folk. We could have some
    arrangement
By which I'd bind myself to keep hands off
Anything special you're a-mind to name.
Though I don't like such things 'twixt those
    that love.
Two that don't love can't live together
    without them.
But two that do can't live together with
    them.'
She moved the latch a little. 'Don't—don't
    go.
Don't carry it to someone else this time.   6c
Tell me about it if it's something human.
Let me into your grief. I'm not so much

Unlike other folks as your standing there
Apart would make me out. Give me my
　　chance.
I do think, though, you overdo it a little.
What was it brought you up to think it the
　　thing
To take your mother-loss of a first child
So inconsolably—in the face of love.
You'd think his memory might be
　　satisfied—'

'There you go sneering now!'   70

　　　　　　　　　'I'm not, I'm not!
You make me angry. I'll come down to
　　you.
God, what a woman! And it's come to
　　this,
A man can't speak of his own child that's
　　dead.'

'You can't because you don't know how to
　　speak.
If you had any feelings, you that dug
With your own hand—how could you?—
　　his little grave;
I saw you from that very window there,
Making the gravel leap and leap in air,
Leap up, like that, like that, and land so
　　lightly   80
And roll back down the mound beside the
　　hole.
I thought, Who is that man? I didn't know
　　you.
And I crept down the stairs and up the
　　stairs
To look again, and still your spade kept
　　lifting.
Then you came in. I heard your rumbling
　　voice
Out in the kitchen, and I don't know why,
But I went near to see with my own eyes.
You could sit there with the stains on your
　　shoes
Of the fresh earth from your own baby's
　　grave
And talk about your everyday concerns.   90
You had stood the spade up against the
　　wall
Outside there in the entry, for I saw it.'

'I shall laugh the worst laugh I ever
　　laughed.
I'm cursed. God, if I don't believe I'm
　　cursed.'

'I can repeat the very words you were
　　saying.
"Three foggy mornings and one rainy day
Will rot the best birch fence a man can
　　build."
Think of it, talk like that at such a time!
What had how long it takes a birch to rot
To do with what was in the darkened
　　parlor.   100
You *couldn't* care! The nearest friends can
　　go
With any one to death, comes so far short
They might as well not try to go at all.
No, from the time when one is sick to death,
One is alone, and he dies more alone.
Friends make pretence of following to the
　　grave,
But before one is in it, their minds are
　　turned
And making the best of their way back to
　　life
And living people, and things they
　　understand.
But the world's evil. I won't have grief so   110
If I can change it. Oh, I won't, I won't!'

'There, you have said it all and you feel
　　better.
You won't go now. You're crying. Close the
　　door.
The heart's gone out of it: why keep it up.
Amy! There's someone coming down the
　　road!'

'*You*—oh, you think the talk is all. I must
　　go—
Somewhere out of this house. How can I
　　make you—'

'If—you—do!' She was opening the door
　　wider.
'Where do you mean to go? First tell me
　　that.
I'll follow and bring you back by force. I
　　will!—'   120
1913   1914

AFTER APPLE–PICKING

My long two-pointed ladder's sticking
　　through a tree
Toward heaven still,
And there's the barrel that I didn't fill
Beside it, and there may be two or three

Apples I didn't pick upon some bough.
But I am done with apple-picking now.
Essence of winter sleep is on the night,
The scent of apples: I am drowsing off.
I cannot rub the strangeness from my sight
I got from looking through a pane of glass
I skimmed this morning from the drinking
    trough   11
And held against the world of hoary grass.
It melted, and I let it fall and break.
But I was well
Upon my way to sleep before it fell,
And I could tell
What form my dreaming was about to take.
Magnified apples appear and disappear,
Stem end and blossom end,
And every fleck of russet showing clear.   20
My instep arch not only keeps the ache,
It keeps the pressure of a ladder-round.
I feel the ladder sway as the boughs bend.
And I keep hearing from the cellar bin
The rumbling sound
Of load on load of apples coming in.
For I have had too much
Of apple-picking: I am overtired
Of the great harvest I myself desired.
There were ten thousand thousand fruit to
    touch,   30
Cherish in hand, lift down, and not let fall.
For all
That struck the earth,
No matter if not bruised or spiked with
    stubble,
Went surely to the cider-apple heap
As of no worth.
One can see what will trouble
This sleep of mine, whatever sleep it is.
Were he not gone,
The woodchuck could say whether it's like
    his   40
Long sleep, as I describe its coming on,
Or just some human sleep.
1913   1914

THE ROAD NOT TAKEN

Two roads diverged in a yellow wood,
And sorry I could not travel both
And be one traveler, long I stood
And looked down one as far as I could
To where it bent in the undergrowth;

Then took the other, as just as fair,
And having perhaps the better claim,

Because it was grassy and wanted wear;
Though as for that the passing there
Had worn them really about the same,   10

And both that morning equally lay
In leaves no step had trodden black.
Oh, I kept the first for another day!
Yet knowing how way leads on to way,
I doubted if I should ever come back.

I shall be telling this with a sigh
Somewhere ages and ages hence:
Two roads diverged in a wood, and I—
I took the one less traveled by,
And that has made all the difference.   20
1915   1916

BIRCHES

WHEN I see birches bend to left and right
Across the lines of straighter darker trees,
I like to think some boy's been swinging
    them.
But swinging doesn't bend them down to
    stay.
Ice-storms do that. Often you must have
    seen them
Loaded with ice a sunny winter morning
After a rain. They click upon themselves
As the breeze rises, and turn many-colored
As the stir cracks and crazes their enamel.
Soon the sun's warmth makes them shed
    crystal shells   10
Shattering and avalanching on the snow-
    crust—
Such heaps of broken glass to sweep away
You'd think the inner dome of heaven had
    fallen.
They are dragged to the withered bracken
    by the load,
And they seem not to break; though once
    they are bowed
So low for long, they never right
    themselves:
You may see their trunks arching in the
    woods
Years afterwards, trailing their leaves on
    the ground
Like girls on hands and knees that throw
    their hair
Before them over their heads to dry in the
    sun.   20
But I was going to say when Truth broke
    in

With all her matter-of-fact about the ice-
   storm
I should prefer to have some boy bend
   them
As he went out and in to fetch the cows—
Some boy too far from town to learn
   baseball,
Whose only play was what he found
   himself,
Summer or winter, and could play alone.
One by one he subdued his father's trees
By riding them down over and over again
Until he took the stiffness out of them,   30
And not one but hung limp, not one was
   left
For him to conquer. He learned all there
   was
To learn about not launching out too soon
And so not carrying the tree away
Clear to the ground. He always kept his
   poise
To the top branches, climbing carefully
With the same pains you use to fill a cup
Up to the brim, and even above the brim.
Then he flung outward, feet first, with a
   swish,
Kicking his way down through the air to
   the ground.   40
So was I once myself a swinger of birches.
And so I dream of going back to be.
It's when I'm weary of considerations,
And life is too much like a pathless wood
Where your face burns and tickles with the
   cobwebs
Broken across it, and one eye is weeping
From a twig's having lashed across it open.
I'd like to get away from earth awhile
And then come back to it and begin over.
May no fate wilfully misunderstand me   50
And half grant what I wish and snatch me
   away
Not to return. Earth's the right place for
   love:
I don't know where it's likely to go better.
I'd like to go by climbing a birch tree,
And climb black branches up a snow-white
   trunk
Toward heaven, till the tree could bear no
   more,
But dipped its top and set me down again.
That would be good both going and coming
   back.
One could do worse than be a swinger of
   birches.
1916   1916

FROM THE HILL WIFE

THE OFT-REPEATED DREAM

SHE had no saying dark enough
   For the dark pine that kept
Forever trying the window-latch
   Of the room where they slept.

The tireless but ineffectual hands
   That with every futile pass
Made the great tree seem as a little bird
   Before the mystery of glass!

It never had been inside the room,
   And only one of the two   10
Was afraid in an oft-repeated dream
   Of what the tree might do.
1916   1916

'OUT, OUT—'

THE buzz-saw snarled and rattled in the
   yard
And made dust and dropped stove-length
   sticks of wood,
Sweet-scented stuff when the breeze drew
   across it.
And from there those that lifted eyes could
   count
Five mountain ranges one behind the other
Under the sunset far into Vermont.
And the saw snarled and rattled, snarled
   and rattled,
As it ran light, or had to bear a load.
And nothing happened: day was all but
   done.
Call it a day, I wish they might have said   10
To please the boy by giving him the half
   hour
That a boy counts so much when saved
   from work.
His sister stood beside them in her apron
To tell them 'Supper.' At the word, the
   saw,
As if to prove saws knew what supper
   meant,
Leaped out at the boy's hand, or seemed to
   leap—
He must have given the hand. However it
   was,
Neither refused the meeting. But the hand!
The boy's first outcry was a rueful laugh.
As he swung toward them holding up the
   hand   20

Half in appeal, but half as if to keep
The life from spilling. Then the boy saw
    all—
Since he was old enough to know, big boy
Doing a man's work, though a child at
    heart—
He saw all spoiled. 'Don't let him cut my
    hand off—
The doctor, when he comes. Don't let him,
    sister!'
So. But the hand was gone already.
The doctor put him in the dark of ether.
He lay and puffed his lips out with his
    breath.
And then—the watcher at his pulse took
    fright.   30
No one believed. They listened at his
    heart.
Little—less—nothing!—and that ended
    it.
No more to build on there. And they, since
    they
Were not the one dead, turned to their
    affairs.
1916   1916

THE SOUND OF THE TREES

I WONDER about the trees.
Why do we wish to bear
Forever the noise of these
More than another noise
So close to our dwelling place?
We suffer them by the day
Till we lose all measure of pace,
And fixity in our joys,
And acquire a listening air.
They are that that talks of going   10
But never gets away;
And that talks no less for knowing,
As it grows wiser and older,
That now it means to stay.
My feet tug at the floor
And my head sways to my shoulder
Sometimes when I watch trees sway,
From the window or the door.
I shall set forth for somewhere,
I shall make the reckless choice   20
Some day when they are in voice
And tossing so as to scare
The white clouds over them on.
I shall have less to say,
But I shall be gone.
1915   1916

THE GRINDSTONE

HAVING a wheel and four legs of its own
Has never availed the cumbersome
    grindstone
To get it anywhere that I can see.
These hands have helped it go, and even
    race;
Not all the motion, though, they ever lent,
Not all the miles it may have thought it
    went,
Have got it one step from the starting place.
It stands beside the same old apple tree.
The shadow of the apple tree is thin
Upon it now, its feet are fast in snow.   10
All other farm machinery's gone in,
And some of it on no more legs and wheel
Than the grindstone can boast to stand or
    go.
(I'm thinking chiefly of the wheelbarrow.)
For months it hasn't known the taste of
    steel,
Washed down with rusty water in a tin.
But standing outdoors hungry, in the cold,
Except in towns at night, is not a sin.
And, anyway, its standing in the yard
Under a ruinous live apple tree   20
Has nothing any more to do with me,
Except that I remember how of old
One summer day, all day I drove it hard,
And someone mounted on it rode it hard,
And he and I between us ground a blade.

I gave it the preliminary spin,
And poured on water (tears it might have
    been;)
And when it almost gayly jumped and
    flowed,
A Father-Time-like man got on and rode,
Armed with a scythe and spectacles that
    glowed.   30
He turned on will-power to increase the
    load
And slow me down—and I abruptly slowed,
Like coming to a sudden railroad station.
I changed from hand to hand in
    desperation.
I wondered what machine of ages gone
This represented an improvement on.
For all I knew it may have sharpened
    spears
And arrowheads itself. Much use for years
Had gradually worn it an oblate
Spheroid that kicked and struggled in its
    gait,   40

Appearing to return me hate for hate;
(But I forgive it now as easily
As any other boyhood enemy
Whose pride has failed to get him
     anywhere.)
I wondered who it was the man thought
     ground—
The one who held the wheel back or the one
Who gave his life to keep it going round?
I wondered if he really thought it fair
For him to have the say when we were done.
Such were the bitter thoughts to which I
     turned.   50

Not for myself was I so much concerned.
Oh no!—although, of course, I could have
     found
A better way to pass the afternoon
Than grinding discord out of a grindstone,
And beating insects at their gritty tune.
Nor was I for the man so much concerned.
Once when the grindstone almost jumped
     its bearing
It looked as if he might be badly thrown
And wounded on his blade. So far from
     caring,
I laughed inside, and only cranked the
     faster,   60
(It ran as if it wasn't greased but glued;)
I'd welcome any moderate disaster
That might be calculated to postpone
What evidently nothing could conclude.
The thing that made me more and more
     afraid
Was that we'd ground it sharp and hadn't
     known,
And now were only wasting precious blade.
And when he raised it dripping once and
     tried
The creepy edge of it with wary touch,
And viewed it over his glasses funny-eyed,
Only disinterestedly to decide   71
It needed a turn more, I could have cried
Wasn't there danger of a turn too much?
Mightn't we make it worse instead of
     better?
I was for leaving something to the whetter.
What if it wasn't all it should be? I'd
Be satisfied if he'd be satisfied.
1921   1923

FIRE AND ICE

SOME say the world will end in fire,
Some say in ice.

From what I've tasted of desire
I hold with those who favor fire.
But if it had to perish twice,
I think I know enough of hate
To say that for destruction ice
Is also great
And would suffice.
1919   1923

DUST OF SNOW

THE way a crow
Shook down on me
The dust of snow
From a hemlock tree

Has given my heart
A change of mood
And saved some part
Of a day I had rued.
1906   1923

THE RUNAWAY

ONCE when the snow of the year was
     beginning to fall,
We stopped by a mountain pasture to say,
     'Whose colt?'
A little Morgan had one forefoot on the
     wall,
The other curled at his breast. He dipped
     his head
And snorted at us. And then he had to bolt.
We heard the miniature thunder where he
     fled,
And we saw him, or thought we saw him,
     dim and grey,
Like a shadow against the curtain of falling
     flakes.
'I think the little fellow's afraid of the snow.
He isn't winter-broken. It isn't play   10
With the little fellow at all. He's running
     away.
I doubt if even his mother could tell him,
     "Sakes,
It's only weather." He'd think she didn't
     know!
Where is his mother? He can't be out
     alone.'
And now he comes again with a clatter of
     stone
And mounts the wall again with whited
     eyes
And all his tail that isn't hair up straight.
He shudders his coat as if to throw off flies

'Whoever it is that leaves him out so late,
When other creatures have gone to stall and
    bin,   20
Ought to be told to come and take him
    in.'
1917   1923

STOPPING BY WOODS ON A
SNOWY EVENING

WHOSE woods these are I think I know.
His house is in the village though;
He will not see me stopping here
To watch his woods fill up with snow.

My little horse must think it queer
To stop without a farmhouse near
Between the woods and frozen lake
The darkest evening of the year.

He gives his harness bells a shake
To ask if there is some mistake.   10
The only other sound's the sweep
Of easy wind and downy flake.

The woods are lovely, dark and deep.
But I have promises to keep,
And miles to go before I sleep,
And miles to go before I sleep.
1923   1923

TO EARTHWARD

LOVE at the lips was touch
As sweet as I could bear;
And once that seemed too much;
I lived on air

That crossed me from sweet things,
The flow of—was it musk
From hidden grapevine springs
Down hill at dusk?

I had the swirl and ache
From sprays of honeysuckle   10
That when they're gathered shake
Dew on the knuckle.

I craved strong sweets, but those
Seemed strong when I was young;
The petal of the rose
It was that stung.

Now no joy but lacks salt
That is not dashed with pain

And weariness and fault;
I crave the stain   20

Of tears, the aftermark
Of almost too much love,
The sweet of bitter bark
And burning clove.

When stiff and sore and scarred
I take away my hand
From leaning on it hard
In grass and sand,

The hurt is not enough:
I long for weight and strength   30
To feel the earth as rough
To all my length.
1914   1923

GOOD–BYE AND KEEP COLD

THIS saying good-bye on the edge of the
    dark
And cold to an orchard so young in the
    bark
Reminds me of all that can happen to harm
An orchard away at the end of the farm
All winter, cut off by a hill from the house.
I don't want it girdled by rabbit and mouse,
I don't want it dreamily nibbled for browse
By deer, and I don't want it budded by
    grouse.
(If certain it wouldn't be idle to call
I'd summon grouse, rabbit, and deer to the
    wall   10
And warn them away with a stick for a gun.)
I don't want it stirred by the heat of the sun
(We made it secure against being, I hope,
By setting it out on a northerly slope.)
No orchard's the worse for the wintriest
    storm;
But one thing about it, it mustn't get warm.
'How often already you've had to be told,
Keep cold, young orchard. Good-bye and
    keep cold.
Dread fifty above more than fifty below.'
I have to be gone for a season or so.   20
My business awhile is with different trees,
Less carefully nurtured, less fruitful than
    these,
And such as is done to their wood with an
    axe—
Maples and birches and tamaracks.
I wish I could promise to lie in the night
And think of an orchard's arboreal plight

When slowly (and nobody comes with a
    light)
Its heart sinks lower under the sod.
But something has to be left to God.
1919   1923

NOT TO KEEP

THEY sent him back to her. The letter came
Saying . . . And she could have him. And
    before
She could be sure there was no hidden ill
Under the formal writing, he was in her
    sight,
Living. They gave him back to her alive—
How else? They are not known to send the
    dead—
And not disfigured visibly. His face?
His hands? She had to look, to ask,
'What is it, dear?' And she had given all
And still she had all—*they* had—they the
    lucky!   10
Wasn't she glad now? Everything seemed
    won,
And all the rest for them permissible ease.
She had to ask, 'What was it, dear?'

                       'Enough,
Yet not enough. A bullet through and
    through,
High in the breast. Nothing but what good
    care
And medicine and rest, and you a week,
Can cure me of to go again.' The same
Grim giving to do over for them both.
She dared no more than ask him with her
    eyes   20
How was it with him for a second trial.
And with his eyes he asked her not to ask.
They had given him back to her, but not to
    keep.
1915   1923

ACQUAINTED WITH THE NIGHT

I HAVE been one acquainted with the night.
I have walked out in rain—and back in rain.
I have outwalked the furthest city light.

I have looked down the saddest city lane.
I have passed by the watchman on his beat
And dropped my eyes, unwilling to explain.

I have stood still and stopped the sound of
    feet

When far away an interrupted cry
Came over houses from another street,

But not to call me back or say good-bye; 10
And further still at an unearthly height,
One luminary clock against the sky

Proclaimed the time was neither wrong nor
    right.
I have been one acquainted with the night.
1925   1928

CANIS MAJOR

THE great Overdog,
That heavenly beast
With a star in one eye,
Gives a leap in the east.

He dances upright
All the way to the west,
And never once drops
On his forefeet to rest.

I'm a poor underdog,
But to-night I will bark   10
With the great Overdog
That romps through the dark.
1925   1928

THE BEAR

THE bear puts both arms around the tree
    above her
And draws it down as if it were a lover
And its choke cherries lips to kiss good-bye,
Then lets it snap back upright in the sky.
Her next step rocks a boulder on the wall
(She's making her cross-country in the fall.)
Her great weight creaks the barbed-wire in
    its staples
As she flings over and off down through the
    maples,
Leaving on one wire tooth a lock of hair.
Such is the uncaged progress of the bear. 10
The world has room to make a bear feel
    free;
The universe seems cramped to you and
    me.
Man acts more like the poor bear in a cage
That all day fights a nervous inward rage,
His mood rejecting all his mind suggests.
He paces back and forth and never rests
The toe-nail click and shuffle of his feet,
The telescope at one end of his beat,

And at the other end the microscope,
Two instruments of nearly equal hope, 20
And in conjunction giving quite a spread.
Or if he rests from scientific tread,
'Tis only to sit back and sway his head
Through ninety odd degrees of arc, it
    seems,
Between two metaphysical extremes.
He sits back on his fundamental butt
With lifted snout and eyes (if any) shut,
(He almost looks religious but he's not,)
And back and forth he sways from cheek to
    cheek,
At one extreme agreeing with one Greek, 30
At the other agreeing with another Greek
Which may be thought, but only so to
    speak.
A baggy figure, equally pathetic
When sedentary and when peripatetic.
1926   1928

TWO TRAMPS IN MUD TIME

OR, A FULL-TIME INTEREST

OUT of the mud two strangers came
And caught me splitting wood in the yard.
And one of them put me off my aim
By hailing cheerily 'Hit them hard!'
I knew pretty well why he dropped behind
And let the other go on a way.
I knew pretty well what he had in mind:
He wanted to take my job for pay.

Good blocks of beech it was I split,
As large around as the chopping block; 10
And every piece I squarely hit
Fell splinterless as a cloven rock.
The blows that a life of self-control
Spares to strike for the common good
That day, giving a loose to my soul,
I spent on the unimportant wood.

The sun was warm but the wind was chill.
You know how it is with an April day
When the sun is out and the wind is still,
You're one month on in the middle of May.
But if you so much as dare to speak, 21
A cloud comes over the sunlit arch,
A wind comes off a frozen peak,
And you're two months back in the middle
    of March.

A bluebird comes tenderly up to alight
And fronts the wind to unruffle a plume,
His song so pitched as not to excite

A single flower as yet to bloom.
It is snowing a flake: and he half knew
Winter was only playing possum. 30
Except in color he isn't blue,
But he wouldn't advise a thing to blossom.

The water for which we may have to look
In summertime with a witching-wand,
In every wheelrut's now a brook,
In every print of a hoof a pond.
Be glad of water, but don't forget
The lurking frost in the earth beneath
That will steal forth after the sun is set
And show on the water its crystal teeth. 40

The time when most I loved my task
These two must make me love it more
By coming with what they came to ask.
You'd think I never had felt before
The weight of an axe-head poised aloft,
The grip on earth of outspread feet,
The life of muscles rocking soft
And smooth and moist in vernal heat.

Out of the woods two hulking tramps
(From sleeping God knows where last
    night, 50
But not long since in the lumber camps.)
They thought all chopping was theirs of
    right.
Men of the woods and lumberjacks,
They judged me by their appropriate tool.
Except as a fellow handled an axe,
They had no way of knowing a fool.

Nothing on either side was said.
They knew they had but to stay their stay
And all their logic would fill my head:
As that I had no right to play 60
With what was another man's work for
    gain.
My right might be love but theirs was
    need.
And where the two exist in twain
Theirs was the better right—agreed.

But yield who will to their separation,
My object in living is to unite
My avocation and my vocation
As my two eyes make one in sight.
Only where love and need are one,
And the work is play for mortal stakes, 70
Is the deed ever really done
For Heaven and the future's sakes.
1934   1936

NEITHER OUT FAR NOR IN
DEEP

THE people along the sand
All turn and look one way.
They turn their back on the land.
They look at the sea all day.

As long as it takes to pass
A ship keeps raising its hull;
The wetter ground like glass
Reflects a standing gull.

The land may vary more;
But wherever the truth may be—   10
The water comes ashore,
And the people look at the sea.

They cannot look out far.
They cannot look in deep.
But when was that ever a bar
To any watch they keep?

1932   1936

A LONE STRIKER

OR, WITHOUT PREJUDICE TO INDUSTRY

THE swinging mill bell changed its rate
To tolling like the count of fate,
And though at that the tardy ran,
One failed to make the closing gate.
There was a law of God or man
That on the one who came too late
The gate for half an hour be locked,
His time be lost, his pittance docked.
He stood rebuked and unemployed.
The straining mill began to shake.   10
The mill, though many, many eyed,
Had eyes inscrutably opaque;
So that he couldn't look inside
To see if some forlorn machine
Was standing idle for his sake.
(He couldn't hope its heart would break.)

And yet he thought he saw the scene:
The air was full of dust of wool.
A thousand yarns were under pull,
But pull so slow, with such a twist,   20

All day from spool to lesser spool,
It seldom overtaxed their strength;
They safely grew in slender length.
And if one broke by any chance,
The spinner saw it at a glance.
The spinner still was there to spin.
That's where the human still came in.
Her deft hand showed with finger rings
Among the harp-like spread of strings.
She caught the pieces end to end   30
And, with a touch that never missed,
Not so much tied as made them blend.
Man's ingenuity was good.
He saw it plainly where he stood,
Yet found it easy to resist.

He knew another place, a wood,
And in it, tall as trees, were cliffs;
And if he stood on one of these,
'Twould be among the tops of trees,
Their upper branches round him
        wreathing,   40
Their breathing mingled with his
        breathing.
If—if he stood! Enough of ifs!
He knew a path that wanted walking;
He knew a spring that wanted drinking;
A thought that wanted further thinking;
A love that wanted re-renewing.
Nor was this just a way of talking
To save him the expense of doing.
With him it boded action, deed.

The factory was very fine;   50
He wished it all the modern speed.
Yet, after all, 'twas not divine,
That is to say, 'twas not a church.
He never would assume that he'd
Be any institution's need.
But he said then and still would say
If there should ever come a day
When industry seemed like to die
Because he left it in the lurch,
Or even merely seemed to pine   60
For want of his approval, why
Come get him—they knew where to search.

1934   1936

VACHEL LINDSAY

1879–1931

FROM A GOSPEL OF BEAUTY

3. ON THE BUILDING OF SPRINGFIELD [1]

LET not our town be large, remembering
That little Athens was the Muses' home,
That Oxford rules the heart of London
    still,
That Florence gave the Renaissance to
    Rome.

Record it for the grandson of your son—
A city is not builded in a day:
Our little town cannot complete her soul
Till countless generations pass away.

Now let each child be joined as to a church
To her perpetual hopes, each man ordained:
Let every street be made a reverent aisle   11
Where Music grows and Beauty is
    unchained.

Let Science and Machinery and Trade
Be slaves of her, and make her all in all,
Building against our blatant, restless time
An unseen, skilful, medieval wall.

Let every citizen be rich toward God.
Let Christ the beggar, teach divinity.
Let no man rule who holds his money
    dear.
Let this, our city, be our luxury.   20

We should build parks that students from
    afar
Would choose to starve in, rather than go
    home,
Fair little squares, with Phidian ornament,
Food for the spirit, milk and honeycomb.

Songs shall be sung by us in that good
    day,
Songs we have written, blood within the
    rhyme
Beating, as when Old England still was
    glad,—
The purple, rich Elizabethan time.

. . . .

1 This poem was one of the three Lindsay recited on his
travels, 'which three in series contain my whole gospel,
directly or by implication.' It is mostly here.

Say, is my prophecy too fair and far?
I only know, unless her faith be high,   30
The soul of this, our Nineveh, is doomed,
Our little Babylon will surely die.

Some city on the breast of Illinois
No wiser and no better at the start
By faith shall rise redeemed, by faith shall
    rise
Bearing the western glory in her heart.

The genius of the Maple, Elm and Oak,
The secret hidden in each grain of corn,
The glory that the prairie angels sing
At night when sons of Life and Love are
    born,   40

Born but to struggle, squalid and alone,
Broken and wandering in their early years.
When will they make our dusty streets their
    goal,
Within our attics hide their sacred tears?

When will they start our vulgar blood
    athrill
With living language, words that set us
    free?
When will they make a path of beauty
    clear
Between our riches and our liberty?

We must have many Lincoln-hearted men.
A city is not builded in a day.   50
And they must do their work, and come
    and go,
While countless generations pass away.
c1908   1912

FROM ALEXANDER CAMPBELL

1. MY FATHERS CAME FROM KENTUCKY

I WAS born in Illinois,—
Have lived there many days.
And I have Northern words,
And thoughts,
And ways.

But my great-grandfathers came
To the west with Daniel Boone,
And taught his babes to read,
And heard the redbird's tune;

And heard the turkey's call,   10
And stilled the panther's cry,
And rolled on the blue-grass
    hills,
And looked God in the eye.

And feud and Hell were theirs;
Love, like the moon's desire,
Love like a burning-mine,
Love like rifle-fire.

I tell tales out of school
Till these Yankees hate my style.
Why should the young cad cry,   20
Shout with joy for a mile?

Why do I faint with love
Till the prairies dip and reel?
My heart is a kicking horse
Shod with Kentucky steel.

No drop of my blood from north
Of Mason and Dixon's line.
And this racer in my breast
Tears my ribs for a sign.

But I ran in Kentucky hills   30
Last week. They were hearth and
    home.
And the church at Grassy Springs,
Under the redbird's wings
Was peace and honeycomb.

                1920

THE LEADEN-EYED

LET not young souls be smothered out be-
    fore
They do quaint deeds and fully flaunt their
    pride.
It is the world's one crime its babes grow
    dull,
Its poor are ox-like, limp and leaden-
    eyed.

Not that they starve, but starve so
    dreamlessly,
Not that they sow, but that they seldom
    reap,
Not that they serve, but have no gods to
    serve,
Not that they die, but that they die like
    sheep.

                1912

THE EAGLE THAT IS FORGOTTEN [1]

(JOHN P. ALTGELD. BORN DECEMBER 30,
1847; DIED MARCH 12, 1902)

SLEEP softly . . . eagle forgotten . . .
    under the stone.
Time has its way with you there, and the
    clay has its own.

'We have buried him now,' thought your
    foes, and in secret rejoiced.
They made a brave show of their mourning,
    their hatred unvoiced.
They had snarled at you, barked at you,
    foamed at you day after day.
Now you were ended. They praised you
    . . . and laid you away.

The others that mourned you in silence and
    terror and truth,
The widow bereft of her crust, and the boy
    without youth,
The mocked and the scorned and the
    wounded, the lame and the
    poor
That should have remembered forever
    . . . remember no more.   10

Where are those lovers of yours, on what
    name do they call,
The lost, that in armies wept over your
    funeral pall?
They call on the names of a hundred high-
    valiant ones,
A hundred white eagles have risen the sons
    of your sons,
The zeal in their wings is a zeal that your
    dreaming began
The valor that wore out your soul in the
    service of man.

Sleep softly . . . eagle forgotten . . .
    under the stone,
Time has its way with you there and the
    clay has its own.
Sleep on, O brave-hearted, O wise man,
    that kindled the flame—

1 Altgeld, as Governor of Illinois, pardoned anarchistic
agitators convicted for their part in the Chicago Hay-
market riot, protested President Cleveland's sending
the regular army to Chicago during the Pullman strike,
and generally championed the down-trodden. It cost
him his governorship, but made him for a time a
symbol.

To live in mankind is far more than to live
    in a name,   20
To live in mankind, far, far more . . .
    than to live in a name.   1912

GENERAL WILLIAM BOOTH ENTERS INTO HEAVEN [1]

(*To be sung to the tune of 'The Blood of the Lamb' with indicated instrument.*)

I

(*Bass drum beaten loudly.*)
Booth led boldly with his big bass drum—
(Are you washed in the blood of the Lamb?)
The Saints smiled gravely and they said:
    'He's come.'
(Are you washed in the blood of the Lamb?)
Walking lepers followed, rank on rank,
Lurching bravos from the ditches dank,
Drabs from the alleyways and drug fiends
    pale—
Minds still passion-ridden, soul-powers
    frail:—
Vermin-eaten saints with moldy breath,   9
Unwashed legions with the ways of Death—
(Are you washed in the blood of the Lamb?)

(*Banjos.*)
Every slum had sent its half-a-score
The round world over. (Booth had groaned
    for more.)
Every banner that the wide world flies
Bloomed with glory and transcendent dyes.
Big-voiced lasses made their banjos bang,
Tranced, fanatical they shrieked and sang:—
'Are you washed in the blood of the Lamb?'
Hallelujah! It was queer to see
Bull-necked convicts with that land make
    free.   20
Loons with trumpets blowed a blare, blare,
    blare
On, on upward thro' the golden air!
(Are you washed in the blood of the Lamb?)

[1] Lindsay's ideal Democracy was to 'come through the services of three kinds of men in wise coöperation: the priests, the statesmen and the artists. Our priests shall be religious men like St. Francis, or John Wesley, or General Booth, or Cardinal Newman.' Lindsay, *Adventures while Preaching* . . . (N.Y., 1914),184–85.
    'In my poem I merely turned into rhyme as well as I could, word for word, General Booth's own account of his life, and the telegraph dispatches of his death after going blind. I set it to the tune that is not a tune, but a speech, a refrain used most frequently in the meetings of the Army on any public square to this day.' Lindsay, *Collected Poems*(N.Y., 1923),22.

2

(*Bass drum slower and softer.*)
Booth died blind and still by faith he trod,
Eyes still dazzled by the ways of God.
Booth led boldly, and he looked the chief
Eagle countenance in sharp relief,
Beard a-flying, air of high command
Unabated in that holy land.   29

(*Sweet flute music.*)
Jesus came from out the court-house door,
Stretched his hands above the passing
    poor.
Booth saw not, but led his queer ones there
Round and round the mighty court-house
    square.
Then, in an instant all that blear review
Marched on spotless, clad in raiment new.
The lame were straightened, withered
    limbs uncurled
And blind eyes opened on a new, sweet
    world.

(*Bass drum louder.*)
Drabs and vixens in a flash made whole!
Gone was the weasel-head, the snout, the
    jowl!
Sages and sibyls now, and athletes clean,   40
Rulers of empires, and of forests green!

(*Grand chorus of all instruments. Tambourines to the foreground.*)
The hosts were sandalled, and their wings
    were fire!
(Are you washed in the blood of the Lamb?)
But their noise played havoc with the
    angel-choir.
(Are you washed in the blood of the Lamb?)
Oh, shout Salvation! It was good to see
Kings and Princes by the Lamb set free.
The banjos rattled and the tambourines
Jing-jing-jingled in the hands of Queens.

(*Reverently sung, no instruments.*)
And when Booth halted by the curb for
    prayer   50
He saw his Master thro' the flag-filled air.
Christ came gently with a robe and crown
For Booth the soldier, while the throng
    knelt down.
He saw King Jesus. They were face to face,
And he knelt a-weeping in that holy place.
Are you washed in the blood of the Lamb?
1912   1913

THE CONGO [1]

A STUDY OF THE NEGRO RACE

1. *Their Basic Savagery*

FAT black bucks in a wine-barrel room,
Barrel-house kings, with feet unstable,
Sagged and reeled and pounded on the table,
Pounded on the table,   *A deep rolling*
Beat an empty barrel with the handle of a broom,   *bass.*
Hard as they were able,
Boom, boom, BOOM,
With a silk umbrella and the handle of a broom,
Boomlay, boomlay, boomlay, BOOM.
THEN I had religion, THEN I had a vision.   10
I could not turn from their revel in derision.
THEN I SAW THE CONGO, CREEPING THROUGH THE BLACK,   *More deliberate.*
CUTTING THROUGH THE FOREST WITH A GOLDEN TRACK.   *Solemnly*
Then along that riverbank   *chanted.*
A thousand miles
Tattooed cannibals danced in files;
Then I heard the boom of the blood-lust song
And a thigh-bone beating on a tin-pan gong.   *A rapidly piling*
And 'BLOOD' screamed the whistles and the fifes of the warriors,   *climax of speed*
'BLOOD' screamed the skull-faced, lean witch-doctors,   20 *and racket.*
'Whirl ye the deadly voo-doo rattle,
Harry the uplands,
Steal all the cattle,
Rattle-rattle, rattle-rattle,
Bing!
Boomlay, boomlay, boomlay, BOOM,'
A roaring, epic, rag-time tune   *With a philosophic*
From the mouth of the Congo   *pause.*
To the Mountains of the Moon.
Death is an Elephant,   30
Torch-eyed and horrible,
Foam-flanked and terrible.   *Shrilly and with*
BOOM, steal the pygmies,   *a heavily accented*
BOOM, kill the Arabs,   *meter.*
BOOM, kill the white men,
HOO, HOO, HOO.
Listen to the yell of Leopold's ghost   *Like the wind in*
Burning in Hell for his hand-maimed host.   *the chimney.*
Hear how the demons chuckle and yell
Cutting his hands off, down in Hell.   40
Listen to the creepy proclamation,
Blown through the lairs of the forest-nation,

1 'The thought of the third section was inspired by a passage in a sermon by my pastor, F.W.Burnham, when he spoke of the death of Ray Eldred, a heroic missionary, who had recently perished on the Congo River. It is logical there should be six lines conforming to the original hymn-theory and set to the tune, "Hark ten thousand harps and voices." But the remainder of "The Congo" is based, however poorly, on the most conventional English tradition of imitative verbal music, going back through Southey's "Cataract of Lodore" to Dryden's "Alexander's Feast." In reciting "The Congo" I unconsciously introduced a new element of chanting, akin to the Gregorian Chant I had heard in the Paulist Fathers' Church, New York. . . . I added this to my usual effort to elaborate the tone-color effects, and as a result of the two "The Congo" became the first recitation of my life to which big conventional gatherings of people would listen. All my sympathetic audiences up to that time had been the fireside sort, with chums, or on the road.' Lindsay, *Letter about My Four Programmes*(Springfield, Ill.,n.d.),5.

Blown past the white-ants' hill of clay,
Blown past the marsh where the butterflies play:—
'Be careful what you do,
Or Mumbo-Jumbo, God of the Congo,
And all of the other
Gods of the Congo,
Mumbo-Jumbo will hoo-doo you,
Mumbo-Jumbo will hoo-doo you,
Mumbo-Jumbo will hoo-doo you.'

*All the o sounds
very golden.
Heavy accents
very heavy.
Light accents
50 very light. Last
line whispered.*

2. *Their Irrepressible High Spirits*

Wild crap-shooters with a whoop and a call
Danced the juba in their gambling-hall
And laughed fit to kill, and shook the town,
And guyed the policemen and laughed them down
With a boomlay, boomlay, boomlay, BOOM.
THEN I SAW THE CONGO, CREEPING THROUGH THE BLACK,
CUTTING THROUGH THE FOREST WITH A GOLDEN TRACK.
A negro fairyland swung into view,
A minstrel river
Where dreams come true.
The ebony palace soared on high
Through the blossoming trees to the evening sky.
The inlaid porches and casements shone
With gold and ivory and elephant-bone.
And the black crowd laughed till their sides were sore
At the baboon butler in the agate door,
And the well-known tunes of the parrot band
That trilled on the bushes of that magic-land.

*Rather shrill and
high.*

*Read exactly as in
first section.*

*Lay emphasis on
60 the delicate ideas.
Keep as light-
footed as possible.*

A troupe of skull-faced witch-men came
Through the agate doorway in suits of flame,
Yea, long-tailed coats with a gold-leaf crust
And hats that were covered with diamond-dust.
And the crowd in the court gave a whoop and a call
And danced the juba from wall to wall.
But the witch-men suddenly stilled the throng
With a stern cold glare, and a stern old song:—
'Mumbo-Jumbo will hoo-doo you.' . . .
Just then from the doorway, as fat as shotes,
Came the cake-walk princes in their long red coats,
Canes with a brilliant lacquer shine,
And tall silk hats that were red as wine.
And they pranced with their butterfly partners there,
Coal-black maidens with pearls in their hair,
Knee-skirts trimmed with the jessamine sweet,
And bells on their ankles and little black feet.
And the couples railed at the chant and the frown
Of the witch-men lean, and laughed them down.
(O rare was the revel, and well worth while
That made those glowering witch-men smile.)

70 *With pomposity.*

*With a great
deliberation and
ghostliness.*

80 *With overwhelm-
ing assurance,
good cheer, and
pomp.*

*With growing
speed and sharply
marked dance-
rhythm.*

90

The cake-walk royalty then began
To walk for a cake that was tall as a man
To the tune of 'Boomlay, boomlay, BOOM,'

While the witch-men laughed, with a sinister air,
And sang with the scalawags prancing there:—
'Walk with care, walk with care,
Or Mumbo-Jumbo, God of the Congo,
And all of the other
Gods of the Congo,
Mumbo-Jumbo will hoo-doo you.   100
Beware, beware, walk with care,
Boomlay, boomlay, boomlay, boom.
Boomlay, boomlay, boomlay, boom,
Boomlay, boomlay, boomlay, boom,
Boomlay, boomlay, boomlay,
Boom.'
Oh rare was the revel, and well worth while
That made those glowering witch-men smile.

*With a touch of
negro dialect, and
as rapidly as
possible toward
the end.*

*Slow philosophic
calm.*

3. *The Hope of Their Religion*

A good old negro in the slums of the town
Preached at a sister for her velvet gown.
Howled at a brother for his low-down ways,   110
His prowling, guzzling, sneak-thief days.
Beat on the Bible till he wore it out,
Starting the jubilee revival shout.
And some had visions, as they stood on chairs,
And sang of Jacob, and the golden stairs.
And they all repented, a thousand strong,
From their stupor and savagery and sin and wrong
And slammed with their hymn books till they shook the room
With 'Glory, glory, glory,'   120
And 'Boom, boom, Boom.'
THEN I SAW THE CONGO, CREEPING THROUGH THE BLACK,
CUTTING THROUGH THE JUNGLE WITH A GOLDEN TRACK.
And the gray sky opened like a new-rent veil
And showed the apostles with their coats of mail.
In bright white steel they were seated round
And their fire-eyes watched where the Congo wound.
And the twelve apostles, from their thrones on high,
Thrilled all the forest with their heavenly cry:—
'Mumbo-Jumbo will die in the jungle;   130
Never again will he hoo-doo you,
Never again will he hoo-doo you.'

*Heavy bass. With
a literal imitation
of camp-meeting
racket, and trance.*

*Exactly as in the
first section.*

*Sung to the tune of
'Hark, ten thou-
sand harps and
voices.'*

Then along that river, a thousand miles,
The vine-snared trees fell down in files.
Pioneer angels cleared the way
For a Congo paradise, for babes at play,
For sacred capitals, for temples clean.
Gone were the skull-faced witch-men lean.
There, where the wild ghost-gods had wailed
A million boats of the angels sailed   140
With oars of silver, and prows of blue
And silken pennants that the sun shone through.
'Twas a land transfigured, 'twas a new creation.
Oh, a singing wind swept the negro nation;
And on through the backwoods clearing flew:—

*With growing
deliberation and
joy.*

*In a rather high
key—as delicately
as possible.*

'Mumbo-Jumbo is dead in the jungle.
Never again will he hoo-doo you.
Never again will he hoo-doo you.'

*To the tune of
'Hark, ten thou-
sand harps and
voices.'*

Redeemed were the forests, the beasts and the men,
And only the vulture dared again   150
By the far, lone mountains of the moon
To cry, in the silence, the Congo tune:—
'Mumbo-Jumbo will hoo-doo you,
Mumbo-Jumbo will hoo-doo you.

*Dying down into a
penetrating,
terrified whisper.*

Mumbo . . . Jumbo . . . will . . . hoo-doo . . . you.'
1913–1914   1914

FROM THE BOOKER WASHINGTON
TRILOGY

I. SIMON LEGREE—A NEGRO SERMON [1]

(To be read in your own variety of negro
dialect.)

LEGREE'S big house was white and green.
His cotton-fields were the best to be seen.
He had strong horses and opulent cattle,
And bloodhounds bold, with chains that
       would rattle.
His garret was full of curious things:
Books of magic, bags of gold,
And rabbits' feet on long twine strings.
But he went down to the Devil.

Legree, he sported a brass-buttoned coat,
A snake-skin necktie, a blood-red shirt.   10
Legree he had a beard like a goat,
And a thick hairy neck, and eyes like dirt.
His puffed-out cheeks were fish-belly
       white,
He had great long teeth, and an appetite.
He ate raw meat, 'most every meal,
And rolled his eyes till the cat would squeal.

His fist was an enormous size
To mash poor niggers that told him lies:
He was surely a witch-man in disguise.
But he went down to the Devil.   20

He wore hip-boots, and would wade all day
To capture his slaves that had fled away.
But he went down to the Devil.

He beat poor Uncle Tom to death
Who prayed for Legree with his last breath.
Then Uncle Tom to Eva flew,
To the high sanctoriums bright and new;
And Simon Legree stared up beneath,
And cracked his heels, and ground his
       teeth:
And went down to the Devil.   30

He crossed the yard in the storm and
       gloom;
He went into his grand front room.
He said, 'I killed him, and I don't care.'
He kicked a hound, he gave a swear;
He tightened his belt, he took a lamp,
Went down cellar to the webs and damp.
There in the middle of the mouldy floor
He heaved up a slab, he found a door—
And went down to the Devil.

His lamp blew out, but his eyes burned
       bright.   40
Simon Legree stepped down all night—
Down, down to the Devil.
Simon Legree he reached the place,
He saw one half of the human race,
He saw the Devil on a wide green throne,
Gnawing the meat from a big ham-bone,
And he said to Mister Devil:

'I see that you have much to eat—
A red ham-bone is surely sweet.
I see that you have lion's feet;   50

---

[1] 'Ideas are raging through the brains of even the duski-
est of the negro leaders, and one can handle for such
an audience almost any large thought he thinks he understands. He can put it into negro poetry, I maintain,
if he is man enough, and still have it negro poetry. But
he must keep his manner bright-colored, full-throated,
relaxed and tropical. By the manner I do not mean dialect. There are innumerable Pullman porters who speak
English in a close approach to the white man's way.
But their thoughts and fancies are still straight from
the jungle. . . . "Simon Legree" is an Afro-American
grotesque, . . . is a serious attempt to record the
devil-fear that haunts the race, though it is written
with a humorous close. . . . Almost any reading negro, whatever his shrewd silence during working hours,
is bound to remember *Uncle Tom's Cabin* with gratitude, and John Brown as well. He is bound to have an
infinite variety of thoughts about them, grave and gay.'
Lindsay, *Poetry: A Magazine of Verse*, VIII,iii,146–47.

I see your frame is fat and fine,
I see you drink your poison wine—
Blood and burning turpentine.'

And the Devil said to Simon Legree:
'I like your style, so wicked and free.
Come sit and share my throne with me,
And let us bark and revel.'
And there they sit and gnash their teeth,
And each one wears a hop-vine wreath.
They are matching pennies and shooting
    craps,   60
They are playing poker and taking naps.
And old Legree is fat and fine:
He heats the fire, he drinks the wine—
Blood and burning turpentine—
    Down, down with the Devil;
    Down, down with the Devil;
    Down, down with the Devil.

                    1917

THE GHOST OF THE BUFFALOES

LAST night at black midnight I woke with a
    cry,
The windows were shaking, there was
    thunder on high,
The floor was atremble, the door was ajar,
White fires, crimson fires, shone from afar.
I rushed to the dooryard. The city was gone.
My home was a hut without orchard or
    lawn.
It was mud-smear and logs near a
    whispering stream,
Nothing else built by man could I see in
    my dream . . .
Then . . .
Ghost-kings came headlong, row upon
    row,   10
Gods of the Indians, torches aglow.

They mounted the bear and the elk and the
    deer,
And eagles gigantic, aged and sere,
They rode long-horn cattle, they cried
    'A-la-la.'
They lifted the knife, the bow, and the
    spear,
They lifted ghost-torches from dead fires
    below,
The midnight made grand with the cry
    'A-la-la.'
The midnight made grand with a red-god
    charge,
A red-god show,

A red-god show,   20
'A-la-la, a-la-la, a-la-la, a-la-la.'

With bodies like bronze, and terrible eyes
Came the rank and the file, with catamount
    cries,
Gibbering, yipping, with hollow-skull
    clacks,
Riding white bronchos with skeleton backs,
Scalp-hunters, beaded and spangled and
    bad,
Naked and lustful and foaming and mad,
Flashing primeval demoniac scorn,
Blood-thirst and pomp amid darkness
    reborn.
Power and glory that sleep in the grass   30
While the winds and the snows and the
    great rains pass.
They crossed the gray river, thousands
    abreast,
They rode in infinite lines to the west,
Tide upon tide of strange fury and foam,
Spirits and wraiths, the blue was their home,
The sky was their goal where the star-flags
    were furled,
And on past those far golden splendors they
    whirled.
They burned to dim meteors, lost in the
    deep.
And I turned in dazed wonder, thinking of
    sleep.

And the wind crept by   40
Alone, unkempt, unsatisfied,
The wind cried and cried—
Muttered of massacres long past,
Buffaloes in shambles vast . . .
An owl said: 'Hark, what is a-wing?'
I heard a cricket carolling,
I heard a cricket carolling,
I heard a cricket carolling.

Then . . .
Snuffing the lightning that crashed from on
    high   50
Rose royal old buffaloes, row upon row.
The lords of the prairie came galloping by.
And I cried in my heart 'A-la-la, a-la-la,
A red-god show,
A red-god show,
A-la-la, a-la-la, a-la-la, a-la-la.'

Buffaloes, buffaloes, thousands abreast,
A scourge and amazement, they swept to
    the west.

With black bobbing noses, with red rolling
    tongues,
Coughing forth steam from their leather-
    wrapped lungs,   60
Cows with their calves, bulls big and vain,
Goring the laggards, shaking the mane,
Stamping flint feet, flashing moon eyes
Pompous and owlish, shaggy and wise.
Like sea-cliffs and caves resounded their
    ranks
With shoulders like waves, and undulant
    flanks.
Tide upon tide of strange fury and foam,
Spirits and wraiths, the blue was their
    home,
The sky was their goal where the star-flags
    are furled,
And on past those far golden splendors they
    whirled.   70
They burned to dim meteors, lost in the
    deep,
And I turned in dazed wonder, thinking of
    sleep.

I heard a cricket's cymbals play,
A scarecrow lightly flapped his rags,
And a pan that hung by his shoulder
    rang,
Rattled and thumped in a listless way,
And now the wind in the chimney sang,
The wind in the chimney,
The wind in the chimney,
The wind in the chimney,   80
    Seemed to say:—
'Dream, boy, dream,
If you anywise can.
To dream is the work
Of beast or man.
Life is the west-going dream-storms'
    breath,
Life is a dream, the sigh of the skies,
The breath of the stars, that nod on their
    pillows
With their golden hair mussed over their
    eyes.'
The locust played on his musical wing,   90
Sang to his mate of love's delight.
I heard the whippoorwill's soft fret.
I heard a cricket carolling,
I heard a cricket carolling,
I heard a cricket say: 'Good-night,
    good-night,
Good-night, good-night, . . .
    good-night.'

1914   1917

THE BRONCHO THAT WOULD NOT BE BROKEN [1]

A LITTLE colt—broncho, loaned to the
    farm
To be broken in time without fury or harm,
Yet black crows flew past you, shouting
    alarm,
Calling 'Beware,' with lugubrious
    singing . . .
The butterflies there in the bush were
    romancing,
The smell of the grass caught your soul in a
    trance,
So why be a-fearing the spurs and the
    traces,
O broncho that would not be broken of
    dancing?

You were born with the pride of the lords
    great and olden
Who danced, through the ages, in corridors
    golden.   10
In all the wide farm-place the person most
    human.
You spoke out so plainly with squealing and
    capering,
With whinnying, snorting, contorting and
    prancing,
As you dodged your pursuers, looking
    askance,
With Greek-footed figures, and Parthenon
    paces,
O broncho that would not be broken of
    dancing.

The grasshoppers cheered. 'Keep
    whirling,' they said.
The insolent sparrows called from the
    shed
'If men will not laugh, make them wish
    they were dead.'
But arch were your thoughts, all malice
    displacing,   20
Though the horse-killers came, with snake-
    whips advancing.
You bantered and cantered away your last
    chance.

1 Lindsay felt something of himself in this broncho
whose breaking he saw on one of his journeys. He
wrote: 'The broncho should not have been called Dick.
He should have been called Daniel Boone, or Davy
Crockett or Custer or Richard, yes, Richard the Lion
Hearted. . . . I think I want on my coat of arms a
broncho, rampant.' Lindsay, *Adventures while Preaching* . . . (N.Y., 1914),136-37.

And they scourged you, with Hell in their
    speech and their faces,
O broncho that would not be broken of
    dancing.

'Nobody cares for you,' rattled the crows,
As you dragged the whole reaper, next day
    down the rows.
The three mules held back, yet you danced
    on your toes.
You pulled like a racer, and kept the mules
    chasing.
You tangled the harness with bright eyes
    side-glancing,
While the drunk driver bled you—a pole
    for a lance—   30
And the giant mules bit at you—keeping
    their places.
O broncho that would not be broken of
    dancing.

In that last afternoon your boyish heart
    broke.
The hot wind came down like a sledge-
    hammer stroke.
The blood-sucking flies to a rare feast
    awoke.
And they searched out your wounds, your
    death-warrant tracing.
And the merciful men, their religion
    enhancing,
Stopped the red reaper, to give you a
    chance.
Then you died on the prairie, and scorned
    all disgraces,
O broncho that would not be broken of
    dancing.   40
                      1917

THE CHINESE NIGHTINGALE [1]

A Song in Chinese Tapestries

'How, how,' he said. 'Friend Chang,' I
    said,
'San Francisco sleeps as the dead—
Ended license, lust and play:
Why do you iron the night away?

Your big clock speaks with a deadly sound,
With a tick and a wail till dawn comes
    round.
While the monster shadows glower and
    creep,
What can be better for man than sleep?'

'I will tell you a secret,' Chang replied;
'My breast with vision is satisfied,   10
And I see green trees and fluttering wings,
And my deathless bird from Shanghai
    sings.'
Then he lit five firecrackers in a pan.
'Pop, pop,' said the firecrackers,
    'cra-cra-crack.'
He lit a joss stick long and black.
Then the proud gray joss in the corner
    stirred;
On his wrist appeared a gray small bird,
And this was the song of the gray small
    bird:
'Where is the princess, loved forever,
Who made Chang first of the kings of
    men?'   20

And the joss in the corner stirred again;
And the carved dog, curled in his arms,
    awoke,
Barked forth a smoke-cloud that whirled
    and broke.
It piled in a maze round the ironing-place,
And there on the snowy table wide
Stood a Chinese lady of high degree,
With a scornful, witching, tea-rose
    face. . . .
Yet she put away all form and pride,
And laid her glimmering veil aside
With a childlike smile for Chang and for
    me.   30

The walls fell back, night was aflower,
The table gleamed in a moonlit bower,
While Chang, with a countenance carved of
    stone,
Ironed and ironed, all alone.
And thus she sang to the busy man Chang:
'Have you forgotten . . .
Deep in the ages, long, long ago,
I was your sweetheart, there on the sand—
Storm-worn beach of the Chinese land?

---

[1] 'Mr. Lindsay wrote "The Chinese Nightingale" in
Springfield and New York, between May and October,
1914, while his father and mother were in China visiting their son-in-law and daughter, who are medical
missionaries at Lu-Chow-Fu. The poet, who has never
seen China himself, says of the poem: "The intention
of the piece is to combine such elements of Chinese
decoration and whim as are to be found by the superficial observer in the curio-store, the chop-suey restaurant, the laundry, the Chinese theatre. To these are to
be added such general ideas of China as may be acquired in any brief résumé of their religion, their cus-
toms and temperament." ' *Poetry: A Magazine of
Verse*, V.v.247.

We sold our grain in the peacock town— 40
Built on the edge of the sea-sands brown—
Built on the edge of the sea-sands
    brown. . . .

When all the world was drinking blood
From the skulls of men and bulls
And all the world had swords and clubs of
    stone,
We drank our tea in China beneath the
    sacred spice-trees,
And heard the curled waves of the harbor
    moan.
And this gray bird, in Love's first spring,
With a bright-bronze breast and a bronze-
    brown wing,
Captured the world with his carolling.   50
Do you remember, ages after,
At last the world we were born to own?
You were the heir of the yellow throne—
The world was the field of the Chinese
    man
And we were the pride of the sons of Han?
We copied deep books and we carved in
    jade,
And wove blue silks in the mulberry
    shade. . . .'

'I remember, I remember
That Spring came on forever,
That Spring came on forever,'   60
Said the Chinese nightingale.

My heart was filled with marvel and dream,
Though I saw the western street-lamps
    gleam,
Though dawn was bringing the western
    day,
Though Chang was a laundryman ironing
    away. . . .
Mingled there with the streets and alleys,
The railroad-yard and the clock-tower
    bright,
Demon clouds crossed ancient valleys;
Across wide lotus-ponds of light
I marked a giant firefly's flight.   70

And the lady, rosy-red,
Flourished her fan, her shimmering fan,
Stretched her hand toward Chang, and
    said:
'Do you remember,
Ages after,
Our palace of heart-red stone?
Do you remember

The little doll-faced children
With their lanterns full of moon-fire,
That came from all the empire   80
Honoring the throne?—
The loveliest fête and carnival
Our world had ever known?
The sages sat about us
With their heads bowed in their beards.
With proper meditation on the sight.
Confucius was not born;
We lived in those great days
Confucius later said were lived aright. . . .
And this gray bird, on that day of spring,   90
With a bright-bronze breast and a bronze-
    brown wing,
Captured the world with his carolling.
Late at night his tune was spent.
Peasants,
Sages,
Children,
Homeward went,
And then the bronze bird sang for you and
    me.
We walked alone. Our hearts were high and
    free.
I had a silvery name, I had a silvery
    name,   100
I had a silvery name—do you remember
The name you cried beside the tumbling
    sea?'

Chang turned not to the lady slim—
He bent to his work, ironing away;
But she was arch, and knowing and
    glowing,
For the bird on his shoulder spoke for him.

'Darling . . . darling . . . darling . . .
    darling . . .'
Said the Chinese nightingale.

. . . .

The great gray joss on the rustic shelf,
Rakish and shrewd, with his collar awry,
Sang impolitely, as though by himself,   111
Drowning with his bellowing the
    nightingale's cry:
'Back through a hundred, hundred years
Hear the waves as they climb the piers,
Hear the howl of the silver seas,
Hear the thunder.
Hear the gongs of holy China
How the waves and tunes combine
In a rhythmic clashing wonder,

Incantation old and fine: 120
   "Dragons, dragons, Chinese dragons,
   Red firecrackers, and green firecrackers,
   And dragons, dragons, Chinese
      dragons." '

Then the lady, rosy-red,
Turned to her lover Chang and said:
'Dare you forget that turquoise dawn
When we stood in our mist-hung velvet
    lawn,
And worked a spell this great joss taught,
Till a God of the Dragons was charmed and
    caught?
From the flag high over our palace home   130
He flew to our feet in rainbow-foam—
A king of beauty and tempest and thunder
Panting to tear our sorrows asunder,
A dragon of fair adventure and wonder.
We mounted the back of that royal slave
With thoughts of desire that were noble and
    grave.
We swam down the shore to the dragon-
    mountains,
We whirled to the peaks and the fiery
    fountains.
To our secret ivory house we were borne.
We looked down the wonderful wing-filled
    regions   140
Where the dragons darted in glimmering
    legions.
Right by my breast the nightingale sang;
The old rhymes rang in the sunlit mist
That we this hour regain—
Song-fire for the brain.
When my hands and my hair and my feet
    you kissed,
When you cried for your heart's new
    pain,
What was my name in the dragon-mist,
In the rings of rainbowed rain?'

'Sorrow and love, glory and love,'   150
Said the Chinese nightingale.
'Sorrow and love, glory and love,'
Said the Chinese nightingale.

And now the joss broke in with his song:
'Dying ember, bird of Chang,
Soul of Chang, do you remember?—
Ere you returned to the shining harbor
There were pirates by ten thousand
Descended on the town
In vessels mountain-high and red and
    brown,   160

Moon-ships that climbed the storms and
    cut the skies.
On their prows were painted terrible bright
    eyes.
But I was then a wizard and a scholar and a
    priest;
I stood upon the sand;
With lifted hand I looked upon them
And sunk their vessels with my wizard
    eyes,
And the stately lacquer-gate made safe
    again.
Deep, deep below the bay, the seaweed and
    the spray,
Embalmed in amber every pirate lies,
Embalmed in amber every pirate lies.'   170

Then this did the noble lady say:
'Bird, do you dream of our home-coming
    day
When you flew like a courier on before
From the dragon-peak to our palace-door,
And we drove the steed in your singing
    path—
The ramping dragon of laughter and
    wrath:
And found our city all aglow,
And knighted this joss that decked it so?
There were golden fishes in the purple river
And silver fishes and rainbow fishes.   180
There were golden junks in the laughing
    river,
And silver junks and rainbow junks:
There were golden lilies by the bay and
    river,
And silver lilies and tiger-lilies,
And tinkling wind-bells in the gardens of
    the town
By the black-lacquer gate
Where walked in state
The kind king Chang
And his sweetheart mate. . . .
With his flag-born dragon   190
And his crown of pearl . . . and . . .
    jade,
And his nightingale reigning in the
    mulberry shade,
And sailors and soldiers on the sea-sands
    brown,
And priests who bowed them down to your
    song—
By the city called Han, the peacock town,
By the city called Han, the nightingale
    town,
   The nightingale town.'

Then sang the bird, so strangely gay,
Fluttering, fluttering, ghostly and
      gray,
A vague, unravelling, final tune,   200
Like a long unwinding silk cocoon;
Sang as though for the soul of him
Who ironed away in that bower dim:—

   'I have forgotten
   Your dragons great,
   Merry and mad and friendly and
      bold.
Dim is your proud lost palace-gate.
I vaguely know
There were heroes of old,
Troubles more than the heart could
      hold,   210
There were wolves in the woods
Yet lambs in the fold,
Nests in the top of the almond tree. . . .
The evergreen tree . . . and the mulberry
      tree . . .
Life and hurry and joy forgotten,

Years on years I but half-remember . . .
Man is a torch, then ashes soon,
May and June, then dead December,
Dead December, then again June.
Who shall end my dream's confusion?   220
Life is a loom, weaving illusion . . .
I remember, I remember
There were ghostly veils and laces . . .
In the shadowy bowery places . . .
With lovers' ardent faces
Bending to one another,
Speaking each his part.
They infinitely echo
In the red cave of my heart.
"Sweetheart, sweetheart, sweetheart,"   230
They said to one another.
They spoke, I think, of perils past.
They spoke, I think, of peace at last.
One thing I remember:
Spring came on forever,
Spring came on forever,'
Said the Chinese nightingale.
1914   1917

EDGAR LEE MASTERS

1869–

FROM SPOON RIVER ANTHOLOGY [1]

THE HILL

WHERE are Elmer, Herman, Bert, Tom and
      Charley,
The weak of will, the strong of arm, the
      clown, the boozer, the fighter?
All, all, are sleeping on the hill.

One passed in a fever,
One was burned in a mine,
One was killed in a brawl,
One died in a jail,
One fell from a bridge toiling for children
      and wife—·
All, all, are sleeping, sleeping, sleeping on
      the hill.

Where are Ella, Kate, Mag, Lizzie and
      Edith,   10
The tender heart, the simple soul, the loud,
      the proud, the happy one?—
All, all, are sleeping on the hill.

One died in shameful childbirth,
One of a thwarted love,
One at the hands of a brute in a brothel,
One of a broken pride, in the search for
      heart's desire,
One after life in far-away London and
      Paris
Was brought to her little space by Ella and
      Kate and Mag—
All, all, are sleeping, sleeping, sleeping on
      the hill.

[1] There are two hundred and forty-four characters in the book, not counting those who figure in the Spooniad and the Epilogue. There are nineteen stories developed by interrelated portraits. Practically every ordinary human occupation is covered, except those of the barber, the miller, the cobbler, the tailor and the garage man . . . and all these were depicted later in the New Spoon River. What critics overlook when they call the Anthology Zolaesque, and by doing so mean to degrade it, is the fact that when the book was put together in its definitive order, . . . the fools, the drunkards, the failures came first, the people of one-birth minds got second place, and the heroes and the enlightened spirits came last, a sort of Divine Comedy, which some critics were acute enough to point out at once.
   'The names I drew from both the Spoon River and the Sangamon river neighborhoods, combining first names here with surnames there, and taking some also from the constitutions and State papers of Illinois.' Masters, 'The Genesis of Spoon River,' *The American Mercury*, XXVIII,cix,50.

Where are Uncle Isaac and Aunt Emily, 20
And old Towny Kincaid and Sevigne
    Houghton,
And Major Walker who had talked
With venerable men of the revolution?—
All, all, are sleeping on the hill.

They brought them dead sons from the war,
And daughters whom life had crushed,
And their children fatherless, crying—
All, all, are sleeping, sleeping, sleeping on
    the hill.

Where is Old Fiddler Jones
Who played with life all his ninety years, 30
Braving the sleet with bared breast,
Drinking, rioting, thinking neither of wife
    nor kin,
Nor gold, nor love, nor heaven?
Lo! he babbles of the fish-frys of long ago,
Of the horse-races of long ago at Clary's
    Grove,
Of what Abe Lincoln said
One time at Springfield.

LUCINDA MATLOCK

I WENT to the dances at Chandlerville,
And played snap-out at Winchester.
One time we changed partners,
Driving home in the moonlight of middle
    June,
And then I found Davis.
We were married and lived together for
    seventy years,
Enjoying, working, raising the twelve
    children,
Eight of whom we lost
Ere I had reached the age of sixty.
I spun, I wove, I kept the house, I nursed
    the sick, 10
I made the garden, and for holiday
Rambled over the fields where sang the
    larks,
And by Spoon River gathering many a
    shell,
And many a flower and medicinal weed—
Shouting to the wooded hills, singing to the
    green valleys.
At ninety-six I had lived enough, that is all,
And passed a sweet repose.
What is this I hear of sorrow and weariness,
Anger, discontent and drooping hopes?
Degenerate sons and daughters, 20
Life is too strong for you—
It takes life to love Life.

THOMAS TREVELYAN

READING in Ovid the sorrowful story of Itys,
Son of the love of Tereus and Procne, slain
For the guilty passion of Tereus for
    Philomela,
The flesh of him served to Tereus by
    Procne,
And the wrath of Tereus, the murderess
    pursuing
Till the gods made Philomela a nightingale,
Lute of the rising moon, and Procne a
    swallow!
Oh livers and artists of Hellas centuries
    gone,
Sealing in little thuribles dreams and
    wisdom,
Incense beyond all price, forever fragrant,
A breath whereof makes clear the eyes of
    the soul! 11
How I inhaled its sweetness here in Spoon
    River!
The thurible opening when I had lived and
    learned
How all of us kill the children of love, and
    all of us,
Knowing not what we do, devour their
    flesh;
And all of us change to singers, although it
    be
But once in our lives, or change—alas!—to
    swallows,
To twitter amid cold winds and falling
    leaves!

FIDDLER JONES

THE earth keeps some vibration going
There in your heart, and that is you.
And if the people find you can fiddle,
Why, fiddle you must, for all your life
What do you see, a harvest of clover?
Or a meadow to walk through to the river?
The wind's in the corn; you rub your hands
For beeves hereafter ready for market;
Or else you hear the rustle of skirts
Like the girls when dancing at Little
    Grove. 10
To Cooney Potter a pillar of dust
Or whirling leaves meant ruinous drouth;
They looked to me like Red-Head Sammy
Stepping it off, to 'Toor-a-Loor.'
How could I till my forty acres
Not to speak of getting more,
With a medley of horns, bassoons and
    piccolos

Stirred in my brain by crows and robins
And the creak of a wind-mill—only these?
And I never started to plow in my life   20
That some one did not stop in the road
And take me away to a dance or picnic.
I ended up with forty acres;
I ended up with a broken fiddle—
And a broken laugh, and a thousand
        memories,
And not a single regret.

BENJAMIN PANTIER

TOGETHER in this grave lie Benjamin
        Pantier, attorney at law,
And Nig, his dog, constant companion,
        solace and friend.
Down the gray road, friends, children, men
        and women,
Passing one by one out of life, left me till I
        was alone
With Nig for partner, bed-fellow, comrade
        in drink.
In the morning of life I knew aspiration and
        saw glory.
Then she, who survives me, snared my
        soul
With a snare which bled me to death,
Till I, once strong of will, lay broken,
        indifferent,
Living with Nig in a room back of a dingy
        office.   10
Under my jaw-bone is snuggled the bony
        nose of Nig—
Our story is lost in silence. Go by, mad
        world!

MRS. BENJAMIN PANTIER

I KNOW that he told that I snared his soul
With a snare which bled him to death.
And all the men loved him,
And most of the women pitied him.
But suppose you are really a lady, and have
        delicate tastes,
And loathe the smell of whiskey and onions.
And the rhythm of Wordsworth's 'Ode'
        runs in your ears,
While he goes about from morning till
        night
Repeating bits of that common thing;
'Oh, why should the spirit of mortal be
        proud?'   10
And then, suppose:
You are a woman well endowed,
And the only man with whom the law and
        morality

Permit you to have the marital relation
Is the very man that fills you with disgust
Every time you think of it—while you think
        of it
Every time you see him?
That's why I drove him away from home
To live with his dog in a dingy room
Back of his office.   20

REUBEN PANTIER

WELL, Emily Sparks, your prayers were not
        wasted,
Your love was not all in vain.
I owe whatever I was in life
To your hope that would not give me up,
To your love that saw me still as good.
Dear Emily Sparks, let me tell you the
        story.
I pass the effect of my father and mother;
The milliner's daughter made me trouble
And out I went in the world,
Where I passed through every peril known
Of wine and women and joy of life.   11
One night, in a room in the Rue de Rivoli,
I was drinking wine with a black-eyed
        cocotte,
And the tears swam into my eyes.
She thought they were amorous tears and
        smiled
For thought of her conquest over me.
But my soul was three thousand miles
        away,
In the days when you taught me in Spoon
        River.
And just because you no more could love
        me,
Nor pray for me, nor write me letters,   20
The eternal silence of you spoke instead.
And the black-eyed cocotte took the tears
        for hers,
As well as the deceiving kisses I gave her.
Somehow, from that hour, I had a new
        vision—
Dear Emily Sparks!

EMILY SPARKS

WHERE is my boy, my boy—
In what far part of the world?
The boy I loved best of all in the school?—
I, the teacher, the old maid, the virgin
        heart,
Who made them all my children.
Did I know my boy aright,
Thinking of him as spirit aflame,
Active, ever aspiring?

Oh, boy, boy, for whom I prayed and
  prayed
In many a watchful hour at night,   10
Do you remember the letter I wrote you
Of the beautiful love of Christ?
And whether you ever took it or not,
My boy, wherever you are,
Work for your soul's sake,
That all the clay of you, all the dross of you,
May yield to the fire of you,
Till the fire is nothing but light! . . .
Nothing but light!

TRAINOR, THE DRUGGIST

ONLY the chemist can tell, and not always
  the chemist,
What will result from compounding
Fluids or solids.
And who can tell
How men and women will interact
On each other, or what children will result?
There were Benjamin Pantier and his wife,
Good in themselves, but evil toward each
  other:
He oxygen, she hydrogen,
Their son, a devastating fire.   10
I Trainor, the druggist, a mixer of
  chemicals,
Killed while making an experiment,
Lived unwedded.

DAISY FRASER

DID you ever hear of Editor Whedon
Giving to the public treasury any of the
  money he received
For supporting candidates for office?
Or for writing up the canning factory
To get people to invest?
Or for suppressing the facts about the bank,
When it was rotten and ready to break?
Did you ever hear of the Circuit Judge
Helping anyone except the 'Q' railroad,
Or the bankers? Or did Rev. Peet or Rev.
  Sibley   10
Give any part of their salary, earned by
  keeping still,
Or speaking out as the leaders wished them
  to do,
To the building of the water works?
But I, Daisy Fraser, who always passed
Along the streets through rows of nods and
  smiles,
And coughs and words such as 'there she
  goes,'
Never was taken before Justice Arnett

Without contributing ten dollars and costs
To the school fund of Spoon River!

ANNE RUTLEDGE

OUT of me unworthy and unknown
The vibrations of deathless music;
'With malice toward none, with charity for
  all.'
Out of me the forgiveness of millions
  toward millions,
And the beneficent face of a nation
Shining with justice and truth.
I am Anne Rutledge who sleep beneath
  these weeds,
Beloved in life of Abraham Lincoln,
Wedded to him, not through union,
But through separation.   10
Bloom forever, O Republic,
From the dust of my bosom!

THE VILLAGE ATHEIST

YE young debaters over the doctrine
Of the soul's immortality,
I who lie here was the village atheist,
Talkative, contentious, versed in the
  arguments
Of the infidels.
But through a long sickness
Coughing myself to death
I read the *Upanishads* and the poetry of
  Jesus.
And they lighted a torch of hope and
  intuition
And desire which the Shadow,   10
Leading me swiftly through the caverns of
  darkness,
Could not extinguish.
Listen to me, ye who live in the senses
And think through the senses only:
Immortality is not a gift,
Immortality is an achievement;
And only those who strive mightily
Shall possess it.

WILLIAM AND EMILY

THERE is something about Death
Like love itself!
If with some one with whom you have know
  passion,
And the glow of youthful love,
You also, after years of life
Together, feel the sinking of the fire,
And thus fade away together,
Gradually, faintly, delicately,
As it were in each other's arms,

Passing from the familiar room—   10
That is a power of unison between souls
Like love itself!
1914–1915   1915

FROM THE NEW SPOON RIVER

ROBERT CHAIN

THERE are two ways in life,
And I tried them both:
First a life of no change,
Life like a gull, which has no dream
But to be a gull, fly over the waters,
Seeking its food, and to nest and sleep!
And then I became a creature that nurses
Growth and mutation in the brain,
Swims to land and turns its fins to legs.
Sensing a shriveled life ahead,   10
And loathing the weary hour,
I changed myself to renew myself,
And lost myself!

FRANCES CORDELL

WHAT a moment of strange dying! Quickly
All my vision girdled earth and showed
        me
Temples in far India, tombs in Persia,
Down the Appian way, and over Florence,
Home of Dante, wandering place of
        Browning.
And how strange, how prying was the
        vision:
For the coffin of old Landor opened;
Showed me what was left of that imperi-
        ous,
Proud and lonely singer of strange beauty.
There he lay, gone down to bits of
        nothing—   10
Just a few stray hairs, a piece of shoulder,
Nothing else of him who wrote these
        verses:
'Proud word you never spoke, but in some
        future
'Day you will keep not speaking of me
        these words,
'Over my open volume you will linger,
'You will say in reading: "This man loved
        me." '
Who was she and where is gone her beauty?
In what place of cypress or of willows,
In what separation from her poet,
Lies the woman, never speaking proud
        words?   20
Only these, as I have said while reading:
'This man loved me,' tears upon the pages!

RICHARD HARNED

GOLDEN bees at the heart of violets,
Heavy with starry wine of the flower,
The lizard lurks for you there in the
        thickets
Armed in mimesis green as the leaves.
The emerald wasp is watching the clay pots,
All day filled with your spoil of the June;
The Fab in terminal scarf of azure,
And breast bedecked in Florentine gold
Thirsts for the fruit of your toil for
        children
Born of her, pressed by the will to life.   10
And the small gray flies come trooping
        after
Wasps and Fabs with shark toothed jaws.
What is it all but a great devouring?
What but Nature that passes us on
From stomach to stomach, till man the
        spirit
Fights against spirit, devouring, devoured?
Golden bees! I died believing
All mounts up to some finest life,
All is love, and the death of loving;
And if there is life that is higher than Art 20
It's peace that shines in God!

HENRY ZOLL, THE MILLER

HAVE you ever noticed the mill pond in the
        dog days?
How it breeds wriggling life,
And seethes and crackles with poisonous
        froth,
Then lies as still as a snake gone blind?
And how can the mill pond know itself
When its water has caked to scum and
        worms?
And how can it know the world or the sky
When it has no mirror with which to see
        them?
But the river above the bend is wise:
Its waters are swift and cold and clear,   10
Always changing and always fresh,
And full of ripples and swirls and waves,
That image a thousand stars by night,
And a thousand phases of sun and clouds,
By a changing movie of forest and hills!
And down in its healthful depths the
        pickerel
Chase each other like silver shadows;
And the swift game fish swim up the
        stream.
Well, this is the soul of a man, my friend:
You brood at first, then froth with regret, 20

Then cake with hatred, and sink to dullness;
Or else you struggle and keep on the move,
Forget and solve and learn and emerge,
Full of sparkle and stars.
And down in your depths there's flashing
    laughter,
Swimming against the current!

1924

JOHNNY APPLESEED [1]

WHEN the air of October is sweet and cold
    as the wine of apples
Hanging ungathered in frosted orchards
    along the Grand River,
I take the road that winds by the resting
    fields and wander
From Eastmanville to Nuncia down to the
    Villa Crossing.

I look for old men to talk with, men as old
    as the orchards,
Men to tell me of ancient days, of those who
    built and planted,
Lichen gray, branch broken, bent and
    sighing,
Hobbling for warmth in the sun and for
    places to sit and smoke.

For there is a legend here, a tale of the
    croaking old ones
That Johnny Appleseed came here,
    planted some orchards around here,
When nothing was here but the pine trees,
    oaks and the beeches,   11
And nothing was here but the marshes,
    lake and the river.

Peter Van Zylen is ninety and this he tells me:
My father talked with Johnny Appleseed
    there on the hill-side,
There by the road on the way to Fruitport,
    saw him
Clearing pines and oaks for a place for an
    apple orchard.

Peter Van Zylen says: He got that name
    from the people
For carrying apple-seed with him and
    planting orchards

[1] John Chapman (c.1775–1847), known as 'Johnny Appleseed,' was a Swedenborgian lover of nature who wandered through the Middle West, planting freely apple-orchards and herbs. His eccentricities and gentle goodness made him even in his own time into a half-legendary personage.

All the way from Ohio, through Indiana
    across here,
Planting orchards, they say, as far as
    Illinois.   20

Johnny Appleseed said, so my father told
    me:
I go to a place forgotten, the orchards will
    thrive and be here
For children to come, who will gather and
    eat hereafter.
And few will know who planted, and none
    will understand.

I laugh, said Johnny Appleseed: Some
    fellow buys this timber
Five years, perhaps from to-day, begins to
    clear for barley.
And here in the midst of the timber is
    hidden an apple orchard.
How did it come here? Lord! Who was it
    here before me?

Yes, I was here before him, to make these
    places of worship,
Labor and laughter and gain in the late
    October.   30
Why did I do it, eh? Some folks say I am
    crazy.
Where do my labors end? Far west, God
    only knows!

Said Johnny Appleseed there on the hill-
    side: Listen!
Beware the deceit of nurseries, sellers of
    seeds of the apple.
Think! You labor for years in trees not
    worth the raising.
You planted what you knew not, bitter or
    sour for sweet.

No luck more bitter than poor seed, but
    one as bitter:
The planting of perfect seed in soil that
    feeds and fails,
Nourishes for a little, and then goes spent
    forever.
Look to your seed, he said, and remember
    the soil.   40

And after that is the fight: the foe curled up
    at the root,
The scale that crumples and deadens, the
    moth in the blossoms,

Becoming a life that coils at the core of a
    thing of beauty:
You bite your apple, a worm is crushed on
    your tongue!

And it's every bit the truth, said Peter Van
    Zylen.
So many things love an apple as well as
    ourselves.
A man must fight for the thing he loves, to
    possess it:
Apples, freedom, heaven, said Peter Van
    Zylen.

1918   1918

BEETHOVEN'S NINTH SYMPHONY
AND THE KING COBRA

I

In the days of steaming swamps and tropic
    ferns,
When life was fermenting and crackling,
    and trying to escape
The trance of Nature, and get beyond itself,
Footless creatures chose legs, and
    conquered the land.
Then they abandoned the conquest, and
    took back to the water,
And became the drooling sea-crocodile,
The laughing mosasaur,
And the silly giant called the ichthyosaur,
And the pleisiosaur, with a mouth like a
    goose,
All flapping, floundering, and laughing to
    be back in the water,   10
Unenvious of their relatives who got wings,
And long tails, and bat-like rudders,
And turtle-beaks, which stood agape,
    grinning like Moloch,
Roosting on sun-hot rocks.

Those were the days when there was
    nothing but demons,
Nothing but horns, hoofs, teeth and fangs.

Somewhere here the crawling, footless,
    coiling
Worm of hell lost his father and mother,
And went on without ancestors, and
    without memory of ancestors,
Or any worship of ancestors, and ended up
    as hell's perfection,   20
Ended as the cobra, crawling forever as
    abandoned diabolism,

As embodied hate and sullen loneliness.
But the footless creatures who clove to the
    land,
And longed till their ears could catch
Something beside this sound and the next
    sound,
Sounds without recurring periods and
    pauses,
Without continuity or rhythm;
The footless creatures which longed
    themselves to claws,
And then longed their claws to fingers,
Which at last could set down the signs of
    eternity for oboes,   30
For clarinets, horns and strings—
These footless creatures started the breed
    which fathered Beethoven at last;
And thus came the finale, the
    consummation:
Beethoven and the King Cobra.

2

Nature is a sleeping spirit.
Nature is a trance, a mass drugged by
    eternity,
A petrifaction, a solid jelly, a self-
    containment,
A contemplation which cannot arise from
    itself,
Or get out of itself, or look upon itself.
Man has escaped from this deep catalepsy:
He has soared up, and can look down;   41
He has flown forward, and can glance back;
He can turn upon the past, and see the
    future.
But as he ages he ceases gradually to be
    outside himself,
Or see himself.
He becomes again all-self-contained,
    reduced to one mood of Nature,
Reduced to the eye which contemplates,
    but does not know.
So he descends to the mind of the cobra,
On the way to the unconsciousness of
    Nature,
Which is Death, the cobra's cousin.   50

Nature is spirit, but the spirit of calm
    swamp-slush;
Nature is unconscious, but it casts upon
    matter
The reflection of what has created Nature.
Nature as the whole of things lies locked in
    the unconsciousness

Which is the primal condition of all
    terraqueous things.
The same power which slumbers in the
    stone,
And dreams in the flower, and sends
    half-legged beings
Out of the water to the land, then back to
    the water,
And into trees, and on to rocks—
This same power awakes in the cobra;   60
It awakes in Beethoven.
It awakes when anything separates itself
    from Nature,
And becomes two instead of one;
And becomes outside as well as inside;
And becomes something more than a
    landscape's mood,
Something more than a motionless eye;
Becomes in truth an eye that knows
    enemies,
And a head that knows that pain is in the
    flesh,
And comes from turning from one to
    two;
And that pain brings something into
    existence   70
Which is an advance upon a mere stare.

It is here that a separation takes place
    between Nature, the creator,
And any mind created.
Pain is the penalty, and fear, both births of
    consciousness.
And thus with this state of being common
    to both Beethoven and the cobra
Beethoven can disturb the cobra
By shocking its ear to be aware of sounds
    and octaves
Too much for an ear which is a tympanum
    and cochlea of mere snake grisle and
    bone,
Murmurous with its swamp nativity, and
    fitted to listen
For enemies and food, nothing else;   80
For the sound of a twig snapping, not
    polyphones.

What but irritation, disturbance,
What but annoyance and pain,
Made the thing at one with Nature
Become the thing escaped and fighting
    Nature,
Both because it resists being jailed again,
And because it resents ever being turned
    loose?

What are irritation, disturbance, annoyance,
    pain?
Are they not evil?
So Beethoven's music must be evil to the
    cobra,   90
For it forces the cobra's ear to do more than
    listen
For enemies and for food.
The cobra evoked from the great trance
Continues as an evil, we say.
But Beethoven so evoked after long aeons
Is he not evil, too?
Is he truth and beauty, yet a sufferer, and
    producing suffering?
Is he truth and beauty, who awakens
    greater consciousness?
Or is he continued evil, bringing pain and
    despair,
And deeper looks into the nothingness
    whence we came,   100
And a forecast of the resumption of sleep
    whither we tend?
Is he then evil as he shows these things to
    the full?
Does he not disturb us, as he does the
    cobra,
Which crawls and writhes and lifts itself
As it hears Beethoven through oboes
Tell of his sorrows and sufferings,
The neglect that the world heaped upon
    him,
His poverty and loneliness,
Loneliness as lonely as this glass-cage of the
    cobra;
All of which Beethoven uttered in music,
    and in the cry: 110
'I have no friend,
'I am alone in the world.
'O God, my Rock, my All,
'Thou Unutterable, hear Thy unhappy,
'Thy most unhappy of mortals.'
Is not the cobra also alone and unhappy?
And these cries of Beethoven
Do they not set vibrating
The unutterable, and the unhappy,
And the loneliness which is the cobra?   120

3

Beethoven was miserable, in agony, in the
    trap of life.
But the king cobra is all misery, all agony,
All embodied evil, being by Nature trapped
    to be within itself,
And by man trapped to be within this glass
    cage.

It is trapped by being fated to be constantly
    aware of its venom genius,
That is the groundwork, the essence and all
    of its being;
And the shape of its head, the stare of its
    eyes show this.
With this goes the sense of enmity between
    the cobra and man,
And fear of man, and fear of the jungle and
    night; and that is being trapped.
Its life is poison, and that is its wisdom also;
    and that is being trapped. 130
Its wisdom is hate for the Power which has
    invented traps,
Hate for the Power which has trapped its
    thought in a shallow skull,
And locked its thought in a trap of
    contemplation,
Where all the traps are contemplated
    dimly.
It is trapped to the life of sensuous
    particulars,
While the whole teases, and is never
    known,
The whole is a slowed-down film.
It is trapped by will without knowledge;
It is trapped by a small speck of brain
    plasm
From which has issued narrow channels 140
Of sight and hearing,
Through which the world of visible and
    audible things:
Man the keeper before the cage, standing
    safe;
And Beethoven with strings, clarinets and
    horns
Gorges through like a freshet, and bursts
    the channels, and tortures the brain.
It is trapped when guessing the life blisses
    of other creatures;
It is trapped, being shut from some realer
    realm of life;
It is trapped, and compelled to crawl and
    coil,
And lick forth a tongue to aid half-eyes;
It is trapped in loneliness, not able to live
    loneliness as the soul can, 150
Not able in loneliness to sink into the trance
    of the ancient swamps;
But by its loneliness made more aware
Of its separateness, and of enemies and
    dangers without—
Such a curse upon anything that can feel!
Such loneliness at the dark bottom-point of
    hell's cone!

It is trapped by dim memory of heredity,
But kept from going back to water,
And kept from taking to the air,
And cut off bitterly from the lineage of
    man:
For man descended not from the snake, 160
But from old, patriarchal, drowsy,
    dreaming reptiles.
It is trapped to the life of the jungle
    forever;
It is trapped by hate of the Cause of
    consciousness,
And it brews venom in revenge.
It is trapped forever to the shape of a
    gorilla's cylindrical excrement;
It is stripped and exposed forever like the
    phallus of Polyphemus,
The horror and disgust of worst and best
    eyes!
It is trapped by regret for vanished æons of
    earth
When there was peace in the pulse of the
    earth mood
Which made a oneness of plants, rocks,
    ooze, and primordial plasm. 170
It is trapped because the chance is now
    gone forever to get feet or wings,
    and fly the jungle.
It is trapped by the will which has made
    this elongated frightfulness,
The will—from what source?—which has
    made
Teeth and fangs and poison,
And the hunger of cannibalism.
For there is a Dual Thing
Which might have made the cobra half
    good,
Not all evil.
And this the cobra feels, and licks forth its
    forked tongue
In hate of this Dual Thing. 180
It is trapped by the power within it
From the Power without it, which has
    implanted in it
This insane will of dealing death.
It is trapped by being the contemplation of
    the motionless eye,
Where no smile lurks, no sense of
    voluptuous content;
But where alert malice sparkles and burns,
    and winks like a half-ashed coal,
And flashes hate and hunger and irritable
    watchfulness.
It is trapped by being engendered and then
    spurned by a superior soul;

It is trapped by being set aside and
    deserted by a soul becoming
    superior as man, as Beethoven;
It is trapped by being life which looks
    neither to what is above,   190
Nor to what is below,
But to what is ahead in the weeds, the
    gopher snake as food.
And thus barred from worlds and worlds of
    life,
And crushed by exultant trumpets,
By horns and strings,
And by drums that echo frightful dangers
    and depths
The cobra lies stretched in the cage with
    motionless eye.
The cobra is a monist. All is Hate,
And the cobra is all hate.
The cobra is the hate of man, made pure
    poison,   200
Condensed in one organism of
    flesh,
For life as horror, as cancer, as war,
As ruin and unreason and madness.

4

It is more than a hundred years past and
    gone
Since Beethoven cried:
'God, O God, my Guardian, my Rock, my
    All!
'Thou seest my heart, and knowest how it
    distresses me
'To do harm to others, though doing right
    to my darling Karl.
'Hear, Thou Unutterable, hear Thy
    unhappy,
'Most unhappy of mortals: 210
'I have no friend, and am alone in the
    world.'

Shall this cry never die out?
Never be hushed as the crackling of weeds
    is hushed
After the giant thunder-lizard has walked
    on?
Shall it never vanish as the rib-marks of the
    serpent in the sand
Are erased by the wind?
It is more than a hundred years now since
    Beethoven
Set down his misery and his ecstasy,
His wounded and baffled spirit,
His climbing and sun-lit and triumphant
    spirit   220

In dots and curves, in numerals and time
    signatures,
In key signatures, in braves and semi-
    braves,
In major and minor keys, and ledger lines
    and clefs,
In bars of duple, triple and quadruple time,
    in rests and scales,
In indications for winds and strings,
Flutes, horns, bassoons, and viols—
All set down, and all to say in harmony:
Alone! Alone! Alone!
All set down so to direct forever the players
    of instruments
How to pass from the earthquake rumble of
    the lost city of the soul   230
To the sunlight and song of the safe slopes;
How to pass with whisperings and
    falterings,
Almost as of children in fear,
To fathomless depths of courage and
    wisdom;
How to pace the harmony of the going-out,
And the returning-in of the blood of the
    Universe,
When the heart of the Great Law opens and
    closes its valves.
And how with plucked strings of
    summoned courage,
And the clamor of drums, to climb, to
    stand
Where no cobra crawls, no devil walks,   240
No charms of hell are worked;
And where the silence of a great summit
Opens out as a flower trembles and unfolds,
Revealing the drone of spheres, the song,
    the infinite music
Of light, which is also sound,
And which is impulse at the root of all
    motion,
And which is without end in space or time.

It is more than a hundred years since the
    secrets
Of Beethoven's soul, of his vision,
Were noted on paper in these cryptograms.
Yet, and because this was done   251
Beethoven's suffering and rapture
    reverberate still,
And by the instantaneous penetration of
    invisible fire
Can pass through granite, through steel,
    through measureless space;
Can pass through the glass of the cobra's
    cage,

And assail the stagnant, green-scum of his
    hate,
Lying sprawled with motionless eye,
Neither immersed in the unconsciousness
    of Nature,
Nor separated from it, and by that truth in
    mastery of it.
So by magnetic waves of fire   260
Does Beethoven enter the cage of the cobra,
And start to torture it with colossal
    mystery,
Which the cobra cannot strike.
The cobra can only weave and writhe and
    stretch,
And lift up long lengths of its body in the
    corner,
And crawl and lie with slight shivers, like
    the flank of a fly-plagued horse—
All before a presence invulnerable to fangs
    and venom.

The king cobra has much attention just
    now:
An oyster-white thickness has overgrown
    his right eye,
So that he sees only with his left eye.   270
The cobra has shed his skin several times,
And each time has failed to slough off
The scale from his right eye.
And now he must be helped by his keeper,
Or the eye will be wholly blind, and that
    will double his loneliness,
As much so as deafness increased the
    loneliness of Beethoven.
The oyster-white thickness is seven-
    layered,
Made up of semi-globular beads,
Half translucent, but massed together
    impenetrable to light.
And the cobra should see, says the cobra's
    keeper.   280
Hence the keeper traps him into a box,
Where the cobra's head is held while the
    oyster scales are snipped off.
The cobra was fierce with anger, and
    fought.
But when the cobra looked from that eye,
And could see the black and white of the
    cage,
Like squares embroidered on canvas,
(Having no yellow spot in either eye),
It acted glad, and glided happily on to the
    floor of the cage again,
And devoured a five-foot gopher snake
Provided for it by the keeper;   290

Devoured the gopher snake as a man kills
    and eats a hog or steer,
Or as men destroy men in business or war.
The cobra took the gopher snake by the
    head,
And swallowed it inch by inch, foot by foot,
All the way down, gurgitating its spasms,
Until only the end of the tail flicked,
And vanished.

5

This is the way Beethoven entered the cage
    of the cobra:
The next day after the seven-fold scale was
    removed,
The next day after the cobra swallowed the
    gopher snake,   300
The Ninth Symphony was played at the
    Park;
And the keeper turned on the radio in the
    reptile room
To see what the cobra would do,
When the sounds of the Scherzo, and the
    Ode to Joy
Echoed and re-echoed about the stone
    walls.
The cobra was lying outstretched with
    motionless eye;
He was not hungry—he had swallowed the
    gopher snake the day before.
He wanted no mate—the rutting season
    was past.
He could see—the seven-fold scale had
    been snipped.
He lay there slick as a gray, glazed cob-web,
Dulled like slimed nacre, and yellow   311
As the inside of a clam-shell, and gray as
    agate.
He was a length of dimmed iridescence of
    saffron and pearl,
And scaled like the permian gar-fish,
Or the legs of the ancient archæopterix.
What but an enemy or music could disturb
    him?
Thus he lay calm as hate which is softly
    seething
When the radio began to sound,
As the musicians at the Park took the soul
    of Beethoven
From the dots, dashes, signs and symbols
    of score sheets,   320
And gave it voice as lettered there, forever
    sealed, and forever unsealed at will
As the echo of Beethoven's soul echoing the
    Great Mystery somewhere,

Not as an imitation of Nature, or of
    anything in Nature,
But as a response to Something,
Even as the agitation of the cobra is a
    response to Beethoven.

The second violins and cellos, the first
    violins, tenors and basses
Begin to whisper their way from the top to
    the bottom of the treble stave
To the bottom of the bass.
A clarinet breaks in like the call of a
    lonesome summer bird;
And one by one the wind-instruments
    enter,   330
And then the flutes and oboes divide the
    lamentation.
They are saying: 'God, O God, my
    Guardian,
'My Rock, my All! Hear Thou,
    Unutterable,
'Hear Thy unhappy, most unhappy of
    mortals.'

6

The cobra stirs;
The cobra sends a ripple of skin down its
    length.
The cobra knows nothing of poverty: it has
    swallowed the gopher snake.
The cobra knows nothing of a nephew's
    ingratitude,
Or the slight of friends, or the neglect of the
    world,
Or the hatefulness of business.   340
But this is restless music, and the cobra
    grows restless.
This is sound which is first impatience, and
    then melancholy;
And the cobra grows impatient, melancholy
    waves stir him.
For fire can burn beings which know not
    what fire is.
This is tenderness, and the cobra resents
    tenderness,
As he would strike the hand that petted his
    head.
These sorrows of Beethoven have found the
    language of sound
Through magnetic waves, which are light
    and vibration,
And vibrating themselves set vibrations
    singing and surging
In the cobra itself, which becomes thus
    vibrating particles.   350

The waves of Beethoven's music advance
    through the cobra's nerves,
Making rhythmic motions of the particles
    in the nerves of the cobra,
And that is like a man in pain before the
    mystery of his fate.

The cobra shifts his place, and licks forth
    his tongue.
He may be shocked into hereditary memory
    of the steaming swamps
When the tyrannosaur and the diplodocus
    went mad,
And trampled the lizards and the crocodiles,
And the first snake one hundred feet long;
And when the pteranodon with twenty-
    four feet of outstretched wings
Flapped in fear among the fronds   360
Of gigantic tree ferns.
This may be the cause of the cobra's
    shifting and moving;
Or it may be only that this sound stirs
    him,
As fire would stir him, or the tap of the
    keeper on the glass of the cage.
But he does not crawl from his place yet.
Like a rope slightly shaken a rhythm goes
    through him
From head to tail, but he keeps his place
Amid the reverberating music of
    Beethoven.

The Scherzo changes all.
Beethoven's soul stepped from darkness to
    brilliant light,   370
From despair to the rapture of strength
Overcoming the world.
Beethoven caught the spirit of a fresh May
    morning,
And it inspired him to exult with trumpets
    and strings,
And drums and trombones.
There are no such mornings in the jungle.
The rhythm of three bars changed to the
    rhythm of four bars
Is nothing less than the secret ecstasy of
    May;
It is nothing less than the thrill of life
Making the worm feel the blisses of
    creation,   380
And making man himself a dweller with
    Eternity.

And now this ecstatic storm of harmony
Is not only the voices of strong men,

And the creak of great pulleys worked by
    them
To lift colossal blocks of granite to the
    terraces
Of timeless pyramids;
It is not merely discords resolved;
It is not the mere toppling and crash of
    colossi,
Followed by the silence of Egyptian palm
    groves;
It is not merely the audible silence   390
Which comes before the hollow sound,
And is followed by the hollow silence
When covers are lifted and placed on great
    earthen jars
Which have been filled with water for
    thirsty villages.
It is not merely the trumpeting of
    mastodons
Amid carboniferous thickets,
Or along level valleys of lava and giant
    cactus—
It is not merely these,
Nor merely Democritus laughing and
    shouting as he chases the
    discovered atom
Near the orbit of Uranus where time and
    space become one;   400
It is not merely any of these.
But it is the song of infinite cranes
Lifting worlds into their orbits;
It is the deep sighing of æons of time;
It is the chuckle of vast ages;
It is the puffing and the halloos of periodic
    cycles
Toiling up the spirals of infinitude;
It is the sound of smooth-lipped lids of
    crystal
Being placed on the huge vials of despair
    and fear,
After their bitter waters have been poured
    into the flaming rivers   410

Of all old Hells to the roar of steam.
It is the sound of ponderable slabs
Being laid and fitted to the sarcophagi of
    dead demi-gorgons;
It is the happy laughter from the cradle of
    the infant Heracles
As he strangled the snakes sent by the
    enmity of Hera;
It is the shout of Heracles despising the
    common kingdom
Of which Hera, the jealous goddess,
    deprived him.
It is the howl of fire from worlds which
    should be burned,
Amid the drift and swirl of apocalyptic
    smoke;
It is the splash of the lake of fire   420
When death is hurled down and engulfed;
It is the thunder of mountain-high gates
    being opened,
Which reveal the landscapes of eternity;
It is the shout and the song of Apollo
As he races and shoots arrows after fleeing
    dragons.
It is the chant of the sun as god of this
    world,
Worthy of worship as the source of life!

7

And now it was that the keeper returned to
    the cage
To see what the cobra was doing.
The cobra had crawled to the corner.   430
It had lifted one third of its length aloft
There in the corner;
It was reaching up with its head, licking out
    its tongue;
It was leaning back unsteadily being unable
    to hold
So much of its length aloft
There in the presence of Beethoven.
1932   1933

CARL SANDBURG
1878–

CHICAGO

Hog Butcher for the World,
Tool Maker, Stacker of Wheat,
Player with Railroads and the
    Nation's Freight Handler;
Stormy, husky, brawling,
City of the Big Shoulders:

They tell me you are wicked, and I believe
    them; for I have seen your painted women
    under the gas lamps luring the farm boys
And they tell me you are crooked, and I
    answer: Yes, it is true I have seen the
    gunman kill and go free to kill again.
And they tell me you are brutal, and my
    reply is: On the faces of women and

children I have seen the marks of wanton
hunger.
And having answered so I turn once more
to those who sneer at this my city, and I
give them back the sneer and say to
them:
Come and show me another city with
lifted head singing so proud to be alive and
coarse and strong and cunning.   10
Flinging magnetic curses amid the toil of
piling job on job, here is a tall bold slugger
set vivid against the little soft cities;
Fierce as a dog with tongue lapping for
action, cunning as a savage pitted against
the wilderness,
     Bareheaded,
     Shovelling,
     Wrecking,
     Planning,
     Building, breaking, rebuilding,
Under the smoke, dust all over his mouth,
laughing with white teeth,
Under the terrible burden of destiny
laughing as a young man laughs,
Laughing even as an ignorant fighter laughs
who has never lost a battle,   20
Bragging and laughing that under his wrist
is the pulse, and under his ribs the heart
of the people,
         Laughing!
Laughing the stormy, husky, brawling
laughter of Youth, half-naked, sweating,
proud to be Hog Butcher, Tool Maker,
Stacker of Wheat, Player with Railroads
and Freight Handler to the Nation.
1913   1916

TO A CONTEMPORARY
BUNKSHOOTER

You come along . . . tearing your shirt
   . . . yelling about Jesus.
    Where do you get that stuff?
    What do you know about Jesus?
Jesus had a way of talking soft and outside
of a few bankers and higher-ups among
the con men of Jerusalem everybody
liked to have this Jesus around because
he never made any fake passes and everything he said went and he helped the sick
and gave the people hope.

You come along squirting words at us,
shaking your fist and call us all dam fools

so fierce the froth slobbers over your lips
. . . always blabbing we're all going to
hell straight off and you know all about
it.

I've read Jesus' words. I know what he
said. You don't throw any scare into me.
I've got your number. I know how much
you know about Jesus.
He never came near clean people or dirty
people but they felt cleaner because he
came along. It was your crowd of bankers
and business men and lawyers hired the
sluggers and murderers who put Jesus
out of the running.
I say the same bunch backing you nailed
the nails into the hands of this Jesus of
Nazareth. He had lined up against him
the same crooks and strong-arm men now
lined up with you paying your way.

This Jesus was good to look at, smelled
good, listened good. He threw out something fresh and beautiful from the skin of
his body and the touch of his hands
wherever he passed along.
You slimy bunkshooter, you put a smut on
every human blossom in reach of your
rotten breath belching about hell-fire and
hiccupping about this Man who lived a
clean life in Galilee.   10
When are you going to quit making the carpenters build emergency hospitals for
women and girls driven crazy with
wrecked nerves from your gibberish
about Jesus?—I put it to you again:
Where do you get that stuff? What do you
know about Jesus?

Go ahead and bust all the chairs you want
to. Smash a whole wagon-load of furniture at every performance. Turn sixty
somersaults and stand on your nutty
head. If it wasn't for the way you scare
the women and kids I'd feel sorry for you
and pass the hat.
I like to watch a good four-flusher work,
but not when he starts people puking and
calling for the doctors.
I like a man that's got nerve and can pull off
a great original performance, but you—
you're only a bug-house pedlar of second-
hand gospel—you're only shoving out a
phoney imitation of the goods this Jesus
wanted free as air and sunlight.

You tell people living in shanties Jesus is
    going to fix it up all right with them by
    giving them mansions in the skies after
    they're dead and the worms have eaten
    'em.
You tell $6 a week department store girls
    all they need is Jesus; you take a steel
    trust wop, dead without having lived,
    grey and shrunken at forty years of age,
    and you tell him to look at Jesus on the
    cross and he'll be all right.
You tell poor people they don't need any
    more money on pay day and even if it's
    fierce to be out of a job, Jesus'll fix that
    up all right, all right—all they gotta do is
    take Jesus the way you say.
I'm telling you Jesus wouldn't stand for the
    stuff you're handing out. Jesus played it
    different. The bankers and lawyers of
    Jerusalem got their sluggers and mur-
    derers to go after Jesus just because Jesus
    wouldn't play their game. He didn't sit in
    with the big thieves.

I don't want a lot of gab from a bunk-
    shooter in my religion.
I won't take my religion from any man
    who never works except with his mouth
    and never cherishes any memory except
    the face of the woman on the American
    silver dollar.   20
I ask you to come through and show me
    where you're pouring out the blood of
    your life.
I've been to this suburb of Jerusalem they
    call Golgotha, where they nailed Him,
    and I know if the story is straight it was
    real blood ran from His hands and the
    nail-holes, and it was real blood spurted
    in red drops where the spear of the
    Roman soldier rammed in between the
    ribs of this Jesus of Nazareth.
1914   1916

FOG

THE fog comes
on little cat feet.

It sits looking
over harbor and city
on silent haunches
and then moves on.

1912   1916

JOY

LET a joy keep you.
Reach out your hands
And take it when it runs by,
As the Apache dancer
Clutches his woman.
I have seen them
Live long and laugh loud,
Sent on singing, singing,
Smashed to the heart
Under the ribs   10
With a terrible love.
Joy always,
Joy everywhere—
Let joy kill you!
Keep away from the little deaths.
1913   1916

NOCTURNE IN A DESERTED
BRICKYARD

STUFF of the moon
Runs on the lapping sand
Out to the longest shadows.
Under the curving willows,
And round the creep of the wave
    Line,
Fluxions of yellow and dusk on the
    waters
Make a wide dreaming pansy of an old pond
    in the night.
1910   1916

GONE

EVERYBODY loved Chick Lorimer in our
    town
        Far off.
    Everybody loved her.
So we all love a wild girl keeping a hold
    On a dream she wants.
Nobody knows now where Chick Lorimer
    went.
Nobody knows why she packed her trunk
    . . . a few old things
And is gone,
        Gone with her little chin
        Thrust ahead of her   10
        And her soft hair blowing careless
        From under a wide hat,
Dancer, singer, a laughing passionate
    lover.

Were there ten men or a hundred hunting
    Chick?
Were there five men or fifty with aching
    hearts?
      Everybody loved Chick Lorimer.
        Nobody knows where she's gone.
1913   1916

I AM THE PEOPLE, THE MOB

I AM the people—the mob—the crowd—
the mass.
Do you know that all the great work of the
world is done through me?
I am the workingman, the inventor, the
maker of the world's food and clothes.
I am the audience that witnesses history.
The Napoleons come from me and the
Lincolns. They die. And then I send
forth more Napoleons and Lincolns.
I am the seed ground. I am a prairie that
will stand for much plowing. Terrible
storms pass over me. I forget. The best
of me is sucked out and wasted. I forget.
Everything but Death comes to me and
makes me work and give up what I have.
And I forget.
Sometimes I growl, shake myself and spat-
ter a few red drops for history to remember. Then—I forget.
When I, the People, learn to remember,
when I, the People, use the lessons of
yesterday and no longer forget who
robbed me last year, who played me for a
fool—then there will be no speaker in all
the world say the name: 'The People,'
with any fleck of a sneer in his voice or
any far-off smile of derision.
The mob—the crowd—the mass—will arrive then.
1914   1916

CABOOSE THOUGHTS

IT's going to come out all right—do you
    know?
The sun, the birds, the grass—they know.
They get along—and we'll get along.

Some days will be rainy and you will sit
    waiting
And the letter you wait for won't come,
And I will sit watching the sky tear off grey
    and grey
And the letter I wait for won't come.

There will be ac-ci-dents.
I know ac-ci-dents are coming.
Smash-ups, signals wrong, washouts,
    trestles rotten,   10
Red and yellow ac-ci-dents.
But somehow and somewhere the end of
    the run
The train gets put together again
And the caboose and the green tail
    lights
Fade down the right of way like a new white
    hope.

I never heard a mocking-bird in Kentucky
Spilling its heart in the morning.

I never saw the snow on Chimborazo.
It's a high white Mexican hat, I hear.

I never had supper with Abe Lincoln.   20
Nor a dish of soup with Jim Hill.

But I've been around.
I know some of the boys here who can go a
    little.
I know girls good for a burst of speed any
    time.

I heard Williams and Walker
Before Walker died in the bughouse.

I knew a mandolin player
Working in a barber shop in an Indiana
    town,
And he thought he had a million dollars.

I knew a hotel girl in Des Moines.   30
She had eyes; I saw her and said to
    myself
The sun rises and the sun sets in her
    eyes.
I was her steady and her heart went pit-a-
    pat.
We took away the money for a prize waltz
    at a Brotherhood dance.
She had eyes; she was safe as the bridge
    over the Mississippi at Burlington;
    I married her.

Last summer we took the cushions going
    west.
Pike's Peak is a big old stone, believe
    me.
It's fastened down; something you can
    count on.

It's going to come out all right—do you
    know?
The sun, the birds, the grass—they know. 40
They get along—and we'll get along.
1916   1918

WILDERNESS

THERE is a wolf in me . . . fangs pointed
for tearing gashes . . . a red tongue for
raw meat . . . and the hot lapping of
blood—I keep this wolf because the wilderness gave it to me and the wilderness
will not let it go.

There is a fox in me . . . a silver-grey fox
. . . I sniff and guess . . . I pick things
out of the wind and air . . . I nose in the
dark night and take sleepers and eat them
and hide the feathers . . . I circle and
loop and double-cross.

There is a hog in me—a snout and a belly
. . . a machinery for eating and grunting
. . . a machinery for sleeping satisfied in
the sun—I got this too from the wilderness and the wilderness will not let it go.

There is a fish in me . . . I know I came
from salt-blue water-gates . . . I scur-
ried with shoals of herring . . . I blew
waterspouts with porpoises . . . before
land was . . . before the water went
down . . . before Noah . . . before the
first chapter of Genesis.

There is a baboon in me . . . clambering-
clawed . . . dog-faced . . . yawping a
galoot's hunger . . . hairy under the
armpits . . . here are the hawk-eyed
hankering men . . . here are the blond
and blue-eyed women . . . here they
hide curled asleep waiting . . . ready to
snarl and kill . . . ready to sing and give
milk . . . waiting—I keep the baboon
because the wilderness says so.

There is an eagle in me and a mocking-bird
. . . and the eagle flies among the Rocky
Mountains of my dreams and fights
among the Sierra crags of what I want
. . . and the mocking-bird warbles in
the early forenoon before the dew is gone,
warbles in the underbrush of my Chat-
tanoogas of hope, gushes over the blue

Ozark foothills of my wishes—And I got
the eagle and the mocking-bird from the
wilderness.

O, I got a zoo, I got a menagerie, inside my
ribs, under my bony head, under my
red-valve heart—and I got something
else: it is a man-child heart, a woman-
child heart: it is a father and mother and
lover: it came from God-Knows-Where:
it is going to God-Knows-Where—For I
am the keeper of the zoo: I say yes and no:
I sing and kill and work: I am a pal of the
world: I came from the wilderness.
1917   1918

SINGING NIGGER

YOUR bony head, Jazbo, O dock walloper,
Those grappling hooks, those wheelbarrow
    handlers,
The dome and the wings of you, nigger,
The red roof and the door of you,
I know where your songs came from.
I know why God listens to your, 'Walk All
    Over God's Heaven.'
I heard you shooting craps, 'My baby's
    going to have a new dress.'
I heard you in the cinders, 'I'm going to
    live anyhow until I die.'
I saw five of you with a can of beer on a
    summer night and I listened to the
    five of you harmonizing six ways to
    sing, 'Way Down Yonder in the
    Cornfield.'
I went away asking where I come from.   10
1917   1918

PRAYERS OF STEEL

LAY me on an anvil, O God.
Beat me and hammer me into a crowbar.
Let me pry loose old walls.
Let me lift and loosen old foundations.

Lay me on an anvil, O God.
Beat me and hammer me into a steel spike.
Drive me into the girders that hold a
    skyscraper together.
Take red-hot rivets and fasten me into the
    central girders.
Let me be the great nail holding a
    skyscraper through blue nights into
    white stars.
1917   1918

COOL TOMBS

WHEN Abraham Lincoln was shoveled into
the tombs, he forgot the copperheads and
the assassin . . . in the dust, in the cool
tombs.

And Ulysses Grant lost all thought of con
men and Wall Street, cash and collateral
turned ashes . . . in the dust, in the cool
tombs.

Pocahontas' body, lovely as a poplar, sweet
as a red haw in November or a pawpaw in
May, did she wonder? does she remember? . . . in the dust, in the cool tombs?

Take any streetful of people buying clothes
and groceries, cheering a hero or throwing confetti and blowing tin horns . . .
tell me if the lovers are losers . . . tell
me if any get more than the lovers . . .
in the dust . . . in the cool tombs.

1915   1918

SHENANDOAH

IN the Shenandoah Valley, one rider grey
and one rider blue, and the sun on the
riders wondering.

Piled in the Shenandoah, riders blue and
riders grey, piled with shovels, one and
another, dust in the Shenandoah taking
them quicker than mothers take children
done with play.

The blue nobody remembers, the grey nobody remembers, it's all old and old nowadays in the Shenandoah.

And all is young, a butter of dandelions
slung on the turf, climbing blue flowers
of the wishing woodlands wondering: a
midnight purple violet claims the sun
among old heads, among old dreams of
repeating heads of a rider blue and a rider
grey in the Shenandoah.

1916   1918

GRASS

PILE the bodies high at Austerlitz and
Waterloo.
Shovel them under and let me work—
I am the grass; I cover all.

And pile them high at Gettysburg
And pile them high at Ypres and Verdun.
Shovel them under and let me work.
Two years, ten years, and passengers ask
the conductor:
What place is this?
Where are we now?

I am the grass.   10
Let me work.

1918   1918

OLD TIMERS

I AM an ancient reluctant conscript.

On the soup wagons of Xerxes I was a
cleaner of pans.

On the march of Miltiades' phalanx I had
a haft and head;
I had a bristling gleaming spear-handle.

Red-headed Cæsar picked me for a
teamster.
He said, 'Go to work, you Tuscan bastard
Rome calls for a man who can drive horses.'

The units of conquest led by Charles the
Twelfth,
The whirling whimsical Napoleonic
columns:
They saw me one of the horseshoers.   10

I trimmed the feet of a white horse
Bonaparte swept the night stars with.

Lincoln said, 'Get into the game; your
nation takes you.'
And I drove a wagon and team, and I had
my arm shot off
At Spotsylvania Court House.

I am an ancient reluctant conscript.

1916   1918

BROKEN–FACE GARGOYLES

ALL I can give you is broken-face gargoyles.
It is too early to sing and dance at funerals,
Though I can whisper to you I am looking
for an undertaker humming a lullaby and
throwing his feet in a swift and mystic
buck-and-wing, now you see it and now
you don't.

Fish to swim a pool in your garden flashing
    a speckled silver,
A basket of wine-saps filling your room
    with flame-dark for your eyes and the
    tang of valley orchards for your nose,
Such a beautiful pail of fish, such a beauti-
    ful peck of apples, I cannot bring you now.
It is too early and I am not footloose yet.

I shall come in the night when I come with
    a hammer and saw.
I shall come near your window, where you
    look out when your eyes open in the
    morning,
And there I shall slam together bird-
    houses and bird-baths for wing-loose
    wrens and hummers to live in, birds with
    yellow wing tips to blur and buzz soft all
    summer,   10
So I shall make little fool homes with doors,
    always open doors for all and each to run
    away when they want to.
I shall come just like that even though now
    it is early and I am not yet footloose,
Even though I am still looking for an un-
    dertaker with a raw, wind-bitten face and
    a dance in his feet.
I make a date with you (put it down) for six
    o'clock in the evening a thousand years
    from now.

All I can give you now is broken-face gar-
    goyles.
All I can give you now is a double gorilla
    head with two fish mouths and four eagle
    eyes hooked on a street wall, spouting
    water and looking two ways to the ends of
    the street for the new people, the young
    strangers, coming, coming, always com-
    ing.

    It is early.
    I shall yet be footloose.
1919   1921

SHIRT

My shirt is a token and symbol,
more than a cover for sun and rain,
my shirt is a signal,
and a teller of souls.

I can take off my shirt and tear it,
and so make a ripping razzly noise,
and the people will say,
'Look at him tear his shirt.'

I can keep my shirt on.
I can stick around and sing like a little
    bird   10
and look 'em all in the eye and never be
    fazed.
    I can keep my shirt on.
1919   1921

JAZZ FANTASIA

Drum on your drums, batter on your ban-
    joes, sob on the long cool winding saxo-
    phones. Go to it, O jazzmen.

Sling your knuckles on the bottoms of the
    happy tin pans, let your trombones ooze,
    and go husha-husha-hush with the slip-
    pery sand-paper.

Moan like an autumn wind high in the
    lonesome tree-tops, moan soft like you
    wanted somebody terrible, cry like a
    racing car slipping away from a motor-
    cycle cop, bang-bang! you jazzmen, bang
    altogether drums, traps, banjoes, horns,
    tin cans—make two people fight on the
    top of a stairway and scratch each other's
    eyes in a clinch tumbling down the
    stairs.

Can the rough stuff . . . now a Missis-
    sippi steamboat pushes up the night
    river with a hoo-hoo-hoo-oo . . . and
    the green lanterns calling to the high
    soft stars . . . a red moon rides on the
    humps of the low river hills . . . go to
    it, O jazzmen.
1919   1921

OSSAWATOMIE

I don' t know how he came,
shambling, dark, and strong.

He stood in the city and told men:
My people are fools, my people are young
    and strong, my people must learn,
    my people are terrible workers and
    fighters.
Always he kept on asking: Where did that
    blood come from?

    They said: You for the fool killer,
            you for the booby hatch
            and a necktie party.

They hauled him into jail.
They sneered at him and spit on him,   10
And he wrecked their jails,
Singing, 'God damn your jails,'
And when he was most in jail
Crummy among the crazy in the dark
Then he was most of all out of jail
Shambling, dark, and strong,
Always asking: Where did that blood come
    from?

They laid hands on him
And the fool killers had a laugh
And the necktie party was a go, by God.   20
They laid hands on him and he was a
    goner.
    They hammered him to pieces and he
        stood up.
They buried him and he walked out of the
        grave, by God,
    Asking again: Where did that blood come
        from?
1919   1921

LOSERS

If I should pass the tomb of Jonah
I would stop there and sit for awhile;
Because I was swallowed one time deep in
    the dark
And came out alive after all.

If I pass the burial spot of Nero
I shall say to the wind, 'Well, well!'—
I who have fiddled in a world on fire,
I who have done so many stunts not worth
    doing.

I am looking for the grave of Sinbad
    too.
I want to shake his ghost-hand and say,   10
'Neither of us died very early, did we?'

And the last sleeping-place of
        Nebuchadnezzar—
When I arrive there I shall tell the
        wind:
'You ate grass; I have eaten crow—
Who is better off now or next year?'

Jack Cade, John Brown, Jesse James,
There too I could sit down and stop for
        awhile.
I think I could tell their headstones:
'God, let me remember all good losers.'

I could ask people to throw ashes on their
        heads   20
In the name of that sergeant at Belleau
        Woods,
Walking into the drumfires, calling his men,
'Come on, you . . . Do you want to live
        forever?'
1919   1921

THREES

I WAS a boy when I heard three red words
a thousand Frenchmen died in the streets
for: Liberty, Equality, Fraternity—I asked
why men die for words.

I was older; men with mustaches, sideburns,
lilacs, told me the high golden words
        are:
Mother, Home, and Heaven—other older
        men with
face decorations said: God, Duty,
        Immortality
—they sang these threes slow from deep
        lungs.

Years ticked off their say-so on the great
        clocks   10
of doom and damnation, soup and nuts:
        meteors flashed
their say-so: and out of great Russia came
        three
dusky syllables workmen took guns and
        went out to die
for: Bread, Peace, Land.

And I met a marine of the U.S.A., a
        leatherneck with
a girl on his knee for a memory in ports
        circling the
earth and he said: Tell me how to say three
        things
and I always get by—gimme a plate of ham
        and eggs—
how much?—and—do you love me,
        kid?
1919   1921

NIGHT STUFF

LISTEN a while, the moon is a lovely woman,
    a lonely woman, lost in a silver dress, lost
    in a circus rider's silver dress.

Listen a while, the lake by night is a lonely
    woman, a lovely woman, circled with
    birches and pines mixing their green and
    white among stars shattered in spray clear
    nights.

I know the moon and the lake have twisted
    the roots under my heart the same as
    a lonely woman, a lovely woman, in
    a silver dress, in a circus rider's silver
    dress.
1917   1921

UPSTREAM

THE strong men keep coming on.
They go down shot, hanged, sick, broken.
They live on fighting, singing, lucky as
    plungers.
The strong mothers pulling them on . . .
The strong mothers pulling them from a
        dark sea, a great prairie, a long
        mountain.
Call hallelujah, call amen, call deep thanks.
The strong men keep coming on.
1920   1922

FROM THE PEOPLE, YES

THE PEOPLE WILL LIVE ON

        The people will live on.
The learning and blundering people will
        live on.
    They will be tricked and sold and again
        sold
And go back to the nourishing earth for
        rootholds,
    The people so peculiar in renewal and
        comeback,
    You can't laugh off their capacity to take
        it.
The mammoth rests between his cyclonic
        dramas.

The people so often sleepy, weary,
enigmatic, is a vast huddle with many units
saying: 10
    'I earn my living.
    I make enough to get by
    and it takes all my time.
    If I had more time
    I could do more for myself
    and maybe for others.
    I could read and study
    and talk things over

and find out about things.
    It takes time.   20
    I wish I had the time.'

The people is a tragic and comic two-face:
hero and hoodlum: phantom and gorilla
twisting to moan with a gargoyle mouth:
'They buy me and sell me . . . it's a
game . . . sometime I'll break loose . . .'

    Once having marched
Over the margins of animal necessity,
Over the grim line of sheer subsistence
    Then man came   30
To the deeper rituals of his bones,
To the lights lighter than any bones,
To the time for thinking things over,
To the dance, the song, the story,
Or the hours given over to dreaming,
    Once having so marched.

Between the finite limitations of the five
senses and the endless yearnings of man
for the beyond the people hold to the
humdrum bidding of work and food while
reaching out when it comes their way for
lights beyond the prison of the five senses,
for keepsakes lasting beyond any hunger or
death.   44
    This reaching is alive.
The panderers and liars have violated and
smutted it.
    Yet this reaching is alive yet
    for lights and keepsakes.

    The people know the salt of the sea   50
    and the strength of the winds
    lashing the corners of the earth.
    The people take the earth
    as a tomb of rest and a cradle of hope.
    Who else speaks for the Family of Man?
    They are in tune and step
    with constellations of universal law.

    The people is a polychrome,
    a spectrum and a prism
    held in a moving monolith,   60
    a console organ of changing themes,
    a clavilux of color poems
    wherein the sea offers fog
    and the fog moves off in rain
    and the labrador sunset shortens
    to a nocturne of clear stars
    serene over the shot spray
    of northern lights.

The steel mill sky is alive.
The fire breaks white and zigzag   70
shot on a gun-metal gloaming.
Man is a long time coming.
Man will yet win.
Brother may yet line up with brother:

This old anvil laughs at many broken
    hammers.
There are men who can't be bought.
The fireborn are at home in fire.   1935

The stars make no noise.
You can't hinder the wind from blowing.
Time is a great teacher.   80
Who can live without hope?

In the darkness with a great bundle of grief
    the people march.
In the night, and overhead a shovel of stars
    for keeps, the people march:
                'Where to? what next?'
                                1936

THEODORE DREISER

1871–1945

FROM AN AMERICAN TRAGEDY

AN AMERICAN PROBLEM [1]

Two incidents which occurred at this time
tended still more to sharpen the contrary
points of view holding between Clyde and
Roberta. One of these was no more than a
glimpse which Roberta had one evening of
Clyde pausing at the Central Avenue curb
in front of the post-office to say a few words   10
to Arabella Stark, who in a large and im-
pressive-looking car, was waiting for her
father who was still in the Stark Building
opposite. And Miss Stark, fashionably out-
fitted according to the season, her world
and her own pretentious taste, was affect-
edly posed at the wheel, not only for the
benefit of Clyde but the public in general.
And to Roberta, who by now was reduced
to the verge of distraction between Clyde's   20
delay and her determination to compel him
to act in her behalf, she appeared to be little
less than an epitome of all the security,
luxury and freedom from responsibility
which so enticed and hence caused Clyde to
delay and be as indifferent as possible to
the dire state which confronted her. For,
alas, apart from this claim of her condition,
what had she to offer him comparable to all
he would be giving up in case he acceded to   30
her request? Nothing—a thought which
was far from encouraging.

Yet, at this moment contrasting her own
wretched and neglected state with that of
this Miss Stark, for example, she found her-

self a prey to an even more complaining
and antagonistic mood than had hitherto
characterized her. It was not right. It was
not fair. For during the several weeks that
had passed since last they had discussed
this matter, Clyde had scarcely said a word
to her at the factory or elsewhere, let alone
called upon her at her room, fearing as he
did the customary inquiry which he could
not satisfy. And this caused her to feel that
not only was he neglecting but resenting
her most sharply.

And yet as she walked home from this
trivial and fairly representative scene, her
heart was not nearly so angry as it was sad
and sore because of the love and comfort
that had vanished and was not likely ever
to come again . . . ever . . . ever . . .
ever. Oh, how terrible, . . . how terrible!

On the other hand, Clyde, and at approximately this same time, was called upon to
witness a scene identified with Roberta,
which, as some might think, only an ironic
and even malicious fate could have intended
or permitted to come to pass. For motoring
north the following Sunday to Arrow Lake
to the lodge of the Trumbulls' to take advantage of an early spring week-end
planned by Sondra, the party on nearing
Biltz, which was in the direct line of the
trip, was compelled to detour east in the
direction of Roberta's home. And coming
finally to a north and south road which ran
directly from Trippettsville past the Alden
farm, they turned north into that. And a
few minutes later, came directly to the corner adjoining the Alden farm, where an
east and west road led to Biltz. Here Tracy

1 The selection, to which the title has been given by the
editors, is Chapter 40 from Book II of *An American
Tragedy*(N.Y., 1925),II,10–14.

Trumbull, driving at the time, requested that some one should get out and inquire at the adjacent farm-house as to whether this road did lead to Biltz. And Clyde, being nearest to one door, jumped out. And then, glancing at the name on the mail-box which stood at the junction and evidently belonged to the extremely dilapidated old farm-house on the rise above, he was not a little astonished to note that the name was that of Titus Alden—Roberta's father. Also, as it instantly came to him, since she had described her parents as being near Biltz, this must be her home. It gave him pause, caused him for the moment to hesitate as to whether to go on or not, for once he had given Roberta a small picture of himself, and she might have shown it up here. Again the mere identification of this lorn, dilapidated realm with Roberta and hence himself, was sufficient to cause him to wish to turn and run.

But Sondra, who was sitting next him in the car and now noting his hesitation, called: 'What's the matter, Clyde? Afraid of the bow-wow?' And he, realizing instantly that they would comment further on his actions if he did not proceed at once, started up the path. But the effect of this house, once he contemplated it thoroughly, was sufficient to arouse in his brain the most troubled and miserable of thoughts. For what a house, to be sure! So lonely and bare, even in this bright, spring weather! The decayed and sagging roof. The broken chimney to the north—rough lumps of cemented field stones lying at its base; the sagging and semi-toppling chimney to the south, sustained in place by a log chain. The unkempt path from the road below, which slowly he ascended! He was not a little dejected by the broken and displaced stones which served as steps before the front door. And the unpainted dilapidated out-buildings, all the more dreary because of these others.

'Gee!' To think that this was Roberta's home. And to think, in the face of all that he now aspired to in connection with Sondra and this social group at Lycurgus, she should be demanding that he marry her! And Sondra in the car with him here to see —if not know. The poverty! The reduced grimness of it all. How far he had traveled away from just such a beginning as this!

With a weakening and sickening sensation at the pit of his stomach, as of some blow administered there, he now approached the door. And then, as if to further distress him, if that were possible, the door was opened by Titus Alden, who, in an old, thread-bare and out-at-elbows coat, as well as baggy, worn, jean trousers and rough, shineless, ill-fitting country shoes, desired by his look to know what he wanted. And Clyde, being taken aback by the clothes, as well as a marked resemblance to Roberta about the eyes and mouth, now as swiftly as possible asked if the east and west road below ran through Biltz and joined the main highway north. And although he would have preferred a quick 'yes' so that he might have turned and gone, Titus preferred to step down into the yard and then, with a gesture of the arm, indicated that if they wanted to strike a really good part of the road, they had better follow this Trippettsville north and south road for at least two more miles, and then turn west. Clyde thanked him briefly and turned almost before he had finished and hurried away.

For, as he now recalled, and with an enormous sense of depression, Roberta was thinking and at this very time, that soon now, and in the face of all Lycurgus had to offer him—Sondra—the coming spring and summer—the love and romance, gayety, position, power—he was going to give all that up and go away with and marry her. Sneak away to some out-of-the-way place! Oh, how horrible! And with a child at his age! Oh, why had he ever been so foolish and weak as to identify himself with her in this intimate way! Just because of a few lonely evenings! Oh, why, why couldn't he have waited and then this other world would have opened up to him just the same? If only he could have waited!

And now unquestionably, unless he could speedily and easily disengage himself from her, all this other splendid recognition would be destined to be withdrawn from him, and this other world from which he sprang might extend its gloomy, poverty-stricken arms to him and envelop him once more, just as the poverty of his family had enveloped and almost strangled him from the first. And it even occurred to him, in a vague way for the first time, how strange it was that this girl and he, whose origin had been strikingly similar, should have been so drawn to each other in the beginning. Why should it have been? How strange life was, anyway? But even more harrowing than this, was the problem of a way out that was before him. And his mind from now on, on this trip, was once more searching for some solution. A word of complaint from Roberta or her parents to his uncle or Gilbert, and assuredly he would be done for.

The thought so troubled him that once in the car, and although previously he had been chattering along with the others about what might be in store ahead in the way of divertissement, he now sat silent. And Sondra, who sat next to him and who previously had been whispering at intervals of her plans for the summer, now, instead of resuming the patter, whispered: 'What come over de sweet phing?' (When Clyde appeared to be the least reduced in mind she most affected this patter with him, since it had an almost electric, if sweetly tormenting effect on him. 'His baby-talking girl,' he sometimes called her.) 'Facey all dark now. Little while ago facey all smiles. Come make facey all nice again. Smile at Sondra. Squeeze Sondra's arm like good boy, Clyde.'

She turned and looked up into his eyes to see what if any effect this baby-worded cajolery was having, and Clyde did his best to brighten, of course. But even so, and in the face of all this amazingly wonderful love on her part for him, the specter of Roberta and all that she represented now in connection with all this, was ever before him—her state, her very recent edict in regard to it, the obvious impossibility of doing anything now but go away with her.

Why—rather than let himself in for a thing like that—would it not be better, and even though he lost Sondra once and for all, for him to decamp as in the instance of the slain child in Kansas City—and be heard of nevermore here. But then he would lose Sondra, his connections here, and his uncle —this world! The loss! The loss! The misery of once more drifting about here and there; of being compelled to write his mother once more concerning certain things about his flight, which some one writing from here might explain to her afterwards—and so much more damagingly. And the thoughts concerning him on the part of his relatives! And of late he had been writing his mother that he was doing so well. What was it about his life that made things like this happen to him? Was this what his life was to be like? Running away from one situation and another just to start all over somewhere else—perhaps only to be compelled to flee from something worse. No, he could not run away again. He must face it and solve it in some way. He must! God!

1925

JAMES BRANCH CABELL

1879–

THE DEMIURGE [1]

—What is man, that his welfare be considered?—an ape who chatters to himself of kinship with the archangels while filthily he digs for groundnuts. . . .
—Yet more clearly do I perceive that this same man is a maimed god. . . . He is under penalty condemned to compute eternity with false weights and to estimate infinity with a yardstick; and he very often does it. . . .

[1] The essay is printed from the author's revised version of Beyond Life in the Storisende Edition (N.Y., 1927).

—There lies the choice which every man must make—or rationally to accept his own limitations? or stupendously to play the fool and swear that he is at will omnipotent?
—DIZAIN DES REINES

I

OFF-HAND (began John Charteris), I would say that books are best insured against oblivion through practise of the auctorial virtues of distinction and clarity, of beauty and symmetry, of tenderness and truth and urbanity. That covers the ground, I think: and so it remains merely to cite supporting instances here and there, by mentioning a few writers who have observed these requirements, and thus to substantiate my formula without unnecessary divagation. . . .

Therefore I shall be very brief. And even so, I imagine, you will not be inclined to listen to much of what I am about to say, if only because, like most of us, you are intimidated by that general attitude toward culture and the humanities which has made of American literature, among foreign penmen, if not precisely an object of despairing envy, at least of feeling comment. In particular, I imagine that my frequent references to the affairs and people of fled years will annoy you, since the American bookpurchaser shies from such pedantic, and indeed from any, allusion to the past, with that distrust peculiar to persons with criminal records. In fact, this murderer, too, is often haunted, I dare say, by memories of his victim, in thinking of the time he has killed, whether with the 'uplifting' or with the 'daring' current novels of yesterday.

But you perceive, I trust, that your personal indifference, and the lazy contempt of America as a whole, toward art matters no more affects the eternal verity and the eternal importance of art than do the religious practises of Abyssinia, say, affect the verity and importance of the New Testament. You perceive, I trust, that you ought to be interested in art matters, whatever is your actual emotion. You understand, in fine— as a mere abstract principle—what your feeling 'ought to be.' Well, it is precisely that tendency to imagine yourself and your emotions as these things 'ought to be' which convicts you, over any verbal disclaimer, of a vital interest in art matters: and it is that tendency about which I propose to speak very briefly. . . .

And yet, so insidious is the influence of general opinion, even when manifested as plain unreason, that, I confess, whenever anyone talks of 'art' and 'æsthetic theories,' I myself am inclined to find him vaguely ridiculous, and to detect in every word he utters a flavor of affectation. So should you prove quite as susceptible as I to the herd-instinct I shall have no ground for complaint. Meanwhile in theory—without of necessity accompanying my friend Felix Kennaston all the way to his conclusion

that the sum of corporeal life represents an essay in romantic fiction,—I can perceive plainly enough that the shape-giving principle of all sentient beings is artistic. That is a mere matter of looking at living creatures and noticing their forms. . . . But the principle goes deeper, in that it shapes too the minds of men, by this universal tendency to imagine—and to think of as in reality existent—all the tenants of earth and all the affairs of earth, not as they are, but 'as they ought to be.' And so it comes about that romance has invariably been the demiurgic and beneficent force, not merely in letters, but in every matter which concerns mankind; and that 'realism,' with its teaching that the mile-posts along the road are as worthy of consideration as the goal, has always figured as man's chief enemy. . . .

2

Indeed, that scathing criticism which Sophocles passed, howsoever anciently on a contemporary, remains no less familiar than significant,—'He paints men as they are: I paint them as they ought to be.' It is aside from the mark that in imputing such veracity to Euripides the singer of Colonos was talking nonsense: the point is that Sophocles saw clearly what was, and what continues to be, the one unpardonable sin against art and human welfare.

For the Greeks, who were nurtured among art's masterworks, recognized, with much of that perturbing candor wherewith children everywhere appraise their associates, that gracefully to prevaricate about mankind and human existence was art's signal function. As a by-product of this perception, Hellenic literature restrained its endeavors, quite naturally, to embroidering events that were incontestable because time had erased the evidence for or against their actual occurrence: and the poets, in their quest of protagonists worth noble handling, evoked them from bright mists of antiquity, wherethrough, as far as went existent proofs, men might in reality have moved 'as they ought to be.' Thus, even Homer, the most ancient of great verbal artists, elected to deal with legends that in his day were venerable: and in Homer when Ajax lifts a stone it is with the strength of ten warriors, and Odysseus, when such a procedure at all promotes the progress of the story, becomes invisible. It seems—upon the whole,—less probable that Homer drew either of these accomplishments from the actual human life about him, than from simple consciousness that it would be very gratifying if men could do these things. And, indeed, as touches enduring art, to write 'with the eye upon the object' appears a relatively modern pretence, perhaps not unconnected with the coetaneous phrase of 'all my eye.'

Then, when the Attic drama came to flowerage, the actors were masked, so that their features might display unhuman perfection; the actors were mounted upon cothurni, to lend impressiveness to man's physical mediocrity; and the actors were clothed in draperies which philanthropically eclipsed humanity's frugal graces. In painting or sculpture, where the human body could be idealized with a free hand, the Greek rule was nakedness: in drama, where the artist's material was incorrigible flesh, there was nothing for it save to disguise the uncaptivating ground-work through some discreet employment of fair apparel. Thus only could the audience be hoodwinked into forgetting for a while what men and women really looked like. In drama, therefore, Theseus declaimed in imperial vestments, and in sculpture wore at the very most a fig-leaf. It is hardly necessary to point out that the Greeks shared few of our delusions concerning 'decency': for, of course, they had no more moral aversion to a man's appearing naked in the street than to a toad's doing so, and objected simply on the ground that both were ugly. So they resolutely wrote about—and carved and painted, for that matter—men 'as they ought to be' doing such things as it would be gratifying for men to do if these feats were humanly possible. . . . And in the twilit evening of Greek literature you will find Theocritus clinging with unshaken ardor to unreality, and regaling the townfolk of Alexandria with tales of an improbable Sicily, where the inhabitants are on terms of friendly intimacy with cyclopes, water-nymphs and satyrs.

3

Equally in the Middle Ages did literature avoid deviation into the credible.

When carpets of brocade were spread in April meadows it was to the end that barons and ladies might listen with delight to peculiarly unplausible accounts of how Sire Roland held the pass at Roncevaux single-handed against an army, and of Lancelot's education at the bottom of a pond by elfin pedagogues, and of how Virgil builded Naples upon eggshells. When English-speaking tale-tellers began to concoct homespun romances they selected such themes as Bevis of Southampton's addiction to giant-killing, and Guy of Warwick's encounter with a man-eating cow eighteen feet long, and the exploits of Thomas of Reading, who exterminated an infinity of dragons and eloped with Prester John's daughter after jilting the Queen of Fairyland. Chaucer, questionless, was so injudicious as to dabble in that muddy stream of contemporaneous happenings which time alone may clarify: but the parts of Chaucer that endure are a Knight's story of mythological events, a Prioress's unsubstantiated account of a miracle, a Nun's Priest's anticipation of Rostand's barnyard fantasy, and a ream or two of other delightful flim-flams. From his contemporaries Chaucer got such matter as the Miller's tale of a clerk's misadventures in osculation.

4

But with the invention of printing, thoughts spread so expeditiously that it became possible to acquire quite serviceable ideas without the trouble of thinking: and very few of us since then have cared to risk impairment of our minds by using them. A consequence was that, with inaction, man's imagination in general grew more sluggish, and demurred, just as mental indolence continues to balk, over the exertion of conceiving an unfamiliar *locale*, in any form of art. The deterioration, of course, was gradual, and for a considerable while theatrical audiences remained receptively illiterate. And it seems at first sight gratifying to note that for a lengthy period Marlowe was the most 'popular' of the Elizabethan playwrights: for in Marlowe's superb verse there is really very little to indicate that the writer had ever encountered any human beings, and certainly nothing whatever to show that he had seriously considered this especial division of fauna: whereas all his

JAMES BRANCH CABELL
'comic' scenes which time has beneficently
Shakespeare's least claim to applause that
Shakespeare was not untainted by the aug-
Othello, and Hamlet, and Macbeth, and
Romeo—to cite only a few instances,—by
For, really, to go mad because a hostess re-
Few of the art-reverencing Elizabethans,

The Roaring Girl and *The New Inn*, by men

Then came the gallant protest of the
Restoration, when Wycherley and his suc-
Railway Station, or of the Capitol at Wash-
Restoration days as now, would have sub-
A great deal of queer nonsense has been
Land alone. And, were there nothing else,

accorded to everybody toward eleven o'clock in the evening.

6

Thus far the illiterate ages, when as yet so few persons could read that literature tended generally toward the acted drama. The stage could supply much illusory assistance, in the way of pads and wigs and grease-paints and soft lightings, toward making men appear heroic and women charming: but, after all, the rôles were necessarily performed by human beings, and the charitable deceit was not continuous. The audience was ever and anon being reminded, against its firm-set will, that men were mediocre creatures.

Now could the poets, howsoever rapidly now multiplied their verse-books, satisfactorily delude their patrons into overlooking this unpleasant fact. For one reason or another, men as a whole have never taken kindlily to printed poetry: most of us are unable to put up with it at all, and even to the exceptional person verse after an hour's reading becomes unaccountably tiresome. Prose—for no very patent cause—is much easier going. So the poets proved ineffectual comforters, who could but rarely be-drug even the few to whom their charms did not seem gibberish.

With the advent of the novel, all this was changed. Not merely were you relieved from metrical fatigue, but there came no commonplace flesh-and-blood to give the lie to the artist's pretensions. It was possible, really for the first time, acceptably to present in literature men 'as they ought to be.' Richardson could dilate as unrestrainedly as he pleased upon the super-eminence in virtue and sin, respectively, of his Grandison and his Lovelace emboldened by the knowledge that there was nothing to check him off save the dubious touchstone of his reader's common-sense. Fielding was not only able to conduct a broad-shouldered young ruffian to fortune and a lovely wife, but could moreover endow Tom Jones with all sorts of heroic and estimable qualities such as (in mere unimportant fact) rascals do not display in actual life. When the novel succeeded the drama it was no longer necessary for the artist to represent human beings with even partial veracity: and this new style of writing at once became emblematic.

And so it has been ever since. Novelists have severally evolved their pleasing symbols wherewith approximately to suggest human beings and the business of human life, much as remote Egyptians drew serrated lines to convey the idea of water and a circle to indicate eternity. The symbols have often varied: but there has rarely been any ill-advised attempt to depict life as it seems in the living of it, or to crystallize the vague notions and feeble sensations with which human beings, actually, muddle through to an epitaph; if only because all sensible persons, obscurely aware that this routine is far from what it ought to be, have always preferred to deny its existence. And moreover, we have come long ago to be guided in any really decisive speech or action by what we have read somewhere; and so, may fairly claim that literature should select (as it does) such speeches and such actions as typical of our essential lives, rather than the gray interstices, which we perforce fill in extempore, and botch.

As concerns the novelists of the day before yesterday, this evasion of veracity is already more or less conceded: the 'platitudinous heroics' of Scott and the 'exaggerated sentimentalism' of Dickens are notorious in quite authoritative circles whose *ducdame* is the honest belief that art is a branch of pedagogy. Thackeray, as has been pointed out elsewhere, avoids many a logical outcome of circumstance, when recognition thereof would be inconvenient, by killing off somebody and blinding the reader with a tear-drenched handkerchief. And when we sanely appraise the most cried-up writer of genteel 'realism,' matters are not conducted much more candidly. Here is a fair sample:—'From the very beginning of my acquaintance with you, your manners, impressing me with the fullest belief of your arrogance, your conceit, and your selfish disdain of the feelings of others, were such as to form that ground-work of disapprobation on which succeeding events have built so immovable a dislike, and I had not known you a month before I felt that you were the last man in the world whom I could ever be prevailed on to marry.' It is Miss Austen's most famous, most beloved, and most 'natural' character replying—not by means of a stilted letter, but colloquially, under the stress of emotion—to a proposal of marriage by the man she loves. This is a crisis which in human life a normal young women simply does not meet with any such rhetorical architecture. . . . So there really seems small ground for wonder that Mr. Darcy observed, 'You have said quite enough, madam'; and no cause whatever for surprise that he hastily left the room, and was heard to open the front-door and quit the house. . . . Yet, be it forthwith added, Scott and Dickens and Thackeray, and even Miss Austen, were in the right, from one or another æsthetic standpoint, in thus variously editing and revising their contemporaries' unsatisfactory disposition of life. Indeed, upon no plea could they be bound to emulate malfeasance.

Criticism as to the veracity of more recent writers is best dismissed with the well-merited commendation that novelists to-day continue rigorously to respect the Second Commandment. Meanwhile it may, with comparative safety, be pointed out that no interred writer of widely conceded genius has ever displayed in depicting the average of human speech and thought and action, and general endowments, such exactness as would be becoming in an affidavit; but rather, when his art touched on these dangerous topics, has regarded romantic prevarication as a necessity. The truth about ourselves is the one truth, above all others, which we are adamantine not to face. And this determination springs, not wholly from vanity, but from a profound race-sense that by such denial we have little to lose, and a great deal to gain.

7

For, as has been said before, an inveterate Sophocles notes clearly that veracity is the one unpardonable sin, not merely against art, but against human welfare. . . . You will observe that the beginnings of fiction everywhere, among all races, take with curious unanimity the same form. It is always the history of the unlooked-for achievements and the ultimate, very public triumph of the ill-used youngest son. From the myth of Zeus, third son of Chronos, to the third prince of the fairy-tale, there is no exception. Everywhere it is to the despised weakling that romance accords the final and very public victory. For in the life-battle for existence it was of course the men of

puniest build who first developed mental ability, since hardier compeers, who took with bloodied hands that which they wanted, had no especial need of less reliable makeshifts: and everywhere this weakling, quite naturally, afforded himself in imagination what the force of circumstance denied him in fact. Competent persons, then as now, had neither the time nor ability for literature.

By and by a staggering stroke of genius improved the tale by adding the handicap of sex-weakness: and Cinderella (whom romance begot and deified as Psyche) straightway led captive every dreamer's hitherto unvoiced desire. This is the most beloved story in the world's library, and, barring a tremendous exception to which I shall presently return, will always remain without rival. Any author anywhere can gain men's love by remodeling (not too drastically) the history of Cinderella: thousands of calligraphic persons have, of course, availed themselves of this fortunate circumstance: and the seeming miracle is that the naïve and the most sophisticated continue to thrill, at each re-telling of the hackneyed story, with the instant response of fiddlestrings, to an interpretation of life which one is tempted to describe as fiddlesticks. Yet an inevitable, very public triumph of the downtrodden—with all imaginable pomp and fanfare—is of necessity a tenet generally acceptable to a world of ineffectual inhabitants, each one of whom is a monarch of dreams incarcerated in a prison of flesh; and each of whom is hourly fretted, no less by the indifference of nature to his plight, than by the irrelevancy thereto of those social orderings he dazedly ballots into existence. . . . Christianity, with its teaching that the oppressed shall be exalted, and the unhappy made free of eternal bliss, thus came in the nick of occasion, to promise what the run of men were eager to believe. Such a delectable prospect, irrespective of its plausibility, could not in the nature of things fail to become popular: as has been strikingly attested by man's wide acceptance of the rather exigent requirements of Christianity, and his honest endeavors ever since to interpret them as meaning whatever happens to be convenient.

In similar fashion, humanity would seem

at an early period to have wrenched comfort from prefiguring man as the hero of the cosmic romance. For it was unpleasantly apparent that man did not excel in physical strength, as set against the other creatures of a planet whereon may be encountered tigers and elephants. His senses were of low development, as compared with the senses of insects: and, indeed, senses possessed by some of these small contemporaries man presently found he did not share, nor very clearly understand. The luxury of wings, and even the common comfort of a caudal appendage, was denied him. He walked painfully, without hoofs, and, created naked as a shelled almond, with difficulty outlived a season of inclement weather. Physically, he displayed in not a solitary trait a product of nature's more ambitious labor. . . . He, thus, surpassed the rest of vital creation in nothing except, as was beginning to be rumored, the power to reason; and even so, was apparently too magnanimous to avail himself of the privilege.

But to acknowledge such disconcerting facts would never do: just as inevitably, therefore, as the peafowl came to listen with condescension to the nightingale, and the tortoise to deplore the slapdash ways of his contemporaries, man probably began very early to regale himself with flattering narratives as to his nature and destiny. Among the countless internecine animals that roamed earth, puissant with claw and fang and sinew, an ape reft of his tail, and grown rusty at climbing, was the most formidable, and in the end would triumph. It was of course considered blasphemous to inquire into the grounds for this belief, in view of its patent desirability, for the race was already human. So the prophetic portrait of man treading among cringing pleosauri to browbeat a frightened dinosaur was duly scratched upon the cave's wall, and art began forthwith to accredit human beings with every trait and destiny which they desiderated. . . .

And so to-day, as always, we delight to hear about invincible men and women of unearthly loveliness—corrected and considerably augmented versions of our family circle,—performing feats illimitably beyond our modest powers. And so to-day no one upon the preferable side of Bedlam wishes to be reminded of what we are in actuality,

even were it possible, by any disastrous miracle, ever to dispel the mist which romance has evoked about all human doings; and to the golden twilight of which old usage has so accustomed us that, like nocturnal birds, our vision grows perturbed in a clearer atmosphere. And we have come very firmly to believe in the existence of men everywhere, not as in fact they are, but 'as they ought to be.'

8

Now art, like all the other noteworthy factors in this remarkable world, serves in the end utilitarian purposes. When a trait is held up as desirable, for a convincingly long while, the average person, out of self-respect, pretends to possess it: with time, he acts letter-perfect as one endowed therewith, and comes unshakably to believe that it has guided him from infancy. For while everyone is notoriously swayed by appearances, this is more especially true of his own appearance: cleanliness is, if not actually next to godliness, so far a promoter of benevolence that no man feels upon quite friendly terms with his fellow-beings when conscious that he needs a shave; and if in grief you resolutely contort your mouth into a smile you somehow do become forthwith aware of a considerable mitigation of misery. . . . So it is that man's vanity and hypocrisy and lack of clear thinking are in a fair way to prove in the outcome his salvation.

All is vanity, quoth the son of David, inverting the truth for popular consumption, as became a wise Preacher who knew that vanity is all. For man alone of animals plays the ape to his dreams. That a dog dreams vehemently is matter of public knowledge: it is perfectly possible that in his more ecstatic visions he usurps the shape of his master, and visits Elysian pantries in human form: with awakening, he observes that in point of fact he is a dog, and as a rational animal, makes the best of canineship. But with man the case is otherwise, in that when logic leads to any humiliating conclusion, the sole effect is to discredit logic.

So has man's indomitable vanity made a harem of his instincts, and walled off a seraglio wherein to beget the virtues and refinements and all ennobling factors in man's long progress from gorillaship. As has been suggested, creative literature would seem to have sprung simply from the instinct of any hurt animal to seek revenge,—and 'to get even,' as the phrase runs, in the field of imagination when such revenge was not feasible in any other arena. . . . Then, too, it is an instinct common to brute creatures that the breeding or even the potential mother must not be bitten,—upon which modest basis a little by a little mankind builded the fair code of domnei, or woman-worship, which for so long a while did yeoman service among legislators toward keeping half our citizens 'out of the mire of politics,' and which still enables any reputable looking married woman to kill whatsoever male she elects with impunity. From the shuddering dread that beasts manifest toward uncomprehended forces, such as wind and thunder and tall waves, man developed religion, and a consoling assurance of divine paternity. And when you come to judge what he made of sexual desire, appraising the deed in view as against the wondrous overture of courtship and that infinity of high achievements which time has seen performed as grace-notes, words fail before his egregious thaumaturgy. For after any such stupendous bit of hocus-pocus, there seems to be no limit fixed to the conjurations of human vanity.

9

And these aspiring notions blended a great while since, into what may be termed the Chivalrous attitude toward life. Thus it is that romance, the real demiurge, the first and loveliest daughter of human vanity, contrives all those dynamic illusions which are used to further the ultimate ends of romance. . . . The cornerstone of Chivalry I take to be the idea of vicarship: for the chivalrous person is, in his own eyes at least, the child of God, and goes about this world as his Father's representative in an alien country. It was very adroitly to human pride, through an assumption of man's personal responsibility in his tiniest action, that Chivalry made its appeal; and exhorted every man to keep faith, not merely with the arbitrary will of a strong god, but with himself. There is no cause for wonder that the appeal was irresistible, when to each man it thus admitted that he himself was

the one thing seriously to be considered. . . . So man became a chivalrous animal; and about this flattering notion of divine vicarship builded his elaborate mediæval code, to which, in essentials, a great number of persons adhere even nowadays. Questionless, however, the Chivalrous attitude does not very happily fit in with modern conditions, whereby the self-elected obligations of the knight-errant toward repressing evil are (in theory at all events) more efficaciously discharged by an organized police and a jury system.

And perhaps it was never, quite, a 'practical' attitude,—no, *mais quel geste!* as was observed by a pre-eminently chivalrous person. At worst, it is an attitude which one finds very taking to the fancy as the posture is exemplified by divers mediæval chroniclers, who had sound notions about portraying men 'as they ought to be.' . . . There is Nicolas de Caen, for instance, who in his *Dizain des Reines* (with which I am familiar, I confess, in the English version alone) presents with some naïveté this notion of divine vicarship, in that he would seem to restrict it to the nobility and gentry. 'For royal persons and their immediate associates,' Dom Nicolas assumes at outset, 'are the responsible stewards of Heaven': and regarding them continuously as such, he selects from the lives of various queens ten crucial moments wherein (as Nicolas phrases it), 'Destiny has thrust her sceptre into the hands of a human being, and left the weakling free to steer the pregnant outcome. Now prove thyself to be at bottom a god or else a beast, saith Destiny, and now eternally abide that choice.' Yet this, and this alone, when you come to think of it, is what Destiny says, not merely to 'royal persons and their immediate associates,' but to everyone. . . . And in his *Roman de Lusignan* Nicolas deals with that quaint development of the Chivalrous attitude to which I just alluded, that took form, as an allied but individual illusion, in domnei, or woman-worship; and found in a man's mistress an ever-present reminder, and sometimes a rival of God. There is something not unpathetic in the thought that this once world-controlling force is restricted to-day to removing a man's hat in an elevator and occasionally compelling a surrender of his seat in a streetcar. . . . But this *Roman de*

Lusignan also has been put into English, with an Afterword by the translator wherein the theories of domnei are rather painstakingly set forth: and thereto I shall presently recur, for further consideration of this illusion of domnei.

Always, of course, the Chivalrous attitude was an intelligent attitude, in which one spun romances and accorded no meticulous attention to mere facts. . . . For thus to spin romances is to bring about, in every sense, man's recreation, since man alone of animals can, actually, acquire a trait by assuming, in defiance of reason, that he already possesses it. To spin romances is, indeed, man's proper and peculiar function in a world wherein he only of created beings can make no profitable use of the truth about himself. For man alone of animals plays the ape to his dreams. So he fares onward chivalrously, led by ignes fatui no doubt, yet moving onward. And that the goal remains ambiguous seems but a trivial circumstance to any living creature who knows, he knows not how, that to stay still can be esteemed a virtue only in the dead.

10

Indeed, when I consider the race to which I have the honor to belong, I am filled with respectful wonder. . . . All about us flows and gyrates unceasingly the material universe,—an endless inconceivable jumble of rotatory blazing gas and frozen spheres and detonating comets, wherethrough spins Earth like a frail midge. And to this blown molecule adhere what millions and millions and millions of parasites just such as I am, begetting and dreaming and slaying and abnegating and

toiling and making mirth, just as did aforetime those countless generations of our forebears, every one of whom was likewise a creature just such as I am! Were the human beings that have been subjected to confinement in flesh each numbered, as is customary in other penal institutes, with what interminable row of digits might one set forth your number, say, or mine?

Nor is this everything. For my reason, such as it is, perceives this race, in its entirety, in the whole outcome of its achievement, to be beyond all wording petty and ineffectual: and no more than thought can estimate the relative proportion to the material universe of our poor Earth, can thought conceive with what quintillionths to express that fractional part which I, as an individual parasite, add to Earth's negligible fretting by ephemeræ.

And still—behold the miracle!—still I believe life to be a personal transaction between myself and Omnipotence; I believe that what I do is somehow of importance; and I believe that I am on a journey toward some very public triumph not unlike that of the third prince in the fairy-tale. . . . Even to-day I believe in this dynamic illusion. For that creed was the first great inspiration of the demiurge,—man's big romantic idea of Chivalry, of himself as his Father's representative in an alien country;—and it is a notion at which mere fact and reason yelp denial unavailingly. For every one of us is so constituted that he knows the romance to be true, and corporal fact and human reason in this matter, as in divers others, to be the suborned and perjured witnesses of 'realism.'

1917–1918   1919

JOHN REED

1887–1920

FROM TEN DAYS THAT SHOOK THE WORLD

Moscow [1]

THE Military Revolutionary Committee, with a fierce intensity, followed up its victory:

[1] The selection is Chapter 10 of *Ten Days That Shook the World* (N.Y., 1919).

NOVEMBER 14TH.

To all Army, corps, divisional and regimental Committees, to all Soviets of Workers', Soldiers' and Peasants' Deputies, to all, all, all.

Conforming to the agreement between the Cossacks, *yunkers*, soldiers, sailors and workers, it has been decided to arraign Alexander Feodorvitch Kerensky before a tribunal of the people. We demand that Kerensky be arrested, and that he be ordered, in the name of the organizations hereinafter mentioned, to come immediately to Petrograd and present himself to the tribunal.

SIGNED,
The Cossacks of the First Division of Ussuri Cavalry; the Committee of Yunkers of the Petrograd detachment of Franc-Tireurs; the delegate of the Fifth Army.

PEOPLE'S COMMISSAR   DYBENKO

The Committee for Salvation, the Duma, the Central Committee of the Socialist Revolutionary party—proudly claiming Kerensky as a member—all passionately protested that he could only be held responsible to the Constituent Assembly.

On the evening of November 16th I watched two thousand Red Guards swing down the Zagorodny Prospekt behind a military band playing the *Marseillaise*—and how appropriate it sounded—with blood-red flags over the dark ranks of workmen, to welcome home again their brothers who had defended 'Red Petrograd.' In the bitter dusk they tramped, men and women, their tall bayonets swaying; through streets faintly lighted and slippery with mud, between silent crowds of bourgeois, contemptuous but fearful. . . .

All were against them—business men, speculators, investors, land-owners, army officers, politicians, teachers, students, professional men, shop-keepers, clerks, agents. The other Socialist parties hated the Bolsheviki with an implacable hatred. On the side of the Soviets were the rank and file of the workers, the sailors, all the undemoralized soldiers, the landless peasants, and a few—a very few—intellectuals. . . .

From the farthest corners of great Russia, whereupon desperate street-fighting burst like a wave, news of Kerensky's defeat came echoing back the immense roar of proletarian victory. Kazan, Saratov, Novgorod, Vinnitza—where the streets had run with blood; Moscow, where the Bolsheviki had

turned their artillery against the last stronghold of the bourgeoisie—the Kremlin.

'They are bombarding the Kremlin!' The news passed from mouth to mouth in the streets of Petrograd, almost with a sense of terror. Travellers from 'white and shining little mother Moscow' told fearful tales. Thousands killed; the Tverskaya and the Kuznetsky Most in flames; the church of Vasili Blazheiny a smoking ruin; Usspensky Cathedral crumbling down; the Spasskaya Gate of the Kremlin tottering; the Duma burned to the ground.

Nothing that the Bolsheviki had done could compare with this fearful blasphemy in the heart of Holy Russia. To the ears of the devout sounded the shock of guns crashing in the face of the Holy Orthodox Church, and pounding to dust the sanctuary of the Russian nation. . . .

On November 15th, Lunatcharsky, Commissar of Education, broke into tears at the session of the Council of People's Commissars, and rushed from the room, crying, 'I cannot stand it! I cannot bear the monstrous destruction of beauty and tradition. . . .'

That afternoon his letter of resignation was published in the newspapers:

I have just been informed, by people arriving from Moscow, what has happened there.

The Cathedral of St. Basil the Blessed, the Cathedral of the Assumption, are being bombarded. The Kremlin, where are now gathered the most important art treasures of Petrograd and of Moscow, is under artillery fire. There are thousands of victims.

The fearful struggle there has reached a pitch of bestial ferocity.

What is left? What more can happen?

I cannot bear this. My cup is full. I am unable to endure these horrors. It is impossible to work under the pressure of thoughts which drive me mad!

That is why I am leaving the Council of People's Commissars.

I fully realize the gravity of this decision. But I can bear no more. . . .

That same day the White Guards and *yunkers* in the Kremlin surrendered, and were allowed to march out unharmed. The treaty of peace follows:

1. The Committee of Public Safety ceases to exist.

2. The White Guard gives up its arms and dissolves. The officers retain their swords and regulation side-arms. In the Military Schools are retained only the arms necessary for instruction; all others are surrendered by the *yunkers*. The Military Revolutionary Committee guarantees the liberty and inviolability of the person.

3. To settle the question of disarmament, as set forth in section 2, a special commission is appointed, consisting of representatives from all organisations which took part in the peace negotiations.

4. From the moment of the signature of this peace treaty, both parties shall immediately give order to cease firing and halt all military operations, taking measures to ensure punctual obedience to this order.

5. At the signature of the treaty, all prisoners made by the two parties shall be released. . . .

For two days now the Bolsheviki had been in control of the city. The frightened citizens were creeping out of their cellars to seek their dead; the barricades in the streets were being removed. Instead of diminishing, however, the stories of destruction in Moscow continued to grow. . . . And it was under the influence of these fearful reports that we decided to go there.

Petrograd, after all, in spite of being for a century the seat of Government, is still an artificial city. Moscow is real Russia, Russia as it was and will be; in Moscow we would get the true feeling of the Russian people about the Revolution. Life was more intense there.

For the past week the Petrograd Military Revolutionary Committee, aided by the rank and file of the Railway Workers, had seized control of the Nicolai Railroad, and hurled trainload after trainload of sailors and Red Guards southwest. . . . We were provided with passes from Smolny, without which no one could leave the capital. . . . When the train backed into the station, a mob of shabby soldiers, all carrying huge sacks of eatables, stormed the doors, smashed the windows, and poured into all the compartments, filling up the aisles and even climbing onto the roof. Three of us managed to wedge our way into a compartment, but almost immediately about twenty soldiers entered. . . . There was room for only four people; we argued, expostulated, and the conductor joined us—but the soldiers merely laughed. Were they to bother about the comfort of a lot of *boorzhui* (bourgeois)? We produced the passes from Smolny; instantly the soldiers changed their attitude.

'Come, comrades,' cried one, 'these are American *tovarishtchi*. They have come thirty thousand versts to see our Revolution, and they are naturally tired. . . .'

With polite and friendly apologies the soldiers began to leave. Shortly afterward we heard them breaking into a compartment occupied by two stout, well-dressed Russians, who had bribed the conductor and locked their door. . . .

About seven o'clock in the evening we drew out of the station, an immense long train drawn by a weak little locomotive burning wood, and stumbled along slowly, with many stops. The soldiers on the roof kicked with their heels and sang whining peasant songs; and in the corridor, so jammed that it was impossible to pass, violent political debates raged all night long. Occasionally the conductor came through, as a matter of habit, looking for tickets. He found very few except ours, and after a half-hour of futile wrangling, lifted his arms despairingly and withdrew. The atmosphere was stifling, full of smoke and foul odours; if it hadn't been for the broken windows we would doubtless have smothered during the night.

In the morning, hours late, we looked out upon a snowy world. It was bitter cold. About noon a peasant woman got on with a basket-full of bread-chunks and a great can of luke warm coffee-substitute. From then on until dark there was nothing but the packed train, jolting and stopping, and occasional stations where a ravenous mob swooped down on the scantily-furnished buffet and swept it clean. . . . At one of these halts I ran into Nogin and Rykov, the seceding Commissars, who were returning to Moscow to put their grievances before their own Soviet; and further along was Bukharin, a short, red-bearded man with the eyes of a fanatic—'more Left than Lenin,' they said of him. . . .

Then the three strokes of the bell and we made a rush for the train, worming our way through the packed and noisy aisle. . . . A good-natured crowd, bearing the discomfort with humorous patience, interminably arguing about everything from the situation in Petrograd to the British Trade-Union system, and disputing loudly with the few boorzhui who were on board. Before we reached Moscow almost every car had organized a Committee to secure and distribute food, and these Committees became divided into political factions, who wrangled over fundamental principles. . . .

The station at Moscow was deserted. We went to the office of the Commissar, in order to arrange for our return tickets. He was a sullen youth with the shoulder-straps of a Lieutenant; when we showed him our papers from Smolny, he lost his temper and declared that he was no Bolshevik, that he represented the Committee of Public Safety. . . . It was characteristic—in the general turmoil attending the conquest of the city, the chief railway station had been forgotten by the victors. . . .

Not a cab in sight. A few blocks down the street, however, we woke up a grotesquely-padded izvostchik asleep upright on the box of his little sleigh. 'How much to the centre of the town?'

He scratched his head. 'The barini won't be able to find a room in any hotel,' he said. 'But I'll take you around for a hundred rubles. . . .' Before the Revolution it cost two! We objected, but he simply shrugged his shoulders. 'It takes a good deal of courage to drive a sleigh nowadays,' he went on. We could not beat him down below fifty. . . . As we sped along the silent, snowy half-lighted streets, he recounted his adventures during the six days' fighting. 'Driving along, or waiting for a fare on the corner,' he said, 'all of a sudden pooff! a cannon ball exploding here, pooff! a cannon ball there, ratt-ratt! a machine-gun. . . . I gallop, the devils shooting all around. I get to a nice quiet street and stop, doze a little, pooff! another cannon ball, ratt-ratt. . . . Devils! Devils! Devils! Brrr!'

In the centre of the town the snow-piled streets were quiet with the stillness of convalescence. Only a few arc-lights were burning, only a few pedestrians hurried along the side-walks. An icy wind blew from the great plain, cutting to the bone. At the first hotel we entered an office illuminated by two candles.

'Yes, we have some very comfortable rooms, but all the windows are shot out. If the gospodin does not mind a little fresh air. . . .'

Down the Tverskaya the shop-windows were broken, and there were shell-holes and torn-up paving stones in the street. Hotel after hotel, all full, or the proprietors still so frightened that all they could say was, 'No, no, there is no room! There is no room!' On the main streets, where the great banking-houses and mercantile houses lay, the Bolshevik artillery had been indiscriminately effective. As one Soviet official told me, 'Whenever we didn't know just where the yunkers and White Guards were, we bombarded their pocket-books. . . .'

At the big Hotel National they finally took us in; for we were foreigners, and the Military Revolutionary Committee had promised to protect the dwellings of foreigners. . . . On the top floor the manager showed us where shrapnel had shattered several windows. 'The animals!' said he, shaking his fist at imaginary Bolsheviki. 'But wait! Their time will come; in just a few days now their ridiculous Government will fall, and then we shall make them suffer!'

We dined at a vegetarian restaurant with the enticing name, 'I Eat Nobody,' and Tolstoy's picture prominent on the walls, and then sallied out into the streets.

The headquarters of the Moscow Soviet was in the palace of the former Governor-General, an imposing white building fronting Skobeliev Square. Red Guards stood sentry at the door. At the head of the wide, formal stairway, whose walls were plastered with announcements of committee-meetings and addresses of political parties, we passed through a series of lofty ante-rooms, hung with red-shrouded pictures in gold frames, to the splendid state salon, with its magnificent crystal lustres and gilded cornices. A low-voiced hum of talk, underlaid with the whirring bass of a score of sewing machines, filled the place. Huge bolts of red and black cotton cloth were unrolled, serpentining across the parqueted floor and over tables, at which sat half a hundred women, cutting and sewing streamers and banners for the Funeral of the Revolutionary Dead. The faces of these women were roughened and scarred with life at its most difficult; they worked now sternly, many of them with eyes red from weeping. . . .The losses of the Red Army had been heavy.

At a desk in one corner was Rogov, an intelligent, bearded man with glasses, wearing the black blouse of a worker. He invited us to march with the Central Executive Committee in the funeral procession next morning. . . .

'It is impossible to teach the Socialist Revolutionaries and the Mensheviki anything!' he exclaimed. 'They compromise from sheer habit. Imagine! They proposed that we hold a joint funeral with the *yunkers!*'

Across the hall came a man in a ragged soldier-coat and *shapka*, whose face was familiar; I recognized Melnichansky, whom I had known as the watch-maker George Melcher in Bayonne, New Jersey, during the great Standard Oil strike. Now, he told me, he was secretary of the Moscow Metal-Workers' Union, and a Commissar of the Military Revolutionary Committee during the fighting. . . .

'You see me!' he cried, showing his decrepit clothing. 'I was with the boys in the Kremlin when the *yunkers* came the first time. They shut me up in the cellar and swiped my overcoat, my money, watch and even the ring on my finger. This is all I've got to wear!'

From him I learned many details of the bloody six-day battle which had rent Moscow in two. Unlike in Petrograd, in Moscow the City Duma had taken command of the *yunkers* and White Guards. Rudnev, the Mayor, and Minor, president of the Duma, had directed the activities of the Committee of Public Safety and the troops. Riabtsev, Commandant of the city, a man of democratic instincts, had hesitated about opposing the Military Revolutionary Committee; but the Duma had forced him. . . . It was the Mayor who had urged the occupation of the Kremlin; 'They will never dare fire on you there,' he said. . . .

One garrison regiment, badly demoralized by long inactivity, had been approached by both sides. The regiment held a meeting to decide what action to take. Resolved, that the regiment remain neutral, and continue its present activities—which consisted in peddling rubbers and sunflower seeds!

'But worst of all,' said Melnichansky, 'we had to organize while we were fighting. The other side knew just what it wanted; but here the soldiers had their Soviet and the workers theirs. . . . There was a fearful wrangle over who should be Commander-in-chief; some regiments talked for days before they decided what to do; and when the officers suddenly deserted us, we had no battle-staff to give orders. . . .'

Vivid little pictures he gave me. On a cold grey day he had stood at a corner of the Nikitskaya, which was swept by blasts of machine-gun fire. A throng of little boys were gathered there—street waifs who used to be newsboys. Shrill, excited as if with a new game, they waited until the firing slackened, and then tried to run across the street. . . . Many were killed, but the rest dashed backward and forward, laughing, daring each other. . . .

Late in the evening I went to the *Dvorianskoye Sobranie*—the Nobles' Club—where the Moscow Bolsheviki were to meet and consider the report of Nogin, Rykov and the others who had left the Council of People's Commissars.

The meeting-place was a theatre, in which, under the old régime, to audiences of officers and glittering ladies, amateur presentations of the latest French comedy had once taken place.

At first the place filled with the intellectuals—those who lived near the centre of the town. Nogin spoke, and most of his listeners were plainly with him. It was very late before the workers arrived; the working-class quarters were on the outskirts of the town, and no street-cars were running. But about midnight they began to clump up the stairs, in groups of ten or twenty—big, rough men, in coarse clothes, fresh from the battle-line, where they had fought like devils for a week, seeing their comrades fall all about them.

Scarcely had the meeting formally opened before Nogin was assailed with a tempest of jeers and angry shouts. In vain he tried to argue, to explain; they would not listen. He had left the Council of People's Commissars; he had deserted his post while the battle was raging. As for the bourgeois press, here in Moscow there was no more bourgeois press; even the City Duma had been dissolved. Bukharin stood up, savage, logical, with a voice which plunged and struck, plunged and struck. . . . Him they listened to with shining eyes. Resolution, to support the action of the Council of People's Commissars, passed by overwhelming majority. So spoke Moscow. . . .

Late in the night we went through the empty streets and under the Iberian Gate to the great Red Square in front of the Kremlin. The church of Vasili Blazheiny loomed fantastic, its bright-coloured, convoluted and blazoned cupolas vague in the darkness. There was no sign of any damage. . . . Along one side of the square the dark towers and walls of the Kremlin stood up. On the high walls flickered redly the light of hidden flames; voices reached us across the immense place, and the sound of picks and shovels. We crossed over.

Mountains of dirt and rock were piled high near the base of the wall. Climbing these we looked down into two massive pits, ten or fifteen feet deep and fifty yards long, where hundreds of soldiers and workers were digging in the light of huge fires.

A young student spoke to us in German. 'The Brotherhood Grave,' he explained. 'To-morrow we shall bury here five hundred proletarians who died for the Revolution.'

He took us down into the pit. In frantic haste swung the picks and shovels, and the earth-mountains grew. No one spoke. Overhead the night was thick with stars, and the ancient Imperial Kremlin wall towered up immeasurably.

'Here in this holy place,' said the student, 'holiest of all Russia, we shall bury our most holy. Here where are the tombs of the Tsars, our Tsar—the People—shall sleep. . . .' His arm was in a sling, from a bullet-wound gained in the fighting. He looked at it. 'You foreigners look down on us Russians because so long we tolerated a mediæval monarchy,' said he. 'But we saw that the Tsar was not the only tyrant in the world; capitalism was worse, and in all the countries of the world capitalism was Emperor. . . . Russian revolutionary tactics are best. . . .'

As we left, the workers in the pit, exhausted and running with sweat in spite of the cold, began to climb wearily out. Across the Red Square a dark knot of men came hurrying. They swarmed into the pits, picked up the tools and began digging, digging, without a word. . . .

So, all the long night volunteers of the People relieved each other, never halting in their driving speed, and the cold light of the dawn laid bare the great Square, white with snow, and the yawning brown pits of the Brotherhood Grave, quite finished.

We rose before sunrise, and hurried through the dark streets to Skobeliev Square. In all the great city not a human being could be seen; but there was a faint sound of stirring, far and near, like a deep wind coming. In the pale half-light a little group of men and women were gathered before the Soviet headquarters, with a sheaf of gold-lettered red banners—the Central Executive Committee of the Moscow Soviets. It grew light. From afar the vague stirring sound deepened and became louder, a steady and tremendous bass. The city was rising. We set out down the Tverskaya, the banners flapping overhead. The little street chapels along our way were locked and dark, as was the Chapel of the Iberian Virgin, which each new Tsar used to visit before he went to the Kremlin to crown himself, and which, day or night, was always open and crowded, and brilliant with the candles of the devout gleaming on the gold and silver and jewels of the ikons. Now, for the first time since Napoleon was in Moscow, they say, the candles were out.

The Holy Orthodox Church had withdrawn the light of its countenance from Moscow, the nest of irreverent vipers who had bombarded the Kremlin. Dark and silent and cold were the churches; the priests had disappeared. There were no popes to officiate at the Red Burial, there had been no sacrament for the dead, nor were any prayers to be said over the grave of the blasphemers. Tikhon, Metropolitan of Moscow, was soon to excommunicate the Soviets. . . .

Also the shops were closed, and the propertied classes stayed at home—but for other reasons. This was the Day of the People, the rumour of whose coming was thunderous as surf. . . .

Already through the Iberian Gate a human river was flowing, and the vast Red Square was spotted with people, thousands of them. I remarked that as the throng passed the Iberian Chapel, where always before the passerby had crossed himself, they did not seem to notice it. . . .

We forced our way through the dense mass packed near the Kremlin wall, and stood upon one of the dirt-mountains. Already several men were there, among them Muranov, the soldier who had been elected Commandant of Moscow—a tall, simple-looking, bearded man with a gentle face.

Through all the streets to the Red Square the torrents of people poured, thousands upon thousands of them, all with the look of the poor and the toiling. A military band came marching up, playing the *Internationale*, and spontaneously the song caught and spread like wind-ripples on a sea, slow and solemn. From the top of the Kremlin wall gigantic banners unrolled to the ground; red, with great letters in gold and in white, saying, 'Martyrs of the Beginning of World Social Revolution,' and 'Long Live the Brotherhood of Workers of the World.'

A bitter wind swept the Square, lifting the banners. Now from the far quarters of the city the workers of the different factories were arriving, with their dead. They could be seen coming through the Gate, the blare of their banners, and the dull red—like blood—of the coffins they carried. These were rude boxes, made of unplaned wood and daubed with crimson, borne high on the shoulders of rough men who marched with tears streaming down their faces, and followed by women who sobbed and screamed, or walked stiffly, with white, dead faces. Some of the coffins were open, the lid carried behind them; others were covered with gilded or silvered cloth, or had a soldier's hat nailed on the top. There were many wreaths of hideous artificial flowers. . . .

Through an irregular lane that opened and closed again the procession slowly moved toward us. Now through the Gate was flowing an endless stream of banners, all shades of red, with silver and gold lettering, knots of crepe hanging from the top—and some Anarchist flags, black with white letters. The band was playing the Revolutionary Funeral March, and against the immense singing of the mass of people, standing uncovered, the paraders sang hoarsely, choked with sobs. . . .

Between the factory-workers came companies of soldiers with their coffins, too, and squadrons of cavalry, riding at salute, and artillery batteries, the cannon wound with red and black—forever, it seemed. Their banners said, 'Long Live the Third International!' or 'We Want an Honest, General, Democratic Peace!'

Slowly the marchers came with their coffins to the entrance of the grave, and the bearers clambered up with their burdens and went down into the pit. Many of them were women—squat, strong proletarian women. Behind the dead came other women—women young and broken, or old, wrinkled women making noises like hurt animals, who tried to follow their sons and husbands into the Brotherhood Grave, and shrieked when compassionate hands restrained them. The poor love each other so!

All the long day the funeral procession passed, coming in by the Iberian Gate and leaving the Square by way of the Nikolskaya, a river of red banners, bearing words of hope and brotherhood and stupendous prophecies, against a back-ground of fifty thousand people,—under the eyes of the world's workers and their descendants forever. . . .

One by one the five hundred coffins were laid in the pits. Dusk fell, and still the banners came drooping and fluttering, the band played the Funeral March, and the huge assemblage chanted. In the leafless branches of the trees above the grave the wreaths were hung, like strange, multi-coloured blossoms. Two hundred men began to shovel in the dirt. It rained dully down upon the coffins with a thudding sound, audible beneath the singing. . . .

The lights came out. The last banners passed, and the last moaning women, looking back with awful intensity as they went. Slowly from the great Square ebbed the proletarian tide. . . .

I suddenly realized that the devout Russian people no longer needed priests to pray them into heaven. On earth they were building a kingdom more bright than any

heaven had to offer, and for which it was a glory to die. . . .

1918

1919

HENRY L. MENCKEN

1880–

BRYAN

HAS it been duly marked by historians that the late William Jennings Bryan's last secular act on this globe of sin was to catch flies? A curious detail, and not without its sardonic overtones. He was the most sedulous fly-catcher in American history, and in many ways the most successful. His quarry, of course, was not *Musca domestica* but *Homo neandertalensis*. For forty years he tracked it with coo and bellow, up and down the rustic backways of the Republic. Wherever the flambeaux of Chautauqua smoked and guttered, and the bilge of Idealism ran in the veins, and Baptist pastors dammed the brooks with the sanctified, and men gathered who were weary and heavy laden, and their wives who were full of Peruna and as fecund as the shad (*Alosa sapidissima*)—there the indefatigable Jennings set up his traps and spread his bait. He knew every country town in the South and West, and he could crowd the most remote of them to suffocation by simply winding his horn. The city proletariat, transiently flustered by him in 1896, quickly penetrated his buncombe and would have no more of him; the cockney gallery jeered him at every Democratic national convention for twenty-five years. But out where the grass grows high, and the horned cattle dream away the lazy afternoons, and men still fear the powers and principalities of the air—out there between the corn-rows he held his old puissance to the end. There was no need of beaters to drive in his game. The news that he was coming was enough. For miles the flivver dust would choke the roads. And when he rose at the end of the day to discharge his Message there would be such breathless attention, such a rapt and enchanted ecstasy, such a sweet rustle of amens as the world had not known since Johann fell to Herod's sardonic ax.

There was something peculiarly fitting in

the fact that his last days were spent in a one-horse Tennessee village, and that death found him there. The man felt at home in such simple and Christian scenes. He liked people who sweated freely, and were not debauched by the refinements of the toilet. Making his progress up and down the Main Street of little Dayton, surrounded by gaping primates from the upland valleys of the Cumberland Range, his coat laid aside, his bare arms and hairy chest shining damply, his bald head sprinkled with dust—so accoutred and on display he was obviously happy. He liked getting up early in the morning, to the tune of cocks crowing on the dunghill. He liked the heavy, greasy victuals of the farmhouse kitchen. He liked country lawyers, country pastors, all country people. He liked country sounds and country smells. I believe that this liking was sincere—perhaps the only sincere thing in the man. His nose showed no uneasiness when a hillman in faded overalls and hickory shirt accosted him on the street, and besought him for light upon some mystery of Holy Writ. The simian gabble of the cross-roads was not gabble to him, but wisdom of an occult and superior sort. In the presence of city folks he was palpably uneasy. Their clothes, I suspect, annoyed him, and he was suspicious of their too delicate manners. He knew all the while that they were laughing at him—if not at his baroque theology, then at least at his alpaca pantaloons. But the yokels never laughed at him. To them he was not the huntsman but the prophet, and toward the end, as he gradually forsook mundane politics for more ghostly concerns, they began to elevate him in their hierarchy. When he died he was the peer of Abraham. His old enemy, Wilson, aspiring to the same white and shining robe, came down with a thump. But Bryan made the grade. His place in the Tennessee hagiography is secure. If the village barber saved any of his hair, then it is curing gall-stones down there to-day. But what label will he bear in more urbane regions? One, I fear, of a far less flattering kind. Bryan lived too long, and descended too deeply into the mud, to be taken seriously hereafter by fully literate men, even of the kind who write school-books. There was a scattering of sweet words in his funeral notices, but it was no more than a response to conventional sentimentality. The best verdict the most romantic editorial writer could dredge up, save in the humorless South, was to the general effect that his imbecilities were excused by his earnestness—that under his clowning, as under that of the juggler of Notre Dame, there was the zeal of a steadfast soul. But this was apology, not praise; precisely the same thing might be said of Mary Baker G. Eddy, the late Czar Nicholas, or Czolgosz. The truth is that even Bryan's sincerity will probably yield to what is called, in other fields, definitive criticism. Was he sincere when he opposed imperialism in the Philippines, or when he fed it with deserving Democrats in Santo Domingo? Was he sincere when he tried to shove the Prohibitionists under the table, or when he seized their banner and began to lead them with loud whoops? Was he sincere when he bellowed against war, or when he dreamed of himself as a tin-soldier in uniform, with a grave reserved among the generals? Was he sincere when he denounced the late John W. Davis, or when he swallowed Davis? Was he sincere when he fawned over Champ Clark, or when he betrayed Clark? Was he sincere when he pleaded for tolerance in New York, or when he bawled for the faggot and the stake in Tennessee?

This talk of sincerity, I confess, fatigues me. If the fellow was sincere, then so was P. T. Barnum. The word is disgraced and degraded by such uses. He was, in fact, a charlatan, a mountebank, a zany without shame or dignity. His career brought him into contact with the first men of his time; he preferred the company of rustic ignoramuses. It was hard to believe, watching him at Dayton, that he had traveled, that he had been received in civilized societies, that he had been a high officer of state. He seemed only a poor clod like those around him, deluded by a childish theology, full of an almost pathological hatred of all learning,

all human dignity, all beauty, all fine and noble things. He was a peasant come home to the barnyard. Imagine a gentleman, and you have imagined everything that he was not. What animated him from end to end of his grotesque career was simply ambition—the ambition of a common man to get his hand upon the collar of his superiors, or, failing that, to get his thumb into their eyes. He was born with a roaring voice, and it had the trick of inflaming half-wits. His whole career was devoted to raising those half-wits against their betters, that he himself might shine. His last battle will be grossly misunderstood if it is thought of as a mere exercise in fanaticism—that is, if Bryan the Fundamentalist Pope is mistaken for one of the bucolic Fundamentalists. There was much more in it than that, as everyone knows who saw him on the field. What moved him, at bottom, was simply hatred of the city men who had laughed at him so long, and brought him at last to so tatterdemalion an estate. He lusted for revenge upon them. He yearned to lead the anthropoid rabble against them, to punish them for their execution upon him by attacking the very vitals of their civilization. He went far beyond the bounds of any merely religious frenzy, however inordinate. When he began denouncing the notion that man is a mammal even some of the hinds at Dayton were agape. And when, brought upon Darrow's cruel hook, he writhed and tossed in a very fury of malignancy, bawling against the baldest elements of sense and decency like a man frantic—when he came to that tragic climax of his striving there were snickers among the hinds as well as hosannas.

Upon that hook, in truth, Bryan committed suicide, as a legend as well as in the body. He staggered from the rustic court ready to die, and he staggered from it ready to be forgotten, save as a character in a third-rate farce, witless and in poor taste. It was plain to everyone who knew him, when he came to Dayton, that his great days were behind him—that, for all the fury of his hatred, he was now definitely an old man, and headed at last for silence. There was a vague, unpleasant manginess about his appearance; he somehow seemed dirty, though a close glance showed him as carefully shaven as an actor, and clad in immaculate linen. All the hair was gone from the dome of his head, and it had begun to fall out, too, behind his ears, in the obscene manner of the late Samuel Gompers. The resonance had departed from his voice; what was once a bugle blast had become reedy and quavering. Who knows that, like Demosthenes, he had a lisp? In the old days, under the magic of his eloquence, no one noticed it. But when he spoke at Dayton it was always audible.

When I first encountered him, on the sidewalk in front of the office of the rustic lawyers who were his associates in the Scopes case, the trial was yet to begin, and so he was still expansive and amiable. I had printed in the *Nation*, a week or so before, an article arguing that the Tennessee anti-evolution law, whatever its wisdom, was at least constitutional—that the rustics of the State had a clear right to have their progeny taught whatever they chose, and kept secure from whatever knowledge violated their superstitions. The old boy professed to be delighted with the argument, and gave the gaping bystanders to understand that I was a publicist of parts. Not to be outdone, I admired the preposterous country shirt that he wore—sleeveless and with the neck cut very low. We parted in the manner of two ambassadors. But that was the last touch of amiability that I was destined to see in Bryan. The next day the battle joined and his face became hard. By the end of the week he was simply a walking fever. Hour by hour he grew more bitter. What the Christian Scientists call malicious animal magnetism seemed to radiate from him like heat from a stove. From my place in the courtroom, standing upon a table, I looked directly down upon him, sweating horribly and pumping his palm-leaf fan. His eyes fascinated me; I watched them all day long. They were blazing points of hatred. They glittered like occult and sinister gems. Now and then they wandered to me, and I got my share, for my reports of the trial had come back to Dayton, and he had read them. It was like coming under fire.

Thus he fought his last fight, thirsting savagely for blood. All sense departed from him. He bit right and left, like a dog with rabies. He descended to demagogy so dreadful that his very associates at the trial table blushed. His one yearning was to keep his yokels heated up—to lead his forlorn mob of imbeciles against the foe. That foe, alas, refused to be alarmed. It insisted upon seeing the whole battle as a comedy. Even Darrow, who knew better, occasionally yielded to the prevailing spirit. One day he lured poor Bryan into the folly I have mentioned: his astounding argument against the notion that man is a mammal. I am glad I heard it, for otherwise I'd never believe in it. There stood the man who had been thrice a candidate for the Presidency of the Republic—there he stood in the glare of the world, uttering stuff that a boy of eight would laugh at! The artful Darrow led him on: he repeated it, ranted for it, bellowed it in his cracked voice. So he was prepared for the final slaughter. He came into life a hero, a Galahad, in bright and shining armor. He was passing out a poor mountebank.

The chances are that history will put the peak of democracy in America in his time; it has been on the downward curve among us since the campaign of 1896. He will be remembered perhaps, as its supreme impostor, the *reductio ad absurdum* of its pretension. Bryan came very near being President. In 1896, it is possible, he was actually elected. He lived long enough to make patriots thank the inscrutable gods for Harding, even for Coolidge. Dullness has got into the White House, and the smell of cabbage boiling, but there is at least nothing to compare to the intolerable buffoonery that went on in Tennessee. The President of the United States may be an ass, but he at least doesn't believe that the earth is square, and that witches should be put to death, and that Jonah swallowed the whale. The Golden Text is not painted weekly on the White House wall, and there is no need to keep ambassadors waiting while Pastor Simpson, of Smithville, prays for rain in the Blue Room. We have escaped something—by a narrow margin, but still we have escaped.

That is, so far. The Fundamentalists, once apparently sweeping all before them, now face minorities prepared for battle even in the South—here and there with some assurance of success. But it is too early, it seems to me, to send the firemen home; the fire is still burning on many a far-flung hill, and it may begin to roar again at any moment. The evil that men do lives after them. Bryan, in his malice, started something that it will not be easy to stop. In ten thousand country towns his old heelers, the evangelical pastors, are propagating his gospel, and everywhere the yokels are ready for it. When he disappeared from the big cities, the big cities made the capital error of assuming that he was done for. If they heard of him at all, it was only as a crimp for real-estate speculators—the heroic foe of the unearned increment hauling it in with both hands. He seemed preposterous, and thence harmless. But all the while he was busy among his old lieges, preparing for a *jacquerie* that should floor all his enemies at one blow. He did his job competently. He had vast skill at such enterprises. Heave an egg out of a Pullman window, and you will hit a Fundamentalist almost everywhere in the United States to-day. They swarm in the country towns, inflamed by their *shamans*, and with a saint, now, to venerate. They are thick in the mean streets behind the gasworks. They are everywhere where learn-ing is too heavy a burden for mortal minds to carry, even the vague, pathetic learning on tap in little red schoolhouses. They march with the Klan, with the Christian Endeavor Society, with the Junior Order of United American Mechanics, with the Epworth League, with all the rococo bands that poor and unhappy folk organize to bring some light of purpose into their lives. They have had a thrill, and they are ready for more.

Such is Bryan's legacy to his country. He couldn't be President, but he could at least help magnificently in the solemn business of shutting off the Presidency from every intelligent and self-respecting man. The storm, perhaps, won't last long, as time goes in history. It may help, indeed, to break up the democratic delusion, now already showing weakness, and so hasten its own end. But while it lasts it will blow off some roofs.

1926

WILLA CATHER

1876–1947

FROM DEATH COMES FOR THE ARCHBISHOP

MISSIONARY JOURNEYS [1]

I

The White Mules

IN mid-March, Father Vaillant was on the road, returning from a missionary journey to Albuquerque. He was to stop at the *rancho* of a rich Mexican, Manuel Lujon, to marry his men and maid servants who were living in concubinage, and to baptize the children. There he would spend the night. To-morrow or the day after he would go on to Santa Fé, halting by the way at the In-

1 'My book was a conjunction of the general and the particular, like most works of the imagination. I had all my life wanted to do something in the style of legend, which is absolutely the reverse of dramatic treatment. Since I first saw the Puvis de Chavannes frescoes of the life of Saint Genèviève in my student days, I have wished that I could try something a little like that in prose; something without accent, with none of the artificial elements of composition. In the Golden Legend the martyrdoms of the saints are no more dwelt upon than are the trivial incidents of their lives; it is as though all human experiences, measured against one supreme spiritual experience, were of about the same importance. The essence of such writing is not to hold the note, not to use an incident for all there is in it—but to touch and pass on. I felt that such writing would be a delightful kind of discipline in these days when the "situation" is made to count for so much in writing, when the general tendency is to force things up. In this kind of writing the mood is the thing—all the little figures and stories are mere improvisation that come out of it. What I got from Father Machebeuf's letters was the mood, the spirit in which they accepted the accidents and hardships of a desert country, the joyful energy that kept them going. To attempt to convey this hardihood of spirit one must use language a little stiff, a little formal, one must not be afraid of the old trite phraseology of the frontier. Some of those time-worn phrases I used as the note from the piano by which the violinist tunes his instrument. Not that there was much difficulty in keeping the pitch. I did not sit down to write the book until the feeling of it had so teased me that I could not get on with other things. The writing of it took only a few months, because the book had all been lived many times before it was written, and the happy mood in which I began never paled. It was like going back and playing the early composers after a surfeit of modern music.' Cather, 'A Letter from Willa Cather,' *The Commonweal*,VII,iii,714. The selection, here printed in the revised version of the 'Autograph Edition,' is Book II of *Death Comes for the Archbishop* (N.Y., 1927).

dian pueblo of Santo Domingo to hold service. There was a fine old mission church at Santo Domingo, but the Indians were of a haughty and suspicious disposition. He had said Mass there on his way to Albuquerque, nearly a week ago. By dint of canvassing from house to house, and offering medals and religious colour prints to all who came to church, he had got together a considerable congregation. It was a large and prosperous pueblo, set among clean sand-hills, with its rich irrigated farm-lands lying just below, in the valley of the Rio Grande. His congregation was quiet, dignified, attentive. They sat on the earth floor, wrapped in their best blankets, repose in every line of their strong, stubborn backs. He harangued them in such Spanish as he could command, and they listened with respect. But bring their children to be baptized, they would not. The Spaniards had treated them very badly long ago, and they had been meditating upon their grievance for many generations. Father Vaillant had not baptized one infant there, but he meant to stop to-morrow and try again. Then back to his Bishop, provided he could get his horse up La Bajada Hill.

He had bought his horse from a Yankee trader and had been woefully deceived. One week's journey of from twenty to thirty miles a day had shown the beast up for a wind-broken wreck. Father Vaillant's mind was full of material cares as he approached Manuel Lujon's place beyond Bernalillo. The *rancho* was like a little town, with all its stables, corrals, and stake fences. The *casa grande* was long and low, with glass windows and bright blue doors, a *portale* running its full length, supported by blue posts. Under this *portale* the adobe wall was hung with bridles, saddles, great boots and spurs, guns and saddle-blankets, strings of red peppers, foxskins, and the skins of two great rattlesnakes.

When Father Vaillant rode in through the gateway, children came running from every direction, some with no clothing but a little shirt, and women with no shawls over their black hair came running after the children. They all disappeared when Manuel Lujon walked out of the great house, hat in hand, smiling and hospitable. He was a man of thirty-five, settled in figure and somewhat full under the chin. He greeted the priest in the name of God and put out a hand to help him alight, but Father Vaillant sprang quickly to the ground.

'God be with you, Manuel, and with your house. But where are those who are to be married?'

'The men are all in the field, Padre. There is no hurry. A little wine, a little bread, coffee, repose—and then the ceremonies.'

'A little wine, very willingly, and bread, too. But not until afterward. I meant to catch you all at dinner, but I am two hours late because my horse is bad. Have someone bring in my saddle-bags, and I will put on my vestments. Send out to the fields for your men, Señor Lujon. A man can stop work to be married.'

The swarthy host was dazed by this dispatch. 'But one moment, Padre. There are all the children to baptize; why not begin with them, if I cannot persuade you to wash the dust from your sainted brow and repose a little.'

'Take me to a place where I can wash and change my clothes, and I will be ready before you can get them here. No, I tell you, Lujon, the marriages first, the baptisms afterward; that order is but Christian. I will baptize the children to-morrow morning, and their parents will at least have been married overnight.'

Father Joseph was conducted to his chamber, and the older boys were sent running off across the fields to fetch the men. Lujon and his two daughters began constructing an altar at one end of the *sala*. Two old women came to scrub the floor, and another brought chairs and stools.

'My God, but he is ugly, the Padre!' whispered one of these to the others. 'He must be very holy. And did you see the great wart he has on his chin? My grandmother could take that away for him if she were alive, poor soul! Somebody ought to tell him about the holy mud at Chimayo. That mud might dry it up. But there is nobody left now who can take warts away.'

'No, the times are not so good any more,' the other agreed. 'And I doubt if all this marrying will make them any better. Of what use is it to marry people after they have lived together and had children? and the man is maybe thinking about another woman, like Pablo. I saw him coming out of the brush with that oldest girl of Trinidad's, only Sunday night.'

The reappearance of the priest upon the scene cut short further scandal. He knelt down before the improvised altar and began his private devotions. The women tiptoed away. Señor Lujon himself went out toward the servants' quarters to hurry the candidates for the marriage sacrament. The women were giggling and snatching up their best shawls. Some of the men had even washed their hands. The household crowded into the *sala*, and Father Vaillant married couples with great dispatch.

'To-morrow morning, the baptisms,' he announced. 'And the mothers see to it that the children are clean, and that there are sponsors for all.'

After he had resumed his travelling-clothes, Father Joseph asked his host at what hour he dined, remarking that he had been fasting since an early breakfast.

'We eat when it is ready—a little after sunset, usually. I have had a young lamb killed for your Reverence.'

Father Joseph kindled with interest. 'Ah, and how will it be cooked?'

Señor Lujon shrugged. 'Cooked? Why, they put it in a pot with chili, and some onions, I suppose.'

'Ah, that is the point. I have had too much stewed mutton. Will you permit me to go into the kitchen and cook my portion in my own way?'

Lujon waved his hand. 'My house is yours, Padre. Into the kitchen I never go—too many women. But there it is, and the woman in charge is named Rosa.'

When the Father entered the kitchen, he found a crowd of women discussing the marriages. They quickly dispersed, leaving old Rosa by her fireplace, where hung a kettle from which issued the savour of cooking mutton fat, all too familiar to Father Joseph. He found a half sheep hanging outside the door, covered with a bloody sack, and asked Rosa to heat the oven for him, announcing that he meant to roast the hind leg.

'But, Padre, I baked before the marriages. The oven is almost cold. It will take an hour to heat it, and it is only two hours till supper.'

'Very well. I can cook my roast in an hour.'

'Cook a roast in an hour!' cried the old woman. 'Mother of God, Padre, the blood will not be dried in it!'

'Not if I can help it!' said Father Joseph fiercely. 'Now hurry with the fire, my good woman.'

When the Padre carved his roast at the supper-table, the serving-girls stood behind his chair and looked with horror at the delicate stream of pink juice that followed the knife. Manuel Lujon took a slice for politeness, but he did not eat it. Father Vaillant had his *gigot* to himself.

All the men and boys sat down at the long table with the host, the women and children would eat later. Father Joseph and Lujon, at one end, had a bottle of white Bordeaux between them. It had been brought from Mexico City on mule-back, Lujon said. They were discussing the road back to Santa Fé, and when the missionary remarked that he would stop at Santo Domingo, the host asked him why he did not get a horse there. 'I am afraid you will hardly get back to Santa Fé on your own. The pueblo is famous for breeding good horses. You might make a trade.'

'No,' said Father Vaillant. 'Those Indians are of a sullen disposition. If I were to have dealings with them, they would suspect my motives. If we are to save their souls, we must make it clear that we want no profit for ourselves, as I told Father Gallegos in Albuquerque.'

Manuel Lujon laughed and glanced down the table at his men, who were all showing their white teeth. 'You said that to the Padre at Albuquerque? You have courage. He is a rich man, Padre Gallegos. All the same, I respect him. I have played poker with him. He is a great gambler and takes his losses like a man. He stops at nothing, plays like an American.'

'And I,' retorted Father Joseph, 'I have not much respect for a priest who either plays cards or manages to get rich.'

'Then you do not play?' asked Lujon. 'I am disappointed. I had hoped we could have a game after supper. The evenings are dull enough here. You do not even play dominoes?'

'Ah, that is another matter!' Father Joseph declared. 'A game of dominoes, there by the fire, with coffee, or some of that excellent grape brandy you allowed me to taste, that I would find refreshing. And tell me, Manuelito, where do you get that brandy? It is like a French liqueur.'

'It is well seasoned. It was made at Bernalillo in my grandfather's time. They make it there still, but it is not so good now.'

The next morning, after coffee, while the children were being got ready for baptism, the host took Father Vaillant through his corrals and stables to show him his stock.

He exhibited with peculiar pride two cream-coloured mules, stalled side by side. With his own hand he led them out of the stable, in order to display to advantage their handsome coats, not bluish-white, as with white horses, but a rich, deep ivory, that in shadow changed to fawn-colour. Their tails were clipped at the ends into the shape of bells.

'Their names,' said Lujon, 'are Contenta and Angelica, and they are as good as their names. It seems that God has given them intelligence. When I talk to them, they look up at me like Christians; they are very companionable. They are always ridden together and have a great affection for each other.'

Father Joseph took one by the halter and led it about. 'Ah, but they are rare creatures! I have never seen a mule or horse coloured like a young fawn before.' To his host's astonishment, the wiry little priest sprang upon Contenta's back with the agility of a grasshopper. The mule, too, was astonished. She shook herself violently, bolted toward the gate of the barnyard, and at the gate stopped suddenly. Since this did not throw her rider, she seemed satisfied, trotted back, and stood placidly beside Angelica.

'But you are a *caballero*, Father Vaillant!' Lujon exclaimed. 'I doubt if Father Gallegos would have kept his seat—though he is something of a hunter.'

'The saddle is to be my home in your country, Lujon. What an easy gait this mule has, and what a narrow back! I notice that especially. For a man with short legs, like me, it is a punishment to ride eight hours a day on a wide horse. And this I must do day after day. From here I go to Santa Fé, and, after a day in conference with the Bishop, I start for Mora.'

'For Mora?' exclaimed Lujon. 'Yes, that is far, and the roads are very bad. On your

mare you will never do it. She will drop dead under you.' While he talked, the Father remained upon the mule's back, stroking her with his hand.

'Well, I have no other. God grant that she does not drop somewhere far from food and water. I can carry very little with me except my vestments and the sacred vessels.'

The Mexican had been growing more and more thoughtful, as if he were considering something profound and not altogether cheerful. Suddenly his brow cleared, and he turned to the priest with a radiant smile, quite boyish in its simplicity.

'Father Vaillant,' he burst out in a slightly oratorical manner, 'you have made my house right with Heaven, and you charge me very little. I will do something very nice for you; I will give you Contenta for a present, and I hope to be particularly remembered in your prayers.'

Springing to the ground, Father Vaillant threw his arms about his host. 'Manuelito!' he cried, 'for this darling mule I think I could almost pray you into Heaven!'

The Mexican laughed, too, and warmly returned the embrace. Arm-in-arm they went in to begin the baptisms.

The next morning, when Lujon went to call Father Vaillant for breakfast, he found him in the barnyard, leading the two mules about and smoothing their fawn-coloured flanks, but his face was not the cheerful countenance of yesterday.

'Manuel,' he said at once, 'I cannot accept your present. I have thought upon it overnight, and I see that I cannot. The Bishop works as hard as I do, and his horse is little better than mine. You know he lost everything on his way out here, in a shipwreck at Galveston—among the rest a fine wagon he had had built for travel on these plains. I could not go about on a mule like this when my Bishop rides a common hack. It would be inappropriate. I must ride away on my old mare.'

'Yes, Padre?' Manuel looked troubled and somewhat aggrieved. Why should the Padre spoil everything? It had all been very pleasant yesterday, and he had felt like a prince of generosity. 'I doubt if she will make La Bajada Hill,' he said slowly, shaking his head. 'Look my horses over and take the one that suits you. They are all better than yours.'

'No, no,' said Father Vaillant decidedly. 'Having seen these mules, I want nothing else. They are the colour of pearls, really! I will raise the price of marriages until I can buy this pair from you. A missionary must depend upon his mount for companionship in his lonely life. I want a mule that can look at me like a Christian, as you said of these.'

Señor Lujon sighed and looked about his barnyard as if he were trying to find some escape from this situation.

Father Joseph turned to him with vehemence. 'If I were a rich *ranchero*, like you, Manuel, I would do a splendid thing; I would furnish the two mounts that are to carry the Word of God about this heathen country, and then I would say to myself: *There go my Bishop and my Vicario, on my beautiful cream-coloured mules.*'

'So be it, Padre,' said Lujon with a mournful smile. 'But I ought to get a good many prayers. On my whole estate there is nothing I prize like those two. True, they might pine if they were parted for long. They have never been separated, and they have a great affection for each other. Mules, as you know, have strong affections. It is hard for me to give them up.'

'You will be all the happier for that, Manuelito,' Father Joseph cried heartily. 'Every time you think of these mules, you will feel pride in your good deed.'

Soon after breakfast Father Vaillant departed, riding Contenta, with Angelica trotting submissively behind, and from his gate Señor Lujon watched them disconsolately until they disappeared. He felt he had been worried out of his mules, and yet he bore no resentment. He did not doubt Father Joseph's devotedness, nor his singleness of purpose. After all, a Bishop was a Bishop, and a Vicar was a Vicar, and it was not to their discredit that they worked like a pair of common parish priests. He believed he would be proud of the fact that they rode Contenta and Angelica. Father Vaillant had forced his hand, but he was rather glad of it.

II

The Lonely Road to Mora

THE Bishop and his Vicar were riding through the rain in the Truchas Mountains.

The heavy, lead-coloured drops were driven slantingly through the air by an icy wind from the peak. These raindrops, Father Latour kept thinking, were the shape of tadpoles, and they broke against his nose and cheeks, exploding with a splash, as if they were hollow and full of air. The priests were riding across high mountain meadows, which in a few weeks would be green, though just now they were slate-coloured. On every side lay ridges covered with blue-green fir trees; above them rose the horny backbones of mountains. The sky was very low; purplish lead-coloured clouds let down curtains of mist into the valleys between the pine ridges. There was not a glimmer of white light in the dark vapours working overhead—rather, they took on the cold green of the evergreens. Even the white mules, their coats wet and matted into tufts, had turned a slaty hue, and the faces of the two priests were purple and spotted in that singular light.

Father Latour rode first, sitting straight upon his mule, with his chin lowered just enough to keep the drive of rain out of his eyes. Father Vaillant followed, unable to see much—in weather like this his glasses were of no use, and he had taken them off. He crouched down in the saddle, his shoulders well over Contenta's neck. Father Joseph's sister, Philomène, who was Mother Superior of a convent in her native town in the Puy-de-Dôme, often tried to picture her brother and Bishop Latour on these long missionary journeys of which he wrote her; she imagined the scene and saw the two priests moving through it in their cassocks, bareheaded, like the pictures of Saint Francis Xavier with which she was familiar. The reality was less picturesque—but for all that, no one could have mistaken these two men for hunters or traders. They wore clerical collars about their necks instead of neckerchiefs, and on the breast of his buckskin jacket the Bishop's silver cross hung by a silver chain.

They were on their way to Mora, the third day out, and they did not know just how far they had still to go. Since morning they had not met a traveller or seen a human habitation. They believed they were on the right trail, for they had seen no other. The first night of their journey they had spent at Santa Cruz, lying in the warm, wide valley of the Rio Grande, where the fields and gardens were already softly coloured with early spring. But since they had left the Española country behind them, they had contended first with wind and sand-storms, and now with cold. The Bishop was going to Mora to assist the Padre there in disposing of a crowd of refugees who filled his house. A new settlement in the Conejos Valley had lately been raided by Indians; many of the inhabitants were killed, and the survivors, who were originally from Mora, had managed to get back there, utterly destitute.

Before the travellers had crossed the mountain meadows, the rain turned to sleet. Their wet buckskins quickly froze, and the rattle of icy flakes struck them and bounded off. The prospect of a night in the open was not cheering. It was too wet to kindle a fire, their blankets would become soaked on the ground. As they were descending the mountain on the Mora side, the grey daylight seemed already beginning to fail, though it was only four o'clock.

Father Latour turned in his saddle and spoke over his shoulder.

'The mules are certainly very tired, Joseph. They ought to be fed.'

'Push on,' said Father Vaillant. 'We will come to shelter of some kind before night sets in.' The Vicar had been praying steadfastly while they crossed the meadows, and he felt confident that Saint Joseph would not turn a deaf ear.

Before the hour was done, they did indeed come upon a wretched adobe house, so poor and mean that they might not have seen it had it not lain close beside the trail, on the edge of a steep ravine. The stable looked more habitable than the house, and the priests thought perhaps they could spend the night in it.

As they rode up to the door, a man came out, bareheaded, and they saw to their surprise that he was not a Mexican, but an American, of a very unprepossessing type. He spoke to them in some drawling dialect they could scarcely understand and asked if they wanted to stay the night. During the few words they exchanged with him, Father Latour felt a growing reluctance to remain even for a few hours under the roof of this ugly, evil-looking fellow. He was tall, gaunt, and ill-formed, with a snake-like neck, ter-

minating in a small, bony head. Under his close-clipped hair this repellent head showed a number of thick ridges, as if the skull joinings were overgrown by layers of superfluous bone. With its small, rudimentary ears, this head had a positively malignant look. The man seemed not more than half human, but he was the only householder on the lonely road to Mora.

The priests dismounted and asked him whether he could put their mules under shelter and give them grain feed.

'As soon as I git my coat on I will. You kin come in.'

They followed him into a room where a piñon fire blazed in the corner, and went toward it to warm their stiffened hands. Their host made an angry, snarling sound in the direction of the partition, and a woman came out of the next room. She was a Mexican.

Father Latour and Father Vaillant addressed her courteously in Spanish, greeting her in the name of the Holy Mother, as was customary. She did not open her lips, but stared at them blankly for a moment, then dropped her eyes and cowered as if she were terribly frightened. The priests looked at each other; it struck them both that this man had been abusing her in some way. Suddenly he turned on her.

'Clear off them cheers fur the strangers. They won't eat ye, if they air priests.'

She began distractedly snatching rags and wet socks and dirty clothes from the chairs. Her hands were shaking so that she dropped things. She was not old, she might have been very young, but she was probably half-witted. There was nothing in her face but blankness and fear.

Her husband put on his coat and boots, went to the door, and stopped with his hand on the latch, throwing over his shoulder a crafty, hateful glance at the bewildered woman.

'Here, you! Come right along, I'll need ye!'

She took her black shawl from a peg and followed him. Just at the door she turned and caught the eyes of the visitors, who were looking after her in compassion and perplexity. Instantly that stupid face became intense, prophetic, full of awful meaning. With her finger she pointed them away, away!—two quick thrusts into the air.

Then, with a look of horror beyond anything language could convey, she threw back her head and drew the edge of her palm quickly across her distended throat—and vanished. The doorway was empty; the two priests stood staring at it, speechless. That flash of electric passion had been so swift, the warning it communicated so vivid and definite, that they were struck dumb.

Father Joseph was the first to find his tongue.

'There is no doubt of her meaning. Your pistol is loaded, Jean?'

'Yes, but I neglected to keep it dry. No matter.'

They hurried out of the house. It was still light enough to see the stable through the grey drive of rain, and they went toward it.

'Señor American,' the Bishop called, 'will you be good enough to bring out our mules?'

The man came out of the stable. 'What do you want?'

'Our mules. We have changed our minds. We will push on to Mora. And here is a dollar for your trouble.'

The man took a threatening attitude. As he looked from one to the other his head played from side to side exactly like a snake's. 'What's the matter? My house ain't good enough for ye?'

'No explanation is necessary. Go into the barn and get the mules, Father Joseph.'

'You dare go into my stable, you——priest!'

The Bishop drew his pistol. 'No profanity, Señor. We want nothing from you but to get away from your uncivil tongue. Stand where you are.'

The man was unarmed. Father Joseph came out with the mules, which had not been unsaddled. The poor things were each munching a mouthful, but they needed no urging to be gone; they did not like this place. The moment they felt their riders on their backs they trotted quickly along the road, which dropped immediately into the arroyo. While they were descending, Father Joseph remarked that the man would certainly have a gun in the house, and that he had no wish to be shot in the back.

'Nor I. But it is growing too dark for that, unless he should follow us on horseback,' said the Bishop. 'Were there horses in the stable?'

'Only a burro.'

Father Vaillant was relying upon the protection of Saint Joseph, whose office he had fervently said that morning. The warning given them by that poor woman, with such scant opportunity, seemed evidence that some protecting power was mindful of them.

By the time they had ascended the far side of the arroyo, night had closed down and the rain was pouring harder than ever.

'I am by no means sure that we can keep in the road,' said the Bishop. 'But at least I am sure we are not being followed. We must trust to these intelligent beasts. Poor woman! He will suspect her and abuse her, I am afraid.' He kept seeing her in the darkness as he rode on, her face in the firelight, and her terrible pantomime.

They reached the town of Mora a little after midnight. The Padre's house was full of refugees, and two of them were put out of a bed in order that the Bishop and his Vicar could get into it.

In the morning a boy came from the stable and reported that he had found a crazy woman lying in the straw, and that she begged to see the two Padres who owned the white mules. She was brought in, her clothing cut to rags, her legs and face and even her hair so plastered with mud that the priests could scarcely recognize the woman who had saved their lives the night before.

She said she had never gone back to the house at all. When the two priests rode away, her husband had run to the house to get his gun, and she had plunged down a washout behind the stable into the arroyo, and had been on the way to Mora all night. She had supposed he would overtake her and kill her, but he had not. She reached the settlement before daybreak, and crept into the stable to warm herself among the animals and wait until the household was awake. Kneeling before the Bishop, she began to relate such horrible things that he stopped her and turned to the native priest.

'This is a case for the civil authorities. Is there a magistrate here?'

There was no magistrate, but there was a retired fur trapper who acted as notary and could take evidence. He was sent for, and in the interval Father Latour instructed the refugee women from Conejos to bathe this poor creature and put decent clothes on her, and to care for the cuts and scratches on her legs.

An hour later the woman, whose name was Magdalena, calmed by food and kindness, was ready to tell her story. The notary had brought along his friend, Saint Vrain, a Canadian trapper who understood Spanish better than he. The woman was known to Saint Vrain, moreover, who confirmed her statement that she was born Magdalena Valdez, at Los Ranchos de Taos, and that she was twenty-four years old. Her husband, Buck Scales, had drifted into Taos with a party of hunters from somewhere in Wyoming. All white men knew him for a dog and a degenerate—but to Mexican girls, marriage with an American meant coming up in the world. She had married him six years ago, and had been living with him ever since in that wretched house on the Mora trail. During that time he had robbed and murdered four travellers who had stopped there for the night. They were all strangers, not known in the country. She had forgot their names, but one was a German boy who spoke very little Spanish and little English; a nice boy with blue eyes, and she had grieved for him more than for the others. They were all buried in the sandy soil behind the stable. She was always afraid their bodies might wash out in a storm. Their horses Buck had ridden off by night and sold to Indians somewhere in the north. Magdalena had borne three children since her marriage, and her husband had killed each of them a few days after birth, by ways so horrible that she could not relate it. After he killed the first baby, she ran away from him, back to her parents at Ranchos. He came after her and made her go home with him by threatening harm to the old people. She was afraid to go anywhere for help, but twice before she had managed to warn travellers away, when her husband happened to be out of the house. This time she had found courage because, when she looked into the faces of these two Padres, she knew they were good men, and she thought if she ran after them they could save her. She could not bear any more killing. She asked nothing better than to die herself, if only she could hide near a church and a priest for a while, to make her soul right with God.

Saint Vrain and his friend got together a search-party at once. They rode out to Scales's place and found the remains of four men buried under the corral behind the stable, as the woman had said. Scales himself they captured on the road from Taos, where he had gone to look for his wife. They brought him back to Mora, but Saint Vrain rode on to Taos to fetch a magistrate.

There was no *calabozo* in Mora, so Scales was put into an empty stable, under guard. This stable was soon surrounded by a crowd of people, who loitered to hear the blood-curdling threats the prisoner shouted against his wife. Magdalena was kept in the Padre's house, where she lay on a mat in the corner, begging Father Latour to take her back to Santa Fé, so that her husband could not get at her. Though Scales was bound, the Bishop felt alarmed for her safety. He and the American notary, who had a pistol of the new revolver model, sat in the *sala* and kept watch over her all night.

In the morning the magistrate and his party arrived from Taos. The notary told him the facts of the case in the plaza, where everyone could hear. The Bishop enquired whether there was any place for Magdalena in Taos, as she could not stay on here in such a state of terror. A man dressed in buckskin hunting-clothes stepped out of the crowd and asked to see Magdalena. Father Latour conducted him into the room where she lay on her mat. The stranger went up to her, removing his hat. He bent down and put his hand on her shoulder. Although he was clearly an American, he spoke Spanish in the native manner.

'Magdalena, don't you remember me?'

She looked up at him as out of a dark well; something became alive in her deep, haunted eyes. She caught with both hands at his fringed buckskin knees.

'Cristobal!' she wailed. 'Oh, Cristobal!'

'I'll take you home with me, Magdalena, and you can stay with my wife. You wouldn't be afraid in my house, would you?'

'No, no, Cristobal, I would not be afraid with you. I am not a wicked woman.'

He smoothed her hair. 'You're a good girl, Magdalena—always were. It will be all right. Just leave things to me.'

Then he turned to the Bishop. 'Señor

Vicario, she can come to me. I live near Taos. My wife is a native woman, and she'll be good to her. That varmint won't come about my place, even if he breaks jail. He knows me. My name is Carson.'

Father Latour had looked forward to meeting the scout. He had supposed him to be a very large man, of powerful body and commanding presence. This Carson was not so tall as the Bishop himself, was very slight in frame, modest in manner, and he spoke English with a soft Southern drawl. His face was both thoughtful and alert; anxiety had drawn a permanent ridge between his blue eyes. Under his blond moustache his mouth had a singular refinement. The lips were full and delicately modelled. There was something curiously unconscious about his mouth, reflective, a little melancholy—and something that suggested a capacity for tenderness.

The Bishop felt a quick glow of pleasure in looking at the man. As he stood there in his buckskin clothes one felt in him standards, loyalties, a code which is not easily put into words, but which is instantly felt when two men who live by it come together by chance. He took the scout's hand.

'I have long wanted to meet Kit Carson,' he said, 'even before I came to New Mexico. I have been hoping you would pay me a visit at Santa Fé.'

The other smiled. 'I'm right shy, sir, and I'm always afraid of being disappointed. But I guess it will be all right from now on.'

This was the beginning of a long friendship.

On their ride back to Carson's ranch, Magdalena was put in Father Vaillant's care, and the Bishop and the scout rode together. Carson said he had become a Catholic merely as a matter of form, as Americans usually did when they married a Mexican girl. His wife was a good woman and very devout; but religion had seemed to him pretty much a woman's affair until his last trip to California. He had been sick out there, and the Fathers at one of the missions took care of him.

'I began to see things different, and thought I might some day be a Catholic in earnest. I was brought up to think priests were rascals, and that the nuns were bad women—all the stuff they talk back in Missouri. A good many of the native priests here bear out that story. Our Padre Martínez at Taos is an old scapegrace, if ever there was one; he's got children and grandchildren in almost every settlement around here. And Padre Lucero at Arroyo Hondo is a miser, takes everything a poor man's got to give him a Christian burial.'

The Bishop discussed the needs of his people at length with Carson. He felt great confidence in his judgment. The two men were about the same age, both a little over forty, and both had been sobered and sharpened by wide experience. Carson had been guide in world-renowned explorations, but he was still almost as poor as in the days when he was a beaver trapper. He lived in a little adobe house with his Mexican wife. The great country of desert and mountain ranges between Santa Fé and the Pacific coast was not yet mapped or charted; the most reliable map of it was in Kit Carson's brain. This Missourian, whose eye was so quick to read a landscape or a human face, could not read a printed page. He could at that time barely write his own name. Yet one felt in him a quick and discriminating intelligence. That he was illiterate was an accident; he had got ahead of books, gone where the printing-press could not follow him. Out of the hardships of his boyhood—from fourteen to twenty picking up a bare living as cook or mule-driver for wagon trains, often in the service of brutal and desperate characters—he had preserved a clean sense of honour and a compassionate heart. In talking to the Bishop of poor Magdalena he said sadly: 'I used to see her in Taos when she was such a pretty girl. Ain't it a pity?'

The degenerate murderer, Buck Scales, was hanged after a short trial. Early in April the Bishop left Santa Fé on horseback and rode to St. Louis, on his way to attend the Provincial Council at Baltimore. When he returned in September, he brought back with him five courageous nuns, Sisters of Loretto, to found a school for girls in letterless Santa Fé. He sent at once for Magdalena and took her into the service of the Sisters. She became housekeeper and manager of the Sisters' kitchen. She was devoted to the nuns, and so happy in the service of the Church that when the Bishop visited the school he used to enter by the kitchen-garden in order to see her serene and handsome face. For she became beautiful, as Carson said she had been as a girl.

After the blight of her horrible youth was over, she seemed to bloom again in the household of God.

1926

OLE RÖLVAAG

1876–1931

FROM GIANTS IN THE EARTH

STRANGELY STILL THE DAYS [1]

I

DURING the first days of October a few white, downy snowflakes hung quivering in the air . . . floated about . . . fell in great oscillating circles. They seemed headed for nowhere; they followed no common course; but finally they reached the ground and disappeared.

The air cleared again. There came a drowsy, sun-filled interval . . . nothing but golden haze . . . quite bereft of all life. . . .

The sun had no strength these days. It peeped out in the morning, glided across the sky as before, yet life it had not until toward evening, as it was nearing the western rim of the prairie. Then it awoke, grew big and blushing, took on a splendour which forced everyone to stop and look; the western sky foamed and flooded with a wanton richness of colour, which ran up in streams to meet the coming night. Folks would walk about in the evenings speaking in low tones. . . . Never in their lives had they seen such sunsets! . . .

. . . Day after day the same . . . evening after evening. Strangely still the days . . . the evenings more mysteriously quiet. How could one lift one's voice against such silence! . . .

Then one morning—October was nearly passed—the sun could not get his eye open at all; the heavens rested close above the plain, grey, dense, and still. The chill of this greyness drove through the air though no wind stirred. People went indoors to put on more clothes, came out again, but froze worse than ever. . . . Bleak,

grey, God-forsaken, the empty desolation stretched on every hand. . . .

Sometime in the afternoon snowflakes began to fall. They came sailing down from the north until the air was a close-packed swarm of greyish-white specks, all bound in the same direction. The evening was short-lived that day, and died in a pitch-black night that weighed down the heart. . . .

. . . Again day came, and brought no other light than that which the greyish-white specks gave. . . . All that day the snow fell—all the next night. . . .

At last it grew light once more—but the day had no sun. A cold wind howled about the huts—left them, and tore down into the white snow blanket, shaking out of it blinding swirls. . . . The swirls vanished and reappeared—died down, flared up again and tore on. . . . New ones constantly rose . . . many. . . .

II

Per Hansa and his boys worked like fire-brands during the last days before winter set in. Every task that came to their hands delighted them; they went from one fairy tale into the next—came out again, and there was a new one at hand; they gave themselves no peace, either by night or by day. . . . But Beret could not share their mood; she would watch them absently as they left the house; or when they were due to return, she would wander about with And-Ongen on her arm, looking for them through the window, and keeping a hot dish in readiness on the stove. They were sure to be cold, poor fellows! . . . Then when they were seated around the table, wrapped up in all their remarkable experiences, the talk would jump from one incident to another, and she would find herself unable to follow it. Their liveliness and loud laughter only drove her heavy thoughts into a still deeper darkness.

---

[1] The selection, to which the title has been given by the editors, is from *Giants in the Earth*(N.Y., 1927),197–208. Book I of the novel, prior to its translation into English, appeared as *I De Dage*(Oslo, Norway, 1924).

She had to admit, however, that Per Hansa could accomplish the most marvellous things; she could not imagine where he had learned it all. . . . There were the walls, for example, of which he himself was especially proud, and which Store-Hans never tired of admiring. He had begun work on these walls immediately after he had returned from the trip east to the Hallings' with the potatoes. The lime had been mixed according to directions, and spread over the walls—three coats of it, no less; now the sod hut shone so brightly inside that it dazzled the eyes. . . . Before the snow came, Beret thought it delightful to have such walls; but after there was nothing but whiteness outside—pure whiteness as far as the eye could see and the thought could reach—she regretted that he had touched them. Her eyes were blinded wherever she looked, either outdoors or indoors; the black-brown earthen floor was the only object on which she could rest them comfortably; and so she always looked down now, as she sat in the house. But hint at it, and thus ruin his pleasure, she could not. . . . And it really didn't matter much to her; she would endure it for the brief time that remained! . . .

She was thankful enough, though, for all the fine fish that he had brought home. Per Hansa had taken both boys with him on the great expedition east to the Sioux River; there they had made a tremendous catch with the help of the net, and Per Hansa had talked with the Trönders about many extraordinary things, and had gained much valuable information. . . . Heaps of frozen fish now lay outside all along the wall; Per Hansa explained to her what a God-send it was that the snow finally had come. Hm! Good Heavens! If it hadn't come soon he would have been obliged to go out and get it! Now he was spared that trouble; with the aid of the snowdrifts they could have fresh fish through the whole winter. . . . 'Hey, woman!' he said with a laugh, whenever she complained of how desolate it was since the snow had come. 'Can't you understand that we could never manage things without the snow? . . . Hey, wife—white and fine, both outdoors and indoors! . . . Wonder if something couldn't be done to the floor, too?'. . .

Now it came to light what had been working in Per Hansa's mind when he had bought all that salt; he salted down quantities of the fish, and packed them away in all the vessels they could spare.

But in the opinion of the boys, the duck hunt with the net was the crowning adventure. Never had there been such an enthusiastic party; the father was almost the worst of the three! Now the great secret of his planning and scheming over the ducks was revealed. While Store-Hans and his brother had only talked about capturing them and wondered what could be done, Per Hansa had figured out every detail in his mind; if the ducks got the best of him on one tack, he would fool them on another; into the net somehow they must go! . . . For three nights they had all stayed out in the swamps to the westward, toiling and fighting among the myriads of birds; in the morning they would come home after daylight, wet as crows, numb all over, and blue in the face with cold. But they always brought a catch! . . . As soon as the evening came they would be off again.

Each time Beret pleaded sadly, both by word and glance, for them to stay at home. . . . They would wear themselves out this way. What could they possibly do with all these fowl? Just wait and see; they might not need so much food—something might happen. . . . The boys only laughed at these objections; their mother sounded just like Sofie; probably all women were alike—they had no sense. Just imagine such a ridiculous idea—catch no more birds! . . . The father joined in with them and poked mild fun at the mother. How silly it would be not to grab good food when it lay right at their door! Suppose the swamps were to freeze up to-night? And after they had picked the ducks, there would be fine feather beds for both herself and Little Per! . . . Per Hansa's voice softened. . . . And besides, there was no more delicate fare than those ducks on any king's table! . . .

But she would not be carried along. . . . 'We won't need them!' she said, dispiritedly . . . and fell into silence.

Dusk settled, the menfolk left—and she was alone with the child again.

But at last winter shut down in earnest; the swamps froze up and duck hunting came to an end for that year.

'I think we ought to carry some soup meat to our neighbours,' said Per Hansa. . . . 'This time it'll be something better than badger stew!'. . .

Every person in the little settlement had been rushed with work during the last days before Father Winter came. They all had a feeling that he wasn't very far away, that old fellow, and thought it best to be well prepared to receive him. Hans Olsa, Tönseten, and the Solum boys had been east to the Sioux River again for wood; they had made two trips, and home had seen very little of them lately. Few visits had been made; everyone had been busy with his own affairs. . . . For other reasons than this, visitors came but seldom to Per Hansa's now; there was something queer about the woman in that place; she said so little; at times people felt that they were unwelcome there. She was apt to break out suddenly with some remark that they could only wonder at; they hardly knew whether to be surprised or offended.

But on the day when the boys carried a gift of ducks to all the houses in the neighbourhood, proud of the dainty food they brought, and relating what sounded like a fairy tale, everyone went over to Per Hansa's to learn how he had gone about catching these birds. For Ole and Store-Hans wouldn't tell, though they plied them with questions. . . . The Solum boys came first, with Tönseten and Kjersti hard upon their heels; last of all came Hans Olsa and Sörine.

Once inside, they completely forgot their curiosity about the duck hunting; they stood with their mouths open, looking up one wall and down the next.

. . . Why . . . why . . . what in the wide world was this? Had they plastered *snow* on the walls? Sam thought it really was snow, and touched it gingerly with his finger. . . . What *was* it, anyway? Could it possibly be paint? . . . My stars, how fine it looked! . . . Per Hansa sat there, sucking his pipe and enjoying his little triumph; it seemed to him that he had never liked his neighbours so well as at this moment. . . . Beret went about listening quietly; in her face was a troubled expression. Not for all the world would she have had the work on the walls undone! . . .

Amazement was universal. . . . Sörine smiled in her pleasant, kindly way; she went over to Beret and said with warm sympathy:

'Now you certainly have got a fine house! . . . You'll thrive all the better for it.' . . . At that, she began to help her with the work. But Kjersti, with an emphatic slap on her thigh, voiced it as her opinion that it was a dirty shame that she and Sörrina had picked up such poor sticks for husbands! Why couldn't *they* ever hatch up some nice scheme? Why was Per Hansa the only man among them with his head on the right end? Yes, they certainly ought to feel ashamed of themselves, sitting there! . . . Tönseten took offence at this; he felt constrained to remind her that he was the fellow who had risen to the occasion and captured the Sognings! She'd better remember that; for what would have become of them all in the long run if the Sognings hadn't joined them? . . . 'And I don't exactly see what this new notion of Per Hansa's is really good for,' he spluttered on. 'It's getting to be so damned swell in here that pretty soon a fellow can't even *spit*!' . . . Tönseten looked accusingly at Beret; it was from her that Per Hansa got these stuck-up airs. She was never willing to be like plain folks, that woman! . . . The Solum boys took great delight in the white walls; this was really beautiful. When they got married they would do the very same thing!

Hans Olsa sucked his pipe and said but little. This seemed very queer to him; he turned it over and over in his mind, but couldn't solve the problem. Was this like Per Hansa, who had always confided everything to him? . . . But here he was going about doing everything alone! When he had learned how a black earthen wall could be made shining white at so small a cost, why hadn't he told the others? There was so little cheer out here; they all sorely needed to share whatever they found. . . . The big, rugged features were very sober; he had to look hard at Per Hansa. No, it was the same good-natured face that one liked so well to have near by! This affair was just one of his many pranks; the longer Hans Olsa gazed at his neighbour, the more plausible grew this solution inside that big head of his.

Awhile later, as the two men stood together outside the door, watching the falling snow, he said, quietly:

'You have made it pretty fine inside, Per Hansa; but He Who is now whitening the outside of your walls does fully as well. . . . You shouldn't be vain in your own strength, you know!'

'Oh, nonsense, Hans Olsa!' laughed Per Hansa. 'What are you prating about? . . . Here, take along a couple more ducks for Sörrina!' . . .

III

It was well enough that winter had come at last, thought Per Hansa; he really needed to lay off and rest awhile. After a good square meal of ducks or fresh fish, he would light his pipe and stretch himself, saying:

'Ha!—now we're really as well off here, my Beret-girl, as anybody could ever wish to be!' . . . He did not always expect an answer, and seldom got one. Then he would throw himself on the bed and take a good after-dinner nap, often sleeping continuously on into the night. . . . Life seemed very pleasant now!

In this fashion he spent quite a number of days; the bad weather still held out. Per Hansa continued to do full justice to the fare. When he had eaten his fill he would point out again to Beret how well off they were, and go to his couch to sleep the sleep of the righteous. It was almost uncanny— he could never seem to get sleep enough! He slept both day and night; and still he felt the need of more rest. . . . Now and then he would go to the door to look out at the weather, and glance across toward the neighbours. No . . . nothing to do outside—the weather was too beastly! He would come in again, and stretch himself, and yawn. . . .

The days wore on.

Yes, they wore on. . . . One exactly like the other. . . . Per Hansa couldn't grasp the strange contradiction that had begun to impress him; he knew that the days were actually growing shorter—were being shorn more closely by every passing night; but— weren't they growing longer?

Indeed they were—no question about it! They finally grew so long that he was at a dead loss to find something to do with which to end them. He assured himself that all this leisure was very fine; that he needed to ease up a bit; during the fall he hadn't spared himself; now it felt like a blessing to sit around and play the gentleman. Times would be strenuous enough for him once more, when spring came with fair weather and his great estate needed to be planted; he would just lay off and rest for a while yet! . . .

The days only grew longer and longer.

In the end, this enforced idleness began to gall him. The landscape showed a monotonous sameness . . . never the slightest change. . . . Grey sky—damp, icy cold. . . . Snow fell . . . snow flew. . . . He could only guess now where the huts of Hans Olsa lay. There wasn't a thing to do outdoors; plenty of wood lay chopped and ready for use; it took but a little while to do the chores. . . . Beyond this, everything took care of itself outside.

Per Hansa sat by the table, or lay down on the bed when he got tired of sitting up; tried to sleep as long as possible; woke up with a start; turned over and tried to sleep again; rose and sat by the table once more, when he grew weary of lying down.

The days wore on, and yet got nowhere. . . . Time had simply come to a standstill! He had never seen the like; this was worse than the deadest lay-up in Lofoten!

The boys were almost as badly off; they too sat restless and idle; and because they had nothing at all to occupy their minds they often came to blows, so that the father had to interfere. . . . But he was never very rough with them; poor boys, what else could they find for amusement? . . . The mother always reminded him of their books. . . . Yes, of course—certainly they must learn to read, the father said; no heathen were going to grow up in his house! He tried to be stern with them over this matter; but then . . . after all, boys were boys, he remembered!

At length he realized that this sort of life could not go on. He didn't give a hang for the weather—put on his coat and bade the boys do the same; then they went out and attacked the woodpile. They sawed and they chopped; they lugged in wood and piled it up; first they stacked up as much chopped wood as they could stow in the odd corners of the house; then they built a curious little fort of chopped wood out in the yard—very neatly and craftily constructed—and piled it full, too; this work cheered them up and kept their minds occupied, though the weather was bitterly cold and inclement. They toiled at it from early morning until late at night, and hardly took time off to eat their dinner; the boys began to get sick of the job and complained of being tired. The woodpile lasted exactly four days; when they had chopped up the last stick there was nothing left for them to do outside.

Then they sat idle again.

The bad spell of weather held out interminably. A cold, piercing wind from the northeast blew the livelong day, and moaned about the corners at night. . . . Snow flew . . . more snow fell.

No sun. . . . No sky. . . . The air was a grey, ashen mist which breathed a deathly chill; it hung around and above them thick and frozen. . . . In the course of time there was a full moon at night, somewhere behind the veil. Then the mist grew luminous and alive—strange to behold. . . . Night after night the ghostly spectacle would return.

Per Hansa would gaze at it and think: Now the trolls are surely abroad! . . . .

One evening Tönseten and Kjersti came over. They sat and talked until it grew very late. One could readily see that Syvert was out of sorts about something; he puffed at his pipe in glum, ill humor, glared at Per Hansa's walls, and didn't have much to say. When he did speak his voice was unnecessarily loud.

Kjersti and Beret sat together on the bed; they seemed to be finding a good deal to chat about.

Kjersti was in an unusually neighbourly mood; she had come over to ask if . . . well, if she couldn't do something for Beret? She had some woollen yarn at home in her chest, very soft and very fine. Would Beret be offended if she knitted a pair of socks for the little newcomer they were all awaiting? . . . It was fine yarn, the very finest! Beret must just try to imagine how lonesome she was, sitting at home all alone with that useless husband of hers—and no little newcomer to wait for! . . . She had plenty of yarn; she could easily make the socks long enough to serve as leggings, too. The work would really bring joy to her—and to Syvert, too, poor fellow, to whom no little newcomer would ever arrive!

. . . Ah, well! . . . God pity us, Syvert wasn't so bad, after all—far be it from her to complain! . . . At that, Kjersti happened to think of a story she had heard, about a couple who couldn't seem to get a child though they wanted one very badly. Here the story was, since they happened to be talking about such matters. . . . This wife had so little sense that she sought the aid of a witch woman, who gave her both *devil's drink* and *beaver-geld*; she rubbed herself with the stuff and drank some of it, too, but no change came; that is, not until one summer when a shoal of herring came into the fjord and with it a fleet of strange fishermen. . . . Alas! desire makes a hot fire, once it has been kindled! But what do you suppose?—her husband became just as fond of that child as if he had been the father of it! . . . Wasn't that a queer thing? . . . But when the boy was a year old and was on the point of being christened —well, on that very Sunday it happened, as they were sailing across the fjord, that the boat capsized and the Lord took both mother and child, right there and then! He had taken away what he had refused to give in honour, and more besides. . . . There was something mysterious about such things, didn't Beret think so? And wasn't it strange that the father should have been so fond of *that* child? . . . Kjersti had known them both very well.

Beret listened attentively to this tale, putting in a word here and there.

Over at the table, the men had pricked up their ears as the story began; they heard it all. Per Hansa looked at Syvert and laughed; Syvert, in turn, glared at the wall and said, angrily:

'I should think you'd be able to find something American to talk about! . . . We're through now with all that troll business over in Norway!' . . . He got up and started to go. . . .

But Per Hansa wouldn't listen to their leaving just yet; since they had braved the weather to make a call they might as well sit awhile longer. . . . 'You'll have the wind astern, Syvert, going home! . . . Come on, sit down and behave yourself!'

On another afternoon all of Hans Olsa's household came over. They stayed till dark; then they began to say that perhaps they'd better be going now—but they made no move to leave. . . . Sörine had brought a gift for Beret. There had been a few bits of cloth lying around the house, for which she could find no use; it had been rather lonesome these days and she had needed something to do, so she had made a little article for this newcomer whom everyone was waiting for! . . . At that, Sörine drew out from her ample bosom a child's cap, of red, white, and blue stripes, with long silk ribbons, all sewed with the greatest care. It was a beautiful cap; all had to see it; there were many warm words of praise. Beret received it in silence; her eyes were wet as she took the cap and laid it carefully in the big chest. . . .

To-night it was Beret who refused to let the visitors leave. She absolutely insisted. Such quantities of food lay outside around the house—far more than they would ever need—that they might as well stay for supper and help to eat it! . . . This proposal overjoyed Per Hansa. It was the plain truth, as Beret said, they had more than they needed—and there was plenty left in the Sioux River, for that matter; to-night they were going to celebrate with fresh fish for supper! . . . He went outside and brought in a generous supply of the frozen fish, which he scaled and cut up; he was in the finest of spirits—it seemed just like the good old days in Lofoten.

. . . That evening was a happy interlude for them all.

1923   1924, 1927

SINCLAIR LEWIS
1885–

FROM MAIN STREET

WELCOME TO OUR CITY! [1]

This is America—a town of a few thousand, in a region of wheat and corn and dairies and little groves.

The town is, in our tale, called 'Gopher Prairie, Minnesota.' But its Main Street is the continuation of Main Streets everywhere. The story would be the same in Ohio or Montana, in Kansas or Kentucky or Illinois, and not very differently would it be told Up York State or in the Carolina hills.

Main Street is the climax of civilization. That this Ford car might stand in front of the Bon Ton Store, Hannibal invaded Rome and Erasmus wrote in Oxford cloisters. What Ole Jenson the grocer says to Ezra Stowbody the banker is the new law for London, Prague, and the unprofitable isles of the sea; whatsoever Ezra does not know and sanction, that thing is heresy, worthless for knowing and wicked to consider.

Our railway station is the final aspiration of architecture. Sam Clark's annual hardware turnover is the envy of the four coun-

ties which constitute God's Country. In the sensitive art of the Rosebud Movie Palace there is a Message, and humor strictly moral.

Such is our comfortable tradition and sure faith. Would he not betray himself an alien cynic who should otherwise portray Main Street, or distress the citizens by speculating whether there may not be other faiths?

I

UNDER the rolling clouds of the prairie a moving mass of steel. An irritable clank and rattle beneath a prolonged roar. The sharp scent of oranges cutting the soggy smell of unbathed people and ancient baggage.

Towns as planless as a scattering of pasteboard boxes on an attic floor. The stretch of faded gold stubble broken only by clumps of willows encircling white houses and red barns.

No. 7, the way-train, grumbling through Minnesota, imperceptibly climbing the giant tableland that slopes in a thousand-mile rise from hot Mississippi bottoms to the Rockies.

It is September, hot, very dusty.

There is no smug Pullman attached to the train, and the day coaches of the East are replaced by free chair cars, with each seat cut into two adjustable plush chairs,

1 The selection, to which the title has been given by the editors, is from *Main Street* (N.Y., 1920), foreword and 20–52.

the head-rests covered with doubtful linen towels. Halfway down the car is a semi-partition of carved oak columns, but the aisle is of bare, splintery, grease-blackened wood. There is no porter, no pillows, no provision for beds, but all today and all tonight they will ride in this long steel box—farmers with perpetually tired wives and children who seem all to be of the same age; workmen going to new jobs; traveling salesmen with derbies and freshly shined shoes.

They are parched and cramped, the lines of their hands filled with grime; they go to sleep curled in distorted attitudes, heads against the window-panes or propped on rolled coats on seat-arms, and legs thrust into the aisle. They do not read; apparently they do not think. They wait. An early-wrinkled, young-old mother, moving as though her joints were dry, opens a suitcase in which are seen creased blouses, a pair of slippers worn through at the toes, a bottle of patent medicine, a tin cup, a paper-covered book about dreams which the news-butcher has coaxed her into buying. She brings out a graham cracker which she feeds to a baby lying flat on a seat and wailing hopelessly. Most of the crumbs drop on the red plush of the seat, and the woman sighs and tries to brush them away, but they leap up impishly and fall back on the plush.

A soiled man and woman munch sandwiches and throw the crusts on the floor. A large brick-colored Norwegian takes off his shoes, grunts in relief, and props his feet in their thick gray socks against the seat in front of him.

An old woman whose toothless mouth shuts like a mud-turtle's, and whose hair is not so much white as yellow like moldy linen, with bands of pink skull apparent between the tresses, anxiously lifts her bag, opens it, peers in, closes it, puts it under the seat, and hastily picks it up and opens it and hides it all over again. The bag is full of treasures and of memories: a leather buckle, an ancient band-concert program, scraps of ribbon, lace, satin. In the aisle beside her is an extremely indignant parrakeet in a cage.

Two facing seats, overflowing with a Slovene iron-miner's family, are littered with shoes, dolls, whisky bottles, bundles wrapped in newspapers, a sewing bag. The oldest boy takes a mouth-organ out of his coat pocket, wipes the tobacco crumbs off, and plays 'Marching through Georgia' till every head in the car begins to ache.

The news-butcher comes through selling chocolate bars and lemon drops. A girl-child ceaselessly trots down to the water-cooler and back to her seat. The stiff paper envelope which she uses for cup drips in the aisle as she goes, and on each trip she stumbles over the feet of a carpenter, who grunts, 'Ouch! Look out!'

The dust-caked doors are open, and from the smoking-car drifts back a visible blue line of stinging tobacco smoke, and with it a crackle of laughter over the story which the young man in the bright blue suit and lavender tie and light yellow shoes has just told to the squat man in garage overalls.

The smell grows constantly thicker, more stale.

2

To each of the passengers his seat was his temporary home, and most of the passengers were slatternly housekeepers. But one seat looked clean and deceptively cool. In it were an obviously prosperous man and a black-haired, fine-skinned girl whose pumps rested on an immaculate horsehide bag.

They were Dr. Will Kennicott and his bride, Carol.

They had been married at the end of a year of conversational courtship, and they were on their way to Gopher Prairie after a wedding journey in the Colorado mountains.

The hordes of the way-train were not altogether new to Carol. She had seen them on trips from St. Paul to Chicago. But now that they had become her own people, to bathe and encourage and adorn, she had an acute and uncomfortable interest in them. They distressed her. They were so stolid. She had always maintained that there is no American peasantry, and she sought now to defend her faith by seeing imagination and enterprise in the young Swedish farmers, and in a traveling man working over his order-blanks. But the older people, Yankees as well as Norwegians, Germans, Finns, Canucks, had settled into submission to poverty. They were peasants, she groaned.

'Isn't there any way of waking them up?

What would happen if they understood scientific agriculture?' she begged of Kennicott, her hand groping for his.

It had been a transforming honeymoon. She had been frightened to discover how tumultuous a feeling could be roused in her. Will had been lordly—stalwart, jolly, impressively competent in making camp, tender and understanding through the hours when they had lain side by side in a tent pitched among pines high up on a lonely mountain spur.

His hand swallowed hers as he started from thoughts of the practise to which he was returning. 'These people? Wake 'em up? What for? They're happy.'

'But they're so provincial. No, that isn't what I mean. They're—oh, so sunk in the mud.'

'Look here, Carrie. You want to get over your city idea that because a man's pants aren't pressed, he's a fool. These farmers are mighty keen and up-and-coming.'

'I know! That's what hurts. Life seems so hard for them—these lonely farms and this gritty train.'

'Oh, they don't mind it. Besides, things are changing. The auto, the telephone, rural free delivery; they're bringing the farmers in closer touch with the town. Takes time, you know, to change a wilderness like this was fifty years ago. But already, why, they can hop into the Ford or the Overland and get into the movies on Saturday evening quicker than you could get down to 'em by trolley in St. Paul.'

'But if it's these towns we've been passing that the farmers run to for relief from their bleakness—Can't you understand? Just *look* at them!'

Kennicott was amazed. Ever since childhood he had seen these towns from trains on this same line. He grumbled, 'Why, what's the matter with 'em? Good hustling burgs. It would astonish you to know how much wheat and rye and corn and potatoes they ship in a year.'

'But they're so ugly.'

'I'll admit they aren't comfy like Gopher Prairie. But give 'em time.'

'What's the use of giving them time unless some one has desire and training enough to plan them? Hundreds of factories trying to make attractive motor cars, but these towns—left to chance. No! That can't be true. It must have taken genius to make them so scrawny!'

'Oh, they're not so bad,' was all he answered. He pretended that his hand was the cat and hers the mouse. For the first time she tolerated him rather than encouraged him. She was staring out at Schoenstrom, a hamlet of perhaps a hundred and fifty inhabitants, at which the train was stopping.

A bearded German and his puckermouthed wife tugged their enormous imitation-leather satchel from under a seat and waddled out. The station agent hoisted a dead calf aboard the baggage-car. There were no other visible activities in Schoenstrom. In the quiet of the halt, Carol could hear a horse kicking his stall, a carpenter shingling a roof.

The business-center of Schoenstrom took up one side of one block, facing the railroad. It was a row of one-story shops covered with galvanized iron, or with clapboards painted red and bilious yellow. The buildings were as ill-assorted, as temporary-looking, as a mining camp street in the motion-pictures. The railroad station was a one-room frame box, a mirey cattle-pen on one side and a crimson wheat-elevator on the other. The elevator, with its cupola on the ridge of a shingled roof, resembled a broad-shouldered man with a small, vicious, pointed head. The only habitable structures to be seen were the florid red-brick Catholic church and rectory at the end of Main Street.

Carol picked at Kennicott's sleeve. 'You wouldn't call this a not-so-bad town, would you?'

'These Dutch burgs *are* kind of slow. Still, at that—See that fellow coming out of the general store there, getting into the big car? I met him once. He owns about half the town, besides the store. Rauskukle, his name is. He owns a lot of mortgages, and he gambles in farm-lands. Good nut on him, that fellow. Why, they say he's worth three or four hundred thousand dollars! Got a dandy great big yellow brick house with tiled walks and a garden and everything, other end of town—can't see it from here—I've gone past it when I've driven through here. Yes sir!'

'Then, if he has all that, there's no excuse whatever for this place! If his three hundred thousand went back into the town, where it belongs, they could burn up these shacks, and build a dream-village, a jewel! Why do the farmers and the townpeople let the Baron keep it?'

'I must say I don't quite get you sometimes, Carrie. Let him? They can't help themselves! He's a dumm old Dutchman, and probably the priest can twist him around his finger, but when it comes to picking good farming land, he's a regular wiz!'

'I see. He's their symbol of beauty. The town erects him, instead of erecting buildings.'

'Honestly, don't know what you're driving at. You're kind of played out, after this long trip. You'll feel better when you get home and have a good bath, and put on the blue negligee. That's some vampire costume, you witch!'

He squeezed her arm, looked at her knowingly.

They moved on from the desert stillness of the Schoenstrom station. The train creaked, banged, swayed. The air was nauseatingly thick. Kennicott turned her face from the window, rested her head on his shoulder. She was coaxed from her unhappy mood. But she came out of it unwillingly, and when Kennicott was satisfied that he had corrected all her worries and had opened a magazine of saffron detective stories, she sat upright.

Here—she meditated—is the newest empire of the world; the Northern Middlewest; a land of dairy herds and exquisite lakes, of new automobiles and tar-paper shanties and silos like red towers, of clumsy speech and a hope that is boundless. An empire which feeds a quarter of the world —yet its work is merely begun. They are pioneers, these sweaty wayfarers, for all their telephones and bank-accounts and automatic pianos and co-operative leagues. And for all its fat richness, theirs is a pioneer land. What is its future? she wondered. A future of cities and factory smut where now are loping empty fields? Homes universal and secure? Or placid châteaux ringed with sullen huts? Youth free to find knowledge and laughter? Willingness to sift the sanctified lies? Or creamy-skinned fat women, smeared with grease and chalk, gorgeous in the skins of beasts and the bloody feathers of slain birds, playing bridge with puffy pink-nailed jeweled fingers, women who after much expenditure of labor and bad temper still grotesquely resemble their own flatulent lap-dogs? The ancient stale inequalities, or something different in history, unlike the tedious maturity of other empires? What future and what hope?

Carol's head ached with the riddle.

She saw the prairie, flat in giant patches or rolling in long hummocks. The width and bigness of it, which had expanded her spirit an hour ago, began to frighten her. It spread out so; it went on so uncontrollably; she could never know it. Kennicott was closeted in his detective story. With the loneliness which comes most depressingly in the midst of many people she tried to forget problems, to look at the prairie objectively.

The grass beside the railroad had been burnt over; it was a smudge prickly with charred stalks of weeds. Beyond the undeviating barbed-wire fences were clumps of golden rod. Only this thin hedge shut them off from the plains—shorn wheatlands of autumn, a hundred acres to a field, prickly and gray near-by but in the blurred distance like tawny velvet stretched over dipping hillocks. The long rows of wheatshocks marched like soldiers in worn yellow tabards. The newly plowed fields were black banners fallen on the distant slope. It was a martial immensity, vigorous, a little harsh, unsoftened by kindly gardens.

The expanse was relieved by clumps of oaks with patches of short wild grass; and every mile or two was a chain of cobalt slews, with the flicker of blackbirds' wings across them.

All this working land was turned into exuberance by the light. The sunshine was dizzy on open stubble; shadows from immense cumulus clouds were forever sliding across low mounds; and the sky was wider and loftier and more resolutely blue than the sky of cities . . . she declared.

'It's a glorious country; a land to be big in,' she crooned.

Then Kennicott startled her by chuckling, 'D' you realize the town after the next is Gopher Prairie? Home!'

3

That one word—home—it terrified her. Had she really bound herself to live, inescapably, in this town called Gopher Prairie? And this thick man beside her, who dared to define her future, he was a stranger! She turned in her seat, stared at him. Who was he? Why was he sitting with her? He wasn't of her kind! His neck was heavy; his speech was heavy; he was twelve or thirteen years older than she; and about him was none of the magic of shared adventures and eagerness. She could not believe that she had ever slept in his arms. That was one of the dreams which you had but did not officially admit.

She told herself how good he was, how dependable and understanding. She touched his ear, smoothed the plane of his solid jaw, and, turning away again, concentrated upon liking his town. It wouldn't be like these barren settlements. It couldn't be! Why, it had three thousand population. That was a great many people. There would be six hundred houses or more. And— The lakes near it would be so lovely. She'd seen them in the photographs. They had looked charming . . . hadn't they?

As the train left Wahkeenyan she began nervously to watch for the lakes—the entrance to all her future life. But when she discovered them, to the left of the track, her only impression of them was that they resembled the photographs.

A mile from Gopher Prairie the track mounts a curving low ridge, and she could see the town as a whole. With a passionate jerk she pushed up the window, looked out, the arched fingers of her left hand trembling on the sill, her right hand at her breast.

And she saw that Gopher Prairie was merely an enlargement of all the hamlets which they had been passing. Only to the eyes of a Kennicott was it exceptional. The huddled low wooden houses broke the plains scarcely more than would a hazel thicket. The fields swept up to it, past it. It was unprotected and unprotecting; there was no dignity in it nor any hope of greatness. Only the tall red grain-elevator and a few tiny church-steeples rose from the mass. It was a frontier camp. It was not a place to live in, not possibly, not conceivably.

The people—they'd be as drab as their houses, as flat as their fields. She couldn't stay here. She would have to wrench loose from this man, and flee.

She peeped at him. She was at once help-less before his mature fixity, and touched by his excitement as he sent his magazine skittering along the aisle, stooped for their bags, came up with flushed face, and gloated, 'Here we are!'

She smiled loyally, and looked away. The train was entering town. The houses on the outskirts were dusky old red mansions with wooden frills, or gaunt frame shelters like grocery boxes, or new bungalows with concrete foundations imitating stone.

Now the train was passing the elevator, the grim storage-tanks for oil, a creamery, a lumber yard, a stock-yard muddy and trampled and stinking. Now they were stopping at a squat red frame station, the platform crowded with unshaven farmers and with loafers—unadventurous people with dead eyes. She was here. She could not go on. It was the end—the end of the world. She sat with closed eyes, longing to push past Kennicott, hide somewhere in the train, flee on toward the Pacific.

Something large arose in her soul and commanded, 'Stop it! Stop being a whining baby!' She stood up quickly; she said, 'Isn't it wonderful to be here at last!'

He trusted her so. She would make herself like the place. And she was going to do tremendous things—

She followed Kennicott and the bobbing ends of the two bags which he carried. They were held back by the slow line of disembarking passengers. She reminded herself that she was actually at the dramatic moment of the bride's home-coming. She ought to feel exalted. She felt nothing at all except irritation at their slow progress toward the door.

Kennicott stooped to peer through the windows. He shyly exulted:

'Look! Look! There's a bunch come down to welcome us! Sam Clark and the missus and Dave Dyer and Jack Elder, and, yes sir, Harry Haydock and Juanita, and a whole crowd! I guess they see us now. Yuh, yuh sure, they see us! See 'em waving!'

She obediently bent her head to look out at them. She had hold of herself. She was ready to love them. But she was embarrassed by the heartiness of the cheering group. From the vestibule she waved to them, but she clung a second to the sleeve of the brakeman who helped her down before she had the courage to dive into the cataract of hand-shaking people, people whom she could not tell apart. She had the impression that all the men had coarse voices, large damp hands, toothbrush mustaches, bald spots, and Masonic watch-charms.

She knew that they were welcoming her. Their hands, their smiles, their shouts, their affectionate eyes overcame her. She stammered, 'Thank you, oh, thank you!'

One of the men was clamoring at Kennicott, 'I brought my machine down to take you home, doc.'

'Fine business, Sam!' cried Kennicott; and, to Carol, 'Let's jump in. That big Paige over there. Some boat, too, believe me! Sam can show speed to any of these Marmons from Minneapolis!'

Only when she was in the motor car did she distinguish the three people who were to accompany them. The owner, now at the wheel, was the essence of decent self-satisfaction; a baldish, largish, level-eyed man, rugged of neck but sleek and round of face —face like the back of a spoon bowl. He was chuckling at her, 'Have you got us all straight yet?'

'Course she has! Trust Carrie to get things straight and get 'em darn quick! I bet she could tell you every date in history!' boasted her husband.

But the man looked at her reassuringly and with a certainty that he was a person whom she could trust she confessed, 'As a matter of fact I haven't got anybody straight.'

'Course you haven't, child. Well, I'm Sam Clark, dealer in hardware, sporting goods, cream separators, and almost any kind of heavy junk you can think of. You can call me Sam—anyway, I'm going to call you Carrie, seein' 's you've been and gone and married this poor fish of a bum medic that we keep round here.' Carol smiled lavishly, and wished that she called people by their given names more easily. 'The fat cranky lady back there beside you, who is pretending that she can't hear me giving her away, is Mrs. Sam'l Clark; and this hungry-looking squirt up here beside me is Dave Dyer, who keeps his drug store running by not filling your hubby's prescriptions right—fact you might say he's the guy that put the "shun" in "prescription." So! Well, leave us take the bonny

bride home. Say, doc, I'll sell you the Candersen place for three thousand plunks. Better be thinking about building a new home for Carrie. Prettiest *Frau* in G.P., if you asks me!'

Contentedly Sam Clark drove off, in the heavy traffic of three Fords and the Minnie-mashie House Free 'Bus.

'I shall like Mr. Clark . . . I *can't* call him "Sam"! They're all so friendly.' She glanced at the houses; tried not to see what she saw; gave way in: 'Why do these stories lie so? They always make the bride's home-coming a bower of roses. Complete trust in noble spouse. Lies about marriage. I'm *not* changed. And this town—O my God! I can't go through with it. This junk-heap!'

Her husband bent over her. 'You look like you were in a brown study. Scared? I don't expect you to think Gopher Prairie is a paradise, after St. Paul. I don't expect you to be crazy about it, at first. But you'll come to like it so much—life's so free here and best people on earth.'

She whispered to him (while Mrs. Clark considerately turned away), 'I love you for understanding. I'm just—I'm beastly over-sensitive. Too many books. It's my lack of shoulder-muscles and sense. Give me time, dear.'

'You bet! All the time you want!'

She laid the back of his hand against her cheek, snuggled near him. She was ready for her new home.

Kennicott had told her that, with his widowed mother as housekeeper, he had occupied an old house, 'but nice and roomy, and well-heated, best furnace I could find on the market.' His mother had left Carol her love, and gone back to Lac-qui-Meurt.

It would be wonderful, she exulted, not to have to live in Other People's Houses, but to make her own shrine. She held his hand tightly and stared ahead as the car swung round a corner and stopped in the street before a prosaic frame house in a small parched lawn.

4

A concrete sidewalk with a 'parking' of grass and mud. A square smug brown house, rather damp. A narrow concrete walk up to it. Sickly yellow leaves in a windrow with dried wings of box-elder seed and snags of wool from the cotton woods. A screened porch with pillars of thin painted pine surmounted by scrolls and brackets and bumps of jigsawed wood. No shrubbery to shut off the public gaze. A lugubrious bay-window to the right of the porch. Window curtains of starched cheap lace revealing a pink marble table with a conch shell and a Family Bible.

'You'll find it old-fashioned—what do you call it?—Mid-Victorian. I left it as is, so you could make any changes you felt were necessary.' Kennicott sounded doubtful for the first time since he had come back to his own.

'It's a real home!' She was moved by his humility. She gaily motioned good-by to the Clarks. He unlocked the door—he was leaving the choice of a maid to her, and there was no one in the house. She jiggled while he turned the key, and scampered in. . . . It was next day before either of them remembered that in their honeymoon camp they had planned that he should carry her over the sill.

In hallway and front parlor she was conscious of dinginess and lugubriousness and airlessness, but she insisted, 'I'll make it all jolly.' As she followed Kennicott and the bags up to their bedroom she quavered to herself the song of the fat little gods of the hearth:

I have my own home,
To do what I please with,
To do what I please with,
My den for me and my mate and my
        cubs,
My own!

She was close in her husband's arms; she clung to him; whatever of strangeness and slowness and insularity she might find in him, none of that mattered so long as she could slip her hands beneath his coat, run her fingers over the warm smoothness of the satin back of his waistcoat, seem almost to creep into his body, find in him strength, find in the courage and kindness of her man a shelter from the perplexing world.

'Sweet, so sweet,' she whispered.

II

'The Clarks have invited some folks to their house to meet us, tonight,' said Kennicott, as he unpacked his suit-case.

'Oh, that is nice of them!'

'You bet. I told you you'd like 'em. Squarest people on earth. Uh, Carrie— Would you mind if I sneaked down to the office for an hour, just to see how things are?'

'Why, no. Of course not. I know you're keen to get back to work.'

'Sure you don't mind?'

'Not a bit. Out of my way. Let me unpack.'

But the advocate of freedom in marriage was as much disappointed as a drooping bride at the alacrity with which he took that freedom and escaped to the world of men's affairs. She gazed about their bedroom, and its full dismalness crawled over her: the awkward knuckly L-shape of it; the black walnut bed with apples and spotty pears carved on the headboard; the imitation maple bureau, with pink-daubed scent-bottles and a petticoated pin-cushion on a marble slab uncomfortably like a gravestone; the plain pine washstand and the garlanded waterpitcher and bowl. The scent was of horsehair and plush and Florida Water.

'How could people ever live with things like this?' she shuddered. She saw the furniture as a circle of elderly judges, condemning her to death by smothering. The tottering brocade chair squeaked, 'Choke her— choke her—smother her.' The old linen smelled of the tomb. She was alone in this house, this strange still house, among the shadows of dead thoughts and haunting repressions. 'I hate it! I hate it!' she panted. 'Why did I ever—'

She remembered that Kennicott's mother had brought these family relics from the old home in Lac-qui-Meurt. 'Stop it! They're perfectly comfortable things. They're— comfortable. Besides—Oh, they're horrible! We'll change them, right away.'

Then, 'But of course he *has* to see how things are at the office—'

She made a pretense of busying herself with unpacking. The chintz-lined, silver-fitted bag which had seemed so desirable a luxury in St. Paul was an extravagant vanity here. The daring black chemise of frail chiffon and lace was a hussy at which the deep-bosomed bed stiffened in disgust, and she hurled it into a bureau drawer, hid it beneath a sensible linen blouse.

She gave up unpacking. She went to the

window, with a purely literary thought of village charm—hollyhocks and lanes and apple-cheeked cottagers. What she saw was the side of the Seventh-Day Adventist Church—a plain clapboard wall of a sour liver color; the ash-pile back of the church; an unpainted stable; and an alley in which a Ford delivery-wagon had been stranded. This was the terraced garden below her boudoir; this was to be her scenery for—

'I mustn't! I mustn't! I'm nervous this afternoon. Am I sick? . . . Good Lord, I hope it isn't that! Not now! How people lie! How these stories lie! They say the bride is always so blushing and proud and happy when she finds that out, but—I'd hate it! I'd be scared to death! Some day but— Please, dear nebulous Lord, not now! Bearded sniffy old men sitting and demanding that we bear children. If *they* had to bear them—! I wish they did have to! Not now! Not till I've got hold of this job of liking the ash-pile out there! . . . I must shut up. I'm mildly insane. I'm going out for a walk. I'll see the town by myself. My first view of the empire I'm going to conquer!'

She fled from the house.

She stared with seriousness at every concrete crossing, every hitching-post, every rake for leaves; and to each house she devoted all her speculation. What would they come to mean? How would they look six months from now? In which of them would she be dining? Which of these people whom she passed, now mere arrangements of hair and clothes, would turn into intimates, loved or dreaded, different from all the other people in the world?

As she came into the small business-section she inspected a broad-beamed grocer in an alpaca coat who was bending over the apples and celery on a slanted platform in front of his store. Would she ever talk to him? What would he say if she stopped and stated, 'I am Mrs. Dr. Kennicott. Some day I hope to confide that a heap of extremely dubious pumpkins as a window-display doesn't exhilarate me much.'

(The grocer was Mr. Frederick F. Ludelmeyer, whose market is at the corner of Main Street and Lincoln Avenue. In supposing that only she was observant Carol was ignorant, misled by the indifference of cities. She fancied that she was slipping through the streets invisible; but when she had passed, Mr. Ludelmeyer puffed into the store and coughed at his clerk, 'I seen a young woman, she come along the side street. I bet she iss Doc Kennicott's new bride, good-looker, nice legs, but she wore a hell of a plain suit, no style, I wonder will she pay cash, I bet she goes to Howland & Gould's more as she does here, what you done with the poster for Fluffed Oats?')

2

When Carol had walked for thirty-two minutes she had completely covered the town, east and west, north and south; and she stood at the corner of Main Street and Washington Avenue and despaired.

Main Street with its two-story brick shops, its story-and-a-half wooden residences, its muddy expanse from concrete walk to walk, its huddle of Fords and lumber-wagons, was too small to absorb her. The broad, straight, unenticing gashes of the streets let in the grasping prairie on every side. She realized the vastness and the emptiness of the land. The skeleton iron windmill on the farm a few blocks away, at the north end of Main Street, was like the ribs of a dead cow. She thought of the coming of the Northern winter, when the unprotected houses would crouch together in terror of storms galloping out of that wild waste. They were so small and weak, the little brown houses. They were shelters for sparrows, not homes for warm laughing people.

She told herself that down the street the leaves were a splendor. The maples were orange; the oaks a solid tint of raspberry. And the lawns had been nursed with love. But the thought would not hold. At best the trees resembled a thinned woodlot. There was no park to rest the eyes. And since not Gopher Prairie but Wakamin was the county-seat, there was no court-house with its grounds.

She glanced through the fly-specked windows of the most pretentious building in sight, the one place which welcomed strangers and determined their opinion of the charm and luxury of Gopher Prairie—the Minniemashie House. It was a tall lean shabby structure, three stories of yellow-streaked wood, the corners covered with sanded pine slabs purporting to symbolize stone. In the hotel office she could see a stretch of bare unclean floor, a line of rickety chairs with brass cuspidors between, a writing-desk with advertisements in mother-of-pearl letters upon the glass-covered back. The dining-room beyond was a jungle of stained table-cloths and catsup bottles.

She looked no more at the Minniemashie House.

A man in cuffless shirt-sleeves with pink arm-garters, wearing a linen collar but no tie, yawned his way from Dyer's Drug Store across to the hotel. He leaned against the wall, scratched a while, sighed, and in a bored way gossiped with a man tilted back in a chair. A lumber-wagon, its long green box filled with large spools of barbed-wire fencing, creaked down the block. A Ford, in reverse, sounded as though it were shaking to pieces, then recovered and rattled away. In the Greek candy-store was the whine of a peanut-roaster, and the oily smell of nuts.

There was no other sound nor sign of life.

She wanted to run, fleeing from the encroaching prairie, demanding the security of a great city. Her dreams of creating a beautiful town were ludicrous. Oozing out from every drab wall, she felt a forbidding spirit which she could never conquer.

She trailed down the street on one side, back on the other, glancing into the cross streets. It was a private Seeing Main Street tour. She was within ten minutes beholding not only the heart of a place called Gopher Prairie, but ten thousand towns from Albany to San Diego:

Dyer's Drug Store, a corner building of regular and unreal blocks of artificial stone. Inside the store, a greasy marble soda-fountain with an electric lamp of red and green and curdled-yellow mosaic shade. Pawed-over heaps of toothbrushes and combs and packages of shaving-soap. Shelves of soap-cartons, teething-rings, garden-seeds, and patent medicines in yellow packages—nostrums for consumption, for 'women's diseases'—notorious mixtures of opium and alcohol, in the very shop to which her husband sent patients for the filling of prescriptions.

From a second-story window the sign 'W. P. Kennicott, Phys. & Surgeon,' gilt on black sand.

A small wooden motion-picture theater called 'The Rosebud Movie Palace.' Lithographs announcing a film called 'Fatty in Love.'

Howland & Gould's Grocery. In the display window, black, overripe bananas and lettuce on which a cat was sleeping. Shelves lined with red crêpe paper which was now faded and torn and concentrically spotted. Flat against the wall of the second story the signs of lodges—the Knights of Pythias, the Maccabees, the Woodmen, the Masons.

Dahl & Oleson's Meat Market—a reek of blood.

A jewelry shop with tinny-looking wrist-watches for women. In front of it, at the curb, a huge wooden clock which did not go.

A fly-buzzing saloon with a brilliant gold and enamel whisky sign across the front. Other saloons down the block. From them a stink of stale beer, and thick voices bellowing pidgin German or trolling out dirty songs—vice gone feeble and unenterprising and dull—the delicacy of a mining-camp minus its vigor. In front of the saloons, farmwives sitting on the seats of wagons, waiting for their husbands to become drunk and ready to start home.

A tobacco shop called 'The Smoke House,' filled with young men shaking dice for cigarettes. Racks of magazines, and pictures of coy fat prostitutes in striped bathing-suits.

A clothing store with a display of 'ox-blood-shade Oxfords with bull-dog toes.' Suits which looked worn and glossless while they were still new, flabbily draped on dummies like corpses with painted cheeks.

The Bon Ton Store—Haydock & Simons'—the largest shop in town. The first-story front of clear glass, the plates cleverly bound at the edges with brass. The second story of pleasant tapestry brick. One window of excellent clothes for men, interspersed with collars of floral piqué which showed mauve daisies on a saffron ground. Newness and an obvious notion of neatness and service. Haydock & Simons. Haydock. She had met a Haydock at the station; Harry Haydock; an active person of thirty-five. He seemed great to her, now, and very like a saint. His shop was clean!

Axel Egge's General Store, frequented

by Scandinavian farmers. In the shallow dark window-space heaps of sleazy sateens, badly woven galateas, canvas shoes designed for women with bulging ankles, steel and red glass buttons upon cards with broken edges, a cottony blanket, a graniteware frying-pan reposing on a sun-faded crêpe blouse.

Sam Clark's Hardware Store. An air of frankly metallic enterprise. Guns and churns and barrels of nails and beautiful shiny butcher knives.

Chester Dashaway's House Furnishing Emporium. A vista of heavy oak rockers with leather seats, asleep in a dismal row.

Billy's Lunch. Thick handleless cups on the wet oilcloth-covered counter. An odor of onions and the smoke of hot lard. In the doorway a young man audibly sucking a tooth-pick.

The warehouse of the buyer of cream and potatoes. The sour smell of a dairy.

The Ford Garage and the Buick Garage, competent one-story brick and cement buildings opposite each other. Old and new cars on grease-blackened concrete floors. Tire advertisements. The roaring of a tested motor; a racket which beat at the nerves. Surly young men in khaki union-overalls. The most energetic and vital places in town.

A large warehouse for agricultural implements. An impressive barricade of green and gold wheels, of shafts and sulky seats, belonging to machinery of which Carol knew nothing—potato-planters, manure-spreaders, silage-cutters, disk-harrows, breaking-plows.

A feed store, its windows opaque with the dust of bran, a patent medicine advertisement painted on its roof.

Ye Art Shoppe, Prop. Mrs. Mary Ellen Wilks, Christian Science Library open daily free. A touching fumble at beauty. A one-room shanty of boards recently covered with rough stucco. A show-window delicately rich in error: vases starting out to imitate tree-trunks but running off into blobs of gilt—an aluminum ash-tray labeled 'Greetings from Gopher Prairie'—a Christian Science magazine—a stamped sofa-cushion portraying a large ribbon tied to a small poppy, the correct skeins of embroidery-silk lying on the pillow. Inside the shop, a glimpse of bad carbon prints of bad and famous pictures, shelves of phonograph records and camera films, wooden toys, and in the midst an anxious small woman sitting in a padded rocking chair.

A barber shop and pool room. A man in shirt sleeves, presumably Del Snafflin the proprietor, shaving a man who had a large Adam's apple.

Nat Hicks's Tailor Shop, on a side street off Main. A one-story building. A fashion-plate showing human pitchforks in garments which looked as hard as steel plate.

On another side street a raw red-brick Catholic Church with a varnished yellow door.

The post-office—merely a partition of glass and brass shutting off the rear of a mildewed room which must once have been a shop. A tilted writing-shelf against a wall rubbed black and scattered with official notices and army recruiting-posters.

The damp, yellow-brick schoolbuilding in its cindery grounds.

The State Bank, stucco masking wood.

The Farmers' National Bank. An Ionic temple of marble. Pure, exquisite, solitary. A brass plate with 'Ezra Stowbody, Pres't.'

A score of similar shops and establishments.

Behind them and mixed with them, the houses, meek cottages or large, comfortable, soundly uninteresting symbols of prosperity.

In all the town not one building save the Ionic bank which gave pleasure to Carol's eyes; not a dozen buildings which suggested that, in the fifty years of Gopher Prairie's existence, the citizens had realized that it was either desirable or possible to make this, their common home, amusing or attractive.

It was not only the unsparing unapologetic ugliness and the rigid straightness which overwhelmed her. It was the planlessness, the flimsy temporariness of the buildings, their faded unpleasant colors. The street was cluttered with electric-light poles, telephone poles, gasoline pumps for motor cars, boxes of goods. Each man had built with the most valiant disregard of all the others. Between a large new 'block' of two-story brick shops on one side, and the fire-brick Overland garage on the other side, was a one-story cottage turned into a millinery shop. The white temple of the Farmer's

Bank was elbowed back by a grocery of glaring yellow brick. One store-building had a patchy galvanized iron cornice; the building beside it was crowned with battlements and pyramids of brick capped with blocks of red sandstone.

She escaped from Main Street, fled home.

She wouldn't have cared, she insisted, if the people had been comely. She had noted a young man loafing before a shop, one unwashed hand holding the cord of an awning; a middle-aged man who had a way of staring at women as though he had been married too long and too prosaically; an old farmer, solid, wholesome, but not clean—his face like a potato fresh from the earth. None of them had shaved for three days.

'If they can't build shrines, out here on the prairie, surely there's nothing to prevent their buying safety-razors!' she raged.

She fought herself: 'I must be wrong. People do live here. It *can't* be as ugly as—as I know it is! I must be wrong. But I can't do it. I can't go through with it.'

She came home too seriously worried for hysteria; and when she found Kennicott waiting for her, and exulting, 'Have a walk? Well, like the town? Great lawns and trees, eh?' she was able to say, with a self-protective maturity new to her, 'It's very interesting.'

3

The train which brought Carol to Gopher Prairie also brought Miss Bea Sorenson.

Miss Bea was a stalwart, corn-colored, laughing young woman, and she was bored by farm-work. She desired the excitements of city-life, and the way to enjoy city-life was, she had decided, to 'go get a yob as hired girl in Gopher Prairie.' She contentedly lugged her pasteboard telescope from the station to her cousin, Tina Malmquist, maid of all work in the residence of Mrs. Luke Dawson.

'Vell, so you come to town,' said Tina.

'Ya. Ay get a yob,' said Bea.

'Vell. . . . You got a fella now?'

'Ya. Yim Yacobson.'

'Vell. I'm glat to see you. How much you vant a veek?'

'Sex dollar.'

'There ain't nobody pay dat. Vait! Dr. Kennicott, I t'ink he marry a girl from de Cities. Maybe she pay dat. Vell. You go take a valk.'

'Ya,' said Bea.

So it chanced that Carol Kennicott and Bea Sorenson were viewing Main Street at the same time.

Bea had never before been in a town larger than Scandia Crossing, which has sixty-seven inhabitants.

As she marched up the street she was meditating that it didn't hardly seem like it was possible there could be so many folks all in one place at the same time. My! It would take years to get acquainted with them all. And swell people, too! A fine big gentleman in a new pink shirt with a diamond, and not no washed out blue denim working-shirt. A lovely lady in a longery dress (but it must be an awful hard dress to wash). And the stores!

Not just three of them, like there were at Scandia Crossing, but more than four whole blocks!

The Bon Ton Store—big as four barns—my! it would simply scare a person to go in there, with seven or eight clerks all looking at you. And the men's suits, on figures just like human. And Axel Egge's, like home, lots of Swedes and Norskes in there, and a card of dandy buttons, like rubies.

A drug store with a soda fountain that was just huge, awful long, and all lovely marble; and on it there was a great big lamp with the biggest shade you ever saw—all different kinds colored glass stuck together; and the soda spouts, they were silver, and they came right out of the bottom of the lampstand! Behind the fountain there were glass shelves, and bottles of new kinds of soft drinks, that nobody ever heard of. Suppose a fella took you *there*!

A hotel, awful high, higher than Oscar Tollefson's new red barn; three stories, one right on top of another; you had to stick your head back to look clear up to the top. There was a swell traveling man in there—probably been to Chicago, lots of times.

Oh, the dandiest people to know here! There was a lady going by, you wouldn't hardly say she was any older than Bea herself; she wore a dandy new gray suit and black pumps. She almost looked like she was looking over the town, too. But you couldn't tell what she thought. Bea would like to be that way—kind of quiet, so no-body would get fresh. Kind of—oh, elegant.

A Lutheran Church. Here in the city there'd be lovely sermons, and church twice on Sunday, *every* Sunday!

And a movie show!

A regular theater, just for movies. With the sign 'Change of bill every evening.' Pictures every evening!

There were movies in Scandia Crossing, but only once every two weeks, and it took the Sorensons an hour to drive in—papa was such a tightwad he wouldn't get a Ford. But here she could put on her hat any evening, and in three minutes' walk be to the movies, and see lovely fellows in dress-suits and Bill Hart and everything!

How could they have so many stores? Why! There was one just for tobacco alone, and one (a lovely one—the Art Shoppy it was) for pictures and vases and stuff, with oh, the dandiest vase made so it looked just like a tree trunk!

Bea stood on the corner of Main Street and Washington Avenue. The roar of the city began to frighten her. There were five automobuls on the street all at the same time—and one of 'em was a great big car that must of cost two thousand dollars—and the 'bus was starting for a train with five elegant-dressed fellows, and a man was pasting up red bills with lovely pictures of washing-machines on them, and the jeweler was laying out bracelets and wrist-watches and *everything* on real velvet.

What did she care if she got six dollars a week? Or two! It was worth while working for nothing, to be allowed to stay here. And think how it would be in the evening, all lighted up—and not with no lamps, but with electrics! And maybe a gentleman friend taking you to the movies and buying you a strawberry ice cream soda!

Bea trudged back.

'Vell? You lak it?' said Tina.

'Ya. Ay lak it. Ay t'ink maybe Ay stay here,' said Bea.

4

The recently built house of Sam Clark, in which was given the party to welcome Carol, was one of the largest in Gopher Prairie. It had a clean sweep of clapboards, a solid squareness, a small tower, and a large screened porch. Inside, it was as shiny, as hard, and as cheerful as a new oak upright piano.

Carol looked imploringly at Sam Clark as he rolled to the door and shouted, 'Welcome, little lady! The keys of the city are yourn!'

Beyond him, in the hallway and the living-room, sitting in a vast circle as though they were attending a funeral, she saw the guests. They were *waiting* so! They were waiting for her! The determination to be all one pretty flowerlet of appreciation leaked away. She begged of Sam, 'I don't dare face them! They expect so much. They'll swallow me in one mouthful—glump!—like that!'

'Why, sister, they're going to love you—same as I would if I didn't think the doc here would beat me up!'

'B-but—I don't dare! Faces to the right of me, faces in front of me, volley and wonder!'

She sounded hysterical to herself; she fancied that to Sam Clark she sounded insane. But he chuckled, 'Now you just cuddle under Sam's wing, and if anybody rubbers at you too long, I'll shoo 'em off. Here we go! Watch my smoke—Sam'l, the ladies' delight and the bridegrooms' terror!'

His arm about her, he led her in and bawled, 'Ladies and worser halves, the bride! We won't introduce her round yet, because she'll never get your bum names straight anyway. Now bust up this star-chamber!'

They tittered politely, but they did not move from the social security of their circle, and they did not cease staring.

Carol had given creative energy to dressing for the event. Her hair was demure, low on her forehead with a parting and a coiled braid. Now she wished that she had piled it high. Her frock was an ingénue slip of lawn, with a wide gold sash and a low square neck, which gave a suggestion of throat and molded shoulders. But as they looked her over she was certain that it was all wrong. She wished alternately that she had worn a spinsterish high-necked dress, and that she had dared to shock them with a violent brick-red scarf which she had bought in Chicago.

She was led about the circle. Her voice mechanically produced safe remarks:

'Oh, I'm sure I'm going to like it here

ever so much,' and 'Yes, we did have the best time in Colorado—mountains,' and 'Yes, I lived in St. Paul several years. Euclid P. Tinker? No, I don't *remember* meeting him, but I'm pretty sure I've heard of him.'

Kennicott took her aside and whispered, 'Now I'll introduce you to them, one at a time.'

'Tell me about them first.'

'Well, the nice-looking couple over there are Harry Haydock and his wife, Juanita. Harry's dad owns most of the Bon Ton, but it's Harry who runs it and gives it the pep. He's a hustler. Next to him is Dave Dyer the druggist—you met him this afternoon—mighty good duck-shot. The tall husk beyond him is Jack Elder—Jackson Elder—owns the planing-mill, and the Minniemashie House, and quite a share in the Farmers' National Bank. Him and his wife are good sports—him and Sam and I go hunting together a lot. The old cheese there is Luke Dawson, the richest man in town. Next to him is Nat Hicks, the tailor.'

'Really? A tailor?'

'Sure. Why not? Maybe we're slow, but we are democratic. I go hunting with Nat same as I do with Jack Elder.'

'I'm glad. I've never met a tailor socially. It must be charming to meet one and not have to think about what you owe him. And do you—Would you go hunting with your barber, too?'

'No but—No use running this democracy thing into the ground. Besides, I've known Nat for years, and besides, he's a mighty good shot and—That's the way it is, see? Next to Nat is Chet Dashaway. Great fellow for chinning. He'll talk your arm off, about religion or politics or books or anything.'

Carol gazed with a polite approximation to interest at Mr. Dashaway, a tan person with a wide mouth. 'Oh, I know! He's the furniture-store man!' She was much pleased with herself.

'Yump, and he's the undertaker. You'll like him. Come shake hands with him.'

'Oh no, no! He doesn't—he doesn't do the embalming and all that—himself? I couldn't shake hands with an undertaker!'

'Why not? You'd be proud to shake hands with a great surgeon, just after he'd been carving up people's bellies.'

She sought to regain her afternoon's calm of maturity. 'Yes. You're right. I want—oh, my dear, do you know how much I want to like the people you like? I want to see people as they are.'

'Well, don't forget to see people as other folks see them as they are! They have the stuff. Did you know that Percy Bresnahan came from here? Born and brought up here!'

'Bresnahan?'

'Yes—you know—president of the Velvet Motor Company of Boston, Mass.—make the Velvet Twelve—biggest automobile factory in New England.'

'I think I've heard of him.'

'Sure you have. Why, he's a millionaire several times over! Well, Perce comes back here for the black-bass fishing almost every summer, and he says if he could get away from business, he'd rather live here than in Boston or New York or any of those places. *He* doesn't mind Chet's undertaking.'

'Please! I'll—I'll like everybody! I'll be the community sunbeam!'

He led her to the Dawsons.

Luke Dawson, lender of money on mortgages, owner of Northern cut-over land, was a hesitant man in unpressed soft gray clothes, with bulging eyes in a milky face. His wife had bleached cheeks, bleached hair, bleached voice, and a bleached manner. She wore her expensive green frock, with its passementeried bosom, bead tassels, and gaps between the buttons down the back, as though she had bought it second-hand and was afraid of meeting the former owner. They were shy. It was 'Professor' George Edwin Mott, superintendent of schools, a Chinese mandarin turned brown, who held Carol's hand and made her welcome.

When the Dawsons and Mr. Mott had stated that they were 'pleased to meet her,' there seemed to be nothing else to say, but the conversation went on automatically.

'Do you like Gopher Prairie?' whimpered Mrs. Dawson.

'Oh, I'm sure I'm going to be ever so happy.'

'There's so many nice people.' Mrs. Dawson looked to Mr. Mott for social and intellectual aid. He lectured:

'There's a fine class of people. I don't like some of these retired farmers who come here to spend their last days—especially the Germans. They hate to pay school-taxes. They hate to spend a cent. But the rest are a fine class of people. Did you know that Percy Bresnahan came from here? Used to go to school right at the old building!'

'I heard he did.'

'Yes. He's a prince. He and I went fishing together, last time he was here.'

The Dawsons and Mr. Mott teetered upon weary feet, and smiled at Carol with crystallized expressions. She went on:

'Tell me, Mr. Mott: Have you ever tried any experiments with any of the new educational systems? The modern kindergarten methods or the Gary system?'

'Oh. Those. Most of these would-be reformers are simply notoriety-seekers. I believe in manual training, but Latin and mathematics always will be the backbone of sound Americanism, no matter what these faddists advocate—heaven knows what they do want—knitting, I suppose, and classes in wiggling the ears!'

The Dawsons smiled their appreciation of listening to a savant. Carol waited till Kennicott should rescue her. The rest of the party waited for the miracle of being amused.

Harry and Juanita Haydock, Rita Simons and Dr. Terry Gould—the young smart set of Gopher Prairie. She was led to them. Juanita Haydock flung at her in a high, cackling, friendly voice:

'Well, this is so nice to have you here. We'll have some good parties—dances and everything. You'll have to join the Jolly Seventeen. We play bridge and we have a supper once a month. You play, of course?'

'N-no, I don't.'

'Really? In St. Paul?'

'I've always been such a book-worm.'

'We'll have to teach you. Bridge is half the fun of life.' Juanita had become patronizing, and she glanced disrespectfully at Carol's golden sash, which she had previously admired.

Harry Haydock said politely, 'How do you think you're going to like the old burg?'

'I'm sure I shall like it tremendously.'

'Best people on earth here. Great hustlers, too. Course I've had lots of chances to go live in Minneapolis, but we like it here. Real he-town. Did you know that Percy Bresnahan came from here?'

Carol perceived that she had been weakened in the biological struggle by disclosing her lack of bridge. Roused to nervous desire to regain her position she turned on Dr. Terry Gould, the young and pool-playing competitor of her husband. Her eyes coquetted with him while she gushed:

'I'll learn bridge. But what I really love most is the outdoors. Can't we all get up a boating party, and fish, or whatever you do, and have a picnic supper afterwards?'

'Now you're talking!' Dr. Gould affirmed. He looked rather too obviously at the cream-smooth slope of her shoulder. 'Like fishing? Fishing is my middle name. I'll teach you bridge. Like cards at all?'

'I used to be rather good at bezique.'

She knew that bezique was a game of cards—or a game of something else. Roulette, possibly. But her lie was a triumph. Juanita's handsome, high-colored, horsey face showed doubt. Harry stroked his nose and said humbly, 'Bezique? Used to be great gambling game, wasn't it?'

While others drifted to her group, Carol snatched up the conversation. She laughed and was frivolous and rather brittle. She could not distinguish their eyes. They were a blurry theater-audience before which she self-consciously enacted the comedy of being the Clever Little Bride of Doc Kennicott:

'These-here celebrated Open Spaces, that's what I'm going out for. I'll never read anything but the sporting-page again. Will converted me on our Colorado trip. There were so many mousey tourists who were afraid to get out of the motor 'bus that I decided to be Annie Oakley, the Wild Western Wampire, and I bought oh! a vociferous skirt which revealed my perfectly nice ankles to the Presbyterian glare of all the Ioway schoolma'ams, and I leaped from peak to peak like the nimble chamoys, and—You may think that Herr Doctor Kennicott is a Nimrod, but you ought to have seen me daring him to strip to his B.V.D.'s and go swimming in an icy mountain brook.'

She knew that they were thinking of becoming shocked, but Juanita Haydock was admiring, at least. She swaggered on:

'I'm sure I'm going to ruin Will as a respectable practitioner—Is he a good doctor, Dr. Gould?'

Kennicott's rival gasped at this insult to professional ethics, and he took an appreciable second before he recovered his social manner. 'I'll tell you, Mrs. Kennicott.' He smiled at Kennicott, to imply that whatever he might say in the stress of being witty was not to count against him in the commercio-medical warfare. 'There's some people in town that say the doc is a fair to middlin' diagnostician and prescription-writer, but let me whisper this to you—but for heaven's sake don't tell him I said so—don't you ever go to him for anything more serious than a pendectomy of the left ear or a strabismus of the cardiograph.'

No one save Kennicott knew exactly what this meant, but they laughed, and Sam Clark's party assumed a glittering lemon-yellow color of brocade panels and champagne and tulle and crystal chandeliers and sporting duchesses. Carol saw that George Edwin Mott and the blanched Mr. and Mrs. Dawson were not yet hypnotized. They looked as though they wondered whether they ought to look as though they disapproved. She concentrated on them:

'But I know whom I wouldn't have dared to go to Colorado with! Mr. Dawson there! I'm sure he's a regular heart-breaker. When we were introduced he held my hand and squeezed it frightfully.'

'Haw! Haw! Haw!' The entire company applauded. Mr. Dawson was beatified. He had been called many things—loan-shark, skinflint, tightwad, pussyfoot—but he had never before been called a flirt.

'He is wicked, isn't he, Mrs. Dawson? Don't you have to lock him up?'

'Oh no, but maybe I better,' attempted Mrs. Dawson, a tint on her pallid face.

For fifteen minutes Carol kept it up. She asserted that she was going to stage a musical comedy, that she preferred café parfait to beefsteak, that she hoped Dr. Kennicott would never lose his ability to make love to charming women, and that she had a pair of gold stockings. They gaped for more. But she could not keep it up. She retired to a chair behind Sam Clark's bulk. The smile-wrinkles solemnly flattened out in the faces of all the other collaborators in having a party, and again they stood about hoping but not expecting to be amused.

Carol listened. She discovered that conversation did not exist in Gopher Prairie. Even at this affair, which brought out the young smart set, the hunting squire set, the respectable intellectual set, and the solid financial set, they sat up with gaiety as with a corpse.

Juanita Haydock talked a good deal in her rattling voice but it was invariably of personalities: the rumor that Raymie Wutherspoon was going to send for a pair of patent leather shoes with gray buttoned tops; the rheumatism of Champ Perry; the state of Guy Pollock's grippe; and the dementia of Jim Howland in painting his fence salmon-pink.

Sam Clark had been talking to Carol about motor cars, but he felt his duties as host. While he droned, his brows popped up and down. He interrupted himself, 'Must stir 'em up.' He worried at his wife, 'Don't you think I better stir 'em up?' He shouldered into the center of the room, and cried:

'Let's have some stunts, folks.'

'Yes, let's!' shrieked Juanita Haydock.

'Say, Dave, give us that stunt about the Norwegian catching a hen.'

'You bet; that's a slick stunt; do that, Dave!' cheered Chet Dashaway.

Mr. Dave Dyer obliged.

All the guests moved their lips in anticipation of being called on for their own stunts.

'Ella, come on and recite "Old Sweetheart of Mine," for us,' demanded Sam.

Miss Ella Stowbody, the spinster daughter of the Ionic Bank, scratched her dry palms and blushed. 'Oh, you don't want to hear that old thing again.'

'Sure we do! You bet!' asserted Sam.

'My voice is in terrible shape tonight.'

'Tut! Come on!'

Sam loudly explained to Carol, 'Ella is our shark at elocuting. She's had professional training. She studied singing and oratory and dramatic art and shorthand for a year, in Milwaukee.'

Miss Stowbody was reciting. As encore to 'An Old Sweetheart of Mine,' she gave a peculiarly optimistic poem regarding the value of smiles.

There were four other stunts: one Jewish, one Irish, one juvenile, and Nat Hicks's parody of Mark Antony's funeral oration.

During the winter Carol was to hear Dave Dyer's hen-catching impersonation seven times, 'An Old Sweetheart of Mine' nine times, the Jewish story and the funeral oration twice; but now she was ardent, and, because she did so want to be happy and simple-hearted, she was as disappointed as the others when the stunts were finished, and the party instantly sank back into coma.

They gave up trying to be festive; they began to talk naturally, as they did at their shops and homes.

The men and women divided, as they had been tending to do all evening. Carol was deserted by the men, left to a group of matrons who steadily pattered of children, sickness, and cooks—their own shop-talk. She was piqued. She remembered visions of herself as a smart married woman in a drawing-room, fencing with clever men. Her dejection was relieved by speculation as to what the men were discussing, in the corner between the piano and the phonograph. Did they rise from these housewifely personalities to a larger world of abstractions and affairs?

She made her best curtsy to Mrs. Dawson; she twittered, 'I won't have my husband leaving me so soon! I'm going over and pull the wretch's ears.' She rose with a *jeune fille* bow. She was self-absorbed and self-approving because she had attained the quality of sentimentality. She proudly dipped across the room and, to the interest and commendation of all beholders, sat on the arm of Kennicott's chair.

He was gossiping with Sam Clark, Luke Dawson, Jackson Elder of the planing-mill, Chet Dashaway, Dave Dyer, Harry Haydock, and Ezra Stowbody, president of the Ionic bank.

Ezra Stowbody was a troglodyte. He had come to Gopher Prairie in 1865. He was a distinguished bird of prey—swooping thin nose, turtle mouth, thick brows, port-wine cheeks, floss of white hair, contemptuous eyes. He was not happy in the social changes of thirty years. Three decades ago, Dr. Westlake, Julius Flickerbaugh the lawyer, Merriman Peedy the Congregational pastor and himself had been the arbiters. That was as it should be; the fine arts—medicine, law, religion, and finance—recognized as aristocratic; four Yankees democratically chatting with but ruling the Ohioans and Illini and Swedes and Germans who had ventured to follow them. But Westlake was old, almost retired; Julius Flickerbaugh had lost much of his practice to livelier attorneys; Reverend (not The Reverend) Peedy was dead; and nobody was impressed in this rotten age of automobiles by the 'spanking grays' which Ezra still drove. The town was as heterogeneous as Chicago. Norwegians and Germans owned stores. The social leaders were common merchants. Selling nails was considered as sacred as banking. These upstarts—the Clarks, the Haydocks—had no dignity. They were sound and conservative in politics, but they talked about motor cars and pump-guns and heaven only knew what new-fangled fads. Mr. Stowbody felt out of place with them. But his brick house with the mansard roof was still the largest residence in town, and he held his position as squire by occasionally appearing among the younger men and reminding them by a wintry eye that without the banker none of them could carry on their vulgar businesses.

As Carol defied decency by sitting down with the men, Mr. Stowbody was piping to Mr. Dawson, 'Say, Luke, when was't Biggins first settled in Winnebago Township? Wa'n't it in 1879?'

'Why no 'twa'n't!' Mr. Dawson was indignant. 'He come out from Vermont in 1867—no, wait, in 1868, it must have been—and took a claim on the Rum River, quite a ways above Anoka.'

'He did not!' roared Mr. Stowbody. 'He settled first in Blue Earth County, him and his father!'

('What's the point at issue?' Carol whispered to Kennicott.

('Whether this old duck Biggins had an English setter or a Llewellyn. They've been arguing it all evening!')

Dave Dyer interrupted to give tidings, 'D' tell you that Clara Biggins was in town couple days ago? She bought a hot-water bottle—expensive one, too—two dollars and thirty cents!'

'Yaaaaaah!' snarled Mr. Stowbody. 'Course. She's just like her grandad was. Never save a cent. Two dollars and twenty—thirty, was it?—two dollars and thirty cents for a hot-water bottle! Brick wrapped up in a flannel petticoat just as good, anyway!'

'How's Ella's tonsils, Mr. Stowbody?' yawned Chet Dashaway.

While Mr. Stowbody gave a somatic and psychic study of them, Carol reflected, 'Are they really so terribly interested in Ella's tonsils, or even in Ella's esophagus? I wonder if I could get them away from personalities? Let's risk damnation and try.'

'There hasn't been much labor trouble around here, has there, Mr. Stowbody?' she asked innocently.

'No, ma'am, thank God, we've been free from that, except maybe with hired girls and farm-hands. Trouble enough with these foreign farmers; if you don't watch these Swedes they turn socialist or populist or some fool thing on you in a minute. Of course, if they have loans you can make 'em listen to reason. I just have 'em come into the bank for a talk, and tell 'em a few things. I don't mind their being democrats, so much, but I won't stand having socialists around. But thank God, we ain't got the labor trouble they have in these cities. Even Jack Elder here gets along pretty well, in the planing-mill, don't you, Jack?'

'Yep. Sure. Don't need so many skilled workmen in my place, and it's a lot of these cranky, wage-hogging, half-baked skilled mechanics that start trouble—reading a lot of this anarchist literature and union papers and all.'

'Do you approve of union labor?' Carol inquired of Mr. Elder.

'Me? I should say not! It's like this: I don't mind dealing with my men if they think they've got any grievances—though Lord knows what's come over workmen, nowadays—don't appreciate a good job. But still, if they come to me honestly, as man to man, I'll talk things over with them. But I'm not going to have any outsider, any of these walking delegates, or whatever fancy names they call themselves now— bunch of rich grafters, living on the ignorant workmen! Not going to have any of those fellows butting in and telling *me* how to run *my* business!'

Mr. Elder was growing more excited, more belligerent and patriotic. 'I stand for freedom and constitutional rights. If any man don't like my shop, he can get up and git. Same way, if I don't like him, he gits. And that's all there is to it. I simply can't understand all these complications and hoop-te-doodles and government reports and wage-scales and God knows what all that these fellows are balling up the labor situation with, when it's all perfectly simple. They like what I pay 'em, or they get out. That's all there is to it!'

'What do you think of profit-sharing?' Carol ventured.

Mr. Elder thundered his answer, while the others nodded, solemnly and in tune, like a shop-window of flexible toys, comic mandarins and judges and ducks and clowns, set quivering by a breeze from the open door:

'All this profit-sharing and welfare work and insurance and old-age pension is simply poppycock. Enfeebles a workman's independence—and wastes a lot of honest profit. The half-baked thinker that isn't dry behind the ears yet, and these suffragettes and God knows what all buttinskis there are that are trying to tell a business man how to run his business, and some of these college professors are just about as bad, the whole kit and bilin' of 'em are nothing in God's world but socialism in disguise! And it's my bounden duty as a producer to resist every attack on the integrity of American industry to the last ditch. Yes—SIR!'

Mr. Elder wiped his brow.

Dave Dyer added, 'Sure! You bet! What they ought to do is simply to hang every one of these agitators, and that would settle the whole thing right off. Don't you think so, doc?'

'You bet,' agreed Kennicott.

The conversation was at last relieved of the plague of Carol's intrusions and they settled down to the question of whether the justice of the peace had sent that hobo drunk to jail for ten days or twelve. It was a matter not readily determined. Then Dave Dyer communicated his carefree adventures on the gipsy trail:

'Yep. I get good time out of the flivver. 'Bout a week ago I motored down to New Wurttemberg. That's forty-three—No, let's see: It's seventeen miles to Belldale, and 'bout six and three-quarters, call it seven, to Torgenquist, and it's a good nineteen miles from there to New Wurttemberg—seventeen and seven and nineteen, that makes, uh, let me see: seventeen and seven 's twenty-four, plus nineteen, well say plus twenty, that makes forty-four, well anyway, say about forty-three or -four miles from here to New Wurttemberg. We got started about seven-fifteen, prob'ly seven-twenty, because I had to stop and fill the radiator, and we ran along, just keeping up a good steady gait—'

Mr. Dyer did finally, for reasons and purposes admitted and justified, attain to New Wurttemberg.

Once—only once—the presence of the alien Carol was recognized. Chet Dashaway leaned over and said asthmatically, 'Say, uh, have you been reading this serial "Two Out" in *Tingling Tales*? Corking yarn! Gosh, the fellow that wrote it certainly can sling baseball slang!'

The others tried to look literary. Harry Haydock offered, 'Juanita is a great hand for reading high-class stuff, like "Mid the Magnolias" by this Sara Hetwiggin Butts, and "Riders of Ranch Reckless." Books. But me,' he glanced about importantly, as one convinced that no other hero had ever been in so strange a plight, 'I'm so darn busy I don't have much time to read.'

'I never read anything I can't check against,' said Sam Clark.

Thus ended the literary portion of the conversation, and for seven minutes Jackson Elder outlined reasons for believing that the pike-fishing was better on the west shore of Lake Minniemashie than on the east—though it was indeed quite true that on the east shore Nat Hicks had caught a pike altogether admirable.

The talk went on. It did go on! Their voices were monotonous, thick, emphatic. They were harshly pompous, like men in the smoking-compartments of Pullman cars. They did not bore Carol. They frightened her. She panted, 'They will be cordial to me, because my man belongs to their tribe. God help me if I were an outsider!'

Smiling as changelessly as an ivory figurine she sat quiescent, avoiding thought, glancing about the living-room and hall, noting their betrayal of unimaginative commercial prosperity. Kennicott said, 'Dandy interior, eh? My idea of how a place ought to be furnished. Modern.' She looked polite, and observed the oiled floors, hardwood staircase, unused fireplace with tiles which resembled brown linoleum, cut-glass vases standing upon doilies, and the

barred, shut, forbidding unit bookcases that were half filled with swashbuckler novels and unread-looking sets of Dickens, Kipling, O. Henry, and Elbert Hubbard.

She perceived that even personalities were failing to hold the party. The room filled with hesitancy as with a fog. People cleared their throats, tried to choke down yawns. The men shot their cuffs and the women stuck their combs more firmly into their back hair.

Then a rattle, a daring hope in every eye, the swinging of a door, the smell of strong coffee, Dave Dyer's mewing voice in a triumphant, 'The eats!' They began to chatter. They had something to do. They could escape from themselves. They fell upon the food—chicken sandwiches, maple cake, drug-store ice cream. Even when the food was gone they remained cheerful. They could go home, any time now, and go to bed!

They went, with a flutter of coats, chiffon scarfs, and good-bys.

Carol and Kennicott walked home.

'Did you like them?' he asked.

'They were terribly sweet to me.'

'Uh, Carrie —You ought to be more careful about shocking folks. Talking about gold stockings, and about showing your ankles to schoolteachers and all!' More mildly: 'You gave 'em a good time, but I'd watch out for that, 'f I were you. Juanita Haydock is such a damn cat. I wouldn't give her a chance to criticize me.'

'My poor effort to lift up the party! Was I wrong to try to amuse them?'

'No! No! Honey, I didn't mean—You were the only up-and-coming person in the bunch. I just mean—Don't get onto legs and all that immoral stuff. Pretty conservative crowd.'

She was silent, raw with the shameful thought that the attentive circle might have been criticizing her, laughing at her.

'Don't, please don't worry!' he pleaded.

Silence.

'Gosh, I'm sorry I spoke about it. I just meant—But they were crazy about you. Sam said to me, "That little lady of yours is the slickest thing that ever came to this town," he said; and Ma Dawson—I didn't hardly know whether she'd like you or not, she's such a dried-up old bird, but she said, "Your bride is so quick and bright, I declare, she just wakes me up." '

Carol liked praise, the flavor and fatness of it, but she was so energetically being sorry for herself that she could not taste this commendation.

'Please! Come on! Cheer up!' His lips said it, his anxious shoulder said it, his arm about her said it, as they halted on the obscure porch of their house.

'Do you care if they think I'm flighty, Will?'

'Me? Why, I wouldn't care if the whole world thought you were this or that or any-thing else. You're my—well, you're my soul!'

He was an undefined mass, as solid-seeming as rock. She found his sleeve, pinched it, cried, 'I'm glad! It's sweet to be wanted! You must tolerate my frivolous-ness. You're all I have!'

He lifted her, carried her into the house, and with her arms about his neck she forgot Main Street.

1920

RING LARDNER

1885–1933

THE GOLDEN HONEYMOON

MOTHER says that when I start talking I never know when to stop. But I tell her the only time I get a chance is when she ain't around, so I have to make the most of it. I guess the fact is neither one of us would be welcome in a Quaker meeting, but as I tell Mother, what did God give us tongues for if He didn't want we should use them? Only she says He didn't give them to us to say the same thing over and over again, like I do, and repeat myself. But I say:

'Well, Mother,' I say, 'when people is like you and I and been married fifty years, do you expect everything I say will be something you ain't heard me say before? But it may be new to others, as they ain't nobody else lived with me as long as you have.'

So she says:

'You can bet they ain't, as they couldn't nobody else stand you that long.'

'Well,' I tell her, 'you look pretty healthy.'

'Maybe I do,' she will say, 'but I looked even healthier before I married you.'

You can't get ahead of Mother.

Yes, sir, we was married just fifty years ago the seventeenth day of last December and my daughter and son-in-law was over from Trenton to help us celebrate the Golden Wedding. My son-in-law is John H. Kramer, the real estate man. He made $12,000 one year and is pretty well thought of around Trenton; a good, steady, hard worker. The Rotarians was after him a long time to join, but he kept telling them his home was his club. But Edie finally made him join. That's my daughter.

Well, anyway, they come over to help us celebrate the Golden Wedding and it was pretty crimpy weather and the furnace don't seem to heat up no more like it used to and Mother made the remark that she hoped this winter wouldn't be as cold as the last, referring to the winter previous. So Edie said if she was us, and nothing to keep us home, she certainly wouldn't spend no more winters up here and why didn't we just shut off the water and close up the house and go down to Tampa, Florida? You know we was there four winters ago and staid five weeks, but it cost us over three hundred and fifty dollars for hotel bill alone. So Mother said we wasn't going no place to be robbed. So my son-in-law spoke up and said that Tampa wasn't the only place in the South, and besides we didn't have to stop at no high price hotel but could rent us a couple rooms and board out somewheres, and he had heard that St. Petersburg, Florida, was *the* spot and if we said the word he would write down there and make inquiries.

Well, to make a long story short, we decided to do it and Edie said it would be our Golden Honeymoon and for a present my son-in-law paid the difference between a section and a compartment so as we could have a compartment and have more privatecy. In a compartment you have an upper and lower berth just like the regular sleeper, but it is a shut in room by itself and got a wash bowl. The car we went in was all compartments and no regular berths at all. It was all compartments.

We went to Trenton the night before and staid at my daughter and son-in-law and we left Trenton the next afternoon at 3.23 p.m.

This was the twelfth day of January. Mother set facing the front of the train, as it makes her giddy to ride backwards. I set facing her, which does not affect me. We reached North Philadelphia at 4.03 p.m. and we reached West Philadelphia at 4.14, but did not go into Broad Street. We reached Baltimore at 6.30 and Washington, D.C., at 7.25. Our train laid over in Washington two hours till another train come along to pick us up and I got out and strolled up the platform and into the Union Station. When I come back, our car had been switched on to another track, but I remembered the name of it, the La Belle, as I had once visited my aunt out in Oconomowoc, Wisconsin, where there was a lake of that name, so I had no difficulty in getting located. But Mother had nearly fretted herself sick for fear I would be left.

'Well,' I said, 'I would of followed you on the next train.'

'You could of,' said Mother, and she pointed out that she had the money.

'Well,' I said, 'we are in Washington and I could of borrowed from the United States Treasury. I would of pretended I was an Englishman.'

Mother caught the point and laughed heartily.

Our train pulled out of Washington at 9.40 p.m. and Mother and I turned in early, I taking the upper. During the night we passed through the green fields of old Virginia, though it was too dark to tell if they was green or what color. When we got up in the morning, we was at Fayetteville, North Carolina. We had breakfast in the dining car and after breakfast I got in conversation with the man in the next compartment to ours. He was from Lebanon, New Hampshire, and a man about eighty years of age. His wife was with him, and two unmarried daughters and I made the remark that I should think the four of them would be crowded in one compartment, but he said they had made the trip every winter for fifteen years and knowed how to keep out of each other's way. He said they was bound for Tarpon Springs.

We reached Charleston, South Carolina, at 12.50 p.m. and arrived at Savannah, Georgia, at 4.20. We reached Jacksonville, Florida, at 8.45 p.m. and had an hour and a quarter to lay over there, but Mother made a fuss about me getting off the train, so we had the darky make up our berths and retired before we left Jacksonville. I didn't sleep good as the train done a lot of hemming and hawing, and Mother never sleeps good on a train as she says she is always worrying that I will fall out. She says she would rather have the upper herself, as then she would not have to worry about me, but I tell her I can't take the risk of having it get out that I allowed my wife to sleep in an upper berth. It would make talk.

We was up in the morning in time to see our friends from New Hampshire get off at Tarpon Springs, which we reached at 6.53 a.m.

Several of our fellow passengers got off at Clearwater and some at Belleair, where the train backs right up to the door of the mammoth hotel. Belleair is the winter headquarters for the golf dudes and everybody that got off there had their bag of sticks, as many as ten and twelve in a bag. Women and all. When I was a young man we called it shinny and only needed one club to play with and about one game of it would of been a-plenty for some of these dudes, the way we played it.

The train pulled into St. Petersburg at 8.20 and when we got off the train you would think they was a riot, what with all the darkies barking for the different hotels.

I said to Mother, I said:

'It is a good thing we have got a place picked out to go to and don't have to choose a hotel, as it would be hard to choose amongst them if every one of them is the best.'

She laughed.

We found a jitney and I give him the address of the room my son-in-law had got for us and soon we was there and introduced ourselves to the lady that owns the house, a young widow about forty-eight years of age. She showed us our room, which was light and airy with a comfortable bed and bureau and washstand. It was twelve dollars a week, but the location was good, only three blocks from Williams Park.

St. Pete is what folks calls the town, though they also call it the Sunshine City, as they claim they's no other place in the country where they's fewer days when Old Sol don't smile down on Mother Earth, and one of the newspapers gives away all their copies free every day when the sun don't shine. They claim to of only give them away some sixty-odd times in the last eleven years. Another nickname they have got for the town is 'the Poor Man's Palm Beach,' but I guess they's men that comes there that could borrow as much from the bank as some of the Willie boys over to the other Palm Beach.

During our stay we paid a visit to the Lewis Tent City, which is the headquarters for the Tin Can Tourists. But maybe you ain't heard about them. Well, they are an organization that takes their vacation trips by auto and carries everything with them. That is, they bring along their tents to sleep in and cook in and they don't patronize no hotels or cafeterias, but they have got to be bona fide auto campers or they can't belong to the organization.

They tell me they's over 200,000 members to it and they call themselves the Tin Canners on account of most of their food being put up in tin cans. One couple we seen in the Tent City was a couple from Brady, Texas, named Mr. and Mrs. Pence, which the old man is over eighty years of age and they had came in their auto all the way from home, a distance of 1,641 miles. They took five weeks for the trip, Mr. Pence driving the entire distance.

The Tin Canners hails from every State in the Union and in the summer time they visit places like New England and the Great Lakes region, but in the winter the most of them comes to Florida and scatters all over the State. While we was down there, they was a national convention of them at Gainesville, Florida, and they elected a Fredonia, New York, man as their president. His title is Royal Tin Can Opener of the World. They have got a song wrote up which everybody has got to learn it before they are a member:

'The tin can forever! Hurrah, boys! Hurrah!
Up with the tin can! Down with the foe!

We will rally round the campfire, we'll
    rally once again,
Shouting, "We auto camp forever!" '

That is something like it. And the members has also got to have a tin can fastened on to the front of their machine.

I asked Mother how she would like to travel around that way and she said:

'Fine, but not with an old rattle brain like you driving.'

'Well,' I said, 'I am eight years younger than this Mr. Pence who drove here from Texas.'

'Yes,' she said, 'but he is old enough to not be skittish.'

You can't get ahead of Mother.

Well, one of the first things we done in St. Petersburg was to go to the Chamber of Commerce and register our names and where we was from as they's great rivalry amongst the different States in regards to the number of their citizens visiting in town and of course our little State don't stand much of a show, but still every little bit helps, as the fella says. All and all, the man told us, they was eleven thousand names registered, Ohio leading with some fifteen hundred-odd and New York State next with twelve hundred. Then come Michigan, Pennsylvania and so on down, with one man each from Cuba and Nevada.

The first night we was there, they was a meeting of the New York-New Jersey Society at the Congregational Church and a man from Ogdensburg, New York State, made the talk. His subject was Rainbow Chasing. He is a Rotarian and a very convicting speaker, though I forget his name.

Our first business, of course, was to find a place to eat and after trying several places we run on to a cafeteria on Central Avenue that suited us up and down. We eat pretty near all our meals there and it averaged about two dollars per day for the two of us, but the food was well cooked and everything nice and clean. A man don't mind paying the price if things is clean and well cooked.

On the third day of February, which is Mother's birthday, we spread ourselves and eat supper at the Poinsettia Hotel and they charged us seventy-five cents for a sirloin steak that wasn't hardly big enough for one.

I said to Mother: 'Well,' I said, 'I guess

it's a good thing every day ain't your birth-day or we would be in the poorhouse.'

'No,' says Mother, 'because if every day was my birthday, I would be old enough by this time to of been in my grave long ago.'

You can't get ahead of Mother.

In the hotel they had a card-room where they was several men and ladies playing five hundred and this new fangled whist bridge. We also seen a place where they was dancing, so I asked Mother would she like to trip the light fantastic toe and she said no, she was too old to squirm like you have got to do now days. We watched some of the young folks at it awhile till Mother got disgusted and said we would have to see a good movie to take the taste out of our mouth. Mother is a great movie heroyne and we go twice a week here at home.

But I want to tell you about the Park. The second day we was there we visited the Park, which is a good deal like the one in Tampa, only bigger, and they's more fun goes on here every day than you could shake a stick at. In the middle they's a big bandstand and chairs for the folks to set and listen to the concerts, which they give you music for all tastes, from Dixie up to classi-cal pieces like Hearts and Flowers.

Then all around they's places marked off for different sports and games—chess and checkers and dominoes for folks that enjoys those kind of games, and roque and horse-shoes for the nimbler ones. I used to pitch a pretty fair shoe myself, but ain't done much of it in the last twenty years.

Well, anyway, we bought a membership ticket in the club which costs one dollar for the season, and they tell me that up to a couple years ago it was fifty cents, but they had to raise it to keep out the riffraff.

Well, Mother and I put in a great day watching the pitchers and she wanted I should get in the game, but I told her I was all out of practice and would make a fool of myself, though I seen several men pitching who I guess I could take their measure without no practice. However, they was some good pitchers, too, and one boy from Akron, Ohio, who could certainly throw a pretty shoe. They told me it looked like he would win the championship of the United States in the February tournament. We come away a few days before they held that

and I never did hear if he win. I forget his name, but he was a clean cut young fella and he has got a brother in Cleveland that's a Rotarian.

Well, we just stood around and watched the different games for two or three days and finally I set down in a checker game with a man named Weaver from Danville, Illinois. He was a pretty fair checker player, but he wasn't no match for me, and I hope that don't sound like bragging. But I always could hold my own on a checker-board and the folks around here will tell you the same thing. I played with this Weaver pretty near all morning for two or three mornings and he beat me one game and the only other time it looked like he had a chance, the noon whistle blowed and we had to quit and go to dinner.

While I was playing checkers, Mother would set and listen to the band, as she loves music, classical or no matter what kind, but anyway she was setting there one day and between selections the woman next to her opened up a conversation. She was a woman about Mother's own age, seventy or seventy-one, and finally she asked Mother's name and Mother told her her name and where she was from and Mother asked her the same question, and who do you think the woman was?

Well, sir, it was the wife of Frank M. Hartsell, the man who was engaged to Mother till I stepped in and cut him out, fifty-two years ago!

Yes, sir!

You can imagine Mother's surprise! And Mrs. Hartsell was surprised, too, when Mother told her she had once been friends with her husband, though Mother didn't say how close friends they had been, or that Mother and I was the cause of Hartsell going out West. But that's what we was. Hartsell left his town a month after the en-gagement was broke off and ain't never been back since. He had went out to Michigan and become a veterinary, and that is where he had settled down, in Hillsdale, Michi-gan, and finally married his wife.

Well, Mother screwed up her courage to ask if Frank was still living and Mrs. Hart-sell took her over to where they was pitch-ing horse-shoes and there was old Frank, waiting his turn. And he knowed Mother as soon as he seen her, though it was over fifty years. He said he knowed her by her eyes.

'Why, it's Lucy Frost!' he says, and he throwed down his shoes and quit the game.

Then they come over and hunted me up and I will confess I wouldn't of knowed him. Him and I is the same age to the month, but he seems to show it more, some way. He is balder for one thing. And his beard is all white, where mine has still got a streak of brown in it. The very first thing I said to him, I said:

'Well, Frank, that beard of yours makes me feel like I was back north. It looks like a regular blizzard.'

'Well,' he said, 'I guess yourn would be just as white if you had it dry cleaned.'

But Mother wouldn't stand that.

'Is that so!' she said to Frank. 'Well, Charley ain't had no tobacco in his mouth for over ten years!'

And I ain't!

Well, I excused myself from the checker game and it was pretty close to noon, so we decided to all have dinner together and they was nothing for it only we must try their cafeteria on Third Avenue. It was a little more expensive than ours and not near as good, I thought. I and Mother had about the same dinner we had been having every day and our bill was $1.10. Frank's check was $1.20 for he and his wife. The same meal wouldn't of cost them more than a dollar at our place.

After dinner we made them come up to our house and we all set in the parlor, which the young woman had give us the use of to entertain company. We begun talking over old times and Mother said she was a-scared Mrs. Hartsell would find it tiresome listening to we three talk over old times, but as it turned out they wasn't much chance for nobody else to talk with Mrs. Hartsell in the company. I have heard lots of women that could go it, but Hartsell's wife takes the cake of all the women I ever seen. She told us the family history of everybody in the State of Michigan and bragged for a half hour about her son, who she said is in the drug business in Grand Rapids, and a Rotarian.

When I and Hartsell could get a word in edgeways we joked one another back and forth and I chafed him about being a horse doctor.

'Well, Frank,' I said, 'you look pretty prosperous, so I suppose they's been plenty of glanders around Hillsdale.'

'Well,' he said, 'I've managed to make more than a fair living. But I've worked pretty hard.'

'Yes,' I said, 'and I suppose you get called out all hours of the night to attend births and so on.'

Mother made me shut up.

Well, I thought they wouldn't never go home and I and Mother was in misery trying to keep awake, as the both of us generally always takes a nap after dinner. Finally they went, after we had made an engagement to meet them in the Park the next morning, and Mrs. Hartsell also invited us to come to their place the next night and play five hundred. But she had forgot that they was a meeting of the Michigan Society that evening, so it was not till two evenings later that we had our first card game.

Hartsell and his wife lived in a house on Third Avenue North and had a private setting room besides their bedroom. Mrs. Hartsell couldn't quit talking about their private setting room like it was something wonderful. We played cards with them, with Mother and Hartsell partners against his wife and I. Mrs. Hartsell is a miserable card player and we certainly got the worst of it.

After the game she brought out a dish of oranges and we had to pretend it was just what we wanted, though oranges down there is like a young man's whiskers; you enjoy them at first, but they get to be a pesky nuisance.

We played cards again the next night at our place with the same partners and I and Mrs. Hartsell was beat again. Mother and Hartsell was full of compliments for each other on what a good team they made, but the both of them knowed well enough where the secret of their success laid. I guess all and all we must of played ten different evenings and they was only one night when Mrs. Hartsell and I come out ahead. And that one night wasn't no fault of hern.

When we had been down there about two weeks, we spent one evening as their guest in the Congregational Church, at a social give by the Michigan Society. A talk was made by a man named Bitting of Detroit, Michigan, on How I was Cured of Story Telling. He is a big man in the Rotarians and give a witty talk.

A woman named Mrs. Oxford rendered some selections which Mrs. Hartsell said was grand opera music, but whatever they was my daughter Edie could of give her cards and spades and not made such a hullaballoo about it neither.

Then they was a ventriloquist from Grand Rapids and a young woman about forty-five years of age that mimicked different kinds of birds. I whispered to Mother that they all sounded like a chicken, but she nudged me to shut up.

After the show we stopped in a drug store and I set up the refreshments and it was pretty close to ten o'clock before we finally turned in. Mother and I would of preferred tending the movies, but Mother said we mustn't offend Mrs. Hartsell, though I asked her had we came to Florida to enjoy ourselves or to just not offend an old chatterbox from Michigan.

I felt sorry for Hartsell one morning. The women folks both had an engagement down to the chiropodist's and I run across Hartsell in the Park and he foolishly offered to play me checkers.

It was him that suggested it, not me, and I guess he repented himself before we had played one game. But he was too stubborn to give up and set there while I beat him game after game and the worst part of it was that a crowd of folks had got in the habit of watching me play and there they all was, looking on, and finally they seen what a fool Frank was making of himself, and they began to chafe him and pass remarks. Like one of them said:

'Who ever told you you was a checker player!'

And:

'You might maybe be good for tiddle-de-winks, but not checkers!'

I almost felt like letting him beat me a couple games. But the crowd would of knowed it was a put up job.

Well, the women folks joined us in the Park and I wasn't going to mention our little game, but Hartsell told about it himself and admitted he wasn't no match for me.

'Well,' said Mrs. Hartsell, 'checkers ain't much of a game anyway, is it?' She said: 'It's more of a children's game, ain't it? At least, I know my boy's children used to play it a good deal.'

'Yes, ma'am,' I said. 'It's a children's game the way your husband plays it, too.'

Mother wanted to smooth things over, so she said:

'Maybe they's other games where Frank can beat you.'

'Yes,' said Mrs. Hartsell, 'and I bet he could beat you pitching horse-shoes.'

'Well,' I said, 'I would give him a chance to try, only I ain't pitched a shoe in over sixteen years.'

'Well,' said Hartsell, 'I ain't played checkers in twenty years.'

'You ain't never played it,' I said.

'Anyway,' says Frank, 'Lucy and I is your master at five hundred.'

Well, I could of told him why that was, but had decency enough to hold my tongue.

It had got so now that he wanted to play cards every night and when I or Mother wanted to go to a movie, any one of us would have to pretend we had a headache and then trust to goodness that they wouldn't see us sneak into the theater. I don't mind playing cards when my partner keeps their mind on the game, but you take a woman like Hartsell's wife and how can they play cards when they have got to stop every couple seconds and brag about their son in Grand Rapids?

Well, the New York-New Jersey Society announced that they was goin to give a social evening too and I said to Mother, I said:

'Well, that is one evening when we will have an excuse not to play five hundred.'

'Yes,' she said, 'but we will have to ask Frank and his wife to go to the social with us as they asked us to go to the Michigan social.'

'Well,' I said, 'I had rather stay home than drag that chatterbox everywheres we go.'

So Mother said:

'You are getting too cranky. Maybe she does talk a little too much but she is good hearted. And Frank is always good company.'

So I said:

'I suppose if he is such good company you wished you had of married him.'

Mother laughed and said I sounded like I was jealous. Jealous of a cow doctor!

Anyway we had to drag them along to the social and I will say that we give them a much better entertainment than they had given us.

Judge Lane of Paterson made a fine talk on business conditions and a Mrs. Newell of Westfield imitated birds, only you could really tell what they was the way she done it. Two young women from Red Bank sung a choral selection and we clapped them back and they gave us Home to Our Mountains and Mother and Mrs. Hartsell both had tears in their eyes. And Hartsell, too.

Well, some way or another the chairman got wind that I was there and asked me to make a talk and I wasn't even going to get up, but Mother made me, so I got up and said:

'Ladies and gentlemen,' I said. 'I didn't expect to be called on for a speech on an occasion like this or no other occasion as I do not set myself up as a speech maker, so will have to do the best I can, which I often say is the best anybody can do.'

Then I told them the story about Pat and the motorcycle, using the brogue, and it seemed to tickle them and I told them one or two other stories, but altogether I wasn't on my feet more than twenty or twenty-five minutes and you ought to of heard the clapping and hollering when I set down. Even Mrs. Hartsell admitted that I am quite a speechifier and said if I ever went to Grand Rapids, Michigan, her son would make me talk to the Rotarians.

When it was over, Hartsell wanted we should go to their house and play cards, but his wife reminded him that it was after 9.30 p.m., rather a late hour to start a card game, but he had went crazy on the subject of cards, probably because he didn't have to play partners with his wife. Anyway, we got rid of them and went home to bed.

It was the next morning, when we met over to the Park, that Mrs. Hartsell made the remark that she wasn't getting no exercise so I suggested that why didn't she take part in the roque game.

She said she had not played a game of roque in twenty years, but if Mother would play she would play. Well, at first Mother wouldn't hear of it, but finally consented, more to please Mrs. Hartsell than anything else.

Well, they had a game with a Mrs. Ryan from Eagle, Nebraska, and a young Mrs. Morse from Rutland, Vermont, who Mother had met down to the chiropodist's. Well, Mother couldn't hit a flea and they all laughed at her and I couldn't help from laughing at her myself and finally she quit and said her back was too lame to stoop over. So they got another lady and kept on playing and soon Mrs. Hartsell was the one everybody was laughing at, as she had a long shot to hit the black ball, and as she made the effort her teeth fell out on to the court. I never seen a woman so flustered in my life. And I never heard so much laughing, only Mrs. Hartsell didn't join in and she was madder than a hornet and wouldn't play no more, so the game broke up.

Mrs. Hartsell went home without speaking to nobody, but Hartsell stayed around and finally he said to me, he said:

'Well, I played you checkers the other day and you beat me bad and now what do you say if you and me play a game of horseshoes?'

I told him I hadn't pitched a shoe in sixteen years, but Mother said:

'Go ahead and play. You used to be good at it and maybe it will come back to you.'

Well, to make a long story short, I give in. I oughtn't to of never tried it, as I hadn't pitched a shoe in sixteen years, and I only done it to humor Hartsell.

Before we started, Mother patted me on the back and told me to do my best, so we started in and I seen right off that I was in for it, as I hadn't pitched a shoe in sixteen years and didn't have my distance. And besides, the plating had wore off the shoes so that they was points right where they stuck into my thumb and I hadn't throwed more than two or three times when my thumb was raw and it pretty near killed me to hang on to the shoe, let alone pitch it.

Well, Hartsell throws the awkwardest shoe I ever seen pitched and to see him pitch you wouldn't think he would ever come nowheres near, but he is also the luckiest pitcher I ever seen and he made some pitches where the shoe lit five and six feet short and then schoonered up and was a ringer. They's no use trying to beat that kind of luck.

They was a pretty fair size crowd watching us and four or five other ladies besides Mother, and it seems like, when Hartsell pitches, he has got to chew and it kept the ladies on the anxious seat as he don't seem to care which way he is facing when he leaves go.

You would think a man as old as him would of learnt more manners.

Well, to make a long story short, I was just beginning to get my distance when I had to give up on account of my thumb, which I showed it to Hartsell and he seen I couldn't go on, as it was raw and bleeding. Even if I could of stood it to go on myself, Mother wouldn't of allowed it after she seen my thumb. So anyway I quit and Hartsell said the score was nineteen to six, but I don't know what it was. Or don't care, neither.

Well, Mother and I went home and I said I hoped we was through with the Hartsells as I was sick and tired of them, but it seemed like she had promised we would go over to their house that evening for another game of their everlasting cards.

Well, my thumb was giving me considerable pain and I felt kind of out of sorts and I guess maybe I forgot myself, but anyhow, when we was about through playing Hartsell made the remark that he wouldn't never lose a game of cards if he could always have Mother for a partner.

So I said:

'Well, you had a chance fifty years ago to always have her for a partner, but you wasn't man enough to keep her.'

I was sorry the minute I had said it and Hartsell didn't know what to say and for once his wife couldn't say nothing. Mother tried to smooth things over by making the remark that I must of had something stronger than tea or I wouldn't talk so silly. But Mrs. Hartsell had froze up like an iceberg and hardly said good night to us and I bet her and Frank put in a pleasant hour after we was gone.

As we was leaving, Mother said to him: 'Never mind Charley's nonsense, Frank. He is just mad because you beat him all hollow pitching horse-shoes and playing cards.'

She said that to make up for my slip, but at the same time she certainly riled me. I tried to keep ahold of myself, but as soon as we was out of the house she had to open up the subject and begun to scold me for the break I had made.

Well, I wasn't in no mood to be scolded. So I said:

'I guess he is such a wonderful pitcher and card player that you wished you had married him.'

'Well,' she said, 'at least he ain't a baby to give up pitching because his thumb has got a few scratches.'

'And how about you,' I said, 'making a fool of yourself on the roque court and then pretending your back is lame and you can't play no more!'

'Yes,' she said, 'but when you hurt your thumb I didn't laugh at you, and why did you laugh at me when I sprained my back?'

'Who could help from laughing!' I said.

'Well,' she said, 'Frank Hartsell didn't laugh.'

'Well,' I said, 'why didn't you marry him?'

'Well,' said Mother, 'I almost wished I had!'

'And I wished so, too!' I said.

'I'll remember that!' said Mother, and that's the last word she said to me for two days.

We seen the Hartsells the next day in the Park and I was willing to apologize, but they just nodded to us. And a couple days later we heard they had left for Orlando, where they have got relatives.

I wished they had went there in the first place.

Mother and I made it up setting on a bench.

'Listen, Charley,' she said. 'This is our Golden Honeymoon and we don't want the whole thing spoilt with a silly old quarrel.'

'Well,' I said, 'did you mean that about wishing you had married Hartsell?'

'Of course not,' she said, 'that is, if you didn't mean that you wished I had, too.'

So I said:

'I was just tired and all wrought up. I thank God you chose me instead of him as they's no other woman in the world who I could of lived with all these years.'

'How about Mrs. Hartsell?' says Mother.

'Good gracious!' I said. 'Imagine being married to a woman that plays five hundred like she does and drops her teeth on the roque court!'

'Well,' said Mother, 'it wouldn't be no worse than being married to a man that expectorates towards ladies and is such a fool in a checker game.'

So I put my arm around her shoulder and she stroked my hand and I guess we got kind of spoony.

They was two days left of our stay in St. Petersburg and the next to the last day Mother introduced me to a Mrs. Kendall from Kingston, Rhode Island, who she had met at the chiropodist's.

Mrs. Kendall made us acquainted with her husband, who is in the grocery business. They have got two sons and five grandchildren and one great-grandchild. One of their sons lives in Providence and is way up in the Elks as well as a Rotarian.

We found them very congenial people and we played cards with them the last two nights we was there. They was both experts and I only wished we had met them sooner instead of running into the Hartsells. But the Kendalls will be there again next winter and we will see more of them, that is, if we decide to make the trip again.

We left the Sunshine City on the eleventh day of February, at 11 a.m. This give us a day trip through Florida and we seen all the country we had passed through at night on the way down.

We reached Jacksonville at 7 p.m. and pulled out of there at 8.10 p.m. We reached Fayetteville, North Carolina, at nine o'clock the following morning, and reached Washington, D.C., at 6.30 p.m., laying over there half an hour.

We reached Trenton at 11.01 p.m. and had wired ahead to my daughter and son-in-law and they met us at the train and we went to their house and they put us up for the night. John would of made us stay up all night, telling about our trip, but Edie said we must be tired and made us go to bed. That's my daughter.

The next day we took our train for home and arrived safe and sound, having been gone just one month and a day.

Here comes Mother, so I guess I better shut up.   1924

LOLA RIDGE
1883–1941

FACES

A LATE snow beats
With cold white fists upon the tenements—
Hurriedly drawing blinds and shutters,
Like tall old slatterns
Pulling aprons about their heads.

Lights slanting out of Mott Street
Gibber out,
Or dribble through bar-room slits,
Anonymous shapes
Conniving behind shuttered panes   10
Caper and disappear . . .
Where the Bowery
Is throbbing like a fistula
Back of her ice-scabbed fronts.

Livid faces
Glimmer in furtive doorways,
Or spill out of the black pockets of
        alleys,
Smears of faces like muddied beads,
Making a ghastly rosary
The night mumbles over   20

And the snow with its devilish and silken
        whisper . . .
Patrolling arcs
Blowing shrill blasts over the Bread Line
Stalk them as they pass,
Silent as though accouched of the
        darkness,
And the wind noses among them
        Like a skunk
That roots about the heart . . .

Colder:
And the Elevated slams upon the silence 30
Like a ponderous door.
Then all is still again,
Save for the wind fumbling over
The emptily swaying faces—
The wind rummaging
Like an old Jew . . .

Faces in glimmering rows . . .
(No sign of the abject life—
Not even a blasphemy . . .)
But the spindle legs keep time   40
To a limping rhythm,

nd the shadows twitch upon the snow
  Convulsively—
s though death played
Vith some ungainly dolls.
917   1918

SONS OF BELIAL

1

'E are old,
ld as song.
efore Rome was
r Cyrene.
Iad nights knew us
nd old men's wives.
'e knew who spilled the sacred oil
or young-gold harlots of the town. . . .
'e knew where the peacocks went
nd the white doe for sacrifice.   10

2

'e were the sons of Belial.
ne black night
enturies ago
'e beat at a door
i Gilead. . . .
'e took the Levite's concubine
'e plucked her hands from off the
        door. . . .
'e choked the cry into her throat
nd stuck the stars among her hair. . . .
'e glimpsed the madly swaying stars   20
etween the rhythms of her hair . . .
nd all our mute and separate strings
velled in a raging symphony. . . .
ur blood sang pæans
ll that night
ill dawn fell like a wounded swan
pon the fields of Gilead.

3

'e are old. . . .
ld as song. . . .
'e are dumb song.   30
pics tingled
our blood
hen we haled Hypatia
ver the stones
Alexandria.)

ruld we loose
he wild rhythms clinched in us. . . .
arch in bands of troubadours. . . .
'e would be of gentle mood.
hen Christ healed us   40

Who were dumb—
When he freed our shut-in song—
We strewed green palms
At his pale feet . . .
We sang hosannas
In Jerusalem.
And all our fumbling voices blent
In a brief white harmony.
(*But a mightier song*
Was in us pent   50
When we nailed Christ
To a four-armed tree.)

4

We are young.
When we rise up with singing roots,
(*Warm rains washing*
Gutters of Berlin
Where we stamped Rosa . . . Luxemburg
On a night in spring.)
Rhythms skurry in our blood.
Little nimble rats of song   60
In our feet run crazily
And all is dust . . . we trample . . . on.

Mad nights when we make ritual
(*Feet running before the sleuth-light . . .*
And the smell of burnt flesh
By a flame-ringed hut
In Missouri,
Sweet as on Rome's pyre. . . .)
We make ropes do rigadoons
With copper feet that jig on air.   70
We are the Mob. . . .
Old as song.
Tyre knew us
And Israel.
1919   1920

REVEILLE

COME forth, you workers!
Let the fires go cold—
Let the iron spill out, out of the troughs—
Let the iron run wild
Like a red bramble on the floors—
Leave the mill and the foundry and the
        mine
And the shrapnel lying on the wharves—
Leave the desk and the shuttle and the
        loom—
Come,
With your ashen lives,   10
Your lives like dust in your hands.

I call upon you, workers.
It is not yet light
But I beat upon your doors.
You say you await the Dawn
But I say you are the Dawn.
Come, in your irresistible unspent force
And make new light upon the mountains.

You have turned deaf ears to others—
Me you shall hear.   20
Out of the mouths of turbines,
Out of the turgid throats of engines,
Over the whistling steam,
You shall hear me shrilly piping.
Your mills I shall enter like the wind,
And blow upon your hearts,
Kindling the slow fire.

They think they have tamed you, workers—
Beaten you to a tool
To scoop up hot honor   30
Till it be cool—
But out of the passion of the red frontiers
A great flower trembles and burns and
     glows
And each of its petals is a people.

Come forth, you workers—
Clinging to your stable
And your wisp of warm straw—
Let the fires grow cold,
Let the iron spill out of the troughs,
Let the iron run wild   40
Like a red bramble on the floors. . . .

As our forefathers stood on the prairies
So let us stand in a ring,
Let us tear up their prisons like grass
And beat them to barricades—
Let us meet the fire of their guns
With a greater fire,
Till the birds shall fly to the mountains
For one safe bough.
1918   1920

FROM FIREHEAD

LIGHT SONG [1]

ON the taut string He was the night bowed
     somberly its ancient music;
And He, attuned to diapasons,
Heard in the conch shell of darkness the
     murmur of many peoples.

[1] Miss Ridge says: 'The passage, from "He," the first
book of *Firehead*, is not, of course, given in its entirety

He felt strange fluxions in him and tender
     and sharp vibrations;
Mob cries, the kisses of the whip that were
     as mouths pressed too close, the
     faltered
Kiss of Judas, faintly malodorous like a
     jonquil that had lain too long on the
     breast of a dead man,
Chill yet on his cheek; the warm kiss of
     Mary and pressure of John's bright
     head
All blent in a vast music, not again
To sound apart in any separate strain
But move in the clear whole wherein He
     whirled
Incandescent, in the pillared flame
Of music that is time made audible
With all its massed formations high in
     air
And wheeling columns streaming out of
     sight—
To what bright conquest or achieved
     despair
Or flaming end past compass or compute?
Music, over time made absolute,
Holding eternal, in the light that moves
From sun to sun, an octave in its flight
The little hatreds and the chiming loves.

Light grew in him like a stalk . . . up and
     up . . . to meet the far shining,
As it was in the beginning . . . the first
     stammering upon the waters . . .
He expanded, treading upon space, through
     him sweetly flowing
The effluvia in which all things move; He
     saw
Earth watching out of her seas, great eyes
     lidded in darkness; sluggishly lifting
The night that drooped upon them, earth
     supine

or even in the exact form in which it appears in the long
poem. For in order to give some kind of unity to the
fragment presented I have separated the central light
theme from its context, very much as one might draw
a single white-thread from a multi-colored weave.
   'Firehead was commenced in August 1927, shortly
after my return from Boston, where like many others
I had gone to protest against the legal killing of Sacco
and Vanzetti—who, as most of us know, were falsely
accused and died for a crime of which they were innocent. In the days following I wrote a number of verses
about the men, and then started to go on with some
other work. Suddenly one day, and without premedita-
tion, I wrote some lyrics on the theme of the Crucif-
ion. Only then did I begin to plan the structure of the
poem and to study my background.' Benét, ed., Fifty
Poets (N.Y., 1933),52–53.

In the vast equations of the night that
    upbore her as on immense wings;
    He heard
Out of the unfathomable arches and
    stretches of the night
The moments falling. Summers endlessly
    uncoiling from off the golden
Spool of the sun and dawns like barefoot
    virgins, with the early   30
Wonder in their eyes, passed him in silvery
    procession . . .
He, privy with the delicate speech of
    things, knowing their infinite
    gestures, telling
Trees by the differing cadences of leaves
    that prattle to the ear sweetly of no
    thing . . .
Knowing the vanity of a rose . . . and how
    stone
Cries at the emergence of great waters . . .
Heard now the feet of centuries . . . in
    these
Enormous footfalls other sounds were lost.
    It was a silent world,
Until into its silence that was as the heart of
    a song or as the quiet at the core of
    hurricanes,

A word out-leapt, an overgrowth
A bloody hand shaped like his own,   40
To a separate life from out his mouth.
(The wind blew salt in each nail-hole
It fanned into a living coal)

In vast semi-circle thrown
Sleeping lay the curved horizon,
Till the hand that spanned the zone,
The streaming hand shaped like his own,
Seized and swung it like a scythe.

He saw the spinning blade divide
The ancient body of the night,   50
A humming scimitar it cleft
The blue deep parts within her nave
No other vaulting thing had reft
And plunged in some high fountain-head
That trumpeted with light.

Light gushed out of the rift and made
A radiance upon the mountains,
Light supernal, turning the rocks to fire,
Holding the seas before it like a glass,
Compelling to its own fabulous desire   60
The small pure waters of his sight
So that for a moment the Omnipotent,

Blazoning his face above the mountains,
Might look therein and be made glad;

Light omnivorous and without mercy
Consuming all things for fuel—
Denying no toad, beast, man, fowl, worm—
Seizing, transfixing the mean norm,
Leaving it starrily, as it left Peter
Pierced with the white crow of dawn,   70
In the arrested moment like a spear
To remain without falling and without
    flight,
A cynosure to burn forever there
Impaled on the implacable light.

Light making bright things its own,
Implicit in it all dark gestations
Of life that terribly flowers and burns again
    to the white bone;
Light no god might blow out with his
    jealous breath
Nor the chained mountains stamp on with
    a ponderous foot,
Informing the night's arteries, swelling the
    great hill-roots,   80
Down,
Full veins of earth, purpling the dim
    strata,
Down
Through the dark declivities, touching the
    riant fire under the world . . .

Until his spirit merging into the light's
    excess
Grew one with that which fed on it . . .
Light, falling on Judea, smiting her rocks to
    song . . .
All things resolving into light and light into
    love . . . love denying
No toad, beast, man, fowl, worm . . .
In one song of monstrous adoration.   90
1927–1929   1929

FROM VIA IGNIS

I

THOU, multi-one, whose contours none
    may mark
In spinning whole, for the brief shapes
    which thrust
Their wilding heads from ferment of this
    dust
Thou leavenest with tumultuous spark,
Art all-equating; no offending part
From part divided but has stance in thee.

The flame consuming and the smoking
    heart
Have place in thy shining advocacy.

Thou, who art termless only in degree
More than the lightnings that of thee
    suspire,   10
Over the lilies and the working grain
And the rumorous epoch of the brain,
Shalt pass with the arrogant caste of fire—
One in the orders of eternity.

3

O lovely Light, look on thy ray perverse!
That makes a puny transit of the night
The generations of the suns traverse.
What star shall be its period of flight?
On what horizon shall the light constrain,
To move, in thy design, in shining order
With docile bodies of the fire, this vain
Brief ray addict to rapine and to murder?

Is there no peace, but heritage of wars,
Here, where we drive to impact on the
    dark,   10
For us, thy progeny, of the fire born
To weave our broken rhythms in the stars—
Is there no rest for this infuriate spark
And the blood singing to the ancient horn?

7

O Light, forsake not thy adoring hills,
Belovèd of the mornings, earliest
To stretch from out the longing of her
    breast
In flight forever theeward. Earth fulfills
Her pact with thee; let not the void engulf
This goodly loam. Though its contentious
    brood
Die in some final dissonance, each self
Hath fumbled toward thee in his solitude.

Though none be left, some spring when
    lilacs close,
Petitioning in fragrance, incomplete,   10
Earth shall attend thee; as in first of days,
In some new Eden with the loam at heat,
Bring forth new eyes to widen on a rose
That could not bear its beauty without
    praise.

8

For thee, the lion and the burning dove,
Earth wears the rose of morning on her brow
With the old iridescent luster. Now

The prostrate horizons toward thee move.
Thy rays attach to each pale trancèd sense,
In bond to shining, until flowers of pain
Of thee begot, grow in all innocence
Through this intrepid dust to light again.

O fount of mornings, functioning through
    time
In dateless ardors, this—before the sea   10
Conceived or rock delivered without cry—
Was in the covenant. The awkward slime
Miscarried a long age till in the first eye
The light streamed upward to identity.

9

Is not this April of our brief desire
That stirs the robins to a twittering
But waste vibration of some vaster spring
Which moves the void to utterance. This
    fire
Once babbled on our hills (that have forgot
Their fiery accents) when the earth was cleft
And flooding in her canyons, raging hot,
Ere this intricate, fair design was left.

Long, long before strange creatures
    overhead
Cast wheeling shadows on the desert, wings
Flamed from out the mountains; radiant
    things,   11
That stood erect upon each blazing rim
Of horned horizons, shone like seraphim
And shook the earth with their enormous
    tread.

13

To leap and having leapt touch privity
Of light . . . and reel back from its edge
    and fall;
This is to be more humbled than a wall
Detowered and left bare before the high-
Browed mornings without loophole. Thus
    the quest
Ends and is begun; the new blood flowing
To lift the sagging spirit in the breast.
But that which shed upon the dark of
    knowing

A lucent beam has sped on, as a ray
Of sunlight when the leaf is shorn away   10
That gave it pattern, to be resolved and soar
Where no clipt vision may identify,
Nor fledgling hand assemble any more
Its lambent dust in form before the eye.

                            1935

SARA TEASDALE

1884–1933

I SHALL NOT CARE

WHEN I am dead and over me bright
    April
  Shakes out her rain-drenched
    hair,
Tho' you should lean above me broken-
    hearted,
  I shall not care.

I shall have peace, as leafy trees are
    peaceful
  When rain bends down the bough,
And I shall be more silent and cold-
    hearted
  Than you are now.

1911   1915

THE ANSWER

  WHEN I go back to earth
  And all my joyous body
  Puts off the red and white
  That once had been so proud,
  If men should pass above
  With false and feeble pity,
  My dust will find a voice
  To answer them aloud:

  'Be still, I am content,
  Take back your poor compassion,   10
  Joy was a flame in me
  Too steady to destroy;
  Lithe as a bending reed
  Loving the storm that sways her—
  I found more joy in sorrow
  Than you could find in joy.'

1914   1915

MORNING

I WENT out on an April morning
  All alone, for my heart was high,
I was a child of the shining meadow,
  I was a sister of the sky.

There in the windy flood of morning
  Longing lifted its weight from me,
Lost as a sob in the midst of cheering,
  Swept as a sea-bird out to sea.

1914   1915

I REMEMBERED

THERE never was a mood of mine,
  Gay or heart-broken, luminous or dull,
But you could ease me of its fever
  And give it back to me more beautiful.

In many another soul I broke the bread,
  And drank the wine and played the
    happy guest,
But I was lonely, I remembered you;
  The heart belongs to him who knew it
    best.

1920   1920

'LET IT BE FORGOTTEN'

LET it be forgotten, as a flower is forgotten,
  Forgotten as a fire that once was singing
    gold,
Let it be forgotten for ever and ever,
  Time is a kind friend, he will make us old.

If anyone asks, say it was forgotten
  Long and long ago,
As a flower, as a fire, as a hushed footfall
  In a long forgotten snow.

1919   1920

ARCTURUS IN AUTUMN

WHEN, in the gold October dusk, I saw you
    near to setting,
  Arcturus, bringer of spring,
Lord of the summer nights, leaving us now
    in autumn,
  Having no pity on our withering;

Oh then I knew at last that my own autumn
    was upon me,
  I felt it in my blood,
Restless as dwindling streams that still
    remember
  The music of their flood.

There in the thickening dark a wind-bent
    tree above me
  Loosed its last leaves in flight—   10
I saw you sink and vanish, pitiless Arcturus,
  You will not stay to share our lengthening
    night.   1926

WITTER BYNNER

1881–

GRENSTONE RIVER

THINGS you heard that blessed be
You shall tell to men like me:

What you heard my lover say
In the golden yesterday,
Leaving me a childish heart,
Glad to revel, quick to start.

And though she awhile is gone
And I come today alone,
'Tis the self-same whisper slips
Through your ripple from her lips.   10

Long shall she and I be dead,
While you whisper what she said;
You, when I no word can give her,
Shall forever whisper, river:

Things you heard that blessed be,
Telling them to men like me.
1905   1907

GRIEVE NOT FOR BEAUTY

GRIEVE not for the invisible transported
     brow
On which like leaves the dark hair grew,
Nor for the lips of laughter that are now
Laughing inaudibly in sun and dew,
Nor for the limbs that, fallen low
And seeming faint and slow,
Shall alter and renew
Their shape and hue
Like birches white before the moon
Or a young apple-tree   10
In spring or the round sea
And shall pursue
More ways of swiftness than the swallow
     dips
Among . . . and find more winds than
     ever blew
The straining sails of unimpeded ships!
1910   1916

A TENT SONG

TILL we watch the last low star,
Let us love and let us take
Of each other all we are.

On some morning with that star
One of us shall lie awake,
Lonely for the other's sake.
1910   1917

PASSING NEAR

I HAD not till today been sure,
     But now I know:
Dead men and women come and go
     Under the pure
     Sequestering snow.

And under the autumnal fern
     And carmine bush,
Under the shadow of a thrush,
     They move and learn;
     And in the rush   10

Of all the mountain-brooks that wake
     With upward fling,
To brush and break the loosening cling
     Of ice, they shake
     The air with spring!

I had not till today been sure,
     But now I know:
Dead youths and maidens come and go
     Beneath the lure
     And undertow   20

Of cities, under every street
     Of empty stress,
Or heart of an adulteress—
     Each loud retreat
     Of lovelessness.

For only by the stir we make
     In passing near
Are we confused and cannot hear
     The ways they take
     Certain and clear.   30

Today I happened in a place
     Where all around
Was silence; until, underground,
     I heard a pace,
     A happy sound—

And people there, whom I could see,
     Tenderly smiled,

While under a wood of silent wild
  Antiquity
    Wandered a child,   40

Leading his mother by the hand,
  Happy and slow,
Teaching his mother where to go
  Under the snow . . .
Not even now I understand.
  I only know.

1915   1917

TILES

CHINESE magicians had conjured their
    chance,
And they hunted, with their hooded birds
    of glee,
The heat that rises from the summer-grass
And shakes against the sea.
And when they had caught a wide expanse
In nets of careful wizardry,
They coloured it like molten glass
For roofs, imperially,
With blue from a cavern, green from a
    morass
And yellow from weeds in the heart of the
    sea,   10
And they laid long rows on the dwellings of
    romance
In perfect alchemy—
And before they ascended like a peal of
    brass,
They and their tiptoeing hawks of glee
Had topped all China with a roof that slants
And shakes against the sea.

1917   1920

THE OLD MEN AND THE YOUNG MEN

SAID the old men to the young men,
  'Who will take arms to be free?'
Said the young men to the old men,
  'We.'

Said the old men to the young men,
  'It is finished. You may go.'
Said the young men to the old men,
  'No.'

Said the old men to the young men,
  'What is there left to do?'   10
Said the young men to the old men,
  'You.'

1919   1925

A DANCE FOR RAIN [1]

(COCHITI)

YOU may never see rain, unless you see
A dance for rain at Cochiti,
Never hear thunder in the air
Unless you hear the thunder there,
Nor know the lightning in the sky
If there's no pole to know it by.
They dipped the pole just as I came,
And I can never be the same
Since those feathers gave my brow
The touch of wind that's on it now,   10
Bringing over the arid lands
Butterfly gestures from Hopi hands
And holding me, till earth shall fail,
As close to earth as a fox's tail.
  I saw them, naked, dance in line
Before the candles of a leafy shrine:
Before a saint in a Christian dress
I saw them dance their holiness,
I saw them reminding him all day long
That death is weak and life is strong   20
And urging the fertile earth to yield
Seed from the loin and seed from the field.
A feather in the hair and a shell at the
    throat
Were lifting and falling with every note
Of the chorus-voices and the drum,
Calling for the rain to come.
A fox on the back, and shaken on the thigh
Rain-cloth woven from the sky,
And under the knee a turtle-rattle
Clacking with the toes of sheep and
    cattle—   30
These were the men, their bodies painted
Earthen, with a white rain slanted;
These were the men, a windy line,
Their elbows green with a growth of pine.
And in among them, close and slow,
Women moved, the way things grow,

1 'Cochiti is a village of Pueblo Indians, whose inhabitants perform each summer rituals which we call dances but which are actually stylized religious ceremonies or prayer dances for rain. It is one of these which I have recorded in my poem, and the events recorded actually happened: the sudden coming of so much rain in the midst of the dance that it formed a lake in the village plaza, into which the koshares, or delight makers—dancers representing the spirits of the dead who return to encourage and inspirit the living—plunged and rolled with frenzied acknowledgment to the gods. Although nominally Catholic, our Indians have been permitted to amalgamate the elements of their old religion with the new; and the old religion would seem, despite their tolerant acceptance of the new, to be far the closer to their marrow.' Author's note.

With a mesa-tablet on the head
And a little grassy creeping tread
And with sprays of pine moved back and
    forth,
While the dance of the men blew from the
    north,   40
Blew from the south and east and west
Over the field and over the breast.
And the heart was beating in the drum,
Beating for the rain to come.
    Dead men out of earlier lives,
Leaving their graves, leaving their wives,
Were partly flesh and partly clay,
And their heads were corn that was dry and
    gray.
They were ghosts of men and once again
They were dancing like a ghost of rain;   50
For the spirits of men, the more they eat,
Have happier hands and lighter feet,
And the better they dance the better they
    know
How to make corn and children grow.
    And so in Cochiti that day,
They slowly put the sun away
And they made a cloud and they made it
    break
And they made it rain for the children's
    sake.
And they never stopped the song or the
    drum

Pounding for the rain to come.   60
    The rain made many suns to shine,
Golden bodies in a line
With leaping feather and swaying pine.
And the brighter the bodies, the brighter
    the rain
Where thunder heaped it on the plain.
Arroyos had been empty, dry,
But now were running with the sky;
And the dancers' feet were in a lake,
Dancing for the people's sake.
And the hands of a ghost had made a cup 70
For scooping handfuls of water up;
And he poured it into a ghostly throat,
And he leaped and waved with every note
Of the dancers' feet and the songs of the
    drum
That had called the rain and made it come.
    For this was not a god of wood,
This was a god whose touch was good,
You could lie down in him and roll
And wet your body and wet your soul;
For this was not a god in a book,   80
This was a god that you tasted and took
Into a cup that you made with your
    hands,
Into your children and into your lands—
This was a god that you could see,
Rain, rain, in Cochiti!
1924   1925

ELINOR WYLIE

1885–1928

FROM MR. HODGE AND
MR. HAZARD

SEPULCHRAL MOTH [1]

MR. Hazard's liveliness had fled away in spectral laughter long before he had cracked a single walnut for the children or refused a single glass of Mr. Hartleigh's port. Annamaria might have forgiven him for not drinking his soup, for then he was 10 talking rather wittily about 'Yarrow Revisited,' but it was impossible to forgive him for not eating his dessert, for then he was silent and listless while Hartleigh chattered about reform. Mr. Hazard seemed to have lost his appetite for politics

together with his appetite for almonds and raisins. His elegance remained to him, but it was a graveyard elegance little to Annamaria's florid taste. 'A moth of which a coffin might have been the chrysalis'; someone had written that from Venice in a letter to Mr. Peacock. Perhaps the writer had been thinking of gondolas, but to Annamaria's mind the words fitted Mr. Hazard like a long black cloak.

'Bitter,' said Annamaria to herself regretfully, 'bitter as gall. And I can remember him when he was the most affectionate, open-hearted boy in the world, with such pretty manners too, and so grateful for the little kindnesses we were able to show him when we lived in the Vale of Health.'

'Hazard,' said Mr. Hartleigh to his friend, 'I think you ought to go back to

1 The selection is Chapter 9 from Book I of *Mr. Hodge and Mr. Hazard, Collected Prose of Elinor Wylie* (N.Y., 1933),675–79.

Spain; the climate of England does not suit you at all. It never did, my dear fellow.'

Mr. Hazard glanced at Mr. Hartleigh with a quick suspicion that he was being impertinent. An affectionate, open-hearted boy would never have harboured this suspicion for an instant, but perhaps while Mr. Hazard's hair had been changing from bronze into silver, the virgin gold of his heart had been mixed with a sad alloy. If a heart is open, iron may very easily enter it, to alter the first purity of its metal.

But even the new Mr. Hazard, whose heart was sealed and seared with fire, could not long suspect Mr. Hartleigh of impertinence. The looming eyes were shabby brown velvet like a pair of bat's-wings. They were too soft for Mr. Hazard's irritable taste; too kind by half, he called them to himself, yet not so kind as Mr. Hartleigh. Mr. Hazard answered him politely, but his voice was a plucked fiddle-string of impatience.

'I cannot go back to Spain,' said Mr. Hazard, 'until I have seen certain people whom I hope to meet in England.'

Both Annamaria and Mr. Hartleigh jumped to the comfortable conclusion that he meant his father and sisters, and even possibly his daughter. His other daughter was dead, of course; dead long since, in a vanished September, and the eldest boy, the one whom his father had taken, was dead of a decline these seven years. The second boy, he who had been so dear to Mr. Hazard, had lain quietly in his grave for so long that only Mr. Hazard remembered that he would have been seventeen years old had he lived. So, since his wife and Lionel were in San Sebastian, and since he had already seen Mr. Piggott and Mr. Bird, Annamaria and Hartleigh fell back on the soft cushioned thought that Mr. Hazard must mean his father, and thence were lulled to a dream of reconciliation and filial joy.

In spite of the sound but inexpensive port now warming their vitals, their hearts would have withered in their bosoms with pure horror had they suspected the truth. Mr. Hazard had no hope of meeting his father, or even the most broadminded of his sisters. It was precisely these same dead children whom Mr. Hazard so im-

probably hoped to meet before leaving England.

Not all the port and brandy in Annamaria's best cut-glass decanters could have removed the chill from their hearts could they have seen this hope within the secret mind of Mr. Hazard. But, even supposing that his mind had suddenly become transparent to their eyes, they would certainly have been so dazzled and amazed that this flying hope must have escaped them. Against the interwoven and concentric circles of his thought, against the colours of fire and crystal which informed its moons and stars, they would surely in their amazement have mistaken this hope for a darting bird or a dead leaf. It must have escaped them, even as it escaped them now in Mr. Hazard's few and casual words.

Deliberately he veiled his eyes against their wonder; he did not speak again for several long minutes. Annamaria was annoyed; she had taken a great deal of pains with the dinner, and had gone to the trouble of making the trifle herself. Mr. Hazard had eaten nothing to speak of, but that was no reason why he should not speak at all. He might have spoken about politics or literature, or the green April leaves waving like seaweed in the pool of the evening sky.

'Then you had better have a month in the country,' said Mr. Hartleigh; he said it as he might have said: 'Then you had better have some hot whisky and water,' and indeed he thought of the country as a medicinal tonic rather than a spring of natural delight, for he was a true Cockney.

'I shall need a month, or even two months,' said Mr. Hazard carelessly; he did not trouble to conceal his secret plan, for he knew that the influenza had done it for him. No one could possibly suspect Mr. Hazard of going to the country to chase wild geese or ghostly swans while he remained so excessively thin. To anyone with an ounce of common sense it must appear that Mr. Hazard was going to the country to eat butter and eggs, or new green peas and ducklings.

'The seaside, I suppose?' asked Annamaria, with kindly interest. 'You wouldn't like Brighton?'

'No,' said Mr. Hazard; the exquisite finality of the word was like a soundless charge of gunpowder to demolish the sea-front and lay the pavilion in ruins.

'The true pastoral country will be your best restorative,' said Mr. Hartleigh. 'The valleys and the verdant hills, the apple blossoms and the lilacs.' Mr. Hartleigh saw no reason why a medicinal tonic should not be flavoured with honey and the extracted juice of flowers.

'Doubtless,' said Mr. Hazard; courtesy drove him to a dissyllable, but he would have preferred a shorter word, or, better still, to be silent. It was too much trouble to unravel the spliced ends of the nerves which bound his body to his brain, but he was either very much bored or very much wearied by the Hartleighs' conversation. Already his laziness was cracking almonds instead of walnuts for the children, and now he began to make a neat and idle list of words of one syllable which might be employed in decent society. 'Yes'; 'no'; 'quite'; 'ah'; 'oh'; 'still' (this might be cleverly prolonged); 'well' (the same rule applied); 'thanks' (that was slightly vulgar); 'so' (that was Germanic); 'good' (excellent); 'but' (French and affected; a shrug was implicit). Really, reflected Mr. Hazard above the litter of papery almond shells upon his plate, it was disgraceful, his native tongue's poverty in those polite monosyllables which may save the weariest breath to cool the bitterest porridge.

The room was a cube of hot bright air, moored fast among the thinner airs of twilight. It did not float, as the trees' branches floated and waved visibly in the green element above them, a sky like a lake reversed, grained and patterned like the surface of water, crossed by cool streams of radiance from the west. The room lay heavy and immovable like a drowned hulk at the bottom of this pool of ether; it did not hang suspended like the tree-tops, it was hopelessly weighed down by the soft imponderable air. It lay like a sunken ship, solid, painted with shining phosphorescence. The evening, so light over the tree-tops, was heavy enough to press upon the room, to crush its thick bright atmosphere closer and closer upon Mr. Hazard's mind. The flame of the lamp and the more gaseous flame of the fire, the dust spangling the bars of brightness with innumerable golden motes, these were emanations too difficult

to breathe, too hot and dense for the delicate rhythm of breathing. Mr. Hazard thought how pleasant it would be if only he might be allowed to lift the black marble clock from the mantelpiece and hurl it through the shut window. The glittering splinters of glass would be neither so thin nor so sharp as the April air rushing in through the broken pane. Of course even to open the window in the old-fashioned way would be better than nothing, but Annamaria would be sure to shut it again. She would remind Mr. Hazard that he ought to be careful; she would pull the shawl about her shoulders and talk about toothache.

'I'll write to you, Hartleigh,' said Mr. Hazard. 'I'll send you an address when I write. Annamaria, I do not know how to thank you for your kindness. . . .'

1928

BEAUTY

SAY not of Beauty she is good,
Or aught but beautiful,
Or sleek to doves' wings of the wood
Her wild wings of a gull.

Call her not wicked; that word's touch
Consumes her like a curse;
But love her not too much, too much,
For that is even worse.

O, she is neither good nor bad,
But innocent and wild!   10
Enshrine her and she dies, who had
The hard heart of a child.

1921

THE EAGLE AND THE MOLE

AVOID the reeking herd,
Shun the polluted flock,
Live like that stoic bird,
The eagle of the rock.

The huddled warmth of crowds
Begets and fosters hate;
He keeps, above the clouds,
His cliff inviolate.

When flocks are folded warm,
And herds to shelter run,   10
He sails above the storm,
He stares into the sun.

If in the eagle's track
Your sinews cannot leap,
Avoid the lathered pack,
Turn from the steaming sheep.

If you would keep your soul
From spotted sight or sound,
Live like the velvet mole;
Go burrow underground.   20

And there hold intercourse
With roots of trees and stones,
With rivers at their source,
And disembodied bones.
                                    1921

WILD PEACHES

1

WHEN the world turns completely upside
      down
You say we'll emigrate to the Eastern Shore
Aboard a river-boat from Baltimore;
We'll live among wild peach trees, miles
      from town,
You'll wear a coonskin cap, and I a gown
Homespun, dyed butternut's dark gold
      colour.
Lost, like your lotus-eating ancestor,
We'll swim in milk and honey till we drown.

The winter will be short, the summer long,
The autumn amber-hued, sunny and hot,
Tasting of cider and of scuppernong;   11
All seasons sweet, but autumn best of all.
The squirrels in their silver fur will fall
Like falling leaves, like fruit, before your
      shot.

2

The autumn frosts will lie upon the grass
Like bloom on grapes of purple-brown and
      gold.
The misted early mornings will be cold;
The little puddles will be roofed with glass.
The sun, which burns from copper into
      brass,
Melts these at noon, and makes the boys
      unfold   20
Their knitted mufflers; full as they can
      hold,
Fat pockets dribble chestnuts as they pass.

Peaches grow wild, and pigs can live in
      clover;

A barrel of salted herrings lasts a year;
The spring begins before the winter's
      over.
By February you may find the skins
Of garter snakes and water moccasins
Dwindled and harsh, dead-white and
      cloudy-clear.

3

When April pours the colours of a shell
Upon the hills, when every little creek   30
Is shot with silver from the Chesapeake
In shoals new-minted by the ocean swell,
When strawberries go begging, and the
      sleek
Blue plums lie open to the blackbird's
      beak,
We shall live well—we shall live very
      well.

The months between the cherries and the
      peaches
Are brimming cornucopias which spill
Fruits red and purple, sombre-bloomed
      and black;
Then, down rich fields and frosty river
      beaches
We'll trample bright persimmons, while
      you kill   40
Bronze partridge, speckled quail, and
      canvasback.

4

Down to the Puritan marrow of my bones
There's something in this richness that I
      hate.
I love the look, austere, immaculate,
Of landscapes drawn in pearly monotones.
There's something in my very blood that
      owns
Bare hills, cold silver on a sky of slate,
A thread of water, churned to milky spate
Streaming through slanted pastures fenced
      with stones.

I love those skies, thin blue or snowy
      gray,
Those fields sparse-planted, rendering
      meagre sheaves;   51
That spring, briefer than apple-blossom's
      breath,
Summer, so much too beautiful to stay,
Swift autumn, like a bonfire of leaves,
And sleepy winter, like the sleep of death.
                                    1921

ESCAPE

WHEN foxes eat the last gold grape,
And the last white antelope is killed,
I shall stop fighting and escape
Into a little house I'll build.

But first I'll shrink to fairy size,
With a whisper no one understands,
Making blind moons of all your eyes,
And muddy roads of all your hands.

And you may grope for me in vain
In hollows under the mangrove root,
Or where, in apple-scented rain,   11
The silver wasp-nests hang like fruit.

                              1921

VELVET SHOES

LET us walk in the white snow
    In a soundless space;
With footsteps quiet and slow,
    At a tranquil pace,
    Under veils of white lace.

I shall go shod in silk,
    And you in wool,
White as a white cow's milk,
    More beautiful
    Than the breast of a gull.   10

We shall walk through the still town
    In a windless peace;
We shall step upon white down,
    Upon silver fleece,
    Upon softer than these.

We shall walk in velvet shoes:
    Wherever we go
Silence will fall like dews
    On white silence below.
    We shall walk in the snow.   20
                              1921

LET NO CHARITABLE HOPE

Now let no charitable hope
Confuse my mind with images
Of eagle and of antelope:
I am in nature none of these.

I was, being human, born alone;
I am, being woman, hard beset;
I live by squeezing from a stone
The little nourishment I get.

In masks outrageous and austere
The years go by in single file;   10
But none has merited my fear,
And none has quite escaped my smile.
                              1923

ON A SINGING GIRL [1]

MUSA of the sea-blue eyes,
Silver nightingale, alone
In a little coffin lies:
A stone beneath a stone.

She, whose song we loved the best,
Is voiceless in a sudden night:
On your light limbs, O loveliest,
May the dust be light!
                              1923

CONFESSION OF FAITH

I LACK the braver mind
That dares to find
The lover friend, and kind.

I fear him to the bone;
I lie alone
By the beloved one,

And, breathless for suspense,
Erect defense
Against love's violence

Whose silences portend   10
A bloody end
For lover never friend.

But, in default of faith,
In futile breath,
I dream no ill of Death.
                              1928

TRUE VINE

THERE is a serpent in perfection tarn-
    ished,
The thin shell pierced, the purity grown
    fainter,

[1] This is paraphrase of Mackail's translation of an epitaph (CIG,6261), of the same title, from the Greek
Anthology. The translation: 'Blue-eyed Musa, the
sweet-voiced nightingale, suddenly this little grave
holds voiceless, and she lies like a stone who was so
accomplished and so famous; fair Musa be this dust
light over thee.' Mackail, Select Epigrams from the
Greek Anthology (London, 1906),164.

The virgin silver shield no longer
    burnished,
The pearly fruit with ruin for its centre.

The thing that sits expectant in our bosoms
Contriving heaven out of very little
Demands such delicate immaculate
    blossoms
As no malicious verity makes brittle.

This wild fastidious hope is quick to
    languish;
Its smooth diaphanous escape is swifter   10
Than the pack of truth; no mortal can
    distinguish
Its trace upon the durable hereafter.

Not so the obdurate and savage lovely
Whose roots are set profoundly upon
    trouble;
This flower grows so fiercely and so bravely
It does not even know that it is noble.

This is the vine to love, whose balsams
    flourish
Upon a living soil corrupt and faulty,
Whose leaves have drunk the skies, and
    stooped to nourish
The earth again with honey sweet and
    salty.   20
                  1928

PETER AND JOHN

TWELVE good friends
Walked under the leaves,
Binding the ends
Of the barley sheaves.

Peter and John
Lay down to sleep
Pillowed upon
A haymaker's heap

John and Peter
Lay down to dream.   10
The air was sweeter
Than honey and cream.

Peter was bred
In the salty cold:
His hair was red
And his eyes were gold.

John had a mouth
Like a wing bent down.

His brow was smooth
And his eyes were brown.   20

Peter to slumber
Sank like a stone,
Of all their number
The bravest one.

John more slowly
Composed himself,
Young and holy
Among the Twelve.

John as he slept
Cried out in grief,   30
Turned and wept
On the golden leaf:

'Peter, Peter,
Stretch me your hand
Across the glitter
Of the harvest land!

'Peter, Peter,
Give me a sign!
This was a bitter
Dream of mine—   40

'Bitter as aloes
It parched my tongue.
Upon the gallows
My life was hung.

'Sharp it seemed
As a bloody sword.
Peter, I dreamed
I was Christ the Lord!'

Peter turned
To holy Saint John: 50
His body burned
In the falling sun.

In the falling sun
He burned like flame:
'John, Saint John,
I have dreamed the same!

'My bones were hung
On an elder tree;
Bells were rung
Over Galilee.   60

'A silver penny
Sealed each of my eyes.

Many and many
A cock crew thrice.'

When Peter's word
Was spoken and done,
'Were you Christ the Lord
In your dream?' said John.

'No,' said the other,
'That I was not.   70
I was our brother
Iscariot.'
                                                              1928

ADDRESS TO MY SOUL

My soul, be not disturbed
By planetary war;
Remain securely orbed
In this contracted star.

Fear not, pathetic flame;
Your sustenance is doubt:
Glassed in translucent dream
They cannot snuff you out.

Wear water, or a mask
Of unapparent cloud;   10
Be brave and never ask
A more defunctive shroud.

The universal points
Are shrunk into a flower;
Between its delicate joints
Chaos keeps no power.

The pure integral form,
Austere and silver-dark,
Is balanced on the storm
In its predestined arc.   20

Small as a sphere of rain
It slides along the groove
Whose path is furrowed plain
Among the suns that move.

The shapes of April buds
Outlive the phantom year:
Upon the void at odds
The dewdrop falls severe.

Five-petalled flame, be cold:
Be firm, dissolving star: 30
Accept the stricter mould
That makes you singular.
                                                              1928

ONE PERSON

Although these words are false, none shall
*   prevail*
To prove them in translation less than true
Or overthrow their dignity, or undo
The faith implicit in a fabulous tale;
The ashes of this error shall exhale
Essential verity, and two by two
Lovers devout and loyal shall renew
The legend, and refuse to let it fail.
Even the betrayer and the fond deceived,
Having put off the body of this death,   1?
Shall testify with one remaining breath,
From sepulchres demand to be believed:
These words are true, although at intervals
The unfaithful clay contrive to make them
*   false.*

I

Now shall the long homesickness have an
    end
Upon your heart, which is a part of all
The past no human creature may recall
Save you, who are persuasive to unbend
The brows of death, and name him for a
    friend:
This ecstasy is supernatural;   20
I have survived to see the heavens fall
Into my hands, which on your hands
    depend.

Time has prepared us an enduring bed
Within the earth of this beloved land;
And, lying side by side and hand in hand,
We sleep coeval with the happy dead
Who are ourselves, a little earlier bound
To one another's bosom in the ground.

2

What other name had half expressed the
    whole
Of that incomparable and touching grace 3(
Which spells the shape of danger in your
    face?
It is the very pattern of your soul;
The eagle's home, above the moon's
    control,
Above the seas, the high precipitate place;
The stairway cut from planetary space;
The crystal steps which climb a steeper
    goal.

The shadow of its light is only this:
That all your beauty is the work of wars

Between the upper and the nether stars;
Its symmetry is perfect and severe   40
Because the barbarous force of agonies
Broke it, and mended it, and made it clear.

3

'Children and dogs are subject to my
          power,'
You said, and smiled, and I beside you
          smiled,
Perceiving my unwisdom of a child,
My courage of a wolf new-taught to cower:
Upon the grass, beneath the falling flower,
I saw my spirit silent and beguiled
Standing at gaze; a brute no longer wild;
An infant wearied by the difficult hour.   50

And am I not your child who has come
          home?
And am I not your hound for faithfulness?
Put forth your hand, put forth your hand to
          bless
A creature stricken timorous and dumb,
Who now regards you with a lover's eyes
And knows that you are merciful and wise.

4

Now am I Orson to your Valentine
Forever, and I choose it shall be so;
For how should the uncivil brier grow
Germane in nature to the noble vine?   60
The savage should be servant to the fine;
The falcon fly superior to the crow;
O dear my lord, believe me that I know
How far your virtues have outnumbered
          mine.

And you have levied final tribute now—
Your chivalry demanding the pretence—
You have constrained your vassal to avow
That we are equals, lest a violence
Be suffered by our love, and so I must
Deny the intrinsic difference in our dust.   70

5

The little beauty that I was allowed—
The lips new-cut and coloured by my sire,
The polished hair, the eyes' perceptive
          fire—
Has never been enough to make me proud:
For I have moved companioned by a cloud,
And lived indifferent to the blood's desire
Of temporal loveliness in vain attire:
My flesh was but a fresh-embroidered
          shroud.

Now do I grow indignant at the fate
Which made me so imperfect to compare 80
With your degree of noble and of fair;
Our elements are the farthest skies apart;
And I enjoin you, ere it is too late,
To stamp your superscription on my heart.

6

I have believed that I prefer to live
Preoccupied by a Platonic mind;
I have believed me obdurate and blind
To those sharp ecstasies the pulses give:
The clever body five times sensitive
I never have discovered to be kind   90
As the poor soul, deceived and half-
          divined,
Whose hopes are water in a witch's sieve.

O now both soul and body are unfit
To apprehend this miracle, my lord!
Not all my senses, striving in accord
With my pure essence, are aware of it
Save as a power remote and exquisite,
Not seen or known, but fervently adored.

7

Would I might make subliminal my flesh
And so contrive a gentle atmosphere   100
To comfort you because I am not there;
Or else incorporate and carve afresh
A lady, from the chilly heaven and clear
Which flows around you like a stream of air,
To warm and wind you in her body's mesh.

So would I cherish you a loving twice;
Once in a mist made matter; once again
In my true substance made ethereal:
And yet I cannot succour you at all
Whose letter cries, 'My hands are cold as
          ice,'   110
The while I kiss the colder air in vain.

8

O love, how utterly am I bereaved
By Time, who sucks the honey of our
          days,
Sets sickle to our Aprils, and betrays
To killing winter all the sun achieved;
Our parted spirits are perplexed and
          grieved
Severed by cold, and change that never
          stays;
And what the clock, and what the season
          says
Is rumour neither valued nor believed.

Thus absence chills us to apparent death 120
And withers up our virtue, but together
We grow beyond vagaries of the weather
And make a summer of our mingled breath
Wherein we flourish, and forget to know
We must lie murdered by predestined
    snow.

9

A subtle spirit has my path attended,
In likeness not a lion but a pard;
And when the arrows flew like hail, and
    hard,
He licked my wounds, and all my wounds
    were mended;   129
And happy I, who walked so well-defended,
With that translucid presence for a guard,
Under a sky reversed and evil-starred;
A woman by an archangel befriended.

Now must I end the knightly servitude
Which made him my preserver, and
    renounce
That heavenly aid forever and at once;
For it were neither courteous nor good
If we, who are but perishable things,
Should hang another weight between his
    wings.

10

When I perceive the sable of your hair   140
Silvered, and deep within those caverns are
Your eyesockets, a double-imaged star,
And your fine substance fretted down by
    care,
Then do I marvel that a woman dare
Prattle of mortal matters near and far
To one so wounded in demonic war
Against some prince of Sirius or Altair.

How is it possible that this hand of clay,
Though white as porcelain, can contrive a
    touch
So delicate it shall not hurt too much?   150
What voice can my invention find to say
So soft, precise, and scrupulous a word
You shall not take it for another sword?

11

'Before I die, let me be happy here.'
The glass of heaven was split, and by that
    token
I knew the bubble of my heart had broken;
The cool and chaste, the iridescent sphere,
Filled, in that vernal season of the year,

With sapling's blood, the beechen and the
    oaken
And the green willow's; when the word was
    spoken   160
This innocence did faint and disappear.

So have I lost my only wedding dower,
The veins of spring, enclosed within my
    heart,
Traced small in silver like a celestial chart;
And I am vanished in the leaf and flower,
Since, at your voice, my body's core and
    pith
Dissolves in air, and is destroyed forthwith.

12

In our content, before the autumn came
To shower sallow droppings on the mould,
Sometimes you have permitted me to fold
Your grief in swaddling-bands, and smile to
    name   171
Yourself my infant, with an infant's claim
To utmost adoration as of old,
Suckled with kindness, fondled from the
    cold,
And loved beyond philosophy or shame.

I dreamt I was the mother of a son
Who had deserved a manger for a crib;
Torn from your body, furbished from your
    rib,
I am the daughter of your skeleton,
Born of your bitter and excessive pain: 180
I shall not dream you are my child again.

13

O, mine is Psyche's heavy doom reversed
Who meet at noon, part by diminished light
But never feel the subtle balm of night
Fall merciful upon a body pierced
By extreme love; and I considered first
That you, a god more prodigally bright
Than the lessor Eros, had enriched my sight
Made your own morning, and the stars
    immersed.

But secondly I saw my soul arise   19
And, in the hushed obscure, presume to
    creep
Tiptoe upon your spirit laid asleep,
And slant the impious beam across your
    eyes;
And I believe I have my just deserts
Lacking the shadow of peace upon our
    hearts.

14

My fairer body and perfected spirit,
Beyond metempsychosis, and beyond
The faults you must forgive me to be fond,
Are yours in any death that I may merit;
Mortality has wearied us who wear it,   200
And they are wiser creatures who have
   shunned
This miry world, this slough of man's
   despond,
To fortify the skies we shall inherit.

I have entreated you to grant me Time
To memorize the pure appointed task;
Today it is Eternity I ask
In which to learn the lesson of this rhyme:
Its liberal periods are not too wide.
To educate me fitly for your bride.

15

My honoured lord, forgive the unruly
   tongue   210
That utters blasphemies; forgive the brain
Borne on a whirlwind of unhallowed pain:
Remember only the intrepid song;
The flag defended and the gauntlet flung;
The love that speech can never render plain;
The mind's resolve to turn and strive
   again;
The fortitude that has endured so long.

My cherished lord, in charity forgive
A starveling hope that may at times desire
To warm its frozen fingers at your fire;   220
'Tis by such trifles that your lovers live,
And so rise up, and in the starlight cold
Frighten the foxes from your loneliest fold.

16

I hereby swear that to uphold your house
I would lay my bones in quick destroying
   lime
Or turn my flesh to timber for all time;
Cut down my womanhood; lop off the
   boughs
Of that perpetual ecstasy that grows
From the heart's core; condemn it as a
   crime
If it be broader than a beam, or climb   230
Above the stature that your roof allows.

I am not the hearthstone nor the
   cornerstone
Within this noble fabric you have builded;

Not by my beauty was its cornice gilded;
Not on my courage were its arches thrown:
My lord, adjudge my strength, and set me
   where
I bear a little more than I can bear.

17

Upon your heart, which is the heart of all
My late discovered earth and early sky,
Give me the dearest privilege to die;   240
Your pity for the velvet of my pall;
Your patience for my grave's inviolate wall;
And for my passing bell, in passing by,
Your voice itself, diminished to a sigh
Above all other sounds made musical.

Meanwhile I swear to you I am content
To live without a sorrow to my name;
To live triumphant, and to die the same,
Upon the fringes of this continent,
This map of Paradise, this scrap of earth 250
Whereon you burn like flame upon a hearth.

18

Let us leave talking of angelic hosts
Of nebulæ, and lunar hemispheres,
And what the days, and what the Uranian
   years
Shall offer us when you and I are ghosts;
Forget the festivals and pentecosts
Of metaphysics, and the lesser fears
Confound us, and seal up our eyes and
   ears
Like little rivers locked below the frosts.

And let us creep into the smallest room 260
That any hunted exile has desired
For him and for his love when he was tired;
And sleep oblivious of any doom
Which is beyond our reason to conceive;
And so forget to weep, forget to grieve,
And wake, and touch each other's hands,
   and turn
Upon a bed of juniper and fern.

1929

O VIRTUOUS LIGHT

A PRIVATE madness has prevailed
Over the pure and valiant mind;
The instrument of reason failed
And the star-gazing eyes struck blind.

Sudden excess of light has wrought
Confusion in the secret place

Where the slow miracles of thought
Take shape through patience into grace.

Mysterious as steel and flint
The birth of this destructive spark   10
Whose inward growth has power to print
Strange suns upon the natural dark.

O break the walls of sense in half
And make the spirit fugitive!
This light begotten of itself
Is not a light by which to live!

The fire of farthing tallow dips
Dispels the menace of the skies
So it illuminate the lips
And enter the discerning eyes.   20

O virtuous light, if thou be man's
Or matter of the meteor stone,
Prevail against this radiance
Which is engendered of its own!

                                    1929

HYMN TO EARTH

FAREWELL, incomparable element,
Whence man arose, where he shall not
          return;
And hail, imperfect urn
Of his last ashes, and his firstborn fruit;
Farewell, the long pursuit,
And all the adventures of his discontent;
The voyages which sent
His heart averse from home:
Metal of clay, permit him that he come
To thy slow-burning fire as to a hearth;   10
Accept him as a particle of earth.

Fire, being divided from the other three,
It lives removed, or secret at the core;
Most subtle of the four,
When air flies not, nor water flows,
It disembodied goes,
Being light, elixir of the first decree,
More volatile than he;
With strength and power to pass
Through space, where never his least atom
          was: 20
He has no part in it, save as his eyes
Have drawn its emanation from the skies.

A wingless creature heavier than air,
He is rejected of its quintessence;
Coming and going hence,

In the twin minutes of his birth and death,
He may inhale as breath,
As breath relinquish heaven's atmosphere,
Yet in it have no share,
Nor can survive therein   30
Where its outer edge is filtered pure and
          thin:
It doth but lend its crystal to his lungs
For his early crying, and his final songs.

The element of water has denied
Its child; it is no more his element;
It never will relent;
Its silver harvests are more sparsely given
Than the rewards of heaven,
And he shall drink cold comfort at its side:
The water is too wide: 40
The seamew and the gull
Feather a nest made soft and pitiful
Upon its foam; he has not any part
In the long swell of sorrow at its heart.

Hail and farewell, beloved element,
Whence he departed, and his parent once;
See where thy spirit runs
Which for so long hath had the moon to
          wife;
Shall this support his life
Until the arches of the waves be bent   50
And grow shallow and spent?
Wisely it cast him forth
With his dead weight of burdens nothing
          worth,
Leaving him, for the universal years,
A little seawater to make his tears.

Hail, element of earth, receive thy own,
And cherish, at thy charitable breast,
This man, this mongrel beast:
He ploughs the sand, and, at his hardest
          need,
He sows himself for seed;   60
He ploughs the furrow, and in this lies
          down
Before the corn is grown;
Between the apple bloom
And the ripe apple is sufficient room
In time, and matter, to consume his love
And make him parcel of a cypress grove.

Receive him as thy lover for an hour
Who will not weary, by a longer stay,
The kind embrace of clay;
Even within thine arms he is dispersed   70
To nothing, as at first;

The air flings downward from its four-
    quartered tower
Him whom the flames devour;
At the full tide, at the flood,
The sea is mingled with his salty
    blood:
The traveller dust, although the dust be
    vile,
Sleeps as thy lover for a little while.

                     1929

THIS CORRUPTIBLE

THE Body, long oppressed
And pierced, then prayed for rest
(Being but apprenticed to the other
    Powers);
And kneeling in that place
Implored the thrust of grace
Which makes the dust lie level with the
    flowers.

Then did that fellowship
Of three, the Body strip;
Beheld his wounds, and none among them
    mortal;
The Mind severe and cool;   10
The Heart still half a fool;
The fine-spun Soul, a beam of sun can
    startle.

These three, a thousand years
Had made adventurers
Amid all villainies the earth can offer,
Applied them to resolve
From the universal gulph
What pangs the poor material flesh may
    suffer.

'This is a pretty pass;
To hear the growing grass   20
Complain; the clay cry out to be
    translated;
Will not this grosser stuff
Receive reward enough
If stabled after labouring, and baited?'

Thus spoke the Mind in scorn:
The Heart, which had outworn
The Body, and was weary of its
    fashion,
Preferring to be dressed
In skin of bird or beast,
Replied more softly, in a feigned
    compassion.   30

'Anatomy most strange
Crying to chop and change;
Inferior copy of a higher image;
While I, the noble guest,
Sick of your second-best
Sigh for embroidered archangelic plumage:

'For shame, thou fustian cloak!'
And then the Spirit spoke;
Within the void it swung securely
    tethered
By strings composed of cloud;   40
It spoke both low and loud
Above a storm no lesser star had weathered.

'O lodging for the night!
O house of my delight!
O lovely hovel builded for my pleasure!
Dear tenement of clay
Endure another day
As coffin sweetly fitted to my measure.

'Take Heart, and call to Mind
Although we are unkind;   50
Although we steal your shelter, strength,
    and clothing;
'Tis you who shall escape
In some enchanting shape
Or be dissolved to elemental nothing.

'You, the unlucky slave,
Are the lily on the grave;
The wave that runs above the bones
    a-whitening;
You are the new-mown grass;
And the wheaten bread of the Mass;
And the fabric of the rain, and the
    lightning.   60

'If one of us elect
To leave the poor suspect
Imperfect bosom of the earth our parent;
And from the world avert
The Spirit or the Heart
Upon a further and essential errand;

'His chain he cannot slough
Nor cast his substance off;
He bears himself upon his flying shoulder;
The Heart, infirm and dull;   70
The Mind, in any skull;
Are captive still, and wearier and colder.

' 'Tis you who are the ghost,
Disintegrated, lost;

The burden shed; the dead who need not
    bear it;
O grain of God in power,
Endure another hour!
It is but for an hour,' said the Spirit.

               1929

FAREWELL, SWEET DUST

Now I have lost you, I must scatter
All of you on the air henceforth;
Not that to me it can ever matter
But it's only fair to the rest of earth.

Now especially, when it is winter
And the sun's not half so bright as he
    was,
Who wouldn't be glad to find a splinter
That once was you, in the frozen grass?

Snowflakes, too, will be softer feathered,
Clouds, perhaps, will be whiter plumed; 10
Rain, whose brilliance you caught and
    gathered,
Purer silver have reassumed.

Farewell, sweet dust; I was never a miser:
Once, for a minute, I made you mine:

Now you are gone, I am none the wiser
But the leaves of the willow are bright as
    wine.

               1929

BIRTHDAY SONNET

TAKE home Thy prodigal child, O Lord of
    Hosts!
Protect the sacred from the secular
    danger;
Advise her, that Thou never needst avenge
    her;
Marry her mind neither to man's nor
    ghost's
Nor holier domination's, if the costs
Of such commingling should transport or
    change her;
Defend her from familiar and stranger
And earth's and air's contagions and rusts.

Instruct her strictly to preserve Thy gift
And alter not its grain in atom sort; 10
Angels may wed her to their ultimate hurt
And men embrace a spectre in a shift
So that no drop of the pure spirit fall
Into the dust: defend Thy prodigal.

               1932

EDNA ST. VINCENT MILLAY
1892–

WHEN THE YEAR GROWS OLD

I CANNOT but remember
    When the year grows old—
October—November—
    How she disliked the cold!

She used to watch the swallows
    Go down across the sky,
And turn from the window
    With a little sharp sigh.

And often when the brown leaves
    Were brittle on the ground, 10
And the wind in the chimney
    Made a melancholy sound.

She had a look about her
    That I wish I could forget—
The look of a scared thing
    Sitting in a net!

Oh, beautiful at nightfall
    The soft spitting snow!
And beautiful the bare boughs
    Rubbing to and fro! 20

But the roaring of the fire,
    And the warmth of fur,
And the boiling of the kettle
    Were beautiful to her!

I cannot but remember
    When the year grows old—
October—November—
    How she disliked the cold!

               1917

I SHALL FORGET YOU PRESENTLY, MY DEAR

I SHALL forget you presently, my dear,
So make the most of this, your little day,
Your little month, your little half a year,

Ere I forget, or die, or move away,
And we are done forever; by and by
I shall forget you, as I said, but now,
If you entreat me with your loveliest lie
I will protest you with my favorite vow.
I would indeed that love were longer-lived,
And vows were not so brittle as they are, 10
But so it is, and nature has contrived
To struggle on without a break thus far,—
Whether or not we find what we are seeking
Is idle, biologically speaking.

1920

THE POET AND HIS BOOK

Down, you mongrel, Death!
    Back into your kennel!
I have stolen breath
    In a stalk of fennel!
You shall scratch and you shall whine
    Many a night, and you shall worry
    Many a bone, before you bury
One sweet bone of mine!

When shall I be dead?
    When my flesh is withered, 10
And above my head
    Yellow pollen gathered
All the empty afternoon?
    When sweet lovers pause and wonder
    Who am I that lie thereunder,
Hidden from the moon?

This my personal death?—
    That my lungs be failing
To inhale the breath
    Others are exhaling? 20
This my subtle spirit's end?—
    Ah, when the thawed winter splashes
    Over these chance dust and ashes,
Weep not me, my friend!

Me, by no means dead
    In that hour, but surely
When this book, unread,
    Rots to earth obscurely,
And no more to any breast,
    Close against the clamorous swelling 30
    Of the thing there is no telling,
Are these pages pressed!

When this book is mould,
    And a book of many
Waiting to be sold
    For a casual penny,

In a little open case,
    In a street unclean and cluttered,
    Where a heavy mud is spattered
From the passing drays, 40

Stranger, pause and look;
    From the dust of ages
Lift this little book,
    Turn the tattered pages,
Read me, do not let me die!
    Search the fading letters, finding
    Steadfast in the broken binding
All that once was I!

When these veins are weeds,
    When these hollowed sockets 50
Watch the rooty seeds
    Bursting down like rockets,
And surmise the spring again,
    Or, remote in that black cupboard,
    Watch the pink worms writhing
        upward
At the smell of rain,

Boys and girls that lie
    Whispering in the hedges,
Do not let me die,
    Mix me with your pledges; 60
Boys and girls that slowly walk
    In the woods, and weep, and quarrel,
    Staring past the pink wild laurel,
Mix me with your talk,

Do not let me die!
    Farmers at your raking,
When the sun is high,
    While the hay is making,
When, along the stubble strewn,
    Withering on their stalks uneaten, 70
    Strawberries turn dark and sweeten
In the lapse of noon;

Shepherds on the hills;
    In the pastures, drowsing
To the tinkling bells
    Of the brown sheep browsing;
Sailors crying through the storm;
    Scholars at your study; hunters
    Lost amid the whirling winter's
Whiteness uniform; 80

Men that long for sleep;
    Men that wake and revel;—
If an old song leap
    To your senses' level

At such moments, may it be
   Sometimes, though a moment only,
   Some forgotten, quaint and homely
Vehicle of me!

Women at your toil,
   Women at your leisure   90
Till the kettle boil,
   Snatch of me your pleasure,
Where the broom-straw marks the leaf;
   Women quiet with your weeping
   Lest you wake a workman sleeping,
Mix me with your grief!

Boys and girls that steal
   From the shocking laughter
Of the old, to kneel
   By a dripping rafter   100
Under the discoloured eaves,
   Out of trunks with hingeless covers
   Lifting tales of saints and lovers,
Travelers, goblins, thieves,

Suns that shine by night,
   Mountains made from valleys,—
Bear me to the light,
   Flat upon your bellies
By the webby window lie,
   Where the little flies are crawling,—   110
   Read me, margin me with scrawling,
Do not let me die!

Sexton, ply your trade!
   In a shower of gravel
Stamp upon your spade!
   Many a rose shall ravel,
Many a metal wreath shall rust
   In the rain, and I go singing
   Through the lots where you are flinging
Yellow clay on dust!   120
              1921

AND YOU AS WELL MUST DIE, BELOVÈD DUST

AND you as well must die, belovèd dust,
And all your beauty stand you in no stead;
This flawless, vital hand, this perfect head,
This body of flame and steel, before the
     gust
Of Death, or under his autumnal frost,
Shall be as any leaf, be no less dead
Than the first leaf that fell,—this wonder
     fled.
Altered, estranged, disintegrated, lost.

Nor shall my love avail you in your hour.
In spite of all my love, you will arise   10
Upon that day and wander down the air
Obscurely as the unattended flower,
It mattering not how beautiful you were,
Or how belovèd above all else that dies.
              1921

LAMENT

LISTEN, children:
Your father is dead.
From his old coats
I'll make you little jackets;
I'll make you little trousers
From his old pants.
There'll be in his pockets
Things he used to put there,
Keys and pennies
Covered with tobacco;   10
Dan shall have the pennies
To save in his bank;
Anne shall have the keys
To make a pretty noise with.
Life must go on,
And the dead be forgotten;
Life must go on,
Though good men die;
Anne, eat your breakfast;
Dan, take your medicine;   20
Life must go on;
I forget just why.
              1921

FROM MEMORIAL TO D.C.

(VASSAR COLLEGE, 1918)

(1921)

Elegy

LET them bury your big eyes
In the secret earth securely,
Your thin fingers, and your fair,
Soft, indefinite-coloured hair,—
All of these in some way, surely,
From the secret earth shall rise;
Not for these I sit and stare,
Broken and bereft completely;
Your young flesh that sat so neatly
On your little bones will sweetly   10
Blossom in the air.

But your voice,—never the rushing
Of a river underground,

Not the rising of the wind
In the trees before the rain,
Not the woodcock's watery call,
Not the note the white-throat utters,
Not the feet of children pushing
Yellow leaves along the gutters
In the blue and bitter fall,   20
Shall content my musing mind
For the beauty of that sound
That in no new way at all
Ever will be heard again.

Sweetly through the sappy stalk
Of the vigorous weed,
Holding all it held before,
Cherished by the faithful sun,
On and on eternally
Shall your altered fluid run,   30
Bud and bloom and go to seed;
But your singing days are done;
But the music of your talk
Never shall the chemistry
Of the secret earth restore.
All your lovely words are spoken.
Once the ivory box is broken,
Beats the golden bird no more.
                                           1921

PITY ME NOT BECAUSE
THE LIGHT OF DAY

PITY me not because the light of day
At close of day no longer walks the sky;
Pity me not for beauties passed away
From field and thicket as the year goes by;
Pity me not the waning of the moon,
Nor that the ebbing tide goes out to sea,
Nor that a man's desire is hushed so soon,
And you no longer look with love on me.
This have I known always: Love is no more
Than the wide blossom which the wind
          assails,   10
Than the great tide that treads the shifting
          shore
Strewing fresh wreckage gathered in the
          gales;
Pity me that the heart is slow to learn
What the swift mind beholds at every turn.
                                           1923

EUCLID ALONE HAS LOOKED
ON BEAUTY BARE

EUCLID alone has looked on Beauty bare.
Let all who prate of Beauty hold their peace,

And lay them prone upon the earth and
          cease
To ponder on themselves, the while they
          stare
At nothing, intricately drawn nowhere
In shapes of shifting lineage; let geese
Gabble and hiss, but heroes seek release
From dusty bondage into luminous air.
O blinding hour, O holy, terrible day,
When first the shaft into his vision shone 10
Of light anatomized! Euclid alone
Has looked on Beauty bare. Fortunate they
Who, though once only and then but far
          away,
Have heard her massive sandal set on stone.
                                           1923

DIRGE WITHOUT MUSIC

I AM not resigned to the shutting away of
          loving hearts in the hard ground.
So it is, and so it will be, for so it has been,
          time out of mind:
Into the darkness they go, the wise and the
          lovely. Crowned
With lilies and with laurel they go; but I am
          not resigned.

Lovers and thinkers, into the earth with
          you.
Be one with the dull, the indiscriminate
          dust.
A fragment of what you felt, of what you
          knew,
A formula, a phrase remains,—but the best
          is lost.

The answers quick and keen, the honest
          look, the laughter, the love,—
They are gone. They are gone to feed the
          roses. Elegant and curled   10
Is the blossom. Fragrant is the blossom. I
          know. But I do not approve.
More precious was the light in your eyes
          than all the roses of the world.

Down, down, down into the darkness of
          the grave
Gently they go, the beautiful, the tender,
          the kind;
Quietly they go, the intelligent, the witty,
          the brave.
I know. But I do not approve. And I am
          not resigned.
                                           1928

THE CAMEO

FOREVER over now, forever, forever gone
That day. Clear and diminished like a
    scene
Carven in cameo, the lighthouse, and the
    cove between
The sandy cliffs, and the boat drawn up on
    the beach;
And the long skirt of a lady innocent and
    young,
Her hand resting on her bosom, her head
    hung;
And the figure of a man in earnest speech.

Clear and diminished like a scene cut in
    cameo
The lighthouse, and the boat on the beach,
    and the two shapes
Of the woman and the man; lost like the
    lost day   10
Are the words that passed, and the pain,—
    discarded, cut away
From the stone, as from the memory the
    heat of the tears escapes.

O troubled forms, O early love unfortunate
    and hard,
Time has estranged you into a jewel cold
    and pure;
From the action of the waves and from the
    action of sorrow forever secure,
White against a ruddy cliff you stand,
    chalcedony on sard.
                                    1928

ON HEARING A SYMPHONY
OF BEETHOVEN

SWEET sounds, oh, beautiful music, do not
    cease!
Reject me not into the world again.
With you alone is excellence and peace,
Mankind made plausible, his purpose plain.
Enchanted in your air benign and shrewd,
With limbs a-sprawl and empty faces pale,
The spiteful and the stingy and the rude
Sleep like the scullions in the fairy-tale.
This moment is the best the world can
    give:
The tranquil blossom on the tortured stem.
Reject me not, sweet sounds! oh, let me
    live,   11
Till Doom espy my towers and scatter
    them,

A city spell-bound under the aging sun,
Music my rampart, and my only one.
                                    1928

FROM FATAL INTERVIEW

16

I DREAMED I moved among the Elysian
    fields,
In converse with sweet women long since
    dead;
And out of blossoms which that meadow
    yields
I wove a garland for your living head.
Danæ, that was the vessel for a day
Of golden Jove, I saw, and at her side,
Whom Jove the Bull desired and bore away,
Europa stood, and the Swan's featherless
    bride.
All these were mortal women, yet all these
Above the ground had had a god for guest;
Freely I walked beside them and at ease, 11
Addressing them, by them again addressed,
And marvelled nothing, for remembering
    you,
Wherefore I was among them well I knew.

52

Oh, sleep forever in the Latmian cave,
Mortal Endymion, darling of the Moon!
Her silver garments by the senseless wave
Shouldered and dropped and on the shingle
    strewn,
Her fluttering hand against her forehead
    pressed,
Her scattered looks that trouble all the sky,
Her rapid footsteps running down the
    west—
Of all her altered state, oblivious lie!
Whom earthen you, by deathless lips
    adored,
Wild-eyed and stammering to the grasses
    thrust,   10
And deep into her crystal body poured
The hot and sorrowful sweetness of the dust:
Whereof she wanders mad, being all unfit
For mortal love, that might not die of it.
                                    1931

THE RETURN

EARTH does not understand her child,
    Who from the loud gregarious town
Returns, depleted and defiled,
    To the still woods, to fling him down.

Earth can not count the sons she bore:
  The wounded lynx, the wounded man
Come trailing blood unto her door;
  She shelters both as best she can.

But she is early up and out,
  To trim the year or strip its bones;   10
She has no time to stand about
  Talking of him in undertones

Who has no aim but to forget,
  Be left in peace, be lying thus
For days, for years, for centuries yet,
  Unshaven and anonymous;

Who, marked for failure, dulled by grief,
  Has traded in his wife and friend
For this warm ledge, this alder leaf:
  Comfort that does not comprehend.   20
                                    1934

A SONNET IN MEMORY

(NICOLA SACCO—BARTOLOMEO VANZETTI)
Executed August 23, 1927

WHERE can the heart be hidden in the
        ground
And be at peace, and be at peace forever,
Under the world, untroubled by the sound
Of mortal tears, that cease from pouring
        never?
Well for the heart, by stern compassion
        harried,
If death be deeper than the churchmen
        say,—
Gone from this world indeed what's
        graveward carried,
And laid to rest indeed what's laid away.
Anguish enough while yet the indignant
        breather
Have blood to spurt upon the oppressor's
        hand;   10
Who would eternal be, and hang in ether
A stuffless ghost above his struggling land,
Retching in vain to render up the groan
That is not there, being aching dust's alone?
                                    1934

HOW NAKED, HOW WITHOUT
A WALL

How naked, how without a wall
  Against the wind and the sharp sleet,
He fares at night, that fares at all
  Forth from the stove's heat.

Or if the moon be in the sky,
  Or if the stars, and the late moon
Not rising till an hour goes by,
  And Libra setting soon,

How naked, how without a stitch
  To shut him from the earnest air,   10
He goes, that by the whispering ditch
  Alone at night will fare.

Nor is it but the rising chill
  From the warm weeds, that strikes him
        cold;
Nor that the stridulant hedge grows still,
  Like what has breath to hold,

Until his tiny foot go past
  At length, with its enormous sound;
Nor yet his helpless shadow cast
  To any wolf around.   20

Bare to the moon and her cold rays
  He takes the road, who by and by
Goes bare beneath the moony gaze
  Of his own awful eye.

He sees his motive, like a fox
  Hid in a badger's hole; he sees
His honour, strangled, in a box,
  Her neck lashed to her knees.

The man who ventures forth alone
  When other men are snug within   30
Walks on his marrow, not his bone,
  And lacks his outer skin.

The draughty caverns of his breath
  Grow visible, his heart shines through:
Surely a thing which only death
  Can have the right to do.
                                    1934

FROM EPITAPH FOR THE
RACE OF MAN

17

ONLY the diamond and the diamond's
        dust
Can render up the diamond unto Man;
One and invulnerable as it began
Had it endured, but for the treacherous
        thrust
That laid its hard heart open, as it must,
And ground it down and fitted it to span
A turbaned brow or fret an ivory fan,

Lopped of its stature, pared of its proper
    crust.
So Man, by all the wheels of heaven
    unscored,
Man, the stout ego, the exuberant mind   10
No edge could cleave, no acid could
    consume,
Being split along the vein by his own kind,
Gives over, rolls upon the palm abhorred,
Is set in brass on the swart thumb of Doom.

18

Here lies, and none to mourn him but the
    sea,
That falls incessant on the empty shore,
Most various Man, cut down to spring no
    more;

Before his prime, even in his infancy
Cut down, and all the clamour that was he,
Silenced; and all the riveted pride he wore,
A rusted iron column whose tall core
The rains have tunnelled like an aspen
    tree.
Man, doughty Man, what power has
    brought you low,
That heaven itself in arms could not
    persuade   10
To lay aside the lever and the spade
And be as dust among the dusts that blow?
Whence, whence the broadside? whose the
    heavy blade? . . .
Strive not to speak, poor scattered mouth;
    I know.

1934

EZRA POUND

1885–

A RETROSPECT [1]

THERE has been so much scribbling about a new fashion in poetry, that I may perhaps be pardoned this brief recapitulation and retrospect.

In the spring or early summer of 1912, 'H.D.,' Richard Aldington and myself decided that we were agreed upon the three principles following:

1. Direct treatment of the 'thing' whether subjective or objective.

2. To use absolutely no word that does not contribute to the presentation.

3. As regarding rhythm: to compose in the sequence of the musical phrase, not in sequence of a metronome.

Upon many points of taste and of predilection we differed, but agreeing upon these three positions we thought we had as much right to a group name, at least as much right, as a number of French 'schools' proclaimed by Mr. Flint in the August number of Harold Munro's magazine for 1911.

This school has since been 'joined' or 'followed' by numerous people who, whatever their merits, do not show any signs of agreeing with the second specification. Indeed vers libre has become as prolix and as verbose as any of the flaccid varieties that preceded it. It has brought faults of its own. The actual language and phrasing is often as bad as that of our elders without even the excuse that the words are shoveled in to fill a metric pattern or to complete the noise of a rhyme-sound. Whether or no the phrases followed by the followers are musical must be left to the reader's decision. At times I can find a marked metre in 'vers libres,' as stale and hackneyed as any pseudo-Swinburnian, at times the writers seem to follow no musical structure whatever. But it is, on the whole, good that the field should be ploughed. Perhaps a few good poems have come from the new method, and if so it is justified.

Criticism is not a circumscription or a set of prohibitions. It provides fixed points of departure. It may startle a dull reader into alertness. That little of it which is good is mostly in stray phrases; or if it be an older artist helping a younger it is in great measure but rules of thumb, cautions gained by experience.

I set together a few phrases on practical working about the time the first remarks on imagisme were published. The first use of the word 'Imagiste' was in my note to

[1] The selection is from a group of Pound's early essays grouped together under this title in *Pavannes and Divisions*(N.Y., 1918).

T.E. Hulme's five poems, printed at the end of my 'Ripostes' in the autumn of 1912. I reprint my cautions from *Poetry* for March, 1913.

A FEW DON'TS

AN 'Image' is that which presents an intellectual and emotional complex in an instant of time. I use the term 'complex' rather in the technical sense employed by the newer psychologists, such as Hart, though we might not agree absolutely in our application.

It is the presentation of such a 'complex' instantaneously which gives that sense of sudden liberation; that sense of freedom from time limits and space limits; that sense of sudden growth, which we experience in the presence of the greatest works of art.

It is better to present one Image in a lifetime than to produce voluminous works.

All this, however, some may consider open to debate. The immediate necessity is to tabulate A LIST OF DON'TS for those beginning to write verses. I can not put all of them into Mosaic negative.

To begin with, consider the three propositions (demanding direct treatment, economy of words, and the sequence of the musical phrase), not as dogma—never consider anything as dogma—but as the result of long contemplation, which, even if it is some one else's contemplation, may be worth consideration.

Pay no attention to the criticism of men who have never themselves written a notable work. Consider the discrepancies between the actual writing of the Greek poets and dramatists, and the theories of the Græco-Roman grammarians, concocted to explain their metres.

LANGUAGE

USE no superfluous word, no adjective, which does not reveal something.

Don't use such an expression as 'dim lands *of peace*.' It dulls the image. It mixes an abstraction with the concrete. It comes from the writer's not realizing that the natural object is always the *adequate* symbol.

Go in fear of abstractions. Do not retell in mediocre verse what has already been done in good prose. Don't think any intelligent person is going to be deceived when you try to shirk all the difficulties of the unspeakably difficult art of good prose by chopping your composition into line lengths.

What the expert is tired of today the public will be tired of tomorrow.

Don't imagine that the art of poetry is any simpler than the art of music, or that you can please the expert before you have spent at least as much effort on the art of verse as the average piano teacher spends on the art of music.

Be influenced by as many great artists as you can, but have the decency either to acknowledge the debt outright, or to try to conceal it.

Don't allow 'influence' to mean merely that you mop up the particular decorative vocabulary of some one or two poets whom you happen to admire. A Turkish war correspondent was recently caught red-handed babbling in his dispatches of 'dove-gray' hills, or else it was 'pearl-pale,' I can not remember.

Use either no ornament or good ornament.

RHYTHM AND RHYME

LET the candidate fill his mind with the finest cadences he can discover, preferably in a foreign language [1] so that the meaning of the words may be less likely to divert his attention from the movement; e.g., Saxon charms, Hebridean Folk Songs, the verse of Dante, and the lyrics of Shakespeare—if he can dissociate the vocabulary from the cadence. Let him dissect the lyrics of Goethe coldly into their component sound values, syllables long and short, stressed and unstressed, into vowels and consonants.

It is not necessary that a poem should rely on its music, but if it does rely on its music that music must be such as will delight the expert.

Let the neophyte know assonance and alliteration, rhyme immediate and delayed, simple and polyphonic, as a musician would expect to know harmony and counterpoint and all the minutiæ of his craft. No time is too great to give to these matters or to any one of them, even if the artist seldom have need of them.

1 'This is for rhythm; his vocabulary must of course be found in his native tongue.' Author's note, ibid., 98.

Don't imagine that a thing will 'go' in verse just because it's too dull to go in prose.

Don't be 'viewy'—leave that to the writers of pretty little philosophic essays. Don't be descriptive; remember that the painter can describe a landscape much better than you can, and that he has to know a deal more about it.

When Shakespeare talks of the 'Dawn in russet mantle clad' he presents something which the painter does not present. There is in this line of his nothing that one can call description; he presents.

Consider the way of the scientists rather than the way of an advertising agent for a new soap.

The scientist does not expect to be acclaimed as a great scientist until he has *discovered* something. He begins by learning what has been discovered already. He goes from that point onward. He does not bank on being a charming fellow personally. He does not expect his friends to applaud the results of his freshman class work. Freshmen in poetry are unfortunately not confined to a definite and recognizable class room. They are 'all over the shop.' Is it any wonder 'the public is indifferent to poetry?'

Don't chop your stuff into separate *iambs*. Don't make each line stop dead at the end, and then begin every next line with a heave. Let the beginning of the next line catch the rise of the rhythm wave, unless you want a definite longish pause.

In short, behave as a musician, a good musician, when dealing with that phase of your art which has exact parallels in music. The same laws govern, and you are bound by no others.

Naturally, your rhythmic structure should not destroy the shape of your words, or their natural sound, or their meaning. It is improbable that, at the start, you will be able to get a rhythm-structure strong enough to affect them very much, though you may fall a victim to all sorts of false stopping due to line ends and cæsuræ.

The musician can rely on pitch and the volume of the orchestra. You can not. The term harmony is misapplied to poetry; it refers to simultaneous sounds of different pitch. There is, however, in the best verse a sort of residue of sound which remains in the ear of the hearer and acts more or less as an organ-base.

A rhyme must have in it some slight element of surprise if it is to give pleasure; it need not be bizarre or curious, but it must be well used if used at all.

Vide further Vildrac and Duhamel's notes on rhyme in 'Technique Poetique.'

That part of your poetry which strikes upon the imaginative *eye* of the reader will lose nothing by translation into a foreign tongue; that which appeals to the ear can reach only those who take it in the original.

Consider the definiteness of Dante's presentation, as compared with Milton's rhetoric. Read as much of Wordsworth as does not seem too unutterably dull.[1]

If you want the gist of the matter go to Sappho, Catullus, Villon, Heine when he is in the vein, Gautier when he is not too frigid; or, if you have not the tongues, seek out the leisurely Chaucer. Good prose will do you no harm, and there is good discipline to be had by trying to write it.

Translation is likewise good training, if you find that your original matter 'wobbles' when you try to rewrite it. The meaning of the poem to be translated can not 'wobble.'

If you are using a symmetrical form, don't put in what you want to say and then fill up the remaining vacuums with slush.

Don't mess up the perception of one sense by trying to define it in terms of another. This is usually only the result of being too lazy to find the exact word. To this clause there are possibly exceptions.

The first three simple proscriptions will throw out nine-tenths of all the bad poetry now accepted as standard and classic; and will prevent you from many a crime of production.

'. . . *Mais d'abord il faut être un poète*,' [2] as MM. Duhamel and Vildrac have said at the end of their little book, 'Notes sur la Technique Poetique.'

Since March, 1913, Ford Madox Hueffer has pointed out that Wordsworth was so intent on the ordinary or plain word that he never thought of hunting for *le mot juste*.

John Butler Yeats has handled or manhandled Wordsworth and the Victorians, and his criticism, contained in letters to his son, is now printed and available.

1 'Vide infra.' Author's note, ibid.,100.
2 'But first one must be a poet.'

I do not like writing *about* art, my first, at least I think it was my first essay on the subject, was a protest against it. . . .

CREDO

Rhythm.—I believe in an 'absolute rhythm,' a rhythm, that is, in poetry which corresponds exactly to the emotion or shade of emotion to be expressed. A man's rhythm must be interpretative, it will be, therefore, in the end, his own, uncounterfeiting, uncounterfeitable.

Symbols.—I believe that the proper and perfect symbol is the natural object, that if a man use 'symbols' he must so use them that their symbolic function does not obtrude; so that *a* sense, and the poetic quality of the passage, is not lost to those who do not understand the symbol as such, to whom, for instance, a hawk is a hawk.

Technique.—I believe in technique as the test of a man's sincerity; in law when it is ascertainable; in the trampling down of every convention that impedes or obscures the determination of the law, or the precise rendering of the impulse.

Form.—I think there is a 'fluid' as well as a 'solid' content, that some poems may have form as a tree has form, some as water poured into a vase. That most symmetrical forms have certain uses. That a vast number of subjects cannot be precisely, and therefore not properly rendered in symmetrical forms.

'Thinking that alone worthy wherein the whole art is employed,'[1] I think the artist should master all known forms and systems of metric, and I have with some persistence set about doing this, searching particularly into those periods wherein the systems came to birth or attained their maturity. It has been complained, with some justice, that I dump my note-books on the public. I think that only after a long struggle will poetry attain such a degree of development, of, if you will, modernity, that it will vitally concern people who are accustomed, in prose, to Henry James and Anatole France, in music to Debussy. I am constantly contending that it took two centuries of Provence and one of Tuscany to develop the media of Dante's masterwork, that it took the latinists of the Renaissance, and the Pleiade, and his own age of painted speech to prepare Shakespeare his tools. It is tremendously important that great poetry be written, it makes no jot of difference who writes it. The experimental demonstrations of one man may save the time of many— hence my furore over Arnaut Daniel—if a man's experiments try out one new rime, or dispense conclusively with one iota of currently accepted nonsense, he is merely playing fair with his colleagues when he chalks up his result.

No man ever writes very much poetry that 'matters.' In bulk, that is, no one produces much that is final, and when a man is not doing this highest thing, this saying the thing once for all and perfectly; when he is not matching Ποικιλόθρον᾽, ἀθανάτ᾽ ᾽Αφρόδιτα,[2] or 'Hist—said Kate the Queen,' he had much better be making the sorts of experiment which may be of use to him in his later work, or to his successors.

'The lyf so short, the craft so long to lerne.' It is a foolish thing for a man to begin his work on a too narrow foundation, it is a disgraceful thing for a man's work not to show steady growth and increasing fineness from first to last.

As for 'adaptations'; one finds that all the old masters of painting recommend to their pupils that they begin by copying masterwork, and proceed to their own composition.

As for 'Every man his own poet.' The more every man knows about poetry the better. I believe in every one writing poetry who wants to; most do. I believe in every man knowing enough of music to play 'God bless our home' on the harmonicum, but I do not believe in every man giving concerts and printing his sin.

The mastery of any art is the work of a lifetime. I should not discriminate between the 'amateur' and the 'professional,' or rather I should discriminate quite often in favour of the amateur, but I should discriminate between the amateur and the expert. It is certain that the present chaos will endure until the Art of poetry has been preached down the amateur gullet, until there is such a general understanding of the fact that poetry is an art and not a pastime; such a knowledge of technique; of tech-

---

1 'Dante, *De Volgari Eloquio*.' Author's note, ibid.,104.

2 'Immortal Aphrodite of the vari-coloured throne.' The first line of Sappho's 'Ode to Aphrodite.'

nique of surface and technique of content, that the amateurs will cease to try to drown out the masters.

If a certain thing was said once for all in Atlantis or Arcadia, in 450 Before Christ or in 1290 after, it is not for us moderns to go saying it over, or to go obscuring the memory of the dead by saying the same thing with less skill and less conviction.

My pawing over the ancients and semi-ancients has been one struggle to find out what has been done, once for all, better than it can ever be done again, and to find out what remains for us to do, and plenty does remain, for if we still feel the same emotions as those which launched the thousand ships, it is quite certain that we come on these feelings differently, through different nuances, by different intellectual gradations. Each age has its own abounding gifts, yet only some ages transmute them into matter of duration. No good poetry is ever written in a manner twenty years old, for to write in such a manner shows conclusively that the writer thinks from books, convention and *cliché*, and not from life, yet a man feeling the divorce of life and his art may naturally try to resurrect a forgotten mode if he find in that mode some leaven, or if he think he sees in it some element lacking in contemporary art which might unite that art again to its sustenance, life.

In the art of Daniel and Cavalcanti, I have seen that precision which I miss in the Victorians—that explicit rendering, be it of external nature, or of emotion. Their testimony is of the eyewitness, their symptoms are first hand.

As for the nineteenth century, with all respect to its achievements, I think we shall look back upon it as a rather blurry, messy sort of a period, a rather sentimentalistic, mannerish sort of a period. I say this without any self-righteousness, with no self-satisfaction.

As for there being a 'movement' or my being of it, the conception of poetry as a 'pure art' in the sense in which I use the term, revived with Swinburne. From the puritanical revolt to Swinburne, poetry had been merely the vehicle—yes, definitely, Arthur Symons' scruples and feelings about the word not withholding—the ox-cart and post-chaise for transmitting thoughts poetic or otherwise. And perhaps

the 'great Victorians,' though it is doubtful, and assuredly the 'nineties' continued the development of the art, confining their improvements, however, chiefly to sound and to refinements of manner.

Mr. Yeats has once and for all stripped English poetry of its perdamnable rhetoric. He has boiled away all that is not poetic— and a good deal that is. He has become a classic in his own lifetime and *nel mezzo del cammin*.[1] He has made our poetic idiom a thing pliable, a speech without inversions.

Robert Bridges, Maurice Hewlett and Frederic Manning are [2] in their different ways seriously concerned with overhauling the metric, in testing the language and its adaptability to certain modes. Ford Hueffer is making some sort of experiments in modernity. The Provost of Oriel continues his translation of the *Divina Commedia*.

As to Twentieth century poetry, and the poetry which I expect to see written during the next decade or so, it will, I think, move against poppy-cock, it will be harder and saner, it will be what Mr. Hewlett calls 'nearer the bone.' It will be as much like granite as it can be, its force will lie in its truth, its interpretative power (of course, poetic force does always rest there); I mean it will not try to seem forcible by rhetorical din, and luxurious riot. We will have fewer painted adjectives impeding the shock and stroke of it. At least for myself, I want it so, austere, direct, free from emotional slither.

1918

SESTINA: ALTAFORTE [3]

Loquitur: '*En' Bertrans de Born.*
　Dante Alighieri put this man in hell for
　　that he was a stirrer up of strife.
　Eccovi!
　Judge ye!
　Have I dug him up again?
The scene is at his castle, Altaforte. 'Papiols'
　　is his jongleur.
'*The Leopard,' the 'device' of Richard Cœur*
　de Lion.

1 'Even by middle-age.'
2 'Dec., 1911.' Author's note, *Pavannes and Divisions* (N.Y., 1918),107.
3 This is a free translation into the sestina form of a Provençal poem, 'In Praise of War,' by Bertrans de Born (c.1140–c.1207), master of the satirical *sirvantes*, who will be most remembered, as Pound says: 'for the goad of his tongue, and for his voiced scorn of sloth,

1

DAMN it all! all this our South stinks peace.
You whoreson dog, Papiols, come! Let's to
  music!
I have no life save when the swords clash.
But ah! when I see the standards gold, vair,
  purple, opposing
And the broad fields beneath them turn
  crimson,
Then howls my heart nigh mad with
  rejoicing.

2

In hot summer have I great rejoicing
When the tempests kill the earth's foul
  peace,
And the lightnings from black heav'n flash
  crimson,
And the fierce thunders roar me their
  music   10
And the winds shriek through the clouds
  mad, opposing,
And through all the riven skies God's
  swords clash.

3

Hell grant soon we hear again the swords
  clash!
And the shrill neighs of destriers in battle
  rejoicing,
Spiked breast to spiked breast opposing!
Better one hour's stour than a year's peace
With fat boards, bawds, wine and frail
  music!
Bah! there's no wine like the blood's
  crimson!

4

And I love to see the sun rise blood-
  crimson.
And I watch his spears through the dark
  clash   20
And it fills all my heart with rejoicing
And pries wide my mouth with fast music
When I see him so scorn and defy peace,
His lone might 'gainst all darkness
  opposing.

5

The man who fears war and squats
  opposing
My words for stour, hath no blood of
  crimson
But is fit only to rot in womanish peace
Far from where worth's won and the
  swords clash
For the death of such sluts I go rejoicing;
Yea, I fill all the air with my music.   30

6

Papiols, Papiols, to the music!
There's no sound like to swords swords
  opposing,
No cry like the battle's rejoicing
When our elbows and swords drip the
  crimson
And our charges 'gainst 'The Leopard's'
  rush clash.
May God damn for ever all who cry
  'Peace!'

7

And let the music of the swords make them
  crimson!
Hell grant soon we hear again the swords
  clash!
Hell blot black for alway the thought
  'Peace'!

1909

FOR E. McC

THAT WAS MY COUNTER-BLADE UNDER
LEONARDO TERRONE, MASTER OF FENCE

GONE while your tastes were keen to you,
Gone where the grey winds call to you,
By that high fencer, even Death,
Struck of the blade that no man parrieth;
Such is your fence, one saith,
  One that hath known you.
Drew you your sword most gallantly
Made you your pass most valiantly
  'Gainst that grey fencer, even Death.

Gone as a gust of breath   10
Faith! no man tarrieth,
'Se il cor ti manca,' but it failed thee not!
'Non ti fidar,' it is the sword that speaks
'In me.' [1]

peace, cowardice, and the barons of the Province.'
Pound, *The Spirit of Romance*(London, 1910),40.
Pound has called the cult of the Province 'a cult of the
emotion,' and described the sestina, which 'like all
fine poetry . . . can be well judged only when heard
spoken,' as 'a form like a thin sheet of flame folding
and infolding upon itself.' Ibid.,18.

[1] 'Sword-rune: "If thy heart fail thee trust not in me." '
Author's note, *Personæ*(N.Y., 1926),19.

Thou trusted'st in thyself and met the
     blade
'Thout mask or gauntlet, and art laid
As memorable broken blades that be
Kept as bold trophies of old pageantry.
As old Toledos past their days of war
     Are kept mnemonic of the strokes thy
          bore,   20
So art thou with us, being good to keep
In our heart's sword-rack, though thy
     sword-arm sleep.

Envoi

STRUCK of the blade that no man parrieth,
Pierced of the point that toucheth lastly all,
'Gainst that grey fencer, even Death,
Behold the shield! He shall not take thee all.
                                          1909

PROVINCIA DESERTA

AT Rochecoart,
Where the hills part
          in three ways,
And three valleys, full of winding roads,
Fork out to south and north,
There is a place of trees . . . grey with
          lichen.
I have walked there
          thinking of old days.

At Chalais
          is a pleached arbour;   10
Old pensioners and old protected women
Have the right there—
          it is charity.
I have crept over old rafters,
          peering down
Over the Dronne,
          over a stream full of lilies.
Eastward the road lies,
          Aubeterre is eastward,
With a garrulous old man at the inn.   20
I know the roads in that place:
Mareuil to the north-east,
          La Tour,
There are three keeps near Mareuil,
And an old woman,
          glad to hear Arnaut,
Glad to lend one dry clothing.

I have walked
          into Perigord,
I have seen the torch-flames, high-leaping,

Painting the front of that church;   31
Heard, under the dark, whirling laughter.
I have looked back over the stream
          and seen the high building,
Seen the long minarets, the white shafts.
I have gone in Ribeyrac
          and in Sarlat,
I have climbed rickety stairs, heard talk of
          Croy,
Walked over En Bertran's old layout,
Have seen Narbonne, and Cahors and
          Chalus,   40
Have seen Excideuil, carefully fashioned.

I have said:
          'Here such a one walked.
'Here Cœur-de-Lion was slain.
          'Here was good singing.
'Here one man hastened his step.
          'Here one lay panting.'
I have looked south from Hautefort,
          thinking of Montaignac,
          southward.
I have lain in Rocafixada,   50
          level with sunset,
Have seen the copper come down
          tingeing the mountains,
I have seen the fields, pale, clear as an
          emerald,
Sharp peaks, high spurs, distant castles.
I have said: 'The old roads have lain here.
'Men have gone by such and such valleys
'Where the great halls were closer
          together.'
I have seen Foix on its rock, seen Toulouse,
          and
          Arles greatly altered,   60
I have seen the ruined 'Dorata.'
          I have said:
'Riquier! Guido.'
          I have thought of the second
          Troy,
Some little prized place in Auvergnat:
Two men tossing a coin, one keeping a
          castle,
One set on the highway to sing.
          He sang a woman.
Auvergne rose to the song;
          The Dauphin backed him.   70
'The castle to Austors!'
          'Pieire kept the singing—
'A fair man and a pleasant.'
          He won the lady,
Stole her away for himself, kept her against
          armed force:

So ends that story.
That age is gone;
Pieire de Mænsac is gone.
I have walked over these roads;
I have thought of them living.   80
                                       1916

THE SEAFARER

(From the Anglo-Saxon)

MAY I for my own self song's truth reckon,
Journey's jargon, how I in harsh days
Hardship endured oft.
Bitter breast-cares have I abided,
Known on my keel many a care's hold,
And dire sea-urge, and there I oft spent
Narrow nightwatch nigh the ship's head
While she tossed close to cliffs. Coldly
     afflicted,
My feet were by frost benumbed.
Chill its chains are; chafing sighs   10
Hew my heart round and hunger begot
Mere-weary mood. Lest man know not
That he on dry land loveliest liveth,
List how I, care-wretched, on ice-cold sea,
Weathered the winter, wretched outcast
Deprived of my kinsmen;
Hung with hard ice-flakes, where hail-scur
     flew,
There I heard naught save the harsh sea
And ice-cold wave, at whiles the swan
     cries,
Did for my games the gannet's clamour, 20
Sea-fowls' loudness was for me laughter,
The mews' singing all my mead-drink.
Storms, on the stone-cliffs beaten, fell on
     the stern
In icy feathers; full oft the eagle screamed
With spray on his pinion.
                       Not any protector
May make merry man faring needy.
This he little believes, who aye in winsome
     life
Abides 'mid burghers some heavy business,
Wealthy and wine-flushed, how I weary oft
Must bide above brine.   31
Neareth nightshade, snoweth from north,
Frost froze the land, hail fell on earth then,
Corn of the coldest. Nathless there
     knocketh now
The heart's thought that I on high streams
The salt-wavy tumult traverse alone.
Moaneth alway my mind's lust
That I fare forth, that I afar hence
Seek out a foreign fastness.

For this there's no mood-lofty man over
     earth's midst,   40
Not though he be given his good, but will
     have in his youth greed;
Nor his deed to the daring, nor his king to
     the faithful
But shall have his sorrow for sea-fare
Whatever his lord will.
He hath not heart for harping, nor in
     ring-having
Nor winsomeness to wife, nor world's
     delight
Nor any whit else save the wave's slash,
Yet longing comes upon him to fare forth
     on the water.
Bosque taketh blossom, cometh beauty of
     berries,
Fields to fairness, land fares brisker,   50
All this admonisheth man eager of mood,
The heart turns to travel so that he then
     thinks
On flood-ways to be far departing.
Cuckoo calleth with gloomy crying,
He singeth summerward, bodeth sorrow,
The bitter heart's blood. Burgher knows
     not—
He the prosperous man—what some
     perform
Where wandering them widest draweth.
So that but now my heart burst from my
     breastlock,
My mood 'mid the mere-flood,   60
Over the whale's acre, would wander wide.
On earth's shelter cometh oft to me,
Eager and ready, the crying lone-flyer,
Whets for the whale-path the heart
     irresistibly,
O'er tracks of ocean; seeing that anyhow
My lord deems to me this dead life
On loan and on land, I believe not
That any earth-weal eternal standeth
Save there be somewhat calamitous
That, ere a man's tide go, turn it to twain.
Disease or oldness or sword-hate   71
Beats out the breath from doom-gripped
     body.
And for this, every earl whatever, for those
     speaking after—
Laud of the living, boasteth some last
     word,
That he will work ere he pass onward,
Frame on the fair earth 'gainst foes his
     malice,
Daring ado, . . .
So that all men shall honour him after

And his laud beyond them remain 'mid the
    English,
Aye, for ever, a lasting life's-blast,   80
Delight 'mid the doughty.
                Days little durable,
And all arrogance of earthen riches,
There come now no kings nor Cæsars
Nor gold-giving lords like those gone.
Howe'er in earth most magnified,
Whoe'er lived in life most lordliest,
Drear all this excellence, delights
    undurable!
Waneth the watch, but the world
    holdeth.
Tomb hideth trouble. The blade is layed
    low.   90
Earthly glory ageth and seareth.
No man at all going the earth's gait,
But age fares against him, his face paleth,
Grey-haired he groaneth, knows gone
    companions,
Lordly men, are to earth o'ergiven,
Nor may he then the flesh-cover, whose
    life ceaseth,
Nor eat the sweet nor feel the sorry,
Nor stir hand nor think in mid heart,
And though he strew the grave with gold,
His born brothers, their buried bodies   100
Be an unlikely treasure hoard.
                    1912

THE RETURN

See, they return; ah, see the tentative
Movements, and the slow feet,
The trouble in the pace and the
    uncertain
Wavering!

See, they return, one, and by one,
With fear, as half-awakened;
As if the snow should hesitate
And murmur in the wind,
    and half turn back;
These were the 'Wing'd-with-Awe,'   10
    Inviolable.

Gods of the wingèd shoe!
With them the silver hounds,
    sniffing the trace of air!

Haie! Haie!
    These were the swift to harry;
These the keen-scented;
These were the souls of blood.

Slow on the leash,
                pallid the leash-men!   20
                    1912

BALLAD OF THE GOODLY FERE [1]

*Simon Zelotes Speaketh It Somewhile
after the Crucifixion*

Ha' we lost the goodliest fere o' all
For the priests and the gallows tree?
Aye lover he was of brawny men,
O' ships and the open sea.

When they came wi' a host to take Our
    Man
His smile was good to see,
'First let these go!' quo' our Goodly Fere,
'Or I'll see ye damned,' says he.

Aye he sent us out through the crossed high
    spears
And the scorn of his laugh rang free,   10
'Why took ye not me when I walked about
Alone in the town?' says he.

Oh we drunk his 'Hale' in the good red
    wine
When we last made company,
No capon priest was the Goodly Fere
But a man o' men was he.

I ha' seen him drive a hundred men
Wi' a bundle o' cords swung free,
That they took the high and holy house
For their pawn and treasury.   20

They'll no' get him a' in a book I think
Though they write it cunningly;
No mouse of the scrolls was the Goodly
    Fere
But aye loved the open sea.

If they think they ha' snared our Goodly
    Fere
They are fools to the last degree.
'I'll go to the feast,' quo' our Goodly Fere,
'Though I go to the gallows tree.'

'Ye ha' seen me heal the lame and blind,
And wake the dead,' says he,   30
'Ye shall see one thing to master all:
'Tis how a brave man dies on the tree.'

1 'Fere = Mate, Companion.' Author's note, *Umbra*
(London, 1920),43.

A son of God was the Goodly Fere
That bade us his brothers be.
I ha' seen him cow a thousand men.
I have seen him upon the tree.

He cried no cry when they drave the nails
And the blood gushed hot and free,
The hounds of the crimson sky gave
    tongue
But never a cry cried he.   40

I ha' seen him cow a thousand men
On the hills o' Galilee,
They whined as he walked out calm
    between,
Wi' his eyes like the grey o' the sea,

Like the sea that brooks no voyaging
With the winds unleashed and free,
Like the sea that he cowed at Genseret
Wi' twey words spoke' suddenly.

A master of men was the Goodly Fere,
A mate of the wind and sea,   50
If they think they ha' slain our Goodly
    Fere
They are fools eternally.

I ha' seen him eat o' the honey-comb
Sin' they nailed him to the tree.
                        1909

FURTHER INSTRUCTIONS

COME, my songs, let us express our baser
    passions,
Let us express our envy of the man with a
    steady job and no worry about the
    future.
You are very idle, my songs.
I fear you will come to a bad end.
You stand about in the streets,
You loiter at the corners and bus-stops,
You do next to nothing at all.

You do not even express our inner
    nobilities,
You will come to a very bad end.

And I?   10
I have gone half cracked,
I have talked to you so much that
        I almost see you about me,
Insolent little beasts, shameless, devoid of
    clothing!

But you, newest song of the lot,
You are not old enough to have done much
    mischief,
I will get you a green coat out of China
With dragons worked upon it,
I will get you the scarlet silk trousers
From the statue of the infant Christ in
    Santa Maria Novella,   20
Lest they say we are lacking in taste,
Or that there is no caste in this family.
                      1916

THE RIVER MERCHANT'S WIFE:

A LETTER [1]

WHILE my hair was still cut straight across
    my forehead
I played about the front gate, pulling
    flowers.
You came by on bamboo stilts, playing
    horse,
You walked about my seat, playing with
    blue plums.
And we went on living in the village of
    Chokan:
Two small people, without dislike or
    suspicion.

At fourteen I married My Lord you.
I never laughed, being bashful.
Lowering my head, I looked at the wall.
Called to, a thousand times, I never looked
    back.   10

At fifteen I stopped scowling,
I desired my dust to be mingled with yours
For ever and for ever and for ever.
Why should I climb the look out?

At sixteen you departed,
You went into far Ku-to-yen, by the river
    of swirling eddies,
And you have been gone five months.
The monkeys make sorrowful noise
    overhead.
You dragged your feet when you went out.
By the gate now, the moss is grown, the
    different mosses,   20
Too deep to clear them away!

1 The poem is a translation from Li Po(701–762), the
Japanese form of whose name Pound has englished.
Li Po, often called the greatest of Chinese poets,
flourished under the Tangs in China's golden age of
poetry. With him, Pound says: 'the visual art in poetry
reached its zenith.' Pound, 'The Island of Paris,' *The
Dial*,LXIX,vi,636.

The leaves fall early this autumn, in wind.
The paired butterflies are already yellow
    with August
Over the grass in the West garden;
They hurt me. I grow older.
If you are coming down through the
    narrows of the river Kiang,
Please let me know beforehand,
And I will come out to meet you
        As far as Cho-fu-Sa.
              By Rihaku.
                 1916

IN A STATION OF THE METRO [1]

THE apparition of these faces in the crowd;
Petals on a wet, black bough.

                 1916

[1] 'Three years ago in Paris I got out of a "metro" train at La Concorde, and saw suddenly a beautiful face, and then another and another, and then a beautiful child's face, and then another beautiful woman, and I tried all that day to find words for what this had meant to me, and I could not find any words that seemed to me worthy, or as lovely as that sudden emotion. And that evening . . . I was still trying and I found, suddenly, the expression. I do not mean that I found words, but there came an equation . . . not in speech, but in little splotches of colour. . . . It was a word, the beginning, for me, of a language in colour. . . . Any mind that is worth calling a mind must have needs beyond the existing categories of language, just as a painter must have pigments or shades more numerous than the existing names of the colours. Perhaps this is enough to explain the words in my "Vortex": "Every concept, every emotion, presents itself to the vivid consciousness in some primary form. It belongs to the art of this form." That is to say, my experience in Paris should have gone into paint. . . . Colour, was, in that instance, the "primary pigment." . . . The Vorticist uses the "primary pigment." Vorticism is art before it has spread itself into flaccidity, into elaboration and secondary applications. . . . All poetic language is the language of exploration. Since the beginning of bad writing, writers have used images as ornaments. The point of Imagisme is that it does not use images *as ornaments*. The image is itself the speech. The image is the word beyond formulated language. . . . One is tired of ornamentations; they are all a trick, and any sharp person can learn them. The Japanese have had the sense of exploration. They have understood the beauty of this sort of knowing. A Chinaman said long ago that if a man can't say what he has to say in twelve lines he had better keep quiet. The Japanese have evolved the still shorter form of *hokku.* . . . The "one image poem" is a form of super-position, that is to say, it is one idea set on top of another. I found it useful in getting out of the impasse in which I had been left by my metro emotion. I wrote a thirty-line poem, and destroyed it because it was what we call work "of second intensity." Six months later I made a poem half that length; a year later I made the following *hokku*-like sentence: [the poem above]. . . .

THE GAME OF CHESS [2]

DOGMATIC STATEMENT CONCERNING THE GAME OF CHESS: THEME FOR A SERIES OF PICTURES

RED knights, brown bishops, bright queens,
Striking the board, falling in strong 'L's of
    colour.
Reaching and striking in angles,
    holding lines in one colour.
This board is alive with light;
    these pieces are living in form,
Their moves break and reform the pattern:
    luminous green from the rooks,
Clashing with 'X's of queens,
    looped with the knight-leaps.

Y' pawns, cleaving, embanking!
Whirl! Centripetal! Mate! King down in the
    vortex,
Clash, leaping of bands, straight strips of
    hard colour,
Blocked lights working in. Escapes.
    Renewal of contest.

                 1916

A VIRGINAL

No, no! Go from me. I have left her lately.
I will not spoil my sheath with lesser
    brightness.
For my surrounding air hath a new
    lightness;
Slight are her arms, yet they have bound
    me straitly
And left me cloaked as with a gauze of
    æther;
As with sweet leaves; as with subtle
    clearness.

In a poem of this sort one is trying to record the precise instant when a thing outward and objective transforms itself, or darts into a thing inward and subjective.' Pound, *Gaudier-Brzeska* (London, 1916), 100–03.

[2] 'The image is not an idea. It is a radiant node or cluster; it is what I can, and must perforce, call a VORTEX, from which, and through which, and into which, ideas are constantly rushing. . . . It is as true for the painting and sculpture as it is for the poetry. Mr. Wadsworth and Mr. Lewis are not using words, they are using shape and colour. Mr. Brzeska and Mr. Epstein are using "planes in relation"; they are dealing with a relation of planes different from the sort of relation of planes dealt with in geometry, hence, what is called "the need of organic forms in sculpture." . . . The organization of forms is a much more energetic and creative action than the copying of light on a haystack. There is undoubtedly a language of form and colour.' Ibid.,106–07.

Oh, I have picked up magic in her nearness
To sheathe me half in half the things that
    sheathe her.
No, no! Go from me. I have still the
    flavour,
Soft as spring wind that's come from
    birchen bowers.   10
Green come the shoots, aye April in the
    branches,
As winter's wound with her sleight hand
    she staunches,
Hath of the trees a likeness of the savour:
As white their bark, so white this lady's
    hours.

                  1912

VILLANELLE: THE
PSYCHOLOGICAL HOUR

I

I HAD over-prepared the event,
    that much was ominous.
With middle-ageing care
    I had laid out just the right books.
I had almost turned down the pages.

    Beauty is so rare a thing.
    So few drink of my fountain.

So much barren regret,
So many hours wasted!
And now I watch, from the window,   10
    the rain, the wandering buses.

'Their little cosmos is shaken'—
    the air is alive with that fact.
In their parts of the city
    they are played on by diverse
        forces.
How do I know?
    Oh, I know well enough.
For them there is something afoot.
    As for me;
I had over-prepared the event—   20

    Beauty is so rare a thing.
    So few drink of my fountain.

Two friends: a breath of the forest . . .
Friends? Are people less friends
    because one has just, at last, found
    them?
Twice they promised to come.

    '*Between the night and morning?*'

Beauty would drink of my mind.
Youth would awhile forget
      my youth is gone from me.   30

2

('Speak up! You have danced so stiffly?
    Some one admired your works,
    And said so frankly.

    'Did you talk like a fool,
    The first night?
    The second evening?'

'*But* they promised again:
      "To-morrow at tea-time." ')

3

Now the third day is here—
    no word from either;   40
No word from her nor him,
Only another man's note:
    'Dear Pound, I am leaving
    England.'

                  1915

HUGH SELWYN MAUBERLEY [1]

(LIFE AND CONTACTS)

Vocat Æstus in Umbram [2]

        Nemesianus Ec. IV.

I

E. P. Ode pour l'Election de son
Sepulchre [3]

FOR three years, out of key with his
    time,
He strove to resuscitate the dead art
Of poetry; to maintain 'the sublime'
In the old sense. Wrong from the start—

1 Of 'Hugh Selwyn Mauberley' T.S.Eliot says: 'This
seems to me a great poem. . . . I know very well
that the apparent roughness and *naïvete* of the verse
and rhyming of "Mauberley" are inevitably the result
of many years of hard work: if you cannot appreciate
the dexterity of "Altaforte" you cannot appreciate the
dexterity of "Mauberley." On the other side, the poem
seems to me, when you have marked the sophistica-
tion and the great variety of the verse, verse of a man
who knows his way about, to be a positive document
of sensibility. It is compact of the experience of a
certain man in a certain place at a certain time; and it
is also a document of an epoch; it is genuine tragedy
and comedy; and it is, in the best sense of Arnold's
worn phrase, "a criticism of life." ' Eliot, ed., *Ezra
Pound, Selected Poems*(London, 1928),xxiii–iv.
2 'The summer calls us into the shade.'
3 'E.P. Ode on the Choice of his Tomb.'

No, hardly, but seeing he had been born
In a half-savage country, out of date;
Bent resolutely on wringing lilies from the
    acorn;
Capaneus; trout for factitious bait;

Ἴδμεν γάρ τοι πάνθ᾽, ὅσ᾽ ἐνὶ Τροίῃ [1]
Caught in the unstopped ear;   10
Giving the rocks small lee-way
The chopped seas held him, therefore, that
    year.

His true Penelope was Flaubert,
He fished by obstinate isles;
Observed the elegance of Circe's hair
Rather than the mottoes on sun-dials.

Unaffected by 'the march of events,'
He passed from men's memory in *l'an
    trentiesme
De son eage*; [2] the case presents
No adjunct to the Muses' diadem.   20

2

The age demanded an image
Of its accelerated grimace,
Something for the modern stage,
Not, at any rate, an Attic grace;

Not, not certainly, the obscure reveries
Of the inward gaze;
Better mendacities
Than the classics in paraphrase!

The 'age demanded' chiefly a mould in
    plaster,
Made with no loss of time,   30
A prose kinema, not, not assuredly, alabaster
Or the 'sculpture' of rhyme.

3

The tea-rose tea-gown, etc.
Supplants the mousseline of Cos,
The pianola 'replaces'
Sappho's barbitos.

Christ follows Dionysus,
Phallic and ambrosial
Made way for macerations;
Caliban casts out Ariel.   40

All things are a flowing,
Sage Heracleitus says;
But a tawdry cheapness
Shall outlast our days.

Even the Christian beauty
Defects—after Samothrace;
We see τὸ καλὸν [3]
Decreed in the market-place.

Faun's flesh is not to us,
Nor the saint's vision.   50
We have the Press for wafer;
Franchise for circumcision.

All men, in law, are equals.
Free of Pisistratus,
We choose a knave or an eunuch
To rule over us.

O bright Apollo,

τίν᾽ ἄνδρα, τίν᾽ ἥρωα, τίνα θεὸν [4]
What god, man, or hero
Shall I place a tin wreath upon!   60

4

These fought in any case,
and some believing,
        pro domo,[5] in any case . . .

Some quick to arm,
some for adventure,
some from fear of weakness,
some from fear of censure,
some for love of slaughter, in
    imagination,
learning later . . .
some in fear, learning love of slaughter;   70

Died some, pro patria,
    non 'dulce' non 'et decor' [6] . . .
walked eye-deep in hell
believing in old men's lies, then
    unbelieving
came home, home to a lie,
home to many deceits,
home to old lies and new infamy;
usury age-old and age-thick
and liars in public places.

---

1 'For we know all the things which are in Troy.'
2 Pound has altered to the third person, Villon's opening line of his *Grand Testament*: 'In the thirtieth year
  of my life.' The phrase has become a contemporary
  cliché, as a cue for poetic retrospection.

3 'The beautiful.'
4 'What man, what hero, what god.'
5 'For the home.'
6 'Dulce et decorum est pro patria mori (It is sweet and
  fitting to die for one's country).' Horace,*C.*III,ii,13.

Daring as never before, wastage as never
    before.   80
Young blood and high blood,
fair cheeks, and fine bodies;

fortitude as never before

frankness as never before,
disillusions as never told in the old days,
hysterias, trench confessions,
laughter out of dead bellies.

5

There died a myriad,
And of the best, among them,
For an old bitch gone in the teeth,   90
For a botched civilization,

Charm, smiling at the good mouth,
Quick eyes gone under earth's lid,

For two gross of broken statues,
For a few thousand battered books.

Yeux Glauques [1]

Gladstone was still respected,
When John Ruskin produced
'King's Treasuries'; Swinburne
And Rossetti still abused.

Fœtid Buchanan lifted up his voice   100
When that faun's head of hers
Became a pastime for
Painters and adulterers.

The Burne-Jones cartons
Have preserved her eyes;
Still, at the Tate, they teach
Cophetua to rhapsodize;

Thin like brook-water,
With a vacant gaze.
The English Rubaiyat was still-born   110
In those days.

The thin, clear gaze, the same
Still darts out faun-like from the half-
    ruin'd face,
Questing and passive. . . .
'Ah, poor Jenny's case' . . .

Bewildered that a world
Shows no surprise

1 'Glaucous Eyes.'

At her last maquero's
Adulteries.

'Siena Mi Fe; Disfecemi Maremma' [2]

Among the pickled fœtuses and bottled
    bones,   120
Engaged in perfecting the catalogue,
I found the last scion of the
Senatorial families of Strasbourg, Monsieur
    Verog.

For two hours he talked of Gallifet;
Of Dowson; of the Rhymers' Club;
Told me how Johnson (Lionel) died
By falling from a high stool in a pub . . .

But showed no trace of alcohol
At the autopsy, privately performed—
Tissue preserved—the pure mind   130
Arose toward Newman as the whisky
    warmed.

Dowson found harlots cheaper than
    hotels;
Headlam for uplift; Image impartially
    imbued
With raptures for Bacchus, Terpsichore and
    the Church.
So spoke the author of 'The Dorian
    Mood,'

M. Verog, out of step with the
    decade,
Detached from his contemporaries,
Neglected by the young,
Because of these reveries.

Brennbaum

The sky-like limpid eyes,   140
The circular infant's face,
The stiffness from spats to collar
Never relaxing into grace;

The heavy memories of Horeb, Sinai and
    the forty years,
Showed only when the daylight fell
Level across the face
Of Brennbaum 'The Impeccable.'

2 'Sienna made me; Maremma was my undoing.' Dante,
Purgatory, V,134. It is said to Dante by Pia de'
Tolomei, one of the souls, who was secretly put to
death by her husband, either because of suspected
infidelity or because he wished another marriage.

Mr. Nixon

In the cream gilded cabin of his steam
    yacht
Mr. Nixon advised me kindly, to advance
    with fewer
Dangers of delay. 'Consider   150
    Carefully the reviewer.

'I was as poor as you are;
When I began I got, of course,
Advance on royalties, fifty at first,' said
    Mr. Nixon,
'Follow me, and take a column,
Even if you have to work free.

'Butter reviewers. From fifty to three
    hundred
I rose in eighteen months;
The hardest nut I had to crack
Was Dr. Dundas.   160

'I never mentioned a man but with the view
Of selling my own works.
The tip's a good one, as for literature
It gives no man a sinecure.

'And no one knows, at sight, a masterpiece.
And give up verse, my boy,
There's nothing in it.'
    · · · · · ·

Likewise a friend of Bloughram's once
    advised me:
Don't kick against the pricks,
Accept opinion. The 'Nineties' tried your
    game   170
And died, there's nothing in it.

10

Beneath the sagging roof
The stylist has taken shelter,
Unpaid, uncelebrated,
At last from the world's welter

Nature receives him;
With a placid and uneducated mistress
He exercises his talents
And the soil meets his distress.

The haven from sophistications and
    contentions   180
Leaks through its thatch;
He offers succulent cooking;
The door has a creaking latch.

11

'Conservatrix of Milésian'
Habits of mind and feeling,
Possibly. But in Ealing
With the most bank-clerkly of English-
    men?

No, 'Milésian' is an exaggeration.
No instinct has survived in her
Older than those her grandmother   190
Told her would fit her station.

12

'Daphne with her thighs in bark
Stretches toward me her leafy hands,'—
Subjectively. In the stuffed-satin drawing-
    room
I await The Lady Valentine's commands,

Knowing my coat has never been
Of precisely the fashion
To stimulate, in her,
A durable passion;

Doubtful, somewhat, of the value   200
Of well-gowned approbation
Of literary effort,
But never of The Lady Valentine's
    vocation:

Poetry, her border of ideas,
The edge, uncertain, but a means of
    blending
With other strata
Where the lower and higher have ending;

A hook to catch the Lady Jane's
    attention,
A modulation toward the theatre,
Also, in the case of revolution,   210
A possible friend and comforter.
    · · · · · ·

Conduct, on the other hand, the soul
'Which the highest cultures have
    nourished'
To Fleet St. where
Dr. Johnson flourished;

Beside this thoroughfare
The sale of half-hose has
Long since superseded the cultivation
Of Pierian roses.

Envoi (1919)

Go, dumb-born book,   220
Tell her that sang me once that song of
              Lawes:
Hadst thou but song
As thou hast subjects known,
Then were there cause in thee that should
              condone
Even my faults that heavy upon me lie,
And build her glories their longevity.

Tell her that sheds
Such treasure in the air,
Recking naught else but that her graces give
Life to the moment,   230
I would bid them live
As roses might, in magic amber laid,
Red overwrought with orange and all made
One substance and one colour
Braving time.

Tell her that goes
With song upon her lips
But sings not out the song, nor knows
The maker of it, some other mouth,
May be as fair as hers,   240
Might, in new ages, gain her worshippers,
When our two dusts with Waller's shall be
              laid,
Siftings on siftings in oblivion,
Till change hath broken down
All things save Beauty alone.

Mauberley

1920

'*Vacuos exercet aera morsus.*' [1]

I

Turned from the 'eau-forte
Par Jaquemart'
To the strait head
Of Messalina:

'His true Penelope   250
Was Flaubert,'
And his tool
The engraver's.

Firmness,
Not the full smile,
His art, but an art
In profile;

Colourless
Pier Francesca,
Pisanello lacking the skill   260
To forge Achaia.

2

'*Qu'est ce qu'ils savent de l'amour, et
qu'est ce qu'ils peuvent comprendre?
      S'ils ne comprennent pas la poésie,
s'ils ne sentent pas la musique, qu'est ce
qu'ils peuvent comprendre de cette passion en
comparaison avec laquelle la rose est grossière
et le parfum des violettes un tonnerre?*' [2]
                                           CAID ALI

For three years, diabolus in the
              scale,
He drank ambrosia,
All passes, ANANGKE [3] prevails.
Came end, at last, to that Arcadia.

He had moved amid her phantasmagoria,
Amid her galaxies,
NUKTOS 'AGALMA [4]

· · · · · ·

Drifted . . . drifted precipitate,
Asking time to be rid of . . .   270
Of his bewilderment; to designate
His new found orchid. . . .

To be certain . . . certain . . .
(Amid aerial flowers) . . . time for
              arrangements—
Drifted on
To the final estrangement;

Unable in the supervening blankness
To sift TO AGATHON [5] from the chaff
Until he found his sieve . . .
Ultimately, his seismograph: 280

—Given that is his 'fundamental
              passion,'
This urge to convey the relation
Of eyelid and cheek-bone
By verbal manifestations;

1 'He bites vainly at the air.' Ovid, *Met.*,VII,786.

2 'What do they know of love, and what can they understand? If they don't understand poetry, if they don't
feel music, what can they understand of this passion,
compared to which the rose is gross and the perfume
of violets a clap of thunder.'
3 'Necessity.'
4 'Night's ornament.'
5 'The good.'

To present the series
Of curious heads in medallion—

He had passed, inconscient, full gaze,
The wide-banded irides
And botticellian sprays implied
In their diastasis;   290

Which anæthesis, noted a year late,
And weighed, revealed his great affect,
(Orchid), mandate
Of Eros, a retrospect.

. . . . . .

Mouths biting empty air,
The still stone dogs,
Caught in metamorphosis, were
Left him as epilogues.

'The Age Demanded'

Vide Poem 2. Page 1278

For this agility chance found
Him of all men, unfit   300
As the red-beaked steeds of
The Cytheræan for a chain bit.

The glow of porcelain
Brought no reforming sense
To his perception
Of the social inconsequence.

Thus, if her colour
Came against his gaze,
Tempered as if
It were through a perfect glaze   310

He made no immediate application
Of this to relation of the state
To the individual, the month was more
    temperate
Because this beauty had been.

    The coral isle, the lion-coloured sand
    Burst in upon the porcelain revery:
    Impetuous troubling
    Of his imagery.

Mildness, amid the neo-Nietzschean
    clatter,
His sense of graduations,   320
Quite out of place amid
Resistance to current exacerbations,

Invitation, mere invitation to perceptivity
Gradually led him to the isolation
Which these presents place
Under a more tolerant, perhaps,
    examination.

By constant elimination
The manifest universe
Yielded an armour
Against utter consternation,   330

A Minoan undulation,
Seen, we admit, amid ambrosiaı
    circumstances,
Strengthened him against
The discouraging doctrine of chances,

And his desire for survival,
Faint in the most strenuous moods,
Became an Olympian *apathein* [1]
In the presence of selected
    perceptions.

A pale gold, in the aforesaid pattern,
The unexpected palms   340
Destroying, certainly, the artist's
    urge,
Left him delighted with the
    imaginary
Audition of the phantasmal sea-surge,

Incapable of the least utterance or
    composition,
Emendation, conservation of the 'better
    tradition,'
Refinement of medium, elimination of
    superfluities,
August attraction or concentration.

Nothing, in brief, but maudlin
    confession,
Irresponse to human aggression,
Amid the precipitation, down-float   35c
Of insubstantial manna,
Lifting the faint susurrus
Of his subjective hosannah.

Ultimate affronts to
Human redundancies;

Non-esteem of self-styled 'his betters'
Leading, as he well knew,
To his final
Exclusion from the world of letters.

1 'Impassivity.'

FROM CANTOS [1]

I

Scattered Moluccas   360
Not knowing, day to day,
The first day's end, in the next noon;
The placid water
Unbroken by the Simoon;

Thick foliage
Placid beneath warm suns,
Tawn foreshores
Washed in the cobalt of oblivions;

Or through dawn-mist
The grey and rose   370
Of the juridical
Flamingoes;

A consciousness disjunct,
Being but this overblotted
Series
Of intermittences;

Coracle of Pacific voyages,
The unforecasted beach;
Then on an oar
Read this: 380

'I was
And I no more exist;
Here drifted
An hedonist.'

Medallion

Luini in porcelain!
The grand piano
Utters a profane
Protest with her clear soprano.

The sleek head emerges
From the gold-yellow frock   390
As Anadyomene in the opening
Pages of Reinach.

Honey-red, closing the face-oval,
A basket-work of braids which seem as if
        they were
Spun in King Minos' hall
From metal, or intractable amber;

The face-oval beneath the glaze,
Bright in its suave bounding-line, as,
Beneath half-watt rays,
The eyes turn topaz.   400
                                      1920

AND then went down to the ship,
Set keel to breakers, forth on the godly sea,
        and
We set up mast and sail on that swart ship,
Bore sheep aboard her, and our bodies also
Heavy with weeping, and winds from
        sternward

1 The clearest statement as to the ultimate structure of the Cantos has been made by William Butler Yeats, based on a conversation with Pound at Rapallo: 'For the last hour we have sat upon the roof which is also a garden, discussing that immense poem of which but seven and twenty Cantos are already published. I have often found there some scene of distinguished beauty but have never discovered why all the suits could not be dealt out in some quite different order. Now at last he explains that it will, when the hundredth Canto is finished, display a structure like that of a Bach Fugue. There will be no plot, no chronicle of events, no logic of discourse, but two themes, the descent into Hades from Homer, a metamorphosis from Ovid, and mixed with these mediæval or modern historical characters. He has tried to produce that picture Porteous commended to Nicholas Poussin in *Le Chef-d'œuvre Inconnu* where everything rounds or thrusts itself without edges, without contours—conventions of the intellect—from a splash of tints and shades, to achieve a work as characteristic of the art of our time as the paintings of Cézanne, avowedly suggested by Porteous, as *Ulysses* and its dream association of words and images, a poem in which there is nothing that can be taken out and reasoned over, nothing that is not a part of the poem itself. He has scribbled on the back of an envelope certain sets of letters that represent emotions or archetypal events—I cannot find any adequate definition—A B C D and then J K L M, and then each set of letters repeated, and then A B C D inverted and this repeated, and then a new element X Y Z, then certain letters that never recur and then all sorts of combinations of X Y Z and J K L M and A B C D and D C B A and all set whirling together. He has shown me upon the wall a photograph of a Cosimo Tura decoration in three compartments, in the upper the Triumph of Love and the Triumph of Chastity, in the middle Zodiacal signs, and in the lower certain events in Cosimo Tura's day. The descent and the metamorphosis—A B C D and J K L M—his fixed elements, took the place of the Zodiac, the archetypal persons—X Y Z—that of the Triumphs, and certain modern events—his letters that do not recur—that of those events in Cosimo Tura's day.

'I may, now that I have recovered leisure, find that the mathematical structure, when taken up into the imagination, is more than mathematical, that seemingly irrelevant details fit together into a single theme, that here is no batch of tone and colour—Hodos Chameliontos—except for some odd corner where one discovers beautiful detail like that finely modelled foot in Porteous' disastrous picture.

'It is almost impossible to understand the art of a generation younger than one's own. I was wrong about *Ulysses* when I had read but some first frag-

Bore us out onward with bellying canvas,
Circe's this craft, the trim-coifed goddess.
Then sat we amidships, wind jamming the
    tiller,
Thus with stretched sail, we went over sea
    till day's end.
Sun to his slumber, shadows o'er all the
    ocean,   10
Came we then to the bounds of deepest
    water,
To the Kimmerian lands, and peopled cities
Covered with close-webbed mist, unpierced
    ever
With glitter of sun-rays
Nor with stars stretched, nor looking back
    from heaven
Swartest night stretched over wretched
    men there.
The ocean flowing backward, came we then
    to the place
Aforesaid by Circe.
Here did they rites, Perimedes and
    Eurylochus,
And drawing sword from my hip   20
I dug the ell-square pitkin;
Poured we libations unto each the dead,
First mead and then sweet wine, water
    mixed with white flour.
Then prayed I many a prayer to the sickly
    death's-heads;
As set in Ithaca, sterile bulls of the best
For sacrifice, heaping the pyre with goods,
A sheep to Tiresias only, black and a bell-
    sheep.
Dark blood flowed in the fosse,
Souls out of Erebus, cadaverous dead, of
    brides
Of youths and of the old who had borne
    much;   30
Souls stained with recent tears, girls tender,
Men many, mauled with bronze lance
    heads,
Battle spoil, bearing yet dreory arms,
These many crowded about me; with
    shouting,
Pallor upon me, cried to my men for more
    beasts;
Slaughtered the herds, sheep slain of
    bronze;
Poured ointment, cried to the gods,

ments, and I do not want to be wrong again—above
all in judging verse. Perhaps when the sudden Italian
spring has come I may have discovered what will
seem all the more, because it is the opposite of all I
have attempted, unique and unforgettable.' Yeats, *A
Packet for Ezra Pound*(Dublin, 1929),2–4.

To Pluto the strong, and praised
    Proserpine;
Unsheathed the narrow sword,
I sat to keep off the impetuous impotent
    dead,   40
Till I should hear Tiresias.
But first Elpenor came, our friend
    Elpenor,
Unburied, cast on the wide earth,
Limbs that we left in the house of Circe,
Unwept, unwrapped in sepulchre, since
    toils urged other.
Pitiful spirit. And I cried in hurried
    speech:
'Elpenor, how art thou come to this dark
    coast?
'Cam'st thou afoot, outstripping seamen?'
    And he in heavy speech:
'Ill fate and abundant wine. I slept in
    Circe's ingle.   50
'Going down the long ladder unguarded,
'I fell against the buttress,
'Shattered the nape-nerve, the soul sought
    Avernus.
'But thou, O King, I bid remember me,
    unwept, unburied,
'Heap up mine arms, be tomb by sea-bord,
    and inscribed:
'*A man of no fortune, and with a name to
    come.*
'And set my oar up, that I swung mid
    fellows.'

And Anticlea came, whom I beat off, and
    then Tiresias Theban,
Holding his golden wand, knew me, and
    spoke first:
'A second time? why? man of ill star,   60
'Facing the sunless dead and this joyless
    region?
'Stand from the fosse, leave me my bloody
    bever
'For soothsay.'
    And I stepped back,
And he strong with the blood, said then:
    'Odysseus
'Shalt return through spiteful Neptune,
    over dark seas,
'Lose all companions.' And then Anticlea
    came.
Lie quiet Divus. I mean, that is Andreas
    Divus,
In officina Wecheli, 1538, out of Homer.
And he sailed, by Sirens and thence
    outward and away   70

And unto Circe.
        Venerandam,[1]
In the Cretan's phrase, with the golden
        crown, Aphrodite,
Cypri munimenta sortita est,[2] mirthful,
        oricalchi,[3] with golden
Girdles and breast bands, thou with dark
        eyelids
Bearing the golden bough of Argicida. So
        that:
                                        1924

2

HANG it all, Robert Browning,
        there can be but the one 'Sordello.'
But Sordello, and my Sordello? [4]
        Lo Sordels si fo di Mantovana.
So-shu churned in the sea.
Seal sports in the spray-whited circles of
        cliff-wash,
Sleek head, daughter of Lir,
        eyes of Picasso
Under black fur-hood, lithe daughter of
        Ocean;
And the wave runs in the beach-groove: 10
'Eleanor, ἑλέναυς and ἑλέπτολις!' [5]
        And poor old Homer blind, blind,
        as a bat,
Ear, ear for the sea-surge, murmur of old
        men's voices:
'Let her go back to the ships,
Back among Grecian faces, lest evil come
        on our own,
Evil and further evil, and a curse cursed on
        our children,
Moves, yes she moves like a goddess
And has the face of a god
        and the voice of Schoeney's
        daughters,
And doom goes with her in walking,   20
Let her go back to the ships,
        back among Grecian voices.'
And by the beach-run, Tyro,
        Twisted arms of the sea-god,
Lithe sinews of water, gripping her,
        cross-hold,
And the blue-gray glass of the wave tents
        them,
Glare azure of water, cold-welter, close
        cover.

1 'To be worshiped.'
2 'She was allotted the protection of Cyprus.'
3 'Of brass.'
4 'Sordello was from around Mantua.'
5 'A hell to ships, a hell to cities.' Æschylus, *Agamemnon*,
689. The epithet was punningly said of Helen.

Quiet sun-tawny sand-stretch,
The gulls broad out their wings,
        nipping between the splay
        feathers;   30
Snipe come for their bath,
        bend out their wing-joints,
Spread wet wings to the sun-film,
And by Scios,
        to left of the Naxos passage,
Naviform rock overgrown,
        algæ cling to its edge,
There is a wine-red glow in the shallows,
        a tin flash in the sun-dazzle.

The ship landed in Scios,   40
        men wanting spring-water,
And by the rock-pool a young boy loggy
        with vine-must,
        'To Naxos? Yes, we'll take you to
        Naxos,
Cum' along lad.' 'Not that way!'
'Aye, that way is Naxos.'
        And I said: 'It's a straight ship.'
And an ex-convict out of Italy
        knocked me into the fore-stays,
(He was wanted for manslaughter in
        Tuscany)
        And the whole twenty against me,   50
Mad for a little slave money.
        And they took her out of Scios
And off her course . . .
        And the boy came to, again, with
        the racket,
And looked out over the bows,
        and to eastward, and to the Naxos
        passage.
        God-sleight then, god-sleight:
        Ship stock fast in sea-swirl,
Ivy upon the oars, King Pentheus,
        grapes with no seed but sea-foam,   60
Ivy in scupper-hole.
Aye, I, Acœtes, stood there,
        and the god stood by me,
Water cutting under the keel,
Sea-break from stern forrards,
        wake running off from the bow,
And where was gunwale, there now was
        vine-trunk,
And tenthril where cordage had been,
        grape-leaves on the rowlocks,
Heavy vine on the oarshafts,   70
And, out of nothing, a breathing,
        hot breath on my ankles,
Beasts like shadows in glass,
        a furred tail upon nothingness.

Lynx-purr, and heathery smell of beasts,
    where tar smell had been,
Sniff and pad-foot of beasts,
    eye-glitter out of black air.
The sky overshot, dry, with no tempest,
Sniff and pad-foot of beasts,   80
    fur brushing my knee-skin,
Rustle of airy sheaths,
    dry forms in the *æther*.
And the ship like a keel in ship-yard,
    slung like an ox in smith's sling,
Ribs stuck fast in the ways,
    grape-cluster over pin-rack,
    void air taking pelt.
Lifeless air become sinewed,
    feline leisure of panthers,   90
Leopards sniffing the grape shoots by
    scupper-hole,
Crouched panthers by fore-hatch,
And the sea blue-deep about us,
    green-ruddy in shadows,
And Lyæus: 'From now, Acœtes, my
    altars,
Fearing no bondage,
    fearing no cat of the wood,
Safe with my lynxes,
    feeding grapes to my leopards,
Olibanum is my incense,   100
    the vines grow in my homage.'

The back-swell now smooth in the rudder-
    chains,
Black snout of a porpoise
    where Lycabs had been,
Fish-scales on the oarsmen.
    And I worship.
I have seen what I have seen.
    When they brought the boy I said:
'He has a god in him,
    though I do not know which god.'   110
And they kicked me into the fore-stays.
I have seen what I have seen:
    Medon's face like the face of a dory,
Arms shrunk into fins. And you, Pentheus,
Had as well listen to Tiresias, and to
    Cadmus,
    or your luck will go out of you.
Fish-scales over groin muscles,
    lynx-purr amid sea . . .

And of a later year,
    pale in the wine-red algæ,   120
If you will lean over the rock,
    the coral face under wave-tinge,
Rose-paleness under water-shift,
    Ileuthyeria, fair Dafne of sea-bords,
The swimmer's arms turned to branches,
Who will say in what year,
    fleeing what band of tritons,
The smooth brows, seen, and half seen,
    now ivory stillness.

And So-shu churned in the sea, So-shu
    also,   130
    using the long moon for a churn-
    stick . . .
Lithe turning of water,
    sinews of Poseidon,
Black azure and hyaline,
    glass wave over Tyro,
Close cover, unstillness,
    bright welter of wave-cords,
Then quiet water,
    quiet in the buff sands,
Sea-fowl stretching wing-joints,   140
    splashing in rock-hollows and
    sand-hollows
In the wave-runs by the half-dune;
Glass-glint of wave in the tide-rips against
    sunlight,
    pallor of Hesperus,
Gray peak of the wave,
    wave, colour of grape's pulp.

Olive gray in the near,
    far, smoke gray of the rock-slide,
Salmon-pink wings of the fish-hawk
    cast gray shadows in water,   150
The tower like a one-eyed great goose
    cranes up out of the olive-grove,

And we have heard the fauns chiding
    Proteus
    in the smell of hay under the olive-
    trees,
And the frogs singing against the fauns
    in the half-light.
And . . .

1924

HILDA DOOLITTLE
(H.D.)
1886–

A NOTE ON POETRY

GLANCING at random over the sheaf of poems in this selection, I fall on 'Lethe' and 'Song.' Those, I know, I wrote in Cornwall, spring-summer 1918. I turn next to 'Fragment 36' and 'The Islands.' Those, definitely, were written at Corfe Castle, in 1916, the year conscription came in. The season was indefinite—rain beat against a high dormer window in a picturesque cobbled street, under the famous ruins of a castle where a young king was done to death while actually reaching, I believe, for the ceremonial stirrup-cup. Anyhow, that town was reputably haunted, as was the actual house I stayed in, in Cornwall.

Poetry? I am to say, why I wrote, when I wrote and how I wrote these fragments. I am to state this simply, for people who may not be altogether in sympathy with my own sort of work. I wish I could do that. I am so afraid I can not. But the inner world of imagination, the ivory tower, where poets presumedly do live, in memory, does stand stark with the sun-lit isles around it, while battle and din of battle and the whole dreary, tragic spectacle of our times seems blurred and sodden and not to be recalled, save in moments of repudiation, historical necessity. I had not the power to repudiate at that time nor to explain. But I do so well remember one shock—a letter from Miss Monroe,[1] timed nicely to arrive to greet me when I had staggered home, exhausted and half-asphyxiated. (I and my companion had been shoved off the pavements, protesting to a special policeman that we would rather be killed on the pavement than suffocated in the underground.) Miss Monroe was one of the first to print and recognize my talent. But how strangely, farcically blind to our predicament! The letter suggested with really staggeringly inept solicitude that H.D. would do so well,—maybe, finally,—if

[1] Harriet Monroe (1860–1936) was the founder and first editor of *Poetry: A Magazine of Verse*, foremost among the many little magazines which were the chief outlet for the renaissance of poetry in the English language during the second decade of this century.

she could get into 'life,' into the rhythm of our time, in touch with events, and so on and so on and so on. I don't know what else she said. I was laughing too much.

Ivory tower?

That was and is still, I believe with many, the final indictment of this sort of poetry.

We don't live. We don't see life. And so on.

In order to speak adequately of my poetry and its aims, I must, you see, drag in a whole deracinated epoch. Perhaps specifically, I might say that the house next door was struck one night. We came home and simply waded through glass, while wind from now unshuttered windows made the house a barn, an unprotected dug-out. What does that sort of shock do to the mind, the imagination—not solely of myself, but of an epoch? One of the group found some pleasure in the sight of the tilted shelves and the books tumbled on the floor. He gave a decisive foot-ball kick with his army boot to the fattest volume. It happened actually to be Browning. He demanded dramatically, 'what is the use of all this—now?' To me, *Fortu* and the *yellow-melon flower* answered by existing. They were in another space, another dimension, never so clear as at that very moment. The *unexpected isle in the far seas* remained. Remains.

Life?

Poetry?

Times and places?

'Leda' was done at the same time as 'Lethe.' Lotus-land, all this. It is nostalgia for a lost land. I call it Hellas. I might, psychologically just as well, have listed the Casco Bay islands off the coast of Maine, but I called my islands Rhodes, Samos and Cos. They are symbols. And, symbolically, the first island of memory was dredged away or lost, like a miniature Atlantis. It was a thickly wooded island in the Lehigh river and, believe it or not, was actually named Calypso's island.

I don't know whether I finally shaped 'Lais,' 'Helen' and 'Fragment 113' in London or in Vaud. I was back and forth those years, usually tempering my dash across the continent with a day or so in Paris. There I saw a few people, picked up a few threads. Those poems belong to 1923-24, roughly. As to the song from the play 'Hippolytus Temporizes,' that is more difficult. I had made a few rough notes and jotted down a few metres in 1920 in the Ionian island of Corfu. I didn't get the play under way or shaped to my satisfaction till many years later. I think I made a rough outline in Vaud, and finally in London (I remember it was a particularly stuffy, dank, damp summer) I got the play finished. So the actual song might be dated Corfu, spring 1920, or London, summer 1926. The times of publication of this and the others were naturally different.

This leaves the early group, 'O, wind,' 'Orchard,' 'Sea Gods,' 'Oread,' 'The Pool.' I let my pencil run riot in those early days of my apprenticeship, in an old-fashioned school copy-book—when I could get one. Then I would select from many pages of automatic or pseudo-automatic writing the few lines that satisfied me. I was doing this anywhere, my first days in a dark London, autumn 1912, then in Italy where I spent that winter, Capri especially, where I had some time and space and found the actual geographical Greece for the first time— Syren isle of the Odyssey. I can not give actual dates to these early finished fragments, but they would be just pre-war and at latest, early-war period. Finished fragments? Yes, I suppose they are that— stylistic slashings, definitely self-conscious, though, as I say, impelled by some inner conflict.

The 'lost' world of the classics and the neo-classics is the world of childhood. 'What are the islands to me?' They are, I suppose, an inner region of defence, escape; these are the poems of escapism—if there is any such word. And of memory— suppressed memory, maybe. (And what about the mother of the Muses? Mnemosene, if I remember?) Actual memory, repressed memory, desire to escape, desire to create (music), intellectual curiosity, a wish to make real to myself what is most real, the fragmentary pages of the early Greek poets,—to tear, if it be even the barest fragment of vibrant, electric parchment from hands not always worthy to touch, to fingers whose sterile 'intellectuality' is so often a

sort of inverted curse of Midas—these are some of the ingredients of my poetry. Times, places, dates don't seem so much to matter. Yet here are the times and places of these fragments, as well as I can time and place them.

And most dramatically, last Sunday I was called to the telephone. 'Your islands were on the air,' I was informed, 'and read beautifully.' 'Where?' I asked. 'Radio City, just a few minutes ago,' was the answer; 'didn't you hear your poem?' No. I did not. I should have liked, in time, in actuality to have heard my 'islands on the air,' here in this island, to have made that link with those other islands, Calypso's island or Catalpa island as some called it, vanished Atlantis in a river in Pennsylvania, sea-islands off the coast of Maine, Aegean islands sensed in passing and the actual Ionian island of Corfu, the early Capri, Syren island of Magna Graecia, and specifically, that island, noted in Phoenician days for its tin (a track ran past the house where I stayed in Cornwall, reputedly first used by the mules carrying tin from the mines to the Phoenician galleys)— England. I should like to have heard my 'islands on the air,' here in this island, the latest in my phantasy of islands, final link and perhaps 'clasp of the white necklace.'

1938

December 12, 1937
New York City

FROM GARDEN

2

O WIND, rend open the heat,
cut apart the heat,
rend it to tatters.

Fruit cannot drop
through this thick air—
fruit cannot fall into heat
that presses up and blunts
the points of pears
and rounds the grapes.

Cut the heat—
plough through it,
turning it on either side
of your path.

1912–1914   1916

ORCHARD

I saw the first pear
as it fell—
the honey-seeking, golden-banded,
the yellow swarm
was not more fleet than I,
(spare us from loveliness)
and I fell prostrate
crying:
you have flayed us
with your blossoms,   10
spare us the beauty
of fruit-trees.

The honey-seeking
paused not,
the air thundered their song,
and I alone was prostrate.

O rough-hewn
god of the orchard,
I bring you an offering—
do you, alone unbeautiful,   20
son of the god,
spare us from loveliness:

these fallen hazel-nuts,
stripped late of their green sheaths,
grapes, red-purple,
their berries
dripping with wine,
pomegranates already broken,
and shrunken figs
and quinces untouched,   30
I bring you as offering.

1912–1914   1916

SEA GODS

1

They say there is no hope—
sand—drift—rocks—rubble of the sea—
the broken hulk of a ship,
hung with shreds of rope,
pallid under the cracked pitch.

They say there is no hope
to conjure you—
no whip of the tongue to anger you—
no hate of words
you must rise to refute.   10

They say you are twisted by the sea,
you are cut apart

by wave-break upon wave-break,
that you are misshapen by the sharp
    rocks,
broken by the rasp and after-rasp.

That you are cut, torn, mangled,
torn by the stress and beat,
no stronger than the strips of sand
along your ragged beach.

2

But we bring violets,   20
great masses—single, sweet,
wood-violets, stream-violets,
violets from a wet marsh.

Violets in clumps from hills,
tufts with earth at the roots,
violets tugged from rocks,
blue violets, moss, cliff, river-violets.

Yellow violets' gold,
burnt with a rare tint—
violets like red ash   30
among tufts of grass.

We bring deep-purple
bird-foot violets.

We bring the hyacinth-violet,
sweet, bare, chill to the touch—
and violets whiter than the in-rush
of your own white surf.

3

For you will come,
you will yet haunt men in ships,
you will trail across the fringe of strait   40
and circle the jagged rocks.

You will trail across the rocks
and wash them with your salt,
you will curl between sand-hills—
you will thunder along the cliff—
break—retreat—get fresh strength—
gather and pour weight upon the beach.

You will draw back,
and the ripple on the sand-shelf
will be witness of your track.   50
O privet-white, you will paint
the lintel of wet sand with froth.

You will bring myrrh-bark
and drift laurel-wood from hot coasts!

when you hurl high—high—
we will answer with a shout.

For you will come,
you will come,
you will answer our taut hearts,
you will break the lie of men's thoughts,   60
and cherish and shelter us.
1912–1914   1916

OREAD

WHIRL up, sea—
whirl your pointed pines,
splash your great pines
on our rocks,
hurl your green over us,
cover us with your pools of fir.
1912–1914   1924

THE POOL

ARE you alive?
I touch you.
You quiver like a sea-fish.
I cover you with my net.
What are you—banded one?
1912–1914   1924

LEDA

WHERE the slow river
meets the tide,
a red swan lifts red wings
and darker beak,
and underneath the purple down
of his soft breast
uncurls his coral feet.

Through the deep purple
of the dying heat
of sun and mist,   10
the level ray of sun-beam
has caressed
the lily with dark breast,
and flecked with richer gold
its golden crest.

Where the slow lifting
of the tide,
floats into the river
and slowly drifts
among the reeds,   20
and lifts the yellow flags,
he floats
where tide and river meet.

Ah kingly kiss—
no more regret
nor old deep memories
to mar the bliss;
where the low sedge is thick,
the gold day-lily
outspreads and rests   30
beneath soft fluttering
of red swan wings
and the warm quivering
of the red swan's breast.
1916   1921

THE ISLANDS

I

WHAT are the islands to me,
what is Greece,
what is Rhodes, Samos, Chios,
what is Paros facing west,
what is Crete?

What is Samothrace,
rising like a ship,
what is Imbros rending the storm-
    waves
with its breast?

What is Naxos, Paros, Milos,   10
what the circle about Lycia,
what, the Cyclades'
white necklace?

What is Greece—
Sparta, rising like a rock,
Thebes, Athens,
what is Corinth?

What is Euboia
with its island violets,
what is Euboia, spread with grass,   20
set with swift shoals,
what is Crete?

What are the islands to me,
what is Greece?

2

What can love of land give to me
that you have not—
what do the tall Spartans know,
and gentler Attic folk?

What has Sparta and her women
more than this?   30

What are the islands to me
if you are lost—
what is Naxos, Tinos, Andros,
and Delos, the clasp
of the white necklace?

3

What can love of land give to me
that you have not,
what can love of strife break in me
that you have not?

Though Sparta enter Athens,   40
Thebes wrack Sparta,
each changes as water,
salt, rising to wreak terror
and fall back.

4

'What has love of land given to you
that I have not?'

I have questioned Tyrians
where they sat
on the black ships,
weighted with rich stuffs,   50
I have asked the Greeks
from the white ships,
and Greeks from ships whose hulks
lay on the wet sand, scarlet
with great beaks.
I have asked bright Tyrians
and tall Greeks—
'what has love of land given you?'
And they answered—'peace.'

5

But beauty is set apart,   60
beauty is cast by the sea,
a barren rock,
beauty is set about
with wrecks of ships,
upon our coast, death keeps
the shallows—death waits
clutching toward us
from the deeps.

Beauty is set apart;
the winds that slash its beach,   70
swirl the coarse sand
upward toward the rocks.

Beauty is set apart
from the islands
and from Greece.

6

In my garden
the winds have beaten
the ripe lilies;
in my garden, the salt
has wilted the first flakes   80
of young narcissus,
and the lesser hyacinth,
and the salt has crept
under the leaves of the white hyacinth.

In my garden
even the wind-flowers lie flat,
broken by the wind at last.

7

What are the islands to me
if you are lost,
what is Paros to me   90
if your eyes draw back,
what is Milos
if you take fright of beauty,
terrible, torturous, isolated,
a barren rock?

What is Rhodes, Crete,
what is Paros facing west,
what, white Imbros?

What are the islands to me
if you hesitate,   100
what is Greece if you draw back
from the terror
and cold splendour of song
and its bleak sacrifice?
1916   1921

SAPPHIC FRAGMENTS

36

I know not what to do:
my mind is divided.
                            —Sappho.

I KNOW not what to do,
my mind is reft:
is song's gift best?
is love's gift loveliest?
I know not what to do,
now sleep has pressed
weight on your eyelids.

Shall I break your rest,
devouring, eager?

is love's gift best?   10
nay, song's the loveliest:
yet were you lost,
what rapture
could I take from song?
what song were left?

I know not what to do:
to turn and slake
the rage that burns,
with my breath burn
and trouble your cool breath?   20
so shall I turn and take
snow in my arms?
(is love's gift best?)
yet flake on flake
of snow were comfortless,
did you lie wondering,
wakened yet unawake.

Shall I turn and take
comfortless snow within my arms?
press lips to lips   30
that answer not,
press lips to flesh
that shudders not nor breaks?

Is love's gift best?
shall I turn and slake
all the wild longing?
O I am eager for you!
as the Pleiads shake
white light in whiter water
so shall I take you?   40

My mind is quite divided,
my minds hesitate,
so perfect matched,
I know not what to do:
each strives with each
as two white wrestlers
standing for a match,
ready to turn and clutch
yet never shake muscle nor nerve nor
    tendon;
so my mind waits   50
to grapple with my mind,
yet I lie quiet,
I would seem at rest.

I know not what to do:
strain upon strain,
sound surging upon sound
makes my brain blind;
as a wave-line may wait to fall

yet (waiting for its falling)
still the wind may take   60
from off its crest,
white flake on flake of foam,
that rises,
seeming to dart and pulse
and rend the light,
so my mind hesitates
above the passion
quivering yet to break,
so my mind hesitates
above my mind,   70
listening to song's delight.

I know not what to do:
will the sound break,
rending the night
with rift on rift of rose
and scattered light?
will the sound break at last
as the wave hesitant,
or will the whole night pass
and I lie listening awake?   80
1916   1924

113
Neither honey nor bee for me.
    —Sappho.

NOT honey,
not the plunder of the bee
from meadow or sand-flower
or mountain bush;
from winter-flower or shoot
born of the later heat:
not honey, not the sweet
stain on the lips and teeth:
not honey, not the deep
plunge of soft belly   10
and the clinging of the gold-edged
pollen-dusted feet;

Not so—
though rapture blind my eyes,
and hunger crisp
dark and inert my mouth,
not honey, not the south,
not the tall stalk
of red twin-lilies,
nor light branch of fruit tree
caught in flexible light branch;   20

Not honey, not the south;
ah flower of purple iris,
flower of white,

or of the iris, withering the grass—
for fleck of the sun's fire,
gathers such heat and power,
that shadow-print is light,
cast through the petals
of the yellow iris flower;

Not iris—old desire—old passion—   30
old forgetfulness—old pain—
not this, nor any flower,
but if you turn again,
seek strength of arm and throat,
touch as the god;
neglect the lyre-note;
knowing that you shall feel
about the frame,
no trembling of the string
but heat, more passionate   40
of bone and the white shell
and fiery tempered steel.

                                    1921

SONG

You are as gold
as the half-ripe grain
that merges to gold again,
as white as the white rain
that beats through
the half-opened flowers
of the great flower tufts
thick on the black limbs
of an Illyrian apple bough.

Can honey distill such fragrance   10
as your bright hair—
for your face is as fair as rain,
yet as rain that lies clear
on white honey-comb,
lends radiance to the white wax,
so your hair on your brow
casts light for a shadow.

1918   1921

LETHE

Nor skin nor hide nor fleece
      Shall cover you,
Nor curtain of crimson nor fine
Shelter of cedar-wood be over you,
      Nor the fir-tree
      Nor the pine.

Nor sight of whin nor gorse
      Nor river-yew,
Nor fragrance of flowering bush,

Nor wailing of reed-bird to waken you,   10
      Nor of linnet,
      Nor of thrush.

Nor word nor touch nor sight
      Of lover, you
Shall long through the night but for this:
The roll of the full tide to cover you
      Without question,
      Without kiss.

1918   1924

LAIS [1]

Let her who walks in Paphos
take the glass,
let Paphos take the mirror
and the work of frosted fruit,
gold apples set
with silver apple-leaf,
white leaf of silver
wrought with vein of gilt.

Let Paphos lift the mirror,
let her look   10
into the polished centre of the disk.

Let Paphos take the mirror;
did she press
flowerlet of flame-flower
to the lustrous white
of the white forehead?
did the dark veins beat
a deeper purple
than the wine-deep tint
of the dark flower?   20

Did she deck black hair
one evening, with the winter-white
flower of the winter-berry,
did she look (reft of her lover)
at a face gone white
under the chaplet
of white virgin-breath?

Lais, exultant, tyrannizing Greece,
Lais who kept her lovers in the porch,
lover on lover waiting,   30
(but to creep
where the robe brushed the threshold
where still sleeps Lais)
so she creeps, Lais,

1 'The poem "Lais" has in italics a translation of the
Plato epigram [Anthol.Pal.,vi,1] in the Greek Anthology.' Author's note, Collected Poems (N.Y., 1925), 214.

to lay her mirror at the feet
of her who reigns in Paphos.

Lais has left her mirror
for she sees no longer in its depth
the Lais' self
that laughed exultant   40
tyrannizing Greece.

Lais has left her mirror,
for she weeps no longer,
finding in its depth,
a face, but other
than dark flame and white
feature of perfect marble.

Lais has left her mirror,
(so one wrote)
to her who reigns in Paphos;   50
Lais who laughed a tyrant over Greece,
Lais who turned the lovers from the porch,
that swarm for whom now
Lais has no use;
Lais is now no lover of the glass,
seeing no more the face as once it was,
wishing to see that face and finding this.
1923–1924   1924

HELEN

ALL Greece hates
the still eyes in the white face,
the lustre as of olives
where she stands,
and the white hands.

All Greece reviles
the wan face when she smiles,

hating it deeper still
when it grows wan and white,
remembering past enchantments   10
and past ills.

Greece sees unmoved,
God's daughter, born of love,
the beauty of cool feet
and slenderest knees,
could love indeed the maid,
only if she were laid,
white ash amid funereal cypresses.
1923–1924   1924

FROM HIPPOLYTUS TEMPORIZES

WHERE is the nightingale,
in what myrrh-wood and dim?
O let the night come black
for we would conjure back
all that enchanted him,
        all that enchanted him.

Where is the bird of fire,
in what packed hedge of rose?
in what roofed ledge of flower?
no other creature knows   10
what magic lurks within,
        what magic lurks within.

Bird, bird, bird, bird we cry,
hear, pity us in pain,
hearts break in the sunlight,
hearts break in daylight rain,
only night heals again,
        only night heals again.
1920–1926   1927

JOHN GOULD FLETCHER

1886–

GREEN SYMPHONY [1]

I

THE glittering leaves of the rhododendrons
Balance and vibrate in the cool air;
While in the sky above them
White clouds chase each other.

Like scampering rabbits,
Flashes of sunlight sweep the lawn;
They fling in passing
Patterns of shadow,
Golden and green.

1 'The material in the "Symphonies" is autobiographic;
they were printed in the order as written, with the exception of "Midsummer Dreams" ("Symphony in
White and Blue") and "Poppies of the Red Year"

("Symphony in Scarlet") which come from the summer following the year 1914 when all the others were
written. Many elements went to their making. The
vivid, luminous colour of Gauguin—the vowel-nuances
of Mallarmé—the shifting, rhythmic diversity of
Debussy—all these I tried to combine with their
emotional and tonal patterns. The "Green Symphony"

With long cascades of laughter,   10
The mating birds dart and swoop to the turf:
'Mid their mad trillings
Glints the gay sun behind the trees.

Down there are deep blue lakes:
Orange blossom droops in the water.

In the tower of the winds,
All the bells are set adrift:
Jingling
For the dawn.

Thin fluttering streamers   20
Of breeze lash through the swaying boughs,
Palely expectant
The earth receives the slanting rain.

I am a glittering raindrop
Hugged close by the cool rhododendron.
I am a daisy starring
The exquisite curves of the close-cropped
         turf.

The glittering leaves of the rhododendron
Are shaken like blue-green blades of grass,
Flickering, cracking, falling: 30
Splintering in a million fragments.

The wind runs laughing up the slope
Stripping off handfuls of wet green leaves,
To fling in peoples' faces.
Wallowing on the daisy-powdered turf,
Clutching at the sunlight,
Cavorting in the shadow.

Like baroque pearls,
Like cloudy emeralds,
The clouds and the trees clash together;   40
Whirling and swirling,
In the tumult
Of the spring,
And the wind.

2

The trees splash the sky with their fingers,
A restless green rout of stars.

With whirling movement
They swing their boughs

is peculiarly a poem of spring—spring seen in three
aspects: morning, noon, and afternoon fading to evening. In general, the "Symphonies" have no meaning
beyond the primary statement of the moods they recall. The identification of self and object was, in them,
deliberately made as close as possible.' Author's note.

About their stems:
Planes on planes of light and shadow   50
Pass among them,
Opening fan-like to fall.

The trees are like a sea;
Tossing,
Trembling,
Roaring,
Wallowing,
Darting their long green flickering fronds
         up at the sky,
Spotted with white blossom-spray.

The trees are roofs: 60
Hollow caverns of cool blue shadow,
Solemn arches
In the afternoons.
The whole vast horizon
In terrace beyond terrace,
Pinnacle above pinnacle,
Lifts to the sky
Serrated ranks of green on green.

They caress the roofs with their fingers,
They sprawl about the river to look into it;
Up the hill they come   71
Gesticulating challenge:
They cower together
In dark valleys;
They yearn out over the fields.

Enamelled domes
Tumble upon the grass,
Crashing in ruin
Quiet at last.

The trees lash the sky with their leaves,   80
Uneasily shaking their dark green
         manes.

3

Far let the voices of the mad wild birds be
         calling me,
I will abide in this forest of pines.

When the wind blows
Battling through the forest,
I hear it distantly,
The crash of a perpetual sea.

When the rain falls,
I watch silver spears slanting downwards
From pale river-pools of sky,   90
Enclosed in dark fronds.

When the sun shines,
I weave together distant branches till they
    enclose mighty circles,
I sway to the movement of hooded
    summits,
I swim leisurely in deep blue seas of
    air.

I hug the smooth bark of stately red pillars
And with cones carefully scattered
I mark the progression of dark dial-
    shadows
Flung diagonally downwards through the
    afternoon.

This turf is not like turf: 100
It is a smooth dry carpet of velvet,
Embroidered with brown patterns of
    needles and cones.
These trees are not like trees:
They are innumerable feathery pagoda-
    umbrellas,
Stiffly ungracious to the wind,
Teetering on red-lacquered stems.

In the evening I listen to the winds' lisping,
While the conflagrations of the sunset
    flicker and clash behind me,
Flamboyant crenellations of glory amid the
    charred ebony boles.

In the night the fiery nightingales   110
Shall clash and trill through the silence:
Like the voices of mermaids crying
From the sea.

Long ago has the moon whelmed this
    uncompleted temple.
Stars swim like gold fish far above the black
    arches.

Far let the timid feet of dawn fly to catch
    me:
I will abide in this forest of pines:
For I have unveiled naked beauty,
And the things that she whispered to me in
    the darkness,
Are buried deep in my heart.   120

Now let the black tops of the pine-trees
    break like a spent wave,
Against the grey sky:
These are tombs and memorials and tem-
    ples and altars sun-kindled for me.

1914   1916

DOWN THE MISSISSIPPI [1]

I

Embarkation

DULL masses of dense green,
The forests range their sombre platforms;
Between them silently, like a spirit,
The river finds its own mysterious path.

Loosely the river sways out, backward,
    forward,
Always fretting the outer side;
Shunning the invisible focus of each
    crescent,
Seeking to spread into shining loops over
    fields.

Like an enormous serpent, dilating,
    uncoiling,
Displaying a broad scaly back of earth-
    smeared gold;   10
Swaying out sinuously between the dull
    motionless forests,
As molten metal might glide down the lip
    of a vase of dark bronze;

It goes, while the steamboat drifting out
    upon it,
Seems now to be floating not only outwards
    but upwards;
In the flight of a petal detached and
    gradually moving skyward
Above the pink explosion of the calyx of the
    dawn.

2

Heat

As if the sun had trodden down the
    sky,
Until it holds living air no more, but only
    humid vapour,

1 'Both these poems ["Midsummer Dreams" and
"Poppies of the Red Year"], in conformity with my
original intentions in the "symphonies," were stated in
terms of subjective vision, rather than as terms of
objective fact. . . . With these two final fusions of
dream and reality I finally put the entire series of
"Symphonies" behind me, and entered a fresh phase
of development. . . . On the trip down I had written
the series of poems, "Down the Mississippi," in which
I gave my new technique of description derived
from natural objects themselves, rather than from my
feelings about them, a full chance to show what it
could do.' Fletcher *Life Is My Song* (N.Y., 1937),
210–11.

Heat pressing upon earth with irresistible
    langour,
Turns all the solid forest into half-liquid
    smudge.   20

The heavy clouds like cargo-boats strain
    slowly against its current;
And the flickering of the haze is like the
    thunder of ten thousand paddles
Against the heavy wall of the horizon, pale-
    blue and utterly windless,
Whereon the sun hangs motionless, a
    brassy disc of flame.

3

Full Moon

Flinging its arc of silver bubbles, quickly
    shifts the moon
From side to side of us as we go down its
    path;
I sit on the deck at midnight and watch it
    slipping and sliding,
Under my tilted chair, like a thin film of
    spilt water.

It is weaving a river of light to take the place
    of this river;
A river where we shall drift all night, then
    come to rest in its shallows;   30
And then I shall wake from my drowsiness
    and look down from some dim
    treetop
Over white lakes of cotton, like moonfields
    on every side.

4

The Moon's Orchestra

When the moon lights up
Its dull red campfire through the
    trees;
And floats out, like a white bal-
    loon,
Into the blue cup of the night, borne by a
    casual breeze;
The moon-orchestra then begins to
    stir.
Jiggle of fiddles commence their crazy
    dance in the darkness.
Crickets churr
Against the stark reiteration of the rusty
    flutes which frogs   40
Puff at from rotted logs
In the swamp.

And then the moon begins her dance of
    frozen pomp
Over the lightly quivering floor of the flat
    and mournful river.
Her white feet slightly twist and swirl.
She is a mad girl
In an old unlit ball room
Whose walls, half-guessed at through the
    gloom,
Are hung with the rusty crape of stark
    black cypress
Which show, through gaps and tatters, red
    stains half hidden away.   50

5

The Stevedores

Frieze of warm bronze that glides with
    catlike movements
Over the gangplank poised and yet
    awaiting,
The sinewy thudding rhythm of forty
    shuffling feet
Falling like muffled drumbeats on the
    stillness.
O roll the cotton down,
Roll, roll the cotton down,
From the further side of Jordan,
O roll the cotton down!

And the river waits,
The river listens,   60
Chuckling little banjo-notes that break
    with a flop on the stillness;
And by the low dark shed that holds the
    heavy freights,
Two lonely cypress trees stand up and
    point with stiffened fingers
Far southward where a single chimney
    stands out aloof in the sky.

6

Night Landing

After the whistle's roar has bellowed and
    shuddered,
Shaking the sleeping town and the
    somnolent river,
The deep toned floating of the pilot's bell
Suddenly warns the engines.

They stop like heart-beats that abruptly
    stop,
The shore glides to us, in a wide low
    curve.   70

And then—supreme revelation of the
    river—
The tackle is loosed—the long gangplank
    swings outwards—
And poised at the end of it, half-naked
    beneath the searchlight,
A blue-black negro with gleaming teeth
    waits for his chance to leap.

7
The Silence

There is a silence I carry about with me
    always;
A silence perpetual, for it is self-created;
A silence of heat, of water, of unchecked
    fruitfulness
Through which each year the heavy
    harvests bloom, and burst and fall.

Deep, matted green silence of my South,
Often within the push and scorn of great
    cities,   80
I have seen that mile-wide waste of water
    swaying out to you,
And on its current glimmering, I am going
    to the sea.

There is a silence I have achieved: I have
    walked beyond its threshold;
I know it is without horizons, boundless,
    fathomless, perfect.
And some day maybe, far away,
I will curl up in it at last and sleep an
    endless sleep.

1915   1921

A NOTE ON POLYPHONIC PROSE

In a recent essay on Shelley, the English critic Herbert Read has said, 'Poetry is mainly a function of language—the exploitation of a medium, a vocal and mental material, in the interests of a personal mood or emotion, or of the thoughts evoked by such moods and emotions. I do not think we can say much more about it; according to our sensitivity we recognize its success. The rest of our reasoning about it is either mere prejudice, ethical anxiety, or academic pride.' Earlier, in one of his critical volumes, the same critic pointed out that there is no hard and fast dividing line to be drawn between poetry and prose. The dividing line, if one is to be sought, must be found not in the form employed, but in the quality of the experience conveyed: 'Poetry is intensive experience, prose is extensive experience.' These remarks, with which I am entirely in agreement, will serve, I think, to illuminate much that has happened in the development of poetry in the English language for the last twenty-five years, including the still vexed question as to the place to be occupied by the unusual form known as polyphonic prose.

The period from 1913 to 1929 was, in England, and still more in America, immensely fecund in technical poetic experiment. It has been followed by a period in which the relation of the poets' ideas to tradition, to society, to dogmatic theology, or to schemes for social justice has been the chief topic debated. As a result both English and American poetry have become progressively more and more intellectualized, while the rich repertory of new forms which the poets, notably the Imagists, of the earlier years evolved has been somewhat overlooked. Whether the process of intellectualization has now reached its limit, it is too early as yet to say. But it is still worth while to reflect for a moment on some of the poetic novelties of twenty years ago and to evaluate their potentialities.

Polyphonic prose is an attempt to employ some of the most time-hallowed rhythmic devices of poetry, such as rhyme, refrain, assonance and alliteration, for the sake of rendering more vividly thereby a range of experience that lies halfway between the domain of poetry and that of prose. In order to describe this range of experience clearly and accurately, one has to go back and examine closely the materials out of which most long poems are composed—inasmuch as polyphonic prose is in itself a form more suitable to extended experience than the stricter kind of Imagism. Somewhat over a century ago Poe declared that the long poem, as such, was a contradiction in terms: being composed of long passages of versified prose interspersed with other passages of poetry. Since then other theorists have raised the issue in another form and have debated the question of 'pure poetry.' Just how much pure poetry exists in any language, and where may it be found? This question, however, as to whether 'pure poetry' does exist, and if so for how long in poems of an extended type, need not detain us. There is sufficient agreement among the critics of all schools that one of the leading character-istics of poetry as distinguished from prose is its compressed, intensive utterance. Or, as T. S. Eliot once remarked, one of the chief reasons for writing poetry today is that it saves space.

Polyphonic prose represents the first at-tempt in English to convey intense poetic experience within a form which takes as its basis that which academic critics, to dis-tinguish it from ordinary prose or from the elaborate and subtly varied prose of Sir Thomas Brown and De Quincey, have called 'oratorical prose.' The difference be-tween this type of 'oratorical prose,' in-tended to be spoken aloud, and ordinary prose is that in the former the cadences are in general more regular and more marked. Anyone who will take the trouble to read aloud some famous oration of the past, such as Webster's reply to Hayne, or Burke's in-dictment of Warren Hastings, will find therein long passages which scan rhythmi-cally. The New England writers of the last century knew this very well, and con-tinually employed passages which in effect are blank verse written as prose, whenever they wanted to be especially eloquent and poetical. One can find such passages in Melville and Hawthorne; and the famous first preface to Walt Whitman's *Leaves of Grass* could be transposed entirely into an oratorical type of versification, akin to Whitman's own, with practically no loss. The only difference, strictly speaking, be-tween such passages and polyphonic prose is that these earlier attempts to write a more poetical and vocal type of prose tend for the most part to recall English blank verse; while the later form of polyphonic prose admits no such constancy. It at-tempts to follow as its basis a rhythm that is kept continually shifting between verse and prose.

It is no derogation to the form itself to say that it was discovered entirely by ac-cident. Miss Amy Lowell, to whom the dis-covery is entirely due, became interested in the form through her admiration for the *Ballades Françaises* of M. Paul Fort. As she pointed out in her introduction to *Can Grande's Castle*, M. Fort's work constantly interspers passages written in prose with others written in the regular classic French measure, the Alexandrine. Inasmuch as the Alexandrine itself is not an easy rhythm for ears attuned to English to sustain over long periods, Miss Lowell realized that some other English rhythm must be devised. Iambic pentameter, the usual alternative, was rejected by Miss Lowell, as she her-self stated, because it was difficult to de-part from and go back to; so she finally hit upon the expedient of basing her form 'on the long, flowing cadence of oratorical prose.'

The two examples printed in this an-thology may give some idea of the possi-bilities of the range and the flexibility in-herent in the form. To take Miss Lowell's contribution, 'The Cross-Roads,' first: Here we have a dramatic narrative, owing some-thing to Browning's dramatic narratives in its mingling of suspense and atmosphere and vivid movement from one episode to another; but owing still more to Miss Lowell's own command over the narrative style, so manifest in many of her other poems; and constantly recalling by its 're-currence of a dominating thought or image, coming in irregularly and in varying words,' the effect of a ballad. My own 'Clipper-Ships' is somewhat different. It attempts to display a verbal panorama of the whole Clipper-Ship era of New England, with a marked refrain based on the combination of an old sea-chantey and the single domi-nating image of the ship, 'beautiful as a tiered cloud.' My poem in short is a brief descriptive epic, while Miss Lowell's is a dramatic ballad.

The form of polyphonic prose is thus flexible enough to permit a considerable variety of subject matter. I can see no rea-son why good polyphonic prose poems should not be written dealing with themes drawn from experiences of love, of personal bereavement, or of religion. But the sur-charging of the prose paragraph with all the possible effects of rhyme, assonance, alliteration and refrain which the form it-self implies makes it only applicable to poems which deal with states of high emotion rather than intellectual tension. I cannot imagine any ultra-modern intellec-tualist-poet using this form for his meta-physical cogitations on the meaning of life, death, the Catholic dogma, or the proletarian revolution.

Since Miss Lowell and I first began to write in polyphonic prose, not many poets have cared to continue with the experiment. It would seem that there is a considerable and general prejudice against the acceptance as poetical of any form which appears typographically to be prose, even though it may possess in ways capable of great variation so many characteristics of fine poetry. Miss Lowell herself referred to this typographical difficulty in her discussion of the form; but she pointed out that if polyphonic prose is read aloud from the page the difficulty immediately disappears. This is indeed the case, though I also fancy that most poetry when not read aloud from the page similarly loses a considerable part of its effect. Nevertheless, polyphonic prose does demand a special effort on the part of the reader to follow. But so does all fine poetry!

Various prose writers seeking for an extension of prose into realms beyond the naturalistic have recently put into their novels long passages of lyrical and emotional description that recall the devices first discovered by the writers of polyphonic prose. One might cite here Thomas Wolfe and his use of the refrain, 'O lost, and by the wind grieved, ghost, come back again,' throughout his *Look Homeward, Angel*; or Conrad Aiken's use in his novel, *Great Circle*, of the 'stream of consciousness' monologue elaborated in a more poetic and rhythmic way than Joyce had allowed himself in *Ulysses*. These attempts, and some others like them, show that variations of polyphonic prose have by no means been abandoned, and that the vein is very far from being worked out.

I myself, however, feel it necessary to warn the reader that I did not continue my writing in polyphonic prose form beyond the year 1920. The few specimens which I was able to produce, all—with one exception which still remains in manuscript— published in my *Breakers and Granite*, cost me so much time and effort, and met with such poor response, that I decided after much thinking to abandon the form in favour of a type of verse which more closely approached the familiar stanzaic forms. Whether I was right or wrong in my direction I cannot say. Sufficient for me to as-

sert that I still believe polyphonic prose to be a medium with very remarkable possibilities; sufficient for me to wish with all my heart that more modern poets would some day try their hands at it.

1937   1938

CLIPPER–SHIPS

BEAUTIFUL as a tiered cloud, skysails set and shrouds twanging, she emerges from the surges that keep running away before day on the low Pacific shore. With the roar of the wind blowing half a gale after, she heels and lunges, and buries her bows in the smother, lifting them swiftly, and scattering the glistening spray-drops from her jibsails with laughter. Her spars are cracking, her royals are half splitting, her lower stunsail booms are bent aside, like bowstrings ready to loose, and the water is roaring into her scuppers, but she still staggers out under a full press of sail, her upper trucks enkindled by the sun into shafts of rosy flame.

Oh, the anchor is up and the sails they are set, and it's 'way Rio; 'round Cape Stiff and up to Boston, ninety days hauling at the ropes: the decks slope and the stays creak as she lurches into it, sending her jib awash at every thrust, and a handful of dust and a thirst to make you weep, are all we get for being two years away to sea.

Topgallant stunsail has carried away! Ease the spanker! The anchor is rusted on the deck. Men in short duck trousers, wide-brimmed straw hats, with brown mahogany faces, pace up and down, spinning the wornout yarns they told a year ago. Some are coiling rope; some smoke; 'Chips' is picking oakum near the boats. Ten thousand miles away lies their last port. In the rigging climbs a hairy monkey, and a green parakeet screams at the masthead. In the dead calm of a boiling noonday near the line, she lifts her spread of shining canvas from heel to truck, from jib o' jib to ringtail, from moonsails to watersails. Men have hung their washing in the stays so she can get more way on her. She ghosts along before an imperceptible breeze, the sails hanging limp in the cross-trees, and clashing against the masts. She is a proud white albatross skimming across the ocean, beautiful as a tiered cloud. Oh, a Yankee ship

omes down the river; blow, boys, blow:
er masts and yards they shine like silver:
low, my bully boys, blow: she's a crack
hip, a dandy clipper, nine hundred miles
rom land; she's a down-Easter from Mas-
achusetts, and she's bound to the Rio
Grande!

Where are the men who put to sea in her
n her first voyage? Some have piled their
ones in California among the hides; some
died frozen off the Horn in snowstorms;
ome slipped down between two greybacks,
when the yards were joggled suddenly.
Still she glistens beautifully, her decks
now-white with constant scrubbing as she
weeps into some empty sailless bay which
leeps all day, where the wild deer skip
way when she fires her eighteen pounder,
he sound reverberating about the empty
ills. San Francisco? No: San Francisco
will not be built for a dozen years to come.
Meanwhile she hums with the tumult of
oading. The mutineers, even, are let out of
heir irons and flogged and fed. Every day
rom when the dawn flares up red amid the
ills to the hour it drops dead to westward,
men walk gawkily, balancing on their heads
he burden of heavy, stiff hides. Now the
anchor is up and the sails they are set and
t's 'way, Rio. Boston girls are pulling at the
opes: only three months of trouble yet:
ime for us to go!

Beautiful as a tiered cloud she flies out
seaward, and on her decks loaf and stumble
a luckless crowd; and filthy sweepings of
he stews. In a week, in a day, they have
spent a year's wages, swilling it away and
letting the waste of it run down among the
gutters. How were these deadbeats bribed
to go? Only the Ann Street runners know.
Dagos, Dutchmen, Souwegians, niggers,
crimp-captured greenhorns, they loaf up on
the after deck, some of them already wrecks,
so sick they wish they had never been born.
Before them all the 'old man' calls for a
bucket of salt water to wash off his shore
face. While he is at it, telling them how he
will haze them till they are dead if they try
soldiering, but it will be good grub and
easy work if they hand, reef and steer and
heave the lead, his officers are below, rummaging through the men's dunnage, pulling
out heavers, prickers, rum bottles, sheath
knives, and pistols. On each grizzled half-
cowed face appears something between a
sheepish grin, a smirk of fear, a threat of
treachery, and the dogged resignation of a
brute. But the mate—Bucko Dougles is his
name—is the very same that booted three
men off the masthead when they were
shortening sail in the teeth of a Cape Horn
snorter. Two of them fell into the sea, and
the third was tossed still groaning into the
water. Only last night the captain stuck his
cigar butt into one poor swabber's face for
not minding the compass, and gave Jim
Baines a taste of ratline hash for coming up
on deck with dirty hands. Meanwhile under
a grand spread of canvas, one hundred feet
from side to side, the ship rides up the
parallels. From aloft through the blue stillness of a tropic night, crammed with stars,
with thunder brewing in the horizon, a
mournful echo rises and swells:

Oh, my name is hanging Johnny,
Hooray, hooray!
Oh, my name is hanging Johnny,
So hang, boys, hang.

The *Great Republic*, launched before
thirty thousand people, her main truck
overlooking the highest steeple of the town,
the eagle at her bows, and colours flying,
now in her first and last port, is slowly
dying. She is a charred hulk, with toppling
masts, seared gilding, and blistered sides.
The *Alert* no more slides pertly through
the bergs of the Horn. The desolate barrens
of Staten Land, where no man was ever
born, hold her bones. The Black Baller
Lightning, that took eighty thousand dollars'
worth of cargo around the world in one
quick trip, was hurled and ripped to pieces
on some unchartered reef or other. The
Dreadnought disappeared in a hurricane's
smother of foam. The *Sovereign of the
Seas*, that never furled her top-sails for ten
years, was sheared clean amidships by the
bows of an iron steamer as she left her last
port. The slaver, *Bald Eagle*, cut an unlucky career short when she parted with her
anchor and piled up on the Paracels where
the pirate junks are waiting for every ship
that swells out over the horizon. The *Antelope* was caught off the Grande Ladrone in
the northeast monsoon; she's gone. The
Flying Cloud, proud as she was of beating
every ship that carried the Stars and Stripes
or the St. George's flag, could not race

faster than a thunder-bolt that fell one
day on her deck and turned her to a cloud
of flame—everything burned away but her
fame! No more will California hear the
little *Pilgrim's* parting cheer. The crew took
to an open boat when their ship was scuttled
by a privateer. So they die out, year after
year.

Sometimes the lookout on a great
steamer wallowing and threshing through
the heavy seas by night, sees far off on his
lee quarter something like a lofty swinging
light. Beautiful as a tiered cloud, a ghostly
clipper-ship emerges from the surges that
keep running away before day on the low
Pacific shore. Her upper works are enkindled by the sun into shafts of rosy
flame. Swimming like a duck, steering like
a fish, easy yet dry, lively yet stiff, she lifts
cloud on cloud of crowded stainless sail.
She creeps abeam, within hail, she dips,
she chases, she outpaces like a mettlesome
racer the lumbering tea-kettle that keeps
her company. Before she fades into the
weather quarter, the lookout cries: 'Holy
Jiggers, are you the *Flying Dutchman*, that
you go two knots to our one?' Hoarsely
comes back this answer from the sail:
'*Challenge* is our name: America our nation: Bully Waterman our master: we can
beat Creation.'

And it's 'way, Rio;
Way—hay—hay, Rio:
O, fare you well, my pretty young girl,
For we're bound to the Rio Grande.

1915   1921

THE SWAN [1]

UNDER a wall of bronze,
Where beeches dip and trail
Thin branches in the water,
With red-tipped head and wings,
A beaked ship under sail,
There glides a great black swan.

1 Fletcher says: 'I recall plainly the circumstances under
which this poem was composed. I was walking along
the Thames, on a beautiful sunny October day, at a
spot where the opposite bank of the river was bordered
by a row of beech trees fringing the water, with long
branches and copper-coloured foliage. Suddenly from a
small creek, appeared a black swan which swam
straight down the river, breaking its perfectly still and
mirror-like surface into wide ripples. The towers of
Oxford University loomed up in the distance, softened
and mellowed by the hazy sunlight of autumn. It was

Under the autumn trees
He goes. The branches quiver,
Dance in the wraith-like water,
Which ripples beneath the sedge   10
With the slackening furrow that glides
In his wake when he is gone:
The beeches bow dark heads.

Into the windless dusk,
Where in mist great towers stand
Guarding a lonely strand
That is bodiless and dim,
He speeds with easy stride;
And I would go beside,
Till the low brown hills divide
At last, for me and him.

1919   1927

ELEGY ON TINTERN ABBEY

THAT 'something far more deeply
          interfused
Whose dwelling is the light of setting suns'
Has changed direction now. And that
          which woke
In one man's vision, fired by the setting sun
Of faith from these old altars, has gone down
Like life-blood trickling from the wounds
          of Christ
Slowly, to the dumb grass. And that which
          stirred
Within the silence of the cemetery
That followed after the proud challenge
          pealed
From lips that loved America and France,
Was a loud mocking hoot from factories   11
Crying, 'Come out; be filled.' And so the
          world
Turned backward from its path and
          followed gold's
False rushlight gleaming from the dismal
          swamp,
Mocking the prophets always and their
          creed.

And thus the music of humanity,
'Of ample power to chasten and subdue,'

this scene and the mood it evoked that I tried to convey in my verse. The mingling of exact rhyme with
assonance (for example "sedge" and "heads" in the
second stanza), the free stanzaic form, the combination of words denoting colour with vowel sounds suggesting the flow of the river, are all effects that may be
found in some of my longer poems, such as the
"Symphonies," but here shortened and compressed.'
Benét, ed., *Fifty Poets*(N.Y., 1933),72–73.

That still sad music breathed from out
    these stones,
Was lost amidst the mounting shriek and
    blare
Of 'sell quick and buy cheap.' And so the
    world   20
Grew one vast Manchester of laisser-
    faire,
Low and victorious, 'mong which
    stranger-folk
Who clinked the spurs of Cavaliers, or
    swore
The oaths of the mad Puritans, went
    down
To drink the stream of Lethe with their
    peers.

God of the world, Who suffers the unjust,
Poured out His potent spell. It fumed like
    wine,
In many brains. One merely spelled out
    words
In some newspaper, and the morning's
    sun
Rose clear to greet them. Long as outward
    white   30
Was inward black, one was content to
    swear
That all was well with earth. Meanwhile
    the wheels.
Turned furious, and the little wheels of
    Time
Beside them, saw they ran the faster as
New nations learned the trick to make them
    turn.

No one can say what happened then, nor
    how.
Men had no time to pause and gather
    thought.
Earth in its furious dance spun one mad
    twirl,
And then beyond the wheels were sudden
    come
The lean grey throats of guns uneasily
    crouching   40
And searching skies for prey. What made
    the world
Grow dark, and then the awful echoes
    start,
Rebounding here and echoing there, none
    knew;
Only the wheels had got at last their way
Not three hours then, but four years
    Calvary.

Meantime the dawn kept to its 'priestlike
    task'
Of waking worlds too brutalized to ask,
Aught but 'how long?' too agonized to
    know
Aught but the need of fitting on anew
One's gas-mask, fixing bayonets again   50
Against attacks unseen. To such a strain
As this now blew 'the misty mountain-
    winds'
That once spoke liberty. And to this came
Songs of man's triumph in the swelling
    main
Full-tide set towards progress. Till, at last,
The sullen guns grew weary riddling earth
To rubbish-heaps and so withdrew again,
Leaving the beaten folk to cower there,
Behind the barrier of an empty word.

And then men saw, as dawn at last released
The last long trenchline furrowing earth
    defiled,   61
That man was fastened hand and foot alike
To his machines; not as Prometheus now
Chained to his sad rock and yet nobler than
The god that doomed him: but Ixion
    cursed,
Who raped great Hera, and hence, self-
    condemned,
Must roll through Hell forever on his wheel.

What then can free our fingers or dispel
The chill delusion of dark crawling
    thoughts
That haunt too close the tomb? Can
    madness save   70
The sanity of the void? Is there a tune
Not torn from man's guts by the fiddling
    bow
Of greed and ignorance hired each day
    anew
To play on them? Well, if there is, not here
May it be found, where, as a numbing
    spell,
Some ancient acquiescence haunts the
    dust;
But rather where the shells and shards are
    piled,
Vain effort, with the souls that strove in
    vain;
There you may find some outcast sons of
    men
Who see, but will not yield to their
    despair.   80

1925   1935

ELEGY ON AN EMPTY
SKYSCRAPER [1]

I

AGAINST the wall of this sky,
Leaden pall threaded with cardboard
    boxes, the pale light of the towers
Flickers unearthly still,
Long leaden streets between them:
Against the wall of this sky, the cream-
    white faces
Of stone blocks bound in glittering steel
    gleam high;
Jut to the sky, and break
Packed huddled ranks of clouds and roofs
    apart
Thrusting their own horizon yet a little
    higher.

Beauty is spread   10
Here over hollow voids; beneath these
    walls
Clamour of traffic slides through
    corridors,
Long elevator-shafts shoot mountainously
    downwards.
Steel on the surface repels
This drizzling daylight; through the inner
    core
Vertical darkness spreads,
Extends its empire upwards,
Forces the tower to tremble with dull
    sound.

Noise of wheels tuned to wheels
Driving the darkness skyward,   20
Forcing the human darkness that should
    hide

The earth in fruitfulness, still bleakly
    upward;
In a stark affirmation,
Stone flanged to steel here to repel the
    daylight;
Void affirmation, since the sky goes higher
And men drift past, unseeing,
Bowed deeper by the weight of locked-in
    stone:—

Balancing bodies against the heat that holds
Its swift course vertically downwards;
Dragging their heavy feet into its molten
    pavements,   30
Swaying their shrinking flesh against its
    reverberant walls;
Noise of wheels tuned to wheels,
Bewildered by the men that move amid
    them;
While still the tower lurches
Upwards with its long shadow,
Flight of white ripples four-square on the
    sky.

Here is this drift against the wall of the sky,
Steel arms that lift,
Tackle that rattles,
Torches that sputter,   40
Chattering hammers that shake the empty
    brain,
The roar and the mutter
Of the swift elevated train;
And the ships at the dockside,
The pencilled lines of the bridges,
The dull green carpet of park,
The wide grey floor of the bay—
Is all this living to-day?
The fuming and looping line of the surly
    river to westward,
Stained by the sunset to red—   50
Is all this living, or dead?
Dead are the twinkling lights and the
    sombre reflections
Of the earth-dwellers stretched
    heavenwards here from below?
Who is there living to know?
Only the wide hollow offices, the corridors
    empty of light,
Tier after tier going downwards here into
    the night.

2

Thick pencil of shadow stretched across the
    street,
If I could lift

1 'The Empire State Building, the tallest in New York
and in the world, was finished in the spring of 1931,
but thanks to the depression has still remained largely
empty on its upper floors. When I first saw it, in
July 1931, on a day of threatening thunderstorms to
north and coppery sunset to westward, I could not
escape the impression that I was standing on the summit of a spot as uninhabited as Everest. I stayed there
three or four hours, filling several pages of a notebook
with such scattered fragments of impression as "leaden
pall threaded with cardboard boxes" to describe the
sky, or "noise of wheels tuned to wheels" to describe
the traffic. It was not until two months and more had
passed, on the return journey to England, that on
going over my notebook I found the fragments I had
assembled could be shaped into a poem. The form is
loosely stanzaic; and the second section aims, by repetition of rhymes from one stanza to another, to give
something of the effect of climbing upwards.' Author's
note.

Your weight and make you write;
Or if at night   60
I could make move that fixed and arrogant
    light
That stands there emptily glaring to
    repeat,
In higher guise, the street-lamp's signal-
    flight;
What against all the words that we repeat
In vain to-day,
What is the one word I would make you
    say?

'Here where once stared in dumb hope to
    the sky
Man by his naked blaze, and saw smoke
    take away
In folds of undulating grey
His prayer, not knowing walls however
    high: 70
Here wall on wall is heaped, steel thread to
    thread
Is riveted to extend the ever-dead:
Vain flight of shadow where the chasms
    cry.'

Is this the word, or is some other thing
That which I seek; the sky gives no reply,
Will man grow wise and grow another
    wing
As powerful as the one that set on high
This thing?
I do not know:
But slow the darkness gathers; echoes
    bring   80
Only the wild cries of mechanic woe.

3

Could I but strip you down,
Tear steel from steel in long peeled strips,
    and break
The interlocking blocks of cream-white
    stone,
Send them like autumn leaves swift
    spinning down,
Or level, near and far,
This city, spread about you greening fields,
Leave you alone, all empty as you are,
Gleaming-nerved flower that no grass
    reveals,

Either I'd do: 90
But it is vain within your walls to go,
To feel in your dead heart the beat and
    strain
Of hopes grown panic-smitten, to and fro
Millions of meaningless lights,
When all about you is the soundless
    night's.

There is wide space between
Man's topmast and his keel, and in it death
Comes without sign or sound or stir of
    breath.
No one shall fill that room, or take his
    place
In it, as stowaway or come-aboard;   100
Nor shall the meagre window-blind be
    lowered,
Nor shall the dark be levelled by a face.
1931   1935

AMY LOWELL

1874-1925

FIREWORKS

You hate me and I hate you,
And we are so polite, we two!

But whenever I see you, I burst apart
And scatter the sky with my blazing heart.
It spits and sparkles in stars and balls,
Buds into roses—and flares, and falls.

Scarlet buttons, and pale green disks,
Silver spirals and asterisks,
Shoot and tremble in a mist
Peppered with mauve and amethyst.   10

I shine in the windows and light up the
    trees,
And all because I hate you, if you please.

And when you meet me, you rend asunder
And go up in a flaming wonder
Of saffron cubes, and crimson moons,
And wheels all amaranths and maroons.

Golden lozenges and spades,
Arrows of malachites and jades,
Patens of copper, azure sheaves.
As you mount, you flash in the glossy
    leaves.   20

Such fireworks as we make, we two!
Because you hate me and I hate you.

1919

PATTERNS

I WALK down the garden paths,
And all the daffodils
Are blowing, and the bright blue squills.
I walk down the patterned garden-paths
In my stiff, brocaded gown.
With my powdered hair and jewelled fan,
I too am a rare
Pattern. As I wander down
The garden paths.

My dress is richly figured,   10
And the train
Makes a pink and silver stain
On the gravel, and the thrift
Of the borders.
Just a plate of current fashion,
Tripping by in high-heeled, ribboned
    shoes.
Not a softness anywhere about me,
Only whalebone and brocade.
And I sink on a seat in the shade
Of a lime tree. For my passion   20
Wars against the stiff brocade.
The daffodils and squills
Flutter in the breeze
As they please.
And I weep;
For the lime-tree is in blossom
And one small flower has dropped upon my
    bosom.

And the plashing of waterdrops
In the marble fountain
Comes down the garden-paths.   30
The dripping never stops.
Underneath my stiffened gown
Is the softness of a woman bathing in a
    marble basin,
A basin in the midst of hedges grown
So thick, she cannot see her lover hiding,
But she guesses he is near,
And the sliding of the water
Seems the stroking of a dear
Hand upon her.
What is Summer in a fine brocaded gown!
I should like to see it lying in a heap upon
    the ground.   41
All the pink and silver crumpled up on the
    ground.

I would be the pink and silver as I ran
    along the paths,
And he would stumble after,
Bewildered by my laughter.
I should see the sun flashing from his
    sword-hilt and the buckles on his
    shoes.
I would choose
To lead him in a maze along the patterned
    paths,
A bright and laughing maze for my heavy-
    booted lover.
Till he caught me in the shade,   50
And the buttons of his waistcoat bruised
    my body as he clasped me,
Aching, melting, unafraid.
With the shadows of the leaves and the
    sundrops,
And the plopping of the waterdrops,
All about us in the open afternoon—
I am very like to swoon
With the weight of this brocade,
For the sun sifts through the shade.

Underneath the fallen blossom
In my bosom,   60
Is a letter I have hid.
It was brought to me this morning by a
    rider from the Duke.
'Madam, we regret to inform you that Lord
    Hartwell
Died in action Thursday se'nnight.'
As I read it in the white, morning sunlight,
The letters squirmed like snakes.
'Any answer, Madam?' said my footman.
'No,' I told him.
'See that the messenger takes some
    refreshment.
No, no answer.'   70
And I walked into the garden,
Up and down the patterned paths,
In my stiff, correct brocade.
The blue and yellow flowers stood up
    proudly in the sun,
Each one.
I stood upright too,
Held rigid to the pattern
By the stiffness of my gown.
Up and down I walked,
Up and down.   80

In a month he would have been my
    husband.
In a month, here, underneath this lime,
We would have broke the pattern;

He for me, and I for him,
He as Colonel, I as Lady,
On this shady seat.
He had a whim
That sunlight carried blessing.
And I answered, 'It shall be as you have
    said.'
Now he is dead.   90

In Summer and in Winter I shall walk
Up and down
The patterned garden-paths
In my stiff, brocaded gown.
The squills and daffodils
Will give place to pillared roses, and to
    asters, and to snow.
I shall go
Up and down,
In my gown.
Gorgeously arrayed,   100
Boned and stayed.
And the softness of my body will be
    guarded from embrace
By each button, hook, and lace.
For the man who should loose me is dead,
Fighting with the Duke in Flanders,
In a pattern called a war.
Christ! What are patterns for?

                1915

LILACS

Lilacs,
False blue,
White,
Purple,
Colour of lilac,
Your great puffs of flowers
Are everywhere in this my New England.
Among your heart-shaped leaves
Orange orioles hop like music-box birds
    and sing
Their little weak soft songs;   10
In the crooks of your branches
The bright eyes of song sparrows sitting on
    spotted eggs
Peer restlessly through the light and
    shadow
Of all Springs.
Lilacs in dooryards
Holding quiet conversations with an early
    moon;
Lilacs watching a deserted house
Settling sideways into the grass of an old
    road;

Lilacs, wind-beaten, staggering under a
    lopsided shock of bloom
Above a cellar dug into a hill.   20
You are everywhere.
You were everywhere.
You tapped the window when the preacher
    preached his sermon,
And ran along the road beside the boy
    going to school.
You stood by pasture-bars to give the cows
    good milking,
You persuaded the housewife that her dish
    pan was of silver
And her husband an image of pure gold.
You flaunted the fragrance of your blossoms
Through the wide doors of Custom
    Houses—
You, and sandal-wood, and tea,   30
Charging the noses of quill-driving clerks
When a ship was in from China.
You called to them: 'Goose-quill men,
    goose-quill men,
May is a month for flitting,'
Until they writhed on their high stools
And wrote poetry on their letter-sheets
    behind the propped-up ledgers.
Paradoxical New England clerks,
Writing inventories in ledgers, reading the
    'Song of Solomon' at night,
So many verses before bed-time,
Because it was the Bible.   40
The dead fed you
Amid the slant stones of graveyards.
Pale ghosts who planted you
Came in the night-time
And let their thin hair blow through your
    clustered stems.
You are of the green sea,
And of the stone hills which reach a long
    distance.
You are of elm-shaded streets with little
    shops where they sell kites and
    marbles,
You are of great parks where everyone
    walks and nobody is at home.
You cover the blind sides of greenhouses   50
And lean over the top to say a hurry-word
    through the glass
To your friends, the grapes, inside.

Lilacs,
False blue,
White,
Purple,
Colour of lilac,

You have forgotten your Eastern origin,
The veiled women with eyes like panthers,
The swollen, aggressive turbans of jeweled
    Pashas.   60
Now you are a very decent flower,
A reticent flower,
A curiously clear-cut, candid flower,
Standing beside clean doorways,
Friendly to a house-cat and a pair of
    spectacles,
Making poetry out of a bit of moonlight
And a hundred or two sharp blossoms.

Maine knows you,
Has for years and years;
New Hampshire knows you,   70
And Massachusetts
And Vermont.
Cape Cod starts you along the beaches to
    Rhode Island;
Connecticut takes you from a river to the
    sea.
You are brighter than apples,
Sweeter than tulips,
You are the great flood of our souls
Bursting above the leaf-shapes of our
    hearts,
You are the smell of all Summers,
The love of wives and children,   80
The recollection of the gardens of little
    children,
You are State Houses and Charters
And the familiar treading of the foot to and
    fro on a road it knows.
May is lilac here in New England,
May is a thrush singing 'Sun up!' on a tip-
    top ash-tree,
May is white clouds behind pine-trees
Puffed out and marching upon a blue sky.
May is a green as no other,
May is much sun through small leaves,
May is soft earth,   90
And apple-blossoms,
And windows open to a South wind.
May is a full light wind of lilac
From Canada to Narragansett Bay.

Lilacs,
False blue,
White,
Purple,
Colour of lilac,
Heart-leaves of lilac all over New England,
Roots of lilac under all the soil of New
    England,   101

Lilac in me because I am New England,
Because my roots are in it,
Because my leaves are of it,
Because my flowers are for it,
Because it is my country
And I speak to it of itself
And sing of it with my own voice
Since certainly it is mine.

                                              1915

THE CROSS–ROADS

A BULLET through his heart at dawn. On the
table a letter signed with a woman's name.
A wind that goes howling round the house,
and weeping as in shame. Cold November
dawn peeping through the windows, cold
dawn creeping over the floor, creeping up
his cold legs, creeping over his cold body,
creeping across his cold face. A glaze of
thin yellow sunlight on the staring eyes.
Wind howling through bent branches. A
wind which never dies down. Howling,
wailing. The gazing eyes glitter in the sunlight. The lids are frozen open and the eyes
glitter.

    The thudding of a pick on hard earth. A
spade grinding and crunching. Overhead,
branches writhing, winding, interlacing,
unwinding, scattering; tortured twinings,
tossings, creakings. Wind flinging branches
apart, drawing them together, whispering
and whining among them. A waning, lob-
sided moon cutting through black clouds.
A stream of pebbles and earth and the
empty spade gleams clear in the moonlight,
then is rammed again into the black earth.
Tramping of feet. Men and horses. Squeaking of wheels.
    'Whoa! Ready, Jim?'
    'All ready.'
    Something falls, settles, is still. Suicides
have no coffin.
    'Give us the stake, Jim. Now.'
    Pound! Pound!
    'He'll never walk. Nailed to the ground.'
    An ash stick pierces his heart, if it buds
the roots will hold him. He is a part of the
earth now, clay to clay. Overhead the
branches sway, and writhe, and twist in the
wind. He'll never walk with a bullet in his
heart, and an ash stick nailing him to the
cold, black ground.

Six months he lay still. Six months. And the water welled up in his body, and soft blue spots chequered it. He lay still, for the ash stick held him in place. Six months! Then her face came out of a mist of green. Pink and white and frail like Dresden china, lilies-of-the-valley at her breast, puce-coloured silk sheening about her. Under the young green leaves, the horse at a foot-pace, the high yellow wheels of the chaise scarcely turning, her face, rippling like grain a-blowing, under her puce-coloured bonnet; and burning beside her, flaming within his correct blue coat and brass buttons, is someone. What has dimmed the sun? The horse steps on a rolling stone; a wind in the branches makes a moan. The little leaves tremble and shake, turn and quake, over and over, tearing their stems. There is a shower of young leaves, and a sudden-sprung gale wails in the trees.

The yellow-wheeled chaise is rocking—rocking, and all the branches are knocking —knocking. The sun in the sky is a flat, red plate, the branches creak and grate. She screams and cowers, for the green foliage is a lowering wave surging to smother her. But she sees nothing. The stake holds firm. The body writhes, the body squirms. The blue spots widen, the flesh tears, but the stake wears well in the deep, black ground. It holds the body in the still, black ground.

Two years! The body has been in the ground two years. It is worn away; it is clay to clay. Where the heart moulders, a greenish dust, the stake is thrust. Late August it is, and night; a night flauntingly jewelled with stars, a night of shooting stars and loud insect noises. Down the road to Tilbury, silence—and the slow flapping of large leaves. Down the road to Sutton, silence—and the darkness of heavy-foli-aged trees. Down the road to Wayfleet, silence—and the whirring scrape of insects in the branches. Down the road to Edgars-town, silence—and stars like stepping-stones in a pathway overhead. It is very quiet at the cross-roads, and the sign-board points the way down the four roads, endlessly points the way where nobody wishes to go. A horse is galloping, galloping up from Sutton. Shaking the wide, still leaves as he goes under them. Striking sparks with his iron shoes; silencing the katydids. Dr. Morgan riding to a child-birth over Til-bury way; riding to deliver a woman of her first-born son. One o'clock from Wayfleet bell tower, what a shower of shooting stars! And a breeze all of a sudden, jarring the big leaves and making them jerk up and down. Dr. Morgan's hat is blown from his head, the horse swerves, and curves away from the sign-post. An oath—spurs—a blurring of grey mist. A quick left twist, and the gelding is snorting and racing down the Tilbury road with the wind dropping away behind him.

The stake has wrenched, the stake has started, the body, flesh from flesh, has parted. But the bones hold tight, socket and ball, and clamping them down in the hard, black ground is the stake, wedged through ribs and spine. The bones may twist, and heave, and twine, but the stake holds them still in line. The breeze goes down, and the round stars shine, for the stake holds the fleshless bones in line.

Twenty years now! Twenty long years! The body has powdered itself away; it is clay to clay. It is brown earth mingled with brown earth. Only flaky bones remain, lain together so long they fit, although not one bone is knit to another. The stake is there too, rotted through, but upright still, and still piercing down between ribs and spine in a straight line.

Yellow stillness is on the cross-roads, yellow stillness is on the trees. The leaves hang drooping, wan. The four roads point four yellow ways, saffron and gamboge rib-bons to the gaze. A little swirl of dust blows up Tilbury road, the wind which fans it has not strength to do more; it ceases, and the dust settles down. A little whirl of wind comes up Tilbury road. It brings a sound of wheels and feet. The wind reels a mo-ment and faints to nothing under the sign-post. Wind again, wheels and feet louder. Wind again—again—again. A drop of rain, flat into the dust. Drop!—Drop! Thick heavy raindrops, and a shrieking wind bending the great trees and wrench-ing off their leaves.

Under the black sky, bowed and drip-ping with rain, up Tilbury road, comes the procession. A funeral procession, bound for the graveyard at Wayfleet. Feet and wheels—feet and wheels. And among them one who is carried.

The bones in the deep, still earth shiver and pull. There is a quiver through the rotted stake. Then stake and bones fall together in a little puffing of dust.

Like meshes of linked steel the rain shuts down behind the procession, now well along the Wayfleet road.

He wavers like smoke in the buffeting wind. His fingers blow out like smoke, his head ripples in the gale. Under the signpost, in the pouring rain, he stands, and watches another quavering figure drifting down the Wayfleet road. Then swiftly he streams after it. It flickers among the trees. He licks out and winds about them. Over, under, blown, contorted. Spindrift after spindrift; smoke following smoke. There is a wailing through the trees, a wailing of fear, and after it laughter—laughter—laughter, skirling up to the black sky. Lightning jags over the funeral procession. A heavy clap of thunder. Then darkness and rain, and the sound of feet and wheels.

                                        1916

THE DINNER–PARTY

FISH

'So . . .' they said,
With their wine-glasses delicately poised,
Mocking at the thing they cannot
        understand.
'So . . .' they said again,
Amused and insolent.
The silver on the table glittered,
And the red wine in the glasses
Seemed the blood I had wasted
In a foolish cause.

GAME

The gentleman with the grey-and-black
        whiskers   10
Sneered languidly over his quail.
Then my heart flew up and laboured,
And I burst from my own holding
And hurled myself forward.
With straight blows I beat upon him,
Furiously, with red-hot anger, I thrust
        against him.
But my weapon slithered over his polished
        surface,

And I recoiled upon myself,
Panting.

DRAWING-ROOM

In a dress all softness and half-tones,   20
Indolent and half-reclined,
She lay upon a couch,
With the firelight reflected in her jewels.
But her eyes had no reflection,
They swam in a grey smoke,
The smoke of smouldering ashes,
The smoke of her cindered heart.

COFFEE

They sat in a circle with their coffee-cups.
One dropped in a lump of sugar,
One stirred with a spoon.   30
I saw them as a circle of ghosts
Sipping blackness out of beautiful china,
And mildly protesting against my
        coarseness
In being alive.

TALK

They took dead men's souls
And pinned them on their breasts for
        ornament;
Their cuff-links and tiaras
Were gems dug from a grave;
They were ghouls battening on exhumed
        thoughts;
And I took a green liqueur from a servant   40
So that he might come near me
And give me the comfort of a living thing.

ELEVEN O'CLOCK

The front door was hard and heavy,
It shut behind me on the house of ghosts.
I flattened my feet on the pavement
To feel it solid under me;
I ran my hand along the railings
And shook them,
And pressed their pointed bars
Into my palms.   50
The hurt of it reassured me,
And I did it again and again
Until they were bruised.
When I woke in the night
I laughed to find them aching,
For only living flesh can suffer.

                                        1916

FROM 1777

2 THE CITY OF FALLING LEAVES

LEAVES fall,
Brown leaves,
Yellow leaves streaked with brown.
They fall,
Flutter,
Fall again.
The brown leaves,
And the streaked yellow leaves,
Loosen on their branches
And drift slowly downwards.   10
One,
One, two, three,
One, two, five.
All Venice is a falling of autumn leaves—
Brown,
And yellow streaked with brown.

'That sonnet, *Abate*,
Beautiful,
I am quite exhausted by it.
Your phrases turn about my heart   20
And stifle me to swooning.
Open the window, I beg.
Lord! What a strumming of fiddles and
        mandolins!
'Tis really a shame to stop indoors.
Call my maid, or I will make you lace me
        yourself.
Fie, how hot it is, not a breath of air!
See how straight the leaves are falling.
Marianna, I will have the yellow satin
        caught up with silver fringe,
It peeps out delightfully from under a
        mantle.
Am I well painted to-day, *caro Abate mio*?
You will be proud of me at the *Ridotto*,
        hey?   31
Proud of being *Cavalier Servente* to such a
        lady?'
'Can you doubt it, *Bellissima Contessa*?
A pinch more rouge on the right cheek,
And Venus herself shines less . . .'
'You bore me, *Abate*;
I vow I must change you!
A letter, Achmet?
Run and look out of the window, *Abate*.
I will read my letter in peace.'   40
The little black slave with the yellow satin
        turban
Gazes at his mistress with strained eyes.
His yellow turban and black skin
Are gorgeous—barbaric.

The yellow satin dress with its silver
        flashings
Lies on a chair
Beside a black mantle and a black mask.
Yellow and black,
Gorgeous—barbaric.
The lady reads her letter,   50
And the leaves drift slowly
Past the long windows.
'How silly you look, my dear *Abate*,
With that great brown leaf in your wig.
Pluck it off, I beg you,
Or I shall die of laughing.'

A yellow wall,
Aflare in the sunlight,
Chequered with shadows,
Shadows of vine-leaves,   60
Shadows of masks.
Masks coming, printing themselves for an
        instant,
Then passing on,
More masks always replacing them.
Masks with tricorns and rapiers sticking
        out behind
Pursuing masks with veils and high
        heels,
The sunlight shining under their insteps.
One,
One, two,
One, two, three,   70
There is a thronging of shadows on the hot
        wall,
Filigreed at the top with moving leaves.
Yellow sunlight and black shadows,
Yellow and black,
Gorgeous—barbaric.
Two masks stand together,
And the shadow of a leaf falls through
        them,
Marking the wall where they are not.
From hat-tip to shoulder-tip,
From elbow to sword-hilt,   80
The leaf falls.
The shadows mingle,
Blur together,
Slide along the wall and disappear.

Gold of mosaics and candles,
And night blackness lurking in the ceiling
        beams.
Saint Mark's glitters with flames and
        reflections.
A cloak brushes aside,
And the yellow of satin

Licks out over the coloured inlays of the
    pavement.   90
Under the gold crucifixes
There is a meeting of hands
Reaching from black mantles.
Sighing embraces, bold investigations,
Hide in confessionals,
Sheltered by the shuffling of feet.
Gorgeous—barbaric
In its mail of jewels and gold,
Saint Mark's looks down at the swarm of
    black masks;
And outside in the palace gardens brown
    leaves fall,   100
Flutter,
Fall.
Brown,
And yellow streaked with brown.

Blue-black the sky over Venice,
With a pricking of yellow stars.
There is no moon,
And the waves push darkly against the prow
Of the gondola,
Coming from Malamocco   110
And streaming toward Venice.
It is black under the gondola hood,
But the yellow of a satin dress
Glares out like the eye of a watching tiger.
Yellow compassed about with darkness,
Yellow and black,
Gorgeous—barbaric.
The boatman sings,
It is Tasso that he sings;
The lovers seek each other beneath their
    mantles,   120
And the gondola drifts over the lagoon,
    aslant to the coming dawn.
But at Malamocco in front,
In Venice behind,
Fall the leaves,
Brown,
And yellow streaked with brown.
They fall,
Flutter,
Fall.

                1916

LITTLE IVORY FIGURES PULLED
WITH STRING

Is it the tinkling of mandolins which
    disturbs you?
Or the dropping of bitter-orange petals
    among the coffee-cups?

Or the slow creeping of the moonlight
    between the olive-trees?
    Drop! drop! the rain
    Upon the thin plates of my heart.

String your blood to chord with this music,
Stir your heels upon the cobbles to the
    rhythm of a dance-tune.
They have slim thighs and arms of silver;
The moon washes away their garments;
They make a pattern of fleeing feet in the
    branch shadows,   10
And the green grapes knotted about them
Burst as they press against one another.
    The rain knocks upon the plates of my
    heart,
    They are crumpled with its beating.

Would you drink only from your brains,
    Old Man?
See, the moonlight has reached your knees,
It falls upon your head in an accolade of
    silver.
Rise up on the music,
Fling against the moon-drifts in a whorl of
    young light bodies:
Leaping grape-clusters,   20
Vine leaves tearing from a grey wall.
You shall run, laughing, in a braid of
    women,
And weave flowers with the frosty spines of
    thorns.
Why do you gaze into your glass,
And jar the spoons with your finger-
    tapping?
    The rain is rigid on the plates of my heart.
    The murmur of it is loud—loud.

                1919

MEETING–HOUSE HILL

I MUST be mad, or very tired,
When the curve of a blue bay beyond a
    railroad track
Is shrill and sweet to me like the sudden
    springing of a tune,
And the sight of a white church above thin
    trees in a city square
Amazes my eyes as though it were the
    Parthenon.
Clear, reticent, superbly final,
With the pillars of its portico refined to a
    cautious elegance,
It dominates the weak trees,
And the shot of its spire

Is cool, and candid,   10
Rising into an unresisting sky.
Strange meeting-house
Pausing a moment upon a squalid hill-top.
I watch the spire sweeping the sky,
I am dizzy with the movement of the sky,
I might be watching a mast
With its royals set full
Straining before a two-reef breeze.
I might be sighting a tea-clipper,
Tacking into the blue bay,   20
Just back from Canton
With her hold full of green and blue
    porcelain,
And a Chinese coolie leaning over the rail
Gazing at the white spire
With dull, sea-spent eyes.

                1925

THE ON-LOOKER

SUPPOSE I plant you
Like wide-eyed Helen

On the battlements
Of weary Troy,
Clutching the parapet with desperate
    hands.
She, too, gazes at a battle-field
Where bright vermilion plumes and metal
    whiteness
Shock and sparkle and go down with
    groans.
Her glances strike the rocking battle,
Again—again—   10
Recoiling from it
Like baffled spear-heads fallen from a
    brazen shield.
The ancients at her elbow counsel patience
    and contingencies;
Such to a woman stretched upon a bed of
    battle,
Who bargained for this only in the
    whispering arras
Enclosed about a midnight of
    enchantment.

                1925

WILLIAM CARLOS WILLIAMS

1883–

A NOTE ON POETRY

THE American writer, insofar as he is child of the Anglo Saxon tradition, uses a language which stems largely from Elizabethan England but which has been modified by time and the accidents of place to acquire a character differing greatly from that of present day english. For the appreciation of American poetry it is necessary [10] that the English reader accept this language difference from the beginning.

Its effects are discernible in many ways. Pace is one of the most important of its manifestations. This is particularly significant in versification since it is the direct forerunner of poetic form. It is by paying attention to the character of the spoken language that form is detected in its beginnings and later refined for exact use.

By listening to the language of his locality the poet begins to learn his craft. It is his function to lift, by use of his imagination and the language he hears, the material conditions and appearances of his environment to the sphere of the intelligence where they will have new currency. Thus anything that the poet can effectively lift from its dull bed by force of the imagination becomes his material. Anything. The commonplace, the tawdry, the sordid all have their poetic uses if the imagination can lighten them. This broadening of the choice in the materials of poetry has great modern significance; there is an older parallel to it in painting, where by dwelling upon light itself the artist has often drawn many otherwise unsightly objects into his works.

Emotion clusters about common things, the pathetic often stimulates the imagination to new patterns—but the job of the poet is to use language effectively, his own language, the only language which is to him authentic. In my own work it has always sufficed that the object of my attention [20] be presented without further comment. This in general might be termed the objective method. But all art is sensual and poetry particularly so. It is directly, that is, of the senses, and since the senses do not exist without an object for their employment all art is necessarily objective. It doesn't declaim or explain; it presents.

But an image is not a poem, for that would leave the language and the form of the poem at loose ends. A poem is a whole, an object in itself, a 'word' with a particular meaning old or new. The whole poem, image and form, that is, constitutes a single meaning. This is the full meaning of the term 'objective' as I employ it.

Times change and forms and their meanings alter. Thus new poems are necessary. Their forms must be discovered in the spoken, the living language of their day, or old forms, embodying exploded concepts, will tyrannize over the imagination, depriving us of its greatest benefits. In the forms of new poems will lie embedded the essences of future enlightenment.

1937   1938

PEACE ON EARTH

THE Archer is wake!
The Swan is flying!
Gold against blue
An Arrow is lying.
There is hunting in heaven—
Sleep safe till to-morrow.

The Bears are abroad!
The Eagle is screaming!
Gold against blue
Their eyes are gleaming!   10
Sleep!
Sleep safe till to-morrow.

The Sisters lie
With their arms intertwining;
Gold against blue
Their hair is shining!
The Serpent writhes!
Orion is listening!
Gold against blue
His sword is glistening!   20
Sleep!
There is hunting in heaven—
Sleep safe till to-morrow.

1911   1913

THE BULL

IT is in captivity—
ringed, haltered, chained
to a drag
the bull is godlike

Unlike the cows
he lives alone, nozzles
the sweet grass gingerly
to pass the time away

He kneels, lies down
and stretching out   10
a foreleg licks himself
about the hoof

then stays
with half-closed eyes,
Olympian commentary on
the bright passage of days.

—The round sun
smooths his lacquer
through
the glossy pinetrees   20

his substance hard
as ivory or glass—
through which the wind
yet plays—
         Milkless

he nods
the hair between his horns
and eyes matted
with hyacinthine curls

1921   1934

THE RED WHEELBARROW

so much depends
upon

a red wheel
barrow

glazed with rain
water

beside the white
chickens

1922   1923

THE SEA–ELEPHANT

TRUNDLED from
the strangeness of the sea—
a kind of
heaven—

Ladies and Gentlemen!
the greatest
sea-monster ever exhibited
alive

the gigantic
sea-elephant——O wallow   10
of flesh where
are

there fish enough for
that
appetite stupidity
cannot lessen?

Sick
of April's smallness
the little
leaves——   20

Flesh has lief of you
enormous sea——
Speak!
Blouaugh! (feed

me) my
flesh is riven——
fish after fish into his maw
unswallowing

to let them glide down
gulching back   30
half spittle half
brine

the
troubled eyes——torn
from the sea.
(In

a practical voice) They
ought
to put it back where
it came from.   40

Gape.
Strange head——
told by old sailors——
rising

bearded
to the surface——and
the only
sense out of them

is that woman's
Yes   50
it's wonderful but they
ought to

put it
back into the sea where
it came from.
Blouaugh!

Swing——ride
walk
on wires——toss balls
stoop and   60

contort yourselves——
But I
am love. I am
from the sea——

Blouaugh!
there is no crime save
the too heavy
body

the sea
held playfully——comes   70
to the surface
the water

boiling
about the head the cows
scattering
fish dripping from

the bounty
of . . . and Spring,
they say
Spring is icummen in——   80

                    1927   1934

RAIN

As the rain falls
so does
          your love

bathe every
          open
Object of the world——

In houses
the priceless dry
          rooms

of illicit love   10
where we live
hear the wash of the
     rain—

There
    paintings
and fine
    metalware
woven stuffs—
all the whoreishness
of our   20
    delight
sees
from its window
the spring wash
of your love
    the falling
rain—

The trees
are become
beasts fresh risen   30
from
    the sea—
water

trickles
from the crevices of
their hides—

So my life is spent
   to keep out love
with which
she rains upon   40

   the world

of spring

   drips

so spreads

   the words

far apart to let in

   her love—

And running in between
the drops

   the rain   50

is a kind physician

   the rain
of her thoughts over
the ocean
    every

where

   walking with
invisible swift feet
over

   the helpless   60
    waves—

Unworldly love
that has no hope
   of the world

   and that
cannot change the world
to its delight—

   The rain

falls upon the earth
and grass and flowers   70
come
   perfectly

into form from its
   liquid

clearness

   But love is
unworldly

   and nothing
comes of it but love

following   80

and falling endlessly
from
   her thoughts

1927   1934

THE BOTTICELLIAN TREES

THE alphabet of
the trees

is fading in the
song of the leaves

the crossing
bars of the thin

letters that spelled
winter

and the cold
have been illumined   10

with
pointed green

by the rain and sun—
The strict simple

principles of
straight branches

are being modified
by pinched out

ifs of color, devout
conditions   20

the smiles of love—
. . . . .

until the stript
sentences

move as a woman's
limbs under cloth

and praise from secrecy
with hot ardor

love's ascendancy
in summer—

In summer the song   30
sings itself

above the muffled words—

1927   1934

NANTUCKET

FLOWERS through the window
lavender and yellow

changed by white curtains—
Smell of cleanliness—

Sunshine of late afternoon—
On the glass tray

a glass pitcher, the tumbler
turned down, by which

a key is lying—And the
immaculate white bed   10

1929   1934

THE RED LILY

To the bob-white's call
and drone of reaper

tumbling daisies in the sun—
one by one

about the smutting panels of
white doors

gray shingles slip and fall—
But you, a loveliness

of even lines
curving to the throat, the   10

crossroads is your home.
You are, upon

your steady stem
one trumpeted wide flower

slightly tilted
above a scale of buds—

Sometimes a farmer's wife
gathers an armful

for her pitcher on the porch—
Topping a stone wall   20

against the shale-ledge
a field full—

By the road, the river
the edge of the woods

—opening in the sun
closing with the dark—

everywhere
Red Lily

in your common cup
all beauty lies—   30
1933   1934

THIS IS JUST TO SAY

I HAVE eaten
the plums
that were in
the icebox

and which
you were probably
saving
for breakfast

Forgive me
they were delicious   10
so sweet
and so cold
1934   1934

THE YACHTS

CONTEND in a sea which the land partly
      encloses
shielding them from the too heavy blows
of an ungoverned ocean which when it
      chooses

tortures the biggest hulls, the best man
      knows
to pit against its beatings, and sinks them
      pitilessly.
Mothlike in mists, scintillant in the
      minute

brilliance of cloudless days, with broad
      bellying sails
they glide to the wind tossing green
      water
from their sharp prows while over them the
      crew crawls

ant-like, solicitously grooming them,
      releasing,   10
making fast as they turn, lean far over and
      having
caught the wind again, side by side, head
      for the mark.

In a well guarded arena of open water
      surrounded by
lesser and greater craft which, sycophant,
      lumbering

and flittering follow them, they appear
      youthful, rare
as the light of a happy eye, live with the
      grace
of all that in the mind is feckless, free and
naturally to be desired. Now the sea which
      holds them

is moody, lapping their glossy sides, as if
      feeling
for some slightest flaw but fails
      completely.
Today no race. Then the wind comes again.
      The yachts   21

move, jockeying for a start, the signal is set
      and they
are off. Now the waves strike at them but
      they are too
well made, they slip through, though they
      take in canvas.

Arms with hands grasping seek to clutch at
      the prows.
Bodies thrown recklessly in the way are cut
      aside.
It is a sea of faces about them in agony, in
      despair

until the horror of the race dawns staggering
      the mind,
the whole sea becomes an entanglement of
      watery bodies
lost to the world, bearing what they cannot
      hold. Broken   30

beaten, desolate, reaching from the dead to
      be taken up
they cry out, failing, failing! their cries
      rising
in waves still as the skillful yachts pass
      over.
1935   1935

FINE WORK WITH PITCH AND COPPER

Now they are resting
in the fleckless light
separately in unison

like the sacks
of sifted stone stacked
regularly by twos

about the flat roof
ready after lunch
to be opened and strewn

down the center at right
angles and lies ready
to edge the coping

The copper in eight   10
foot strips has been
beaten lengthwise

One still chewing
picks up a copper strip
and runs his eye along it

1936

1936

MARIANNE MOORE

1887–

A NOTE ON POETRY

I TEND to write in a patterned arrangement, with rhymes; stanza as it follows
stanza being identical in number of syllables
and rhyme-plan, with the first stanza. (Regarding the stanza as the unit, rather than
the line, I sometimes divide a word at the
end of a line, relying on a general straight-
forwardness of treatment to counteract the
mannered effect.) I have a liking for the
long syllable followed by three (or more)   10
short syllables,—'ly*ing on the* air *there is a*
bird,' and for the inconspicuous or light
rhyme,—'let' in flageolet, for instance,
being rhymed with 'set' in the lines,

Its leaps should be set
to the flageolet.

I try to secure an effect of flowing continuity and am more and more impressed
by the many correspondences between
verse and instrumental music. I am against 20
the stock phrase and an easier use of words
in verse than would be tolerated in prose. I
feel that the form is the outward equivalent
of a determining inner conviction, and that
the rhythm is the person.

FROM THE JERBOA [1]

ABUNDANCE

AFRICANUS meant
the conqueror sent
   from Rome. It should mean the

untouched: the sand-brown jumping-rat
   —free-born; and
   the blacks, that choice race with an
      elegance
   ignored by one's ignorance.

Part terrestrial,
and part celestial,
   Jacob saw, cudgel staff
   in claw-hand—steps of air and air
      angels; his   10
   friends were the stones. The
      translucent mistake
   of the desert, does not make

hardship for one who
can rest and then do
   the opposite—launching
   as if on wings, from its match-thin hind
      legs, in
   daytime or at night; that departs with
      great
   speed, followed by, as a weight,

a double length, thin
tail furred like the skin;   20
   that curls round it when it
   sleeps 'round'—the nose nested in fur,
      a hind leg
   at each side of the head—or lies
      lengthwise,
   in view, when the body lies

flat. Seen by daylight,
the body is white
   in front; and on the back,
   buffy-brown like the breast of the fawn-
      breasted
      bower-bird. It hops like the fawn-
      breast, but has
   chipmunk contours—perceived as   30

1 ' "There are little rats called jerboas which run on
long hind-legs as thin as a match. The forelimbs are
mere tiny hands." Dr.R.L.Ditmars: p.274, *Strange
Animals I Have Known.*' Author's note, *Collected
Poems*(N.Y., 1935),109.

it turns its bird head—
the nap directed
  neatly back and blending
    with the ear which reiterates the slimness
      of the body. The fine hairs on the tail,
      repeating the other pale

markings, lengthen till
at the tip they fill
  out in a tuft—black and
  white; strange detail of the simplified
    creature,   40
    fish-shaped and silvered to steel by the
    force
    of the large desert moon. Course

the jerboa, or
plunder its food store,
  and you will be cursed. It
  honours the sand by assuming its colour;
    closed upper paws seeming one with
    the fur
    in its flight from a danger.

By fifths and sevenths,
in leaps of two lengths, 50
  like the uneven notes
  of the Bedouin flute, it stops its gleaning
    on little wheel castors, and makes
    fern-seed
    foot-prints with kangaroo speed.

Its leaps should be set
to the fiageolet;
  pillar body erect
  on a three-cornered smooth-working
    Chippendale
    claw—propped on hind legs, and tail
    as third toe,
    between leaps to its burrow. 60
            1935

NO SWAN SO FINE [1]

'No water so still as the
  dead fountains of Versailles.' No swan,
with swart blind look askance
and gondoliering legs, so fine
  as the chintz china one with fawn-
brown eyes and toothed gold
collar on to show whose bird it was.

1 ' "There is no water so still as the dead fountains of
Versailles." Percy Phillip, *New York Times Magazine*,
10thMay,1931.
  'A pair of Louis XV candelabra with Dresden figures
of swans belonging to Lord Balfour.' Author's note,
ibid.,110.

Lodged in the Louis Fifteenth
  candelabrum-tree of cockscomb-
tinted buttons, dahlias, 10
sea-urchins, and everlastings,
  it perches on the branching foam
of polished sculptured
flowers—at ease and tall. The king is
  dead.

           1935

THE FRIGATE PELICAN [2]

RAPIDLY cruising or lying on the air there is
    a bird
  that realizes Rasselas's friend's project
  of wings uniting levity with strength.
    This
    hell-diver, frigate-bird, hurricane-
bird; unless swift is the proper word
  for him, the storm omen when
  he flies close to the waves, should be seen
    fishing, although oftener
    he appears to prefer

to take, on the wing, from industrious
    cruder-winged species 10
  the fish they have caught, and is seldom
    successless.
  A marvel of grace, no matter how fast his
    victim may fly or how often may
turn, the dishonest pelican's ease
  in pursuit, bears him away
  with the fish that the badgered bird
    drops.
    A kind of superlative
    swallow, that likes to live

on food caught while flying, he is not a
    pelican. The toe
  with slight web, air-boned body, and
    very long wings 20
  with the spread of a swan's—
    duplicating a
    bow-string as he floats overhead—feel
the changing V-shaped scissor swallow-
    tail direct the rigid keel.
  And steering beak to windward always,
    the fleetest foremost fairy
    among birds, outflies the

2 '*Fregata aquila*. The Frigate Pelican of Audubon.
  '*Giant tame armadillo*. Photograph and description
by W.StephenThomas of New York.
  '*Red-spotted orchids*. The blood, supposedly, of na-
tives slain by Pizarro.
  ' "If I do well, I am blessed," etc. Hindoo saying.' Author's note,ibid.,111.

aeroplane which cannot flap its wings nor
    alter any quill-
  tip. For him, the feeling in a hand, in
    fins, is
in his unbent downbent crafty oar. With
    him   30
    other pelicans aimlessly soar
as he does; separating, until
    not flapping they rise once more,
closing in without looking and move
    outward again to the top
    of the circle and stop

and blow back, allowing the wind to reverse
    their direction.
  This is not the stalwart swan that can
    ferry the
woodcutter's two children home; no.
    Make hay; keep
    the shop; I have one sheep; were a
    less
limber animal's mottoes. This one   41
    finds sticks for the swan's-down
    dress
of his child to rest upon and would
    not know Gretel from Hänsel.
    As impassioned Handel—

meant for a lawyer and a masculine German
    domestic
career—clandestinely studied the
    harpsichord
and never was known to have fallen in
    love,
    the unconfiding frigate-bird
    hides
in the height and in the majestic   50
    display of his art. He glides
a hundred feet or quivers about
    as charred paper behaves—full
    of feints; and an eagle

of vigilance, earns the term aquiline;
    keeping at a height
so great the feathers look black and the
    beak does not
show. It is not retreat but exclusion
    from
    which he looks down and observes
    what went
secretly, as it thought, out of sight
    among dense jungle plants. Sent   60
ahead of the rest, there goes the true
    knight in his jointed coat that
    covers all but his bat

ears; a-trot, with stiff pig gait—our tame
    armadillo, loosed by
his master and as pleased as a dog.
    Beside the
spattered blood—that orchid which the
    native fears—
    the fer-de-lance lies sleeping;
    centaur-
like, this harmful couple's amity
    is apropos. A jaguar
and crocodile are fighting. Sharp-
    shinned   70
    hawks and peacock-freckled small
    cats, like the literal

merry-go-round, come wandering within
    the circular view
of the high bird for whom from the air
    they are ants
keeping house all their lives in the crack
    of a
    crag with no view from the top. And
    here,
unlikely animals learning to
    dance, crouch on two steeds that rear
behind a leopard with a frantic
    face, tamed by an Artemis   80
    who wears a dress like his,

and hampering haymaker's hat. *Festina
    lente*. Be gay
civilly. How so? 'If I do well I am
    blessed
whether any bless me or not, and if I do
    ill I am cursed.' We watch the moon
    rise
on the Susquehanna. In his way
    this most romantic bird, flies
to a more mundane place, the mangrove
    swamp, to sleep. He wastes the
    moon.
    But he, and others, soon   90

rise from the bough, and though flying are
    able to foil the tired
moment of danger, that lays on heart and
    lungs the
weight of the python that crushes to
    powder.
    The tune's illiterate footsteps fail;
the steam hacks are not to be admired.
    These, unturbulent, avail
themselves of turbulence to fly—pleased
    with the faint wind's varyings,
    on which to spread fixed wings.

The reticent lugubrious ragged immense
        minuet   100
  descending to leeward, ascending to
     windward
  again without flapping, in what seems to
     be
     a way of resting, are now nearer,
but as seemingly bodiless yet
     as they were. Theirs are sombre
  quills for so wide and lightboned a bird
     as the frigate pelican
     of the Carribean.

                       1935

THE FISH

wade
through black jade.
  Of the crow-blue mussel-shells, one
    keeps
  adjusting the ash-heaps;
    opening and shutting itself like

an
injured fan.
  The barnacles which encrust the side
  of the wave, cannot hide
    there for the submerged shafts of
    the   10

sun,
split like spun
  glass, move themselves with spotlight
    swiftness
  into the crevices—
    in and out, illuminating

the
turquoise sea
  of bodies. The water drives a wedge
  of iron through the iron edge
    of the cliff; whereupon the stars,   20

pink
rice-grains, ink
  bespattered jelly-fish, crabs like green
  lilies, and submarine
    toadstools, slide each on the other.

All
external
  marks of abuse are present on this
  defiant edifice—
    all the physical features of   30

ac-
cident—lack
  of cornice, dynamite grooves, burns, and
  hatchet strokes, these things stand
    out on it; the chasm-side is

dead.
Repeated
  evidence has proved that it can live
  on what cannot revive
    its youth. The sea grows old in it.   40

                       1921

POETRY [1]

I, TOO, dislike it: there are things that are
     important beyond all this fiddle.
  Reading it, however, with a perfect
     contempt for it, one discovers in
  it after all, a place for the genuine.
    Hands that can grasp, eyes
    that can dilate, hair that can rise
     if it must, these things are important
     not because a

high-sounding interpretation can be put
     upon them but because they are
  useful. When they become so derivative
     as to become unintelligible,
  the same thing may be said for all of us,
    that we
    do not admire what   10
    we cannot understand: the bat
     holding on upside down or in quest
     of something to

eat, elephants pushing, a wild horse taking
     a roll, a tireless wolf under
  a tree, the immovable critic twitching his
     skin like a horse that feels a flea,
     the base-

1 'Diary of Tolstoy(Dutton),p.84. "Where the boundary
between prose and poetry lies, I shall never be able to
understand. The question is raised in manuals of style,
yet the answer to it lies beyond me. Poetry is verse:
prose is not verse. Or else poetry is everything with
the exception of business documents and school
books." '
  ' "Literalists of the imagination." Yeats: *Ideas of
Good and Evil*(A.H.Bullen),p.182. "The limitation of
his view was from the very intensity of his vision; he
was a too literal realist of imagination, as others are of
nature; and because he believed that the figures seen
by the mind's eye, when exalted by inspiration were
'eternal existences,' symbols of divine essences, he
hated every grace of style that might obscure their
lineaments." ' Author's note, ibid.,112–13.

ball fan, the statistician—
     nor is it valid
          to discriminate against 'business
          documents and

school-books'; all these phenomena are
          important. One must make a
          distinction
     however: when dragged into promi-
          nence by half poets, the
          result is not poetry,
     nor till the poets among us can be   20
     'literalists of
          the imagination'—above
               insolence and triviality and can
               present

for inspection, imaginary gardens with real
          toads in them, shall we have
     it. In the meantime, if you demand on the
          one hand,
     the raw material of poetry in
          all its rawness and
          that which is on the other hand
               genuine, then you are interested in
               poetry.

                                        1921

THE MONKEYS

winked too much and were afraid of
          snakes. The zebras, supreme
          in
their abnormality; the elephants with their
          fog-coloured skin
     and strictly practical appendages
          were there, the small cats; and the
               parrakeet—
          trivial and humdrum on
               examination, destroying
          bark and portions of the food it could
          not eat.

I recall their magnificence, now not more
          magnificent
than it is dim. It is difficult to recall the
          ornament,
     speech, and precise manner of what one
          might
          call the minor acquaintances
               twenty   10
          years back; but I shall not forget him
               —that Gilgamesh among
          the hairy carnivora—that cat with the

wedge-shaped, slate-gray marks on its
          forelegs and the resolute tail,
astringently remarking, 'They have
          imposed on us with their pale
     half-fledged protestations, trembling
          about
     in inarticulate frenzy, saying
          it is not for us to understand art;
          finding it
     all so difficult, examining the thing

as if it were inconceivably arcanic, as
          symmet-
rically frigid as if it had been carved out of
          chrysoprase   20
     or marble—strict with tension, malignant
          in its power over us and deeper
          than the sea when it proffers flattery
          in exchange for hemp,
     rye, flax, horses, platinum, timber, and
          fur.'
1916   1921

A GRAVE [1]

MAN looking into the sea,
taking the view from those who have as
          much right to it as you have to it
          yourself,
it is human nature to stand in the middle of
          a thing,
but you cannot stand in the middle of this;
the sea has nothing to give but a well
          excavated grave.
The firs stand in a procession, each with an
          emerald turkey-foot at the top,
reserved as their contours, saying nothing;
repression, however, is not the most
          obvious characteristic of the sea;
the sea is a collector, quick to return a
          rapacious look.
There are others besides you who have
          worn that look—   10
whose expression is no longer a protest; the
          fish no longer investigate them
for their bones have not lasted:
men lower nets, unconscious of the fact
          that they are desecrating a grave,

[1] Miss Moore writes: 'As for "A Grave," it has a significance strongly apart from the literal origin, which
was a man who placed himself between my mother and
me, and surf we were watching from a middle ledge
of rocks on Monhegan Island after a storm. ("Don't
be annoyed," my mother said. "It is human nature to
stand in the middle of a thing.")' Benét, ed., Fifty
Poets (N.Y., 1933),84–85.

and row quickly away—the blades of the
        oars
moving together like the feet of water-
        spiders as if there were no such
        thing as death.
The wrinkles progress upon themselves in a
        phalanx—beautiful under networks
        of foam,
and fade breathlessly while the sea rustles in
        and out of the seaweed;
the birds swim through the air at top speed,
        emitting cat-calls as heretofore—
the tortoise-shell scourges about the feet of
        the cliffs, in motion beneath them;
and the ocean, under the pulsation of
        lighthouses and noise of bell-buoys,
advances as usual, looking as if it were not
        that ocean in which dropped things
        are bound to sink—   21
in which if they turn and twist, it is neither
        with volition nor consciousness.
                                        1924

IS YOUR TOWN NINEVEH?

WHY so desolate?
        In phantasmagoria about fishes,
        what disgusts you? Could
        not all personal upheaval in
                the name of freedom, be tabooed?

Is it Nineveh
        and are you Jonah
        in the sweltering east wind of your
                wishes?
        I myself have stood
                there by the Aquarium, looking 10
                at the Statue of Liberty.
                                        1921

TO A SNAIL [1]

IF 'compression is the first grace of
        style,'
you have it. Contractility is a virtue
as modesty is a virtue.
It is not the acquisition of any one thing
that is able to adorn,
or the incidental quality that occurs
as a concomitant of something well said,
that we value in style,
but the principle that is hid:

in the absence of feet, 'a method of
        conclusions';   10
'a knowledge of principles,'
in the curious phenomenon of your
        occipital horn.
1915   1924

THE PAST IS THE PRESENT [2]

IF external action is effete
        and rhyme is outmoded,
        I shall revert to you,
        Habakkuk, as on a recent occasion I was
                goaded
                into doing by XY, who was speaking
                of unrhymed verse.
This man said—I think that I repeat
        his identical words:
        'Hebrew poetry is
        prose with a sort of heightened
                consciousness.' Ecstasy affords
                the occasion and expediency
                determines the form.   10
                                        1924

SILENCE [3]

MY father used to say,
'Superior people never make long visits,
have to be shown Longfellow's grave
or the glass flowers at Harvard.
Self-reliant like the cat—
that takes its prey to privacy,
the mouse's limp tail hanging like a
        shoelace from its mouth—
they sometimes enjoy solitude,
and can be robbed of speech
by speech which has delighted them.   10
The deepest feeling always shows itself in
        silence;
not in silence, but restraint.'
Nor was he insincere in saying, 'Make my
        house your inn.'
Inns are not residences.
                                        1924

1 'The author of the anonymous *De Elocutione* says,
"The first grace of style is that which results from
compression." ' Author's note.

2 ' "Hebrew poetry is prose with a sort of heightened
consciousness." The Reverend E.H.Kellogg.' Author's note, *Collected Poems* (N.Y., 1935), 123–24.

3 ' "My father used to say, 'Superior people never make
long visits. When I am visiting, I like to go about by
myself. I never had to be shown Longfellow's grave or
the glass flowers at Harvard.' " ' Miss A.M.Homans.
    'Edmund Burke, in *Burke's Life*, by Prior. " 'Throw
yourself into a coach,' said he. 'Come down and
make my house your inn.' " ' Author's note, ibid., 124.

WALLACE STEVENS

1879–

A NOTE ON POETRY

MY intention in poetry is to write poetry: to reach and express that which, without any particular definition, everyone recognizes to be poetry, and to do this because I feel the need of doing it.

There is such a complete freedom now-a-days in respect to technique that I am rather inclined to disregard form so long as I am free and can express myself freely. I don't know of anything, respecting form, that makes much difference. The essential thing in form is to be free in whatever form is used. A free form does not assure freedom. As a form, it is just one more form. So that it comes to this, I suppose, that I believe in freedom regardless of form.

1937   1938

THE WORMS AT HEAVEN'S GATE

OUT of the tomb, we bring Badroulbadour,
Within our bellies, we her chariot.
Here is an eye. And here are, one by one,
The lashes of that eye and its white lid.
Here is the cheek on which that lid declined,
And, finger after finger, here, the hand,
The genius of that cheek. Here are the lips,
The bundle of the body and the feet.

Out of the tomb we bring Badroulbadour.
                                        1923

THE EMPEROR OF ICE-CREAM [1]

CALL the roller of big cigars,
The muscular one, and bid him whip
In kitchen cups concupiscent curds.
Let the wenches dawdle in such dress
As they are used to wear, and let the boys
Bring flowers in last month's newspapers.
Let be be finale of seem.
The only emperor is the emperor of
        ice-cream.

[1] Stevens says of the poem: 'This wears a deliberately commonplace costume, and yet it seems to contain something of the essential gaudiness of poetry; that is the reason why I like it.' Benét, ed., *Fifty Poets*,(N.Y., 1933),46.

Take from the dresser of deal,
Lacking the three glass knobs, that sheet
On which she embroidered fantails once
And spread it so as to cover her face.
If her horny feet protrude, they come
To show how cold she is, and dumb.
Let the lamp affix its beam.
The only emperor is the emperor of
        ice-cream.

                                        1923

SUNDAY MORNING

1

COMPLACENCIES of the peignoir, and late
Coffee and oranges in a sunny chair,
And the green freedom of a cockatoo
Upon a rug mingle to dissipate
The holy hush of ancient sacrifice.
She dreams a little, and she feels the dark
Encroachment of that old catastrophe,
As a calm darkens among water-lights.
The pungent oranges and bright, green
        wings
Seem things in some procession of the dead,
Winding across wide water, without sound,
The day is like wide water, without sound,
Stilled for the passing of her dreaming feet
Over the seas, to silent Palestine,
Dominion of the blood and sepulchre.

2

Why should she give her bounty to the
        dead?
What is divinity if it can come
Only in silent shadows and in dreams?
Shall she not find in comforts of the sun,
In pungent fruit and bright, green wings,
        or else
In any balm or beauty of the earth,
Things to be cherished like the thought of
        heaven?
Divinity must live within herself:
Passions of rain, or moods in falling snow;
Grievings in loneliness, or unsubdued
Elations when the forest blooms; gusty
Emotions on wet roads on autumn nights;
All pleasures and all pains, remembering
The bough of summer and the winter
        branch.
These are the measures destined for her
        soul.

3

Jove in the clouds had his inhuman birth.
No mother suckled him, no sweet land gave
Large-mannered motions to his mythy
    mind.
He moved among us, as a muttering king,
Magnificent, would move among his hinds,
Until our blood, commingling, virginal,
With heaven, brought such requital to
    desire
The very hinds discerned it, in a star.
Shall our blood fail? Or shall it come to be
The blood of paradise? And shall the earth
Seem all of paradise that we shall know?   41
The sky will be much friendlier then than
    now,
A part of labor and a part of pain,
And next in glory to enduring love,
Not this dividing and indifferent blue.

4

She says, 'I am content when wakened
    birds,
Before they fly, test the reality
Of misty fields, by their sweet questionings;
But when the birds are gone, and their
    warm fields
Return no more, where, then, is paradise?'
There is not any haunt of prophecy,   51
Nor any old chimera of the grave,
Neither the golden underground, nor isle
Melodious, where spirits gat them home,
Nor visionary south, nor cloudy palm
Remote on heaven's hill, that has endured
As April's green endures; or will endure
Like her remembrance of awakened birds,
Or her desire for June and evening, tipped
By the consummation of the swallow's
    wings.   60

5

She says, 'But in contentment I still feel
The need of some imperishable bliss.'
Death is the mother of beauty; hence from
    her,
Alone, shall come fulfilment to our dreams
And our desires. Although she strews the
    leaves
Of sure obliteration on our paths,
The path sick sorrow took, the many paths
Where triumph rang its brassy phrase, or
    love
Whispered a little out of tenderness,
She makes the willow shiver in the sun   70

For maidens who were wont to sit and gaze
Upon the grass, relinquished to their feet.
She causes boys to pile new plums and
    pears
On disregarded plate. The maidens taste
And stray impassioned in the littering
    leaves.

6

Is there no change of death in paradise?
Does ripe fruit never fall? Or do the boughs
Hang always heavy in that perfect sky,
Unchanging, yet so like our perishing earth,
With rivers like our own that seek for seas
They never find, the same receding shores
That never touch with inarticulate pang?   82
Why set the pear upon those river-banks
Or spice the shores with odors of the plum?
Alas, that they should wear our colors
    there,
The silken weavings of our afternoons,
And pick the strings of our insipid lutes!
Death is the mother of beauty, mystical,
Within whose burning bosom we devise
Our earthly mothers waiting, sleeplessly.   90

7

Supple and turbulent, a ring of men
Shall chant in orgy on a summer morn
Their boisterous devotion to the sun,
Not as a god, but as a god might be,
Naked among them, like a savage source.
Their chant shall be a chant of paradise,
Out of their blood, returning to the sky;
And in their chant shall enter, voice by
    voice,
The windy lake wherein their lord delights,
The trees, like serafin, and echoing hills,
That choir among themselves long
    afterward.   101
They shall know well the heavenly
    fellowship
Of men that perish and of summer morn.
And whence they came and whither they
    shall go
The dew upon their feet shall manifest.

8

She hears, upon that water without sound,
A voice that cries, 'The tomb in Palestine
Is not the porch of spirits lingering.
It is the grave of Jesus, where he lay.'
We live in an old chaos of the sun,   110
Or old dependency of day and night,
Or island solitude, unsponsored, free,

Of that wide water, inescapable.
Deer walk upon our mountains, and the
    quail
Whistle about us their spontaneous cries;
Sweet berries ripen in the wilderness;
And, in the isolation of the sky,
At evening, casual flocks of pigeons make
Ambiguous undulations as they sink,
Downward to darkness, on extended
    wings.   120
                                              1923

THE BIRD WITH THE
COPPERY, KEEN CLAWS

ABOVE the forest of the parakeets,
A parakeet of parakeets prevails,
A pip of life amid a mort of tails.

(The rudiments of tropics are around,
Aloe of ivory, pear of rusty rind.)
His lids are white because his eyes are blind.

He is not paradise of parakeets,
Of his gold ether, golden alguazil,
Except because he broods there and is still.

Panache upon panache, his tails deploy   10
Upward and outward, in green-vented
    forms,
His tip a drop of water full of storms.

But though the turbulent tinges undulate
As his pure intellect applies its laws,
He moves not on his coppery, keen claws.

He munches a dry shell while he exerts
His will, yet never ceases, perfect cock,
To flare, in the sun-pallor of his rock.
                                              1923

TO THE ONE OF FICTIVE
MUSIC

SISTER and mother and diviner love,
And of the sisterhood of the living dead
Most near, most clear, and of the clearest
    bloom,
And of the fragrant mothers the most dear
And queen, and of diviner love the day
And flame and summer and sweet fire, no
    thread
Of cloudy silver sprinkles in your gown
Its venom of renown, and on your head
No crown is simpler than the simple hair.

Now, of the music summoned by the birth
That separates us from the wind and sea,   11
Yet leaves us in them, until earth becomes,
By being so much of the things we are,
Gross effigy and simulacrum, none
Gives motion to perfection more serene
Than yours, out of our imperfections
    wrought,
Most rare, or ever of more kindred air
In the laborious weaving that you wear.

For so retentive of themselves are men
That music is intensest which proclaims   20
The near, the clear, and vaunts the clearest
    bloom,
And of all vigils musing the obscure,
That apprehends the most which sees and
    names,
As in your name, an image that is sure,
Among the arrant spices of the sun,
O bough and bush and scented vine, in
    whom
We give ourselves our likest issuance.

Yet not too like, yet not so like to be
Too near, too clear, saving a little to endow
Our feigning with the strange unlike,
    whence springs   30
The difference that heavenly pity brings.
For this, musician, in your girdle fixed
Bear other perfumes. On your pale head
    wear
A band entwining, set with fatal stones.
Unreal, give back to us what once you gave:
The imagination that we spurned and crave.
                                              1923

PETER QUINCE AT THE CLAVIER

I

JUST as my fingers on these keys
Make music, so the self-same sounds
On my spirit make a music, too.

Music is feeling, then, not sound;
And thus it is that what I feel,
Here in this room, desiring you,

Thinking of your blue-shadowed silk,
Is music. It is like the strain
Waked in the elders by Susanna.

Of a green evening, clear and warm,   10
She bathed in her still garden, while
The red-eyed elders watching, felt

The basses of their beings throb
In witching chords, and their thin
    blood
Pulse pizzicati of Hosanna.

2

In the green water, clear and warm,
Susanna lay.
She searched
The touch of springs,
And found   20
Concealed imaginings.
She sighed,
For so much melody.

Upon the bank, she stood
In the cool
Of spent emotions.
She felt, among the leaves,
The dew
Of old devotions.

She walked upon the grass,   30
Still quavering.
The winds were like her maids,
On timid feet,
Fetching her woven scarves,
Yet wavering.

A breath upon her hand
Muted the night.
She turned—
A cymbal clashed,
And roaring horns.   40

3

Soon, with a noise like tambourines,
Came her attendant Byzantines.

They wondered why Susanna cried
Against the elders by her side;

And as they whispered, the refrain
Was like a willow swept by rain.

Anon, their lamps' uplifted flame
Revealed Susanna and her shame.

And then, the simpering Byzantines
Fled, with a noise like tambourines.   50

4

Beauty is momentary in the mind—
The fitful tracing of a portal;
But in the flesh it is immortal.

The body dies; the body's beauty lives.
So evenings die, in their green going,
A wave, interminably flowing.
So gardens die, their meek breath scenting
The cowl of winter, done repenting.
So maidens die to the auroral
Celebration of a maiden's choral.   60

Susanna's music touched the bawdy
    strings
Of those white elders; but, escaping,
Left only Death's ironic scraping.
Now in its immortality, it plays
On the clear viol of her memory,
And makes a constant sacrament of
    praise.

                          1923

SEA SURFACE FULL OF CLOUDS

1

In that November off Tehuantepec,
The slopping of the sea grew still one night
And in the morning summer hued the deck

And made one think of rosy chocolate
And gilt umbrellas. Paradisal green
Gave suavity to the perplexed machine

Of ocean, which like limpid water lay.
Who, then, in that ambrosial latitude
Out of the light evolved the moving
    blooms,

Who, then, evolved the sea-blooms from
    the clouds   10
Diffusing balm in that Pacific calm?
C'était mon enfant, mon bijou, mon âme.[1]

The sea-clouds whitened far below the
    calm
And moved, as blooms move, in the
    swimming green
And in its watery radiance, while the hue

Of heaven in an antique reflection rolled
Round those flotillas. And sometimes the
    sea
Poured brilliant iris on the glistening blue.

2

In that November off Tehuantepec   19
The slopping of the sea grew still one night
At breakfast jelly yellow streaked the deck

1 'It was my child, my darling, and my soul.'

And made one think of chop-house
  chocolate
And sham umbrellas. And a sham-like
  green
Capped summer-seeming on the tense
  machine

Of ocean, which in sinister flatness lay.
Who, then, beheld the rising of the clouds
That strode submerged in that malevolent
  sheen,

Who saw the mortal massives of the blooms
Of water moving on the water-floor?
C'était mon frère du ciel, ma vie, mon or.[1] 30

The gongs rang loudly as the windy booms
Hoo-hooed it in the darkened
  ocean-blooms.
The gongs grew still. And then blue heaven
  spread

Its crystalline pendentives on the sea
And the macabre of the water-glooms
In an enormous undulation fled.

3

In that November off Tehuantepec,
The slopping of the sea grew still one night
And a pale silver patterned on the deck 39

And made one think of porcelain chocolate
And pied umbrellas. An uncertain green,
Piano-polished, held the tranced machine

Of ocean, as a prelude holds and holds.
Who, seeing silver petals of white blooms
Unfolding in the water, feeling sure

Of the milk within the saltiest spurge,
  heard, then,
The sea unfolding in the sunken clouds?
Oh! C'était mon extase et mon amour.[2]

So deeply sunken were they that the
  shrouds,
The shrouding shadows, made the petals
  black 50
Until the rolling heaven made them blue,

A blue beyond the rainy hyacinth,
And smiting the crevasses of the leaves
Deluged the ocean with a sapphire blue.

4

In that November off Tehuantepec
The night-long slopping of the sea grew
  still.
A mallow morning dozed upon the deck

And made one think of musky chocolate
And frail umbrellas. A too-fluent green
Suggested malice in the dry machine 60

Of ocean, pondering dank stratagem.
Who then beheld the figures of the
  clouds
Like blooms secluded in the thick marine?

Like blooms? Like damasks that were
  shaken off
From the loosed girdles in the spangling
  must.
C'était ma foi, la nonchalance divine.[3]

The nakedness would rise and suddenly
  turn
Salt masks of beard and mouths of
  bellowing,
Would—But more suddenly the heaven
  rolled

Its bluest sea-clouds in the thinking green,
And the nakedness became the broadest
  blooms, 71
Mile-mallows that a mallow sun cajoled.

5

In that November off Tehuantepec
Night stilled the slopping of the sea. The
  day
Came, bowing and voluble, upon the deck,

Good clown. . . . One thought of Chinese
  chocolate
And large umbrellas. And a motley green
Followed the drift of the obese machine

Of ocean, perfected in indolence.
What pistache one, ingenious and droll, 80
Beheld the sovereign clouds as jugglery

And the sea as turquoise-turbaned Sambo,
  neat
At tossing saucers—cloudy-conjuring sea?
C'était mon esprit bâtard, l'ignominie.[4]

---

1 'It was my heavenly brother, my life, my gold.'
2 'Oh! It was my ecstasy and my love.'
3 'It was my faith, divine nonchalance.'
4 'It was ignominy, my hybrid mind.'

The sovereign clouds came clustering. The
    conch
Of loyal conjuration trumped. The wind
Of green blooms turning crisped the
    motley hue

To clearing opalescence. Then the sea   88
And heaven rolled as one and from the two
Came fresh transfigurings of freshest blue.

                        1931

THE IDEA OF ORDER AT KEY WEST

SHE sang beyond the genius of the sea.
The water never formed to mind or voice,
Like a body wholly body, fluttering
Its empty sleeves; and yet its mimic
    motion
Made constant cry, caused constantly a
    cry,
That was not ours although we
    understood,
Inhuman, of the veritable ocean.

The sea was not a mask. No more was she.
The song and water were not medleyed
    sound
Even if what she sang was what she heard,
Since what she sang was uttered word by
    word.   11
It may be that in all her phrases stirred
The grinding water and the gasping wind;
But it was she and not the sea we heard.

For she was the maker of the song she sang.
The ever-hooded, tragic-gestured sea
Was merely a place by which she walked to
    sing.
Whose spirit is this? we said, because we
    knew
It was the spirit that we sought and knew
That we should ask this often as she sang.

If it was only the dark voice of the sea   21
That rose, or even colored by many waves;
If it was only that outer voice of sky
And cloud, of the sunken coral
    water-walled,
However clear, it would have been deep air,
The heaving speech of air, a summer sound
Repeated in a summer without end
And sound alone. But it was more than that,
More even than her voice, and ours, among
The meaningless plungings of water and
    the wind,   30

Theatrical distances, bronze shadows
    heaped
On high horizons, mountainous
    atmospheres
Of sky and sea.

                    It was her voice that made
The sky acutest at its vanishing.
She measured to the hour its solitude.
She was the single artificer of the world
In which she sang. And when she sang, the
    sea,
Whatever self it had, became the self
That was her song, for she was the maker.
    Then we,   40
As we beheld her striding there alone,
Knew that there never was a world for her
Except the one she sang and, singing,
    made.

Ramon Fernandez, tell me, if you know,
Why, when the singing ended and we
    turned
Toward the town, tell why the glassy
    lights,
The lights in the fishing boats at anchor
    there,
As the night descended, tilting in the air,
Mastered the night and portioned out the
    sea,   49
Fixing emblazoned zones and fiery poles,
Arranging, deepening, enchanting night.

Oh! Blessed rage for order, pale Ramon,
The maker's rage to order words of the
    sea,
Words of the fragrant portals,
    dimly-starred,
And of ourselves and of our origins,
In ghostlier demarcations, keener sounds.

                        1935

A POSTCARD FROM THE VOLCANO

CHILDREN picking up our bones
Will never know that these were once
As quick as foxes on the hill;

And that in autumn, when the grapes
Made sharp air sharper by their smell
These had a being, breathing frost;

And least will guess that with our bones
We left much more, left what still is
The look of things, left what we felt

At what we saw. The spring clouds blow 10
Above the shuttered mansion-house,
Beyond our gate and the windy sky

Cries out a literate despair.
We knew for long the mansion's look
And what we said of it became

A part of what it is . . . Children,
Still weaving budded aureoles,
Will speak our speech and never know,

Will say of the mansion that it seems
As if he that lived there left behind 20
A spirit storming in blank walls,

A dirty house in a gutted world,
A tatter of shadows peaked to white,
Smeared with the gold of the opulent sun.

1935

FROM OWL'S CLOVER
V. SOMBRE FIGURATION

1

THERE is a man whom rhapsodies of change,
Of which he is the cause, have never
    changed
And never will, a subman under all
The rest, to whom in the end the rest
    return,
The man below the man below the man,
Steeped in night's opium, evading day.

2

We have grown weary of the man that
    thinks.
He thinks and it is not true. The man
    below
Imagines and it is true, as if he thought
By imagining, anti-logician, quick 10
With a logic of transforming certitudes.
It is not that he was born in another land,
Powdered with primitive lights, and lives
    with us
In glimpses, on the edge or at the tip.
He was born within us as a second self,
A self of parents who have never died,
Whose lives return, simply, upon our lips,
Their word and ours; in what we see, their
    hues
Without a season, unstinted in livery,
And ours, of rigid measure, a miser's paint;
And most in what we hear, sound brushed
    away, 21

A mumbling at the elbow, turgid tunes,
As of insects or cloud-stricken birds,
    away
And away, dialogues between incognitos.
He dwells below, the man below, in less
Than body and in less than mind, ogre,
Inhabitant, in less than shape, of shapes
That are dissembled in vague memory
Yet still retain resemblances, remain 2?
Remembrances, a place of a field of lights,
As a church is a bell and people are an
    eye,
A cry, the pallor of a dress, a touch.
He turns us into scholars, studying
The masks of music. We perceive each
    mask
To be the musician's own and, thence,
    become
An audience to mimics glistening
With meanings, doubled by the closest
    sound,
Mimics that play on instruments discerned
In the beat of the blood.
                    Green is the path we take 40
Between chimeras and garlanded the way,
The down-descent into November's void.
The spontaneities of rain or snow
Surprise the sterile rationalist who sees
Maidens in bloom, bulls under sea, the lark
On urns and oak-leaves twisted into
    rhyme.
The man, but not the man below, for whom
The pheasant in a field was pheasant,
    field,
Until they changed to eagle in white air,
Lives in a fluid, not on solid rock. 50
The solid was an age, a period
With appropriate, largely English,
    furniture,
Barbers with charts of the only possible
    modes,
Cities that would not wash away in the
    mist,
Each man in his asylum maundering,
Policed by the hope of Christmas. Summer
    night,
Night gold, and winter night, night silver,
    these
Were the fluid, the cat-eyed atmosphere, in
    which
The man and the man below were
    reconciled,
The east wind in the west, order
    destroyed, 60
The cycle of the solid having turned.

3

High up in heaven a sprawling portent
   moves,
As if it bears all darkness in its bulk.
But this we cannot see. The shaggy top
Broods in tense meditation, constantly,
On the city, on which it leans, the people
   there,
Its shadow on their houses, on their walls,
Their beds, their faces drawn in distant
   sleep.
This is invisible.   The supporting arms
Reach from the horizons, rim to rim,   70
While the shaggy top collects itself to do
And the shoulders turn, breathing
   immense intent.
All this is hidden from sight.
                  It is the form
Of a generation that does not know itself,
Still questioning if to crush the soaring
   stacks.
The man below beholds the portent
   poised,
An image of his making, beyond the eye.
The year's dim elongations stretch below
To tumbled rock, its bright projections lie
The shallowest iris on the emptiest eye.   81
The future must bear within it every past,
Not least the pasts destroyed, magniloquent
Syllables, pewter on ebony, yet still
A board for bishops' grapes, the happy
   form
That revolution takes for connoisseurs:
The portent may itself be memory;
And memory may itself be time to come
And must be, when the portent, changed,
   takes on
A mask up-gathered brilliantly from the
   dirt,   90
And memory's lord is the lord of prophesy
And steps forth, priestly in severity,   .
Yet lord, a mask of flame, the darkest form
A wandering orb upon a path grown clear.

4

High up in heaven the sprawling portent
   moves.
The statue in a crow's perspective of trees
Stands brimming white, chiaroscuro
   scaled
To space. To space? The statue scaled to
   space
Would be a ring of heads and haunches,
   torn

From size, backs larger than the eye, not
   flesh   100
In marble, but marble massive as the thrust
Of that which is not seen and cannot be.
The portent would become man-haggard to
A race of dwarfs, the meditative arms
And head a shadow trampled under hoofs,
Man-misty to a race star-humped, astride
In a clamor thudding up from central
   earth.
Not the space in camera of the man below,
Immeasurable, the space in which he knows
The locust's titter and the turtle's sob.   110
The statue stands in true perspective.
     Crows
Give only their color to the leaves. The
   trees
Are full of fanfares of farewell, as night
And the portent end in night, composed,
   before
Its wheel begins to turn.
               The statue stands
In hum-drum space, farewell, farewell, by
   day
The green, white, blue of the ballad-eye,
   by night
The mirror of other nights combined in
   one.
The spring is hum-drum like an
   instrument,   120
That a man without passion plays in an
   aimless way.
Even imagination has an end,
When the statue is not a thing imagined, a
   stone,
The flight of emblemata through his mind,
Thoughts by descent. To flourish the great
   cloak we wear
At night, to turn away from the
   abominable
Farewells and, in the darkness, to feel
   again
The reconciliation, the rapture of a time
Without imagination, without past   129
And without future, a present time, is that
The passion, indifferent to the poets' hum,
That we conceal? A passion to fling the
   cloak,
Adorned for a multitude, in a gesture spent
In the gesture's whim, a passion merely to
   be
For the gaudium of being, Jocundus
   instead
Of the black-blooded scholar, the man of
   the cloud, to be

The medium man among other medium
 men,
The cloak to be clipped, the night to be
 re-designed,
Its land-breath to be stifled, its color
 changed,
Night and the imagination being one. 140
1936   1937

FROM A THOUGHT REVOLVED

III. ROMANESQUE AFFABULATION

HE sought an earthly leader who could
 stand
Without panache, without cockade,
Son only of man and sun of men,
The outer captain, the inner saint,

The pine, the pillar and the priest,
The voice, the book, the hidden well,

The faster's feast and heavy-fruited star,
The father, the beater of the rigid drums,

He that at midnight touches the guitar,
The solitude, the barrier, the Pole 10
In Paris, celui qui chante et pleure,[1]
Winter devising summer in its breast,

Summer assaulted, thundering, illumed,
Shelter yet thrower of the summer spear,
With all his attributes no god but man
Of men whose heaven is in themselves,

Or else whose hell, foamed with their
 blood
And the long echo of their dying cry,
A fate intoned, a death before they die,
The race that sings and weeps and knows
  not why.   20
1936   1937

CONRAD AIKEN
1889–

DISCORDANTS [2]

I

MUSIC I heard with you was more than
 music,
And bread I broke with you was more than
 bread;
Now that I am without you, all is desolate;
All that was once so beautiful is dead.

Your hands once touched this table and this
 silver,
And I have seen your fingers hold this glass.

These things do not remember you,
 belovèd,—
And yet your touch upon them will not
 pass.

For it was in my heart you moved among
 them,
And blessed them with your hands and
 with your eyes; 10
And in my heart they will remember
 always,—
They knew you once, O beautiful and wise.
1914   1916

THE HOUSE OF DUST [3]

IV
iii

WELL, as you say, we live for small
 horizons:
We move in crowds, we flow and talk
 together,   101

1 'He who sings and weeps.'

2 ' "Music I Heard with You," from "Discordants"
(1914), the first of a group of five lyrics, is an early and
experimental specimen of a form which has since attracted me: the presentation of poems in a series or sequence. Other similar series in my later work are
"Variations" (1916), "Improvisations: Lights and
Snow" (1917), "Priapus and the Pool" (1922), and the
two recent volumes of preludes, "Preludes for Memnon" and "Time in the Rock." What interested me
was the possibility of variation, whether by contrast of
tone, theme, or form, within the frame of a unifying
reference. As early as these rather rudimentary "Discordants" I had begun to harbor dangerous notions of
dividing poetry, as one would divide music, into alternating and contrasting movements. The five symphonic poems which I was to do later—"The Charnel
Rose," "The Jig of Forslin," "Senlin," "The House
of Dust," and "The Pilgrimage of Festus"—were
more elaborate developments of the same idea.' Author's note.

3 'The theme of "The House of Dust" might be described as an extended analogy between the multicellular activity and nature of a great city, and the
multicellular activity and nature of the human consciousness. The approach to it—as in the other symphonies also—might be said to be *spiral*: by a series of
contrasted narrative or lyric or analytic sections, moving slowly forward, but now and again looping back,
the juxtaposition of the different modes being as care-

Seeing so many eyes and hands and faces,
So many mouths, and all the secret
    meanings,—
Yet know so little of them; only seeing
The small bright circle of our
    consciousness,
Beyond which lies the dark. Some few we
    know—
Or think we know. . . . Once, on a sun-
    bright morning,
I walked in a certain hallway, trying to find
A certain door: I found one, tried it,
    opened,
And there in a spacious chamber, brightly
    lighted,   110
A hundred men played music, loudly,
    swiftly,
While one tall woman sent her voice above
    them
In powerful sweetness. . . . Closing then
    the door
I heard it die behind me, fade to whisper,—
And walked in a quiet hallway as before.
Just such a glimpse, as through that
    opened door,
Is all we know of those we call our
    friends. . . .
We hear a sudden music, see a playing
Of ordered thoughts—and all again is
    silence.
The music, we suppose, (as in ourselves) 120
Goes on forever there, behind shut doors,—
As it continues after our departure,
So, we divine, it played before we
    came . . .
What do you know of me, or I of you? . . .
Little enough. . . . We set these doors
    ajar

Only for chosen movements of the music:
This passage, (so I think—yet this is
    guesswork)
Will please him,—it is in a strain he
    fancies,—
More brilliant, though, than his; and while
    he likes it
He will be piqued. . . . He looks at me
    bewildered   130
And thinks (to judge from self—this too is
    guesswork)
The music strangely subtle, deep in
    meaning,
Perplexed with implications; he suspects
    me
Of hidden riches, unexpected wisdom. . . .
Or else I let him hear a lyric passage,—
Simple and clear; and all the while he
    listens
I make pretence to think my doors are
    closed.
This too bewilders him. He eyes me
    sidelong
Wondering 'Is he such a fool as this?
Or only mocking?' —There I let it
    end. . . .   140
Sometimes, of course, and when we least
    suspect it—
When we pursue our thoughts with too
    much passion,
Talking with too great zeal—our doors fly
    open
Without intention; and the hungry watcher
Stares at the feast, carries away our secrets,
And laughs . . . but this, for many
    counts, is seldom.
And for the most part we vouchsafe our
    friends,
Our lovers too, only such few clear notes
As we shall deem them likely to admire:
'Praise me for this' we say, or 'laugh at
    this,'   150
Or 'marvel at my candor' . . . all the
    while
Withholding what's most precious to
    ourselves,—
Some sinister depth of lust or fear or
    hatred,
The sombre note that gives the chord its
    power;
Or a white loveliness—if such we know—
Too much like fire to speak of without
    shame.

. . . .

fully calculated as possible to produce an effect as of contrapuntal richness in music. In the circumstances, many sections of the symphonies must suffer greatly if detached from their context, to which they are bound *affectively* rather than logically: their own tone is partly the overtone (the remembered emotion-mass) of the preceding section; and this too will change in retrospect when the *next* section has been read. That, at any rate, was my theory. The present selection from "The House of Dust" stands better by itself than most, simply because it is the climax and arcanum of the poem, in the attempt of consciousness to be, as it were, conscious of itself. But even here it may be interesting to notice that it is set, for better effect, between a rather hard little narrative movement and an elegiac section. The reflective blank verse, too, perhaps gains something in character from its contrast with the rhymed and stanzaed movements—the one rapid, the other slow—which precede and follow it.' Author's note.

1916–1917   1920

FROM PRIAPUS AND THE POOL

III [1]

WHEN trout swim down Great Ormond
     Street,
And sea-gulls cry above them lightly,
And hawthorns heave cold flagstones
     up
To blossom whitely,

Against old walls of houses there,
Gustily shaking out in moonlight
Their country sweetness on sweet air;
And in the sunlight,

By the green margin of that water,
Children dip white feet and shout,   10
Casting nets in the braided water
To catch the trout:

Then I shall hold my breath and die,
Swearing I never loved you; no,
'You are not lovely!' I shall cry,
'I never loved you so.'

IV [2]

THIS is the shape of the leaf, and this of the
     flower,
And this the pale bole of the tree
Which watches its bough in a pool of
     unwavering water
In a land we never shall see.

The thrush on the bough is silent, the dew
     falls softly,
In the evening is hardly a sound.
And the three beautiful pilgrims who come
     here together
Touch lightly the dust of the ground,

Touch it with feet that trouble the dust but
     as wings do,
Come shyly together, are still,   10

Like dancers who wait, in a pause of the
     music, for music
The exquisite silence to fill.

This is the thought of the first, and this of
     the second,
And this the grave thought of the third:
'Linger we thus for a moment, palely
     expectant,
And silence will end, and the bird

'Sing the pure phrase, sweet phrase, clear
     phrase in the twilight
To fill the blue bell of the world;
And we, who on music so leaflike have
     drifted together,
Leaflike apart shall be whirled.'   20

XVI [3]

SEE, as the carver carves a rose,
A wing, a toad, a serpent's eye,
In cruel granite, to disclose
The soft things that in hardness lie,

So this one, taking up his heart,
Which time and change had made a stone,
Carved out of it with dolorous art,
Labouring yearlong and alone,

The thing there hidden—rose, toad, wing?
A frog's hand on a lily pad?   10
Bees in a cobweb—? No such thing!
A girl's head was the thing he had,

Small, shapely, richly crowned with hair,
Drowsy, with eyes half closed, as they
Looked through you and beyond you,
     clear
To something farther than Cathay:

Saw you, yet counted you not worth
The seeing, thinking all the while
How, flower-like, beauty comes to birth;
And thinking this, began to smile.   20

Medusa! For she could not see
The world she turned to stone and ash.
Only herself she saw, a tree
That flowered beneath a lightning-flash.

---

1 'This is perhaps interesting for the shift after the second stanza from masculine-feminine endings to fem-
inine-masculine, and then in the final stanza, wholly
masculine. An effect as of modulation from minor to
major.' Author's note.

2 'This, originally called "Portrait of a Girl," when published out of series, may be compared with number IX
of "Priapus and the Pool," of which it is the companion-piece. The latter was originally called "Portrait
of a Man," and both are *whole-poem* analogies; the one
envisaging the girl as a meeting of three pilgrims under
a tree, the other envisaging the man as a desert over
which blows a fragrant wind from another land.' Author's note.

3 'It may be worth noting in this how the theme of the
"carver" is reënforced by the introduction of a series
of small concrete objects, without qualifications, and
all monosyllabic: rose, wing, toad, serpent's eye, and
so on.' Author's note.

Thus dreamed her face—a lovely thing,
To worship, weep for, or to break.
Better to carve a claw, a wing,
Or, if the heart provide, a snake.
1920   1922

SEA HOLLY [1]

BEGOTTEN by the meeting of rock with
        rock,
The mating of rock and rock, rocks
        gnashing together;
Created so, and yet forgetful, walks
The seaward path, puts up her left hand,
        shades
Blue eyes, the eyes of rock, to see better
In slanting light the ancient sheep (which
        kneels
Biting the grass) the while her other hand,
Hooking the wicker handle, turns the basket
Of eggs. The sea is high to-day. The eggs
Are cheaper. The sea is blown from the
        southwest,   10
Confused, taking up sand and mud in
        waves,
The waves break, sluggish, in brown foam,
        the wind
Disperses (on the sheep and hawthorn)
        spray,—
And on her cheeks, the cheeks engendered
        of rock,
And eyes, the colour of rock. The left hand
Falls from the eyes, and undecided slides
Over the left breast on which muslin
        lightly
Rests, touching the nipple, and then down
The hollow side, virgin as rock, and bitterly
Caresses the blue hip.   20

1 ' "Sea Holly" is a curiosity in the technique of mere
repetition. In forty-eight lines, the word "rock" is repeated twenty-two times. Not a method wholly to be
recommended, but here perhaps excusable, in conjunction with the harshness and staccato qualities of
the verse, for its obvious contribution of bleakness and
monotony to the theme of barrenness. This poem, together with "The Room" and "Sound of Breaking"
and ten others, constituted a series of experiments in
blank verse. The great flexibility of the form attracted
me, with its range all the way from lyric or narrative
to contemplative or analytic; and in addition to seeking
a medium somewhat hard on the surface, metallic and
ironic, I was also interested in using a "parable" form,
a thing that might be called a narrative symbol, or
symbolic narrative. It was my idea to keep the *terms*
as simple as possible, and merely to let the chosen
theme *act itself*: a mere reporting of a thing done and
seen. In "The Room," for example, the statement is
of the barest, and in "Sound of Breaking" little more
so.' Author's note

                                  It was for this,
This obtuse taking of the seaward path,
This stupid hearing of larks, this hooking
Of wicker, this absent observation of sheep
Kneeling in harsh sea-grass, the cool hand
        shading
The spray-stung eyes—it was for this the
        rock
Smote itself. The sea is higher to-day,
And eggs are cheaper. The eyes of rock take
        in
The seaward path that winds toward the
        sea,
The thistle-prodder, old woman under a
        bonnet,   30
Forking the thistles, her back against the
        sea,
Pausing, with hard hands on the handle,
        peering
With rock eyes from her bonnet.

                                  It was for this,
This rock-lipped facing of brown waves,
        half sand
And half water, this tentative hand that
        slides
Over the breast of rock, and into the hollow
Soft side of muslin rock, and then fiercely
Almost as rock against the hip of rock—
It was for this in midnight the rocks met, 40
And dithered together, cracking and
        smoking.

                                  It was for this
Barren beauty, barrenness of rock that
        aches
On the seaward path, seeing the fruitful
        sea,
Hearing the lark of rock that sings, smelling
The rock-flower of hawthorn, sweetness of
        rock—
It was for this, stone pain in the stony
        heart,
The rock loved and laboured; and all is lost.
1924   1925

THE ROOM

THROUGH that window—all else being
        extinct
Except itself and me—I saw the struggle
Of darkness against darkness. Within the
        room
It turned and turned, dived downward.
        Then I saw

How order might—if chaos wished—
    become:
And saw the darkness crush upon itself,
Contracting powerfully; it was as if
It killed itself: slowly: and with much pain.
Pain. The scene was pain, and nothing but
    pain.
What else, when chaos draws all forces
    inward   10
To shape a single leaf? . . .

                For the leaf came,
Alone and shining in the empty room;
After a while the twig shot downward from
    it;
And from the twig a bough; and then the
    trunk,
Massive and coarse; and last the one black
    root.
The black root cracked the walls. Boughs
    burst the window:
The great tree took possession.

                    Tree of trees!
Remember (when time comes) how chaos
    died   20
To shape the shining leaf. Then turn, have
    courage,
Wrap arms and roots together, be
    convulsed
With grief, and bring back chaos out of
    shape.
I will be watching then as I watch now.
I will praise darkness now, but then the
    leaf.
1924   1925

SOUND OF BREAKING

WHY do you cry out, why do I like to hear
    you
Cry out, here in the dewless evening, sitting
Close, close together, so close that the
    heart stops beating
And the brain its thought? Wordless,
    worthless mortals
Stumbling, exhausted, in this wilderness
Of our conjoint destruction! Hear the
    grass
Raging about us! Hear the worms applaud!
Hear how the ripples make a sound of
    chaos!
Hear now, in these and the other sounds of
    evening,
The first brute step of God!   10

                    About your elbow,
Making a ring of thumb and finger, I
Slide the walled blood against the less-
    walled blood,
Move down your arm, surmount the wrist-
    bone, shut
Your long slim hand in mine. Each
    finger-tip
Is then saluted by a finger-tip;
The hands meet back to back, then face to
    face;
Then lock together. And we, with eyes
    averted,
Smile at the evening sky of alabaster,
See nothing, lose our souls in the
    maelstrom, turning   20
Downward in rapid circles.

                    Bitter woman,
Bitter of heart and brain and blood, bitter
    as I
Who drink your bitterness—can this be
    beauty?
Do you cry out because the beauty is cruel?
Terror, because we downward sweep so
    swiftly?
Terror of darkness?

                It is a sound of breaking,
The world is breaking, the world is a sound
    of breaking,
Many-harmonied, diverse, profound,   30
A shattering beauty. See, how together we
    break,
Hear what a crashing of disordered chords
    and discords
Fills the world with falling, when we thus
    lean
Our two mad bodies together!

                    It is a sound
Of everlasting grief, the sound of weeping,
The sound of disaster and misery, the
    sound
Of passionate heartbreak at the centre of
    the world.
1924   1925

THE POMECITRON TREE [1]

HERE the skeleton leaf, between
Eglantine and celandine,
Harries an hour (that seems an age)

[1] ' "The Pomecitron Tree" is an extension of the same
    notion in more lyric terms, and in the strict form of

The snail's deliberate pilgrimage.
And in that same stupendous hour,
While royally unfolds the flower
Magniloquent in the sunlight, She
Dreams by the pomecitron tree.

Not lust alone is in her mind,
Nor the sad shapes of humankind.   10
What ant is this, with horns, who comes
Exploring huge geraniums?
Up the green-jointed column stalks,
And into halls of scarlet walks;
Boldly intrudes, partakes, then goes
—Alas!—to eat her favorite rose.

Not lust alone; yet this was lust,
And lust was that deliberate gust
That warmly roused the leaves, caressed
The lawn, and on her open breast   20
Blew, from the pomecitron tree,
One ravished petal, and a bee . . .
Into her bosom flew, from this,
The fiery-winged wounding kiss.

Into her bosom. Deeper then,
It startles to that world of men,
Who, in the kingdom of her mind,
Awake, arise, begin to wind
Along the subterranean road
That leads from their abhorred abode. . . .
They move and murmur, while the ant   31
Climbs an enormous rhubarb plant.

And then it is her voice that cries,
While still beneath the tree she lies:
Maker of gardens, let me be
Turned to a pomecitron tree!
Within his veins no longings rise;
He turns no concupiscent eyes;
Nor hears, in the infernal mind,
The lustful army wake and wind.   40

He, though his roots are in the grave,
Is placid and unconscious, save

an eight-line stanza. The theme, as will be seen, is a
metaphysical one, but is presented dramatically, is
acted and spoken. To bring the abstractions alive there
is a continuous emphasis on the sensory aspects of the
situation, and all the more because as the theme is itself in part a questioning of the *nature* of the senses
and of sensory experience. The light formality of the
octasyllabic couplets is intended as a further aid in giving
a note as of almost gaiety to a mood of tragic self-anal-
ysis. Both the form and the word "pomecitron" were
suggested by George Sandys' verse translation of the
"Song of Solomon" in the seventeenth century.' Author's note.

Of burning light, or rain, that slides
On dripping leaves and down his sides
In his cool thought the sparrow nests;
A leaf, among more leaves she rests;
Or, if she sings, her watery voice
Is joined with countless that rejoice.

What bliss is his! what deep delight!
To face, with his own dark, the night!   50
With his own sunrise meet the sun!
Or whistle with the wind, and run!
Why, Lord, was it ordained that I
Must turn an inward-roving eye?
Why must I know, unlike this tree,
What lusts and murders nourish me?

To him, no doubt, most innocent
Seems, in this sunlight, my intent:
No primrose ever lightlier breathed
Than my tall body, flower-enwreathed.   60
Soft as lilies the sunlight rests
Upon my pollen-powdered breasts.
My two hands, of their own sweet will,
Can stir like leaves, or stand as still.

What stems can match this throat of gold
And ivory? What stalks uphold
So lightly, in this garden, such
Delirious flowers to taste and touch?
What pistilled mouth can rival here
My mouth, what leaves outvie my hair   70
In mindless beauty? . . . Yet, behind
This mindless beauty lurks a mind.

Ah, while the rhubarb leaf is spread
Broad as a salver by my head:
And the green aphis pastures on
This tall green tower of Solomon:
The mind, within my flower's bell,
Conceals its black concentric hell.
There at this minute swarms the host,
And lewd ghost speaks with furious
          ghost.

There the sad shapes of humankind   81
Through brown defiles in sorrow wind;
And, if they speak, their arid speech
Is of that land they cannot reach.
There the defeated warrior lies,
And westward turns defrauded eyes.
Deformed and monstrous are those men;
They climb, and do not turn again.

It is to me each lifts his face!
It is to me, with footsore pace,   90

Summoned once more, they creep and
    come,
Pointing toward me as to home.
What love is in their eyes! Alas,
That love so soon to lust should pass!
The hands they lift are stumps; they stir
The rank leaves where their faces were.

Maker of gardens, let me be
Turned to a pomecitron tree;
Or let me be this rhubarb plant,
Whose lavish love is ignorant;   100
Or let me be this daffodil,
Which lusts and murders, yet is still
All-in-itself, a golden All
Concentred in one burning ball!

. . . She sighs; and it is in her thought
That grief so desperate may be fraught
With tears; and tears were sweet, displayed
Here, in the pomecitron shade;
And grief is pleasant, when beguiled
By mindless garden, or a child;   110
But the few tears are thought, not shed;
She claps her hands, and laughs, instead.
1925   1930

FROM PRELUDES FOR MEMNON [1]

XLV [2]

THE dead man spoke to me and begged a
    penny,
For god's sake, and for yours and mine, he
    said,

Slowly under the streetlamp turned his
    head,
I saw his eyes wide open and he stared
Through me as if my bones and flesh were
    nothing,
Through me and through the earth and
    through the void,
His eyes were dark and wide and cold and
    empty
As if his vision had become a grave
Larger than bones of any world could fill,
But crystal clear and deep and deeply still.

Poor devil—why, he wants to close his eyes,
He wants a charity to close his eyes,   12
And follows me with outstretched palm,
    from world to world
And from house to house and street to
    street,
Under the streetlamps and along dark
    alleys,
And sits beside me in my room, and sleeps
Upright with eyes wide open by my bed,
Circles the Pleiades with a glance, returns
From cold Orion with a slow turn of the
    head,
Looks north and south at once, and all the
    while   20
Holds, in that void of an unfocused stare,
My own poor footsteps, saying

                         I have read
Time in the rock and in the human heart,
Space in the bloodstream, and those lesser
    works
Written by rose and windflower on the
    summer, sung
By water and snow, deciphered by the eye,
Translated by the slaves of memory,
And all that you be you, and I be I,
Or all that by imagination, aping   30
God, the supreme poet of despair,
I may be you, you me, before our time
Knowing the rank intolerable taste of death,
And walking dead on the still living earth.

---

1 'The two selections from "Preludes for Memnon" and three from "Time in the Rock" are really, in effect, all parts of one poem, or one such "series" as mentioned earlier in these notes. Originally, I planned to entitle the two companion groups "Preludes to Attitude" ("Memnon") and "Preludes to Definition" ("Time in the Rock"), and I have always regarded them as belonging together and as constituting one unit. Together, they form the most extended use of "series" I have attempted, and the most complex. The range offered by the theme—with its paired questions of "what attitude shall we take towards the world, external and internal, which we see; and what definitions can we find for a world of experience so fluid"—was naturally much greater than that available in the earlier series, where usually a single tone prevailed throughout, though of course with variations. (Viz., "autumn" in "Variations"; "winter" in "Improvisations: Lights and Snow.") Here, as in the symphonies, I was free to rove farther afield, but without so much check of symphonic form; such check as was necessary lay in the relative freedom of the theme and, of course, as in the earlier use of "series," in the play of one movement or idea against another, repetition in elaboration, repetition by inversion, cross-reference, and so on. The majority of the movements are in blank verse, but as in the symphonies there is occasional recourse to stanza or rhyme or other formal device. For the most part, the tone is kept down to what is almost a conversational level, and a quiet type of poetry is aimed at, such as will move readily from the barest of statement or directest of analysis to the more obviously "poetic." ' Author's note.

2 'No. XLV of "Memnon" is a companion-piece of No. LVIII in the same volume, which begins with the same line and is a variant of the same theme Author's note.

. . . I rose and dressed and descended the
    stair
Into the sunlight, and he came with me,
Staring the skeleton from the daffodil,
Freezing the snowflake in the blackbird's
    whistle,
And with that cold profound unhating
    eye
He moved the universe from east to west,
Slowly, disastrously,—but with such
    splendor   41
As god, the supreme poet of delight, might
    envy,—
To the magnificent sepulchre of sleep.

LVI [1]

RIMBAUD and Verlaine, precious pair of
    poets,
Genius in both (but what is genius?)
    playing
Chess on a marble table at an inn
With chestnut blossom falling in blond
    beer
And on their hair and between knight and
    bishop—
Sunlight squared between them on the
    chess-board
Cirrus in heaven, and a squeal of music
Blown from the leathern door of Sainte
    Sulpice—

Discussing, between moves, iamb and
    spondee
Anacoluthon and the open vowel   10
God the great peacock with his angel
    peacocks
And his dependent peacocks the bright
    stars:
Disputing too of fate as Plato loved it,
Or Sophocles, who hated and admired,
Or Socrates, who loved and was amused:

Verlaine puts down his pawn upon a leaf
And closes his long eyes, which are
    dishonest,
And says 'Rimbaud, there is one thing to
    do:

We must take rhetoric, and wring its
    neck! . . .'
Rimbaud considers gravely, moves his
    Queen;   20
And then removes himself to Timbuctoo.

And Verlaine dead,—with all his jades and
    mauves;
And Rimbaud dead in Marseilles with a
    vision,
His leg cut off, as once before his heart;
And all reported by a later lackey,
Whose virtue is his tardiness in time.

Let us describe the evening as it is:—
The stars disposed in heaven as they are:
Verlaine and Shakspere rotting, where they
    rot,
Rimbaud remembered, and too soon
    forgot;   30

Order in all things, logic in the dark;
Arrangement in the atom and the spark;
Time in the heart and sequence in the
    brain—

Such as destroyed Rimbaud and fooled
    Verlaine.
And let us then take godhead by the neck—

And strangle it, and with it, rhetoric.
1927–1931   1931

FROM TIME IN THE ROCK [2]

XXII

IF man, that angel of bright consciousness,
that wingless mind and brief epitome
of god's forgetfulness, will be going forth
into the treacherous envelope of sunlight—
why, the poor fool, does he expect, does he
    expect
to return at evening? or to return the
    same?
Those who have put on, in the morning,
that cloak of light, that sheath of air,
wrapped themselves suddenly, on the
    exit,
in the wild wave of daybreak, which has
    come   10

---

1 ' "Rimbaud and Verlaine" is one of several sections
in the two series which deal with the problem of communication itself, and may be compared with the section which follows it. It is something of an oddity of
form, each stanza being a line shorter than that preceding it, and the end falling into couplets, by way of
ironic comment on the accompanying dismissal of
"rhetoric." ' Author's note.

2 'Two of the sections from "Time in the Rock"—"If
man, that angel" and "What without speech"—
again touch on the problem of communication, which
indeed is one of the recurring themes of the two books
of preludes.' Author's note.

from cruel Alpha,—what has become of
    them?
They will return as the sons of darkness.

If woman, that demon of unconsciousness,
that wingèd body of delightful chaos,
that quick embodied treason and deceit,
will go forth sinuously from the opening
    door
and take to herself the garment of
    daylight—
who will vouch for her, go her surety,
who will her bondsman be, or swear by the
    cloud
that she, who thus went forth, will thus
    come back?   20
If she took darkness with her, will she
    return
with luminous heart, and a soft light
    within?
For that which goes forth comes back
    changed or dead.

If the child, that frail mirror of the sky,
that little room of foolish laughter and
    grief,
transient toucher and taster of the surface,
assembler and scatterer of light,—if he go
    forth
into the simple street to count its stones,
its walls, its houses, its weeds and
    grassblades,
so, in the numbered, to sum the infinite—
infant compendium of the terrible—:   31
will the changed man, and the changed
    woman,
await him, with full knowledge, in the
    evening—
salute him gravely, with a kiss or
    handshake,
oblique embrace of the young wingless
    shoulders—
will they, unknowing, unknown, know this
    Unknown?

All three at evening, when they return
    once more
from the black ocean of dark Omega,
by those wild waves washed up with stars
    and hours,
brought home at last from nowhere to
    nothing—   40
all three will pause in the simple light,
and speak to each other, slowly, with such
    queer speech

as dead men use among the asphodels;
nor know each other; nor understand each
    other;
but tread apart on the wind, like dancers
borne by unearthly music to unearthly
    peace.

The house of evening, the house of clouds,
    vast hall
of which the walls are walls of everywhere,
enfolds them, like a wind which blows out
    lights.
And they are there, lying apart, lying
    alone,   50
those three who went forth suddenly in the
    morning
and now return, estranged and changed;
each is alone, with his extinguished lamp;
each one would weep, if he had time to
    weep;
but, before tears can fall, they are
    asleep.

XLVI

WHAT without speech we knew and could
    not say
what without thought we did and could not
    change
violence of the hand which the mind
    thought strange
let us take these things into another world,
    another dream

what without love we touched pronouncing
    good
what without touch we loved and gave no
    sign
violence of spirit which only spirit knew
    divine
let us take these things into another world,
    another sleep   10

walk with me heliotrope fly with me
    sparrow
come beating of my heart and learn how
    life is narrow
how little, and ill, will be remembered by
    tomorrow
let us give our lives into another world
    another hand

where like old rocks we shall be heaped
    forgetful;
or waste away like stars in fiery
    stillness;

no clock with mortal cry to speak our
    illness;
let us take our deaths into another time
        another god   20

come girl, come golden-breasted girl, and
    walk
on the so silent and sun-sandalled path
between the foremath and the aftermath
let us hurl our joy into another chaos,
    another wrath
        and make it love

what without speech we know we then
    shall say
and all our violence will there be gay
what without thought we do will be but
    play
and our unspoken love as bright as day
        and we shall live.   30

LXXXIV

WHAT face she put on it, we will not
    discuss:
she went hence an hour since. Where she
    went,
is another matter. To the north, to the
    south,
as the man whistled, or the whim bade, she
    went,
or even—who can say—following a star.
Her heart is like an hourglass, from which
    the sand runs—
no sooner run than tilted to run again;
her mind, a mirror, which reflects always
    the last moment;

her face, you would know it anywhere, it
    gives you back
your own light, like the moon. Tell her a
    lie,   10
threefold she reflects it; tell her the truth,
and its returned brilliance will strike you
    dead.
She is of quicksilver. You might as well
pillow your head on a cloud, as on that
    breast,
or strive to sleep with a meteor: when you
    wake,
she is gone, your own hand is under your
    cheek.

Yet she is of the material that earth is made
    of:
will breed as quick as a fly: bloom like the
    cherry,
fearless of frost: and has a nimble fancy
as tropic in pattern as a fernleaf. She walks
as naturally as a young tree might walk: 21
with no pretence: picks up her roots and
    goes
out of your world, and into the secret
    darkness,
as a lady with lifted train will leave a
    ballroom,
and who knows why.

        Wherefor do you love her, gentlemen?
Because, like the spring earth, she is
    fruitfulness?
and you are seed? you need no other
    reason?
and she no other than her perpetual season.
1931–1936   1936

E. E. CUMMINGS

1894–

FOURTEEN POEMS

I

All in green went my love riding
on a great horse of gold
into the silver dawn.

four lean hounds crouched low and smiling
the merry deer ran before.

Fleeter be they than dappled dreams
the swift sweet deer
the red rare deer.

Four red roebuck at a white water
the cruel bugle sang before.

Horn at hip went my love riding
riding the echo down
into the silver dawn.

four lean hounds crouched low and smiling
the level meadows ran before.

Softer be they than slippered sleep
the lean lithe deer
the fleet flown deer.

Four fleet does at a gold valley
the famished arrow sang before.

Bow at belt went my love riding
riding the mountain down
into the silver dawn.

four lean hounds crouched low and smiling
the sheer peaks ran before.

Paler be they than daunting death
the sleek slim deer
the tall tense deer.

Four tall stags at a green mountain
the lucky hunter sang before.

All in green went my love riding
on a great horse of gold
into the silver dawn.

four lean hounds crouched low and smiling
my heart fell dead before.

1923

2

of evident invisibles
exquisite the hovering

at the dark portals

of hurt girl eyes

sincere with wonder

a poise a wounding
a beautiful suppression

the accurate boy mouth

    now droops the faun head

    now the intimate flower dreams   10

    of parted lips
    dim upon the syrinx

                                       1923

3

Buffalo Bill's
defunct
      who used to
      ride a watersmooth-silver
                 stallion
and break onetwothreefourfive pigeonsjustlikethat
                                  Jesus

he was a handsome man
                 and what i want to know is
how do you like your blueeyed boy   10
Mister Death

                                       1923

4

it is at moments after i have dreamed
of the rare entertainment of your eyes,
when (being fool to fancy) i have deemed

with your peculiar mouth my heart my heart made wise;
at moments when the glassy darkness holds

the genuine apparition of your smile
(it was through tears always) and silence moulds
such strangeness as was mine a little while;

moments when my once more illustrious arms
are filled with fascination, when my breast   10
wears the intolerant brightness of your charms:

one pierced moment whiter than the rest

—turning from the tremendous lie of sleep
i watch the roses of the day grow deep.

                                     1923

5

Picasso
you give us Things
which
bulge:grunting lungs pumped full of sharp thick mind

you make us shrill
presents always
shut in the sumptuous screech of
simplicity

(out of the
black unbunged
Something gushes vaguely a squeak of planes
                                                            10
or

between squeals of
Nothing grabbed with circular shrieking tightness
solid screams whisper.)
Lumberman of The Distinct

your brain's
axe only chops hugest inherent
Trees of Ego,from
whose living and biggest   20

bodies lopped
of every
prettiness

you hew form truly

                                                            1925

6

    Humanity i love you
    because you would rather black the boots of
    success than enquire whose soul dangles from his
    watch-chain which would be embarassing for both

    parties and because you
    unflinchingly applaud all
    songs containing the words country home and
    mother when sung at the old howard

    Humanity i love you because
    when you're hard up you pawn your   10
    intelligence to buy a drink and when
    you're flush pride keeps

    you from the pawn shop and
    because you are continually committing
    nuisances but more
    especially in your own house

    Humanity i love you because you
    are perpetually putting the secret of
    life in your pants and forgetting
    it's there and sitting down   20

    on it
    and because you are
    forever making poems in the lap
    of death Humanity

    i hate you

                                                            1925

7

O Thou to whom the musical white spring

offers her lily inextinguishable,
taught by thy tremulous grace bravely to fling

Implacable death's mysteriously sable
robe from her redolent shoulders,
                Thou from whose
feet reincarnate song suddenly leaping
flameflung, mounts, inimitably to lose
herself where the wet stars softly are keeping

their exquisite dreams—O Love! upon thy dim   10
shrine of intangible commemoration,
(from whose faint close as some grave languorous hymn

pledged to illimitable dissipation
unhurried clouds of incense fleetly roll)

i spill my bright incalculable soul.

                                   1925

8

this is the garden:colours come and go,
frail azures fluttering from night's outer wing
strong silent greens serenely lingering,
absolute lights like baths of golden snow.
This is the garden:pursed lips do blow
upon cool flutes within wide glooms,and sing
(of harps celestial to the quivering string)
invisible faces hauntingly and slow.

This is the garden. Time shall surely reap,
and on Death's blade lie many a flower curled,   10
in other lands where other songs be sung;
yet stand They here enraptured, as among
the slow deep trees perpetual of sleep
some silver-fingered fountain steals the world.

                                   1925

9

gee i like to think of dead it means nearer because deeper
firmer since darker than little round water at one end of
the well   it's too cool to be crooked and it's too firm
to be hard but it's sharp and thick and it loves,   every
old thing falls in rosebugs and jackknives and kittens and
pennies they all sit there looking at each other having the
fastest time because they've
never met before

dead's more even than how many ways of sitting on
your head your unnatural hair has in the morning   10

dead's clever too like POF goes the alarm off and the
little striker having the best time tickling away everybody's brain so everybody just puts out their finger
and they stuff the poor thing all full of fingers

dead has a smile like the nicest man you've never met
who maybe winks at you in a streetcar and you pretend
you don't but really you do see and you are My how
glad he winked and hope he'll do it again

or if it talks about you somewhere behind your back
it makes your neck feel pleasant and stoopid   and if   20
dead says may i have this one and was never intro-
duced you say Yes because you know you want it to
dance with you and it wants to and it can dance and
Whocares

dead's fine like hands do you see that water flowerpots
in windows but they live higher in their house than
you so that's all you see but you don't want to

dead's happy like the way underclothes All so differently solemn and inti and sitting on one string

dead never says my dear,Time for your musiclesson   30
and you like music and to have somebody play who
can but you know you never can and why have to?

dead's nice like a dance where you danced simple hours
and you take all your prickley-clothes off and squeeze-
into-largeness without one word   and you lie still as
anything   in largeness and this largeness begins to
give you,the dance all over again and you,feel all again
all over the way men you liked made you feel when they
touched you(but that's not all)because largeness tells
you so you can feel what you made, men feel when,you   40
touched,them

dead's sorry like a thistlefluff-thing which goes landing away all by himself on somebody's roof or something where who-ever-heard-of-growing and nobody
expects you to anyway

dead says come with me he says(andwhyevernot)into
the round well and see the kitten and the penny and
the jackknife and the rosebug
                              and you say Sure you
say   (like that)   sure i'll come with you you say for i   50
like kittens i do and jackknives i do and pennies i do
and rosebugs i do

                                                         1925

                         10

it really must
be Nice, never to

have no imagination)or never
never to wonder about guys you used to(and them
slim hot queens with dam next to nothing

on)tangoing
(while a feller tries
to hold down the fifty bucks per
job with one foot and rock a

cradle with the other)it Must be   10
nice never to have no doubts about why you
put the ring
on(and watching her
face grow old and tired to which

you're married and hands get red washing
things and dishes)and to never, never really wonder i
mean about the smell
of babies and how you

know the dam rent's going to and everything and never, never
Never to stand at no window   20
because i can't sleep(smoking sawdust

cigarettes in the
middle of the night

                                                                  1926

                                     II
                   here's a little mouse)and
                   what does he think about, i
                   wonder as over this
                   floor(quietly with

                   bright eyes)drifts(nobody
                   can tell because
                   Nobody knows, or why
                   jerks Here &, here,
                   gr(oo)ving the room's Silence)this like
                   a littlest   10
                   poem a
                   (with wee ears and see?

                   tail frisks)
                             (gonE)
                   'mouse',
                             We are not the same you and

                   i, since here's a little he
                   or is
                   it It
                   ? (or was something we saw in the mirror)?   20

                   therefore we'll kiss;for mayne
                   what was Disappeared

into ourselves
who   (look).   ,startled

1926

12

along the brittle treacherous bright streets
of memory comes my heart, singing like
an idiot, whispering like a drunken man

who(at a certain corner, suddenly)meets
the tall policeman of my mind.
                        awake
being not asleep, elsewhere our dreams began
which now are folded:but the year completes
his life as a forgotten prisoner

—'Içi?'—'Ah non, mon cheri; il fait trop froid'—   10
they are gone: along these gardens moves a wind bringing
rain and leaves, filling the air with fear
and sweetness. . . . pauses.   (Halfwhispering. . . . halfsinging

stirs the always smiling chevaux de bois)

when you were in Paris we met here

1926

13

since feeling is first
who pays any attention
to the syntax of things
will never wholly kiss you;

wholly to be a fool
while Spring is in the world

my blood approves,
and kisses are a better fate
than wisdom
lady i swear by all flowers. Don't cry   10
—the best gesture of my brain is less than
your eyelids' flutter which says

we are for each other: then
laugh, leaning back in my arms
for life's not a paragraph

And death i think is no parenthesis

1926

14

somewhere i have never travelled,gladly beyond
any experience, your eyes have their silence:
in your most frail gesture are things which enclose me,
or which i cannot touch because they are too near

your slightest look easily will unclose me
though i have closed myself as fingers,
you open always petal by petal myself as Spring opens
(touching skilfully,mysteriously)her first rose

or if your wish be to close me,i and
my life will shut very beautifully,suddenly,   10
as when the heart of this flower imagines
the snow carefully everywhere descending;

nothing which we are to perceive in this world equals
the power of your intense fragility:whose texture
compels me with the colour of its countries,
rendering death and forever with each breathing

(i do not know what it is about you that closes
and opens;only something in me understands
the voice of your eyes is deeper than all roses)
nobody,not even the rain,has such small hands

1931

THORNTON WILDER

1897–

FROM THE WOMAN OF ANDROS

AEGEAN MOODS [1]

BRYNOS rose with the dawn, and it was not
many hours later that the morning's work
was over. . . . Pamphilus, having helped
his father in the warehouse and being in no
mood for exercising in the field, started out
to walk to the highest point on the island.
It was early Spring. A strong wind had   10
blown every cloud from the sky and the sea
lay covered with flying white-tipped waves.
His garments leapt and billowed about him
and his very hair tugged at his head. The
gulls themselves, leaning upon the gusts,
were caught unawares from time to time
and blown with ruffled feathers and scan-
dalized cries towards the violet-blue zenith.
Pamphilus led his life with much worry
and self-examination and all the exhilara-   20
tion of wind and sun could not drive from
his mind the anxious affection with which

1 The selection, to which the title has been given by the
editors, is from *The Woman of Andros*(N.Y., 1930),
62–81. In a prefatory note, the author says: 'The first
part of this novel is based upon the *Andria*, a comedy
of Terence who in turn based his work upon two
Greek plays, now lost to us, by Menander.' The section used above is one of Wilder's amplifications.

he now turned over his thoughts of Chrysis
and Philumena and of the four members
of his family. He was straying among the
rocks and the lizards and the neglected
dwarfed olive-trees, when his attention was
suddenly caught by an incident on the
hillside to his left. A group of boys from
the town was engaged in tormenting a
young girl. She was retreating backwards
up the slope through a disused orchard,
shouting haughtily back at her pursuers.
The boys' malice had turned to anger; they
were retorting hotly and letting fly about
her a few harmless stones. Pamphilus
strode over to the group and with a gesture
ordered the boys down the hill. The girl,
her face still flushed and distrustful, stood
with her back against a tree and waited for
him to come towards her. They looked at
one another for a moment in silence. Finally Pamphilus said:

'What is the matter?'

'They're just country fools, that's all.
They've never seen anyone before who
didn't come from their wretched Brynos.'
And then from rage and disappointment
she began to cry uncontrollably and despairingly.

Pamphilus watched her for a time and then asked her where she had been going.

'Nowhere. I was just going for a walk and they followed me from the town. I can't do anything. I can't go anywhere. . . . I wasn't hurting them. I was just going for a walk alone and they called names after me. They followed me way up here; I called names at them and then they started throwing things at me. That's all.'

'I thought I knew everyone on the island,' said Pamphilus thoughtfully, 'but I have never seen you before. Have you been here long?'

'Yes, I've been here almost a year,' she replied, adding indistinctly, '. . . but I hardly ever go out or anything.'

'You hardly ever go out?'

'No,' and she fumbled with her dress and stared at the sea, frowning.

'You should try to know some of the other girls and go out for walks with them.'

This time she turned and looked into his face. 'I don't know any of the other girls. I . . . I live at home and they don't let me go out of the house, except when I go out for walks nights with . . . well, with Mysis.' She continued to be shaken with sobs, but she was adjusting her hair and the folds of her dress. 'I don't see why they have to throw stones at me,' she added.

Pamphilus looked at her in silence, gravely. Presently he collected himself and said: 'There's a big smooth stone over there. Will you go over there and sit down?'

She followed him to the stone, still busy with her hair and drawing her fingers across her eyes and cheeks.

'I have a sister just about your age,' said Pamphilus. 'You can begin by knowing her. You can go for walks with her and then you wouldn't be a stranger any more. Her name is Argo. You'd like one another, I know. My sister is weaving a large mantle for my mother and she'd like you to help her with it and she could help you with yours. Are you making a mantle?'

'Yes.'

'That would be fine,' said Pamphilus, and from that moment Glycerium loved him forever.

'I probably know your father, don't I?' he asked.

'I have no father,' she replied, looking up at him weakly, 'I am the sister of the woman from Andros.'

'Oh . . . oh . . . ,' said Pamphilus, more astonished than he had ever been in his life. 'I know your sister well.'

'Yes,' said Glycerium. Her bright wet eyes strayed over the streaked sea and the blown birds. 'She doesn't want anyone to know that I'm there. All day I stay up on the top of the house or work in the court. Only at night I'm allowed to go for a walk with Mysis. Even now I'm supposed to be in the house, but I broke my promise. She has gone to the market and so I broke my promise. I wanted to see what the island and the sea look like by day. And I wanted to look across to Andros where I come from. But the boys followed me here and threw stones at me and I can never come again.'

Here she fell to weeping even more despairingly than before and Pamphilus could do nothing but say 'Well' several times and 'Yes.' At last he asked her what her name was.

'Glycerium. Chrysis went away from home a long time ago and I was living with my brother and he died and I couldn't live with him any more. And I had nowhere to go or anything, and one day she came back and took me to live with her. That's all.'

'Have you any brothers or sisters?'

'Oh, no.'

'Who is Mysis?'

'Mysis isn't Greek. She is from Alexandria. Chrysis found her. All of them in the house,—she just found them somewhere. That's what she does. Mysis was a slave in the cloth mills. Sometimes she tells me about it.'

Pamphilus still gazed at her, and bringing back her wandering evasive glance from the sea she looked at him from her thin face and enormous hungry eyes. Even a long glance did not now embarrass them.

'Do you want me to ask Chrysis to let you go about the island by day?' he asked.

'If she doesn't want it, we mustn't change her. Chrysis knows best.' She turned away from him and said in a lower voice, dreamy and embittered: 'But what can become of me? Am I always to stay locked up? I am fifteen already. The world is full of wonderful things and people that I might never know about. I know it was wrong of me to break my promise; but to live for years without ever knowing new people,—to hear them passing the door all day, and to see them a long ways off. Do you think I did very wrong?'

'No.'

'I don't know anyone. I don't know anyone.'

'Well . . . well, you'll come to know my sister. That will be a beginning,' he said, taking her fingertips thoughtfully and wonderingly in his.

'Yes,' she said.

'Everything is beginning over again. I'm your friend. Then my sister. Soon you will have a great many. You'll see.'

'But where will I be five years from now and ten years from now,' she cried, staring about her wildly. 'I don't know. I'm afraid. I'm unhappy. Everyone in the world is happy except me.'

The caress of the hands in first love, and never so simply again, seems to be a sharing of courage, an alliance of two courages against a confusing world. As his hand passed from her hair to her shoulder, she turned to him with parted lips and hesitant eyes, then suddenly bound both her arms about his neck. Into his ears her lips wildly and all but meaninglessly repeated: 'Yes. Yes. Yes. I can't stay there forever. I should never know anyone. I should never see anybody.'

'She will let you come to see me,' he said.

'No,' said Glycerium. 'But I'll come by myself. I mustn't ask her. She would not let me come. She always knows best. And the boys can throw their stones. I don't mind if you're here. What . . . what is your name?'

'My name is Pamphilus, Glycerium.'

'Can . . . can I call you by it?'

It was not at this meeting, nor at their next, but at the third, beneath the dwarfed olive-trees, that those caresses that seemed to be for courage, for pity and for admiration, were turned by Nature to her own uses.

These conversations took place in the early Spring. One afternoon in the late Summer Chrysis slipped out of her house and climbed the hill behind it. She was filled with a great desire to be alone and to think. She looked out over the glittering sea. The winds were moderate on that afternoon and before them the innumerable neat waves hurried towards the shore, running up the sands with a long whisper, or discreetly lifting against the rocks a scarf of foam. In the distance a school of dolphins engaged at their eternal games led the long procession of curving backs. The water was marbled at intervals with the strange fields and roadways of a lighter blue; and behind all she beheld with love the violet profile of Andros. For a time she strayed about upon the crest of the hill, making sure that no one was watching or following her, then descending the further side she sought out her favorite retreats, a point of rock that projected into the sea and a sheltered cove beside it. As she drew near the place, she stumbled forward, almost running, and as she went she murmured soothingly to herself: 'We are almost there. Look, we are almost there now.' At last, climbing over the boulders she let herself down into an amphitheatre of hot dry sand. She started unbinding her hair, but stopped herself abruptly: 'No, no. I must think. I should fall asleep here. I must think first. I shall come back soon,' she muttered to the amphitheatre, and continuing her journey she reached the furthermost heap of stones and sat down. She rested her chin upon her hand and fixing her eyes upon the horizon she waited for the thoughts to come.

The first thing to think about was her new illness. Several times she had been awakened by a wild fluttering in her left side that continued, deepening, until it seemed to her as though a great stake were being driven into her heart. And all the day the sensation would remain with her as of a heavy object burdening the place where this trouble lay. 'Probably . . . very likely,' she said to herself, 'the next time I shall die of it.' At the thought a wave of anticipation passed over her. 'I shall probably die of it,' she repeated cheerfully and became interested in some crayfish in the pool at her feet. She plucked some grasses behind her and started dragging them before the eyes of the indignant animals. 'Nothing in life could make me abandon my sheep, but if I die they will have to fall back on Circumstance as I did. Glycerium, what will become of you? Apraxine, Mysis . . .? There are times when we cannot see one step ahead of us, but five years later we are eating and sleeping somewhere.' (It was humorous, pretending that one's heart was as hard as that.) 'Yes,' she said aloud, to the pain that trembled within her, 'only come quickly.' She leaned forward still dragging the stems before the shell-fish: 'I have lived thirty-five years. I have lived enough. *Stranger, near this spot lies Chrysis, daughter of Arches of Andros: the ewe that has strayed from the flock lives many years in one day and dies at a great age when the sun sets.*' She laughed at the deceptive comforts of self-pity and taking off a sandal put her foot into the water. She drew herself up for a moment, asking herself what there was left in the house for the colony's supper; then recollecting some fish and some salad on the shelf, she returned to her thoughts. She repeated her epitaph, making it a song and emphasizing, for self-mockery, its false sentiment. 'O Andros, O Poseidon, how happy I am. I have no right to be happy like this. . . .'

And she knew as she gazed at the frieze of dolphins still playing in the distance that her mind was avoiding another problem that awaited her. 'I am happy because I love this Pamphilus,—Pamphilus the anxious, Pamphilus the stupid. Why cannot someone tell him that it is not necessary to suffer so about living.' And the low exasperated sigh escaped her, the protest we make at the preposterous, the incorrigible beloved. 'He thinks he is failing. He thinks he is inadequate to life at every turn. Let him rest some day, O ye Olympians, from pitying those who suffer. Let him learn to look the other way. This is something new in the world, this concern for the unfit and the broken. Once he begins that, there's no end to it, only madness. It leads nowhere. That is some god's business.' Whereupon he discovered that she was weeping; but when she had dried her eyes he was still thinking about him. 'Oh, such people are unconscious of their goodness. They strike their foreheads with their hands because of their failure, and yet the rest of us are made glad when we remember their faces. Pamphilus, you are another herald from the future. Some day men will be like you. Do not frown so. . . .'

But these thoughts were very fatiguing. She arose and, returning to the amphi-theatre, laid herself down upon the sand. She murmured some fragments from the Euripidean choruses and fell asleep. She had always been an islander and this hot and impersonal sun playing upon a cold and impersonal sea was not unfriendly to her. And now for two hours the monotony of sun and sea played about her and wove itself into the mood of her sleeping mind. As once the gray-eyed Athena stood guarding Ulysses—she leaning upon her spear, her great heart full of concern and of those long divine thoughts that are her property —even so, now, the hour and the place all but gathered itself into a presence and shed its influence upon her. When her eyes finally opened she listened for a time to the calm in her heart. 'Some day,' she said, 'we shall understand why we suffer. I shall be among the shades underground and some wonderful hand, some Alcestis, will touch me and will show me the meaning of all these things; and I shall laugh softly for hours as I do now . . . as I do now.'

She arose and binding up her hair prepared to ascend the slope. But just as she turned to leave the place, there visited her the desire to do something ceremonial, to mark the hour. She stood up straightly and held out her arms to the setting sun: 'If you still hear prayers from the lips of mortals, if our longings touch you at all, hear me now. Give to this Pamphilus some assurance—even some assurance such as you have given to me, unstable though I am— that he is right. And oh! (but I do not say this from vanity or pride, O Apollo,—but perhaps this is weak, this is childish of me, perhaps this renders the whole prayer powerless!) if it is possible, let the thought of me or of something I have said be comforting to him some day. And . . . and . . .'

But her arms fell to her side. The world seemed empty. The sun went down. The sea and sky became suddenly remote and she was left with only the tears in her eyes and the longing in her heart. She closed her lips and turned her head aside. 'I suppose there is no god,' she whispered. 'We must do these things ourselves. We must drag ourselves through life as best we can.'

1930

ROBINSON JEFFERS

1887–

THE TOWER BEYOND TRAGEDY [1]

I

You'd never have thought the Queen was
Helen's sister—Troy's burning-flower
from Sparta, the beautiful sea-flower
Cut in clear stone, crowned with the fragrant golden mane, she the ageless, the
uncontaminable—
This Clytemnestra was her sister, low-

statured, fierce-lipped, not dark nor
blond, greenish-gray-eyed,
Sinewed with strength, you saw, under the
purple folds of the queen-cloak, but
craftier than queenly,
Standing between the gilded wooden porch-
pillars, great steps of stone above the
steep street,
Awaiting the King.
                Most of his men were
quartered on the town; he, clanking
bronze, with fifty
And certain captives, came to the stair.
The Queen's men were a hundred in the
street and a hundred
Lining the ramp, eighty on the great flags
of the porch; she raising her white arms
the spear-butts
Thundered on the stone, and the shields
clashed; eight shining clarions   10
Let fly from the wide window over the
entrance the wild-birds of their metal
throats, air-cleaving
Over the King come home. He raised his
thick burnt-colored beard and smiled;
then Clytemnestra,
Gathering the robe, setting the golden-
sandaled feet carefully, stone by stone,
descended
One half the stair. But one of the captives
marred the comeliness of that embrace
with a cry
Gull-shrill, blade-sharp, cutting between
the purple cloak and the bronze plates,
then Clytemnestra:
Who was it? The King answered: A piece
of our goods out of the snatch of Asia, a
daughter of the king,
So treat her kindly and she may come into
her wits again.
Eh, you keep state here my queen.
You've not been the poorer for me.—
In heart, in the widowed chamber,
dear, she pale replied, though the
slaves
Toiled, the spearmen were faithful. What's
her name, the slave-girl's?
AGAMEMNON Come up the stair. They tell
me my kinsman's   20
Lodged himself on you.
CLYTEMNESTRA Your cousin Ægisthus? He

1 The poem is based on the *Agamemnon* and the *Libation Bearers* of Aeschylus. In a letter to Alberts, 13 May 1929, Jeffers says: 'We turn to the classic stories, I suppose, as to Greek sculpture, for a more ideal and also more normal beauty, because the myths of our own race were never developed, and have been alienated from us.' Alberts, *A Bibliography of . . . Jeffers* (N.Y., 1933), 24.

Of the symbolism, Jeffers wrote, n.d., to Louis Adamic: 'In "Tamar" a little and vaguely, in "The Tower Beyond Tragedy" and "The Women at Point Sur" consciously and definitely, incest is symbolized racial introversion—man regarding man exclusively—founding his values, desires, his picture of the universe, all on his own humanity. With the thickening of civilization, science reforms the picture of the universe and makes it inhuman, but the values and desires are ever more fixed inward. People living in cities hardly look at or think of anything but each other and each other's amusements and works.' Adamic, *Robinson Jeffers* (Seattle, 1929), 28.

Of his metrical intention, Jeffers wrote, n.d., in a letter to Klein: 'People talked about my "free verse" and I never protested, but now I am quite touched that someone has at last discovered the metrical intention in it. . . . Of course you have noticed that (chiefly in my narrative poems) many lines are of irregular length —"free" no doubt, as are many lines in Elizabethan dramatic verse—but it seems to me that there is a metrical pattern, if only, and most irregular, as a background from which to measure departures from the pattern. . . . It seems to me . . . that the counting of stresses is not enough, without some regard to the quantities of the unstressed syllables, to make well-sounding lines. But there I can't propose any rule; it is more a matter of ear and rhythmic sense. A line made up of syllables like "many" or "easy" couldn't balance rhythmically with a line made up of syllables like "storm-bent," "oak-trees," though the number of syllables were the same. . . . Several modern poets have caught Coleridge's and Bridge's thought, or found it out for themselves, but it seems to me that there remains an infinite field of rhythm as yet untouched or hardly touched. English as a language of very diverse and tolerably stable quantities, beside being a strongly accented language, great and new things might be done in it if we had time and ear.' Quoted, Alberts, *A Bibliography of . . . Jeffers* (N.Y., 1933), 150–51.

was out of refuge, flits between here and
Tiryns.
Dear: the girl's name?
AGAMEMNON   Cassandra. We've a
hundred or so other captives; besides
two hundred
Rotted in the hulls,—they tell odd stories
about you and your guest: eh? no matter:
—the ships
Ooze pitch and the August road smokes
dirt, I smell like an old shepherd's goat-
skin, you'll have bath-water?
CLYTEMNESTRA
They're making it hot. Come, my lord. My
hands will pour it.
                         (*They enter the palace.*)
CASSANDRA
In the holy city,
In Troy, when the stone was standing walls
and the ash
Was painted and carved wood and pictured
curtains,   30
And those lived that are dead, they had
caged a den
Of wolves out of the mountain, and I a
maiden
Was led to see them: it stank and
snarled,
The smell was the smell here, the eyes were
the eyes
Of steep Mycenæ: O God guardian of wan-
derers
Let me die easily.
So cried Cassandra the daughter of King
Priam, treading the steps of the palace at
Mycenæ,
Swaying like a drunken woman, drunk with
the rolling of the ship, and with tears, and
with prophecy.
The stair may yet be seen, among the old
stones that are Mycenæ; tall dark Cassandra, the prophetess,
The beautiful girl with whom a God bargained for love, high-nurtured, captive,
shamefully stained   40
With the ship's filth and the sea's, rolled
her dark head upon her shoulders like a
drunken woman
And trod the great stones of the stair. The
captives, she among them, were ranked
into a file
On the flagged porch, between the parapet
and the spearmen. The people below
shouted for the King,
King Agamemnon, returned conqueror,

after the ten years of battle and death in
Asia.
Then cried Cassandra:
Good spearmen you did not kill my father,
not you
Violated my mother with the piercing
That makes no life in the womb, not you
defiled
My tall blond brothers with the masculine
lust
That strikes its loved one standing,   50
And leaves him what no man again nor a
girl
Ever will gaze upon with the eyes of desire:
Therefore you'll tell me
Whether it's an old custom in the Greek
country
The cow goring the bull, break the inner
door back
And see in what red water how cloaked your
King
Bathes, and my brothers are avenged a little.
One said: Captive be quiet. And she: What
have I to be quiet for, you will not be-
lieve me.
Such wings my heart spreads when the red
runs out of any Greek, I must let the
bird fly. O soldiers
He that mishandled me dies! The first, one
of your two brute Ajaxes, that threw me
backward   60
On the temple flagstones, a hard bride-bed,
I enduring him heard the roofs of my
city breaking,
The roar of flames and spearmen: what
came to Ajax? Out of a cloud the loud-
winged falcon lightning
Came on him shipwrecked, clapped its
wings about him, clung to him, the violent flesh burned and the bones
Broke from each other in that passion; and
now this one, returned safe, the Queen is
his lightning.
While she yet spoke a slave with haggard
eyes darted from the door; there were
hushed cries and motions
In the inner dark of the great hall. Then
the Queen Clytemnestra issued, smiling.
She drew
Her cloak up, for the brooch on the left
shoulder was broken; the fillet of her hair
had come unbound;
Yet now she was queenly at length; and
standing at the stair-head spoke: Men
of Mycenæ, I have made

Sacrifice for the joy this day has brought to
us, the King come home, the enemy
fallen, fallen,
In the ashes of Asia. I have made sacrifice.
I made the prayer with my own lips, and
struck the bullock   70
With my own hand. The people murmured
together, She's not a priestess, the Queen
is not a priestess,
What has she done there, what wild sayings
Make wing in the Queen's throat?

CLYTEMNESTRA   I have
something to tell you.   Too much joy is
a message-bearer of misery.
A little is good; but come too much and it
devours us.   Therefore we give of a great
harvest
Sheaves to the smiling Gods; and therefore
out of a full cup we pour the quarter. No
man
Dare take all that God sends him, whom
God favors, or destruction
Rides into the house in the last basket. I
have been twelve years your shepherdess,
I the Queen have ruled you
And I am accountable for you.

CASSANDRA
Why should a man kill his own mother?   80
The cub of the lion being grown
Will fight with the lion, but neither lion nor
wolf
Nor the unclean jackal
Bares tooth against the womb that he
dropped out of:
Yet I have seen—

CLYTEMNESTRA
Strike that captive woman with your hand,
spearman; and then if the spirit
Of the she-wolf in her will not quiet, with
the butt of the spear.

CASSANDRA   —the blade in the
child's hand
Enter the breast that the child sucked—
that woman's—
The left breast that the robe has dropped
from, for the brooch is broken,   90
That very hillock of whiteness, and she
crying, she kneeling—
          (*The spearman who is nearest* CASSANDRA
          covers her mouth with his hand.)

CLYTEMNESTRA
My sister's beauty entered Troy with too
much gladness. They forgot to make
sacrifice.
Therefore destruction entered; therefore

the daughters of Troy cry out in strange
dispersals, and this one
Grief has turned mad. I will not have that
horror march under the lion-gate of
Mycenæ
That split the citadel of Priam. Therefore I
say I have made sacrifice; I have sub-
tracted
A fraction from immoderate joy. For con-
sider, my people,
How unaccountably God has favored the
city and brought home the army. King
Agamemnon,
My dear, my husband, my lord and yours,
Is yet not such a man as the Gods love; but
insolent, fierce, overbearing, whose folly
Brought many times many great evils   100
On all the heads and fighting hopes of the
Greek force. Why, even before the fleet
made sail,
While yet it gathered on Bœotian Aulis,
this man offended. He slew one of the
deer
Of the sacred herd of Artemis, out of pure
impudence, hunter's pride that froths in
a young boy
Laying nock to string of his first bow: this
man, grown, a grave king, leader of the
Greeks.
The angry Goddess
Blew therefore from the horn of the Trojan
shore storm without end, no slackening,
no turn, no slumber
Of the eagle bound to break the oars of the
fleet and split the hulls venturing: you
know what answer
Calchas the priest gave: his flesh must pay
whose hand did the evil—his flesh! mine
also. His? My daughter.
They knew that of my three there was one
that I loved.
Blameless white maid, my Iphigenia, whose
throat the knife,   110
Whose delicate soft throat the thing that
cuts sheep open was drawn across by a
priest's hand
And the soft-colored lips drained bloodless
That had clung here—here—Oh!
          (*Drawing the robe from her breasts.*)
These feel soft, townsmen; these are red at
the tips, they have neither blackened nor
turned marble.
King Agamemnon hoped to pillow his
black-haired breast upon them, my husband, that mighty conqueror,

Come home with glory. He thought they
were still a woman's, they appear a
woman's. I'll tell you something.

Since fawn slaughtered for slaughtered
fawn evened the debt these that feel soft
and warm are wounding ice,

They ache with their hardness . . .

Shall I go on and count the other follies of
the King? The insolences to God and
man

That brought down plague, and brought
Achilles' anger against the army? Yet
God brought home a remnant   120

Against all hope: therefore rejoice.

But lest too much rejoicing slay us I have
made sacrifice. A little girl's brought you
over the sea.

What could be great enough for safe return?
A sheep's death? A bull's? What thank-
offering?

All these captives, battered from the ships,
bruised with captivity, damaged flesh and
forlorn minds?

God requires wholeness in the victim. You
dare not think what he demands. I dared.
I, I,

Dared.

Men of the Argolis, you that went over
the sea and you that guarded the home
coasts

And high stone war-belts of the cities:
remember how many spearmen these
twelve years have called me

Queen, and have loved me, and been faithful, and remain faithful. What I bring you
is accomplished.

VOICES

King Agamemnon. The King. We will hear
the King.   130

CLYTEMNESTRA   What I bring you
is accomplished.

Accept it, the cities are at peace, the ways
are safe between them, the Gods favor
us. Refuse it . . .

You will not refuse it . . .

VOICES   The King. We
will hear the King.   Let us see the King.

CLYTEMNESTRA

You will not refuse it; I have my faithful.
They would run, the red rivers,

From the gate and by the graves through
every crooked street of the great city,
they would run in the pasture

Outside the walls: and on this stair:
stemmed at this entrance—

CASSANDRA

Ah, sister, do you also behold visions? I was
watching red water—

CLYTEMNESTRA

Be wise, townsmen. As for the King: slaves
will bring him to you when he has
bathed; you will see him.

The slaves will carry him on a litter, he has
learned Asian ways in Asia, too great a
ruler   140

To walk, like common spearmen.

CASSANDRA   Who is
that, standing behind you, Clytemnestra?
What God

Dark in the doorway?

CLYTEMNESTRA   Deal you with your
own demons. You know what I have
done, captive. You know

I am holding lions with my two eyes: if I
turn and loose them . . .

CASSANDRA It is . . . the King. There!
There! Ah!

CLYTEMNESTRA

Or if I should make any move to increase
confusion. If I should say for example,
Spearman

Kill that woman. I cannot say it this moment; so little as from one spear wound
in your body

A trickle would loose them on us.

CASSANDRA   Yet he
stands behind you. A-ah! I can bear it.
I have seen much lately   150

Worse.

A CAPTAIN (down the stair; standing
forward from his men) O Queen, there
is no man in the world, but one
(if that one lives), may ask you to
speak

Otherwise than you will. You have spoken
in riddles to the people . . .

CASSANDRA   Not me!
Why will you choose

Me! I submitted to you living, I was forced,
you entered me . . .

THE CAPTAIN   Also there was a
slave here,

Whose eyes stood out from his chalk face,
came buzzing from the palace postern
gate, whimpering

A horrible thing. I killed him. But the men
have heard it.

CASSANDRA   You were the king, I was
your slave.

Here you see, here, I took the black-haired

breast of the bull, I endured it, I opened
my thighs, I suffered   160
The other thing besides death that you
Greeks have to give us . . .

THE CAPTAIN   Though this
one raves and you are silent,

O Queen, terrible-eyed . . .

CASSANDRA   That was the
slave's part: but this time . . . dead
King . . .

I . . . will . . . not submit. Ah! Ah! No!
If you will steal the body of someone living take your wife's, take that soldier's
there—

THE CAPTAIN

I pray you Queen command the captive
woman be quieted in a stone chamber;
she increases confusion,

The soldiers cannot know some terrible
thing may not have happened; your men
and the King's grin

Like wolves over the kill, the whole city
totters on a sword-edge over sudden—

CASSANDRA (screaming)

Drive him off me! Pity, pity!   170
I have no power; I thought when he was
dead another man would use me, your
Greek custom,

Not he, he, newly slain.

He is driving me out, he enters, he possesses, this is my last defilement. Ah . . .
Greeks . . .

Pity Cassandra!
                         With the voice the spirit
seemed to fly out. She upflung her
shining

Arms with the dreadful and sweet gesture
of a woman surrendering utterly to force
and love,

She in the eyes of the people, like a shameless woman, and fell writhing, and the
dead King's soul

Entered her body. In that respite the
Queen:
                Captain: and you, soldiers, that
shift unsoldierly

The weapons that should be upright, at attention, like stiff grass-blades: and you,
people of Mycenæ: 180

While this one maddened, and you muttered, echoing together, and you, soldier,
with anxious questions

Increased confusion: who was it that stood
firm, who was it that stood silent, who
was it that held

With her two eyes the whole city from splitting wide asunder? Your Queen was it?
I am your Queen,

And now I will answer what you asked.
. . . It is true. . . . He has died. . . .
I am the Queen.

My little son Orestes will grow up and
govern you.
                    While she spoke the body
of Cassandra

Arose among the shaken spears, taller than
the spears, and stood among the waving
spears

Stone-quiet, like a high war-tower in a
windy pinewood, but deadly to look at,
with blind and tyrannous

Eyes; and the Queen: All is accomplished;
and if you are wise, people of Mycenæ:
quietness is wisdom.

No tumult will call home a dead man out of
judgment. The end is the end. Ah,
soldiers! Down spears!   190

What, now Troy's fallen you think there's
not a foreigner in the world bronze may
quench thirst on? Lion-cubs,

If you will tear each other in the lair
happy the wolves, happy the hook-nose
vultures.

Call the eaters of carrion? I am your queen,
I am speaking to you, you will hear me
out before you whistle

The foul beaks from the mountain nest. I
tell you I will forget mercy if one man
moves now.

I rule you, I.

The Gods have satisfied themselves in this
man's death; there shall not one drop of
the blood of the city

Be shed further. I say the high Gods are
content; as for the lower,

And the great ghost of the King: my slaves
will bring out the King's body decently
before you

And set it here, in the eyes of the city: spices
the ships bring from the south will comfort his spirit;

Mycenæ and Tiryns and the shores will
mourn him aloud; sheep will be slain for
him; a hundred beeves   200

Spill their thick blood into the trenches;
captives and slaves go down to serve him,
yes all these captives

Burn in the ten-day fire with him, un-
measured wine quench it, urned in pure
gold the gathered ashes

Rest forever in the sacred rock; honored; a
  conqueror. . . . Slaves, bring the King
  out of the house.
Alas my husband! she cried, clutching the
  brown strands of her hair in both her
  hands, you have left me
A woman among lions! Ah the King's
  power, ah the King's victories! Weep for
  me, Mycenæ!
Widowed of the King!
                    The people stood
  amazed, like sheep that snuff at their dead
  shepherd, some hunter's
Ill-handled arrow having struck him from
  the covert, all by mischance; he is fallen
  on the hillside
Between the oak-shadow and the stream;
  the sun burns his dead face, his staff lies
  by him, his dog
Licks his hand, whining. So, like sheep, the
  people   210
Regarded that dead majesty whom the
  slaves brought out of the house on a gold
  bed, and set it
Between the pillars of the porch. His royal
  robe covered his wounds, there was no
  stain
Nor discomposure.
                    Then that captain who
  had spoken before: O Queen, before the
  mourning
The punishment: tell us who has done this.
  She raised her head, and not a woman
  but a lioness
Blazed at him from her eyes: Dog, she answered, dog of the army,
Who said Speak dog, and you dared speak?
  Justice is mine. Then he was silent; but
  Cassandra's
Body standing tall among the spears, over
  the parapet, her body but not her spirit
Cried with a man's voice: Shall not even the
  stones of the stair, shall not the stones
  under the columns
Speak, and the towers of the great wall of
  my city come down against the murder-
  ess? O Mycenæ   220
I yearned to night and day under the tents
  by Troy, O Tiryns, O Mycenæ, the
  door
Of death, and the gate before the door!
CLYTEMNESTRA   That
  woman lies, or the spirit of a lie cries
  from her. Spearman,
Kill that woman!

                    But Cassandra's body
  set its back against the parapet, its face
Terribly fronting the raised knife; and
  called the soldier by his name, in the
  King's voice, saying,
Sheathe it; and the knife lowered, and the
  soldier
Fell on his knees before the King in the
  woman's body; and the body of Cassandra cried from the parapet:
Horrible things, horrible things this house
  has witnessed: but here is the most vile,
  that hundreds
Of spears are idle while the murderess,
  Clytemnestra the murderess, the snake
  that came upon me   230
Naked and bathing, the death that lay with
  me in bed, the death that has borne children to me,
Stands there unslain.
CLYTEMNESTRA Cowards, if the bawling of
  that bewildered heifer from Troy fields
  has frightened you
How did you bear the horns of her brothers? Bring her to me.
THE BODY OF CASSANDRA
                    Let no man
  doubt, men of Mycenæ,
She has yet the knife hid in her clothes, the
  very blade that stabbed her husband and
  the blood is on it.
Look, she handles it now. Look, fellows.
  The hand under the robe. Slay her not
  easily, that she-wolf.
Do her no honor with a spear! Ah! If I
  could find the word, if I could find it,
The name of her, to say husband-slayer and
  bed-defiler, bitch and wolf-bitch, king's
  assassin
And beast, beast, beast, all in one breath, in
  one word: spearmen   240
You would heap your shields over this
  woman and crush her slowly, slowly,
  while she choked and screamed,
No, you would peel her bare and on the
  pavement for a bride-bed with a spear-
  butt for husband
Dig the lewd womb until it burst: this for
  Agamemnon, this for Ægisthus—Agh,
  cowards of the city
Do you stand quiet?
CLYTEMNESTRA Truly, soldiers,
I think it is he verily. No one could invent
  the abominable voice, the unspeakable
  gesture,

The actual raging insolence of the tyrant. I
am the hand ridded the Argolis of him.
I here, I killed him, I, justly.

THE BODY OF CASSANDRA   You have
heard her, you have heard her, she has
made confession.

Now if she'll show you the knife too—   250
CLYTEMNESTRA   Here.
I kept it for safety.
And, as that beast said, his blood's yet on it.
Look at it, with so little a key I unlocked
the kingdom of destruction. Stand firm,
till a God
Lead home this ghost to the dark country
So many Greeks have peopled, through his
crimes, his violence, his insolence, stand
firm till that moment
And through the act of this hand and of this
point no man shall suffer anything again
forever
Of Agamemnon.

THE BODY OF CASSANDRA
                I say if you let this woman
live, this crime go unpunished, what man
among you
Will be safe in his bed? The woman ever
envies the man, his strength, his freedom, his loves.
Her envy is like a snake beside him, all his
life through, her envy and hatred: law
tames that viper: 260
Law dies if the Queen die not: the viper is
free then,
It will be poison in your meat or a knife to
bleed you sleeping. They fawn and slaver
over us
And then we are slain.

CLYTEMNESTRA (*to one of the slaves that
carried the King's body*)
                Is my lord Ægisthus
Slain on the way? How long? How long?
                    (*To the people*) He
came, fat with his crimes.
Greek valor broke down Troy, your valor,
soldiers, and the brain of Odysseus, the
battle-fury of Achilles,
The stubborn strength of Menelaus, the excellence of you all: this dead man here,
his pride
Ruined you a hundred times: he helped
nowise, he brought bitter destruction:
but he gathered your glory
For the cloak of his shoulders. I saw him
come up the stair, I saw my child Iphigenia   270

Killed for his crime; I saw his harlot, the
captive woman there, crying out behind
him, I saw . . .
I saw . . . I saw . . . how can I speak
what crowd of the dead faces of the faithful Greeks,
Your brothers, dead of his crimes; those
that perished of plague and those that
died in the lost battles
After he had soured the help of Achilles—
for another harlot—those dead faces of
your brothers,
Some black with the death-blood, many
trampled under the hooves of horses,
many spotted with pestilence,
Flew all about him, all lamenting, all crying
out against him,—horrible—horrible—I
gave them
Vengeance; and you freedom.
                    (*To the slave*) Go
up and look, for God's sake, go up to
the parapets,
Look toward the mountain. Bring me word
quickly, my strength breaks,
How can I hold all the Argolis with my
eyes forever? I alone? Hell cannot hold
her dead men,   280
Keep watch there—send me word by
others—go, go!
                    (*To the people*) He came
triumphing.
Magnificent, abominable, all in bronze.
I brought him to the bath; my hands undid
the armor;
My hands poured out the water;
Dead faces like flies buzzed all about
us;
He stripped himself before me, loathsome,
unclean, with laughter;
The labors of the Greeks had made him fat,
the deaths of the faithful had swelled his
belly;
I threw a cloak over him for a net and
struck, struck, struck,
Blindly, in the steam of the bath; he bel-
lowed, netted,   290
And bubbled in the water;
All the stone vault asweat with steam bel-
lowed;
And I undid the net and the beast was
dead, and the broad vessel
Stank with his blood.

THE BODY OF CASSANDRA
                The word! the word
O burning mind of God,

If ever I gave you bulls teach me that word,
the name for her, the name for her!

A SLAVE (*running from the door; to* CLYTEM-
NESTRA)

My lord Ægisthus has come down the
mountain, Queen, he approaches the
Lion-gate.

CLYTEMNESTRA   It is time. I am tired now.

Meet him and tell him to come in the postern doorway.

THE CAPTAIN (*on the stair: addressing the
soldiers and the people below*)

Companions: before God, hating the smell
of crimes, crushes the city into gray ashes

We must make haste. Judge now and act.
For the husband-slayer   301

I say she must die, let her pay forfeit. And
for the great ghost of the King, let all
these captives,

But chiefly the woman Cassandra, the crier
in a man's voice there, be slain upon his
pyre to quiet him.

He will go down to his dark place and God
will spare the city.

(*To the soldiers above, on the ramp and
the porch*)

Comrades: Mycenæ is
greater

Than the Queen of Mycenæ. The King is
dead: let the Queen die: let the city live.
Comrades,

We suffered something in Asia, on the
stranger's coast, laboring for you. We
dreamed of home there

In the bleak wind and drift of battle; we
continued ten years, laboring and dying;
we accomplished

The task set us; we gathered what will make
all the Greek cities glorious, a name
forever;

We shared the spoil, taking our share to enrich Mycenæ. O but our hearts burned
then, O comrades   310

But our hearts melted when the great oars
moved the ships, the water carried us,
the blue sea-waves

Slid under the black keel; I could not see
them, I was blind with tears, thinking of
Mycenæ.

We have come home. Behold the dear
streets of our longing,

The stones that we desired, the steep ways
of the city and the sacred doorsteps

Reek and steam with pollution, the accursed vessel

Spills a red flood over the floors.

The fountain of it stands there and calls herself the Queen. No queen, no queen, that
husband-slayer,

A common murderess. Comrades join us

We will make clean the city and sweeten it
before God. We will mourn together at
the King's burying,

And a good year will come, we will rejoice
together.   320

CLYTEMNESTRA Dog, you dare something.
Fling no spear, soldiers,

He has a few fools back of him would attempt the stair if the dog were slain: I
will have no one

Killed out of need.

ONE OF HER MEN ON THE PORCH (*flinging his
spear*)

Not at him: at you
Murderess!

But some God, no lover of
justice, turned it; the great bronze tip
grazing her shoulder

Clanged on the stone behind: the gong of a
change in the dance: now Clytemnestra,
none to help her,

One against all, swayed raging by the
King's corpse, over the golden bed: it is
said that a fire

Stood visibly over her head, mixed in the
hair, pale flames and radiance.

CLYTEMNESTRA   Here am I,
thieves, thieves,

Drunkards, here is my breast, a deep white
mark for cowards to aim at: kings have
lain on it.   330

No spear yet, heroes, heroes?

See, I have no blemish, the arms are white,
the breasts are deep and white, the whole
body is blemishless:

You are tired of your brown wives, draw
lots for me, rabble, thieves, there is loot
here, shake the dice, thieves, a game yet!

One of you will take the bronze and one the
silver,

One the gold, and one me,

Me Clytemnestra a spoil worth having:

Kings have kissed me, this dead dog was a
king, there is another

King at the gate: thieves, thieves, would not
this shining

Breast brighten a sad thief's hut, roll in his
bed's filth

Shiningly? You could teach me to draw
water at the fountain,   340

A dirty child on the other hip: where are
the dice? Let me throw first, if I throw
sixes
I choose my masters: closer you rabble, let
me smell you.
Don't fear the knife, it has king's blood on
it, I keep it for an ornament,
It has shot its sting.
THE BODY OF CASSANDRA   Fools, fools,
strike!
Are your hands dead?
CLYTEMNESTRA   You would see all
of me
Before you choose whether to kill or dirtily
cherish? If what the King's used needs
commending
To the eyes of thieves for thieves' use: give
me room, give me room, fellows, you'll
see it is faultless.
The dress . . . there . . .   350
THE BODY OF CASSANDRA   Fools this wide
whore played wife
When she was going about to murder me
the King; you, will you let her trip you
With the harlot's trick? Strike! Make an
end!
CLYTEMNESTRA   I have not my sister's,
Troy's flame's beauty, but I have some-
thing.
This arm, round, firm, skin without hair,
polished like marble: the supple-jointed
shoulders:
Men have praised the smooth neck, too,
The strong clear throat over the deep wide
breasts . . .
THE BODY OF CASSANDRA   She is
buying an hour: sheep: it may be
Ægisthus
Is at the Lion-gate.
CLYTEMNESTRA   If he were here, Ægisthus,
I'd not be the peddler of what trifling
charms I have for an hour of life yet.
You have wolves' eyes: 361
Yet there is something kindly about the
blue ones there—yours, young soldier,
young soldier. . . . The last,
The under-garment? You won't buy me
yet? This dead dog,
The King here, never saw me naked: I had
the night for nurse: turn his head side-
ways, the eyes
Are only half shut. If I should touch him,
and the blood came, you'd say I had
killed him. Nobody, nobody,
Killed him: his pride burst.

Ah, no one has pity!
I can serve well, I have always envied your
women, the public ones.
Who takes me first? Tip that burnt log onto
the flagstones,
This will be in a king's bed then. Your eyes
are wolves' eyes: 370
So many, so many, so famishing—
I will undo it, handle me not yet, I can
undo it . . .
Or I will tear it.
And when it is off me then I will be de-
livered to you beasts . . .
THE BODY OF CASSANDRA
Then strip her and use her to the bones,
wear her through, kill her with it.
CLYTEMNESTRA
When it is torn
You'll say I am lovely: no one has seen
before . . .
It won't tear: I'll slit it with this knife—
          (ÆGISTHUS, with many spearmen, issues
          from the great door. CLYTEMNESTRA
          stabs right and left with the knife; the
          men are too close to strike her with their
          long spears.)
CLYTEMNESTRA
It's time. Cowards, goats, goats. Here!
Ægisthus!
ÆGISTHUS
I am here. What have they done?   380
CLYTEMNESTRA
Nothing: clear the porch: I have done some-
thing. Drive them on the stair!
Three of them I've scarred for life: a rough
bridegroom, the rabble, met a fierce
bride.   (She catches up her robe.)
I held them with my eyes, hours, hours. I
am not tired. . . . My lord, my lover:
I have killed a twelve-point stag for a pres-
ent for you: with my own hands: look, on
the golden litter.
You arrive timely.
THE BODY OF CASSANDRA   Tricked, stabbed,
shamed, mocked at, the spoil of a lewd
woman, despised
I lie there ready for her back-stairs darling
to spit on. Tricked, stabbed, sunk in the
drain
And gutter of time. I that thundered the
assault, I that mustered the Achæans.
Cast out of my kingdom,
Cast out of time, out of the light.
CLYTEMNESTRA   One of
the captives, dear. It left its poor wits   390

Over the sea. If it annoys you I'll quiet it.
But post your sentinels.
All's not safe yet, though I am burning with
joy now.

THE BODY OF CASSANDRA   O single-
eyed glare of the sky
Flying southwest to the mountain: sun,
through a slave's eyes,
My own broken, I see you this last day; my
own darkened, no dawn forever; the
adulterers
Will swim in your warm gold, day after
day; the eyes of the murderess will possess you;
And I have gone away down: knowing that
no God in the earth nor sky loves justice;
and having tasted
The toad that serves women for heart.
From now on may all bridegrooms
Marry them with swords. Those that have
borne children
Their sons rape them with spears.   400

CLYTEMNESTRA   More
yet, more, more, more, while my hand's
in? It's not a little
You easily living lords of the sky require of
who'd be like you, who'd take time in the
triumph,
Build joy solid. Do we have to do everything? I have killed what I hated:
Kill what I love? The prophetess said it,
this dead man says it: my little son, the
small soft image
That squirmed in my arms be an avenger?
—Love, from your loins
Seed: I begin new, I will be childless for
you. The child my son, the child my
daughter!
Though I cry I feel nothing.

ÆGISTHUS   O strongest
spirit in the world. We have dared
enough, there is an end to it.
We may pass nature a little, an arrow-flight,
But two shots over the wall you come in a
cloud upon the feasting Gods, lightning
and madness.   410

CLYTEMNESTRA
Dear: make them safe. They may try to run
away, the children. Set spears to watch
them: no harm, no harm,
But stab the nurse if they go near a door.
Watch them, keep the gates, order the
sentinels,
While I make myself queen over this people
again. I can do it.

THE BODY OF CASSANDRA   The sun's gone;
that glimmer's
The moon of the dead. The dark God calls
me. Yes, God,
I'll come in a moment.

CLYTEMNESTRA   (at the head of the great
stairs)
Soldiers: townsmen: it seems
I am not at the end delivered to you: dogs,
for the lion came: the poor brown and
spotted women
Will have to suffice you. But is it nothing to
have come within handling distance of
the clear heaven
This dead man knew when he was young
and God endured him? Is it nothing to
you?   420
It is something to me to have felt the fury
And concentration of you: I will not say
I am grateful: I am not angry: to be
desired
Is wine even to a queen. You bathed me in
it, from brow to foot-sole, I had nearly
enough.
But now remember that the dream is over.
I am the Queen: Mycenæ is my city. If
you grin at me
I have spears: also Tiryns and all the country people of the Argolis will come
against you and swallow you,
Empty out these ways and walls, stock them
with better subjects. A rock nest for new
birds here, townsfolk:
You are not essential.

THE BODY OF CASSANDRA   I hear him calling through the she-wolf's noise, Agamemnon, Agamemnon,
The dark God calls. Some old king in a
fable is it?

CLYTEMNESTRA   So choose.
What choices? To reënter my service   430
Unpunished, no thought of things past,
free of conditions. . .
Or—dine at this man's table, have new
mouths made in you to eat bronze with.

THE BODY OF CASSANDRA   Who is Agamemnon?

CLYTEMNESTRA
You letting go of the sun: is it dark the land
you are running away to?

THE BODY OF CASSANDRA   It is dark.

CLYTEMNESTRA   Is it sorrowful?

THE BODY OF CASSANDRA
There is nothing but misery.

CLYTEMNESTRA   Has any man

ever come back thence? Hear *me*, not the dark God.

THE BODY OF CASSANDRA   No man has ever.

CLYTEMNESTRA

Go then, go, go down. You will not choose to follow him, people of the rock-city? No one   440

Will choose to follow him. I have killed: it is easy: it may be I shall kill nearer than this yet:

But not you, townsfolk, you will give me no cause; I want security; I want service, not blood.

I have been desired of the whole city, publicly; I want service, not lust. You will make no sign

Of your submission; you will not give up your weapons; neither shall your leaders be slain;

And he that flung the spear, I have forgotten his face.

ÆGISTHUS (*entering*)   Dearest, they have gone, the nurse and the children,

No one knows where.

CLYTEMNESTRA   I am taming this people: send men after them. If any harm comes to the children

Bring me tokens. I will not be in doubt, I will not have the arch fall on us. I dare

What no one dares. I envy a little the dirty mothers of the city. O, O!   450

Nothing in me hurts. I have animal waters in my eyes, but the spirit is not wounded. Electra and Orestes

Are not to live when they are caught. Bring me sure tokens.

CASSANDRA   Who is this woman like a beacon

Lit on the stair, who are these men with dogs' heads?

I have ranged time and seen no sight like this one.

CLYTEMNESTRA

Have you returned, Cassandra? . . . The dead king has gone down to his place, we may bury his leavings.

CASSANDRA

I have witnessed all the wars to be; I am not sorrowful

For one drop from the pail of desolation

Spilt on my father's city; they were carrying it forward

To water the world under the latter starlight.   460

CLYTEMNESTRA (*to her slaves*)

Take up the poles of the bed; reverently; careful on the stair; give him to the people. (*To the people.*) O soldiers

This was your leader; lay him with honor in the burial-chapel; guard him with the spears of victory;

Mourn him until to-morrow, when the pyre shall be built.

Ah, King of men, sleep, sleep, sleep!

. . . But when shall I? . . . They are after their corpse, like dogs after the butcher's cart. Cleomenes, that captain

With the big voice: Neobulus was the boy who flung the spear and missed. *I* shall not miss

When spear-flinging-time comes. . . . Captive woman, you have seen the future, tell me my fortune.

(ÆGISTHUS *comes from the doorway.*) Ægisthus,

Have your hounds got them?

ÆGISTHUS   I've covered every escape with men, they'll not slip through me. But commanded

To bring them here living.   470

CLYTEMNESTRA   That's hard: tigresses don't do it: I have some strength yet: don't speak of it

And I shall do it.

ÆGISTHUS   It is a thing not to be done: we'll guard them closely: but mere madness

Lies over the wall of too-much.

CLYTEMNESTRA   King of Mycenæ, new-crowned king, who was your mother?

ÆGISTHUS   Pelopia.

What mark do you aim at?

CLYTEMNESTRA   And your father?

ÆGISTHUS   Thyestes.

CLYTEMNESTRA   And her father?   480

ÆGISTHUS   The same man, Thyestes.

CLYTEMNESTRA

See, dearest, dearest? They love what men call crime, they have taken her crime to be the king of Mycenæ.

Here is the stone garden of the plants that pass nature: there is no too-much here: the monstrous

Old rocks want monstrous roots to serpent among them. I will have security. I'd burn the standing world

Up to this hour and begin new. You think

I am too much used for a new brood? Ah, lover,

I have fountains in me. I had a fondness for the brown cheek of that boy, the curl of his lip,

The widening blue of the doomed eyes . . . I will be spared nothing. Come in, come in, they'll have news for us.

CASSANDRA

If anywhere in the world

Were a tower with foundations, or a treasure-chamber

With a firm vault, or a walled fortress   490

That stood on the years, not staggering, not moving

As the mortar were mixed with wine for water

And poppy for lime: they reel, they are all drunkards,

The piled strengths of the world: no pyramid

In bitter Egypt in the desert

But skips at moonrise; no mountain

Over the Black Sea in awful Caucasus

But whirls like a young kid, like a bud of the herd,

Under the hundredth star: I am sick after steadfastness

Watching the world cataractlike   500

Pour screaming onto steep ruins: for the wings of prophecy

God once my lover give me stone sandals

Planted on stone: he hates me, the God, he will never

Take home the gift of the bridleless horse

The stallion, the unbitted stallion: the bed

Naked to the sky on Mount Ida,

The soft clear grass there,

Be blackened forever, may vipers and Greeks

In that glen breed

Twisting together, where the God   510

Come golden from the sun

Gave me for a bride-gift prophecy and I took it for a treasure:

I a fool, I a maiden,

I would not let him touch me though love of him maddened me

Till he fed me that poison, till he planted that fire in me,

The girdle flew loose then.

The Queen considered this rock, she gazed on the great stone blocks of Mycenæ's acropolis;

Monstrous they seemed to her, solid they appeared to her, safe rootage for monstrous deeds: Ah fierce one

Who knows who laid them for a snare? What people in the world's dawn breathed on chill air and the vapor

Of their breath seemed stone and has stood and you dream it is established? These also are a foam on the stream   520

Of the falling of the world: there is nothing to lay hold on:

No crime is a crime, the slaying of the King was a meeting of two bubbles on the lip of the cataract,

One winked . . . and the killing of your children would be nothing: I tell you for a marvel that the earth is a dancer,

The grave dark earth is less quiet than a fool's fingers,

That old one, spinning in the emptiness, blown by no wind in vain circles, light-witted and a dancer.

CLYTEMNESTRA (entering)

You are prophesying: prophesy to a purpose, captive woman. My children, the boy and the girl,

Have wandered astray, no one can find them.

CASSANDRA   Shall I tell the lioness

Where meat is, or the she-wolf where the lambs wander astray?

CLYTEMNESTRA   But look into the darkness   530

And foam of the world: the boy has great tender blue eyes, brown hair, disdainful lips, you'll know him

By the gold stripe bordering his garments; the girl's eyes are my color, white her clothing—

CASSANDRA   Millions

Of shining bubbles burst and wander

On the stream of the world falling . . .

CLYTEMNESTRA   These are my children!

CASSANDRA   I see mountains, I see no faces.

CLYTEMNESTRA

Tell me and I make you free; conceal it from me and a soldier's spear finishes the matter.

CASSANDRA

I am the spear's bride, I have been waiting, waiting for that ecstasy—

CLYTEMNESTRA (striking her)   Live then. It will not be unpainful.   540

(CLYTEMNESTRA goes in.)

CASSANDRA

O fair roads north where the land narrows
Over the mountains between the great gulfs,
O that I too with the King's children
Might wander northward hand in hand.
Mine are worse wanderings:
They will shelter on Mount Parnassus,
For me there is no mountain firm enough,
The storms of light beating on the head-
    lands,
The storms of music undermine the moun-
    tains, they stumble and fall inward,
Such music the stars   550
Make in their courses, the vast vibration
Plucks the iron heart of the earth like a
    harp-string.
Iron and stone core, O stubborn axle of the
    earth, you also
Dissolving in a little time like salt in water,
What does it matter that I have seen Mace-
    don
Roll all the Greek cities into one billow and
    strand in Asia
The anthers and bracts of the flower of the
    world?
That I have seen Egypt and Nineveh
Crumble, and a Latian village
Plant the earth with javelins? It made laws
    for all men, it dissolved like a cloud.   560
I have also stood watching a storm of wild
    swans
Rise from one river-mouth . . . O force
    of the earth rising,
O fallings of the earth: forever no rest, not
    forever
From the wave and the trough, from the
    stream and the slack, from growth and
    decay: O vulture-
Pinioned, my spirit, one flight yet, last,
    longest, unguided,
Try into the gulf,
Over Greece, over Rome, you have space
O my spirit for the years

II

Are not few of captivity: how many have I
    stood here
Among the great stones, while the Queen's
    people
Go in and out of the gate, wearing light
    linen   570
For summer and the wet spoils of wild
    beasts
In the season of storms: and the stars have
    changed, I have watched

The grievous and unprayed-to constella-
    tions
Pile steaming spring and patient autumn
Over the enduring walls: but you over the
    walls of the world,
Over the unquieted centuries, over the
    darkness-hearted
Millenniums wailing thinly to be born, O
    vulture-pinioned
Try into the dark,
Watch the north spawn white bodies and
    red-gold hair,
Race after race of beastlike warriors; and
    the cities   580
Burn, and the cities build, and new lands
    be uncovered
In the way of the sun to his setting . . . go
    on farther, what profit
In the wars and the toils? but I say
Where are prosperous people my enemies
    are, as you pass them O my spirit
Curse Athens for the joy and the marble,
    curse Corinth
For the wine and the purple, and Syracuse
For the gold and the ships; but Rome,
    Rome,
With many destructions for the corn and
    the laws and the javelins, the insolence,
    the threefold
Abominable power: pass the humble
And the lordships of darkness, but far
    down   590
Smite Spain for the blood on the sunset
    gold, curse France
For the fields abounding and the running
    rivers, the lights in the cities, the laugh-
    ter, curse England
For the meat on the tables and the terrible
    gray ships, for old laws, far dominions,
    there remains
A mightier to be cursed and a higher for
    malediction
When America has eaten Europe and takes
    tribute of Asia, when the ends of the
    world grow aware of each other
And are dogs in one kennel, they will tear
The master of the hunt with the mouths of
    the pack: new fallings, new risings, O
    winged one
No end of the fallings and risings? An end
    shall be surely,
Though unnatural things are accomplished,
    they breathe in the sea's depth,   599
They swim in the air, they bridle the cloud-
    leaper lightning to carry their messages:

Though the eagles of the east and the west
    and the falcons of the north were not
    quieted, you have seen a white cloth
Cover the lands from the north and the eyes
    of the lands and the claws of the hunters,
The mouths of the hungry with snow
Were filled, and their claws
Took hold upon ice in the pasture, a morsel
    of ice was their catch in the rivers,
That pure white quietness
Waits on the heads of the mountains, not
    sleep but death, will the fire
Of burnt cities and ships in that year warm
    you my enemies? The frost, the old frost,
Like a cat with a broken-winged bird it
    will play with you,
It will nip and let go; you will say it is gone,
    but the next   610
Season it increases: O clean, clean,
White and most clean, colorless quietness,
Without trace, without trail, without stain
    in the garment, drawn down
From the poles to the girdle. . . . I have
    known one Godhead
To my sore hurt: I am growing to come to
    another: O grave and kindly
Last of the lords of the earth, I pray you
    lead my substance
Speedily into another shape, make me
    grass, Death, make me stone,
Make me air to wander free between the
    stars and the peaks; but cut humanity
Out of my being, that is the wound that
    festers in me,
Not captivity, not my enemies: you will
    heal the earth also,   620
Death, in your time; but speedily Cassan-
    dra.
You rock-fleas hopping in the clefts of
    Mycenæ,
Suckers of blood, you carrying the scepter
    farther, Persian, Emathian,
Roman and Mongol and American, and you
    half-gods
Indian and Syrian and the third, emperors
    of peace, I have seen on what stage
You sing the little tragedy; the column of
    the ice that was before on one side flanks
    it,
The column of the ice to come closes it up
    on the other: audience nor author
I have never seen yet: I have heard the
    silence: it is I Cassandra,
Eight years the bitter watch-dog of these
    doors,   630

Have watched a vision
And now approach to my end. Eight years
    have I seen the phantoms
Walk up and down this stair; and the rocks
    groan in the night, the great stones move
    when no man sees them.
And I have forgotten the fine ashlar ma-
    sonry of the courts of my father. I am
    not Cassandra
But a counter of sunrises, permitted to live
    because I am crying to die; three thou-
    sand,
Pale and red, have flowed over the towers
    in the wall since I was here watching; the
    deep east widens,
The cold wind blows, the deep earth sighs,
    the dim gray finger of light crooks at the
    morning star.
The palace feasted late and sleeps with its
    locked doors; the last drunkard from the
    alleys of the city
Long has reeled home. Whose foot is this
    then, what phantom
Toils on the stair?
A VOICE BELOW Is someone watching
    above? Good sentinel I am only a girl
    beggar.   640
I would sit on the stair and hold my bowl.
CASSANDRA   I here
    eight years have begged for a thing and
    not received it.
THE VOICE
You are not a sentinel? You have been
    asking some great boon, out of all reason.
CASSANDRA   No: what the meanest
Beggar disdains to take.
THE GIRL BEGGAR   Beggars disdain
    nothing: what is it that they refuse you?
CASSANDRA   What's given
Even to the sheep and to the bullock.
THE GIRL   Men
    give them salt, grass they find out for
    themselves.
CASSANDRA   Men give them   650
The gift that you though a beggar have
    brought down from the north to give my
    mistress.
THE GIRL   You speak riddles.
I am starving, a crust is my desire.
CASSANDRA   Your
    voice is young though winds have hoars-
    ened it, your body appears
Flexible under the rags: have you some
    hidden sickness, the young men will not
    give you silver?

THE GIRL
I have a sickness: I will hide it until I am cured. You are not a Greek woman?

CASSANDRA   But you
Born in Mycenæ return home. And you bring gifts from Phocis: for my once master who's dead
Vengeance; and for my mistress peace, for my master the King peace, and, by-shot of the doom's day,   659
Peace for me also. But I have prayed for it.

THE GIRL   I know you, I knew you before you spoke to me, captive woman,
And I unarmed will kill you with my hands if you babble prophecies.
That peace you have prayed for, I will bring it to you
If you utter warnings.

CASSANDRA   To-day I shall have peace, you cannot tempt me, daughter of the Queen, Electra.
Eight years ago I watched you and your brother going north to Phocis: the Queen saw knowledge of you
Move in my eyes: I would not tell her where you were when she commanded me: I will not betray you
To-day either: it is not doleful to me
To see before I die generations of destruction enter the doors of Agamemnon.
Where is your brother?   670

ELECTRA   Prophetess: you see all: I will tell you nothing.

CASSANDRA He has well chosen his ambush,
It is true Ægisthus passes under that house to-day, to hunt in the mountain.

ELECTRA   Now I remember
Your name. Cassandra.

CASSANDRA   Hush: the gray has turned yellow, the standing beacons
Stream up from the east; they stir there in the palace; strange, is it not, the dawn of one's last day's
Like all the others? Your brother would be fortunate if to-day were also
The last of his.

ELECTRA   He will endure his destinies; and Cassandra hers; and Electra mine.   680
He has been for years like one tortured with fire: this day will quench it.

CASSANDRA   They are opening the gates: beg now.

To your trade, beggar-woman.

THE PORTER (coming out) Eh, pillar of miseries,
You still on guard there? Like a mare in a tight stall, never lying down. What's this then?
A second ragged one? This at least can bend in the middle and sit on a stone.

ELECTRA   Dear gentleman
I am not used to it, my father is dead and hunger forces me to beg, a crust or a penny.

THE PORTER
This tall one's licensed in a manner. I think they'll not let two bundles of rag
Camp on the stair: but if you'd come to the back door and please me nicely: with a little washing   690
It'd do for a pastime.

ELECTRA   I was reared gently: I will sit here, the King will see me,
And none mishandle me.

THE PORTER   I bear no blame for you.
I have not seen you: you came after the gates were opened.   (He goes in.)

CASSANDRA
O blossom of fire, bitter to men,
Watchdog of the woeful days,
How many sleepers
Bathing in peace, dreaming themselves delight,
All over the city, all over the Argolid plain, all over the dark earth,   700
(Not me, a deeper draught of peace
And darker waters alone may wash me)
Do you, terrible star, star without pity,
Wolf of the east, waken to misery.
To the wants unaccomplished, to the eating desires,
To unanswered love, to hunger, to the hard edges
And mold of reality, to the whips of their masters.
They had flown away home to the happy darkness,
They were safe until sunrise.
        (KING ÆGISTHUS, with his retinue, comes from the great door.)

ÆGISTHUS
Even here, in the midst of the city, the early day   710
Has a clear savor. (To ELECTRA) What, are you miserable, holding the bowl out?
We'll hear the lark to-day in the wide hills

and smell the mountain. I'd share happiness with you.
What's your best wish, girl beggar?

ELECTRA   It is covered, my lord, how should a beggar
Know what to wish for beyond a crust and
a dark corner and a little kindness?

ÆGISTHUS   Why do you tremble?

ELECTRA
I was reared gently; my father is dead.

ÆGISTHUS   Stand up: will you take
service here in the house? What country
Bred you gently and proved ungentle to you?

ELECTRA   I have wandered north
from the Eurotas, my lord,   720
Begging at farmsteads.

ÆGISTHUS   The Queen's coun-
trywoman then, she'll use you kindly.
She'll be coming
In a moment, then I'll speak for you.—Did
you bid them yoke the roans into my
chariot, Menalcas,
The two from Orchomenus?

ONE OF THE RETINUE   Yesterday
evening, my lord,
I sent to the stable.

ÆGISTHUS   They cost a pretty
penny, we'll see how they carry it.—
She's coming: hold up your head, girl.
    (CLYTEMNESTRA, *with two serving-
    women, comes from the door.*)

CLYTEMNESTRA
Good hunt, dearest. Here's a long idle day
for me to look to. Kill early, come home
early.

ÆGISTHUS
There's a poor creature on the step who's
been reared nicely and slipped into
misery. I said you'd feed her,
And maybe find her a service. Farewell,
sweet one.   730

CLYTEMNESTRA   Where did she come from?
How long have you been here?

ÆGISTHUS   She says she has begged her
way up from Sparta. The horses are
stamping on the cobbles, good-by, good-
by.
    (*He goes down the stair with his hunts-
    men.*)

CLYTEMNESTRA   Good-by, dearest. Well.
Let me see your face.

ELECTRA   It is filthy to look at. I am
ashamed.

CLYTEMNESTRA   (*to one of her serving-
women*)   Leucippe do you think this is a

gayety of my lord's, he's not used to be
so kindly to beggars?
—Let me see your face.

LEUCIPPE   She is very dirty, my lady. It is
possible one of the house-boys . . .

CLYTEMNESTRA   I say draw that rag back,
let me see your face. I'd have him
whipped then.

ELECTRA   It was only in hope that someone
would put a crust in the bowl, your
majesty, for I am starving. I didn't think
your majesty would see me.

CLYTEMNESTRA   Draw back the rag.   740

ELECTRA   I am very faint and starving but
I will go down; I am ashamed.

CLYTEMNESTRA   Stop her, Corinna. Fetch
the porter, Leucippe. You will not go so
easily. (ELECTRA *sinks down on the steps
and lies prone, her head covered.*) I am
aging out of queenship indeed, when
even the beggars refuse my bidding.
(LEUCIPPE *comes in with the porter.*) You
have a dirty stair, porter. How long has
this been here?

THE PORTER   O my lady it has crept up
since I opened the doors, it was not here
when I opened the doors.

CLYTEMNESTRA   Lift it up and uncover its
face. What is that cry in the city? Stop:
silent: I heard a cry . . .
Prophetess, your nostrils move like a dog's,
what is that shouting? . . .
I have grown weak, I am exhausted, things
frighten me . . .
Tell her to be gone, Leucippe, I don't wish
to see her, I don't wish to see her.
                    (ELECTRA *rises.*)

ELECTRA   Ah, Queen, I will show you my
face.

CLYTEMNESTRA   No . . . no . . . be gone.

ELECTRA (*uncovering her face*)
Mother: I have come home: I am humbled.
This house keeps a dark welcome   750
For those coming home out of far coun-
tries.

CLYTEMNESTRA   I won't look: how
could I know anyone? I am old and
shaking.
He said, Over the wall beyond nature
Lightning, and the laughter of the Gods. I
did not cross it, I will not kill what I
gave life to.
Whoever you are, go, go, let me grow
downward to the grave quietly now.

ELECTRA   I cannot

Go: I have no other refuge. Mother! Will
you not kiss me, will you not take me
into the house,
Your child once, long a wanderer? Electra
my name. I have begged my way from
Phocis, my brother is dead there,
Who used to care for me.

CLYTEMNESTRA   Who is dead,
who?   760

ELECTRA   My brother Orestes,
Killed in a court quarrel.

CLYTEMNESTRA (*weeping*)   Oh, you lie! The
widening blue blue eyes,
The little voice of the child . . . Liar.

ELECTRA   It
is true. I have wept long, on every mountain. You, mother,
Have only begun weeping. Far off, in a far
country, no fit burial . . .

CLYTEMNESTRA   And do you bringing
Bitterness . . . or lies . . . look for a
welcome? I have only loved two:
The priest killed my daughter for a lamb
on a stone and now you say the boy too
. . . dead, dead?
The world's full of it, a shoreless lake of
lies and floating rumors . . . pack up
your wares, peddler,   770
Too false for a queen. Why, no, if I
believed you . . . Beast, treacherous
beast, that shouting comes nearer,
What's in the City?

ELECTRA   I am a stranger, I
know nothing of the city, I know only
My mother hates me, and Orestes my
brother
Died pitifully, far off.

CLYTEMNESTRA   Too many things,
too many things call me, what shall I do?
Electra,
Electra help me. This comes of living
softly, I had a lion's strength
Once.

ELECTRA   Me for help? I am utterly helpless, I had help in my brother and he is
dead in Phocis.
Give me refuge: but each of us two must
weep for herself, one sorrow. An end of
the world were on us   780
What would it matter to us weeping? Do
you remember him,
Mother, mother?

CLYTEMNESTRA   I have dared too much:
never dare anything, Electra, the ache is
afterward,

At the hour it hurts nothing. Prophetess,
you lied.
You said he would come with vengeance on
me: but now he is dead, this girl says:
and because he was lovely, blue-eyed,
And born in a most unhappy house I will
believe it. But the world's fogged with
the breath of liars,
And if she has laid a net for me . . .
I'll call up the old lioness lives yet in my
body, I have dared, I have dared, and
tooth and talon
Carve a way through. Lie to me?

ELECTRA   Have I
endured for months, with feet bleeding,
among the mountains,   790
Between the great gulfs alone and starving,
to bring you a lie now? I know the worst
of you, I looked for the worst,
Mother, mother, and have expected nothing but to die of this home-coming: but
Orestes
Has entered the cave before; he is gathered
up in a lonely mountain quietness, he is
guarded from angers
In the tough cloud that spears fall back
from.

CLYTEMNESTRA   Was he still
beautiful? The brown mothers down in
the city
Keep their brats about them; what it is to
live high! Oh!
Tell them down there, tell them in Tiryns,
Tell them in Sparta,
That water drips through the Queen's fin-
gers and trickles down her wrists, for
the boy, for the boy
Born of her body, whom she, fool, fool,
fool,   800
Drove out of the world. Electra,
Make peace with me.
Oh, Oh, Oh!
I have labored violently all the days of my
life for nothing—nothing—worse than
anything—this death
Was a thing I wished. See how they make
fools of us.
Amusement for them, to watch us labor
after the thing that will tear us in pieces.
. . . Well, strength's good.
I am the Queen; I will gather up my frag-
ments
And not go mad now.

ELECTRA   Mother, what are
the men

With spears gathering at the stair's foot?
Not of Mycenæ by their armor, have you
mercenaries   810
Wanting pay? Do they serve . . . Ægisthus?

CLYTEMNESTRA   What men? I
seem not to know . . .
Who has laid a net for me, what fool
For me, me? Porter, by me.
Leucippe, my guards; into the house, rouse
them. I am sorry for him,
I am best in storm. You, Electra?
The death you'll die, my daughter. Guards,
out! Was it a lie? No matter, no matter,
no matter,
Here's peace. Spears, out, out! They bun-
gled the job making me a woman. Here's
youth come back to me,
And all the days of gladness.

LEUCIPPE (*running back from the door*) O,
Queen, strangers . . .   820

ORESTES (*a sword in his hand, with spearmen
following, comes from the door*) Where is
that woman
The Gods utterly hate?

ELECTRA   Brother: let her
not speak, kill quickly. Is the other one
safe now?

ORESTES   That dog
Fell under his chariot, we made sure of him
between the wheels and the hooves,
squealing. Now for this one.

CLYTEMNESTRA
Wait. I was weeping, Electra will tell you,
my hands are wet still,
For your blue eyes that death had closed
she said away up in Phocis. I die now,
justly or not
Is out of the story, before I die I'd tell you
—wait, child, wait. Did I quiver
Or pale at the blade? I say, caught in a net,
netted in by my enemies, my husband
murdered,
Myself to die, I am joyful knowing she lied,
you live, the only creature   830
Under all the spread and arch of daylight
That I love, lives.

ELECTRA   The great fangs drawn
fear craftiness now, kill quickly.

CLYTEMNESTRA   As for
her, the wife of the shepherd
Suckled her, but you
These very breasts nourished: rather one of
your northern spearmen do what's needful; not you

Draw blood where you drew milk. The
Gods endure much, but beware them.

ORESTES   This, a God in his temple
Openly commanded.

CLYTEMNESTRA   Ah, child, child,
who has mistaught you and who has betrayed you? What voice had the God? 840
How was it different from a man's and did
you see him? Who sent the priest presents? They fool us,
And the Gods let them. No doubt also the
envious King of Phocis has lent you
counsel as he lent you
Men: let one of them do it. Life's not jewel
enough
That I should plead for it: this much I
pray, for your sake, not with your hand,
not with your hand, or the memory
Will so mother you, so glue to you, so embracing you,
Not the deep sea's green day, no cleft of a
rock in the bed of the deep sea, no ocean
of darkness
Outside the stars, will hide nor wash you.
What is it to me that I have rejoiced
knowing you alive,
O child, O precious to me, O alone loved,
if now dying by my manner of death
I make nightmare the heir, nightmare, horror, in all I have of you;
And you haunted forever, never to sleep
dreamless again, never to see blue
cloth   850
But the red runs over it; fugitive of dreams,
madman at length, the memory of a
scream following you houndlike,
Inherit Mycenæ? Child, for this has not
been done before, there is no old fable,
no whisper
Out of the foundation, among the people
that were before our people, no echo has
ever
Moved among these most ancient stones,
the monsters here, nor stirred under any
mountain, nor fluttered
Under any sky, of a man slaying his mother.
Sons have killed fathers—

ORESTES   And a woman
her son's father—

CLYTEMNESTRA
O many times: and these old stones have seen
horrors: a house of madness and blood
I married into: and worse was done on this
rock among the older people before: but
not this,

Not the son his mother; this the silent ones,
The old hard ones, the great bearers of
burden have not seen yet,   860
Nor shall, to-day nor yet to-morrow, nor
ever in the world. Let her do it, it is not
unnatural,
The daughter the mother; the little liar
there,
Electra do it. Lend her the blade.

ELECTRA   Brother
though the great house is silent hark the
city,
That buzzes like the hive one has dipped a
wand in. End this. Then look to our
safety.

ORESTES   Dip in my sword
Into my fountain? Did I truly, little and
helpless,
Lie in the arms, feed on the breast there?

ELECTRA   Another, a greater,
lay in them, another kissed the breast
there,
You forget easily, the breaker of Asia, the
over-shadower, the great memory, under
whose greatness   870
We have hung like hawks under a storm,
from the beginning,—and he when this
poison destroyed him
Was given no room to plead in.

ORESTES   Dip my
wand into my fountain?

CLYTEMNESTRA   Men do not kill the meanest
Without defence heard—

ELECTRA   Him—Agamemnon?

CLYTEMNESTRA   But you, O
my son, my son,
Molded in me, made of me, made of my
flesh, built with my blood, fed with my
milk, my child
I here, I and no other, labored to bear,
groaning—

ELECTRA   This that makes beastlike
lamentation   880
Hunted us to slay us, we starving in the
thicket above the stream three days and
nights watched always
Her hunters with spears beating the field:
prophetess was it for love that she looked
after us?

CASSANDRA   That love
The King had tasted; that was her love.

ELECTRA   And
mourning for our father on the mountain
we judged her;

And the Gods condemned her, what more,
what more? Strike.

ORESTES   If they'd give me time, the pack
there—how can I think,
And all the whelps of Mycenæ yelling at the
stair-foot? Decision: a thing to be decided:
The arm's lame, dip in, dip in? Shut your
mouths, rabble.

CLYTEMNESTRA   There is one thing no man
can do.   890

ORESTES   What, enter his fountain?

ELECTRA
O coward!

ORESTES   I will be passive, I'm blunted.
She's not this fellow's mother.

ELECTRA   O spearman, spearman, do it!
One stroke: it is just.

THE SPEARMAN   As for me, my
lord . . .

CLYTEMNESTRA (calling loudly)   Help,
help, men of Mycenæ, to your Queen.
Break them.
Rush the stair, there are only ten hold it.
Up, up, kill.

ORESTES   I will kill.   899

CLYTEMNESTRA (falling on her knees)   Child,
Spare me, let me live! Child! Ai! . . .

ELECTRA   You have done well.

ORESTES   I have done . . . I have
done . . .
Who ever saw such a flow . . . was I
made out of this, I'm not red, am I?
See, father?
It was someone else did it but I told him
to. Drink, drink, dog. Drink dog.
He reaches up a tongue between the stones,
lapping it. So thirsty old dog, uh?
Rich and sticky.

CLYTEMNESTRA (raising herself a little) Sleep
. . . for me . . . yes.
Not you . . . any   more . . . Orestes
. . . I shall be there. You will beg death
. . . vainly as I have begged . . . life.
Ah . . . beast that I unkennelled! 910
                                  (She dies.)

ORESTES (crouching by her)   Ooh . . .
ooh . . .

ELECTRA
The face is lean and terrible. Orestes!
They are fighting on the stair. Man yourself. Come. Pick up the sword.
Let her be, two of ours are down, they
yield on the stair. Stand up, speak or
fight, speak to the people

Or we go where she is.

ORESTES   There's a red and
sticky sky that you can touch here.
And though it's unpleasant we are at peace.

ELECTRA (*catching up the sword*) Agamemnon failed here. Not in me. Hear, Mycenæans.
I am Agamemnon's daughter, we have
avenged him, the crime's paid utterly.
You have not forgotten the great King—
what, in eight years? I am Electra, I am
his daughter.   920
My brother is Orestes. My brother is your
king and has killed his murderers. The
dog Ægisthus is dead,
And the Queen is dead: the city is at peace.

ORESTES (*standing up*)   Must I dip
my wand into my fountain, give it to
me.
The male plaything.
      (*He catches* ELECTRA'S *arm, snatching at
      the sword.*)

ELECTRA   For what? Be quiet,
they have heard me.

ORESTES You said I must do it, I will do it.

ELECTRA   It is done!
Brother, brother? (ORESTES *takes the sword
from her by force.*) O Mycenæ
With this sword he did justice, he let it fall,
he has retaken it,
He is your King.   930

ORESTES   Whom must I pierce,
the girl that plotted with me in the
mountain? There was someone to
kill . . .
Sweet Electra?

ELECTRA   It is done, it is finished!

CASSANDRA   The nearest, the
most loved, her, truly. Strike!—Electra,
My father has wanted vengeance longer.

THE PEOPLE BELOW   Orestes, Orestes!

ELECTRA (*pointing to* CASSANDRA)   Her
—your mother—she killed him.

ORESTES (*turning and striking*) How tall
you have grown, mother.

CASSANDRA (*falling*) I . . . waited long
for it . . .

ORESTES
I have killed my mother and my mother—
two mothers—see, there they lie—I have
gone home twice. You put it in   940
And the flesh yields to it . . . (*He goes
down the stair.*) Now, to find her again
All through the forest . . .

ELECTRA   Let him pass,

Mycenæans. Avoid his sword. Let him
pass, pass. The madness of the house
Perches on him.

A LEADER OF THE MYCENÆANS   Daughter of
Agamemnon,
You with constancy and force
In the issueless thing have found an issue.
Now it is for us the kingless city
To find a ruler. Rest in the house. As for
the young man,
Though he has done justice, and no hand
in Mycenæ is raised against him, for him
there is no issue.
We let him go on; and if he does not slay
himself with the red sword he will die in
the mountain.   950
With us be peace. Rest in the house,
daughter of Agamemnon. The old mad-
ness, with your brother,
Go out of our gates.

ELECTRA   A house to rest in!
. . . Gather up the dead: I will go in; I
have learned strength.

III

They carried the dead down the great stair;
the slaves with pails of water and sand
scoured the dark stains.
The people meeting in another place to
settle the troubled city the stair was left
vacant,
The porch untrampled, and about twilight
one of the great stones: The world is
younger than we are,
Yet now drawing to an end, now that the
seasons falter. Then another, that had
been spared the blood-bath:
What way do they falter?—There fell
warm rain, the first answered, in the
midst of summer. A little afterward
Cold rain came down; and sand was rubbed
over me as when the winds blow. This in
the midst of summer.
—I did not feel it, said the second sleepily.
And a third: The noisy and very mobile
creatures   960
Will be quieted long before the world's
end.—What creatures?—The active
ones, that have two ends let downward,
A mongrel race, mixed of soft stone with
fugitive water. The night deepened, the
dull old stones
Droned at each other, the summer stars
wheeled over above them. Before dawn
the son of Agamemnon

Came to the stair-foot in the darkness.

ORESTES   O stones of the house:
I entreat hardness: I did not live with
you
Long enough in my youth. . . . I will go
up to where I killed her. . . . We must
face things down, mother,
Or they'd devour us. . . . Nobody? . . .
Even the stones have been scrubbed. A
keen housekeeper, sweet Electra.
. . . It would be childish to forget it; the
woman has certainly been killed, and I
think it was I
Her son did it. Something not done before
in the world. Here is the penalty:
You gather up all your forces to the act, and
afterward   970
Silence, no voice, no ghost, vacancy, but
all's not expended. Those powers want
bitter action. No object.
Deeds are too easy. Our victims are too fragile, they ought to have thousands of lives,
you strike out once only
The sky breaks like a bubble. . . . No,
wife of Ægisthus,—Why should I mask
it?—mother, my mother,
The one soft fiber that went mad yesterday's
Burnt out of me now, there is nothing you
could touch if you should come; but you
have no power, you dead
Are a weak people. This is the very spot: I
was here, she here: and I walk over it not
trembling,
Over the scrubbed stones to the door. (*He
knocks with the sword-hilt.*) They sleep
well. But my sister having all her desire
Better than any.   (*He knocks again.*)
THE PORTER (*through the door*) Who is
there?
ORESTES   The owner of the house. Orestes.
THE PORTER   Go away, drunkard.   981
ORESTES   Shall I tell my servants to break
in the door and whip the porter?
THE PORTER   Oh, Oh! You men from
Phocis, stand by me while I speak to the
door. (*Having opened the door, holding a
torch.*) Is it you truly, my lord? We
thought, we thought . . . we pray you
to enter the house, my lord Orestes.
ORESTES   You are to waken my sister.
I'll speak with her here.
ELECTRA (*at the door*) Oh! You are safe,
you are well! Did you think I could be
sleeping? But it is true,

I have slept soundly. Come, come.
ORESTES   A fellow
in the forest
Told me you'd had the stone scrubbed
. . . I mean, that you'd entered the
house, received as Agamemnon's daughter
In the honor of the city. So I free to go
traveling have come with—what's the
word, Electra?—farewell.   990
Have come to bid you farewell.
ELECTRA   It means
—you are going somewhere? Come into
the house, Orestes, tell me . . .
ORESTES
The cape's rounded. I have not ship-
wrecked.
ELECTRA   Around the rock we have
passed safely is the hall of this house,
The throne in the hall, the shining lordship
of Mycenæ.
ORESTES   No: the open world, the
sea and its wonders.
You thought the oars raked the headland
in the great storm—what, for Mycenæ?
ELECTRA   Not meanest of the Greek cities:
Whose king captained the world into Asia.
Have you suddenly become . . . a God,
brother, to over-vault
Agamemnon's royalty? O come in, come
in. I am cold, cold. I pray you.   1000
ORESTES   Fetch a cloak, porter.
If I have outgrown the city a little—I have
earned it. Did you notice, Electra, she
caught at the sword
As the point entered: the palm of her right
hand was slashed to the bone before the
mercy of the point
Slept in her breast: the laid-open palm it
was that undermined me . . . Oh, the
cloak. It's a blond night,
We'll walk on the stones: no chill, the stars
are mellow. If I dare remember
Yesterday . . . because I have conquered,
the soft fiber's burnt out.
ELECTRA   You have conquered: possess:
enter the house,
Take up the royalty.
ORESTES   You were in my
vision to-night in the forest, Electra, I
thought I embraced you   1009
More than brotherwise . . . possessed,
you call it . . . entered the fountain—
ELECTRA   Oh, hush.
Therefore you would not kill her!

ORESTES
I killed. It is foolish to darken things with
  words. I was here, she there, screaming.
  Who if not I?
ELECTRA
The hidden reason: the bitter kernel of
  your mind that has made you mad: I
  that learned strength
Yesterday, I have no fear.
ORESTES   Fear? The city
  is friendly and took you home with
  honor, they'll pay
Phocis his wage, you will be quiet.
ELECTRA   Are you
  resolved to understand nothing, Orestes?
I am not Agamemnon, only his daughter.
  You are Agamemnon. Beggars and the
  sons of beggars
May wander at will over the world, but
  Agamemnon has his honor and high
  Mycenæ
Is not to be cast.   1020
ORESTES   Mycenæ for a ship: who
  will buy kingdom
And sell me a ship with oars?
ELECTRA   Dear: listen.
  Come to the parapet where it hangs over
  the night:
The ears at the door hinder me. Now, let
  the arrow-eyed stars hear, the night, not
  men, as for the Gods
No one can know them, whether they be
  angry or pleased, tall and terrible, stand-
  ing apart,
When they make signs out of the darkness.
  . . . I cannot tell you. . . . You will
  stay here, brother?
ORESTES   I'll go
To the edge and over it. Sweet sister, if
  you've got a message for them, the dark
  ones?
ELECTRA   You do not mean
Death; but a wandering; what does it mat-
  ter what you mean? I know two ways
  and one will quiet you.   1030
You shall choose either.
ORESTES   But I am quiet.
  It is more regular than a sleeping child's:
  be untroubled,
Yours burns, it is you trembling.
ELECTRA   Should
  I not tremble? It is only a little to offer,
But all that I have.
ORESTES   Offer?
ELECTRA   It is accom-

plished: my father is avenged: the fates
  and the body of Electra
Are nothing. But for Agamemnon to rule
  in Mycenæ: that is not nothing. O my
  brother
You are Agamemnon: rule: take all you
  will: nothing is denied you. The Gods
  have redressed evil
And clamped the balance.   1040
ORESTES   No doubt they
  have done what they desired.
ELECTRA   And yours,
  yours? I will not suffer her
Justly punished to dog you over the end of
  the world. Your desire? Speak it openly,
  Orestes.
She is to be conquered: if her ghost were
  present on the stones—let it hear you. I
  will make war on her
With my life, or with my body.
ORESTES   What strange
  martyrdom, Electra, what madness for
  sacrifice
Makes your eyes burn like two fires on a
  watch-tower, though the night darkens?
ELECTRA   What you want you shall have:
And rule in Mycenæ. Nothing, nothing is
  denied you. If I knew which of the two
  choices
Would quiet you, I would do and not speak,
  not ask you. Tell me, tell me. Must I
  bear all the burden,   1050
I weaker, and a woman? You and I were
  two hawks quartering the field for living
  flesh, Orestes,
Under the storm of the memory
Of Agamemnon: we struck: we tore the
  prey, that dog and that woman. Suddenly since yesterday
You have shot up over me and left me,
You are Agamemnon, you are the storm of
  the living presence, the very King, and I,
  lost wings
Under the storm, would die for you. . . .
  You do not speak yet? . . . Mine to say
  it all? . . . You know me a maiden,
  Orestes,
You have always been with me, no man has
  even touched my cheek. It is not easy for
  one unmarried
And chaste, to name both choices. The first
  is easy. That terrible dream in the forest:
  if fear of desire
Drives you away: it is easy for me not to be.
  I never have known

Sweetness in life: all my young days were
  given—   1060
ORESTES   I thought to be silent was better,
And understand you: afterwards I'll speak.
ELECTRA   —to the noise of
  blood crying for blood, a crime to be
  punished,
A house to be emptied: these things are
  done: and now I am lonely, and what
  becomes of me is not important.
There's water, and there are points and
  edges, pain's only a moment: I'd do it
  and not speak, but nobody knows
Whether it would give you peace or madden
  you again, I'd not be leagued with that
  bad woman against you,
And these great walls sit by the crater, terrible desires blow through them. O
  brother, I'll never blame you,
I share the motherhood and the father-
  hood, I can conceive the madness, if you
  desire too near
The fountain: tell me: I also love *you*: not
  that way, but enough to suffer. What
  needs to be done
To make peace for you, tell me. I shall so
  gladly die to make it for you: or so gladly
  yield you   1070
What you know is maiden. You are the
  King; have all your will: only remain in
  steep Mycenæ,
In the honor of our father. Not yet: do not
  speak yet. You have said it is not
Remorse drives you away: monsters require
  monsters, to have let her live a moment
  longer
Would have been the crime: therefore it
  cannot be but desire drives you: or the
  fear of desire: dearest,
It is known horror unlocks the heart, a
  shower of things hidden: if that which
  happened yesterday unmasked
A beautiful brother's love and showed
  more awful eyes in it: all that our Gods
  require is courage.
Let me see the face, let the eyes pierce me.
  What, dearest? Here in the stiff cloth of
  the sacred darkness
Fold over fold hidden, above the sleeping
  city,
By the great stones of the door, under the
  little golden falcons that swarm before
  dawn up yonder,
In the silence . . . must I dare to woo
  you,   1080

I whom man never wooed? to let my hand
  glide under the cloak. . . . O you will
  stay! these arms
Making so soft and white a bond around
  you . . . I also begin to love—that way,
  Orestes,
Feeling the hot hard flesh move under the
  loose cloth, shudder against me. . . .
  Ah, your mouth, Ah,
The burning—kiss me—
ORESTES   We shall never
  ascend this mountain. So it might come
  true: we have to be tough against them,
Our dreams and visions, or they true themselves into flesh. It is sweet: I faint for
  it: the old stones here
Have seen more and not moved. A custom
  of the house. To accept you, little Electra, and go my journey
To-morrow: you'd call cheating. Therefore: we shall not go up this mountain
  dearest, dearest,
To-night nor ever. It's Clytemnestra in
  you. But the dead are a weak tribe. If I
  had Agamemnon's
We'd live happily sister and lord it in
  Mycenæ—be a king like the others—
  royalty and incest   1090
Run both in the stream of the blood. Who
  scrubbed the stones there?
ELECTRA   Slaves. O
  fire burn me! Enter and lay waste,
Deflower, trample, break down, pillage the
  little city,
Make what breach you will, with flesh or a
  spear, give it to the spoiler. See, as I tear
  the garment.
What if I called it cheating? Be cruel and
  treacherous: I'll run my chances
On the bitter mercies of to-morrow.
ORESTES   Bitter they would be. No.
ELECTRA   It's clear that for
  this reason
You'd sneak out of Mycenæ and be lost
  outward. Taste first, bite the apple, once
  dared and tried
Desire will be not terrible. It's doglike to
  run off whining. Remember it was I that
  urged   1100
Yesterday's triumph. You: life was enough:
  let them live. I drove on, burning; your
  mind, reluctant metal,
I dipped it in fire and forged it sharp, day
  after day I beat and burned against you,
  and forged

A sword: I the arm. Are you sorry it's done?
  Now again with hammer and burning
  heat I beat against you,
You will not be sorry. We two of all the
  world, we alone,
Are fit for each other, we have so wrought
  . . . O eyes scorning the world, storm-
  feathered hawk my hands
Caught out of the air and made you a king
  over this rock, O axe with the gold
  helve, O star
Alone over the storm, beacon to men over
  blown seas, you will not flee fate, you
  will take
What the Gods give. What is a man not
  ruling? An ant in the hill: ruler or slave
  the choice is,
—Or a runaway slave, your pilgrim portion, buffeted over the borders of the
  lands, publicly
Whipped in the cities. But you, you will
  bind the north-star on your forehead,
  you will stand up in Mycenæ   1110
Stone, and a king.
ORESTES   I am stone enough not
  to be changed by words, nor by the
  sweet and burning flame of you,
Beautiful Electra.
ELECTRA   Well then: we've
  wasted our night. See, there's the morning star
I might have draggled into a metaphor of
  you. A fool: a boy: no king.
ORESTES   It would have
  been better
To have parted kindlier, for it is likely
We shall have no future meeting.
ELECTRA   You will
  let this crime (the God commanded) that
  dirtied the old stones here
Make division forever?   1120
ORESTES   Not the crime, the
  wakening. That deed is past, it is finished, things past
Make no division afterward, they have no
  power, they have become nothing at all:
  this much
I have learned at a crime's knees.
ELECTRA   Yet we are divided.
ORESTES   Because I have suddenly
  awakened, I will not waste inward
Upon humanity, having found a fairer
  object.
ELECTRA   Some nymph of the field? I
  knew this coldness

Had a sick root: a girl in the north told me
  about the hill-shepherds who living in
  solitude
Turn beast with the ewes, their oreads baa
  to them through the matted fleece and
  they run mad, what madness
Met you in the night and sticks to you? 1130
ORESTES   I left
  the madness of the house, to-night in the
  dark, with you it walks yet.
How shall I tell you what I have learned?
  Your mind is like a hawk's or like a lion's,
  this knowledge
Is out of the order of your mind, a stranger
  language. To wild beasts and the blood
  of kings
A verse blind in the book.
ELECTRA   At least my
  eyes can see dawn graying: tell and not
  mock me, our moment
Dies in a moment.
ORESTES   Here is the last labor
To spend on humanity. I saw a vision of us
  move in the dark: all that we did or
  dreamed of
Regarded each other, the man pursued the
  woman, the woman clung to the man,
  warriors and kings
Strained at each other in the darkness, all
  loved or fought inward, each one of the
  lost people   1140
Sought the eyes of another that another
  should praise him; sought never his own
  but another's; the net of desire
Had every nerve drawn to the center, so
  that they writhed like a full draught of
  fishes, all matted
In the one mesh; when they look backward
  they see only a man standing at the beginning,
Or forward, a man at the end; or if upward,
  men in the shining bitter sky striding and
  feasting,
Whom you call Gods . . .
It is all turned inward, all your desires
  incestuous, the woman the serpent, the
  man the rose-red cavern,
Both human, worship forever . . .
ELECTRA   You have dreamed
  wretchedly.
ORESTES   I have
  seen the dreams of the people and not
  dreamed them.
As for me, I have slain my mother.   1150
ELECTRA   No more?

ORESTES   And the gate's
open, the gray boils over the mountain,
I have greater
Kindred than dwell under a roof. Didn't I
say this would be dark to you? I have cut
the meshes
And fly like a freed falcon. To-night, lying
on the hillside, sick with those visions,
I remembered
The knife in the stalk of my humanity; I
drew it and it broke; I entered the life of
the brown forest
And the great life of the ancient peaks, the
patience of stone, I felt the changes in
the veins
In the throat of the mountain, a grain in
many centuries, we have our own time,
not yours; and I was the stream
Draining the mountain wood; and I the
stag drinking; and I was the stars,
Boiling with light, wandering alone, each
one the lord of his own summit; and I
was the darkness
Outside the stars, I included them, they
were a part of me. I was mankind also, a
moving lichen   1160
On the cheek of the round stone . . . they
have not made words for it, to go behind
things, beyond hours and ages,
And be all things in all time, in their returns and passages, in the motionless and
timeless center,
In the white of the fire . . . how can I
express the excellence I have found, that
has no color but clearness;
No honey but ecstasy; nothing wrought
nor remembered; no undertone nor
silver second murmur
That rings in love's voice, I and my loved
are one; no desire but fulfilled; no passion but peace,
The pure flame and the white, fierier than
any passion; no time but spheral eternity: Electra,
Was that your name before this life
dawned—
ELECTRA   Here is mere death. Death
like a triumph I'd have paid to keep
you
A king in high Mycenæ: but here is shameful death, to die because I have lost you.
They'll say
*Having done justice Agamemnon's son ran
mad and was lost in the mountain; but
Agamemnon's daughter*   1170

*Hanged herself from a beam of the house: O
bountiful hands of justice!* This horror
draws upon me
Like stone walking.
ORESTES   What fills men's
mouths is nothing; and your threat is
nothing; I have fallen in love outward.
If I believed you—it is I that am like stone
walking.
ELECTRA   I can endure even to hate
you,
But that's no matter. Strength's good. You
are lost. I here remember the honor of
the house, and Agamemnon's.

She turned and entered the ancient house.
Orestes walked in the clear dawn; men
say that a serpent
Killed him in high Arcadia. But young or
old, few years or many, signified less
than nothing
To him who had climbed the tower beyond
time, consciously, and cast humanity,
entered the earlier fountain.
1924–1925   1925

NOON

THE pure air trembles, O pitiless God,
The air aches with flame on these gaunt
rocks
Over the flat sea's face, the forest
Shakes in gales of piercing light.

But the altars are behind and higher
Where the great hills raise naked heads,
Pale agonists in the reverberance
Of the pure air and the pitiless God.

On the domed skull of every hill
Who stand blazing with spread vans,   10
The arms uplifted, the eyes in ecstasy?

What wine has the God drunk, to sing
Violently in heaven, what wine his
worshipers
Whose silence blazes? The light that is
over
Light, the terror of noon, the eyes
That the eagles die at, have thrown
down
Me and my pride, here I lie naked
In a hollow of the shadowless rocks,
Full of the God, having drunk fire.
c.1920   1930

NIGHT

The ebb slips from the rock, the sunken
Tide-rocks lift streaming shoulders
Out of the slack, the slow west
Sombering its torch; a ship's light
Shows faintly, far out,
Over the weight of the prone ocean
On the low cloud.

Over the dark mountain, over the dark
    pinewood,
Down the long dark valley along the
    shrunken river,
Returns the splendor without rays, the
    shining of shadow,   10
Peace-bringer, the matrix of all shining and
    quieter of shining.
Where the shore widens on the bay she
    opens dark wings
And the ocean accepts her glory. O soul
    worshipful of her
You like the ocean have grave depths
    where she dwells always,
And the film of waves above that takes the
    sun takes also
Her, with more love. The sun-lovers have
    a blond favorite,
A father of lights and noises, wars, weeping
    and laughter,
Hot labor, lust and delight and the other
    blemishes. Quietness
Flows from her deeper fountain; and he
    will die; and she is immortal.

Far off from here the slender   20
Flocks of the mountain forest
Move among stems like towers
Of the old redwoods to the stream,
No twig crackling; dip shy
Wild muzzles into the mountain water
Among the dark ferns.

O passionately at peace you being secure
    will pardon
The blasphemies of glowworms, the lamp
    in my tower, the fretfulness
Of cities, the crescents of the planets, the
    pride of the stars.
This August night in a rift of cloud Antares
    reddens,   30
The great one, the ancient torch, a lord
    among lost children,
The earth's orbit doubled would not girdle
    his greatness, one fire

Globed, out of grasp of the mind enormous;
    but to you O Night
What? Not a spark? What flicker of a spark
    in the faint far glimmer
Of a lost fire dying in the desert, dim coals
    of a sand-pit the Bedouins
Wandered from at dawn . . . Ah singing
    prayer to what gulfs tempted
Suddenly are you more lost? To us the
    near-hand mountain
Be a measure of height, the tide-worn cliff
    at the sea-gate a measure of
    continuance.

The tide, moving the night's
Vastness with lonely voices,   40
Turns, the deep dark-shining
Pacific leans on the land,
Feeling his cold strength
To the outmost margins: you Night will
    resume
The stars in your time.

O passionately at peace when will that tide
    draw shoreward?
Truly the spouting fountains of light,
    Antares, Arcturus,
Tire of their flow, they sing one song but
    they think silence.
The striding winter giant Orion shines, and
    dreams darkness.
And life, the flicker of men and moths and
    the wolf on the hill,   50
Though furious for continuance,
    passionately feeding, passionately
Remaking itself upon its mates, remembers
    deep inward
The calm mother, the quietness of the
    womb and the egg,
The primal and the latter silences: dear
    Night it is memory
Prophesies, prophecy that remembers, the
    charm of the dark.
And I and my people, we are willing to love
    the four-score years
Heartily; but as a sailor loves the sea, when
    the helm is for harbor.

Have men's minds changed,
Or the rock hidden in the deep of the
    waters of the soul
Broken the surface? A few centuries   60
Gone by, was none dared not to people
The darkness beyond the stars with harps
    and habitations.

But now, dear is the truth. Life is grown
    sweeter and lonelier,
And death is no evil.
1924   1925

FROM TAMAR

INVOCATION [1]

V

O SWIFTNESS of the swallow and strength
Of the stone shore, brave beauty of falcons,
Beauty of the blue heron that flies
Opposite the color of evening
From the Carmel River's reed-grown
    mouth
To her nest in the deep wood of the deer
Cliffs of peninsular granite engirdle,
O beauty of the fountains of the sun
I pray you enter a little chamber,
I have given you bodies, I have made you
    puppets,   10
I have made idols for God to enter
And tiny cells to hold your honey.
I have given you a dotard and an idiot,
An old woman puffed with vanity, youth
    but botched with incest,
O blower of music through the crooked
    bugles,
You that make signs of sins and choose the
    lame for angels,
Enter and possess. Being light you have
    chosen the dark lamps,
A hawk the sluggish bodies: therefore God
    you chose
Me; and therefore I have made you idols
    like these idols
To enter and possess.   20
  . . . .
1923   1925

ANTE MORTEM

IT is likely enough that lions and scorpions
Guard the end; life never was bonded to be
    endurable nor the act of dying
Unpainful; the brain burning too often
Earns, though it held itself detached from
    the object, often a burnt age.
No matter, I shall not shorten it by hand.
Incapable of body or unmoved of brain is
    no evil, one always went envying
The quietness of stones. But if the striped
    blossom

[1] The title is given by the editors.

Insanity spread lewd splendors and
    lightning terrors at the end of the
    forest;
Or intolerable pain work is known
    miracle,
Exile the monarch soul, set a sick monkey
    in the office . . . remember me 10
Entire and balanced when I was
    younger,
And could lift stones, and comprehend in
    the praises the cruelties of life.
c.1925   1930

TOR HOUSE

IF you should look for this place after a
    handful of lifetimes:
Perhaps of my planted forest a few
May stand yet, dark-leaved Australians or
    the coast cypress, haggard
With storm-drift; but fire and the axe are
    devils.
Look for foundations of sea-worn granite,
    my fingers had the art
To make stone love stone, you will find
    some remnant.
But if you should look in your idleness after
    ten thousand years:
It is the granite knoll on the granite
And lava tongue in the midst of the bay, by
    the mouth of the Carmel
River-valley, these four will remain 10
In the change of names. You will know it
    by the wild sea-fragrance of wind
Though the ocean may have climbed or
    retired a little;
You will know it by the valley inland that
    our sun and our moon were born
    from
Before the poles changed; and Orion in
    December
Evenings was strung in the throat of the
    valley like a lamp-lighted bridge.
Come in the morning you will see white gulls
Weaving a dance over blue water, the wane
    of the moon
Their dance-companion, a ghost walking
By daylight, but wider and whiter than any
    bird in the world.
My ghost you needn't look for; it is
    probably   20
Here, but a dark one, deep in the granite,
    not dancing on wind
With the mad wings and the day moon.
c.1927   1928

FROM CAWDOR

The Death of the Eagle [1]

XV

WHILE George went to the house
For his revolver, Michal climbed up the
  hill
Weeping; but when he came with death in
  his hand
She'd not go away, but watched. At the one
  shot
The great dark bird leaped at the roof of the
  cage   70
In silence and struck the wood; it fell, then
  suddenly
Looked small and soft, muffled in its folded
  wings.

The nerves of men after they die dream
  dimly
And dwindle into their peace; they are not
  very passionate,
And what they had was mostly spent while
  they lived.
They are sieves for leaking desire; they
  have many pleasures
And conversations; their dreams too are
  like that.
The unsocial birds are a greater race;
Cold-eyed, and their blood burns. What
  leaped up to death,
The extension of one storm-dark wing
  filling its world,   80
Was more than the soft garment that fell.
  Something had flown away. Oh
  cage-hoarded desire,
Like the blade of a breaking wave reaped by
  the wind, or flame rising from fire,
  or cloud-coiled lightning
Suddenly unfurled in the cave of heaven: I
  that am stationed, and cold at heart,
  incapable of burning,
My blood like standing sea-water lapped in
  a stone pool, my desire to the rock,
  how can I speak of you?
Mine will go down to the deep rock.

      This rose,
Possessing the air over its emptied prison,
The eager powers at its shoulders waving
  shadowless
Unwound the ever-widened spirals of
  flight

As a star light, it spins the night-stabbing
  threads   90
From its own strength and substance: so
  the aquiline desire
Burned itself into meteor freedom and
  spired
Higher still, and saw the mountain-
  dividing
Canyon of its captivity (that was to Cawdor
Almost his world) like an old crack in a wall,
Violet-shadowed and gold-lighted; the
  little stain
Spilt on the floor of the crack was the
  strong forest;
The grain of sand was the Rock. A speck,
  an atomic
Center of power clouded in its own smoke
Ran and cried in the crack; it was Cawdor;
  the other   100
Points of humanity had neither weight nor
  shining
To prick the eyes of even an eagle's passion.

This burned and soared. The shining ocean
  below lay on the shore
Like the great shield of the moon come
  down, rolling bright rim to rim with
  the earth. Against it the multiform
And many-canyoned coast-range hills were
  gathered into one carven mountain,
  one modulated
Eagle's cry made stone, stopping the
  strength of the sea. The beaked and
  winged effluence
Felt the air foam under its throat and saw
The mountain sun-cup Tassajara, where
  fawns
Dance in the steam of the hot fountains at
  dawn,
Smoothed out, and the high strained ridges
  beyond Cachagua,   110
Where the rivers are born and the last
  condor is dead,
Flatten, and a hundred miles toward
  morning the Sierras
Dawn with their peaks of snow, and
  dwindle and smooth down
On the globed earth.

      It saw from the height and desert
  space of unbreathable air
Where meteors make green fire and die, the
  ocean dropping westward to the
  girdle of the pearls of dawn
And the hinder edge of the night sliding

toward Asia; it saw far under
    eastward the April-delighted
Continent; and time relaxing about it now,
    abstracted from being, it saw the
    eagles destroyed,
Mean generations of gulls and crows taking
    their world: turn for turn in the air,
    as on earth
The white faces drove out the brown. It
    saw the white decayed and the
    brown from Asia returning;   120
It saw men learn to outfly the hawk's brood
    and forget it again; it saw men cover
    the earth and again
Devour each other and hide in caverns, be
    scarce as wolves. It neither
    wondered nor cared, and it saw
Growth and decay alternate forever, and
    the tides returning.

It saw, according to the sight of its kind, the
    archetype
Body of life a beaked carnivorous desire
Self-upheld on storm-broad wings: but the
    eyes
Were spouts of blood; the eyes were gashed
    out; dark blood
Ran from the ruinous eye-pits to the hook
    of the beak
And rained on the waste spaces of empty
    heaven.
Yet the great Life continued; yet the great
    Life   130
Was beautiful, and she drank her defeat,
    and devoured
Her famine for food.

      There the eagle's phantom
      perceived
Its prison and its wound were not its
    peculiar wretchedness,
All that lives was maimed and bleeding,
    caged or in blindness,
Lopped at the ends with death and
    conception, and shrewd
Cautery of pain on the stumps to stifle the
    blood, but not
Refrains for all that; life was more than its
    functions
And accidents, more important than its
    pains and pleasures,
A torch to burn in with pride, a necessary
Ecstasy in the run of the cold substance, 141
And scape-goat of the greater world. (But
    as for me,

I have heard the summer dust crying to be
    born
As much as ever flesh cried to be quiet.)
Pouring itself on fulfilment the eagle's
    passion
Left life behind and flew at the sun, its
    father.
The great unreal talons took peace for prey
Exultantly, their death beyond death;
    stooped upward, and struck
Peace like a white fawn in a dell of fire.
1927   1928

LOVE THE WILD SWAN

'I HATE my verses, every line, every word.
Oh pale and brittle pencils ever to try
One grass-blade's curve, or the throat of
    one bird
That clings to twig, ruffled against white sky.
Oh cracked and twilight mirrors ever to
    catch
One color, one glinting flash, of the
    splendor of things.
Unlucky hunter, Oh bullets of wax,
The lion beauty, the wild-swan wings, the
    storm of the wings.'
—This wild swan of a world is no hunter's
    game.
Better bullets than yours would miss the
    white breast,   10
Better mirrors than yours would crack in
    the flame.
Does it matter whether you hate your . . .
    self? At least
Love your eyes that can see, your mind that
    can
Hear the music, the thunder of the wings.
    Love the wild swan.
1934   1935

SELF CRITICISM IN FEBRUARY

THE bay is not blue but somber yellow
With wrack from the battered valley, it is
    speckled with violent foam-heads
And tiger-striped with long lovely
    storm-shadows.
You love this better than the other mask;
    better eyes than yours
Would feel the equal beauty in the blue.
It is certain you have loved the beauty of
    storm disproportionately.
But the present time is not pastoral, but
    founded

On violence, pointed for more massive
   violence: perhaps it is not
Perversity but need that perceives the
   storm-beauty.
Well, bite on this: your poems are too full of
   ghosts and demons,   10
And people like phantoms—how often life's
   are—
And passion so strained that the clay mouths
   go praying for destruction—
Alas, it is not unusual in life;
To every soul at some time. *But why insist*
   on it? And now

For the worst fault: you have never
   mistaken
Demon nor passion nor idealism for the real
   God.
Then what is most disliked in those verses
Remains most true. *Unfortunately. If only*
   you could sing
That God is love, or perhaps that social
Justice will soon prevail. I can tell lies in
   prose.   20
1937   1937

EUGENE O'NEILL

1888–

LAZARUS LAUGHED [1]

A PLAY FOR AN IMAGINATIVE THEATRE

ACT ONE:
   Scene One: Lazarus' home in Bethany—
   a short time after the miracle.
   Scene Two: Months later. Outside the
   House of Laughter in Bethany. Late
   evening.

ACT TWO:
   Scene One: A street in Athens. A night
   months later.
   Scene Two: A temple immediately inside
   the walls of Rome. Midnight. Months
   later.

ACT THREE:
   Scene One: Garden of Tiberius' palace.
   A night a few days later.

Scene Two: Inside the palace. Immediately after.

ACT FOUR:
   Scene One: The same. A while after.
   Scene Two: Interior of a Roman theatre.
   Dawn of the same night.

CHARACTERS

LAZARUS OF BETHANY
HIS FATHER
HIS MOTHER
MARTHA } his sisters
MARY
MIRIAM, his wife
SEVEN GUESTS, neighbors of Lazarus
CHORUS OF OLD MEN
AN ORTHODOX PRIEST
CHORUS OF LAZARUS' FOLLOWERS
A CENTURION
GAIUS CALIGULA
CRASSUS, a Roman General
CHORUS OF GREEKS
SEVEN CITIZENS OF ATHENS
CHORUS OF ROMAN SENATORS
SEVEN SENATORS
CHORUS OF LEGIONARIES
FLAVIUS, a centurion
MARCELLUS, a patrician
CHORUS OF THE GUARD
TIBERIUS CÆSAR
POMPEIA
CHORUS OF YOUTHS AND GIRLS
CHORUS OF THE ROMAN POPULACE
CROWDS

[1] To Arthur Quinn, O'Neill wrote, May 1927, concerning the theme of *Lazarus Laughed*: 'The fear of death is the root of all evil, the cause of all man's blundering unhappiness. Lazarus knows there is no death, there is only change. He is reborn without that fear. Therefore he is the first and only man who is able to laugh affirmatively. His laughter is a triumphant Yes to life in its entirety and its eternity. His laughter affirms God, it is too noble to desire personal immortality, it wills its own extinction, it gives its life for the sake of Eternal Life (patriotism carried to its logical ultimate). His laughter is the direct expression of joy in the Dionysian sense, the joy of a celebrant who is at the same time a sacrifice in the eternal process of change and growth and transmutation which is life, of which his life is an insignificant manifestation, soon to be reabsorbed. And life itself is the self-affirmative joyous laughter of God.' Quinn, *A History of the American Drama* (N.Y., 1936), 252–53.

ACT ONE

SCENE ONE

SCENE: *Exterior and interior of* LAZARUS'
*home at Bethany. The main room at the
front end of the house is shown—a long,
low-ceilinged, sparely furnished chamber,
with white walls gray in the fading daylight that enters from three small windows
at the left. To the left of center several long* 10
*tables placed lengthwise to the width of the
room, around which many chairs for guests
have been placed. In the rear wall, right,
a door leading into the rest of the house.
On the left, a doorway opening on a road
where a crowd of men has gathered. On the
right, another doorway leading to the yard
where there is a crowd of women.*
*Inside the house, on the men's side, seven
male Guests are grouped by the door,* 20
watching LAZARUS *with frightened awe,
talking hesitantly in low whispers. The
Chorus of Old Men, seven in number, is
drawn up in a crescent, in the far corner,
right, facing* LAZARUS.
[*All of these people are masked in accord-
ance with the following scheme: There are
seven periods of life shown: Boyhood (or
Girlhood), Youth, Young Manhood (or
Womanhood), Manhood (or Womanhood),* 30
*Middle Age, Maturity and Old Age; and
each of these periods is represented by
seven different masks of general types of
character as follows: The Simple, Ignorant; the Happy, Eager; the Self-Tortured,
Introspective; the Proud, Self-Reliant;
the Servile, Hypocritical; the Revengeful,
Cruel; the Sorrowful, Resigned. Thus in
each crowd (this includes among the men
the Seven Guests who are composed of one* 40
*male of each period-type as period one—
type one, period two—type two, and so on
up to period seven—type seven) there are
forty-nine different combinations of period
and type. Each type has a distinct predominant color for its costumes which varies
in kind according to its period. The masks
of the Chorus of Old Men are double the
size of the others. They are all seven in the
Sorrowful, Resigned type of Old Age.*] 50
*On a raised platform at the middle of the
one table placed lengthwise at center sits*
LAZARUS, *his head haloed and his body
illumined by a soft radiance as of tiny
phosphorescent flames.*

LAZARUS, *freed now from the fear of death,
wears no mask.*
In appearance LAZARUS *is tall and powerful, about fifty years of age, with a mass of
gray-black hair and a heavy beard. His
face recalls that of a statue of a divinity of
Ancient Greece in its general structure and
particularly in its quality of detached serenity. It is dark-complected, ruddy and
brown, the color of rich earth upturned by
the plow, calm but furrowed deep with the
marks of former suffering endured with a
grim fortitude that had never softened into
resignation. His forehead is broad and
noble, his eyes black and deep-set. Just now
he is staring straight before him as if his
vision were still fixed beyond life.*
*Kneeling beside him with bowed heads are
his wife,* MIRIAM, *his sisters,* MARTHA *and*
MARY, *and his* FATHER *and* MOTHER.
MIRIAM *is a slender, delicate woman of
thirty-five, dressed in deep black, who holds
one of his hands in both of hers, and keeps
her lips pressed to it. The upper part of her
face is covered by a mask which conceals
her forehead, eyes and nose, but leaves her
mouth revealed. The mask is the pure pallor of marble, the expression that of a
statue of Woman, of her eternal acceptance
of the compulsion of motherhood, the inevitable cycle of love into pain into joy and
new love into separation and pain again
and the loneliness of age. The eyes of the
mask are almost closed. Their gaze turns
within, oblivious to the life outside, as they
dream down on the child forever in memory
at her breast. The mouth of* MIRIAM *is
sensitive and sad, tender with an eager, understanding smile of self-forgetful love, the
lips still fresh and young. Her skin, in contrast to the mask, is sunburned and earth-
colored like that of* LAZARUS. MARTHA,
MARY *and the two parents all wear full
masks which broadly reproduce their own
characters.* MARTHA *is a buxom middle-
aged housewife, plain and pleasant.* MARY
*is young and pretty, nervous and high-
strung. The* FATHER *is a small, thin, feeble
old man of over eighty, meek and pious.
The* MOTHER *is tall and stout, over sixty-
five, a gentle, simple woman.*
*All the masks of these Jews of the first two
scenes of the play are pronouncedly Semitic.
A background of twilight sky. A dissolving
touch of sunset still lingers on the horizon.*

It is some time after the miracle and Jesus has gone away.

CHORUS OF OLD MEN

[*In a quavering rising and falling chant —their arms outstretched toward* LAZARUS]

Jesus wept!
Behold how he loved him!
He that liveth,
He that believeth,
Shall never die!

CROWD

[*On either side of house, echo the chant*]

He that believeth
Shall never die!
Lazarus, come forth!

FIRST GUEST

[*A Simple Boy—in a frightened whisper after a pause of dead silence*]

That strange light seems to come from within him!
[*With awe*]
Think of it! For four days he lay in the 20
tomb!
[*Turns away with a shudder*]

SECOND GUEST

[*A Happy Youth—with reassuring conviction*]

It is a holy light. It came from Jesus.

FIFTH GUEST

[*An Envious, Middle-Aged Man*]

Maybe if the truth were known, our friend there never really died at all!

FOURTH GUEST

[*A Defiant Man, indignantly*]

Do you doubt the miracle? I tell you I was here in this house when Lazarus died!

SEVENTH GUEST

[*An Aged, Sorrowful Man*]

And I used to visit him every day. He knew himself his hour was near.

FOURTH GUEST

He wished for death! He said to me one day: 'I have known my fill of life and the sorrow of living. Soon I shall know peace.' And he smiled. It was the first time I had seen him smile in years.

THIRD GUEST

[*A Self-Tortured Man—gloomily*]

Yes, of late years his life had been one long misfortune. One after another his children died—

SIXTH GUEST

[*A Mature Man with a cruel face— with a harsh laugh*]

They were all girls. Lazarus had no luck.

SEVENTH GUEST

The last was a boy, the one that died at birth. You are forgetting him.

THIRD GUEST

Lazarus could never forget. Not only did his son die but Miriam could never bear him more children.

FIFTH GUEST

[*Practically*]

But he could not blame bad luck for everything. Take the loss of his father's wealth since he took over the management. That was his own doing. He was a bad farmer, a poor breeder of sheep, and a bargainer so easy to cheat it hurt one's conscience to trade with him!

SIXTH GUEST

[*With a sneer—maliciously*]

You should know best about that!
[*A suppressed laugh from those around him*]

FIRST GUEST

[*Who has been gazing at* LAZARUS— *softly*]

Ssssh! Look at his face!
[*They all stare. A pause*]

SECOND GUEST

[*With wondering awe*]

Do you remember him, neighbors, before he died? He used to be pale even when he worked in the fields. Now he seems as brown as one who has labored in the earth all day in a vineyard beneath the hot sun!
[*A pause*]

FOURTH GUEST

The whole look of his face has changed. He is like a stranger from a far land. There is no longer any sorrow in his eyes. They must have forgotten sorrow in the   10
grave.

FIFTH GUEST

[*Grumblingly*]

I thought we were invited here to eat—and all we do is stand and gape at him!

FOURTH GUEST

[*Sternly*]

Be silent! We are waiting for him to speak.

THIRD GUEST

[*Impressively*]

He did speak once. And he laughed!   20

ALL THE GUESTS

[*Amazed and incredulous*]

Laughed?

THIRD GUEST

[*Importantly*]

Laughed! I heard him! It was a moment after the miracle—

MIRIAM   30

[*Her voice, rich with sorrow, exultant now*]

Jesus cried, 'Lazarus, come forth!'
[*She kisses his hand. He makes a slight movement, a stirring in his vision. The* GUESTS *stare. A frightened pause*]

FIFTH GUEST

[*Nudging the* SECOND—*uneasily*]

Go on with your story!

THIRD GUEST

Just as he appeared in the opening of the tomb, wrapped in his shroud—

SECOND GUEST

[*Excitedly—interrupting*]

My heart stopped! I fell on my face! And all the women screamed!
[*Sceptically*]
You must have sharp ears to have heard him laugh in that uproar!

THIRD GUEST

I helped to pry away the stone so I was right beside him. I found myself kneeling, but between my fingers I watched Jesus and Lazarus. Jesus looked into his face for what seemed a long time and suddenly Lazarus said 'Yes' as if he were answering a question in Jesus' eyes.

ALL THE GUESTS

[*Mystified*]

Yes? What could he mean by yes?

THIRD GUEST

Then Jesus smiled sadly but with tenderness, as one who from a distance of years of sorrow remembers happiness. And then Lazarus knelt and kissed Jesus' feet and both of them smiled and Jesus blessed him and called him 'My Brother' and went away; and Lazarus, looking after Him, began to laugh softly like a man in love with God! Such a laugh I never heard! It made my ears drunk! It was like wine! And though I was half-dead with fright I found myself laughing, too!

MIRIAM

[*With a beseeching summons*]

Lazarus, come forth!

CHORUS

[*Chanting*]

Lazarus! Come forth!

CROWD

[*On either side of the house—echoing the chant*]

Come forth! Come forth!

LAZARUS

[*Suddenly in a deep voice—with a wonderful exultant acceptance in it*]

Yes!

[*The GUESTS in the room, the CROWDS outside all cry out in fear and joy and fall on their knees*]

CHORUS

[*Chanting exultantly*]

The stone is taken away!
The spirit is loosed!
The soul let go!

LAZARUS

[*Rising and looking around him at everyone and everything—with an all-embracing love—gently*]

Yes!

[*His family and the GUESTS in the room now throng about LAZARUS to embrace him. The CROWDS of men and women on each side push into the room to stare at him. He is in the arms of his MOTHER and MIRIAM while his SISTERS and FATHER kiss and press his hands. The five are half hysterical with relief and joy, sobbing and laughing*]

FATHER

My son is reborn to me!

CHORUS

Hosannah!

ALL

[*With a great shout*]

Hosannah!

FATHER

Let us rejoice! Eat and drink! Draw up your chairs, friends! Music! Bring wine!

[*Music begins in the room off right, rear —a festive dance tune. The company sit down in their places, the FATHER and MOTHER at LAZARUS' right and left, MIRIAM next to the MOTHER, MARTHA and MARY beside the FATHER. But LAZARUS remains standing. And the CHORUS OF OLD MEN remain in their formation at the rear. Wine is poured and all raise their goblets toward LAZARUS—then suddenly they stop, the music dies out, and an awed and frightened stillness prevails, for LAZARUS is a strange, majestic figure whose understanding smile seems terrible and enigmatic to them*]

FATHER

[*Pathetically uneasy*]

You frighten us, my son. You are strange—standing there—

[*In the midst of a silence more awkward than before he rises to his feet, goblet in hand—forcing his voice, falteringly*]

A toast, neighbors!

CHORUS

[*In a forced echo*]

A toast!

ALL

[*Echoing them*]

A toast!

FATHER

To my son, Lazarus, whom a blessed miracle has brought back from death!

LAZARUS

[*Suddenly laughing softly out of his vision, as if to himself, and speaking with a strange unearthly calm in a voice that is like a loving whisper of hope and confidence*]

No! There is no death!

[*A moment's pause. The people remain with goblets uplifted, staring at him. Then all repeat after him questioningly and frightenedly*]

ALL

There—is—no—death?

SIXTH GUEST

[*Suddenly blurts out the question which is in the minds of all*]

What did you find beyond there, Lazarus? [*A pause of silence*]

LAZARUS

[*Smiles gently and speaks as if to a group of inquisitive children*]

O Curious Greedy Ones, is not one world in which you know not how to live enough for you?

SIXTH GUEST

[*Emboldened*]

Why did you say yes, Lazarus?

FOURTH GUEST

Why did you laugh?

ALL THE GUESTS

[*With insistent curiosity but in low awed tones*]

What is beyond there, Lazarus?

CHORUS

[*In a low murmur*]

What is beyond there? What is beyond?

CROWD

[*Carrying the question falteringly back into silence*]

What is beyond?

LAZARUS

[*Suddenly again—now in a voice of loving exaltation*]

There is only life! I heard the heart of Jesus

laughing in my heart; 'There is Eternal Life in No,' it said, 'and there is the same Eternal Life in Yes! Death is the fear between!' And my heart reborn to love of life cried 'Yes!' and I laughed in the laughter of God!

[HE *begins to laugh, softly at first—a laugh so full of a complete acceptance of life, a profound assertion of joy in living, so devoid of all self-consciousness or fear, that it is like a great bird song triumphant in depths of sky, proud and powerful, infectious with love, casting on the listener an enthralling spell. The crowd in the room are caught by it. Glancing sideways at one another, smiling foolishly and self-consciously, at first they hesitate, plainly holding themselves in for fear of what the next one will think*]

CHORUS

[*In a chanting murmur*]

Lazarus laughs!
Our hearts grow happy!
Laughter like music!
The wind laughs!
The sea laughs!
Spring laughs from the earth!
Summer laughs in the air!
Lazarus laughs!

LAZARUS

[*On a final note of compelling exultation*]

Laugh! Laugh with me! Death is dead! Fear is no more! There is only life! There is only laughter!

CHORUS

[*Chanting exultingly now*]

Laugh! Laugh!
Laugh with Lazarus!
Fear is no more!
There is no death!

[*They laugh in a rhythmic cadence dominated by the laughter of* LAZARUS]

CROWD

[*Who, gradually, joining in by groups or one by one—including* LAZARUS' *fam-*

ily with the exception of MIRIAM, *who does not laugh but watches and listens to his laughter with a tender smile of being happy in his happiness—have now all begun to laugh in rhythm with the* CHORUS—*in a great, full-throated pæan as the laughter of* LAZARUS *rises higher and higher*]

Laugh! Laugh!
Fear is no more!
There is no death!

CHORUS

Laugh! Laugh!
There is only life!
There is only laughter!
Fear is no more!
Death is dead!

CROWD

[*In a rhythmic echo*]

Laugh! Laugh!
Death is dead!
There is only laughter!

[*The room rocks, the air outside throbs with the rhythmic beat of their liberated laughter—still a bit uncertain of its freedom, harsh, discordant, frenzied, desperate and drunken, but dominated and inspired by the high, free, aspiring, exulting laughter of* LAZARUS]

CURTAIN

ACT ONE

SCENE TWO

SCENE: *Some months later. Exterior of* LAZARUS' *home in Bethany, now known as the House of Laughter. It is a clear bright night, the sky sparkling with stars. At the extreme front is a road. Between this and the house is a small raised terrace. The house is low, of one story only, its walls white. Four windows are visible with a closed door in the middle of the wall. Steps lead up to this door, and to the left of door a flight of stairs goes up to the balustraded roof. The windows shine brilliantly with the flickering light of many candles which gives them a throbbing star-like*

effect. From within comes the sound of flutes and dance music. The dancers can be seen whirling swiftly by the windows. There is continually an overtone of singing laughter emphasizing the pulsing rhythm of the dance.

On the road in the foreground, at left and right, two separate groups of Jews are gathered. They are not divided according to sex as in the previous scene. Each is composed about equally of men and women, forty-nine in each, masked and costumed as before. It is religious belief that now divides them. The adherents of Jesus, the Nazarenes, among whom may be noted MARTHA *and* MARY, *are on the left; the Orthodox, among whom are* LAZARUS' FATHER *and* MOTHER *and a* PRIEST, *are at right. Between the two hostile groups is the same* CHORUS OF OLD MEN, *in a formation like a spearhead, whose point is placed at the foot of the steps leading to the terrace. All these people are staring fascinatedly at the house, listening entranced, their feet moving, their bodies swaying to the music's beat, stiffly, constrainedly, compelled against their wills. Then the music suddenly stops and the chant of youthful voices is heard:*

FOLLOWERS OF LAZARUS

[*From within the house*]

Laugh! Laugh!
There is only life!
There is only laughter!

CHORUS OF OLD MEN

[*As if they were subjects moved by hypnotic suggestion—miserably and discordantly*]

Ha-ha-ha-ha!
There is only laughter!
Ha-ha—

CROWD

[*In the same manner*]

Ha-ha—

MARY

Ha—

[*Then frantically—half-weeping with indignant rage—to the Nazarenes*]

Stop! Oh, how can we laugh! We are betraying Jesus! My brother Lazarus has become a devil!

THE ORTHODOX PRIEST

[*His mask is that of a religious fanatic. He is sixty or so*]

Ha—ha—
[*Tearing his beard and stamping with rage*]
Stop it, you fools! It is a foul sin in the sight   10
of Jehovah! Why do you come here every
night to listen and watch their abominations? The Lord God will punish you!

MARY

[*Echoing him—to her people*]

Jesus will never forgive you!

THE PRIEST

[*Angrily*]

Jesus?
[*He turns to look at the Nazarenes disdainfully and spits on the ground insultingly*]
[*The members of the two groups begin to glare at each other. The* CHORUS *falls back, three on each side, leaving one neutral figure before the steps. The* PRIEST *goes on tauntingly*]
Did you hear her, friends? These renegade
Nazarenes will soon deny they are Jews   20
at all! They will begin to worship in filthy
idolatry the sun and stars and man's body—
as Lazarus in there,
[*Points to the house*]
the disciple of their Jesus, has so well set
them the example!
[*This is followed by an outburst of insulting shouts of accusation and denial from both sides*]

A NAZARENE

[*The* FOURTH GUEST *of Scene One*]

You lie! Lazarus is no disciple! He is a   30
traitor to Jesus! We scorn him!

PRIEST

[*Sneeringly*]

But your pretended Messiah did not scorn
him. According to your stupid lies, he
raised him from the dead! And answer me,
has your Jesus ever denied Lazarus, or denounced his laughter? No! No doubt he is
laughing, too, at all you credulous fools—
for if Lazarus is not his disciple, in the
matter of the false miracle he was his accomplice!
[*This provokes a furious protest from the Nazarenes and insulting hoots and jeers from the Orthodox, penetrated by a piercing scream from* LAZARUS' MOTHER, *who, crushed in the crowd, sinks fainting to the ground. The* FATHER *bends over her. The group of the Orthodox falls back from them. With frightened cries* MARTHA *and* MARY *run from the group of Nazarenes and kneel beside her*]

FATHER

[*Pitifully*]

Rachel! Darling! Speak to me!

MARTHA

[*Practically*]

She has only fainted.

MARY

She is opening her eyes! Mother, dear!

MOTHER

[*Weakly*]

Did I fall?
[*Recognizing* MARTHA *and* MARY]
Martha—and Mary—my dear ones!
[*They embrace her, weeping*]
I have not kissed you since you left home
to follow that Jesus—Oh, if we were only
at home again—and if, also, my poor boy,
Lazarus—
[*She sobs*]

FATHER

[*Gruffly*]

You must not speak of him!

MARTHA

Do not worry your head about Lazarus.
He is not worth it!

MARY

[*With surprising vindictiveness*]

He is accursed! He has betrayed our Lord!

PRIEST

[*To those around him—mockingly*]

Do you hear? They already call the Nazarene 'Lord!' A Lord who is in the common prison at Jerusalem, I heard today! A fine Lord whom our High Priests have had arrested like a thief!

MARY

[*With fanatic fervor*]

He is a king! Whenever He chooses He will gather a great army and He will seize His kingdom and all who deny Him shall be crucified! 10

PRIEST

[*Tauntingly*]

Now their jail-bird is a king, no less! Soon they will make him a god, as the Romans do their Cæsars!

MARY

[*Her eyes flashing*]

He is the Messiah!

PRIEST

[*Furiously*]

The Messiah! May Jehovah smite you in your lies! Step back among your kind! You defile us!
[*As she stands defiantly ne appeals to the* FATHER]
Have you no authority? She called him the 20 Messiah—that common beggar, that tramp! Curse her!

FATHER

[*Confused, pitifully harried, collecting his forces*]

Wait! Go back, Mary! You chose to follow that impostor—

MARY

[*Defiantly*]

The Messiah!

MARTHA

[*Trying to calm her*]

Ssssh! Remember he is our father!

MARY

[*Fanatically*]

I deny him! I deny all who deny Jesus!

MOTHER

[*Tearfully*]

And me, darling?

MARY

You must come to us, Mother! You must believe in Jesus and leave all to follow Him!

FATHER

[*Enraged*]

So! You want to steal your mother away, to leave me lonely in my old age! You are an unnatural daughter! I disown you! Go, before I curse—

MOTHER

[*Beseechingly*]

Father!

MARTHA

[*Pulling* MARY *away*]

Mary! Jesus teaches to be kind.

MARY

[*Hysterically*]

He teaches to give up all and follow Him! I want to give Him everything! I want my father to curse me!

FATHER

[*Frenziedly*]

Then I do curse you! No—not you—but the devil in you! And the devil in Martha! And the great mocking devil that dwells in Lazarus and laughs from his mouth! I curse these devils and that Prince of Devils, that false prophet, Jesus! It is he who has brought division to my home and many homes that were happy before. I curse him! I curse the day he called my good son, Lazarus, from the grave to walk again with a devil inside him! It was not my son who came back but a devil! My son is dead! And you, my daughters, are dead! I am the father only of devils!

[*His voice has risen to a wailing lament*] My children are dead!

LAZARUS

[*His voice rings from within the house in exultant denial*]

Death is dead! There is only laughter!   10
[*He laughs*]
[*The voices of all his* FOLLOWERS *echo his laughter. They pour in a laughing rout from the doorway onto the terrace. At the same moment the* CHORUS OF FOLLOWERS *appears on the roof and forms along the balustrade, facing front*]
[*These* FOLLOWERS OF LAZARUS, *forty-nine in number, composed about equally of both sexes, wear a mask that, while recognizably Jewish, is a* LAZARUS *mask, resembling him in its expression of fearless faith in life, the mouth shaped by laughter. The* CHORUS OF FOLLOWERS, *seven in number, all men, have identical masks of double size, as before. The Period of all these masks is anywhere between Youth and Manhood (or Womanhood)*]
[*The music continues to come from within. Laughing, the* FOLLOWERS *dance to it in weaving patterns on the terrace. They are dressed in bright-colored diaphanous robes. Their chorused laughter, now high and clear, now dying to a humming murmur, stresses the rhythmic flow of the dance*]

CHORUS OF FOLLOWERS

Laugh! Laugh!
There is no death!
There is only laughter!

FOLLOWERS

There is only laughter!   20
Death is dead!
Laugh! Laugh!

CROWD

[*The two groups of Nazarenes and Orthodox, on the appearance of the* FOLLOWERS, *immediately forget their differences and form into one mob, led by their* CHORUS OF OLD MEN, *whose jeering howls they echo as one voice*]

Yaah! Yaah! Yaah!
[*But they cannot keep it up. The music and laughter rise above their hooting. They fall into silence. Then they again begin to feel impelled by the rhythm and laughter, their feet move, their bodies sway. Their lips quiver, their mouths open as if to laugh. Their* CHORUS OF OLD MEN *are the first to be affected. It is as if this reaction were transmitted through the* CHORUS *to the* CROWD]

PRIEST

[*His mouth twitching—fighting against the compulsion in him—stammers*]

Brothers—listen—we must unite—in one cause—to—stamp out—this abomination!
[*It is as if he can no longer control his speech. He presses his hand over his mouth convulsively*]

AN AGED ORTHODOX JEW

[*The* SEVENTH GUEST *of Scene One— starts to harangue the crowd. He fights the spell but cannot control his jerking body nor his ghastly, spasmodic laughter*]

Neighbors! Our young people are corrupted! They are leaving our farms—to dance and sing! To laugh! Ha—! Laugh at everything! Ha-ha—!
[*He struggles desperately to control himself*]

CHORUS OF OLD MEN

[*A barking laugh forced from them*]
Ha-ha—!

CROWD

[*Echoing this*]
Ha-ha—!

THE AGED JEW

They have no respect for life! When I said in kindness, 'You must go back to work,' they laughed at me! Ha—! 'We desire joy. We go to Lazarus,' they said—and left my fields! I begged them to stay—with tears in my eyes! I even offered them more money! They laughed! 'What is money? Can the heart eat gold?' They laughed at money! Ha-ha—!

[He chokes with exasperated rage]

CHORUS OF OLD MEN

[Echoing him]

Ha-ha—!

CROWD

[Echoing the CHORUS*]*

Ha-ha—!

AGED JEW

[Shaking his fist at LAZARUS' FOLLOW-ERS*]*

That loafer taught them that! They come to him and work for nothing! For nothing! And they are glad, these undutiful ones! While they sow, they dance! They sing to the earth when they are plowing! They tend his flocks and laugh toward the sun! Ha-ha-ha—!

[He struggles again]

CHORUS OF OLD MEN

[As before]

Ha-ha-ha—

CROWD

[As before]

Ha-ha-ha—

AGED JEW

How can we compete with labor for laughter! We will have no harvest. There will be no food! Our children will starve! Our race will perish! And he will laugh! Ha-ha-ha-ha!

[He howls with furious, uncontained laughter]

CHORUS OF OLD MEN

[Echoing his tone]

Our children will starve!
Our race will perish!
Lazarus laughs!
Ha-ha-ha-ha! Ha-ha-ha-ha!

CROWD

[As before]

10 Ha-ha-ha-ha! Ha-ha-ha-ha!

[Their former distinctions of Nazarenes and Orthodox are now entirely forgotten. The members of LAZARUS' *family are grouped in the center as if nothing had ever happened to separate them. The* CHORUS OF OLD MEN *is again joined in its spearhead formation at the stairs. Apparent first in this* CHORUS, *a queer excitement begins to pervade this mob. They begin to weave in and out, clasping each other's hands now and then, moving mechanically in jerky steps to the music in a grotesque sort of marionettes' country dance. At first this is slow but it momentarily becomes more hectic and peculiar. They raise clenched fists or hands distended into threatening talons. Their voices sound thick and harsh and animal-like with anger as they mutter and growl, each one aloud to himself or herself]*

CHORUS OF OLD MEN

20 *[Threateningly, gradually rising to hatred]*

Hear them laugh!
See them dance!
Shameless! Wanton!
Dirty! Evil!
Infamous! Bestial!
Madness! Blood!
Adultery! Murder!
We burn!
We kill!
30 We crucify!
Death! Death!
Beware, Lazarus!

[This last in a wild frenzy]

CROWD

[*Frenziedly*]

Beware, Lazarus!
We burn! We kill!
We crucify!
Death! Death!

[*They crowd toward the gateway, their
arms stretched out as if demanding
LAZARUS for a sacrificial victim.
Meanwhile they never cease to hop*   10
*up and down, to mill around, to twist
their bodies toward and away from
each other in bestial parody of the
dance of the* FOLLOWERS]

[*The tall figure of* LAZARUS, *dressed in a
white robe, suddenly appears on the
roof of the house. He stands at the
balustrade in the middle of the*
CHORUS. *Beside him, a little behind,*
MIRIAM *appears dressed in black, her
face upturned, her lips praying. She*   20
*appears to have grown older, to be
forty now.* LAZARUS' *body is softly
illumined by its inner light. The
change in him is marked. He seems ten
years younger, at the prime of forty.
His body has become less angular and
stiff. His movements are graceful and
pliant. The change is even more noticeable in his face, which has filled
out, become purer in outline, more
distinctly Grecian. His complexion is
the red-brown of rich earth, the gray
in his black, curly beard has almost
disappeared*]

[*He makes a sign and the music ceases.
His* FOLLOWERS *remain fixed in their
dancing attitudes like figures in a
frieze. Each member of the mob remains frozen in a distorted posture.
He stares down at the mob pityingly,
his face calm*]

LAZARUS

[*Speaks amid a profound silence. His
voice releases his own dancers and the
mob from their fixed attitudes. The
music begins to play again within the
house, very soft and barely audible,
swelling up and down like the sound
of an organ from a distant church*]

You laugh, but your laughter is guilty! It
laughs a hyena laughter, spotted, howling

its hungry fear of life! That day I returned
did I not tell you your fear was no more,
that there is no death? You believed then—
for a moment! You laughed—discordantly,
hoarsely, but with a groping toward joy.
What! Have you so soon forgotten, that now
your laughter curses life again as of old?

[*He pauses—then sadly*]

That is your tragedy! You forget! You forget the God in you! You wish to forget!
Remembrance would imply the high duty
to live as a son of God—generously!—with
love!—with pride!—with laughter! This is
too glorious a victory for you, too terrible
a loneliness! Easier to forget, to become
only a man, the son of a woman, to hide
from life against her breast, to whimper your
fear to her resigned heart and be comforted
by her resignation! To live by denying life!

[*Then exhortingly*]

Why are your eyes always either fixed on
the ground in weariness of thought, or
watching one another with suspicion?
Throw your gaze upward! To Eternal Life!
To the fearless and deathless! The everlasting! To the stars!

[*He stretches out his arms to the sky—
then suddenly points*]

See! A new star has appeared! It is the one
that shone over Bethlehem!

[*His voice becomes a little bitter and
mocking*]

The Master of Peace and Love has departed this earth. Let all stars be for you
henceforth symbols of Saviors—Sons of   30
God who appeared on worlds like ours to
tell the saving truth to ears like yours, inexorably deaf!

[*Then exaltedly*]

But the greatness of Saviors is that they may
not save! The greatness of Man is that no
god can save him—until he becomes a god!

[*He stares up at the stars, rapt in contemplation, oblivious to all around
him now*]

[*Rapidly approaching from the left a
man's voice jarring in high-pitched
cruel laughter is heard. They all listen,
huddled together like sheep*]

MESSENGER

[*The* THIRD GUEST *of Scene One rushes
in breathlessly, shouting*]

The Nazarene has been crucified!

PRIEST

[*With fierce triumph*]

Jehovah is avenged! Hosannah!

ORTHODOX

Hosannah! The false prophet is dead! The pretended Messiah is dead!
[*They jump and dance, embracing one another. The* NAZARENES *stand paralyzed and stunned. The two groups mechanically separate to right and left again, the* CHORUS OF OLD MEN *dividing itself as before*]

MARY

[*In a frenzy of grief*]

Do not believe him! Jesus could not die!
[*But at this moment a Nazarene youth, exhausted by grief and tears, staggers in from the left*]

MESSENGER

[SECOND GUEST *of Scene One*]

Jesus is dead! Our Lord is murdered!
[*He sinks on his knees sobbing. All the* NAZARENES *do likewise, wailing, rending their garments, tearing their hair, some even beating their heads on the ground in the agony of their despair*]

MARY

[*Insane with rage now*]

They have murdered Him!
[*To her followers—savagely*]
An eye for an eye! Avenge the Master!
[*Their frenzy of grief turned into rage, the* NAZARENES *leap to their feet threateningly. Concealed swords and knives are brought out by both sides*]

MIRIAM

[*Leaning over the balustrade—in a voice of entreaty*]

Mary! Brothers!
[*But none heed her or seem to see her.* LAZARUS *and his* FOLLOWERS *remain oblivious to men, arms upstretched toward the stars, their heads thrown back*]

MARY

[*Wildly*]

Vengeance! Death to His murderers!

PRIEST

[*Fiercely to his followers*]

Death to the Nazarenes!
[*With cries of rage the two groups rush on one another. There is a confused tumult of yells, groans, curses, the shrieks of women, the sounds of blows as they meet in a pushing, whirling, struggling mass in which individual figures are indistinguishable. Knives and swords flash above the heads of the mass, hands in every tense attitude of striking, clutching, tearing are seen upraised. As the fight is at its height a* ROMAN CENTURION *and a squad of eight* SOLDIERS *come tramping up at the double-quick. They all are masked. These Roman masks now and henceforth in the play are carried out according to the same formula of Seven Periods, Seven Types, as those of the Jews seen previously, except that the basis of each face is Roman— heavy, domineering, self-complacent, the face of a confident dominant race. The* CENTURION *differs from his soldiers only in being more individualized. He is middle-aged, his soldiers belong to the Period of Manhood. All are of the Simple, Ignorant Type*]

CENTURION

[*Shouts commandingly*]

Disperse!
[*But no one hears him—with angry disgust to his* SOLDIERS]
Charge! Cut them down!
[*The* SOLDIERS *form a wedge and charge with a shout. They soon find it necessary to use their swords, and strike down everyone in their way*]

MIRIAM

Mercy, Romans!
[*As they pay no attention to her, in desperation she embraces* LAZARUS *beseechingly, forcing his attention back to earth*]
10 Lazarus! Mercy!

LAZARUS

[*Looks down upon the struggling mass and cries in a ringing voice*]

Hold!

[*Each person stands transfixed, frozen in the last movement, even the Roman soldiers and the* CENTURION *himself. Ten dead and mortally wounded lie on the ground, trampled by the feet of friend and foe alike.* LAZARUS *looks at the* CROWD. *To each he seems to look at him or her alone. His eyes are accusing and stern. As one head, the heads of all are averted. Even the* CENTURION *stares at the ground humbly, in spite of himself. Finally* LAZARUS *speaks in a voice of infinite disdain*]

Sometimes it is hard to laugh—even *at* men!

[*He turns his eyes from them, staring straight before him. This seems to release them from their fixed positions. The* NAZARENES *and the* ORTHODOX *separate and slink guiltily apart. The* CHORUS OF OLD MEN *forms again, the apex at the center of the steps as before. A low wail of lamentation arises from them. The two crowds of Nazarenes and Orthodox echo this*]

CHORUS OF OLD MEN

[*In a wailing chant*]

Woe unto Israel!
Woe unto thee, Jerusalem!
O divided house,
Thou shalt crumble to dust,
And swine shall root
Where thy Temple stood!
Woe unto us!

CROWD

[*In a great echoing cry*]

Woe unto us!

CENTURION

[*Gruffly to hide his embarrassment at being awed by* LAZARUS]

Here, you! Drag your carcasses away!

[*From each side men and women come forward to identify and mourn their*

dead. *The wail of lamentation rises and falls. The* CENTURION *looks up at* LAZARUS—*harshly*]

You, there! Are you he whom they call the Laugher?

LAZARUS

[*Without looking at him—his voice seeming to come from some dream within him*]

I am Lazarus.

CENTURION

Who was brought back from death by enchantment?

LAZARUS

[*Looking down at him now—with a smile, simply*]

No. There is no death!

CHORUS OF FOLLOWERS

[*Chanting joyously*]

There is no death!

FOLLOWERS

[*Echoing*]

There is no death!

AN ORTHODOX MAN

[*Bending beside the body of* LAZARUS' FATHER]

Here is your father, Lazarus. He is dead.

AN ORTHODOX WOMAN

This is your mother, Lazarus. She is dead.

A NAZARENE

Here is your sister, Martha, Lazarus. She is dead.

A NAZARENE WOMAN

And this is Mary, Lazarus. She is dead.

MIRIAM

[*Suddenly—with deep grief*]

And Jesus who was the Son of Man, who

loved you and gave you life again has died, Lazarus—has died!

LAZARUS

[*In a great triumphant voice*]

Yes! Yes!! Yes!!! Men die! Even a Son of Man must die to show men that Man may live! But there is no death!

CENTURION

[*At first in a tone of great awe—to his* SOLDIERS]

Is he a god?
[*Then gruffly, ashamed of his question*]
Come down, Jew! I have orders to bring   10
you to Rome to Cæsar!

LAZARUS

[*As if he were answering not the* CENTURION *but the command of his fate from the sky*]

Yes!

[*He walks down the narrow stairs and,* MIRIAM *following him, comes down the path to the road. He goes and kneels for a moment each beside the bodies of his* FATHER, MOTHER, *and* SISTERS *and kisses each in turn on the forehead. For a moment the struggle with his grief can be seen in his face. Then he looks up to the stars and, as if answering a question, again says simply and acceptingly*]
Yes!
[*Then exultantly*]
Yes!!   20
[*And begins to laugh from the depths of his exalted spirit. The laughter of his* CHORUS *and then of his* FOLLOWERS *echoes his. The music and dancing begin again*]
[*The* CENTURION *grins sheepishly. The* SOLDIERS *chuckle. The* CENTURION *laughs awkwardly. The* SOLDIERS *laugh. The music from the house and the laughter of the* FOLLOWERS *grow louder. The infection spreads to the* CHORUS OF OLD MEN *whose swaying grief falls into the rhythm of the laughter and music as does that of the mourners*]

LAZARUS' FOLLOWERS

[*Led by their* CHORUS]

Laugh! Laugh!

CHORUS OF OLD MEN

[*Torn by the conflict—torturedly*]

Ha-ha-ha—
Woe to us, woe!

CROWD

[*Beside the bodies*]

Woe to us, woe!
Ha-ha—!

CENTURION

[*Laughingly*]

You are brave, you Laugher! Remember Tiberius never laughs! And boast not to Cæsar there is no death, or he will invent a new one for you!

LAZARUS

[*With a smile*]

But all death is men's invention! So laugh!
[*He laughs and the* CENTURION *and* SOLDIERS *laugh with him, half dancing clumsily now to the beat of the music*]

CHORUS OF LAZARUS' FOLLOWERS

Laugh! Laugh!
Fear is no more!
There is no death!
There is only life!
There is only laughter!

FOLLOWERS

[*Dancing*]

Laugh! Laugh!
Fear is no more!
Death is dead!

CHORUS OF OLD MEN

[*Forgetting their grief—their eyes on* LAZARUS *now, their arms outstretched to him as are those of the crowd*]

*grouped around the bodies but for-
getting them*]

Death is no more!
Death is dead!
Laugh!

CROWD

Laugh! Laugh!
Death is no more!

CENTURION

[*Laughing, to his laughing* SOLDIERS]

Forward!
[*They tramp, dancing, off*]
[LAZARUS *and* MIRIAM *start to follow*]

MIRIAM

[*Suddenly pointing to his* FOLLOWERS
*who are dancing and laughing oblivi-
ously—pityingly*]

But your faithful ones who love you, Laz-   10
arus?

LAZARUS

[*Simply, with a trace of a sad sternness*]

This is their test. Their love must remember—or it must forget. Come!
[*With a last gesture back like a blessing
on all he is leaving, he goes. The
laughter of the* SOLDIERS *recedes.
That of the* CHORUS OF OLD MEN
and of the CROWD *falters and breaks
into lamenting grief again, guilt-
stricken because of its laughter*]   20

CHORUS OF OLD MEN

Laugh! Laugh!
Death is dead!
Laugh!—But woe!
There lie our dead!
Oh shame and guilt!
We forget our dead!

CROWD

[*With fierce remorseful grief*]

Woe to us, woe!
There lie our dead!   30

CHORUS OF LAZARUS' FOLLOWERS

[*Their voices and the music growing
more and more hesitating and faint*]

Laugh! Laugh!
There is only life!
There is only—
Laugh—
[*Their dance is faltering and slow now*]
Fear is no—
Death is—
Laugh—
[*The music and dancing and voices cease.
The lights in the windows, which have
been growing dim, go out. There is a
second of complete, death-like silence.
The mourning folk in the foreground
are frozen figures of grief. Then a
sudden swelling chorus of forlorn be-
wilderment, a cry of lost children
comes from the* CHORUS OF FOL-
LOWERS *and the* FOLLOWERS *them-
selves. They huddle into groups on the
roof and on the terrace. They stretch
their arms out in every direction
supplicatingly*]

CHORUS OF FOLLOWERS

Oh, Lazarus, laugh!
Do not forsake us!
We forget!
Where is thy love fled?
Give back thy laughter,
Thy fearless laughter!
We forget!

FOLLOWERS

Give back thy laughter!
We forget!

CHORUS OF FOLLOWERS

[*With dull, resigned terror now*]

Death slinks out
Of his grave in the heart!
Ghosts of fear
Creep back in the brain!
We remember fear!
We remember death!

FOLLOWERS

Death in the heart!
Fear in the brain!

We remember fear!
We remember death!

CHORUS OF FOLLOWERS

[*Wailing hopelessly now*]

Forgotten is laughter! .
We remember
Only death!
Fear is God!
Forgotten is laughter!
Life is death!

FOLLOWERS

Forgotten is laughter!
Life is death!   10

ALL

[*The* CHORUS OF OLD MEN *and the*
CROWD *joining in*]

Life is a fearing,
A long dying,
From birth to death!
God is a slayer!
Life is death!

CURTAIN

ACT TWO

SCENE ONE

SCENE: *Some months later. A square in
Athens about ten o'clock at night. In the
rear, pure and beautiful in the light of a
full moon, is the façade of a temple. An
excited crowd of Greeks of both sexes is
gathered in the square as if for some public
festival. They are masked according to the
scheme of Seven Periods in Seven Types
of Character for each sex. Here, of course,
the foundation of the mask is the Grecian
type of face.*

On the left, the CHORUS OF GREEKS *is
grouped, seven in number, facing front, in
the spearhead formation. As before the*
CHORUS *wears masks double the life size
of the* CROWD *masks. They are all of the
Proud Self-Reliant type, in the period of
Young Manhood.*

*These seven are clad in goat skins, their
tanned bodies and masks daubed and*

*stained with wine lees, in imitation of the
old followers of* DIONYSUS. *Rumor has led
them to hope and believe that* LAZARUS
may be the reincarnation of this deity.

*The people in the crowd are holding them-
selves in restraint with difficulty; they stir
and push about restlessly with an eager
curiosity and impatience. All eyes are
fixed off left. A buzz of voices hums in the
air.*

*Acting as police, a number of Roman le-
gionaries (masked like the soldiers of Scene
Two) armed with staves, keep back the
crowd from the line of the street that runs
from left to right, front. They resent this
duty, which has already kept them there a
long time, and are surly and quick-tem-
pered with the Greeks.*

*At front, pacing impatiently up and down,
is a young Roman noble of twenty-one, clad
richly, wearing beautifully wrought armor
and helmet. This is* GAIUS, *the heir of
Tiberius Cæsar, nicknamed* CALIGULA *by
the soldiers in whose encampments he was
born and where he spent his childhood. His
body is bony and angular, almost mal-
formed, with wide, powerful shoulders and
long arms and hands, and short, skinny,
hairy legs like an ape's. He wears a half-
mask of crimson, dark with a purplish
tinge, that covers the upper part of his face
to below the nose. This mask accentuates
his bulging, prematurely wrinkled forehead, his hollow temples and his bulbous,
sensual nose. His large troubled eyes, of a
glazed greenish-blue, glare out with a
shifty feverish suspicion at everyone. Below
his mask his own skin is of an ænemic
transparent pallor. Above it, his hair is
the curly blond hair of a child of six or
seven. His mouth also is childish, the red
lips soft and feminine in outline. Their expression is spoiled, petulant and self-
obsessed, weak but domineering. In combination with the rest of the face there is an
appalling morbid significance to his mouth
One feels that its boyish cruelty, encouraged as a manly attribute in the coarse
brutality of camps, has long ago become
naïvely insensitive to any human suffering
but its own.*

Walking with CALIGULA *is* CNEIUS CRAS-
SUS, *a Roman general—a squat, muscular
man of sixty, his mask that of a heavy
battered face full of coarse humor.*

CHORUS OF GREEKS

[*Intoning solemnly*]

Soon the God comes!
Redeemer and Savior!
Dionysus, Son of Man and a God!

GREEK CROWD

[*Echoing*]

Soon the God comes
Redeemer and Savior!   10
Dionysus!

FIRST GREEK

They say an unearthly flame burns in this
Lazarus!

SECOND GREEK

The sacred fire! He must be the Fire-born,
the son of Zeus!   20

THIRD GREEK

Many who have seen him swear he is
Dionysus, rearisen from Hades!

FOURTH GREEK

[*Importantly*]

I saw Lazarus at Antioch where the galley
on which they were taking him to Rome
had been thrice blown back by a storm.
Fear of this warning omen is why they now
march with him by land.   30

FIRST GREEK

Does he truly resemble a god?

FOURTH GREEK

[*Impressively*]

One look in his eyes while his laughter sings
in your ears and you forget sorrow! You
dance! You laugh! It is as if a heavy weight
you had been carrying all your life without
knowing it suddenly were lifted. You are
like a cloud, you can fly, your mind reels
with laughter, you are drunk with joy!
    [*Solemnly*]
Take my word for it, he is indeed a god.   40
Everywhere the people have acclaimed

him. He heals the sick, he raises the dead,
by laughter.

SEVENTH GREEK

But I have heard that when he has gone
people cannot remember his laughter, that
the dead are dead again and the sick die,
and the sad grow more sorrowful.

FIFTH GREEK

Well, we shall soon see with our own eyes.
But why should the God return in the body
of a Jew?

SIXTH GREEK

What better disguise if he wishes to remain
unknown? The fools of Romans will never
suspect him!

THIRD GREEK

[*Laughing*]

Never! They are beginning to claim he is a
Roman!

FIFTH GREEK

So much the better! He will be in their confidence!

FOURTH GREEK

He will lead us against Rome! He will
laugh our tyrants into the sea! Ha!
    [*He turns toward the Romans and laughs
    sneeringly. This is taken up by the
    CROWD—unpleasant, resentful laugh-
    ter. They push forward aggressively
    and almost sweep the soldiers from
    their feet*]

CRASSUS

[*Angrily*]

Drive them back!

CALIGULA

[*Suddenly with a distorted warped
    smile*]

Order them to use their swords, Cneius.
Let the scum look at their dead and learn
respect for us!

SOLDIERS

[*Shoving and whacking*]

Back! Step back! Back there!

[*The crowd push back to their former line. There are muttered curses, groans, protests, which subside into the former hum of expectancy*]

CALIGULA

[*With the same smile*]

The sword, my old hyena! Corpses are so educational!

CRASSUS

[*Surlily*]

I would like to, I promise you! When I see how they hate us—!

CALIGULA

[*Carelessly*]

Let them hate—so long as they fear us! We must keep death dangling

[*He makes the gesture of doing so*]

before their eyes!

[*He gives a soft, cruel laugh*]

Will you not sacrifice in my honor? What are a few Greeks?

[*Queerly*]

I like to watch men die.

CRASSUS

I dare not, Caligula. Cæsar has forbidden bloodshed.

CALIGULA

Tiberius is a miser. He wants to hoard all of death for his own pleasure!

[*He laughs again*]

CRASSUS

[*With rough familiarity*]

I wager no one will make that complaint against you when you are Cæsar!

[*He chuckles*]

CALIGULA

[*With the sudden grandiose posturing of a bad actor unintentionally burlesquing grandeur*]

When I, Gaius Caligula, am Cæsar, I—

[*Then superstitiously looking up at the sky with cringing foreboding*]

But it brings bad luck to anticipate fate.

[*He takes off his helmet and spits in it—then with a grim smile*]

The heirs of a Cæsar take sick so mysteriously! Even with you who used to ride me on your knee, I do not eat nor drink until you have tasted first.

CRASSUS

[*Nodding approvingly*]

You are sensible. I suppose I, too, have my price—if they were only clever enough to discover it!

[*He laughs hoarsely*]

CALIGULA

[*Steps back from him with an uneasy shudder*]

You are honest, at least—too honest, Cneius!

[*Grimly*]

If my father Germanicus had had you for his counselor, he might have escaped their poison.

[*Then gloomily*]

I must fear everyone. The world is my enemy.

CRASSUS

Kill it then!

[*He laughs again*]

CHORUS

[*Stretching out their arms in the direction from which* LAZARUS *is expected —supplicatingly*]

Son of the Lightning!
Deadly thy vengeance!
Swift thy deliverance!
Beholding thy Mother,
Greece, our Mother,
Her beauty in bondage,
Her pride in chains!
Hasten, Redeemer!

CROWD

[*As before—echoing the chant*]

Hasten, Redeemer!
Son of the Lightning!
Deadly thy vengeance!
Swift thy deliverance!

CALIGULA

[*Disdainfully*]

What clods! Mob is the same everywhere,
eager to worship any new charlatan! They
have already convinced themselves this
Lazarus is a reincarnation of Dionysus! A
Jew become a god! By the breasts of Venus
that *is* a miracle!
[*He laughs*]

CRASSUS

[*Seriously*]

But he must be expert in magic. He was
buried four days and came out unharmed.
Maybe he is not a Jew. Some say his father
was really a legionary of our garrison in
Judea. And he teaches people to laugh at
death. That smacks of Roman blood!

CALIGULA

[*Ironically*]

Better still! He tells them there is no death
at all! Hence the multitude of fools who
have acclaimed him everywhere since he
left his own country—and why Tiberius
has begun to fear his influence.

CRASSUS

[*Sententiously*]

Whom Cæsar fears—disappears!

CALIGULA

Yes, the dupes who follow Lazarus will be
killed. But Tiberius believes this Lazarus
may know a cure for death or for renewing
youth, and the old lecher hopes he can
worm the secret out of him—before he kills
him.
[*He laughs ironically, then disgustedly*]
That is why I must escort this Jew to
Rome—as a special honor!
[*With fierce, haughty resentment*]

I, the heir of Cæsar!
[*Savagely*]
Oh, if I were Cæsar—!

CRASSUS

[*With a coarse, meaning smirk*]

Patience. Tiberius is old.

CALIGULA

[*Suddenly becoming terribly uneasy at
some thought*]

Cneius! What if this Lazarus has really discovered a cure for old age and should reveal
it to Tiberius!
[*His lips tremble, his eyes are terrified,
he shrinks against* CRASSUS *for protection—with boyish pleading*]
Oh, Cneius, what could I do then?

CRASSUS

[*Matter-of-factly*]

Kill him before Cæsar can talk to him.

CALIGULA

[*Almost in tears*]

But if he knows a charm against death how
could he be slain, old fool?

CRASSUS

[*Gruffly*]

Bah!
[*Then with grim humor*]
Death in bed I suspect, but when men are
killed I know they stay dead!
[*Disgustedly*]
A moment ago you were laughing at him!
[*Scornfully*]
Do you fear him now?

CALIGULA

[*Rather shamefacedly pulls himself together—then broodingly*]

I fear everyone who lives. Even you. As
you advised me.
[*He turns away*]

CRASSUS

[*Contemptuously*]

Well, maybe he can teach you to laugh at

fear. You would welcome him then, eh, cry baby?

CALIGULA

[*With sudden passionate intensity but only half aloud as if to himself*]

I would love him, Cneius! As a father! As a god!
[*He stands staring before him strangely. There is a new stir from the crowd who again push forward*]

CRASSUS

[*Pointing off right*]

Look! I see a great crowd! Your Lazarus must be coming at last!

CHORUS

[*Chanting in a deep, rhythmic monotone like the rising and falling cadences of waves on a beach*]

He comes, the Redeemer and Savior!
Laughing along the mountains!
To give back our lost laughter
To raise from the dead our freedom
To free us from Rome!

CROWD

[*Echoing this chant*]

Fire-born! Redeemer! Savior!
Raise from the dead our freedom!
Give back our lost laughter!
Free us from Rome!
[*They have been pushing forward, more and more fiercely and defiantly. The ROMAN SOLDIERS in spite of their efforts are pushed backward step by step*]

SOLDIERS

[*Angrily*]

Back! Back!
[*The SOLDIERS work with a will, dealing out blows with their staves at everyone in reach. But now these blows seem only to infuriate the CROWD which steadily pushes them back into the street. At the same time the distant sound of exultant music, singing and laughter becomes steadily louder.*

Both SOLDIERS and CROWD are inspired to battle by these strains without their knowing it. CALIGULA is listening spell-bound, his mouth open, his body swaying and twitching. Even CRASSUS stares off at the oncomers, forgetful of the growing plight of his SOLDIERS]

CROWD

[*Led by their CHORUS—angrily*]

Cowards! Pigs!
Strike! Hit!
Stones! Knives!
Stab! Kill!
Death to the Romans!
Death!

A SOLDIER

[*Alarmed, calls to CRASSUS*]

General! Let us use our swords!

SOLDIERS

[*Enraged—eagerly*]

Yes! Swords!

CROWD

Death!

CRASSUS

[*Turning—uneasy but afraid to give any drastic order*]

Bah! Staves are enough. Crack their skulls!

CROWD

[*Led by the CHORUS—defiantly*]

Death to Crassus!
Drunkard! Coward!
Death to him!
[*They continue to push forward, hooting and jeering*]

CRASSUS

[*Exploding for a second*]

By the gods—!
[*To the SOLDIERS*]
Draw your swords!
[*The troops do so eagerly. The CROWD

*sag back momentarily with exclama-
tions of fear*]

CALIGULA

[*Listening as in a trance to the music and
what is going on behind him—in a
queer whisper*]

Kill, Cneius! Let me dance! Let me sing!
[*The music and crashing of cymbals and
the ferment of passions around him
cause him to lose all control over himself. He gives a crazy leap in the air
and begins to dance grotesquely and
chant in a thick voice*]
He is coming! Death, the Deliverer! Kill,
soldiers! I command you! I, Caligula! I will
be Cæsar! Death!

CROWD

[*Led by the* CHORUS—*savage now*]

Beast! Cur!
Death to Caligula!
[*They crowd forward*]

CALIGULA

[*Drawing his sword and flourishing it
drunkenly—his eyes glazed*]

Death!

CRASSUS

[*Drawing his own sword in a frenzy*]

Strike! Death!
[*His* SOLDIERS *raise their swords. The*
CROWD *have raised whatever weapons they have found—knives, clubs,
daggers, stones, bare fists*]

CHORUS

[*Chanting fiercely*]

Death!

ALL

[ROMANS *and* GREEKS *alike as one great
voice*]

Death!
[*The chorused word beats down all sound
into a stricken silence. The wild joyous music ceases. The Romans and
Greeks seem to lean back from one*

*another and collect strength to leap
forward. At this moment the voice of*
LAZARUS *comes ringing through the
air like a command from the sky*]

LAZARUS

There is no death!
[*The* SOLDIERS *and* GREEKS *remain
frozen in their attitudes of murderous
hate. Following his words the laughter
of* LAZARUS *is heard, exultant and
gaily mocking, filling them with the
sheepish shame of children caught in
mischief. Their hands hang, their arms
sink to their sides. The music starts
once more with a triumphant clash of
cymbals,* LAZARUS' *laughter is echoed
from the throats of the multitude of his*
FOLLOWERS *who now come dancing
into the square, preceded by a band
of masked musicians and by their*
CHORUS.
[*This* CHORUS *wears, in double size, the
laughing mask of* LAZARUS' FOLLOW-
ERS *in the same Period and Type as in
the preceding scene, except that here
the mask of each member of the*
CHORUS *has a different racial basis—
Egyptian, Syrian, Cappadocian,
Lydian, Phrygian, Cilician, Parthian.
The* FOLLOWERS *are costumed and
masked as in the preceding scene,
seven Types in seven Periods, except
that, as in the* CHORUS, *racially there
are many nations represented. All
have wreaths of ivy in their hair and
flowers in their hands which they
scatter about. They whirl in between
the* SOLDIERS *and* CROWD, *forcing
them back from each other, teasing
them, sifting into the* CROWD, *their*
CHORUS *in a half circle, confronting
the* CHORUS OF GREEKS]

CHORUS OF FOLLOWERS

Laugh! Laugh!
There is no death!
There is only life!
There is only laughter!

FOLLOWERS

[*Echoing*]

Laugh! Laugh!

10

There is no death!

[CALIGULA *and* CRASSUS *are swept to one side, left. Then the cries and laughter of all become mingled into one exclamation:*

ALL

Lazarus! Lazarus!

[*The squad of* ROMAN SOLDIERS *led by the* CENTURION, *who had taken* LAZARUS *prisoner, march in with dancers' steps, like a proud guard of honor now, laughing, pulling a chariot in which* LAZARUS *stands dressed in a tunic of white and gold, his bronzed face and limbs radiant in the halo of his own glowing light*]

[LAZARUS *now looks less than thirty-five. His countenance now might well be that of the positive masculine Dionysus, closest to the soil of the Grecian Gods, a Son of Man, born of a mortal. Not the coarse, drunken Dionysus, nor the effeminate God, but Dionysus in his middle period, more comprehensive in his symbolism, the soul of the recurring seasons, of living and dying as processes in eternal growth, of the wine of life stirring forever in the sap and blood and loam of things.* MIRIAM *is beside him, dressed in black, smiling the same sad tender smile, holding* LAZARUS' *arm as if for protection and in protection. She appears older, a woman over forty-five*]

CHORUS OF GREEKS

[*Rushing to* LAZARUS' *car*]

Hail, Dionysus!
Iacchus!
Lazarus!
Hail!

[*They surround him, throw over his shoulders and head the finely dressed hide of a bull with great gilded horns, force into his right hand the mystic rod of Dionysus with a pine cone on top, then prostrate themselves*]

Hail, Savior!
Redeemer!
Conqueror of Death!

ALL

[*In a repeated chorus which finally in-*

cludes even the ROMAN SOLDIERS, *raising their arms to him*]

Hail, Lazarus!
Redeemer!
Hail!

[*They are silent.* LAZARUS *looks at them, seeming to see each and all at the same time, and his laughter, as if in answer to their greetings, is heard rising from his lips like a song*]

CRASSUS

[*Awed*]

Look! He is more than man!

CALIGULA

[*Trembling, in a queer agitation*]

I dare not look!

CRASSUS

Do you hear his laughter?

CALIGULA

[*Chokingly—puts his hands over his ears*]

I will not hear!

CRASSUS

But you must welcome him in Cæsar's name!

CALIGULA

[*His teeth chattering*]

I must kill him!

LAZARUS

[*Looking directly at him—gaily mocking*]

Death is dead, Caligula!
[*He begins to laugh again softly*]

CALIGULA

[*With an hysterical cry of defiant terror*]

You lie!
[*Sword in hand he whirls to confront* LAZARUS, *but at the first sight of his face he stops in his tracks, trembling,*

held fascinated by LAZARUS' *eyes,
mumbling with a last pitiful remainder
of defiance*]
But—you lie—whatever you are! I say
there *must* be death!
[*The sword has fallen to his side. He
stares open-mouthed at* LAZARUS.
*There is something of a shy, wonder-
ing child about his attitude now.*
LAZARUS *looks at him, laughing
with gentle understanding.* CALIGULA
*suddenly drops his sword and covering
his face with his hands weeps like a
boy who has been hurt*]
You have murdered my only friend, Lazarus! Death would have been my slave
when I am Cæsar. He would have been my
jester and made me laugh at fear!
[*He weeps bitterly*]

LAZARUS

[*Gaily*]

Be your own jester instead, O Caligula!
Laugh at yourself, O Cæsar-to-be!
[*He laughs. The* CROWD *now all join
in with him*]
[CALIGULA *suddenly uncovers his face,
grins his warped grin, gives a harsh
cackle which cracks through the other
laughter with a splitting discord, cuts
a hopping caper like some grotesque
cripple which takes him to the side of*
LAZARUS' *chariot where he squats on
his hams and, stretching out his hand,
fingers* LAZARUS' *robe inquisitively
and stares up into his face in the attitude of a chained monkey*]

CALIGULA

[*With a childish, mischievous curiosity*]

Then if there is no death, O Teacher, tell
me why I love to kill?

LAZARUS

Because you fear to die!
[*Then gaily mocking*]
But what do you matter, O Deathly-Im-
portant One? Put yourself that question—
as a jester!
[*Exultantly*]
Are you a speck of dust danced in the wind?
Then laugh, dancing! Laugh yes to your

insignificance! Thereby will be born your
new greatness! As Man, Petty Tyrant of
Earth, you are a bubble pricked by death
into a void and a mocking silence! But as
dust, you are eternal change, and everlasting growth, and a high note of laughter
soaring through chaos from the deep heart
of God! Be proud, O Dust! Then you may
love the stars as equals!
[*Then mockingly again*]
And then perhaps you may be brave enough
to love even your fellow men without fear
of their vengeance!

CALIGULA

[*Dully*]

I cannot understand. I hate men. I am
afraid of their poison and their swords and
the cringing envy in their eyes that only
yields to fear!

LAZARUS

[*Gaily mocking*]

Tragic is the plight of the tragedian whose
only audience is himself! Life is for each
man a solitary cell whose walls are mirrors.
Terrified is Caligula by the faces he makes!
But I tell you to laugh in the mirror, that
seeing your life gay, you may begin to live
as a guest, and not as a condemned one!
[*Raising his hands for silence—with a
playful smile*]
Listen! In the dark peace of the grave the
man called Lazarus rested. He was still
weak, as one who recovers from a long illness—for, living, he had believed his life
a sad one!
[*He laughs softly, and softly they all
echo his laughter*]
He lay dreaming to the croon of silence,
feeling as the flow of blood in his own veins
the past reënter the heart of God to be renewed by faith into the future. He thought:
'Men call this death'—for he had been dead
only a little while and he still remembered.
Then, of a sudden, a strange gay laughter
trembled from his heart as though his life,
so long repressed in him by fear, had found
at last its voice and a song for singing. 'Men
call this death,' it sang. 'Men call life death
and fear it. They hide from it in horror.
Their lives are spent in hiding. Their fear
becomes their living. They worship life as
death!'

CHORUS OF FOLLOWERS

[*In a chanting echo*]

Men call life death and fear it.
They hide from it in horror.
Their lives are spent in hiding.
Their fear becomes their living.
They worship life as death!

LAZARUS

And here the song of Lazarus' life grew pitiful. 'Men must learn to live,' it mourned.   10
'Before their fear invented death they
knew, but now they have forgotten. They
must be taught to laugh again!' And Lazarus answered 'Yes!'
   [*He now addresses the crowd—especially*
      CALIGULA, *directly*, *laughingly*]
Thus sang his life to Lazarus while he lay
dead! Man must learn to live by laughter!
   [*He laughs*]

CHORUS OF FOLLOWERS

Laugh! Laugh!
There is only life!   20
There is only laughter!
Fear is no more!
Death is dead!

CHORUS OF GREEKS

Laugh! Laugh!
Hail, Dionysus!
Fear is no more!
Thou hast conquered death!

ALL

[*Laughing—in a great laughing chorus*]

Laugh! Laugh!
Fear is no more!
Death is dead!   30

LAZARUS

[*As to a crowd of children—laughingly*]

Out with you! Out into the woods! Upon
the hills! Cities are prisons wherein man
locks himself from life. Out with you under
the sky! Are the stars too pure for your sick
passions? Is the warm earth smelling of
night too desirous of love for your pale introspective lusts? Out! Let laughter be   40
your new clean lust and sanity! So far man

has only learned to snicker meanly at his
neighbor! Let a laughing away of self be
your new right to live forever! Cry in your
pride, 'I am Laughter, which is Life, which
is the Child of God!'
   [*He laughs and again his voice leads and
      dominates the rhythmic chorus of
      theirs. The music and dancing begin
      again*]

THE TWO CHORUSES

[*Chanting in unison*]

Laugh! Laugh!
There is only God!
We are His Laughter!

ALL

[*Echoing*]

There is only God!
We are His Laughter!
Laugh! Laugh!
   [*They take hold of his chariot traces,
      and as he had come, in the midst of a
      happy multitude, now augmented by
      all the* GREEKS, *and the* ROMAN
      SOLDIERS *who had awaited him,
      dancing, playing, singing, laughing,
      he is escorted off. The noise of their
      passing recedes.* CALIGULA *and* CRAS-
      SUS *are left in the empty square, the
      former squatting on his hams, monkey-
      wise, and brooding somberly*]

CRASSUS

[*Is swaying and staggering, like a man
   in a drunken stupor, in a bewildered,
   stubborn struggle to control himself.
   He stammers after the* SOLDIERS]

Ha-ha-ha—Halt! Halt, I say! No use—
they are gone—mutiny—Halt!
   [*He continues to stumble toward left*]
Ha-ha—Stop it, curse you! Am I laughing?
Where am I going? After Lazarus? Thirty
years of discipline and I—Halt, traitor!
Remember Cæsar! Remember Rome! Halt,
traitor!
   [*He faints with the violence of his strug-
      gle and falls in a limp heap*]

CALIGULA

[*Startled by his fall, terrified, hops to his*

*feet and snatches up his sword de-
fensively, glancing over his shoulder
and whirling around as if he expected
someone to stab him in the back. Then,
forcing a twisted grin of self-contempt
—harshly]*

Coward! What do I fear—if there is no
death?

*[As if he had to cut something, he
snatches up a handful of flowers—
desperately]*

You must laugh, Caligula!

*[He starts to lop off the flowers from
their stems with a savage intentness]*

Laugh! Laugh! Laugh!

*[Finally, impatiently, he cuts off all the
remaining with one stroke]*

Laugh!

*[He grinds the petals under his feet and
breaks out into a terrible hysterical
giggle]*

Ha-ha—

CURTAIN

ACT TWO

SCENE TWO

SCENE: *A midnight, months later. Immediately inside the walls of Rome. In the
foreground is the portico of a temple between whose massive columns one looks
across a street on a lower level to the high
wall of Rome at the extreme rear. In the
center of the wall is a great metal gate.
The night is thick and oppressive. In the
sky overhead lightning flashes and thunder
rumbles and crashes but there is no rain.
Within the portico on rows of chairs placed
on a series of wide steps which are on each
side, members of the Senate are seated in
their white robes. High hanging lamps cast
a wan light over their faces. They are all
masked in the Roman mask, refined in
them by nobility of blood but at the same
time with strength degenerated, corrupted
by tyranny and debauchery to an exhausted cynicism. The three periods of
Middle Age, Maturity and Old Age are
represented in the types of the Self-Tortured, Introspective; Proud, Self-Reliant;
the Servile, Hypocritical; the Cruel, Revengeful; and the Resigned, Sorrowful.
The SENATORS are divided into two groups
on each side, thirty in each. Seated in the*

*middle of the lower of the three high broad
stairs that lead to the level from which
the columns rise is the* CHORUS OF SEN-
ATORS, *seven in number, facing front, in
double-sized masks of the Servile, Hypocritical type of Old Age.*

LAZARUS, *in his robe of white and gold, the
aura of light surrounding his body seeming
to glow more brightly than ever, stands in
the rear at the edge of the portico, center,
gazing upward into the pall of sky beyond
the wall. His figure appears in its immobility to be the statue of the god of the
temple. Near him, but to the rear and to
the left of him, facing right,* MIRIAM *is
kneeling in her black robes, swaying backward and forward, praying silently with
moving lips like a nun who asks mercy for
the sins of the world. She has grown much
older, her hair is gray, her shoulders are
bowed.*

*On the other side, placed similarly in re-
lation to* LAZARUS *and facing* MIRIAM,
CALIGULA *is squatting on his hams on a
sort of throne-chair of ivory and gold. He is
dressed with foppish richness in extreme
bright colors, a victory wreath around his
head. He stares blinkingly and inquisitively
at* LAZARUS, *then at* MIRIAM. *He is half-
drunk. A large figured goblet of gold is in
his hand. A slave with an amphora of wine
crouches on the steps by his chair. The
slave wears a black negroid mask.*

*At the opening of the scene there is heard
the steady tramp of departing troops,
whose masks, helmets and armored shoulders can be seen as they pass through the
street before* LAZARUS *to the gate beyond.
Finally with a metallic clash the gate is
shut behind them and there is a heavy and
oppressive silence in which only the murmured prayers of* MIRIAM *are heard.*

CHORUS OF THE SENATE

*[Intones wearily, as if under a boring
compulsion]*

The Roman Senate
Is the Roman Senate
The Mighty Voice
10   Of the Roman People
As long as Rome is Rome.

CALIGULA

[As if he hadn't heard—sings hoarsely

*an old camp song of the Punic Wars,
pounding with his goblet*]

A bold legionary am I!
March, oh march on!
A Roman eagle was my daddy,
My mother was a drunken drabby
Oh, march on to the wars!

Since lived that Lady Leda
March, oh march on!
Women have loved high-fliers
And we are eagles of Rome!
Oh march on to the wars!

Comrades, march to the wars!
There's pretty girls in Carthage
And wine to swill in Carthage,
So we must capture Carthage
And fight for Mother Rome!
[*Holds out his goblet to be refilled. There
is silence again. He stares at* LAZARUS
*with a somber intentness. He says
thickly*]
The legions have gone, Lazarus.
[LAZARUS *gives no evidence of having
heard him.* CALIGULA *gulps at his
wine. The* SENATORS *begin to talk to
each other in low voices*]

FIRST SENATOR

How does that Jew make that light come
from him, I wonder? It is a well-contrived
bit of magic.

SECOND SENATOR

What are we waiting for? A messenger came
to me with Cæsar's command that the
Senate meet here at midnight.

THIRD SENATOR

[*Bored*]

Some new whim of Tiberius, naturally—
[*With a meaning titter*]
—or rather I should say, unnaturally!

FOURTH SENATOR

Perhaps Cæsar has decided to abolish our
august body by a massacre in mass!

THIRD SENATOR

[*Yawning*]

There was a feast at Cinna's last night that

lasted until this evening. I could welcome
my own murder as an excuse for sleeping!

FIFTH SENATOR

[*Pompously*]

Tiberius would not dare harm the Senate.
He may mistreat individual Senators, but
the Roman Senate is the Roman Senate!

CHORUS OF THE SENATE

[*As before—wearily as if under a boring
compulsion—intones*]

While Rome is Rome
The Senate is the Senate
The Mighty Voice of the Roman People.

FIRST SENATOR

[*With the ghost of a laugh—wearily*]

The Senate is an empty name—a pack of
degenerate cowards with no trace of their
ancient nobility or courage remaining—
that and no more!

THIRD SENATOR

[*Flippantly*]

You are too severe with yourself, Lucius!
[*A titter of laughter*]

FIRST SENATOR

[*Wearily*]

A degenerate coward. I am, I confess it.
So are you too, Sulpicius—a hundred fold!
—whether you admit it or not.
[SULPICIUS *laughs weakly without taking offense*]

SIXTH SENATOR

[*After a pause—sighing*]

In truth, the Senate is not what it used to
be. I can remember—

FIRST SENATOR

Let us forget, if we can!
[*Then impatiently*]
What are we doing here?

SECOND SENATOR

I imagine it has something to do with the

followers of this Lazarus encamped outside the wall. Probably the legions are to
butcher them in their sleep.

SEVENTH SENATOR

And what part do we play—official witnesses? But how can we witness at night
and through a wall?
[*With bored resignation*]
Ah well, the moods of Tiberius are strange,
to say the least. But Cæsar is Cæsar.

CHORUS

[*Again with bored weariness as before*]

Hail!
Cæsar is Cæsar
The August One
Prince of the Senate
Tribune over Tribunes
Consul of Consuls
Supreme Pontiff
Emperor of Rome
God among Gods
Hail!

FIRST SENATOR

[*After a pause of silence—dryly*]

Cæsar is a beast—and a madman!

FIFTH SENATOR

[*Pompously*]

Respect, sir! More respect for Cæsar!

THIRD SENATOR

[*Mockingly*]

Or caution, Lucius. One of us might repeat your opinion to him.

FIRST SENATOR

You would if it would pay you. But all my
money is squandered. My death is worthless to Tiberius. He would not reward you.
Moreover, you would not be revenged on
me, for I long for death.

THIRD SENATOR

[*Dryly*]

Your stomach must be out of order.

FIRST SENATOR

The times are out of order. But let us
change the subject. Is it true Tiberius has
fled to Capri?

FOURTH SENATOR

Yes. He was terrified by the multitude of
laughing idiots who appeared today with
that charlatan.
[*He points to* LAZARUS]

SECOND SENATOR

There are thousands of them outside the
wall. Cæsar refused to let them enter the
city. The story is, this Lazarus was dead
four days and then restored himself to life
by magic.

FIRST SENATOR

I have a mind to question him.
[*Calls as to a slave*]
You, there! Jew, turn round! In the name
of the Senate!
[LAZARUS *seems not to hear him.*
LUCIUS *remarks with a weary smile*]
So much for our authority!

SIXTH SENATOR

[*With injured dignity*]

What insolence!
[*In a rage*]
Ho, barbarian cur, turn round! The Senate
commands you!
[LAZARUS *does not seem to hear, but*
CALIGULA *turns on them fiercely*]

CALIGULA

Silence! Leave him alone!
[*With insulting scorn*]
I, Caligula, command *you*!
[*The* SENATORS *seem to shrink back
from him in fear, all but* LUCIUS, *who
answers with a mocking servility*]

FIRST SENATOR

At least, grant us the boon to see this
corpse's face, O Gracious Gaius!

CALIGULA

[*Fixing his cruel, burning eyes on him—softly*]

I heard you wish for death, Lucius. When I am Cæsar you shall scream and pray for it!

FIRST SENATOR

[*Dryly and haughtily*]

You were bred in camp, Gaius. You should have learned more courage there along with your coarseness. But accept my gratitude for your warning. I shall take care to die before you become Cæsar—and life becomes too idiotic!

CALIGULA

[*His grin becoming ferocious with cruelty*]

No. You are too weak to kill yourself. Look at me, Lucius! I am imagining what I shall have done to you!
[*The* SENATORS *are now trembling. Even* LUCIUS *cannot repress a shudder of horror at the face glaring at him. Suddenly* CALIGULA *throws the cup from him and springs to his feet*]
What good is wine if it cannot kill thought? Lazarus! It is time. I must give the signal! The legions are waiting. It is Cæsar's command that they spare none of your followers.
[*He has walked toward* LAZARUS]

MIRIAM

[*Stretches out her hands to* CALIGULA *imploringly*]

Mercy! Spare them who are so full of life and joy!

CALIGULA

[*Harshly*]

For their joy I will revenge myself upon them! Mercy? If there is no death, then death is a mercy! Ask that man!
[*He points accusingly to* LAZARUS]
And why should you plead for them, Jewess? There are few Jews among them. They are mostly those whom your people call idolaters and would gladly see murdered.

MIRIAM

[*With deep grief*]

I am a mother of dead children. I plead for the mothers of those about to die.

CALIGULA

[*Contemptuously*]

Pah!
[*He turns from her and puts his hand on* LAZARUS' *shoulder*]
Lazarus! Do you hear? I must signal to the legions!

LAZARUS

[*Turns. He has grown more youthful. He seems no more than thirty. His face is exalted and calm and beautiful. His eyes shine with an unearthly glory. The* SENATORS *lean forward in their seats, fascinated by his face. A low murmur of admiration comes from them.* LAZARUS *speaks commandingly*]

Wait! I will awaken my beloved ones that their passing may be a symbol to the world that there is no death!
[*He turns, throwing back his head and stretching up his arms, and begins to laugh low and tenderly, like caressing music at first but gradually gaining in volume, becoming more and more intense and insistent, finally ending up on a triumphant, blood-stirring call to that ultimate attainment in which all prepossession with self is lost in an ecstatic affirmation of Life. The voices of his* FOLLOWERS *from beyond the wall, at first one by one, then several at a time, then multitudes, join in his laughter. Even the* SENATORS *are drawn into it. Now every one of these is standing up, stretching out his arms toward* LAZARUS, *laughing harshly and discordantly and awkwardly in his attempt to laugh. Terrific flashes of lightning and crashes of thunder seem a responsive accompaniment from the heavens to this laughter of thousands which throbs in beating waves of sound in the air. Mingled with the laughing from beyond the wall comes the sound of*]

singing and the music of flutes and cymbals. MIRIAM has crawled on her knees to the edge of the portico where her black figure of grief is outlined below and to the left of LAZARUS, her arms raised outward like the arms of a cross

FOLLOWERS OF LAZARUS

[In a great chanting singing chorus]

Laugh! Laugh!
There is only God!
Life is His Laughter!
We are His Laughter!
Fear is no more!
Death is dead!

CHORUS OF SENATORS

[Taking it up in a tone between chanting and their old solemn intoning]

Laugh! Laugh!
Fear is no more!
Death is dead!

ALL

[The multitude beyond the wall, all the SENATORS, everyone except the never-laughing MIRIAM and CALIGULA and the MEN OF THE LEGIONS]

Laugh! Laugh!
Death is dead!

CALIGULA

[In a queer state of mingled exaltation and fear—hopping restlessly about from foot to foot—shouting]

The signal! Shall I give the signal to kill, Lazarus?

MEN OF THE LEGIONS

[Following a brazen trumpet call, are suddenly heard from beyond the wall beginning to laugh their hoarse, bass laughter, a deeper note than all the others]

Laugh! Laugh!

CALIGULA

[Listening—with dismay]

I hear the legions, Lazarus! They are laughing with them!

[He cries with a strange pitifulness and beseeching]

You are playing me false, Lazarus! You are trying to evade death! You are trying to spare your people! You are small and weak like other men when the test comes! You give way to pity! Your great laughter becomes pitiful!

[Working himself into a rage]

You are a traitor, Lazarus! You betray Cæsar! Have you forgotten I will be Cæsar? You betray me, Lazarus!

[He rushes to the edge and, making a megaphone of his hands, bellows]

You on the wall! Sentry! It is I, Caligula! Kill!

[The brazen trumpets of the LEGIONS sound from beyond the wall. He springs near LAZARUS again, in a fiendish ecstasy, dancing a hopping grotesque sword dance behind him, chanting as he does so]

Kill! Kill laughter! Kill those who deny Cæsar! I will be Cæsar! Kill those who deny Death! I will be Death! My face will be bright with blood! My laughing face, Lazarus! Laughing because men fear me! My face of victorious Fear! Look at me! I am laughing, Lazarus! *My* laughter! Laughter of Gods and Cæsars! Ha-ha-ha-ha!

[He laughs, his laughter fanatically cruel and savage, forced from his lips with a desperate, destroying abandon. For a moment, above all the chorus of other sounds, his voice fights to overcome that of LAZARUS, whose laughter seems now to have attained the most exultant heights of spiritual affirmation. Then CALIGULA's breaks into a cry of fear and a sob, and, casting his sword aside, he hides his face in his hands and cries beseechingly]

Forgive me! I love you, Lazarus! Forgive me!

[At this second the blaring trumpets of the LEGIONS are heard approaching and their great bass chorus of marching tramping laughter]

MEN OF THE LEGIONS

[*Chanting*]

Laugh! Laugh! Laugh!
Fear, no more!
Death, no more!
Death is dead!

[*There is now no sound of the singing or the laughter or music of* LAZARUS' FOLLOWERS. MIRIAM *rocks to and fro and raises a low wail of lamentation. The* SENATORS *cheer and shout as at a triumph*]

CHORUS OF SENATORS

[*Saluting* LAZARUS]

Hail, Victor!
Hail, Divine One!
Thou hast slain fear!
Thou hast slain death!   10
Hail! Triumph!

SENATORS

Hail! Hail!
Slayer of Fear!
Slayer of Death!

[*The gate in the wall is clanged open. The returning* LEGIONS *burst through and gather in a dense mob in the street below* LAZARUS, *who looks down upon them, silent but smiling gently now. They stare at him with admiration. Only a sea of their masks can be seen, their eyes shining exultantly.* CRASSUS, *their general, ascends the steps until he stands a little below* LAZARUS. *Their* CHORUS OF LEGIONARIES *in double-sized masks climb to the step below* CRASSUS, *forming behind him. They are in the Period of Manhood, of the Simple, Ignorant Type. No weapons can be seen—only their masks and helmets* 20 *and armor gleaming in the lightning flashes and in the flickering light of torches. Their laughter seems to shake the walls and make the pillars of the temple dance*]

CHORUS OF THE LEGIONS

Fear, no more!
Death, no more!
Death is dead!

LEGIONARIES

[*Echoing*]

Laugh! Laugh! Laugh!
Death is dead!

CRASSUS

[*Raising his hand*]

Silence!

[*They obey. He turns to* LAZARUS *and bows his head, falling on one knee, raising his right arm*]

Hail!

LEGIONARIES

[*As one man—raising their arms*]

Hail!

CALIGULA

[*Suddenly pushes forward impudently and strikes a grandiose attitude*]

I am here, my brave ones!

[*There is a roar of mocking laughter from the* LEGIONARIES]

CRASSUS

[*Not unkindly*]

Not you, Little Killer! We hail the Great Laugher!

CALIGULA

[*Harshly*]

Have you killed all his followers?

CRASSUS

No. They died. They did not wait for our attack. They charged upon us, laughing! They tore our swords away from us, laughing, and we laughed with them! They stabbed themselves, dancing as though it were a festival! They died, laughing, in one another's arms! We laughed, too, with joy because it seemed it was not they who died but death itself they killed!

[*He stops uncertainly, bowing to* LAZARUS, *awkwardly*]

I do not understand this. I am a soldier. But there is a god in it somewhere! For I know they were drunk, and so were we, with a happiness no mortal ever felt on earth before! And death was dead!

[*In a sudden outburst as if he were drunk with excitement, he takes off his helmet and waves it*]

Hail, Deliverer! Death is dead! We left our swords with them! What virtue in killing when there is no death? Your foe laughs. The joke is on you. What a fool's game, eh? One can only laugh! Now we want peace to laugh in—to laugh at war! Let Cæsars fight—that is all they are good 10 for—and not much good for that!

CALIGULA

[*Frenziedly*]

Silence, impious traitor!

CRASSUS

[*Smiling drunkenly*]

Shut up, yourself, camp-brat! Though you were Cæsar this minute I would laugh at you! Your death is dead! We will make Lazarus Cæsar! What say you?

[*He appeals to the* SOLDIERS]

CALIGULA

No!   20

CHORUS OF THE LEGIONS

[*With laughing intoxication*]

Hail, Lazarus Cæsar! Hail!

LEGIONARIES

Lazarus Cæsar, hail!

CRASSUS

[*Appealing to* SENATE]

And you, Senators!

CHORUS OF SENATORS

[*With the same joyous intoxication as* 30 *the* SOLDIERS]

Hail, Lazarus Cæsar! Hail!

SENATORS

Lazarus Cæsar, hail!

CALIGULA

[*Piteously*]

No, Lazarus! Say no for my sake!

LAZARUS

[*With gay mockery*]

What is—Cæsar?

[*He begins to laugh with mockery. All except* CALIGULA *and* MIRIAM *join in this laughter*]

CRASSUS

Ha-ha! What is Cæsar? You are right! You deserve better from us. A god? How is that? We will build you a temple, Lazarus, and make you a god!

LAZARUS

[*Laughingly*]

When men make gods, there is no God!

[*He laughs. They all laugh*]

CRASSUS

[*With puzzled good-nature*]

I do not understand. But there is a god in it somewhere—a god of peace—a god of happiness! Perhaps you are already he, eh? Are you? Well, never mind now, remember our offer. Give us your answer tomorrow. Good night to you!

LAZARUS

[*As the* SOLDIERS *start to march away behind* CRASSUS, *and the* SENATORS *turn to retire, he stops them all for a moment with a gesture—with a deep earnestness*]

Wait! When you awake tomorrow, try to remember! Remember that death is dead! Remember to laugh!

ALL

[*As if taking an oath wit   e voice*]

We will remember, Lazaru

CRASSUS

[*Making a sign to the regimental musicians jovially*]

And we will laugh! Play there!
[*The bands crash out. The* LEGIONS *tramp away*]

CHORUS OF THE LEGIONS

[*Chanting to the music*]

Laugh! Laugh! Laugh!
Cæsar, no more!
War, no more!
Wounds, no more!
Death is dead!
Dead! Dead! Dead!

LEGIONARIES

Laugh! Laugh! Laugh!
Death is dead!
Dead! Dead! Dead!

CHORUS OF SENATORS

[*Following them*]

Cæsar, no more!
Fear, no more!
Death, no more!
Laugh! Laugh! Laugh!

SENATE

[*Elated, excited as a crowd of schoolboys going on a vacation. Marching after them*]

Laugh! Laugh! Laugh!
Death is dead!
[LAZARUS, MIRIAM *and* CALIGULA *remain*]

LAZARUS

[*With a great yearning*]

If men would remember! If they could!
[*He stares after them compassionately*]

CALIGULA

[*Crouching beside* LAZARUS. *Plucks at his robe humbly*]

You will n̶t laugh at Cæsar, Lazarus, will you—whe̶ ̶m Cæsar? You will not laugh at gods w̶ ̶ey make me a god?

[LAZARUS *does not answer.* CALIGULA *forces a cruel vindictive smile*]
I swear you shall not laugh at death when I am Death! Ha-ha—
[*He starts to laugh harshly—then suddenly, terrified, slinks away and sidles off at right*]

MIRIAM

[*From where she kneels bowed with grief—brokenly*]

Those who have just died were like your children, Lazarus. They believed in you and loved you.

LAZARUS

10 And I loved them!

MIRIAM

Then how could you laugh when they were dying?

LAZARUS

[*Exultingly*]

Did they not laugh? That was their victory and glory!
[*With more and more of a passionate, proud exultation*]
Eye to eye with the Fear of Death, did
20 they not laugh with scorn? 'Death to old Death,' they laughed! 'Once as squirming specks we crept from the tides of the sea. Now we return to the sea! Once as quivering flecks of rhythm we beat down from the sun. Now we reënter the sun! Cast aside is our pitiable pretense, our immortal egohood, the holy lantern behind which cringed our Fear of the Dark! Flung off is that impudent insult to life's nobility
30 which gibbers: "I, this Jew, this Roman, this noble or this slave, must survive in my pettiness forever!" Away with such cowardice of spirit! We will to die! We will to change! Laughing we lived with our gift, now with laughter give we back that gift to become again the Essence of the Giver! Dying we laugh with the Infinite. We are the Giver and the Gift! Laughing, we will our own annihilation! Laughing
40 we give our lives for Life's sake!'
[*He laughs up to heaven ecstatically*]

This must Man will as his end and his new beginning! He must conceive and desire his own passing as a mood of eternal laughter and cry with pride, 'Take back, O God, and accept in turn a gift from me, my grateful blessing for Your gift—and see, O God, now I am laughing with You! I am Your laughter—and You are mine!'

[*He laughs again, his laughter dying lingeringly and tenderly on his lips like a strain of music receding into the silence over still waters*]

MIRIAM

[*With a sigh—meekly*]

I cannot understand, Lazarus.
[*Sadly*]
They were like your children—and they 10
have died. Must you not mourn for them?

LAZARUS

[*Gently*]

Mourn? When they laughed?

MIRIAM

[*Sadly*]

They are gone from us. And their mothers weep.

LAZARUS

[*Puts his arm around her and raises her to her feet—tenderly*]

But God, their Father, laughs!
[*He kisses her on the forehead*]

CURTAIN

ACT THREE
SCENE ONE

SCENE: *Some days later—exterior of* TI-BERIUS' *villa-palace at Capri. It is about two in the morning of a clear black night. In the rear, the walls of the villa, which is built entirely of marble on the brow of a cliff, loom up with a startling clarity against the sky. The rear foreground is a marble terrace at the middle of which is a triumphal arch. On each side, leading up to it, are massive marble columns standing like the mummies of legionaries at*

attention. In the exact centre of the arch itself a cross is set up on which a full grown male lion has been crucified. A lamp reflecting downward has been fixed at the top of the cross to light up an inscription placed over the lion's head. Below the steps to the terrace, in a line facing front, on each side of the cross, is the CHORUS OF THE GUARD *in their double masks and gorgeous uniforms and armor. Their masks are the same as the* LEGIONARY CHORUS *of the previous scene.*
The windows of the palace glow crimson-purple with the reflection of many shaded lamps. The sound of music in a strained theme of that joyless abandon which is vice is heard above a confused drunken clamor of voices, punctuated by the high, staccato laughter of women and youths. A squad of the GUARD *in the same uniforms as the* CHORUS, *masked as all the* ROMAN SOLDIERS *previously, enter from the left, front, climbing up from the beach below. They are commanded by a Centurion,* FLAVIUS. *His mask is that of a typical young patrician officer. They are followed by* LAZARUS *and* MIRIAM. CALIGULA *walks behind, his drawn sword in his hand. He is in a state of queer conflicting emotion, seeming to be filled with a nervous dread and terror of everything about him, while at the same time perversely excited and elated by his own morbid tension.* LAZARUS, *looking no more than twenty-five, haloed in his own mystic light, walks in a deep, detached serenity.* MIRIAM, *in black, her hair almost white now, her figure bowed and feeble, seems more than ever a figure of a sad, resigned mother of the dead. The soldiers form in line with the columns.*

FLAVIUS

[*Saluting* CALIGULA—*with an awed glance at* LAZARUS]

I will announce your coming—
[*As if in spite of himself he bows awkwardly to* LAZARUS]
—and that of this man. Cæsar was not expecting you so soon, I think.

CALIGULA

[*Forcing a light tone*]

Lazarus laughed and the gall[...]es forgot

heir fetters and made their oars fly as if
hey were bound for the Blessed Isles of
Liberty!

[*Then with an ironic smile*]

But you need not tell Tiberius that, good
Flavius. Say it was due to my extreme
zeal.

FLAVIUS

[*Smiles with respectful understanding.*
CALIGULA *nods in dismissal.* FLAVIUS
turns to go—apologetically]

You may have to wait. I dare not speak
before he questions me.

[FLAVIUS *salutes and hastens to the
villa, walking under an arm of the
cross unconcernedly without an upward glance. As they follow him
with their eyes* CALIGULA *and* MIR-
IAM *see the lion for the first time. He
steps back with a startled exclamation. She gives a cry of horror and
covers her eyes with her hands to shut
out the sight*]

LAZARUS

[*Immediately puts his arms around her
protectingly*]

What is it, Beloved?

[*She hides her face on his breast, pointing toward the lion with a trembling
hand*]

CALIGULA

[*Pointing—curiously now, but with entire callousness*]

This lion they have crucified. Are you
frightened, Jewess?

[*With a cruel laugh*]

My grandfather frequently plants whole
orchards of such trees, but usually they
bear human fruit!

MIRIAM

[*With a shudder*]

Monster!

CALIGULA

[*With genuine surprise—turning to her*]

Who? Why?

[*He approaches the cross and stares at
it moodily*]

But why did he have it placed here where
he knew you must pass? Tiberius does not
go to such pains to frighten women.

[*His eyes fasten on the inscription above
the lion's head*]

Aha! I see!

[*He reads*]

'From the East, land of false gods and
superstition, this lion was brought to Rome
to amuse Cæsar.'

[*A silence.* CALIGULA *shrugs his shoulders, turning away—lightly*]

A lesson for you, Lazarus. An example for
other lions—not to roar—or laugh—at
Cæsar!

[*He gives a harsh laugh*]

Tiberius must be terribly afraid of you.

[*Then sombrely*]

You should never have come here. I would
have advised you not to—but what are you
to me? My duty, if I wish to become
Cæsar, is to Cæsar. Besides, you are no
fool. Evidently you must desire your own
death. Last night *you* might have been
Cæsar. The legions were yours.

LAZARUS

[*Smiling without bitterness—with a sad
comprehension*]

But this morning the legions had forgotten.
They only remembered—to go out and
pick up their swords. They also pillaged
the bodies a little, as their right, believing
now that they had slain them!

[*This last a bit bitterly*]

CALIGULA

[*Tauntingly*]

The legions did slay them! It was only by
some magician's trick you made them
think your followers killed themselves.

LAZARUS

[*Not answering him—ironically to himself*]

It is too soon. Men still need their swords
to slash at ghosts in the dark. Men, those
haunted heroes!

[*He laughs softly*]

CALIGULA

[*Irritably*]

What are you laughing at?

LAZARUS

At Lazarus when I find him feeling
wronged because men are men!
[*He laughs again, softly and musically*]

CALIGULA

[*Again taunting brutally*]

You may be in his place soon!
[*He points to the lion*]
Will you laugh then?
[MIRIAM *gives a cry of terror*]

LAZARUS

[*Calmly*]

Yes.
[*Then humbly, bowing his head*]
I will laugh with the pride of a beggar set
upon the throne of Man!

CALIGULA

[*Sneeringly*]

You boast.
[*Then as* LAZARUS *does not answer,
touching the lion with intentional
provoking brutality*]
This one from Africa seems almost gone.
They do not last as long as men.

LAZARUS

[*Walks up the steps to the cross and,
stretching to his full height, gently
pushes the lion's hair out of its eyes—
tenderly*]

Poor brother! Cæsar avenges himself on
you because of me. Forgive me your suffering!

CALIGULA

[*With a start backward—with frightened awe*]

Gods! He licks your hand! I could swear
he smiles—with his last breath!
[*Then with relief*]
Now he is dead!

LAZARUS

[*Gently*]

There is no death.

CALIGULA

[*Pointing to the lion*]

What is that then?

LAZARUS

Your fear of life.

CALIGULA

[*Impatiently*]

Bah!
[*Then sombrely*]
A little fear is useful even for lions—or
teachers of laughter if they wish to laugh
long!
[*Then with a sudden exasperation*]
Escape now, you fool, while there is still
time!

LAZARUS

[*Laughing softly*]

Escape—what?

CALIGULA

[*In a frenzy*]

You know, you ass, you lunatic! Escape
death! Death! Death!
[*To* MIRIAM]
You, woman! Talk to him! Do you want
him nailed up like that?

MIRIAM

[*With a pitiful cry*]

Lazarus! Come! Caligula will help us!

CALIGULA

[*Harshly*]

You presume, Jewess! I have no wish to
die!
[*Then with his wry smile*]
But I will turn my back—and shut my
eyes—
[*He walks away to left*]

MIRIAM

[*Beseechingly*]

Lazarus! I could not bear that aching hunger of my empty heart if you should die again!

LAZARUS

[*Coming to her—tenderly*]

I will not leave you! Believe in me!
[*He kisses her forehead tenderly*]

MIRIAM

[*After a pause—slowly and lamentingly*]

I wish we were home, Lazarus. This Roman world is full of evil. These skies threaten. These hearts are heavy with hatred. There is a taint of blood in the air that poisons the breath of the sea. These columns and arches and thick walls seem waiting to fall, to crush these rotten men and then to crumble over the bones that raised them until both are dust. It is a world deadly to your joy, Lazarus. Its pleasure is a gorging of dirt, its fulfilled desire a snoring in a sty in the mud among swine. Its will is so sick that it must kill in order to be aware of life at all. I wish we were home, Lazarus. I begin to feel horror gnawing at my breast. I begin to know the torture of the fear of death, Lazarus—not of my death but of yours—not of the passing of your man's body but of the going away from me of your laughter which is to me as my son, my little boy!

LAZARUS

[*Soothing her*]

Be comforted, Beloved. Your fear shall never be!

MIRIAM

On the hills near Bethany you might pray at noon and laugh your boy's laughter in the sun and there would be echoing laughter from the sky and up from the grass and distantly from the shining sea. We would adopt children whose parents the Romans had butchered, and their laughter would be around me in my home where I cooked and weaved and sang. And in the dawn at your going out, and in the evening on your return, I would hear in the hushed air the bleating of sheep and the tinkling of many little bells and your voice. And my heart would know peace.

LAZARUS

[*Tenderly*]

Only a little longer! There is God's laughter on the hills of space, and the happiness of children, and the soft healing of innumerable dawns and evenings, and the blessing of peace!

CALIGULA

[*Looks around at* LAZARUS *impatiently. Then he makes a beckoning gesture to* MIRIAM]

Ssstt!
[*Wonderingly she leaves* LAZARUS' *side and follows him.* LAZARUS *remains, his eyes fixed on the cross, directly in front of it.* CALIGULA *speaks gruffly to* MIRIAM *with a sneer*]

Jewess, your Lazarus is mad, I begin to think.
[*Then confusedly but helplessly inquisitive and confiding—bursting out*]

What is it troubles me about him? What makes me dream of him? Why should I—love him, Jewess? Tell me! You love him, too. I do not understand this. Why, wherever he goes, is there joy? You heard even the galley slaves laugh and clank time with their chains!
[*Then with exasperation*]

And yet why can I not laugh, Jewess?

MIRIAM

[*In a tone of hushed grief*]

I may not laugh either. My heart remains a little dead with Lazarus in Bethany. The miracle could not revive all his old husband's life in my wife's heart.

CALIGULA

[*Disgustedly*]

What answer is that to me?
[*Then brusquely*]

But I called you to put you on your guard.
[*He points*]

There is death in there—Tiberius' death,
a kind from which no miracles can recall
one!

[*He smiles his twisted smile*]

Since Lazarus will not help himself, you
must protect him. I will not, for once in
there I am

[*Mockingly*]

the heir of Cæsar, and you are scum whom
I will kill at his order as I would two
beetles! So keep watch! Taste first of what he
eats—even were I the one to give it to him!   10

LAZARUS

[*Suddenly laughs softly*]

Why do you delight in believing evil of
yourself, Caligula?

CALIGULA

[*Flying into a queer rage*]

You lie! I am what I am!

[*With grandiose pride*]

What could you know of a Cæsar?

LAZARUS

[*Still laughing with an affectionate
understanding*]

What—I know!

[*As he finishes speaking all the sound of
music and voices from the house ceases
abruptly and there is a heavy silence*]

MIRIAM

[*Shaking her head and turning away
sadly*]

That is too far, Lazarus. Let us go home.   20

CALIGULA

[*Harshly*]

Sst! Do you hear? Flavius has told Cæsar.

[*Grimly forcing a harsh snicker*]

Now we will soon know—

[*There is the sudden blaring of a trumpet from within the palace. A wide
door is flung open and a stream of
reddish light comes out against which
the black figures of several men are
outlined. The door is shut again
quickly. Several SLAVES bearing
lamps on poles escort the patrician,*

MARCELLUS, *forward to the arch. He
passes under the crucified lion without
a glance—then stands, cool and disdainful, to look about him. He is a
man of about thirty-five, wearing the
type mask of a Roman patrician to
which are added the dissipated cour-
tier's characteristics of one who leans
to evil more through weakness than
any instinctive urge. He is dressed
richly. His smile is hypocritical and
his eyes are hard and cold but when
they come to rest on LAZARUS he gives
a start of genuine astonishment*]

CALIGULA

[*Who has moved to LAZARUS' side de-
fensively—in a quick whisper*]

Beware of this man, Lazarus!

[*Then advancing—with a condescending
hauteur*]

Greeting, Marcellus!

MARCELLUS

[*In an ingratiating tone*]

Greeting, Gaius. I have a message from
Cæsar for the man called Lazarus.

LAZARUS

[*Calmly*]

I am Lazarus.

MARCELLUS

[*Makes a deep bow—flatteringly*]

I had surmised it, sir. Although I cannot
pretend to virtue in myself at least I may
claim the merit of recognizing it in others.

[*He advances toward LAZARUS, smiling,
with one hand kept hidden beneath his
cloak*]

CALIGULA

[*Stepping between them—sharply*]

What is your message?

MARCELLUS

[*Surprised—placatingly*]

I am sorry, Gaius, but it was Cæsar's command I speak to Lazarus alone.

CALIGULA

[*Fiercely*]

And then, Marcellus?

[MARCELLUS *shrugs his shoulders and smiles deprecatingly*]

LAZARUS

[*With a compelling dignity*]

Let him speak.

[*Inclining his head to* MARCELLUS— *strangely*]

Over here where it is dark you will not be seen—nor see yourself.

[*He walks to the darkness at right*]

CALIGULA

[*Turning his back on them, with angry boyish resentfulness that is close to tears*]

Idiot! Go and die, then!

MIRIAM

[*With a terrified cry*]

Lazarus!   10

[*She starts to go to him*]

LAZARUS

[*Motioning her to remain where she is— gently*]

Believe, Beloved!

[*He turns his back on them all and stands waiting*]

MARCELLUS

[*Stares at* LAZARUS—*then over his shoulder at* CALIGULA—*uncertainly*]

What does he mean, Gaius?

[*Then suddenly putting on a brave front, he strides up behind* LAZARUS]

Cæsar wished me to bid you welcome, to tell you how much regard he has for you, but he desired me to ask whether you propose to laugh here—in Cæsar's palace? He has heard that you laugh at death—that you have caused others to laugh—even his   20 legionaries.

[*A pause,* MARCELLUS *remains behind* LAZARUS' *back, the latter standing like a victim*]

Briefly, Cæsar requires your pledge that you will not laugh. Will you give it?

[*He frees his dagger from under his robe. A pause. Arrogantly*]

I am waiting! Answer when Cæsar commands!

[*Then angrily, baffled*]

I will give you while I count three—or take your silence as a refusal! One! Two! Three!

[*He raises his hand to stab* LAZARUS *in the back.* MIRIAM *stifles a scream. At the same instant,* LAZARUS *begins to laugh, softly and affectionately.* MARCELLUS *stops, frozen in mid-action, the dagger upraised.* CALIGULA *has whirled around and stands staring, a smile gradually coming to his face.* LAZARUS *turns, his laughter grown a trifle louder, and faces* MARCELLUS. *The latter steps back from him, staring open-mouthed, fascinated. His arm sinks to his side. The dagger falls from his fingers. He smiles back at* LAZARUS—*the curious, sheepish, bashful smile of one who has fallen in love and been discovered*]

LAZARUS

[*Going to him, puts both hands on his shoulders and looks in his eyes, laughing affectionately—then quizzically*]

Here is another one who believes in death! But soon you will laugh with life! I see it in your eyes. Farewell, Marcellus!

[*He turns away from him and walks, laughing, toward the arch in rear. With bowed head the black-robed figure of* MIRIAM *follows him.* MARCELLUS *hides his face in his hands, half-sobbing, and half-laughing hysterically.* LAZARUS *pauses before the cross for a moment—raises his hand as if blessing the dead lion, then passes below it, moving slowly on toward the palace in the rear. His laughter rises with more and more summoning power. The files of the* GUARD, *as he passes them, two by two join in his laughter, saluting him as if in spite of themselves*]

CALIGULA

[*Sidling up to* MARCELLUS, *cruel and mocking*]

Are you weeping, Marcellus? Laugh at that blundering fool, yourself! What will Cæsar say? Will he laugh when he has your body broken one bone at a time with hammers? Why did you not kill? For shame! A patrician exposed to laughter by a Jew! Poor craven! Why could you not strike? There *must* be death! Coward! Why did you not stab? 10

[*Then in a queer awed whisper*]
I know! Was it not because of a sudden you loved him and could not?

MARCELLUS

[*Suddenly—eagerly*]

Yes! That was it! I loved him!

CALIGULA

[*Craftily and cruelly*]

You were about to murder him!

MARCELLUS

[*Tortured with remorse*]

No! No! How could I? What infamy! 20
[*Cries tearfully*]
Forgive me, Lazarus!

CALIGULA

[*With vindictive insistence*]

Judge yourself!
[*He takes up the dagger*]
Here is your dagger! Avenge him on yourself!

MARCELLUS

[*Trying to laugh*]

Ha-ha—Yes!
[*He stabs himself and falls. Suddenly his laughter is released*]
I laugh! You are a fool, Caligula! There is no death!
[*He dies, laughing up at the sky*] 30

CALIGULA

[*Kicks his body with savage cruelty*]

You lie!

[*Then suddenly kneels and bends over it imploringly*]
Tell me you lie, Marcellus! Do me that mercy!—and when I am Cæsar, I—
[*He begins to weep like a frightened boy, his head in his hands. Meanwhile* LAZARUS *has arrived with* MIRIAM *at the steps before the door of the palace. As he starts to ascend these, the crimson-purple lights of the many windows of the palace go out one by one as if fleeing in terror from the laughter which now beats at the walls*]

CHORUS OF THE GUARD

Fear, no more!
Death, no more!
Laugh! Laugh! Laugh!
Death is dead!

ALL THE GUARDS

[*Now all in a great chorus, raising their spears aloft and saluting* LAZARUS *as if they were his own triumphal body guard*]
Laugh! Laugh! Laugh!
Death is dead!
[LAZARUS *has ascended the steps. He walks into the black archway of the darkened palace, his figure radiant and unearthly in his own light.* MIRIAM *follows him. They disappear in the darkness. There is a pause of dead silence*]

CALIGULA

[*Raises his head uneasily, looks back toward the palace, jumps to his feet in a panic of terror, and runs toward the palace door, calling*]

Lazarus! Wait! I will defend you! There is death inside there—death! Beware, Lazarus!

CHORUS OF THE GUARD

[*As the laughter of* LAZARUS *is heard again from the dark palace*]

Laugh! Laugh! Laugh!
Death is dead!

ALL THE GUARDS

Dead! Dead! Dead!
Death is dead!

CURTAIN

ACT THREE

SCENE TWO

SCENE: *The banquet hall in the palace of* TIBERIUS—*an immense high-ceilinged room. In the rear, center, is a great arched doorway. Smaller arches in the middle of the side walls lead into other rooms. Long couches are placed along the walls at right and left, and along the rear wall on either side of the arch. Before these couches, a series of narrow tables is set. In the center of the room on a high dais is the ivory and gold chair of* CÆSAR, *a table in front of it, couches for him to recline on at either side. On this table, and on all the tables for his guests, gold lamps with shades of crimson-purple are placed.*

Reclining on the couches on the right are young women and girls, on the left, youths of an equal number.

[*The masks are based on the Roman masks of the periods of Boyhood (or Girlhood), Youth, and Young Manhood (or Womanhood) and there are seven individuals of each period and sex in each of the three types of the Introspective, Self-Tortured; the Servile, Hypocritical; and the Cruel, Revengeful—a crowd of forty-two in all. There is a distinctive character to the masks of each sex, the stamp of an effeminate corruption on all the male, while the female have a bold, masculine expression. The male masks are a blotched heliotrope in shade. These youths wear female wigs of curled wire like frizzed hair of a yellow gold. They are dressed in women's robes of pale heliotrope, they wear anklets and bracelets and necklaces. The women are dressed as males in crimson or deep purple. They also wear wire wigs but of straight hair cut in short boyish mode, dyed either deep purple or crimson. Those with crimson hair are dressed in purple, and vice versa. The female voices are harsh, strident, mannish—those of the youths affected, lisping, effeminate. The whole effect of these two groups is of sex corrupted and warped, of invented lusts and artificial vices.*

The CHORUS *in this scene and the next is composed of three males and four females —the males in the period of Youth, one in each of the types represented, and three of the females in similar type-period masks.*

The fourth female is masked in the period of Womanhood in the Proud, Self-Reliant type. They sit, facing front in their double-sized masks, on the side steps of the dais, four on right, three on left.]

POMPEIA, *a Roman noblewoman, the favorite mistress of* CÆSAR, *sits at front, right.*

She wears a half-mask on the upper part of her face, olive-colored with the red of blood smoldering through, with great, dark, cruel eyes—a dissipated mask of intense evil beauty, of lust and perverted passion. Beneath the mask, her own complexion is pale, her gentle, girlish mouth is set in an expression of agonized self-loathing and weariness of spirit. Her body is strong and beautiful. Her wig and dress are purple.

TIBERIUS CÆSAR *stands on the dais, dressed in deep purple, fringed and ornamented with crimson and gold. An old man of seventy-six, tall, broad and corpulent but of great muscular strength still despite his age, his shiny white cranium rises like a polished shell above his half-masked face. This mask is a pallid purple blotched with darker color, as if the imperial blood in his veins had been sickened by age and debauchery. The eyes are protuberant, leering, cynical slits, the long nose, once finely modeled, now gross and thickened, the forehead lowering and grim. Beneath the mask, his own mouth looks as incongruous as* CALIGULA'S. *The lips are thin and stern and self-contained—the lips of an able soldier-statesman of rigid probity. His chin is forceful and severe. The complexion of his own skin is that of a healthy old campaigner.*

As the curtain rises, slaves are hurriedly putting out the many lamps. From outside, the laughter of LAZARUS *rises on the deep ground swell of the* GUARD'S *laughter. The walls and massive columns seem to reverberate with the sound. In the banquet room all are listening fascinatedly. Every reaction, from the extreme of panic fear or hypnotized ecstasy to a feigned cynical amusement or a pretended supercilious indifference, is represented in their frozen attitudes.* TIBERIUS *stands, shrinking back, staring at the doorway in the rear with superstitious dread. A squad of the* GUARD *surround the dais, commanded by* FLAVIUS.

TIBERIUS

[*In a strained voice shaken by apprehension and awe*]

Marcellus! Strike him down! Stab him!

SOLDIERS OF THE GUARD

[*From without*]

Laugh! Laugh! Laugh!
Death is dead!

TIBERIUS

[*As he suddenly sees the shining figure of LAZARUS appear at the end of the dark hall beyond the archway*]

Gods! Flavius, look!
[*He points with a shaking finger. FLAVIUS has leaped up to his side*]

FLAVIUS

[*Not without dread himself*]

That is the man, Cæsar.

TIBERIUS

Man? Say a dæmon!
[*To the slaves who are turning out the few remaining lamps*]
Quick! Darkness!
[*He puts out the lamp on his table himself. Then as nothing is seen but the light from the approaching LAZARUS*]
Flavius! Stand here in my place! It will think you are Cæsar!
[*He clumps heavily down the steps of the dais*]
Guards! Here! Cover me with your shields!
[*He goes to the extreme right corner, front, and crouches there. His GUARDS follow him. They hold their shields so that they form a wall around him and half over him. Then CALIGULA's voice is heard screaming above the chorus of laughter as he enters the hall behind LAZARUS*]

CALIGULA

Beware of death! I will defend you, Lazarus!
[*He is seen to rush past LAZARUS, flourishing his sword and comes running into the room, shouting*]
Cæsar! Dare not to murder Lazarus!

[*He leaps to the dais and up its steps in a frenzy*]
Dare not, I say!
[*He stabs FLAVIUS with a savage cry*]
Ah!
[*Then, as the body of FLAVIUS falls heavily and rolls down the steps at right, he begins to laugh, at first a clear laughter of selfless joy, sounding startlingly incongruous from him*]
I have saved you, Lazarus—at the risk of my own life—and now, hear me, I can laugh!
[*LAZARUS appears in the archway, MIRIAM behind him. He stops laughing and immediately there is silence, except for CALIGULA. LAZARUS casts a luminous glow over the whole room in which the masked faces appear distorted and livid. CALIGULA stands with upraised sword by the chair of CÆSAR. Suddenly his laughter cracks, changes, becomes full of his old fear and blood-lust*]

CALIGULA

Ha-ha-ha! See, Lazarus!
[*He points to the body of FLAVIUS with his sword*]
Welcome in the name of Cæsar, now Cæsar is slain and I am Cæsar!
[*He assumes the absurd grandiose posture of his imperial posing. No one looks at him or hears him. Their eyes are on LAZARUS as he moves directly to where TIBERIUS crouches behind the shields of the GUARDS. MIRIAM follows him. CALIGULA turns and stares toward him, and then down at the body of FLAVIUS and back, in a petrified, bewildered stupor. LAZARUS steps up beside TIBERIUS. The GUARDS make way for him fearfully*]

TIBERIUS

[*Feeling his nearness—straightening himself with a certain dignity*]

Strike! I have been a soldier. Thou canst not make me fear death, Dæmon!
[*He draws his toga over his face*]

LAZARUS

[*Smiling gently*]

Then fear not fear, Tiberius!

[*He reaches out and pulls back the toga from his face.* TIBERIUS *looks into his eyes, at first shrinkingly, then with growing reassurance, his own masked face clearly revealed now in the light from* LAZARUS]

TIBERIUS

[*At first falteringly*]

So—thou art not evil? Thou art not come to contrive my murder?

[*As* LAZARUS *smilingly shakes his head,* TIBERIUS *frowns*]

Then why dost thou laugh against Cæsar?

[*Then bitterly—with a twisted attempt at a smile*]

Yet I like thy laughter. It is young. Once I laughed somewhat like that—so I pardon thee. I will even laugh at thee in return. Ha-ha! 10

[*His laughter is cold, cruel and merciless as the grin of a skeleton*]

CALIGULA

[*Who has been staring in a bewildered stupor from* TIBERIUS, *whom he thought he had killed, to the body of* FLAVIUS—*quaking with terror now as if this laugh was meant for him, drops to his knees, his sword clattering down the steps to the floor*]

Mercy, Tiberius! I implore you forgive your Caligula! 20

TIBERIUS

[*Not understanding. Fixing his eyes on* CALIGULA *with a malevolent irony*]

Come down from my throne, Caligula.

[CALIGULA *slinks down warily*]

You are too impatient. But I must pardon you, too—for where could I find another heir so perfect for serving my spite upon mankind?

[*He has walked toward the throne while he is speaking,* CALIGULA *backing away from him.* LAZARUS *remains where he is,* MIRIAM *beside and to the rear of him.* TIBERIUS, *his eyes fixed on* CALIGULA, *stumbles against the body of* FLAVIUS. *He gives a startled gasp and shrinks back, calling*] 30

Lights! A light here!

[*A crowd of masked slaves obey his orders. One runs to him with a lantern. He looks down at* FLAVIUS' *corpse—half to himself*]

I did wisely to stand him in my place.

[*To* CALIGULA—*with sinister emphasis*]

Too impatient, my loving grandchild! Take care lest I become impatient also—with your impatience!

[CALIGULA *shudders and backs away to the extreme left corner, front, where he crouches on his haunches as inconspicuously as possible.* TIBERIUS *suddenly whirls around as if he felt a dagger at his back*]

TIBERIUS

Where—?

[*Seeing* LAZARUS *where he had been— with relief—staring at his face now that the room is flooded with the purplish-crimson glow from all the lamps*]

Ah, you are there. More lights! Darkness leads men into error. My heir mistakes a man for Cæsar and Cæsar, it appears, has mistaken a man for a dæmon!

[*Scrutinizing him—with sinister finality*]

I can deal with men. I know them well. Too well!

[*He laughs grimly*]

Therefore I hate them.

[*He mounts the steps of the dais and sits on the couch at left of table—staring at* LAZARUS, *wonderingly*]

But you seem—something other than man! That light!

[*Then he forces a harsh laugh*]

A trick! I had forgotten you are a magician.

[*Arrogantly*]

Stand there, Jew. I would question you about your magic.

[*Smilingly* LAZARUS *ascends to where* TIBERIUS *points at the top of the dais.* MIRIAM *remains standing at the foot.* TIBERIUS *stares for a while with somber intensity at* LAZARUS]

They say you died and have returned from death?

LAZARUS

[*Smiling—as if he were correcting a child*]

There is no death, Cæsar.

TIBERIUS

[*With a sneer of scepticism but with an underlying eagerness*]

I have heard you teach that folly.
[*Then threateningly*]
You shall be given full opportunity to prove it!
[*A pause—then in a low voice, bending down toward* LAZARUS]
Do you foretell the future?
[*Trembling but with a pretense of carelessness*]
Must I die soon?

LAZARUS

[*Simply*]

Yes, Cæsar.

TIBERIUS

[*Jumping up with a shuddering start*]

Soon? Soon?
[*Then his fear turning to rage*]
What do you say? Vile Jew, do you dare threaten me with death!
[LAZARUS, *looking into his eyes, begins to laugh softly.* TIBERIUS *sinks back on his couch, fighting to control himself—confusedly*]
Laugh not, I ask you. I am old. It is not seemly.
[LAZARUS *ceases his low laughter. A pause.* TIBERIUS *broods—then suddenly*]
And you were really dead?
[*He shudders*]
Come nearer. I need to watch your face. I have learned to read the lies in faces. A Cæsar gets much practice—from childhood on—too much!
[*With awe*]
Your eyes are dark with death. While I watch them, answer me, what cured thee of death?

LAZARUS

[*Gently*]

There is only life, Cæsar.
[*Then gaily mocking but compellingly*]
And laughter! Look! Look well into my eyes, old Reader of Lies, and see if you can find aught in them that is not life—and laughter!

[*He laughs softly. A ripple of soft laughter from the motionless figures about the room echoes his.* TIBERIUS *stares into his eyes. In the silence that ensues* POMPEIA *gets up and walks over to the dais. She stops to stare for a moment with cruel contempt at* MIRIAM, *then stands and looks up at* LAZARUS, *trying in vain to attract his or* CÆSAR'S *attention. Failing in this, she passes over and sits beside* CALIGULA, *whose attention is concentrated on* LAZARUS]

POMPEIA

I admire your strange magician, Caligula.

CALIGULA

[*Without looking at her*]

He is no magician. He is something like a god.

POMPEIA

[*Longingly*]

His laughter is like a god's. He is strong. I love him.

CALIGULA

[*Turning to her—coarsely*]

Do not waste your lust. He is faithful to his wife, I warn you.

POMPEIA

[*She points to* MIRIAM]

Not that ugly slave?

CALIGULA

Yes. And yet, on our journey, whole herds of women—and many as beautiful as you, Pompeia—threw themselves on him and begged for his love.

POMPEIA

[*Her voice hardening*]

And he?

CALIGULA

He laughed—and passed on.
[*She starts.* CALIGULA *goes on wonderingly*]

But they seemed as happy as if his laughter had possessed them! You are a woman. Tell me, how could that be?

POMPEIA

[*Her voice cruel*]

He shall not laugh at me!

CALIGULA

[*Tauntingly*]

I will bet a string of pearls against your body for a night that he does.

POMPEIA

[*Defiantly*]

Done!
[*Then she laughs—a low, cruel laugh—
staring at* MIRIAM]
So he loves that woman?

CALIGULA

[*Curiously*]

What are you planning?

POMPEIA

I shall offer her the fruit Cæsar preserves for those he fears.

CALIGULA

[*With a careless shrug*]

You will not win his love by killing her.

POMPEIA

I no longer want his love. I want to see him   20
suffer, to hear his laughter choke in his throat with pain!
[*She speaks with more and more volup-
tuous satisfaction*]
Then *I* shall laugh!
[*She laughs softly and steps forward*]

CALIGULA

[*Concernedly*]

Stop. I am his protector.
[*Then suddenly*]
But what is the Jewess to me?
[*With more and more of a spirit of per-
verse cruelty*]
Do it, Pompeia! His laughter is too cruel to us! We must save death from him!

POMPEIA

[*Walks to the dais which she ascends
slowly until she stands by* CÆSAR'S
couch behind him, confronting LAZ-
ARUS. *But the two men remain unmindful of her presence.* TIBERIUS
continues to stare into LAZARUS' *eyes.
His whole body is now relaxed, at
rest, a dreamy smile softens his thin,
compressed mouth.* POMPEIA *leans
over and takes a peach from the bowl
of fruit on* CÆSAR'S *table and, taking*
TIBERIUS' *hand in her other, she
kisses it and calls insistently*]

Cæsar. It is I, Pompeia.
[LAZARUS *does not look at her. She
stares at him defiantly.* TIBERIUS
blinks his eyes in a daze]

TIBERIUS

[*Dreamily*]

10   Yes! A cloud came from a depth of sky—around me, softly, warmly, and the cloud dissolved into the sky, and the sky into peace!
[*Suddenly springing to his feet and star-
ing about him in a confused rage—
clutching* POMPEIA *by the shoulder
and forcing her to her knees*]
What are you doing here?

POMPEIA

Forgive your loving slave! I grew afraid this magician had put you under a spell.
[*She stares at* LAZARUS, *her words chal-
lenging him*]

TIBERIUS

[*Confusedly, sinking back on his couch
and releasing her*]

A spell? Could it be he laid a dream of death upon me, leading me to death?
[*He trembles timorously—appealing to*
LAZARUS]
Whatever magic thou didst to me, Dæmon, I beseech thee undo it!

LAZARUS

[*Smiling*]

30   Do you fear peace?

POMPEIA

[*Harshly and insolently*]

Mock not at Cæsar, dog!

[LAZARUS *continues to smile. His eyes remain on* CÆSAR. *He seems absolutely unaware of* POMPEIA. *This enrages her the more against him. She speaks tauntingly to* TIBERIUS]

Surely, Cæsar, this magician must have powerful charms since he dares to mock Tiberius to his face!

TIBERIUS

[*Stung*]

Be still!

[*Then in a low tone to her*]

Do you not know this Lazarus died and 10 then by his magic rose from his tomb?

POMPEIA

[*Scornfully*]

To believe that, I must have seen it, Cæsar!

TIBERIUS

[*Impatiently*]

Do you think I would believe without good evidence? I have had them take the statements of many witnesses. The miracle was 20 done in conjunction with another Jew acting as this man's tool. This other Jew, the report states, could not possibly have possessed any magic power Himself, for Pilate crucified Him a short time after and He died in pain and weakness within a few hours. But this Lazarus laughs at death!

LAZARUS

[*Looks up, smiling with ironical bitterness*]

Couldst Thou but hear, Jesus! And men shall keep on in panic nailing Man's soul 30 to the cross of their fear until in the end they do it to avenge Thee, for Thine Honor and Glory!

[*He sighs sadly—then after a struggle overcoming himself—with exultance*]

Yes!

[*His eyes fall again to* TIBERIUS *and he smiles*]

Yes! Yes to the stupid as to the wise! To what is understood and to what cannot be understood! Known and unknown! Over and over! Forever and ever! Yes!

[*He laughs softly to himself*]

TIBERIUS

[*With superstitious dread*]

What dost thou mean, Dæmon?

POMPEIA

[*With indignant scorn*]

Let him prove there is no death, Cæsar!

[*She appeals to the company who straighten up on their couches with interest*]

CHORUS

[*Chant demandingly*]

Let him prove there is no death!
We are bored!

CROWD

[*Echoing*]

Prove there is no death!
We are bored, Cæsar!

TIBERIUS

[*Waits to see what* LAZARUS *will say—then as he says nothing, plucking up his courage—his cruelty aroused*]

Do you hear, Lazarus?

POMPEIA

Make him perform his miracle again!

CHORUS

[*As before*]

Let him perform a miracle!
We are bored, Cæsar!

CROWD

[*They now stand up and coming from behind their tables, move forward toward the dais*]

A miracle!
We are bored!

POMPEIA

Let him raise someone from the dead!

CHORUS

[*Chanting with a pettish insistence*]

Raise the dead!
We are bored!

CROWD

[*Echoing—grouping in a big semicircle as of spectators in a theatre, around and to the sides of the dais, one sex on each side. CALIGULA moves in from the left in front of them. They form in three ranks, the first squatting on their hams like savages (as CALIGULA does), the second rank crouching over them, the third leaning over the second, all with a hectic, morbid interest*]

10

We are bored!
Raise the dead!

POMPEIA

[*With a cruel smile*]

I have thought of a special test for him, Cæsar.
[*She whispers in CÆSAR'S ear and points to MIRIAM and the fruit in her hand*] 20
And he must laugh!

TIBERIUS

[*With a harsh, cruel chuckle*]

Yes, I shall command him to laugh!
[*Then disgustedly*]
But she is sad and old. I will be only doing him a favor.

CALIGULA

[*Rocking back and forth on his haunches—looking at LAZARUS with taunting cruelty*] 30

No, Cæsar! I know he loves her!

LAZARUS

Yes!
[*He steps down from the dais to MIRIAM'S side and taking her head in*

both his hands, he kisses her on the lips]

TIBERIUS

[*With a malignant grin*]

Give her the fruit!

POMPEIA

[*Advances and offers the peach to MIRIAM—with a hard, cruel little laugh*]

Cæsar invites you to eat!

MIRIAM

[*To LAZARUS—requesting meekly but longingly*]

May I accept, Lazarus? Is it time at last? My love has followed you over long roads among strangers and each league we came from home my heart has grown older. Now it is too old for you, a heart too weary for your loving laughter. Ever your laughter has grown younger, Lazarus! Upward it springs like a lark from a field, and sings! Once I knew your laughter was my child, my son of Lazarus; but then it grew younger and I felt at last it had returned to my womb—and ever younger and younger—until, tonight, when I spoke to you of home, I felt new birth-pains as your laughter, grown too young for me, flew back to the unborn—a birth so like a death!
[*She sobs and wipes her eyes with her sleeve—then humbly, reaching out for the fruit*]
May I accept it, Lazarus? You should have newborn laughing hearts to love you. My old one labors with memories and its blood is sluggish with the past. Your home on the hills of space is too far away. My heart longs for the warmth of close walls of earth baked in the sun. Our home in Bethany, Lazarus, where you and my children lived and died. Our tomb near our home, Lazarus, in which you and my children wait for me. Is it time at last?

LAZARUS

[*Deeply moved*]

Poor lonely heart! It has been crueler for you than I remembered. Go in peace—to peace!
[*His voice trembles in spite of himself*]

I shall be lonely, dear one.
[*With a note of pleading*]
You have never laughed with my laughter.
Will you call back—Yes!—when you know
—to tell me you understand and laugh with
me at last?

MIRIAM

[*Not answering him, to* POMPEIA, *taking
the peach and making a humble courtesy before her*]

I thank you, pretty lady.
[*She raises the peach toward her mouth.
Involuntarily one of* LAZARUS' *hands
half-reaches out as if to stop her*]

POMPEIA

[*With savage triumph, pointing*]

See! He would stop her! He is afraid of
death!

CHORUS

[*Pointing—jeeringly*]

He is afraid of death! Ha-ha-ha-ha!

CROWD

[*Jeeringly*]

Ha-ha-ha-ha!

MIRIAM

[*Bites into the peach and, chewing, begins, as if immediately affected, to
talk like a garrulous old woman, her
words coming quicker and quicker as
her voice becomes fainter and fainter*]

Say what you like, it is much better I should
go home first, Lazarus. We have been away
so long, there will be so much to attend to
about the house. And all the children will
be waiting. You would be as helpless as a
child, Lazarus. Between you and the children, things would soon be in a fine state!
[*More and more confused*]
No, no! You cannot help me, dearest one.
You are only in my way. No, I will make
the fire. When you laid it the last time, we
all had to run for our lives, choking, the
smoke poured from the windows, the
neighbors thought the house was burning!
[*She laughs—a queer, vague little inward laugh*]

You are so impractical. The neighbors all
get the best of you. Money slips through
your fingers. If it was not for me—
[*She sighs—then brightly and lovingly*]
But, dearest husband, why do you take it
so to heart? Why do you feel guilty because
you are not like other men? That is why
I love you so much. Is it a sin to be born a
dreamer? But God, He must be a dreamer,
too, or how would we be on earth? Do not
keep saying to yourself so bitterly, you are
a failure in life! Do not sit brooding on the
hilltop in the evening like a black figure of
Job against the sky!
[*Her voice trembling*]
Even if God has taken our little ones—yes,
in spite of sorrow—have you not a good
home I make for you, and a wife who loves
you?
[*She forces a chuckle*]
Be grateful, then—for me! Smile, my sad
one! Laugh a little once in a while! Come
home, bringing me laughter of the wind
from the hills!
[*Swaying, looking at the peach in her
hand*]
What a mellow, sweet fruit! Did you bring
it home for me?
[*She falls back into his arms. Gently
he lets her body sink until it rests
against the steps of the dais.* TIBERIUS
*rises from his couch to bend over with
cruel gloating.* POMPEIA *steps nearer
to* LAZARUS, *staring at him mockingly.*
CALIGULA *hops to her side, looking
from* LAZARUS *to* MIRIAM. *The half-
circle of masked figures moves closer,
straining forward and downward as if
to overwhelm the two figures at the
foot of the dais with their concentrated death wish*]

TIBERIUS

[*Thickly*]

She is dead, and I do not hear you laugh!

LAZARUS

[*Bending down—supplicatingly*]

Miriam! Call back to me! Laugh!
[*He pauses. A second of dead silence.
Then, with a sound that is very like a
sob, he kisses her on the lips*]
I am lonely!

POMPEIA

[*With savage malice—jeeringly*]

See! He weeps, Cæsar!
[*She bursts into strident laughter*]
Ha-ha-ha-ha!

CHORUS

[*Echoing her laughter*]

Ha-ha-ha-ha!
There is fear!
There is death!

CROWD

There is death!
Ha-ha-ha-ha!

CALIGULA

[*In a frenzy of despairing rage, hopping up and down*]

Liar! Charlatan! Weakling! How you have cheated Caligula!
[*He suddenly slaps* LAZARUS *viciously across the face*]
There is death! Laugh, if you dare!   10

TIBERIUS

[*Standing—in a sinister cold rage, the crueler because his dream of a cure for death is baffled, yet feeling his power as* CÆSAR *triumphant nevertheless*]

And I thought you might be a dæmon. I thought you might have a magic cure—
[*With revengeful fury*]
But death is, and death is mine! I shall make you pray for death! And I shall make Death laugh at you! Ha-ha-ha-ha!
[*In a frenzy as* LAZARUS *neither makes a sound nor looks up*]   20
Laugh, Lazarus! Laugh at yourself! Laugh with me!
[*Then to his soldiers*]
Scourge him! Make him laugh!

CALIGULA

[*Running to soldiers—fiercely*]

Give me a scourge!

POMPEIA

[*Running to the soldiers—hysterically*]

Ha-ha-ha-ha! Let me beat him, Cæsar!

[*They group behind him. The rods and scourges are uplifted over his back to strike, when in the dead expectant silence,* MIRIAM'S *body is seen to rise in a writhing tortured last effort*]

MIRIAM

[*In a voice of unearthly sweetness*]

Yes! There is only life! Lazarus, be not lonely!
[*She laughs and sinks back and is still*]
[*A shuddering murmur of superstitious fear comes from them as they shrink back swiftly from* LAZARUS, *remaining huddled one against the other.* POMPEIA *runs to the feet of* TIBERIUS *and crouches down on the steps below him, as if for protection, her terrified eyes on* MIRIAM. CALIGULA *runs to her and crouches beside and beneath her*]

LAZARUS

[*Kisses* MIRIAM *again and raises his head. His face is radiant with new faith and joy. He smiles with happiness and speaks to himself with a mocking affection as if to an amusing child*]

That much remained hidden in me of the sad old Lazarus who died of self-pity—his loneliness! Lonely no more! Man's loneliness is but his fear of life! Lonely no more! Millions of laughing stars there are around me! And laughing dust, born once of woman on this earth, now freed to dance! New stars are born of dust eternally! The old, grown mellow with God, burst into flaming seed! The fields of infinite space are sown—and grass for sheep springs up on the hills of earth! But there is no death, nor fear, nor loneliness! There is only God's Eternal Laughter! His Laughter flows into the lonely heart!
[*He begins to laugh, his laughter clear and ringing—the laughter of a conqueror arrogant with happiness and the pride of a new triumph. He bends and picks up the body of* MIRIAM *in his arms and, his head thrown back, laughing, he ascends the dais and places her on the table as on a bier. He touches one hand on her breast, as*

if he were taking an oath to life on her heart, looks upward and laughs, his voice ringing more and more with a terrible unbearable power and beauty that beats those in the room into an abject submissive panic]

[TIBERIUS grovels half under the table, his hands covering his ears, his face on the floor; he is laughing with the agony and terror of death. POMPEIA lies face down on the first step and beats it with her fists; she is laughing with horror and self-loathing. CA-LIGULA, his hands clutching his head, pounds it against the edge of the steps; he is laughing with grief and remorse. The rest, soldiers, slaves and the prostitutes of both sexes, writhe and twist distractedly, seeking to hide their heads against each other, beat-ing each other and the floor with clenched hands. An agonized moan of supplicating laughter comes from them all]

ALL

Ha-ha-ha-ha! Ha-ha-ha-ha!
Let us die, Lazarus!
Mercy, Laughing One!
Mercy of death!
Ha-ha-ha-ha! Ha-ha-ha-ha!
[But the laughter of LAZARUS is as re-mote now as the laughter of a god]

CURTAIN

ACT FOUR
SCENE ONE

SCENE: The same as previous Scene—the same night a short while later. All the lamps are out except the one on the table on the dais which, placed beside the head of MIRIAM, shines down upon the white mask of her face. In the half-darkness, the walls are lost in shadow, the room seems immense, the dais nearer.

LAZARUS sits on the couch at the right on the dais. His face is strong and proud although his eyes are fixed down on the face of MIRIAM. He seems more youthful still now, like a young son who keeps watch by the body of his mother, but at the same time retaining the aloof serenity of the statue of

a god. His face expresses sorrow and a happiness that transcends sorrow.

On the other side of the table, at the end of the couch, TIBERIUS sits facing front, his elbows on his knees, his large hands with bloated veins hanging loosely. He keeps his gaze averted from the corpse. He talks to LAZARUS half over his shoulder.

On the top step, POMPEIA sits, facing right, her hands clasped about one knee, the other leg stretched down to the lower step. Her head is thrown back and she is gazing up into LAZARUS' face.

On the step below her, CALIGULA squats on his haunches, his arms on his knees, his fists pressed to his temples. He is staring straight before him.

Only these four people are in the room now.

TIBERIUS

[Gloomily]

Was she dead, Dæmon, and was it thy power that recalled life to her body for that moment? Or was she still living and her words only the last desire of her love to comfort you, Lazarus?
[LAZARUS does not repy]
If thou dost not tell me, I must always doubt thee, Dæmon.

POMPEIA

[With a sigh of bewildered happiness, turns to CALIGULA]

10   I am glad he laughed, Caligula! Did I say I loved him before? Then it was only my body that wanted a slave. Now it is my heart that desires a master! Now I know love for the first time in my life!

CALIGULA

[Bitterly]

Fool! What does he care for love?
[Somberly]
He loves everyone—but no one—not even me!
[He broods frowningly]

POMPEIA

[Following her own thoughts]

And now that hag is dead he will need a woman, young and beautiful, to protect and comfort him, to make him a home and bear his children!

[*She dreams, her eyes again fixed on* LAZARUS—*then suddenly turning to* CALIGULA]

I am glad I lost our bet. But you must accept some other payment. Now I know love, I may not give myself to any man save him!

CALIGULA

I do not want you! What are you but another animal! Faugh!

[*With a grimace of disgust*]

Pleasure is dirty and joyless! Or we who seek it are, which comes to the same thing.

[*Then grimly*]

But our bet can rest. This is not the end. There may still be a chance for you to laugh at him!

POMPEIA

No! Now I could not! I should weep for his defeat!

TIBERIUS

[*Gloomily arguing, half to himself*]

His laughter triumphed over me, but he has not brought her back to life. I think he knows no cure for another's death, as I had hoped. And I must always doubt that it was not some trick—

[*Harshly*]

until I have tested him with his own life! He cannot cheat me then!

[*A pause—arguing to himself*]

But he was dead—that much has been proved—and before he died he was old and sad. What did he find beyond there?

[*Suddenly—turning to* LAZARUS *now*]

What did you find beyond death, Lazarus?

LAZARUS

[*Exaltedly*]

Life! God's Eternal Laughter!

TIBERIUS

[*Shaking his head*]

I want hope—for me, Tiberius Cæsar.

LAZARUS

What is—you? But there is hope for Man! Love is Man's hope—love for his life on earth, a noble love above suspicion and distrust! Hitherto Man has always suspected his life, and in revenge and self-torture his love has been faithless! He has even betrayed Eternity, his mother, with his slave he calls Immortal Soul!

[*He laughs softly, gaily, mockingly—then to* TIBERIUS *directly*]

Hope for you, Tiberius Cæsar? Then dare to love Eternity without your fear desiring to possess her! Be brave enough to be possessed!

TIBERIUS

[*Strangely*]

My mother was the wife of Cæsar.

[*Then dully*]

I do not understand.

LAZARUS

Men are too cowardly to understand! And so the worms of their little fears eat them and grow fat and terrible and become their jealous gods they must appease with lies!

TIBERIUS

[*Wearily*]

Your words are meaningless, Lazarus. You are a fool. All laughter is malice, all gods are dead, and life is a sickness.

LAZARUS

[*Laughs pityingly*]

So say the race of men, whose lives are long dyings! They evade their fear of death by becoming so sick of life that by the time death comes they are too lifeless to fear it! Their disease triumphs over death—a noble victory called resignation! 'We are sick,' they say, 'therefore there is no God in us, therefore there is no God!' Oh, if men would but interpret that first cry of man fresh from the womb as the laughter of one who even then says to his heart, 'It is my pride as God to become Man. Then let it be my pride as Man to recreate the God in me!'

[*He laughs softly but with exultant pride*]

POMPEIA

[*Laughing with him—proudly*]

He will create a god in me! I shall be proud!

CALIGULA

[*Pounding his temples with his fists—tortured*]

I am Caligula. I was born in a camp among soldiers. My father was Germanicus, a hero, as all men know. But I do not understand this—and though I burst with pride, I cannot laugh with joy!

TIBERIUS

[*Gloomily*]

Obscurities! I have found nothing in life that merits pride. I am not proud of being Cæsar—and what is a god but a Cæsar over Cæsars? If fools kneel and worship me because they fear me, should I be proud? But Cæsar is a fact, and Tiberius, a man, is one, and I cling to these certainties—and I do not wish to die! If I were sure of eternal sleep beyond there, deep rest and forgetfulness of all I have ever seen or heard or hated or loved on earth, I would gladly die! But surely, Lazarus, nothing is sure— peace the least sure of all—and I fear there is no rest beyond there, that one remembers there as here and cannot sleep, that the mind goes on eternally the same—a long insomnia of memories and regrets and the ghosts of dreams one has poisoned to death passing with white bodies spotted by the leprous fingers of one's lusts.

[*Bitterly*]

I fear the long nights now in which I lie awake and listen to Death dancing round me in the darkness, prancing to the drum beat of my heart!

[*He shudders*]

And I am afraid, Lazarus—afraid that there is no sleep beyond there, either!

LAZARUS

There is peace!

[*His words are like a benediction he pronounces upon them. Soothed in a mysterious, childlike way, they repeat the word after him, wonderingly*]

POMPEIA

Peace?

CALIGULA

Peace?

TIBERIUS

Peace?

[*For a long moment there is complete silence. Then TIBERIUS sighs heavily, shaking his head*]

Peace! Another word blurred into a senseless sigh by men's longing! A bubble of froth blown from the lips of the dying toward the stars! No!

[*He grins bitterly—then looks at LAZARUS—somberly contemptuous and threatening*]

You are pleased to act the mysterious, Jew, but I shall solve you!

[*Then with a lawyer-like incisiveness*]

There is one certainty about you and I must know the cause—for there must be a cause and a rational explanation! You were fifty when you died—

LAZARUS

[*Smiling mockingly*]

Yes. When I died.

TIBERIUS

[*Unheeding*]

And now your appearance is of one younger by a score. Not alone your appearance! You *are* young. I see the fact, the effect. And I demand an explanation of the cause without mystic nonsense or evasion.

[*Threateningly*]

And I warn you to answer directly in plain words—and not to laugh, you understand! —not to dare!—or I shall lose patience with you and—

[*With a grim smile*]

I can be terrible!

[*LAZARUS smiles gently at him. He turns away with confused annoyance, then back to LAZARUS, resuming his lawyer-like manner*]

What was it restored your youth? How did you contrive that your body reversed the natural process and grows younger? Is it a charm by which you invoke a supernatural force? Or is it a powder you dissolve in wine? Or a liquid? Or an unguent you rub into the skin to revitalize the old bones and tissues? Or—what is it, Lazarus?

LAZARUS

[*Gently*]

I know that age and time are but timidities of thought.

TIBERIUS

[*Broodingly—as if he had not heard—persuasively*]

Perhaps you ask yourself, what would Tiberius do with youth? Then, because you must have heard rumors of my depravity, you will conclude the old lecher desires youth for his lusts!

[*He laughs harshly*]

Ha! Why, do not my faithful subjects draw pictures of an old buck goat upon the walls   10 and write above them, Cæsar? And they are just. In self-contempt of Man I have made this man, myself, the most swinish and contemptible of men! Yes! In all this empire there is no man so base a hog as I!

[*He grins bitterly and ironically*]

My claim to this excellence, at least, is not contested! Everyone admits therein Tiberius is by right their Cæsar!

[*He laughs bitterly*]

Ha! So who would believe Tiberius if he   20 said, I want youth again because I loathe lust and long for purity!

LAZARUS

[*Gently*]

I believe you, Cæsar.

TIBERIUS

[*Stares at him—deeply moved*]

You—believe—?

[*Then gruffly*]

You lie! You are not mad—and only a madman would believe another man!

[*Then confidingly, leaning over toward* LAZARUS]

I know it is folly to speak—but—one gets old, one becomes talkative, one wishes to confess, to say the thing one has always   40 kept hidden, to reveal one's unique truth—and there is so little time left—and one is alone! Therefore the old—like children—talk to themselves, for they have reached that hopeless wisdom of experience which knows that though one were to cry it in the streets to multitudes, or whisper it in the kiss to one's beloved, the only ears that can ever hear one's secret are one's own!

[*He laughs bitterly*]

And so I talk aloud, Lazarus! I talk to my   50 loneliness!

LAZARUS

[*Simply*]

I hear, Tiberius.

TIBERIUS

[*Again moved and confused—forcing a mocking smile*]

Liar! Eavesdropper! You merely—listen!

[*Then he turns away*]

My mother, Livia, that strong woman, giving birth to me, desired not a child, but a Cæsar—just as, married to Augustus, she loved him not but loved herself as Cæsar's wife. She made me feel, in the proud questioning of her scornful eyes, that to win her mother love I must become Cæsar. She poisoned Prince Marcellus and young Gaius and Lucius that the way might be clear for me. I used to see their blood dance in red specks before my eyes when   20 I looked at the sky. Now—

[*He brushes his hand before his eyes*]

it is all a red blot! I cannot distinguish. There have been too many. My mother—her blood is in that blot, for I revenged myself on her. I did not kill her, it is true, but I deprived her of her power and she died, as I knew she must, that powerful woman who bore me as a weapon! The murder was subtle and cruel—how cruel   30 only that passionate, deep-breasted woman unslaked by eighty years of devoured desires could know! Too cruel! I did not go to her funeral. I was afraid her closed eyes might open and look at me!

[*Then with almost a cry*]

I want youth, Lazarus, that I may play again about her feet with the love I felt for her before I learned to read her eyes!

[*He half sobs, bowing his head. A pause*]

CALIGULA

[*Nudging* POMPEIA—*with a crafty whisper*]

Do you hear? The old lecher talks to himself. He is becoming senile. He will soon die. And I shall be Cæsar. Then I shall laugh!

POMPEIA

[*Staring up at* LAZARUS' *face, hearing*

only CALIGULA'S *words without their meaning*]

No. My Lazarus does not laugh now. See. His mouth is silent—and a little sad, I think.

LAZARUS

[*Gently and comfortingly*]

I hear, Tiberius.

TIBERIUS

[*Harshly*]

I hated that woman, my mother, and I still hate her! Have you ever loved, Lazarus?
    [*Then with a glance at MIRIAM'S body and a shuddering away from it—vaguely*]
I was forgetting her. I killed your love, too, did I not? Well, I must! I envy those who are loved. Where I can, I kill love—for retribution's sake—but much of it escapes me.
    [*Then harshly again*]
I loved Agrippina. We were married. A son was born to us. We were happy. Then that proud woman, my mother, saw my happiness. Was she jealous of my love? Or did she know no happy man would wish to be Cæsar? Well, she condemned my happiness to death. She whispered to Augustus and he ordered me to divorce Agrippina. I should have opened her veins and mine, and died with her. But my mother stayed by me, Agrippina was kept away, my mother spoke to me and spoke to me and even wept, that tall woman, strong as a great man, and I consented that my love be murdered. Then my mother married me to a whore. Why? The whore was Cæsar's daughter, true—but I feel that was not all of it, that my mother wished to keep me tortured that I might love her alone and long to be Cæsar!
    [*He laughs harshly*]
Ha! In brief, I married the whore, she tortured me, my mother's scheming prospered—that subtle and crafty woman!—and many years passed in being here and there, in doing this and that, in growing full of hate and revengeful ambition to be Cæsar. At last, Augustus died. I was Cæsar. Then I killed that whore, my wife,

and I starved my mother's strength to death until she died, and I began to take pleasure in vengeance upon men, and pleasure in taking vengeance on myself.
    [*He grins horribly*]
It is all very simple, as you see!
    [*He suddenly starts to his feet—with harsh arrogance and pride, threateningly*]
Enough! Why do I tell you these old tales? Must I explain to you why I want youth? It is my whim! I am Cæsar! And now I must lie down and try to sleep! And it is my command that you reveal the secret of your youth to me when I awake, or else—
    [*With malignant cruelty*]
I will have to revenge the death of a hope on you—and a hope at my age demands a terrible expiation on its slayer!
    [*He walks down and starts to go off, right—then turns and addresses LAZARUS with grim irony*]
Good night to you, Lazarus. And remember there shall be death while I am Cæsar!
    [*He turns to go*]

LAZARUS

[*Smiling affectionately at him, shakes his head*]

Cæsar must believe in death. But does the husband of Agrippina?

TIBERIUS

[*Stops short and stares at LAZARUS, confused and stuttering*]

What—what—do you mean, Lazarus?

LAZARUS

I have heard your loneliness.

TIBERIUS

[*Cruelly and grimly again*]

So much the more reason why my pride should kill you! Remember that!
    [*He turns and strides off into the darkness at right*]

CALIGULA

[*Peers after him until sure he is gone—then gets up and begins o grotesque, hopping dance, singing a verse of the legionary's song*]

A bold legionary am I
March, oh march on!
A Roman eagle was my daddy
My mother was a drunken drabby
Oh march on to the wars!

[*He laughs gratingly, posturing and gesticulating up at* LAZARUS]

Ha-ha-ha! He is gone! I can breathe! His breath in the same air suffocates me! The gods grant mine do the same for him! But he is failing! He talks to himself like a man in second childhood. His words are a thick babble I could not hear. They well from his lips like clots of blood from a reopened wound. I kept listening to the beating of his heart. It sounded slow, slower than when I last heard it. Did you detect that, Lazarus? Once or twice I thought it faltered—

[*He draws in his breath with an avid gasp—then laughs gratingly*]

Ha-ha-ha—

[*Grandiloquently*]

Tiberius, the old buck goat, will soon be gone, my friends, and in his place you will be blessed with the beautiful young god, Caligula! Hail to Caligula! Hail! Ha-ha-ha—

[*His laughter suddenly breaks off into a whimper and he stands staring around him in a panic of fear that he has been overheard. He slinks noiselessly up the steps of the dais and squats coweringly at* LAZARUS' *feet, blinking up at his face in monkey-wise, clutching* LAZARUS' *hand in both of his. His teeth can be heard chattering together in nervous fear*]

[POMPEIA, *whose gaze has remained fixed on* LAZARUS' *throughout, has gradually moved closer to him until she, too, is at his feet, half-kneeling beneath the table on which* MIRIAM *lies, side by side with* CALIGULA *but as oblivious of him as he is of her*]

[*Having grown calmer now,* CALIGULA *speaks again—mournful and bewildered*]

CALIGULA

Why should I love you, Lazarus? Your laughter taunts me! It insults Cæsar! It denies Rome! But I will warn you again. Escape! Tonight Tiberius' mood is to play sentimental, but tomorrow he will jeer while hyenas gnaw at your skull and lick your brain. And then—there is pain, Lazarus! There is pain!

POMPEIA

[*Pressing her hand to her own heart—with a shudder*]

Yes, there is pain!

LAZARUS

[*Smiling down on them—gently*]

If you can answer Yes to pain, there is no pain!

POMPEIA

[*Passionately*]

Yes! Yes! I love Lazarus!

CALIGULA

[*With a bitter grin*]

Do not take pain away from us! It is our one truth. Without pain there is nothing—a nothingness in which even your laughter, Lazarus, is swallowed at one gulp like a whining gnat by the cretin's silence of immensity! Ha-ha! No, we must keep pain! Especially Cæsar must! Pain must twinkle with a mad mirth in a Cæsar's eyes—men's pain—or they would become dissatisfied and disrespectful! Ha-ha!

[*He stops his grating laughter abruptly and continues mournfully*]

I am sick, Lazarus, sick of cruelty and lust and human flesh and all the imbecilities of pleasure—the unclean antics of half-witted children!

[*With a mounting agony of longing*]

I would be clean! If I could only laugh your laughter, Lazarus! That would purify my heart. For I could wish to love all men, as you love them—as I love you! If only I did not fear them and despise them! If I could only believe—believe in them—in life—in myself!—believe that one man or woman in the world knew and loved the real Caligula—then I might have faith in Caligula myself—then I might laugh your laughter!

LAZARUS

[*Suddenly, in a quiet but compelling voice*]

I, who know you, love you, Caligula.
[*Gently patting his head*]
I love Caligula.

CALIGULA

[*Staring up at him in pathetic confusion*]

You? You? You, Lazarus?
[*He begins to tremble all over as if in a seizure—chokingly*]
Beware! It is not good—not just—to make fun of me—to laugh at my misery—saying you love—
[*In a frenzy, he jumps to his feet threatening LAZARUS*]
Are you trying to fool me, hypocrite? Do you think I have become so abject that you dare—? Because I love you, do you presume—? Do you think I am your slave, dog of a Jew, that you can—insult—to my face—the heir of Cæsar—
[*He stutters and stammers with rage, hopping up and down grotesquely, shaking his fist at LAZARUS, who smiles at him affectionately as at a child in a tantrum*]

LAZARUS

[*Catching his eyes and holding them with his glance—calmly*]

Believe, Caligula!

CALIGULA

[*Again overcome—stuttering with strange terror*]

Believe? But I cannot! I must not! You cannot know me, if—You are a holy man! You are a god in a mortal body—you can laugh with joy to be alive—while I—Oh, no, you cannot love me! There is nothing in me at bottom but a despising and an evil eye! You cannot! You are only being kind!
[*Hysterically*]
I do not want your kindness! I hate your pity! I am too proud! I am too strong!
[*He collapses weepingly, kneeling and clutching LAZARUS' hand in both of his*]

LAZARUS

[*Smiling*]

You are so proud of being evil! What if there is no evil? What if there are only health and sickness? Believe in the healthy god called Man in you! Laugh at Caligula, the funny clown who beats the backside of his shadow with a bladder and thinks thereby he is Evil, the Enemy of God!
[*He suddenly lifts the face of CALIGULA and stares into his eyes*]
Believe! What if you are a man and men are despicable? Men are also unimportant! Men pass! Like rain into the sea! The sea remains! Man remains! Man slowly arises from the past of the race of men that was his tomb of death! For Man death is not! Man, Son of God's Laughter, *is*!
He begins to laugh triumphantly, staring deep into CALIGULA's eyes]
Is, Caligula! Believe in the laughing god within you!

CALIGULA

[*Bursting suddenly into choking, joyful laughter—like a visionary*]

I believe! I believe there is love even for Caligula! I can laugh—now—Lazarus! Free laughter! Clean! No sickness! No lust for death! My corpse no longer rots in my heart! The tomb is full of sunlight! I am alive! I who love Man, I who can love and laugh! Listen, Lazarus! I dream! When I am Cæsar, I will devote my power to your truth. I will decree that there must be kindness and love! I will make the Empire one great Blessed Isle! Rome shall know happiness, it shall believe in life, it shall learn to laugh your laughter, Lazarus, or I—
[*He raises his hand in an imperial autocratic gesture*]

LAZARUS

[*Gaily mocking*]

Or you will cut off its head?

CALIGULA

[*Fiercely*]

Yes! I will—!
[*Then meeting LAZARUS' eyes, he beats his head with his fists crazily*]
Forgive me! I forget! I forget!

LAZARUS

Go out under the sky! Let your heart climb on laughter to a star! Then make it iook down at earth, and watch Caligula commanding Life under pain of death to do his will!

[*He laughs*]

CALIGULA

[*Laughing*]

I will! I do! I laugh at him! Caligula is a trained ape, a humped cripple! Now I take him out under the sky, where I can watch his monkey tricks, where there is space for laughter and where this new joy, your love of me, may dance!

[*Laughing clearly and exultantly, he runs out through the arched doorway at rear*]

LAZARUS

[*Stops laughing—shaking his head, almost sadly*]

They forget! It is too soon for laughter!

[*Then grinning at himself*]

What, Lazarus? Are you too, thinking in terms of time, old fool so soon to reënter infinity?

[*He laughs with joyous self-mockery*]

POMPEIA

[*Who has crept to his feet, kisses his hand passionately*]

I love you, Lazarus!

LAZARUS

[*Stops laughing, and looks down at her gently*]

And I love you, woman.

POMPEIA

[*With a gasp of delight*]

You?

[*She stares up into his eyes doubtingly, raising her face toward his*]

Then—put your arms around me.

[*He does so, smiling gently*]

And hold me to you.

[*He presses her closer to him*]

And kiss me.

[*He kisses her on the forehead*]

No, on the lips!

[*He kisses her. She flings her arms about his neck passionately and kisses him again and again—then slowly draws away—remains looking into his eyes a long time, shrinking back from him with bewildered pain which speedily turns to rage and revengeful hatred*]

No! No! It is *my* love, not Love! I want you to know *my* love, to give me back love —for me—only for me—Pompeia—my body, my heart—me, a woman—not Woman, women! Do I love Man, men? I hate men! I love you, Lazarus—a man—a lover—a father to children! I want love— as you loved that woman there

[*She points to* MIRIAM]

that I poisoned for love of you! But did you love her—or just Woman, wife and mother of men?

[*She stares—then as if reading admission in his eyes, she springs to her feet*]

Liar! Cheat! Hypocrite! Thief!

[*Half hysterical with rage, pain and grief, she bends over* MIRIAM *and smoothes the hair back from her forehead*]

Poor wife! Poor woman! How he must have tortured you! Now I remember the pity in your eyes when you looked at me! Oh, how his soothing gray words must have pecked at the wound in your heart like doves with bloody beaks!

[*Then with sudden harshness*]

But perhaps you were too dull to understand, too poor and tired and ugly and old to care, too slavish—! Pah!

[*She turns away with contempt and faces* LAZARUS *with revengeful hatred*]

Did you think I would take her place—become your slave, wait upon you, give you love and passion and beauty in exchange for phrases about man and gods—you who are neither a man nor a god but a dead thing without desire! You dared to hope I would give my body, my love, to you!

[*She spits in his face and laughs harshly*]

You insolent fool! I shall punish you! You shall be tortured as you have tortured!

[*She laughs wildly—then steps down from the dais and goes off right, crying distractedly*]

Cæsar! This man has made you a fool before all the world! Torture him, Cæsar!
Now! Let the people witness! Send heralds
to wake them! Torture him, Cæsar, the
man who laughs at you! Ha-ha-ha-ha!

[*Her laughter is caught up by all the
GIRLS and YOUTHS of the palace,
who, as she disappears, led by their
CHORUS, pour in from each side of
the room and dance forward to group
themselves around the dais as in the
previous scene, staring at LAZARUS,
laughing cruelly, falsely, stridently*]

CHORUS

[*Tauntingly*]

Ha-ha-ha-ha!
Laugh now, Lazarus!   10
Let us see you laugh!
Ha-ha-ha-ha!

CROWD

[*Echoing*]

Ha-ha-ha-ha!
Ha-ha-ha-ha!

LAZARUS

[*Moves, and immediately there is silence.
He bends down and kisses MIRIAM
and picks her up in his arms. Talking
down to her face—with a tender smile*]

Farewell! You are home! And now I will
take your body home to earth! Space is
too far away, you said! Home in the earth!
There will be so much for you to do there!
Home! Earth!   20

[*His voice trembling a bit*]
Farewell, body of Miriam. My grief is a
lonely cry wailing in the home in my heart
that you have left forever!

[*Then exultantly*]
But what am I? Now your love has become
Eternal Love! Now, since your life passed,
I feel Eternal Life made nobler by your
selflessness! Love has grown purer! The
laughter of God is more profoundly tender!

[*He looks up in an ecstasy and descends
the dais, carrying her*]
Yes, that is it! That is it, my Miriam!

[*Laughing softly and tenderly, he walks
around the dais and carries the body
out through the doorway in rear*]

[*The CHORUS and YOUTHS and GIRLS
make way for him in awed silence—
then scurry around to right and left,
forming an aisle through which he
passes—then after he has gone out
through the arch, they close into a
semicircular group again, staring
after him, and a whisper of strange,
bewildered, tender laughter comes from
them*]

CHORUS

[*In this whisper*]

That is it!
Love is pure!
Laughter is tender!
Laugh!

CROWD

[*Echoing*]

Laugh! Laugh!

CURTAIN

ACT FOUR
SCENE TWO

SCENE: *The arena of an amphitheatre. It is
just before dawn of the same night. Cæsar's
throne is on the left at the extreme front,
facing right, turned a little toward front.
It is lighted by four immense lamps. In
front of the throne is a marble railing that
tops the wall that encloses the arena. In
the rear the towering pile of the circular
amphitheatre is faintly outlined in deeper
black against the dark sky.*

TIBERIUS *sits on the throne, his eyes fixed
on the middle of the arena off right, where,
bound to a high stake after he had been
tortured,* LAZARUS *is now being burnt alive
over a huge pile of faggots. The crackling
of the flames is heard. Their billowing rise
and fall is reflected on the masked faces
of the multitude who sit on the banked
tiers of marble behind and to the rear
of the throne, with their* CHORUS, *seven
men masked in Middle Age in the Servile,
Hypocritical type, grouped on each side
of the throne of Cæsar on a lower tier.
Half-kneeling before* TIBERIUS, *her chin
resting on her hands on top of the marble
rail,* POMPEIA *also stares at* LAZARUS.

*Before the curtain, the crackle of the flames
and an uproar of human voices from the
multitude, jeering, hooting, laughing at*
LAZARUS *in cruel mockery of his laughter.
This sound has risen to its greatest volume
as the curtain rises.*

CHORUS

[*Chanting mockingly*]

Ha-ha-ha-ha!
Burn and laugh!
Laugh now, Lazarus!
Ha-ha-ha-ha!

CROWD

[*Chanting with revengeful mockery*]

Ha-ha-ha-ha!

TIBERIUS

Who laughs now, Lazarus—thou or Cæsar?
Ha-ha—!
[*With awe*]
His flesh melts in the fire but his eyes
shine with peace!

POMPEIA

How he looks at me!
[*Averting her eyes with a shudder*]
Command them to put out his eyes, Cæsar!

TIBERIUS

[*Harshly*]

No. I want to read his eyes when they see
death!
[*Then averting his face—guiltily*]
He is looking at me, not you. I should not
have listened to your cries for his death.

POMPEIA

[*Turning to him again with a shudder
of agony—beseechingly*]

Have them put out his eyes, Cæsar! They
call to me!

TIBERIUS

[*As if not hearing her—to himself*]

Why do I feel remorse? His laughter dies
and is forgotten, and the hope it raised
dies—
[*With sudden excitement*]

And yet—he must know something—and
if he would—even now he could tell—
[*Suddenly rising to his feet he calls imploringly*]
Lazarus!

CHORUS

[*Chanting in a great imploring chorus
now*]
Lazarus!

CROWD

[*Echoing*]
Lazarus!

SOLDIER'S VOICE

[*Calling from off beside the stake*]

You had us gag him, Cæsar, so he might
not laugh. Shall we cut away the gag?

POMPEIA

[*In terror*]

No, Cæsar! He will laugh! And I will go to
him!
[*Desperately*]
He will laugh at you, Cæsar—and the mob
will laugh with him!

TIBERIUS

[*Struggles with himself—then calls*]

Lazarus! If you hear let your eyes answer,
and I will grant the mercy of death to end
your agony! Is there hope of love somewhere for men on earth?

CHORUS

[*Intoning as before*]

Is there hope of love
For us on earth?

CROWD

Hope of love
For us on earth!

SOLDIER'S VOICE

His eyes laugh, Cæsar!

TIBERIUS

[*In a strange frenzy now*]

Hear me, thou Dæmon of Laughter! Hear

and answer, I beseech thee, who alone
hath known joy!
[*More and more wildly*]
How must we live? Wherein lies happiness?

CHORUS

Wherein lies happiness?

CROWD

Wherein, happiness?

TIBERIUS

Why are we born? To what end must we
die?

CHORUS

Why are we born to die?

CROWD

Why are we born?

SOLDIER'S VOICE

His eyes laugh, Cæsar! He is dying! He
would speak!

CHORUS AND CROWD

[*In one great cry*]

Cæsar! Let Lazarus speak!

POMPEIA

[*Terrified*]

No, Cæsar! He will laugh—and you will
die—and I will go to him!

TIBERIUS

[*Torn—arguing with his fear*]

But—he may know some hope—
[*Then making his decision, with grim
fatalism*]
Hope—or nothing!
[*Calls to the* SOLDIERS]
Let him speak!

CHORUS AND CROWD

[*Cheering*]

Hail, Cæsar!

LAZARUS

[*His voice comes, recognizably the
voice of* LAZARUS, *yet with a strange,
fresh, clear quality of boyhood, gaily
mocking with life*]

Hail, Cæsar!

CROWD

[*Frantic with hope*]

Hail, Lazarus!

TIBERIUS

Pull away the fire from him! I see death in
his eyes!
[*The flaming reflections in the banked,
masked faces dance madly as the
SOLDIERS rake back the fire from the
stake. With a forced, taunting
mockery*]
What do you say now, Lazarus? You are
dying!

CHORUS AND CROWD

[*Taking his tone—mockingly*]

You are dying, Lazarus!

LAZARUS

[*His voice a triumphant assertion of the
victory of life over pain and death*]

Yes!

TIBERIUS

[*Triumphant yet disappointed—with
scorn and rage*]

Ha! You admit it, do you, coward! Craven!
Knave! Duper of fools! Clown! Liar! Die!
I laugh at you! Ha-ha-ha-ha—
[*His voice breaks chokingly*]

CROWD

[*Led by their* CHORUS—*in the same
frenzy of disappointment, with all
sorts of grotesque and obscene gestures and noises, thumbing their fingers to their noses, wagging them at
their ears, sticking out their tongues,
slapping their behinds, barking, crowing like roosters, howling, and hooting in every conceivable manner*]

Yah! Yah! Yellow Gut! Bungkisser! Muck-

heel! Scumwiper! Liar! Pig! Jackal! Die!
We laugh at you! Ha-ha-ha—
[*Their voices, too, break*]

POMPEIA

[*Rising to her feet like one in a trance,
staring toward* LAZARUS]

They are tormenting him. I hear him crying to me!
[*She moves to the top of the steps leading
to the arena*]

LAZARUS

[*His voice thrilling with exultance*]

O men, fear not life! You die—but there is
no death for Man!
[*He begins to laugh, and at the sound
of his laughter, a great spell of silence
settles upon all his hearers—then as
his laughter rises, they begin to laugh
with him*]

POMPEIA

[*Descending the steps like a sleep-walker*]

I hear his laughter calling. I must go to him.

TIBERIUS

[*As if he realized something was happening that was against his will—
trying feebly to be imperial*]

I command you not to laugh! Cæsar com-
mands—
[*Calling feebly to the* SOLDIERS]
Put back—the gag! Stop his laughter!
[*The laughter of* LAZARUS *gaily and
lovingly mocks back at him*]

SOLDIER'S VOICE

[*His voice gently remonstrating*]

We may not, Cæsar. We love his laughter!
[*They laugh with him*]

CHORUS AND CROWD

[*In a soft, dreamy murmur*]

We love his laughter!
We laugh!

TIBERIUS

[*Dreamily*]
Then—pile the fire back around him. High

and higher! Let him blaze to the stars! I
laugh with him!

SOLDIER'S VOICE

[*Gently and gravely*]

That is just, Cæsar. We love men flaming
toward the stars! We laugh with him!

CHORUS AND CROWD

[*As the flames, piled back and fed anew
by the* SOLDIERS, *flare upward and
are reflected on their masks in dancing waves of light*]

We love men flaming toward the stars!
We laugh!

POMPEIA

[*In the arena*]

The fire calls me. My burning heart calls
for the fire!
[*She laughs softly and passes swiftly
across the arena toward* LAZARUS]

TIBERIUS

[*In a sort of childish complaint*]

You must pardon me, Lazarus. This is my
Cæsar's duty—to kill you! You have no
right to laugh—before all these people—
at Cæsar. It is not kind.
[*He sobs snuffingly—then begins to
laugh at himself*]
[*Suddenly the flames waver, die down,
then shoot up again and* POMPEIA'S
*laughter is heard for a moment, rising
clear and passionately with that of*
LAZARUS, *then dying quickly out*]

SOLDIER'S VOICE

A woman has thrown herself in the flames,
Cæsar! She laughs with Lazarus!

TIBERIUS

[*In a sudden panicky flurry—feverishly*]

Quick, Lazarus! You will soon be silent!
Speak!—in the name of man's solitude—
his agony of farewell—what is beyond
there, Lazarus?
[*His voice has risen to a passionate entreaty*]

CHORUS

[*In a great pleading echo*]

What is beyond there, Lazarus?

CROWD

What is beyond?

LAZARUS

[*His voice speaking lovingly, with a surpassing clearness and exaltation*]

Life! Eternity! Stars and dust! God's
Eternal Laughter!

> [*His laughter bursts forth now in its
> highest pitch of ecstatic summons to
> the feast and sacrifice of Life, the
> Eternal*]
>
> [*The crowds laugh with him in a fren-
> zied rhythmic chorus. Led by the
> CHORUS, they pour down from the
> banked walls of the amphitheatre
> and dance in the flaring reflection of
> the flames strange wild measures of
> liberated joy. TIBERIUS stands on the
> raised dais laughing great shouts of
> clear, fearless laughter*]

CHORUS

[*Chanting as they dance*]

Laugh! Laugh!
We are stars!
We are dust!
We are gods!
We are laughter!

CROWD

We are dust!
We are gods!
Laugh! Laugh!

CALIGULA

[*Enters from behind TIBERIUS. His aspect is wild, his hair disheveled, his
clothes torn, he is panting as if exhausted by running. He stares toward
the flames stupidly—then screams
despairingly above the chant*]

Lazarus! I come to save you! Do you still
live, Lazarus?

TIBERIUS

[*Has been speaking. His words are now*

heard as the tumult momentarily dies
down*]

I have lived long enough! I will die with
Lazarus! I no longer fear death! I laugh!
I laugh at Cæsar! I advise you, my brothers,
fear not Cæsars! Seek Man in the brother-
hood of the dust! Cæsar is your fear of
Man! I counsel you, laugh away your
Cæsars!

CALIGULA

[*With resentful jealousy and rage—in a
voice rising to a scream*]

What do I hear, Lazarus? You laugh with
your murderer? You give him your laughter? You have forgotten me—my love—
you make him love you—you make him
laugh at Cæsars—at me!

> [*Suddenly springs on TIBERIUS in a
> fury and grabbing him by the throat
> chokes him, forcing him back on the
> throne—screaming*]

Die, traitor! Die!

> [*TIBERIUS' body relaxes in his hands,
> dead, and slips from the chair.
> CALIGULA rushes madly down the
> stairs into the midst of the oblivious,
> laughing, dancing crowd, screaming*]

You have betrayed me, dog of a Jew! You
have betrayed Cæsar!

> [*Beginning to be caught by the contagion
> of the laughter*]

Ha-ah—No! I will not laugh! I will kill
you! Give me a spear!

> [*He snatches a spear from a soldier and
> fights his way drunkenly toward the
> flames, like a man half overcome by
> a poisonous gas, shouting, half-laugh-
> ing in spite of himself, half-weeping
> with rage*]

Ha-ah—The gods be with Cæsar Caligula!
O Immortal Gods, give thy brother
strength! You shall die, Lazarus—die—
Ha-ah—!

> [*He disappears toward the flames, his
> spear held ready to stab*]

CHORUS AND CROWD

[*Who have been entirely oblivious of him
—chanting*]

Laugh! Laugh!
We are gods!
We are dust!

LAZARUS

[At his first word there is a profound silence in which each dancer remains frozen in the last movement]

Hail, Caligula Cæsar! Men forget!
[He laughs with gay mockery as at a child]

CHORUS AND CROWD

[Starting to laugh]

Laugh! Laugh!
[Then there is a fierce cry of rage from CALIGULA *and* LAZARUS' *laughter ceases, and with it the laughter of the crowd turns to a wail of fear and lamentation]*

CALIGULA

[Dashes back among them waving his bloody spear and rushing up to the throne stands on it and strikes a grandiose pose]

I have killed God! I am Death! Death is Cæsar!

CHORUS AND CROWD

[Turning and scurrying away—huddled in fleeing groups, crouching close to the ground like a multitude of terrified rats, their voices squeaky now with fright]

Hail, Cæsar! Hail to Death!
[They are gone]

CALIGULA

[Keeping his absurd majestic pose, turns and addresses with rhetorical intoning, and flowing gestures, the body of LAZARUS, *high upon its stake, the flames below it now flickering fitfully]*

Hail, Caligula! Hero of heroes, conqueror of the Dæmon, Lazarus, who taught the treason that fear and death were dead! But I am Lord of Fear! I am Cæsar of Death! And you, Lazarus, are carrion!
[Then in a more conversational tone, putting aside his grandiose airs, confidentially]
I had to kill you, Lazarus! Surely your good sense tells you—You heard what the old

fool, Tiberius, told the mob. A moment more and there would have been a revolution—no more Cæsars—and my dream—!
[He stops—bewilderedly]
My dream? Did I kill laughter? I had just learned to laugh—with love!
[More confusedly]
I must be a little mad, Lazarus. It was one terror too many, to have been laughing your laughter in the night, to have been dreaming great yearning dreams of all the good my love might do for men when I was Cæsar—and then, to hear the old howling of mob lust, and to run here—and there a high white flame amidst the fire—you, Lazarus!—dying!—laughing with him—Tiberius—betraying me—who loved you, Lazarus! Yes, I became mad! I am mad! And I can laugh my own mad laughter, Lazarus—my own! Ha-ha-ha-ha!
[He laughs with a wild triumphant madness and again rhetorically, with sweeping gestures and ferocious capers]
And all of men are vile and mad, and I shall be their madmen's Cæsar!
[He turns as if addressing an amphitheatre full of his subjects]
O my good people, my faithful scum, my brother swine, Lazarus is dead and we have murdered great laughter, and it befits our madness to have done so, and it is befitting above all to have Caligula for Cæsar!
[Then savagely]
Kneel down! Abase yourselves! I am your Cæsar and your God! Hail!
[He stands saluting himself with a crazy intensity that is not without grandeur. A pause. Suddenly the silence seems to crush down upon him; he is aware that he is alone in the vast arena; he whirls about, looking around him as if he felt an assassin at his back; he lunges with his spear at imaginary foes, jumping, dodging from side to side, yelping]
Ho, there! Help! Help! Your Cæsar calls you! Help, my people! To the rescue!
[Suddenly throwing his spear away and sinking on his knees, his face toward LAZARUS, *supplicatingly]*
Lazarus! Forgive me! Help me! Fear kills me! Save me from death!
[He is groveling in a paroxysm of terror, grinding his face in his fists as if to hide it]

LAZARUS

[*His voice is heard in a gentle, expiring sigh of compassion, followed by a faint dying note of laughter that rises and is lost in the sky like the flight of his soul back into the womb of Infinity*]

Fear not, Caligula! There is no death!

CALIGULA

[*Lifts his head at the first sound and rises with the laughter to his feet, until, as it is finally lost, he is on tip-toes, his arms straining upward to the sky, a tender, childish laughter of love on his lips*]

I laugh, Lazarus! I laugh with you!
[*Then grief-stricken*]
Lazarus!
[*He hides his face in his hands, weeping*]
No more!
[*Then beats his head with his fists*]
I will remember! I will!
[*Then suddenly, with a return to grotesqueness—harshly*]
All the same, I killed him and I proved there is death!
[*Immediately overcome by remorse, groveling and beating himself*]
Fool! Madman! Forgive me, Lazarus! Men forget!

CURTAIN

1925–1926   1927

GERTRUDE STEIN

1874–1946

HOW WRITING IS WRITTEN [1]

WHAT I want to talk about to you is just the general subject of how writing is written. The beginning of it is what everybody has to know: everybody is contemporary with his period. A very bad painter once said to a very great painter, 'Do what you like, you cannot get rid of the fact that we are contemporaries.' That is what goes on in writing. The whole crowd of you are contemporary to each other, and the whole business of writing is the question of living in that contemporariness. Each generation has to live in that. The thing that is important is that nobody knows what the contemporariness is. In other words, they don't know where they are going, but they are on their way.

Each generation has to do with what you would call the daily life: and a writer, painter, or any sort of creative artist, is not at all ahead of his time. He is contemporary. He can't live in the past, because it is gone. He can't live in the future, because no one knows what it is. He can live only in the present of his daily life. He is expressing the thing that is being expressed by everybody else in their daily lives. The thing you have to remember is that everybody lives a contemporary daily life. The writer lives it, too, and expresses it imperceptibly. The fact remains that in the act of living, everybody has to live contemporarily. But in the things concerning art and literature they don't have to live contemporarily, because it doesn't make any difference; and they live about forty years behind their time. And that is the real explanation of why the artist or painter is not recognized by his contemporaries. He is expressing the time-sense of his contemporaries, but nobody is really interested. After the new generation has come, after the grandchildren, so to speak, then the opposition dies out: because after all there is then a new contemporary expression to oppose.

That is really the fact about contemporariness. As I see the whole crowd of you, if there are any of you who are going to express yourselves contemporarily, you will do something which most people won't want to look at. Most of you will be so busy living the contemporary life that it will be like the tired business man: in the things of the mind you will want the things you know. And too, if you don't live contemporarily, you are a nuisance. That

[1] The text is a transcript of a talk by Miss Stein in 1935 before the students at The Choate School, Wallingford, Conn. In a slightly different version it appeared in *The Choate Literary Magazine*,XXI,ii,5–14.

is why we live contemporarily. If a man goes along the street with horse and carriage in New York in the snow, that man is a nuisance; and he knows it, so now he doesn't do it. He would not be living, or acting, contemporarily: he would only be in the way, a drag.

The world can accept me now because there is coming out of *your* generation somebody they won't like, and therefore they accept me because I am sufficiently past in having been contemporary so they don't have to dislike me. So thirty years from now I shall be accepted. And the same thing will happen again: that is the reason why every generation has the same thing happen. It will always be the same story, because there is always the same situation presented. The contemporary thing in art and literature is the thing which doesn't make enough difference to the people of that generation so that they can accept it or reject it.

Most of you know that in a funny kind of way you are nearer your grandparents than your parents. Since this contemporariness is always there, nobody realizes that you cannot follow it up. That is the reason people discover—those interested in the activities of other people—that they cannot understand their contemporaries. If you kids started in to write, I wouldn't be a good judge of you, because I am of the third generation. What you are going to do I don't know any more than anyone else. But I created a movement of which you are the grandchildren. The contemporary thing is the thing you can't get away from. That is the fundamental thing in all writing.

Another thing you have to remember is that each period of time not only has its contemporary quality, but it has a time-sense. Things move more quickly, slowly, or differently, from one generation to another. Take the Nineteenth Century. The Nineteenth Century was roughly the Englishman's Century. And their method, as they themselves, in their worst moments, speak of it, is that of 'muddling through.' They begin at one end and hope to come out at the other: their grammar, parts of speech, methods of talk, go with this fashion. The United States began a different phase when, after the Civil War, they dis-

covered and created out of their inner need a different way of life. They created the Twentieth Century. The United States, instead of having the feeling of beginning at one end and ending at another, had the conception of assembling the whole thing out of its parts, the whole thing which made the Twentieth Century productive. The Twentieth Century conceived an automobile as a whole, so to speak, and then created it, built it up out of its parts. It was an entirely different point of view from the Nineteenth Century's. The Nineteenth Century would have seen the parts, and worked towards the automobile through them.

Now in a funny sort of way this expresses, in different terms, the difference between the literature of the Nineteenth Century and the literature of the Twentieth. Think of your reading. If you look at it from the days of Chaucer, you will see that what you might call the 'internal history' of a country always affects its use of writing. It makes a difference in the expression, in the vocabulary, even in the handling of grammar. In an amusing story in your *Literary Magazine*, when the author speaks of the fact that he is tired of using quotation marks and isn't going to use them any more, with him that is a joke; but when I began writing, the whole question of punctuation was a vital question. You see, I had this new conception: I had this conception of the whole paragraph, and in *The Making of Americans* I had this idea of a whole thing. But if you think of contemporary English writers, it doesn't work like that at all. They conceive of it as pieces put together to make a whole, and I conceived it as a whole made up of its parts. I didn't know what I was doing any more than you know, but in response to the need of my period I was doing this thing. That is why I came in contact with people who were unconsciously doing the same thing. They had the Twentieth Century conception of a whole. So the element of punctuation was very vital. The comma was just a nuisance. If you got the thing as a whole, the comma kept irritating you all along the line. If you think of a thing as a whole, and the comma keeps sticking out, it gets on your nerves; because, after all, it destroys the reality of the whole. So

I got rid more and more of commas. Not because I had any prejudice against commas; but the comma was a stumbling-block. When you were conceiving a sentence, the comma stopped you. That is the illustration of the question of grammar and parts of speech, as part of the daily life as we live it.

The other thing which I accomplished was the getting rid of nouns. In the Twentieth Century you feel like movement. The Nineteenth Century didn't feel that way. The element of movement was not the predominating thing that they felt. You know that in your lives movement is the thing that occupies you most—you feel movement all the time. And the United States had the first instance of what I call Twentieth Century writing. You see it first in Walt Whitman. He was the beginning of movement. He didn't see it very clearly, but there was a sense of movement that the European was much influenced by, because the Twentieth Century has become the American Century. That is what I mean when I say that each generation has its own literature.

There is a third element. You see, everybody in his generation has his sense of time which belongs to his crowd. But then, you always have the memory of what you were brought up with. In most people that makes a double time, which makes confusion. When one is beginning to write he is always under the shadow of the thing that is just past. And that is the reason why the creative person always has the appearance of ugliness. There is this persistent drag of the habits that belong to you. And in struggling away from this thing there is always an ugliness. That is the other reason why the contemporary writer is always refused. It is the effort of escaping from the thing which is a drag upon you that is so strong that the result is an apparent ugliness; and the world always says of the new writer, 'It is so ugly!' And they are right, because it *is* ugly. If you disagree with your parents, there is an ugliness in the relation. There is a double resistance that makes the essence of this thing ugly.

You always have in your writing the resistance outside of you and inside of you, a shadow upon you, and the thing which you must express. In the beginning of your writing, this struggle is so tremendous that that result is ugly; and that is the reason why the followers are always accepted before the person who made the revolution. The person who has made the fight probably makes it seem ugly, although the struggle has the much greater beauty. But the followers die out; and the man who made the struggle and the quality of beauty remains in the intensity of the fight. Eventually it comes out all right, and so you have this very queer situation which always happens with the followers: the original person has to have in him a certain element of ugliness. You know that is what happens over and over again: the statement made that it is ugly—the statement made against me for the last twenty years. And they are quite right, because it *is* ugly. But the essence of that ugliness is the thing which will always make it beautiful. I myself think it is much more interesting when it seems ugly, because in it you see the element of the fight. The literature of one hundred years ago is perfectly easy to see, because the sediment of ugliness has settled down and you got the solemnity of its beauty. But to a person of my temperament, it is much more amusing when it has the vitality of the struggle.

In my own case, the Twentieth Century, which America created after the Civil War, and which had certain elements, had a definite influence on me. And in *The Making of Americans*, which is a book I would like to talk about, I gradually and slowly found out that there were two things I had to think about; the fact that knowledge is acquired, so to speak, by memory; but that when you know anything, memory doesn't come in. At any moment that you are conscious of knowing anything, memory plays no part. When any of you feels anybody else, memory doesn't come into it. You have the sense of the immediate. Remember that my immediate forebears were people like Meredith, Thomas Hardy, and so forth, and you will see what a struggle it was to do this thing. This was one of my first efforts to give the appearance of one time-knowledge, and not to make it a narrative story. This is what I mean by immediacy of description: you will find it in *The Mak-*

ing of Americans: 'It happens very often that a man has it in him, that a man does something, that he does it very often that he does many things, when he is a young man when he is an old man, when he is an older man.' Do you see what I mean? And here is a description of a thing that is very interesting: 'One of such of these kind of them had a little boy and this one, the little son wanted to make a collection of butter- flies and beetles and it was all exciting to him and it was all arranged then and then the father said to the son you are certain this is not a cruel thing that you are wanting to be doing, killing things to make collec- tions of them, and the son was very dis- turbed then and they talked about it to- gether the two of them and more and more they talked about it then and then at last the boy was convinced it was a cruel thing and he said he would not do it and the father said the little boy was a noble boy to give up pleasure when it was a cruel one. The boy went to bed then and then the father when he got up in the early morning saw a wonderfully beautiful moth in the room and he caught him and he killed him and he pinned him and he woke up his son then and showed it to him and he said to him "see what a good father I am to have caught and killed this one," the boy was all mixed up inside him and then he said he would go on with his collecting and that was all there was then of discussing and this is a little description of something that happened once and it is very interesting.'

I was trying to get this present imme- diacy without trying to drag in anything else. I had to use present participles, new constructions of grammar. The grammar- constructions are correct, but they are changed, in order to get this immediacy. In short, from that time I have been trying in every possible way to get the sense of immediacy, and practically all the work I have done has been in that direction.

In *The Making of Americans* I had an idea that I could get a sense of immediacy if I made a description of every kind of human being that existed, the rules for re- semblances and all the other things, until really I had made a description of every human being—I found this out when I was at Harvard working under William James.

Did you ever see that article that came out in *The Atlantic Monthly* a year or two ago, about my experiments with auto- matic writing? It was very amusing. The experiment that I did was to take a lot of people in moments of fatigue and rest and activity of various kinds, and see if they could do anything with automatic writing. I found they could not do anything with automatic writing, but I found out a great deal about how people act. I found there a certain kind of human being who acted in a certain way, and another kind who acted in another kind of way, and their resem- blances and their differences. And then I wanted to find out if you could make a history of the whole world, if you could know the whole life history of everyone in the world, their slight resemblances and lack of resemblances. I made enormous charts, and I tried to carry these charts out. You start in and you take everyone that you know, and then when you see anybody who has a certain expression or turn of the face that reminds you of some one, you find out where he agrees or disagrees with the character, until you build up the whole scheme. I got to the place where I didn't know whether I knew people or not. I made so many charts that when I used to go down the streets of Paris I wondered whether they were people I knew or ones I didn't. That is what *The Making of Ameri- cans* was intended to be. I was to make a description of every kind of human being until I could know by these variations how everybody was to be known. Then I got very much interested in this thing, and I wrote about nine hundred pages, and I came to a logical conclusion that this thing could be done. Anybody who has patience enough could literally and entirely make of the whole world a history of human nature. When I found it could be done, I lost interest in it. As soon as I found def- initely and clearly and completely that I could do it, I stopped writing the long book. It didn't interest me any longer. In doing the thing, I found out this ques- tion of resemblances, and I found in mak- ing these analyses that the resemblances were not of memory. I had to remember what person looked like the other person. Then I found this contradiction: that the resemblances were a matter of memory.

There were two prime elements involved, the element of memory and the other of immediacy.

The element of memory was a perfectly feasible thing, so then I gave it up. I then started a book which I called *A Long Gay Book* to see if I could work the thing up to a faster tempo. I wanted to see if I could make that a more complete vision. I wanted to see if I could hold it in the frame. Ordinarily the novels of the Nineteenth Century live by association; they are wont to call up other pictures than the one they present to you. I didn't want, when I said 'water,' to have you think of running water. Therefore I began limiting my vocabulary, because I wanted to get rid of anything except the picture within the frame. While I was writing I didn't want, when I used one word, to make it carry with it too many associations. I wanted as far as possible to make it exact, as exact as mathematics; that is to say, for example, if one and one make two, I wanted to get words to have as much exactness as that. When I put them down they were to have this quality. The whole history of my work, from *The Making of Americans*, has been a history of that. I made a great many discoveries, but the thing that I was always trying to do was this thing.

One thing which came to me is that the Twentieth Century gives of itself a feeling of movement, and has in its way no feeling for events. To the Twentieth Century events are not important. You must know that. Events are not exciting. Events have lost their interest for people. You read them more like a soothing syrup, and if you listen over the radio you don't get very excited. The thing has got to this place, that events are so wonderful that they are not exciting. Now you have to remember that the business of an artist is to be exciting. If the thing has its proper vitality, the result must be exciting. I was struck with it during the War: the average dough-boy standing on a street corner doing nothing— (they say, at the end of their doing nothing, 'I guess I'll go home')—was much more exciting to people than when the soldiers went over the top. The populace were passionately interested in their standing on the street corners, more so than in the St. Mihiel drive. And it is a perfectly natural thing. Events had got so continuous that the fact that events were taking place no longer stimulated anybody. To see three men, strangers, standing, expressed their personality to the European man so much more than anything else they could do. That thing impressed me very much. But the novel which tells about what happens is of no interest to anybody. It is quite characteristic that in *The Making of Americans*, Proust, *Ulysses*, nothing much happens. People are interested in existence. Newspapers excite people very little. Sometimes a personality breaks through the newspapers—Lindbergh, Dillinger—when the personality has vitality. It wasn't what Dillinger *did* that excited anybody. The feeling is perfectly simple. You can see it in my *Four Saints*. Saints shouldn't do anything. The fact that a saint is there is enough for anybody. The *Four Saints* was written about as static as I could make it. The saints conversed a little, and it all did something. It did something more than the theatre which has tried to make events has done. For our purposes, for our contemporary purposes, events have no importance. I merely say that for the last thirty years events are of no importance. They may make a great many people unhappy, they may cause convulsions in history, but from the standpoint of excitement, the kind of excitement the Nineteenth Century got out of events doesn't exist.

And so what I am trying to make you understand is that every contemporary writer has to find out what is the inner time-sense of his contemporariness. The writer or painter, or what not, feels this thing more vibrantly, and he has a passionate need of putting it down; and that is what creativeness does. He spends his life in putting down this thing which he doesn't know is a contemporary thing. If he doesn't put down the contemporary thing, he isn't a great writer, for he has to live in the past. That is what I mean by 'everything is contemporary.' The minor poets of the period, or the precious poets of the period, are all people who are under the shadow of the past. A man who is making a revolution has to be contemporary. A minor person can live in the imagination. That tells the story pretty completely.

The question of repetition is very important. It is important because there is no such thing as repetition. Everybody tells every story in about the same way. You know perfectly well that when you and your roommates tell something, you are telling the same story in about the same way. But the point about it is this. Everybody is telling the story in the same way. But if you listen carefully, you will see that not all the story is the same. There is always a slight variation. Somebody comes in, and you tell the story over again. Every time you tell that story it is told slightly differently. All my early work was a careful listening to all the people telling their story, and I conceived the idea which is, funnily enough, the same as the idea of the cinema. The cinema goes on the same principle: each picture is just infinitesimally different from the one before. If you listen carefully, you say something, the other person says something; but each time it changes just a little, until finally you come to the point where you convince him or you don't convince him. I used to listen very carefully to people talking. I had a passion for knowing just what I call their 'insides.' And in *The Making of Americans* I did this thing; but of course to my mind there is no repetition. For instance, in these early 'Portraits,' and in a whole lot of them in this book (*Portraits and Prayers*) you will see that every time a statement is made about someone being somewhere, that statement is different. If I had repeated, nobody would listen. Nobody could be in the room with a person who said the same thing over and over and over. He would drive everybody mad. There has to be a very slight change. Really listen to the way you talk, and every time you change it a little bit. That change, to me, was a very important thing to find out. You will see that when I kept on saying something was something or somebody was somebody, I changed it just a little bit until I got a whole portrait. I conceived the idea of building this thing up. It was all based upon this thing of everybody's slightly building this thing up. What I was after was this immediacy. A single photograph doesn't give it. I was trying for this thing, and so to my mind there is no repetition. The only thing that is repetition is when

somebody tells you what he has learned. No matter how you say it, you say it differently. It was this that led me in all that early work.

You see, finally, after I got this thing as completely as I could, then, of course, it being my nature, I wanted to tear it down. I attacked the problem from another way. I listened to people. I condensed it in about three words. There again, if you read those later 'Portraits,' you will see that I used three or four words instead of making a cinema of it. I wanted to condense it as much as possible and change it around, until you could get the movement of a human being. If I wanted to make a picture of you as you sit there, I would wait until I got a picture of you as individuals and then I'd change them until I got a picture of you as a whole.

I did these 'Portraits,' and then I got the idea of doing plays. I had the 'Portraits' so much in my head that I would almost know how you differ one from the other. I got this idea of the play, and put it down in a few words. I wanted to put them down in that way, and I began writing plays and I wrote a great many of them. The Nineteenth Century wrote a great many plays, and none of them are now read, because the Nineteenth Century wanted to put their novels on the stage. The better the play the more static. The minute you try to make a play a novel, it doesn't work. That is the reason I got interested in doing these plays.

When you get to that point there is no essential difference between prose and poetry. This is essentially the problem with which your generation will have to wrestle. The thing has got to the point where poetry and prose have to concern themselves with the static thing. That is up to you.

1935   1935

THE LIFE OF JUAN GRIS [1]

THE LIFE AND DEATH OF JUAN GRIS

JUAN GRIS was one of the younger children of a well-to-do merchant of Madrid. The

[1] Juan Gris(1887–1927) was, with Bracque and Picasso, one of the front-guard of cubism. Like his contemporaries, he passed through a number of phases: from pure representation to a concentration on composition,

earliest picture he has of himself is at about five years of age dressed in a little lace dress standing beside his mother who was very sweet and pleasantly maternal-looking. When he was about seven years old his father failed in business honorably and the family fell upon very hard times but in one way and another two sons and a daughter lived to grow up well educated and on the whole prosperous. Juan went to the school of engineering at Madrid and when about seventeen came to Paris to study. He tells delightful stories of his father and Spanish ways which strangely enough he never liked. He had very early a very great attraction and love for French culture. French culture has always seduced me he was fond of saying. It seduces me and then I am seduced over again. He used to tell how Spaniards love not to resist temptation. In order to please them the better class merchants such as his father would always have to leave many little things about everything else being packages carefully tied up and in the back on shelves. He used to dwell upon the lack of trust and comradeship in Spanish life. Each one is a general or does not fight and if he does not fight each one is a general. No one that is no Spaniard can help any one because no one no Spaniard can help any one. And this being so and it is so Juan Gris was a brother and comrade to every one being one as no one ever had been one. That is the proportion. One to any one number of millions. That is any proportion. Juan Gris was that one. French culture was always a seduction. Bracque who was such a one was always a seduction seducing French culture seducing again and again. Josette equable intelligent faithful spontaneous delicate courageous delightful forethoughtful the school of Fointainebleau delicate deliberate measured and free all these things seduced. I am seduced and then I am seduced over again he was fond of saying. He had his own Spanish gift of intimacy. We were intimate. Juan knew what he did. In the beginning he did all sorts of things he used to

draw for humorous illustrated papers he had a child a boy named George he lived about he was not young and enthusiastic. The first serious exhibition of his pictures was at the Galerie Kahnweiler rue Vignon in 1914. As a Spaniard he knew cubism and had stepped through into it. He had stepped through it. There was beside this perfection. To have it shown you. Then came the war and desertion. There was little aid. Four years partly illness much perfection and rejoining beauty and perfection and then at the end there came a definite creation of something. This is what is to be measured. He made something that is to be measured. And that is that something.

Therein Juan Gris is not everything but more than anything. He made that thing. He made the thing. He made a thing to be measured.

Later having done it he could be sorry it was not why they like it. And so he made it very well loving and he made it very plainly playing. And he liked a knife and all but reasonably. This is what is made to be and he then did some stage setting. We liked it but nobody else could see that something is everything. It is everything if it is what is it. Nobody can ask about measuring. Unfortunately. Juan could go on living. No one can say that Henry Kahnweiler can be left out of him. I remember he said Kahnweiler goes on but no one buys anything and I said it to him and he smiled so gently and said I was everything. This is the history of Juan Gris.
1927   1934

FROM A LONG GAY BOOK

WHEN THEY ARE A LITTLE OLDER [1]

WHEN they are very little just a baby they cannot know that thing. When they are a little bigger they can know that other ones are older and younger. When they are a little bigger they can remember that they were littler. When they are a little older they can know that they are then not what any one is describing, they are knowing then that they are older than the description, than every description of the age they

---

to an intensive use of decorative color, and to analytical abstraction. In addition to his work on smaller canvases he designed sets for the ballet, to which Miss Stein refers. Her portrait was written at the time of his death, and appeared soon after in *Transition*, no. 4, 160–62.

1 The selection, to which the title has been given by the editors, is from *A Long Gay Book*, printed in *Matisse, Picasso & G. S.* (Paris, 1933), 25–26.

are then. When they are older they are beginning to remember their reading, they
are beginning to believe a description. of
them. When they are a little older they are
knowing then that they just have been
younger. When they are a little older they
are beginning to know they will be older.
When they are a little older they know they
are old enough to know that age is a different thing it has been. When they are a 10
little older they are knowing they are beginning then to be young to some who are
much older and they are beginning to be
old to some who are much younger. When
they are a little older they know they are
beginning to be afraid of changing thinking
about ageing, they are beginning then to
know something of being uncertain about
what is being young and what is being old,
they are beginning then to be afraid of 20
everything. When they are a little older
they are coming to be certain that they
have been younger. When they are a little
older they are beginning to be certain that
age has no meaning. When they are coming
to be a little older they are coming to be
saying that they are beginning to be wondering if age has not some meaning. When
they are a little older they are certainly beginning to be believing what they remem- 30
bered reading about being young and older

and middle aged and older and almost old
and old. When they are a little older they
are commencing to be certain that ageing
has meaning. When they are a little older
they are certain that they can be older and
that being older will sometime be coming.
When they are a little older they are commencing mentioning ageing to prepare any
one for some such thing being something
that will be showing in them. When they
are a little older they are commencing mentioning that they are expecting anything.
When they are a little older they are commencing mentioning any such thing quite
often. When they are a little older they are
not mentioning being an older one, they
are then mentioning that many are existing
who are being young ones. When they are
a little older they are mentioning anything
and mentioning it quite often. When they
are a little older any one is mentioning that
thing and not mentioning everything and
they are mentioning being a little older and
they are mentioning everything. When they
are a little older it depends then on how
much longer they will be being living just
how long they will be mentioning anything
again and again. They are then completely
old ones and not any one is knowing everything of that thing.
1909–1912   1933

SHERWOOD ANDERSON

1876–1941

DEATH IN THE WOODS [1]

I

SHE was an old woman and lived on a farm
near the town in which I lived. All country

and small-town people have seen such old
women, but no one knows much about
them. Such an old woman comes into town
driving an old worn-out horse or she comes
afoot carrying a basket. She may own a
few hens and have eggs to sell. She brings

[1] 'It seems to me that the theme of this story is the persistent animal hunger of man. There are these women
who spend their whole lives, rather dumbly feeding
this hunger. For years I wanted to write this story.

'As for the technique, it was quite definitely thought
out. Over a period of several years I made several attempts that had to be thrown aside. For example I
thought it necessary to definitely lift the animal hunger, I wanted to get at, out of the realm of sex. Therefore my tired-out, sexless old woman, the dogs feeding
from the food attached to her body after her own
death. And there is always the desire to get your story
imbedded in the whole life of a community.

'The story has its particular form, attempts at flashes
out of a community life, the young man and the German fighting over the girl in the road, the son bringing

his mistress to his mother's house, the butcher, half-
grudgingly and yet out of pity, giving her the meat
bones, the dogs circling in the mysterious moonlit
night in the forest, the men and boys of the town
hurrying out of town to find the body . . . all of this
to get a certain effect. It is a little hard to define. What
is wanted is something beyond the horizon, to retain
the sense of mystery in life while showing, at the same
time, at what cost our ordinary animal hungers are
sometimes fed.' Author's note.

Anderson mentions the theme of this tale in *A Story
Teller's Story* N.Y., 1924). Its first complete version,
differing slightly from that printed above, is in *Tar: A
Midwest Childhood* (N.Y., 1926).

them in a basket and takes them to a grocer. There she trades them in. She gets some salt pork and some beans. Then she gets a pound or two of sugar and some flour.

Afterwards she goes to the butcher's and asks for some dog-meat. She may spend ten or fifteen cents, but when she does she asks for something. Formerly the butchers gave liver to any one who wanted to carry it away. In our family we were always hav- ing it. Once one of my brothers got a whole cow's liver at the slaughter-house near the fair grounds in our town. We had it until we were sick of it. It never cost a cent. I have hated the thought of it ever since.

The old farm woman got some liver and a soup bone. She never visited with any one, and as soon as she got what she wanted she lit out for home. It made quite a load for such an old body. No one gave her a lift. People drive right down a road and never notice an old woman like that.

There was such an old woman who used to come into town past our house one Sum- mer and Fall when I was a young boy and was sick with what was called inflammatory rheumatism. She went home later carrying a heavy pack on her back. Two or three large gaunt-looking dogs followed at her heels.

The old woman was nothing special. She was one of the nameless ones that hardly any one knows, but she got into my thoughts. I have just suddenly now, after all these years, remembered her and what happened. It is a story. Her name was Grimes, and she lived with her husband and son in a small unpainted house on the bank of a small creek four miles from town.

The husband and son were a tough lot. Although the son was but twenty-one, he had already served a term in jail. It was whispered about that the woman's husband stole horses and ran them off to some other county. Now and then, when a horse turned up missing, the man had also dis- appeared. No one ever caught him. Once, when I was loafing at Tom Whitehead's livery-barn, the man came there and sat on the bench in front. Two or three other men were there, but no one spoke to him. He sat for a few minutes and then got up and went away. When he was leaving he turned around and stared at the men. There was a look of defiance in his eyes.

'Well, I have tried to be friendly. You don't want to talk to me. It has been so wherever I have gone in this town. If, some day, one of your fine horses turns up missing, well, then what?' He did not say anything actu- ally. 'I'd like to bust one of you on the jaw,' was about what his eyes said. I re- member how the look in his eyes made me shiver.

The old man belonged to a family that had had money once. His name was Jake Grimes. It all comes back clearly now. His father, John Grimes, had owned a sawmill when the country was new, and had made money. Then he got to drinking and run- ning after women. When he died there wasn't much left.

Jake blew in the rest. Pretty soon there wasn't any more lumber to cut and his land was nearly all gone.

He got his wife off a German farmer, for whom he went to work one June day in the wheat harvest. She was a young thing then and scared to death. You see, the farmer was up to something with the girl—she was, I think, a bound girl and his wife had her suspicions. She took it out on the girl when the man wasn't around. Then, when the wife had to go off to town for supplies, the farmer got after her. She told young Jake that nothing really ever happened, but he didn't know whether to believe it or not.

He got her pretty easy himself, the first time he was out with her. He wouldn't have married her if the German farmer hadn't tried to tell him where to get off. He got her to go riding with him in his buggy one night when he was threshing on the place, and then he came for her the next Sunday night.

She managed to get out of the house without her employer's seeing, but when she was getting into the buggy he showed up. It was almost dark, and he just popped up suddenly at the horse's head. He grabbed the horse by the bridle and Jake got out his buggy-whip.

They had it out all right! The German was a tough one. Maybe he didn't care whether his wife knew or not. Jake hit him over the face and shoulders with the buggy- whip, but the horse got to acting up and he had to get out.

Then the two men went for it. The girl didn't see it. The horse started to run away and went nearly a mile down the road before the girl got him stopped. Then she managed to tie him to a tree beside the road. (I wonder how I know all this. It must have stuck in my mind from small-town tales when I was a boy.) Jake found her there after he got through with the German. She was huddled up in the buggy seat, crying, scared to death. She told Jake a lot of stuff, how the German had tried to get her, how he chased her once into the barn, how another time, when they happened to be alone in the house together, he tore her dress open clear down the front. The German, she said, might have got her that time if he hadn't heard his old woman drive in at the gate. She had been off to town for supplies. Well, she would be putting the horse in the barn. The German managed to sneak off to the fields without his wife seeing. He told the girl he would kill her if she told. What could she do? She told a lie about ripping her dress in the barn when she was feeding the stock. I remember now that she was a bound girl and did not know where her father and mother were. Maybe she did not have any father. You know what I mean.

Such bound children were often enough cruelly treated. They were children who had no parents, slaves really. There were very few orphan homes then. They were legally bound into some home. It was a matter of pure luck how it came out.

II

She married Jake and had a son and daughter, but the daughter died.

Then she settled down to feed stock. That was her job. At the German's place she had cooked the food for the German and his wife. The wife was a strong woman with big hips and worked most of the time in the fields with her husband. She fed them and fed the cows in the barn, fed the pigs, the horses and the chickens. Every moment of every day, as a young girl, was spent feeding something.

Then she married Jake Grimes and he had to be fed. She was a slight thing, and when she had been married for three or four years, and after the two children were born, her slender shoulders became stooped.

Jake always had a lot of big dogs around the house, that stood near the unused saw-mill near the creek. He was always trading horses when he wasn't stealing something and had a lot of poor bony ones about. Also he kept three or four pigs and a cow. They were all pastured in the few acres left of the Grimes place and Jake did little enough work.

He went into debt for a threshing outfit and ran it for several years, but it did not pay. People did not trust him. They were afraid he would steal the grain at night. He had to go a long way off to get work and it cost too much to get there. In the Winter he hunted and cut a little firewood, to be sold in some nearby town. When the son grew up he was just like the father. They got drunk together. If there wasn't anything to eat in the house when they came home the old man gave his old woman a cut over the head. She had a few chickens of her own and had to kill one of them in a hurry. When they were all killed she wouldn't have any eggs to sell when she went to town, and then what would she do?

She had to scheme all her life about getting things fed, getting the pigs fed so they would grow fat and could be butchered in the Fall. When they were butchered her husband took most of the meat off to town and sold it. If he did not do it first the boy did. They fought sometimes and when they fought the old woman stood aside trembling.

She had got the habit of silence anyway —that was fixed. Sometimes, when she began to look old—she wasn't forty yet—and when the husband and son were both off, trading horses or drinking or hunting or stealing, she went around the house and the barnyard muttering to herself.

How was she going to get everything fed?—that was her problem. The dogs had to be fed. There wasn't enough hay in the barn for the horses and the cow. If she didn't feed the chickens how could they lay eggs? Without eggs to sell how could she get things in town, things she had to have to keep the life of the farm going? Thank heaven, she did not have to feed her husband—in a certain way. That hadn't lasted long after their marriage and after the babies came. Where he went on his long trips she did not know. Sometimes he was gone from home for weeks, and after the boy grew up they went off together.

They left everything at home for her to

manage and she had no money. She knew no one. No one ever talked to her in town. When it was Winter she had to gather sticks of wood for her fire, had to try to keep the stock fed with very little grain.

The stock in the barn cried to her hungrily, the dogs followed her about. In the Winter the hens laid few enough eggs. They huddled in the corners of the barn and she kept watching them. If a hen lays an egg in the barn in the Winter and you do not find it, it freezes and breaks.

One day in Winter the old woman went off to town with a few eggs and the dogs followed her. She did not get started until nearly three o'clock and the snow was heavy. She hadn't been feeling very well for several days and so she went muttering along, scantily clad, her shoulders stooped. She had an old grain bag in which she carried her eggs, tucked away down in the bottom. There weren't many of them, but in Winter the price of eggs is up. She would get a little meat in exchange for the eggs, some salt pork, a little sugar, and some coffee perhaps. It might be the butcher would give her a piece of liver.

When she had got to town and was trading in her eggs the dogs lay by the door outside. She did pretty well, got the things she needed, more than she had hoped. Then she went to the butcher and he gave her some liver and some dog-meat.

It was the first time any one had spoken to her in a friendly way for a long time. The butcher was alone in his shop when she came in and was annoyed by the thought of such a sick-looking old woman out on such a day. It was bitter cold and the snow, that had let up during the afternoon, was falling again. The butcher said something about her husband and her son, swore at them, and the old woman stared at him, a look of mild surprise in her eyes as he talked. He said that if either the husband or the son were going to get any of the liver or the heavy bones with scraps of meat hanging to them that he had put into the grain bag, he'd see him starve first.

Starve, eh? Well, things had to be fed. Men had to be fed, and the horses that weren't any good but maybe could be traded off, and the poor thin cow that hadn't given any milk for three months.

Horses, cows, pigs, dogs, men.

III

The old woman had to get back before darkness came if she could. The dogs followed at her heels, sniffing at the heavy grain bag she had fastened on her back. When she got to the edge of town she stopped by a fence and tied the bag on her back with a piece of rope she had carried in her dress-pocket for just that purpose. That was an easier way to carry it. Her arms ached. It was hard when she had to crawl over fences and once she fell over and landed in the snow. The dogs went frisking about. She had to struggle to get to her feet again, but she made it. The point of climbing over the fences was that there was a short cut over a hill and through a woods. She might have gone around by the road, but it was a mile farther that way. She was afraid she couldn't make it. And then, besides, the stock had to be fed. There was a little hay left and a little corn. Perhaps her husband and son would bring some home when they came. They had driven off in the only buggy the Grimes family had, a rickety thing, a rickety horse hitched to the buggy, two other rickety horses led by halters. They were going to trade horses, get a little money if they could. They might come home drunk. It would be well to have something in the house when they came back.

The son had an affair on with a woman at the county seat, fifteen miles away. She was a rough enough woman, a tough one. Once, in the Summer, the son had brought her to the house. Both she and the son had been drinking. Jake Grimes was away and the son and his woman ordered the old woman about like a servant. She didn't mind much; she was used to it. Whatever happened she never said anything. That was her way of getting along. She had managed that way when she was a young girl at the German's and ever since she had married Jake. That time her son brought his woman to the house they stayed all night, sleeping together just as though they were married. It hadn't shocked the old woman, not much. She had got past being shocked early in life.

With the pack on her back she went painfully along across an open field, wading in the deep snow, and got into the woods.

There was a path, but it was hard to follow. Just beyond the top of the hill, where the woods was thickest, there was a small clearing. Had some one once thought of building a house there? The clearing was as large as a building lot in town, large enough for a house and a garden. The path ran along the side of the clearing, and when she got there the old woman sat down to rest at the foot of a tree.

It was a foolish thing to do. When she got herself placed, the pack against the tree's trunk, it was nice, but what about getting up again? She worried about that for a moment and then quietly closed her eyes.

She must have slept for a time. When you are about so cold you can't get any colder. The afternoon grew a little warmer and the snow came thicker than ever. Then after a time the weather cleared. The moon even came out.

There were four Grimes dogs that had followed Mrs. Grimes into town, all tall gaunt fellows. Such men as Jake Grimes and his son always keep just such dogs. They kick and abuse them, but they stay. The Grimes dogs, in order to keep from starving, had to do a lot of foraging for themselves, and they had been at it while the old woman slept with her back to the tree at the side of the clearing. They had been chasing rabbits in the woods and in adjoining fields and in their ranging had picked up three other farm dogs.

After a time all the dogs came back to the clearing. They were excited about something. Such nights, cold and clear and with a moon, do things to dogs. It may be that some old instinct, come down from the time when they were wolves and ranged the woods in packs on Winter nights, comes back into them.

The dogs in the clearing, before the old woman, had caught two or three rabbits and their immediate hunger had been satisfied. They began to play, running in circles in the clearing. Round and round they ran, each dog's nose at the tail of the next dog. In the clearing, under the snow-laden trees and under the wintry moon they made a strange picture, running thus silently, in a circle their running had beaten in the soft snow. The dogs made no sound. They ran around and around in the circle.

It may have been that the old woman saw them doing that before she died. She may have awakened once or twice and looked at the strange sight with dim old eyes.

She wouldn't be very cold now, just drowsy. Life hangs on a long time. Perhaps the old woman was out of her head. She may have dreamed of her girlhood, at the German's, and before that, when she was a child and before her mother lit out and left her.

Her dreams couldn't have been very pleasant. Not many pleasant things had happened to her. Now and then one of the Grimes dogs left the running circle and came to stand before her. The dog thrust his face close to her face. His red tongue was hanging out.

The running of the dogs may have been a kind of death ceremony. It may have been that the primitive instinct of the wolf, having been aroused in the dogs by the night and the running, made them somehow afraid.

'Now we are no longer wolves. We are dogs, the servants of men. Keep alive, man! When man dies we become wolves again.'

When one of the dogs came to where the old woman sat with her back against the tree and thrust his nose close to her face he seemed satisfied and went back to run with the pack. All the Grimes dogs did it at some time during the evening, before she died. I knew all about it afterward, when I grew to be a man, because once in a woods in Illinois, on another Winter night, I saw a pack of dogs act just like that. The dogs were waiting for me to die as they had waited for the old woman that night when I was a child, but when it happened to me I was a young man and had no intention whatever of dying.

The old woman died softly and quietly. When she was dead and when one of the Grimes dogs had come to her and had found her dead all the dogs stopped running.

They gathered about her.

Well, she was dead now. She had fed the Grimes dogs when she was alive, what about now?

There was the pack on her back, the grain bag containing the piece of salt pork, the liver the butcher had given her, the dog-meat, the soup bones. The butcher in town, having been suddenly overcome with a feeling of pity, had loaded her grain bag heavily. It had been a big haul for the old woman.

It was a big haul for the dogs now.

IV

One of the Grimes dogs sprang suddenly out from among the others and began worrying the pack on the old woman's back. Had the dogs really been wolves that one would have been the leader of the pack. What he did, all the others did.

All of them sank their teeth into the grain bag the old woman had fastened with ropes to her back.

They dragged the old woman's body out into the open clearing. The worn-out dress was quickly torn from her shoulders. When she was found, a day or two later, the dress had been torn from her body clear to the hips, but the dogs had not touched her body. They had got the meat out of the grain bag, that was all. Her body was frozen stiff when it was found, and the shoulders were so narrow and the body so slight that in death it looked like the body of some charming young girl.

Such things happened in towns of the Middle West, on farms near town, when I was a boy. A hunter out after rabbits found the old woman's body and did not touch it. Something, the beaten round path in the little snow-covered clearing, the silence of the place, the place where the dogs had worried the body trying to pull the grain bag away or tear it open—something startled the man and he hurried off to town.

I was in Main street with one of my brothers who was town newsboy and who was taking the afternoon papers to the stores. It was almost night.

The hunter came into a grocery and told his story. Then he went to a hardware-shop and into a drugstore. Men began to gather on the sidewalks. Then they started out along the road to the place in the woods.

My brother should have gone on about his business of distributing papers but he didn't. Every one was going to the woods. The undertaker went and the town marshal. Several men got on a dray and rode out to where the path left the road and went into the woods, but the horses weren't very sharply shod and slid about on the slippery roads. They made no better time than those of us who walked.

The town marshal was a large man whose leg had been injured in the Civil War. He carried a heavy cane and limped rapidly along the road. My brother and I followed at his heels, and as we went other men and boys joined the crowd.

It had grown dark by the time we got to where the old woman had left the road but the moon had come out. The marshal was thinking there might have been a murder. He kept asking the hunter questions. The hunter went along with his gun across his shoulders, a dog following at his heels. It isn't often a rabbit hunter has a chance to be so conspicuous. He was taking full advantage of it, leading the procession with the town marshal. 'I didn't see any wounds. She was a beautiful young girl. Her face was buried in the snow. No, I didn't know her.' As a matter of fact, the hunter had not looked closely at the body. He had been frightened. She might have been murdered and some one might spring out from behind a tree and murder him. In a woods, in the late afternoon, when the trees are all bare and there is white snow on the ground, when all is silent, something creepy steals over the mind and body. If something strange or uncanny has happened in the neighborhood all you think about is getting away from there as fast as you can.

The crowd of men and boys had got to where the old woman had crossed the field and went, following the marshal and the hunter, up the slight incline and into the woods.

My brother and I were silent. He had his bundle of papers in a bag slung across his shoulder. When he got back to town he would have to go on distributing his papers before he went home to supper. If I went along, as he had no doubt already determined I should, we would both be late. Either mother or our older sister would have to warm our supper.

Well, we would have something to tell. A boy did not get such a chance very often. It was lucky we just happened to go into the grocery when the hunter came in. The hunter was a country fellow. Neither of us had ever seen him before.

Now the crowd of men and boys had got to the clearing. Darkness comes quickly on such Winter nights, but the full moon made everything clear. My brother and I stood near the tree, beneath which the old woman had died.

She did not look old, lying there in that light, frozen and still. One of the men turned her over in the snow and I saw everything. My body trembled with some strange mystical feeling and so did my brother's. It might have been the cold.

Neither of us had ever seen a woman's body before. It may have been the snow, clinging to the frozen flesh, that made it look so white and lovely, so like marble. No woman had come with the party from town; but one of the men, he was the town blacksmith, took off his overcoat and spread it over her. Then he gathered her into his arms and started off to town, all the others following silently. At that time no one knew who she was.

V

I had seen everything, had seen the oval in the snow, like a miniature race-track, where the dogs had run, had seen how the men were mystified, had seen the white bare young-looking shoulders, had heard the whispered comments of the men.

The men were simply mystified. They took the body to the undertaker's, and when the blacksmith, the hunter, the marshal and several others had got inside they closed the door. If father had been there perhaps he could have got in, but we boys couldn't.

I went with my brother to distribute the rest of his papers and when we got home it was my brother who told the story.

I kept silent and went to bed early. It may have been I was not satisfied with the way he told it.

Later, in the town, I must have heard other fragments of the old woman's story. She was recognized the next day and there was an investigation.

The husband and son were found somewhere and brought to town and there was an attempt to connect them with the woman's death, but it did not work. They had perfect enough alibis.

However, the town was against them. They had to get out. Where they went I never heard.

I remember only the picture there in the forest, the men standing about, the naked girlish-looking figure, face down in the snow, the tracks made by the running dogs and the clear cold Winter sky above. White fragments of clouds were drifting across the sky. They went racing across the little open space among the trees.

The scene in the forest had become for me, without my knowing it, the foundation for the real story I am now trying to tell. The fragments, you see, had to be picked up slowly, long afterwards.

Things happened. When I was a young man I worked on the farm of a German. The hired-girl was afraid of her employer. The farmer's wife hated her.

I saw things at that place. Once later, I had a half-uncanny, mystical adventure with dogs in an Illinois forest on a clear, moon-lit Winter night. When I was a schoolboy, and on a Summer day, I went with a boy friend out along a creek some miles from town and came to the house where the old woman had lived. No one had lived in the house since her death. The doors were broken from the hinges; the window lights were all broken. As the boy and I stood in the road outside, two dogs, just roving farm dogs no doubt, came running around the corner of the house. The dogs were tall, gaunt fellows and came down to the fence and glared through at us, standing in the road.

The whole thing, the story of the old woman's death, was to me as I grew older like music heard from far off. The notes had to be picked up slowly one at a time. Something had to be understood.

The woman who died was one destined to feed animal life. Anyway, that is all she ever did. She was feeding animal life before she was born, as a child, as a young woman working on the farm of the German, after she married, when she grew old and when she died. She fed animal life in cows, in chickens, in pigs, in horses, in dogs, in men. Her daughter had died in childhood and with her one son she had no articulate relations. On the night when she died she was hurrying homeward, bearing on her body food for animal life.

She died in the clearing in the woods and even after her death continued feeding animal life.

You see it is likely that, when my brother told the story, that night when we got home and my mother and sister sat listening, I did not think he got the point. He was too young and so was I. A thing so complete has its own beauty.

I shall not try to emphasize the point. I am only explaining why I was dissatisfied then and have been ever since. I speak of that only that you may understand why I have been impelled to try to tell the simple story over again.

1933

ERNEST HEMINGWAY

1898–

THE UNDEFEATED

MANUEL GARCIA climbed the stairs to Don Miguel Retana's office. He set down his suitcase and knocked on the door. There was no answer. Manuel, standing in the hallway, felt there was someone in the room. He felt it through the door.

'Retana,' he said, listening.

There was no answer.

He's there, all right, Manuel thought.

'Retana,' he said and banged the door.

'Who's there?' said someone in the office.

'Me, Manolo,' Manuel said.

'What do you want?' asked the voice.

'I want to work,' Manuel said.

Something in the door clicked several times and it swung open. Manuel went in, carrying his suitcase.

A little man sat behind a desk at the far side of the room. Over his head was a bull's head, stuffed by a Madrid taxidermist; on the walls were framed photographs and bull-fight posters.

The little man sat looking at Manuel.

'I thought they'd killed you,' he said.

Manuel knocked with his knuckles on the desk. The little man sat looking at him across the desk.

'How many corridas you had this year?' Retana asked.

'One,' he answered.

'Just that one?' the little man asked.

'That's all.'

'I read about it in the papers,' Retana said. He leaned back in the chair and looked at Manuel.

Manuel looked up at the stuffed bull. He had seen it often before. He felt a certain family interest in it. It had killed his brother, the promising one, about nine years ago. Manuel remembered the day.

There was a brass plate on the oak shield the bull's head was mounted on. Manuel could not read it, but he imagined it was in memory of his brother. Well, he had been a good kid.

The plate said: 'The Bull "Mariposa" of the Duke of Veragua, which accepted 9 varas for 7 caballos, and caused the death of Antonio Garcia, Novillero, April 27, 1909.'

Retana saw him looking at the stuffed bull's head.

'The lot the Duke sent me for Sunday will make a scandal,' he said. 'They're all bad in the legs. What do they say about them at the Café?'

'I don't know,' Manuel said. 'I just got in.'

'Yes,' Retana said. 'You still have your bag.'

He looked at Manuel, leaning back behind the big desk.

'Sit down,' he said. 'Take off your cap.'

Manuel sat down; his cap off, his face was changed. He looked pale, and his coleta pinned forward on his head, so that it would not show under the cap, gave him a strange look.

'You don't look well,' Retana said.

'I just got out of the hospital,' Manuel said.

'I heard they'd cut your leg off,' Retana said.

'No,' said Manuel. 'It got all right.'

Retana leaned forward across the desk and pushed a wooden box of cigarettes toward Manuel.

'Have a cigarette,' he said.

'Thanks.'

Manuel lit it.

'Smoke?' he said, offering the match to Retana.

'No,' Retana waved his hand, 'I never smoke.'

Retana watched him smoking.

'Why don't you get a job and go to work?' he said.

'I don't want to work,' Manuel said. 'I am a bull-fighter.'

'There aren't any bull-fighters any more,' Retana said.

'I'm a bull-fighter,' Manuel said.

'Yes, while you're in there,' Retana said.

Manuel laughed.

Retana sat, saying nothing and looking at Manuel.

'I'll put you in a nocturnal if you want,' Retana offered.

'When?' Manuel asked.

'To-morrow night.'

'I don't like to substitute for anybody,' Manuel said. That was the way they all got killed. That was the way Salvador got killed. He tapped with his knuckles on the table.

'It's all I've got,' Retana said.

'Why don't you put me on next week?' Manuel suggested.

'You wouldn't draw,' Retana said. 'All they want is Litri and Rubito and La Torre. Those kids are good.'

'They'd come to see me get it,' Manuel said, hopefully.

'No, they wouldn't. They don't know who you are any more.'

'I've got a lot of stuff,' Manuel said.

'I'm offering to put you on to-morrow night,' Retina said. 'You can work with young Hernandez and kill two novillos after the Charlots.'

'Whose novillos?' Manuel asked.

'I don't know. Whatever stuff they've got in the corrals. What the veterinaries won't pass in the daytime.'

'I don't like to substitute,' Manuel said.

'You can take it or leave it,' Retana said. He leaned forward over the papers. He was no longer interested. The appeal that Manuel had made to him for a moment when he thought of the old days was gone. He would like to get him to substitute for Larita because he could get him cheaply. He could get others cheaply too. He would like to help him though. Still he had given him the chance. It was up to him.

'How much do I get?' Manuel asked. He was still playing with the idea of refusing. But he knew he could not refuse.

'Two hundred and fifty pesetas,' Retana said. He had thought of five hundred, but when he opened his mouth it said two hundred and fifty.

'You pay Villalta seven thousand,' Manuel said.

'You're not Villalta,' Retana said.

'I know it,' Manuel said.

'He draws it, Manolo,' Retana said in explanation.

'Sure,' said Manuel. He stood up. 'Give me three hundred, Retana.'

'All right,' Retana agreed. He reached in the drawer for a paper.

'Can I have fifty now?' Manuel asked.

'Sure,' said Retana. He took a fifty peseta note out of his pocket-book and laid it, spread out flat, on the table.

Manuel picked it up and put it in his pocket.

'What about a cuadrilla?' he asked.

'There's the boys that always work for me nights,' Retana said. 'They're all right.'

'How about picadors?' Manuel asked.

'They're not much,' Retana admitted.

'I've got to have one good pic,' Manuel said.

'Get him then,' Retana said. 'Go and get him.'

'Not out of this,' Manuel said. 'I'm not paying for any cuadrilla out of sixty duros.'

Retana said nothing but looked at Manuel across the big desk.

'You know I've got to have one good pic,' Manuel said.

Retana said nothing but looked at Manuel from a long way off.

'It isn't right,' Manuel said.

Retana was still considering him, leaning back in his chair, considering him from a long way away.

'There're the regular pics,' he offered.

'I know,' Manuel said. 'I know your regular pics.'

Retana did not smile. Manuel knew it was over.

'All I want is an even break,' Manuel said reasonably. 'When I go out there I want to be able to call my shots on the bull. It only takes one good picador.'

He was talking to a man who was no longer listening.

'If you want something extra,' Retana

said, 'go and get it. There will be a regular cuadrilla out there. Bring as many of your own pics as you want. The charlotada is over by 10.30.'

'All right,' Manuel said. 'If that's the way you feel about it.'

'That's the way,' Retana said.

'I'll see you to-morrow night,' Manuel said.

'I'll be out there,' Retana said.

Manuel picked up his suitcase and went out.

'Shut the door,' Retana called.

Manuel looked back. Retana was sitting forward looking at some papers. Manuel pulled the door tight until it clicked.

He went down the stairs and out of the door into the hot brightness of the street. It was very hot in the street and the light on the white buildings was sudden and hard on his eyes. He walked down the shady side of the steep street toward the Puerta del Sol. The shade felt solid and cool as running water. The heat came suddenly as he crossed the intersecting streets. Manuel saw no one he knew in all the people he passed.

Just before the Puerto del Sol he turned into a café.

It was quiet in the café. There were a few men sitting at tables against the wall. At one table four men played cards. Most of the men sat against the wall smoking, empty coffee-cups and liqueur-glasses before them on the tables. Manuel went through the long room to a small room in back. A man sat at a table in the corner asleep. Manuel sat down at one of the tables.

A waiter came in and stood beside Manuel's table.

'Have you seen Zurito?' Manuel asked him.

'He was in before lunch,' the waiter answered. 'He won't be back before five o'clock.'

'Bring me some coffee and milk and a shot of the ordinary,' Manuel said.

The waiter came back into the room carrying a tray with a big coffee-glass and a liqueur-glass on it. In his left hand he held a bottle of brandy. He swung these down to the table and a boy who had followed him poured coffee and milk into the glass from two shiny, spouted pots with long handles.

Manuel took off his cap and the waiter noticed his pigtail pinned forward on his head. He winked at the coffee-boy as he poured out the brandy into the little glass beside Manuel's coffee. The coffee-boy looked at Manuel's pale face curiously.

'You fighting here?' asked the waiter, corking up the bottle.

'Yes,' Manuel said. 'To-morrow.'

The waiter stood there, holding the bottle on one hip.

'You in the Charlie Chaplin's?' he asked.

The coffee-boy looked away, embarrassed.

'No. In the ordinary.'

'I thought they were going to have Chaves and Hernandez,' the waiter said.

'No. Me and another.'

'Who? Chaves or Hernandez?'

'Hernandez, I think.'

'What's the matter with Chaves?'

'He got hurt.'

'Where did you hear that?'

'Retana.'

'Hey, Looie,' the waiter called to the next room, 'Chaves got cogida.'

Manuel had taken the wrapper off the lumps of sugar and dropped them into his coffee. He stirred it and drank it down, sweet, hot, and warming in his empty stomach. He drank off the brandy.

'Give me another shot of that,' he said to the waiter.

The waiter uncorked the bottle and poured the glass full, slopping another drink into the saucer. Another waiter had come up in front of the table. The coffee-boy was gone.

'Is Chaves hurt bad?' the second waiter asked Manuel.

'I don't know,' Manuel said, 'Retana didn't say.'

'A hell of a lot he cares,' the tall waiter said. Manuel had not seen him before. He must have just come up.

'If you stand in with Retana in this town, you're a made man,' the tall waiter said. 'If you aren't in with him, you might just as well go out and shoot yourself.'

'You said it,' the other waiter who had come in said. 'You said it then.'

'You're right I said it,' said the tall waiter. 'I know what I'm talking about when I talk about that bird.'

'Look what he's done for Villalta,' the first waiter said.

'And that ain't all,' the tall waiter said.
'Look what he's done for Marcial Lalanda.
Look what he's done for Nacional.'

'You said it, kid,' agreed the short
waiter.

Manuel looked at them, standing talking
in front of his table. He had drunk his
second brandy. They had forgotten about
him. They were not interested in him.

'Look at that bunch of camels,' the tall
waiter went on. 'Did you ever see this
Nacional II?'

'I seen him last Sunday didn't I?' the
original waiter said.

'He's a giraffe,' the short waiter said.

'What did I tell you?' the tall waiter
said. 'Those are Retana's boys.'

'Say, give me another shot of that,'
Manuel said. He had poured the brandy
the waiter had slopped over in the saucer
into his glass and drank it while they were
talking.

The original waiter poured his glass full
mechanically, and the three of them went
out of the room talking.

In the far corner the man was still asleep,
snoring slightly on the intaking breath,
his head back against the wall.

Manuel drank his brandy. He felt sleepy
himself. It was too hot to go out into the
town. Besides there was nothing to do. He
wanted to see Zurito. He would go to sleep
while he waited. He kicked his suitcase
under the table to be sure it was there.
Perhaps it would be better to put it back
under the seat, against the wall. He leaned
down and shoved it under. Then he leaned
forward on the table and went to sleep.

When he woke there was someone sitting
across the table from him. It was a big man
with a heavy brown face like an Indian.
He had been sitting there some time. He
had waved the waiter away and sat reading
the paper and occasionally looking down at
Manuel, asleep, his head on the table. He
read the paper laboriously forming the
words with his lips as he read. When it
tired him he looked at Manuel. He sat
heavily in the chair, his black Cordoba hat
tipped forward.

Manuel sat up and looked at him.

'Hello, Zurito,' he said.

'Hello, kid,' the big man said.

'I've been asleep.' Manuel rubbed his
forehead with the back of his fist.

'I thought maybe you were.'

'How's everything?'

'Good. How is everything with you?'

'Not so good.'

They were both silent. Zurito, the picador, looked at Manuel's white face. Manuel
looked down at the picador's enormous
hands folding the paper to put away in his
pocket.

'I got a favor to ask you, Manos,' Manuel said.

Manosduros was Zurito's nickname. He
never heard it without thinking of his huge
hands. He put them forward on the table
self-consciously.

'Let's have a drink,' he said.

'Sure,' said Manuel.

The waiter came and went and came
again. He went out of the room looking
back at the two men at the table.

'What's the matter, Manolo?' Zurito set
down his glass.

'Would you pic two bulls for me to-
morrow night?' Manuel asked, looking up
at Zurito across the table.

'No,' said Zurito. 'I'm not pic-ing.'

Manuel looked down at his glass. He
had expected that answer; now he had it.
Well, he had it.

'I'm sorry, Manolo, but I'm not pic-ing.'
Zurito looked at his hands.

'That's all right,' Manuel said.

'I'm too old,' Zurito said.

'I just asked you,' Manuel said.

'Is it the nocturnal to-morrow?'

'That's it. I figured if I had just one
good pic, I could get away with it.'

'How much are you getting?'

'Three hundred pesetas.'

'I get more than that for pic-ing.'

'I know,' said Manuel. 'I didn't have any
right to ask you.'

'What do you keep on doing it for?'
Zurito asked. 'Why don't you cut off your
coleta, Manolo?'

'I don't know,' Manuel said.

'You're pretty near as old as I am,'
Zurito said.

'I don't know,' Manuel said. 'I got to do
it. If I can fix it so that I get an even break,
that's all I want. I got to stick with it,
Manos.'

'No, you don't.'

'Yes, I do. I've tried keeping away from
it.'

'I know how you feel. But it isn't right. You ought to get out and stay out.'

'I can't do it. Besides, I've been going good lately.'

Zurito looked at his face.

'You've been in the hospital.'

'But I was going great when I got hurt.'

Zurito said nothing. He tipped the cognac out of his saucer into his glass.

'The papers said they never saw a better faena,' Manuel said.

Zurito looked at him.

'You know when I get going I'm good,' Manuel said.

'You're too old,' the picador said.

'No,' said Manuel. 'You're ten years older than I am.'

'With me it's different.'

'I'm not too old,' Manuel said.

They sat silent, Manuel watching the picador's face.

'I was going great till I got hurt,' Manuel offered.

'You ought to have seen me, Manos,' Manuel said, reproachfully.

'I don't want to see you,' Zurito said. 'It makes me nervous.'

'You haven't seen me lately.'

'I've seen you plenty.'

Zurito looked at Manuel, avoiding his eyes.

'You ought to quit it, Manolo.'

'I can't,' Manuel said. 'I'm going good now, I tell you.'

Zurito leaned forward, his hands on the table.

'Listen. I'll pic for you and if you don't go big to-morrow night, you'll quit. See? Will you do that?'

'Sure.'

Zurito leaned back, relieved.

'You got to quit,' he said. 'No monkey business. You got to cut the coleta.'

'I won't have to quit,' Manuel said. 'You watch me. I've got the stuff.'

Zurito stood up. He felt tired from arguing.

'You got to quit,' he said. 'I'll cut your coleta myself.'

'No, you won't,' Manuel said. 'You won't have a chance.'

Zurito called the waiter.

'Come on,' said Zurito. 'Come on up to the house.'

Manuel reached under the seat for his suitcase. He was happy. He knew Zurito would pic for him. He was the best picador living. It was all simple now.

'Come on up to the house and we'll eat,' Zurito said.

Manuel stood in the patio de caballos waiting for the Charlie Chaplins to be over. Zurito stood beside him. Where they stood it was dark. The high door that led into the bull-ring was shut. Above them they heard a shout, then another shout of laughter. Then there was silence. Manuel liked the smell of the stables about the patio de caballos. It smelt good in the dark. There was another roar from the arena and then applause, prolonged applause, going on and on.

'You ever seen these fellows?' Zurito asked, big and looming beside Manuel in the dark.

'No,' Manuel said.

'They're pretty funny.' Zurito said. He smiled to himself in the dark.

The high, double, tight-fitting door into the bull-ring swung open and Manuel saw the ring in the hard light of the arc-lights, the plaza, dark all the way around, rising high; around the edge of the ring were running and bowing two men dressed like tramps, followed by a third in the uniform of a hotel bell-boy who stooped and picked up the hats and canes thrown down onto the sand and tossed them back up into the darkness.

The electric light went on in the patio.

'I'll climb onto one of those ponies while you collect the kids,' Zurito said.

Behind them came the jingle of the mules, coming out to go into the arena and be hitched onto the dead bull.

The members of the cuadrilla, who had been watching the burlesque from the runway between the barrera and the seats, came walking back and stood in a group talking, under the electric light in the patio. A good-looking lad in a silver-and-orange suit came up to Manuel and smiled.

'I'm Hernandez,' he said and put out his hand.

Manuel shook it.

'They're regular elephants we've got to-night,' the boy said cheerfully.

'They're big ones with horns,' Manuel agreed.

'You drew the worst lot,' the boy said.

'That's all right,' Manuel said. 'The bigger they are, the more meat for the poor.'

'Where did you get that one?' Hernandez grinned.

'That's an old one,' Manuel said. 'You line up your cuadrilla, so I can see what I've got.'

'You've got some good kids,' Hernandez said. He was very cheerful. He had been on twice before in nocturnals and was beginning to get a following in Madrid. He was happy the fight would start in a few minutes.

'Where are the pics?' Manuel asked.

'They're back in the corrals fighting about who gets the beautiful horses,' Hernandez grinned.

The mules came through the gate in a rush, the whips snapping, bells jangling and the young bull ploughing a furrow of sand.

They formed up for the paseo as soon as the bull had gone through.

Manuel and Hernandez stood in front. The youths of the cuadrillas were behind, their heavy capes furled over their arms. In back, the four picadors, mounted, holding their steel-tipped push-poles erect in the half-dark of the corral.

'It's a wonder Retana wouldn't give us enough light to see the horses by,' one picador said.

'He knows we'll be happier if we don't get too good a look at these skins,' another pic answered.

'This thing I'm on barely keeps me off the ground,' the first picador said.

'Well, they're horses.'

'Sure, they're horses.'

They talked, sitting their gaunt horses in the dark.

Zurito said nothing. He had the only steady horse of the lot. He had tried him, wheeling him in the corrals and he responded to the bit and the spurs. He had taken the bandage off his right eye and cut the strings where they had tied his ears tight shut at the base. He was a good, solid horse, solid on his legs. That was all he needed. He intended to ride him all through the corrida. He had already, since he had mounted, sitting in the half-dark in the big, quilted saddle, waiting for the paseo, pic-ed through the whole corrida in his mind. The other picadors went on talking on both sides of him. He did not hear them.

The two matadors stood together in front of their three peones, their capes furled over their left arms in the same fashion. Manuel was thinking about the three lads in back of him. They were all three Madrilenos, like Hernandez, boys about nineteen. One of them, a gypsy, serious, aloof, and dark-faced, he liked the look of. He turned.

'What's your name, kid?' he asked the gypsy.

'Fuentes,' the gypsy said.

'That's a good name,' Manuel said.

The gypsy smiled, showing his teeth.

'You take the bull and give him a little run when he comes out,' Manuel said.

'All right,' the gypsy said. His face was serious. He began to think about just what he would do.

'Here she goes,' Manuel said to Hernandez.

'All right. We'll go.'

Heads up, swinging with the music, their right arms swinging free, they stepped out, crossing the sanded arena under the arc-lights, the cuadrillas opening out behind, the picadors riding after, behind came the bull-ring servants and the jingling mules. The crowd applauded Hernandez as they marched across the arena. Arrogant, swinging, they looked straight ahead as they marched.

They bowed before the president, and the procession broke up into its component parts. The bull-fighters went over to the barrera and changed their heavy mantles for the light fighting capes. The mules went out. The picadors galloped jerkily around the ring, and two rode out the gate they had come in by. The servants swept the sand smooth.

Manuel drank a glass of water poured for him by one of Retana's deputies, who was acting as his manager and sword-handler. Hernandez came over from speaking with his own manager.

'You got a good hand, kid,' Manuel complimented him.

'They like me,' Hernandez said happily.

'How did the paseo go?' Manuel asked Retana's man.

'Like a wedding,' said the handler. 'Fine. You came out like Joselito and Belmonte.'

Zurito rode by, a bulky equestrian statue. He wheeled his horse and faced him toward the toril on the far side of the ring where the bull would come out. It was strange under the arc-light. He pic-ed in the hot afternoon sun for big money. He didn't like this arc-light business. He wished they would get started.

Manuel went up to him.

'Pic him, Manos,' he said. 'Cut him down to size for me.'

'I'll pic him, kid,' Zurito spat on the sand. 'I'll make him jump out of the ring.'

'Lean on him, Manos,' Manuel said.

'I'll lean on him,' Zurito said. 'What's holding it up?'

'He's coming now,' Manuel said.

Zurito sat there, his feet in the box-stirrups, his great legs in the buckskin-covered armor gripping the horse, the reins in his left hand, the long pic held in his right hand, his broad hat well down over his eyes to shade them from the lights, watching the distant door of the toril. His horse's ears quivered. Zurito patted him with his left hand.

The red door of the toril swung back and for a moment Zurito looked into the empty passageway far across the arena. Then the bull came out in a rush, skidding on his four legs as he came out under the lights, then charging in a gallop, moving softly in a fast gallop, silent except as he woofed through wide nostrils as he charged, glad to be free after the dark pen.

In the first row of seats, slightly bored, leaning forward to write on the cement wall in front of his knees, the substitute bull-fight critic of El Heraldo scribbled: 'Campagnero, Negro, 42, came out at 90 miles an hour with plenty of gas—'

Manuel, leaning against the barrera, watching the bull, waved his hand and the gypsy ran out, trailing his cape. The bull, in full gallop, pivoted and charged the cape, his head down, his tail rising. The gypsy moved in a zigzag, and as he passed, the bull caught sight of him and abandoned the cape to charge the man. The gyp sprinted and vaulted the red fence of the barrera as the bull struck it with his horns. He tossed into it twice with his horns, banging into the wood blindly.

The critic of El Heraldo lit a cigarette and tossed the match at the bull, then wrote in his note-book, 'large and with enough horns to satisfy the cash customers, Campagnero showed a tendency to cut into the terrane of the bull-fighters.'

Manuel stepped out on the hard sand as the bull banged into the fence. Out of the corner of his eye he saw Zurito sitting the white horse close to the barrera, about a quarter of the way around the ring to the left. Manuel held the cape close in front of him, a fold in each hand, and shouted at the bull. 'Huh! Huh!' The bull turned, seemed to brace against the fence as he charged in a scramble, driving into the cape as Manuel side-stepped, pivoted on his heels with the charge of the bull, and swung the cape just ahead of the horns. At the end of the swing he was facing the bull again and held the cape in the same position close in front of his body, and pivoted again as the bull recharged. Each time, as he swung, the crowd shouted.

Four times he swung with the bull, lifting the cape so it billowed full, and each time bringing the bull around to charge again. Then, at the end of the fifth swing, he held the cape against his hip and pivoted, so the cape swung out like a ballet dancer's skirt and wound the bull around himself like a belt, to step clear, leaving the bull facing Zurito on the white horse, come up and planted firm, the horse facing the bull, its ears forward, its lips nervous, Zurito, his hat over his eyes, leaning forward, the long pole sticking out before and behind in a sharp angle under his right arm, held halfway down, the triangular iron point facing the bull.

El Heraldo's second-string critic, drawing on his cigarette, his eyes on the bull, wrote: 'the veteran Manolo designed a series of acceptable veronicas, ending in a very Belmontistic recorte that earned applause from the regulars, and we entered the tercio of the cavalry.'

Zurito sat his horse, measuring the distance between the bull and the end of the pic. As he looked, the bull gathered himself together and charged, his eyes on the horse's chest. As he lowered his head to hook, Zurito sunk the point of the pic in the swelling hump of muscle above the bull's shoulder, leaned all his weight on the shaft, and with his left hand pulled the white horse into the air, front hoofs pawing, and swung him to the right as he pushed the bull under and through so the horns passed safely under the horse's belly and the horse came down, quivering, the bull's tail brushing his chest as he charged the cape Hernandez offered him.

Hernandez ran sideways, taking the bull out and away with the cape, toward the other picador. He fixed him with a swing of the cape, squarely facing the horse and rider, and stepped back. As the bull saw the horse he charged. The picador's lance slid along his back, and as the shock of the charge lifted the horse, the picador was already half-way out of the saddle, lifting his right leg clear as he missed with the lance and falling to the left side to keep the horse between him and the bull. The horse, lifted and gored, crashed over with the bull driving into him, the picador gave a shove with his boots against the horse and lay clear, waiting to be lifted and hauled away and put on his feet.

Manuel let the bull drive into the fallen horse; he was in no hurry, the picador was safe; besides, it did a picador like that good to worry. He'd stay on longer next time. Lousy pics! He looked across the sand at Zurito a little way out from the barrera, his horse rigid, waiting.

'Huh!' he called to the bull, 'Tomar!' holding the cape in both hands so it would catch his eye. The bull detached himself from the horse and charged the cape, and Manuel, running sideways and holding the cape spread wide, stopped, swung on his heels, and brought the bull sharply around facing Zurito.

'Campagnero accepted a pair of varas for the death of one rosinante, with Hernandez and Manolo at the quites,' *El Heraldo's* critic wrote. 'He pressed on the iron and clearly showed he was no horse-lover. The veteran Zurito resurrected some of his old stuff with the pike-pole, notably the suerte—'

'Olé! Olé!' the man sitting beside him shouted. The shout was lost in the roar of the crowd, and he slapped the critic on the back. The critic looked up to see Zurito, directly below him, leaning far out over his horse, the length of the pic rising in a sharp angle under his armpit, holding the pic

almost by the point, bearing down with all his weight, holding the bull off, the bull pushing and driving to get at the horse, and Zurito, far out, on top of him, holding him, holding him, and slowly pivoting the horse against the pressure, so that at last he was clear. Zurito felt the moment when the horse was clear and the bull could come past, and relaxed the absolute steel lock of his resistance, and the triangular steel point of the pic ripped in the bull's hump of shoulder muscle as he tore loose to find Hernandez's cape before his muzzle. He charged blindly into the cape and the boy took him out into the open arena.

Zurito sat patting his horse and looking at the bull charging the cape that Hernandez swung for him out under the bright light while the crowd shouted.

'You see that one?' he said to Manuel.

'It was a wonder,' Manuel said.

'I got him that time,' Zurito said. 'Look at him now.'

At the conclusion of a closely turned pass of the cape the bull slid to his knees. He was up at once, but far out across the sand Manuel and Zurito saw the shine of the pumping flow of blood, smooth against the black of the bull's shoulder.

'I got him that time,' Zurito said.

'He's a good bull,' Manuel said.

'If they gave me another shot at him, I'd kill him,' Zurito said.

'They'll change the thirds on us,' Manuel said.

'Look at him now,' Zurito said.

'I got to go over there,' Manuel said, and started on a run for the other side of the ring, where the monos were leading a horse out by the bridle toward the bull, whacking him on the legs with rods and all, in a procession, trying to get him toward the bull, who stood, dropping his head, pawing, unable to make up his mind to charge.

Zurito, sitting his horse, walking him toward the scene, not missing any detail, scowled.

Finally the bull charged, the horse leaders ran for the barrera, the picador hit too far back, and the bull got under the horse, lifted him, threw him onto his back.

Zurito watched. The monos, in their red shirts, running out to drag the picador clear. The picador, now on his feet, swearing and flopping his arms. Manuel and

Hernandez standing ready with their capes. And the bull, the great, black bull, with a horse on his back, hooves dangling, the bridle caught in the horns. Black bull with a horse on his back, staggering short-legged, then arching his neck and lifting, thrusting, charging to slide the horse off, horse sliding down. Then the bull into a lunging charge at the cape Manuel spread for him.

The bull was slower now, Manuel felt. He was bleeding badly. There was a sheen of blood all down his flank.

Manuel offered him the cape again. There he came, eyes open, ugly, watching the cape. Manuel stepped to the side and raised his arms, tightening the cape ahead of the bull for the veronica.

Now he was facing the bull. Yes, his head was going down a little. He was carrying it lower. That was Zurito.

Manuel flopped the cape; there he comes; he side-stepped and swung in another veronica. He's shooting awfully accurately, he thought. He's had enough fight, so he's watching now. He's hunting now. Got his eye on me. But I always give him the cape.

He shook the cape at the bull; there he comes; he side-stepped. Awful close that time. I don't want to work that close to him.

The edge of the cape was wet with blood where it had swept along the bull's back as he went by.

All right, here's the last one.

Manuel, facing the bull, having turned with him each charge, offered the cape with his two hands. The bull looked at him. Eyes watching, horns straight forward, the bull looked at him, watching.

'Huh!' Manuel said, 'Toro!' and leaning back, swung the cape forward. Here he comes. He side-stepped, swung the cape in back of him, and pivoted, so the bull followed a swirl of cape and then was left with nothing, fixed by the pass, dominated by the cape. Manuel swung the cape under his muzzle with one hand, to show the bull was fixed, and walked away.

There was no applause.

Manuel walked across the sand towards the barrera, while Zurito rode out of the ring. The trumpet had blown to change the act to the planting of the banderillos while Manuel had been working with the bull. He had not consciously noticed it. The monos were spreading canvas over the two dead horses and sprinkling sawdust around them.

Manuel came up to the barrera for a drink of water. Retana's man handed him the heavy porous jug.

Fuentes, the tall gypsy, was standing holding a pair of banderillos, holding them together, slim, red sticks, fish-hook points out. He looked at Manuel.

'Go on out there,' Manuel said.

The gypsy trotted out. Manuel set down the jug and watched. He wiped his face with his handkerchief.

The critic of *El Heraldo* reached for the bottle of warm champagne that stood between his feet, took a drink, and finished his paragraph.

'—the aged Manolo rated no applause for a vulgar series of lances with the cape and we entered the third of the palings.'

Alone in the centre of the ring the bull stood, still fixed. Fuentes, tall, flat-backed, walking toward him arrogantly, his arms spread out, the two slim, red sticks, one in each hand, held by the fingers, points straight forward. Fuentes walked forward. Back of him and to one side was a peon with a cape. The bull looked at him and was no longer fixed.

His eyes watched Fuentes, now standing still. Now he leaned back, calling to him. Fuentes twitched the two banderillos and the light on the steel points caught the bull's eye.

His tail went up and he charged.

He came straight, his eyes on the man. Fuentes stood still, leaning back, the banderillos pointing forward. As the bull lowered his head to hook, Fuentes leaned backward, his arms came together and rose, his two hands touching, the banderillos two descending red lines, and leaning forward drove the points into the bull's shoulder, leaning far in over the bull's horns and pivoting on the two upright sticks, his legs tight together, his body curving to one side to let the bull pass.

'Olé!' from the crowd.

The bull was hooking wildly, jumping like a trout, all four feet off the ground. The red shafts of the banderillos tossed as he jumped.

Manuel standing at the barrera, noticed that he hooked always to the right.

'Tell him to drop the next pair on the right,' he said to the kid who started to run out to Fuentes with the new banderillos.

A heavy hand fell on his shoulder. It was Zurito.

'How do you feel, kid?' he asked.

Manuel was watching the bull.

Zurito leaned forward on the barrera, leaning the weight of his body on his arms. Manuel turned to him.

'You're going good,' Zurito said.

Manuel shook his head. He had nothing to do now until the next third. The gypsy was very good with the banderillos. The bull would come to him in the next third in good shape. He was a good bull. It had all been easy up to now. The final stuff with the sword was all he worried over. He did not really worry. He did not even think about it. But standing there he had a heavy sense of apprehension. He looked out at the bull, planning his faena, his work with the red cloth that was to reduce the bull, to make him manageable.

The gypsy was walking out toward the bull again, walking heel-and-toe, insultingly, like a ball-room dancer, the red shafts of the banderillos twitching with his walk. The bull watched him, not fixed now, hunting him, but waiting to get close enough so he could be sure of getting him, getting the horns into him.

As Fuentes walked forward the bull charged. Fuentes ran across the quarter of a circle as the bull charged and, as he passed running backward, stopped, swung forward, rose on his toes, arms straight out, and sunk the banderillos straight down into the tight of the big shoulder muscles as the bull missed him.

The crowd were wild about it.

'That kid won't stay in this night stuff long,' Retana's man said to Zurito.

'He's good,' Zurito said.

'Watch him now.'

They watched.

Fuentes was standing with his back against the barrera. Two of the cuadrilla were back of him, with their capes ready to flop over the fence to distract the bull.

The bull, with his tongue out, his barrel heaving, was watching the gypsy. He thought he had him now. Back against the red planks. Only a short charge away. The bull watched him.

The gypsy bent back, drew back his arms, the banderillos pointing at the bull. He called to the bull, stamped one foot. The bull was suspicious. He wanted the man. No more barbs in the shoulder.

Fuentes walked a little closer to the bull. Bent back. Called again. Somebody in the crowd shouted a warning.

'He's too damn close,' Zurito said.

'Watch him,' Retina's man said.

Leaning back, inciting the bull with the banderillos, Fuentes jumped, both feet off the ground. As he jumped the bull's tail rose and he charged. Fuentes came down on his toes, arms straight out, whole body arching forward, and drove the shafts straight down as he swung his body clear of the right horn.

The bull crashed into the barrera where the flopping capes had attracted his eye as he lost the man.

The gypsy came running along the barrera toward Manuel, taking the applause of the crowd. His vest was ripped where he had not quite cleared the point of the horn. He was happy about it, showing it to the spectators. He made the tour of the ring. Zurito saw him go by, smiling, pointing at his vest. He smiled.

Somebody else was planting the last pair of banderillos. Nobody was paying any attention.

Retana's man tucked a baton inside the red cloth of a muleta, folded the cloth over it, and handed it over the barrera to Manuel. He reached in the leather sword-case, took out a sword, and holding it by its leather scabbard, reached it over the fence to Manuel. Manuel pulled the blade out by the red hilt and the scabbard fell limp.

He looked at Zurito. The big man saw he was sweating.

'Now you get him, kid,' Zurito said.

Manuel nodded.

'He's in good shape,' Zurito said.

'Just like you want him,' Retana's man assured him.

Manuel nodded.

The trumpeter, up under the roof, blew for the final act, and Manuel walked across the arena toward where, up in the dark boxes, the president must be.

In the front row seats the substitute bull-fight critic of *El Heraldo* took a long drink of the warm champagne. He had decided it was not worth while to write a running story and would write up the corrida back in the office. What the hell was it anyway? Only a nocturnal. If he missed anything he would get it out of the morning papers. He took another drink of the champagne. He had a date at Maxim's at twelve. Who were these bull-fighters anyway? Kids and bums. A bunch of bums. He put his pad of paper in his pocket and looked over toward Manuel, standing very much alone in the ring, gesturing with his hat in a salute toward a box he could not see high up in the dark plaza. Out in the ring the bull stood quiet, looking at nothing.

'I dedicate this bull to you, Mr. President, and to the public of Madrid, the most intelligent and generous of the world,' was what Manuel was saying. It was a formula. He said it all. It was a little long for nocturnal use.

He bowed at the dark, straightened, tossed his hat over his shoulder, and, carrying the muleta in his left hand and the sword in his right, walked out toward the bull.

Manuel walked toward the bull. The bull looked at him; his eyes were quick. Manuel noticed the way the banderillos hung down on his left shoulder and the steady sheen of blood from Zurito's pic-ing. He noticed the way the bull's feet were. As he walked forward, holding the muleta in his left hand and the sword in his right, he watched the bull's feet. The bull could not charge without gathering his feet together. Now he stood square on them, dully.

Manuel walked toward him, watching his feet. This was all right. He could do this. He must work to get the bull's head down, so he could go in past the horns and kill him. He did not think about the sword, not about killing the bull. He thought about one thing at a time. The coming things oppressed him, though. Walking forward, watching the bull's feet, he saw successively his eyes, his wet muzzle, and the wide, forward-pointing spread of his horns. The bull had light circles about his eyes. His eyes watched Manuel. He felt he was going to get this little one with the white face.

Standing still now and spreading the red cloth of the muleta with the sword, pricking the point into the cloth so that the sword, now held in his left hand, spread the red flannel like the jib of a boat, Manuel noticed the points of the bull's horns. One of them was splintered from banging against the barrera. The other was sharp as a porcupine quill. Manuel noticed while spreading the muleta that the white base of the horn was stained red. While he noticed these things he did not lose sight of the bull's feet. The bull watched Manuel steadily.

He's on the defensive now, Manuel thought. He's reserving himself. I've got to bring him out of that and get his head down. Always get his head down. Zurito had his head down once, but he's come back. He'll bleed when I start him going and that will bring it down.

Holding the muleta, with the sword in his left hand widening it in front of him, he called to the bull.

The bull looked at him.

He leaned back insultingly and shook the wide-spread flannel.

The bull saw the muleta. It was a bright scarlet under the arc-light. The bull's legs tightened.

Here he comes. Whoosh! Manuel turned as the bull came and raised the muleta so that it passed over the bull's horns and swept down his broad back from head to tail. The bull had gone clean up in the air with the charge. Manuel had not moved.

At the end of the pass the bull turned like a cat coming around a corner and faced Manuel.

He was on the offensive again. His heaviness was gone. Manuel noted the fresh blood shining down the black shoulder and dripping down the bull's leg. He drew the sword out of the muleta and held it in his right hand. The muleta held low down in his left hand, leaning toward the left, he called to the bull. The bull's legs tightened, his eyes on the muleta. Here he comes, Manuel thought. Yuh!

He swung with the charge, sweeping the muleta ahead of the bull, his feet firm, the sword following the curve, a point of light under the arcs.

The bull recharged as the pase natural finished and Manuel raised the muleta for a pase de pecho. Firmly planted, the bull came by his chest under the raised muleta. Manuel leaned his head back to avoid the clattering banderillo shafts. The hot, black bull body touched his chest as it passed.

Too damn close, Manuel thought. Zurito, leaning on the barrera, spoke rapidly to the gypsy, who trotted out toward Manuel with a cape, Zurito pulled his hat down low and looked out across the arena at Manuel.

Manuel was facing the bull again, the muleta held low and to the left. The bull's head was down as he watched the muleta.

'If it was Belmonte doing that stuff, they'd go crazy,' Retana's man said.

Zurito said nothing. He was watching Manuel out in the centre of the arena.

'Where did the boss dig this fellow up?' Retana's man asked.

'Out of the hospital,' Zurito said.

'That's where he's going damn quick,' Retana's man said.

Zurito turned on him.

'Knock on that,' he said, pointing to the barrera.

'I was just kidding, man,' Retana's man said.

'Knock on the wood.'

Retana's man leaned forward and knocked three times on the barrera.

'Watch the faena,' Zurito said.

Out in the centre of the ring, under the lights, Manuel was kneeling, facing the bull, and as he raised the muleta in both hands the bull charged, tail up.

Manuel swung his body clear and, as the bull recharged, brought around the muleta in a half-circle that pulled the bull to his knees.

'Why, that one's a great bull-fighter,' Retana's man said.

'No, he's not,' said Zurito.

Manuel stood up and, the muleta in his left hand, the sword in his right, acknowledged the applause from the dark plaza.

The bull had humped himself up from his knees and stood waiting, his head hung low.

Zurito spoke to two of the other lads of the cuadrilla and they ran out to stand back of Manuel with their capes. There were four men back of him now. Hernandez had followed him since he first came out with the muleta. Fuentes stood watching, his cape held against his body, tall, in repose, watching lazy-eyed. Now the two came up. Hernandez motioned them to stand one at each side. Manuel stood alone, facing the bull.

Manuel waved back the men with the capes. Stepping back cautiously, they saw his face was white and sweating.

Didn't they know enough to keep back? Did they want to catch the bull's eye with the capes after he was fixed and ready? He had enough to worry about without that kind of thing.

The bull was standing, his four feet square, looking at the muleta. Manuel furled the muleta in his left hand. The bull's eyes watched it. His body was heavy on his feet. He carried his head low, but not too low.

Manuel lifted the muleta at him. The bull did not move. Only his eyes watched.

He's all lead, Manuel thought. He's all square. He's framed right. He'll take it.

He thought in bull-fight terms. Sometimes he had a thought and the particular piece of slang would not come into his mind and he could not realize the thought. His instincts and his knowledge worked automatically, and his brain worked slowly and in words. He knew all about bulls. He did not have to think about them. He just did the right thing. His eyes noted things and his body performed the necessary measures without thought. If he thought about it, he would be gone.

Now, facing the bull, he was conscious of many things at the same time. There were the horns, the one splintered, the other smoothly sharp, the need to profile himself toward the left horn, lance himself short and straight, lower the muleta so the bull would follow it, and, going in over the horns, put the sword all the way into a little spot about as big as a five-peseta piece straight in back of the neck, between the sharp pitch of the bull's shoulders. He must do all this and must then come out from between the horns. He was conscious he must do all this, but his only thought was in words: 'Corto y derecho.'

'Corto y derecho,' he thought, furling the muleta. Short and straight. Corto y derecho, he drew the sword out of the muleta, profiled on the splintered left horn, dropped the muleta across his body, so his right hand with the sword on the level with his eye made the sign of the cross, and, rising on his toes, sighted along the dipping blade of the sword at the spot high up between the bull's shoulders.

Corto y derecho he lanced himself on the bull.

There was a shock, and he felt himself go up in the air. He pushed on the sword as he went up and over, and it flew out of his hand. He hit the ground and the bull was on him. Manuel, lying on the ground, kicked at the bull's muzzle with his slippered feet. Kicking, kicking, the bull after him, missing him in his excitement, bumping him with his head, driving the horns into the sand. Kicking like a man keeping a ball in the air, Manuel kept the bull from getting a clean thrust at him.

Manuel felt the wind on his back from the capes flopping at the bull, and then the bull was gone, gone over him in a rush. Dark, as his belly went over. Not even stepped on.

Manuel stood up and picked up the muleta. Fuentes handed him the sword. It was bent where it had struck the shoulderblade. Manuel straightened it on his knee and ran toward the bull, standing now beside one of the dead horses. As he ran, his jacket flopped where it had been ripped under his armpit.

'Get him out of there,' Manuel shouted to the gypsy. The bull had smelled the blood of the dead horse and ripped into the canvas cover with his horns. He charged Fuentes's cape, with the canvas hanging from his splintered horn, and the crowd laughed. Out in the ring, he tossed his head to rid himself of the canvas. Hernandez, running up from behind him, grabbed the end of the canvas and neatly lifted it off the horn.

The bull followed it in a half-charge and stopped still. He was on the defensive again. Manuel was walking toward him with the sword and muleta. Manuel swung the muleta before him. The bull would not charge.

Manuel profiled toward the bull, sighting along the dipping blade of the sword. The bull was motionless, seemingly dead on his feet, incapable of another charge.

Manuel rose to his toes, sighting along the steel, and charged.

Again there was the shock and he felt himself being borne back in a rush, to strike hard on the sand. There was no chance of kicking this time. The bull was on top of him. Manuel lay as though dead, his head on his arms, and the bull bumped him. Bumped his back, bumped his face in the sand. He felt the horn go into the sand between his folded arms. The bull hit him in the small of the back. His face drove into the sand. The horn drove through one of his sleeves and the bull ripped it off. Manuel was tossed clear and the bull followed the capes.

Manuel got up, found the sword and muleta, tried the point of the sword with his thumb, and then ran toward the barrera for a new sword.

Retana's man handed him the sword over the edge of the barrera.

'Wipe off your face,' he said.

Manuel, running again toward the bull, wiped his bloody face with his handkerchief. He had not seen Zurito. Where was Zurito?

The cuadrilla had stepped away from the bull and waited with their capes. The bull stood, heavy and dull again after the action.

Manuel walked toward him with the muleta. He stopped and shook it. The bull did not respond. He passed it right and left, left and right before the bull's muzzle. The bull's eyes watched it and turned with the swing, but he would not charge. He was waiting for Manuel.

Manuel was worried. There was nothing to do but go in. Corto y derecho. He profiled close to the bull, crossed the muleta in front of his body and charged. As he pushed in the sword, he jerked his body to the left to clear the horn. The bull passed him and the sword shot up in the air, twinkling under the arc-lights, to fall red-hilted on the sand.

Manuel ran over and picked it up. It was bent and he straightened it over his knee.

As he came running toward the bull, fixed again now, he passed Hernandez standing with his cape.

'He's all bone,' the boy said encouragingly.

Manuel nodded, wiping his face. He put the bloody handkerchief in his pocket.

There was the bull. He was close to the barrera now. Damn him. Maybe he was all bone. Maybe there was not any place for the sword to go in. The hell there wasn't! He'd show them.

He tried a pass with the muleta and the bull did not move. Manuel chopped the muleta back and forth in front of the bull. Nothing doing.

He furled the muleta, drew the sword out, profiled and drove in on the bull. He felt the sword buckle as he shoved it in, leaning his weight on it, and then it shot high in the air, end-over-ending into the crowd. Manuel had jerked clear as the sword jumped.

The first cushions thrown down out of the dark missed him. Then one hit him in the face, his bloody face looking toward the crowd. They were coming down fast. Spotting the sand. Somebody threw an empty champagne-bottle from close range. It hit Manuel on the foot. He stood there watching the dark, where the things were coming from. Then something whished through the air and struck by him. Manuel leaned over and picked it up. It was his sword. He straightened it over his knee and gestured with it to the crowd.

'Thank you,' he said. 'Thank you.'

Oh, the dirty bastards! Dirty bastards! Oh, the lousy, dirty bastards! He kicked into a cushion as he ran.

There was the bull. The same as ever. All right, you dirty, lousy bastard!

Manuel passed the muleta in front of the bull's black muzzle.

Nothing doing.

You won't! All right. He stepped close and jammed the sharp peak of the muleta into the bull's damp muzzle.

The bull was on him as he jumped back and as he tripped on a cushion he felt the horn go into him, into his side. He grabbed the horn with his two hands and rode backward, holding tight onto the place. The bull tossed him and he was clear. He lay still. It was all right. The bull was gone.

He got up coughing and feeling broken and gone. The dirty bastards!

'Give me the sword,' he shouted. 'Give me the stuff.'

Fuentes came up with the muleta and the sword.

Hernandez put his arm around him.

'Go on to the infirmary, man,' he said. 'Don't be a damn fool.'

'Get away from me,' Manuel said. 'Get to hell away from me.'

He twisted free. Hernandez shrugged his shoulders. Manuel ran toward the bull.

There was the bull standing, heavy, firmly planted.

All right, you bastard! Manuel drew the sword out of the muleta, sighted with the same movement, and flung himself on to the bull. He felt the sword go in all the way. Right up to the guard. Four fingers and his thumb into the bull. The blood was hot on his knuckles, and he was on top of the bull.

The bull lurched with him as he lay on, and seemed to sink; then he was standing clear. He looked at the bull going down slowly over on his side, then suddenly four feet in the air.

Then he gestured at the crowd, his hand warm from the bull blood.

All right, you bastards! He wanted to say something, but he started to cough. It was hot and choking. He looked down for the muleta. He must go over and salute the president. President hell! He was sitting down looking at something. It was the bull. His four feet up. Thick tongue out. Things crawling around on his belly and under his legs. Crawling where the hair was thin. Dead bull. To hell with the bull! To hell with them all! He started to get to his feet and commenced to cough. He sat down again, coughing. Somebody came and pushed him up.

They carried him across the ring to the infirmary, running with him across the sand, standing blocked at the gate as the mules came in, then around under the dark passageway, men grunting as they took him up the stairway, and then laid him down.

The doctor and two men in white were waiting for him. They laid him out on the table. They were cutting away his shirt. Manuel felt tired. His whole chest felt scalding inside. He started to cough and they held something to his mouth. Everybody was very busy.

There was an electric light in his eyes. He shut his eyes.

He heard someone coming very heavily up the stairs. Then he did not hear it. Then he heard a noise far off. That was the crowd. Well, somebody would have to kill his other bull. They had cut away all his shirt. The doctor smiled at him. There was Retana.

'Hello, Retana!' Manuel said. He could not hear his voice.

Retana smiled at him and said something. Manuel could not hear it.

Zurito stood beside the table, bending over where the doctor was working. He was in his picador clothes, without his hat.

Zurito said something to him. Manuel could not hear it.

Zurito was speaking to Retana. One of the men in white smiled and handed Retana a pair of scissors. Retana gave them to Zurito. Zurito said something to Manuel. He could not hear it.

To hell with this operating-table! He'd been on plenty of operating-tables before. He was not going to die. There would be a priest if he was going to die.

Zurito was saying something to him. Holding up the scissors.

That was it. They were going to cut off his coleta. They were going to cut off his pigtail.

Manuel sat up on the operating-table. The doctor stepped back, angry. Someone grabbed him and held him.

'You couldn't do a thing like that, Manos,' he said.

He heard suddenly, clearly, Zurito's voice.

'That's all right,' Zurito said. 'I won't do it. I was joking.'

'I was going good,' Manuel said. 'I didn't have any luck. That was all.'

Manuel lay back. They had put something over his face. It was all familiar. He inhaled deeply. He felt very tired. He was very, very tired. They took the thing away from his face.

'I was going good,' Manuel said weakly. 'I was going great.'

Retana looked at Zurito and started for the door.

'I'll stay here with him,' Zurito said.

Retana shrugged his shoulders.

Manuel opened his eyes and looked at Zurito.

'Wasn't I going good, Manos?' he asked, for confirmation.

'Sure,' said Zurito. 'You were going great.'

The doctor's assistant put the cone over Manuel's face and he inhaled deeply. Zurito stood awkwardly, watching.

1927

JOHN DOS PASSOS

1896–

FROM U.S.A.

TIN LIZZIE [1]

'Mr. Ford the automobileer,' the feature-writer wrote in 1900,

'Mr. Ford the automobileer began by giving his steed three or four sharp jerks with the lever at the righthand side of the seat; that is, he pulled the lever up and down sharply in order, as he said, to mix air with gasoline and drive the charge into the exploding cylinder. . . . Mr. Ford slipped a small electric switch handle and there followed a puff, puff, puff. . . . The puffing of the machine assumed a higher key. She was flying along about eight miles an hour. The ruts in the road were deep, but the machine certainly went with a dreamlike smoothness. There was

___
[1] The selection is one of the biographical interludes from *The Big Money*(N.Y., 1936),47–57, reprinted in the trilogy *U.S.A.*(N.Y., 1937).

none of the bumping common even to a streetcar. . . . By this time the boulevard had been reached, and the automobileer, letting a lever fall a little, let her out. Whiz! She picked up speed with infinite rapidity. As she ran on there was a clattering behind, the new noise of the automobile.

For twenty years or more,

ever since he'd left his father's farm when he was sixteen to get a job in a Detroit machineshop, Henry Ford had been nuts about machinery. First it was watches, then he designed a steamtractor, then he built a horseless carriage with an engine adapted from the Otto gasengine he'd read about in *The World of Science*, then a mechanical buggy with a onecylinder four-cycle motor, that would run forward but not back;

at last, in nineteight, he felt he was far enough along to risk throwing up his job with the Detroit Edison Company, where he'd worked his way up from night fireman to chief engineer, to put all his time into working on a new gasoline engine,

(in the late eighties he'd met Edison at a meeting of electriclight employees in Atlantic City. He'd gone up to Edison after Edison had delivered an address and asked him if he thought gasoline was practical as a motor fuel. Edison had said yes. If Edison said it, it was true. Edison was the great admiration of Henry Ford's life);

and in driving his mechanical buggy, sitting there at the lever jauntily dressed in a tightbuttoned jacket and a high collar and a derby hat, back and forth over the level illpaved streets of Detroit,

scaring the big brewery horses and the skinny trotting horses and the sleekrumped pacers with the motor's loud explosions,

looking for men scatterbrained enough to invest money in a factory for building automobiles.

He was the eldest son of an Irish immigrant who during the Civil War had married the daughter of a prosperous Pennsylvania Dutch farmer and settled down to farming near Dearborn in Wayne County, Michigan;

like plenty of other Americans, young Henry grew up hating the endless sogging through the mud about the chores, the hauling and pitching manure, the kerosene lamps to clean, the irk and sweat and solitude of the farm.

He was a slender, active youngster, a good skater, clever with his hands; what he liked was to tend the machinery and let the others do the heavy work. His mother had told him not to drink, smoke, gamble or go into debt, and he never did.

When he was in his early twenties his father tried to get him back from Detroit, where he was working as mechanic and repairman for the Drydock Engine Company that built engines for steamboats, by giving him forty acres of land.

Young Henry built himself an uptodate square white dwellinghouse with a false mansard roof and married and settled down on the farm,

but he let the hired men do the farming;

he bought himself a buzzsaw and rented a stationary engine and cut the timber off the woodlots.

He was a thrifty young man who never drank or smoked or gambled or coveted his neighbor's wife, but he couldn't stand living on the farm.

He moved to Detroit, and in the brick barn behind his house tinkered for years in his spare time with a mechanical buggy that would be light enough to run over the clayey wagonroads of Wayne County, Michigan.

By 1900 he had a practicable car to promote.

He was forty years old before the Ford Motor Company was started and production began to move.

Speed was the first thing the early automobile manufacturers went after. Races advertised the makes of cars.

Henry Ford himself hung up several records at the track at Grosse Pointe and on the ice on Lake St. Clair. In his 999 he did the mile in thirtynine and fourfifths seconds.

But it had always been his custom to hire others to do the heavy work. The speed he was busy with was speed in production, the records records in efficient output. He hired Barney Oldfield, a stunt bicyclerider from Salt Lake City, to do the racing for him.

Henry Ford had ideas about other things than the designing of motors, carburetors, magnetos, jigs and fixtures, punches and dies; he had ideas about sales,

that the big money was in economical quantity production, quick turnover, cheap interchangeable easilyreplaced standardized parts;

it wasn't until 1909, after years of arguing with his partners, that Ford put out the first Model T.

Henry Ford was right.

That season he sold more than ten thousand tin lizzies, ten years later he was selling almost a million a year.

In these years the Taylor Plan was stirring up plantmanagers and manufacturers all over the country. Efficiency was the word. The same ingenuity that went into improving the performance of a machine could go into improving the performance of the workmen producing the machine.

In 1913 they established the assemblyline at Ford's. That season the profits were something like twentyfive million dollars, but they had trouble in keeping the men on the job, machinists didn't seem to like it at Ford's.

Henry Ford had ideas about other things than production.

He was the largest automobile manufacturer in the world; he paid high wages; maybe if the steady workers thought they were getting a cut (a very small cut) in the profits, it would give trained men an inducement to stick to their jobs,

wellpaid workers might save enough money to buy a tin lizzie; the first day Ford's announced that cleancut properlymarried American workers who wanted jobs had a chance to make five bucks a day (of course it turned out that there were strings to it; always there were strings to it)

such an enormous crowd waited outside the Highland Park plant

all through the zero January night

that there was a riot when the gates were opened; cops broke heads, jobhunters threw bricks; property, Henry Ford's own property, was destroyed. The company dicks had to turn on the firehose to beat back the crowd.

The American Plan; automotive prosperity seeping down from above; it turned out there were strings to it.

But that five dollars a day
paid to good, clean American workmen
who didn't drink or smoke cigarettes or read or think,
and who didn't commit adultery
and whose wives didn't take in boarders,
made America once more the Yukon of the sweated workers of the world;
made all the tin lizzies and the automotive age, and incidentally,
made Henry Ford the automobileer, the admirer of Edison, the birdlover,
the great American of his time.

But Henry Ford had ideas about other things besides assemblylines and the livinghabits of his employees. He was full of ideas. Instead of going to the city to make

his fortune, here was a country boy who'd made his fortune by bringing the city out to the farm. The precepts he'd learned out of McGuffey's Reader, his mother's prejudices and preconceptions, he had preserved clean and unworn as freshprinted bills in the safe in a bank.

He wanted people to know about his ideas, so he bought the *Dearborn Independent* and started a campaign against cigarettesmoking.

When war broke out in Europe, he had ideas about that too. (Suspicion of armymen and soldiering were part of the midwest farm tradition, like thrift, stickativeness, temperance and sharp practice in money matters.) Any intelligent American mechanic could see that if the Europeans hadn't been a lot of ignorant underpaid foreigners who drank, smoked, were loose about women and wasteful in their methods of production, the war could never have happened.

When Rosika Schwimmer broke through the stockade of secretaries and servicemen who surrounded Henry Ford and suggested to him that he could stop the war,

he said sure they'd hire a ship and go over and get the boys out of the trenches by Christmas.

He hired a steamboat, the *Oscar II*, and filled it up with pacifists and socialworkers,

to go over to explain to the princelings of Europe

that what they were doing was vicious and silly.

It wasn't his fault that Poor Richard's commonsense no longer rules the world and that most of the pacifists were nuts,

goofy with headlines.

When William Jennings Bryan went over to Hoboken to see him off, somebody handed William Jennings Bryan a squirrel in a cage; William Jennings Bryan made a speech with the squirrel under his arm. Henry Ford threw American Beauty roses to the crowd. The band played *I Didn't Raise My Boy to Be a Soldier*. Practical jokers let loose more squirrels. An eloping couple was married by a platoon of ministers in the saloon, and Mr. Zero, the flophouse humanitarian, who reached the dock too late to sail,

dove into the North River and swam after the boat.

The *Oscar II* was described as a floating Chautauqua; Henry Ford said it felt like a middlewestern village, but by the time they reached Christiansand in Norway, the reporters had kidded him so that he had gotten cold feet and gone to bed. The world was too crazy outside of Wayne County, Michigan. Mrs. Ford and the management sent an Episcopal dean after him who brought him home under wraps,

and the pacifists had to speechify without him.

Two years later Ford's was manufacturing munitions, Eagle boats; Henry Ford was planning oneman tanks, and oneman submarines like the one tried out in the Revolutionary War. He announced to the press that he'd turn over his war profits to the government,

but there's no record that he ever did.

One thing he brought back from his trip was the Protocols of the Elders of Zion.

He started a campaign to enlighten the world in the *Dearborn Independent*; the Jews were why the world wasn't like Wayne County, Michigan, in the old horse and buggy days;

the Jews had started the war, Bolshevism, Darwinism, Marxism, Nietzsche, short skirts and lipstick. They were behind Wall Street and the international bankers, and the whiteslave traffic and the movies and the Supreme Court and ragtime and the illegal liquor business.

Henry Ford denounced the Jews and ran for senator and sued the *Chicago Tribune* for libel,

and was the laughingstock of the kept metropolitan press;

but when the metropolitan bankers tried to horn in on his business

he thoroughly outsmarted them.

In 1918 he had borrowed on notes to buy out his minority stockholders for the picayune sum of seventyfive million dollars.

In February, 1920, he needed cash to pay off some of these notes that were coming due. A banker is supposed to have called on him and offered him every facility if the bankers' representative could be made a member of the board of directors. Henry Ford handed the banker his hat,

and went about raising the money in his own way:

he shipped every car and part he had in his plant to his dealers and demanded immediate cash payment. Let the other fellow do the borrowing had always been a cardinal principle. He shut down production and canceled all orders from the supplyfirms. Many dealers were ruined, many supplyfirms failed, but when he reopened his plant,

he owned it absolutely,

the way a man owns an unmortgaged farm with the taxes paid up.

In 1922 there started the Ford boom for President (high wages, waterpower, industry scattered to the small towns) that was skillfully pricked behind the scenes

by another crackerbarrel philosopher,

Calvin Coolidge;

but in 1922 Henry Ford sold one million three hundred and thirtytwo thousand two hundred and nine tin lizzies; he was the richest man in the world.

Good roads had followed the narrow ruts made in the mud by the Model T. The great automotive boom was on. At Ford's production was improving all the time; less waste, more spotters, strawbosses, stoolpigeons (fifteen minutes for lunch, three minutes to go to the toilet, the Taylorized speedup everywhere, reach under, adjust washer, screw down bolt, shove in cotterpin, reachunder adjustwasher, screwdown bolt, reachunderadjustscrewdownreachunderadjust until every ounce of life was sucked off into production and at night the workmen went home grey shaking husks).

Ford owned every detail of the process from the ore in the hills until the car rolled off the end of the assemblyline under its own power, the plants were rationalized to the last tenthousandth of an inch as measured by the Johansen scale;

in 1926 the production cycle was reduced to eightyone hours from the ore in the mine to the finished salable car proceeding under its own power,

but the Model T was obsolete.

New Era prosperity and the American Plan

(there were strings to it, always there were strings to it)

had killed Tin Lizzie.

Ford's was just one of many automobile plants.

When the stockmarket bubble burst,

Mr. Ford the crackerbarrel philosopher said jubilantly,

'I told you so.

Serves you right for gambling and getting in debt.

The country is sound.'

But when the country on cracked shoes, in frayed trousers, belts tightened over hollow bellies,

idle hands cracked and chapped with the cold of that coldest March day of 1932,

started marching from Detroit to Dearborn, asking for work and the American Plan, all they could think of at Ford's was machineguns.

The country was sound, but they mowed the marchers down.

They shot four of them dead.

Henry Ford as an old man
is a passionate antiquarian,

(lives besieged on his father's farm embedded in an estate of thousands of millionaire acres, protected by an army of servicemen, secretaries, secret agents, dicks under orders of an English exprizefighter,

always afraid of the feet in broken shoes on the roads, afraid the gangs will kidnap his grandchildren,

that a crank will shoot him,

that Change and the idle hands out of

work will break through the gates and the high fences;

protected by a private army against

the new America of starved children and hollow bellies and cracked shoes stamping on souplines,

that has swallowed up the old thrifty farmlands

of Wayne County, Michigan,

as if they had never been).

Henry Ford as an old man
is a passionate antiquarian.

He rebuilt his father's farmhouse and put it back exactly in the state he remembered it in as a boy. He built a village of museums for buggies, sleighs, coaches, old plows, waterwheels, obsolete models of motorcars. He scoured the country for fiddlers to play old-fashioned square-dances.

Even old taverns he bought and put back into their original shape, as well as Thomas Edison's early laboratories.

When he bought the Wayside Inn near Sudbury, Massachusetts, he had the new highway where the newmodel cars roared and slithered and hissed oilily past (*the new noise of the automobile*),

moved away from the door,

put back the old bad road,

so that everything might be

the way it used to be,

in the days of horses and buggies.

1936

T. S. ELIOT

1888–

TRADITION AND THE INDIVIDUAL TALENT

· I

In English writing we seldom speak of tradition, though we occasionally apply its name in deploring its absence. We cannot refer to 'the tradition' or to 'a tradition'; at most, we employ the adjective in saying that the poetry of So-and-so is 'traditional' or even 'too traditional.' Seldom, perhaps, does the word appear except in a phrase of censure. If otherwise, it is vaguely approbative, with the implication, as to the work approved, of some pleasing archæological

reconstruction. You can hardly make the word agreeable to English ears without this comfortable reference to the reassuring science of archæology.

Certainly the word is not likely to appear in our appreciations of living or dead writers. Every nation, every race, has not only its own creative, but its own critical turn of mind; and is even more oblivious of the shortcomings and limitations of its critical habits than of those of its creative genius. We know, or think we know, from the enormous mass of critical writing that has appeared in the French language the critical method or habit of the French; we only conclude (we are such unconscious people) that the French are 'more critical' than we, and sometimes even plume ourselves a little with the fact, as if the French were the less spontaneous. Perhaps they are; but we might remind ourselves that criticism is as inevitable as breathing, and that we should be none the worse for articulating what passes in our minds when we read a book and feel an emotion about it, for criticizing our own minds in their work of criticism. One of the facts that might come to light in this process is our tendency to insist, when we praise a poet, upon those aspects of his work in which he least resembles anyone else. In these aspects or parts of his work we pretend to find what is individual, what is the peculiar essence of the man. We dwell with satisfaction upon the poet's difference from his predecessors, especially his immediate predecessors; we endeavour to find something that can be isolated in order to be enjoyed. Whereas if we approach a poet without this prejudice we shall often find that not only the best, but the most individual parts of his work may be those in which the dead poets, his ancestors, assert their immortality most vigorously. And I do not mean the impressionable period of adolescence, but the period of full maturity.

Yet if the only form of tradition, of handing down, consisted in following the ways of the immediate generation before us in a blind or timid adherence to its successes, 'tradition' should positively be discouraged. We have seen many such simple currents soon lost in the sand; and novelty is better than repetition. Tradition is a matter of much wider significance. It cannot be inherited, and if you want it you must obtain it by great labour. It involves, in the first place, the historical sense, which we may call nearly indispensable to anyone who would continue to be a poet beyond his twenty-fifth year; and the historical sense involves a perception, not only of the pastness of the past, but of its presence; the historical sense compels a man to write not merely with his own generation in his bones, but with a feeling that the whole of the literature of Europe from Homer and within it the whole of the literature of his own country has a simultaneous existence and composes a simultaneous order. This historical sense, which is a sense of the timeless as well as of the temporal and of the timeless and of the temporal together, is what makes a writer traditional. And it is at the same time what makes a writer most acutely conscious of his place in time, of his own contemporaneity.

No poet, no artist of any art, has his complete meaning alone. His significance, his appreciation is the appreciation of his relation to the dead poets and artists. You cannot value him alone; you must set him, for contrast and comparison, among the dead. I mean this as a principle of æsthetic, not merely historical, criticism. The necessity that he shall conform, that he shall cohere, is not onesided; what happens when a new work of art is created is something that happens simultaneously to all the works of art which preceded it. The existing monuments form an ideal order among themselves, which is modified by the introduction of the new (the really new) work of art among them. The existing order is complete before the new work arrives; for order to persist after the supervention of novelty, the *whole* existing order must be, if ever so slightly, altered; and so the relations, proportions, values of each work of art toward the whole are readjusted; and this is conformity between the old and the new. Whoever has approved this idea of order, of the form of European, of English literature will not find it preposterous that the past should be altered by the present as much as the present is directed by the past. And the poet who is aware of this will be aware of great difficulties and responsibilities.

In a peculiar sense he will be aware also that he must inevitably be judged by the standards of the past. I say judged, not amputated, by them; not judged to be as good as, or worse or better than, the dead; and certainly not judged by the canons of dead critics. It is a judgment, a comparison, in which two things are measured by each other. To conform merely would be for the new work not really to conform at all; it would not be new, and would therefore not be a work of art. And we do not quite say that the new is more valuable because it fits in; but its fitting in is a test of its value—a test, it is true, which can only be slowly and cautiously applied, for we are none of us infallible judges of conformity. We say: it appears to conform, and is perhaps individual, or it appears individual, and may conform; but we are hardly likely to find that it is one and not the other.

To proceed to a more intelligible exposition of the relation of the poet to the past: he can neither take the past as a lump, an indiscriminate bolus, nor can he form himself wholly on one or two private admirations, nor can he form himself wholly upon one preferred period. The first course is inadmissible, the second is an important experience of youth, and the third is a pleasant and highly desirable supplement. The poet must be very conscious of the main current, which does not at all flow invariably through the most distinguished reputations. He must be quite aware of the obvious fact that art never improves, but that the material of art is never quite the same. He must be aware that the mind of Europe—the mind of his own country—a mind which he learns in time to be much more important than his own private mind—is a mind which changes, and that this change is a development which abandons nothing *en route*, which does not superannuate either Shakespeare, or Homer, or the rock drawing of the Magdalenian draughtsmen. That this development, refinement perhaps, complication certainly, is not, from the point of view of the artist, any improvement. Perhaps not even an improvement from the point of view of the psychologist or not to the extent which we imagine; perhaps only in the end based upon a complication in economics and machinery. But the difference between the present and the past is that the conscious present is an awareness of the past in a way and to an extent which the past's awareness of itself cannot show.

Someone said: 'The dead writers are remote from us because we *know* so much more than they did.' Precisely, and they are that which we know.

I am alive to a usual objection to what is clearly part of my programme for the *métier* of poetry. The objection is that the doctrine requires a ridiculous amount of erudition (pedantry), a claim which can be rejected by appeal to the lives of poets in

any pantheon. It will even be affirmed that much learning deadens or perverts poetic sensibility. While, however, we persist in believing that a poet ought to know as much as will not encroach upon his necessary receptivity and necessary laziness, it is not desirable to confine knowledge to whatever can be put into a useful shape for examinations, drawing-rooms, or the still more pretentious modes of publicity. Some can absorb knowledge, the more tardy must sweat for it. Shakespeare acquired more essential history from Plutarch than most men could from the whole British Museum. What is to be insisted upon is that the poet must develop or procure the consciousness of the past and that he should continue to develop this consciousness throughout his career.

What happens is a continual surrender of himself as he is at the moment to something which is more valuable. The progress of an artist is a continual self-sacrifice, a continual extinction of personality.

There remains to define this process of depersonalization and its relation to the sense of tradition. It is in this depersonalization that art may be said to approach the condition of science. I therefore invite you to consider, as a suggestive analogy, the action which takes place when a bit of finely filiated platinum is introduced into a chamber containing oxygen and sulphur dioxide.

2

Honest criticism and sensitive appreciation is directed not upon the poet but upon the poetry. If we attend to the confused cries of the newspaper critics and the susurrus of popular repetition that follows, we shall hear the names of poets in great numbers; if we seek not Blue-book knowledge but the enjoyment of poetry, and ask for a poem, we shall seldom find it. I have tried to point out the importance of the relation of the poem to other poems by other authors, and suggested the conception of poetry as a living whole of all the poetry that has ever been written. The other aspect of this Impersonal theory of poetry is the relation of the poem to its author. And I hinted, by an analogy, that the mind of the mature poet differs from that of the immature one not precisely in any valuation of 'personality,' not being necessarily more interesting, or having 'more to say,' but rather by being a more finely perfected medium in which special, or very varied, feelings are at liberty to enter into new combinations.

The analogy was that of the catalyst. When the two gases previously mentioned are mixed in the presence of a filament of platinum, they form sulphurous acid. This combination takes place only if the platinum is present; nevertheless the newly formed acid contains no trace of platinum, and the platinum itself is apparently unaffected: has remained inert, neutral, and unchanged. The mind of the poet is the shred of platinum. It may partly or exclusively operate upon the experience of the man himself; but, the more perfect the artist, the more completely separate in him will be the man who suffers and the mind which creates; the more perfectly will the mind digest and transmute the passions which are its material.

The experience, you will notice, the elements which enter the presence of the transforming catalyst, are of two kinds: emotions and feelings. The effect of a work of art upon the person who enjoys it is an experience different in kind from any experience not of art. It may be formed out of one emotion, or may be a combination of several; and various feelings, inhering for the writer in particular words or phrases or images, may be added to compose the final result. Or great poetry may be made without the direct use of any emotion whatever: composed out of feelings solely. Canto XV of the *Inferno* (Brunetto Latini) is a working up of the emotion evident in the situation; but the effect, though single as that of any work of art, is obtained by considerable complexity of detail. The last quatrain gives an image, a feeling attaching to an image, which 'came,' which did not develop simply out of what precedes, but which was probably in suspension in the poet's mind until the proper combination arrived for it to add itself to. The poet's mind is in fact a receptacle for seizing and storing up numberless feelings, phrases, images, which remain there until all the particles which can unite to form a new compound are present together.

If you compare several representative passages of the greatest poetry you see how great is the variety of types of combination, and also how completely any semi-ethical criterion of 'sublimity' misses the mark. For it is not the 'greatness,' the intensity, of the emotions, the components, but the intensity of the artistic process, the pressure, so to speak, under which the fusion takes place, that counts. The episode of Paolo and Francesca employs a definite emotion, but the intensity of the poetry is something quite different from whatever intensity in the supposed experience it may give the impression of. It is no more intense, furthermore, than Canto XXVI, the voyage of Ulysses, which has not the direct dependence upon an emotion. Great variety is possible in the process of transmutation of emotion: the murder of Agamemnon, or the agony of Othello, gives an artistic effect apparently closer to a possible original than the scenes from Dante. In the *Agamemnon*, the artistic emotion approximates to the emotion of an actual spectator; in *Othello* to the emotion of the protagonist himself. But the difference between art and the event is always absolute; the combination which is the murder of Agamemnon is probably as complex as that which is the voyage of Ulysses. In either case there has been a fusion of elements. The ode of Keats contains a number of feelings which have nothing particular to do with the nightingale, but which the nightingale, partly perhaps because of its attractive name, and partly because of its reputation, served to bring together.

The point of view which I am struggling to attack is perhaps related to the metaphysical theory of the substantial unity of the soul: for my meaning is, that the poet has, not a 'personality' to express, but a particular medium, which is only a medium and not a personality, in which impressions and experiences combine in peculiar and unexpected ways. Impressions and experiences which are important for the man may take no place in the poetry, and those which become important in the poetry may play quite a negligible part in the man, the personality.

I will quote a passage which is unfamiliar enough to be regarded with fresh attention in the light—or darkness—of these observations:

And now methinks I could e'en chide
    myself
For doating on her beauty, though her
    death
Shall be revenged after no common action.
Does the silkworm expend her yellow
    labours
For thee? For thee does she undo herself?
Are lordships sold to maintain ladyships
For the poor benefit of a bewildering
    minute?
Why does yon fellow falsify highways,
And put his life between the judge's lips,
To refine such a thing—keeps horse and
    men
To beat their valours for her? . . .

In this passage (as is evident if it is taken in its context) there is a combination of positive and negative emotions: an intensely strong attraction toward beauty and an equally intense fascination by the ugliness which is contrasted with it and which destroys it. This balance of contrasted emotion is in the dramatic situation to which the speech is pertinent, but that situation alone is inadequate to it. This is, so to speak, the structural emotion, provided by the drama. But the whole effect, the dominant tone, is due to the fact that a number of floating feelings, having an affinity to this emotion by no means superficially evident, have combined with it to give us a new art emotion.

It is not in his personal emotions, the emotions provoked by particular events in his life, that the poet is in any way remarkable or interesting. His particular emotions may be simple, or crude, or flat. The emotion in his poetry will be a very complex thing, but not with the complexity of the emotions of people who have very complex or unusual emotions in life. One error, in fact, of eccentricity in poetry is to seek for new human emotions to express; and in this search for novelty in the wrong place it discovers the perverse. The business of the poet is not to find new emotions, but to use the ordinary ones and, in working them up into poetry, to express feelings which are not in actual emotions at all. And emotions which he has never experienced will serve his turn as well as those familiar to him. Consequently, we must believe that 'emotion recollected in tranquillity' is an inexact formula. For it is neither emotion, nor recollection, nor, without distortion of meaning, tranquillity. It is a concentration, and a new thing resulting from the concentration, of a very great number of experiences which to the practical and active person would not seem to be experiences at all; it is a concentration which does not happen consciously or of deliberation. These experiences are not 'recollected,' and they finally unite in an atmosphere which is 'tranquil' only in that it is a passive attending upon the event. Of course this is not quite the whole story. There is a great deal, in the writing of poetry, which must be conscious and deliberate. In fact, the bad poet is usually unconscious where he ought to be conscious, and conscious where he ought to be unconscious. Both errors tend to make him 'personal.' Poetry is not a turning loose of emotion, but an escape from emotion; it is not the expression of personality, but an escape from personality. But, of course, only those who have personality and emotions know what it means to want to escape from these things.

3

ὁ δὲ νοῦς ἴσως θειότερόν τι καὶ ἀπαθές
ἐστιν.[1]

This essay proposes to halt at the frontier of metaphysics or mysticism, and confine itself to such practical conclusions as can be applied by the responsible person interested in poetry. To divert interest from the poet to the poetry is a laudable aim: for it would conduce to a juster estimation of actual poetry, good and bad. There are many people who appreciate the expression of sincere emotion in verse, and there is a smaller number of people who can appreciate technical excellence. But very few know when there is an expression of *significant* emotion, emotion which has its life in the poem and not in the history of the poet. The emotion of art is impersonal. And the poet cannot reach this impersonality without surrendering himself wholly to the work to be done. And he is not likely to know what is to be done unless he lives in what is not merely the present,

---

[1] 'The mind seems to be something more divine and unaffected.'

but the present moment of the past, unless he is conscious, not of what is dead, but of what is already living.

1920

RELIGION AND LITERATURE

WHAT I have to say is largely in support of the following propositions: Literary criticism should be completed by criticism from a definite ethical and theological standpoint. In so far as in any age there is common agreement on ethical and theological matters, so far can literary criticism be substantive. In ages like our own, in which there is no such common agreement, it is the more necessary for Christian readers to scrutinize their reading, especially of works of imagination, with explicit ethical and theological standards. The 'greatness' of literature cannot be determined solely by literary standards; though we must remember that whether it is literature or not can be determined only by literary standards.[1]

We have tacitly assumed, for some centuries past, that there is *no* relation between literature and theology. This is not to deny that literature—I mean, again, primarily works of imagination—has been, is, and probably always will be judged by some moral standards. But moral judgements of literary works are made only according to the moral code accepted by each generation, whether it lives according to that code or not. In an age which accepts some precise Christian theology, the common code may be fairly orthodox: though even in such periods the common code may exalt such concepts as 'honour,' 'glory' or 'revenge' to a position quite intolerable to Christianity. The dramatic ethics of the Elizabethan Age offers an interesting study. But when the common code is detached from its theological background, and is consequently more and more merely a matter of habit, it is exposed both to prejudice and to change. At such times morals are open to being altered *by* literature; so that we find in practice that what is 'objectionable'

in literature is merely what the present generation is not used to. It is a commonplace that what shocks one generation is accepted quite calmly by the next. This adaptability to change of moral standards is sometimes greeted with satisfaction as an evidence of human perfectibility: whereas it is only evidence of what unsubstantial foundations people's moral judgements have.

I am not concerned here with religious literature but with the application of our religion to the criticism of any literature. It may be as well, however, to distinguish first what I consider to be the three senses in which we can speak of 'religious literature.' The first is that of which we say that it is 'religious literature' in the same way that we speak of 'historical literature' or of 'scientific literature.' I mean that we can treat the Authorized translation of the Bible, or the works of Jeremy Taylor, as literature, in the same way that we treat the historical writing of Clarendon or of Gibbon—our two great English historians —as literature; or Bradley's *Logic*, or Buffon's *Natural History*. All of these writers were men who, incidentally to their religious, or historical, or philosophic purpose, had a gift of language which makes them delightful to read to all those who can enjoy language well written, even if they are unconcerned with the objects which the writers had in view. And I would add that though a scientific, or historical, or theological, or philosophic work which is also 'literature,' may become superannuated as anything but literature, yet it is not likely to be 'literature' unless it had its scientific or other value for its own time. While I acknowledge the legitimacy of this enjoyment, I am more acutely aware of its abuse. The persons who enjoy these writings *solely* because of their literary merit are essentially parasites; and we know that parasites, when they become too numerous, are pests. I could easily fulminate for a whole hour against the men of letters who have gone into ecstasies over 'the Bible as literature,' the Bible as 'the noblest monument of English prose.' Those who talk of the Bible as a 'monument of English prose' are merely admiring it as a monument over the grave of Christianity. I must try to avoid the by-paths of my

[1] 'As an example of literary criticism given greater significance by theological interests, I would call attention to Theodor Haecker: *Virgil* . . . [London,1934].' Author's note, *Essays Ancient and Modern* (London, 1936), 93.

discourse: it is enough to suggest that just as the work of Clarendon, or Gibbon, or Buffon, or Bradley would be of inferior literary value if it were insignificant as history, science and philosophy respectively, so the Bible has had a *literary* influence upon English literature *not* because it has been considered as literature, but because it has been considered as the report of the Word of God. And the fact that men of letters now discuss it as 'literature' probably indicates the *end* of its 'literary' influence.

The second kind of relation of religion to literature is that which is found in what is called 'religious' or 'devotional' poetry. Now what is the usual attitude of the lover of poetry—and I mean the person who is a genuine and first-hand enjoyer and appreciator of poetry, not the person who follows the admirations of others—towards this department of poetry? I believe, all that may be implied in his calling it a *department*. He believes, not always explicitly, that when you qualify poetry as 'religious' you are indicating very clear limitations. For the great majority of people who love poetry, *'religious* poetry' is a variety of *minor* poetry: the religious poet is not a poet who is treating the whole subject matter of poetry in a religious spirit, but a poet who is dealing with a confined part of this subject matter: who is leaving out what men consider their major passions, and thereby confessing his ignorance of them. I think that this is the real attitude of most poetry lovers towards such poets as Vaughan, or Southwell, or Crashaw, or George Herbert, or Gerard Hopkins.

But what is more, I am ready to admit that up to a point these critics are right. For there is a kind of poetry, such as most of the work of the authors I have mentioned, which is the product of a special religious awareness, which may exist without the general awareness which we expect of the major poet. In some poets, or in some of their works, this general awareness may have existed; but the preliminary steps which represent it may have been suppressed, and only the end-product presented. Between these, and those in which the religious or devotional genius represents the *special* and limited awareness, it may be very difficult to discriminate. I do not pretend to offer Vaughan, or Southwell, or George Herbert, or Hopkins as major poets: I feel sure that the first three, at least, are poets of this limited awareness. They are not great religious poets in the sense in which Dante, or Corneille, or Racine, even in those of their plays which do not touch upon Christian themes, are great Christian religious poets. Or even in the sense in which Villon and Baudelaire, with all their imperfections and delinquencies, are Christian poets. Since the time of Chaucer, Christian poetry (in the sense in which I shall mean it) has been limited in England almost exclusively to minor poetry.

I repeat that when I am considering Religion and Literature, I speak of these things only to make clear that I am not concerned primarily with Religious Literature, I am concerned with what should be the relation between Religion and all Literature. Therefore the third type of 'religious literature' may be more quickly passed over. I mean the literary works of men who are sincerely desirous of forwarding the cause of religion: that which may come under the heading of Propaganda. I am thinking, of course, of such delightful fiction as Mr. Chesterton's *Man Who Was Thursday*, or his *Father Brown*. No one admires and enjoys these things more than I do; I would only remark that when the same effect is aimed at by zealous persons of less talent than Mr. Chesterton the effect is negative. But my point is that such writings do not enter into any serious consideration of the relation of Religion and Literature: because they are conscious operations in a world in which it is assumed that Religion and Literature are not related. It is a conscious and limited relating. What I want is a literature which should be *un*consciously, rather than deliberately and defiantly, Christian: because the work of Mr. Chesterton has its point from appearing in a world which is definitely not Christian.

I am convinced that we fail to realize how completely, and yet how irrationally, we separate our literary from our religious judgements. If there could be a complete separation, perhaps it might not matter: but the separation is not, and never can be, complete. If we exemplify literature by the novel—for the novel is the form in which literature affects the greatest number—we may remark this gradual secularization of literature during at least the last three hundred years. Bunyan, and to some extent Defoe, had moral purposes: the former is beyond suspicion, the latter may be suspect. But since Defoe the secularization of the novel has been continuous. There have been three chief phases. In the first, the novel took the Faith, in its contemporary version, for granted, and omitted it from its picture of life. Fielding, Dickens and Thackeray belong to this phase. In the second, it doubted, worried about, or contested the Faith. To this phase belong George Eliot, George Meredith and Thomas Hardy. To the third phase, in which we are living, belong nearly all contemporary novelists except Mr. James Joyce. It is the phase of those who have never heard the Christian Faith spoken of as anything but an anachronism.

Now, do people in general hold a definite opinion, that is to say religious or anti-religious; and do they read novels, or poetry for that matter, with a separate compartment of their minds? The common ground between religion and fiction is behaviour. Our religion imposes our ethics, our judgement and criticism of ourselves, and our behaviour towards our fellow men. The fiction that we read affects our behaviour towards our fellow men, affects our patterns of ourselves. When we read of human beings behaving in certain ways, with the approval of the author, who gives his benediction to this behaviour by his attitude towards the result of the behaviour arranged by himself, we can be influenced towards behaving in the same way.[1] When the contemporary novelist is an individual thinking for himself in isolation, he may have something important to offer to those who are able to receive it. He who is alone may speak to the individual. But the majority of novelists are persons drifting in the stream, only a little faster. They have some sensitiveness, but little intellect.

We are expected to be broadminded about literature, to put aside prejudice or conviction, and to look at fiction as fiction and at drama as drama. With what is inaccurately called 'censorship' in this country—with what is much more difficult to cope with than an official censorship, because it represents the opinions of individuals in an irresponsible democracy, I have very little sympathy; partly because it so often suppresses the wrong books, and partly because it is little more effective than Prohibition of Liquor; partly because it is one manifestation of the desire that state control should take the place of decent domestic influence; and wholly because it acts only from custom and habit, not from decided theological and moral principles. Incidentally, it gives people a false sense of security in leading them to believe that books which are *not* suppressed are harmless. Whether there *is* such a thing as a harmless book I am not sure: but there very likely are books so utterly unreadable as to be incapable of injuring anybody. But it is certain that a book is not harmless merely because no one is consciously offended by it. And if we, as readers, keep our religious and moral convictions in one compartment, and take our reading merely for entertainment, or on a higher plane, for æsthetic pleasure, I would point out that the author, whatever his conscious intentions in writing, in practice recognizes no such distinctions. The author of a work of imagination is trying to affect us wholly, as human beings, whether he knows it or not; and we are affected by it, as human beings, whether we intend to be or not. I suppose that everything we eat has some other effect upon us than merely the pleasure of taste and mastication; it affects us during the process of assimilation and digestion; and I believe that exactly the same is true of anything we read.

The fact that what we read does not concern merely something called our *literary taste*, but that it affects directly, though only amongst many other influences, the whole of what we are, is best elicited, I think, by a conscientious examination of the history of our individual literary education. Consider the adolescent reading of any person with some literary sensibility. Everyone, I believe, who is at all sensible to the seductions of poetry, can remember some moment in youth when he

---

1 'Here and later I am indebted to Montgomery Belgion. *The Human Parrot*(chapter on The Irresponsible Propagandist)[London, 1931].' Author's note, ibid., 100.

or she was completely carried away by the work of one poet. Very likely he was carried away by several poets, one after the other. The reason for this passing infatuation is not merely that our sensibility to poetry is keener in adolescence than in maturity. What happens is a kind of inundation, of invasion of the undeveloped personality, the empty (swept and garnished) room, by the stronger personality of the poet. The same thing may happen at a later age to persons who have not done much reading. One author takes complete possession of us for a time; then another; and finally they begin to affect each other in our mind. We weigh one against another; we see that each has qualities absent from others, and qualities incompatible with the qualities of others: we begin to be, in fact, critical; and it is our growing critical power which protects us from excessive possession by any one literary personality. The good critic—and we should all try to be critics, and not leave criticism to the fellows who write reviews in the papers—is the man who, to a keen and abiding sensibility, joins wide and increasingly discriminating reading. Wide reading is not valuable as a kind of hoarding, an accumulation of knowledge, or what sometimes is meant by the term 'a well-stocked mind.' It is valuable because in the process of being affected by one powerful personality after another, we cease to be dominated by any one, or by any small number. The very different views of life, cohabiting in our minds, affect each other, and our own personality asserts itself and gives each a place in some arrangement peculiar to ourself.

It is simply not true that works of fiction, prose or verse, that is to say works depicting the actions, thoughts and words and passions of imaginary human beings, *directly* extend our knowledge of life. Direct knowledge of life is knowledge directly in relation to ourselves, it is our knowledge of *how* people behave in general, of *what* they are like in general, in so far as that part of life in which we ourselves have participated gives us material for generalization. Knowledge of life obtained through fiction is only possible by another stage of self-consciousness. That is to say, it can only be a knowledge of other people's knowledge of life, not of life itself. So far as we are taken up with the happenings in any novel in the same way in which we are taken up with what happens under our eyes, we are acquiring at least as much falsehood as truth. But when we are developed enough to say: 'This is the view of life of a person who was a good observer within his limits, Dickens, or Thackeray, or George Eliot, or Balzac; but he looked at it in a different way from me, because he was a different man; he even selected rather different things to look at, or the same things in a different order of importance, because he was a different man; so what I am looking at is the world as seen by a particular mind'—then we are in a position to gain something from reading fiction. We are learning *something* about life from these authors direct, just as we learn something from the reading of history direct; but these authors are only really helping us when we can see, and allow for, their differences from ourselves.

Now what we get, as we gradually grow up and read more and more, and read a greater diversity of authors, is a variety of views of life. But what people commonly assume, I suspect, is that we gain this experience of other men's views of life only by 'improving reading.' This, it is supposed, is a reward we get by applying ourselves to Shakespeare, and Dante, and Goethe, and Emerson, and Carlyle, and dozens of other respectable writers. The rest of our reading for amusement is merely killing time. But I incline to come to the alarming conclusion that it is just the literature that we read for 'amusement,' or 'purely for pleasure' that may have the greatest and least suspected influence upon us. It is the literature which we read with the least effort that can have the easiest and most insidious influence upon us. Hence it is that the influence of popular novelists, and of popular plays of contemporary life, requires to be scrutinized most closely. And it is chiefly *contemporary* literature that the majority of people ever read in this attitude of 'purely for pleasure,' of pure passivity.

The relation of what I have been saying to the subject announced for my discourse should now be a little more apparent. Though we may read literature merely for pleasure, of 'entertainment' or of 'æsthetic enjoyment,' this reading never affects simply a sort of special sense: it affects us as entire human beings; it affects our moral and religious existence. And I say that while individual modern writers of eminence can be improving, contemporary literature as a whole tends to be degrading. And that even the effect of the better writers, in an age like ours, may be degrading to some readers; for we must remember that what a writer does to people is not necessarily what he intends to do. It may be only what people are capable of having done to them. People exercise an unconscious selection, in being influenced. A writer like D. H. Lawrence may be in his effect either beneficial or pernicious. I am not even sure that I have not had some pernicious influence myself.

At this point I anticipate a rejoinder from the liberal-minded, from all those who are convinced that if everybody says what he thinks, and does what he likes, things will somehow, by some automatic compensation and adjustment, come right in the end. 'Let everything be tried,' they say, 'and if it is a mistake, then we shall learn by experience.' This argument might have some value, if we were always the same generation upon earth; or if, as we know to be not the case, people ever learned much from the experience of their elders. These liberals are convinced that only by what is called unrestrained individualism will truth ever emerge. Ideas, views of life, they think, issue distinct from independent heads, and in consequence of their knocking violently against each other, the fittest survive, and truth rises triumphant. Anyone who dissents from this view must be either a mediævalist, wishful only to set back the clock, or else a fascist, and probably both.

If the mass of contemporary authors were really individualists, every one of them inspired Blakes, each with his separate vision, and if the mass of the contemporary public were really a mass of *individuals* there might be something to be said for this attitude. But this is not, and never has been, and never will be. It is not only that the reading individual to-day (or at any day) is not enough an individual to be able to absorb all the 'views of life' of all the authors pressed upon us by the publishers' advertisements and reviewers, and to be able to arrive at wisdom by considering one against another. It is that the contemporary authors are not individuals enough either. It is not that the world of separate individuals of the liberal democrat is undesirable; it is simply that this world does not exist. For the reader of contemporary literature is not, like the reader of the established great literature of all time, exposing himself to the influence of divers and contradictory personalities; he is exposing himself to a mass movement of writers who, each of them, think that they have something individually to offer, but are really all working together in the same direction. And there never was a time, I believe, when the reading public was so large, or so helplessly exposed to the influences of its own time. There never was a time, I believe, when those who read at all, read so many more books by living authors than books by dead authors; there never was a time so completely parochial, so shut off from the past. There may be too many publishers; there are certainly too many books published; and the journals ever incite the reader to 'keep up' with what is being published. Individualistic democracy has come to high tide: and it is more difficult to-day to be an individual than it ever was before.

Within itself, modern literature has perfectly valid distinctions of good and bad, better and worse: and I do not wish to suggest that I confound Mr. Bernard Shaw with Mr. Noel Coward, Mrs. Woolf with Miss Mannin. On the other hand, I should like it to be clear that I am not defending a 'high'-brow against a 'low'-brow literature. What I do wish to affirm is that the whole of modern literature is corrupted by what I call Secularism, that it is simply unaware of, simply cannot understand the meaning of, the primacy of the supernatural over the natural life: of something which I assume to be our primary concern.

I do not want to give the impression that I have delivered a mere fretful jeremiad against contemporary literature. Assuming a common attitude between you, or some of you, and myself, the question is not so much, what is to be done about it? as, how should we behave towards it?

I have suggested that the liberal attitude towards literature will not work. Even if the writers who make their attempt to impose their 'view of life' upon us were really distinct individuals, even if we as readers were distinct individuals, what would be the result? It would be, surely, that each reader would be impressed, in his reading, merely by what he was previously prepared to be impressed by; he would follow the 'line of least resistance,' and there would be no assurance that he would be made a better man. For literary judgement we need to be acutely aware of two things at once: of 'what we like,' and of 'what we *ought* to like.' Few people are honest enough to know either. The first means knowing what we really feel: very few know that. The second involves understanding our shortcomings; for we do not really know what we ought to like unless we also know why we ought to like it, which involves knowing why we don't yet like it. It is not enough to understand what we ought to be, unless we know what we are; and we do not understand what we are, unless we know what we ought to be. The two forms of self-consciousness, knowing what we are and what we ought to be, must go together.

It is our business, as readers of literature, to know what we like. It is our business, as Christians, *as well as* readers of literature, to know what we ought to like. It is our business as honest men not to assume that whatever we like is what we ought to like; and it is our business as honest Christians not to assume that we do like what we ought to like. And the last thing I would wish for would be the existence of two literatures, one for Christian consumption and the other for the pagan world. What I believe to be incumbent upon all Christians is the duty of maintaining consciously certain standards and criteria of criticism over and above those applied by the rest of the world; and that by these criteria and standards everything that we read must be tested. We must remember that the greater part of our current reading matter is written for us by people who have no real belief in a supernatural order, though some of it may be written by people with individual notions of a supernatural order which are not ours. And the greater part of our reading matter is coming to be written by people who not only have no such belief, but are even ignorant of the fact that there are still people in the world so 'backward' or so 'eccentric' as to continue to believe. So long as we are conscious of the gulf fixed between ourselves and the greater part of contemporary literature, we are more or less protected from being harmed by it, and are in a position to extract from it what good it has to offer us.

There are a very large number of people in the world to-day who believe that all ills are fundamentally economic. Some believe that various specific economic changes alone would be enough to set the world right; others demand more or less drastic changes in the social as well, changes chiefly of two opposed types. These changes demanded, and in some places carried out, are alike in one respect, that they hold the assumptions of what I call Secularism: they concern themselves only with changes of a temporal, material, and external nature; they concern themselves with morals only of a collective nature. In an exposition of one such new faith I read the following words:

'In our morality the one single test of any moral question is whether it impedes or destroys in any way the power of the individual to serve the State. [The individual] must answer the questions: "Does this action injure the nation? Does it injure other members of the nation? Does it injure my ability to serve the nation?" And if the answer is clear on all those questions, the individual has absolute liberty to do as he will.'

Now I do not deny that this is a kind of morality, and that it is capable of great good within limits; but I think that we should all repudiate a morality which had no higher ideal to set before us than that. It represents, of course, one of the violent reactions we are witnessing, against the view that the community is solely for the benefit of the individual; but it is equally a gospel of this world, and of this world alone. My complaint against modern literature is of the same kind. It is not that modern literature is in the ordinary sense 'immoral' or even 'amoral'; and in any case to prefer that charge would not be enough

It is simply that it repudiates, or is wholly ignorant of, our most fundamental and important beliefs; and that in consequence its tendency is to encourage its readers to get what they can out of life while it lasts, to miss no 'experience' that presents itself, and to sacrifice themselves, if they make any sacrifice at all, only for the sake of tangible benefits to others in this world either now or in the future. We shall certainly continue to read the best of its kind, of what our time provides; but we must tirelessly criticize it according to our own principles, and not merely according to the principles admitted by the writers and by the critics who discuss it in the public press.

1935

THE LOVE SONG OF
J. ALFRED PRUFROCK

S'io credesse che mia risposta fosse
A persona che mai tornasse al mondo,
Questa fiamma staria senza piu scosse.
Ma perciocche giammai di questo fondo
Non torno vivo alcun, s'i' odo il vero,
Senza tema d'infamia ti rispondo. [1]

LET us go then, you and I,
When the evening is spread out against the
    sky
Like a patient etherized upon a table;
Let us go, through certain half-deserted
    streets,
The muttering retreats
Of restless nights in one-night cheap
    hotels
And sawdust restaurants with oyster-
    shells:
Streets that follow like a tedious argument
Of insidious intent
To lead you to an overwhelming
    question. . .   10
Oh, do not ask, 'What is it?'
Let us go and make our visit.

In the room the women come and go
Talking of Michelangelo.

[1] 'If I could believe that my answer might be to a person who should ever return into the world, this flame would stand without more quiverings; but inasmuch as, if I hear the truth, never from this depth did any living man return, without fear of infamy I answer thee.' (trans., C.E.Norton). The passage is spoken by a soul in hell to Dante, in his *Inferno,*XXVII,61–66.

The yellow fog that rubs its back upon the
    window-panes,
The yellow smoke that rubs its muzzle on
    the window-panes
Licked its tongue into the corners of the
    evening,
Lingered upon the pools that stand in
    drains,
Let fall upon its back the soot that falls
    from chimneys,
Slipped by the terrace, made a sudden
    leap,   20
And seeing that it was a soft October night,
Curled once about the house, and fell
    asleep.

And indeed there will be time
For the yellow smoke that slides along the
    street,
Rubbing its back upon the window-panes:
There will be time, there will be time
To prepare a face to meet the faces that you
    meet;
There will be time to murder and create,
And time for all the works and days of
    hands
That lift and drop a question on your plate;
Time for you and time for me,   31
And time yet for a hundred indecisions,
And for a hundred visions and revisions,
Before the taking of a toast and tea.

In the room the women come and go
Talking of Michelangelo.

And indeed there will be time
To wonder, 'Do I dare?' and, 'Do I dare?'
Time to turn back and descend the stair,
With a bald spot in the middle of my hair—
[They will say: 'How his hair is growing
    thin!']   41
My morning coat, my collar mounting
    firmly to the chin,
My necktie rich and modest, but asserted
    by a simple pin—
[They will say: 'But how his arms and legs
    are thin!']
Do I dare
Disturb the universe?
In a minute there is time
For decisions and revisions which a minute
    will reverse.

For I have known them all already, known
    them all:—

Have known the evenings, mornings,
    afternoons,   50
I have measured out my life with coffee
    spoons;
I know the voices dying with a dying fall
Beneath the music from a farther room.
    So how should I presume?

And I have known the eyes already, known
    them all—
The eyes that fix you in a formulated
    phrase,
And when I am formulated, sprawling on a
    pin,
When I am pinned and wriggling on the
    wall,
Then how should I begin
To spit out all the butt-ends of my days and
    ways?   60
    And how should I presume?

And I have known the arms already, known
    them all—
Arms that are braceleted and white and
    bare
[But in the lamplight, downed with light
    brown hair!]
Is it perfume from a dress
That makes me so digress?
Arms that lie along a table, or wrap about a
    shawl.
    And should I then presume?
    And how should I begin?

    . . . . . .

Shall I say, I have gone at dusk through
    narrow streets   70
And watched the smoke that rises from the
    pipes
Of lonely men in shirt-sleeves, leaning out
    of windows? . . .

I should have been a pair of ragged claws
Scuttling across the floors of silent seas.

    . . . . . .

And the afternoon, the evening, sleeps so
    peacefully!
Smoothed by long fingers,
Asleep . . . tired . . . or it malingers,
Stretched on the floor, here beside you and
    me.
Should I, after tea and cakes and ices,
Have the strength to force the moment to
    its crisis?   80

But though I have wept and fasted, wept
    and prayed,
Though I have seen my head [grown
    slightly bald] brought in upon a
    platter,
I am no prophet—and here's no great
    matter;
I have seen the moment of my greatness
    flicker,
And I have seen the eternal Footman hold
    my coat, and snicker,
And in short, I was afraid.

And would it have been worth it, after all,
After the cups, the marmalade, the tea,
Among the porcelain, among some talk of
    you and me,
Would it have been worth while,   90
To have bitten off the matter with a smile,
To have squeezed the universe into a ball
To roll it toward some overwhelming
    question,
To say: 'I am Lazarus, come from the dead,
Come back to tell you all, I shall tell you
    all'—
If one, settling a pillow by her head,
    Should say: 'That is not what I
      meant at all,
    That is not it, at all.'

And would it have been worth it, after all,
Would it have been worth while,   100
After the sunsets and the dooryards and the
    sprinkled streets,
After the novels, after the teacups, after the
    skirts that trail along the floor—
And this, and so much more?—
It is impossible to say just what I mean!
But as if a magic lantern threw the nerves
    in patterns on a screen:
Would it have been worth while
If one, settling a pillow or throwing off a
    shawl,
And turning toward the window, should
    say:
    'That is not it at all,
    That is not what I meant, at all.'   110

    . . . . . .

No! I am not Prince Hamlet, nor was meant
    to be;
Am an attendant lord, one that will do
To swell a progress, start a scene or two,
Advise the prince; no doubt, an easy tool,
Deferential, glad to be of use,

Politic, cautious, and meticulous;
Fuil of high sentence, but a bit obtuse;
At times, indeed, almost ridiculous—
Almost, at times, the Fool.

I grow old . . . I grow old . . .   120
I shall wear the bottoms of my trousers
    rolled.

Shall I part my hair behind? Do I dare to
    eat a peach?
I shall wear white flannel trousers, and walk
    upon the beach.
I have heard the mermaids singing, each to
    each.

I do not think that they will sing to me.

I have seen them riding seaward on the waves
Combing the white hair of the waves blown
    back
When the wind blows the water white and
    black.

We have lingered in the chambers of the sea
By sea-girls wreathed with seaweed red and
    brown   130
Till human voices wake us, and we drown.
                                    1915

LA FIGLIA CHE PIANGE [1]

O quam te memorem virgo . . . [2]

STAND on the highest pavement of the
    stair—
Lean on a garden urn—
Weave, weave the sunlight in your hair—
Clasp your flowers to you with a pained
    surprise—
Fling them to the ground and turn
With a fugitive resentment in your eyes:
But weave, weave the sunlight in your hair.

So I would have had him leave,
So I would have had her stand and grieve,
So he would have left   10
As the soul leaves the body torn and
    bruised,
As the mind deserts the body it has used.
I should find
Some way incomparably light and deft,
Some way we both should understand,

Simple and faithless as a smile and shake of
    the hand.

She turned away, but with the autumn
    weather
Compelled my imagination many days,
Many days and many hours:
Her hair over her arms and her arms full of
    flowers.   20
And I wonder how they should have been
    together!
I should have lost a gesture and a pose.
Sometimes these cogitations still amaze
The troubled midnight and the noon's
    repose.

                                    1917

THE HIPPOPOTAMUS [3]

*Similiter et omnes revereantur Diaconos, ut
mandatum Jesu Christi; et Episcopum, ut
Jesum Christum, existentem filium Patris;
Presbyteros autem, ut concilium Dei et
conjunctionem Apostolorum. Sine his
Ecclesia non vocatur; de quibus suadeo vos
sic habeo.*

                S. IGNATII AD TRALLIANOS. [4]

*And when this epistle is read among you,
cause that it be read also in the church of
the Laodiceans.* [5]

THE broad-backed hippopotamus
Rests on his belly in the mud;
Although he seems so firm to us
He is merely flesh and blood.

Flesh and blood is weak and frail,
Susceptible to nervous shock;
While the True Church can never fail
For it is based upon a rock.

The hippo's feeble steps may err
In compassing material ends,   10
While the True Church need never stir
To gather in its dividends.

3 'The Hippopotamus' is a free, satirical paraphrase of a
  poem of the same title by Theophile Gautier (1811–
  1872).
4 'In like manner, let all reverence the Deacons as Jesus
  Christ, and the Bishop as the Father; and the Presby-
  ters as the council of God, and the assembly of the
  Apostles. Without these there is no Church. Concerning all which I am persuaded that ye think after the
  same manner.' Chevallier, trans., 'The Epistle of
  Ignatius to the Trallians,' *Epistles . . . of Ignatius*
  (London, 1833),96.
5 *Colossians.*4:16.

1 'The Weeping Maiden.'
2 'O—how shall I address you, O maiden!' Virgil,
  Æneid,I,327.

The 'potamus can never reach
The mango on the mango-tree;
But fruits of pomegranate and peach
Refresh the Church from over sea.

At mating time the hippo's voice
Betrays inflexions hoarse and odd,
But every week we hear rejoice
The Church, at being one with God.   20

The hippopotamus's day
Is passed in sleep; at night he hunts;
God works in a mysterious way—
The Church can sleep and feed at once.

I saw the 'potamus take wing
Ascending from the damp savannas,
And quiring angels round him sing
The praise of God, in loud hosannas.

Blood of the Lamb shall wash him
        clean
And him shall heavenly arms enfold,   30
Among the saints he shall be seen
Performing on a harp of gold.

He shall be washed as white as snow,
By all the martyr'd virgins kist,
While the True Church remains below
Wrapt in the old miasmal mist.

                    1919

WHISPERS OF IMMORTALITY

WEBSTER was much possessed by death
And saw the skull beneath the skin;
And breastless creatures underground
Leaned backward with a lipless grin.

Daffodil bulbs instead of balls
Stared from the sockets of the eyes!
He knew that thought clings round dead
        limbs
Tightening its lusts and luxuries.

Donne, I suppose, was such another
Who found no substitute for sense,   10
To seize and clutch and penetrate;
Expert beyond experience,

He knew the anguish of the marrow
The ague of the skeleton;
No contact possible to flesh
Allayed the fever of the bone.

. . . . . .

Grishkin is nice: her Russian eye
Is underlined for emphasis;
Uncorseted, her friendly bust
Gives promise of pneumatic bliss.   20

The couched Brazilian jaguar
Compels the scampering marmoset
With subtle effluence of a cat;
Grishkin has a maisonette:

The sleek Brazilian jaguar
Does not in his arboreal gloom
Distil so rank a feline smell
As Grishkin in a drawing-room.

And even the Abstract Entities
Circumambulate her charm;   30
But our lot crawls between dry ribs
To keep our metaphysics warm.

                    1919

SWEENEY AMONG THE NIGHTINGALES [1]

ὤμοι πέπληγμαι καιρίαν πληγὴν ἔσω.[2]

APENECK Sweeney spreads his knees
Letting his arms hang down to laugh,
The zebra stripes along his jaw
Swelling to maculate giraffe.

The circles of the stormy moon
Slide westward to the River Plate,
Death and the Raven drift above
And Sweeney guards the hornèd gate.

Gloomy Orion and the Dog
Are veiled; and hushed the shrunken seas;
The person in the Spanish cape   11
Tries to sit on Sweeney's knees

[1] 'Eliot once remarked that all he consciously set out to create in "Sweeney Among the Nightingales" was a sense of foreboding. Yet the very exactitude with which he has built up his impression by means of the close details of his night-town scene, as well as by the way he underlines his effect both through a reference in the epigraph and in the final stanza to another scene of foreboding that ended in the murder of Agamemnon, inevitably causes his delineation to take on wider implications. The sharp contrast that seems at first simply to be mocking a debased present as it juxtaposes Sweeney with the hero of antiquity, ends in establishing also an undercurrent of moving drama: for a sympathetic feeling for Sweeney is set up by the realization that he is a man as well as Agamemnon, and that his plotted death is therefore likewise a human tragedy.' Matthiessen, *The Achievement of T.S.Eliot* (Boston, 1935),129–30.

[2] 'Alas! I am stricken by a timely blow within.'

Slips and pulls the table cloth
Overturns a coffee-cup,
Reorganized upon the floor
She yawns and draws a stocking up;

The silent man in mocha brown
Sprawls at the window-sill and gapes;
The waiter brings in oranges
Bananas figs and hothouse grapes;   20

The silent vertebrate in brown
Contracts and concentrates, withdraws;
Rachel *née* Rabinovitch
Tears at the grapes with murderous paws;

She and the lady in the cape
Are suspect, thought to be in league;
Therefore the man with heavy eyes
Declines the gambit, shows fatigue,

Leaves the room and reappears
Outside the window, leaning in,   30
Branches of wistaria
Circumscribe a golden grin;

The host with someone indistinct
Converses at the door apart,
The nightingales are singing near
The Convent of the Sacred Heart,

And sang within the bloody wood
When Agamemnon cried aloud,
And let their liquid siftings fall
To stain the stiff dishonoured shroud.   40

1919

GERONTION [1]

Thou hast nor youth nor age
But as it were an after dinner sleep
Dreaming of both.[2]

HERE I am, an old man in a dry month,
Being read to by a boy, waiting for rain.

I was neither at the hot gates
Nor fought in the warm rain
Nor knee deep in the salt marsh, heaving a
      cutlass,
Bitten by flies, fought.
My house is a decayed house,
And the jew squats on the window sill, the
      owner,
Spawned in some estaminet of Antwerp,
Blistered in Brussels, patched and peeled in
      London.   10
The goat coughs at night in the field
      overhead;
Rocks, moss, stonecrop, iron, merds.
The woman keeps the kitchen, makes tea,
Sneezes at evening, poking the peevish
      gutter.
                    I an old man,
A dull head among windy spaces.

Signs are taken for wonders. 'We would see
      a sign!'
The word within a word, unable to speak a
      word,
Swaddled with darkness. In the juvescence
      of the year
Came Christ the tiger   20
In depraved May, dogwood and chestnut,
      flowering judas,
To be eaten, to be divided, to be drunk
Among whispers; by Mr. Silvero
With caressing hands, at Limoges
Who walked all night in the next room;

By Hakagawa, bowing among the Titians;
By Madame de Tornquist, in the dark room
Shifting the candles; Fräulein von Kulp
Who turned in the hall, one hand on the
      door. Vacant shuttles
Weave the wind. I have no ghosts,   30
An old man in a draughty house
Under a windy knob.

After such knowledge, what forgiveness?
      Think now
History has many cunning passages,
      contrived corridors
And issues, deceives with whispering
      ambitions,

---

[1] 'The poem opens with what is to be a recurrent theme of Mr. Eliot's: the mixing of "memory and desire" in present barrenness. The old man in his "dry month," waiting for the life-giving 'rain' that he knows will never come, is stirred to envy, then to poignant recollection by the story of hot-blooded vitality, which contrasts with the squalour of his actual surrounding. Youthful desire mingles in memory with the most exalted emotions, those associated with the mysteries of religion.' Leavis, *New Bearings in English Poetry* (London, 1932),84.

    'As he [Eliot] said once in conversation, the images here are "consciously concrete;" they correspond as closely as possible to something he has actually seen and remembered. But he also believes that if they are clearly rendered, they will stand for something larger than themselves; they will not depend for their apprehension upon any private reference, but will become "unconsciously general." ' Matthiessen, *The Achievement of T.S.Eliot*(Boston, 1935),62.

[2] Shakespeare, *Measure for Measure*,III,i,32–34.

Guides us by vanities. Think now
She gives when our attention is distracted
And what she gives, gives with such supple
      confusions
That the giving famishes the craving. Gives
      too late
What's not believed in, or if still believed, 40
In memory only, reconsidered passion.
      Gives too soon
Into weak hands, what's thought can be
      dispensed with
Till the refusal propagates a fear. Think
Neither fear nor courage saves us.
      Unnatural vices
Are fathered by our heroism. Virtues
Are forced upon us by our impudent
      crimes.
These tears are shaken from the wrath-
      bearing tree.

The tiger springs in the new year. Us he
      devours. Think at last
We have not reached conclusion, when I
Stiffen in a rented house. Think at last   50
I have not made this show purposelessly
And it is not by any concitation
Of the backward devils
I would meet you upon this honestly.
I that was near your heart was removed
      therefrom
To lose beauty in terror, terror in
      inquisition.
I have lost my passion: why should I need
      to keep it
Since what is kept must be adulterated?
I have lost my sight, smell, hearing, taste
      and touch:
How should I use them for your closer
      contact?   60

These with a thousand small deliberations
Protract the profit of their chilled delirium,
Excite the membrane, when the sense has
      cooled,
With pungent sauces, multiply variety
In a wilderness of mirrors. What will the
      spider do,
Suspend its operations, will the weevil
Delay? De Bailhache, Fresca, Mrs.
      Cammel, whirled
Beyond the circuit of the shuddering Bear
In fractured atoms. Gull against the wind,
      in the windy straits
Of Belle Isle, or running on the Horn,   70
White feathers in the snow, the Gulf claims,

And an old man driven by the Trades
To a sleepy corner.

                        Tenants of the house,
Thoughts of a dry brain in a dry season.
                                         1920

ASH-WEDNESDAY [1]

I

BECAUSE I do not hope to turn again
Because I do not hope
Because I do not hope to turn
Desiring this man's gift and that man's
      scope
I no longer strive to strive towards such
      things
(Why should the agèd eagle stretch its
      wings?)
Why should I mourn
The vanished power of the usual
      reign?

Because I do not hope to know again
The infirm glory of the positive hour   10
Because I do not think
Because I know I shall not know
The one veritable transitory power
Because I cannot drink
There, where trees flower, and springs
      flow, for there is nothing again

Because I know that time is always
      time
And place is always and only place
And what is actual is actual only for one
      time
And only for one place
I rejoice that things are as they are and   20
I renounce the blessèd face
And renounce the voice

[1] ' . . . The balance that is sustained in "Ash-Wednesday" between knowledge of the desert and perception
of the garden gives a full tone of authority to both, and
thus to the range of experience which they encompass.
This poem is not an escape from the problem of life into
an easy dream world. The most urgent notes are suggested by the connotations of its title. On Ash-Wednesday is performed the ritual of anointing the forehead
with ashes, while the priest recites: "Remember, man,
that thou art dust, and unto dust thou shalt return."
. . . By the time we reach the last poem of the series,
we have a full sense of the wavering of an individual
spirit, its desire to lose itself in the universal Will, and
yet its continual distraction back to the world of desire
and loss.' Matthiessen, The Achievement of T.S.Eliot
(Boston, 1935),120–22.

Because I cannot hope to turn again
Consequently I rejoice, having to construct
    something
Upon which to rejoice

And pray to God to have mercy upon us
And I pray that I may forget
These matters that with myself I too much
    discuss
Too much explain
Because I do not hope to turn again   30
Let these words answer
For what is done, not to be done again
May the judgement not be too heavy upon
    us

Because these wings are no longer wings to
    fly
But merely vans to beat the air
The air which is now thoroughly small and
    dry
Smaller and dryer than the will
Teach us to care and not to care
Teach us to sit still.

Pray for us sinners now and at the hour of
    our death   40
Pray for us now and at the hour of our
    death.

2

Lady, three white leopards sat under a
    juniper-tree
In the cool of the day, having fed to satiety
On my legs my heart my liver and that
    which had been contained
In the hollow round of my skull. And God
    said
Shall these bones live? shall these
Bones live? And that which had been
    contained
In the bones (which were already dry) said
    chirping:
Because of the goodness of this Lady
And because of her loveliness, and
    because   50
She honours the Virgin in meditation,
We shine with brightness. And I who am
    here dissembled
Proffer my deeds to oblivion, and my love
To the posterity of the desert and the fruit
    of the gourd.
It is this which recovers
My guts the strings of my eyes and the
    indigestible portions

Which the leopards reject. The Lady is
    withdrawn
In a white gown, to contemplation, in a
    white gown.
Let the whiteness of bones atone to
    forgetfulness.   59
There is no life in them. As I am forgotten
And would be forgotten, so I would forget
Thus devoted, concentrated in purpose.
    And God said
Prophesy to the wind, to the wind only for
    only
The wind will listen. And the bones sang
    chirping
With the burden of the grasshopper,
    saying

Lady of silences
Calm and distressed
Torn and most whole
Rose of memory
Rose of forgetfulness   70
Exhausted and life-giving
Worried resposeful
The single Rose
Is now the Garden
Where all loves end
Terminate torment
Of love unsatisfied
The greater torment
Of love satisfied
End of the endless   80
Journey to no end
Conclusion of all that
Is inconclusible
Speech without word and
Word of no speech
Grace to the Mother
For the Garden
Where all love ends.

Under a juniper-tree the bones sang,
    scattered and shining
We are glad to be scattered, we did little
    good to each other,   90
Under a tree in the cool of the day, with the
    blessing of sand,
Forgetting themselves and each other,
    united
In the quiet of the desert. This is the land
    which ye
Shall divide by lot. And neither division
    nor unity
Matters. This is the land. We have our
    inheritance.

3[1]

At the first turning of the second stair
I turned and saw below
The same shape twisted on the banister
Under the vapour in the fetid air
Struggling with the devil of the stairs who
    wears   100
The deceitful face of hope and of despair.

At the second turning of the second
    stair
I left them twisting, turning below;
There were no more faces and the stair was
    dark,
Damp, jaggèd, like an old man's mouth
    drivelling, beyond repair,
Or the toothed gullet of an agèd shark.·

At the first turning of the third stair
Was a slotted window bellied like the fig's
    fruit
And beyond the hawthorn blossom and a
    pasture scene
The broadbacked figure drest in blue and
    green   110
Enchanted the maytime with an antique
    flute.
Blown hair is sweet, brown hair over the
    mouth blown,
Lilac and brown hair;
Distraction, music of the flute, stops and
    steps of the mind over the third
    stair,
Fading, fading; strength beyond hope and
    despair
Climbing the third stair.

1 'It is more than likely that he [Eliot] meant the turn-
ings of his stair to represent something even more
definite, to remind the reader that they correspond in
general to the three divisions of Dante's hill of Purgatory. At the foot of the hill were those whose sin had
been the greatest, who had been guilty of love distorted, those who had loved evil things instead of God,
those whose self-absorbed pride had shut them off
from Him. Higher up were those whose love of God
had been defective; higher still, the least gravely sinful,
those who had loved excessively things which should
take only a secondary place in the affections, among
them the sensual and lustful. (A hint of the correspondence between these particular qualities of excess and
Eliot's third stair is underscored by the image describing the window itself "bellied like the fig's fruit").
Such a reminder that the stages of the soul which Eliot
is depicting correspond also to a completely developed
pattern of philosophic and religious thought, would
remove the experience entirely from anything purely
personal, and would thus enable it to possess a more
universal significance.' Matthiessen, ibid.,65–66.

Lord, I am not worthy
Lord, I am not worthy

    but speak the word only.

4

Who walked between the violet and the
    violet   120
Who walked between
The various ranks of varied green
Going in white and blue, in Mary's colour,
Talking of trivial things
In ignorance and in knowledge of eternal
    dolour
Who moved among the others as they
    walked,
Who then made strong the fountains and
    made fresh the springs

Made cool the dry rock and made firm the
    sand
In blue of larkspur, blue of Mary's colour,
Sovegna vos [2]   130

Here are the years that walk between,
    bearing
Away the fiddles and the flutes, restoring
One who moves in the time between sleep
    and waking, wearing

White light folded, sheathed about her,
    folded.
The new years walk, restoring
Through a bright cloud of tears, the years,
    restoring
With a new verse the ancient rhyme.
    Redeem
The time. Redeem
The unread vision in the higher dream
While jewelled unicorns draw by the gilded
    hearse.   140
The silent sister veiled in white and blue
Between the yews, behind the garden god,
Whose flute is breathless, bent her head and
    signed but spoke no word

But the fountain sprang up and the bird
    sang down
Redeem the time, redeem the dream
The token of the word unheard, unspoken

Till the wind shake a thousand whispers
    from the yew

And after this our exile

2 'Remember.'

5

If the lost word is lost, if the spent word is
    spent
If the unheard, unspoken   150
Word is unspoken, unheard;
Still is the unspoken word, the Word
    unheard,
The Word without a word, the Word
    within
The world and for the world;
And the light shone in darkness and
Against the Word the unstilled world still
    whirled
About the centre of the silent Word.

    O my people, what have I done unto thee.

Where shall the word be found, where will
    the word
Resound? Not here, there is not enough
    silence   160
Not on the sea or on the islands, not
On the mainland, in the desert or the rain
    land,
For those who walk in darkness
Both in the day time and in the night time
The right time and the right place are not
    here
No place of grace for those who avoid the
    face
No time to rejoice for those who walk
    among noise and deny the voice

Will the veiled sister pray for
Those who walk in darkness, who chose
    thee and oppose thee,
Those who are torn on the horn between
    season and season, time and time,
    between   170
Hour and hour, word and word, power and
    power, those who wait
In darkness? Will the veiled sister pray
For children at the gate
Who will not go away and cannot pray:
Pray for those who chose and oppose

    O my people, what have I done unto thee.

Will the veiled sister between the slender
Yew trees pray for those who offend her
And are terrified and cannot surrender
And affirm before the world and deny
    between the rocks   180
In the last desert between the last blue rocks

The desert in the garden the garden in the
    desert
Of drouth, spitting from the mouth the
    withered apple-seed.

    O my people.

6

Although I do not hope to turn again
Although I do not hope
Although I do not hope to turn

Wavering between the profit and the loss
In this brief transit where the dreams cross
The dreamcrossed twilight between birth
    and dying   190
(Bless me father) though I do not wish to
    wish these things
From the wide window towards the granite
    shore
The white sails still fly seaward, seaward
    flying
Unbroken wings

And the lost heart stiffens and rejoices
In the lost lilac and the lost sea voices
And the weak spirit quickens to rebel
For the bent golden-rod and the lost sea
    smell
Quickens to recover
The cry of quail and the whirling plover 200
And the blind eye creates
The empty forms between the ivory gates
And smell renews the salt savour of the
    sandy earth

This is the time of tension between dying
    and birth
The place of solitude where three dreams
    cross
Between blue rocks
But when the voices shaken from the yew-
    tree drift away
Let the other yew be shaken and reply.

Blessèd sister, holy mother, spirit of the
    fountain, spirit of the garden,
Suffer us not to mock ourselves with
    falsehood   210
Teach us to care and not to care
Teach us to sit still
Even among these rocks,
Our peace in His will
And even among these rocks
Sister, mother

And spirit of the river, spirit of the sea,
Suffer me not to be separated

And let my cry come unto Thee.

1930

MARINA [1]

Quis hic locus, quae regio, quae mundi plaga? [2]

WHAT seas what shores what grey rocks and
      what islands
What water lapping the bow
And scent of pine and the woodthrush
      singing through the fog
What images return
O my daughter.

Those who sharpen the tooth of the dog,
      meaning
Death
Those who glitter with the glory of the
      hummingbird, meaning
Death
Those who sit in the stye of contentment,
      meaning   10
Death
Those who suffer the ecstasy of the animals,
      meaning
Death

Are become unsubstantial, reduced by a
      wind,
A breath of pine, and the woodsong fog
By this grace dissolved in place

What is this face, less clear and clearer
The pulse in the arm, less strong and
      stronger—
Given or lent? more distant than stars and
      nearer than the eye

Whispers and small laughter between leaves
      and hurrying feet   20

1 'It is Marina, who was lost and found again, who becomes the symbol for the new realization striven after.
. . . "Marina" belongs, like "Ash-Wednesday," to
"the time of tension between dying and birth," and
exhibits an even more subtle ambiguity than anything
in the sequence. The liturgical note is absent, and one
may indicate the change in rhythm by saying that it
has about it nothing of ritual, yet the poem expresses
something nearer to assurance than anything in "Ash-
Wednesday." ' Leavis, *New Bearings in English
Poetry*(London, 1932),129–30.
2 'What is this place, what region, what part of the
world?'

Under sleep, where all the waters meet.

Bowsprit cracked with ice and paint
      cracked with heat.
I made this, I have forgotten
And remember.
The rigging weak and the canvas rotten
Between one June and another September.
Made this unknowing, half conscious,
      unknown, my own.
The garboard strake leaks, the seams need
      caulking.
This form, this face, this life
Living to live in a world of time beyond me;
      let me   30
Resign my life for this life, my speech for
      that unspoken,
The awakened, lips parted, the hope, the
      new ships.

What seas what shores what granite islands
      towards my timbers
And woodthrush calling through the fog
My daughter.

1930

FROM CORIOLAN

TRIUMPHAL MARCH [3]

STONE, bronze, stone, steel, stone, oakleaves
      horses' heels
Over the paving.
And the flags. And the trumpets. And so
      many eagles.

3 In the context of the lines at the end of 'Triumphal
March,' 'the central figure of the poem is seen to be
neither Corialanus nor a modern statesman alone, no
more an Elizabethan than a Roman general; not even a
symbol for leadership so much as the embodiment of
qualities of spiritual perception and mastery that are
integral to any deep apprehension of the meaning of
life, and thus also to the existence of any adequate
society. The hidden sources of inner life, the reserved
balance, which sustain this individual and mark him
off from the shallow chaotic flux of mere externalized
rootless existence, make him almost a symbol for the
harmonious union of emotion and thought that Eliot
has so frequently stressed as characteristic of a "firm
grasp of human experience"; these qualities likewise
demand a sustained equilibrium in the relations between the individual and the social structure. The
ripely developed human being has gained the integrity
that comes from mature self-knowledge, and he therefore understands that no wholeness exists in isolation,
that the individual cannot find fulfillment except
through also giving himself to society—a truth none
the less implied in "Difficulties of a Statesman" [the
remaining section of "Coriolan"] by the fact that what
is presented there is the break-down of the relation
between the leader and the state in the hopeless con-

How many? Count them. And such a press
    of people.
We hardly knew ourselves that day, or knew
    the City.
This is the way to the temple, and we so
    many crowding the way.
So many waiting, how many waiting? what
    did it matter, on such a day?
Are they coming? No, not yet. You can see
    some eagles. And hear the trumpets.
Here they come. Is he coming?
The natural wakeful life of our Ego is a
    perceiving.   10
We can wait with our stools and our
    sausages.
What comes first? Can you see? Tell us. It is

  5,800,000 rifles and carbines,
    102,000 machine guns,
     28,000 trench mortars,
     53,000 field and heavy guns,
I cannot tell how many projectiles, mines
    and fuses,

    13,000 aeroplanes,
    24,000 aeroplane engines,
    50,000 ammunition waggons,   20
now 55,000 army waggons,
    11,000 field kitchens,
     1,150 field bakeries.

What a time that took. Will it be he now?
    No,
Those are the golf club Captains, these the
    Scouts,
And now the *société gymnastique de Poissy*
And now come the Mayor and the
    Liverymen. Look
There he is now, look:
There is no interrogation in his eyes
Or in the hands, quiet over the horse's
    neck,   30
And the eyes watchful, waiting, perceiving,
    indifferent.
O hidden under the dove's wing, hidden in
    the turtle's breast,
Under the palmtree at noon, under the
    running water
At the still point of the turning world. O
    hidden.

Now they go up to the temple. Then the
    sacrifice.
Now come the virgins bearing urns, urns
    containing
Dust
Dust
Dust of dust, and now
Stone, bronze, stone, steel, stone, oakleaves,
    horses' heels   40
Over the paving.

That is all we could see. But how many
    eagles! and how many trumpets!
(And Easter Day, we didn't get to the
    country,
So we took young Cyril to church. And
    they rang a bell
And he said right out loud, *crumpets*.)
        Don't throw away that sausage,
It'll come in handy. He's artful. Please, will
    you
Give us a light?
Light
Light   50
Et les soldats faisaient la haie? ILS LA
    FAISAIENT.[1]

                     1931

---

fusion of bureaucracy.' Matthiessen, *The Achievement of T.S.Eliot*(Boston, 1935),140–41.

  'It happens that I have recently come across an interesting example of how Eliot's own feeling for syllable and rhythm, encountering a passage in prose seems to have started the movement of his "Triumphal March," and hence gives an illuminating glimpse of his own "auditory imagination" in action. I began reading Charles Maurras's *L'Avenir de l'Intelligence* largely because Eliot had recommended it as one of the standard expositions of the classical point of view. It opens with an ironic account of how each new tawdry journalistic triumph is now greeted in the streets with procession and applause. A mediocre writer is represented as talking excitedly: "—Y avez-vous pris garde? dit-il, les yeux serrés, le chef de l'Etat s'était fait représenter. Nous avions la moitié du Conseil des ministres et les deux préfets. Tant de généraux! Des régiments avec drapeau, des musiciens et leur bannière. Sans compter beaucoup de magistrats en hermine et de professeurs, ces derniers sans leur toge, ce qui est malheureux.—Et les soldats faisaient la haie?— Ils la faisaient.—En armes? Vous l'avez dit.—Mais que disait le peuple?—Il n'en croyait pas ses cent yeux!"

  'I have given a whole paragraph in order that the reader can also sense the possible way in which Eliot's ear quickened at "Tant de généraux"; and can perceive not only the source from which he took his final marching line: "Et les soldats faisaient la haie? ILS LA FAISAIENT"; but, more importantly, the source from which he also incorporated something of the whole sensation of movement that he transformed into the rhythms of his verse. In calculating what elements a poet's ear takes from the sources of his inspiration, it should also be observed that Eliot transformed the context here into quite a new pattern of his own, utilizing, however, a suggestion of the futile bustle of the crowd to contrast with the momentary vision of the serenity of his hero.' Matthiessen, ibid.,82–83.

[1] 'So the soldiers drew up a cordon?' 'They did!'

FROM THE ROCK

10

. . . .

O LIGHT Invisible, we praise Thee!
Too bright for mortal vision.
O Greater Light, we praise Thee for the
    less;
The eastern light our spires touch at
    morning,   20
The light that slants upon our western
    doors at evening,
The twilight over stagnant pools at
    batflight,
Moon light and star light, owl and moth
    light,
Glow-worm glowlight on a grassblade.
O Light Invisible, we worship Thee!

We thank Thee for the lights that we have
    kindled,
The light of altar and of sanctuary;
Small lights of those who meditate at
    midnight
And lights directed through the coloured
    panes of windows
And light reflected from the polished
    stone,   30
The gilded carven wood, the coloured
    fresco.
Our gaze is submarine, our eyes look
    upward
And see the light that fractures through
    unquiet water.

We see the light but see not whence it comes.
O Light Invisible, we glorify Thee!

In our rhythm of earthly life we tire of light.
    We are glad when the day ends,
    when the play ends; and ecstasy is
    too much pain.
We are children quickly tired: children
    who are up in the night and fall
    asleep as the rocket is fired; and the
    day is long for work or play.
We tire of distraction or concentration, we
    sleep and are glad to sleep,
Controlled by the rhythm of blood and the
    day and the night and the seasons.
And we must extinguish the candle, put
    out the light and relight it;   40
Forever must quench, forever relight the
    flame.
Therefore we thank Thee for our little
    light, that is dappled with shadow.
We thank Thee who hast moved us to
    building, to finding, to forming at
    the ends of our fingers and beams of
    our eyes.
And when we have built an altar to the
    Invisible Light, we may set thereon
    the little lights for which our bodily
    vision is made.
And we thank Thee that darkness reminds
    us of light.
O Light Invisible, we give Thee thanks for
    Thy great glory!

    1934

ARCHIBALD MACLEISH

1892–

NOTE BY A. MACL.

THE one man who should never attempt an explanation of a poem is its author. If the poem can be improved by its author's explanations it never should have been published, and if the poem cannot be improved by its author's explanations the explanations are scarcely worth reading. The following brief notes therefore are offered not by way of interpretation of the poems but by way of illustration of the materials out of which the poems came. They are excerpts from note-books kept at the time.

    'Ars Poetica' was written in 1924. Notebook references to its subject read as fol-

lows: 'The purpose of the expression of emotion in a poem is not to recreate the poet's emotion in some one else. . . . Art is not a pandar. . . . The poem itself is a finality, an end, a creation—not a stimulant.'

    'Fenellosa says truly that metaphor "the revealer of nature" is the very essence of poetry. But metaphor is not exegesis or demonstration. Metaphor is experience: it is the conviction of the senses and the conviction of the senses is experience.'

    'The essential fact about form in poetry is that poetry is an art in and of time and that its form is the line of a succession.'

    'You Andrew Marvell' (so-called in reference to the famous 'Ever at my back' lines from Marvell's 'To His Coy Mistress') was written in the fall of 1926 after a return from Persia. It originated with a phrase in the following note written on the Mediterranean. 'The unforeseen experience —consciousness now of the other side of the earth: the always westward coming on of night—Teheran dark—Pa-i-Tak—the Tigris—the house at Rutba Wells—the Levant shore—Crete—Messina—the Garoupe Light—Saragossa the round domes —ocean.'

'L'An Trentiesme de Mon Eage' was written in France in December 1924. A note made in Paris reads: 'The curious fact that significance in our time has fallen from the sun and the stars and the vast words with the resounding vowels to light upon the minute facets of minute experience—the door knob, the coat buttons and the bannisters. And this would not be strange were it not that we retain so strongly the sense of mortality.'

'Conquistador' was begun in 1929. The first note referring to the project runs: ' "The Conquest of the New World" which is the metaphor not only of our continent but (and most movingly) of our time—as "America" is the metaphor of all human hope—as "west" is the metaphor of the dreamed-of future. . . . The reports of the existence of this world: the rumors of its riches; the discovery of its coast, of its mountains westward; the arduous journey; the hopeless battles; the beautiful city; the victory which yields defeat. . . . The heroism and the nobility and the pathos of our indestructible belief in that kingdom in the west, our search for it, our discovery of it; our conquest of it and its forever loss. . .'

Of the other poems selected it is perhaps only necessary to give the dates. 'Not Marble, Nor the Gilded Monuments' was written in New York about 1926, 'The End of the World' in Normandy in 1924, the 'Too-Late Born' at the end of 1924, the 'Frescoes for Mr. Rockefeller's City' (the reference being to the fresco Diego Rivera painted for Mr. Rockefeller's Radio City, and was compelled to paint out) in 1932, the 'Speech to Those Who Say Comrade' and 'Pole Star for This Year' in 1935, 'Pony Rock' in 1929.

1937 1938

ARS POETICA

A POEM should be palpable and mute
As a globed fruit

Dumb
As old medallions to the thumb

Silent as the sleeve-worn stone
Of casement ledges where the moss has
grown—

A poem should be wordless
As the flight of birds

. . . . . .

A poem should be motionless in time
As the moon climbs

Leaving, as the moon releases
Twig by twig the night-entangled trees,

Leaving, as the moon behind the winter
leaves,
Memory by memory the mind—

A poem should be motionless in time
As the moon climbs

. . . . . .

A poem should be equal to:
Not true

For all the history of grief
An empty doorway and a maple leaf

For love
The leaning grasses and two lights above
the sea—

A poem should not mean
But be
1924 1926

YOU, ANDREW MARVELL

AND here face down beneath the sun
And here upon earth's noonward height
To feel the always coming on
The always rising of the night

To feel creep up the curving east
The earthy chill of dusk and slow
Upon those under lands the vast
And ever climbing shadow grow

And strange at Ecbatan the trees
Take leaf by leaf the evening strange   10
The flooding dark about their knees
The mountains over Persia change

And now at Kermanshah the gate
Dark empty and the withered grass
And through the twilight now the late
Few travelers in the westward pass

And Baghdad darken and the bridge
Across the silent river gone
And through Arabia the edge
Of evening widen and steal on   20

And deepen on Palmyra's street
The wheel rut in the ruined stone
And Lebanon fade out and Crete
High through the clouds and overblown

And over Sicily the air
Still flashing with the landward gulls
And loom and slowly disappear
The sails above the shadowy hulls

And Spain go under and the shore
Of Africa the gilded sand   30
And evening vanish and no more
The low pale light across that land

Nor now the long light on the sea

And here face downward in the sun
To feel how swift how secretly
The shadow of the night comes on. . .
1926   1930

'NOT MARBLE
NOR THE GILDED MONUMENTS'

THE praisers of women in their proud and
          beautiful poems
Naming the grave mouth and the hair and
          the eyes
Boasted those they loved should be forever
          remembered
These were lies

The words sound but the face in the Istrian
          sun is forgotten
The poet speaks but to her dead ears no
          more
The sleek throat is gone—and the breast
          that was troubled to listen
Shadow from door

Therefore I will not praise your knees nor
          your fine walking
Telling you men shall remember your name
          as long   10
As lips move or breath is spent or the iron
          of English
Rings from a tongue

I shall say you were young and your arms
          straight and your mouth scarlet
I shall say you will die and none will
          remember you
Your arms change and none remember the
          swish of your garments
Nor the click of your shoe

Not with my hand's strength not with
          difficult labor
Springing the obstinate words to the bones
          of your breast
And the stubborn line to your young stride
          and the breath to your breathing
And the beat to your haste   20
Shall I prevail on the hearts of unborn men
          to remember

(What is a dead girl but a shadowy ghost
Or a dead man's voice but a distant and
          vain affirmation
Like dream words most)

Therefore I will not speak of the undying
          glory of women
I will say you were young and straight and
          your skin fair
And you stood in the door and the sun was
          a shadow of leaves on your shoulders
And a leaf on your hair

I will not speak of the famous beauty of
          dead women
I will say the shape of a leaf lay once on
          your hair   30
Till the world ends and the eyes are out and
          the mouths broken
Look! It is there!
1926   1930

THE END OF THE WORLD

QUITE unexpectedly as Vasserot
The armless ambidextrian was lighting
A match between his great and second toe
And Ralph the lion was engaged in biting
The neck of Madame Sossman while the
          drum

Pointed, and Teeny was about to cough
In waltz-time swinging Jocko by the
    thumb—
Quite unexpectedly the top blew off:

And there, there overhead, there, there,
    hung over
Those thousands of white faces, those
    dazed eyes,   10
There in the starless dark the poise, the
    hover,
There with vast wings across the canceled
    skies,
There in the sudden blackness the black
    pall
Of nothing, nothing, nothing—nothing at
    all.
1925   1926

L'AN TRENTIESME DE MON EAGE

AND I have come upon this place
By lost ways, by a nod, by words,
By faces, by an old man's face
At Morlaix lifted to the birds,

By hands upon the tablecloth
At Aldebori's, by the thin
Child's hands that opened to the moth
And let the flutter of the moonlight in,

By hands, by voices, by the voice
Of Mrs. Whitman on the stair,   10
By Margaret's 'If we had the choice
To choose or not—' through her thick hair,

By voices, by the creak and fall
Of footsteps on the upper floor,
By silence waiting in the hall
Between the doorbell and the door,

By words, by voices, a lost way—
And here above the chimney stack
The unknown constellations sway—
And by what way shall I go back?   20
1924   1926

THE TOO–LATE BORN

WE too, we too, descending once again
The hills of our own land, we too have
    heard
Far off—Ah, que ce cor a longue haleine—
The horn of Roland in the passages of
    Spain,

The first, the second blast, the failing third,
And with the third turned back and
    climbed once more
The steep road southward, and heard faint
    the sound
Of swords, of horses, the disastrous war,
And crossed the dark defile at last, and
    found
At Roncevaux upon the darkening plain   10
The dead against the dead and on the silent
    ground
The silent slain—
1924   1926

PONY ROCK

ONE who has loved the hills and died, a man
Intimate with them—how their profiles
    fade
Large out of evening or through veils of
    rain
Vanish and reappear or how the sad
Long look of moonlight troubles their
    blind stones—
One who has loved them does not utterly,
Letting his fingers loosen and the green
Ebb from his eyeballs, close his eyes and go:

But other men long after he is dead
Seeing those hills will catch their breath
    and stare   10
As one who reading in a book some word
That calls joy back but can recall not
    where—
Only the crazy sweetness in the head—
Will stare at the black print till the page is
    blurred.
1929   1933

FROM FRESCOES FOR MR. ROCKEFELLER'S CITY

I

LANDSCAPE AS A NUDE

SHE lies on her left side her flank golden:
Her hair is burned black with the strong
    sun:
The scent of her hair is of rain in the dust
    on her shoulders:
She has brown breasts and the mouth of no
    other country:

Ah she is beautiful here in the sun where
    she lies:

She is not like the soft girls naked in
    vineyards
Nor the soft naked girls of the English
    islands
Where the rain comes in with the surf on an
    east wind:

Hers is the west wind and the sunlight: the
    west
Wind is the long clean wind of the
    continents—   10
The wind turning with earth: the wind
    descending
Steadily out of the evening and following on:

The wind here where she lies is west: the
    trees
Oak ironwood cottonwood hickory:
    standing in
Great groves they roll on the wind as the
    sea would:
The grasses of Iowa Illinois Indiana

Run with the plunge of the wind as a wave
    tumbling:

Under her knees there is no green lawn of
    the Florentines:
Under her dusty knees is the corn stubble:
Her belly is flecked with the flickering light
    of the corn: 20

She lies on her left side her flank golden:
Her hair is burned black with the strong
    sun:
The scent of her hair is of dust and of
    smoke on her shoulders:
She has brown breasts and the mouth of no
    other country:

2

WILDWEST

THERE were none of my blood in this battle:
There were Minneconjous: Sans Arcs:
    Brules:
Many nations of Sioux: they were few men
    galloping:

This would have been in the long days in
    June:
They were galloping well deployed under
    the plum-trees:
They were driving riderless horses:
    themselves they were few:

Crazy Horse had done it with few numbers:
Crazy Horse was small for a Lakota:
He was riding always alone thinking of
    something:

He was standing alone by the picket lines
    by the ropes: 10
He was young then: he was thirty when he
    died:
Unless there were children to talk he took
    no notice:

When the soldiers came for him there on
    the other side
On the Greasy Grass in the villages we
    were shouting
'Hoka Hey! Crazy Horse will be riding!'

They fought in the water: horses and men
    were drowning:
They rode on the butte: dust settled in
    sunlight:
Hoka Hey! they lay on the bloody ground:

No one could tell of the dead which man
    was Custer. . .   19
That was the end of his luck: by that river:
The soldiers beat him at Slim Buttes once:

They beat him at Willow Creek when the
    snow lifted:
The last time they beat him was the
    Tongue:
He had only the meat he had made and of
    that little:

Do you ask why he should fight? It was his
    country:
My God should he not fight? It was his:
But after the Tongue there were no herds
    to be hunting:

He cut the knots of the tails and he led
    them in:
He cried out 'I am Crazy Horse! Do not
    touch me!'
There were many soldiers between and the
    gun glinting. . .   30

And a Mister Josiah Perham of Maine had
    much of the
land Mister Perham was building the
    Northern Pacific
railroad that is Mister Perham was saying
    at lunch that

forty say fifty millions of acres in gift and
government grant outright ought to be
    worth a
wide price on the Board at two-fifty and

later a Mister Cooke had relieved Mister
    Perham and
later a Mister Morgan relieved Mister
    Cooke:
Mister Morgan converted at prices current:

It was all prices to them: they never looked
    at it: 40
why should they look at the land: they were
    Empire Builders:
it was all in the bid and the asked and the
    ink on their books. . .

When Crazy Horse was there by the Black
    Hills
His heart would be big with the love he had
    for that country
And all the game he had seen and the
    mares he had ridden

And how it went out from you wide and
    clean in the sunlight

3

Burying Ground by the Ties

Ayee! Ai! This is heavy earth on our
    shoulders:
There were none of us born to be buried in
    this earth:
Niggers we were Portuguese Magyars
    Polacks:

We were born to another look of the sky
    certainly:
Now we lie here in the river pastures:
We lie in the mowings under the thick
    turf:

We hear the earth and the all-day rasp of
    the grasshoppers:
It was we laid the steel on this land from
    ocean to ocean:
It was we (if you know) put the U. P.
    through the passes

Bringing her down into Laramie full load 10
Eighteen mile on the granite anticlinal
Forty-three foot to the mile and the grade
    holding:

It was we did it: hunkies of our kind:
It was we dug the caved-in holes for the
    cold water:
It was we built the gully spurs and the
    freight sidings:

Who would do it but we and the Irishmen
    bossing us?
It was all foreign-born men there were in
    this country:
It was Scotsmen Englishmen Chinese
    Squareheads Austrians. . .

Ayee! but there's weight to the earth under
    it:
Not for this did we come out—to be lying
    here   20
Nameless under the ties in the clay cuts:

There's nothing good in the world but the
    rich will buy it:
Everything sticks to the grease of a gold
    note—
Even a continent—even a new sky!

Do not pity us much for the strange grass
    over us:
We laid the steel to the stone stock of these
    mountains:
The place of our graves is marked by the
    telegraph poles!

It was not to lie in the bottoms we came
    out
And the trains going over us here in the dry
    hollows . . .

5

Empire Builders

The Museum Attendant:

This is *The Making of America in Five
    Panels:*

This is Mister Harriman making America:
Mister-Harriman-is-buying-the-Union-
    Pacific-at-Seventy:
The Sante Fe is shining on his hair:

This is Commodore Vanderbilt making
    America:
Mister-Vanderbilt-is-eliminating-the-
    short-interest-in-Hudson:
Observe the carving on the rocking chair:

This is J.P.Morgan making America:
(The Tennessee Coal is behind to the left
    of the Steel Company:)   9
Those in mauve are braces he is wearing:

This is Mister Mellon making America:
Mister-Mellon-is-represented-as-a-
    symbolical-figure-in-aluminum-
Strewing-bank-stocks-on-a-burnished-
    stair:

This is the Bruce is the Barton making
    America:
Mister-Barton-is-selling-us-Doctor's-
    Deliciousest-Dentifrice:
This is he in beige with the canary:

You have just beheld the Makers making
    America:
This is *The Making of America in Five
Panels:*
America lies to the west-southwest of the
    Switch-Tower:
There is nothing to see of America but
    land: 20

*The Original Document
under the Panel Paint:*
'To Thos. Jefferson Esq. his obd't serv't
M. Lewis: captain: detached:

                Sir:

Having in mind your repeated commands
    in this matter:
And the worst half of it done and the
    streams mapped:

And we here on the back of this beach
    beholding the
Other ocean—two years gone and the cold

Breaking with rain for the third spring
    since St. Louis:
The crows at the fishbones on the frozen
    dunes: 30

The first cranes going over from south
    north:
And the river down by a mark of the pole
    since the morning:

And time near to return, and a ship
    (Spanish)
Lying in for the salmon: and fearing chance
    or the

Drought or the Sioux should deprive you
    of these discoveries—
Therefore we send by sea in this writing:

                Above the
Platte there were long plains and a clay
    country:
Rim of the sky far off: grass under it:

Dung for the cook fires by the sulphur licks
After that there were low hills and the
    sycamores: 40

And we poled up by the Great Bend in the
    skiffs:
The honey bees left us after the Osage
    River:

The wind was west in the evenings and no
    dew and the
Morning Star larger and whiter than
    usual—

The winter rattling in the brittle haws:
The second year there was sage and the
    quail calling:

All that valley is good land by the river:
Three thousand miles and the clay cliffs
    and

Rue and beargrass by the water banks
And many birds and the brant going over
    and tracks of   50

Bear elk wolves marten: the buffalo
Numberless so that the cloud of their dust
    covers them:

The antelope fording the fall creeks: and
    the mountains and
Grazing lands and the meadow lands and
    the ground

Sweet and open and well-drained:
                We advise you to
Settle troops at the forks and to issue
    licenses:

Many men will have living on these lands:
There is wealth in the earth for them all
    and the wood standing

And wild birds on the water where they
    sleep:

There is stone in the hills for the towns of
    a great people . . .'   60

You have just beheld the Makers making
    America:

They screwed her scrawny and gaunt with
    their seven-year panics:
They bought her back on their mortgages
    old-whore-cheap:
They fattened their bonds at her breasts
    till the thin blood ran from them:

Men have forgotten how full clear and deep
The Yellowstone moved on the gravel and
    grass grew
When the land lay waiting for her westward
    people!
1932   1933

FROM CONQUISTADOR

TENTH BOOK

O Halcyon! O sea-conceiving bird!
The bright surf breaking on thy silver
    beaches

And the life goes out of us leaving the
    chucked sherds!

Leaving an old man's memories to leach
Like a cock's jewels of gravel and worn
    thin
With the sleepless caul of the heart and
    hard and clean:

Leaving within the eyes behind the fingers
Back of the soft lid and the scarlet vein
The harsh flash of the steel where the light
    lingers! . . .

Leaving the slag in us. . . .   10
               leaving us those days. . . .

And I see well as from dark into light lying
    here:
The lint of the broom-straw turns in the
    sun's ray:

The cocks sing in the heat: there are cakes
    frying:
The drinking water drops from the hung
    gourd:
The rafters circle with the dozing flies:

The dogs rise and cross to the cool of the
    urine:

I see well in the dark of the room—as
    through shutters the
Sun is white on a street and the shadows
    sure—

As men move under tree-boughs and the
    sunlight   20
Leaps like a cat on their gilt capes and
    clings
And is swept off by the next branch:
    shunted. . . .

So I remember it: yes: and the evening
    bringing the
Doves down from the air: their wings steep
    to it!
And thou Colúa! and the paddles rinsed in
    the

Clear pools of thy sun! I cannot sleep for
    the
Light under my lids of thy bitter water:
I cannot sleep for thy cries and the walls
    keeping the

Leaning weight of thy sun by night and the
    autumn
Smelling of flowers as spring does: (wearing
    the   30
Cotton sleeves we were drunk and the wind
    caught in them):

And the girls they gave us for love with the
    scented hair:
The green light through the leaves: the
    slow awakening:
How there were many and small birds in
    the air then. . . .

We were like those that in their lands they
    say
The steers of the sun went up through the
    wave-lit orchards
Shaking the water drops and those gold
    naked

Girls before them at their dripping horns!
And they ate the sea-doused figs with the
    salt taste:
And all their time was of kine and of sea
    and of morning: 40

So did we lie in that land in the long days:
And they gave us a king's house to our
    heads and we dwelt in it:
And the house was smooth and of clean
    walls and so spacious

And well made and with lime and the stone
    set there was
Place for us all and the guns and our goods
    and our Indians:
Each man his mat under him smelling of

Lake grass and of leeks and an ell in width
And his painted cloth with the corn and the
    cones and the aloes
(For in that land there were men skilled in
    these images—

Such as sit with a day's sun in their laps   50
And they stare in the eyes of the trapped
    hare in the stubble:)
And the rooms smelled of the sweet wood
    like a chapel:

And all were of plank and were ceiled and
    of pinned lumber
And painted with scarlet beams and their
    out-walls burnished
And made to shine as a good coin: and
    some were

Build to the water and the light returned
And spilled up from the float of the ripples
    and ran on the
Wall's glare as a flame where the sunlight
    blurs it:

And some were shadowed to the cool
    canals:
And they poled in with their slow skiffs
    and their melons   60
Leaning against the gaff's end and the slash
    and

Drip of the stroke came back: and the cries
    sending the
Sun-bright birds up—and the beat of
    sound
Would pass and float on the stream and the
    wings settle:

(For all the isle was channeled as that
    ground
That takes its stars from Istria and their
    eyes

See first the new moon toward the Tuscan
    Mountain:)

And the town rang with the clang of oars
    and the cries:
And they brought the corn through the
    water-streets and the faggots:
They poled in with the heaped fish: the
    hides   70

Smelling of oak: the bowls slobbered with
    maguey:
They stood in the cool of the dark arcades
    in the market:
Many there were of them: tall men with
    the hank of the

Coarse skein on their wrists and their
    thumbs parting it:
Sellers of split fruits: of blue stones:
Of brass: of the nubile slaves—their hands
    bargaining:

Stroking the breasts up: and the thing was
    shown:
Merchants of sweet nuts and of chives and
    of honey:
Of leaves of dock for the eyes: of a calf's
    bone for the

Gloss of the hair as the hand draws it: of
    dung   80
For salt for the tanning of leather: sellers of
    yarn:
Old men with the sun-bleached hair and
    the bunches of

Herbs: of lettuces washed cool: of
    garlic
Dried brown on a withy of plaited grass:
Sellers of cooked dough by the coal-fires
    larding the

Stained skirt with the spittle of burning
    fat:
Those the makers of ropes: those that
    shredded the
Silken down of a seed and their fingers
    fastened the

Stone to the twist of it turning the scarlet
    thread:
Sellers of good dreams: of blue clay for the
Baking of gods: of quills of the gold: of
    hennequin: 90

Sellers of beetles for red dyes: makers of
Stone masks of the dead and of stone
    mirrors:
Makers of fortunate knots: magistrates in
    the

Swept porch—and they kept the names of
    the year:
They took the tax on the red stones and the
    herons:
They judged of the levies of salt: venders of
    syrups:

Of harsh drugs for the old from the
    coupling of hares:
Of dry seeds: of sweet straws . . . . many
    and
Strange cries that they had . . . . and they
    stood wearing the   100

Knotted and white cloths like capes and
    they went with
Strong knees through the heat of the sun
    and their thighs were
Straight and their bellies like knuckles of
    bronze: and they set their

Heels in the sand of the earth as a man
    riding a
Wave's back in the sea and their sex was
    naked
And stained with the salt of the sun like a
    golden hide:

And the tall girls there were in the wind
    and the way of the
Sun was under their knees and the way of
    the wind
Like a hand over them: smoothing the
    scarves out: shaking an

Odor of noon from their skirts like the odor
    at midday of   110
Clean cloths to bleach on the water stones
(And the butterfly opens his slow wings:)
    and their skin like the

Rain's fragrance of water: (one alone
Returns from a shadow of plantains and
    her mouth
Secret with lust as the honey of black
    combs):

And their loins were heavy with love and
    they laid them down

Under the lids of their eyes as under a
    garment:
They gave themselves in the green herb
    and the flowers:

Ah how the throat of a girl and a girl's arms
    are
Bright in the riding sun and the young sky
And the green year of our lives where the
    willows are!   121

How they were slender with strong breasts
    and the light of the
Leaves over them! How there were tall men
And the wading lake to their wrists and
    their wet thighs

Dabbled with sunlight: and they drew the
    nets
In the green sedge of the shore and they
    came singing:
The sea-film silvered in the lifting web:

Ah how the land was a good land! and the
    king of it
Rich and with young wives and with gold
    and his gardens
Sounding with water: and he went to drink

At noon at the grooved stone by the sheds
    and the jars were   131
Choked with the float of the sun: and he ate
    simnel
And sweet cakes he ate and a kind of
    partridges:

And none knew his ways or his times with
    women:
Silent he was and not seen and he came by
Dark: and his desire was in their limbs as an

Odor of plums in the night air and they
    wakened
Stretching their arms out and between
    their knees
Delight like the sun's mouth and the
    water's weight:

And all his house was sounding as of trees
And the leaves of the trees were dark and a
    dew came down from them: 141
Even at noon the dew fell like an ease of

Dusk to comfort a man's eyes: and the
    ground was

Trodden with naked heels: and he kept
    beasts:
And birds he kept in a grove and the green
    loud with the

Locusts and golden and shrill wrens and
    the bees
In the split hive of the wall and the names
    of serpents
Curled in the painted vessels at his feet:

And he kept marks on a stone for the sky's
    turning—
For the way of stars in the trees and the
    moon's toil: 150
Niter and salt he ate from the quick earth:

They brought baskets of sweetened seeds
    and of oil to him:
They cried to him Lord! my Lord! my
    great Lord!
They came with naked feet and the small
    voices:

Ah how the land was a good land! and the
    doors with
Morning with many leaves with the clean
    odor of
Water sluiced on the night stones: (and the
    core of the

Broken melon smelled of a girl's robe:)
We woke scenting the slot of the heat on the
    air:
We rinsed our mouths in the sun: by the
    listed boats   160

Purging ourselves to the coarse sand the
    glare of the
Sun was a cleanness of pebbles: far out
The fisherman leaned to his line and the
    silent herons:

And we lay under a lift of the green and
    their gowns were of
Spun twist in our hands: the hollow groin
Beat with a small heart: we heard the
    trowels

Strike on the brick of the roofs like silver
    coins:
We heard the whistle of tamed birds: to our
    tongues
Our mouths were sweetened with the
    scented ointment:

And we drank of the milk of the aloe and
    were drunk: 170
And the words hived in the heap of our
    bones and we praised the
Taste of a bitter leaf: we praised the sun

And the earth for the odor of men in its hot
    days—
For a woman's color of pink shell or the
    pock of the
Purple vein at her breast as a bruise made
    in it:

We praised the trampling of sun as a gilt
    cock:
Our hearts were singing as hammered
    bronze and our mouths with
Sound as the corn is where the wind goes:
    and we mocked the

Shape of love with our thumbs: we cried
    aloud of the
Great sky: of the salt rock: of the land. . . .

And nevertheless it was not so: for the
    ground was   181

Silent against us: on our foreign hands
The dust was a solemn and red stain: our
    tongues were
Unskilled to the pulp of their fruits as a
    language of

Sullen stones in our mouths: we heard the
    sun in the
Crackle of live trees with the ears of
    strangers. . . .

And they passed with their cries at dawn
    and their deep drums:

And we saw them go by the stone courts
    and the cages:
And all clean and with coarse lime and the
    temple
Steep in the reach of the sky. . .   190
            and the boy was slain!

The belly arched to the stone knife: I
    remember
They sang and were glad as a small child in
    the sunlight
And they ate the limbs for a feast and the
    flesh trembled. . . .

1929   1932

SPEECH TO THOSE WHO SAY COMRADE

THE brotherhood is not by the blood
    certainly:
But neither are men brothers by speech—
    by saying so:
Men are brothers by life lived and are hurt
    for it:

Hunger and hurt are the great begetters of
    brotherhood:
Humiliation has gotten much love:
Danger I say is the nobler father and
    mother:

Those are as brothers whose bodies have
    shared fear
Or shared harm or shared hurt or indignity.
Why are the old soldiers brothers and
    nearest?

For this: with their minds they go over the
    sea a little   10
And find themselves in their youth again as
    they were in
Soissons and Meaux and at Ypres and
    those cities:

A French loaf and the girls with their
    eyelids painted
Bring back to aging and lonely men
Their twentieth year and the metal odor of
    danger:

It is this in life which of all things is
    tenderest—
To remember together with unknown men
    the days
Common also to them and perils ended:

It is this which makes of many a
    generation—
A wave of men who having the same years
Have in common the same dead and the
    changes.   21

The solitary and unshared experience
Dies of itself like the violations of love
Or lives on as the dead live eerily:

The unshared and single man must cover
    his
Loneliness as a girl her shame for the way of
Life is neither by one man nor by suffering.

Who are the born brothers in truth? The
    puddlers
Scorched by the same flame in the same
    foundries:
Those who have spit on the same boards
    with the blood in it: 30

Ridden the same rivers with green logs:
Fought the police in the parks of the same
    cities:
Grinned for the same blows: the same
    flogging:

Veterans out of the same ships—factories—
Expeditions for fame: the founders of
    continents:
Those that hid in Geneva a time back:

Those that have hidden and hunted and all
    such—
Fought together: labored together: they
    carry the
Common look like a card and they pass
    touching.

Brotherhood! No word said can make you
    brothers!   40
Brotherhood only the brave earn and by
    danger or
Harm or by bearing hurt and by no other.

Brotherhood here in the strange world is
    the rich and
Rarest giving of life and the most valued:
Not to be had for a word or a week's wishing.
1935   1936

POLE STAR FOR THIS YEAR

WHERE the wheel of light is turned:
Where the axle of the night is
Turned: is motionless: where holds
And has held ancient sureness always:

Where of faring men the eyes
At oar bench at the rising bow
Have seen—torn shrouds between—the
    Wain
And that star's changelessness: not
    changing:

There upon that intent star:
Trust of wandering men: of truth   10
The most reminding witness: we
Fix our eyes also: waylost: the wanderers:

We too turn now to that star:
We too in whose trustless hearts
All truth alters and the lights
Of earth are out now turn to that star:

Liberty of man and mind
That once was mind's necessity
And made the West blaze up has burned
To bloody embers and the lamp's out: 20

Hope that was a noble flame
Has fanned to violence and feeds
On cities and the flesh of men
And chokes where unclean smoke
    defiles it:

Even the small spark of pride
That taught the tyrant once is dark
Where gunfire rules the starving street
And justice cheats the dead of honor:

Liberty and pride and hope
And every guide-mark of the mind   30

That led our blindness once has vanished.
This star will not. Love's star will not.

Love that has beheld the face
A man has with a man's eyes in it
Bloody from the slugger's blows
Or heard the cold child cry for hunger—

Love that listens where the good:
The virtuous: the men of faith:
Proclaim the paradise on earth
And murder starve and burn to make it—

Love that cannot either sleep   41
Or keep rich music in the ear
Or lose itself for the wild beat
The anger in the blood makes raging—

Love that hardens into hate—
Love like hatred and as bright—
Love is that one waking light
That leads now when all others darken.
1935   1936

JOHN CROWE RANSOM

1888–

SPECTRAL LOVERS

By night they haunted a thicket of April mist,
As out of the rich ground strangely come to
    birth,
Else two immaculate angels fallen on earth.
Lovers they knew they were, but why
    unclasped, unkissed?
Why should two lovers go frozen asunder
    in fear?
And yet they were, they were.

Over the shredding of an April blossom
Her thrilling fingers touched him quick
    with care;
Of many delicate postures she cast a snare;
But for all the red heart beating in the bale
    bosom,   10
Her face as of cunningly tinctured ivory
Was hard with an agony.

Stormed by the little batteries of an April
    night,
Passionate being the essences of the field,
Should the penetrable walls of the
    crumbling prison yield

And open her treasure to the first
    clamourous knight?
'This is the mad moon, and must I
    surrender all?
If he but ask it, I shall.'

And gesturing largely to the very moon of
    Easter,
Mincing his steps, and swishing the
    jubilant grass,   20
And beheading some field-flowers that had
    come to pass,
He had reduced his tributaries faster,
Had not considerations pinched his heart
Unfitly for his art.

'Am I reeling with the sap of April like a
    drunkard?
Blessed is he that taketh this richest of cities;
But it is so stainless, the sack were a
    thousand pities;
This is that marble fortress not to be
    conquered,
Lest its white peace in the black flame turn
    to tinder
And an unutterable cinder.'   30

They passed me once in April, in the
    mist.
No other season is it, when one walks and
    discovers
Two clad in the shapes of angels, being
    spectral lovers,
Trailing a glory of moon-gold and
    amethyst,
Who touch their quick fingers fluttering
    like a bird
Whose songs shall never be heard.

                        1924

OLD MAN PLAYING WITH
CHILDREN

A DISCREET householder exclaims on the
    grandsire
In war-paint and feathers, with fierce
    grandsons and axes,
Dancing around a backyard fire of boxes,
'Watch grandfather, he'll set the house on
    fire.'

But I will unriddle for you the thought of
    his mind,
An old one you cannot open with
    conversation.
What animates those thin legs in risky
    motion?
Mixes the snow on the head with snow on
    the wind?

'Grandson, grandsire. We are equally boy
    and boy.
Do not offer me your reclining-chair and
    slippers   10
With tedious old women talking in
    wrappers.
This life is not good but in danger and in
    joy.

'It is you who are elder to these and
    younger to me
That are penned as slaves by your
    properties and causes
And never walk out of your shaped
    insupportable houses,
And shamefully, when boys shout, go in
    and flee.

'God forgive me, I know too well your
    middling ways,
Having taken care and performed
    ignominies unreckoned

Between the first brief childhood and the
    brief second,
But I will be more honourable in these
    days.'   20

                        1924

PHILOMELA

PROCNE, Philomela, and Itylus,
Your names are liquid, your improbable
    tale
Is recited in the classic numbers of the
    nightingale.
Ah, but our numbers are not felicitous,
It goes not liquidly for us.

Perched on a Roman ilex, and duly
    apostrophized,
The nightingale descanted unto Ovid;
She has even appeared to the Teutons, the
    swilled and gravid;
At Fontainebleau it may be the bird was
    gallicized;
Never was she baptized.   10

To England came Philomela with her pain,
Fleeing the hawk her husband; querulous
    ghost,
She wanders when he sits heavy on his
    roost,
Utters herself in the original again,
The untranslatable refrain.

Not to these shores she came! this other
    Thrace,
Environ barbarous to the royal Attic;
How could her delicate dirge run
    democratic,
Delivered in a cloudless boundless public
    place
To an inordinate race?   20

I pernoctated with the Oxford students
    once,
And in the quadrangles, in the cloisters, on
    the Cher,
Precociously knocked at antique doors ajar,
Fatuously touched the hems of the
    hierophants,
Sick of my dissonance.

I went out to Bagley Wood, I climbed the
    hill;
Even the moon had slanted off in a
    twinkling,

I heard the sepulchral owl and a few bells
    tinkling,
There was no more villainous day to
    unfulfil,
The diuternity was still.   30

Up from the darkest wood where Philomela
    sat,
Her fairy numbers issued. What then ailed
    me?
My ears are called capacious but they
    failed me,

Her classics registered a little flat!
I rose, and venomously spat.

Philomela, Philomela, lover of song,
I am in despair if we may make us
    worthy,
A bantering breed sophistical and
    swarthy;
Unto more beautiful, persistently more
    young
Thy fabulous provinces belong.   41

1924

ALLEN TATE

1899–

ELEGY [1]

JEFFERSON DAVIS: 1808–1889

No more the white refulgent streets,
Never the dry hollows of the mind
Shall he in fine courtesy walk
Again, for death is not unkind.

A civil war cast on his fame,
The four years' odium of strife
Unbodies his dust; love cannot warm
His tall corpuscles to this life.

What did we gain? What did we lose?
Be still; grief for the pious dead   10
Suspires from bosoms of kind souls
Lavender-wise, propped up in bed.

Our loss put six feet under ground
Is measured by the magnolia's root;
Our gain's the intellectual sound
Of death's feet round a weedy tomb.

In the back chambers of the State
(Just preterition for his crimes)
We curse him to our busy sky
Who's busy in hell a hundred times   20

A day, though profitless his task,
Heedless what Belial may say—
He who wore out the perfect mask
Orestes fled in night and day.
1922–1931   1928

ODE TO THE CONFEDERATE DEAD [2]

Row after row with strict impunity
The headstones yield their names to the
    element,

1 'The first version of this poem, just four stanzas, was written in 1921, and called "Euthanasia"; the first I ever had in print. It wasn't good and it had nothing to do with Jefferson Davis. I forgot it until, one day in 1930, in the way things begin to run about loose in one's head, the first two lines came back to me, with the original "gutter" automatically changed to "hollows." The man walking the street became an elegant figure. He was unmistakably Jefferson Davis. I wrote the new poem in a very few minutes. From the original only four lines were carried over without change into the new poem, though a good deal of the imagery, slightly altered, was still useful. I ignore Davis' pathetic old age, and conceive him as a tragic person, as he would have been had the Federal Government executed him for "treason." I often think of my poems as commentaries on those human situations from which there is no escape.' Author's note.

2 'The structure of the "Ode" is simple. Figure to yourself a man stopping at the gate of a Confederate graveyard on a late autumn afternoon. The leaves are falling; his first impressions bring him the "rumor of mortality"; and the desolation barely allows him, at the beginning of the second stanza, the heroically conventional surmise that the dead will enrich the earth, "where these memories grow." From those quoted words to the end of that passage he pauses for a baroque meditation on the ravages of time, concluding with the figure of the "blind crab." This creature has mobility but no direction, energy but no purposeful world to use it in: in the entire poem there are only two explicit symbols for the locked-in ego; the crab is the first and less explicit symbol, a mere hint, a planting of the idea that will become overt in its second instance—the jaguar towards the end. The crab is the first intimation of the nature of the moral conflict upon which the drama of the poem develops: the cut-offness of the modern "intellectual man" from the world.

'The next long passage or strophe, beginning "You know who have waited by the wall," states the other term of the conflict. It is the theme of heroism, not merely moral heroism, but heroism in a grand style,

The wind whirrs without recollection;
In the riven troughs the splayed leaves
Pile up, of nature the casual sacrament
To the seasonal eternity of death;
Then driven by the fierce scrutiny
Of heaven to their election in the vast
    breath,
They sough the rumor of mortality.

Autumn is desolation in the plot   10
Of a thousand acres where these memories
    grow
From the inexhaustible bodies that are not
Dead, but feed the grass row after rich
    row.
Think of the autumns that have come and
    gone!—
Ambitious November with the humors of
    the year,
With a particular zeal for every slab,
Staining the uncomfortable angels that rot
On the slabs, a wing chipped here, an arm
    there:
The brute curiosity of an angel's stare
Turns you, like them, to stone,   20
Transforms the heaving air
Till plunged to a heavier world below
You shift your sea-space blindly
Heaving, turning like the blind crab.

    Dazed by the wind, only the wind
    The leaves flying, plunge

You know who have waited by the wall
The twilight certainty of an animal,
Those midnight restitutions of the blood
You know—the immitigable pines, the
    smoky frieze   30
Of the sky, the sudden call: you know the
    rage,
The cold pool left by the mounting flood,

Of muted Zeno and Parmenides.
You who have waited for the angry
    resolution
Of those desires that should be yours
    tomorrow,
You know the unimportant shrift of death
And praise the vision
And praise the arrogant circumstance
Of those who fall
Rank upon rank, hurried beyond
    decision—   40
Here by the sagging gate, stopped by the
    wall.

    Seeing, seeing only the leaves
    Flying, plunge and expire

Turn your eyes to the immoderate past,
Turn to the inscrutable infantry rising
Demons out of the earth—they will not last.
Stonewall, Stonewall, and the sunken fields
    of hemp,
Shiloh, Antietam, Malvern Hill, Bull Run.
Lost in that orient of the thick and fast
You will curse the setting sun.   50

    Cursing only the leaves crying
    Like an old man in a storm

You hear the shout, the crazy hemlocks
    point
With troubled fingers to the silence which
Smothers you, a mummy, in time.

                    The hound bitch
Toothless and dying, in a musty cellar
Hears the wind only.

            Now that the salt of their blood
Stiffens the saltier oblivion of the sea,   60
Seals the malignant purity of the flood,
What shall we who count our days and bow
Our heads with a commemorial woe
In the ribboned coats of grim felicity,
What shall we say of the bones, unclean,
Whose verdurous anonymity will grow?
The ragged arms, the ragged heads and
    eyes
Lost in these acres of the insane green?
The gray lean spiders come, they come and
    go;

elevating even death from mere physical dissolution
into a formal ritual: this heroism is a formal ebullience
of the human spirit in an entire society, not private,
romantic illusion—something better than moral
heroism, great as that may be, for moral heroism,
being personal and individual, may be achieved by
certain men in all ages, even ages of decadence. But
the late Hart Crane's commentary is better than any
I can make: "The theme of chivalry, a tradition of
excess (not literally excess, rather active faith) which
cannot be perpetuated in the fragmentary cosmos of
today—'those desires that should be yours tomorrow,'
but which, you know, will not persist nor find any
way into action." ' Tate, 'Narcissus as Narcissus,'
The Virginia Quarterly Review,XIV,i,113–14. The
essay also contains a valuable analysis of the poetics of
his 'Ode.'

In a tangle of willows without light   70
The singular screech-owl's tight
Invisible lyric seeds the mind
With the furious murmur of their chivalry.

We shall say only the leaves
Flying, plunge and expire

We shall say only the leaves whispering
In the improbable mist of nightfall
That flies on multiple wing:
Night is the beginning and the end
And in between the ends of distraction   80
Waits mute speculation, the patient curse
That stones the eyes, or like the jaguar leaps
For his own image in a jungle pool, his
     victim.

What shall we say who have knowledge
Carried to the heart? Shall we take the act
To the grave? Shall we, more hopeful, set
     up the grave
In the house? The ravenous grave?

                                   Leave now
The shut gate and the decomposing wall:
The gentle serpent, green in the mulberry
     bush,   90
Riots with his tongue through the hush—
Sentinel of the grave who counts us all!
1926–1936   1928

MOTHER AND SON [1]

Now all day long the man who is not dead
Hastens the dark with inattentive eyes,
The lady of the white hand, of the erect
     head,
Stares at the cover, leans for the son's
     replies

[1] 'This poem was written in Paris in 1928, one morning
when suddenly the first line came to mind, without
warning of what the poem would be about; the first
draft was very rapid. But it has been retouched many
times. I think there is little in it to interpret. The cuttlefish, symbol of memory, has puzzled a few readers.
This disagreeable creature blinds its prey by squirting
a black fluid into the water, in which it then hides: a
man in emotional danger withdraws into his private
mind where not even maternal love can follow him and
where he becomes mysterious and menacing. I speak
of this dark place as "beams of memory" because I
want the blackness to shine. Milton and Dante in two
famous phrases make you see darkness, but I cannot
without subterfuge: of course Dante cheats a little too
by calling it *perso*. At the end of the poem the spider
is not a symbol, merely an image of horror.' Author's
note.

At last to her importunate womanhood—
That hand of death laid on the living bed;
Such is the fierce compositor of blood.

She waits; he lies upon the bed of sin
Where greed, avarice, anger writhed and
     slept
Till to their silence they were gathered in:
There, fallen with time, his tall and wicked
     kin   1
Once fired the passions that were never
     kept
In the permanent heart, and there his
     mother lay
To bear him on the impenetrable day.

The falcon mother cannot will her hand
Up to the bed, nor break the manacle
That exile sets upon her harsh command
That he should say the time is beautiful—
Transfigured with her own devouring
     light:
The sick man craves the impalpable night.

Loosed betwixt eye and lid, the swimming
     beams   2
Of memory, that school of cuttlefish,
Rise to the air, plunge to the cold streams—
Rising and plunging the half-forgotten
     wish
To tear his heart out in a slow disgrace
And freeze the hue of terror to her face.

Hate, misery, and fear beat off his heart
To the dry fury of the woman's mind,
The son prone in his autumn moves apart
A seed blown upon a returning wind.   30
O child, be vigilant till towards the south
On the flowered wall all the sweet
     afternoon,
That reach of sun, swift as the
     cottonmouth,
Strikes at the black crucifix on her breast
Where the cold dusk comes suddenly to
     rest—
Mortality will speak the victor soon!

The dreary flies lazy and casual
Stick to the ceiling, buzz along the wall,
O heart, the spider shuffles from the mould
Weaving, between the pinks and grapes, his
     pall.   40
The bright wallpaper, imperishably old,
Uncurls and flutters, it will never fall.
1928   1928

TO THE ROMANTIC
TRADITIONISTS [1]

I HAVE looked at them long,
My eyes blur; sourceless light
Keeps them forever young
Before our aging sight.

You see them too—strict forms
Of will, the secret dignity
Of our dissolute storms;
They grow too bright to be.

What were they like? What mark
Can signify their charm?   10
They never saw the dark;
Rigid, they never knew alarm.

Do not the scene rehearse!
The perfect eyes enjoin
A contemptuous verse;
We speak the crabbed line.

Immaculate race! to yield   1934

Us final knowledge set
In a cold frieze, a field
Of war but no blood let.   20

Are they quite willing,
Do they ask to pose
Naked and simple, chilling
The very wind's nose?

They ask us how to live!
We answer: Again try
Being the drops we sieve.
What death it is to die!

Therefore because they nod
Being too full of us   30
I look at the turned sod
Where it is perilous

And yawning all the same
As if we knew them not
And history had no name—
No need to name the spot!   1936

STEPHEN VINCENT BENÉT

1898–1943

KING DAVID [2]

I

DAVID sang to his hook-nosed harp:
'The Lord God is a jealous God!
His violent vengeance is swift and sharp!
And the Lord is King above all gods!

'Blest be the Lord, through years untold,
The Lord Who has blessed me a thousand
     fold!

'Cattle and concubines, corn and
     hives
Enough to last me a dozen lives.

'Plump, good women with noses flat,
Marrowful blessings, weighty and fat.   10

'I wax in His peace like a pious gourd,
The Lord God is a pleasant God,

1 'This poem is addressed to people who destroy the
past by trying to live it, but it might have been written
to persons who give the same allegiance to the future.
This kind of romantic character imagines a life from
which evil, and so the life, is removed. At bottom the
heresy like other romantic attitudes however finespun,
is pragmatical and secular, putting its faith in the
externals of a system. The poem is like a speech from
a conversation; one of the talkers takes the floor to
admonish his friends; but he appears to have the grace
to include himself in the censure. For after he addresses the romantics as "you" in the second stanza,
he speaks of "we" from then on, and it may not be
mere politeness. "Them" in the first line alludes to
the perfect men of a perfect past. They cannot shield
us from death, the "turned sod," which is the goal and
meaning of the eternal evil in life. (Of course, there
ought to be a poem some time on the barbarians of the
pure present, who think they can ignore the past
entirely.)' Author's note.
2 ' "King David" and "The Mountain Whippoorwill"
are both ballads, and written as such: "King David"

in the strict ballad-form with refrain; "The Mountain
Whippoorwill" with variations. A ballad ought to have
pace. I hope they both have it. In "The Mountain
Whippoorwill" I was trying to adapt the strict ballad
form to a contemporary American subject, vary it as I
chose, and use colloquial speech—get the note of the
boxwood fiddle into it, if it could be done. I had heard
the mountain fiddlers in the North Carolinas, and
their tunes stuck in my mind. Of course I didn't draw
up these rules on paper before I wrote the poem, any
more than you say to yourself: "I will now have a
blue-eyed child with a Roman nose and a hare-lip."
But I was trying to think back to the fiddle music and
the speech.' Author's note.

Break mine enemy's jaw, O Lord!
For the Lord is King above all gods!'

His hand dropped slack from the tunable
strings,
A sorrow came on him—a sorrow of kings.

A sorrow sat on the arm of his throne,
An eagle sorrow with claws of stone.

'I am merry, yes, when I am not thinking,
But life is nothing but eating and drinking.

'I can shape my psalms like daggers of
jade,   21
But they do not shine like the first I made.

'I can harry the heathen from North to
South,
But no hot taste comes into my mouth.

'My wives are comely as long-haired goats,
But I would not care if they cut their
throats!

'Where are the maids of the desert tents
With lips like flagons of frankincense?

'Where is Jonathan? Where is Saul?
The captain-towers of Zion wall?   30

'The trees of cedar, the hills of Nod,
The kings, the running lions of God?

'Their words were a writing in golden dust,
Their names are myrrh in the mouths of the
just.

'The sword of the slayer could never divide
them—
Would God I had died in battle beside them!'

The Lord looked down from a thunder-
clap.
(The Lord God is a crafty God.)
He heard the strings of the shrewd harp
snap.
(The Lord who is King above all gods.)   40

He pricked the king with an airy thorn,
It burnt in his body like grapes of scorn.

The eyelids roused that had drooped like
lead.
David lifted his heavy head.

The thorn stung at him, a fiery bee,
'The world is wide. I will go and see
From the roof of my haughty palace,' said
he.

2

Bathsheba bathed on her vine-decked roof.
(The Lord God is a mighty God.)
Her body glittered like mail of proof.   50
(And the Lord is King above all gods.)

Her body shimmered, tender and white
As the flesh of aloes in candlelight.

King David forgot to be old or wise.
He spied on her bathing with sultry eyes.

A breath of spice came into his nose.
He said, 'Her breasts are like two young
roes.'

His eyes were bright with a crafty gleam.
He thought, 'Her body is soft as cream.'

He straightened himself like an unbent bow
And called a servant and bade him go.   61

3

Uriah the Hittite came to his lord,
Dusty with war as a well-used sword.

A close, trim man like a belt, well-buckled;
A jealous gentleman, hard to cuckold.

David entreated him, soft and bland,
Offered him comfits from his own hand.

Drank with him deep till his eyes grew red,
And laughed in his beard as he went to
bed.

The days slipped by without hurry or
strife,   70
Like apple-parings under a knife.
And still Uriah kept from his wife.

Lean fear tittered through David's psalm,
'This merry husband is far too calm!'

David sent for Uriah then,
They greeted each other like pious men.

'Thou hast borne the battle, the dust and
the heat.
Go down to thy house and wash thy feet!'

Uriah frowned at the words of the king.
His brisk, hard voice had a leaden ring.　80

'While the hosts of God still camp in the
　field,
My house to me is a garden sealed.

'How shall I rest while the arrow yet flies?
The dust of the war is still in my eyes.'

David spoke with his lion's roar.
'If Peace be a bridle that rubs you sore,
You shall fill your belly with blood and
　war!'

Uriah departed, calling him kind.
His eyes were serpents in David's mind.

He summoned a captain, a pliable man.　90
'Uriah the Hittite shall lead the van.

'In the next assault when the fight roars
　high,
And the Lord God is a hostile God,
Retire from Uriah that he may die.
For the Lord is King above all gods.'

4

The messenger came while King David
　played
The friskiest ditty ever made.

'News, O King, from our dubious war!
The Lord of Hosts hath prevailed once
　more!

'His foes are scattered like chirping
　sparrows,　100
Their kings lie breathless, feathered with
　arrows.

'Many are dead of your captains tall.
Uriah the Hittite was first to fall.'

David turned from the frolicsome strings
And rent his clothes for the death of kings.

Yet, as he rent them, he smiled for joy,
The sly, wide smile of a wicked boy.

'The powerful grace of the Lord prevails!
He has cracked Uriah between His nails!

'His blessings are mighty, they shall not
　cease!　110

And my days henceforth shall be days of
　peace!'

His mind grew tranquil, smoother than
　fleece.
He rubbed his body with scented grease.
And his days thenceforward were days of
　peace.

His days were fair as the flowering lime
—For a little time, for a little time.

And Bathsheba lay in his breast like a dove,
A vessel of amber, made for love.

5

When Bathsheba was great with child,
(The Lord God is a jealous God!)　120
Portly and meek as a moon grown mild,
(The Lord is King above all gods!)

Nathan, the prophet, wry and dying,
Preached to the king like a locust crying:

'Hearken awhile to a doleful thing!
There were two men in thy land, O King!

'One was rich as a gilded ram.
One had one treasure, a poor ewe-lamb.

'Rich man wasted his wealth like spittle.
Poor man shared with his lamb spare
　victual.　130

'A traveler came to the rich man's door.
"Give me to eat, for I hunger sore!"

'Rich man feasted him fatly, true,
But the meat that he gave him was fiends'
　meat, too,
Stolen and roasted, the poor man's ewe!

'Hearken, my lord, to a deadly thing!
What shall be done with these men, O
　King?'

David hearkened, seeing it plain,
His heart grew heavy with angry pain:
'Show me the rich man, that he be slain!'

Nathan barked as a jackal can.　141
'Just, O King! And thou art the man!'

David rose as the thunders rise
When some one in Heaven is telling lies.

But his eyes were weaker than Nathan's
    eyes.

His huge bulk shivered like quaking sod,
Shoulders bowing to Nathan's rod,
Nathan, the bitter apple of God.

His great voice shook like a runner's, spent.
'My sin has found me! Oh, I repent!'   150

Answered Nathan, that talkative Jew:
'For many great services, comely and true,
The Lord of Mercy will pardon you.

'But the child in Bathsheba, come of your
    seed,
Shall sicken and die like a blasted weed.'

David groaned when he heard him speak.
The painful tears ran hot on his cheek.

Ashes he cast on his kingly locks.
All night long he lay on the rocks.

Beseeching his Lord with a howling cry: 160
'O Lord God, O my jealous God,
Be kind to the child that it may not die,
For thou art King above all gods!'

6

Seven long nights he lay there, howling,
A lion wounded, moaning and growling.

Seven long midnights, sorrowing greatly,
While Sin, like a dead man, embraced him
    straitly.

Till he was abased from his lust and pride
And the child was born and sickened and
    died.

He arose at last. It was ruddy Day.   170
And his sin like water had washed away.

He cleansed and anointed, took fresh
    apparel,
And worshiped the Lord in a tuneful carol.

His servants, bearing the child to bury,
Marveled greatly to see him so merry.

He spoke to them mildly as mid-May
    weather:
'The child and my sin are perished
    together.

'He is dead, my son. Though his whole
    soul yearn to me,
I must go to him, he may not return to
    me.

'Why should I sorrow for what was
    pain?   180
A cherished grief is an iron chain.'

He took up his harp, the sage old
    chief,
His heart felt clean as a new green
    leaf.

His soul smelt pleasant as rain-wet
    clover.
'I have sinned and repented and that's all
    over.

'In his dealings with heathen, the Lord is
    hard.
But the humble soul is his spikenard.'

His wise thoughts fluttered like doves in the
    air.
'I wonder is Bathsheba still so fair?

'Does she weep for the child that our sin
    made perish?   190
I must comfort my ewe-lamb, comfort and
    cherish.

'The justice of God is honey and balm.
I will soothe her heart with a little
    psalm.'

He went to her chamber, no longer sad,
Walking as light as a shepherd lad.

He found her weeping, her garments
    rent,
Trodden like straw by God's punishment.
He solaced her out of his great content.

Being but a woman, a while she grieved,
But at last she was comforted, and
    conceived.   200

Nine months later she bore him a son.
(The Lord God is a mighty God!)
The name of that child was SOLOMON.
He was God's tough staff till his days were
    run!
(And the Lord is King above all gods!)
1923   1923

THE MOUNTAIN WHIPPOORWILL

(OR, HOW HILL-BILLY JIM WON THE GREAT
FIDDLERS' PRIZE)

(A Georgia Romance)

Up in the mountains, it's lonesome all the
    time,
(Sof' win' slewin' thu' the sweet-potato
    vine.)

Up in the mountains, it's lonesome for a
    child,
(Whippoorwills a-callin' when the sap runs
    wild.)

Up in the mountains, mountains in the fog,
Everythin's as lazy as an old houn' dog.

Born in the mountains, never raised a pet,
Don't want nuthin' an' never got it yet.

Born in the mountains, lonesome-born,
Raised runnin' ragged thu' the cockleburrs
    and corn.   10

Never knew my pappy, mebbe never
    should.
Think he was a fiddle made of mountain
    laurel-wood.

Never had a mammy to teach me pretty-
    please.
Think she was a whippoorwill, a-skitin'
    thu' the trees.

Never had a brother ner a whole pair of
    pants,
But when I start to fiddle, why, yuh got to
    start to dance!

Listen to my fiddle—Kingdom Come—
    Kingdom Come!
Hear the frogs a-chunkin' 'Jug o' rum, Jug
    o' rum!'
Hear that mountain-whippoorwill be
    lonesome in the air,
An' I'll tell yuh how I traveled to the Essex
    County Fair.   20

Essex County has a mighty pretty fair,
All the smarty fiddlers from the South come
    there.

Elbows flyin' as they rosin up the bow
For the First Prize Contest in the Georgia
    Fiddlers' Show.

Old Dan Wheeling, with his whiskers in his
    ears,
King-pin fiddler for nearly twenty years.

Big Tom Sargent, with his blue wall-eye,
An' Little Jimmy Weezer that can make a
    fiddle cry.

All sittin' roun', spittin' high an' struttin'
    proud,
(Listen, little whippoorwill, yuh better bug
    yore eyes!)   30
Tun-a-tun-a-tunin' while the jedges told the
    crowd
Them that got the mostest claps'd win the
    bestest prize.

Everybody waitin' for the first tweedle-dee,
When in comes a-stumblin'—hill-billy me!

Bowed right pretty to the jedges an' the
    rest,
Took a silver dollar from a hole inside my
    vest,

Plunked it on the table an' said 'There's my
    callin' card!
An' anyone that licks me—well, he's got to
    fiddle hard!'

Old Dan Wheeling, he was laughin' fit to
    holler,
Little Jimmy Weezer said, 'There's one
    dead dollar!'   40

Big Tom Sargent had a yaller-toothy grin,
But I tucked my little whippoorwill spang
    underneath my chin,
An' petted it an' tuned it till the jedges
    said, 'Begin!'

Big Tom Sargent was the first in line;
He could fiddle all the bugs off a sweet-
    potato-vine.

He could fiddle down a possum from a
    mile-high tree.
He could fiddle up a whale from the bottom
    of the sea.

Yuh could hear hands spankin' till they
    spanked each other raw,

When he finished variations on 'Turkey in
   the Straw.'

Little Jimmy Weezer was the next to play;
He could fiddle all night, he could fiddle all
   day.   51

He could fiddle chills, he could fiddle fever,
He could make a fiddle rustle like a lowland
   river.

He could make a fiddle croon like a lovin'
   woman.
An' they clapped like thunder when he'd
   finished strummin'.

Then came the ruck of the bob-tailed
   fiddlers,
The let's-go-easies, the fair-to-middlers.

They got their claps an' they lost their
   bicker,
An' settled back for some more corn-
   licker.

An' the crowd was tired of their no-count
   squealing,   60
When out in the center steps Old Dan
   Wheeling.

He fiddled high and he fiddled low,
(Listen, little whippoorwill; yuh got to spread
   yore wings!)
He fiddled with a cherrywood bow.
(Old Dan Wheeling's got bee-honey in his
   strings.)

He fiddled the wind by the lonesome
   moon,
He fiddled a most almighty tune.

He started fiddling like a ghost,
He ended fiddling like a host.

He fiddled north an' he fiddled south,   70
He fiddled the heart right out of yore
   mouth.

He fiddled here an' he fiddled there.
He fiddled salvation everywhere.

When he was finished, the crowd cut loose,
(Whippoorwill, they's rain on yore breast.)
An' I sat there wonderin' 'What's the use?'
(Whippoorwill, fly home to yore nest.)

But I stood up pert an' I took my bow,
An' my fiddle went to my shoulder, so.

An'—they wasn't no crowd to get me
   fazed—   80
But I was alone where I was raised.

Up in the mountains, so still it makes yuh
   skeered,
Where God lies sleepin' in his big white
   beard.

An' I heard the sound of the squirrel in the
   pine,
An' I heard the earth a-breathin' thu' the
   long night-time.

They've fiddled the rose, an' they've
   fiddled the thorn,
But they haven't fiddled the mountain-
   corn.

They've fiddled sinful an' fiddled moral,
But they haven't fiddled the breshwood-
   laurel.

They've fiddled loud, an' they've fiddled
   still,   90
But they haven't fiddled the whippoorwill.

I started off with a *dump-diddle-dump,*
(Oh, hell's broke loose in Georgia!)
Skunk-cabbage growin' by the bee-gum
   stump,
(Whippoorwill, yo're singin' now!)

Oh, Georgia booze is mighty fine booze,
The best yuh ever poured yuh,
But it eats the soles right offen yore shoes,
For Hell's broke loose in Georgia.

My mother was a whippoorwill pert,   100
My father, he was lazy,
But I'm Hell broke loose in a new store shirt
To fiddle all Georgia crazy.

Swing yore partners—up an' down the
   middle!
Sashay now—oh, listen to that fiddle!
Flapjacks flippin' on a red-hot griddle,
An' Hell broke loose,
Hell broke loose,
Fire on the mountains—snakes in the grass.
Satan's here a-bilin'—oh, Lordy, let him
   pass!   110

Go down Moses, set my people free,
Pop goes the weasel thu' the old Red Sea!
Jonah sittin' on a hickory-bough,
Up jumps a whale—an' where's yore
    prophet now?
Rabbit in the pea-patch, possum in the pot,
Try an' stop my fiddle, now my fiddle's
    gettin' hot!
Whippoorwill, singin' thu' the mountain
    hush,
Whippoorwill, shoutin' from the burnin'
    bush,
Whippoorwill, cryin' in the stable-door,
Sing tonight as yuh never sang before!   120
Hell's broke loose like a stompin'
    mountain-shoat,
Sing till yuh bust the gold in yore throat!
Hell's broke loose for forty miles aroun'
Bound to stop yore music if yuh don't sing
    it down.
Sing on the mountains, little whippoorwill,
Sing to the valleys, an' slap 'em with a hill,
For I'm struttin' high as an eagle's quill,
An' Hell's broke loose,
Hell's broke loose,
Hell's broke loose in Georgia!   130

They wasn't a sound when I stopped
    bowin',
(*Whippoorwill, yuh can sing no more.*)
But, somewhere or other, the dawn was
    growin',
(*Oh, mountain whippoorwill!*)

An' I thought, 'I've fiddled all night an' lost.
Yo're a good hill-billy, but yuh've been
    bossed.'

So I went to congratulate old man Dan,
—But he put his fiddle into my han'—
An' then the noise of the crowd began.
1923   1923

FROM JOHN BROWN'S BODY [1]

INVOCATION

AMERICAN muse, whose strong and diverse
    heart
So many men have tried to understand

But only made it smaller with their art,
Because you are as various as your land,

As mountainous-deep, as flowered with
    blue rivers,
Thirsty with deserts, buried under snows,
As native as the shape of Navajo quivers,
And native, too, as the sea-voyaged rose.

Swift runner, never captured or subdued,
Seven-branched elk beside the mountain
    stream,   10
That half a hundred hunters have pursued
But never matched their bullets with the
    dream,

Where the great huntsmen failed, I set my
    sorry
And mortal snare for your immortal quarry.

You are the buffalo-ghost, the broncho-
    ghost
With dollar-silver in your saddle-horn,
The cowboys riding in from Painted Post,
The Indian arrow in the Indian corn,

And you are the clipped velvet of the lawns
Where Shropshire grows from
    Massachusetts sods,   20
The grey Maine rocks—and the war-
    painted dawns
That break above the Garden of the Gods.

The prairie-schooners crawling toward the
    ore
And the cheap car, parked by the station-
    door.

Where the skyscrapers lift their foggy plumes
Of stranded smoke out of a stony mouth
You are that high stone and its arrogant
    fumes,
And you are ruined gardens in the South

And bleak New England farms, so winter-
    white
Even their roofs look lonely, and the deep
The middle grainland where the wind of
    night   31
Is like all blind earth sighing in her sleep.

1 'The method of *John Brown's Body* is an expansion of
the method used in *Five Men and Pompey*. The "Invocation" was, originally, the start of the Third Book.
Then, when finished, it seemed to go more naturally
as the beginning of the whole poem. The incidental
lyrics, of which "The Hider's Song" is one, are in the
poem for relief, change of mood, etc.; but I wanted
them to be an essential part of the poem, not just stuck
in like currants in a cake. They are part of the building,
not removable ornaments. "Pickett's Charge" was a
try for an unrhymed form that would carry ballad
narrative.' Author's note.

A friend, an enemy, a sacred hag
With two tied oceans in her medicine-bag.

They tried to fit you with an English song
And clip your speech into the English tale.
But, even from the first, the words went
        wrong,
The catbird pecked away the nightingale.

The homesick men begot high-
        cheekboned things
Whose wit was whittled with a different
        sound   40
And Thames and all the rivers of the kings
Ran into Mississippi and were drowned.

They planted England with a stubborn
        trust.
But the cleft dust was never English dust.

Stepchild of every exile from content
And all the disavouched, hard-bitten pack
Shipped overseas to steal a continent
With neither shirts nor honor to their back.

Pimping grandee and rump-faced regicide,
Apple-cheeked younkers from a windmill-
        square,   50
Puritans stubborn as the nails of Pride,
Rakes from Versailles and thieves from
        County Clare,

The black-robed priests who broke their
        hearts in vain
To make you God and France or God and
        Spain.

These were your lovers in your buckskin-
        youth.
And each one married with a dream so
        proud
He never knew it could not be the truth
And that he coupled with a girl of cloud.

And now to see you is more difficult yet
Except as an immensity of wheel   60
Made up of wheels, oiled with inhuman
        sweat
And glittering with the heat of ladled steel.

All these you are, and each is partly you,
And none is false, and none is wholly true.

So how to see you as you really are,
So how to suck the pure, distillate, stored

Essence of essence from the hidden star
And make it pierce like a riposting sword.

For, as we hunt you down, you must
        escape
And we pursue a shadow of our own   70
That can be caught in a magician's cape
But has the flatness of a painted stone.

Never the running stag, the gull at wing,
The pure elixir, the American thing.

And yet, at moments when the mind was
        hot
With something fiercer than joy or grief,
When each known spot was an eternal spot
And every leaf was an immortal leaf,

I think that I have seen you, not as one,   79
But clad in diverse semblances and powers,
Always the same, as light falls from the sun,
And always different, as the differing hours.

Yet, through each altered garment that you
        wore
The naked body, shaking the heart's core.

All day the snow fell on that Eastern town
With its soft, pelting, little, endless sigh
Of infinite flakes that brought the tall sky
        down
Till I could put my hands in the white sky

And taste cold scraps of heaven on my
        tongue
And walk in such a changed and luminous
        light   90
As gods inhabit when the gods are young.
All day it fell. And when the gathered night

Was a blue shadow cast by a pale glow
I saw you then, snow-image, bird of the
        snow.

And I have seen and heard you in the dry
Close-huddled furnace of the city street
When the parched moon was planted in the
        sky
And the limp air hung dead against the heat.

I saw you rise, red as that rusty plant,
Dizzied with lights, half-mad with senseless
        sound,   100
Enormous metal, shaking to the chant
Of a triphammer striking iron ground.

Enormous power, ugly to the fool,
And beautiful as a well-handled tool.

These, and the memory of that windy day
On the bare hills, beyond the last barbed
    wire,
When all the orange poppies bloomed one
    way
As if a breath would blow them into fire,

I keep forever, like the sea-lion's tusk
The broken sailor brings away to land,   110
But when he touches it, he smells the musk,
And the whole sea lies hollow in his hand.

So, from a hundred visions, I make one,
And out of darkness build my mocking sun.

And should that task seem fruitless in the
    eyes
Of those a different magic sets apart
To see through the ice-crystal of the wise
No nation but the nation that is Art,

Their words are just. But when the
    birchbark-call
Is shaken with the sound that hunters make
The moose comes plunging through the
    forest-wall   121
Although the rifle waits beside the lake.

Art has no nations—but the mortal sky
Lingers like gold in immortality.

This flesh was seeded from no foreign grain
But Pennsylvania and Kentucky wheat,
And it has soaked in California rain
And five years tempered in New England
    sleet

To strive at last, against an alien proof
And by the changes of an alien moon,   130
To build again that blue, American roof
Over a half-forgotten battle-tune

And call unsurely, from a haunted ground,
Armies of shadows and the shadow-sound.

In your Long House there is an attic-place
Full of dead epics and machines that rust,
And there, occasionally, with casual face,
You come awhile to stir the sleepy dust;

Neither in pride nor mercy, but in vast
Indifference at so many gifts unsought,   140

The yellowed satins, smelling of the past,
And all the loot the lucky pirates brought.

I only bring a cup of silver air,
Yet, in your casualness, receive it there.

Receive the dream too haughty for the
    breast,
Receive the words that should have walked
    as bold
As the storm walks along the mountain-
    crest
And are like beggars whining in the cold.

The maimed presumption, the unskilful
    skill,
The patchwork colors, fading from the first,
And all the fire that fretted at the will   151
With such a barren ecstasy of thirst.

Receive them all—and should you choose
    to touch them
With one slant ray of quick, American light,
Even the dust will have no power to smutch
    them,
Even the worst will glitter in the night.

If not—the dry bones littered by the way
May still point giants toward their golden
    prey.

               1928

THE HIDER'S SONG

THIS is the hidden place that hiders know.
This is where hiders go.
Step softly, the snow that falls here is
    different snow,
The rain has a different sting.
Step softly, step like a cloud, step softly as
    the least
Whisper of air against the beating wing,
And let your eyes be sealed
With two blue muscadines
Stolen from secret vines,
Or you will never find in the lost field   10
The table spread, the signs of the hidden
    feast.

This is where hiders live.
This is the tentative
And outcast corner where hiders steal away
To bake their hedgehogs in a lump of clay,
To raise their crops and children wild and
    shy,

And let the world go by
In accidental marches of armed wrath
That stumble blindly past the buried path.
Step softly, step like a whisper, but do not
    speak   20
Or you will never see
The furriness curled within the hollow tree,
The shadow-dance upon the wilderness
    creek.
This is the hiders' house.
This is the ark of pine-and-willow-boughs.
This is the quiet place.
You may call now, but let your call be
    sweet
As clover-honey strained through silver
    sieves
And delicate as the dust upon the moth
Or you will never find your fugitives.   30
Call once, and call again,
Then, if the lifted strain
Has the true color and substance of the
    wild,
You may perceive, if you have lucky eyes,
Something that ran away from being wise
And changed silk ribbons for a greener
    cloth,
Some budding-horned and deer-milk-
    suckled child
Some lightness, moving toward you on
    light feet,
Some girl with indolent passion in her face.
                        1928

PICKETT'S CHARGE

THE cannonade fell still. All along the fish-
    hook line,
The tired men stared at the smoke and
    waited for it to clear;
The men in the centre waited, their rifles
    gripped in their hands,
By the trees of the riding fate, and the low
    stone wall, and the guns.

These were Hancock's men, the men of the
    Second Corps,
Eleven States were mixed there, where
    Minnesota stood
In battle-order with Maine, and Rhode
    Island beside New York,
The metals of all the North, cooled into an
    axe of war.

The strong sticks of the North, bound into
    a fasces-shape,   1070

The hard winters of snow, the wind with
    the cutting edge,
And against them came that summer that
    does not die with the year,
Magnolia and honeysuckle and the blue
    Virginia flag.

Tall Pickett went up to Longstreet—his
    handsome face was drawn.
George Pickett, old friend of Lincoln's in
    days gone by with the blast.
When he was a courteous youth and
    Lincoln the strange shawled man
Who would talk in a Springfield street with
    a boy who dreamt of a sword.

Dreamt of a martial sword, as swords are
    martial in dreams,
And the courtesy to use it, in the old bright
    way of the tales.
Those days are gone with the blast. He has
    his sword in his hand.   1080
And he will use it today, and remember
    that using long.

He came to Longstreet for orders, but
    Longstreet would not speak.
He saw Old Peter's mouth and the thought
    in Old Peter's mind.
He knew the task that was set and the men
    that he had to lead
And a pride came into his face while
    Longstreet stood there dumb.

'I shall go forward, sir,' he said and turned
    to his men.
The commands went down the line. The
    grey ranks started to move.
Slowly at first, then faster, in order,
    stepping like deer,
The Virginians, the fifteen thousand, the
    seventh wave of the tide.

There was a death-torn mile of broken
    ground to cross,   1090
And a low stone wall at the end, and behind
    it the Second Corps,
And behind that force another, fresh men
    who had not yet fought.
They started to cross that ground. The
    guns began to tear them.

From the hill they say that it seemed more
    like a sea than a wave,

A sea continually torn by stones flung out
    of the sky,
And yet, as it came, still closing, closing and
    rolling on,
As the moving sea closes over the flaws and
    rips of the tide.

You could mark the path that they took by
    the dead that they left behind,
Spilled from that deadly march as a cart
    spills meal on a road,
And yet they came on unceasing, the fifteen
    thousand no more,   1100
And the blue Virginia flag did not fall, did
    not fall, did not fall.

They halted but once to fire as they came.
    Then the smoke closed down
And you could not see them, and then, as it
    cleared again for a breath,
They were coming still but divided,
    gnawed at by blue attacks,
One flank half-severed and halted, but the
    centre still like a tide.

Cushing ran down the last of his guns to the
    battle-line,
The rest had been smashed to scrap by
    Lee's artillery fire.
He held his guts in his hand as the charge
    came up to the wall
And his gun spoke out for him once before
    he fell to the ground.

Armistead leapt the wall and laid his hand
    on the gun,   1110
The last of the three brigadiers who
    ordered Pickett's brigades,
He waved his hat on his sword and 'Give
    'em the steel!' he cried,
A few men followed him over. The rest
    were beaten or dead.

A few men followed him over. There had
    been fifteen thousand
When that sea began its march toward the
    fish-hook ridge and the wall.
So they came on in strength, light-footed,
    stepping like deer,
So they died or were taken. So the iron
    entered their flesh.

Lee, a mile away, in the shade of a little
    wood,

Stared, with his mouth shut down, and saw
    them go and be slain,
And then saw for a single moment, the blue
    Virginia flag   1120
Planted beyond the wall, by that other
    flag that he knew.

The two flags planted together, one instant,
    like hostile flowers.
Then the smoke wrapped both in a mantle
    —and when it had blown away,
Armistead lay in his blood, and the rest
    were dead or down,
And the valley grey with the fallen and the
    wreck of the broken wave.

Pickett gazed around him, the boy who had
    dreamt of a sword
And talked with a man named Lincoln.
    The sword was still in his hand.
He had gone out with fifteen thousand. He
    came back to his lines with five.
He fought well till the war was over, but a
    thing was cracked in his heart.
            1928

LITANY FOR DICTATORSHIPS [1]

FOR all those beaten, for the broken heads,
The fosterless, the simple, the oppressed,
The ghosts in the burning city of our
    time . . .

For those taken in rapid cars to the house
    and beaten
By the skilful boys, the boys with the
    rubber fists,
—Held down and beaten, the table cutting
    their loins,
Or kicked in the groin and left, with the
    muscles jerking
Like a headless hen's on the floor of the
    slaughter-house
While they brought the next man in with
    his white eyes staring.
For those who still said 'Red Front!' or
    'God Save the Crown!'   10

[1] ' "Litany for Dictatorships" began with the obvious
idea: "For all those . . .," "For all those, who . . .,"
and developed, starting with the general statement,
widening out, and coming back to general statement
again. It was meant to hurt, and, again, I hope it does.
The last lines are as flat and definite a statement as I
could get—each line ends with a period, and the voice
is not raised.' Author's note

And for those who were not courageous
But were beaten nevertheless.
For those who spit out the bloody stumps
    of their teeth
Quietly in the hall,
Sleep well on stone or iron, watch for the
    time
And kill the guard in the privy before they
    die,
Those with the deep-socketed eyes and the
    lamp burning.

For those who carry the scars, who walk
    lame—for those
Whose nameless graves are made in the
    prison-yard
And the earth smoothed back before
    morning and the lime scattered.   20

For those slain at once. For those living
    through months and years
Enduring, watching, hoping, going each
    day
To the work or the queue for meat or the
    secret club,
Living meanwhile, begetting children,
    smuggling guns,
And found and killed at the end like rats in
    a drain.

For those escaping
Incredibly into exile and wandering there.
For those who live in the small rooms of
    foreign cities
And who yet think of the country, the long
    green grass,
The childhood voices, the language, the
    way wind smelt then,   30
The shape of rooms, the coffee drunk at
    the table,
The talk with friends, the loved city, the
    waiter's face,
The gravestones, with the name, where
    they will not lie
Nor in any of that earth. Their children are
    strangers.

For those who planned and were leaders
    and were beaten
And for those, humble and stupid, who had
    no plan
But were denounced, but grew angry, but
    told a joke,
But could not explain, but were sent away
    to the camp,

But had their bodies shipped back in the
    sealed coffins,
'Died of pneumonia.' 'Died trying to
    escape.'   40

For those growers of wheat who were shot
    by their own wheat-stacks,
For those growers of bread who were sent
    to the ice-locked wastes,
And their flesh remembers their fields.

For those denounced by their smug,
    horrible children
For a peppermint-star and the praise of the
    Perfect State,
For all those strangled or gelded or merely
    starved
To make perfect states; for the priest
    hanged in his cassock,
The Jew with his chest crushed in and his
    eyes dying,
The revolutionist lynched by the private
    guards
To make perfect states, in the names of the
    perfect states.   50

For those betrayed by the neighbors they
    shook hands with
And for the traitors, sitting in the hard
    chair
With the loose sweat crawling their hair and
    their fingers restless
As they tell the street and the house and the
    man's name.

And for those sitting at table in the house
With the lamp lit and the plates and the
    smell of food,
Talking so quietly; when they hear the cars
And the knock at the door, and they look at
    each other quickly
And the woman goes to the door with a stiff
    face,
Smoothing her dress.   60
            'We are all good citizens here.
We believe in the Perfect State.'
                    And that was the last
Time Tony or Karl or Shorty came to the
    house
And the family was liquidated later.

It was the last time.
            We heard the shots in the night
But nobody knew next day what the trouble
    was

And a man must go to his work. So I didn't
    see him
For three days, then, and me near out of my
    mind   70
And all the patrols on the streets with their
    dirty guns
And when he came back, he looked drunk,
    and the blood was on him.

For the women who mourn their dead in
    the secret night,
For the children taught to keep quiet, the
    old children,
The children spat-on at school.
                        For the wrecked laboratory,
The gutted house, the dunged picture, the
    pissed-in well,
The naked corpse of Knowledge flung in
    the square
And no man lifting a hand and no man
    speaking.

For the cold of the pistol-butt and the
    bullet's heat,   80
For the rope that chokes, the manacles that
    bind,
The huge voice, metal, that lies from a
    thousand tubes
And the stuttering machine-gun that
    answers all.

For the man crucified on the crossed
    machine-guns
Without name, without resurrection,
    without stars,
His dark head heavy with death and his
    flesh long sour

With the smell of his many prisons—John
    Smith, John Doe,
John Nobody—oh, crack your mind for his
    name!
Faceless as water, naked as the dust,
Dishonored as the earth the gas-shells
    poison   90
And barbarous with portent.
                                    This is he.
This is the man they ate at the green table
Putting their gloves on ere they touched
    the meat.
This is the fruit of war, the fruit of peace,
The ripeness of invention, the new lamb,
The answer to the wisdom of the wise.
And still he hangs, and still he will not die,
And still, on the steel city of our years
The light fails and the terrible blood
    streams down.   100

We thought we were done with these things
    but we were wrong.
We thought, because we had power, we had
    wisdom.
We thought the long train would run to the
    end of Time.
We thought the light would increase.
Now the long train stands derailed and the
    bandits loot it.
Now the boar and the asp have power in
    our time.
Now the night rolls back on the West and
    the night is solid.
Our fathers and ourselves sowed dragon's
    teeth.
Our children know and suffer the armed men.
1935   1936

LÉONIE ADAMS

1899–

AN OLD SPELL

HEARTS may not bend in course, but toward
    its loves,
Through heaping time, shall run the simple
    river;
And that enchantment that I lightly took
Out of the lovely April is for ever.

O falsely hearing, since of lying tunes,
Three notes were solitary, three apart,
That made of all the insolent armour wax,

Sank in the breast, and pierced the sensible
    heart;

And eyes forsworn, that, busied with your
    cheats,
Were fixed with tears, is not that only need,
Beauty's, the desolate wanderer of waste
    earth,   11
The sower in darkness of an exquisite seed?

These dropped like dew upon a dreaming
    flower

That in my breast stirred with delicious
    morn,
And breathed upon its colour the bleak air,
And felt along its lovely side the thorn.

Not now will I turn from comfortless love
    again,
Nor, heart, forget the burden that you hold,
And flesh, though it harry you unto the last,
Go ridden through darkness to an end of
    gold.   20
1923   1925

SAID OF THE EARTH AND THE MOON

Now moony light
The dews drink over the black turf,
And earth, at bottom darkness lying,
Looks up on heaven and heavenly night;
Stares on the glittering lady climbing
Her airy arch away,
Till a cold humour of her breast
Infests her clay.

The huntress of the air lets fly,
The beast of earth receives her arrow,   10
And by those silver arrows maimed,
The bones course with watery marrow.

Now fever-bright the dead moon goes,
The mistress to the sun, that crept
From starveling death, and on his breath
Has fed her lustre while her lover slept.

For the swart earth has breeded of her
    loves,
But the moon spent upon her withered shell;
And though the moon is barren, she's not
    cursed,
Nor the fruit unholy to be beautiful.   20

The stars were scattered at the edge of even,
Clouds may not snare her glittering heels
    tonight,
And still the amorous gold sun is sleeping,
The earth lies moored, she mounts the
    brink of heaven.
1925   1925

THE RIVER IN THE MEADOWS [1]

CRYSTAL parting the meads,
A boat drifted up like a swan;

Tranquil, dipping his bright front to the
    waters,
A slow swan is gone.

Full water, O flowing silver,
Clear, level with the clover,
It will stain drowning a star,
With the moon it will brim over.

Runner through lands dewy and shorn,
Cattle stoop at its brink,   10
And every fawny-coloured throat
Will sway its bells and drink.

I saw a boat sailing the meadows
With a tranced gait; it seemed
Loosed by a spell from its moorings,
By a thing the helmsman dreamed.

And I saw it could carry no traveller,
For the vessel would go down
If a heart were heavy winged
Or the bosom it dwelt in stone.   20
1925   1929

COUNTRY SUMMER

Now the rich cherry whose sleek wood
And top with silver petals traced
Like a strict box its gems encased
Has spilt from out that cunning lid,
All in an innocent green round
Those melting rubies which it hid;
With moss ripe-strawberry encrusted
So birds get half and lips are merry
To taste that deep-red, lark'sbite berry;
And blackcap bloom meal-yellow dusted.

The wren that thieved it in the eaves   11
A trailer of the rose could catch
To her poor droopy sloven thatch;
And side by side with the wren's brood—
O quarry Rour of beggars' luck!—
Opens the quaint and hairy bud;
And full, and golden is the yield
Of cows that never have to house,
But all night nibble under boughs
Or cool their sides in the moist field.   20

Into the rooms flow meadow airs,
The warm farm-baking smell's blown
    round;

Summer,' and 'Word for Harvest' are the revised
versions to be included in Miss Adams's forthcoming
volume of selected poems.

Inside and out, and sky and ground
Are much the same: the wishing star,
Hesperus, kind and early-born,
Is risen only finger-far;
All stars are close in summer air,
And tremble, and beam mild as amber,
And wicks in the blue evening chamber
Shine hushed as stars which settled there.

Now straightening from the flowery hay
Down the still light the mowers look,   32
Then turn, as they in slumber shook
And stirred, half-waked, to later days
When left alone in the yellow stubble
The rusty-coated mare would graze;
Yet thick the lazy dreams are born;
A second thought will come to mind
Small as the shivering of the wind
Morning and evening in the corn.   40
1926   1929

THE MOUNT

No, I have tempered haste,
The joyous traveller said,
The steed has passed me now
Whose hurrying hooves I fled.
My spectre rides thereon,
I learned what mount he has,
Upon what summers fed,
And wept to know again,
Beneath the saddle swung,
Treasure for whose great theft   10
This breast was wrung.
His bridle bells sang out,
I could not tell their chime,
So brilliantly he rings,

But called his name as Time.
His bin was morning light,
Those straws which gild his bed
Are of the fallen West.
Although green lands consume
Beneath their burning tread,   20
In everlasting bright
His hooves have rest.
1929   1929

WORD FOR HARVEST

The year turns to its rest;
Up from the earth, the fields, the early-
        fallen dew
Moves the large star with evening,
        Arcturus, low with autumn,
And summer calls in her many voices upon
        the frost.

I, who have not seen for weeping
The plum ripen and fall or the yellowing
        sheaf,
Am not unmindful now of the season
        which came and went,
The hours which told off sweetness,
The bud, and the rich leaf.   9

Though I turned aside before the summer,
And weathered a gaunt season of the
        mind,
Let me sit among you when the husk is
        stripped,
Let me weigh by the bright grain
Those labours in an acre of cloud and the
        reap of the wind.
1927   1929

WILLIAM FAULKNER

1897–

DRY SEPTEMBER

Through the bloody September twilight,
aftermath of sixty-two rainless days, it had
gone like a fire in dry grass—the rumor, the
story, whatever it was. Something about
Miss Minnie Cooper and a Negro. Attacked, insulted, frightened: none of them,
gathered in the barber shop on that Saturday evening where the ceiling fan stirred,   10
without freshening it, the vitiated air, sending back upon them, in recurrent surges of
stale pomade and lotion, their own stale
breath and odors, knew exactly what had
happened.

'Except it wasn't Will Mayes,' a barber
said. He was a man of middle age; a thin,
sand-colored man with a mild face, who
was shaving a client. 'I know Will Mayes.
He's a good nigger. And I know Miss
Minnie Cooper, too.'

'What do you know about her?' a second
barber said.

'Who is she?' the client said. 'A young
girl?'

'No,' the barber said. 'She's about forty,

I reckon. She aint married. That's why I dont believe—'

'Believe, hell!' a hulking youth in a sweat-stained silk shirt said. 'Wont you take a white woman's word before a nigger's?'

'I dont believe Will Mayes did it,' the barber said. 'I know Will Mayes.'

'Maybe you know who did it, then. Maybe you already got him out of town, you damn niggerlover.'

'I dont believe anybody did anything. I dont believe anything happened. I leave it to you fellows if them ladies that get old without getting married dont have notions that a man cant—'

'Then you are a hell of a white man,' the client said. He moved under the cloth. The youth had sprung to his feet.

'You dont?' he said. 'Do you accuse a white woman of lying?'

The barber held the razor poised above the half-risen client. He did not look around.

'It's this durn weather,' another said. 'It's enough to make a man do anything. Even to her.'

Nobody laughed. The barber said in his mild, stubborn tone: 'I aint accusing nobody of nothing. I just know and you fellows know how a woman that never—'

'You damn niggerlover!' the youth said.

'Shut up, Butch,' another said. 'We'll get the facts in plenty of time to act.'

'Who is? Who's getting them?' the youth said. 'Facts, hell! I—'

'You're a fine white man,' the client said. 'Aint you?' In his frothy beard he looked like a desert rat in the moving pictures. 'You tell them, Jack,' he said to the youth. 'If there aint any white men in this town, you can count on me, even if I aint only a drummer and a stranger.'

'That's right, boys,' the barber said. 'Find out the truth first. I know Will Mayes.'

'Well, by God!' the youth shouted. 'To think that a white man in this town—'

'Shut up, Butch,' the second speaker said. 'We got plenty of time.'

The client sat up. He looked at the speaker. 'Do you claim that anything excuses a nigger attacking a white woman? Do you mean to tell me you are a white man and you'll stand for it? You better go back North where you came from. The South dont want your kind here.'

'North what?' the second said. 'I was born and raised in this town.'

'Well, by God!' the youth said. He looked about with a strained, baffled gaze, as if he was trying to remember what it was he wanted to say or to do. He drew his sleeve across his sweating face. 'Damn if I'm going to let a white woman—'

'You tell them, Jack,' the drummer said. 'By God, if they—'

The screen door crashed open. A man stood in the floor, his feet apart and his heavy-set body poised easily. His white shirt was open at the throat; he wore a felt hat. His hot, bold glance swept the group. His name was McLendon. He had commanded troops at the front in France and had been decorated for valor.

'Well,' he said, 'are you going to sit there and let a black son rape a white woman on the streets of Jefferson?'

Butch sprang up again. The silk of his shirt clung flat to his heavy shoulders. At each armpit was a dark halfmoon. 'That's what I been telling them! That's what I—'

'Did it really happen?' a third said. 'This aint the first man scare she ever had, like Hawkshaw says. Wasn't there something about a man on the kitchen roof, watching her undress, about a year ago?'

'What?' the client said. 'What's that?' The barber had been slowly forcing him back into the chair; he arrested himself reclining, his head lifted, the barber still pressing him down.

McLendon whirled on the third speaker. 'Happen? What the hell difference does it make? Are you going to let the black sons get away with it until one really does it?'

'That's what I'm telling them!' Butch shouted. He cursed, long and steady, pointless.

'Here, here,' a fourth said. 'Not so loud. Dont talk so loud.'

'Sure,' McLendon said; 'no talking necessary at all. I've done my talking. Who's with me?' He poised on the balls of his feet, roving his gaze.

The barber held the drummer's face down, the razor poised. 'Find out the facts first, boys. I know Willy Mayes. It wasn't him. Let's get the sheriff and do this thing right.'

McLendon whirled upon him his furious, rigid face. The barber did not look away. They looked like men of different races. The other barbers had ceased also above their prone clients. 'You mean to tell me,' McLendon said, 'that you'd take a nigger's word before a white woman's? Why, you damn niggerloving—'

The third speaker rose and grasped Mc-Lendon's arm; he too had been a soldier. 'Now, now. Let's figure this thing out. Who knows anything about what really happened?'

'Figure out hell!' McLendon jerked his arm free. 'All that're with me get up from there. The ones that aint—' He roved his gaze, dragging his sleeve across his face.

Three men rose. The drummer in the chair sat up. 'Here,' he said, jerking at the cloth about his neck; 'get this rag off me. I'm with him. I dont live here, but by God, if our mothers and wives and sisters—' He smeared the cloth over his face and flung it to the floor. McLendon stood in the floor and cursed the others. Another rose and moved toward him. The remainder sat uncomfortable, not looking at one another, then one by one they rose and joined him.

The barber picked the cloth from the floor. He began to fold it neatly. 'Boys, dont do that. Will Mayes never done it. I know.'

'Come on,' McLendon said. He whirled. From his hip pocket protruded the butt of a heavy automatic pistol. They went out. The screen door crashed behind them reverberant in the dead air.

The barber wiped the razor carefully and swiftly, and put it away, and ran to the rear, and took his hat from the wall. 'I'll be back as soon as I can,' he said to the other barbers. 'I cant let—' He went out, running. The two other barbers followed him to the door and caught it on the rebound, leaning out and looking up the street after him. The air was flat and dead. It had a metallic taste at the base of the tongue.

'What can he do?' the first said. The second one was saying 'Jees Christ, Jees Christ' under his breath. 'I'd just as lief be Will Mayes as Hawk, if he gets McLendon riled.'

'Jees Christ, Jees Christ,' the second whispered.

'You reckon he really done it to her?' the first said.

II

She was thirty-eight or thirty-nine. She lived in a small frame house with her invalid mother and a thin, sallow, unflagging aunt, where each morning between ten and eleven she would appear on the porch in a lace-trimmed boudoir cap, to sit swinging in the porch swing until noon. After dinner she lay down for a while, until the afternoon began to cool. Then, in one of the three or four new voile dresses which she had each summer, she would go downtown to spend the afternoon in the stores with the other ladies, where they would handle the goods and haggle over the prices in cold, immediate voices, without any intention of buying.

She was of comfortable people—not the best in Jefferson, but good people enough—and she was still on the slender side of ordinary looking, with a bright, faintly haggard manner and dress. When she was young she had had a slender, nervous body and a sort of hard vivacity which had enabled her for a time to ride upon the crest of the town's social life as exemplified by the high school party and church social period of her contemporaries while still children enough to be unclassconscious.

She was the last to realize that she was losing ground; that those among whom she had been a little brighter and louder flame than any other were beginning to learn the pleasure of snobbery—male—and retaliation—female. That was when her face began to wear that bright, haggard look. She still carried it to parties on shadowy porticoes and summer lawns, like a mask or a flag, with that bafflement of furious repudiation of truth in her eyes. One evening at a party she heard a boy and two girls, all schoolmates, talking. She never accepted another invitation.

She watched the girls with whom she had grown up as they married and got homes and children, but no man ever called on her steadily until the children of the other girls had been calling her 'aunty' for several years, the while their mothers told them in bright voices about how popular Aunt Minnie had been as a girl. Then the town began to see her driving on Sunday afternoons with the cashier in the bank. He was a widower of about forty—a high-colored man, smelling always faintly of the barber shop or of whisky. He owned the first automobile in town, a red runabout; Minnie had the first motoring bonnet and veil the town ever saw. Then the town began to say: 'Poor Minnie.' 'But she is old enough to take care of herself,' others said. That was when she began to ask her old schoolmates that their children call her 'cousin' instead of 'aunty.'

It was twelve years now since she had been relegated into adultery by public opinion, and eight years since the cashier had gone to a Memphis bank, returning for one day each Christmas, which he spent at an annual bachelors' party at a hunting club on the river. From behind their curtains the neighbors would see the party pass, and during the over-the-way Christmas day visiting they would tell her about him, about how well he looked, and how they heard that he was prospering in the city, watching with bright, secret eyes her haggard, bright face. Usually by that hour there would be the scent of whisky on her breath. It was supplied her by a youth, a clerk at the soda fountain: 'Sure; I buy it for the old gal. I reckon she's entitled to a little fun.'

Her mother kept to her room altogether now; the gaunt aunt ran the house. Against that background Minnie's bright dresses, her idle and empty days, had a quality of furious unreality. She went out in the evenings only with women now, neighbors, to the moving pictures. Each afternoon she dressed in one of the new dresses and went downtown alone, where her young 'cousins' were already strolling in the late afternoons with their delicate, silken heads and thin, awkward arms and conscious hips, clinging to one another or shrieking and giggling with paired boys in the soda fountain when she passed and went on along the serried store fronts, in the doors of which the sitting and lounging men did not even follow her with their eyes any more.

III

The barber went swiftly up the street where the sparse lights, insect-swirled, glared in rigid and violent suspension in the lifeless air. The day had died in a pall of dust; above the darkened square, shrouded by the spent dust, the sky was as clear as the inside of a brass bell. Below the east was a rumor of the twice-waxed moon.

When he overtook them McLendon and three others were getting into a car parked in an alley. McLendon stooped his thick head, peering out beneath the top. 'Changed your mind, did you?' he said. 'Damn good thing; by God, tomorrow when this town hears about how you talked tonight—'

'Now, now,' the other ex-soldier said. 'Hawkshaw's all right. Come on, Hawk; jump in.'

'Will Mayes never done it, boys,' the barber said. 'If anybody done it. Why, you all know well as I do there aint any town where they got better niggers than us. And you know how a lady will kind of think things about men when there aint any reason to, and Miss Minnie anyway—'

'Sure, sure,' the soldier said. 'We're just going to talk to him a little; that's all.'

'Talk hell!' Butch said. 'When we're through with the—'

'Shut up, for God's sake!' the soldier said. 'Do you want everybody in town—'

'Tell them, by God!' McLendon said. 'Tell every one of the sons that'll let a white woman—'

'Let's go; let's go: here's the other car.' The second car slid squealing out of a cloud of dust at the alley mouth. McLendon started his car and took the lead. Dust lay like fog in the street. The street lights hung nimbused as in water. They drove on out of town.

A rutted lane turned at right angles. Dust hung above it too, and above all the land. The dark bulk of the ice plant, where the Negro Mayes was night watchman, rose against the sky. 'Better stop here, hadn't we?' the soldier said. McLendon did not reply. He hurled the car up and slammed to a stop, the headlights glaring on the blank wall.

'Listen here, boys,' the barber said; 'if he's here, dont that prove he never done it? Dont it? If it was him, he would run. Dont you see he would?' The second car came up and stopped. McLendon got down; Butch sprang down beside him. 'Listen, boys,' the barber said.

'Cut the lights off!' McLendon said. The breathless dark rushed down. There was no sound in it save their lungs as they sought air in the parched dust in which for two months they had lived; then the diminishing crunch of McLendon's and Butch's feet, and a moment later McLendon's voice:

'Will! . . . Will!'

Below the east the wan hemorrhage of the moon increased. It heaved above the ridge, silvering the air, the dust, so that they seemed to breathe, live, in a bowl of molten lead. There was no sound of nightbird nor insect, no sound save their breathing and a faint ticking of contracting metal about the cars. Where their bodies touched one another they seemed to sweat dryly, for no more moisture came. 'Christ!' a voice said; 'let's get out of here.'

But they didn't move until vague noises began to grow out of the darkness ahead; then they got out and waited tensely in the breathless dark. There was another sound: a blow, a hissing expulsion of breath and McLendon cursing in undertone. They stood a moment longer, then they ran forward. They ran in a stumbling clump, as though they were fleeing something. 'Kill him, kill the son,' a voice whispered. McLendon flung them back.

'Not here,' he said. 'Get him into the car.' 'Kill him, kill the black son!' the voice murmured. They dragged the Negro to the car. The barber had waited beside the car. He could feel himself sweating and he knew he was going to be sick at the stomach.

'What is it, captains?' the Negro said. 'I aint done nothing. 'Fore God, Mr. John.' Someone produced handcuffs. They worked busily about the Negro as though he were a post, quiet, intent, getting in one another's way. He submitted to the handcuffs, looking swiftly and constantly from dim face to dim face. 'Who's here, captains?' he said, leaning to peer into the faces until they could feel his breath and smell his sweaty reek. He spoke a name or two. 'What you all say I done, Mr. John?'

McLendon jerked the car door open. 'Get in!' he said.

The Negro did not move. 'What you all going to do with me, Mr. John? I aint done nothing. White folks, captains, I aint done nothing: I swear 'fore God.' He called another name.

'Get in!' McLendon said. He struck the Negro. The others expelled their breath in a dry hissing and struck him with random blows and he whirled and cursed them, and swept his manacled hands across their faces and slashed the barber upon the mouth, and the barber struck him also. 'Get him in there,' McLendon said. They pushed at him. He ceased struggling and got in and sat quietly as the others took their places. He sat between the barber and the soldier, drawing his limbs in so as not to touch them, his eyes going swiftly and constantly from face to face. Butch clung to the running board. The car moved on. The barber nursed his mouth with his handkerchief.

'What's the matter, Hawk?' the soldier said.

'Nothing,' the barber said. They regained the highroad and turned away from town. The second car dropped back out of the dusk. They went on, gaining speed; the final fringe of houses dropped behind.

'Goddamn, he stinks!' the soldier said.

'We'll fix that,' the drummer in front beside McLendon said. On the running board Butch cursed into the hot rush of air. The barber leaned suddenly forward and touched McLendon's arm.

'Let me out, John,' he said.

'Jump out, niggerlover,' McLendon said without turning his head. He drove swiftly. Behind them the sourceless lights of the second car glared in the dust. Presently McLendon turned into a narrow road. It was rutted with disuse. It led back to an abandoned brick kiln—a series of reddish mounds and weed- and vine-choked vats without bottom. It had been used for pasture once, until one day the owner missed one of his mules. Although he prodded carefully in the vats with a long pole, he could not even find the bottom of them.

'John,' the barber said.

'Jump out, then,' McLendon said, hurling the car along the ruts. Beside the barber the Negro spoke:

'Mr Henry.'

The barber sat forward. The narrow tunnel of the road rushed up and past. Their motion was like an extinct furnace blast: cooler, but utterly dead. The car bounded from rut to rut.

'Mr Henry,' the Negro said.

The barber began to tug furiously at the door. 'Look out, there!' the soldier said, but the barber had already kicked the door open and swung onto the running board. The soldier leaned across the Negro and grasped at him, but he had already jumped. The car went on without checking speed.

The impetus hurled him crashing through dust-sheathed weeds, into the ditch. Dust puffed about him, and in a thin, vicious crackling of sapless stems he lay choking and retching until the second car passed and died away. Then he rose and limped on until he reached the highroad and turned toward town, brushing at his clothes with his hands. The moon was higher, riding high and clear of the dust at last, and after a while the town began to glare beneath the dust. He went on, limping. Presently he heard cars and the glow of them grew in the dust behind him and he left the road and crouched again in the weeds until they passed. McLendon's car came last now. There were four people in it and Butch was not on the running board.

They went on; the dust swallowed them; the glare and the sound died away. The dust of them hung for a while, but soon the eternal dust absorbed it again. The barber climbed back onto the road and limped on toward town.

IV

As she dressed for supper on that Saturday evening, her own flesh felt like fever. Her hands trembled among the hooks and eyes, and her eyes had a feverish look, and her hair swirled crisp and crackling under the comb. While she was still dressing the friends called for her and sat while she donned her sheerest underthings and stockings and a new voile dress. 'Do you feel strong enough to go out?' they said, their eyes bright too, with a dark glitter. 'When you have had time to get over the shock, you must tell us what happened. What he said and did; everything.'

In the leafed darkness, as they walked toward the square, she began to breathe deeply, something like a swimmer preparing to dive, until she ceased trembling, the four of them walking slowly because of the terrible heat and out of solicitude for her. But as they neared the square she began to tremble again, walking with her head up, her hands clinched at her sides, their voices about her murmurous, also with that feverish, glittering quality of their eyes.

They entered the square, she in the center of the group, fragile in her fresh dress. She was trembling worse. She walked slower and slower, as children eat ice cream, her head up and her eyes bright in the haggard banner of her face, passing the hotel and the coatless drummers in chairs along the curb looking around at her: 'That's the one: see? The one in pink in the middle.' 'Is that her? What did they do with the nigger? Did they—?' 'Sure. He's all right.' 'All right, is he?' 'Sure. He went on a little trip.' Then the drug store, where even the young men lounging in the doorway tipped their hats and followed with their eyes the motion of her hips and legs when she passed.

They went on, passing the lifted hats of the gentlemen, the suddenly ceased voices, deferent, protective. 'Do you see?' the friends said. Their voices sounded like long, hovering sighs of hissing exultation. 'There's not a Negro on the square. Not one.'

They reached the picture show. It was like a miniature fairyland with its lighted lobby and colored lithographs of life caught in its terrible and beautiful mutations. Her lips began to tingle. In the dark, when the picture began, it would be all right; she could hold back the laughing so it would not waste away so fast and so soon. So she hurried on before the turning faces, the undertones of low astonishment, and they took their accustomed places where she could see the aisle against the silver glare and the young men and girls coming in two and two against it.

The lights flicked away; the screen glowed silver, and soon life began to unfold, beautiful and passionate and sad, while still the young men and girls entered, scented and sibilant in the half dark, their paired backs in silhouette delicate and sleek, their slim, quick bodies awkward, divinely young, while beyond them the silver dream accumulated, inevitably on and on. She began to laugh. In trying to suppress it, it made more noise than ever;

heads began to turn. Still laughing, her friends raised her and led her out, and she stood at the curb, laughing on a high, sustained note, until the taxi came up and they helped her in.

They removed the pink voile and the sheer underthings and the stockings, and put her to bed, and cracked ice for her temples, and sent for the doctor. He was hard to locate, so they ministered to her with hushed ejaculations, renewing the ice and fanning her. While the ice was fresh and cold she stopped laughing and lay still for a time, moaning only a little. But soon the laughing welled again and her voice rose screaming.

'Shhhhhhh! Shhhhhhhhhh!' they said, freshening the icepack, smoothing her hair, examining it for gray; 'poor girl!' Then to one another: 'Do you suppose anything really happened?' their eyes darkly aglitter, secret and passionate. 'Shhhhhhhhhh! Poor girl! Poor Minnie!'

V

It was midnight when McLendon drove up to his neat new house. It was trim and fresh as a birdcage and almost as small, with its clean green-and-white paint. He locked the car and mounted the porch and entered. His wife rose from a chair beside the reading lamp. McLendon stopped in the floor and stared at her until she looked down.

'Look at that clock,' he said, lifting his arm, pointing. She stood before him, her face lowered, a magazine in her hands. Her face was pale, strained, and weary-looking. 'Haven't I told you about sitting up like this, waiting to see when I come in?'

'John,' she said. She laid the magazine down. Poised on the balls of his feet, he glared at her with his hot eyes, his sweating face.

'Didn't I tell you?' He went toward her. She looked up then. He caught her shoulder. She stood passive, looking at him.

'Dont, John. I couldn't sleep. . . . The heat; something. Please, John. You're hurting me.'

'Didn't I tell you?' He released her and half struck, half flung her across the chair, and she lay there and watched him quietly as he left the room.

He went on through the house, ripping off his shirt, and on the dark, screened porch at the rear he stood and mopped his head and shoulders with the shirt and flung it away. He took the pistol from his hip and laid it on the table beside the bed, and sat on the bed and removed his shoes, and rose and slipped his trousers off. He was sweating again already, and he stooped and hunted furiously for the shirt. At last he found it and wiped his body again, and, with his body pressed against the dusty screen, he stood panting. There was no movement, no sound, not even an insect. The dark world seemed to lie stricken beneath the cold moon and the lidless stars.

1931

THOMAS WOLFE

1900–1938

FROM OF TIME AND THE RIVER

THE DEATH OF STONEMAN GANT [1]

I

THE news that Gant was dying had spread rapidly through the town and, as often happens, that news had brought him back to life again in the heart and living memory of men who had known him, and who had scarcely thought of him for years. That night—the night of his death—the house was filled with some of the men who had known him best since he came to the town forty years before.

Among these people were several of the prominent and wealthy business men of the community: these included, naturally, Eliza's brothers, William and James Pentland, both wealthy lumber dealers, as well as one of her younger brothers, Crockett, who was Will Pentland's bookkeeper, a pleasant, ruddy, bucolic man of fifty years. Among the other men of wealth and influence who had been Gant's friends there

[1] The selection is from *Of Time and the River*(N.Y., 1935),246–273. The title is that originally given by Wolfe to this section, when writing the novel.

was Fagg Sluder, who had made a fortune as a contractor and retired to invest his money in business property, and to spend his time seated in an easy creaking chair before the fire department, in incessant gossip about baseball with the firemen and the young professional baseball players whose chief support he was, whose annual deficit he cheerfully supplied, and to whom he had given the local baseball park, which bore his name. He had been one of Gant's best friends for twenty years, he was immensely fond of him, and now, assembled in the broad front hall in earnest discussion with the Pentlands and Mike Fogarty, another of Gant's friends, and armed with the invariable cigar (despite his doctor's orders he smoked thirty or forty strong black cigars every day), which he chewed on, took out of his mouth, and put back again, with quick, short, unconscious movements, he could be heard saying in the rapid, earnest, stammering tone that was one of the most attractive qualities of his buoyant and constantly hopeful nature:

'I-I-I-I just believe he's going to pull right out of this and-and-and-get well! Why-why-why-why-when I went in there tonight he spoke right up and-and-and knew me right away!' he blurted out, sticking the cigar in his mouth and chewing on it vigorously a moment—'why-why-why his mind is-is-is-is just as clear—as it always was—spoke right up, you know, says "Sit down, Fagg"—shook hands with me—knew me right away—talked to me just the same way he always talked—says "Sit down, Fagg. I'm glad to see you. How have you been?" he says—and-and-and—I just believe he's going to pull right out of this,' Mr. Sluder blurted out,—'be damned if I don't—what do you say, Will?' and snatching his chewed cigar butt from his mouth he turned eagerly to Will Pentland for confirmation. And Will, who, as usual, had been paring his stubby nails during the whole course of the conversation, his lips pursed in their characteristic family grimace, now studied his clenched fingers for a moment, pocketed his knife and turning to Fagg Sluder, with a little bird-like nod and wink, and with the incomparable Pentland drawl, at once precise, and full of the relish of self-satisfaction, said:

'Well, if any man alive can do it, W.O. is that man. I've seen him time and again when I thought every breath would be his last—and he's got over it every time. I've always said,' he went on precisely, and with a kind of deadly directness in his small compact and almost wizened face, 'that he has more real vitality than any two men that I ever knew—he's got out of worse holes than this before—and he may do it again.' He was silent a moment, his small packed face pursed suddenly in its animal-like grimace that had an almost savage ferocity and a sense of deadly and indomitable power.

Even more astonishing and troubling was the presence of these four older members of the Pentland family gathered together in his mother's hall. As they stood there talking—Eliza with her hands held in their loose and powerful clasp across her waist, Will intently busy with his finger-nails, Jim listening attentively to all that was said, his solid porcine face and small eyes wincing from time to time in a powerful but unconscious grimace, and Crockett, gentlest, ruddiest, most easy-going and dreamy of them all, speaking in his quiet drawling tone and stroking his soft brown mustaches in a gesture of quiet and bucolic meditation, Luke could not recall having seen so many of them together at one time and the astonishing enigma of their oneness and variety was strikingly apparent.

What was it?—this indefinable tribal similarity that united these people so unmistakably. No one could say: it would have been difficult to find four people more unlike in physical appearance, more strongly marked by individual qualities. Whatever it was—whether some chemistry of blood and character, or perhaps some physical identity of broad and fleshy nose, pursed reflective lips and flat wide cheeks, or the energies of powerfully concentrated egotisms—their kinship with one another was astonishing and instantly apparent.

2

In a curious and indefinable way the two groups of men in the hallway had become divided: the wealthier group of prominent citizens, which was composed of the brothers William, James, and Crockett Pentland, Mr. Sluder and Eliza, stood in a group near the front hall door, engaged in earnest conversation. The second group, which was composed of working men, who had known Gant well, and worked for or with him—a group composed of Jannadeau the jeweller, old Alec Ramsay and Saul Gudger, who were stonecutters, Gant's nephew, Ollie Gant, who was a plasterer, Ernest Pegram, the city plumber, and Mike Fogarty, who was perhaps Gant's closest friend, a build-ing contractor—this group, composed of men who had all their lives done stern labor with their hands, and who were really the men who had known the stonecutter best, stood apart from the group of prominent and wealthy men who were talking so earnestly to Eliza.

And in this circumstance, in this uncon-scious division, in the air of constraint, vague uneasiness and awkward silence that was evident among these working men, as they stood there in the hallway dressed in their 'good clothes,' nervously fingering their hats in their big hands, there was something immensely moving. The men had the look that working people the world over have always had when they found themselves suddenly gathered together on terms of social intimacy with their employ-ers or with members of the governing class.

And Helen, coming out at this instant from her father's room into the hall, sud-denly saw and felt the awkward division between these two groups of men, as she had never before felt or noticed it, as sharply as if they had been divided with a knife.

And, it must be admitted, her first feel-ing was an unworthy one—an instinctive wish to approach the more 'important' group, to join her life to the lives of these 'influential' people who represented to her a 'higher' social level. She found herself walking towards the group of wealthy and prominent men at the front of the hall, and away from the group of working men who had really been Gant's best friends.

But seeing the brick-red face of Alec Ramsay, the mountainous figure of Mike Fogarty, suddenly with a sense of disbe-lief, and almost terrified revelation of the truth, she thought: 'Why-why-why—these men are really the closest friends he's got—not rich men like Uncle Will or Uncle Jim or even Mr. Sluder—but men like Mike Fogarty—and Jannadeau—and Mr. Dun-

can—and Alec Ramsay—and Ernest Peg-ram—and Ollie Gant—but—but—good heavens, no!' she thought, almost desper-ately—'surely these are not his closest friends—why-why—of course, they're de-cent people—they're honest men—but they're only common people—I've always considered them as just *working* men—and-and-and—my God!' she thought, with that terrible feeling of discovery we have when we suddenly see ourselves as others see us —'do you suppose that's the way people in this town think of Papa? Do you suppose they have always thought of him as just a common working man—oh, no! but of course not!' she went on impatiently, trying to put the troubling thought out of her mind. 'Papa's not a working man—Papa is a *business* man—a well thought of business man in this community. Papa has always owned property since he came here—he has always had his own shop'—she did not like the sound of the word shop, and in her mind she hastily amended it to 'place'— 'he's always had his own place, up on the public square—he's—he's rented places to other people—he's—he's—oh, of course not!—Papa is different from men like Ernest Pegram, and Ollie, and Jannadeau and Alec Ramsay—why, they're just work-ing men—they work with their hands— Ollie's just an ordinary plasterer—and-and —Mr. Ramsay is nothing but a stone-cutter.'

And a small insistent voice inside her said most quietly: 'And your father?'

And suddenly Helen remembered Gant's great hands of power and strength, and how they now lay quietly beside him on the bed, and lived and would not die, even when the rest of him had died, and she remembered the thousands of times she had gone to his shop in the afternoon and found the stone-cutter in his long striped apron bending with delicate concentration over a stone in-scription on a trestle, holding in his great hands the chisel and the heavy wooden mallet the stonecutters use, and remember-ing, the whole rich and living compact of the past came back to her, in a rush of ten-derness and joy and terror, and on that flood a proud and bitter honesty returned. She thought: 'Yes, he was a stonecutter, no different from these other men, and these men were his real friends.'

And going directly to old Alec Ramsay she grasped his blunt thick fingers, the nails of which were always whitened a little with stone dust, and greeted him in her large and spacious way:

'Mr. Ramsay,' she said, 'I want you to know how glad we are that you could come. And that goes for all of you—Mr. Jannadeau, and Mr. Duncan, and Mr. Fogarty, and you, Ernest, and you, too, Ollie—you are the best friends Papa has, there's no one he thinks more of, and no one he would rather see.'

Mr. Ramsay's brick-red face and brick-red neck became even redder before he spoke, and beneath his grizzled brows his blue eyes suddenly were smoke blue. He put his blunt hand to his mustache for a moment, and tugged at it, then he said in his gruff, quiet, and matter-of-fact voice:

'I guess we know Will about as well as any one, Miss Helen. I've worked for him off and on for thirty years.'

At the same moment, she heard Ollie Gant's easy, deep, and powerful laugh, and saw him slowly lift his cigarette in his coarse paw; she saw Jannadeau's great yellow face and massive domy brow, and heard him laugh with guttural pleasure, saying, 'Ah-h! I tell you vat! Dat girl has alvays looked out for her datty—she's de only vun dat coult hantle him; efer since she vas ten years olt it has been de same.' And she was overwhelmingly conscious of that immeasurable mountain of a man, Mike Fogarty, beside her, the sweet clarity of his blue eyes, and the almost purring music of his voice as he gently laid his mutton of a hand upon her shoulder for a moment, saying,

'Ah, Miss Helen, I don't know how Will could have got along all these years without ye—for he has said the same himself a thousand times—aye! that he has!'

And instantly, having heard these words, and feeling the strong calm presences of these powerful men around her, it seemed to Helen she had somehow re-entered a magic world that she thought was gone forever. And she was immensely content.

At the same moment, with a sense of wonder, she discovered an astonishing thing, that she had never noticed before, but that she must have heard a thousand times;—this was that of all these people,

who knew Gant best, and had a deep and true affection for him, there were only two —Mr. Fogarty and Mr. Ramsay—who had ever addressed him by his first name. And so far as she could now remember, these two men, together with Gant's mother, his brothers, his sister Augusta, and a few of the others who had known him in his boyhood in Pennsylvania, were the only people who ever had. And this revelation cast a strange, a lonely and a troubling light upon the great gaunt figure of the stonecutter, which moved her powerfully and which she had never felt before. And most strange of all was the variety of names by which these various people called her father.

As for Eliza, had any of her children ever heard her address her husband as anything but 'Mr. Gant'—had she ever called him by one of his first names—their anguish of shame and impropriety would have been so great that they could hardly have endured it. But such a lapse would have been incredible: Eliza could no more have addressed Gant by his first name, than she could have quoted Homer's Greek; had she tried to address him so, the muscles of her tongue would have found it physically impossible to pronounce the word. And in this fact there was somehow, now that Gant was dying, an enormous pathos. It gave to Eliza's life with him a pitiable and moving dignity, the compensation of a proud and wounded spirit for all the insults and injuries that had been heaped upon it. She had been a young country woman of twenty-four when she had met him, she had been ignorant of life, and innocent of the cruelty, the violence, the drunkenness and abuse of which men are capable, she had borne this man fifteen children, of whom eight had come to life, and had for forty years eaten the bread of blood and tears and joy and grief and terror, she had wanted affection and had been given taunts, abuse, and curses, and somehow her proud and wounded spirit had endured with an anguished but unshaken fortitude all the wrongs and cruelties and injustices of which he had been guilty toward her. And now at the very end her pride still had this pitiable distinction, her spirit still preserved this last integrity: she had not betrayed her wounded soul to a shameful familiarity, he had remained to her—ir mind and heart and living word—what he had been from the first day that she met him; the author of her grief and misery, the agent of her suffering, the gaunt and lonely stranger who had come into her hills from a strange land and a distant people— that furious, gaunt, and lonely stranger with whom by fatal accident her destiny—past hate or love or birth or death or human error and confusion—had been insolubly enmeshed, with whom for forty years she had lived, a wife, a mother, and a stranger —and who would to the end remain to her a stranger—'Mr. Gant.'

What was it? What was the secret of this strange and bitter mystery of life that had made of Gant a stranger to all men, and most of all a stranger to his wife? Perhaps some of the answer might have been found in Eliza's own unconscious words when she described her meeting with him forty years before:

'It was not that he was old,' she said,— 'he was only thirty-three—but he *looked* old—his *ways* were old—he had lived so much among old people.—Pshaw!' she continued, with a little puckered smile, 'if any one had told me that night I saw him sitting there with Lydia and old Mrs. Mason—that was the very day they moved into the house, the night he gave the big dinner—and Lydia was still alive and, of course, she was ten years older than he was, and that may have had something to do with it—but I got to studying him as he sat there, of course, he was tired and run down and depressed and worried over all that trouble that he'd had in Sidney before he came up here, when he lost everything, and he knew that Lydia was dying, and that was preyin' on his mind—but he *looked* old, thin as a rake you know, and sallow and run down, and with those *old* ways he had acquired, I reckon, from associatin' with Lydia and old Mrs. Mason and people like that—but I just sat there studying him as he sat there with them and I said—"Well, you're an old man, aren't you, sure enough?"—pshaw! if any one had told me that night that some day I'd be married to him I'd have laughed at them—I'd have considered that I was marrying an old man —and that's just exactly what a lot of people thought, sir, when the news got out that I was goin' to marry him—I know Martha

Patton came running to me, all excited and out of breath—said, "Eliza! You're not going to marry that old man—you know you're not!"—you see, his *ways* were old, he *looked* old, *dressed* old, *acted* old—every-thing he did was old; there was always, it seemed, something strange and old-like about him, almost like he had been born that way.'

And it was at this time that Eliza met him, saw him first—'Mr. Gant'—an im-mensely tall, gaunt, cadaverous-looking man, with a face stern and sad with care, lank, drooping mustaches, sandy hair, and cold-gray staring eyes—'not so old, you know—he was only thirty-three—but he *looked* old, he *acted* old, his *ways* were old —he had lived so much among older people he seemed older than he was—I thought of him as an old man.'

This, then, was 'Mr. Gant' at thirty-three, and since then, although his fortunes and position had improved, his character had changed little. And now Helen, faced by all these working men, who had known, liked, and respected him, and had now come to see him again before he died— suddenly knew the reason for his loneliness, the reason so few people—least of all, his wife—had ever dared address him by his first name. And with a swift and piercing revelation, his muttered words, which she had heard him use a thousand times when speaking of his childhood—'We had a tough time of it—I tell you what, we did!' —now came back to her with the unutter-able poignancy of discovery. For the first time she understood what they meant. And suddenly, with the same swift and name-less pity, she remembered all the pictures which she had seen of her father as a boy and a young man. There were a half dozen of them in the big family album, together with pictures of his own and Eliza's family: they were the small daguerreotypes of fifty years before, in small frames of faded plush, with glass covers, touched with the faint pale pinks with which the photogra-phers of an earlier time tried to paint with life the sallow hues of their photography. The first of these pictures showed Gant as a little boy; later, a boy of twelve, he was standing in a chair beside his brother Wesley, who was seated, with a wooden smile upon his face. Later, a picture of

Gant in the years in Baltimore, standing, his feet crossed, leaning elegantly upon a marble slab beside a vase; later still, the young stonecutter before his little shop in the years at Sidney; finally, Gant, after his marriage with Eliza, standing with gaunt face and lank drooping mustaches before his shop upon the square, in the company of Will Pentland, who was at the time his business partner.

And all these pictures, from first to last, from the little boy to the man with the lank drooping mustaches, had been marked by the same expression: the sharp thin face was always stern and sad with care, the shallow cold-gray eyes always stared out of the bony cage-formation of the skull with a cold mournfulness—the whole impression was always one of gaunt sad loneliness. And it was not the loneliness of the dreamer, the poet, or the misjudged prophet, it was just the cold and terrible loneliness of man, of every man, and of the lost American who has been brought forth naked under immense and lonely skies, to 'shift for himself,' to grope his way blindly through the confusion and brutal chaos of a life as naked and unsure as he, to wander blindly down across the continent, to hunt forever for a goal, a wall, a dwelling place of warmth and certitude, a light, a door.

And for this reason, she now understood something about her father, this great gaunt figure of a stonecutter that she had never understood or thought about before: she suddenly understood his order, sense of decency and dispatch; his love of cleanness, roaring fires, and rich abundance, his foul drunkenness, violence, and howling fury, his naked shame and trembling penitence, his good clothes of heavy monumental black that he always kept well pressed, his clean boiled shirts, wing collars, and his love of hotels, ships, and trains, his love of gardens, new lands, cities, voyages. She knew suddenly that he was unlike any other man that ever lived, and that every man that ever lived was like her father. And remembering the cold and mournful look in his shallow staring eyes of cold hard gray, she suddenly knew the reason for that look, as she had never known it before, and understood now why so few men had ever called him by his first name

—why he was known to all the world as 'Mr. Gant.'

Having joined this group of working men, Helen immediately felt an indefinable but powerful sense of comfort and physical well-being which the presence of such men as these always gave to her. And she did not know why; but immediately, once she had grasped Mr. Ramsay by the hand, and was aware of Mike Fogarty's mountainous form and clear-blue eye above her, and Ollie Gant's deep and lazy laugh, and the deliberate and sensual languor with which he raised his cigarette to his lips with his powerful plasterer's hand, drawing the smoke deep into his strong lungs and letting it trickle slowly from his nostrils as he talked—she was conscious of a feeling of enormous security and relief which she had not known in years.

And this feeling, as with every person of strong sensuous perceptions, was literal, physical, chemical, astoundingly acute. She not only felt an enormous relief and joy to get back to these working people, it even seemed to her that everything they did— the way Mr. Duncan held his strong cheap cigar in his thick dry fingers, the immense satisfaction with which he drew on it, the languid and sensual trickling of cigarette smoke from Ollie Gant's nostrils, his deep, good-natured, indolently lazy laugh, even the perceptible bulge of tobacco-quid in Alec Ramsay's brick-red face, his barely perceptible rumination of it—all these things, though manlike in their nature, seemed wonderfully good and fresh and living to her—the whole plain priceless glory of the earth restored to her—and gave her a feeling of wonderful happiness and joy.

And later that night when all these men, her father's friends, had gone into his room, filling it with their enormous and full-blooded vitality, as she saw him lying there, wax-pale, bloodless, motionless, yet with a faint grin at the edge of his thin mouth as he received them, as she heard their deep full-fibred voices, Mike Fogarty's lilting Irish, Mr. Duncan's thick Scotch burr, Ollie Gant's deep and lazy laugh, and the humor of Alec Ramsay's deep, gruff and matter-of-fact tone, relating old times—'God, Will!' he said, 'at your worst, you weren't in it compared to Wes! He was a holy terror when he drank! Do you remember the day he drove his fist through your plate-glass window right in the face of Jannadeau—and went home then and tore all the plumbing out of the house and pitched the bathtub out of the second-story window into Orchard Street —God! Will!—you weren't in it compared to Wes'—as she heard all this, and saw Gant's thin grin and heard his faint and rusty cackle, his almost inaudible 'E'God! Poor Wes!'—she could not believe that he was going to die, the great full-blooded working men filled the room with the vitality of a life which had returned in all its rich and living flood, and seemed intolerably near and familiar—and she kept thinking with a feeling of wonderful happiness and disbelief: 'Oh, but Papa's not going to die! It's not possible! He can't! He can't!'

3

The dying man himself was no longer to be fooled and duped by hope; he knew that he was done for, and he no longer cared. Rather, as if that knowledge had brought him a new strength—the immense and measureless strength that comes from resignation, and that has vanquished terror and despair—Gant had already consigned himself to death, and now was waiting for it, without weariness or anxiety, and with a perfect and peaceful acquiescence.

This complete resignation and tranquillity of a man whose life had been so full of violence, protest, and howling fury stunned and silenced them, and left them helpless. It seemed that Gant, knowing that often he had lived badly, was now determined to die well. And in this he succeeded. He accepted every ministration, every visit, every stammering reassurance, or frenzied activity, with a passive gratefulness which he seemed to want every one to know. On the evening of the day after his first hemorrhage, he asked for food and Eliza, bustling out, pathetically eager to do something, killed a chicken and cooked it for him.

And as if, from that infinite depth of death and silence from which he looked at her, he had seen, behind the bridling brisk activity of her figure, forever bustling back and forth, saying confusedly— 'Why,

yes! The very thing! This very minute, sir!'—had seen the white strained face, the stricken eyes of a proud and sensitive woman who had wanted affection all her life, had received for the most part injury and abuse, and who was ready to clutch at any crust of comfort that might console or justify her before he died—he ate part of the chicken with relish, and then looking up at her, said quietly:

'I tell you what—that was a good chicken.'

And Helen, who had been sitting beside him on the bed, and feeding him, now cried out in a tone of bantering and good-humored challenge:

'What! Is it better than the ones *I* cook for you! You'd better not say it is—I'll beat you if you do.'

And Gant, grinning feebly, shook his head, and answered:

'Ah-h! Your mother is a good cook, Helen. You're a good cook, too—but there's no one else can cook a chicken like your mother!'

And stretching out his great right hand, he patted Eliza's worn fingers with his own.

And Eliza, suddenly touched by that word of unaccustomed praise and tenderness, turned and rushed blindly from the room at a clumsy bridling gait, clasping her hands together at the wrist, her weak eyes blind with tears—shaking her head in a strong convulsive movement, her mouth smiling a pale tremulous smile, ludicrous, touching, made unnatural by her false teeth, whispering over and over to herself, 'Poor fellow! Says, "There's no one else can cook a chicken like your mother." Reached out and patted me on the hand, you know. Says "I tell you what, there's no one who can cook a chicken like your mother." I reckon he wanted to let me know, to tell me, but says, "The rest of you have all been good to me, Helen's a good cook, but there's no one else can cook like your mother." '

'Oh, here, here, here,' said Helen, who, laughing uncertainly had followed her mother from the room when Eliza had rushed out, and had seized her by the arms, and shook her gently, 'good heavens! *Here!* You mustn't carry on like this! You mustn't take it this way! Why, he's all right!' she cried out heartily and shook

Eliza again. 'Papa's going to be all right! Why, what are you crying for?' she laughed. 'He's going to get well now—don't you know that?'

And Eliza could say nothing for a moment but kept smiling that false trembling and unnatural smile, shaking her head in a slight convulsive movement, her eyes blind with tears.

'I tell you what,' she whispered, smiling tremulously again and shaking her head, 'there was something about it—you know, the way he said it—says, "There's no one who can come up to your mother"—there was something in the way he said it! Poor fellow, says, "None of the rest of you can cook like her"—says, "I tell you what, that was certainly a good chicken"— Poor fellow! It wasn't so much what he said as the way he said it—there was something about it that went through me like a knife —I tell you what it did!'

'Oh, here, here, here!' Helen cried again, laughing. But her own eyes were also wet, the bitter possessiveness that had dominated all her relations with her father, and that had thrust Eliza away from him, was suddenly vanquished. At that moment she began to feel an affection for her mother that she had never felt before, a deep and nameless pity and regret, and a sense of sombre satisfaction.

'Well,' she thought, 'I guess it's all she's had, but I'm glad she's got that much to remember. I'm glad he said it: she'll always have that now to hang on to.'

And Gant lay looking up from that sunken depth of death and silence, his great hands of living power quiet with their immense and passive strength beside him on the bed.

4

Towards one o'clock that night Gant fell asleep and dreamed that he was walking down the road that led to Spangler's Run. And although he had not been along that road for fifty years everything was as fresh, as green, as living and familiar as it had ever been to him. He came out on the road from Schaefer's farm, and on his left he passed by the little white frame church of the United Brethren, and the graveyard about the church where his friends and family had been buried. From the road he could see the line of family gravestones which he himself had carved and set up after he had returned from serving his apprenticeship in Baltimore. The stones were all alike: tall flat slabs of marble with plain rounded tops, and there was one for his sister Susan, who had died in infancy, and one for his sister Huldah, who had died in childbirth while the war was on, and one for Huldah's husband, a young farmer named Jake Lentz who had been killed at Chancellorsville, and one for the husband of his oldest sister, Augusta, a man named Martin, who had been an itinerant photographer and had died soon after the war, and finally one for Gant's own father. And since there were no stones for his brother George or for Elmer or for John, and none for his mother or Augusta, Gant knew that he was still a young man, and had just recently come home. The stones which he had put up were still white and new, and in the lower right hand corner of each stone, he had carved his own name: W.O. Gant.

It was a fine morning in early May and everything was sweet and green and as familiar as it had always been. The graveyard was carpeted with thick green grass, and all around the graveyard and the church there was the incomparable green velvet of young wheat. And the thought came back to Gant, as it had come to him a thousand times, that the wheat around the graveyard looked greener and richer than any other wheat that he had ever seen. And beside him on his right were the great fields of the Schaefer farm, some richly carpeted with young green wheat, and some ploughed, showing great bronze-red strips of fertile nobly swelling earth. And behind him on the great swell of the land, and commanding that sweet and casual scene with the majesty of its incomparable lay was Jacob Schaefer's great red barn and to the right the neat brick house with the white trimming of its windows, the white picket fence, the green yard with its rich tapestry of flowers and lilac bushes and the massed leafy spread of its big maple trees. And behind the house the hill rose, and all its woods were just greening into May, still smoky, tender and unfledged, gold-yellow with the magic of young green. And before the woods began there was the apple orchard halfway up the hill; the trees were heavy with the blossoms and stood there in all their dense still bloom incredible.

And from the greening trees the bird-song rose, the grass was thick with the dense gold glory of the dandelions, and all about him were a thousand magic things that came and went and never could be captured. Below the church, he passed the old frame house where Elly Spangler, who kept the church keys, lived, and there were apple trees behind the house, all dense with bloom, but the house was rickety, unpainted and dilapidated as it had always been, and he wondered if the kitchen was still buzzing with a million flies, and if Elly's half-wit brothers, Jim and Willy, were inside. And even as he shook his head and thought, as he had thought so many times 'Poor Elly,' the back door opened and Willy Spangler, a man past thirty wearing overalls, and with a fond, foolish witless face, came galloping down across the yard toward him, flinging his arms out in exuberant greeting, and shouting to him the same welcome that he shouted out to every one who passed, friends and strangers all alike— 'I've been lookin' fer ye! I've been lookin' fer ye, Oll,' using, as was the custom of the friends and kinsmen of his Pennsylvania boyhood, his second name—and then, anxiously, pleadingly, again the same words that he spoke to every one: 'Ain't ye goin' to stay?'

And Gant, grinning, but touched by the indefinable sadness and pity which that kind and witless greeting had always stirred in him since his own childhood, shook his head, and said quietly:

'No, Willy. Not to-day. I'm meeting some one down the road'—and straightway felt, with thudding heart, a powerful and nameless excitement, the urgency of that impending meeting—why, where, with whom, he did not know—but all-compelling now, inevitable.

And Willy, still with wondering, foolish, kindly face followed along beside him now, saying eagerly, as he said to every one: 'Did ye bring anythin' fer me? Have ye got a chew?'

And Gant, starting to shake his head in refusal, stopped suddenly, seeing the look of disappointment on the idiot's face, and putting his hand in the pocket of his coat, took out a plug of apple-tobacco, saying:

'Yes. Here you are, Willy. You can have this.'

And Willy, grinning with foolish joy, had clutched the plug of tobacco and, still kind and foolish, had followed on a few steps more, saying anxiously:

'Are ye comin' back, Oll? Will ye be comin' back real soon?'

And Gant, feeling a strange and nameless sorrow, answered:

'I don't know, Willy'—for suddenly he saw that he might never come this way again.

But Willy, still happy, foolish, and contented, had turned and galloped away toward the house, flinging his arms out and shouting as he went:

'I'll be waitin' fer ye. I'll be waitin' fer ye, Oll.'

And Gant went on then, down the road, and there was a nameless sorrow in him that he could not understand, and some of the brightness had gone out of the day.

When he got to the mill, he turned left along the road that went down by Spangler's Run, crossed by the bridge below, and turned from the road into the wood-path on the other side. A child was standing in the path, and turned and went on ahead of him. In the wood the sunlight made swarming moths of light across the path, and through the leafy tangle of the trees: the sunlight kept shifting and swarming on the child's gold hair, and all around him were the sudden noises of the wood, the stir, the rustle, and the bullet thrum of wings, the cool broken sound of hidden water.

The wood got denser, darker as he went on and coming to a place where the path split away into two forks, Gant stopped, and turning to the child said, 'Which one shall I take?' And the child did not answer him.

But some one was there in the wood before him. He heard footsteps on the path, and saw a footprint in the earth, and turning took the path where the footprint was, and where it seemed he could hear some one walking.

And then, with the bridgeless instancy of dreams, it seemed to him that all of the bright green-gold around him in the wood grew dark and sombre, the path grew darker, and suddenly he was walking in a strange and gloomy forest, haunted by the brown and tragic light of dreams. The forest shapes of great trees rose around him, he could hear no bird-song now, even his own feet on the path were soundless, but he always thought he heard the sound of some one walking in the wood before him. He stopped and listened: the steps were muffled, softly thunderous, they seemed so near that he thought that he must catch up with the one he followed in another second, and then they seemed immensely far away, receding in the dark mystery of that gloomy wood. And again he stopped and listened, the footsteps faded, vanished, he shouted, no one answered. And suddenly he knew that he had taken the wrong path, that he was lost. And in his heart there was an immense and quiet sadness, and the dark light of the enormous wood was all around him; no birds sang.

5

Gant awoke suddenly and found himself looking straight up at Eliza who was seated in a chair beside the bed.

'You were asleep,' she said quietly with a grave smile, looking at him in her direct and almost accusing fashion.

'Yes,' he said, breathing a little hoarsely, 'what time is it?'

It was a few minutes before three o'clock in the morning. She looked at the clock and told him the time: he asked where Helen was.

'Why,' said Eliza quickly, 'she's right here in this hall room: I reckon she's asleep, too. Said she was tired, you know, but that if you woke up and needed her to call her. Do you want me to get her?'

'No,' said Gant. 'Don't bother her. I guess she needs the rest, poor child. Let her sleep.'

'Yes,' said Eliza, nodding, 'and that's exactly what you must do, too, Mr. Gant. You try to go on back to sleep now,' she said coaxingly, 'for that's what we all need. There's no medicine like sleep—as the fellow says, it's Nature's sovereign remedy,' said Eliza, with that form of sententiousness that she was very fond of— 'so you go on, now, Mr. Gant, and get a good night's sleep, and when you wake up in the morning, you'll feel like a new man. That's half the battle—if you can get your sleep, you're already on the road to recovery.'

'No,' said Gant, 'I've slept enough.'

He was breathing rather hoarsely and heavily and she asked him if he was comfortable and needed anything. He made no answer for a moment, and then muttered something under his breath that she could not hear plainly, but that sounded like 'little boy.'

'Hah? What say? What is it, Mr. Gant?' Eliza said. 'Little boy?' she said sharply, as he did not answer.

'Did you see him?' he said.

She looked at him for a moment with troubled eyes, then said:

'Pshaw, Mr. Gant, I guess you must have been dreaming.'

He did not answer, and for a moment there was no sound in the room but his breathing, hoarse, a little heavy. Then he muttered:

'Did some one come into the house?'

She looked at him sharply, inquiringly again, with troubled eyes:

'Hah? What say? Why, no, I think not,' she said doubtfully, 'unless you may have heard Gilmer come in an' go up to his room.'

And Gant was again silent for several moments, breathing a little heavily and hoarsely, his hands resting with an enormous passive strength, upon the bed. Presently he said quietly:

'Where's Bacchus?'

'Hah? Who's that?' Eliza said sharply, in a startled kind of tone. 'Bacchus? You mean Uncle Bacchus?'

'Yes,' said Gant.

'Why, pshaw, Mr. Gant!' cried Eliza laughing—for a startled moment she had wondered if 'his mind was wanderin',' but one glance at his quiet eyes, the tranquil sanity of his quiet tone, reassured her——

'Pshaw!' she said, putting one finger up to her broad nose-wing and laughing slyly. 'You must have been havin' queer dreams, for a fact!'

'Is he here?'

'Why, I'll vow, Mr. Gant!' she cried again. 'What on earth is in your mind? You know that Uncle Bacchus is way out West in Oregon—it's been ten years since he came back home last—that summer of the reunion at Gettysburg.'

'Yes,' said Gant. 'I remember now.'

And again he fell silent, staring upward in the semi-darkness, his hands quietly at rest beside him, breathing a little hoarsely, but without pain. Eliza sat in the chair watching him, her hands clasped loosely at her waist, her lips pursed reflectively, and a puzzled look in her eyes: 'Now I wonder what ever put that in his mind?' she thought. 'I wonder what made him think of Bacchus. Now his mind's not wanderin' —that's one thing sure. He knows what he's doing just as well as I do—I reckon he must have dreamed it—that Bacchus was here—but that's certainly a strange thing, that he should bring it up like this.'

He was so silent that she thought he might have gone to sleep again, he lay motionless with his eyes turned upward in the semi-darkness of the room, his hands immense and passive at his side. But suddenly he startled her again by speaking, a voice so quiet and low that he might have been talking to himself.

'Father died the year before the war,' he said, 'when I was nine years old. I never got to know him very well. I guess Mother had a hard time of it. There were seven of us—and nothing but that little place to live on—and some of us too young to help her much—and George away at war. She spoke pretty hard to us sometimes—but I guess she had a hard time of it. It was a tough time for all of us,' he muttered, 'I tell you what, it was.'

'Yes,' Eliza said, 'I guess it was. I know she told me—I talked to her, you know, the time we went there on our honeymoon— whew! what about it?' she shrieked faintly, and put her finger up to her broad nose-wing with the same sly gesture—'it was all I could do to keep a straight face sometimes—why, you know, the way she had of talkin'—the expressions she used—oh! came right out with it, you know—sometimes I'd have to turn my head away so she wouldn't see me laughin'—says, you know, "I was left a widow with seven children to bring up, but I never took charity from no one; as I told 'em all, I've crawled under the dog's belly all my life; now I guess I can get over its back."'

'Yes,' said Gant with a faint grin. 'Many's the time I've heard her say that.'

'But she told it then, you know,' Eliza went on in explanatory fashion, 'about your father and how he'd done hard labor on a farm all his life and died—well, I reckon you'd call it consumption.'

'Yes,' said Gant. 'That was it.'

'And,' Eliza said reflectively, 'I never asked—of course, I didn't want to embarrass her—but I reckon from what she said, he may have been—well, I suppose you might say he was a drinkin' man.'

'Yes,' said Gant, 'I guess he was.'

'And I know she told it on him,' said Eliza, laughing again, and passing one finger slyly at the corner of her broad nose-wing, 'how he went to town that time—to Brant's Mill, I guess it was—and how she was afraid he'd get to drinkin', and she sent you and Wes along to watch him and to see he got home again—and how he met up with some fellers there and, sure enough, I guess he started drinkin' and stayed away too long—and then, I reckon he was afraid of what she'd say to him when he got back—and that was when he bought the clock—it's that very clock upon the mantel, Mr. Gant—but that was when he got the clock, all right—I guess he thought it would pacify her when she started out to scold him for gettin' drunk and bein' late.'

'Yes,' said Gant, who had listened without moving, staring at the ceiling, and with a faint grin printed at the corners of his mouth, 'well do I remember: that was it, all right.'

'And then,' Eliza went on, 'he lost the way comin' home—it had been snowin', and I reckon it was getting dark, and he had been drinkin'—and instead of turnin' in on the road that went down by your place he kept goin' on until he passed Jake Schaefer's farm—an' I guess Wes and you, poor child, kept follerin' where he led, thinkin' it was all right—and when he realized his mistake he said he was tired an' had to rest a while and—I'll vow! to think he'd go and do a thing like that,' said Eliza, laughing again—'he lay right down in the snow, sir, with the clock beside him—and went sound to sleep.'

'Yes,' said Gant, 'and the clock was broken.'

'Yes,' Eliza said, 'she told me about that

too—and how she heard you all come creepin' in real quiet an' easy-like about nine o'clock that night, when she and all the children were in bed—an' how she could hear him whisperin' to you and Wes to be quiet—an' how she heard you all come creepin' up the steps—and how he came tip-toein' in real easy-like an' laid the clock down on the bed—I reckon the glass had been broken out of it—hopin' she'd see it when she woke up in the morning an' wouldn't scold him then for stayin' out——'

'Yes,' said Gant, still with the faint attentive grin, 'and then the clock began to strike.'

'Whew-w!' cried Eliza, putting her finger underneath her broad nose-wing—'I know she had to laugh about it when she told it to me—she said that all of you looked so sheepish when the clock began to strike that she didn't have the heart to scold him.'

And Gant, grinning faintly again, emitted a faint rusty cackle that sounded like 'E'God!' and said: 'Yes, that was it. Poor fellow.'

'But to think,' Eliza went on, 'that he would have no more sense than to do a thing like that—to lay right down there in the snow an' go to sleep with you two children watchin' him. And I know how she told it, how she questioned you and Wes next day, and I reckon started in to scold you for not takin' better care of him, and how you told her, "Well, Mother, I thought that it would be all right. I kept steppin' where he stepped, I thought he knew the way." And said she didn't have the heart to scold you after that—poor child, I reckon you were only eight or nine years old, and boy-like thought you'd follow in your father's footsteps and that everything would be all right.'

'Yes,' said Gant, with the faint grin again, 'I kept stretchin' my legs to put my feet down in his tracks—it was all I could do to keep up with him. . . . Ah, Lord,' he said, and in a moment said in a faint low voice, 'how well I can remember it. That was just the winter before he died.'

'And you've had that old clock ever since,' Eliza said. 'That very clock upon the mantel, sir—at least, you've had it ever since I've known you, and I reckon you had

it long before that—for I know you told me how you brought it South with you. And that clock must be all of sixty or seventy years old—if it's a day.'

'Yes,' said Gant, 'it's all of that.'

And again he was silent, and lay so still and motionless that there was no sound in the room except his faint and labored breathing, the languid stir of the curtains in the cool night breeze, and the punctual tocking of the old wooden clock. And presently, when she thought that he might have gone off to sleep again, he spoke, in the same remote and detached voice as before:

'Eliza,'—he said—and at the sound of that unaccustomed word, a name he had spoken only twice in forty years—her white face and her worn brown eyes turned toward him with the quick and startled look of an animal—'Eliza,' he said quietly, 'you have had a hard life with me, a hard time. I want to tell you that I'm sorry.'

And before she could move from her white stillness of shocked surprise, he lifted his great right hand and put it gently down across her own. And for a moment she sat there bolt upright, shaken, frozen, with a look of terror in her eyes, her heart drained of blood, a pale smile trembling uncertainly and foolishly on her lips. Then she tried to withdraw her hand with a clumsy movement, she began to stammer with an air of ludicrous embarrassment, she bridled, saying—'Aw-w, now, Mr. Gant. Well, now, I reckon,'—and suddenly these few simple words of regret and affection did what all the violence, abuse, drunkenness and injury of forty years had failed to do. She wrenched her hand free like a wounded creature, her face was suddenly contorted by that grotesque and pitiable grimace of sorrow that women have had in moments of grief since the beginning of time, and digging her fist into her closed eye quickly with the pathetic gesture of a child, she lowered her head and wept bitterly:

'It was a hard time, Mr. Gant,' she whispered, 'a hard time, sure enough. . . . It wasn't all the cursin' and the drinkin'— I got used to that. . . . I reckon I was only an ignorant sort of girl when I met you and I guess,' she went on with a pathetic and unconscious humor, 'I didn't know what married life was like . . . but I could have stood the rest of it . . . the bad names an' all the things you called me when I was goin' to have another child . . . but it was what you said when Grover died . . . accusin' me of bein' responsible for his death because I took the children to St. Louis to the Fair—' and at the words as if an old and lacerated wound had been re-opened raw and bleeding, she wept hoarsely, harshly, bitterly—'that was the worst time that I had—sometimes I prayed to God that I would not wake up—he was a fine boy, Mr. Gant, the best I had—like the write-up in the paper said he had the sense an' judgment of one twice his age . . . an' somehow it had grown a part of me, I expected him to lead the others— when he died it seemed like everything was gone . . . an' then to have you say that I had—' her voice faltered to a whisper, stopped: with a pathetic gesture she wiped the sleeve of her old frayed sweater across her eyes and already ashamed of her tears, said hastily:

'Not that I'm blamin' you, Mr. Gant. . . . I reckon we were both at fault . . . we were both to blame . . . if I had it to do all over I know I could do better . . . but I was so young and ig-norant when I met you, Mr. Gant . . . knew nothing of the world . . . there was always something strange-like about you that I didn't understand.'

Then, as he said nothing, but lay still and passive, looking at the ceiling, she said quickly, drying her eyes and speaking with a brisk and instant cheerfulness, the un-daunted optimism of her ever-hopeful nature:

'Well, now, Mr. Gant, that's all over, and the best thing we can do is to forget about it. . . . We've both made our mis-takes—we wouldn't be human if we didn't —but now we've got to profit by expe-rience—the worst of all this trouble is all over—you've got to think of getting well now, that's the only thing you've got to do, sir,' she said pursing her lips and winking briskly at him—'just set your mind on getting well—that's all you've got to do now, Mr. Gant—and the battle is half won. For half our ills and troubles are all imag-ination,' she said sententiously, 'and if

you'll just make up your mind now that you're going to get well—why, sir, you'll do it,' and she looked at him with a brisk nod. 'And we've both got years before us, Mr. Gant—for all we know, the best years of our life are still ahead of us—so we'll both go on and profit by the mistakes of the past and make the most of what time's left,' she said. 'That's just exactly what we'll do!'

And quietly, kindly, without moving, and with the impassive and limitless regret of a man who knows that there is no re-turn, he answered:

'Yes, Eliza. That is what we'll do.'

'And now,' she went on coaxingly, 'why don't you go on back to sleep now, Mr. Gant? There's nothin' like sleep to restore a man to health—as the feller says, it's Nature's sovereign remedy, worth all the doctors and all the medicine on earth,' she winked at him, and then concluded on a note of cheerful finality, 'so you go on and get some sleep now, and to-morrow you will feel like a new man.'

And again he shook his head in an almost imperceptible gesture of negation:

'No,' he said, 'not now. Can't sleep.'

He was silent again, and presently, his breath coming somewhat hoarse and la-bored, he cleared his throat, and put one hand up to his throat, as if to relieve him-self of some impediment.

Eliza looked at him with troubled eyes and said:

'What's the matter, Mr. Gant? There's nothing hurtin' you?'

'No,' he said. 'Just something in my throat. Could I have some water?'

'Why, yes, sir! That's the very thing!' She got up hastily, and looking about in a somewhat confused manner, saw behind her a pitcher of water and a glass upon his old walnut bureau, and saying 'This very minute, sir!' started across the room.

And at the same moment, Gant was aware that some one had entered the house, was coming towards him through the hall, would soon be with him. Turning his head towards the door he was conscious of something approaching with the speed of light, the instancy of thought, and at that moment he was filled with a sense of in-expressible joy, a feeling of triumph and security he had never known. Something immensely bright and beautiful was converging in a flare of light, and at that instant, the whole room blurred around him, his sight was fixed upon that focal image in the door, and suddenly the child was standing there and looking towards him.

And even as he started from his pillows, and tried to call his wife he felt something thick and heavy in his throat that would not let him speak. He tried to call to her again but no sound came, then something wet and warm began to flow out of his mouth and nostrils, he lifted his hands up to his throat, the warm wet blood came pouring out across his fingers; he saw it and felt joy.

For now the child—or some one in the house was speaking, calling to him; he heard great footsteps, soft but thunderous, imminent, yet immensely far, a voice well-known, never heard before. He called to it, and then it seemed to answer him; he called to it with faith and joy to give him rescue, strength, and life, and it answered him and told him that all the error, old age, pain and grief of life was nothing but an evil dream; that he who had been lost was found again, that his youth would be restored to him and that he would never die, and that he would find again the path he had not taken long ago in a dark wood.

And the child still smiled at him from the dark door; the great steps, soft and powerful, came ever closer, and as the instant imminent approach of that last meeting came intolerably near, he cried out through the lake of jetting blood, 'Here, Father, here!' and heard a strong voice answer him, 'My son!'

At that instant he was torn by a rending cough, something was wrenched loose in him, the death gasp rattled through his blood, and a mass of greenish matter foamed out through his lips. Then the world was blotted out, a blind black fog swam up and closed above his head, some one seized him, he was held, supported in two arms, he heard some one's voice saying in a low tone of terror and of pity, 'Mr. Gant! Mr. Gant! Oh, poor man, poor man! He's gone!' And his brain faded into night. Even before she lowered him back upon the pillows, she knew that he was dead.

Eliza's sharp scream brought three of her children—Daisy, Steve, and Luke, and the nurse, Bessie Gant, who was the wife of Gant's nephew Ollie—running from the kitchen. At the same moment Helen, who had taken an hour's sleep—her first in two days—in the little hall-bedroom off the porch, was wakened by her mother's cry, the sound of a screen-door slammed, and the sound of footsteps running past her window on the porch. Then, for several minutes she had no consciousness of what she did, and later she could not remember it. Her actions were those of a person driven by a desperate force, who acts from blind intuition, not from reason. Instantly, the moment that she heard her mother scream, the slam of the screen-door, and the running feet, she knew what had happened, and from that moment she knew only one frenzied desire; somehow to get to her father before he died.

The breath caught hoarse and sharp in her throat in a kind of nervous sob, it seemed that her heart had stopped beating and that her whole life-force was paralyzed; but she was out of her bed with a movement that left the old springs rattling, and she came across the back-porch with a kind of tornado-like speed that just came instantly from nowhere: in a moment she was standing in the open door with the sudden bolted look of a person who has been shot through the heart, staring at the silent group of people, and at the figure on the bed, with a dull strained stare of disbelief and horror.

All the time, although she was not conscious of it, her breath kept coming in a kind of hoarse short sob, her large big-boned face had an almost animal look of anguish and surprise, her mouth was partly open, her large chin hung down, and at this moment, as they turned towards her she began to moan, 'Oh-h, oh-h, oh-h, oh-h!' in the same unconscious way, like a person who has received a heavy blow in the pit of the stomach. Then her mouth gaped open, a hoarse and ugly cry was torn from her throat—a cry not of grief but loss—and she rushed forward like a mad woman. They tried to stop her, to restrain her, she flung them away as if they had been rag dolls and hurled herself down across the body on the bed, raving like a maniac.

'Oh, Papa, Papa. . . . Why didn't they

tell me? . . . Why didn't they let me know? . . . Why didn't they call me? . . . Oh, Papa, Papa, Papa! . . . dead, dead, dead . . . and they didn't tell me . . . they didn't let me know . . . they let you die . . . and I wasn't here! . . . I wasn't here!'—and she wept harshly, horribly, bitterly, rocking back and forth like a mad woman, with a dead man in her arms. She kept moaning, '. . . They didn't tell me . . . they let you die without me . . . I wasn't here . . . I wasn't here . . .'

And even when they lifted her up from the bed, detached her arms from the body they had held in such a desperate hug, she still kept moaning in a demented manner, as if talking to the corpse, and oblivious of the presence of these living people:

'They never told me . . . they never told me. . . . They let you die here all by yourself . . . and I wasn't here . . . I wasn't here.'

All of the women, except Bessie Gant, had now begun to weep hysterically, more from shock, exhaustion, and the nervous strain than from grief, and now Bessie Gant's voice could be heard speaking to them sharply, coldly, peremptorily, as she tried to bring back order and calmness to the distracted scene:

'Now, you get out of here—all of you! . . . There's nothing more any of you can do—I'll take care of all the rest of it! . . . Get out, now . . . I can't have you in the room while there's work to do. . . . Helen, go on back to bed and get some sleep. . . . You'll feel better in the morning.'

'They never told me! . . . They never told me,' she turned and stared stupidly at Bessie Gant with dull glazed eyes. 'Can't you do something? . . . Where's Mc-Guire? Has any one called him yet?'

'No,' said the nurse sharply and angrily, 'and no one's going to. You're not going to get that man out of bed at this hour of the night when there's nothing to be done. . . . Get out of here, now, all of you,' she began to push and herd them towards the door. 'I can't be bothered with you. . . . Go somewhere—anywhere—get drunk—only don't come back in here.'

The whole house had come to life; in the excitement, shock, and exhaustion of their nerves the dead man still lying there in such a grotesque and twisted position, was forgotten. One of Eliza's lodgers, a man named Gilmer, who had been in the house for years, was wakened, went out, and got a gallon of corn whiskey; every one drank a great deal, became, in fact, somewhat intoxicated; when the undertakers came to take Gant away, none of the family was present. No one saw it. They were all in the kitchen seated around Eliza's battered old kitchen table, with the jug of whiskey on the table before them. They drank and talked together all night long until dawn came.

6

The morning of Gant's funeral the house was filled with people who had known him and the air was heavy with the sweet, cloying fragrance of the funeral flowers: the odors of lilies, roses, and carnations. His coffin was banked with flowers, but in the centre there was a curious and arresting plainness, a simple wreath of laurel leaves. Attached to the wreath was a small card on which these words were written: 'Hugh McGuire.'

And people passing by the coffin paused for a moment and stared at the name with a feeling of unspoken wonder in their hearts. Eliza stood looking at the wreath a moment with hands clasped across her waist, and then turned away, shaking her head rapidly, with a short convulsive pucker of her lips, as she spoke to Helen in a low voice:

'I tell you what—it's pretty strange when you come to think of it—it gives you a queer feeling—I tell you what, it does.'

And this expressed the emotion that every one felt when they saw the wreath. For Hugh McGuire had been found dead at his desk at six o'clock that morning, the news had just spread through the town, and now, when people saw the wreath upon Gant's coffin, there was something in their hearts they could not utter.

Gant lay in the splendid coffin, with his great hands folded quietly on his breast. Later, the boy could not forget his father's hands. They were the largest, most powerful, and somehow the most shapely hands he had ever seen. And even though his great right hand had been so crippled and stiffened by an attack of inflammatory rheumatism ten years before that he had never regained the full use of it, and since that time could only hold the great wooden mallet that the stonecutters use in a painful and clumsy half-clasp between the thumb and the big stiffened fingers, his hands had never lost their character of life, strength, and powerful shapeliness.

The hands had given to the interminable protraction of his living death a kind of concrete horror that it otherwise would not have had. For as his powerful gaunt figure waned and wasted under the ravages of the cancer that was consuming him until he had become only the enfeebled shadow of his former self, his gaunt hands, on which there was so little which death could consume, lost none of their former rocklike heaviness, strength and shapely power. Thus, even when the giant figure of the man had become nothing but a spectral remnant of itself, sunk in a sorrow of time, awaiting death, those great, still-living hands of power and strength hung incredibly, horribly, from that spectral form of death to which they were attached.

And for this reason those powerful hands of life evoked, as nothing else could have done, in an instant searing flash of memory and recognition the lost world of his father's life of manual power, hunger, fury, savage abundance and wild joy, the whole enchanted structure of that lost life of magic he had made for them. Constantly, those great hands of life joined, with an almost grotesque incongruity, to that scarecrow form of wasting death would awake for them, as nothing else on earth could do, all of the sorrowful ghosts of time, the dream-like spell and terror of the years between, the years of phantom death, the horror of unreality, strangeness, disbelief, and memory, that haunted them.

So was it now, even in death, with his father's hands. In their powerful, gaunt and shapely clasp, as he lay dead in his coffin, there seemed to be held and gathered, somehow, all of his life that could never die—a living image of the essential quality of his whole life with its fury and unrest, desire and hunger, the tremendous sweep and relish of its enormous appetites and the huge endowment of its physical and sensual powers.

Thus, one could suppose that on the face of a dead poet there might remain—how, where or in what way we could not tell, a kind of flame, a light, a glory,—the magic and still living chrysm of his genius. And on the face of the dead conqueror we might still see living, arrogant, and proud with all its dark authorities the frown of power, the inflexible tyranny of stern command, the special infinitude of the invincible will that would not die with life, and that incredibly remains, still dark and living in its scorn and mockery of time.

Then, on the face of an old dead prophet or philosopher there would live and would not die the immortality of proud, lonely thought. We could not say just where that spirit rested. Sometimes it would seem to rest upon the temples of the grand and lonely head. Sometimes we would think it was a kind of darkness in the shadows of the closed and sunken eyes, sometimes the marsh fire of a dark and lambent flame that hovered round the face, that could never be fixed, but that we always knew was there.

And just as poet, prophet, priest and conqueror might each retain in death some living and fitting image of his whole life's truth, so would the strength, the skill, all of the hope, hunger, fury, and unrest that had lashed and driven on through life the gaunt figure of a stonecutter be marvellously preserved in the granite power and symmetry of those undying hands.

Now the corpse was stretched out on the splendid satin cushions of the expensive coffin. It has been barbered, powdered, disembowelled, and pumped full of embalming fluid. And as it lay there with its waxen head set forward in its curious gaunt projectiveness, the pale lips firmly closed and with a little line of waxen mucous in the lips, the women came forward with their oily swollen faces, and a look of ravenous eagerness in their eyes, stared at it hard and long, lifted their sodden handkerchiefs slowly to their oily mouths, and were borne away, sobbing hysterically, by their equally oily, ravenous, sister orgiasts in sorrow.

Meanwhile his father's friends, the stonecutters, masons, building contractors, butchers, business men and male relatives were standing awkwardly about, dressed in their good, black clothes which they seemed not to wear so much as to inhabit with a kind of unrestful itchiness, lowering their eyes gravely and regretfully as the women put on their revolting show, talking together in low voices, and wondering when it would all be over.

These circumstances, together with the heavy unnatural languor of the funeral smells, the sweet-sick heaviness of the carnations, the funereal weepy blacks in which the women had arrayed themselves, the satiny sandalwood scent that came from the splendid coffin, and the fragrant faintly acrid odor of embalmed flesh, particularly when blended with the smell of cooking turnip greens, roast pork and apple sauce out in the kitchen, combined to create an atmosphere somewhat like a dinner party in a comfortably furnished morgue.

In all this obscene pomp of burial there was something so grotesque, unnatural, disgusting, and remote from all he could remember of the dead man's life and personality that everything about him—even the physical horror of his bloody death— now seemed so far away he could hardly believe it ever happened. Therefore, he stared at this waxen and eviscerated relic in the coffin with a sense of weird disbelief, unable to relate it to the living man who had bled great lakes of blood the night before.

Yet, even in his death, his father's hands still seemed to live, and would not die. And this was the reason why the memory of those hands haunted him then and would haunt him forever after. This was the reason why, when he would try to remember how he looked when dead, he could remember nothing clearly except the powerful sculptured weight and symmetry of his tremendous hands as they lay folded on his body in the coffin. The great hands had a stony, sculptured and yet living strength and vitality, as if Michelangelo had carved them. They seemed to rest there upon the groomed, bereft and vacant horror of the corpse with a kind of terrible reality as if there really is, in death, some energy of life that will not die, some element of man's life that must persist and that resumes into a single feature of his life the core and essence of his character.

1934   1935

HART CRANE

1899–1932

GENERAL AIMS AND THEORIES [1]

WHEN I started writing Faustus & Helen it was my intention to embody in modern terms (words, symbols, metaphors) a contemporary approximation to an ancient human culture or mythology that seems to have been obscured rather than illumined with the frequency of poetic allusions made to it during the last century. The name of Helen, for instance, has become an all-too-easily employed crutch for evocation whenever a poet felt a stitch in his side. The real evocation of this (to me) very real and absolute conception of beauty seemed to consist in a reconstruction in these modern terms of the basic emotional attitude toward beauty that the Greeks had. And in so doing I found that I was really building a bridge between so-called classic experience and many divergent realities of our seething, confused cosmos of today, which has no formulated mythology yet for classic poetic reference or for religious exploitation.

So I found 'Helen' sitting in a street car; the Dionysian revels of her court and her seduction were transferred to a Metropolitan roof garden with a jazz orchestra; and the katharsis of the fall of Troy I saw approximated in the recent World War. The importance of this scaffolding may easily be exaggerated, but it gave me a series of correspondences between two widely separated worlds on which to sound some major themes of human speculation— love, beauty, death, renascence. It was a kind of grafting process that I shall doubt-

1 This explanatory essay was given by Crane to his friend Miss Laura Riding, and remained unpublished until its inclusion in Philip Horton's Hart Crane (N.Y., 1937).

less not be interested in repeating, but which is consistent with subsequent theories of mine on the relation of tradition to the contemporary creating imagination.

It is a terrific problem that faces the poet today—a world that is so in transition from a decayed culture toward a reorganization of human evaluations that there are few common terms, general denominators of speech that are solid enough or that ring with any vibration or spiritual conviction. The great mythologies of the past (including the Church) are deprived of enough façade to even launch good raillery against. Yet much of their traditions are operative still—in millions of chance combinations of related and unrelated detail, psychological reference, figures of speech, precepts, etc. These are all a part of our common experience and the terms, at least partially, of that very experience when it defines or extends itself.

The deliberate program, then, of a 'break' with the past or tradition seems to me to be a sentimental fallacy. . . . The poet has a right to draw on whatever practical resources he finds in books or otherwise about him. He must tax his sensibility and his touchstone of experience for the proper selections of these themes and details, however,—and that is where he either stands, or falls into useless archeology.

I put no particular value on the simple objective of 'modernity.' The element of the temporal location of an artist's creation is of very secondary importance; it can be left to the impressionist or historian just as well. It seems to me that a poet will accidentally define his time well enough simply by reacting honestly and to the full extent of his sensibilities to the states of passion, experience and rumination that fate forces on him, first hand. He must, of course, have a sufficiently universal basis of experience to make his imagination selective and valuable. His picture of the 'period,' then, will simply be a by-product of his curiosity and the relation of his experience to a postulated 'eternity.'

I am concerned with the future of America, but not because I think that America has any so-called par value as a state or as a group of people. . . . It is only because I feel persuaded that here are destined to be discovered certain as yet undefined spiritual quantities, perhaps a new hierarchy of faith not to be developed so completely elsewhere. And in this process I like to feel myself as a potential factor; certainly I must speak in its terms and what discoveries I may make are situated in its experience.

But to fool one's self that definitions are being reached by merely referring frequently to skyscrapers, radio antennæ, steam whistles, or other surface phenomena of our time is merely to paint a photograph. I think that what is interesting and significant will emerge only under the conditions of our submission to, and examination and assimilation of the organic effects on us of these and other fundamental factors of our experience. It can certainly not be an organic expression otherwise. And the expression of such values may often be as well accomplished with the vocabulary and blank verse of the Elizabethans as with the calligraphic tricks and slang used so brilliantly at times by an impressionist like Cummings.

It may not be possible to say that there is, strictly speaking, any 'absolute' experience. But it seems evident that certain æsthetic experience (and this may for a time engross the total faculties of the spectator) can be called absolute, inasmuch as it approximates a formally convincing statement of a conception or apprehension of life that gains our unquestioning assent, and under the conditions of which our imagination is unable to suggest a further detail consistent with the design of the æsthetic whole.

I have been called an 'absolutist' in poetry, and if I am to welcome such a label it should be under the terms of the above definition. It is really only a *modus operandi*, however, and as such has been used organically before by at least a dozen poets such as Donne, Blake, Baudelaire, Rimbaud, etc. I may succeed in defining it better by contrasting it with the impressionistic method. The impressionist is interesting as far as he goes—but his goal has been reached when he has succeeded in projecting certain selected factual details into his reader's consciousness. He is really not interested in the *causes* (metaphysical) of his materials, their emotional derivations or their utmost spiritual consequences. A kind of retinal registration is enough, along with a certain psychological stimulation. And this is also true of your realist (of the Zola type), and to a certain extent of the classicist, like Horace, Ovid, Pope, etc.

Blake meant these differences when he wrote:

> We are led to believe in a lie
> When we see *with* not *through* the eye.

The impressionist creates only with the eye and for the readiest surface of the consciousness, at least relatively so. If the effect has been harmonious or even stimulating, he can stop there, relinquishing entirely to his audience the problematic synthesis of the details into terms of their own personal consciousness.

It is my hope to go *through* the combined materials of the poem, using our 'real' world somewhat as a spring-board, and to give the poem *as a whole* an orbit or predetermined direction of its own. I would like to establish it as free from my own personality as from any chance evaluation on the reader's part. (This is, of course, an impossibility, but it is a characteristic worth mentioning.) Such a poem is at least a stab at a truth, and to such an extent may be differentiated from other kinds of poetry and called 'absolute.' Its evocation will not be toward decoration or amusement, but rather toward a state of consciousness, an 'innocence' (Blake) or absolute beauty. In this condition there may be discoverable under new forms certain spiritual illuminations, shining with a morality essentialized from experience directly, and not from previous precepts or preconceptions. It is as though a poem gave the reader as he left it a single, new *word*, never before spoken and impossible to actually enunciate, but self-evident as an active principle in the reader's consciousness henceforward.

As to technical considerations: the motivation of the poem must be derived from the implicit emotional dynamics of the materials used, and the terms of expression employed are often selected less for their logical (literal) significance than for their associational meanings. Via this and their metaphorical inter-relationships, the entire construction of the poem is raised on the organic principle of a 'logic of metaphor,' which antedates our so-called pure logic, and which is the genetic basis of all speech, hence consciousness and thought-extension.

These dynamics often result, I'm told, in certain initial difficulties in understanding my poems. But on the other hand I find them at times the only means possible for expressing certain concepts in any forceful or direct way whatever. To cite two examples:—when, in Voyages (II), I speak of 'adagios of islands,' the reference is to the motion of a boat through islands clustered thickly, the rhythm of the motion, etc. And it seems a much more direct and creative statement than any more logical employment of words such as 'coasting slowly through the islands,' besides ushering in a whole world of music. Similarly in Faustus and Helen (III) the speed and tense altitude of an aeroplane are much better suggested by the idea of 'nimble blue plateaus'—*implying* the aeroplane and its speed against a contrast of stationary elevated earth. Although the statement is pseudo in relation to formal logic—it *is* completely logical in relation to the truth of the imagination, and there is expressed a concept of speed and space that could not be handled so well in other terms.

In manipulating the more imponderable phenomena of psychic motives, pure emotional crystallizations, etc., I have had to rely even more on these dynamics of inferential mention, and I am doubtless still very unconscious of having committed myself to what seems nothing but obscurities to some minds. A poem like Possessions really cannot be technically explained. It must rely (even to a large extent with myself) on its organic impact on the imagination to successfully imply its meaning. This seems to me to present an exceptionally difficult problem, however, considering the real clarity and consistent logic of many of the other poems.

I know that I run the risk of much criticism by defending such theories as I have, but as it is part of a poet's business to risk not only criticism—but folly—in the conquest of consciousness I can only say that I attach no intrinsic value to what means I use beyond their practical service in giving form to the living stuff of the imagination.

New conditions of life germinate new

forms of spiritual articulation. And while I feel that my work includes a more consistent extension of traditional literary elements than many contemporary poets are capable of appraising, I realize that I am utilizing the gifts of the past as instruments principally; and that the voice of the present, if it is to be known, must be caught at the risk of speaking in idioms and circumlocutions sometimes shocking to the scholar and historians of logic. Language has built towers and bridges, but itself is inevitably as fluid as always.

1925   1937

FOR THE MARRIAGE OF FAUSTUS AND HELEN [1]

> *'And so we may arrive by Talmud skill*
> *And profane Greek to raise the building up*
> *Of Helen's house against the Ismaelite,*
> *King of Thogarma, and his habergeons*
> *Brimstony, blue and fiery; and the force*
> *Of King Abaddon, and the beast of Cittim;*
> *Which Rabbi David Kimchi, Onkelos,*
> *And Aben Ezra do interpret Rome.'*
>
> —THE ALCHEMIST

I

THE mind has shown itself at times
Too much the baked and labeled dough
Divided by accepted multitudes.
Across the stacked partitions of the day—
Across the memoranda, baseball scores,
The stenographic smiles and stock
      quotations
Smutty wings flash out equivocations.

---

1 Horton says of this poem: 'Arranged in three parts, which he conceived as spanning a rising scale from the "quotidian" to the universal, this work was his first attempt to deal with the major problems of poetry. That parts as he described them were colorless abstractions: first, "Meditation, Evocation, Love, Beauty"; second, "Dance, Humor, Satisfaction"; and third, "Tragedy, War (the eternal soldier), Résumé, Ecstasy, Final Declaration." But the symbolism he chose provided a concrete, even a dramatic, framework. Once it is known that Helen is "the symbol of this abstract 'sense of beauty'—Faustus the symbol of myself, the poetic or imaginative man of all time," the action of the poem and its philosophical implications become perfectly apparent. Crane imagined the poem as a kind of prothalamion celebrating his pursuit and capture of the Platonic idea of beauty, and at the same time defining his relation not only to his art, but also to the world of tradition in which beauty had sometimes lived as a vital principle.' Horton, *Hart Crane* (N.Y., 1937), 119–20.

The mind is brushed by sparrow wings;
Numbers, rebuffed by asphalt, crowd   9
The margins of the day, accent the curbs,
Convoying divers dawns on every corner
To druggist, barber and tobacconist,
Until the graduate opacities of evening
Take them away as suddenly to somewhere
Virginal perhaps, less fragmentary, cool.

> *There is the world dimensional*
> *for those untwisted by the love of*
> *things irreconcilable . . .*

And yet, suppose some evening I forgot
The fare and transfer, yet go by that way
Without recall,—lost yet poised in traffic.
Then I might find your eyes across an
      aisle,
Still flickering with those prefigurations—
Prodigal, yet uncontested now,   21
Half-riant before the jerky window frame.

There is some way, I think, to touch
Those hands of yours that count the nights
Stippled with pink and green
      advertisements.
And now, before its arteries turn dark,
I would have you meet this bartered blood.
Imminent in his dream, none better knows
The white wafer cheek of love, or offers
      words
Lightly as moonlight on the eaves meets
      snow.   30

Reflective conversion of all things
At your deep blush, when ecstasies thread
The limbs and belly, when rainbows spread
Impinging on the throat and sides . . .
Inevitable, the body of the world
Weeps in inventive dust for the hiatus
That winks above it, bluet in your breasts.

The earth may glide diaphanous to death;
But if I lift my arms it is to bend
To you who turned away once, Helen,
      knowing   40
The press of troubled hands, too alternate
With steel and soil to hold you endlessly.
I meet you, therefore, in that eventual
      flame
You found in final chains, no captive then—
Beyond their million brittle, bloodshot
      eyes;
White, through white cities passed on to
      assume

That world which comes to each of us
    alone.

Accept a lone eye riveted to your plane,
Bent axle of devotion along companion
    ways   49
That beat, continuous, to hourless days—
One inconspicuous, glowing orb of praise.

II

Brazen hypnotics glitter here;
Glee shifts from foot to foot,
Magnetic to their tremolo.
This crashing opéra bouffe,
Blest excursion! this ricochet
From roof to roof—
Know, Olympians, we are breathless
While nigger cupids scour the stars!

A thousand light shrugs balance us   60
Through snarling hails of melody.
White shadows slip across the floor
Splayed like cards from a loose hand;
Rhythmic ellipses lead into canters
Until somewhere a rooster banters.

Greet naïvely—yet intrepidly
New soothings, new amazements
That cornets introduce at every turn—
And you may fall downstairs with me
With perfect grace and equanimity.   70
Or, plaintively scud past shores
Where, by strange harmonic laws
All relatives, serene and cool,
Sit rocked in patent armchairs.

O, I have known metallic paradises
Where cuckoos clucked to finches
Above the deft catastrophes of drums.
While titters hailed the groans of death
Beneath gyrating awnings I have seen
The incunabula of the divine grotesque.   80
This music has a reassuring way.

The siren of the springs of guilty song—
Let us take her on the incandescent wax
Striated with nuances, nervosities
That we are heir to: she is still so young,
We cannot frown upon her as she smiles,
Dipping here in this cultivated storm
Among slim skaters of the gardened skies.

III

Capped arbiter of beauty in this street
That narrows darkly into motor dawn,—   90

You, here beside me, delicate ambassador
Of intricate slain numbers that arise
In whispers, naked of steel;
                religious gunman!
Who faithfully, yourself, will fall too soon,
And in other ways than as the wind settles
On the sixteen thrifty bridges of the city:
Let us unbind our throats of fear and pity.

                We even,
Who drove speediest destruction   100
In corymbulous formations of
    mechanics,—
Who hurried the hill breezes, spouting
    malice
Plangent over meadows, and looked down
On rifts of torn and empty houses
Like old women with teeth unjubilant
That waited faintly, briefly and in vain:

We know, eternal gunman, our flesh
    remembers
The tensile boughs, the nimble blue
    plateaus,
The mounted, yielding cities of the air!
That saddled sky that shook down vertical
Repeated play of fire—no hypogeum   111
Of wave or rock was good against one hour.

We did not ask for that, but have survived,
And will persist to speak again before
All stubble streets that have not curved
To memory, or known the ominous lifted
    arm
That lowers down the arc of Helen's brow
To saturate with blessing and dismay.

A goose, tobacco and cologne—
Three-winged and gold-shod prophecies of
    heaven,   120
The lavish heart shall always have to leaven
And spread with bells and voices, and atone
The abating shadows of our conscript dust.

Anchises' navel, dripping of the sea,—
The hands Erasmus dipped in gleaming
    tides,
Gathered the voltage of blown blood and
    vine;
Delve upward for the new and scattered
    wine,
O brother-thief of time, that we recall.
Laugh out the meager penance of their days
Who dare not share with us the breath
    released,   130

The substance drilled and spent beyond
    repair
For golden, or the shadow of gold hair.

Distinctly praise the years, whose volatile
Blamed bleeding hands extend and thresh
    the height
The imagination spans beyond despair,
Outpacing bargain, vocable and prayer.
1923   1926

BLACK TAMBOURINE

THE interests of a black man in a cellar
Mark tardy judgment on the world's closed
    door.
Gnats toss in the shadow of a bottle,
And a roach spans a crevice in the
    floor.

Æsop, driven to pondering, found
Heaven with the tortoise and the hare;
Fox brush and sow ear top his grave
And mingling incantations on the air.

The black man, forlorn in the cellar,
Wanders in some mid-kingdom, dark, that
    lies,   10
Between his tambourine, stuck on the
    wall,
And, in Africa, a carcass quick with flies.
1921   1926

PRAISE FOR AN URN

IN MEMORIAM: ERNEST NELSON

IT was a kind and northern face
That mingled in such exile guise
The everlasting eyes of Pierrot
And, of Gargantua, the laughter.

His thoughts, delivered to me
From the white coverlet and pillow,
I see now, were inheritances—
Delicate riders of the storm.

The slant moon on the slanting hill
Once moved us toward presentiments 10
Of what the dead keep, living still,
And such assessments of the soul

As, perched in the crematory lobby,
The insistent clock commented on,
Touching as well upon our praise
Of glories proper to the time.

Still, having in mind gold hair,
I cannot see that broken brow
And miss the dry sound of bees
Stretching across a lucid space.   20

Scatter these well-meant idioms
Into the smoky spring that fills
The suburbs, where they will be lost.
They are no trophies of the sun.
1922   1926

FROM VOYAGES

2

AND yet this great wink of eternity,
Of rimless floods, unfettered leewardings,
Samite sheeted and processioned where
Her undinal vast belly moonward bends,
Laughing the wrapt inflections of our
    love;

Take this Sea, whose diapason knells
On scrolls of silver snowy sentences,
The sceptred terror of whose sessions
    rends
As her demeanors motion well or ill,
All but the pieties of lovers' hands.   10

And onward, as bells off San Salvador
Salute the crocus lustres of the stars,
In these poinsettia meadows of her
    tides,—
Adagios of islands, O my Prodigal,
Complete the dark confessions her veins
    spell.

Mark how her turning shoulders wind the
    hours,
And hasten while her penniless rich
    palms
Pass superscription of bent foam and
    wave,—
Hasten, while they are true,—sleep, death,
    desire,
Close round one instant in one floating
    flower.   20

Bind us in time, O Seasons clear, and
    awe.
O minstrel galleons of Carib fire,
Bequeath us to no earthly shore until
Is answered in the vortex of our grave
The seal's wide spindrift gaze toward
    paradise.
1924–1925   1926

FROM THE BRIDGE

PROEM:

TO BROOKLYN BRIDGE [1]

How many dawns, chill from his rippling
    rest
The seagull's wings shall dip and pivot him,
Shedding white rings of tumult, building
    high
Over the chained bay waters Liberty—

Then, with inviolate curve, forsake our eyes
As apparitional as sails that cross
Some page of figures to be filed away;
—Till elevators drop us from our day . . .

I think of cinemas, panoramic sleights
With multitudes bent toward some flashing
    scene   10
Never disclosed, but hastened to again,
Foretold to other eyes on the same screen;

And Thee, across the harbor, silver-paced
As though the sun took step of thee, yet left
Some motion ever unspent in thy stride,—
Implicitly thy freedom staying thee!

Out of some subway scuttle, cell or loft
A bedlamite speeds to thy parapets,
Tilting there momently, shrill shirt
    ballooning,
A jest falls from the speechless caravan.   20

Down Wall, from girder into street noon
    leaks,
A rip-tooth of the sky's acetylene;
All afternoon the cloud-flown derricks
    turn . . .
Thy cables breathe the North Atlantic still.

And obscure as that heaven of the Jews,
Thy guerdon . . . Accolade thou dost
    bestow
Of anonymity time cannot raise:
Vibrant reprieve and pardon thou dost show.

O harp and altar, of the fury fused,
(How could mere toil align thy choiring
    strings!)   30
Terrific threshold of the prophet's pledge,
Prayer of pariah, and the lover's cry,—

Again the traffic lights that skim thy swift
Unfractioned idiom, immaculate sigh of
    stars,
Beading thy path—condense eternity:
And we have seen night lifted in thine arms.

Under thy shadow by the piers I waited;
Only in darkness is thy shadow clear.
The City's fiery parcels all undone,
Already snow submerges an iron year . . .

O Sleepless as the river under thee,   41
Vaulting the sea, the prairies' dreaming sod,
Unto us lowliest sometime sweep, descend
And of the curveship lend a myth to God.
1926   1930

II.4

THE DANCE [2]

THE swift red flesh, a winter king—
Who squired the glacier woman down the
    sky?
She ran the neighing canyons all the spring;
She spouted arms; she rose with maize—to
    die.

And in the autumn drouth, whose
    burnished hands

1 Crane wrote, 18 Feb. 1923, to a friend: 'Very roughly,
it [The Bridge] concerns a mystical synthesis of America. History and fact, location etc. all have to be transfigured into abstract form that would almost function
independently of its subject matter. The initial impulses of our people will have to be gathered up toward
the climax of the bridge, symbol of our constructive
future, our unique identity, in which is also included
our scientific hopes and achievements of the future.'
Ibid.,142.

2 'The Dance' is from Part II: 'Powhatan's Daughter.'
Crane wrote, 12 Sept. 1927, of it to Otto Kahn:
'Powhatan's daughter, or Pocahontas, is the mythological nature-symbol chosen to represent the physical
body of the continent, or the soil. . . . The five sub-
sections of Part II are mainly concerned with a gradual
exploration of this "body" whose first possessor was
the Indian. . . . [Section] 4. "The Dance": Here one
is on the pure mythical and smoky soil at last! Not
only do I describe the conflict between the two races
in this dance—I also become identified with the
Indian and his world before it is over, which is the
only method possible of ever really possessing the
Indian and his world as a cultural factor. I think I
really succeed in getting under the skin of this glorious
and dying animal, in terms of expression, in symbols,
which he, himself, would comprehend. Pocahontas
(the continent) is the common basis of our meeting,
she survives the extinction of the Indian, who finally,
after being assumed into the elements of nature (as
he understood them) persists only as a kind of "eye"
in the sky, or as a star that hangs between day
and night—"the twilight's dim perpetual throne." '
Ibid.,335-38.

With mineral wariness found out the stone
Where prayers, forgotten, streamed the
    mesa sands?
He holds the twilight's dim, perpetual
    throne.

Mythical brows we saw retiring—loth,   9
Disturbed and destined, into denser green.
Greeting they sped us, on the arrow's oath:
Now lie incorrigibly what years
    between . . .

There was a bed of leaves, and broken play;
There was a veil upon you, Pocahontas,
    bride—
O princess whose brown lap was virgin
    May;
And bridal flanks and eyes hid tawny pride.

I left the village for dogwood. By the canoe
Tugging below the mill-race, I could see
Your hair's keen crescent running, and the
    blue   19
First moth of evening take wing stealthily.

What laughing chains the water wove and
    threw!
I learned to catch the trout's moon
    whisper; I
Drifted how many hours I never knew,
But, watching, saw that fleet young crescent
    die,—

And one star, swinging, take its place,
    alone,
Cupped in the larches of the mountain
    pass—
Until, immortally, it bled into the dawn.
I left my sleek boat nibbling margin
    grass . . .

I took the portage climb, then chose
A further valley-shed; I could not stop.   30
Feet nozzled wat'ry webs of upper flows;
One white veil gusted from the very top.

O Appalachian Spring! I gained the ledge;
Steep, inaccessible smile that eastward
    bends
And northward reaches in that violet
    wedge
Of Adirondacks!—wisped of azure wands,

Over how many bluffs, tarns, streams I
    sped!

—And knew myself within some boding
    shade:—
Grey tepees tufting the blue knolls ahead,
Smoke swirling through the yellow
    chestnut glade . . .   40

A distant cloud, a thunder-bud—it grew,
That blanket of the skies: the padded foot
Within,—I heard it; 'til its rhythm drew,
—Siphoned the black pool from the heart's
    hot root!

A cyclone threshes in the turbine crest,
Swooping in eagle feathers down your
    back;
Know, Maquokeeta, greeting; know death's
    best;
—Fall, Sachem, strictly as the tamarack!

A birch kneels. All her whistling fingers fly.
The oak grove circles in a crash of leaves;   50
The long moan of a dance is in the sky.
Dance, Maquokeeta: Pocahontas
    grieves . . .

And every tendon scurries toward the
    twangs
Of lightning deltaed down your saber hair,
Now snaps the flint in every tooth; red
    fangs
And splay tongues thinly busy the blue
    air . . .

Dance, Maquokeeta! snake that lives
    before,
That casts his pelt, and lives beyond!
    Sprout, horn!
Spark, tooth! Medicine-man, relent,
    restore—   59
Lie to us,—dance us back the tribal morn!

Spears and assemblies: black drums
    thrusting on—
O yelling battlements,—I, too, was liege
To rainbows currying each pulsant bone:
Surpassed the circumstance, danced out
    the siege!

And buzzard-circleted, screamed from the
    stake;
I could not pick the arrows from my side.
Wrapped in that fire, I saw more escorts
    wake—
Flickering, sprint up the hill groins like a
    tide.

I heard the hush of lava wrestling your
          arms,   69
And stag teeth foam about the raven throat;
Flame cataracts of heaven in seething
          swarms
Fed down your anklets to the sunset's
          moat.

O, like the lizard in the furious noon,
That drops his legs and colors in the sun,
—And laughs, pure serpent, Time itself,
          and moon
Of his own fate, I saw thy change begun!

And saw thee dive to kiss that destiny
Like one white meteor, sacrosanct and
          blent
At last with all that's consummate and free
There, where the first and last gods keep
          thy tent.   80

. . . . . .

Thewed of the levin, thunder-shod and
          lean,
Lo, through what infinite seasons dost thou
          gaze—
Across what bivouacs of thin angered
          slain,
And see'st thy bride immortal in the maize!

Totem and fire-gall, slumbering pyramid—
Though other calendars now stack the sky,
Thy freedom is her largesse, Prince, and
          hid
On paths thou knewest best to claim her by.

High unto Labrador the sun strikes free
Her speechless dream of snow, and stirred
          again,   90
She is the torrent and the singing tree;
And she is virgin to the last of men . . .

West, west and south! winds over
          Cumberland
And winds across the llano grass resume
Her hair's warm sibilance. Her breasts are
          fanned
O stream by slope and vineyard—into
          bloom!

And when the caribou slant down for salt
Do arrows thirst and leap? Do antlers shine
Alert, star-triggered in the listening vault
Of dusk?—And are her perfect brows to
          thine?   100

We danced, O Brave, we danced beyond
          their farms,
In cobalt desert closures made our
          vows . . .
Now is the strong prayer folded in thine
          arms,
The serpent with the eagle in the boughs.
1926   1930

III

CUTTY SARK [1]

O, the navies old and oaken,
O, the Temeraire no more!
          —MELVILLE.

I met a man in South Street, tall—
a nervous shark tooth swung on his
          chain.
His eyes pressed through green grass
—green glasses, or bar lights made them
so—
          shine—
                    GREEN—
                              eyes—
stepped out—forgot to look at you
or left you several blocks away—   10

in the nickel-in-the-slot piano jogged
'Stamboul Nights'—weaving somebody's
          nickel—sang—

O Stamboul Rose—dreams weave the
*   rose!*

          Murmurs of Leviathan he spoke,
          and rum was Plato in our heads . . .

1 In the same letter to Kahn, Crane wrote: ' "Cutty
Sark" is a phantasy on the period of the whalers and
clipper ships. It also starts in the present and "progresses backwards." The form of the poem may seem
erratic, but is meant to present the hallucinations incident to rum-drinking in a South Street dive, as well as
reminiscent lurchings of a boat in heavy seas, etc. So
I allow myself something of the same freedom of
punctuation which E.E.Cummings employs.
    ' "Cutty Sark" is arranged on the plan of a fugue.
Two voices—that of the world of Time, and that of
the World of Eternity—are interwoven in the action.
The Atlantis theme (Eternity, or the Absolute) is the
transmuted voice of the nickel-in-the-slot piano, and
this voice alternates with that of the derelict sailor and
the description of the action. It is into this Absolute
that the finale to the whole poem (Atlantis) projects
at the close of the book.
    'The calligramme of ships, seen as a phantom regatta
from Brooklyn Bridge on the way "home" is simply a
lyrical apostrophe to a world of loveliness forever
vanished.' Ibid.,339.

'It's S.S.*Ala*—Antwerp—now remember
    kid
to put me out at three she sails on time.
I'm not much good at time any more
    keep
weakeyed watches sometimes snooze—' his
    bony hands   19
got to beating time . . . 'A whaler
    once—
I ought to keep time and get over it—I'm a
Democrat—I know what time it is—No
I don't want to know what time it is—that
damned white Arctic killed my time . . .'

    O Stamboul Rose—drums weave—

'I ran a donkey engine down there on the
    Canal
in Panama—got tired of that—
then Yucatan selling kitchenware—
    beads—
have you seen Popocatepetl—birdless
    mouth
with ashes sifting down—?   30
          and then the coast again . . .'

    Rose of Stamboul O coral Queen—
    teased remnants of the skeletons of cities—
    and galleries, galleries of watergutted lava
    snarling stone—green—drums—drown
Sing!
'—that spiracle!' he shot a finger out the
    door . . .
'O life's a geyser—beautiful—my lungs—
No—I can't live on land—!'

I saw the frontiers gleaming of his mind; 40
or are there frontiers—running sands
    sometimes
running sands—somewhere—sands
    running . . .
Or they may start some white machine that
    sings.
Then you may laugh and dance the
    axletree—
steel—silver—kick the traces—and know—

    ATLANTIS ROSE drums wreathe the
    rose,
    the star floats burning in a gulf of tears
    and sleep another thousand—

               interminably
long since somebody's nickel—stopped—
playing—   51

A wind worried those wicker-neat lapels, the
swinging summer entrances to cooler
    hells . . .
Outside a wharf truck nearly ran him down
—he lunged up Bowery way while the dawn
was putting the Statue of Liberty out—that
torch of hers you know—

I started walking home across the
    Bridge . . .

    . . . . . .

Blithe Yankee vanities, turreted sprites,
    winged   59
          British repartees, skil-
ful savage sea-girls
that bloomed in the spring—Heave, weave
those bright designs the trade winds
    drive . . .

    Sweet opium and tea, Yo-ho!
    Pennies for porpoises that bank the keel!
    Fins whip the breeze around Japan!

Bright skysails ticketing the line, wink
    round the Horn
to Frisco, Melbourne . . .
            Pennants, parabolas—
clipper dreams indelible and ranging, 70
baronial white on lucky blue!
Perennial-*Cutty*-trophied-*Sark*!

Thermopylæ, Black Prince, Flying Cloud
    through Sunda
—scarfed of foam, their bellies veered
    green esplanades,
locked in wind-humors, ran their eastings
    down;

    at Java Head freshened the nip
    (sweet opium and tea!)
    and turned and left us on the lee . . .

Buntlines tusseling (91 days, 20 hours and
    anchored!)   79
          Rainbow, Leander
(last trip a tragedy)—where can you be
Nimbus? and you rivals two—

    a long tack keeping—

               Taeping?
               Ariel?

1926   1930

VII

THE TUNNEL [1]

To Find the Western path
Right thro' the Gates of Wrath.
                    —BLAKE.

PERFORMANCES, assortments, résumés—
Up Times Square to Columbus Circle
        lights
Channel the congresses, nightly sessions,
Refractions of the thousand theatres,
        faces—
Mysterious kitchens. . . . You shall search
        them all.
Some day by heart you'll learn each famous
        sight
And watch the curtain lift in hell's despite;
You'll find the garden in the third act dead,
Finger your knees—and wish yourself in bed
With tabloid crime-sheets perched in easy
        sight.   10

        Then let you reach your hat
        and go.
        As usual, let you—also
        walking down—exclaim
        to twelve upward leaving
        a subscription praise
        for what time slays.

Or can't you quite make up your mind to
        ride;
A walk is better underneath the L a brisk
Ten blocks or so before? But you find
        yourself   20
Preparing penguin flexions of the arms,—
As usual you will meet the scuttle yawn:
The subway yawns the quickest promise
        home.

Be minimum, then, to swim the hiving
        swarms
Out of the Square, the Circle burning
        bright—
Avoid the glass doors gyring at your right,
Where boxed alone a second, eyes take
        fright
—Quite unprepared rush naked back to
        light:

And down beside the turnstile press the
        coin
Into the slot. The gongs already rattle.   30

        And so
        of cities you bespeak
        subways, rivered under streets
        and rivers. . . . In the car
        the overtone of motion
        underground, the monotone
        of motion is the sound
        of other faces, also underground—

'Let's have a pencil Jimmy—living now
at Floral Park   40
Flatbush—on the fourth of July—
like a pigeon's muddy dream—potatoes
to dig in the field—travlin the town—too—
night after night—the Culver line—the
girls all shaping up—it used to be—'

Our tongues recant like beaten weather
        vanes.
This answer lives like verdigris, like hair
Beyond extinction, surcease of the bone;
And repetition freezes—'What

'what do you want? getting weak on the
        links?
fandaddle daddy don't ask for change—IS   50
        THIS
FOURTEENTH? it's half past six she
        said—if
you don't like my gate why did you
swing on it, why *didja*
swing on it
anyhow—'
                And somehow anyhow swing—

The phonographs of hades in the brain
Are tunnels that re-wind themselves, and
        love
A burnt match skating in a urinal—   60
Somewhere above Fourteenth TAKE
        THE EXPRESS
To brush some new presentiment of pain—

'But I want service in this office SERVICE
I said—after
the show she cried a little afterwards
        but—'

Whose head is swinging from the swollen
        strap?
Whose body smokes along the bitten rails,

---

1 In an earlier letter to Kahn, 18 March 1926, Crane
spoke of 'The Tunnel' as 'the encroachment of machinery on humanity; a kind of purgatory in relation
to the open sky of the last section.' *Hound and Horn*,
VII,iv,678.

Bursts from a smouldering bundle far
    behind
In back forks of the chasms of the
    brain,—
Puffs from a riven stump far out behind   70
In interborough fissures of the mind . . . ?

And why do I often meet your visage here,
Your eyes like agate lanterns—on and on
Below the toothpaste and the dandruff ads?
—And did their riding eyes right through
    your side,
And did their eyes like unwashed platters
    ride?
And Death, aloft—gigantically down
Probing through you—toward me, O
    Evermore!
And when they dragged your retching
    flesh,
Your trembling hands that night through
    Baltimore—   80
That last night on the ballot rounds, did
    you
Shaking, did you deny the ticket, Poe?

For Gravesend Manor change at Chambers
    Street.
The platform hurries along to a dead stop.

The intent escalator lifts a serenade
Stilly
Of shoes, umbrellas, each eye attending its
    shoe, then
Bolting outright somewhere above where
    streets
Burst suddenly in rain. . . . The gongs
    recur:
Elbows and levers, guard and hissing door.
Thunder is galvothermic here below. . . .
    The car   91
Wheels off. The train rounds, bending to a
    scream,
Taking the final level for the dive
Under the river—
And somewhat emptier than before,
Demented, for a hitching second, humps;
    then
Lets go. . . . Toward corners of the floor
Newspapers wing, revolve and wing.
Blank windows gargle signals through the
    roar.

And does the Dæmon take you home, also,
Wop washerwoman, with the bandaged
    hair?   101

After the corridors are swept, the
    cuspidors—
The gaunt sky-barracks cleanly now, and
    bare,
O Genoese, do you bring mother eyes and
    hands
Back home to children and to golden hair?

Dæmon, demurring and eventful yawn!
Whose hideous laughter is a bellows
    mirth
—Or the muffled slaughter of a day in
    birth—
O cruelly to inoculate the brinking dawn
With antennæ toward worlds that glow
    and sink;—   110
To spoon us out more liquid than the dim
Locution of the eldest star, and pack
The conscience navelled in the plunging
    wind,
Umbilical to call—and straightway die!

O caught like pennies beneath soot and
    steam,
Kiss of our agony thou gatherest;
Condensed, thou takest all—shrill ganglia
Impassioned with some song we fail to
    keep.
And yet, like Lazarus, to feel the slope,
The sod and billow breaking,—lifting
    ground,   120
—A sound of waters bending astride the sky
Unceasing with some Word that will not
    die . . . !

    . . . . . .

A tugboat, wheezing wreaths of steam,
Lunged past, with one galvanic blare stove
    up the River.
I counted the echoes assembling, one after
    one,
Searching, thumbing the midnight on the
    piers.
Lights, coasting, left the oily tympanum of
    waters;
The blackness somewhere gouged glass on
    a sky.
And this thy harbor, O my City, I have
    driven under,
Tossed from the coil of ticking towers. . . .
    Tomorrow,   130
And to be. . . . Here by the River that is
    East—
Here at the waters' edge the hands drop
    memory;

Shadowless in that abyss they unaccounting
    lie.
How far away the star has pooled the sea—
Or shall the hands be drawn away, to die?   1926

Kiss of our agony Thou gatherest,
    O Hand of Fire
      gatherest—
          1930

HORACE GREGORY

1898–

A NOTE ON POETRY

THE language of modern poetry is best explained by Wallace Stevens in his introduction to William Carlos Williams's *Collected Poems*: I cannot presume to say more than he has said in that significant essay. But there is perhaps something to be said about my technic of recreating images, for it is often closely related to the physical environment in which I live. The motion picture has deeply influenced our visual consciousness, quite as a speech heard over the radio enters our conception of the spoken word. And certain other means of mechanical invention, as well as the sciences of physical-chemistry, have greatly altered our conceptions of time and space. In so far as these actually enter our lives and become part of human consciousness, they become important and from them 'new' sensations are aroused, so much so, that it may be said that we see and feel things in a 'new' perspective. Some few of my poems reveal the direct influence of *montage*, particularly, 'New York, Cassandra' in which images are superimposed one upon the other in rapid succession, in the order of their emotional intensity. This poem must not be read as one might read a narrative, nor should the Emerson section of *Chorus For Survival*, nor 'It is Later Than You Think.' In these poems the visual technic owes a debt to the consciousness of living in a world in which human emotions are deeply affected by 'new' sensations. It is my hope always to convey precise emotion which is the function of poetry, no matter where or when it happens to be written.

NEW YORK, CASSANDRA

CASSANDRA, the world's on fire; the harvest's sour:
from Salem into China, an old sailor's song
sung to the yellow sea that pours
oceans of grain over us, fire and flood;
it will be hard to sleep.

Macbeth has murder'd sleep, sleep festering
under his eyelids, Cassandra, like an old wound split wide.
Macbeth shall sleep no more—good night, Macbeth—
wake well tonight:
          spring (naked mind)   10
arms, sheets, window curtains pushed aside
to see the fire, hear the guns.

Breakfast will be delayed beyond Canopus,
lunch clean, untouched by human hands, embalmed in cellophane,
revolving in an automat, will wait . . .

Somebody said that Macbeth went insane,
leaped thirty stories down to Birnam wood
                  (inane,
O Dunsinane, your palaces are empty)

The king bled through the sheets (cock crow) Macbeth   20
grew sick, cracked the eternal verities
engraved upon his heart in rock:

        Pick me sweet verities,
                        sweet verities;
        where shall we find again such girls as these?
        Nightingale Venus, bright Beatrice shall sing tonight,
        silverlipped requiem Mary shall answer them,
        clothed in the blood of Christ down to her knees.
        Pick me sweet verities,
                        sweet verities.   30

                              They stand,
a row of broken statues from Alexandria (B.C.)
to Salt Lake City.

II

Give Cerberus a non-employment wage, the dog is hungry.
This head served in the war, Cassandra, it lost an eye;
that head spits fire, for it lost its tongue licking the paws
of lions caged in Wall Street and their claws
were merciless.

        Follow, O follow him, loam-limbed Apollo, crumbling before
        Tiffany's window; he must buy   40
        himself earrings for he meets his love tonight,
        (Blossoming Juliet
        emptied her love into her true love's lap)
        dies in his arms.
                        He is a poet,
        kiss him, Socrates.

They say the red arm of the Proletariat swings,
Hammer and Sickle, a quarter moon in the sky,
The dogstar comets leap . . .
They say Macbeth embezzled funds, the market   50
fell too soon, too soon the hands of Christ
withered on the cross.
                    His wife was barren
(her eyes are flowers
blowing in the field down where the Lackawanna railroad runs:
flow softly rivers of coal and steam)
His life insurance went to the banks.

III

There are five limousines, unbought, rotting behind plate glass,
delicate worms in leather and sharp April grass
piercing steel joints . . .   60
Talk to the guns, Cassandra, tell them this is peace,
not war, not war,
              peace,
                  PEACE.

IV

We came to you with a city in our hands;
we said:
            Destroy this city, by God, we hate this city.
You heard us and your house was a tower of flames . . .
Remember there was once a king, an old king with an iron beard,
Whose life was like your house, a floor of ashes.   70

He put out his eyes, Cassandra.
                        We shall keep
our eyes though we learn nothing . . .
                            The night is cold,
Cassandra.
1932   1933

POEM FOR MY DAUGHTER

TELL her I love
                she will remember me
always, for she
is of my tissues made;
                    she will remember
these streets where the moon's shade
falls and my shadow mingles
with shadows sprung
from a midnight tree.

Tell her I love that I   10
am neither in earth nor sky,
stone nor cloud,
but only this
walled garden she knows well
and which her body is.

Her eyes alone shall make
me blossom for her sake;
contained within her, all
my days shall flower or die,
birthday or funeral   20
concealed where no man's eye
finds me unless she says:
He is my flesh and I
am what he was.
1932   1933

FROM CHORUS FOR SURVIVAL

VI

UNDER the stone I saw them flow,
express Times Square at five o'clock
eyes set in darkness, trampling down
all under, limbs and bodies driven

in crowds, crowds over crowds, the street
exit in starlight and dark air
to empty rooms, to empty arms,
wall paper gardens flowering there,
error and loss upon the walls.

I saw each man who rode alone   10
prepare for sleep in deeper sleep
and there to ride, sightless, unknown,
to darkness that no day recalls.

Riderless home, shoulder to head,
feet on concrete and steel to ride
Times Square at morning and repeat
tomorrow's five o'clock in crowds
(red light and green for speed) descend:
break entrance home to love or hate
(I read the answer at the door)   20
the destination marked 'Return,
no stop till here; this is the end.'
1934–1935   1935

XIII

THROUGH streets where crooked Wicklow flows
I saw a man with broken nose:
His venomous eyes turned full on me
And cursed the ancient poverty
That scarred his limbs and mired his clothes.

O cursed, wind-driven poverty
That breaks the man and mires his clothes.

Beyond the street, beyond the town,
Rose hill and tree and sea and down:
O drear and shadowy green ash-tree,   10
O hills that neither sleep nor rest
But are like waves in that dark sea
That rides the wind, nor-east, nor-west,

O cursed, wind-driven poverty!

Below the hill, below the town,
Deep, whispering voices everywhere
Break quiet in the morning air
And mount the skies to pierce the sun.

I saw the naked, cowering man
Shrink in the midnight of his eye,   20
There, to eat bitterness within,
And close the door and hide the sin
That made his withering heart run dry.
O venomous, dark, unceasing eye
That turned on street and town and me,
Between the waves of hill and sea
Until his eyelid closed the sky.

The rain-rilled, shaken, green ash-tree
Spread roots to gather him and me
In downward pull of earth that drains   30
The blood that empties through men's veins
Under the churchyard, under stone
Until the body lies alone
And will not wake: nor wind, nor sky
Bring sunlight into morning air
And breathe disquiet everywhere
Into the heart of hill and town.

O heart whose heart is like my own
And not to rest or sleep but climb
Wearily out of earth again   40
To feed again that venomous eye
That is the manhood of my time,
Whether at home or Wicklow town.

This is my street to walk again,
O cursed, wind-driven poverty,
              I hear the coming of the rain.

1934   1935

XIV

After a year's travel Emerson recrosses the Atlantic and is back home in Concord, 1833.

'THE voyage crossed, the firmament one star,
New found New England, home:
              Now meet me there
In Concord's orchard where the apple bough
Swings over shoulder at the window-pane
In the green season . . .
              Wake my limbs again
Adam-Ralph Emerson, the first man here;
Eden, the gate unlatched, this place my own.

And I have seen the world, heard the lark climbing   10
His golden sinuous music in dark air,
That speech unknown but to the subtlest ear
Echo through morning over St. Paul's dome,
Wing following through April's hemisphere,
Not less familiar now than earth at home:
England, the colosseum of great minds

He recalls London:

Under deep trees, the bright-eyed mariner,
Coleridge, speaking and the music gone:
Miraculous white hair, the oracle
Voice descending, flowing on,   20

Visits Coleridge,

Knowing, perhaps, that I would understand:
Me, in a vision, under visionary eyes,
My pale, frail body and the profile spare,

Visible the wedding guest who must depart,
Must go like youth before the day is done,
Saying "good-bye" and clasp an aged hand.

Perhaps he knew, perhaps he saw . . .

then Carlyle.

Perhaps Carlyle

Read something in my veins.

Mary, 'the aunt
of genius' speaks.

We are a little mad,   30

The Emersons, blood thin but deep and the quick body given
To God at bed-time, clipped within the spirit
In sleep, in prayers, the candle lit at dark
In homage to the sun.
Dissolve the body and the light is gone:
The stars expire and angels lose their glory,
The vertebræ within a nest of quiet
Between the sheets to fear the wind that stirs
Cypress and willow over us. . . .

Essential   40

I, the boy, the curious scientific dreaming eye
Fixed on the landscape ash-tree, elm,
And rippling grass like water at low tide:
Trees' branches spars of Salem's ships that rode
Jewel-edged at sunset into Asia's side,
Her night our noon, her noon-day our tomorrow,
The tropic desert silence under snow. . . .

The Emerson
family fireside.

Lyceum

Lectures at the hearth at home, and in the fire there,
My boyhood saw
Greek islands floating over Harvard Square: 50
Homer, the blind head sleeping
In celestial seas;
Everett, the voice, asking whose lips were these
Come out of time to breathe our native air?
State House, the fallen stone Acropolis. . . .

The Emerson
poets: Dante, the
old poet,

And at my hearth, the family Lyceum:
Feed the soul's sepulture, they said, and hear
Dante the Florentine who walked to heaven,
Spiring in golden cages out of hell   60
To hail unearthly love, the Beatrice
Lady and bride,
spirit on the last hill
Of that high world,
O Paradiso!
And the last desire
Turned in a crystal image on the stair:
More beautiful than dress that angels wear
Was hers, whose waking limbs were cloaked with fire.

*and Thomas Gray,
the new.*

Read Thomas Gray, the grave-yard nightingale,   70
The cold rhyme out of season, raven-dark
November-piercing death at April's core:
Love, fame, Cromwell or Milton sleep at last
In dust that circles at the cottage door. . . .
Worship and heresy: God's food, the devil's meat,
Black cloth and ashes where I sit to eat—

*The rejection of
the ministry and
Calvinism.*

To be divine
              (and through my heart great goodness flows)
To walk in India at a Concord shrine.

            Bitter the thinking man who sees   80
            The careful millionaire, the red frontier
            In city walls closed; and the hot mills pour
            Iron for guns, starvation, war:
            To know too well, to think too long:

The bitter hours into seasons pass
Until the soul fills up,
Breaks, scatters backward into that better time that never was.
We are alive this hour and survive:
            Then, walk with me alone an orchard mile
            Into the twilight end of Concord days,   90
            Know in my face the acquiescent smile,
            Dissention always deepest in mild gaze
            To look down darkness toward the trembling light—

*Prince Arthur in
the Tower: No
more the eyes of
youth.*

Lights out! and the globe broken, *And with hot irons
Put out both mine eyes?*,
Still gaze toward music where the light
Was and the song:

*The last memory
of Europe:*

            Swing chariot philomel in midnight skies!
            Broken, yet not unheard.
                        Say in my heart I am   100
That angry ancient legend of a bird
Who walked alive
                  eating the ashes of his funeral urn,
Alive to walk until the memory fails
In clapboard lecture halls.

Phoenix

            O my America,
            And not to speak of you except in praise,
            The midland ocean at my heart,
            Thou art Atlantis risen from the seas,
            Bride of the Indian Summer and the corn,   110

The mountain forest, slow, unwinding plain:
The many footed cities at thy side . . .

I am thy husband to divorce thee never:
Never-forever is a long, long time
For faith in blindness and the memory gone.

This place an orchard and no roads,
Yet every step I take shall be my own
Till houses fall in houses, cities fall:
Still floats the wedding caul, the oversoul,
My name the hydrographic written on   120
This stone that crumbles with the garden wall.

        Cheerful, the actual smile is permanent,
        I turn my head always to face the sun.'

1933–1935   1935

XV

The meek shall disinherit the earth

From Furnished Rooms at twilight through the rain,—
Traffic in asphalt mirrors on the Square
Gathers before it mounts Fifth Avenue,
North through the white-arc'd victory in stone,
Toward five o'clock, past Forty Second Street,—
Midnight at Riverside and no return . . .
                              The voices out of air,
The dying echoes of a bitter year:
'Come talk to me at 61, my attic   10
An antique stairway-landing in the sky,
My heart, your friend . . .'
                      O poet, dying at this year's end,
An old man in the mirror's calendar!

The house, an old ship harbored into alien time,
Dry-docked in broken timber, the bricks fallen,
Steel hawsers split, the cornice sprung:
Here, the brass plate, another poet's name,
'Where Allen Seeger lived,' but read no more,
See this man leaning from the top flight floor,   20
Unfolding light from the quick eye,
Mid-darkness, down.

His body was a shadow on the stair,
The resurrection from a wax museum
In X-ray photographs against the wall,
The voice, Isaiah's noise at heaven's throne.

'I have been ill, been poor, the menopause
Too long and all gestation ceased, yet in my dreams alive
With poetry, the long wave coiling
In my blood, and after it, the tide.   30

I am the poet of the golden bird,

The winged bough whose day is always spring,
Whose fiery chariot is the song unheard
Leaping the ashes of time's Illium
From dark to dark . . .
                              Perhaps no one will hear

Me when I say "It is impossible to die,"
Seeing men starve at street corners in rain,
(My face reflected in each eye,
The soul's glass inward down the vertebræ),   40
When there's a word unsaid that I must find
Written across the bottom of my brain,
There, in the long quietus after pain,
In sleep, in memories . . .
Shakespeare and Dante singing in the shade,
Perpetual oak and olive sheltering
The delicate laurel of middle-aged spring—
May in October and an early frost . . .
The dream still warm—
                              Will no one hear my dream?   50
Before the words are lost
In speech of men unborn on foreign shores?

Weeping in gas-lit solitudes of fame,
I saw the naked goddess of the sky
Open her lips to mine
Until I waked "Good morning" to the sun,
And no one knew my name . . .
                              I had been gone
Too long, revolving doors, no entrance, here's the street,
We'll take your finger prints next time we meet,   60
The face is unfamiliar—
                              And old friends
Stored all my letters in forgotten drawers.

Then my book perished
At second-hand, old stock, unsold in dust,
The leaf uncut, unfallen from the tree.
Who touches it unfolds my heart, heart, body
Trembling between sheets in a cold room
On winter mornings and the sun gone out
To pace the park with nursemaids in the Square . . .   70

O my America, in me discover
Thy face in darkness and thy road disseverred,
The hundred million souls unknown, unknown
Bright in oblivion and yet unseen,
Each house an institution for the blind,
A local habitation with no name,
Until the blow-torch splinters stone . . .
                              I saw the flame
Leap fifty stories high in elevators
Riding through the sky.   80
Will someone speak? There is no requiem.'
1933   1935

IT IS LATER THAN YOU THINK
ABIGAIL TO MINERVA

SAVE us, O save us, cries Abigail to Minerva:
Do you see what time it is
On the clock's face, full moon half-risen in July,
Bells chiming? Look at time, Minerva, O come in from the tomb,
That orchard where the apple tree's last century
Now blooms underground, its dry roots spreading
Across the graveyard whose only flower is thin grass
Of lost New Milford. I am here on the top stair
Holding the banister to keep from falling.

Come, come to me, Minerva, before the clock strikes,   10
Before we dissolve in night wind, the pure darkness that has no name.
Do not wait now until I call no more,
Until the voice itself is gone, when hands lose hold on oak,
When stays in calico no longer hold weak body.
Is that your footstep at the door?
Is your hand raised to knock, have you come quietly
As you once did as a child, deceiving me, stealing the young heart
Out of my clumsy flesh, perfect cool fingers closing over the rich heart?
My body trembling, my lips saying: 'No, this is not my sister,
This gold-haired girl, whose pale skin is delight,   20
Clear water in crystal as the noon sun shines through it,
She is not my sister,' but someone seen
As a vision in a noon-tide dream, naked and faintly smiling,
Small hand of love extended from thin arm,
The bare feet scarcely pressing grass
And love's hand offering new-picked buttercups.

Come, come, O come, Minerva, both of us must be here
To meet this hour in an old empty house
Where the clock strikes everywhere, even between its walls,
Through coverlet, through pillow: 'One, two; one, two'   30
As though distant owls called us awake to tell us the actual dream had fled:
That we could not return to what we were
In the old orchard on a summer noon,
There, quite alone, locked in each other's arms in prayer;
That a third face had slipped between us
And a third pair of eyes looked down
From heaven unmoving, piercing sun's rays at noon,
Entering even the darkness of the night that has no moon.

If I were calling someone who had no name, she would come sooner, Minerva!
If my voice were a voice without words,   40
Would you hear me calling, calling as a bird calls
After the trap has sprung and will call again
After he has been set free, knowing the cage is always there,
Even in the topmost branches of the tallest elm?
Would you hear me then, Minerva, would you know the voice was I,
A tired woman, who has lived fifty years too long
Beyond noon when we met and from that hour had no need of love?

This white house is no longer white, but gray rain-beaten,

Difficult to see at night unless the lamp
Is lit at kitchen window or the moon carries our iron   50
Cock-crowing weather vane across her face.
Do not step from the path, Minerva, clear road between our hearts,
Sun-lit, moon-lit, for the orchard grass
Uncut so long conceals the treacherous dead grape vine, apple root,
Rose brier, rusty scythe and the half-dug pit that was to be a grave.
Come to the door, say without words through faintly smiling lips:
'Yes, we have lived too long and there is danger everywhere'
Because the clock's hands move across the full moon's face,
Because Grandfather Colby died before the hour struck,
And the whole town knew the clock was slow,   60
Retarding time that I could not set right:
Loss of a million hours in our blood.
I heard him scream in the same voice that I call now:
'It's late, it's very late'
And after him banks closed, crops failed,
And the workmen starved like varnished rats between factory walls
And the food store failed.
'It's late,' he said, 'will someone break the clock that's always late!'

Come to me, child Minerva, like the child Christ
In a vision to his dying mother,   70
Thorn-free and body whole, the cross forgotten,
Eyes wide and beautiful, forever piercing death.
Come, come, Minerva, close the door softly as I no longer wait,
Feeling the earth downplunging in darkness, sink in deeper earth,
I saying quietly: 'It is very late;
It is later than you think.'
1936

COMMENTARIES

VOLUME II

WALT WHITMAN (1819–1892)

'THE United States themselves are essentially the greatest poem.' Whitman's early life was his best preparation for expressing this poem in *Leaves of Grass*. He was born on Long Island in 1819, the son of a carpenter. He became first an office boy for a lawyer, then printer's devil, then schoolmaster, and finally newspaper editor. Off and on he returned to carpentering with his father. The countryside and seashore of Brooklyn and the crowded streets of New York became familiar to him; he even wandered as far afield as New Orleans and Chicago. As an editorial writer he understood the enthusiasms and aspirations of the people, and as a constant reader and reviewer he absorbed something from articulate philosophies. Tentatively, as early as 1847, he began to sketch poems which should give form to the body, the sense of fraternity, and the soul of the American people.

Leaves of Grass, first set in type by his own hands, was issued in 1855 as a slender volume of twelve poems. In each of the numerous, successive editions it grew larger, as he included new volumes, some of which were first separately published.

'The want for something finished, completed, and technically beautiful will certainly not be supplied by this writer, as it is by existing esthetic works. For the best poems both the old ones and later ones now accepted as first class are polished, rhymed regular, with all the elegance of fine conceits, carefully elaborated, showing under all the restraints of art, language and phrase chosen after very much has been rejected, and only the best admitted, and then all joined and cemented together, and finally presenting the beauty of some architectural temple—some palace, proudly rising in proportions of marble, entered from superb porticos and adorned with statuary satisfying the art sense and that of form, fulfilling beauty and inviting criticism. Not so his poetry. Its likeness is not the solid stately palace, nor the sculpture that adorns it, nor the paintings on its walls. Its analogy is *the Ocean*. Its verses are the liquid, billowy waves, ever rising and falling, perhaps sunny and smooth, perhaps wild with storm, always moving, always alike in their nature as rolling waves, but hardly any two exactly alike in size or measure (meter), never having the sense of something finished and fixed, always suggesting something beyond.'

The form of Whitman's poetry came from its subject; the freeness of his verse was an expression of the freeness of nature and the people, seen, however, through his own personality.

Whitman's early *Leaves of Grass* was the exuberant outgrowth of an almost adolescent enthusiasm for body and brotherhood. The Civil War matured him. In 1862 he began to nurse the wounded; day after day he passed tirelessly from bedside to bedside, his sensitive hands cooling fevered brows, his strong arms about the shoulders of dying men. Whitman had always been fascinated by death, as 'Out of the Cradle Endlessly Rocking' indicates; 'When Lilacs Last in the Dooryard Bloom'd,' however, was written not from the single incident of the assassination of President Lincoln, but soberly drawn from the suffering and deaths of countless common soldiers.

The poems which Whitman wrote after the Civil War were chiefly concerned with the soul. Whitman grew to understand that any significance attached to the American people meant little as a lusty cry of nationalism, and carried weight only as a thoughtful expression of mankind. His ear for poetry also developed and became more sensitive; and it is in his later work that he became a great poet.

Whitman was often criticized for the lengthy cataloguings to be found in poems like his 'Song of Myself.' He intended the mass effect of such *pointillisme* to blend the individual citations into a single gigantic impression, full of life. Similarly impressionistic is the effect of his prose jottings in *Specimen Days and Collect*(Philadelphia, 1882–83), except that here the greater individual length and his increased sensibility gave to each its own life.

Whitman's influence has not always been direct, but it has been profound. Such widely different English writers as Robert Louis Stevenson and Gerard Manley Hopkins were indebted to him. 'French poetry,'

said Richard Aldington, 'from about 1908 to 1914, was largely Whitman.' In America his influence was not widely felt until after 1910. To poets everywhere, once the lesson had sunk in, Whitman's pioneer work meant the extension of territory and the possibility of individual expression. He seemed to be 'The Poet' for whom Emerson had called.

H.L.Traubel and others, eds., *The Complete Writings of Walt Whitman*, 10 vols.(N.Y., 1902).

Emory Holloway, ed., *Leaves of Grass*, Inclusive Edition(N.Y., 1925).

Floyd Stovall, ed., *Walt Whitman*, Representative Selections, with Introduction, Bibliography, and Notes in American Writers Series(N.Y., 1934).

C.J.Furness, ed., *Walt Whitman's Workshop*(Cambridge, Mass., 1928).

Emory Holloway, *Whitman: An Interpretation in Narrative*(N.Y., 1926).

Bliss Perry, *Walt Whitman*, in American Men of Letters Series(Boston, 1906).

John Burroughs, *Whitman: A Study*(Boston, 1896).

Newton Arvin, *Whitman*(N.Y., 1938).

K.Campbell, 'The Evolution of Whitman as an Artist,' *American Literature*,VI, 254–63.

C.F.Strauch, 'The Structure of Walt Whitman's "Song of Myself," ' *English Journal*(College Ed.),XXVII,597–607.

Carolyn Wells and Alfred F.Goldsmith, *A Concise Bibliography of the Works of Walt Whitman*(Boston, 1922).

EMILY DICKINSON (1830–1886)

QUIETLY and perceptively, in a corner of Massachusetts, Emily Dickinson was writing poetry. Like Thoreau, she had 'business with a drop of dew.' She centered her attention not on the unusual, but on customary things seen unusually.

Her life was confined to her red-brick home in Amherst, to the flowers in her garden, and to the thick trees which shut both in. She seldom saw those outside of her immediate family, yet she seemed perfectly happy. She had no regrets at having given up the gaiety of her life as a young girl in a college town. 'I am small,' she wrote to a friend, 'like the wren; and my hair is

bold, like the chestnut burr; and my eyes, like the sherry in the glass that the guest leaves.' 'I find ecstasy in living; the mere sense of living is joy enough.'

She expressed her rapture in a thousand brief poems, charged with the highest emotion, familiarity, and wit. Her quick perception delighted in provocative incongruities. God was a next-door neighbor to talk pleasantly with; the burdens of human existence were to be expressed in terms of the trivialities of a household. She liked piquancy of rhyme as well as of thought, and deliberately sought the effect of assonance, half-rhymes, or no rhyme at all.

10

Emily Dickinson was perfectly sure of herself; she would never change a line for the sake of convention.

She sought also to escape from the tired language of poetry. The hummingbird among the blossoms followed 'a route of evanescence,' and she saw the railway train, like the sun, 'lap the miles.' She weeded and trimmed the diction of her poetry with the busy fingers of a woman in her garden. Like a good housewife she kept words from standing idle, and her sense of economy of expression brought sharpness and distinction.

'Are you too deeply occupied to say if my verse is alive?' With this intelligent query, and definition of her aim, she sent four poems in 1862 to Thomas Wentworth Higginson, a contributor to the *Atlantic Monthly*, whose work she admired. Higginson became her friend and critic, though she never changed one line to please him, and neither he nor the few who knew she was writing could persuade her to publish her work. Her poems were meant to be sent with a letter, to be tucked into a cluster of flowers for a friend, or to be lowered in a basket from her room to children at play.

'If fame belonged to me, I could not escape her,' she said; nor could she, even by death. In 1890, 1891, and 1896, three series of her poems were published. Gradually the public came to understand that one of America's finest poets had lived without their having known her. It was not, however, until in the nineteen-twenties, with her inclusion in various anthologies and with the publication of *The Life and Letters of Emily Dickinson* by her niece, that there was true appreciation of her poetic significance.

M.D.Bianchi and A.L.Hampson, eds., *The Collected Poems of Emily Dickinson*(Boston, 1937), with a biographical introduction by A.L.Hampson.

M.D.Bianchi, ed., *The Single Hound, Poems of a Lifetime*, by Emily Dickinson (Boston, 1914), with an introduction by her niece, Martha Dickinson Bianchi.

A.L.Hampson, ed., *Poems for Youth*, by Emily Dickinson(Boston, 1934), with a foreword by May Lamberton Becker and illustrations by George and Doris Hauman.

M.D.Bianchi and A.L.Hampson, eds., *Further Poems of Emily Dickinson*(Boston, 1929), with an introduction by A.L.Hampson.

——, *The Unpublished Poems of Emily Dickinson*(Boston, 1935).

M.L.Todd, ed., *Letters of Emily Dickinson*, 2 vols.(N.Y., 1931).

M.D.Bianchi, *The Life and Letters of Emily Dickinson*(Boston, 1924).

M.D.Bianchi, *Emily Dickinson Face to Face* (Boston, 1932), with a foreword by A.L.Hampson.

J.Pollitt, *Emily Dickinson: The Human Background of Her Poetry*(N.Y., 1930).

G.Taggard, *The Life and Mind of Emily Dickinson*(N.Y., 1930).

G.F.Whicher, *This Was a Poet: A Critical Biography of Emily Dickinson*(N.Y., 1938).

C.Aiken, 'Emily Dickinson,' *Dial*,LXXVI, 301–08.

A.L.Hampson, *Emily Dickinson: A Bibliography*(Northampton, Mass., 1930).

THOMAS BAILEY ALDRICH (1836–1907)

THOMAS BAILEY ALDRICH's first book of poems, *The Bells*(N.Y., 1855), appeared in the same year as Whitman's *Leaves of Grass*, but their futures as poets could hardly have been more widely different. Aldrich had been born in Portsmouth, New Hampshire, and was in 1855 a clerk in a New York counting-room. Through the success of his romantic and sentimental poems he soon became an editor, and in 1866 moved to Boston, which he found delightful. Within a few months he wrote to Bayard Taylor:

'The humblest man of letters has a position here which he doesn't have in New York. To be known as an able writer is to have the choicest society opened to you. . . . A knight of the quill here is supposed necessarily to be a gentleman. In New York— he's a Bohemian!'

Aldrich was no Bohemian, and became a very good editor of the *Atlantic Monthly*. He was never very original, but was a man of great taste and a writer of considerable skill. Certain of his short stories, such as

'Marjorie Daw,' were extremely popular in their day, while the reminiscences of his childhood, in *The Story of a Bad Boy*(Boston, 1870), became a minor classic of juvenile literature.

His best work is to be found in the poetry of his later years. Here he wrote with all the precision of an engraver upon silver. He used to like to say of himself, 'Though I am not genuine Boston, I am Boston-plated.' Most people agreed that it was excellent plate.

The Writings of T.B.Aldrich, 9 vols.(Boston, 1896).

A Book of Songs and Sonnets Selected from the Poems of Thomas Bailey Aldrich(Boston, 1906). This represents Aldrich's own selection from his poetry.

Ponkapog Papers(Boston, 1903).

Ferris Greenslet, *The Life of T.B.Aldrich* (Boston, 1908). Contains a bibliography.

Lilian W.Aldrich, *Crowding Memories*(Boston, 1920).

BAYARD TAYLOR (1825–1878)

BAYARD TAYLOR described his *Views A-Foot* (N.Y., 1846) as 'a new voice from the track where thousands had been before him.' This account of a pilgrimage through Europe made him famous at the age of twenty-one. Most of his poetry was a similarly romantic pilgrimage where thousands had been, and was equally popular. Taylor wrote several novels and dramas, a fine translation of Goethe's *Faust*, and innumerable travel books and volumes of poetry. Few, however, have any literary distinction.

Taylor was born in 1825 in Chester County, Pennsylvania, and was largely self-educated. In 1844 he published his first book of poems; partly with the meagre proceeds from it, and partly with the financial assistance of editors who were willing to print accounts of his travels, he immediately went abroad for two years. In 1849 he journeyed to California to report the gold rush, his impressions of which are to be found in *Eldorado*(N.Y., 1850) and *A Book of Romances, Lyrics and Songs*(Boston, 1851). In 1851 he made another trip to Europe, and continued his travels to the Near East and the Orient. His *Poems of the Orient*(N.Y., 1854), and particularly the 'Bedouin Song,' brought a sensuous titilla-

tion similar to that occasioned by Melville's *Typee*. The public looked on him as the ideal romantic, and whether he grasped an Alpine stock, swung a miner's pick, or stood clad in Bedouin robes, they thronged to hear him lecture on his travels.

The exoticism of his experiences, the charm of his personality, and the great seriousness with which he undertook deeper and deeper themes of poetry blinded critics, as well as the public, to the shallowness of his achievement. It was, perhaps, because he felt so strongly that a poet 'must pitch his tent on many a distant field' that his work lacks any definite integrity.

M.H.Taylor, ed., *B.Taylor, Poetical Works* (Boston, 1907).

J.R.Schultz, ed., *The Unpublished Letters of Bayard Taylor in the Huntington Library* (San Marino, Calif., 1937).

Marie Hansen-Taylor and H.E.Scudder, *Life and Letters of Bayard Taylor*, 2 vols. (Boston, 1884).

A.H.Smyth, *Bayard Taylor*(Boston, 1896). Contains bibliography.

R.C.Beatty, *Bayard Taylor: Laureate of the Gilded Age*(Norman, Okla., 1936).

EDMUND CLARENCE STEDMAN (1833–1908)

THE leader of the American late-Victorian poets was Edmund Clarence Stedman. He was brought up in Norwich, Connecticut, and was a student at Yale until he was expelled in 1852 after his second year. Following periods as newspaper editor, manufacturer, war correspondent, and assistant in the office of the Attorney-General of the United States, in 1863 he entered

Wall Street. The rest of his life was divided between Bears, Bulls, and the Muse of Poetry. 'You know that *all* my writing is done after a long day's work.'

Stedman's own poetry of consequence is confined to a few lyrics and ballads. His chief significance to the historian of American literature comes through his immense influence as an editor and as the friend and critic of almost every contemporary poet from Taylor to Robinson. He wrote a critical study of British verse in his *Victorian Poets*(Boston, 1875) and, to supplement it, edited *A Victorian Anthology* (Boston, 1895); to cover the American scene he wrote *Poets of America*(Boston, 1885) and edited *An American Anthology* (Boston, 1900). Each is an important summary of the general taste formed by an admiration of the technique and aims of Tennyson.

Stedman realized that 'a new land calls for a new song,' and he sensed that the poetry of his time should bear a direct and vigorous relationship to contemporary thought. Yet he wrote: 'To my notion, metaphysics and transcendentalism are at the opposite pole from the divine and clear spirit of poetry.' 'The traits . . . which I have deprecated earnestly are in the first place obscurity and hardness. . . .' By the rejection of attempts to grapple with the problem of expression, Stedman encouraged poetry which dealt more with mood than with the mind. He failed to understand that a clear lyric spirit not only cannot express the uncertain and troubled times of intellectual change, but does not arise from them. Stedman's chief concern was with conventional craftsmanship, and he helped to stifle any potential vigor by too great an emphasis on traditional forms. If poetry was truly to express his transitional age, it should have been allowed to develop its own strength and to find its own forms.

The Poems of Edmund Clarence Stedman (Boston, 1908).
The Nature and Elements of Poetry(Boston, 1892).
Laura Stedman and G.M.Gould, *Life and Letters of Edmund Clarence Stedman*, 2 vols.(N.Y., 1910). Contains bibliography.

BRET HARTE (1836–1902)

THE literary exploitation of the frontier received its first great impetus from Francis Bret Harte. He was born in 1836 in Albany, New York, and in 1854 followed his widowed mother to California. Harte tried his hand at numerous occupations which took him into the mining country, but what he really wanted to do was to write. When he was twenty-one he began contributing to the *Golden Era* and finally became one of its editors, then editor of the *Californian*, and finally of the *Overland Monthly*, all local magazines. His earliest literary attempts were, in the manner of Irving, to make use of the romantic Spanish civilization of California's past, and 'The Legend of Monte del Diablo' appeared in the *Atlantic Monthly* in 1863. It was, however, through stories like 'The Outcasts of Poker Flat' and poems like 'Plain Language from Truthful James' that he became by 1870 famous throughout the country. In 1871 he left for the East, where for a few years he was the darling of publishers and the public. In 1878, his funds growing low, he went as consul to Crefield in Germany, and after two years of service there and five years as consul in Glasgow, he settled in England for the rest of his life.

It was altogether fitting for Bret Harte to lay a sprig of western pine at the grave of Dickens. From him he learned the trick of making unusual characters seem typical, and of providing reality with an atmosphere of sentiment. Harte had a fine eye for the colorful and a keen sense of dramatic form, to both of which the development of the short story owed much. Rudyard Kipling, in 1881, when he was editing *The Pioneer* in India, queried, 'Why buy Bret Harte . . . when I was prepared to supply home-grown fiction on the hoof?' It was exactly what Harte himself had done with Dickens.

Harte wrote on the same theme for the rest of his life, but he never developed his art beyond that of his earliest successes, nor did he ever have much understanding of anything but the obvious dramatic significance of his material. Harte was an Easterner who had struck it rich by stumbling on a vein of free gold. Unfortunately for him it petered out.

The Writings of Bret Harte, 19 vols.(Boston, 1896–1903).
G.R.Stewart, Jr., *Bret Harte, Argonaut and Exile*(Boston, 1931).
H.C.Merwin, *The Life of Bret Harte, with*

Some Account of the California Pioneers (Boston, 1911).

T.E.Pemberton, *The Life of Bret Harte* (London, 1903).

F.L.Pattee, *The Development of the American Short Story*(New York, 1923),220–44.

JOHN HAY (1838–1905)

JOHN HAY is best known in political history as a suave and brilliant statesman, but in literature he is remembered for his coarse *Pike County Ballads*(Boston, 1871). Hay knew the Pikes, who were the chief stock figures of early frontier literature, from having lived among them on the edge of the Mississippi, in the village of Warsaw, Illinois, where he spent most of his boyhood, and from his school days in Pike County, Illinois. He attended a small college in Springfield, but finished his studies at Brown University in Rhode Island. It was his ambition, as his close friend Henry Adams later observed, 'to fill in the social gaps of a class which, as yet, showed but thin ranks and little cohesion.'

The fact that his uncle's law office, where he studied after graduation, was next to Lincoln's in Springfield, Illinois, led, through the persuasion of John G. Nicolay, to Hay's being made an assistant private secretary to the President in Washington. The ten-volume chronicle of these years, which he wrote with Nicolay, *Abraham Lincoln: A History*(N.Y., 1890), became famous.

Hay's career included the role of historian, novelist, journalist, and diplomat, but only incidentally that of poet. After several years in minor diplomatic posts he became an editorial writer and night editor of the New York *Tribune,* for which he wrote poems like 'Jim Bludsoe.' In these rough-hewn ballads his work was original and native, but he was unfortunately turned to conventional and unimportant versifying both by the misdirected criticism of his time and his own conception of the expression of a gentleman. This ideal he achieved as Ambassador to the Court of St. James's, a post which he filled with 'completeness,' 'harmony,' and 'perfect ease.'

The Complete Poetical Works of John Hay (Boston, 1916).

Tyler Dennett, *John Hay: From Poetry to Politics*(N.Y., 1930).

F.L.Pattee, 'The Discovery of Pike County,' *A History of American Literature Since* 1870(N.Y., 1915).

Henry Adams, *The Education of Henry Adams*, in Modern Library(N.Y., 1931).

JOAQUIN MILLER (1839–1913)

JOAQUIN MILLER loved dash, and he lived picturesquely. 'My cradle was a covered wagon, pointed west.' He was a son of the open. His parents, who named him Cincinnatus Hiner Miller, were restless pioneers; his first years were spent on the Mississippi frontier, and in 1852 he travelled with them in a covered wagon to Oregon. He at one time attended a mission school at Eugene, but what he preferred to remember from his youth were his adventures as a runaway boy in California mining camps, his establishment of a pony express, and his life among the Indians. What he did not actually experience he later imagined, and an exciting legend grew up around him. In

1868 he published his first volume of poems, and in 1869 his second. In 1870 he went to San Francisco, where he met Bret Harte and his circle, and had a taste of what the public liked. He moved east to New York, and on to London. There, in 1871, he published his *Songs of the Sierras*, which caused a literary sensation. William Michael Rossetti, in particular, took him under his wing and introduced him to everyone. In his spurred boots and sombrero, Miller became at once for the British a symbol of the 'picturesqueness' of America. 'It helps sell the poems, boys! And it tickles the duchesses!'

Miller lived with dash, and he wrote with

dash. 'All life, all action that is beautiful and grand and good is poetry waiting for expression. The world is one great poem, because it is very grand, very good, and very beautiful.' This optimism helped him to find heroic elements wherever he turned, but particularly in the West. Byron and, later, Browning influenced him poetically, but his vigor and sense of natural grandeur are particularly his own.

Miller returned to America in September 1871, and after other sojourns in England, South America, and Italy, and brief returns to America, he settled for three years in a log cabin outside of Washington, D.C. Then he moved in 1886 to Oakland, California, where for the rest of his life he lived at 'The Hights,' a frame hut which he built above the city. There as a sage and eccentric he became a Californian phenomenon, representing a mysticism that was still popular and a West that had passed.

Joaquin Miller's Poems, 6 vols.(San Francisco, 1909–10).
Memorie and Rime(N.Y., 1884).
S.G.Firman, ed., *Overland in a Covered Wagon: An Autobiography of Joaquin Miller*(N.Y., 1930).
Martin S. Peterson, *Joaquin Miller: Literary Frontiersman*(Stanford University, Calif., 1937).

SAMUEL CLEMENS (1835–1910)

SAMUEL CLEMENS was born in Florida, Missouri, and moved when he was four to the Mississippi river town of Hannibal. In *Tom Sawyer*(Hartford, 1876) and *The Adventures of Huckleberry Finn*(N.Y., 1885) he made out of a somewhat romanticized Hannibal that which came to be the common scene of American childhood. In 1848 he became a printer, and two years later made a start as a newspaper man. In 1853 he left Hannibal to go down the river to St. Louis, and during the next few years travelled as far afield in his work as New York and Philadelphia. In 1857 he set out for South America, but on reaching New Orleans decided instead to become a river pilot. When the river traffic was closed at the outbreak of the Civil War, he moved on to Nevada to join his brother. There, in reporting for the Virginia City *Enterprise*, he began to develop his power as a writer.

Samuel Clemens became 'Mark Twain' at Virginia City. In the lusty and exaggerated language of the men who thronged there at the discovery of the Comstock Lode he found expression for his genius. No matter how greatly he later refined his vocabulary for the public, the richness and vitality of frontier speech remained with him.

'The humorous story is American, the comic story is English, the witty story is French. The humorous story depends for its effect upon the *manner* of the telling; the comic story and the witty story upon the *matter*. The humorous story may be spun out to great length, and may wander around as much as it pleases, and arrive nowhere in particular; but the comic and witty stories must be brief and end with a point. . . . The humorous story is told gravely; the teller does his best to conceal the fact that he even dimly suspects that there is anything funny about it . . .' This was Mark Twain's analysis of his 'Jumping Frog,' and was the basis of all his humorous and satiric writings. It was exaggeration of one sort, as 'Huck Finn on the Raft' was of the opposite. Less fortunately, it was also the cause of his continued insensitivity to form.

'The Jumping Frog of Calaveras County,' written in 1865 when he was a reporter in California, made him nationally known. *Innocents Abroad*(Hartford, 1869) heightened his popularity. Mark Twain travelled to the Holy Land, and poked, en route, into the same shadowy corners which had lured authors from the time of Irving to that of Taylor. He roared with scornful delight at what he discovered, and Americans howled with him. It was the beginning of another declaration of independence on the part of the people.

Shortly after his return, in 1870, he married, and became editor of the Buffalo *Express*. In 1872 he published *Roughing It*, one of the few books worthy of the frontier life it portrayed. *Life on the Mississippi*(Boston, 1883) was a somewhat more polished, but equally worthy, account of flush times on the river. These and the stories of Tom Sawyer and Huck Finn are, in every important sense, classics.

In 1872 he moved to Hartford, Connecticut, and guided by his wife's conventional touch settled down to a quiet and on the whole conventional life. Emotionally, however, he rebelled, and he developed a bitter cynicism towards most of the opinions and beliefs which his fellow citizens held proper. His Voltairean dialogue on Little Bessie is a far cry from his account of the Jumping Frog.

The Writings of Mark Twain, 25 vols.(N.Y., 1899–1910).

F.L.Pattee, ed., Mark Twain, Representative Selections, with Introduction and Bibliography, in American Writers Series (N.Y., 1935).

A.B.Paine, Mark Twain: A Biography, 3 vols.(N.Y., 1912).

——, ed., Mark Twain's Letters, 2 vols. (N.Y., 1917).

——, ed., Mark Twain's Autobiography, 2 vols.(N.Y., 1924).

——, ed., Mark Twain's Notebook(N.Y., 1935).

Gamaliel Bradford, 'Mark Twain,' American Portraits(Boston, 1922), 1–28.

Van Wyck Brooks, The Ordeal of Mark Twain(N.Y., rev. ed., 1933).

Bernard De Voto, Mark Twain's America (Boston, 1932).

E.C.Wagenknecht, Mark Twain: The Man and His Work(New Haven, 1935).

Merle Johnson, comp., A Bibliography of the Works of Mark Twain(N.Y., rev. ed., 1935).

HENRY TIMROD (1828–1867)

HENRY TIMROD was born in Charleston, South Carolina. In this Cambridge of the South he became a friend of Paul Hayne, when they were boys together at Mr. Coate's school. The two later joined the group which gathered about the aging William Gilmore Simms, and were filled with Simms' ambition for a Southern literature.

Timrod, who was the son of a literary editor and minor poet, studied for a time at what is now the University of Georgia, tried law, and finally became a private tutor. Most of his poetry was published in The Southern Literary Messenger, or in Russell's Magazine which succeeded it as the voice of the South. A volume of his poems was published in Boston in 1860, and was favorably reviewed, but no other volume appeared until Hayne edited, with a laudatory preface, the posthumous Poems of Henry Timrod (N.Y., 1873).

'The Cotton Boll' and 'Charleston' are given significance by their sense of the impending Civil War, but have a poetical strength and independence of their own. The greater part of his work, however, was merely a languorous blending of Wordsworth and Tennyson. As much as Timrod admired Poe, he could not accept the latter's insistence on Beauty as the sole criterion of poetry. He preferred Wordsworth's lesson, 'first, that the materials and stimulants of poetry might be found in the commonest things about us; and second, behind the sights, sounds, and hues of external nature there is "something more than meets the senses, something undefined and unutterable which must be felt and perceived by the soul" in its moments of rapt contemplation.' 'When I stand in the presence of Truth, Beauty, and Power I recognize poetry.' As a poetic principle it ought to have been enough, and was, at least, responsible for 'The Cotton Boll.'

It was not Timrod's continued poverty, illness, and early death which explain the mediocrity of the greater number of his poems. He was on the whole too imitative and too easily seduced by poetic diction and rhyme. Not even his tenderness and sincerity could redeem his poetry from its conventionality.

Poems of Henry Timrod(Richmond, Va., 1901).

Henry Timrod, 'A Theory of Poetry,' Atlantic Monthly,XCVI,313–26.

G.A.Wauchope, Henry Timrod, Man and Poet: A Critical Study(Columbia, S.C., 1915).

G.P.Voigt, 'Timrod's Essays in Literary Criticism,' American Literature,VI, 163–7.

——, 'Timrod in the Light of Newly Revealed Letters,' South Atlantic Quar., XXXVII,263–9.

PAUL HAMILTON HAYNE (1830–1886)

PAUL HAMILTON HAYNE achieved much wider fame than did his friend Timrod. The son of an American naval officer who died when the boy was young, he was cared for by his mother and by an uncle who was the Hayne of Webster's famous address in the United States Senate. He was graduated from Charleston College and then took up law, which he dropped for journalism and poetry. His chief position and most brilliant success was as editor of *Russell's Magazine* during its brief existence from 1857 to 1860. *Poems*(Boston, 1855), *Sonnets and Other Poems*(Boston, 1857), and *Avolio*(Boston, 1860) helped establish his reputation as a poet.

At the beginning of the Civil War, Hayne was an aide on the staff of Governor Picken, but being physically frail was soon forced to retire. Like Timrod, but not so successfully, he wrote patriotic verse. The bombardment of Charleston and the ravages of Sherman's army caused him to lose his home and his possessions, and after the war he retired with his wife to Copse Hill, a shanty in the pine barrens near Augusta,

Georgia, where they lived romantically and in poverty. 'Perhaps you know,' Lanier wrote to a friend, 'that, with us of the younger generation in the South since the War, pretty much of the whole of life has been merely not dying.'

Hayne's poetry attracted such friends in England as Tennyson, Swinburne, and Jean Ingelow; and in America the New England coterie all paid him tribute. They respected his skill, but mostly they admired a certain romantic sentimentality which we are accustomed to associate with his period and particularly with the poetry of the South.

Poems of Paul Hamilton Hayne(Boston, 1882). Contains biographical sketch by Margaret J.Preston.
A.H.Starke, 'Sidney Lanier and Paul Hamilton Hayne: Three Unpublished Letters,' *American Literature*,I,32–9.
E.Mims, 'Paul Hamilton Hayne,' *Library of Southern Literature*,V,2265–71.
Sidney Lanier, *Music and Poetry*(N.Y., 1898),197–211.

SIDNEY LANIER (1842–1881)

SIDNEY LANIER's perception that verse is a phenomenon of sound, and his attempts to write poetical harmony instead of mere melody make him one of the important figures of American poetry in the nineteenth century. Lanier was the greatest virtuoso flautist of his day, and his training as a musician is responsible for his accomplishment as a poet. 'Whatever turn I have for art,' he said, 'is purely musical.' His taste for Mendelssohn in preference to Bach may weaken his musically imitative verse, but it does not alter the correctness of his initial perception.

Lanier was born in 1842 in Macon, Georgia, and was graduated from Oglethorpe College at the age of eighteen. He was appointed a tutor there, but in 1861, during the first year of the Civil War, he enlisted in the Confederate Army. Finally, near the end of the war, he was captured and imprisoned. He tried teaching again, and law, but his health was broken and he

went to Texas in what proved at last to be a vain fight against consumption. In Texas he resumed his study of the flute, which he had played since boyhood, and attempted to secure a position in a symphony orchestra in New York. From there he went in 1873 to Baltimore as a member of the Peabody Symphony Orchestra. Later, in 1879, as a result of his intensive study of English literature, he was appointed a member of the faculty of Johns Hopkins. It was in this post that he wrote *The Science of English Verse*(N.Y., 1880) and *Music and Poetry* (N.Y., 1898).

Tiger Lilies(N.Y., 1867), Lanier's only novel, is a backwoods account of the Civil War, and is important as an early example of local color. His keen ear enlivens the dialogue, uneven in quality though it is, and his sensibility accounts for innumerable passages of great poetic beauty. Unfortunately the book appears never to have been reprinted.

In all his writing, Lanier is an admirable representative of the agricultural romantic tradition of the post-war South, sharing the common and deep-rooted antagonism to Northern industrialism which lingers on even today in the magnolia metaphysics of many who take their Southern stand. Lanier's particular position was reinforced by an overwhelming reliance on the spirit of brotherhood, and the concluding line of 'The Symphony' best summarizes both his philosophical and his poetical creeds:

Music is love in search of a word.

It has often been argued that Lanier confused two mediums of expression in stressing the relationship between music and poetry. This may be partially true in his practice, but not in his theory. What he actually said was that each was a phenomenon of sound. It is not without significance that Lanier was fond of *Piers Plowman,* nor that he returned to the oldest tradition of English poetry in 'The Revenge of Hamish.' Lanier's emphasis foreshadowed the modern poets' reliance on the ear. Despite the inadequacy of his system of indicating metrics through musical notation, *The Science of English Verse* is one of the few important American contributions to the theory of poetry.

Poems of Sidney Lanier(N.Y., 1929).

A.H.Starke, *Sidney Lanier: A Biographical and Critical Study*(Chapel Hill, N.C., 1933). Contains a bibliography.

E.Mims, *Sidney Lanier,* in American Men of Letters Series(Boston, 1905).

H.W.Lanier, ed., *Letters of Sidney Lanier: Selections from His Correspondence, 1866–1881*(N.Y., 1899).

N.B.Fagin, 'Sidney Lanier: Poet of the South,' *Johns Hopkins Alumni Magazine,* XX,232–41.

R.P.Warren, 'The Blind Poet: Sidney Lanier,' *American Review,*II,27–45.

S.T.Williams, 'Lanier,' in Macy, J., ed., *American Writers on American Literature* (N.Y., 1931), 327–41.

Gay W.Allen, 'Sidney Lanier as a Literary Critic,' *Phil.Quar.,*XVII,121–38.

GEORGE WASHINGTON CABLE (1844–1925)

THE most popular American literature during the last quarter of the nineteenth century dealt with unfamiliar and romantic sections of the country. George Washington Cable became famous for his tales of New Orleans. He was born there in 1844, and was brought up in close familiarity with its neighboring plantations, its great town houses, its French Quarter, and the soft patois of the Creoles. He served in the Confederate Army during the Civil War, then became a reporter, and after 1869 worked as a clerk in a firm of cotton factors for as long as he lived in New Orleans. His first use of local material was in his column for the New Orleans *Picayune,* but it was not until 1873 that his first tale appeared in a magazine. 'Belles Demoiselles Plantation' appeared in 1874, and in 1879 his stories were collected in *Old Creole Days.* This and his novel, *The Grandissimes*(N.Y., 1880), were his best work.

Cable himself considered that his greatest literary influences came from the work, somewhat oddly grouped, of Dickens, Thackeray, Poe, and Irving. To Poe he apparently owed his fine sense of structure, but his style seems closer to the leisurely but crisp exposition of Prosper Merimée, one of the many Frenchmen whom he read. Cable's chief interest was psychological rather than dramatic, and his characterizations, though penetrating, are indicated lightly rather than in the probing manner of a Hawthorne.

Cable's research into the social history of New Orleans disclosed certain details which made him unpopular in the South. In 1885 he moved to Northampton, Massachusetts, where he lived for the rest of his life. He continued to write, but increasingly it became difficult to recognize in the pious man who went to seed among home-culture clubs, garden plans, and Northampton society, the author who had once written with the verve and apparent worldliness of a Frenchman.

The Creoles of Louisiana(N.Y., 1884).

M.E.Burt and L.L.Cable, eds., *The Cable Story Book*(N.Y., 1899).

L.L.C.Bikle, *George W.Cable, His Life and*

Letters(N.Y., 1928). Contains a check-list of Cable's writings.

E.W.Bowen, 'George W.Cable: An Ap-preciation,' *South Atlantic Quarterly*, XVIII,145–55.

E.L.Tinker, 'Cable and the Creoles,' *American Literature*,V,313–26.

JOEL CHANDLER HARRIS (1848–1908)

JOEL CHANDLER HARRIS extended the use of regional material into that of folk-lore. Harris was born in 1848 in Eatonton, Georgia, and as a boy was trained as a printer. He began contributing to the paper in whose printing office he worked, and after the Civil War was a reporter on papers in Macon, in New Orleans, and in Savannah. In 1876 he became an editor of the Atlanta *Constitution*, a position which he retained for the next twenty-five years. Harris' first sketches of Negro life were written to fill a column for this paper. In these local stories he was particularly concerned with an accurate transmission of Negro speech.

An article by William Owens, 'Folk-Lore of the Southern Negroes,' in *Lippincott's Magazine* for December 1877, apparently opened Harris' eyes to the wealth that lay near at hand. Owens, after discussing the folk-lore of all tribes and peoples, laid particular stress on that of Africo-Americans, which he described as 'a medley of fables, songs, sayings, incantations, charms and superstitious traditions brought from various tribes along the West African coasts.' 'Almost without exception the actors in these fables are brute animals endowed with speech and reason, in whom mingle strangely and with ludicrous incongruity, the human and brute characteristics. The dramatis personæ are always honored with the title of Buh, which is generally supposed to be an abbreviation of the word "brother" . . . Of the Buh fables, that which is by all odds the greatest favorite, and which appears in the greatest variety of forms, is the "Story of Buh Rabbit and the Tar Baby."'

Harris took immediate advantage of the suggestion, and became an avid collector of Negro fables. His first volume, *Uncle Remus: His Songs and Sayings*(N.Y., 1881), had an immediate popularity. Parallel stories poured in on him from all lands, and his work took on a significance somewhat similar to that of the collection of Chaucerian analogues or to the assembling of English and Scottish ballads by Professor Francis Child of Harvard.

'The story of the Rabbit and the Fox, as told by the Southern Negroes,' said Harris, 'is artistically dramatic in this: it progresses in an orderly way from a beginning to a well-defined conclusion, and is full of striking episodes that suggest the culmination. It seems to me to be to a certain extent allegorical, albeit such an interpretation may be unreasonable. At least it is a fable thoroughly characteristic of the Negro; and it needs no scientific investigation to show why he selects as his hero the weakest and most harmless of all animals, and brings him out victorious in contests with the bear, the wolf, and the fox. It is not virtue that triumphs, but helplessness; it is not malice, but mischievousness.'

Uncle Remus: His Songs and Sayings(N.Y., 1881).
Nights with Uncle Remus(N.Y., 1883).
J.C.Harris, ed., *Joel Chandler Harris, Editor and Essayist*(Chapel Hill, N.C., 1931).
Julia C.Harris, *The Life and Letters of Joel Chandler Harris*(Boston, 1918). Contains a bibliography.
E.C.Parsons, 'Joel Chandler Harris and Negro Folklore,' *Dial*,LXVI,491–93.

LAFCADIO HEARN (1850–1904)

LAFCADIO HEARN'S life was as exotically romantic as the tinge he gave to his writing. He was born on the Ionian island of Leu-cadia, from which he received his Christian name, and was the son of an Irish army surgeon and a Greek mother. He was brought up by a great-aunt in Ireland, and attended for a time Roman Catholic seminaries in France and England. At the age of sixteen he ran away, spent three years in poverty in London, and in 1869 drifted to New York. 'I was nineteen years old and a stranger in the great strange world of America, and grievously tormented by grim realities. As I did not know how to face those realities, I tried to forget them as much as possible; and romantic dreams, daily nourished at a public library helped me to forget.' He left New York for Cincinnati, where he became a reporter, and in 1877 went on to New Orleans in his 'worship of the Odd, the Queer, the Strange, the Exotic, the Monstrous' to which he pledged himself. His search led him to the West Indies, and finally to Japan, where he married and lived for the rest of his life.

'His idea of work was to illustrate with a mosaic of rare and richly-coloured words. But there is a wonderful tenderness, a nervous sensibility of feeling, an Oriental sensuousness of warmth in his creations . . .' This was Hearn's description of Théophile Gautier, but it might as well have been of his own writing. Hearn translated and was enormously impressed with the work of French romanticists, particularly that of Gautier and Loti. It was the spirit of these impressionists that led him to state: 'I write for beloved friends who can see colour in words, can smell the perfume of syllables in blossoms, can be shocked with the fine elfish electricity of words. And in the eternal order of things, words will eventually have their rights recognized by the people.'

'The Legend of L'Île Dernière' is the first section, and background, of the account of a child saved from the storm which swept Lost Island in 1856. Hearn's familiarity with the scene came from his visit in 1884 to the near-by Grand Island, near the mouth of the Mississippi, which possessed, he wrote to a friend, 'subjects innumerable for artistic studies—a hybrid population from all the ends of heaven, white, yellow, red, brown, cinnamon-color, and the tints of bronze and gold. Basques, Andalusians, Portugese, Malays, Chinamen, etc.' On Hearn's return to New Orleans, his tale was printed in the columns of the local *Times-Democrat*, and some years later was expanded into *Chita*(N.Y., 1888). 'My work is ornamental—my dream is poetical prose.'

Interpretations of Literature(N.Y., 1915).
An American Miscellany(N.Y., 1924).
K.Koizumi, *Father and I*(Boston, 1935).
S.Koizumi(Mrs. Hearn), *Reminiscences of Lafcadio Hearn*(Boston, 1918).
Y.Noguchi, *Lafcadio Hearn in Japan*(N.Y., 1911).
J.Temple, *Blue Ghost*(N.Y., 1931).
E.L.Tinker, *Lafcadio Hearn's American Days*(N.Y., 1924).

SARAH ORNE JEWETT (1849–1909)

THE finest local writing of this period is to be found in Sarah Orne Jewett's *The Country of the Pointed Firs*(Boston, 1896). 'People talk about dwelling upon trivialities and commonplaces in life,' she said, 'but a master writer gives everything weight, and makes you feel the distinction and importance of it, and count upon the right or the wrong side of a life's account.' Her sketches of the country people of Maine, among whom she was brought up, are full of quiet and sympathetic charm, and mellow with Miss Jewett's own ripeness of spirit. By understatement and indirection, faintly flavored with the dialect her keen ear caught, she was able to capture the mood and character of New Englanders as no one else has done, before her time or since.

At the back of her desk she kept pinned, as a constant reminder, 'those two wonderful little bits of Flaubert,—*Écrire la vie ordinaire comme on écrit l'histoire;* and the other *Ce n'est pas de faire rire—mais d'agir a la façon de la nature, c'est à dire de faire rêver.*'

Sarah Orne Jewett achieved the goal of all local-colorists of her time; that if a writer can faithfully portray human nature, the characters of his particular region will be in reality universal. The common error of local colorists, as of most regional writers, was, however, as Carl Van Doren has observed, that in actuality they 'thought first of color and then of form, first of the piquant surfaces and then—if at all—of the stubborn deeps of human life.'

Miss Jewett learned to know the people about South Berwick, where she was born, during the many rides about the countryside which she took with her father, who was a country doctor. She never travelled widely nor led an exciting life. She never needed to, for like Thoreau she discovered that the world was close at hand.

Deephaven(Boston, 1877).

A Country Doctor(Boston, 1884).

A White Heron and Other Stories(Boston, 1886).

Willa Cather, ed., *The Best Stories of Sarah Orne Jewett*, 2 vols.(Boston, 1925). With introduction.

Annie Fields, ed., *Letters of Sarah Orne Jewett*(Boston, 1911).

F.O.Matthiessen, *Sarah Orne Jewett*(Boston, 1929).

WILLIAM DEAN HOWELLS (1837–1920)

WILLIAM DEAN HOWELLS' chief contribution to American literature was the advancement of realism, but his long career as a writer included most of the literary phases of the nineteenth and early twentieth centuries. Howells was born in 1837 in Martin's Ferry, a small Ohio village. The village life meant little to him, however, and his first book, *Poems of Two Friends*(Columbus, Ohio, 1860) was the reflection of his reading of early romanticists. A biography of Abraham Lincoln for the campaign of 1860 earned him an appointment to the consularship at Venice, where he remained for four years. This experience was expressed in *Venetian Life*(N.Y., 1866) and *Italian Journeys*(N.Y., 1867), graceful travel sketches in the tradition of Bayard Taylor. In 1866 he became an assistant editor of the *Atlantic Monthly*, in what he called 'his Holy Land of Boston.' For a time he wrote little but innocuous verse, and it was not until his novels of New England life that he entered the field of 'reticent realism,' the boundaries of which he describes in the selection titled 'The Novel.' 'Ah! poor Real Life, which I love,' he wrote, 'can I make others share the delight I find in thy foolish and insipid face?' Of these novels the best are *A Modern Instance*(Boston, 1882) and *The Rise of*

Silas Lapham(Boston, 1885). Balzac and, later, the Russians became his models, or at least his admirations. From 1871 to 1881 he was the editor of the *Atlantic*, and then settled in New York, the new literary capital, for the remainder of his life. In *A Traveler from Altruria*(N.Y., 1894) he wrote a mildly socialistic and Utopian novel which reflected his increasing discontent with the structure of capitalistic society. It is difficult to determine whether Howells was a little ahead of or a little behind his times, but he kept close to them.

Criticism and Fiction(N.Y., 1891).

My Literary Passions(N.Y., 1895).

Impressions and Experiences(N.Y., 1896).

Literary Friends and Acquaintances(N.Y., 1900).

Mildred Howells, ed., *Life in Letters of William Dean Howells*, 2 vols.(Garden City, N.Y., 1928).

D.G.Cooke, *William Dean Howells*(N.Y., 1922). Contains bibliography.

O.W.Firkins, *William Dean Howells*(Cambridge, Mass., 1924). Contains bibliography.

Herbert Edwards, 'Howells and the Controversy over Realism in American Fiction,' *American Literature*,III,237–48.

FREDERICK GODDARD TUCKERMAN (1821–1873)

FREDERICK GODDARD TUCKERMAN'S sonnets seem to have been written ahead of their time. To a form which poetasters customarily rendered silken and sleek he dared to give homeliness and rough strength. He did not care, however, to publish, and his poetic skill was known to his contemporaries only through his occasionally sensitive but generally orthodox volume, *Poems*, published in 1860, 1864, and 1869. It was not until 1908 when Walter Prichard Eaton discovered several sonnets in an unpublished anthology by Louis How, looked up *Poems*, and wrote an article on Tuckerman's verse that he was at all remembered; and not until 1931, when Witter Bynner edited a collection of Tuckerman's published and hitherto unpublished sonnets, did he become well known.

The subject matter of his sonnets comes close to what the nineteenth century would have considered anti-poetic. As to their form Bynner says, 'In the light of Tuckerman's obvious familiarity with the classics, in the light of recent experiment with variations in verse, in the light of present knowledge that Walt Whitman and Emily Dickinson had ears more sensitive than their contemporaries had, we may be sure that Tuckerman knew what he was doing when he ended a sonnet with an Alexandrine or shortened the last line by a foot, or when he shuffled the rhyme-scheme to suit the rise and fall of his meaning. He was aware of his irregularity, as was George Meredith in "Modern Love," adding to the sonnet the two extra lines. He was as tenderly conscious of his form as was ever any maker of the sonnet. Instead of bungling or staling the sonnet-form he renewed it and, moulding it to his emotion, made it inevitable.'

Tuckerman was born of a distinguished Boston family, and entered Harvard at the age of sixteen. Because of trouble with his eyes he quit college and never returned. Later he studied law and in 1844 was admitted to the bar. During a visit to Europe he was the guest of Lord Tennyson, who, as a token of admiration, presented him with the manuscript of 'Locksley Hall.' Most of his life, however, was passed in seclusion from the world, in his home at Greenfield, Massachusetts, where he settled in 1847 and where he remained until his death.

The Sonnets of Frederick Goddard Tuckerman(N.Y., 1931). Edited, with an introduction by Witter Bynner.

EDWARD ROWLAND SILL (1841–1887)

THE poetry of Edward Rowland Sill has its chief importance in his effort to bring into his verse some sense of the intellectual currents of his time. Sill was for the *idea*. 'I almost feel like despising and violating all *form*, when I see the fools that worship it. I always understood why Emerson made his poems rough—and I sympathize more than ever.' To a publisher he wrote: 'You cannot, of course, realize (till you have come to teach the subject) how all our best literature in this century—and a good deal of it in the last century—dips continually into this underlying stream of philosophical thought, and ethical feeling. "In Memoriam," for example, is one of the poems I read with my senior classes. You may discuss its rhythms, its epithets, its metaphors, its felicities and infelicities of Art,—you are still on the surface of it. The fact is that a thinking man puts a lot of his views in general into it—and those views and his feelings about them are precisely the "literature" there is in the thing. And the study of it, as literature, should transfer these views and feelings straight and clear to the brain of the student.'

Josiah Royce, the philosopher and his friend, wrote of him: 'As for Sill's ideal itself, it was an ideal of the highest manhood, an ideal towards which he desired all his friends to strive. His ideal future man was the combination of the truth-seeker and the doer of good into the one person of the true poet. He would never admit any real opposition between the scientific and the poetical spirit, or between either and the capacity for simple practical devotion to one's daily tasks. We ourselves, he taught, make in our false one-sidedness the so-called oppositions of these ideals. In themselves they are one. Science is, or ought to be, poetry, and poetry is knowledge, and the humanity of the future will not divide life, but will unite it.'

Sill was born in Connecticut, and was educated at Phillips Exeter Academy and at Yale. In 1861, after his graduation, he travelled by sea to California, where he taught first in the Oakland High School, and from 1874 to 1882 as professor of English at the University of California. In 1868 he published *The Hermitage and Other Poems*, the only book of his poems made public during his life. In protest against the increasing vocationalism of the University of California he resigned his position in 1882 and moved back to the East. Thereafter he became a fairly regular contributor of both prose and poetry to the leading magazines. An exceptionally shy man, he seldom published over his own name; and it may have been his general lack of self-confidence which kept him from striking out as boldly in the form of his verse as he did in its ideas.

The Poetical Works of Edward Rowland Sill (N.Y., 1906).
The Prose of Edward Rowland Sill(N.Y., 1900).
W.B.Parker, *Edward Rowland Sill: His Life and Work*(Boston, 1915).
Newton Arvin, 'The Failure of E.R.Sill,' *Bookman*,LXXII,581–89.

JOHN BANISTER TABB (1845–1909)

THE memorable quality of the verse written by 'Father Tabb' lies in its orthodox devotion to Roman Catholicism and the warmth of its kindly, if unsophisticated, wit. Some few of his contemporaries likened his verse to the poetry of Robert Herrick, George Herbert, and William Blake. With characteristic modesty he refuted their claims in a letter to his friend Browne, dated 25 December 1906:

I am getting, dear Doctor, from England the very kindest notices of my book [*A Selection from the Verses of John B. Tabb* (London, 1906)]. . . . From the *Tribune* comes a clipping so like your own estimate and worded so like it, that were you in London, I should lay it to your charge. 'A Modern Herrick,' it is headed. Of this poet, the *Golden Treasury* has all that I know. With Herbert and Blake I am even less familiar; and yet it is to these three that they compare me. Nothing, I am glad to observe, is detected of my worship of Keats, whom I know best of the gods. . . .

His verse, however, bears traces of a literary influence exerted by a reading of Edgar Allan Poe, and in the humorous poems, as well as in those written obviously for the enjoyment of small children, one finds a clear resemblance to the punning of Thomas Hood and the charm of Robert Louis Stevenson.

'Father Tabb' was born at 'The Forest,' the family estate at Mattoax, in Amelia County, Virginia, in 1845. He served in the Confederate cause during the Civil War, and after the War, he was appointed to an instructorship at the Episcopal St. Paul's School for Boys in Baltimore, Maryland. In 1872 he entered St. Charles College, Maryland, to study for the Catholic priesthood. In 1884 he was ordained priest in the Baltimore Cathedral, and from then onward until his death in 1909 he was a member of the faculty at St. Charles.

Francis E.A. Litz, ed., *The Poetry of Father Tabb*(N.Y., 1928).
J.M.Tabb, *Father Tabb, His Life and Work*(Boston, 1921).
F.E.A.Litz, *Father Tabb—A Study of His Life and Works*(Baltimore, 1923).

RICHARD HOVEY (1864–1900)

DESPITE Richard Hovey's ambition to recreate the Arthurian legends in the form of poetic drama, his abilities as a poet are chiefly remembered through his collaboration with Bliss Carmen in writing *Songs from Vagabondia*(Boston, 1894) and *More Songs from Vagabondia*(Boston, 1896). The collaboration also included the work of Tom Buford Meteyard, who designed with a touch of Pre-Raphaelite craftsmanship

the covers and end papers of the Vagabondia volumes which were to attain such
widespread popularity. The three friends
had spent a holiday together, including a
winter in New York, a trip to Arcadie, and
an autumn tour to Washington, D.C. The
early winter of 1894 was to bring to fruition
the ideal of spiritual vagrancy and literary
Bohemianism in the first *Songs from Vagabondia.*

Hovey's education at Dartmouth College, where he emerged as a class poet,
author of 'Men of Dartmouth,' a song still
sung today at Hanover, and subsequent
journeys across the Atlantic to Paris and
Avignon, furnished the background for the
kind of lyricism which was to become
known as the poetry of Vagabondia. However far he travelled, he was never to lose
the spirit of:

The campus is reborn in us to-day;
The old grip stirs our hearts with new-old
joy;
Again bursts bonds for madcap holiday
The eternal boy.

Hovey attempted to combine the Transcendentalism of Emerson and Whitman
with his admiration for the ecstatic utterances of the French Symbolists and Parnas-
sians, particularly as he interpreted them
in the work of Mallarmé, Verlaine and
Verhaeren. The exuberance of Bliss Carmen's

All the world is Vagabondia
To him who is a vagabond

overrode whatever contradictions may

have been felt in an equal love for Paul
Verlaine, Hovey's 'Prince of Vagabonds,'
and Walt Whitman, his 'King of Free-
Versists.'

Some hint of the historical importance of
the *Songs from Vagabondia* is indicated by
Muriel Miller's *Bliss Carmen: A Portrait*
(Toronto, 1935), in which she wrote:

However, the two poets did not mean
their Vagabondian scheme to be a mere
idle pastime of a summer's day; it represented far more to them: It was their
joint protest against the warped conven-
tion-bound lives of the material, money-
making American citizen of their
day . . .

Hovey was to intersperse his songs from
Vagabondia with translations of Maurice
Maeterlinck, more songs for Dartmouth
and the Psi Upsilon fraternity, *Seaward:
An Elegy*, in memory of Thomas Williams
Parsons, as well as further experiments in
the writing of poetic drama. His brief
career which came to an end at the age of
thirty-six in 1900 was to symbolize for the
American reading public the promise and
vitality of a hybrid Bohemianism which had
taken root in the literary circles of New
York and San Francisco.

Along the Trail(Boston, 1898).
The Birth of Galahad(Boston, 1898).
Taliesin: A Masque(Boston, 1900).
The Holy Grail and Other Fragments(Bos-
ton, 1900).
Last Songs from Vagabondia(Boston, 1901).
To the End of the Trail(N.Y., 1908).

LOUISE IMOGEN GUINEY (1861–1920)

LIKE her contemporary, Lizette Woodward
Reese, Louise Imogen Guiney turned to
the poetry of the seventeenth century to
find a criterion for the writing of her own
verse. But unlike Miss Reese's verse her
work bears traces of a wide, yet specific
reading of the Cavalier poets. 'I owe much
to the minor lyricists of King Charles I.'s
time,' she wrote, 'and to Sidney and Spencer before them. . . . The great prose
writers who taught me my little prose are

Sir Thomas Browne, Jeremy Taylor, Burke,
Lamb, Hazlitt, Newman and Stevenson.'
Among her lyrics one finds evidence of
her reading the poetry of Marvell, Cam-
pion, Vaughan, Lovelace and Suckling, yet
whatever literary influences marked her
style, she retained throughout her work the
stronger impress of an individual discrimination in its choice of diction. As she
wrote in her 'A Talisman:'

For better than fortune's best
Is mastery in the using,
And sweeter than anything sweet
The art to lay it aside!

The distinct quality of her literary admirations as well as the quickened perceptions of her own poetic gifts may be found in the first stanza of her poem, 'Written in my Lord Clarendon his History of the Rebellion:'

How life hath cheapen'd, and how blanke
The Worlde is! like a fen
Where long ago unstained sanke
The starrie gentlemen:

Since Marston Moor and Newbury dranke
King Charles his gentlemen.

Happy Ending(Boston, 1927). Collected Lyrics, new edition.
Grace Guiney, ed., *Letters of Louise Imogen Guiney*(N.Y., 1926), 2 vols.
Alice Brown, *Louise Imogen Guiney*(Boston, 1921).
E.M.Tenison, *Louise Imogen Guiney, Her Life and Works*, 1861–1920(London, 1923).
E.M.Tenison (comp.), 'A Bibliography of Louise Imogen Guiney,' *Bookman's Journal and Print Collector*, December 1922–January, March 1923.

LIZETTE REESE (1856–1936)

THE lyricism of Lizette Reese owed a confessed indebtedness to the English lyric of the early seventeenth century and in particular to the poetry of Robert Herrick. To this marked literary influence she contributed her own art of understatement as well as a singular perception into the physical beauty of the gardens and countryside of suburban Baltimore. Something of her attitude toward her contemporaries of the later nineteenth century may be found in *A Victorian Village*(New York, 1929):

The Victorians had a full cup and it spilled over. I think that this is the reason that their faults, worst among which were their over elaboration and sentimentality, are so apparent. They had so much material on hand, so much creative ability, that at times and too often they were mastered by them. If they had been poor and idle, they might have had fewer defects. . . . To judge their poetry and prose a critic must have a poetic sense and a sense of humor.

The criterion that Miss Reese set for her own work is also suggested by her commentary on poetry: 'The novelists must

stand by their creation of character, which is the decisive test of the artist, the poets by their perpetuation in word and phrase of beauty, that readjusted of the changes and chances, the confusions and rancors of life.'

As Harriet Monroe once wrote of her:

Miss Reese's method was always simple. If the personal poems in her early books confess a few Victorian frailties of diction and sentiment—faint whiffs of faded perfume, a bit trite like pressed flowers—her best work, even of the 80's and 90's escaped that softness; and her latest style is free of archaism, as her motives of sentimentality. Her poems considered as a whole have a rare unity and harmony. . . . Always carefully studied, they do not try to say or do anything startlingly original; but they sing, with austere taste and musical precision, a clear minor tune all in the same key.

Selected Poems(N.Y., 1926).
White April(N.Y., 1930).
The York Road(N.Y., 1931).
Pastures(N.Y., 1933).

GEORGE STERLING (1869–1926)

THE career of George Sterling and his influence upon the writers of the Pacific

Coast comprise one of the most spectacular, if not one of the most notable, chapters in American literary history. Born at Sag Harbor, New York, in 1869, at the age of twenty-six he moved to California, where under the patronage of Ambrose Bierce and within the environment of the Bohemian Club he combined political Socialism with an aesthetic that ran parallel to the *Yellow Book* doctrines of Ernest Dowson and the later Oscar Wilde. His verse, however, revealed the uses of a Miltonic rhetoric that overweighted the latter-day Romanticism which entered the phrasing of the titles of his books: *A Wine of Wizardry, The Triumph of Bohemia, The House of Orchids, The Caged Eagle, The Binding of the Beast.*

His friends in writing of him had much to say of his physical appearance. They spoke of his 'long-featured mediaeval face' or with equal freedom of his seeming to be 'a reincarnation perhaps from the Athens of the fourth or third century B.C.' Jack London said, 'He looks like a Greek coin run over by a Roman chariot'—all of which was testimony to the fact that his personal character contributed its share to his literary influence.

He was among the first to recognize the abilities of younger Californian writers and in 1926 he wrote of Robinson Jeffers under the title *Robinson Jeffers, the Man and the Artist,* paying tribute to a quality in Jeffers which most closely resembled his own emotion as he once wrote:

I stand as one whose feet at noontide gain
A lonely shore; who feels his soul set free,
And hears the blind sea chanting to the sun.

George Sterling died by his own hand in 1926.

Selected Poems(San Francisco, 1923).
Poems to Vera(N.Y., 1938).
R.G.Berkelman, 'George Sterling on "The Black Vulture," ' *American Literature*,X, 223–4.
Cecil Johnson (comp.), *A Bibliography of the Works of George Sterling*(San Francisco, 1931).

AMBROSE BIERCE (1842–1914?)

AMBROSE BIERCE wrote a few of the finest short stories in American literature, and some of its most trenchant cynicism. He was born in Pomery, Meiggs County, Ohio, in 1842. During the Civil War he served in the Union Army, and took part in the battles of Chickamauga, Shiloh, Kenesaw Mountain, and others. After the war was concluded, he travelled to San Francisco where he finally became a newspaper editor. In 1871 he went to London where he contributed to humorous magazines and became a fellow of minor literary circles. In 1876 he returned to San Francisco. Here, the combination of his talent and his sarcasm made his 'Prattle,' a column which he conducted for the *San Francisco Examiner,* read and feared by the public. Admiration of this kind of power continued among bright and ambitious newspapermen until it culminated in the schools of H.L.Mencken and Ben Hecht. However widely the public read him in newspapers, Bierce's published volumes had no great success. Toward the end of the year 1913 he disappeared, presumably to fight with Villa in Mexico. Nothing more was heard of him.

Tales of Soldiers and Civilians(N.Y., 1891), later titled *In the Midst of Life,* and *Can Such Things Be?*(N.Y., 1893) contain his best short stories. Of the first volume, Boynton has said: 'The constant factor in the book is extreme emotional tension. Sometimes the characters are pathological and the situations abnormal. The people and the events are barely within the reach of credibility. Bierce thus often turned naturally to war episodes, because, though actual, they were farthest from the even tenor of normal life. In these it was the rarest occurrence for him to reveal a sense of humankind in general. The mass, the herd, the crowd, served as a dim background for one man living at the highest pitch and often enough dying of the tension; and the individual himself was less a character than a piece of susceptibility played on by overwhelming emotions.' This is the character not only of such tales as 'An Occurrence at Owl Creek Bridge,' but of the mystery stories of *Can Such Things Be?*

The quality of his emotion which made him known as 'Bitter Bierce' can be seen in the admirable compression of his *Fantastic Fables*(N.Y., 1899) and *The Cynic's Word Book*(N.Y., 1906), later titled *The Devil's Dictionary*. Poor Richard had undergone a remarkable transformation.

Collected Works(N.Y., 1909–12). 12 vols.
B.C.Pope, ed., *The Letters of Ambrose Bierce*(San Francisco, 1922).
Vincent Starrett, *Ambrose Bierce*(Chicago, 1920).
Walter Neale, *The Life of Ambrose Bierce* (N.Y., 1929).

C.Hartley Grattan, *Bitter Bierce*(N.Y., 1929).
Cary McWilliams, *Ambrose Bierce*(N.Y., 1929).
A.M.Miller, 'The Influence of Edgar Allan Poe on Ambrose Bierce,' *American Literature*,IV,130–50.
George Sterling, 'The Shadow Maker,' *American Mercury*,VI,10–19.
N.Wilt, 'Ambrose Bierce and the Civil War,' *American Literature*,I,260–85.
Vincent Starrett, *A Bibliography of the Writings of Ambrose Bierce*(Philadelphia, 1929).

STEPHEN CRANE (1871–1900)

THE brilliant precocity of Stephen Crane's *The Red Badge of Courage*(N.Y., 1895) placed him in the foreground of a new generation of writers who came of age in the closing years of the nineteenth century. It was as though his admirers were waiting for the very type of psychological fiction that *The Red Badge of Courage* was to introduce. His earlier novel *Maggie*(N.Y., 1892), which had been rejected by magazine editors and publishing houses of the day, has left its impress as one of the first experiments in naturalistic prose written in America.

Upon reading the poems of Emily Dickinson, and under the stimulus of his 'discovery' of a highly original American genius, he wrote his first book of poems, *The Black Riders*, which he issued in 1895. Harriet Monroe, in her introduction to *The New Poetry*(N.Y., 1917), quoted the title poem of his second book of verse, *War Is Kind*, to illustrate the character of a kind of poetry which she regarded as being in the line of a tradition that foreshadowed the work of the Imagist and the 'free verse writers' of the poetic Renaissance in 1912.

Stephen Crane was born in Newark, New Jersey, in 1871. He entered Lafayette College, but before receiving a degree left at the age of sixteen to test his skill at journalism. The spectacular success of *The Red Badge of Courage*, with its vivid detail of character and situations on the battlefield, insured the further success of his journalistic career. He was sent as war correspondent to the Greco-Turkish War in 1897 and in the following year to the Spanish-American War.

His success also brought with it the rapid expenditure of his remarkable nervous energy which seemed to produce at white heat the impressionistic vividness of such short stories as 'The Open Boat' and 'The Upturned Face,' as well as the highly-keyed output of many reportorial sketches, stories for children, and new poems. No less energetic was his invasion of England during the last two years of his life, where he moved toward the center of a literary group that included such men as Joseph Conrad, Henry James, and Ford Madox Ford. He died in the Black Forest, Germany, in 1900.

W.Follett, ed., *The Work of Stephen Crane* (N.Y., 1925–26), 12 vols.
——,*The Collected Poems of Stephen Crane* (N.Y., 1930).
T.Beer, *Stephen Crane, A Study in American Letters*(N.Y., 1923).
Joseph Conrad, 'Stephen Crane: A Note without Dates,' *Bookman*,L,529–31.
Hamlin Garland, 'Stephen Crane as I Knew Him,' *Yale Review*,n.s.III,494–506.
W.Follett, 'The Second Twenty-Eight Years,' *Bookman*,LXVIII,532–37.
V.Starrett, *Stephen Crane: A Bibliography* (Philadelphia, 1923).

FRANK NORRIS (1870–1902)

FRANK NORRIS brought force to American fiction. 'Give us stories now, give us men, strong, brutal men, with red-hot blood in 'em, with unleashed passions rampant in 'em . . .' *Moran of the Lady Letty*(N.Y., 1898), a novel of the tigers of the sea, and *McTeague*(N.Y., 1899), the story of the disintegration of a brute of society, displayed a type of romantic materialism. But Norris began to perceive a deeper significance to force:

Men were naught, death was naught, life was naught; FORCE only existed— FORCE that brought men into the World, FORCE that crowded them out of it to make way for the succeeding generation, FORCE that made the wheat grow, FORCE that garnered it from the soul to give place to the succeeding crop.

It was the mystery of creation, the stupendous mystery of re-creation; the vast rhythm of the seasons, measured, alternative, the sun and the stars keeping time as the eternal symphony of reproduction swung its tremendous cadences, like the colossal pendulum of an almighty machine—primordial energy flung out from the hand of the Lord God himself, immortal, calm, infinitely strong.

On this concept Norris patterned his uncompleted trilogy on wheat, his symbol of world force, the scheme of which is described in the annotation to the selection 'Wheat' from its first two novels. It was not, however, solely the display of force which gave these books their significance, but Norris' increasing implication that such force must be understood and controlled by man.

Frank Norris was born in 1870 in Chicago, the son of a wealthy wholesale jeweler, and spent a great part of his youth in San Francisco. For about two years Nor-

ris studied art in Paris, filled with the spirit of romantic mediaevalism which had marked the nineteenth century. He returned home in 1890 and entered the University of California, but left after four years without graduating, and spent a year at Harvard. It was during his college years that he began *McTeague*. Later he became a newspaper correspondent, was sent to South Africa to cover the Boer War, and later to Cuba for the Spanish-American War. His last years were spent in New York in the office of a publisher. Before he could either complete his trilogy on wheat or commence his projected trilogy on the Battle of Gettysburg as a symbol of the spirit of America, he died of peritonitis.

'Every novel,' Norris wrote, 'must do one of three things—it must (1) tell something, (2) show something, or (3) prove something. Some novels do all three of these; some do only two; all must do at least one . . . . The third and what we hold to be the best class, proves something, draws conclusions from a whole congeries of forces, social tendencies, race impulses, devotes itself not to a study of men but of man.' It is this perception on Norris' part of the function of a novelist which brings regret that he did not live long enough truly to fulfill it.

The Responsibilities of the Novelist(N.Y., 1903).
The Complete Works of Frank Norris, 10 vols.(Garden City, N.Y., 1928).
Stories and Sketches from the San Francisco Weekly, 1893 to 1897, with a Foreword by Charles G. Norris(San Francisco, 1931).
F.Walker, *Frank Norris*(Garden City, N.Y., 1932).
Frank Norris: Two Poems and 'Kim' Reviewed, with a Bibliography by Harvey Taylor(San Francisco, 1930).

EDWIN MARKHAM (1852–1940)

EDWIN MARKHAM's reputation rests almost solely upon the publication of a single poem, 'The Man with The Hoe,' which

appeared in the *San Francisco Examiner* on 15 January 1899. Its long worked-over and rhetorical plea for social justice was inspired by Markham's admiration for Millet's famous painting from which he borrowed the title of the poem and dramatized the figure of a French peasant, 'Bowed by the weight of centuries . . . Stolid and stunned, a brother to the ox.'

Markham was born in Oregon City, Oregon, in 1852, and was the youngest son in a family that had moved westward across the continent. He was educated at the State Normal at San Jose, California, and graduated from the College at Santa Rosa. His verse was written in the Byronic convention that had been established by Joaquin Miller on the Pacific Coast and which marked the dramatic mannerisms of everything he wrote. The publication of *The Man with the Hoe and Other Poems* in 1899 was followed two years later by a second volume, *Lincoln, and Other Poems*, in

which the same Populist note of eloquence was struck. The character of Markham's Populism at the turn of the nineteenth century was to be reflected later in the literature of 'Muck-raking' and in the journalism of the 'Trust-busting' era.

He moved to New York in 1901, making his home on Staten Island.

The Man with the Hoe and Other Poems (Garden City, N.Y., 1899).
Lincoln, and Other Poems(N.Y., 1901).
New Poems(Garden City, N.Y., 1932).
'The Man with the Hoe' and other poems. (Timely Recording Co., Nos. 1000–02.) A recording of selected poems by Markham.
W.L.Stidger, *Edwin Markham*(N.Y., 1933).
A Wreath for Edwin Markham(Chicago, 1922).

CHARLES ERSKINE SCOTT WOOD (1852–1944)

THE life of Charles Erskine Scott Wood has been that of the complete man. Trained at West Point, he served in many Indian campaigns, then left the army to study law, receiving the degrees of Ph.B. and LL.B. from Columbia in 1883. He settled in Portland, Oregon, and became widely known in the Northwest as an attorney. Soon he began to lead his own kind of double life: in one of his two offices he met corporation clients, and in the other greeted poets, artists, rebels, hoboes, and dreamers. At one time, when he was still in Oregon, he took over the editorship of *The Pacific Monthly*, and almost single-handed wrote the entire magazine, under various pseudonyms, at the same time that he was carrying on his work in law. His practice became more and more that of defending the downtrodden, and his best writing has come out of his intense sympathy and understanding of their plight.

His most important works in prose are

his satirical *Heavenly Discourse*(N.Y., 1927) and *Earthly Discourse*(N.Y., 1937), which deftly remove the epidermis from contemporary shams and illustrate his burning passion for social justice. In poetry he has made of *The Poet in the Desert*(Portland, Oregon, 1915) both a rhapsody and a vehement protest against the man-made ills of life. So frequently has he revised this work, and so completely does it include his attitude toward life that it becomes something of a modern *Leaves of Grass*. Its free verse and sweep are vaguely suggestive of Whitman, but the voice is that of Wood.

With his wife, Sarah Bard Field, the poet, he has made his home at Los Gatos, California, into a haven and salon for writers on the Pacific Coast.

A Masque of Love(Chicago, 1904).
The Poet in the Desert(N.Y., 1928).
Poems from the Ranges(N.Y., 1929).

TRUMBULL STICKNEY (1874–1904)

TRUMBULL STICKNEY was perhaps the most gifted and certainly the most precocious member of a 'tragic generation' in America

which came of age in the years immediately preceding the end of the nineteenth century. William Vaughn Moody himself has said that Stickney's 'Prometheus Pyrphoros' antedated his own 'The Fire Bringer' by several years. It was at Stickney's own request that Moody did not then acknowledge the other's priority in the use of the material and what Moody calls 'my deep obligation to his work.' The sources of Stickney's poem were in the account given by Hesiod. Stickney also left a splendid fragment, begun in the first half of the year 1901, of a drama on the life of the Emperor Julian.

Trumbull Stickney was born in Geneva, Switzerland, in 1874. He was graduated with high classical honors from Harvard in 1895 and in France studied for seven years at the Sorbonne and at the Collège de France. He was the first American ever to receive the degree of *docteur ès lettres* from a French university. His *Les Sentences dans la Poésie Grecque* was accepted as one of the best of modern studies in Hellenic literature. In the autumn of 1903 he became an instructor of Greek at Harvard. He died in the fall of 1904.

As E.K.Rand wrote of Stickney in the *Harvard Graduates' Magazine:* 'A rare intellectual leadership a command of affections and enthusiasms, was in store for him' in his teaching at the time of his death. Considering the nature of his death, for he died of a tumor in the brain, the lines his editors place at the end of his *Poems* are significant:

Sir, say no more,
Within me 'tis as if
The green and climbing eyesight of a cat
Crawled near my mind's poor birds.

Dramatic Verses(Boston, 1902).
Poems(Boston, 1905).

WILLIAM VAUGHN MOODY (1869–1910)

In the year 1900 no poet in America occupied as significant a position as William Vaughn Moody. In 'An Ode in Time of Hesitation' and in his 'Gloucester Moors' he spoke directly to the literary public of his day. He was a leader in what might well be called America's 'tragic generation' in literature, a generation which after the death of Longfellow, Lanier, and Whitman faced the not unconscious danger of failure in a concerted effort to revive the power of poetic drama in English verse and to make their creation flourish on American soil.

William Vaughn Moody was born in Spencer, Indiana, in 1869, and after leaving high school did some local newspaper work and studied drawing and painting. By teaching and tutoring he earned his way through Riverview Academy, New York, and then through Harvard, from which he received an A.B. in 1893 and an A.M. in 1894. In 1895 he was appointed to an instructorship at the University of Chicago, at which he wrote, in collaboration with Robert Morss Lovett, a *History of English Literature.*

While in Chicago he began his ambitious projects in poetic drama, choosing as a central theme the union of God with man and the incompleteness of either without the other. The very diction of his verse became possessed by the desire to recreate Miltonic grandeur and was typified by his writing such lines as

I am the Woman, ark of the law and its
    breaker.

His very consciousness that America was 'the eagle nation Milton saw Mewing its mighty youth' seemed to lead him further toward the creation of awe-inspiring themes in epic phrasing. Yet, as Percy H. Boynton remarked, 'His love for America, however, did not dull his sense of the dangers that threatened its youth. Within its boundaries he was well aware of the economic evils which menaced it . . . . In "Gloucester Moors" he was disturbed, if not made fearful. . . . There was no hope in the poem, only speculation and distress.' And that distress was only partially relieved by the satire which animated his convictions in 'The Menagerie.'

The commercial success of his play in prose, *The Great Divide*(N.Y., 1906), fell far short of the goal that he had sought in his rejection of materialism and his deeply felt need for a transcendental salvation. He was to follow this success with another play in prose, *The Faith Healer*(Boston, 1909), the year before his death, still seeking the adequate medium for the expression of a neo-transcendental philosophy in a world that his friend Edwin Arlington Robinson described in 'The Valley of the Shadow.'

R.M.Lovett, ed., *Selected Poems of William Vaughn Moody*, in Riverside College Classics(Boston, 1931).

J.M.Manly, ed., *The Poems and Plays of William Vaughn Moody*, 2 vols.(Boston, 1912).

P.MacKaye, ed., *Letters to Harriet*(Boston, 1936).

D.G.Mason, ed., *Some Letters of William Vaughn Moody*(Boston, 1913).

D.D.Henry, *William Vaughn Moody*(Boston, 1934). Contains bibliography.

N.F.Adkins, 'The Poetic Philosophy of William V. Moody,' *Texas Review*,IX, 97–112.

A.H.Quinn, *A History of the American Drama from the Civil War to the Present Day*(N.Y., 1927),II,1-26.

HENRY ADAMS (1838–1918)

HENRY ADAMS brought the problem of Force into American letters with infinitely more subtlety and importance than had Frank Norris. 'Like his masters, since thought began,' Adams wrote of himself, in his account of his education, 'he was handicapped by the eternal mystery of Force—the sink of all science.' 'Any schoolboy could see that man as a force must be measured by motion, from a fixed point. Psychology helped here by suggesting a unit—the point of history where man held the highest idea of himself in a unified universe. Eight or ten years of study had led Adams to think he might use the century 1150–1250, expressed in Amiens Cathedral and the Works of Thomas Aquinas, as the unit from which he might measure motion down to his own time, without assuming anything as true or untrue, except relation. The movement might be studied at once in philosophy and mechanics. Setting himself to the task, he began a volume which he mentally knew as *Mont-Saint-Michel and Chartres: a Study of Thirteenth-Century Unity*. From that point he proposed to fix a position for himself, which he could label: *The Education of Henry Adams: a Study of Twentieth-Century Multiplicity*. With the help of these two points of relation, he hoped to project his lines forward and backward indefinitely, subject to correction from anyone who should know better.'

Adams' life was spent in this education. He was the son of an Ambassador to the Court of St. James's and the grandson of a President of the United States. He was graduated from Harvard in 1858, and for seven years afterwards was his father's secretary in London. He tried newspaper reporting of the sessions of Congress; he tried serving as professor of history at Harvard; he was editor for a time of *The North American Review*; he travelled widely in Europe; he journeyed to the islands of the Pacific; he passed most of his life in Washington as a friend of the near-great. He wrote biographies of Albert Gallatin and John Randolph, two men who had helped to fashion their age; he wrote two novels, *Democracy*(Boston, 1880) and *Esther*(Boston, 1884), the first of which treated society in terms of politics, and the second, in terms of religion; he wrote a brilliant nine-volume social and political history of the administrations of Jefferson and Madison in his *History of the United States of America*, 1801–1817(Boston 1889–91). Each was a probing.

His conclusion was: 'To educate—one's self to begin with—had been the effort of one's life for sixty years; and the difficulties of education had gone on doubling with the coal-output, until the prospect of waiting on another ten years, in order to face a seventh doubling of complexities, allured one's mind but slightly. The law of acceleration was definite, and did not require ten years' more study except to show whether it held good. No scheme could be suggested to the new American, and no fault needed to be found, or complaint made; but the next great influx of new forces seemed near at hand, and its style of education promised to be violently coercive. The movement from unity into multiplicity, between 1200 and 1900, was unbroken in sequence, and rapid in acceleration. Prolonged one generation longer, it would require a new social mind. As though thought were common salt in indefinite solution it must enter a new phase subject to new laws.'

In summing up Adams' education, R.P.Blackmur has observed: 'Again and again he describes unifying conceptions as working principles; without them no work could be done; with them, even at the expense of final failure, every value could be provisionally ascertained. That is the value of Adams for us: the double value of his scrupulous attitude towards his unifying notions and of the human aspirations he was able to express under them. To feel that value as education is a profound deliverance: the same deliverance Adams felt in the Gothic Cathedral. "The delight of its aspiration is flung up to the sky. The pathos of its self-distrust and anguish of doubt is buried in the earth as its last secret." The principles asserted are nothing,

though desperate and necessary; the values expressed because of the principles are everything. For Adams, as for everyone, the principle of unity carried to failure showed the most value by the way, and the value was worth the expense.'

Historical Essays(N.Y., 1891).

Mont St. Michel and Chartres(Boston, 1913). Privately printed, Washington, 1904.

The Education of Henry Adams(Boston, 1918). Privately printed, Washington, 1904.

The Degradation of the Democratic Dogma (N.Y., 1919).

Letters to a Niece and Prayer to the Virgin of Chartres(Boston, 1920).

W.C.Ford, ed., *A Cycle of Adams Letters*, 1861–1865(Boston, 1920).

——, *Letters of Henry Adams*, 1858–1891 (Boston, 1930).

Gamaliel Bradford, 'Henry Adams,' in *American Portraits*(Boston, 1920).

R.P.Blackmur, 'The Expense of Greatness. Three Emphases on Henry Adams,' *The Virginia Quarterly Review*,XII,396–415.

WILLIAM SYDNEY PORTER (O. HENRY) (1862–1910)

WILLIAM SYDNEY PORTER developed the structure of the plot of the short story to the breaking point. The tricks of Bret Harte, Thomas Bailey Aldrich, and Frank Stockton served him to supply the incessant demands of newspapers and magazines, and his formula left little freshness either to sentiment or to the surprise ending.

Porter was born in Greensboro, North Carolina, in 1862. At the age of fifteen he began working in his uncle's drugstore, but after five years of this left for Texas. He drifted from one occupation to another, and finally became teller in the First National Bank in Austin. He quit this to begin newspaper work. When he was accused of embezzling from the bank, he fled to Honduras, but returned because of his wife's illness, and served three years in prison. During the period of his sentence he continued writing, and began to sell under the pseudonym of O. Henry to magazines in New York. Shortly after his re-

lease he went there, and there he stayed until his death.

Porter had begun to know small-town folk when he first stood behind a drugstore counter, and these characters he used in his stories of metropolitan life. Even his description of New York as 'Bagdad' is typical of his approach, and it is doubtful if he is deserving of his repeated praise as 'the narrator and supreme celebrant of the life of the great city.' It is understandable that the most nationally popular writers and columnists on New York life should be those who come from the village and who pretend to find little difference between New York life and that of their own Main Streets.

Not all of Porter's stories deal with city life, and many are drawn from his experiences in the South, in the West, and in Central America. Occasionally in each group he was successful, for within the limitations of his formula Porter had great ability. It is not surprising, however, that future American writers of the short story were to react against a predominant emphasis on plot.

The Complete Works of O. Henry(N.Y., 1912).

C.A.Smith, *O. Henry*(N.Y., 1916).

R.H.Davis and A.B.Maurice, *The Caliph of Bagdad*(N.Y., 1931).

P.S.Clarkson, *A Bibliography of William Sidney Porter*(Caldwell, Idaho, 1938).

HENRY JAMES (1843–1916)

DURING the latter half of the nineteenth century, it was Henry James, the American expatriate, who revived the virtues of sensibility in English fiction. Since the publication of Jane Austen's *Sense and Sensibility*, no writer of prose had had a keener perception into the conventions which sustained yet ruled society than Henry James. Not the least interest in reading his work is to observe the development of his sensibility from its earliest demonstration through the obvious juxtaposition of contrary elements until its mature expression in the dramatization of apparently static situations.

The rudimentary practice of James is to be found in what has come to be known as the 'international novel.' Writing in this manner, James developed the technique of what he called 'reflectors,' by which both Americans and Europeans stood out in mutual chiaroscuro, not only in differentiations of racial characteristics but of individual characteristics among themselves. In its theory it was an unwitting expansion of the principle of James Fenimore Cooper's *Homeward Bound*. Brilliant examples of this type of James' fiction are to be found in such novels as *The American*(Boston, 1877), *Daisy Miller*(N.Y., 1879), and *The Portrait of a Lady*(Boston, 1882).

The Portrait of a Lady serves as a bridge between his early and his later, and more mature, writing. In its preface may be found, as R.P.Blackmur has pointed out, 'the genius and intention of James the novelist.'

There is, I think, no more nutritive or suggestive truth in this connection than that of the perfect dependence of the 'moral' sense of a work of art on the amount of felt life concerned in producing it. The question comes back thus, obviously, to the kind and degree of the artist's prime sensibility, which is the soil out of which his subject springs. The quality and capacity of that soil, its capacity to 'grow' with due freshness and straightness any vision of life, represents, strongly or weakly, the projected morality. . . . Here we get exactly the high price of the novel as a literary form with closeness, to range through all the differences of the individual relation to its general subject-matter, all the varieties of outlook on life, of disposition to reflect and project, created by conditions that are never the same from man to man (or, as far as that goes, from woman to woman), but positively to appear more true to its character in proportion as it strains, or tends to burst, with a latent extravaganza, its mould.

James was not merely interested in emotion or in plot, but rather in the mind and its complex revelation of the character of 'the fine intelligence, either as agent or as the object of action or as both, . . . at the heart of James' work.' Only by penetration, minute examination, and scrupulous exegesis on the part of the author was such complex revelation possible. Consequently James is best read, as it were, from his own creative position within his material, for only by this inner approach can the remarkable subtlety and the perfect order of his works of art be felt.

James' own rootless life is perhaps one reason for his lack of interest in the variety of physical realism which increasingly occupied the attention of American writers during his lifetime. His father, Henry James, Sr., was a wealthy litterateur who trained Henry James and his brother William James, the psychologist, like highly bred race horses. They were tutored, sent abroad for education, and primed for the expression of genius. Fortunately both possessed it. Henry James was never able to be completely contented anywhere, but after 1869 he lived abroad, and shortly after the onset of the World War became a British subject in protest against America's failure to enter on the side of the Allies.

His life was entirely devoted to the art of writing, not only its practice but its theory. 'The Art of Fiction' is an early example of the latter. His finest discussions of this subject occur, however, in the prefaces which he wrote for the collected edition of his work. Unfortunately these must be read in entirety for any satisfactory understanding, and only recently, in *The Art of the Novel*, have they been brought together and made generally accessible. 'No man of our time,' said Ezra Pound in 1918, in one of the first, and few, intelligent essays on James, 'has so laboured to create means of communication as did the late Henry James. The whole of great art is a struggle for communication.' It was for his advancement of the means of communication through prose that James had his greatest importance to literature.

The Novels and Tales of Henry James, 26 vols.(N.Y., 1907-17).

The American Scene(N.Y., 1907).

The Finer Grain(N.Y., 1910).

Notes on Novelists(N.Y., 1914).

Notes of a Son and Brother(N.Y., 1914).

The Ivory Tower(N.Y., 1917).

The Middle Years(N.Y., 1917).

The Sense of the Past(N.Y., 1917).

Notes and Reviews(Cambridge, Mass., 1921).

The Art of the Novel: Critical Prefaces by Henry James, with an Introduction by R.P.Blackmur(N.Y., 1934).

P.Lubbock, ed., *The Letters of Henry James*, 2 vols.(N.Y., 1920).

C.H.Grattan, *The Three Jameses*(N.Y., 1932).

J.W.Beach, *The Method of Henry James* (New Haven, 1918).

Marianne Moore and others, 'Homage to Henry James,' *Hound & Horn*,VII, 361-562.

Le R. Phillips, *A Bibliography of the Writings of Henry James*(N.Y., 1930).

EDITH WHARTON (1862-1937)

EDITH WHARTON was born an aristocrat, and wisely wrote about the life she knew best. She was aware of the structure of Society, for during the years she had spent in New York, Long Island, Newport, Lenox, and Paris she had had ample opportunity to observe both its advantages and its limitations. The resultant, shrewd commentary is unique and valuable.

Her greatest literary influence was from the early work and personal criticisms of Henry James. It is in fact doubtful if the literary significance of James' early period can be as well grasped from his own work as from that of his pupil.

Mrs. Wharton was extraordinarily successful in both the short story and the novel. 'The chief technical difference between the short story and the novel may . . .' she says, 'be summed up by saying that situation is the main concern of the short story, character of the novel; and it follows that the effect produced by the short story depends almost entirely upon its form, or presentation.' Nowhere better than in 'The Other Two' is there a defter illustration of her perfect control of form and her ability to draw by implication from a single situation a penetrating analysis of Society.

The Valley of Decision(N.Y., 1902), *The House of Mirth*(N.Y., 1905), and *The Age of Innocence*(N.Y., 1922) best illustrate her particular combination of the novel of manners and that of character (or psychology). As with her short stories, these works keep within the scope of her experience. If Mrs. Wharton is to be criticized it must not be on the ground that she did not write about other groups of society but that, even within her own province, she too frequently succumbed to literary fashions.

The Writing of Fiction(N.Y., 1925).

A Backward Glance, an autobiography (N.Y., 1934).

W.L.Cross, 'Edith Wharton,' *Bookman*, LXIII,641-46.

Henry James, *Notes on Novelists*(N.Y., 1914),353-56.

Edmund Wilson, 'Justice to Edith Wharton,' *New Republic*,XCV,209-13.

L.Davis, *A Bibliography of the Writings of Edith Wharton*(Portland, Me., 1933).

PAUL ELMER MORE (1864–1937)

PAUL ELMER MORE was the most articulate leader of the group of neo-humanists which began to develop in the first years of the present century and attracted most attention during the nineteen-twenties. Its chief significance lay in its attempt to bring order to an increasingly chaotic world, the particular approach being through the precepts of tradition. Its earliest teacher was Irving Babbitt, a professor at Harvard, who found in the languishing ideal of Rousseau an easy straw dummy for a target. Through his students and his associates the movement spread.

More was born in St. Louis, Missouri, in 1864, and was educated at Washington University in that city, and at Harvard where he was an associate of Babbitt. He taught Sanscrit there and at Bryn Mawr, and then became literary editor, first of *The Independent* in 1901, and afterwards of *The New York Evening Sun* in 1903 and of *The Nation* from 1909 to 1914. After resigning from this position he became a lecturer at Princeton University. His principal writings are collected in the six volumes of *The Greek Tradition*(N.Y., 1917–27), in the eleven volumes of *The Shelburne*

Essays(N.Y., 1904–21), and in the three supplementary volumes of *The New Shelburne Essays*(N.Y., 1928–35). The range of *The Shelburne Essays* includes all literature, and their quality is the finest of that of any American critic. In the advancement of the appreciation of American literature More's criticism has been of the greatest importance. Whittier, Longfellow, and others have received a new and deserved artistic dignity through his commentary, and few approaches to the backgrounds of Hawthorne and Poe have been keener than his. If More's essays on American writers were to be brought together into one collection, he would receive the general recognition which is his due.

The Religion of Plato(N.Y., 1921).
Hellenistic Philosophies(N.Y., 1923).
The Catholic Faith(N.Y., 1931).
R.Shafer, *Paul Elmer More and American Criticism*(New Haven, Conn., 1935).
H.P.Parkes, 'Paul Elmer More: Manichean,' *Hound & Horn*,V,477–83.
H.W.Peck, 'Some Aspects of the Criticism of Paul Elmer More,' *Sewanee Review*, XXVI,63–84.

GEORGE SANTAYANA (1863–)

IN the preface to his *Collected Poems*, George Santayana wrote:

Of impassioned tenderness or Dionysiac frenzy I have nothing, nor even of that magic and pregnancy of phrase—really the creation of a fresh idiom—which marks the high light of poetry. Even if my temperament had been naturally warmer, the fact that the English language (and I can write no other with assurance) was not my mother-tongue would of itself preclude any inspired use of it on my part; its roots do not quite reach to my center. I never drank in in childhood the homely cadences and ditties which in pure spontaneous poetry set the essential key.

And in writing of poetry in *The Life of Reason* he remarked:

For poetry, while truly poetical, never loses sight of initial feelings and underlying appeals; it is incorrigibly transcendental, and takes every present passion and every private dream in turn for the core of the universe. . . . Lying is a privilege of poets because they have not yet reached the level on which truth and error are discernible. Veracity and significance are not ideals for a primitive mind; we learn to value them as we learn to live, when we discover that the spirit cannot be wholly free and solipsistic.

The significance of these statements rests on the fact that they contain less modesty than a suggestion of finely tempered irony which marks the best of his highly conventionalized poetic utterance. His sonnet 'On the Death of a Metaphysician,' and his consciously poetical prose are perhaps the best expression of the 'Genteel Tradition' in America: their purified nineteenth-century diction, their intellectual charm, their clear, if not specific, visual imagery—all serve to illustrate the importance of George Santayana's contribution to American literature.

George Santayana was born in Madrid, Spain, in 1863 and came to America at the age of nine. He was educated at Harvard, receiving his Ph.D. from that institution in 1889. As a lecturer at Harvard he became one of its most distinguished philosophers, and while at the University, 1889 to 1912, he wrote his four notable contributions to American philosophy and letters: *The Sense of Beauty*(N.Y., 1896), *Interpretations of Poetry and Religion*(N.Y., 1900),

The Life of Reason(N.Y., 1905–06), and *Three Philosophical Poets*(N.Y., 1910). In 1912 he left America and since then has lived in England, France, and Italy.

Poems, selected by the author and revised (N.Y., 1923).
Winds of Doctrine(N.Y., 1913).
Scepticism and Animal Faith(N.Y., 1923).
The Realm of Essence(N.Y., 1927).
The Genteel Tradition at Bay(N.Y., 1931).
The Last Puritan(N.Y., 1936).
Realm of Truth(N.Y., 1938).
I.Edman, 'Santayana at Seventy,' *Saturday Review of Literature*,X,349–50.
G.W.Howgate, *George Santayana*(Philadelphia, 1938).

EDWIN ARLINGTON ROBINSON (1869–1935)

EDWIN ARLINGTON ROBINSON stripped poetry of the florid diction typical of the late nineteenth century and turned it toward straight-forward and hard speech. His first volume, *The Torrent and the Night Before*, was published in 1896. It was a sign for the direction which modern poetry was to take. His earliest poems, greatly influenced by the poetry of Thomas Hardy, were cryptic portraits of the people of Tilbury Town, reminiscent of Gardiner, Maine, where he was brought up. They have the dryness of New England and the dramatic quality which was always characteristic of his verse. This dramatic quality he extended to longer and even more effective results in such brilliant poems as 'Ben Johnson Entertains a Man from Stratford,' 'The Man Against the Sky,' and 'Mr. Flood's Party.' Increasingly he became fixed upon the idea that man must stand in darkness in order to see the light, and with this perhaps Puritan heritage he was always content.

'You must think of me as a disappointed playwright,' he once remarked to a friend. During the first decade of the twentieth century he became deeply interested in the vigorous movement for a poetic drama which was led by William Vaughn Moody and Percy MacKaye. Out of this interest came such plays in verse as his *Van Zorn*

and *Porcupine*. The movement dwindled, and in 1910 and 1911 Robinson undertook to rewrite his plays in the form of novels. The results he tore up and burned; the effect, however, was lasting. His plays were originally closet drama, and any attempts to novelize them must have intellectualized and spun them out even more. Thus when at last he turned to the composition of the long narrative poems which chiefly occupied him for the rest of his life he appeared to be confused between the provinces of the novel and of poetry. Little narrative verse is successful unless it moves through the force of highly charged emotion. This, unfortunately, Robinson's highly psychological narratives never did.

It was not until the publication of *Tristram*(N.Y., 1927) that he met with anything like a popular success. The subject was reasonably enough within the Victorian conventions in poetry to be acceptable to the public, though there is no apparent reason why they should have welcomed this and have rejected his similar *Merlin* of a decade before. Of his poems written on the Arthurian legends, Robinson felt that '*Merlin, Lancelot,* and *Tristram*— taken together as a sort of unit—appear to me as likely to last as anything I have written.' General opinion, however, seems to favor his earlier work.

Collected Poems of Edwin Arlington Robinson(N.Y., 1937).

Mark Van Doren, *Edwin Arlington Robinson*(N.Y., 1927).

B.R.Redman, *Edwin Arlington Robinson* (N.Y., 1926).

Hermann Hagedorn, *Edwin Arlington Robinson*(N.Y., 1938).

Amy Lowell, *Tendencies in Modern American Poetry*(Boston, 1917),3–75.

Harriet Monroe, *Poets & Their Art*(N.Y., 1926),1–11.

E.E.Pipkin, 'The Arthur of Edwin Arlington Robinson,' *English Journal*,XIX, 183–95.

F.I.Carpenter, 'Tristram the Transcendent,' *New England Quarterly*,XI,501–23.

C.B.Hogan, *A Bibliography of Edwin Arlington Robinson*(New Haven, Conn., 1936).

WILLIAM ELLERY LEONARD (1876–1944)

THE poetic conventions which mark the characteristic style of William Ellery Leonard's verse are those of the Miltonic tradition as it was exemplified in the work of the English Romantic poets. Leonard's narrative poem *Two Lives* (1925) displays at length the impress of the conventions which have given his style its Romantic quality. In subject the work resembles Richard Dehmel's *Zwei Menschen*, and in form the work is an avowed experiment in the use of the sonnet as a standard form in narrative poetry.

William Ellery Leonard was born in Plainfield, New Jersey, in 1876. After receiving his A.M. in Harvard, in 1899 he extended his research in Philology at the University of Göttingen and Bonn. He has been a professor of English at the University of Wisconsin since 1906.

His translations of Beowulf and Empedocles and Lucretius are among the best of

their kind in the English language. For the last ten years Leonard's remarkable literary insights and energies have been devoted to his researches in Anglo-Saxon, Middle English, and the Romance Languages.

Byron and Byronism in America(N.Y., 1905).

The Vaunt of Man and Other Poems(N.Y., 1912).

The Lynching Bee and Other Poems(N.Y., 1920).

A Son of Earth(N.Y., 1928). Collected poems.

The Poet of Galilee(N.Y., 1928).

The Locomotive God(N.Y., 1927).

Two Lives(N.Y., 1930).

'The Poetic Process from the Inside,' *Bookman*,LXXV,327–33.

Ludwig Lewisohn, 'Poet and Scholar,' *Nation*,CXVI,660–61.

ROBERT FROST (1875–)

THE plain speech of Robert Frost was a parallel to Edwin Arlington Robinson's in the reform of poetic diction. His manner of speech is as crisp and fresh as the taste of a good apple, and his wit and wisdom have the New England manner of cracker-box philosophy. 'The style is the man,' Frost has said. 'Rather say the style is the way the man takes himself; and to be at all charming or even bearable, the way is almost rigidly prescribed. If it is with outer seriousness, it must be with inner humor. If it is with outer humor, it must be with inner seriousness.' There need be no better proof that Frost is a New Englander.

Actually, he was born in San Francisco, California, but after his father's death,

when Frost was nine, he returned with his mother to Lawrence, Massachusetts. For a few months in 1892 he was a student at Dartmouth, and from 1897 to 1899 he was enrolled in Harvard University. Thereafter he farmed in New Hampshire and taught school, until in 1912 he sailed with his wife and children for England. His first two books, *A Boy's Will*(London, 1913) and *North of Boston*(London, 1914), were published there, though he had been writing poetry for a decade before. It is an interesting commentary on the state of publishing and public taste in America. When he returned to America in 1915, however, many prejudices had been stripped away and his way made easier. In time it became easy.

Frost, like Edwin Arlington Robinson, had a predilection for the dramatic. In the preface to a one-act play that he wrote, he said: 'A dramatic necessity goes deep into the nature of the sentence. Sentences are not different enough to hold the attention unless they are dramatic. No ingenuity of varying structure will do. All that can save them is the speaking tone of voice somehow entangled in the words and fastened to the page for the ear of the imagination. That is all that can save poetry from sing-song, all that can save prose from itself.' And 'Everything written is as good as it is dramatic. It need not declare itself in form, but it is dramatic or nothing.' This perhaps natural tendency of poets intent on bringing the speaking voice of dramatic action into verse is clearly seen in such of Frost's work as 'The Death of the Hired Man' and 'Home Burial,' and is present in nearly all of his work.

Frost has always managed to exercise the greatest control over his verse, and the flatness of his lines becomes a perfect setting for his subdued imagery. 'A poem begins with a lump in the throat; a homesickness or a lovesickness. It is a reaching-out toward expression; an effort to find fulfilment.' This 'effort to find fulfilment' may be regarded as the work of a poet's lifetime. Frost has followed his own advice by evident care in the writing of his verse and by infrequent publication of its slender volumes.

Collected Poems of Robert Frost(N.Y., 1930).

A Further Range(N.Y., 1936).

G.B.Munson, *Robert Frost*(N.Y., 1927).

Robert S. Newdick, 'Robert Frost and the Dramatic,' *New England Quarterly*,X, 262–69.

——, 'Robert Frost and the Sound of Sense,' *American Literature*,IX,290–300.

Richard Thornton, ed., *Recognition of Robert Frost*(N.Y., 1937). A collection of reviews and essays in homage to Frost.

W.B.S.Clymer and C.R.Green, *Robert Frost:A Bibliography*(Amherst, Mass., 1937).

'The Tuft of Flowers,' 'A Peck of Gold,' 'Fire and Ice,' 'The Death of the Hired Man,' 'The Runaway,' 'The Road Not Taken,' 'Neither Out Far nor In Deep,' 'Two Tramps in Mud Time,' 'Mending Wall,' 'Dust of Snow,' 'Birches.' (Erpi Picture Consultants, SS 9608–6 to 9614–6). Recordings by Robert Frost for the National Council of Teachers of English.

VACHEL LINDSAY (1879–1931)

IN his introduction to *The Congo*(N.Y., 1916) Lindsay wrote: 'Mr. Yeats asked me recently in Chicago, "What are we going to do to restore the primitive singing voice of poetry?"' This was another appeal for returning the cadence of the poetic line to that of the voice. Lindsay's response, already made, was with what he called the 'Higher Vaudeville imagination.' 'America needs the flamboyant to save her soul.' The public received his first flamboyant note in 1913 when Harriet Monroe published 'General William Booth Enters into Heaven' in her recently founded *Poetry: A Magazine of Verse*.

Lindsay was a boy when he began his campaign to save souls, for if he was not born with the spirit of a missionary, his parents drilled the importance of such an obligation into him. From the age of six he had been trained as an artist, and after quitting Hiram College, Ohio, in 1900 he pondered a career of 'Christian cartooning.' His high seriousness, which came from the Campbellite religion of his parents, was reinforced and decorated by his unrelinquished devotion to the precepts of the Pre-Raphaelites and the Christian socialist doctrines of William Morris. Their amalgamation of the arts he himself first sought to express through poems which illustrated his drawings:

In the shade of a lantern unlighted
Awaits us a heathen benighted
He drinks Inspiration from a jar decoration
His exquisite taste is delighted.

It was a bad poetic beginning. After periods of studying art in New York, lecturing before a Y.M.C.A., and working for the Anti-Saloon League in the section of Illinois about Springfield, his birthplace, he made in 1912 his long and famous journey on foot from Illinois to New Mexico, with a packet of pamphlets, *Poems to be Traded for Bread*, and a bundle of his cartoons.

Like a troubadour circuit-rider he travelled from house to house, carrying on his 'warfare for Beauty and Democracy,' by showing his drawings and reading such poems as one

To Those That Would Mend These Times

Go plant the arts that woo the weariest,
Bold arts that simple workmen understand,
That make no poor men and keep all men rich,
And throne our Lady Beauty in the land!

It was during this extension of the Ruskinesque revival with which he had hoped to bring about a 'Golden Springfield' that he formulated the 'bold arts' of his poem on Booth. This he sent in to Miss Monroe while he was still en route. Independently, and to an extent unwittingly, he joined the new movement of poetry.

Lindsay discovered that others besides simple workmen understood and liked verse, 'where every line may be two-thirds spoken and one-third sung, the entire rendering, musical and elocutionary, depending upon the improvising power and sure instinct of the performer.' Women's Clubs for the rest of his life insisted that he write

and read only poems like 'The Congo,' 'Simon Legree,' and 'General William Booth,' until Lindsay could not bear even the thought of them.

His creative life was constantly buffeted between vaudeville and Ruskin. By instinct he was abreast of his time; emotionally he was behind it. The resulting conflict he could never resolve. One group of Lindsay's works is unforgettable for its vigorous movement and vital individuality; another is commonplace through its limp and sentimental unreality. As a result his verse is an exaggerated symbol both of what poetry was striving for and fighting against.

Collected Poems (N.Y., 1925).
Selected Poems(N.Y., 1931). Edited, with an introduction, by Hazleton Spencer.
Adventures While Preaching the Gospel of Beauty(N.Y., 1914).
A Handy Guide for Beggars(N.Y., 1916).
The Congo(Columbia University Phonograph Record No. 2). A recording by Lindsay.
John L.Sullivan(Columbia University Phonograph Record No. 3). A recording by Lindsay.
E.L.Masters, *Vachel Lindsay: A Poet in America*(N.Y., 1935).
H.Monroe, *Poets & Their Art*(N.Y., 1926), 21-28.
H.Spencer, 'The Life and Death of a Bard,' *American Mercury*,XXV,455-62.
Thelma Wiles Thalinger, 'Vachel Lindsay: Pen and Ink Symbolist,' *Magazine of Art*, XXXI,450-56.

EDGAR LEE MASTERS (1869-)

EDGAR LEE MASTERS' contribution to American literature is best represented by his *Spoon River Anthology* (N.Y., 1915) which first appeared in the pages of William Marion Reedy's magazine, *Reedy's Mirror*. In its unrhymed verse forms, its penetration into the lives of those who lived in a middle western community, its naturalism, its obvious veracity—all combined to make Edgar Lee Masters the personification of the small town freethinker. Like Sinclair Lewis' *Main Street*, Masters' *Anthology* is a landmark in American literature.

Edgar Lee Masters was born in Garnett, Kansas, in 1869. During his early adolescence, his family moved to Lewistown, Illinois, where he studied law in his father's office. He then left Lewistown for Chicago where for many years he practiced law. Not unlike the work of many of his contemporaries, Masters' early work included two experiments in poetic drama, the first a play on Benedict Arnold written in 1895, and the second *Maximilian* published in 1902. Between 1898 and 1937 Masters has published many volumes of poetry, but of these only the *Spoon River* volumes, the *Domesday*

Book(N.Y., 1920), and *The Fate of the Jury* (N.Y., 1929) have contributed materially to his poetic reputation. Of · recent years Masters' work in prose has been no less prolific, yet of it all only his autobiography, *Across Spoon River*(N.Y., 1936) seems to hold more than a transitory interest for his readers. *Across Spoon River* resembles Dreiser's *Dawn* in its evident desire to record faithfully the experiences of the author's life.

Selected Poems(N.Y., 1925).
Invisible Landscapes(N.Y., 1935).
Mitch Miller(N.Y., 1920).

Skeeters Kirby(N.Y., 1923).
'The Genesis of Spoon River,' *American Mercury*,XXVIII,38–55.
J.C.Chandler, 'The Spoon River Country,' *Journal of the Illinois State Historical Society*,XIV,252–329.
Conrad Aiken, *Scepticisms*(N.Y., 1919), 65–75.
Amy Lowell, *Tendencies in Modern American Poetry*(Boston, 1917),139–200.
Harriet Monroe, *Poets & Their Art*(N.Y., 1926),46–55.
Louis Untermeyer, *American Poetry Since 1900*(N.Y., 1923), 163–80.

CARL SANDBURG (1878–)

SANDBURG's poem 'Chicago' was, when it first appeared in 1914, the apparent epitome of the anti-poetic. Its subject was not the only aspect which aroused opposition, for Sandburg had taken its language out of the mouths of the people rather than of the poets. His own life seemed in itself anti-poetic. He had had almost no schooling as a boy; he was a newspaper reporter, had driven a milk-wagon, had been a porter and a dishwasher, had worked in a brickyard, had harvested, been a soldier,—had in fact, by circumstance, combined the experiences of the people in himself.

It was the people from whom he got his strength, and their apostle, Whitman, from whom he received his directions on subject matter and freedom of expression. Sandburg was, however, not an imitator. 'The difference between Whitman and Sandburg,' Morton Zabel has observed,

is primarily a difference between a visionary imagination and a realistic one, between a prophet who deals in the racial and social aspects of humanitarianism and a historian who handles the specific facts of industrial life and labor. Whitman, given his sympathies and cause and with his greater imaginative vision, might have written his book without any immediate contact with its materials, whereas Sandburg, so denied, could have written none of his. The two poets join only at the point which is their common weakness: in the rhap-

sodic cries and flights that are the diffused and prevalent bane of the one and the merely incidental weakness of the other. Sandburg is saved from this pretension by his plain verbal sanity. He does not discard the lyric imagination; it filters through his pages and produces many short passages of characteristic fancy:

Alive yet the spillover of last night's
    moonrise
    brought returns of peculiar cash
    a cash of thin air alive yet.

But it is seldom allowed to develop into vague apostrophe or inflated allegory, any more than his language is allowed to use the pompous phrases, French or Latin counterfeit, and hollow pedantry of Whitman's style.

Sandburg's imagination and expression is realistic, but his faith in the people is the vague mysticism of Christian socialism which he absorbed during the years 1910 to 1912 when he was secretary to the Social-Democratic mayor of Milwaukee.

His first volume of poetry was privately printed in 1904, but it was not until after the success of 'Chicago' and the publication of *Chicago Poems*(N.Y., 1916) that he became a poet by profession. Succeeding volumes, *Cornhuskers*(N.Y., 1918), *Smoke and Steel*(N.Y., 1920), *Slabs of the Sunburnt West*(N.Y., 1923), *Good Morning*

America(N.Y., 1928), and *The People, Yes* (N.Y., 1936) indicate his fidelity to his theme. These volumes of poetry he has interspersed with such fanciful books for children as *Rootabaga Stories*(N.Y., 1922) and with his extended work on the biography of Lincoln, of which the first volume, *Abraham Lincoln: The Prairie Years* (N.Y., 1926), has been unsurpassed by any other biographer. The common bond of all his works is indicated by his description of *The People, Yes* as 'a footnote to the Gettysburg Address.' His range has been extended into the field of balladry and folk songs, a large number of which he collected in *The American Songbag*(N.Y., 1927). From such varied interests, as well as from his personal experience, comes the richness of his vocabulary which is his chief strength.

Sandburg's poetry shows little development from his earliest volumes to his latest.

He found a form of expression admirably suited to his thought, and his thought has changed but little.

R.West, ed., *Selected Poems of Carl Sandburg*(N.Y., 1926).

Carl Sandburg, *A Recital of Authentic American Folksongs from his collection 'The American Songbag,'* (Musicraft, Album II,207–10). A recording of eight folksongs.

H.Hansen, *Carl Sandburg: The Man and His Poetry*(Girard, Kan., 1925).

H.Monroe, *Poets & Their Art*(N.Y., 1926), 29–38.

M.D.Zabel, 'Sandburg's Testament,' in *Literary Opinion in America*(N.Y., 1937), 406–15.

William P. Schenk (comp.), 'Carl Sandburg—A Bibliography,' *Bulletin of Bibliography*,XVI,4–7.

THEODORE DREISER (1871–1945)

STEPHEN CRANE'S *Maggie*(N.Y., 1892) and Theodore Dreiser's *Sister Carrie*(N.Y., 1900) are indicative of the recognition in the American novel of naturalism. It is significant that it was Frank Norris, full of his comprehension of the 'responsibility of the novelist,' who arranged for the publication of Dreiser's *Sister Carrie*. Once issued, the book was sabotaged by its own publisher. It was not republished in America until 1914. The position of novelists at that time has been reminiscently described by Dreiser:

I think it nothing less than tragic that these men, or boys, fresh, forceful, imbued with a burning desire to present life as they saw it, were thus completely overawed by the moral hypocrisy of the American mind and did not even dare to think of sending their novel to an American publisher. . . . You couldn't write about life as it was; you had to write about it as somebody else thought it was, the ministers and farmers and dullards of the home.

Dreiser learned to see life with the eyes of a newspaper reporter. He was born at

Terre Haute, Indiana, in 1871, and attended first the public schools and later Indiana University. Then he worked for newspapers in Chicago, St. Louis, Pittsburg, and New York. Chicago excited him, with its tonic clatter, its black factories and its spacious mansions, as later it excited Sandburg. Said Dreiser, 'I think I grasped Chicago in its larger material if not in its more complicated mental aspects.' But the task of having to cover in the course of a single day both a wedding and a suicide or to write impartially of both the well-fed and the starving taught him the carelessness of life. He came out of this experience with a lack of confidence: 'Man, as I was beginning to find—all of us—were small, irritable, nasty in their struggle for life.' 'Life is a god-damned stinking game.'

Nevertheless he developed his enormous capacity for sympathy which has marked all his writing.

I was filled with an intense sympathy for the woes of others, life in all its helpless degradation and poverty, the unsatisfied dreams of people, their sweaty labors, the things they were compelled to endure—nameless impositions, curses, brutalities—the things they would never have, their hungers, thirsts, half-formed dreams of pleasures, their glittering insanities and beaten resolutions at the end. I have sobbed dry sobs looking into what I deemed to be broken faces and the eyes of human failures.

Dreiser's novels have been based on the give and take of these impositions and on the lives of human failures. He has always written best when he has described actual material. The Titan(N.Y., 1914) was based on the career of Charles Yerkes, the Chicago grain dealer about whom Norris wrote in The Pit; The Genius(N.Y., 1915), the story of a painter who became a magazine editor, was based on the career of Ben Hampton; and An American Tragedy (N.Y., 1925) was in spots an almost verbatim account of an upper New York State murder. Dreiser's genius lies in his ability to grasp many of the implications of these lives. Essentially Dreiser is an individualist as well as a materialist, and the tragedy of his characters comes from the failures of their material lives. The result is an admirable portrait of his age. From even a single chapter such as that titled by the editors 'An American Problem' one can grasp the legitimate quandary which faced Clyde Griffith.

Dreiser's prose stumbles along its path, eager, impetuous, awkward, and psychologically perfect. Dreiser's work was both revolutionary and unforgettable in American prose. As Sherwood Anderson has remarked:

Theodore Dreiser is old—he is very, very old. . . . Something grey and bleak and hurtful, that has been in the world perhaps forever, is personified in him. . . . When Dreiser is gone men shall write books, many of them, and in the books they shall write there will be so many of the qualities Dreiser lacks. The new, the younger men shall have a sense of humor, and everyone knows Dreiser has no sense of humor. More than that, American prose writers shall have grace, lightness of touch, a dream of beauty breaking through the husks of life. . . . Heavy, heavy, the feet of Theodore. How easy to pick some of his books to pieces, to laugh at him for so much of his heavy prose. These feet are making a path, and the children who follow after will run quickly and nimbly because the path has been made. The fellows of the ink-pots, the prose writers of America who follow Dreiser will have much to do that he has never done. Their road is long, but, because of him, those who follow will never have to face the road through the wilderness of Puritan denial, the road that Dreiser faced alone.

Sister Carrie(N.Y., 1900).
Jennie Gerhardt(N.Y., 1911).
The Financier(N.Y., 1912).
A Traveler at Forty(N.Y., 1913).
Twelve Men(N.Y., 1919).
A Book about Myself(N.Y., 1922).
An American Tragedy(N.Y., 1925).
Dawn(N.Y., 1931).
D.Dudley, Forgotten Frontiers(N.Y., 1932).
Sherwood Anderson, Horses and Men (N.Y., 1923),xi–xii.
R.Bourne, History of a Literary Radical (N.Y.,1920),195–204.
H.L.Mencken, A Book of Prefaces(N.Y., 1917),67–148.
C.Fadiman, 'Dreiser and the American Dream,' Nation,CXXXV,364–65.

JAMES BRANCH CABELL (1879–)

JAMES BRANCH CABELL learned to see life through the veil of romantic mediaevalism. In his earliest writing, at the beginning of the century, he saw only the veil; then with The Rivet in Grandfather's Neck (N.Y., 1915) he began to cast his serious attention on American life. In his later work he did not throw aside the veil. 'It comes almost to saying that the novel of contemporary life, via the typewriter of the serious artist, will return to the oldest of forms, and become more or less an allegory. . . . Art, I repeat, must deal with contemporary life by means of symbols. And the creative writer should handle facts religiously, in that particular mood of piety which holds that incomplete accord with a creator's will is irreligious. . . . Facts must be kept in their proper place, outside of which they lose veracity.' Such was Cabell's demiurge.

He was born a Southern gentleman, and his attitude was shaped by the period in which he taught French and Greek at William and Mary, from which he had been graduated. These two factors combined to make him into something of an American Anatole France, whose ironic commentary on his contemporary civilization had been written in his fabular *L'Île des Penguins*. Cabell's island was the imaginary French province of Poictesme. Within its boundaries he carried on his skirmishes against the forces of Philistia. Of these, *Jurgen*(N.Y., 1919) was best known. Puritan prudery and middle-class gaucheries were to be stung by his barbed satire, but the barb was so deftly concealed by the elaborated brilliance of his style that its wound was scarcely felt by the majority of his readers. They were not hurt but titillated.

The seriousness underlying his writing differed only in manner from the blatancy of the 'Menckenoids,' as Cabell called them, who were his fellow contributors to the *Smart Set* and the *American Mercury* in a general age of criticism. On his standards of Southern gentility, younger writers of his section first modelled their own attacks.

The Works of James Branch Cabell(N.Y., 1927–30), 18 vols.
These Restless Heads(N.Y., 1934).
Smirt: an Urbane Nightmare(N.Y., 1934).
Smith: a Sylvan Interlude(N.Y., 1935).
H.L.Mencken, *James Branch Cabell*(N.Y., 1927).
Carl Van Doren, *James Branch Cabell* (N.Y., 1925).
Ellen Glasgow, 'The Biography of Manuel,' *Saturday Review of Literature*,VI, 1108–09.
J.Hergesheimer, 'James Branch Cabell,' *American Mercury*,XIII,38–47.
Leon Howard, 'Figures of Allegory,' *Sewanee Review*,XXXVII,193–203.
R.M.Lovett, 'Mr. James Branch Cabell,' *New Republic*,XXVI,187–89.
H.Walpole, *The Art of James Branch Cabell* (N.Y., 1920). ·
I.R.Brussel, *A Bibliography of the Writings of James Branch Cabell* (Philadelphia, 1932).

JOHN REED (1887–1920)

JOHN REED, in 1917, wrote of himself:

I am twenty-nine years old, and I know that this is the end of a part of my life, the end of youth. Sometimes it seems to me the end of the world's youth too; certainly the Great War has done something to us all. But it is also the beginning of a new phase of life; and the world we live in is so full of swift change and color and meaning that I can hardly keep from imagining the splendid and terrible possibilities of the time to come. The last ten years I've gone up and down the earth drinking in experience, fighting and loving, seeing and hearing and testing things. I've traveled all over Europe, and to the borders of the East, and down in Mexico, having adventures; seeing men killed and broken, victorious and laughing, men with visions and men with a sense of humor. I've watched civilization change and broaden and sweeten in my lifetime; and I've watched it wither and crumble in the red blast of war. And war I have seen, too, in the trenches, with the armies. I'm not quite sick of seeing yet, but soon I will be—I know that. My future life will not be what it has been. And I so want to stop a minute, and look back, and get my bearings.

Reed was born in Portland, Oregon, of well-to-do parents, and was educated at Harvard during the stimulating decade when men like Walter Lippmann, Heywood Broun, T.S.Eliot, Conrad Aiken, and Joseph Ferdinand Gould were students there. After a Vagabondian tour abroad, Reed went to New York and entered its literary Bohemia. During this period he contributed verse to *Poetry* and to the *Masses*, and issued privately a long poem on life in Greenwich Village. In 1914, when Villa had captured Chihahua, he left for Mexico as a correspondent for the *Metropolitan Magazine*. His articles were the most dramatic contributions to the journalistic literature of America since Richard Harding Davis' reports of the battle of San Juan hill. During the World War he was abroad as a foreign correspondent. It was after his return to America for an operation that he wrote the reminiscence quoted above. In August of that year he sailed for Russia where he arrived in time to witness the October revolution. As a friend of Lenin he was granted access to important documents, and was encouraged to write a history of what he had seen. This he did in *Ten Days that Shook the World* (N.Y., 1919), after his return to New York. 'I have to see,' Reed said. His history was a step toward the heightened reportorial sketches of Ernest Hemingway and John Dos Passos.

Later in the year of its publication Reed was forced to flee from America to escape charges of sedition, and went again to Russia. There he died of the typhus and was buried in the Kremlin. In a review of Reed's biography, Max Lerner wrote:

He was no thinker but a man of action. But it was his good fortune to be led to the most desirable of all fates for a man of action who is also a writer and a poet—the chance at once to write history and to make it.

It is this emphasis on freedom and action and joyousness—almost its obsession of Reed's with them—that gives his life its importance for us and makes the incidents of it credible. Reed died thinking he had found in communism a solution not only for himself but for the workers and the creative everywhere. How deep his communism was is a question that is difficult to answer. He probably understood communism only as he understood everything else—as a verifiable part of his own experience.

'Almost Thirty,' *The New Republic*, LXXXVI,267–70, 332–36.
Ten Days that Shook the World(N.Y., 1926). With an introduction by Lenin.
Granville Hicks, *John Reed: The Making of a Revolutionary*(N.Y., 1936).
Max Lerner, 'John Reed: No Legend,' *Nation*,CXLII,552–53.

HENRY L. MENCKEN (1880–)

THE popular rhetorician of post-war America was Henry Louis Mencken, and the textbooks were his series of *Prejudices*, made up of his editorials for the *Smart Set* and for the *American Mercury*. Such magazines represented the supreme national self-consciousness indicated at its best by Van Wyck Brooks' *America's Coming of Age*(N.Y., 1915). This self-consciousness found expression in a post-adolescent urge to hit out at everything and to applaud the blows.

Mencken's first series of *Prejudices* attacked the pedantries of professors, the utopianism of H.G.Wells; the social philosophies of Henry George and Thorsten Veblen; and sociology, psychology, and theology. His attitude toward the contemporary scene is indicated in the following quotation:

But how, then, explain the fact that the populace is constantly ravished and

set aflame by fresh brigades of moral, political and sociological revolutionists—that it is forever playing the eager victim to new mountebanks? The explanation lies in the simple circumstance that these performers upon the public midriff are always careful to ladle out nothing actually alarming and accursed. What they offer is always the same old panacea with an extra-gaudy label—the tried, tasted and much-loved dose, the colic cure that mother used to make. Superficially, the United States seems to suffer from an endless and astounding neophilism; actually all its thinking is done within the boundaries of a very small group of political, economic and religious ideas, most of them unsound. For example, there is the fundamental idea of democracy—the idea that all political power should remain in the hands of the populace, that its exercise by superior men is intrinsically immoral. Out of this idea spring innumerable notions and crazes that are no more, at bottom, than restatements of it in sentimental terms: rotation in office, direct elections, the initiative and referendum, the recall, the popular primary, and so on. Again, there is the primary doctrine that the possession of great wealth is a crime—a doctrine half a religious heritage and half the product of mere mob envy. Out of it have come free silver, trust-busting, government ownership, muck-raking, Populism, Bleaseism, Progressivism, the milder forms of Socialism, the whole gasconade of 'reform' politics. Yet again, there is the ineradicable peasant suspicion of the man who is having a better time in the world—a suspicion grounded, like the foregoing, partly upon undisguised envy and partly upon archaic and barbaric religious taboos. Out of it have come all the glittering pearls of the uplift, from Abolition to Prohibition, and from the crusade against horseracing to the Mann Act. The whole political history of the United States is a history of these three ideas.

Mencken's vigorous style is in consciously direct antithesis to John Dryden's remarks on the art of satire: 'How easy it is to call rogue and villain, and that wittily! But how hard to make a man appear a fool, a blockhead, or a knave, without using any of those opprobrious terms! To spare the grossness of the names, and to do the thing yet more severely, is to draw a full face, and to make the nose and cheeks stand out, and yet not to employ any depth of shadowing. This is the mystery of that noble trade, which yet no master can teach to his apprentice; he may give the rules, but the scholar is never the nearer in his practice.'

Damn! A Book of Calumny(N.Y., 1918).
Prejudices(N.Y.,1919,1920,1922,1924,1926, 1927).
Selected Prejudices(N.Y., 1930).
The American Language(N.Y., 1936).
I.Goldberg, *The Man Mencken*(N.Y., 1925).
E.Boyd, *H.L.Mencken*(N.Y., 1925).
J.B.Cabell, *Some of Us*(N.Y., 1930).
S.P.Sherman, *Americans*(N.Y., 1922),1-12.

WILLA CATHER (1876–1947)

DESPITE her early experience as a journalist, Willa Cather has turned elsewhere for a model of expression. 'If the novel is a form of imaginative art, it cannot be at the same time a vivid and brilliant form of journalism. . . . Whatever is felt upon the page without being specifically named there—that, one might say, is created. It is the inexplicable presence of the thing not named, of the overtone divined by the ear but not heard by it, the verbal mood, the emotional aura of fact or the thing or the deed, that gives high quality to the novel or the drama, as well as to poetry itself.'

This manner she has expressed most successfully in such of her novels as *The Professor's House*(N.Y., 1925), *Death Comes for the Archbishop*(N.Y., 1925), and *Shadows on the Rock*(N.Y., 1931). It is not the only mood to be found in her writing, but it is uniquely successful in contemporary American prose. That it should suit so admirably her pictures of frontier life comes from her concept of the moral certitude of

pioneers. 'The generation that subdued the wild land and broke up the virgin prairie is passing, but there is still there, a group of rugged figures in the background which inspire respect, compel admiration. With these old men and women the attainment of material prosperity was a moral victory, because it was wrung from hard conditions, was the result of a struggle that tested character. They can look out over those broad stretches of fertility and say: "We made this, with our backs and hands." ' This 'moral victory' brings a calm to her successful characters which is admirably expressed through the quietness of her style. It was this same calm which was characteristic of the characters of Sarah Orne Jewett's *Country of the Pointed Firs*, to whom Miss Cather avowedly owes so much.

In *Death Comes for the Archbishop* the first Archbishop of Santa Fé could say, in a spiritual sense, that the land was being won. 'We made this, with our backs and hands.' Thus Death, when it came in the manner of Holbein's series of woodcuts, could be welcomed with composure. The character of Bishop Latour was based on that of the Rev. John Baptist Lamy, and that of Father Vaillant on Padre Joseph Machebeuf who became first Bishop of Denver. The incident of the pearl-grey mules was one actually related in outline by Machebeuf in a letter to his sister in France.

Miss Cather was born in Virginia, but was taken by her parents to Nebraska when she was nine. It was there that she observed and became friends with the immigrants whom she described in *My Ántonia*(N.Y., 1918). In her descriptions she has been careful to maintain her own position as an outsider, familiar with but not actually a part of the life she describes.

Novels and Stories(Boston, 1937–38), 12 vols.
Not Under Forty(N.Y., 1936). Contains 'The Novel Demeuble.'
'A Letter from Willa Cather,' *Commonweal*, VII,713–14. On the composition of *Death Comes for the Archbishop*.
'Shadows on the Rock: A Letter,' *Saturday Review of Literature*,VIII,216.
R.Rapin, *Willa Cather*(N.Y., 1930). Contains a bibliography.
L.Carroll, 'Willa Sibert Cather,' *Bookman*, LIII,212–16.
H.Gregory, 'Review of *Shadows on the Rock*,' *Symposium*,II,551–54.
W.J.Howlett, *Life of the Right Reverend Joseph P. Machebeuf, D.D.*(Pueblo, Colo., 1908).
L.H.Warner, *Archbishop Lamy, An Epoch Maker*(Santa Fé, N.M., 1936).

OLE RÖLVAAG (1876–1931)

OLE EDVART RÖLVAAG was himself an immigrant, and one of the few American writers able to write from within such experience. He was born in the village of Rölvaag, on an island just south of the Arctic Circle off the coast of Norway. It was from this village that he took his name after his arrival in America. Rölvaag was a fisherman, and as the result of a storm in the winter of 1893 resolved to emigrate to America. He finally arrived in 1896 and went immediately to his uncle's farm in South Dakota. He worked on the land for three years, and then entered a preparatory school in Canton, South Dakota. In 1905 he was graduated from St. Olaf's College in Minnesota, studied for a year in Norway, and became a member of the St. Olaf's faculty until his retirement in 1931.

His first book was *Amerika-Breve* [*Letters from America*](Minneapolis, 1912), and like all of his work was written in Norwegian. He wrote, however, comparatively little except textbooks until after 1920 when his third novel, *To Tullinger*[*Two Fools*] was published. In 1922 appeared *Længeslens Baat*[*The Boat of Longing*]. These were widely read by Norwegian-speaking Americans. In 1923, stimulated by the report that Johan Bojer, the Norwegian novelist, was about to visit America to write a novel

about immigrant life, Rölvaag set immediately at work to compose his own. *Giants in the Earth* was first printed in Norway, and was then translated into English by Rölvaag, in collaboration with Lincoln Colcord. It was the first of a trilogy, of which *Peder Victorious*(N.Y., 1929) and *Their Father's God*(N.Y., 1931) were the remaining volumes.

Other writers have been able to indicate the psychological situation of immigrants who penetrated the American frontier, but Rölvaag's great gift was his ability to reproduce its effect. Such is the scene in which he describes the oncoming of winter to a woman like Beret, a scene differing from but as essentially American as that described by De Crêvecœur or by Whittier.

Paa Glemte Veie [*The Forgotten Path*](Minneapolis, 1914).
The Boat of Longing(N.Y., 1933).
Peder Seier [*Peder Victorious*](Oslo, Norway, 1928).
Den Signede Dag [*Their Father's God*] (Oslo, Norway, 1931).
L.Colcord, 'Rölvaag the Fisherman Shook His Fist at Fate,' *American Magazine*, CV,37,188–92.
P.H.Boynton, 'O.E.Rölvaag and the Con-

quest of the Pioneer,' *English Journal*, XVIII,535–42.

E.I.Haugen, 'Rölvaag: Norwegian-American,' *Norwegian-American Studies and Records*,VII,53–73.

J.E.Olson, 'Rölvaag's Novels of Norwegian Pioneer Life in the Dakotas,' *Scandinavian Studies and Notes*,IX,45–55.

V.L.Parrington, *Main Currents in American Thought*(N.Y., 1927–30),III,387–96.

SINCLAIR LEWIS (1885–)

THE overwhelming success of Sinclair Lewis' novel, *Main Street* (N.Y., 1920), came in the period which accepted Mencken as its schoolmaster. Lewis was born in 1885 in Sauk Center, Minnesota, the son of a country doctor, went east to Yale, and afterwards worked in numerous editorial offices. *Main Street* is usually thought of as his first novel; actually it was his seventh. The earlier novels had been more or less slight, but serious in intent.

According to Lewis he began to plan *Main Street* when he was a sophomore in college. It broke on the Sauk Centers of America like a torrent of rain after a thunderclap. Writers had been accusing them indirectly for years, but now there was a man to speak to them in their own language. The Jim Blausers always gave their extravagant praise, but here was Lewis dressed up as Carol Kennicott to explain that these things were not so. The novel was the sermon of a speaker who used their own technique of ridiculing through mimicry. Lewis' greatest power is as a mimic. He has an acute and sympathetic perception of the nuances of ordinary conversation, and a blindness for the nuances of landscape. Despite 'the broom-swish of Aunt Bessie's voice, and the mop-pounding of Uncle Whittier's grumble,' *Main Street* is more of a landmark than a work of art.

In *Babbitt*(N.Y., 1922), Lewis gave another word to the language, through his description of the American Everyman of the Nineteen-Twenties. The scope was wider than that of *Main Street*, the application was more universal, and the cure was less specific. Lewis realized the cultural deficiencies of George F. Babbitt, but recognized also the spiritual yearnings which drew Babbitt to Tavis, his mistress; which caused him to support Doane, the radical, to refuse to join the Good Citizen's League, and to support Paul Riesling when

Paul shot his wife, Zilla. He sympathized with Myra's humdrum life and her temporary turn to New Thought. Lewis admitted the force of Babbitt's world to draw him back into its pattern, but allowed him enough of his former yearning to assert himself at moments of crisis, and to say at his son's marriage: 'Go ahead, old man! The world is yours!' It was easy enough for Carol to criticize Main Street, since she came freshly to it; Babbitt's criticism of himself was infinitely more significant.

Arrowsmith(N.Y., 1925), an account of the struggle of a doctor to keep the path of pure research, is perhaps his best work technically. It is not however the most interesting, for Arrowsmith is not personally so common a denominator. *Elmer Gantry* (N.Y., 1927), a satire on evangelism, was a cannonade directed against a toy figure. Lewis can hardly be called a distinguished writer of prose, but he has always possessed a sense of the timely, and his biting power of mimicry has won him approval in Europe and embarrassment and applause in America. In 1930 he became the first American to be awarded the Nobel Prize in literature.

Dodsworth(N.Y., 1929).

Ann Vickers(N.Y., 1933).

Selected Short Stories of Sinclair Lewis (N.Y., 1935).

It Can't Happen Here(N.Y., 1935).

O.Harrison, *Sinclair Lewis*(N.Y., 1925).

Carl Van Doren, *Sinclair Lewis*(N.Y., 1933). With a Bibliography by Harvey Taylor.

W.R.Benét, 'The Earlier Lewis,' *Saturday Review of Literature*,X,421–22.

H.S.Canby, 'Sinclair Lewis's Art of Work,' *Saturday Review of Literature*,X,465–473.

E.M.Forster, *Sinclair Lewis Interprets America*(N.Y., 1932).

RING LARDNER (1885–1933)

AN important aspect of modern prose, coincidental to the practice of modern poetry, has been an increasing sensitivity to the value of the spoken word. The exact phonetic reproduction of dialect by writers like Joel Chandler Harris was extended to common speech, and an increasing awareness of the relationship between the words and thoughts of characters has helped to remove from prose the artificial diction which marked much of the writing of the previous century. The work of few authors demonstrates this awareness better than that of Ring Lardner.

Lardner was born in 1885 at Niles, Michigan, and after two years at the Armour Institute of Technology in Chicago, became in 1905 a reporter for the South Bend, Indiana, *Times*. In 1907 he re-turned to Chicago where he was a sportswriter and columnist. It was while writing for the *Tribune* that he published *You Know Me Al*(N.Y., 1916) in the racy vernacular of the baseball player. In later stories like 'The Golden Honeymoon' he widened his gallery of American portraits.

Lardner's complete understanding of the people about whom he wrote accounts for the accuracy with which their speech expresses both their characters and their situations. Thus dialogue alone is sufficient, and in this economy he represents an increasing tendency among contemporary writers to discard that which is purely descriptive.

Round Up(N.Y., 1929).
First and Last(N.Y., 1934).

LOLA RIDGE (1871–1941)

THERE can be little doubt of the sincere and unified intention which lies behind the poetry of Lola Ridge. From the publication of her first book, *The Ghetto and Other Poems*(N.Y., 1918), to the writing of her *Dance of Fire*(N.Y., 1935), the theme of human martyrdom, particularly the martyrdom of the poor and disenfranchised has been the subject of her verse. *The Ghetto*, with its vivid, imagistic portraits of life in a lower Manhattan city street, illustrated her sincerity of feeling in the statement of her theme.

She was born in Dublin, Ireland, and spent her childhood in Australia and in New Zealand. Her early ambition was to be a painter, and she studied art at the Academie Julienne in Sydney. She came to the United States in 1907. For three years she wrote fiction for popular magazines. She took over the editorship of Alfred Kreymborg's magazine, *Others*, and was on the staff of *Broom*. She later lived in New York City.

The technical development of her work is shown by her uses of light and fire symbolism in the most recent of her books of poetry, *The Dance of Fire*.

Sun-Up(N.Y., 1920).
Red Flag(N.Y., 1927).
Firehead(N.Y., 1929).

SARA TEASDALE (1884–1933)

THE reiteration of the Arthurian legend symbolism in American poetry was again made evident in the early verse of Sara Teasdale. During the year 1907, in which her first book, *Sonnets to Duse*, appeared, she also published her poem, 'Guinevere,' in William Marion Reedy's magazine, *Reedy's Mirror*. Although her first book preceded the excitement and enthusiasms of the 'poetic renaissance' of 1912, it was not until the 'renaissance' was five years old, that her characteristic *Love Songs* brought her work to the attention of a phenomenally large reading public. During the decade that was to 'discover' the poetry of Edna St. Vincent Millay, the verse of Sara Teasdale created a standard for feminine lyricism; and in this connection her greapopularity contributed its influence toward the publicity given to the feminist movement in America during the World War.

Sara Teasdale was born in 1884 in St. Louis, Missouri, and, after her education in that city, travelled in southern Europe and in the Near East. On her return to this continent in 1907 she began to make friends in literary circles in New York and in 1916 moved from her home in St. Louis to live there permanently.

In commenting on *The Collected Poems of Sara Teasdale*, Morton Dauwen Zabel wrote in *The Southern Review*,

. . . careful selection offers its rewards here; fifty or sixty poems, instead of 350, should some day be bound together as among the best lyrics of the older tradition that America has produced. Miss Teasdale was known as an admirer of Christina Rossetti, of whose life and verse she was preparing a study when she died. Christina Rossetti is the mistress of the particular art in which poets of the sentimental tendency have written, from Laetitia Landon and Felicia Hemans down, but there is no question that she was a secure and impassioned mistress, particularly in the range of her resources, extending from the imaginative skill of 'Goblin Market' and 'Sing-Song' to the Elizabethan intensity of 'The Convent Threshold.' Miss Teasdale reached neither of these distances in her development. She moved in fact hardly at all from her initial attitude. All she could do was to refine and perfect that attitude to the utmost degree of sincerity she had in her. This refinement appears at its best in her volume *Dark of the Moon* in 1926, where may be found not only some love-songs of exquisite artistry like 'The Flight,' 'Arcturus in Autumn' and 'Words for an Old Air' but several lyrics of a more detached, laconic, and sophisticated nature which promised a richer maturity for her talents. . . . She was a poet whose work, with its easy sentiment and human appeal, can easily be mistaken for a distasteful kind of popular verse-journalism; it requires discriminating selection; but when it is given that . . . an art of unmistakable charm is retrieved, and it should always hold a place in American lyric verse.

The Collected Poems of Sara Teasdale (N.Y., 1937).
Harriet Monroe, *Poets & Their Art* (N.Y., 1926), 72–7.
Morton Zabel, 'Varieties of Poetic Experience,' *The Southern Review*, III, 806–07.

WITTER BYNNER (1881–)

WITTER BYNNER is one of the few men writing poetry today in whose work may be found any considerable body of the simple lyric. He defines poetry as 'passionate patience,' but this definition is amplified by his conviction that: 'Primarily, poetry like music—as a matter of fact with music—came out of the heart and lips of simple mankind.' For Bynner, modern poetry began with Kipling and Housman, and has continued with Alfred Noyes and Masefield. He has on the whole been content to remain aloof from other techniques, though he has indulged himself in numerous tilts in opposition. The best known of these forays occurred when with Arthur Davison Ficke, under the respective pen-names of Emanuel Morgan and Anne Knish, he perpetrated the hoax of the school of *Spectra* (N.Y., 1915). His own experimentation has been largely in the practice of a kind of rhymed free verse, demonstrated in his first volume, *An Ode to Harvard and Other Poems* (Boston, 1907), and later expanded into a characteristic medium of his own.

Bynner has been a great admirer of the poetry and philosophy of the Chinese, and with Dr. Kiang Kang-hu has published in *The Jade Mountain* (N.Y., 1929) translations of some three hundred of the finest poems of the T'ang dynasty. In this interest, at least, he was in sympathy with the imagists in their general respect for the concentrated economy and simplicity of Chinese verse. Yet he is specific in limiting the influence on his own work: 'I am not referring to the superficial tricks by which a Chinese poet makes his words balanced and melodious. The discovery which has largely undone my early convictions as to the way of writing poetry has really to do with use of substance rather than with turns of expression.'

Selected Poems by Witter Bynner(N.Y.,

1936). With an editor's foreword by Robert Hunt, and a critical preface by Paul Horgan.

Eden Tree(N.Y., 1931).

The Persistence of Poetry(San Francisco, 1929).

ELINOR WYLIE (1885–1928)

FEW writers have been so essentially permeated with the spirit of a predecessor as was Elinor Wylie with that of Shelley. She read him first in her *Third Reader*, and at the age of eleven, when she read Trelawny's recollections of Shelley, she describes herself as so filled with emotion that she was

> afraid to move, afraid to cry for fear the scene within the pages of the book might be hidden from her eyes, wondering and wondering why the bright creature who had lived within that scene should have died and fallen into dust no stronger than the golden leaves blowing in at the window.

This enthusiasm remained with her, and she became a close student of his life. Two of her novels, *The Orphan Angel*(N.Y., 1926) and *Mr. Hodge and Mr. Hazard* (N.Y., 1928), were concerned, directly or indirectly, with him. Something within the Puritan marrow of her bones caused her to reject the richness of Keats and to ally herself with Shelley. She did not imitate his poetry; she was merely, to borrow a phrase from 'One Person,' 'a woman by an archangel befriended.'

Her life as a poet was spent in stern self-discipline to attain clarity and sharpness of utterance within traditional verse-forms. Her first book of poems, *Incidental Numbers*, her mother had anonymously published at London in 1912 in an edition of sixty numbers for private distribution. She included no poems from it in her subsequent volumes. These were *Nets to Catch the Winds*(N.Y., 1921), *Black Armour* (N.Y., 1923), *Trivial Breath*(N.Y., 1928), and *Angels and Earthly Creatures*(N.Y., 1929). Each shows a steady advance over her previous work. It was in a sense as

though she had been training herself for the time when she should have something to say. This came in the poetry of her last volume, and particularly in 'One Person,' one of the finest sonnet sequences in the English language.

Her prose illustrated the qualities which caused James Branch Cabell to characterize her as a 'Dresden china shepherdess.' Of *Mr. Hodge and Mr. Hazard*, Isabel Paterson has said:

> The whole story of *Mr. Hodge and Mr. Hazard* is the absence of Shelley. This is England after it rejected Shelley; England revisited by a melancholy stranger in 1833. Mr. Hazard, described as returning from years of exile in the East, was variously described as Byron or Trelawny; but he is rather a ghost, the Last of the Romantics. And he cut a very strange figure ten years after Byron expired at Missolonghi. . . .
>
> So this 'symbolic romance of the mind' is the epilogue of that great drama of a lost cause, dedicated to the burning heart of Shelley and the perverse ego of Byron. . . .
>
> This is also her best prose. Here she chastened the abundance of her imagery and disciplined her luxuriant talent. *Jennifer Lorn*[N.Y., 1923] is a dish of curds and cream flavoured with saffron. *The Venetian Glass Nephew*[N.Y., 1925] has the brittle exquisiteness of its title. *The Orphan Angel* is Shelley's own prose! In *Mr. Hodge and Mr. Hazard*, at moments perhaps Lady Clara's muslins billow about her too ethereally; she all but floats away in an Angelica Kauffman apotheosis. But the common little man, Mr. Hartleigh, and his petulant shallow vulgar Annamaria are clothed in sentences of the most austere distinc-

tion. The course-grained matter-of-fact Mr. Hodge is depicted in his most stultifying aspect without resort to hyperbole or emphasis. He speaks, and he is there. This is the very object of prose, to render the substance of things so that the spirit is implicit. The prose of poets usually tends to a 'false gallop,' as the verse of the born prose-writer seldom quickens or lifts above a footpace. Elinor Wylie had both gifts; and she never once let a pedestrian line intrude into her verse, but at first her prose occasionally escaped restraint. Here at the last she compelled it to its true function.

She was born in Somerville, New Jersey, and spent much of her girlhood in Washington, D.C., where her father was Assistant Attorney-General under Theodore Roosevelt. For some years she lived abroad with her second husband, Horace Wylie, principally in rural England. Her third marriage was with William Rose Benét. Her health during her brief literary career was precarious, and she died instantly of a stroke in 1928, having just prepared for the printer her last volume of poems.

Collected Poems of Elinor Wylie(N.Y., 1932). Edited, with a foreword, by William Rose Benét.

Collected Prose of Elinor Wylie(N.Y., 1934). With prefaces by Carl Van Doren, Carl Van Vechten, Stephen Vincent Benét, Isabel Paterson, and William Rose Benét.

Nancy Hoyt, *Elinor Wylie: the Portrait of an Unknown Lady*(Indianapolis, 1935).

J.B.Cabell, *Some of Us*(N.Y., 1930),13–26.

M.M.Colum, 'O Virtuous Light!' *Saturday Review of Literature*,V,1043–44.

——, 'In Memory of Elinor Wylie,' *New Republic*,LVII,316–19.

W.R.Benét, *The Prose and Poetry of Elinor Wylie*(Norton, Massachusetts, 1934).

M.D.Zabel, 'The Pattern of the Atmosphere,' *Poetry*,XL,273–82.

EDNA ST. VINCENT MILLAY (1892–)

EDNA ST. VINCENT MILLAY is indubitably the most popular American poet, and she has retained this popularity during the many phases of her verse. She began writing with comparative triviality, save for her fine 'Renascence,' but expressing with pith and salty phrases the plight of the modern sophisticated woman. The quatrain in which she burned her candle at both ends became the 'Psalm of Life' of the Nineteen-Twenties. Although her verse remained essentially conventional, she has achieved a manner and an idiom essentially her own. Both in lyrics and in the sonnet form she has succeeded as have few others of our time.

A publisher's announcement of her first volume, *Renascence*(N.Y., 1917), stated in regard to her verses:

> They deal, as poetry should deal, primarily with emotion; with the sense of tears and laughter, in mortal things; with beauty and passion; with having and losing; with discoveries and inventions.

Miss Millay has, however, increasingly concerned herself with social problems. The trial of Sacco and Vanzetti stirred her, as it did so many, and her most recent volume, *Conversation at Midnight* (N.Y., 1937) was an attempt to capture the flavor of political and social opinion of a few years past.

The magnificence of her language has been generously applauded, but the charm of her purely lyric lines has blinded many to the fact that her ear has always been closely tuned to the roughness of common speech. This is hardly surprising in view of her long interest in drama. For some years she worked with the Provincetown Playhouse in New York, and in 1921 three of her plays were published. In 1927 appeared *The King's Henchman*, the libretto of an operetta which was produced at the Metropolitan Opera House.

Recently she has said of herself, in a published interview:

> 'I, for instance, am moving naturally in the direction of dramatic poetry—by

which I don't mean that I've given up writing lyric poetry. Really, the public is very stern with the artist—it looks upon him as an inspired scatter-brain, yet expects him to proceed in more rigidly methodical fashion than any banker! I've given up nothing. . . .

'If you don't change and develop between your first book and your 10th, then you just keep on re-writing yourself. And it seems to me that life should do more for you than just keep you alive. After all, a child is not merely fed with the food he eats; he is strengthened, and he grows. It's the same with the poet—that is to say, if he has a heart appetite for life. It's no good nibbling at it.' Then she added with a smile:

'He must also, of course, have an excellent digestion.'

A Few Figs from Thistles(N.Y., 1920).
The Lamp and the Bell(N.Y., 1921).
Aria da Capo(N.Y., 1921).
Second April(N.Y., 1921).
Two Slatterns and a King(N.Y., 1921).
The Ballad of the Harp-Weaver(N.Y., 1922).
The Harp-Weaver and Other Poems(N.Y., 1923).
The King's Henchman(N.Y., 1927).
The Buck in the Snow and Other Poems (N.Y., 1928).
Fatal Interview(N.Y., 1931).
The Princess Marries the Page(N.Y., 1932).
Wine from These Grapes(N.Y., 1934).
Elizabeth Atkins, *Edna St. Vincent Millay and Her Times*(Chicago, 1936).
E.Davison, 'Edna St. Vincent Millay,' *English Journal*,XVI,671–82.
J.H.Preston, 'Edna St. Vincent Millay,' *Sewanee Review*,XXXVIII,42–49.

EZRA POUND (1885–)

WHAT poetry needed at the turn of the last century was not new fields to conquer but a fresh manual of arms. This Ezra Pound helped, more than any other poet, to provide. Like Picasso he has been at the same time a critic and an artist.

Pound was born in Hailey, Idaho, in 1885, studied at the University of Pennsylvania, and was an instructor there from 1905 to 1907. No group in America's literary history has proved so significant as that in which, at this time, Ezra Pound, Hilda Doolittle, William Carlos Williams, and Marianne Moore moved as friends. Pound taught for a time in Indiana, but in 1908 sailed for Italy where he published his first book of poems, *A Lume Spento* (Venice, 1908). Within a few months he left for England where he published a second volume, *Personæ*(London, 1909).

It was in April of 1909 when Pound first joined the group led by T.E.Hulme, which met in a Soho restaurant to discuss and experiment with verse whose 'great aim is,' as Hulme expressed it, 'accurate, precise and definite description.' Hulme saw the necessity for a strict discipline in the expression of art, in contrast to the various forms of flabbiness which had come in the old age of nineteenth-century Romanti-

cism. He recognized that a new youthfulness had brought about 'a change in sensibility,' and that the proper expression of art 'will culminate, not so much in the simple geometric forms found in archaic art, but in the more complicated ones associated in our minds with the age of machinery.' The group died out, but Pound carried on its spirit, gave the name 'Imagisme' to an important aspect of their experimentation, and with his particularly vigorous and common-sense commentaries brought their issues squarely before the literary world.

'Poetry,' said Pound, 'is the statement of overwhelming emotional values': but he also added that 'poetry is a sort of inspired mathematics, which gives us equations, not for abstract figures, triangles, spheres and the like, but equations for the human emotions.' It was in this way that he extended the province of what might be termed the relatively static quality of early Imagism into the dynamic imagery of Vorticism. The limitations of the early manner of Imagism were what caused most poets to relinquish it after its discipline had been absorbed.

Pound's comment on a poem from the Provençal, that 'like all fine poetry it can be well judged only when heard spoken,' indicates his awareness of the importance of sound in the practice of a medium which had become predominantly visual. The common relationship of verse and music to sound he has amplified by his observation in *Antheil and the Treatise on Harmony* (Paris, 1924) that apparent discords in sound may be resolved by sufficient periods of rest. In a passage, unwittingly similar to the problem which had been faced by Lanier, Pound indicated some of the difficulties consequent to a return to the oral tradition in English verse:

> Everyone has been annoyed by the difficulty of indicating the *exact* tone and rhythm with which one's verse is to be read. One questions the locus of degrees, *sic*: at what point is it more expeditious to learn musical notation and to set one's words to, or print them with the current musical notation, rather than printing them hind-side-to and topsy-turvy on the page.

This problem of a visual indication of both sound and necessary periods of rest has been largely solved through typography and the arrangement of poetical lines.

These various comprehensions gave force and significance to Pound's searches through early literatures for examples of perfection in various techniques. His extraordinarily wide familiarity with the past was sufficient to give him a sense of the support of tradition. His objective increasingly became fixed ahead rather than behind, and in this respect he differed radically from the apparently similar utilization of the past on the part of such nineteenth-century Romantics as the Pre-Raphaelites, with whom he seemed as a youth to have been joined in spirit.

Pound has always had an acute sense of what is fresh in literature. Not only have his commentaries on recognized literature been provocative and illuminating, but it was he who sent to Harriet Monroe for *Poetry:A Magazine of Verse* the poems of Frost, Eliot, H.D., Aldington, Lawrence, Joyce, Tagore, Flint, Yeats, and others; and it was he who made Margaret Anderson's *Little Review* into a magazine into which

James Joyce's *Ulysses* found its first and congenial appearance.

The greatest importance must be attached to Pound's readiness to relinquish a position once its immediate potentialities have been exhausted by himself. This following of an Emersonian precept has given his poetry its steady progression, and solved in his case the dilemma later expressed by Zabel, that 'the greatest difficulty of being a pioneer is in remaining a contemporary.' It is in respect to this malleability of Pound's that 'Hugh Selwyn Mauberley' becomes not only an important technical demonstration but an equally significant personal document.

For the past two decades, Pound's most important work has been in the creation of a flexible yet definite stanza. These 'Cantos' proceed directly out of Pound's profound knowledge of the past, and are a direct reflection both of his own historical awareness and the modern sense of the mutual impingements of various flashes of memory and of contemporary consciousness. They are the speech of a brilliant and somewhat pedantic man. No one could possibly understand all his references, though footnotes will in time blind us into thinking that we did understand them from the beginning. The Cantos give the excitement of listening to a brilliant and rapid conversationalist who presents keys to the imagination and hurries his listener from door to door. It is perhaps idle to quibble about the plan before the series is completed. Pound has sensed potentialities in his medium not recognizable at first, and is presenting to poets, even now, as much stimulation as he gave in 1912 to the so-called Poetic Renaissance.

Exultations(London, 1909).
Provença(Boston, 1910).
The Spirit of Romance(London, 1910).
Canzoni(London, 1911).
Ripostes(London, 1912).
Des Imagistes(N.Y., 1914). Editor.
Gaudier-Brzeska: A Memoir(N.Y., 1916).
Lustra(N.Y., 1917).
Pavannes and Divisions(N.Y., 1918).
Instigations(N.Y., 1920).
A Draft of XXX Cantos(London, 1933).
Eleven New Cantos. XXXI–XLI(N.Y., 1934).

Make It New(New Haven, Conn., 1935).
[T.S.Eliot.] *Ezra Pound: His Metric Poetry* (N.Y., 1917).
R.P.Blackmur, *The Double Agent*(N.Y., 1935), 30–67.

D.Fitts, 'Music Fit for the Odes,' *Hound & Horn*,IV,278–89.
F.R.Leavis, *New Bearings in English Poetry*(London,1932),133–57.
L.Zukofsky, 'The Cantos of Ezra Pound,' *Criterion*,X,424–40.

H.D. (1886–)

OF the poets who were moved by the need for greater clarity and precision, H.D. has kept closest to the tenets which were formulated in definitions of Imagism; and her poem, 'Oread,' has on all sides been accepted as its classical example.

When Pound first sent her poems in 1912 to Harriet Monroe, he wrote of them:

> Objective—no slither; direct—no excessive use of adjectives, no metaphors that won't permit examination. It's straight talk, straight as the Greek!

While Pound had turned from one literature to another in rapid succession, H.D.'s interest has remained consistently Hellenic. The purity of the best Greek tradition is to be felt in the poems of her first book, *Sea Gardens*(London, 1916), and her most recent work has been the translation of the *Ion of Euripides*(Boston, 1937). With her, however, it is a matter of affinity with the Greek tradition rather than a pedantic adaptation of its forms. H.D. has simply used the past as an overtone to the expression of her own personality. Although she speaks of herself in terms of 'escapism,' even the ivory tower of her inner world of imagination has had its window from which she has looked out and recorded her observation. Certainly it was not mere chance which caused her to translate the *Ion* at a moment when Europe seemed again to be on the verge of war.

She has proved herself a modern again in her poetic diction, which might be characterized as a revolt against the school of Swinburne and Gilbert Murray. Nowhere is this more apparent than in her sparing use of adjectives, on which Pound commented, or in the stern discipline of her poetic lines. Her remarkably acute ear is always evident in the subtleties of her strict, yet original forms. She is herself the classicist whom so many admirers have vulgarized in imitation.

Hilda Doolittle was born in Bethlehem, Pennsylvania, but passed most of her childhood in Philadelphia, where her father was Director of the Flower Observatory. She attended Bryn Mawr College, and it was as a student there that she was a friend of Williams, Pound, and Miss Moore. In 1911 she went to London, which she has made her home.

Collected Poems of H.D.(N.Y., 1925).
Palimpsest(London, 1926). A novel.
Hippolytus Temporizes(Boston, 1927).
Red Roses for Bronze(Boston, 1931).
Hedylus(London, 1928). A novel.
G.Hughes, *Imagism & the Imagists*(Stanford University,1931).
R.P.Blackmur, 'The Lesser Satisfactions,' *Poetry*,XLI,94–100.
W.Bryher, 'Spear-Shaft and Cyclamen-Flower,' *Poetry*, XIX,333–37.
F.S.Flint, 'The Poetry of H.D.,' *Egoist*,II, 72–73.
M.Sinclair, 'The Poems of H.D.,' *Fortnightly Review*,n.s.CXXI, 329–45.
L.Untermeyer, 'The Perfect Imagist,'*Saturday Review of Literature*,I,260.
H.P.Collins, *Modern Poetry*(London, n.d.), 154–202.

JOHN GOULD FLETCHER (1886–)

JOHN GOULD FLETCHER is one of the many Americans who, early in the century, quit America in order to escape the conventionalities that were ready to strangle any creative expression which did not fit the norm. Fletcher was born at Little Rock, Arkansas, in 1886, and was sent north by his parents to complete his preparation for Harvard at Phillips Academy in Andover, Massachusetts. He left Harvard before his graduation, and after a brief excursion with an archaeological expedition into the Southwest, sailed in 1908 for Italy. Finally, drawn by the newly-stirring poetical activity in London, he went to England, where he remained for many years. Without ever quite being at the center of any of the movements, he was interested in most of them, and certain of his poems appeared in Miss Lowell's first collection of Imagist poetry in 1915.

Fletcher has always been an experimentalist, and with greater ability than any of his contemporaries he was able to bring into English verse the transmutations of color practised by the French Symbolists. This ability he combined with an analogy of verse to music, in what he called 'a presentation of daily life in terms of highly-orchestrated and colored words.' Examples of this impressionistic method are to be found in his 'Symphonies,' the technique of which his annotation indicates in more detail. 'Fletcher,' Robert Penn Warren has pointed out, 'was the first, or one of the first, to develop in English a type of imagery which Edith Sitwell has since erected into something like an oblique technique of vision.'

His experimentation was further carried on, in conjunction with Amy Lowell, in the development of polyphonic prose; and his 'Clipper Ships' is perhaps the most successful example of this extension of the provinces of both prose and poetry. Of late years, and particularly since his return to America, he has interested himself more and more in conventional forms, the best expressions of which are to be found in *XXIV Elegies* (Santa Fé, N.M., 1935). In contrast with his earlier concentration on 'pure poetry,' these elegies also illustrate his increasing concern with contemporary life. Such an elegy as that on Tintern Abbey should not be thought of as an imitation of Wordsworth's lyric, but merely as a poet's attempt at utilizing it as a frame of reference to his own observation.

Fletcher has worked in other fields besides poetry. He has been a translator, critic, and biographer; and his autobiography, *Life Is My Song* (N.Y., 1937), is a revealing portrait of a sensitive and troubled mind.

Selected Poems (N.Y., 1938).
Paul Gauguin, his Life and Art (N.Y., 1921).
John Smith—Also Pocahontas (N.Y., 1928).
The Two Frontiers; a Study in Historical Psychology (N.Y., 1930).
C.Aiken, *Scepticisms* (N.Y., 1919), 105–14.
D.Fitts, 'Poet and Theorist,' *Poetry*, IX, 43–47.
A.Lowell, *Tendencies in Modern American Poetry* (N.Y., 1917), 280–343.
H.Monroe, *Poets & Their Art* (N.Y., 1926).
R.P.Warren, 'A Note on Three Southern Poets,' *Poetry*, XL, 105–08.

AMY LOWELL (1874–1925)

AFTER some eight years of writing in the conventional 'poetic jargon' of nineteenth-century verse, Amy Lowell, on a visit to London in 1913, was among the first to recognize the value of the new poetic idiom which bore the name of Imagism. She had come to London armed with a letter of introduction from Harriet Monroe to Ezra Pound, and after meeting him as well as H.D., John Gould Fletcher, and Richard Aldington, and entering into correspondence with other young and promising poets who had welcomed a poetic renaissance in England, she returned to Boston as an enthusiastic convert to the doctrines of what she called 'Some Imagists.' Her particular enthusiasm, however, had its source in her discovery of Paul Fort, the French poet, and her early experiments in Imagistic verse were written in a vein that clearly showed his influence upon her imagination.

Her sincere desire to extend her recognition of the importance of the new poetry and its poets to the American public led her to carry her enthusiasms to the lecture platform where she faced ridicule with the utmost good humor as long as she was permitted the right to say:

As a matter of fact the poet must learn his trade in the same manner, and with the same painstaking care, as the cabinet maker . . . a workman may be pardoned, therefore, for spending a few moments to explain and describe the technique of his trade. A work of beauty which cannot stand an intimate examination is a poor and jerry-built thing. . . . Only a vigorous tree has the vitality to put forth new branches. The poet with originality and power is always seeking to give his readers the same poignant feeling which he has himself. To do this he must constantly find new and striking images, delightful and unexpected forms.

Quite as Theodore Roosevelt gave vitality and color to such phrases as 'the big stick' and 'the strenuous life,' so Amy Lowell endowed the phrases 'polyphonic prose' and 'imagist poetry' with the forces of her seemingly inexhaustible energy. Yet throughout the decade in which she wrote so valiantly for the cause of Imagism, she retained her early admiration for the personality and poetry of John Keats. The influence of Keats and Tennyson had left its traces on her first book of poems, and as she neared the completion of her biography of Keats in 1924, her own poetry reassumed the discipline of nineteenth-century lyric form. Although her poems 'Fireworks' and 'Patterns' are among the best known examples of her poetry and are often quoted as representative of the 'free verse' movement in America from 1912 to 1916, it is valuable to observe the unpretentious charm and simplicity of her later verse.

After many years of ill health she died at her home, 'Sevenells,' in Boston in 1925.

Selected Poems of Amy Lowell(Boston, 1928). Edited by John Livingston Lowes.
Six French Poets(N.Y., 1915).
Tendencies in Modern American Poetry (N.Y., 1917).
John Keats(Boston, 1925), 2 vols.
Poetry and Poets: Essays(Boston, 1930).
Some Imagist Poets (Boston, 1915, 1916, 1917). Editor.
S.Foster Damon, Amy Lowell (Boston, 1935). Contains a bibliography.
W.Bryher, Amy Lowell: A Critical Appreciation(London, 1918).
A.MacLeish, 'Amy Lowell and the Art of Poetry,' North American Review, CCXXI,508–21.
W.T.Scott,'Amy Lowell After Ten Years,' New England Quarterly,VIII,320–30.
J.W.Tupper,'The Poetry of Amy Lowell,' Sewanee Review,XXVIII,37–53.
J.G.Fletcher, Life is My Song(N.Y., 1937): passim.

WILLIAM CARLOS WILLIAMS (1883–)

THE most characteristic thing about my life, I suppose, is that I still live, working for my living, in the same suburb of New York City where I was born on the 17th of September, 1883. Whereas, my forebears seem to have been restless souls, never long in the same place. My father was born in Birmingham, England, and my mother in Mayaguez, Puerto Rico. I went to the public schools here in Rutherford, N.J., until I was about twelve years old, then to a New York City high school, finally to the University of Pennsylvania for my degree in Medicine. Among these years was one when with my brother, I attended a school in Switzerland, living also in Paris for six months at that time. Later I studied Medicine at the University of Leipzig and took my internship in two hospitals in New York. Writing has been my constant companion during these years.

No American has written cleaner verse, stripped to the elements of poetry, than has William Carlos Williams: yet an even more significant contribution to American literature has been his demonstration that the elements of poetry may be found anywhere, if the poet only charge the objects of his attention with their maximum emotional content. The importance of Williams' statement that he has lived always in the same locality lies in his consequent familiarity with the common things on which he bases his poetry. 'To each thing its special quality,' Williams has said, 'its special value that will enable it to stand alone. When each poem has achieved its particular form unlike any other, when it shall stand alone—then we have achieved our language. We have said what it is in our minds to say.'

Williams is a romantic and somewhat of a sentimentalist. Of this quality, Wallace Stevens wrote in his introduction to Williams' *Collected Poems* 1921–1931:

> Sentiment has such an abhorrent name that one hesitates. But if what vitalizes Williams has an abhorrent name, its obviously generative function in his case may help to change its reputation. What Williams gives, on the whole, is not sentiment but the reaction from sentiment, or, rather, a little sentiment, very little, together with acute reaction.
>
> His passion for the anti-poetic is a blood passion and not a passion of the inkpot. The anti-poetic is his spirit's cure. He needs it as a naked man needs shelter or as an animal needs salt. To a man with a sentimental side the anti-poetic is that truth, that reality to which all of us are forever fleeing.
>
> The anti-poetic has many aspects. The aspect to which a poet is addicted is a test of his validity. Its merely rhetorical aspect is valueless. As an affectation, it is a commonplace. As a scourge, it has a little more meaning. But as a phase of a man's spirit, as a source of salvation, now, in the midst of a baffled genera-

tion, as one looks out of the window at Rutherford or Passaic, or as one walks the streets of New York, the anti-poetic acquires an extraordinary potency, especially if one's nature possesses that side so attractive to the Furies.

> Something of the unreal is necessary to fecundate the real; something of the sentimental is necessary to fecundate the anti-poetic. Williams, by nature, is more of a realist than is commonly true in the case of a poet.

The qualities of Williams' poetry are also those of his prose, of which *The White Mule* (Norfolk, Conn., 1937) and short stories like 'Old Doc Rivers' and 'The Girl with the Pimply Face' are perhaps his best examples. His introduction, 'A Note on Poetry,' is a sufficient explanation of his intent in both mediums.

The Tempers(London, 1913).
Al Que Quiere(Boston, 1917).
The Complete Collected Poems of William Carlos Williams, 1906–1938(Norfolk, Conn., 1938).
An Early Martyr(N.Y., 1935).
Adam & Eve and The City(Peru, Vt., 1936).
'A Tentative Statement,' *The Little Review*,XII,95–98.
Life Along the Passaic River(Norfolk, Conn., 1938). Short stories.

MARIANNE MOORE (1887–)

IN his introduction to Marianne Moore's *Selected Poems*, T.S.Eliot wrote:

> My conviction, for what it is worth, has remained unchanged for the last fourteen years: that Miss Moore's poems form part of the small body of durable poetry written in our time; of that small body of writings, among what passes for poetry, in which an original sensibility and alert intelligence and deep feeling have been engaged in maintaining the life of the English language.

Of poetry, Miss Moore herself has written:

> I, too, dislike it: there are things that are important beyond all this fiddle.

> Reading it, however, with a perfect contempt for it, one discovers in
> it after all, a place for the genuine.

Of the poetic imagination, she has also written:

> nor till the poets among us can be
> 'literalists of
> the imagination'—above
> insolence and triviality and can present
>
> for inspection, imaginary gardens with real
> toads
> in them, shall we have
> it.

Marianne Moore was born in St. Louis,

Missouri, in 1887 and received her B.A. at Bryn Mawr College in 1909. She taught stenography at the Carlisle Indian School from 1911 to 1915. Her first book, *Poems*, was published in London in 1921 and upon publication of her second book of poems in 1924 she received the Dial award for 'distinguished service to American letters.' She was an assistant in the Hudson Park Branch of the New York Public Library until she assumed her four-year editorship of *The Dial* from 1925 to 1929.

Starting with the first publication of her verse in an issue of *The Egoist* in London in 1915, Miss Moore's poetry has been associated with the work of H.D., T.S.Eliot, Ezra Pound, and William Carlos Williams. With Williams, she shares the distinction of being one of the few American poets in her generation whose work has undergone the discipline of a slow maturity. As does the verse of Emily Dickinson, Miss Moore's

verse combines acute and accurate perception of a physical world with the resourcefulness of poetic wit. 'No Swan So Fine' illustrates her mastery of a firm, yet subtle lyric form, and her most recent version of 'A Grave' again displays her sensibility to the tonal variations of verbal sound and visual image. The quality of Miss Moore's power to observe the detail of a richly varied physical world, both active and inanimate, suggests the very quality of a twentieth-century civilization in America that readily accepted the material aspects of William James' pragmatism.

Selected Poems by Marianne Moore(N.Y., 1935). With an introduction by T.S.Eliot.
Pangolin, and Other Verse(London, 1936).
R.P.Blackmur, *The Double Agent*(N.Y., 1935), 141–71.

WALLACE STEVENS (1879–)

NOT the least of the contributions made by Harriet Monroe's *Poetry: A Magazine of Verse* was its early publication of the poetry of Wallace Stevens. His poetry is the work of a singularly sensitive imagination and the impression it conveys to the reader is one of a subdued elegance created by his choice of the precise visual image and an equally distinguished vocabulary. No less important than the poems themselves are their decorative titles placed in exact juxtaposition to what each poem has to say. If one looks for an analogy to Stevens' verse in painting, one thinks of Whistler, but it is Whistler who has come to life again with a peculiarly sharp-cued eye. The poetry of Wallace Stevens reveals not merely the connoisseur of fine rhythms and the nuances of the lyrical line, but a trained

observer who gazes with an intelligent eye upon the decadence of a civilized world that follows the rapid acquisition of wealth and power.

Wallace Stevens was born in Pennsylvania, in 1879, and was educated at Harvard. In 1923 the first collection of his poems, *Harmonium* was published. This was followed by a second collection, including fourteen new poems, under the same title in 1931. Twelve years later a third book of poems *Ideas of Order* appeared, and in 1937 he published a fourth book, *The Man with the Blue Guitar*. He lives in Hartford, Connecticut.

R.P.Blackmur, *The Double Agent*(N.Y., 1935), 68–102.

CONRAD AIKEN (1889–)

SINCE the publication of his first book of poems, *Earth Triumphant and Other Tales and Verse*(N.Y., 1914), the poetry of Conrad Aiken has been written very near the center of each succeeding movement in American poetry. The tonal quality of Aiken's sensibility is apparent to even the most casual reader, and that sensibility is

again apparent in the critical sensitivity of his anthologies of American verse.

His *Selected Poems*(N.Y., 1929) displayed the wide range of his poetic facilities, but it is in *The Morning Song from Senlin* that one finds the counters of his style which extend into his latest volume of Preludes: *Time in the Rock*. The title,

Preludes, which he has chosen as the general title for his work since 1930 is indicative of its character; for within the flexible stanza form he has created the poems in circular progression, never—like an unfinished symphony—quite reaching the conclusion of what he has to say.

Aiken said of himself that he was 'in quest of a sort of absolute poetry, a poetry in which the intention is not so much to arouse an emotion, or to persuade of a reality, as to employ such emotion or sense of reality (tangentially struck) with the same cool detachment with which a composer strikes notes or chords.'

Conrad Aiken was born in Savannah, Georgia, in 1889. He was educated at Harvard, from which he received his A.B. in 1912. Since then, he has lived alternately in Rye, England, and in Boston.

Aside from his books of poems he has published two novels, *Blue Voyage*(N.Y., 1927) and *Great Circle*(N.Y., 1933), which possess something of the same preoccupation with psychoanalysis which may be found in his later poetry.

Selected Poems by Conrad Aiken(N.Y., 1929).
John Deth, a Metaphysical Legend, and Other Poems(N.Y., 1930).
Preludes for Memnon(N.Y., 1931).
Landscape West of Eden(N.Y., 1935).
Time in the Rock(N.Y., 1936).
Scepticisms: Notes on Contemporary Poetry (N.Y., 1919).
Marianne Moore, 'If a Man Die,' *Hound & Horn*,V,313–20.
Louis Untermeyer, *American Poetry Since 1900* (N.Y., 1923), 170–82.

E. E. CUMMINGS (1894–)

THE one true wit among modern poets is Edward Estlin Cummings. He alone has understood the poetical conceit, and has employed it in the expression of the preoccupation with death, the materialism, and the sentiment of the 'War Generation.'

Cummings was born in Cambridge, Massachusetts, in 1894, and after receiving his master's degree at the age of twenty-two became one of the ambulance boys in France. It was this exposure to war which for him, as for so many other writers of his generation, concentrated attention upon the individual and through increased tension heightened all emotional values. His war novel, *The Enormous Room*(N.Y., 1922), was based on the sensibilities of an individual under such strain. There have been few novels of the World War to equal it.

Cummings had printed numerous conventional poems in *The Harvard Advocate* during his student days. The effect of the war on him as a poet is to be found expressed in his introduction to a later edition of *The Enormous Room*(N.Y., 1934):

Did it ever occur to you that people in this socalled world of ours are not interested in art?
Da da.

But Cummings was already too essentially a conventional poet to adopt the complete nihilism of the movement of dadaism, and the expression of his emotion was changed only in his attitude. This change of attitude found its outlet in inverted imagery, occasional preciosity, and in true conceit. The fundamental position of a lyric poet was not, however, altered; and his erotic poetry is the finest written by an American.

He was also preoccupied with the general problem of sound in poetics, and found his solution partly through his keen ear for the nuances of hard-boiled speech and most spectacularly through his experimentations with the serviceability of typography. The use of print to indicate the values of sound has been recognized for centuries, and it was because of the indicated stress of capitalization, black letters, and italics, that Thomas Prince could observe of the sermons of a preacher like Cotton Mather, that his style 'like his manner of speaking was very emphatical.' Similarly, Cummings has given specific directions for what must be heard in his poems. But so sensitive has been his ear, that through his use of tmeses, or the word-splitting practices of certain Greek and Latin poets, his readers can hear only through their eyes.

Collected Poems(N.Y., 1938).

Him(N.Y., 1927).

Eimi(N.Y., 1933).

'Seven Poems' (Decca Records and Harcourt, Brace & Co., N.Y., unnumbered). A recording by Cummings of 'Poem, or Beauty Hurts Mr. Vinal,' 'Item,' 'Buffalo Bill,' 'In Just Spring,' 'Oh Sweet Spontaneous Earth,' 'Since Feeling is First,' and 'Somewhere I have Never Traveled.'

R.P.Blackmur, *The Double Agent*(N.Y., 1935),1-29.

John Peale Bishop, 'The Poems and Prose of E.E.Cummings,' *Southern Revue*,IV, 173-86.

THORNTON WILDER (1897–)

THE popularity of Thornton Wilder's second novel, *The Bridge of San Luis Rey* (N.Y., 1928), was so spectacular that it acted as a disservice to its author. His first novel, *The Cabala*(N.Y., 1926), introduced the work of a young novelist who had accepted the conventions of French prose and who was interested primarily in reflecting what he conceived to be the classical clarity of expression that he had found in French literature. His *Bridge of San Luis Rey* was, in fact, a literary acknowledgment of his debt to the *Letters of Madame de Sévigné*. Even *The Woman of Andros*(N.Y., 1930), his delicately wrought reconstruction of the mood of paganism, reflected the quality of style to be found in the French letter writers of the eighteenth century.

From the character of his early prose, it was obvious that Wilder had little intention or desire to become a 'popular' American novelist of the later 1920's. His work seemed all to consciously removed from the realistic tendencies in the American novel of the twentieth century. With characteristic candor and honesty, he said to an interviewer from the *Saturday Review of Literature*, June 11, 1938:

For years I shrank from describing the modern world. I was alarmed at finding a way of casting into generalization the world of doorbells and telephones. And now, though many of the subjects will often be of the past, I like to feel that I accept the twentieth century, not only as a fascinating age to live in, but as assimilable stuff to think with.

His excursions into the life of the past were followed by a satire in the form of a novel, *Heaven Is My Destination* (1935). This experiment in the writing of a contemporaneous and realistic satire showed Wilder's sensitivity to the criticism he had received for too sedulously reconstructing the themes and forms of the literature that belonged to an age other than his own. It was also characteristic of Wilder to attempt an answer to his critics in his own way.

No less remarkable than his popularity as a novelist was his sustained and at last successful development as a playwright. His earlier plays, *The Angel That Troubled the Waters, and Other Plays*(N.Y., 1928), and *The Long Christmas Dinner, and Other Plays in One Act*(N.Y., 1931) were first steps in the training which enabled him to write *Our Town*(N.Y., 1938). The seriousness of his intention is again significant in an interview by a reporter from the New York *Herald Tribune*. Wilder said:

As drama students know, the French inherited from the Romans a great sense of economy of play structure and an urgent desire for unification. Only essentials occupied the classic French playwright and nothing not utterly necessary to the progress and motivation of the script was allowed to intrude upon it.

The devices of *Our Town* owe their precedence to an English adaptation of the Chinese play, *Yellow Jacket*, which was produced in America at a time when the 'Little Theater' movement was at its height. The essential materials of Wilder's play, however, seem to stem from another tradition in American culture. In its attempt to reproduce the universalities of American life, *Our Town* recalls the prose drama of William Vaughn Moody, which met with approval three decades before. The tradition was American.

Thornton Wilder was born in 1897 at Madison, Wisconsin, and at the age of nine accompanied his family to China, where his father was consul-general at Hongkong and at Shanghai. After his return to America in 1914, Wilder studied at the Berkeley, California, public schools and at the Thacher School in the same state. In 1920, after an interlude of service in the Coast Artillery during the World War, he was graduated from Yale. For two years after that he was a student at the American Academy at Rome. From 1921 to 1928 he was a master at Lawrenceville Academy, in New Jersey, and later was for several years a member of the faculty of the University of Chicago.

R.P.Blackmur, 'Thornton Wilder,' *Hound & Horn*,III,586–89.

E.K.Brown, 'A Christian Humanist: Thornton Wilder,' *University of Toronto Quarterly*,IV,356–70.

M.Gold, 'Wilder: Prophet of the Genteel Christ,' *New Republic*,LXIV,266–67.

R.McNamara, 'Phases of American Religion in Thornton Wilder and Willa Cather,' *Catholic World*,CXXXV,641–49.

W.L.Phelps, 'Men Now Famous,' *Delineator*,CXVII,94–96.

E.G.Twitchett, 'Mr. Thornton Wilder,' *The London Mercury*,XXII,32–39.

ROBINSON JEFFERS (1887–)

IN a sense Robinson Jeffers is the obverse of Walt Whitman. Witter Bynner took up Whitman's philosophy of love for one's fellow men, and Carl Sandburg carried on Whitman's function as a poet of the people; but Jeffers has definitely said that he regards humanity as an excrescence on nature, and that the love of man is merely 'the trap that catches noblest spirits, that caught—they say—God, when he walked on earth.' If Whitman was the Yea-Sayer, Jeffers is the Nay-Sayer. And the expression of his dark philosophy, though nihilistic, is extraordinarily powerful. The man himself is like a force of nature. The reason he has dealt so much with the ugly theme of incest in his long poems in free verse is explained thus: 'In *Tamar* a little and in *The Women at Point Sur* consciously and definitely, incest is symbolized racial introversion: man regarding man exclusively—founding his values, desires, a picture of the universe, all on his own humanity. . . . The tendency to romanticize unmoral freedom leads to destruction—often of the individual but always of the social organism. One of the intentions of *Point Sur* was to indicate the destruction and strip everything but its natural ugliness from the unmorality.' If Jeffers seems to draw poison from life, he is like the King Mithridates that A.E.Housman celebrated by telling how he accustomed himself to poison to such an extent that he remained quite hale and hearty.

His *Roan Stallion* and his *Tower Beyond*

Tragedy are generally regarded as his masterpieces. In commenting on the origin of the latter poem, Jeffers himself has said:

My father gave me a good start in Latin and Greek when I was quite young, both at school and at college I took them as they came, and that was never profoundly. I think most of whatever acquaintance I have with the classic spirit came from reading English poetry.

The origin of *The Tower Beyond Tragedy* was probably in the rich voice and Amazon stature of a German-Jewish actress with whom we were casually acquainted a few years ago. She recited one of the more barbaric Scotch ballads magnificently in private, and her voice suggested Clytemnestra and Cassandra to me, all the more because she rather failed in the usual sort of play.

I had no thought of production when I wrote, and for that reason began with some lines of narrative, but of course your advanced class is free to give a private performance if they should wish to.

We turn to the classic stories, I suppose, as to Greek sculpture, for a more ideal and also more normal beauty, because the myths of our own race were never developed, and have been alienated from us.

The long, powerful rhythms that he has made his own, like the welter and assault of waves on his own Carmel coast, the evocative strength of description, the right metaphor, the illuminating epithet, will be found throughout his work. In his shorter poems he reveals an ironic wit, some of which resembles the epigrammatic forcefulness of the Nay-saying paradoxes found in Nietzsche's *Thus Spake Zarathustra*. And in some of his shorter pieces there are also passages of descriptive brilliance, particularly in his 'Love the Wild Swan,' which are characteristic of the insight that illumines Jeffers' use of natural phenomena in the symbolism of his more ambitious poems. Despite his tendency to overstress the mere show of power in his vivid imagery, and despite his seemingly endless repetition of the theme of incest in his poetic narratives, he is justly regarded today as one of the major figures in American poetry.

Son of a scholar who taught him poetry, Jeffers went to school during his travels abroad as a child, was graduated from Occidental College in Los Angeles, California, and spent some time at the Universities of Zurich and Southern California, and at the Los Angeles Medical School. He now lives at Tor House, which he built with own hands at Mount Carmel in California.

Flagons and Apples(Los Angeles, Calif., 1912).
Californians(N.Y., 1916).
Tamar, and Other Poems(N.Y., 1924).
Roan Stallion, Tamar and Other Poems (N.Y., 1925).
The Women at Point Sur(N.Y., 1927).
Cawdor, and Other Poems(N.Y., 1928).
Dear Judas, and Other Poems(N.Y., 1928).
Descent to the Dead(N.Y., 1931).
Thurso's Landing(N.Y., 1932).
Give Your Heart to the Hawks, and Other Poems(N.Y., 1933).
Solstice and Other Poems(N.Y., 1935).
Such Counsels You Gave to Me(N.Y., 1937).
The Selected Poetry of Robinson Jeffers (N.Y., 1938).
L.Adamic, *Robinson Jeffers; a Portrait* (Seattle, Wash., 1929).
L.C.Powell, *Robinson Jeffers, the Man and His Work*(Los Angeles, Calif., 1934). Foreword by Robinson Jeffers.
G.Sterling, *Robinson Jeffers, the Man and the Artist*(N.Y., 1926).
H.Hatcher, 'The Torches of Violence,' *English Journal*,XXIII, 91–99.
R.Humphries, 'Robinson Jeffers,' *Modern Monthly*,VIII,680–89,748–53.
S.S.Alberts, *A Bibliography of the Works of Robinson Jeffers*(N.Y., 1933). Contains invaluable commentary by Jeffers on his poetry.

EUGENE O'NEILL (1888–)

EUGENE O'NEILL is the first American dramatist of importance, and with his plays the American theatre became something more than an expensive diversion for its audience. His first one-act plays of the sea were produced in 1916 on the wharves of Provincetown, Massachusetts, later in the stables of Greenwich Village, and finally in the gilt theatres of Broadway. O'Neill's success marked that of a concerted effort to bring a native dignity to the stage.

His father was the famous actor James O'Neill, who during the 'nineties played the role of the Count of Monte Cristo throughout America. Eugene O'Neill was brought up in the theatre, and has never lost his sense either of the dramatic or of the potentialities of the grandiose from which he ostensibly reacted. He has been a

continual pioneer and experimenter in the technique of the theatre, and has brought into it most of the themes which had interested writers of his time.

O'Neill's first plays were based on his own experiences as a sailor in the Caribbean; they demonstrated both his sense of realism and his keen ear for common speech. The theatre needed such gifts. *Desire Under the Elms*, produced in 1924, was a brilliant example of his talents. The psychological value of sound he indicated through the tom-toms in his *Emperor Jones*, 1920. The force of psychological knowledge in its revelation of man's duality was brought out, in combination with man's spiritual and material ambiguity, by the use of the masks of *The Great God Brown*, 1925, the theme of which is in many ways the most significant of O'Neill's plays. The interest in the dominating impulsions of sex was in his *Strange Interlude*, 1928, whose nine acts were an indication of his impatience with the restrictions of time in relation to theatrical production. Even the use of parallel overtones, which Pound and Eliot had used in poetry and James Joyce had employed in prose, were brought to the theatre in *Mourning Becomes Electra*, 1931, a modern application of the problems raised in the Agamemnon trilogy of Aeschylus. This awareness of the possibilities of the stage has been no small part of O'Neill's contribution. In recognition of his accomplishment, he was given in 1937 the Nobel Prize in literature.

O'Neill's desire to extend the boundaries of the stage has on occasion caused him to look beyond it. It is on these terms that *Lazarus Laughed*(N.Y., 1926), 'a play for the imaginary theatre,' should be read. The Lucretian laughter of Lazarus is the triumphant *Yes!* of modern materialism. But the significance of the play does not lie entirely in its summation of post-war belief. For both in its rhythmical language and in its use of the chorus it is an important milestone in a determined effort (since the era of William Vaughn Moody) to give life to poetical drama. O'Neill added what Moody's followers lacked: a sense of the theatre.

Thirst and Other One Act Plays(Boston, 1914).
The Moon of the Caribbees, and Six Other Plays of the Sea(N.Y., 1919).

Beyond the Horizon(N.Y., 1920).
Gold(N.Y., 1920).
The Emperor Jones, Diff'rent, The Straw (N.Y., 1921).
The Hairy Ape: Anna Christie: The First Man(N.Y., 1922).
All God's Chillun Got Wings, and Welded (N.Y., 1924).
Desire Under the Elms(N.Y., 1925).
The Great God Brown: The Fountain: The Moon of the Caribbees and Other Plays (N.Y., 1926).
Marco Millions(N.Y., 1927).
Lazarus Laughed(N.Y., 1927).
Strange Interlude(N.Y., 1928).
Dynamo(N.Y., 1929).
Mourning Becomes Electra(N.Y., 1931).
Ah, Wilderness!(N.Y., 1933).
Days Without End(N.Y., 1934).
The Plays of Eugene O'Neill(N.Y., 1934–35). 12 vols.
Nine Plays of Eugene O'Neill (N.Y., 1932).
B.H.Clark, *Eugene O'Neill; the Man and His Plays*(N.Y., 1936).
A.H.Quinn, *A History of the American Drama from the Civil War to the Present Day*(N.Y., 1927),II,165–206.
A.D.Mickle, *Six Plays of Eugene O'Neill* (N.Y., 1929).
J.T.Shipley, *The Art of Eugene O'Neill* (Seattle, Washington, 1928).
R.D.Skinner, *Eugene O'Neill*(N.Y. and Toronto, 1935).
S.K.Winther, *Eugene O'Neill*(N.Y., 1934).
F.Fergusson, 'Eugene O'Neill,' *Hound & Horn*,III,145–60.

GERTRUDE STEIN (1874–1946)

THE publication in 1909 of Gertrude Stein's *Three Lives* marked the appearance of a significant literary pioneer. These stories of Swedish and German peasants and of a Negress were Miss Stein's first attempts in what has been her constant aim, 'to get to the very core of the communication of the intuition.' She brought about this communication through words and rhythms particularly suited to the intelligences of her characters. Her discovery was an important step in realism.

Her work was an example of the in-creased sensitivity on the part of writers to the revelations of psychological research. She was herself a trained psychologist, and had been one of William James' favorite students when she attended Radcliffe College. This study she continued at Johns Hopkins until 1903, when she left America, to settle first in London and then in Paris. It was under James that she first began her research in the problem of automatic writing, out of which came her understanding of its value in the expression of character.

Out of her knowledge of psychology

came also her perception of the values attached to individual words, and the ambiguities which arise from the varying attachments of meaning by individuals. This led to her concentration upon the essence of words, and to a consequent simplification and clarity in their use. It was this aspect of her work which caused Sherwood Anderson to remark concerning her:

> Miss Stein is a worker in words with the same loving touch in her strong fingers that was characteristic of the women of the kitchens of the brick houses in the town of my boyhood. She is an American woman of the old sort, one who cares for the handmade goodies and who scorns the factory-made foods, and in her own great kitchen she is making something with her materials, something sweet to the tongue and fragrant to the nostrils.

And it was as a result of the encouragement and stimulation which her example gave to writers like Ernest Hemingway and Sherwood Anderson, that she could say of the latter: 'Sherwood Anderson had a genius for using the sentence to convey a direct emotion.' Such direct conveyance is an important characteristic of modern American prose.

In her essay, 'How Writing Is Written,' Miss Stein sums up the progress of her experimentation. That she had completed both *Three Lives* and *The Making of Americans*(Paris, 1924) during the first decade of the century demonstrates that much fine writing is unsuspected by its own age.

Tender Buttons(N.Y., 1914).
The Making of Americans(N.Y., 1934). Abridged, with a preface by Bernard Faÿ.
Three Lives(N.Y., 1933).
Lectures in America(N.Y., 1935).
Four Saints in Three Acts(N.Y., 1934).
The Autobiography of Alice B. Toklas (N.Y., 1933).
Everybody's Autobiography(N.Y., 1937).
Portraits and Prayers(N.Y., 1934).

SHERWOOD ANDERSON (1876–1941)

THE career of few writers better illustrates the common literary desire to attain the morality of form than does that of Sherwood Anderson. When as a middle-aged, fairly prosperous factory-owner, he walked out of his office to learn the craft of writing, he became as much a symbol of America's spiritual uneasiness as the factory was of America's urge for material achievement.

In the first years of Anderson's groping revolt he formulated his 'Apology for Crudity' which became a creed for lesser men and a stamp for himself.

> For a long time I have believed that crudity is an inevitable quality in the production of a really significant present-day American literature. How indeed is one to escape the obvious fact that there is as yet no native subtlety of thought or living among us? And if we are a crude and childlike people, how can our literature hope to escape the influence of that fact? Why indeed should we want it to escape?

Anderson recognized in other men a groping similar to his own. Mankind was represented in his symbol of the teacher whose sensitive hands had the artist's urge to create form or at least to touch beauty. The teacher was misunderstood and driven out. 'Men had erected walls about themselves and . . . all men were perhaps destined to stand forever behind the walls—on which they constantly beat with their fists, or with whatever tools they could get hold of. Wanted to break through to something, you understand. One couldn't quite make out whether there was just one great wall or many little individual walls.'

The highest wall, in the period when America was somewhat belatedly reading Freud, seemed to be Sex. Anderson's realistic stories of American village life in *Winesburg, Ohio*(N.Y., 1919) were chiefly concerned with this frustration. *Many Marriages*(N.Y., 1923) and *Dark Laughter* (N.Y., 1925) were novels based on the same, perhaps at the time unconscious, symbol of incompleteness.

'One who thinks a great deal about people and what they are up to in the world comes inevitably in time to relate them to experiences connected with his own life.' This notation in *Sherwood Anderson's Notebook*(N.Y., 1926) indicates both the structural method and the fuller comprehension demonstrated in his story 'Death in the Woods.' The nucleus of the story was an incident which he had witnessed as a boy, and which had haunted him by his initial perception of the incompleteness of his understanding. Reminiscently, in *A Story Teller's Story*(N.Y., 1924), he wrote:

There are so many people in that land of whom I should like to tell you. I should like to take you with me through the gate into the land, let you wander there with me. There are people there with whom I should like you to talk. There is the old woman accompanied by the gigantic dogs who died alone in a wood on a winter day, the stout man with the gray eyes and with the pack on his back, who stands talking to the beautiful woman as she sits in her carriage, the little dark woman with the boyish husband who lives in a small house by a dusty road far out in the country.

These and many other figures, all having a life of their own, all playing forever in the field of my fancy. The fanciful shadowy life striving to take on flesh, to live as you and I live, to come out of the shadowy world of the fancy into the actuality of accomplished art.

Gradually, as Anderson had his own experiences, he was able to relate them to the story of the old woman, and to express them in a series of convolutions from the central incident which represents the increasing circumference of his own comprehension. This is the formulation of all writing.

'I believe,' says Anderson, 'that, in this matter of form, it is largely a matter of depth of feeling.' The conclusion of 'Death in the Woods' is significant: 'A thing so complete has its own beauty.' It was Anderson's own answer to crudity.

He answered it as well in the bare beauty of his style. Anderson has contrived an idiom of his own, which at its best has the qualities of great prose. He has almost a poet's ear for rhythm, which he is able to control and turn to fit either the emotion or the idea with which he is concerned. 'The writer,' he says, 'is seeking a certain tune, a rhythm. When he has caught it the words and sentences flow freely. There is a new cunning, a new majesty to his thoughts.' This new cunning and majesty is apparent in 'Death in the Woods.'

Sherwood Anderson was born at Camden, Ohio, and brought up in an environment similar to that which he describes in the stories of his childhood: *Tar; a Midwest Childhood* (N.Y., 1926) and *Windy McPherson's Son* (N.Y., 1916). His later life of escape from the conventional life of a manufacturer and his development as a writer is told in *A Story Teller's Story* (N.Y., 1924). More recently he lived at Marion, Virginia, where he was the owner of a newspaper.

Poor White(N.Y., 1920).

The Triumph of the Egg(N.Y., 1921).

Horses and Men(N.Y., 1923).

Hello Towns!(N.Y., 1929).

Death in the Woods and Other Stories(N.Y., 1933).

C.B.Chase, *Sherwood Anderson* (N.Y., 1927).

C.Fadiman, 'Sherwood Anderson: the Search for Salvation,' *Nation*,CXXXV, 454–56.

N.B.Fagin, *The Phenomenon of Sherwood Anderson*(Baltimore, 1927). Contains a bibliography.

R.Smith, 'Sherwood Anderson,' *Sewanee Review*,XXXVII,159–63.

C.Van Doren, 'Sinclair Lewis and Sherwood Anderson,' *Century*,CX, 362–69.

ERNEST HEMINGWAY (1898–)

THE influence of Ernest Hemingway's prose upon the younger short-story writers of the post-war period in American literature may be said to be as marked as the influence of T.S.Eliot's verse upon the younger poets of the same era. Hemingway, like many other novelists of his generation, has acknowledged a debt to the early prose of Gertrude Stein. Yet Hemingway's earliest writing, exhumed from school publications, reveals the fact that his hard-hitting short sentences in prose preceded whatever literary influences his later work may possess.

During the World War he belonged to a group of writers which included John Dos Passos, Archibald MacLeish, and Malcolm Cowley. These men, who had served in the War, and who afterwards went to Paris to assimilate their War experiences, were the acknowledged leaders of what Gertrude Stein called 'the lost generation.' One of the best examples of the literature which was to define the character of 'America's Post-War Period' is Hemingway's short story, 'Hills Like White Elephants.' Another example of Hemingway's application of an extraordinary craftsmanship is 'The Undefeated.'

His second book, *In Our Time*, was published in Paris in 1924. It was followed by three novels, *The Sun Also Rises*(N.Y., 1926), *A Farewell to Arms*(N.Y., 1929), and *To Have and To Have Not*(N.Y., 1937); and two books of short stories *Men Without Women*(N.Y., 1926) and *Winner Take Nothing*(N.Y., 1933). No less important than the appearance of these books is the influence exerted by Hemingway's point of view towards literature—an influence which is exemplified in his short stories and which was stated in his *Death in the Afternoon*(N.Y., 1932):

This too to remember. If a man writes clearly enough any one can see if he fakes. If he mystifies to avoid a straight statement, which is very different from breaking so-called rules of syntax or grammar to make an effect which can be obtained in no other way, the writer takes a longer time to be known as a fake and other writers who are afflicted by the same necessity will praise him in their own defense. True mysticism should not be confused with incompetence in writing which seeks to mystify where there is no mystery but is really only the necessity to fake to cover lack of knowledge or the inability to state clearly. Mysticism implies a mystery and there

are many mysteries; but incompetence is not one of them; nor is overwritten journalism made literature by the injection of a false epic quality. Remember this too: all bad writers are in love with the epic.

Hemingway's preoccupation with the theme of death, which so frequently enters the violent action of his stories, is also characteristic of the group of writers in which he assumed leadership. It was as though the great sacrifice of the lives of young men during the World War had given Hemingway a particularly keen awareness to the precariousness of living. But this awareness also left its mark upon the elements of his prose style, which, in its effort to convey emotion in the fewest possible words, stripped naked the very core of the sentimentality that was characteristic of the men and women who were brought to life in his fiction.

Ernest Hemingway was born at Oak Park, Illinois, in 1898. He attended the public schools of Michigan, where he was brought up. He was a reporter in Kansas City at the outbreak of the World War, and he left to join the volunteer ambulance unit in France. Later he served with the Italian army, and after the war remained abroad as correspondent for the Toronto *Star*. He lived for some years in Paris as a correspondent for the Hearst papers, and while there came to know Gertrude Stein and to concentrate on his own writing. Of recent years he has lived at Key West, Florida.

Three Stories & Ten Poems(Dijon, France, 1923).
The Torrents of Spring(N.Y., 1926).
Green Hills of Africa(N.Y., 1935).
The Fifth Column and the First Forty-Nine (N.Y., 1938). Collected short stories.
M.Cowley, 'A Farewell to Spain,' *New Republic*,LXXIII, 76–77.
R.M.Lovett, 'Ernest Hemingway,' *English Journal*,XXI,609–17.
L.Kirstein, 'The Canon of Death,' *Hound & Horn*,V,519–39.
C.Fadiman, 'Ernest Hemingway: an American Byron,' *Nation*,CXXXVI,63–64.
L.H.Cohn, *A Bibliography of the writings of Ernest Hemingway*(N.Y., 1931).

JOHN DOS PASSOS (1896–)

ALTHOUGH John Dos Passos' first novel, *One Man's Initiation—1917* (London, 1920), was the story based on his experiences in the World War, it was not until 1921, when his second novel of the War, *Three Soldiers*, was published in America that his abilities as a realistic prose writer were widely recognized. In 1927 his third novel, *Manhattan Transfer*, introduced a novelist whose experiments in the writing of prose are of first importance.

The extraverted energy which marks the prose of John Dos Passos has its origins in his boyhood reading of the novels of Captain Marryat as well as in his experiences in the writing of nervous, brilliant, liberal journalism. To these may be added his admiration for the poetry of Cendrars, a contemporary French poet, whose verse is characterized by its extraordinary velocity and vivid impressionism.

Upon completion of his trilogy, *The 42nd Parallel*(N.Y., 1930), *Nineteen Nineteen*(N.Y., 1932), and *The Big Money* (N.Y., 1936), brought together as *U.S.A.* (N.Y., 1937), John Dos Passos emerged as a major figure in contemporary American fiction. No less remarkable than his assimilation of the historical events and situations which characterized the years of the World War and the decade immediately following it was his ability to create a new technique in the writing of a social novel. It may be said that the technique of *U.S.A.* bears a close relationship to the technique of the cinema. John Dos Passos' method of telling a story has within it all the devices which have made the uses of montage so effective to audiences in a motion picture theater. His broken narrative of the lives of his characters, his 'news reels' which are direct quotations of headlines and fragments of items clipped from newspapers, his 'camera eye' which records his personal impressions of the events which dominate the lives of his characters, his biographies of the leading figures in contemporary American life, written in unrhymed and syncopated prose, a prose which closely resembles the verse of Carl Sandburg and Edgar Lee Masters, —all combine to create a visual impression of remarkable vividness and unquestionable veracity. The social philosophy which underlies the theme of *U.S.A.* is indicated by his sympathetic and penetrating biography of Thorsten Veblen in *The Big Money*, the last novel of his trilogy.

John Dos Passos was born in Chicago in 1896. During his adolescence, Gibbon's *Decline and Fall of the Roman Empire* was his Bible. He was educated at Harvard, where he received the degree of A.B. in 1916. In a news item in *Time*, August 10, 1936, it is reported that though he was graduated *cum laude* from Harvard he thinks he got little out of college and regards his four years there as largely wasted. His latest book is *Journeys Between Wars* (N.Y., 1938), a collection of the reportorial travel sketches which he has been writing since 1922.

A Pushcart at the Curb(N.Y., 1922).
Three Plays(N.Y., 1934).
M.Cowley, 'The Poet and the World,' *New Republic*,LXX,303–05.
G.Hicks, 'John Dos Passos,' *Bookman*, LXXV,32–42.

T. S. ELIOT (1888–)

THE general acceptance of modern verse has come very largely through the poetry of T.S.Eliot. This has been brought about not because other men have in general agreed with what Eliot has had to say at various stages of his development, but because his continued preoccupation with, and articulated solutions of, the problem of communication have both clarified his own expression and given the means to other poets to clarify theirs.

The position of the poet and of the critic today is indicated by Eliot in the first of the Charles Eliot Norton Lectures which he gave at Harvard University in the winter of 1932–33:

When I speak of modern poetry as being extremely critical, I mean that the contemporary poet, who is not merely a composer of graceful verses—is forced to ask himself such questions as 'what is poetry for?'; not merely 'what am I to say?' but rather 'how and to whom am I to say it?' We have to communicate—if it is communication, for the word may beg the question—an experience which is not an experience in the ordinary sense, for it may only exist, formed out of many personal experiences ordered in some way which may be very different from the way of valuation of practical life, in the expression of it. *If* poetry is a form of 'communication,' yet that which is to be communicated is the poem itself, and only incidentally the experience and the thought which have gone into it. The poem's existence is somewhere between the writer and the reader; it has a reality which is not simply the reality of what the writer is trying to 'express,' or of his experience of writing it, or of the experience of the reader or of the writer as reader.

Thomas Stearns Eliot was born at St. Louis, Missouri, in 1888. In 1909 he was graduated from Harvard University, and in the next year was given his master's degree. During the winter of 1911–12 he was at the Sorbonne in Paris and from 1912 to 1914 was a student at Merton College, Oxford. Since then he has remained in England, where he has become a British subject.

In an introduction to *This American World* (London, 1928) by Edgar A. Mowrer, Eliot has discussed his past:

I have a background which Mr. Mowrer would recognize, and which is different from that of the native European and from that of many Americans. My family were New Englanders, who had been settled—my branch of it—for two generations in the South West—which was, in my own time, rapidly becoming merely the Middle West. The family guarded jealously its connections with New England; but it was not until years of maturity that I perceived that I myself had always been a New Englander in the South West, and a South Westerner in

New England; when I was sent to school in New England I lost my southern accent without ever acquiring the accent of the native Bostonian. In New England I missed the long dark river, the ailanthus trees, the flaming cardinal birds, the high limestone bluffs where we searched for fossil shell-fish; in Missouri I missed the fir trees, the bay and goldenrod, the song-sparrows, the red granite and the blue sea of Massachusetts. I remember a friend of my school-days, whose family had lived in the same New England seaport for two hundred and fifty years. In some ways his background was as different from mine as that of any European. My grandmother—one of my grandmothers—had shot her own wild turkeys for dinner; his had collected Chinese pottery brought home by the Salem clippers. It was perhaps easier for the grandson of pioneers to migrate eastward than it would have been for my friend to migrate in any direction.

'The Love Song of J. Alfred Prufrock' was written while Eliot was still an undergraduate at Harvard, and its reflection of Laforgue is indicative of his early and independent recognition of the importance of French poetry to English verse. Eliot said in 1918: 'It is exactly as wasteful for a poet to do what has been done already, as for a biologist to rediscover Mendel's discoveries. The French poets in question have made "discoveries" in verse of which we cannot afford to be ignorant, discoveries which are not merely a concern for French syntax. To remain with Wordsworth is equivalent to ignoring the whole of science subsequent to Erasmus Darwin.' Eliot's receptivity to the lessons of the French, of the Elizabethan dramatists, as well as to the Pound of 'Hugh Selwyn Mauberley' and the 'Cantos' has given him the technical strength of tradition.

Eliot has also been one of the first to recognize in poetry the importance of anthropology as a frame of reference to the modern mind. The investigation of variant civilizations and religions has brought forth certain common denominators which can serve as fresh symbols of interrelationship. '*The Golden Bough*,' Eliot said in 1921, 'can be read in two ways: as a collection of entertaining myths, or as a revelation of that vanished mind of which our mind is a continuation.' Eliot has chosen the second way, and utilized it in accord with his observation that 'in art there should be interpenetration and metamorphosis.' In this way he has managed to combine timeliness with timelessness.

The dramatic quality of Eliot's earliest verse makes it easy to understand why he has become more and more interested in dramatic poetry, until he might say in the last of the Charles Eliot Norton Lectures:

The ideal medium for poetry, to my mind, and the most direct means of social 'usefulness' for poetry, is the theatre. In a play of Shakespeare you get several levels of significance. For the simplest auditors there is the plot, for the more thoughtful the character and conflict of character, for the more literary the words and phrasing, for the musically sensitive the rhythm, and for auditors of greater sensitiveness and understanding a meaning which reveals itself gradually. And I do not believe that the classification of audience is so clear-cut as this; but rather that the sensitiveness of every auditor is acted upon by all these elements at once, though in different degrees of consciousness. At none of these levels is the auditor bothered by the presence of that which he does not understand, or by the presence of that in which he is not interested.

The development of Eliot's attitudes and beliefs has been always fresh and consistent. The uncertainty and timidity of J. Alfred Prufrock resulted naturally enough in the sterility of Gerontion, which he epitomized in his contemporary picture of 'The Waste Land.' Then, standing as it were at the edge of a precipice, and faced with the necessity of belief and advancement, Eliot turned to the right, as others were to turn to the left. Because he moved with the utmost seriousness and sincerity, the expression of his own progress has been vitally useful for the expression of any progress, and the implications of his essay on 'Religion and Literature' can serve many masters.

But above all Eliot is a poet.

Collected Poems, 1909–1935(N. Y., 1936).
The Rock(N.Y., 1934).
Murder in the Cathedral(N.Y., 1935).
Selected Essays, 1917–1932(N.Y., 1932).
The Use of Poetry and the Use of Criticism (N.Y., 1933).
After Strange Gods(N.Y., 1934).
Essays, Ancient and Modern(N.Y., 1936).
'Gerontion' and 'The Hollow Men'(Harvard University Phonograph Records, No.3, SS–5053). A recording by Eliot.
F.O.Matthiessen, *The Achievement of T.S. Eliot*(Boston, 1935).
C.Aiken, 'After Ash Wednesday,' *Poetry*, XLV,161–65.
R.P.Blackmur, *The Double Agent*(N.Y., 1935),184–218.
F.R.Leavis, *New Bearings in English Poetry*(London, 1932),75–132.
T.McGreevy, *Thomas Stearns Eliot*(London, 1931).
J.C.Ransom, 'T.S.Eliot on Criticism,' *Saturday Review of Literature*,X,574.
I.A.Richards, 'The Poetry of T.S.Eliot,' *Living Age*,CCCXXIX,112–15.
A.Tate, 'Irony and Humility,' *Hound & Horn*,IV,290–97.
E.Wilson, *Axel's Castle*(N.Y., 1931),93–131.
H.R.Williamson, *The Poetry of T.S.Eliot* (London, 1932).
M.D.Zabel, 'T.S.Eliot in Mid-Career,' *Poetry*,XXXVI,330–37.

ARCHIBALD MACLEISH (1892–)

ARCHIBALD MACLEISH's *New Found Land* (Boston, 1930) was the first articulate expression in poetry of a post-war generation, whose emotions had been reflected in the novels of Ernest Hemingway and John Dos Passos. MacLeish's conversation with Andrew Marvell represented the synthesis of the time-space relationship which, when crystallized in poetic form, represented the unity which the World War had seemed to deny. Its comprehension was demonstrated in the substance given to MacLeish's already characteristic smoothness and control of the lyric line.

It was at this time, when he was past thirty, that MacLeish says that he began his real writing. The verve with which he had been able to express his travels in Persia, where after quitting his law practice he had wandered from the central cities of Bushire to Ispahan and Teheran, is still evident in a similar synthesis of the American scene in 'Frescoes for Mr. Rockefeller's City.' In addition to this verve, the brilliance and clarity of his visual imagery and his sensitivity to light and color contribute towards the success of his translation of Bernáe Díaz del Castillo's *True History of the Conquest of New Spain* into the narrative poem, *Conquistador*(Boston, 1932).

MacLeish's consistent experimentations within conventional verse forms have been extended into the forms of poetic drama in *Panic*(N.Y., 1935), of the radio play in *The Fall of the City*(N.Y., 1936), and into the newsreel sound-track technique of *Land of the Free*(N.Y., 1938). This willingness to explore the potentialities of contemporary media has been MacLeish's greatest strength, and promises his greatest contribution to American verse.

Archibald MacLeish was educated at the Hotchkiss School in Connecticut, at Yale University, and at the Harvard Law School. After a period during which he taught at Harvard and practised law, he went abroad in order to devote himself to writing. For some years he was an editor of *Fortune*.

Poems 1924–1933(Boston, 1933).

Union Pacific—A Ballet(N.Y., 1934).

Public Speech(N.Y., 1936).

D.Fitts, 'To Karthage Then I Came,' *Hound & Horn*,IV,637–41.

L.Jones, 'Archibald MacLeish: a Modern Metaphysical,' *English Journal*,XXIV, 441–51.

M.D.Zabel, 'The Cinema of Hamlet,' *Literary Opinion in America*(N.Y., 1937), 415–26.

JOHN CROWE RANSOM (1888–)

Of particular significance in modern American poetry was that group of Southern poets who issued, from the spring of 1922 to the winter of 1925, a co-operative journal of poetry, called *The Fugitive*, published at Nashville, Tennessee. The leader of this group of seven was John Crowe Ransom, who was graduated from Vanderbilt University, taught there for many years, and is now a member of the faculty of Kenyon College in Ohio. The magazine grew from the discussions of the original members, all friends. They included Allen Tate, Donald Davidson, and others. At first the poets contributing to the magazine used pseudonyms, and the foreword to its first number indicated, in an amusing fashion, a change in Southern literature. It said in part:

> *The Fugitive* flees from nothing faster than from the highcaste Brahmins of the Old South. Without raising the question of whether the blood in the veins of its editors runs red, they at any rate are not advertising it as blue; indeed, as to pedigree, they cheerfully invite the most unfavorable inference from the circumstances of their anonymity.

An anthology gathered from the poetry of this group and called *Fugitives* was published in 1928. It represents the South's most distinguished contribution to modern regional poetry.

Ransom is one of the most truly original poets of our time. His approach is tangential, and his verse is always sophisticated in its use of formal, lyrical device. Mark Van Doren has spoken of his 'almost acid gaiety' and of his use of 'fresh realistic words.' In general, it may be said that his verse suggests the very quality of ironic disillusionment that many writers of the South, who are less gifted than he, have attempted to convey.

A Tennesseean by birth, Ransom, after graduating from Vanderbilt, was a Rhodes scholar at Christ Church, Oxford, from 1910 to 1913, when he received his B.A. Six years later, in 1919 his first book, *Poems About God*, appeared, with an introduction by Christopher Morley. After five more years his second volume, *Chills and Fever*(1924), showed the maturity of his craftsmanship, for it contains within it some of the best poetry, and certainly the most distinguished lyricism that the South has produced in its present generation.

Grace After Meat(N.Y., 1924).
Two Gentlemen in Bonds(N.Y., 1927).
God Without Thunder(N.Y., 1930).
The World's Body(N.Y., 1938).
'The Aesthetic of Regionalism,' *The American Review*,II,290–310.
R.P.Warren, 'John Crowe Ransom, a Study in Irony,' *Virginia Quarterly Review*,XI,93–112.

ALLEN TATE (1899–)

ALLEN TATE'S work is best known for its representation of culture to be found south of the Mason-Dixon line. Tate is the most eloquent member of the South's 'new generation' since the close of the World War. Perhaps the best known of his poems is 'The Ode to the Confederate Dead,' which is a brilliant exercise in the uses of twentieth-century rhetoric.

He has written exhaustively of his own work in an essay characteristically entitled 'Narcissus as Narcissus' in *The Virginia Quarterly Review*. Concerning his 'Ode to the Confederate Dead' he wrote:

That poem is 'about' solipsism or Narcissism, or any other *ism* that denotes the failure of the human personality to function properly in nature and society. Society (and 'nature' as modern society constructs it) appears to offer limited fields for the exercise of the whole man, who wastes his energy piecemeal over separate functions that ought to come under a unity of being. (Until the last generation, only certain women were whores, having been set aside as special instances of sex amid a social scheme that held the general belief that sex must be part of a whole; now the general belief is that sex must be special.) Without

unity we get the remarkable self-consciousness of our age.

The number of Greek and Latin derivatives in Tate's vocabulary indicates to his readers his admiration for the frequently elaborate sonorous and at times archaic word. His most enduring claims to originality, however, are to be found in the quality of his wit. This is used for the expression of mingled anger and disillusionment which characterizes the attitude of the post war Southerner who is all too conscious of the defects existing in contemporary American civilization.

Allen Tate was born in Winchester, Kentucky, in 1899. He received his A.B. from Vanderbilt University in 1922. Under the leadership of John Crowe Ransom he edited the *Fugitive*. His first book of poems, *Mr. Pope and Other Poems*, appeared in 1928. *Poems: 1928–1931* was published in 1932. In 1936 he published *The Mediterranean and Other Poems*, and in 1937 his *Selected Poems*. He now lives in Tennessee in a large house overlooking the Cumberland River.

Reactionary Essays on Poetry and Ideas (N.Y., 1936).
The Fathers(N.Y., 1938). A novel.

STEPHEN VINCENT BENÉT (1898–1943)

THE appearance of Stephen Vincent Benét's fourth book of poems, *Tiger Joy* (N.Y., 1925), gave character to his rising reputation as a young and felicitous American poet. Three years later, his epic of the Civil War, *John Brown's Body*, brought with its publication the recognition of a wide

reading public. The poem contained a great variety of diversification, extending from loose, long rhythms approximating prose to short passages of lyric eloquence. In his latest book of poems, *Burning City* (N.Y., 1936), he extended his range into free verse with powerful impact in his

'Litany for Dictatorships.' His octave of sonnets in 'The Golden Corpse' and the dedicatory sonnets to *John Brown's Body* paint purely American backgrounds in a manner fresh and new; and the recent series of 'Nightmares,' devoted to commentary on our possible future, seems little more fantastic than certain developments in the history of our own time.

Benét has come a long way since he overcame the early influence of Robert Browning, William Morris, and Gilbert K. Chesterton, which was at different times evident in his earliest work in verse. But even his first small book, published at the age of seventeen, presented a series of Roman portraits with remarkable vigor. The variety of his poetry, from bizarre and humorous to trenchantly grave and dramatic, may be safely left to the audit of the future. In prose, his work in the novel, always full of vitality, has steadily improved; and today his best short stories are recognized as of unusual originality.

Stephen Vincent Benét was born in Bethlehem, Pennsylvania, in 1898. He received his A.B. from Yale in 1919. He married Rosemary Carr of Chicago in 1921. He lives in New York City.

Ballads and Poems, 1915–1930(N.Y., 1931).
Spanish Bayonet(N.Y., 1926).
W.R.Benét, 'Round About Parnassus,' *Saturday Review of Literature*,VII,491.
L.Bacon, 'Stephen Vincent Benét,' *Saturday Review of Literature*,X,608.
S.R.Daniels, 'A Saga of the American Civil War,' *Contemporary Review*,CXLVI, 466–71.

LÉONIE ADAMS (1899–)

WITH the publication of her first book of poems, *Those Not Elect*(N.Y., 1925), Léonie Adams was immediately recognized as one of the few distinguished lyricists of the day. The quality of her imagination, which so closely resembles the characteristics of seventeenth-century devotional verse, caused her to be classified as a 'metaphysical poet.' Her lyricism, however, more closely resembles the tonal quality of the poetry of William Butler Yeats and Walter de la Mare; and the character of her 'metaphysics' has something of the same quickening influence upon contemporary poetry as the verse of Gerard Manley Hopkins.

As Babette Deutsch wrote in her critical study of modern verse, *This Modern Poetry:*

None of her contemporaries has recorded with more delicate precision the motions of the hours and the seasons as sky and earth body them forth.

Miss Adams was born in Brooklyn, New York, in 1899. She was graduated from Barnard College in 1922, and from 1928 to 1929 lived in London. She returned to New York City in 1930 and was appointed to an instructorship in English at New York University. Her second book, *High Falcon*, appeared in 1929. She is now a member of the English faculty of Bennington College, Bennington, Vermont.

WILLIAM FAULKNER (1897–)

No American writer has assimilated the various techniques of modern symbolism with greater ingenuity than has William Faulkner. Although *Sanctuary*(N.Y., 1931) is his best known novel, *As I Lay Dying* (N.Y., 1930) is his finest achievement. A kind of terrible awareness of death has been the theme he uses to symbolize the sense of decay which has preoccupied the South since the Reconstruction Period. The necessity of linking this emotion with its symbol has resulted in a brutal distortion of the incident on which he has based such stories as 'Dry September.'

Faulkner was born in 1897, and was brought up in Oxford, Mississippi. His undergraduate life at the University of Mississippi, which he had entered as a special student at the age of sixteen, was broken by his enlistment in the Canadian Flying Corps. During his station in Oxford, England, he listened to the university lec-

tures, and after the Armistice re-entered the University of Mississippi, where he remained from 1919 to 1921. His first publication was a volume of pastoral poetry, *The Marble Faun*(Boston, 1924). The appearance of *The Green Bough* in 1933 is evidence of his awareness of the value of the techniques of contemporary poetry to a writer of psychological fiction. His novel, *The Sound and the Fury*(N.Y., 1929), is an illustration of his application of those techniques to prose.

These 13(N.Y., 1931).
Light in August(N.Y., 1932).
Doctor Martino and Other Stories(N.Y., 1934).
Pylon(N.Y., 1935).

The Unvanquished(N.Y., 1938).
The Wild Palms(N.Y., 1939).
A.Buttitta, 'William Faulkner: That Writin' Man of Oxford,' *Saturday Review of Literature*,XVIII,6–8.
W.R.Benét, 'Faulkner as a Poet,' *Saturday Review of Literature*,IX,565.
H.S.Canby, 'The School of Cruelty,' *Saturday Review of Literature*,VII,673–74.
G.Hicks, 'The Past and Future of William Faulkner,' *Bookman*,LXXIV,17–24.
E.Scott, *On William Faulkner's 'The Sound and the Fury'*(N.Y., 1929).
A.R.Thompson, 'The Cult of Cruelty,' *Bookman*,LXXIV,477–87.
A.Starke, 'An American Comedy: an Introduction to a Bibliography of William Faulkner,' *Colophon*, Part XIX.

THOMAS WOLFE (1900–1938)

THE consciousness of disintegration which characterized the writing of the early nineteen-twenties changed to a general recognition of the necessity for some form of integration. The novels of Thomas Wolfe express through the sensibilities of a single man a synthesis of human experience.

The first two of Wolfe's projected series of six novels, *Look Homeward Angel*(N.Y., 1930) and *Of Time and the River*(N.Y., 1935), succeed in re-creating the essential emotions out of the physical reality of American life: such as a newsboy's life in a small town; the all-night restaurant; the death of one's father; a journey in a train; the introduction to university life; and an American's discovery of Europe. The emphasis which Wolfe placed on emotional values accounts for the extraordinary vividness with which he was able to reconstruct the remembrance of things past in American life.

The same emphasis on emotion accounts for Wolfe's approximation of poetry in the writing of his prose. The energy that this released resulted in one of the most spontaneous examples of prose ever written in this or any country. It is this spontaneity

which brings to the reader those sensations which have been identified with the poetry of Whitman.

Wolfe's prose shows a duality of purpose in the creation of both the starkly realistic and the fabulous character of human experience. In the latter, in particular, he represented what promises to be a new and vigorous development of American prose.

Thomas Wolfe was born at Ashville, North Carolina, and attended both the University of North Carolina and Harvard University, where he was a student in Professor George Baker's '47 Workshop.' For a brief period he was an instructor in English literature at New York University. The manuscript of his third long novel, *The Web and the Rock*(N.Y., 1939), was delivered to his publishers just before his death in Baltimore in September 1938.

From Death to Morning(N.Y., 1935).
The Story of a Novel(N.Y., 1936).
H.S.Canby, 'The River of Youth,' *Saturday Review of Literature*,XI,1–2.
R.P.Warren, 'A Note on the Hamlet of Thomas Wolfe,' *American Review*,V, 191–208.

HART CRANE (1899–1932)

THE publication of Hart Crane's *The Bridge* in 1930 was an event comparable to the appearance of T.S.Eliot's *The Waste*

Land in 1922. This ambitious poem was an attempt to synthesize the variety of poetic experience which during the preceding decade had been subject to analysis. As Crane wrote in 1929:

> The poet's concern must be, as always, self-discipline toward a formal integration of experience. For poetry is an architectural art, based not on Evolution or the idea of progress, but on the articulation of the contemporary human consciousness *sub specie æternitatis*, and inclusive of all readjustments incident to science and other shifting factors related to that consciousness. The key to the process of free creative activity which Coleridge gave us in his *Lectures on Shakespeare* exposes the responsibilities of every poet, modern or ancient, and cannot be improved upon. 'No work of true genius,' he says, 'dares want its appropriate form, neither indeed is there any danger of this. As it must not, so genius cannot, be lawless: for it is even this that constitutes its genius—the power of acting creatively under laws of its own origination.'

No less important was his statement concerning the more technical problems of the post-war poet who sought to assimilate what had been regarded as a conflict between the imagery of the machine and the imagery of natural phenomena:

> For unless poetry can absorb the machine, i.e., *acclimatize* it as naturally and casually as trees, cattle, galleons, castles and all other human associations of the past, then poetry has failed of its full contemporary function.

It was Crane's intention in writing *The Bridge* to recreate the *Myth of America*.

His choices of Brooklyn Bridge, of Pocahontas, of Cutty Sark, and of the subway train for the symbolic representation of the American myth were deliberate: they represented the poet's effort to recreate the beauty and intensity of living close to the very heart of American civilization.

Despite the fact that *The Bridge* remains an unfinished poem, one must seek for an analogy to the work of Rimbaud to find poetry of like intensity and power. As in the work of Rimbaud, Crane's mysticism found its expression through the medium of concrete and realistic imagery and language. Perhaps no poet of his time so closely approximated the sensuous qualities of word, image, and tonal music that are generally regarded as characteristic of the poetry of John Keats.

Hart Crane was born in Garrettsville, Ohio, in 1899. He was educated in the public schools of Ohio and wrote copy in advertising offices in Cleveland and New York. Like other members of his generation, he crossed the Atlantic for a brief stay in Paris. In 1932 he committed suicide by leaping from the deck of a north-bound steamer on the Gulf of Mexico.

White Buildings(N.Y., 1926). With a foreword by Allen Tate.
The Collected Poems of Hart Crane(N.Y., 1933). Edited with an introduction by Waldo Frank.
Philip Horton, *Hart Crane*(N.Y., 1937).
A.Tate, 'In Memoriam: Hart Crane,' *Hound & Horn*,V,612–19.
——, 'Hart Crane and the American Mind,' *Poetry*,XL,210–16.
G.B.Munson, *Destinations*(N.Y., 1928), 160–77.

HORACE GREGORY (1898–)

A COLLECTED edition of the poems of Horace Gregory should bear its own title, for his three books of poems are a single expression of his search to know himself at the same time that he has been learning to understand the world in which he lives.

Chelsea Rooming House(N.Y., 1930) is a geographical illustration of the ultimately clarifying effect on the sensibilities of an unsatisfied and romantic mind of a plunge

from the academic milieu of home and university into the coarse vitality of lower West Side Manhattan life. The toughening effect of this new milieu on his thought appears to have been paralleled by that of Thomas Hardy on his poetry. Somewhat belatedly, hence more eclectically, Gregory has increasingly learned the lessons of modern poetics.

The initial shock over, Gregory's subsequent volumes, *No Retreat* (N.Y., 1933) and *Chorus for Survival*(N.Y., 1935) indicate through their titles his own optimistic position. He has not written directly about himself so much as about that which he sees; and the implication of his work is not to be found in particular poems but rather through their relationship to his central theme. The characters of Chelsea have been increasingly supplemented by others which have come into Gregory's widening experience, as well as by a judicious utilization of his literary heritage. This heritage he has also developed by distinguished criticism. It is by these ways that he has achieved success in his expressed desire 'to combine the idiom of contemporary life with my early (and entirely literary) influences.' Or, as he has expressed the same thought in verse,

Envy the great but do not enter where they
     go.

Gregory's first volume demonstrated his admirable acuteness of ear both for idiom and rhythm, his clarity of expression, and his live fancy. His later work, however, has shown a greater imaginative insight and a heightened power of vivid expression which has given force and individuality to his poetry. His natural gift for the lyric, somewhat stifled by the uncertainties of his adjustment, is becoming stronger and clearer. In his own approaching maturity he indicates a promise of a general poetical maturity.

Horace Gregory was born in Milwaukee in 1898, and was educated at the German-English Academy in that city and at the University of Wisconsin. He now lectures on poetry and criticism at Sarah Lawrence College.

The necessity for a poet of this day to bear a conscious relationship to the age in which he lives has been recognized by many other poets besides Gregory. He stands alone with Crane, however, in his knowledge of America's past—not so much of its pageantry and color but of its spiritual tradition. It is in this way that he makes Emerson not only a figure of the past but of the present, and gives to American writers the much-needed lesson that America's future lies behind as well as ahead.

The Poems of Catullus(N.Y., 1931). A translation.
Pilgrim of the Apocalypse; a Critical Study of D.H.Lawrence(N.Y., 1933).
New Letters in America(N.Y., 1937). Editor.

BIBLIOGRAPHY

BACKGROUND

Historical, Social, Intellectual

ANDREWS,C.M., *The Colonial Period of American History*, 3 vols.(New Haven, 1934-7).

BARTHOLOMEW,J.G., *A Literary and Historical Atlas of America*, Everyman's Library(London, 1911).

Beer, Thomas, *The Mauve Decade: American Life at the End of the Nineteenth Century* (N.Y.,1926).

EGGLESTON,E., *The Transit of Civilization from England to America in the Seventeenth Century*(N.Y.,1901).

FAŸ,B., *The Revolutionary Spirit in France and America*(N.Y.,1927).

Frothingham,O.B., *Transcendentalism in New England*(N.Y.,1876).

GABRIEL,R.H., ed., *The Pageant of America: a Pictorial History of the United States*, 15 vols.(New Haven, 1926-9).

HORNBERGER,T., 'Science and the New World,' *Catalogue of Huntington Library*, 3-18(1937).

JOHNSON,Allen, and Malone, Dumas, eds., *Dictionary of American Biography*, 20 vols. (N.Y.,1928-36).

Jones,H.M., *America and French Culture*, 1750-1848(Chapel Hill, N.C.,1927).

KITTREDGE,G.L., *Witchcraft in Old and New England*(Cambridge,Mass., 1929).

Koch,G.A., *Republican Religion: The American Revolution and the Cult of Reason*(N.Y., 1933).

McMASTER,J.B., *A History of the People of the United States, from the Revolution to the Civil War*, 8 vols.(N.Y., 1833-1913).

Morais,H.M., *Deism in Eighteenth Century America*(N.Y.,1934).

Morison,S.E., *The Puritan Pronaos: Studies in the Intellectual Life of New England in the Seventeenth Century*(N.Y.,1936).

Morison,S.E., and Commager,H.S., *The Growth of the American Republic*, 2 vols., rev.ed.(N.Y.,1937).

Mumford,L., *The Brown Decades: A Study of the Arts in America*, 1865-1895(N.Y., 1931).
——, *The Golden Day: A Study in American Experience and Culture*(N.Y.,1926).

PARRINGTON,V.L., *Main Currents in American Thought*, 3 vols.(N.Y.,1927-30). I, *The Colonial Mind*, 1620-1800; II, *The Romantic Revolution*, 1800-1860; III, *The Beginnings of Critical Realism*, 1860-1920.

Paxson,F.L., *The History of the American Frontier*, 1763-1893(Boston, 1924).

Phillips,U.B., *Life and Labor in the Old South* (Boston, 1929).

RILEY,I.W., *American Thought, from Puritanism to Pragmatism*(N.Y., 1915,1923).

SCHLESINGER,A.N., and Fox,D.R., eds., *A History of American Life*, 12 vols.(N.Y., 1927—). I, Priestley,H.I., *The Coming of the White Man*, 1492-1848. II, Wertenbaker, T.J., *The First Americans*, 1607-1690. III, Adams,J.T., *Provincial Society*, 1690-1763. VI, Fish,C.R., *The Rise of the Common Man*, 1830-1850. VII, Cole,A.C., *The Irrepressible Conflict*, 1850-1865. VIII, Nevins,A., *The Emergence of Modern America*, 1865-1878. IX, Tarbell,Ida M., *The Nationalizing of Business*, 1878-1898. X, Schlesinger,A.M., *The Rise of the City*, 1878-1898. XI, Faulkner,H.U., *The Quest for Social Justice*, 1898-1914. XII, Slosson, P.W., *The Great Crusade and After*, 1914-1928. (Vols. IV, V, not announced.)

Schneider,H.W., *The Puritan Mind*(N.Y., 1930).

Scholes,Percy B., *The Puritans and Music in England and New England*(London, 1934).

Sibley,John L. and Shipton,C.K., *Biographical Sketches of Graduates of Harvard University*, 5 vols., complete for 1642-1712 (Cambridge, Mass., 1873-1937).

Sullivan,M., *Our Times: The United States*, 1900-1925, 6 vols.(N.Y.,1926-35).

Swift,L., *Brook Farm*(N.Y.,1900).

THWAITES,R.G., ed., *Early Western Travels*, 1748-1846, 32 vols.(Cleveland, 1904-7).

Townsend,H.G., *Philosophical Ideas in the United States*(N.Y.,1934).

Turner,F.J., *The Frontier in American History* (N.Y.,1920).

WECTER,D., *The Saga of American Society: A Record of Social Aspiration, 1607–1937* (N.Y.,1937).

Wright,Luella, *Literary Life of the Early Friends*(N.Y.,1932).
Wright,T.G., *Literary Culture in Early New England, 1620–1730*(New Haven, 1920).

LITERARY HISTORY AND CRITICISM

GENERAL
AMERICAN Literature, A Journal of Literary History, Criticism, and Bibliography (1929—).

BOYNTON,P.H., *Literature and American Life*(Boston, 1936).
Brawley,B., *The Negro in Literature and Art in the United States*(N.Y.,1918).
——, *Early Negro American Writers*(Chapel Hill, N.C.,1935).

CAIRNS,W.B., *A History of American Literature*, rev.ed.(N.Y.,1930).
Calverton,V.F., *The Liberation of American Literature*(N.Y.,1932).
Christy,A., *The Orient in American Transcendentalism*(N.Y.,1932).
Clark,H.H., 'Nationalism in American Literature,' *University of Toronto Quarterly*, II,492–519.
Cowley,M., ed., *After the Genteel Tradition: American Writers Since 1910*(N.Y.,1937).

DAVIDSON,D., 'Regionalism and Nationalism in American Literature,' *American Review*, v,48–61.
Dondore,D.A., *The Prairie and the Making of Middle America*(Cedar Rapids, Ia.,1926).
Duyckinck,E.A. and G.L., *Cyclopaedia of American Literature*, ed. to date by M.L.Simons, 2 vols.(Philadelphia, 1875).

EASTMAN,M., *The Literary Mind*(N.Y., 1931).

FOERSTER,N., *Nature in American Literature* (N.Y.,1923).
——, ed., *The Reinterpretation of American Literature*(N.Y.,1928).

HAZARD,L.L., *The Frontier in American Literature*(N.Y.,1927).
Hicks,G., *The Great Tradition*(N.Y.,1933).

KEISER,A., *The Indian in American Literature*(N.Y.,1933).

LAWRENCE,D.H., *Studies in Classic American Literature*(N.Y.,1923).
Lewisohn,Ludwig, *Expression in America* (N.Y.,1932).

McCLOSKEY,J.C., 'The Campaign of Periodicals after the War of 1812 for National American Literature,' *PMLA*, L,262–73.
Mencken,H.L., *The American Language*, 4th ed.(N.Y.,1936).
Miller,Perry, and Johnson,T.H., eds., *The Puritans*, American Writers Series(N.Y., 1937).
More,P.E., *Shelburne Essays*, 11 vols.(N.Y., 1904–21).
Mott,F.L., *A History of American Magazines*, Vol.I, 1741–1850(N.Y.,1930); Vol.II, 1850–65 and Vol.III, 1865–85(Cambridge, Mass., 1938).

PATTEE,F.L., *The First Century of American Literature: 1770–1870*(N.Y.,1935).
——, *A History of American Literature Since 1870*(N.Y.,1915).
Perry,Bliss, *The American Spirit in Literature* (New Haven, 1918).

ROURKE,C.M., *American Humor*(N.Y.,1931).
Rusk,R.L., *The Literature of the Middle Western Frontier*, 2 vols.(N.Y.,1925).

SHERMAN,S.P., *Americans*(N.Y.,1924).

TANDY,J.R., *Crackerbox Philosophers in American Humor and Satire*(N.Y.,1925).
Taylor, Walter F., *A History of American Letters*(N.Y.,1936). Contains the best select bibliographies, by Harry Hartwick.
Thompson,Ralph, *American Literary Annuals and Gift Books, 1825–1865*(N.Y.,1936).
Trent,W.P., Erskine,John, Sherman,S.P., and Van Doren,Carl, eds., *The Cambridge History of American Literature*, 4 vols.(N.Y., 1917–21, 1927); 3 vols., 1933, without bibliographies.
Twelve Southerners, *I'll Take My Stand: The South and the Agrarian Tradition*(N.Y., 1930).
Tyler,M.C., *A History of American Literature During the Colonial Time*, 2 vols., rev.ed. (N.Y.,1897).
——, *The Literary History of the American Revolution, 1763–1783*, 2 vols.(N.Y.,1897).

VAN DOREN,Carl and Mark, *American and British Literature Since 1890*(N.Y.,1925).

WENDELL, Barrett, *A Literary History of America*, 6th ed.(N.Y.,1911).

Williams,S.T., *American Literature*, Hour Library(Philadelphia, 1933).

ZABEL,Morton, ed., *Literary Opinion in America*(N.Y.,1937).

PROSE

BABBITT,Irving, and others, *Criticism in America, Its Function and Status*(N.Y., 1924).

Bement,Douglas, *Weaving the Short Story* (N.Y.,1931).

Brownell,W.C., *American Prose Masters*(N.Y., 1909).

CANBY,H.S., *A Study of the Short Story* (N.Y.,1913).

Charvat,William, *The Origins of American Critical Thought*, 1810–1835(Philadelphia, 1936).

Conway,A.M., *The Essay in American Literature*, in *New York University Series of Graduate School Studies*(1914), No.3.

FOERSTER,N., *American Criticism*(Boston, 1928).

HARTWICK,H., *The Foreground of American Fiction*(N.Y.,1934).

Hatcher,Harlan, *Creating the Modern American Novel*(N.Y.,1935).

Hicks,P.M., *The Development of the Natural History Essay in American Literature* (Philadelphia, 1924).

JONES,H.M., 'American Prose Style: 1700– 1770,' *Huntington Library Bulletin* (November 1934), No.6,115–51.

LEE,J.M., *History of American Journalism* (Boston, 1917,1923).

Leisy,Ernest E., 'The Novel in America: Notes for a Survey,' *Southwest Review*, XXII,88–99(1936).

Loshe,Lillie D., *The Early American Novel* (N.Y.,1907,1930).

MULLER,Herbert J., *Modern Fiction: A Study of Values*(N.Y.,1937).

O'BRIEN,E.J., *The Advance of the American Short Story*, rev.ed.(N.Y.,1931).

——, ed., *The Best Short Stories of 1915—and The Yearbook of the American Short Story* (Boston, annually since 1915).

PATTEE,F.L., *The Development of the American Short Story*(N.Y.,1923).

QUINN,Arthur H., *American Fiction: An Historical and Critical Survey*(N.Y., 1936).

SHURTER,R.L., 'The Utopian Novel in America, 1888–1910,' *South Atlantic Quarterly*,XXXIV,137–44.

Speare,M.E., *The Political Novel: Its Development in England and in America* (N.Y.,1924).

VAN DOREN,Carl, *The American Novel* (N.Y.,1921).

——, *Contemporary American Novelists*, 1900– 1920(N.Y.,1922).

WILLIAMS,B.C., *Our Short Story Writers* (N.Y.,1920).

POETRY

ALLEN,G.W., *American Prosody*(N.Y., 1935).

BEACH,J.W., *The Concept of Nature in Nineteenth-Century Poetry*(N.Y.,1936).

Blackmur,R.P., *The Double Agent: Essays in Craft and Elucidation*(N.Y.,1936).

HOWARD,Leon, 'The Influence of Milton on Colonial American Poetry,' *Huntington Library Bulletin*, No.9,63–89.

Hulme,T.E., *Speculations*, ed. by Herbert Read(N.Y.,1924).

LOWELL,A., *Tendencies in Modern American Poetry*(Boston, 1917).

MacNEICE,Louis, *Modern Poetry*, A Personal Essay(N.Y., 1938).

Morris,Amos R., *The Orchestration of the Metrical Line*, 2nd ed.(Boston, 1935).

Murdock,K.B., *Handkerchiefs from Paul* (Cambridge, Mass.,1927).

OTIS,W.B., *American Verse*, 1625–1807 (N.Y.,1909).

POETRY: A Magazine of Verse, ed. by Harriet Monroe(Chicago, 1912—). Its early numbers provide the best history of the poetic renascence of about 1912.

RIDING,L., and Graves,R., *A Survey of Modernist Poetry*(London, 1927).

STEDMAN,E.C., *Poets of America*(Boston, 1885).

Stedman,E.C. and Hutchinson,E.M., eds., *A Library of American Literature from the Earliest Settlement to the Present Time*, 11 vols.(N.Y.,1889–90).

TAUPIN,René, *L'Influence du symbolisme française sur la poésie américaine*(Paris, 1929).

UNTERMEYER,Louis, *American Poetry Since* 1900(N.Y.,1923).

WILSON,Edmund, *Axel's Castle*(N.Y., 1931).
Winters,Yvor, *Primitivism and Decadence: A Study of American Experimental Poetry* (N.Y.,1937).

DRAMA
DUNLAP,W., *History of the American Theatre* (N.Y.,1832).

HORNBLOW,A., *A History of the Theatre in America from its Beginnings to the Present Time*, 2 vols.(Philadelphia, 1919).

MOSES,M.J., ed., *Representative Plays by American Dramatists*, 3 vols.(N.Y.,1918–21).

ODELL,G.C.D., *Annals of the New York Stage*, 9 vols. to date(N.Y.,1927–37).

QUINN,A.H., *A History of the American Drama from the Beginning to the Civil War* (N.Y.,1923).
——, *A History of the American Drama from The Civil War to the Present Day*, 2 vols. (N.Y.,1927).
——, ed., *Representative American Plays, from 1767 to the Present Day*(N.Y.,1938).

BIBLIOGRAPHIES

EVANS,C., *American Bibliography*, 12 vols. to date, 1639–1799(Chicago, 1903–34).

FOLEY,P.K., *American Authors*, 1795–1895, a Bibliography of First and Notable Editions Chronologically Arranged with Notes (Boston, 1897).

HILL,F.P., *American Plays Printed* 1714–1830: *a Bibliographical Record*(Stanford University, Calif.,1934).

TRENT,W.P., Erskine,John, Sherman,S.P., and Van Doren,Carl, eds., *The Cambridge History of American Literature*, 4 vols. (N.Y.,1917–21).

WEGELIN,Oscar, *Early American Fiction*, 1774–1830: *a Compilation of the Titles of Works of Fiction*, rev. ed.(N.Y.,1929).
——, *Early American Poetry: a Compilation of the Titles of Verse and Broadsides*, 2nd ed. (N.Y.,1930).

Lists of current books and articles on American Literature may be found in the March issues of *PMLA*(since 1923), and lists of current articles in each issue of *American Literature*.

References to individual authors will be found under the commentaries.

INDEX OF FIRST LINES

Sleep softly . . . eagle forgotten . . . under the stone, 1148

so much depends, 1314

So that soldierly legend is still on its journey, 858

'So . . . ' they said, 1310

Some say the world will end in fire, 1142

Something there is that doesn't love a wall, 1134

somewhere i have never travelled, gladly beyond, 1349

Somewhere—in desolate wind-swept space, 854

Stand on the highest pavement of the stair, 1491

Stone, bronze, stone, steel, stone, oakleaves, horses' heels, 1498

Stuff of the moon, 1173

Suddenly out of its stale and drowsy lair, the lair of slaves, 820

Suppose I plant you, 1313

Surgeons must be very careful, 851

Sweet sounds, oh, beautiful music, do not cease! 1264

Take home Thy prodigal child, O Lord of Hosts! 1260

Tall, sombre, grim, against the morning sky, 909

Tell her I love, 1567

'Tell me what you're doing over here, John Gorham,' 1124

Thank God my brain is not inclined to cut, 1026

That afternoon the Postman brought, among, 1131

That 'something far more deeply interfused,' 1302

That such have died enables us, 853

The alphabet of, 1316

The apparition of these faces in the crowd, 1276

The Archer is wake! 1314

The bay is not blue but sombre yellow, 1382

The bear puts both arms around the tree above her, 1144

The Body, long oppressed, 1259

The breath of dew and twilight's grace, 983

The broad-backed hippopotamus, 1491

The brotherhood is not by the blood certainly, 1511

The buzz-saw snarled and rattled in the yard, 1140

The cannonade fell still. All along the fish-hook line, 1526

The cows are bawling in the mountains, 1021

The dead man spoke to me and begged a penny, 1339

The desert murmurs to the sun a strange murmur, 1022

The earth keeps some vibration going, 1160

The ebb slips from the rock, the sunken, 1379

The fog comes, 1173

The glittering leaves of the rhododendrons, 1294

The great Overdog, 1144

The increasing moonlight drifts across my bed, 854

The interests of a black man in a cellar, 1558

The last night that she lived, 851

The little beauty that I was allowed, 1255

The man Flammonde, from God knows where, 1120

The meek shall disinherit the earth, 1572

The mind has shown itself at times, 1556

The people along the sand, 1146

The people will live on, 1179

The praisers of women in their proud and beautiful poems, 1502

The pure air trembles, O pitiless God, 1378

The royal feast was done; the King, 978

The sky is low, the clouds are mean, 853

The sky-like limpid eyes, 1279

The soul selects her own society, 848

The strong men keep coming on, 1179

The swift red flesh, a winter king, 1559

The swinging mill bell changed its rate, 1146

The thought beneath so slight a film, 853

The trees in the garden rained flowers, 1010

'The voyage crossed, the firmament one star,' 1569

The way a crow, 1142

The wayfarer, 1009

The year turns to its rest, 1531

Thee for my recitative, 843

Their mouths have drunken Death's eternal wine, 984

Their noonday never knows, 979

There are two ways in life, 1163

There is a man whom rhapsodies of change, 1331

There is a serpent in perfection tarnished, 1252

There is a silence I carry about with me always, 1298

There is a wolf in me . . . fangs pointed, 1175

There is something about Death, 1162

There never was a mood of mine, 1245

There was a child went forth every day, 833

There was never a sound beside the wood but one, 1133

There were none of my blood in this battle, 1504

Thereafter I found these Greek lines underscored, 1131

'They called it Annandale—and I was there,' 1113

They say that 'time assuages,' 848

They say there is no hope, 1289

They sent him back to her. The letter came, 1144

Things you heard that blessed be, 1246

This I beheld, or dreamed it in a dream, 978

INDEX OF TITLES

Titles which repeat the first line of poems, chapter titles, and titles of fragments, have not been included in this index